About this book

Rough Guides are designed to be good to read and easy to use. The book is divided into the following sections, and you should be able to find whatever you need in one of them.

The introductory **colour section** gives you a feel for Thailand, suggesting when to go and what not to miss, and includes a full list of **contents**. Then comes **basics**, for pre-departure information and other practicalities.

The **guide** chapters cover Thailand in depth, each starting with a highlights panel, introduction and a map to help you plan your route.

Contexts fills you in on history, the environment and hill tribes, while individual **colour sections** introduce Thai food, temples and the festival of Loy Krathong. **Language** gives you an extensive menu reader and enough Thai to get by.

The book concludes with all the **small print**, including details of how to send in updates and corrections, and a comprehensive **index**.

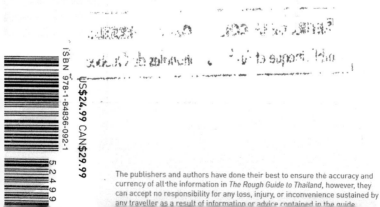

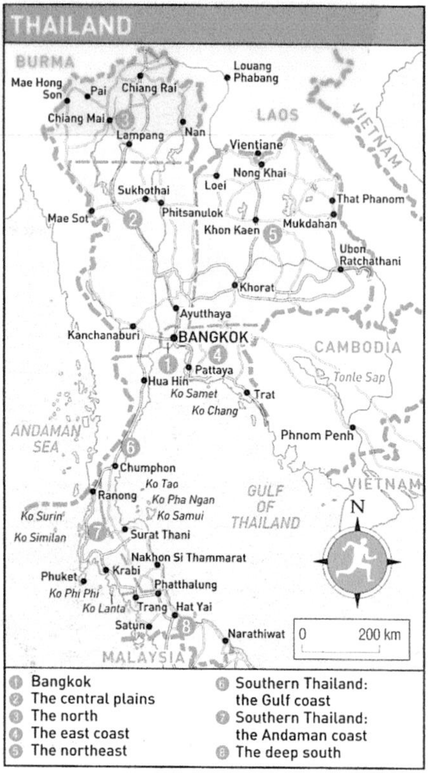

1. Bangkok
2. The central plains
3. The north
4. The east coast
5. The northeast
6. Southern Thailand: the Gulf coast
7. Southern Thailand: the Andaman coast
8. The deep south

This seventh edition published October 2009.

ISBN 978-1-84836-092-1
US$24.99 CAN$29.99
52499

The **Rough Guide** to

Thailand

written and researched by

Paul Gray and Lucy Ridout

with additional contributions from

John Clewley and Ron Emmons

ROUGH GUIDES

www.roughguides.com

Contents

◀◀ Ko Wua Talap, Ang Thong Marine Park ◀ Longtail boat and riverside temple, Thonburi, Bangkok

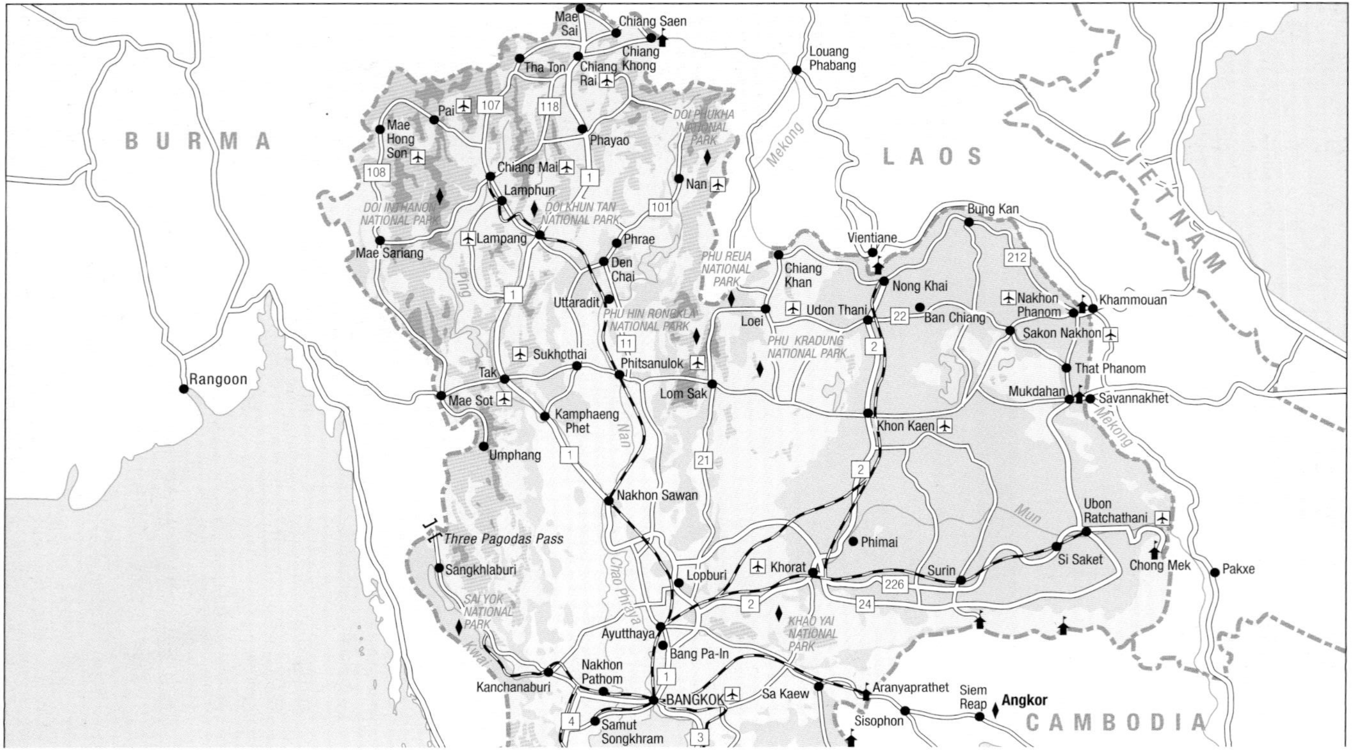
BURMA
LAOS
VIETNAM
CAMBODIA
Rangoon
Mae Sai
Chiang Saen
Chiang Khong
Tha Ton
Chiang Rai
Louang Phabang
Pai
107
118
Mae Hong Son
Phayao
DOI PHUKHA NATIONAL PARK
Mekong
108
Chiang Mai
1
Nan
Lamphun
DOI INTHANON NATIONAL PARK
DOI KHUN TAN NATIONAL PARK
101
Bung Kan
Lampang
Phrae
Mae Sariang
Vientiane
Den Chai
PHU REUA NATIONAL PARK
212
Ping
Chiang Khan
Nong Khai
Nakhon Phanom
Khammouan
Uttaradit
PHU HIN RONGKLA NATIONAL PARK
Loei
Udon Thani
22
Ban Chiang
11
Sakon Nakhon
PHU KRADUNG NATIONAL PARK
2
Sukhothai
Phitsanulok
That Phanom
Tak
Mukdahan
Savannakhet
Lom Sak
Mae Sot
Kamphaeng Phet
Khon Kaen
Nan
Umphang
21
Nakhon Sawan
Mun
Ubon Ratchathani
Three Pagodas Pass
Phimai
Chong Mek
Pakxe
Sangkhlaburi
Khorat
Si Saket
Surin
Lopburi
226
Chao Phraya
SAI YOK NATIONAL PARK
24
KHAO YAI NATIONAL PARK
Ayutthaya
Kwai
Bang Pa-In
Nakhon Pathom
Kanchanaburi
Aranyaprathet
Siem Reap
Angkor
BANGKOK
Sa Kaew
Sisophon
4
Samut Songkhram
3

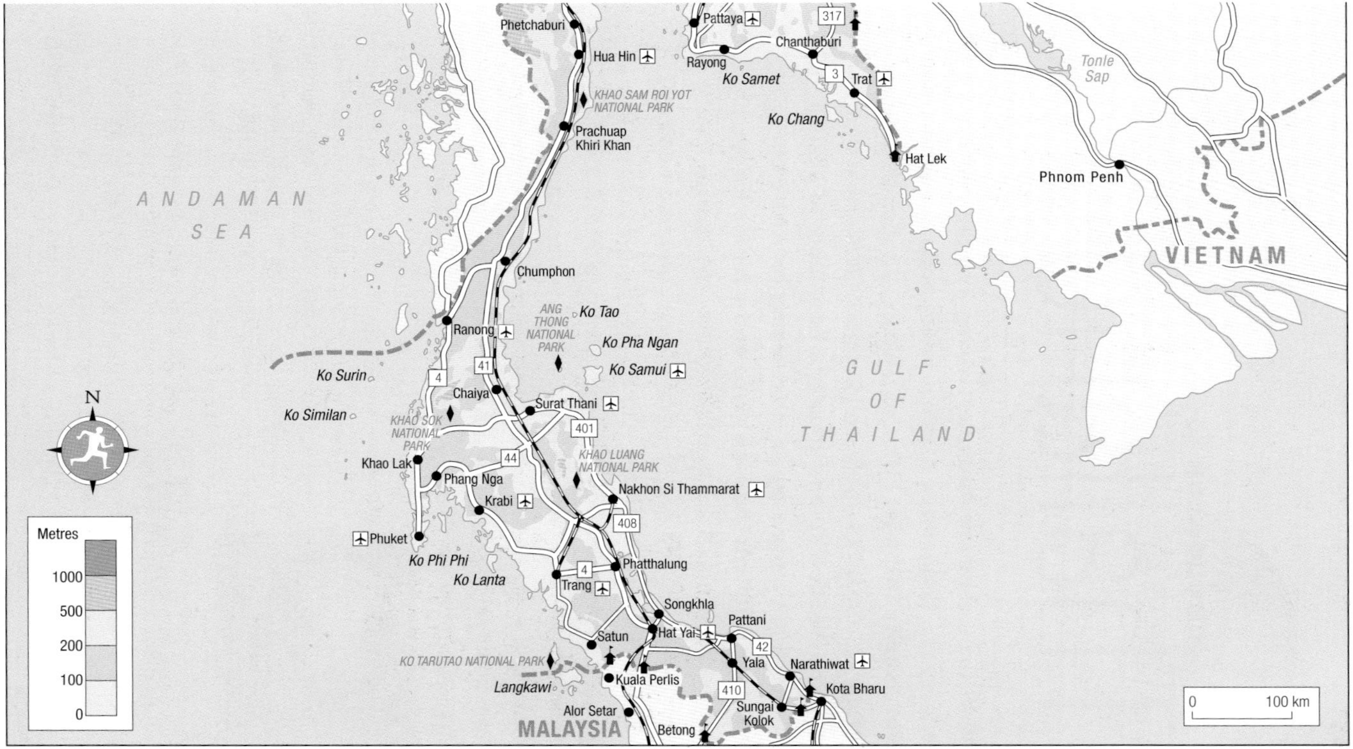
Pattaya
317
Phetchaburi
Hua Hin
Rayong
Chanthaburi
Tonle Sap
Ko Samet
3
Trat
KHAO SAM ROI YOT NATIONAL PARK
Ko Chang
Prachuap Khiri Khan
Hat Lek
Phnom Penh
ANDAMAN SEA
VIETNAM
Chumphon
ANG THONG NATIONAL PARK
Ko Tao
Ranong
Ko Pha Ngan
41
Ko Samui
GULF OF THAILAND
Ko Surin
4
Chaiya
N
Surat Thani
Ko Similan
KHAO SOK NATIONAL PARK
401
44
KHAO LUANG NATIONAL PARK
Khao Lak
Phang Nga
Nakhon Si Thammarat
Krabi
408
Metres
Phuket
Ko Phi Phi
Phatthalung
1000
4
Ko Lanta
Trang
500
Songkhla
Pattani
200
Satun
Hat Yai
42
KO TARUTAO NATIONAL PARK
Yala
Narathiwat
100
Kuala Perlis
Langkawi
410
Kota Bharu
0
Alor Setar
Sungai Kolok
0
100 km
MALAYSIA
Betong

Introduction to

Thailand

With twelve million foreigners flying into the country each year, Thailand is Asia's primary holiday destination. Yet despite this vast influx of visitors, Thailand's cultural integrity remains largely undamaged – a country that adroitly avoided colonization has been able to absorb Western influences while maintaining its own rich heritage. Though the high-rises and neon lights occupy the foreground of the tourist picture, the typical Thai community is still the farming village, and you need not venture far to encounter a more traditional scene of fishing communities, rubber plantations and Buddhist temples. Around forty percent of Thais earn their living from the land, based around the staple rice, which forms the foundation of the country's unique and famously sophisticated cuisine.

Tourism has been just one factor in the country's development which, since the deep-seated regional uncertainties surrounding the Vietnam War faded, has been free, for the most part, to proceed at death-defying pace – for a time in the 1980s and early 1990s, Thailand boasted the fastest-expanding economy in the world. Politics in Thailand, however, has not been able to keep pace. Since World War II, coups d'état have been as common a method of changing government as general elections. The malnourished democratic system is characterized by corruption and cronyism, while in recent years, opposing mass movements, with ill-defined aims, have found it necessary to take to the streets to try to get their voices heard.

Through all the changes of the last sixty years, the much-revered constitutional monarch, King Bhumibol, who sits at the pinnacle of an elaborate hierarchical system of deference covering the whole of Thai society, has lent a large measure of stability. Furthermore, some 85 percent of the population are still practising Theravada Buddhists, a unifying faith that colours all aspects of daily life – from the tiered temple rooftops that dominate every skyline, to the omnipresent saffron-robed monks and the packed calendar of festivals.

Where to go

The clash of tradition and modernity is most intense in **Bangkok**, the first stop on almost any itinerary. Within its historic core you'll find resplendent temples, canalside markets and the opulent indulgence of the eighteenth-century

▲ Elephant in Pai

Fact file

- Known as **Siam** until 1939, Thailand lies wholly within the tropics, covering an **area** of 511,770 square kilometres and divided into 76 provinces or *changwat*.
- The **population** of 63 million is made up of ethnic Thais (75 percent) and Chinese (14 percent), with the rest comprising mainly immigrants from neighbouring countries as well as hill-tribespeople; the national language is *phasaa Thai*.
- Buddhism is the national **religion**, with some 85 percent followers, and Islam the largest minority religion.
- Average **life expectancy** is 72 years.
- Since 1932 the country has been a **constitutional monarchy**; King Bhumibol, also known as Rama IX (being the ninth ruler of the Chakri dynasty), has been on the throne since 1946. The elected **National Assembly** (Rathasapha) has five hundred MPs in the House of Representatives (Sapha Phuthaen Ratsadon), led by a prime minister, and two hundred members of the Senate (Wuthisapha).
- Tourism is the country's main **industry**, and its biggest **exports** are computers and components, vehicles and vehicle parts, textiles and rubber.

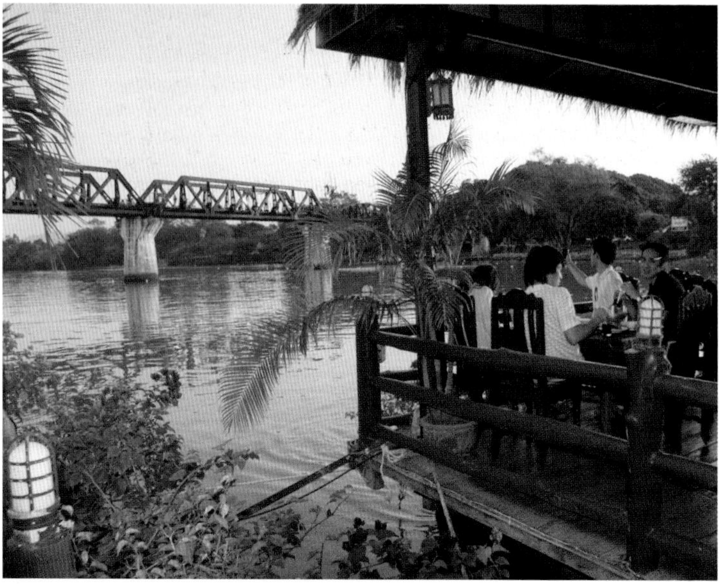

◀ Floating restaurant near the Bridge over River Kwai

Grand Palace, while downtown Bangkok's forest of skyscrapers shelters cutting-edge fashion and decor boutiques and some achingly hip bars and clubs. After touchdown in Bangkok, much of the package-holiday traffic flows east to **Pattaya**, the country's seediest resort, but for prettier beaches you're better off venturing just a little further, to the islands of **Ko Samet** and the **Ko Chang archipelago**, with their squeaky white sand and shorefront bungalows.

Few tourists visit **Isaan**, the poorest and in some ways the most traditionally Thai region. Here, a trip through the gently modulating landscapes of the **Mekong River** valley, which defines Thailand's northeastern extremities, takes in archetypal agricultural villages and a fascinating array of religious sites, while the southern reaches of Isaan hold some of Thailand's best-kept secrets – the magnificent stone temple complexes of **Phimai**, **Phanom Rung** and **Khao Phra Viharn**, all built by the Khmers of Cambodia almost ten centuries ago. Closer to the capital, **Khao Yai National Park** encapsulates the phenomenal diversity of Thailand's flora and fauna, which here range from wild orchids to strangling figs, elephants to hornbills.

At the heart of the northern uplands, **Chiang Mai** is both an attractive historic city and a vibrant cultural centre, with a strong tradition of arts, crafts and festivals. It does a burgeoning line in self-improvement courses – from ascetic meditation to the more earthly pleasures of Thai cookery classes – while the overriding enticement of the surrounding region is the

Thai boxing

Such is the national obsession with *muay thai*, or Thai boxing, that when Wijan Ponlid returned home from the Sydney 2000 Olympics with the country's only gold medal (for international flyweight boxing), he was paraded through town at the head of a procession of 49 elephants, given a new house and over 20 million baht, and offered a promotion in the police force. Belatedly perhaps, *muay thai* has recently entered the canon of martial-arts cinema: *Ong Bak* (2003), *Tom Yum Goong* (2005) and *Ong Bak 2* (2008) were global box-office hits, and their all-punching, all-kicking star, Tony Jaa, who performed all his own stunts, has been appointed Cultural Ambassador for Thailand.

Though there are boxing venues all around the country, the very best fights are staged at Bangkok's two biggest stadiums, Rajdamnoen and Lumphini, and are well worth attending as a cultural experience even if you have no interest in the sport itself; see p.193 for times and ticket prices and p.69 for more on the rules and rituals of *muay thai*.

prospect of **trekking** through villages inhabited by a richly mixed population of tribal peoples. Plenty of outdoor activities and courses, as well as hot springs and massages, can be enjoyed at **Pai**, a surprisingly cosmopolitan hill station for travellers, four hours northwest of Chiang Mai.

With Chiang Mai and the north so firmly planted on the independent tourist trail, the intervening **central plains** tend to get short shrift. Yet there is rewarding trekking around **Umphang**, near the Burmese border, and the elegant ruins of former capitals **Ayutthaya** and **Sukhothai** embody a glorious artistic heritage, displaying Thailand's distinctive ability to absorb influences from quite different cultures. **Kanchanaburi**, stunningly located on the **River Kwai**, tells of a much darker episode in Thailand's past, for it was along the course of this river that the Japanese army built the Thailand–Burma Railway during World War II, at the cost of thousands of POW lives.

Sand and sea are what most Thai holidays are about,

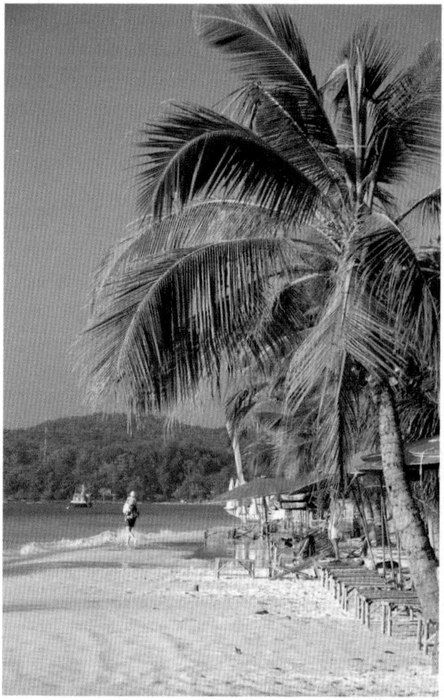

▲ Hat Sai Kaew, Ko Samet

Hill-tribe trekking

Trekking in northern Thailand isn't just about walking through beautiful, rainforested mountain scenery, it also brings you into contact with the hill tribes or *chao khao*, fascinating ethnic minorities who are just clinging on to their traditional ways of life. Scattered around this part of Southeast Asia, the hill tribes have developed sophisticated customs, laws and beliefs to harmonize relationships between individuals and their environment. Despite the disturbance caused by trekking, most *chao khao* are genuinely hospitable to foreigners, but it's important that you go with a knowledgeable guide who has the interests of the local people at heart – and that you act as a sensitive guest in the face of their hospitality. For more on the hill tribes, see p.845; for trekking practicalities, see p.315.

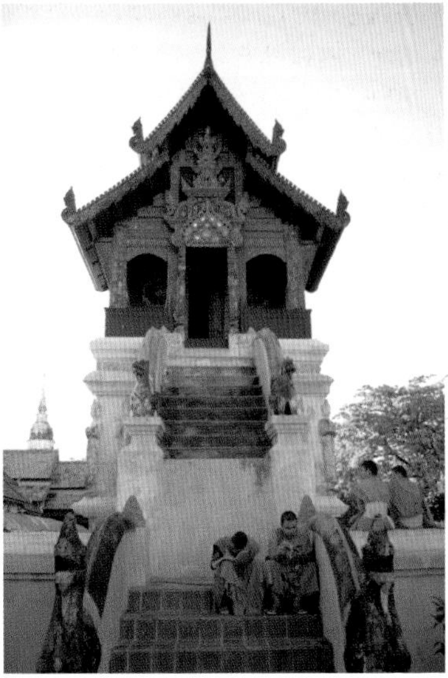

◀ Wat Phra Singh, Chiang Mai

though, and the pick of the coasts are in southern Thailand, where the Samui archipelago off the **Gulf coast** is one of the highlights. **Ko Samui** itself has the most sweeping white-sand beaches, and the greatest variety of accommodation and facilities to go with them. **Ko Pha Ngan** next door is still pure backpacker territory, where you have a stark choice between desolate coves and **Hat Rin**, Thailand's party capital. The remotest island, rocky **Ko Tao**, is acquiring increasing sophistication as Southeast Asia's largest dive-training centre.

Across on the other side of the peninsula, the **Andaman coast** boasts even more exhilarating scenery and the finest coral reefs in the country, in particular around the **Ko Surin** and **Ko Similan** island chains, which rank among the best dive sites in the world.

The largest Andaman coast island, **Phuket**, is one of Thailand's top tourist destinations and graced with a dozen fine beaches, though several have been overdeveloped with a glut of high-rises and tacky nightlife. Breathtakingly beautiful little **Ko Phi Phi** is a major party hub, surrounded by the turquoise seas and dramatic limestone cliffs that characterize the coastline throughout **Krabi province**. Large, forested **Ko Lanta** is, for the moment at least, a calmer alternative for families, but for genuine jungle you'll need to head inland, to the rainforests of **Khao Sok National Park**.

Further down the Thai peninsula, in the provinces of the **deep south**, the teeming sea life and unfrequented sands of the **Trang islands** and **Ko Tarutao National Marine Park** are the main draws. There's now the intriguing possibility of **island-hopping** your way down through them – in fact, all the way from Phuket to Penang in Malaysia – without setting foot on the mainland.

When to go

The **climate** of most of Thailand is governed by three seasons: rainy (roughly May–Oct), caused by the southwest monsoon dumping moisture gathered from the Andaman Sea and the Gulf of Thailand; cool (Nov–Feb); and hot (March–May). The **rainy season** is the least predictable of the three, varying in length and intensity from year to year, but usually it gathers force between June and August, coming

▲ Ao Nang

Spirit houses

Although the vast majority of Thais are Buddhist, nearly everyone also believes that the physical world is inhabited by **spirits**. These spirits can cause trouble if not given enough care and attention, and are apt to wreak havoc when made homeless. Therefore, whenever a new building is constructed – be it a traditional village house or a multi storey office block – the owners will also construct a home for the spirits who previously occupied that land. Crucially, these spirit houses must be given the best spot on the site – which in Bangkok often means on the roof – and must also reflect the status of the building in question, so their architecture can range from the simplest wooden structure to an elaborate scale-model of a particularly ornate temple or even a sleek little icon of modernism. Daily **offerings** of flowers, incense and candles are set inside the spirit house, sometimes with morsels of food. For an introduction to animist and Buddhist practices in Thailand, see p.811.

to a peak in September and October, when unpaved roads are reduced to mud troughs and whole districts of Bangkok are flooded. The **cool season** is the pleasantest time to visit, although temperatures can still reach a broiling 30°C in the middle of the day. In the **hot season**, when temperatures often rise to 35°C in Bangkok, the best thing to do is to hit the beach.

Within this scheme, slight variations are found from region to region. The upland, less humid **north** experiences the greatest range of temperatures: at night in the cool season the thermometer dips markedly, occasionally approaching zero on the higher slopes, and this region is often hotter than the central plains between March and May. It's

▲ Siam Square, Bangkok

the **northeast** that gets the very worst of the hot season, with clouds of dust gathering above the parched fields, and humid air too. In **southern Thailand**, temperatures are more consistent throughout the year, with less variation the closer you get to the equator. The rainy season hits the **Andaman coast** of the southern peninsula harder than anywhere else in the country: heavy rainfall usually starts in May and persists until November.

One area of the country, the **Gulf coast** of the southern peninsula, lies outside this general pattern. With the sea immediately to the east, this coast and its offshore islands feel the effects of the northeast monsoon, which

Rat or raja?

There's no standard system of **transliterating** Thai script into Roman, so you're sure to find that the Thai words in this book don't always match the versions you'll see elsewhere. Maps and street signs are the biggest sources of confusion, so we've generally gone for the transliteration that's most common on the spot; where it's a toss-up between two equally popular versions, we've used the one that helps best with pronunciation. However, sometimes you'll need to do a bit of lateral thinking, bearing in mind that a classic variant for the town of Ayutthaya is Ayudhia, while among street names, Thanon Rajavithi could come out as Thanon Ratwithi – and it's not unheard of to find one spelling posted at one end of a road, with another at the opposite end. See p.861 for an introduction to the Thai language.

Bungalows on Ko Phi Phi

brings rain between October and January, especially in November, but suffers less than the Andaman coast from the southwest monsoon.

Overall, the **cool season** is generally the **best time** to come to Thailand: as well as having more manageable temperatures and less rain, it offers waterfalls in full spate and the best of the upland flowers in bloom. Bear in mind, however, that it's also the busiest season, so forward planning is essential.

Thailand's climate

Average daily temperatures (°C) and monthly rainfall (mm)

	Jan	Feb	Mar	Apr	May	Jun	Jul	Aug	Sep	Oct	Nov	Dec
Bangkok												
Max temp (°C)	26	28	29	30	30	29	29	28	28	28	27	26
Rainfall (mm)	11	28	31	72	190	152	158	187	320	231	57	9
Chiang Mai												
Max temp (°C)	21	23	26	29	29	28	27	27	27	26	24	22
Rainfall (mm)	8	6	15	45	153	136	167	227	251	132	44	15
Pattaya												
Max temp (°C)	26	28	29	30	30	29	29	28	28	28	27	26
Rainfall (mm)	12	23	41	79	165	120	166	166	302	229	66	10
Ko Samui												
Max temp (°C)	26	26	28	29	29	28	28	28	28	27	26	25
Rainfall (mm)	38	8	12	63	186	113	143	123	209	260	302	98
Phuket												
Max temp (°C)	27	28	28	29	28	28	28	28	27	27	27	27
Rainfall (mm)	35	31	39	163	348	213	263	263	419	305	207	52

35

things not to miss

It's not possible to see everything that Thailand has to offer in one trip – and we don't suggest you try. What follows is a selective taste of the country's highlights: beautiful beaches, outstanding national parks, magnificent temples and mouthwatering food, arranged in five colour-coded categories to help you find the very best things to see, do and experience. All entries have a page reference to take you straight into the Guide, where you can find out more.

01 The Grand Palace, Bangkok Page **130** • No visitor should miss this huge complex, which encompasses the country's holiest and most beautiful temple, Wat Phra Kaeo, and its most important image, the Emerald Buddha.

02 Sukhothai Page **277** • Stay in one of the many welcoming guest houses in New Sukhothai and hire a bicycle to explore the elegant ruins of the nearby old city, Thailand's thirteenth-century capital.

03 Ayutthaya Page **253** • River boats and bicycles are the perfect way to explore the scattered temple ruins of this former capital.

04 Traditional massage Page **70** • Combining elements of acupressure and yoga, a pleasantly brutal way to help shed jet lag, or simply to end the day.

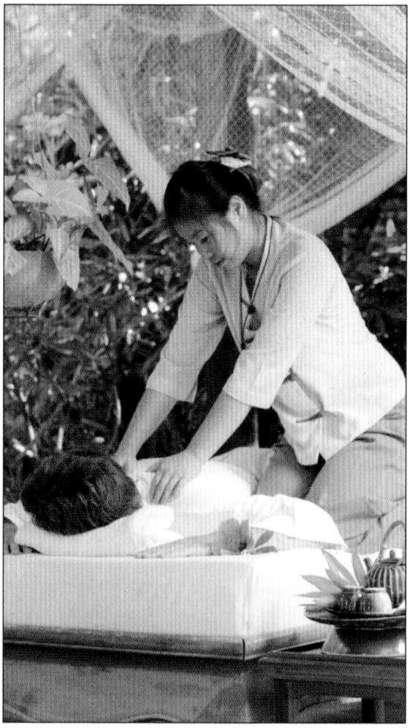

05 Night markets Page **55** • Evening gatherings of pushcart kitchens, which are usually the best-value and most entertaining places to eat in any Thai town.

06 Vegetarian festival, Phuket Page **686** • During Taoist Lent, fasting Chinese devotees test their spiritual resolve with acts of gruesome self-mortification.

07 Jim Thompson's House, Bangkok Page **162** • The house of the legendary American adventurer, entrepreneur and art collector is a small, personal museum of Thai crafts and architecture.

08 Wat Phra That Doi Suthep, Chiang Mai
Page **351** • One of the most harmonious ensembles of temple architecture in the country, with mountaintop views over half of northern Thailand thrown in.

10 The Mae Hong Son loop
Page **377** • A spectacular 600km trip, winding over steep forested mountains and through tightly hemmed farming valleys.

09 Khao Sok National Park
Page **665** • Mist-clad outcrops, jungle trails serenaded by whooping gibbons, and the vast Cheow Lan lake all make Khao Sok a rewarding place to explore.

11 The National Museum, Bangkok Page **141** • A colossal hoard of Thailand's artistic treasures.

12 Silk Page **514** • Weavers from the northeast produce the country's most exquisite designs, though high-quality silk is sold all over Thailand.

13 Riding the Death Railway, River Kwai Page **240** • Thailand's most scenic train journey is also its most historic, using the track constructed by World War II POWs, whose story is movingly told in the nearby Hellfire Pass Museum.

14 Ko Tao Page **624** • Take a dive course, or just explore this remote island's contours by boat or on foot.

15 Thai cookery classes in Chiang Mai Page **332** • Of the many courses now on offer in the town, cookery classes are the most instantly gratifying and popular.

16 Snorkelling off Ko Surin Page **664** • Camp out on this remote chain of national park islands to make the most of the spectacular shallow reefs.

17 Chatuchak Weekend Market, Bangkok Page **171** • Thailand's top shopping experience features over 8000 stalls selling everything from cooking pots to designer lamps.

18 The Mekong River Page **542** • Forming 750km of the border between Thailand and Laos, the mighty Mekong provides an endlessly fascinating scenic backdrop to travels in the northeast.

19 Khmer ruins Page **508** • The neighbouring Khmers left a chain of magnificent Angkorian temple complexes across the northeast, including this one at Phanom Rung.

20 Ko Lanta Page **751** • A popular choice for families, with its many long beaches and plentiful but still reasonably low-key resort facilities.

21 Khao Yai National Park Page **494** • Easy trails, dramatic waterfalls and a healthy cast of hornbills and gibbons: Khao Yai is Thailand's most popular national park.

22 Nakhon Si Thammarat Page **634** • Superb food and excellent-value hotels to accompany the chief religious and cultural riches of the south.

23 Tom yam kung See *Thai cuisine* colour section • Delicious hot and sour soup with prawns and lemon grass, which typifies the strong, fresh flavours of Thai food.

24 Nan Page **371** • Few travellers make the trip out to Nan, but it's set in rich mountain scenery, with a strong handicraft tradition and some intriguing temples, including the beautiful murals at Wat Phumin.

25 Umphang treks Page **304** • The best way to reach mighty Tee Lor Su Falls from Umphang is by rafting and hiking your way through the jungle.

26 Full moon party at Hat Rin, Ko Pha Ngan Page **615** • *Apocalypse Now* without the war . . .

27 Ko Tarutao National Marine Park Page **783** • Spectacular and relatively peaceful islands, sheltering a surprising variety of landscapes and fauna.

28 Ko Kood Page **481** • An untamed beauty, fringed by very pretty beaches.

29 Ko Samet Page **446** • Petite and pretty, Ko Samet is hugely popular for its gorgeous white sand and its seafood dinners on the beach.

30 Folklore Museum, Phitsanulok Page **275** • One of Thailand's best ethnology museums, complete with a reconstructed village home and a fascinating array of traditional kitchen implements.

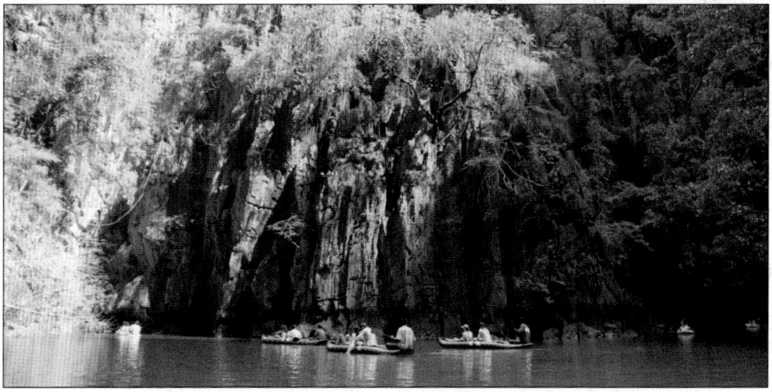

31 Sea-canoeing in Ao Phang Nga Page **714** • Low-impact paddling is the best way to explore the secret island-lagoons and mangrove swamps of this extraordinary bay.

32 Rock-climbing on the Railay peninsula Page **736** • Even novice climbers can scale the cliffs here for unbeatable views of the Andaman coastline.

33 Songkhran Page **66** • Thai New Year is the excuse for a national waterfight – don't plan on getting much done in mid-April, just join in.

34 Wat Pho, Bangkok Page **137** • A lively and lavish temple, encompassing the awesome Reclining Buddha and a great massage school.

35 Wat Phu Tok Page **554** • A uniquely atmospheric meditation temple on a steep, wooded outcrop – clamber around for the spectacular views, if nothing else.

Basics

Basics

Getting there

Thailand currently has six international airports, in Bangkok, Chiang Mai, Hat Yai, Krabi, Phuket and Ko Samui. The vast majority of travellers fly into Bangkok's Suvarnabhumi Airport (see p.95).

Air fares to Thailand generally depend on the **season**, with the highest being approximately mid-November to mid-February, when the weather is best (with premium rates charged for flights between mid-Dec and New Year), and in July and August to coincide with school holidays. You will need to book several months in advance to get reasonably priced tickets during these peak periods.

The cheapest way of getting to most **regional Thai airports** is usually to buy a flight to Bangkok and then a domestic add-on; see p.45 for details of domestic airlines. However, for flights to **Phuket** you also have the option of flying nonstop from Sydney (with Jetstar) as well as on a through-ticket from any international departure point via Kuala Lumpur (with Malaysia Airlines or Air Asia), Singapore (Singapore/Silk Air), Seoul (Korean Air) or Hong Kong (Cathay Pacific/Dragonair), and from Penang with Firefly. For **Ko Samui** there are flights from Singapore, Hong Kong (both Bangkok Airways), KL (Berjaya Airlines and Firefly) and Penang (Firefly); for **Krabi** you can fly via KL with Air Asia, or nonstop from Oslo and Munich with Krabi Airline; and for **Chiang Mai** Singapore/Silk Air fly via Singapore, Air Asia via KL

Flights from the UK and Ireland

The fastest and most comfortable way of reaching Thailand **from the UK** is to fly nonstop from London to Bangkok with Qantas/British Airways, Thai Airways or Eva Airways, a journey time of about eleven and a half hours. These airlines usually keep their prices competitive, at around £500/730 plus tax in low/high season. Fares on indirect scheduled flights to Bangkok are always cheaper than nonstop flights and start at £380/550 plus tax, though these journeys can take anything from two to twelve hours longer.

There are no nonstop flights from any **regional airports** in Britain or from any **Irish airports**, and rather than routing via London, you may find it convenient to fly to another hub such as Frankfurt (with Lufthansa), Zurich (with Swiss), Abu Dhabi (with Etihad) or Dubai (with Emirates), and take a connecting flight from there. Return flights from Newcastle upon Tyne with Emirates, for example, with good connections in Dubai, currently start at around £530, including taxes, from Dublin via Amsterdam with Aer Lingus and China Airlines, at around €800.

Flights from the US and Canada

There are no nonstop flights from North America to Bangkok, as Thai Airways recently abandoned its "ultra-long-haul" services from New York and Los Angeles and now only flies from LA via Osaka (5 weekly). However, plenty of other airlines run daily flights to Bangkok from major East and West Coast cities with only **one stop** en route; it's generally easier to find a reasonable fare on flights via Asia than via Europe, even if you're departing from the East Coast. From New York expect to pay around US$1150/1350 return in low season/high season, including taxes, from LA US$950/1150. Air Canada has the most convenient service to Bangkok from the largest number of Canadian cities; from Vancouver, expect to pay around Can$1450/1600 in low season/high season; from Toronto, Can$1650/1825. Cheaper rates are often available if you're prepared to make two or three stops and take more time.

Minimum **flying times**, including stopovers, are twenty hours from New York or Toronto (westbound or eastbound), nineteen hours thirty minutes from LA, eighteen hours from Vancouver.

Six steps to a better kind of travel

At Rough Guides we are passionately committed to travel. We feel strongly that only through travelling do we truly come to understand the world we live in and the people we share it with – plus tourism has brought a great deal of **benefit** to developing economies around the world over the last few decades. But the extraordinary growth in tourism has also damaged some places irreparably, and of course **climate change** is exacerbated by most forms of transport, especially flying. This means that now more than ever it's important to **travel thoughtfully** and **responsibly**, with respect for the cultures you're visiting – not only to derive the most benefit from your trip but also to preserve the best bits of the planet for everyone to enjoy. At Rough Guides we feel there are six main areas in which you can make a difference:

- Consider what you're contributing to the **local economy**, and how much the services you use do the same, whether it's through employing local workers and guides or sourcing locally grown produce and local services.
- Consider the **environment** on holiday as well as at home. Water is scarce in many developing destinations, and the biodiversity of local flora and fauna can be adversely affected by tourism. Try to patronize businesses that take account of this.
- Travel with a purpose, not just to tick off experiences. Consider **spending longer** in a place, and getting to know it and its people.
- Give thought to how often you **fly**. Try to avoid short hops by air and more harmful night flights.
- Consider **alternatives to flying**, travelling instead by bus, train, boat and even by bike or on foot where possible.
- Make your trips **"climate neutral"** via a reputable carbon-offset scheme. All Rough Guide flights are offset, and every year we donate money to a variety of charities devoted to combating the effects of climate change.

Flights from Australia and New Zealand

There's no shortage of **scheduled flights** to Bangkok **from Australia**, with direct services from major cities operated by Thai Airways, Qantas/British Airways, Jetstar and Emirates (around nine hours from Sydney and Perth), and plenty of indirect flights via Asian hubs, which take at least eleven and a half hours. You can also fly nonstop to Phuket from Sydney (with Jetstar) and Perth (on Thai). There's often not much difference between the fares on nonstop and indirect flights, which start from around Aus$700/1200 (excluding taxes) in low/high season from Sydney and most major eastern Australian cities. Fares from Perth and Darwin are up to Aus$100/200 cheaper.

From **New Zealand**, Thai Airways runs nonstop twelve-hour flights between Auckland and Bangkok, charging from NZ$1100/1700 (excluding taxes) in low/high season. BA/Qantas and Emirates flights from Auckland make brief stops in Sydney, adding at least a couple of hours to the trip, and other major Asian airlines offer indirect flights via their hubs (from 17hr): fares for indirect flights also start at about NZ$1100/1700. From Christchurch and Wellington you'll pay NZ$150–300 more than from Auckland.

Flights from South Africa

From South Africa, Thai Airways, code-sharing with South African Airways, operate three nonstop flights a week from Johannesburg to Bangkok, taking eleven and a half hours and costing around ZAR10,500 return in low season, ZAR12,000 in high season, including taxes. Otherwise, you'll be making a stop either in the Middle East or in Hong Kong or Southeast Asia, with fares starting at around ZAR7500/10,000 low/high season.

Airlines

Aer Lingus Ⓦwww.aerlingus.com
Air Canada Ⓦwww.aircanada.com

Air New Zealand www.airnewzealand.com
Bangkok Airways www.bangkokair.com
Berjaya Air www.berjaya-air.com
British Airways www.ba.com
Cathay Pacific www.cathaypacific.com
Emirates www.emirates.com
Etihad Airways www.etihadairways.com
EVA Air www.evaair.com
Firefly www.fireflyz.com.my
Jetstar www.jetstar.com
Korean Air www.koreanair.com
Krabi Airline www.krabi-airline.com
Lufthansa www.lufthansa.com
Malaysia Airlines www.malaysiaairlines.com
Qantas Airways www.qantas.com
Qatar Airways www.qatarairways.com
Silk Air www.silkair.com
Singapore Airlines www.singaporeair.com
South African Airways www.flysaa.com
Swiss www.swiss.com
Thai Airways www.thaiair.com
Tiger Airways www.tigerairways.com

Travel agents and tour operators worldwide

Adventure Center US 1-800/228-8747 or 510/654-1879, www.adventurecenter.com. Hiking and "soft adventure" specialist agent, offering dozens of packages to Thailand with well-regarded tour operators from all over the world.
All Points East (formerly Gecko Travel) UK 023/9225 8859, Thailand 081 885 9490; www.allpointseast.com. Southeast Asia specialist operating small-group adventure holidays with off-the-beaten-track itineraries. Also offers motorbike tours and family-oriented tours.
Andaman Discoveries Thailand www.andamandiscoveries.com. Village-based homestay community tourism programmes around Khuraburi on the north Andaman coast that allow visitors to experience daily activities such as batik making, cashew-nut farming and roof thatching.
Asian Trails Thailand www.asiantrails.net. Well-regarded company that does self-drive tours, cycling and motorcycling adventures, homestay programmes, river and sea cruises, plus more typical package tours.
Creative Events Asia Thailand www.creativeeventsasia.com. Wedding specialists for everything from paperwork to the ceremony and guest accommodation.
Crooked Trails US 206/383-9828, www.crookedtrails.com. Not-for-profit community-based tourism organization offering homestays in hill-tribe villages and along the Andaman coast, usually featuring volunteer work as well as cultural tours.
ETC (Educational Travel Centre) Thailand www.etc.co.th. Unusual tour programmes including Thai cooking holidays, rice-barge cruises to Ayutthaya and the River Kwai, and Meaningful Thailand options featuring homestays and/or short-term English teaching.
Flight Centre US 1-866/967/5351, Canada 1-877/967 5302, UK 0870/499 0040, Australia 13 31 33, New Zealand 0800/243 544, South Africa 0860 400 727; www.flightcentre.com. Guarantees to offer the lowest international air fares.
Grasshopper Adventures Thailand 087 929 5208, UK 020/8123 8144, US 818/921-7101, Australia 03/9016 3172; www.grasshopperadventures.com. Cycling tours around Bangkok and Chiang Mai and longer rides to Kanchanaburi and Krabi.
Hands Up Holidays UK 0800/783 3554 or 020/8871 0341, US & Canada 201/984-5372, New Zealand 06/347 1189; www.handsupholidays.com. Mostly two-week trips (or tailor-mades) combining luxury sightseeing with three to five days' volunteering in a hill-tribe village, at an orphanage, caring for elephants or teaching English.
Intrepid Travel US 1-800/970 7299, Canada 1-866/360-1151, UK 020 3147 7777, Ireland 01/524 0071, Australia 1300/364 512, New Zealand 0800/600 610; www.intrepidtravel.com. Well-regarded small-group adventure tour operator that uses local transport and travellers'-style accommodation.
Nature Trails Thailand www.naturetrailsthailand.com. Specialist bird-watching tours in Thailand's national parks.
North South Travel UK 01245/608 291, www.northsouthtravel.co.uk. Competitive travel agency, offering discounted fares worldwide. Profits are used to support projects in the developing world, especially the promotion of sustainable tourism.
Origin Asia Thailand www.alex-kerr.com. Cultural programmes that teach and explain living Thai arts such as dance, music, martial arts, textiles, flower offerings and cooking. Courses last from one day to a week and are held in Bangkok and Chiang Mai.
Responsible Travel UK 01273/600030, www.responsibletravel.com. One-stop shop for scores of fair-trade, ethically inclined holidays in Thailand, including trips that focus on wildlife, meditation, family activities and village life
Spice Roads Thailand www.spiceroads.com. Escorted bike tours through north, central and southern Thailand.
STA Travel US 1-800/781-4040, UK 0871/230/0040, Australia 134 782, New Zealand 0800/474 400, South Africa 0861/781 781; www.statravel.com. Worldwide specialists in

independent travel. Good discounts for students and under-26s.
Symbiosis UK ⓣ0845/123 2844, US ⓣ1-866/723-7903, ⓦwww.symbiosis-travel.com. Upmarket, off-the-beaten-track tours with an environmentally sensitive, fair-trade focus, including visiting hill tribes by mountain bike, as well as homestays on the Andaman coast and kayaking at Khao Sok and Ko Tarutao.
Telltale Travel UK ⓣ0800/011 2571, ⓦwww.telltaletravel.co.uk. Tailor-made tours that aim to offer as authentic an experience as possible, with accommodation mainly in upscale homestays in Bangkok and beyond.
Trailfinders UK ⓣ0845/058 5858, Ireland ⓣ01/677 7888, Australia ⓣ1300/780 212; ⓦwww.trailfinders.com. One of the best-informed and most efficient agents for independent travellers.
Travel Cuts US ⓣ1-800/592-CUTS, Canada ⓣ1-866/246-9762; ⓦwww.travelcuts.com. Popular, long-established specialists in budget travel, including student and youth discount offers.
USIT Ireland ⓣ01/602 1906, Northern Ireland ⓣ028/9032 7111, with branches in Athlone, Belfast, Cork, Dublin, Galway, Limerick and Waterford; ⓦwww.usit.ie. Ireland's main outlet for discounted, youth and student fares.

Travel via neighbouring countries

Sharing land borders with Burma, Laos, Cambodia and Malaysia, Thailand works well as part of many overland itineraries, both across Asia and between Europe and Australia. Bangkok is also one of the major regional flight hubs for Southeast Asia.

The main restrictions on overland routes in and out of Thailand are determined by where the permitted land crossings lie and by **visas**. For a guide to Thai visa rules see p.36. Details of visa requirements for travel to Thailand's immediate neighbours are outlined below, but should be double-checked before you travel. All **Asian embassies** are located in Bangkok (see p.207), but waiting times can be shorter at visa-issuing consulates outside the capital: China and India run consulates in Chiang Mai (see p.349), and Laos and Vietnam have consulates in Khon Kaen (see p.534). In Bangkok, many Khao San tour agents offer to get your visa for you, but beware: some are reportedly **faking the stamps**, which could get you in to pretty serious trouble, so it's safer to go to the embassy yourself.

The right paperwork is also crucial if you're planning to **drive your own car or motorbike** into Thailand; see the Golden Triangle Rider website (ⓦwww.gt-rider.com) for advice.

Burma

There is no overland access from **Burma** into Thailand and access in the opposite direction is restricted. Western tourists are only allowed to make limited-distance trips into Burma, usually just for the day, at Mae Sai, at Myawaddy near Mae Sot, and at Kaw Thaung (Victoria Point) near Ranong. The crossing at Three Pagodas Pass near Kanchanaburi was closed in 2007 and at the time of writing still had not reopened. At these borders you generally enter Burma on a temporary US$10 **visa** and then get a new fifteen-day visa when returning to Thailand; see relevant accounts for details. Tourists who intend to enter Burma by air can buy four-week tourist visas at the Burmese embassy in Bangkok for B800; apply to the embassy and you can collect the next day.

Cambodia

At the time of writing, six overland crossings on the **Thai–Cambodia border** are open to non-Thais. See the relevant town accounts for specific details on all the border crossings; for travellers' up-to-the-minute experiences, plus an account of the common **scam** on through-transport from Bangkok to Siem Reap, consult ⓦwww.talesofasia.com/cambodia-overland.htm.

Most travellers use either the crossing at Poipet, which has transport connections to Sisophon, Siem Reap and Phnom Penh and lies just across the border from the Thai town of Aranyaprathet (see p.457), with its transport to Chanthaburi and Bangkok; or they follow the route from Sihanoukville in Cambodia via Koh Kong and Hat Lek to Trat (see p.461), which is near Ko Chang on Thailand's east coast. The Trat route is the fastest option if you're travelling nonstop from Bangkok to Cambodia.

The crossings in northeast Thailand include the Chong Chom–O'Smach border pass, near Kap Choeng in Thailand's Surin province (see p.512), and the Sa Ngam–Choam border in Si Saket province (see p.520); from both these borders there's transport to Anlong Veng and Siem Reap. There are also two crossings in Chanthaburi province (see p.457), with transport to and from Pailin in Cambodia.

Visas for Cambodia are issued to travellers on arrival at Phnom Penh and Siem Reap airports, and at all the above-listed land borders; you need US$20 and two photos for this. If you do need to buy an advance thirty-day visa, you can do so online or from the Cambodian Embassy in Bangkok. This costs about B1000; apply before noon and you can collect your visa the following day after 5pm.

Laos and Vietnam

There are five main points along the **Lao border** where tourists can cross into Thailand: Houayxai (for Chiang Khong; see p.424); Vientiane (for Nong Khai; see p.548); Khammouan (aka Tha Khaek, for Nakhon Phanom; see p.555); Savannakhet (for Mukdahan; see p.558); and Pakxe (for Chong Mek; see p.527). All these borders can also be used as exits into Laos; see relevant town account for transport details.

Visas are required for all non-Thai visitors to Laos. A thirty-day **visa on arrival** can be bought for US$30–42 (depending on your nationality), plus one photo, at Vientiane, Louang Phabang and Pakxe airports, and all the above-listed land borders. Or you can buy one in advance from either the Lao Embassy in Bangkok or the Lao Consulate in Khon Kaen for B400–1700; these visas can be collected the following day – or in less than an hour if you pay an extra B200.

If you have the right Lao visa and Vietnamese exit stamp, you can travel **from Vietnam** to Thailand via Savannakhet in a matter of hours; you'll need to use Vietnam's Lao Bao border crossing, west of Dong Ha, where you can catch a bus to Savannakhet and then another bus across the new Mekong bridge to Mukdahan. All travellers into Vietnam need to buy a visa in advance. Thirty-day visas can take up to four working days to process at the embassy in Bangkok and cost B1000; the same visas are usually issued in 24 hours at the Vietnamese consulate in Khon Kaen.

Malaysia and Singapore

Travelling between Thailand and **Malaysia and Singapore** has in the past been a straightforward and very commonly used overland route, with plentiful connections by bus, minibus, share-taxi and train, most of them routed through the southern Thai city and transport hub of Hat Yai. However, because of the ongoing **violence in Thailand's deep south** (see p.771), all major Western governments are currently advising people not to travel to or through Songkhla, Pattani, Yala and Narathiwat provinces, unless essential (and consequently most insurance companies are not covering travel there). This encompasses Hat Yai and the following border crossings to and from Malaysia: at Padang Besar, on the main rail line connecting Butterworth in Malaysia (and, ultimately, Kuala Lumpur and Singapore) with Hat Yai and Bangkok; at Sungai Kolok, terminus of a railway line from Hat Yai and Bangkok, and at adjacent Ban Taba, both of which are connected by road to nearby Kota Bharu in Malaysia; and at the road crossings at Sadao, south of Hat Yai, and at Betong, south of Yala. (The routes towards Kota Bharu and Betong pass through particularly volatile territory, with martial law declared in Pattani, Yala and Narathiwat provinces; however, martial law is not in effect in Hat Yai itself nor the districts of Songkhla province through which the Bangkok–Butterworth rail line and the Hat Yai–Sadao road pass.)

Nevertheless, the provinces of Trang and Satun on the west coast are not affected, and it's still perfectly possible to travel

overland via Satun: by ferry between Satun's Thammalang pier and Kuala Perlis or the island of Langkawi, or by air-con minibus between Ban Khuan and Kangar (see p.789); or by boat between Ko Lanta, Ko Lipe and Langkawi (see p.784). For up-to-the-minute advice, consult your government travel advisory (see p.63).

Most Western tourists can spend thirty days in Malaysia and fourteen days in Singapore without having bought a visa beforehand, and there are useful Thai embassies or consulates in Kuala Lumpur, Kota Bharu, Penang and Singapore (see opposite).

Visas

There are three main entry categories for visitors to Thailand; for all of them, under International Air Travel Association rules, your passport should be valid for at least six months. As visa requirements are subject to frequent change, you should always consult before departure a Thai embassy or consulate, a reliable travel agent, or the Thai Ministry of Foreign Affairs' website at ⓦwww.mfa.go.th/web/2637.php. For further, unofficial but usually reliable, details on all visa matters, go to ⓦwww.thaivisa.com and especially their various moderated forums.

Most Western passport holders (that includes citizens of the UK, Ireland, the US, Canada, Australia, New Zealand and South Africa) are allowed to enter the country for short **stays** without having to apply for a visa – officially termed the **tourist visa exemption**. You'll be granted a thirty-day stay at an international airport but, in a recent change, only fifteen days at an overland border; the period of stay will be stamped into your passport by immigration officials upon entry. You're supposed to be able to somehow show proof of means of living while in the country (B10,000 per person, B20,000 per family), and in theory you may be put back on the next plane without it or sent back to get a sixty-day tourist visa from the nearest Thai embassy, but this is unheard of. You are also required to show proof of tickets to leave Thailand again within the allotted time. This is rarely checked by Thai immigration authorities, though there have been a few cases recently, mostly at the Cambodian border. However, if you have a one-way air ticket to Thailand and no evidence of onward travel arrangements, it's best to buy a tourist visa in advance: some airlines will stop you boarding the plane without one, as they would be liable for flying you back to your point of origin if you did happen to be stopped.

If you're fairly certain you may want to stay longer than fifteen/thirty days, then from the outset you should apply for a **sixty-day tourist visa** from a Thai embassy or consulate, accompanying your application – which generally takes several days to process – with your passport and two photos. The sixty-day visa currently costs, for example, US$35 or £28 in the UK; multiple-entry versions are available, costing US$35 or £28 per entry, which may be handy if you're going to be leaving and re-entering Thailand. Ordinary tourist visas are valid for three months, ie you must enter Thailand within three months of the visa being issued by the Thai embassy or consulate, while multiple-entry versions are valid for six months. Visa application forms can be downloaded from, for example, the Thai Ministry of Foreign Affairs' website.

Thai embassies also consider applications for **ninety-day non-immigrant visas** (£45 or US$65, for example, single entry, £100 or US$175 multiple-entry) as long as you can offer a reason for your visit, such as study, business or visiting family/friends (there are different categories of non-immigrant visa for which different levels of proof are needed). As it can be a hassle to organize a ninety-day visa, it's generally easier to apply for a thirty-day extension to your sixty-day visa once inside Thai borders.

It's not a good idea to **overstay** your visa limits. Once you're at the airport or the border, you'll have to pay a fine of B500 per day before you can leave Thailand. More importantly, however, if you're in the country with an expired visa and you get involved with police or immigration officials for any reason, however trivial, they are obliged to take you to court, possibly imprison you, and deport you.

Border runs, extensions and re-entry permits

Setting aside the caveats about proof of funds and onward tickets above, it's generally easy to get a new fifteen-day tourist visa exemption by hopping **across the border** into a neighbouring country and back. Such tourist visa exemptions can be **extended** within Thailand for up to a further ten days, sixty-day tourist visas for a further thirty days, at the discretion of immigration officials; extensions cost B1900 and are issued over the counter at immigration offices (*kaan khao muang*; ⓣ1111 for 24hr information in English, ⓦwww.immigration.go.th) in nearly every provincial capital – most offices ask for one or two photos as well, plus two photocopies of the main pages of your passport including your Thai arrival card, arrival stamp and visa. Many Khao San tour agents offer to get your visa extension for you, but beware: some are reportedly faking the stamps, which could get you into serious trouble. Immigration offices in Bangkok and at Suvarnabhumi Airport, as well as at border checkpoints, also issue **re-entry permits** (B1000 single re-entry, B3800 multiple) if you want to leave the country and come back again while maintaining the validity of your existing visa.

Thai embassies and consulates abroad

For a full listing of Thai diplomatic missions abroad, consult the Thai Ministry of Foreign Affairs' website at ⓦwww.mfa.go.th/web/10.php.

Australia 111 Empire Circuit, Yarralumla, Canberra ACT 2600 ⓣ02/6206 0100, ⓦcanberra.thaiembassy.org; plus consulate at 131 Macquarrie St, Sydney, NSW 2000 ⓣ02/9241 2542–3, ⓦthaiconsulatesydney.org.
Burma 94 Pyay Rd, Dagon Township, Rangoon ⓣ01/226721.
Cambodia 196 Preah Norodom Blvd, Sangkat Tonle Bassac, Khan Chamcar Mon, Phnom Penh ⓣ023/726306–10, ⓦwww.thaiembassy.org/phnompenh.
Canada 180 Island Park Drive, Ottawa, ON, K1Y 0A2 ⓣ613/722-4444, ⓦwww.magma.ca/~thaiott; plus consulate at 1040 Burrard St, Vancouver, BC, V6Z 2R9 ⓣ604/687-1143, ⓦwww.thaicongenvancouver.org.
Laos Vientiane, ⓦwww.thaiembassy.org/vientiane: embassy at Avenue Kaysone Phomvihane, Saysettha District ⓣ021/214581–2, consular section at Unit 15 Bourichane Road, Ban Phone Si Nuan, Muang Si Sattanak ⓣ021/453916; plus consulate at Khanthabouly District, Savannakhet Province, PO Box 513 ⓣ041/212373.
Malaysia 206 Jalan Ampang, 50450 Kuala Lumpur ⓣ03/2148 8222, ⓦwww.thaiembassy.org/kualalumpur; plus consulates at 4426 Jalan Pengkalan Chepa, 15400 Kota Bharu ⓣ09/748 2545; and 1 Jalan Tunku Abdul Rahman, 10350 Penang ⓣ04/226 9484.
New Zealand 2 Cook St, PO Box 17226, Karori, Wellington ⓣ04/476 8616–9, ⓦwww.thaiembassynz.org.nz.
Singapore 370 Orchard Road, Singapore 238870 ⓣ6737 2158, ⓦwww.thaiembassy.sg.
South Africa 428 Pretorius/Hill St, Arcadia, Pretoria 0083 ⓣ012/342 5470, ⓦwww.thaiembassy.co.za.
UK & Ireland 29–30 Queens Gate, London SW7 5JB ⓣ020/7589 2944, ⓦwww.thaiembassyuk.org.uk. Visa applications by post are not accepted here, but can be sent to various honorary consulates, including those in Hull (ⓦwww.thaiconsul-uk.com) and Dublin (ⓦwww.thaiconsulateireland.com).
US 1024 Wisconsin Ave NW, Suite 401, Washington, DC 20007 ⓣ202/944-3600, ⓦwww.thaiembdc.org; plus consulates at 700 North Rush St, Chicago, IL 60611 ⓣ312/664-3129, ⓦwww.thaichicago.net; 611 North Larchmont Blvd, 2nd Floor, Los Angeles, CA 90004 ⓣ323/962-9574, ⓦwww.thai-la.net; and 351 E 52nd St, New York, NY 10022 ⓣ212/754-1770, ⓦwww.thaiconsulnewyork.com.
Vietnam 63–65 Hoang Dieu St, Hanoi ⓣ04/823-5092–3; plus consulate at 77 Tran Quoc Thao St, District 3, Ho Chi Minh City ⓣ08/932-7637–8, ⓦwww.thaiembassy.org/hochiminhcity.

Health

Although Thailand's climate, wildlife and cuisine present Western travellers with fewer health worries than in many Asian destinations, it's as well to know in advance what the risks might be, and what preventive or curative measures you should take.

For a start, there's no need to bring huge supplies of non-prescription medicines with you, as Thai **pharmacies** (*raan khai yaa*; typically open daily 8.30am–8pm) are well stocked with local and international branded medicaments, and of course they are generally much less expensive than at home. Nearly all pharmacies are run by trained English-speaking pharmacists, who are usually the best people to talk to if your symptoms aren't acute enough to warrant seeing a doctor. The British pharmacy chain, Boots, now has branches in many big cities and operates a 24-hour health advice line (☎1800/200444 or 02 233 0575). These are the best place to stock up on some Western products such as **tampons** (which Thai women do not use).

Hospital (*rong phayabaan*) cleanliness and efficiency vary, but generally hygiene and healthcare standards are good and the ratio of medical staff to patients is considerably higher than in most parts of the West. As with head pharmacists, doctors speak English. Several Bangkok hospitals are highly regarded (see p.207), and all provincial capitals have at least one hospital: if you need to get to one, ask at your accommodation for advice on, and possibly transport to, the nearest or most suitable. In the event of a major health crisis, get someone to contact your embassy (see p.207) and insurance company – it may be best to get yourself transported to Bangkok or even home.

There have been outbreaks of **Avian Influenza** (**bird flu**) in domestic poultry and wild birds in Thailand which have led to a small number of human fatalities, believed to have arisen through close contact with infected poultry. There has been no evidence of human-to-human transmission in Thailand, and the risk to humans is believed to be very low. However, as a precaution, you should avoid visiting live-animal markets and other places where you may come into close contact with birds, and ensure that poultry and egg dishes are thoroughly cooked.

Inoculations

There are no compulsory **inoculation** requirements for people travelling to Thailand from the West, but you should consult a doctor or other health professional, preferably at least four weeks in advance of your trip, for the latest information on recommended immunizations. Most doctors strongly advise vaccinations or boosters against polio, tetanus, diphtheria, hepatitis A and, in many cases, typhoid, and in some cases they might also recommend protecting yourself against cholera, Japanese B encephalitis, rabies, hepatitis B and tuberculosis. There is currently no vaccine against malaria; for information on prophylaxis, see opposite. If you forget to have all your inoculations before leaving home, or don't leave yourself sufficient time, you can get them in Bangkok at, for example, the Thai Red Cross Society's Queen Saovabha Institute or Global Doctor; see p.207 for details.

Mosquito-borne diseases

Mosquitoes in Thailand spread not only malaria, but also diseases such as dengue fever, especially during the rainy season. The main message, therefore, is to **avoid being bitten** by mosquitoes. You should smother yourself and your clothes in **mosquito repellent** containing the chemical compound DEET, reapplying regularly (shops, guest houses and department stores all over Thailand stock it, but if you want the highest-strength repellent, or convenient roll-ons or sprays, do your shopping before you leave home). DEET is strong stuff, and if you have sensitive skin, a natural alternative is citronella (available in the UK as Mosi-guard), made from a blend of eucalyptus oils; the Thai version is made with lemon grass.

At night you should sleep either under a **mosquito net** sprayed with DEET or in a bedroom with **mosquito screens** across the windows (or in an enclosed air-con room). Accommodation in tourist spots nearly always provides screens or a net (check both for holes), but if you're planning to go way off the beaten track or want the security of having your own mosquito net just in case, wait until you get to Bangkok to buy one, where department stores sell them for much less than you'd pay in the West. Plug-in insecticide vaporizers, knock-down insect sprays and mosquito coils – also widely available in Thailand – help keep the insects at bay; electronic "buzzers" are useless.

Malaria

Thailand is **malarial**, with the disease being carried by mosquitoes that bite from dusk to dawn, but the risks involved vary across the country.

There is a significant risk of malaria, mainly in rural and forested areas, in a narrow strip along the **borders with Burma** (excluding, for example, Chiang Rai and Kanchanaburi towns, and resorts and road and rail routes along the Gulf coast), **Laos** and **Cambodia** (including Ko Chang). The only anti-malarial drugs that are currently likely to be effective in these areas are **Doxycycline** and **Malarone**, whose use should be discussed with your travel health adviser, especially as prophylaxis advice can change from year to year. Doxycycline is sold across the counter in Thai branches of Boots but Malarone is not currently available in Thailand.

Elsewhere in Thailand the risk of malaria is considered to be so low that anti-malarial tablets are not advised.

The **signs of malaria** are often similar to flu, but are very variable. The incubation period for malignant malaria, which can be fatal, is usually 7–28 days, but it can take up to a year for symptoms of the benign form to occur. The most important symptom is a raised temperature of at least 38°C beginning a week or more after the first potential exposure to malaria: if you suspect anything, go to a hospital or clinic immediately.

Dengue fever

Dengue fever, a debilitating and occasionally fatal viral disease that is particularly prevalent during and just after the rainy season, is on the increase throughout tropical Asia, and is endemic to many areas of Thailand, especially in the south. Unlike malaria, dengue fever is spread by mosquitoes that can bite during daylight hours, so you should also use mosquito repellent during the day. Symptoms include fever, headaches, fierce joint and muscle pain ("breakbone fever" is another name for dengue), and possibly a rash, and usually develop between five and eight days after being bitten.

There is no vaccine against dengue fever; the only treatment is lots of rest, liquids and paracetamol (or any other acetaminophen painkiller, not aspirin), though more serious cases may require hospitalization.

Rabies

Rabies is widespread in Thailand, mainly carried by dogs (between four and seven percent of stray dogs in Bangkok are reported to be rabid), but also cats and monkeys. It is transmitted by bites, scratches or even occasionally licks. Dogs are everywhere in Thailand and even if kept as pets they're never very well cared for; hopefully their mangy appearance will discourage the urge to pat them, as you should steer well clear of them. Rabies is invariably fatal if the patient waits until symptoms begin, though modern vaccines and treatments are very effective and deaths are rare. The important thing is, if you are bitten, licked or scratched by an animal, to vigorously clean the wound with soap and disinfect it, preferably with something containing iodine, and to seek medical advice regarding treatment right away.

Other bites and stings

Thailand's seas are home to a few dangerous creatures that you should look out for, notably **jellyfish**, which tend to be washed towards the beach by rough seas during the monsoon season but can appear at any time of year. All manner of stinging and non-stinging jellyfish can be found in Thailand – as a general rule, those with the longest tentacles tend to have the worst stings – but reports of serious incidents are rare; ask around at your resort or at a local dive shop to see if there have been any sightings of poisonous varieties. You also need to be wary of poisonous **sea snakes**, **sea urchins** and a couple of less conspicuous species – **stingrays**, which often lie buried in the sand, and **stonefish**, whose potentially lethal venomous spikes are easily stepped on because the fish look like stones and lie motionless on the sea bed.

If **stung or bitten** you should always seek medical advice as soon as possible, but there are a few ways of alleviating the pain or administering your own first-aid in the meantime. If you're stung by a jellyfish, wash the affected area with salt water (not fresh water) and, if possible, with vinegar (failing that, ammonia, citrus fruit juice or even urine may do the trick), and try to remove the fragments of tentacles from the skin with a gloved hand, forceps, thick cloth or credit card. The best way to minimize the risk of stepping on the toxic spines of sea urchins, stingrays and stonefish is to wear thick-soled shoes, though these cannot provide total protection; sea urchin spikes should be removed after softening the skin with ointment, though some people recommend applying urine to help dissolve the spines; for stingray and stonefish stings, alleviate the pain by immersing the wound in hot water while awaiting help.

In the case of a **poisonous snake bite**, don't try sucking out the poison or applying a tourniquet: wrap up and immobilize the bitten limb and try to stay still and calm until medical help arrives; all provincial hospitals in Thailand carry supplies of antivenins. For more on Thai snakes, see p.830.

Some of Thailand's wilder, less developed beaches are plagued by **sandflies**, tiny, barely visible midges whose bites can trigger an allergic response, leaving big red weals and an unbearable itch, and possible infection if scratched too vigorously. Many islanders say that slathering yourself in (widely available) coconut oil is the best deterrent as sandflies apparently don't like the smell. Applying locally made camphor-based yellow oil (see p.467) quells the itch, but you may need to resort to antihistamines for the inflammation. **Leeches** aren't dangerous but can be a bother when walking in forested areas, especially during and just after the rainy season. The most effective way to get leeches off your skin is to burn them with a lighted cigarette, or douse them in salt; oily suntan lotion or insect repellent sometimes makes them lose their grip and fall off.

Worms and flukes

Worms can be picked up through the soles of your feet, so avoid going barefoot. They can also be ingested by eating undercooked meat, and liver **flukes** by eating raw or undercooked freshwater fish. Worms which cause schistosomiasis (bilharziasis) by attaching themselves to your bladder or intestines can be found in freshwater rivers and lakes. The risk of contracting this disease is low, but you should avoid swimming in the southern reaches of the Mekong River and in most freshwater lakes.

Digestive problems

By far the most common travellers' complaint in Thailand, **digestive troubles** are often caused by contaminated food and water, or sometimes just by an overdose of unfamiliar foodstuffs. For advice on food and water hygiene, see pp.53 and 56.

Stomach trouble usually manifests itself as simple **diarrhoea**, which should clear up without medical treatment within three to seven days and is best combated by drinking lots of fluids. If this doesn't work, you're in danger of getting **dehydrated** and should take some kind of rehydration solution, either a commercial sachet of ORS (oral rehydration solution), sold in all Thai pharmacies, or a do-it-yourself version, which can be made by adding a handful of sugar and a pinch of salt to every litre of boiled or bottled water (soft drinks are not a viable alternative). If you can eat, avoid fatty foods.

Anti-diarrhoeal agents such as Imodium are useful for blocking you up on long bus journeys, but only attack the symptoms and may prolong infections; an antibiotic such as ciprofloxacin, however, can often reduce a typical attack of traveller's diarrhoea to one day. If the diarrhoea persists for a week or more, or if you have blood or mucus in your stools, or an accompanying fever, go to a doctor or hospital.

HIV and AIDS

AIDS is widespread in Thailand, primarily because of the sex trade (see p.168). **Condoms** (*meechai*) are sold in pharmacies, convenience stores, department stores, hairdressers and even street markets.

Should you need to have treatment involving an **injection** at a hospital, try to check that the needle has been sterilized first; this is not always practicable, however, so you might consider carrying your own syringes. Due to rigorous screening methods, Thailand's medical blood supply is now considered safe from HIV/AIDS infection.

Medical resources for travellers

UK and Ireland

Hospital for Tropical Diseases Travel Clinic London ⓣ0845/155/5000 or 020/7387 4411, ⓦwww.thehtd.org.

MASTA (Medical Advisory Service for Travellers Abroad) UK ⓣ0870/606 2782 or ⓦwww.masta.org for the nearest clinic.

NHS Travel Health Website ⓦwww.fitfortravel.scot.nhs.uk.

Travel Medicine Services Belfast ⓣ028/9031 5220.

Tropical Medical Bureau Dublin ⓣ1850/487674, ⓦwww.tmb.ie.

US and Canada

Canadian Society for International Health ⓣ613/241-5785, ⓦwww.csih.org. Extensive list of travel health centres.

CDC ⓦwwwn.cdc.gov/travel. Official US government travel health site.

International Society for Travel Medicine ⓣ1-770/736-7060, ⓦwww.istm.org. Has a full list of travel health clinics.

Australia, New Zealand and South Africa

Travellers' Medical and Vaccination Centre ⓦwww.tmvc.com.au, in Australia ⓣ1300/658 844. Travel clinics in Australia, New Zealand and South Africa.

Getting around

Travel in Thailand is both inexpensive and efficient, if not always speedy. Unless you travel by plane, long-distance journeys in Thailand can be arduous, especially if a shoestring budget restricts you to hard seats and no air-conditioning.

Nonetheless, the wide range of transport options makes travelling around Thailand easier than elsewhere in Southeast Asia. **Buses** are fast and frequent, and can be quite luxurious; **trains** are slower but safer and offer more chance of sleeping during overnight trips; moreover, if travelling by day you're likely to follow a more scenic route by rail than by road. Inter-town **songthaews**, **share-taxis** and air-con **minibuses** are handy, and **ferries** provide easy access to all major islands. Local transport comes in all sorts of permutations, both public and chartered.

For an idea of the frequency and duration of transport services, check the **travel details** section at the end of each chapter.

Inter-town buses

Buses, overall the most convenient way of getting around the country, come in two main categories: **ordinary** (*rot thammadaa*;

usually orange-coloured) and **air-con** (*rot air* or *rot thua*; usually blue). Ordinary and many air-con buses are run by Baw Khaw Saw (BKS), the government-controlled transport company, while privately owned air-con buses, some of which operate from Baw Khaw Saw terminals, also ply the most popular long-distance routes. Be warned that long-distance overnight buses, particularly the private air-con buses, seem to be involved in more than their fair share of accidents; because of this, some travellers prefer to do the overnight journeys by train and then make a shorter bus connection to their destination.

Ordinary buses

Ordinary buses are incredibly inexpensive and generally cover short-range routes between main towns (up to 150km), running frequently during daylight hours. Each bus is staffed by a team of two or three – the driver, the fare collector and the optional "stop" and "go" yeller – who often personalize the vehicle with stereo systems, stickers, jasmine garlands and the requisite Buddha image or amulet. With an entertaining team and eye-catching scenery, journeys can be fun, but there are drawbacks. For a start, the teams work on a commission basis, so they pack as many people in as possible and might hang around for thirty minutes after they're due to leave in the hope of cramming in a few extra. They also stop so often that their average speed of 60km/hr can only be achieved by hurtling along at breakneck speeds between pick-ups, often propelled by amphetamine-induced craziness. To flag down an ordinary bus from the roadside you should wait at the nearest **bus shelter**, or **sala**, usually located at intervals along the main long-distance bus route through town or on the fringes of any decent-sized settlement, for example on the main highway that skirts the edge of town. Where there is only a bus shelter on the "wrong" side of the road, you can be sure that buses travelling in both directions will stop there for any waiting passengers; simply leave your bag on the right side of the road to alert the bus driver and wait in the shade. If you're in the middle of nowhere with no *sala* in sight, any ordinary bus should stop for you if you flag it down.

Air-con buses

Most Thais making journeys of 100km or more choose to travel by **air-con bus**, and on many routes, including most services out of Bangkok, non-air-con options have been replaced by second-class air-con vehicles. On the busiest routes air-con services depart every twenty to thirty minutes, while on less popular journeys there may be only three or four a day. Whatever the frequency, passengers are often allotted specific seats, and on the longest journeys may get blankets, snacks and nonstop DVDs.

On some routes you have a choice of three or even four classes of air-con bus, with the **second-class** service being the cheapest, slowest (with the most frequent stops), and least comfortable (no toilets, for instance), and the **VIP** (or even "super VIP") services having the fewest seats (generally 24–32 instead of 44) and more leg room for reclining.

Air-con services can cost up to twice as much as the ordinary buses (two or three times as much for VIP buses). Not all air-con buses have toilets, so it's always worth using bus-station facilities before you board; and make sure you have some warm clothes, as temperatures can get chilly, even with the blanket.

On a lot of long-distance routes **private air-con buses** are indistinguishable from government ones and operate out of the same Baw Khaw Saw bus terminals. The major private companies, such as Nakhonchai (☎02 936 0009) and Sombat Tour (☎02 570 9030), have roughly similar fares, though naturally with more scope for price variation, and offer comparable facilities and standards of service. The opposite is unfortunately true of a number of the smaller, private, unlicensed companies, several of which have a poor reputation for service and comfort, but gear themselves towards *farang* (foreigners) customers with bargain fares and convenient timetables. The long-distance tour buses that run **from Thanon Khao San** in Banglamphu to Chiang Mai and Surat Thani are a case in point; travellers on these routes frequently complain about shabby furnishings, ineffective air-conditioning, unhelpful (even aggressive) drivers, lateness and a frightening lack of safety awareness – and there are frequent reports of theft from luggage on these routes, too, and even the spraying of "sleeping gas" so that hand luggage can be rifled without interruption. Generally it's best to travel with the government or licensed private bus companies from the main bus terminals (who have a reputation with their regular Thai customers to maintain) or to go by train instead – the extra comfort and peace of mind are well worth the extra baht.

Tickets and timetables

Tickets for all buses can be bought from the departure terminals, but for ordinary buses it's normal to buy them on board. Air-con buses may operate from a separate station or office, and tickets for the more popular routes should be booked a day in advance. As a rough indication of **fares**, a trip from Bangkok to Surat Thani, a distance of 640km, costs B500–800 for VIP, B490 for first-class air-con and B400 for second-class air-con.

Long-distance buses often depart in clusters around the same time (early morning or late at night for example), leaving a gap of five or more hours during the day with no services at all. Local TAT offices sometimes keep up-to-date bus **timetables** in English, or go to the bus terminal the day before you want to leave and check with staff there. That said, if you turn up at a bus terminal in the morning for a medium-length journey (150–300km), you're almost always guaranteed to be on your way within two hours.

Songthaews, share-taxis and air-conditioned minibuses

In rural areas, the bus network is often supplemented by **songthaews** (literally "two rows"), which are open-ended vans (or occasionally cattle-trucks) onto which the drivers squash as many passengers as possible on two facing benches, leaving latecomers to swing off the running board at the back. As well as their essential role within towns (see p.46), songthaews ply set routes from larger towns out to their surrounding suburbs and villages, and, where there's no call for a regular bus service, between small towns: some have destinations written on in Thai, but few are numbered. In most towns you'll find the songthaew "terminal" near the market; to pick one up between destinations just flag it down. To indicate to the driver that you want to get out, the normal practice is to rap hard with a coin on the metal railings as you approach the spot (or press the bell if there is one).

In the deep south (see p.770) they do things with a little more style – **share-taxis** connect many of the major towns, though they are inexorably being replaced by more comfortable **air-conditioned minibuses**. Many similar private air-con minibuses are now cropping up on popular routes elsewhere in the country (eg Ayutthaya–Bangkok, Trat–Hat Lek and Chiang Mai–Pai); they generally depart frequently and cover the distance faster than the ordinary bus service, but can be uncomfortably cramped when full and are not ideal for travellers with huge rucksacks, who may be required to pay extra. As with full-sized buses (see opposite), be wary of unlicensed private companies that offer minibuses solely for farangs from Bangkok's Thanon Khao San.

In many cases, long-distance songthaews and air-con minibuses will drop you at an exact address (for example a particular guest house) if you warn them far enough in advance. As a rule, the **cost** of inter-town songthaews is comparable to that of air-con buses, that of air-con minibuses perhaps a shade more.

Trains

Managed by the State Railway of Thailand (SRT), the **rail** network consists of four main lines and a few branch lines. The **Northern**

Train information

For 24hr **train information**, phone the State Railway of Thailand (SRT) in Bangkok on ⓣ02 220 4444, or on its free hotline ⓣ1690. The SRT website (ⓦwww.railway.co.th) carries English-language timetables, a breakdown of ticket prices from Bangkok and a link to the new booking website, ⓦwww.thairailwayticket.com.

Line connects Bangkok with Chiang Mai via Ayutthaya, Lopburi, Phitsanulok and Lampang. The **Northeastern Line** splits into two just beyond Ayutthaya, the lower branch running eastwards to Ubon Ratchathani via Khorat and Surin, the more northerly branch linking the capital with Nong Khai (with a short extension over the Mekong into Laos; see p.548) via Khon Kaen and Udon Thani. The **Eastern Line** also has two branches, one of which runs from Bangkok to Aranyaprathet on the Cambodian border, the other of which connects Bangkok with Si Racha and Pattaya. The **Southern Line** extends via Hua Hin, Chumphon and Surat Thani, with spurs off to Trang and Nakhon Si Thammarat, to Hat Yai (see the travel warning on p.769), where it branches: one line continues down the west coast of Malaysia, via Butterworth, where you change trains for Kuala Lumpur and Singapore; the other heads down the eastern side of the peninsula to Sungai Kolok on the Thailand–Malaysia border (20km from Pasir Mas on Malaysia's interior railway). At Nakhon Pathom a branch of this line veers off to Nam Tok via Kanchanaburi – this is all that's left of the Death Railway, of *Bridge on the River Kwai* notoriety (see p.231).

Fares depend on the class of seat, whether or not you want air-conditioning, and on the speed of the train; those quoted here exclude the "speed" supplements, which are discussed below. Hard, wooden or thinly padded third-class seats are a bit cheaper than buses (Bangkok–Surat Thani B297, or B397 with air-con), and are fine for about three hours, after which numbness sets in. For longer journeys you'd be wise to opt for the padded and often reclining seats in second class (Bangkok–Surat B438, or B578 with air-con). On long-distance trains, you also usually have the option of second-class berths (Bangkok–Surat B498–548, or B758–848 with air-con), with day seats that convert into comfortable curtained-off bunks in the evening; lower bunks, which are more expensive than upper, have a few cubic centimetres more of space, a little more shade from the lights in the carriage, and a window. Female passengers can sometimes request a berth in an all-female section of a carriage. Travelling first class (Bangkok–Surat B1279) means a two-person air-con sleeping compartment, complete with washbasin.

There are several different **types of train**: slowest of all is the third-class-only Ordinary service, which is generally (but not always) available only on short and medium-length journeys and has no speed supplement. Next comes the misleadingly named Rapid train (B50–110 supplement), a trip on which from Bangkok to Surat Thani, for example, takes twelve or thirteen hours; the Express (B150 supplement) which does the same route in around twelve hours; and the Special Express (B170 supplement) which covers the ground in between nine and eleven hours. Among the last-mentioned, fastest of all are the mostly daytime Special Express Diesel Railcars, which can generally be relied on to run on time. Nearly all long-distance trains have **dining cars**, and rail staff will also bring meals to your seat.

Booking at least one day in advance is strongly recommended for second- and first-class seats on all lengthy journeys, and sleepers should be booked as far in advance as possible (reservations open sixty days before departure). You can make bookings for any journey in Thailand at the train station in any major town, as well as by phone, though you have to pay for the tickets before 4pm the next day at a train station. It's now also possible to book online, at least three days in advance, at Ⓦwww.thairailwayticket.com, though currently the website is allocated only ten percent of available seats. Otherwise, you can arrange advance bookings over the internet with reputable Thai travel agencies such as Traveller 2000 (Ⓦwww.traveller2000.com) or Thai Focus (Ⓦwww.thaifocus.com). For details on how to book trains out of Bangkok **in person**, see p.202.

The SRT publishes clear and fairly accurate free **timetables** in English, detailing types of trains and classes available on each route, as well as fares; the best place to get hold of them is over the counter at Bangkok's Hualamphong Station or, if you're lucky, the TAT office in Bangkok. These English-only timetables cover the services that the SRT think will appeal to tourists; other, slow trains covering short- and medium-length routes are also shown on mostly Thai national timetables, and there are more detailed local timetables covering, for example, the Bangkok–Ayutthaya route.

The SRT also sells twenty-day **rail passes** (available only in Thailand), covering unlimited train journeys in second- (or third-) class seats for B1500, or B3000 with all supplements thrown in. However, unless you're on a whistle-stop tour of all four corners of the country, the rail network is not really extensive enough to make them pay.

Ferries

Regular **ferries** connect all major islands with the mainland, and for the vast majority of crossings you simply buy your ticket on board. Safety standards are generally just about adequate but there have been a small number of sinkings in recent years – avoid travelling on boats that are clearly overloaded or in poor condition. In tourist areas competition ensures that prices are kept low, and fares tend to vary with the speed of the crossing, if anything: thus Chumphon–Ko Tao costs between B200 (6hr) and B550 (1hr 30min).

On the east coast and the Andaman coast boats generally operate a reduced service during the monsoon season (May–Oct), when the more remote spots become inaccessible. Ferries in the Samui archipelago are fairly constant year-round. Details on island connections are given in the relevant chapters.

Flights

The domestic arm of **Thai Airways** (Ⓣ02 356 1111, Ⓦwww.thaiair.com) offers the widest choice of internal flights, flying from Bangkok to Chiang Mai, Chiang Rai, Hat Yai, Khon Kaen, Ko Samui, Krabi, Phitsanulok, Phuket, Surat Thani, Ubon Ratchathani and Udon Thani, as well as from Chiang Mai to Mae Hong Son and Phuket. However, with deregulation, several smaller airlines have recently broken into the volatile market, including one or two cheap, no-frills companies. **Bangkok Airways** (Ⓣ02 265 5555, Ⓦwww.bangkokair.com) is Thai Airways' main competitor at home, covering major destinations from Bangkok such as Chiang Mai, Ko Samui, Phuket, Sukhothai and Trat, as well as Chiang Mai–Ko Samui, a Pattaya–Ko Samui–Phuket triangle and Ko Samui–Krabi.

Among the newcomers on the scene, **Air Asia** (Ⓣ02 515 9999, Ⓦwww.airasia.com) currently flies from Bangkok to Chiang Mai, Chiang Rai, Hat Yai, Krabi, Phuket, Ranong, Surat Thani, Ubon Ratchathani and Udon Thani; **Nok Air** (Ⓣ1318 or 02 900 9955, Ⓦwww.nokair.com), part-owned by Thai Airways, covers Bangkok to Chiang Mai, Hat Yai, Nakhon Si Thammarat, Phuket, Trang and Udon Thani, and, in partnership with SGA Airlines, Bangkok to Hua Hin and Chiang Mai to Chiang Rai, Mae Hong Son and Pai; **One-Two-Go** (Ⓣ1126 or 02 229 4100–1, Ⓦwww.fly12go.com), operated by Orient Thai Airlines, has flights from Bangkok to Chiang Mai, Chiang Rai, Hat Yai, Phuket and Trang; and **PB Air** (Ⓣ02 261 0222, Ⓦwww.pbair.com), in partnership with Thai Airways, flies from Bangkok to Buriram, Lampang, Mae Hong Son, Nakhon Phanom, Nan, Roi-Et and Sakon Nakhon. These routings change surprisingly frequently and at the very minor airports, schedules are erratic and flights are sometimes cancelled, so always check ahead.

In some instances a flight can save you days of travelling: a flight from Chiang Mai to Phuket with Thai Airways, for example, takes two hours, as against a couple of days by meandering train and/or bus. To give an idea of **fares**, on the Bangkok–Chiang Mai route Bangkok Airways charges around B3700 one way, while advanced-purchase, inflexible tickets with Thai cost around B2400 and as little as B1790 with Nok Air or B1350 (plus B50 per checked-in bag) with Air Asia.

If you're planning to use the internal network a lot, you might want to consider buying an **airpass**, although certain taxes and fees are extra and the passes must be bought outside Thailand from one of the airlines' offices or a travel agent. Of the two available, Bangkok Airways' Discovery Airpass is the easier to use: you buy between three and six flight coupons, generally for US$60 each, confirming the first flight before departure, though the others (valid for two months after the first flight) can be left open; a coupon for Bangkok–Ko Samui costs US$75, while the coupons are not valid on the Chiang Mai–Ko Samui route. (Similar coupons are available for international flights by Bangkok Airways and flights with its partners, Siem

Reap Airways and Lao Airlines.) Thai Airways' Discover Thailand pass covers three one-way flights within a three-month period for US$199; you fix the routes when you buy the pass, but dates of travel can be changed in Thailand. Up to five additional flights can be added for US$59 each.

Local transport

Most sizeable towns have some kind of **local transport system**, comprising a network of buses, songthaews or even longtail boats, with set fares and routes but not rigid timetabling – in many cases vehicles wait until they're full before they leave.

Buses and songthaews

Larger cities such as Bangkok, Khorat, Ubon Ratchathani and Phitsanulok have a **local bus** network which usually extends to the suburbs and operates from dawn till dusk (through the night in Bangkok). Most vehicles display route numbers in Western numerals, and you pay the conductor B6–15 depending on your destination (on some routes you can choose to take air-con buses, for which you pay a few baht extra).

Within medium-sized and large towns, the main transport role is often played by **songthaews**. The size and shape of vehicle used varies from town to town – and in some places they're known as "tuk-tuks" from the noise they make, not to be confused with the smaller tuk-tuks, described below, that operate as private taxis – but all have the tell-tale two facing benches in the back. In some towns, especially in the northeast, songthaews follow fixed routes; in others such as Chiang Mai, they act as communal taxis, picking up a number of people who are going in roughly the same direction and taking each of them right to their destination. To hail a songthaew just flag it down, and to indicate that you want to get out, either rap hard with a coin on the metal railings, or ring the bell if there is one. Fares within towns are around B10–20, depending on distance.

Longtail boats

Wherever there's a decent public waterway, there'll be a **longtail boat** ready to ferry you along it. Another great Thai trademark, these elegant, streamlined boats are powered by deafening diesel engines – sometimes custom-built, more often adapted from cars or trucks – which drive a propeller mounted on a long shaft that is swivelled for steering. Longtails carry between eight and twenty passengers: generally you'll have to charter the whole boat, but on popular fixed routes, for example between small, inshore islands and the mainland, it's cheaper to wait until the boatman gets his quorum.

Taxi services

Taxis also come in many guises, and in bigger towns you can often choose between taking a tuk-tuk, a samlor and a motorbike taxi. The one thing common to all modes of chartered transport, bar Bangkok's metered taxis, is that you must establish the **fare** beforehand: although drivers nearly always pitch their first offers too high, they do calculate with traffic and time of day in mind, as well as according to distance – if successive drivers scoff at your price, you know you've got it wrong.

Tuk-tuks

Named after the noise of its excruciatingly unsilenced engine, the three-wheeled, open-sided **tuk-tuk** is the classic Thai vehicle. Painted in primary colours, tuk-tuks blast their way round towns and cities on two-stroke engines, zipping around faster than any car and taking corners on two wheels. They aren't as dangerous as they look though, and can be an exhilarating way to get around, as long as you're not too fussy about exhaust fumes. Fares come in at around B50 for a medium-length journey (over B100 in Bangkok) regardless of the number of passengers – three is the safe maximum, though six is not uncommon. See p.110 for advice on how to avoid being ripped off by Bangkok tuk-tuk drivers.

Samlors

Tuk-tuks are also sometimes known as samlors (literally "three wheels"), but the original **samlors** are tricycle rickshaws propelled by pedal power alone. Slower and a great deal more stately than tuk-tuks, samlors still operate in one or two towns around the country.

A further permutation are the motorized samlors (often called "skylabs" in northeastern Thailand), where the driver relies on a motorbike rather than a bicycle to propel passengers to their destination. They look much the same as cycle samlors, but often sound as noisy as tuk-tuks.

Motorbike taxis

Even faster and more precarious than tuk-tuks, **motorbike taxis** feature both in towns and in out-of-the-way places. In towns – where the drivers are identified by coloured, numbered vests – they have the advantage of being able to dodge traffic jams, but are obviously only really suitable for the single traveller, and motorbike taxis aren't the easiest mode of transport if you're carrying luggage. In remote spots, on the other hand, they're often the only alternative to hitching or walking, and are especially useful for getting between bus stops on main roads, around car-free islands and to national parks or ancient ruins.

Within towns motorbike-taxi fares can start at B10 for very short journeys, but for trips to the outskirts the cost rises steeply – about B200 for a twenty-kilometre round trip.

Vehicle rental

Despite first impressions, a high accident rate and the obvious mayhem that characterizes Bangkok's roads, **driving** yourself around Thailand can be fairly straightforward. Many roads, particularly in the northeast and the south, are remarkably uncongested. Major routes are clearly signed in English, though this only applies to some minor roads; unfortunately there is no perfect English-language map to compensate (see p.84).

Outside the capital, its immediate environs and the eastern seaboard, local drivers are generally considerate and unaggressive; they very rarely use their horns for example, and will often indicate and even swerve away when it's safe for you to overtake. The most inconsiderate and dangerous road-users in Thailand are bus drivers and lorry drivers, many of whom drive ludicrously fast, hog the road, race round bends on the wrong side of the road and use their horns remorselessly; worse still, many of them are tanked up on amphetamines, which makes them quite literally fearless.

Bus and lorry drivers are at their worst after dark (many of them only drive then), so you are strongly advised **never to drive at night** – a further hazard being the inevitable stream of unlit bicycles and mopeds in and around built-up areas, as well as poorly signed roadworks, which are often not made safe or blocked off from unsuspecting traffic. Orange signs, or sometimes just a couple of tree branches or a pile of stones on the road, warn of hazards ahead.

As for local **rules of the road**, Thais drive on the left, and the speed limit is 60km per hr within built-up areas and 90km per hr outside them. Beyond that, there are few rules that are generally followed – you'll need to keep your concentration up and expect the unexpected from fellow road-users. Watch out especially for vehicles pulling straight out of minor roads, when you might expect them to give way. An oncoming vehicle flashing its lights means it's coming through no matter what; a right indicator signal from the car in front usually means it's not safe for you to overtake, while a left indicator signal usually means that it is safe to do so.

Theoretically, foreigners need an international **driver's licence** to rent any kind of vehicle, but most car-rental companies accept national licences, and the smaller operations have been known not to ask for any kind of proof whatsoever; motorbike renters very rarely bother. A popular current rip-off, notably on Ko Pha Ngan and Ko Tao, is for small agents to charge renters exorbitant amounts for any minor damage to a jeep or motorbike, even paint chips, that they find on return – they'll claim that it's very expensive to get a new part shipped over from the mainland. Check out any vehicle carefully before renting; on the two islands mentioned, we've tried to recommend agents who don't indulge in this practice.

Petrol (*nam man*, which can also mean oil) currently costs around B20 a litre, though it's been as high as B43 in recent years. The big fuel stations are the least costly places to fill up (*hai tem*), and many of these also have toilets and simple restaurants, though some of the more decrepit-looking fuel stations on the main highways only sell diesel. Most small villages have easy-to-spot roadside huts where the fuel is pumped out of a large barrel.

Renting a car

If you decide to **rent a car**, go to a reputable dealer, such as Avis, Budget or SMT National (see below), or a rental company recommended by TAT, and make sure you get insurance from them. There are international car-rental places at many airports, including Bangkok's Suvarnabhumi, which is not a bad place to kick off, as you're on the edge of the city and within fairly easy, signposted reach of the major regional highways.

Car-rental places in provincial capitals and resorts are listed in the relevant accounts in this book. The price of a small car at a reputable company is generally about B1500 per day. In some parts of the country, where there are no dedicated car-rental agencies, you'll still be able to rent a car or air-con minibus with driver, for around B1800 per day.

Jeeps or basic four-wheel drives are a lot more popular with farangs, especially on beach resorts and islands like Pattaya, Phuket and Ko Samui, but they're notoriously **dangerous**; a huge number of tourists manage to roll their jeeps on steep hillsides and sharp bends. Jeep rental usually works out somewhere between B900 and B1200 per day.

International companies will accept your credit-card details as surety, but smaller agents will usually want to hold on to your passport.

Car rental agencies

Avis Ⓦ www.avisthailand.com
Budget Ⓦ www.budget.co.th
Master Ⓦ www.mastercarrental.com
SMT National Ⓦ www.nationalcar.com or www.smtrentacar.com
Thai Rentacar Ⓦ www.thairentacar.com

Renting a motorbike

One of the best ways of exploring the countryside is to **rent a motorbike**, an especially popular option in the north of the country. Bikes of around 100c, either fully automatic or with step-through gears, are best if you've never ridden a motorbike before, but aren't really suited for long slogs. If you're going to hit the dirt roads you'll certainly need something more powerful, like a 125–250cc trail bike. These have the edge in gear choice and are the best bikes for steep slopes, though an inexperienced rider may find these machines a handful; the less widely available 125–250cc road bikes are easier to control and much cheaper on fuel.

Rental **prices** for the day usually work out at somewhere around B150–200 for a small bike and B500 for a good trail bike, though you can bargain for a discount on a long rental. Renters will often ask for a deposit and your passport or credit-card details; insurance is not often available, so it's a good idea to make sure your travel insurance covers you for possible mishaps.

Before signing anything, **check the bike** thoroughly – test the brakes, look for oil leaks, check the treads and the odometer, and make sure the chain isn't stretched too tight (a tight chain is more likely to break) – and preferably take it for a test run. As you will have to pay an inflated price for any damage when you get back, make a note on the contract of any defects such as broken mirrors, indicators and so on. Make sure you know what kind of fuel the bike takes as well.

As far as **equipment** goes, a helmet is essential – most rental places provide poorly made ones, but they're better than nothing. Helmets are obligatory on all motorbike journeys, and the law is often rigidly enforced with on-the-spot fines in major tourist resorts. You'll need sunglasses if your helmet doesn't have a visor. Long trousers, a long-sleeved top and decent shoes will provide a second skin if you go over, which most people do at some stage. Pillions should wear long trousers to avoid getting nasty burns from the exhaust. For the sake of stability, leave most of your luggage in baggage storage and pack as small a bag as possible, strapping it tightly to the bike with bungy cords – these are usually provided. Once on the road, oil the chain at least every other day, keep the radiator topped up and fill up with oil every 300km or so.

For expert **advice** on motorbike travel in Thailand, check out David Unkovich's website (Ⓦ www.gt-rider.com).

Cycling

The options for **cycling** in Thailand are numerous, whether you choose to ride the length of the country from the Malaysian border to Chiang Rai, or opt for a dirt-road adventure in the mountains north of Chiang Mai. Most Thai roads are in good condition and clearly signposted; although the western and northern borders are mountainous, the rest of the country is surprisingly flat. The secondary **roads** (distinguished by their three-digit numbers) are paved but carry far less traffic than the main arteries and are the preferred cycling option. Traffic is reasonably well behaved and personal safety is not a major concern as long as you "ride to survive"; dogs, however, can be a nuisance on minor roads so it's probably worth having rabies shots before your trip. There are bike shops in nearly every town, and basic equipment and repairs are cheap. Unless you head into the remotest regions around the Burmese border you are rarely more than 25km from food, water and accommodation. Overall, the best time to cycle is during the cool, dry season from November to February and the least good from April to July (see p.11 for climate information).

The traffic into and out of Bangkok is dense so it's worth hopping on a bus or train for the first 50–100km to your starting point. The Bangkok Skytrain and intercity air-con buses, taxis and most Thai domestic planes (no bike box required) will **carry your bike** free of charge. The Bangkok subway does not allow bikes. Intercity trains will only transport your bike (for a fare – about the price of a person) if there is a luggage carriage attached, unless you dismantle it and carry it as luggage in the compartment with you. Intercity non-air-con buses and songthaews will carry your bike on the roof for a fare (about the price of a person).

Local one-day cycle tours and **bike-rental outlets** (B30–100 per day) are listed throughout this book. For details of organized **cycle tours** nationwide see p.29, in northern Thailand, p.322. For detailed accounts of cycling in Thailand see Biking Southeast Asia with Mr Pumpy at Ⓦwww.mrpumpy.net.

Cycling practicalities

Strong, light, quality **mountain bikes** are the most versatile choice. 26-inch wheels are standard throughout Thailand and are strongly recommended; dual-use (combined road and off-road) tyres are best for touring. As regards panniers and **equipment**, the most important thing is to travel light. Carry a few spare spokes, but don't overdo it with too many tools and spares; parts are cheap in Thailand and most problems can be fixed quickly at any bike shop.

Bringing your bike from home is the best option as you are riding a known quantity. **Importing** it by plane should be straightforward, but check with the airlines for details. Most Asian airlines do not charge extra.

Buying in Thailand is also a possibility: the range is reasonable and prices tend to be cheaper than in the West or Australia. In Bangkok, the best outlet is Probike at 237/2 Thanon Rajdamri (actually off Soi Sarasin next to Lumphini Park; Ⓣ02 253 3384, Ⓦwww.probike.co.th); Velo Thailand (see p.104) also sell international-brand aluminium-frame bikes, as well as renting mountain bikes for B300 per day. You can also rent good mountain bikes through the Bangkok cycle-tour operator Spice Roads (Ⓣ02 712 5305, Ⓦwww.spiceroads.com), for B280–400 per day. There are a few good outlets in Chiang Mai, too (see also Ⓦwww.chiangmaicycling.org): Cacti (see p.323), who also **rent** all manner of mountain and city bikes; Chaitawat, on Thanon Phra Pokklao, south off Thanon Ratchamankha, on the right (Ⓣ053 279890); and Canadian-owned Top Gear, 173 Thanon Chang Moi (Ⓣ053 233450).

Hitching

Public transport being so inexpensive, you should only have to resort to **hitching** in the most remote areas, in which case you'll probably get a lift to the nearest bus or songthaew stop quite quickly. On routes served by buses and trains, hitching is not standard practice, but in other places locals do rely on regular passers-by (such as national park officials), and you can make use of this "service" too. As with hitching anywhere in the world, think twice about hitching solo or at night, especially if you're female. Like bus drivers, truck drivers are notorious users of amphetamines, so you may want to wait for a safer offer.

Accommodation

For the simplest double room prices start at a bargain B150 in the outlying regions, B200 in Bangkok, and B400 in the pricier resorts. Tourist centres invariably offer a tempting range of more upmarket choices but in these areas rates fluctuate according to demand, plummeting during the off-season, peaking over the Christmas fortnight and, in some places, rising at weekends throughout the year.

Guest houses, bungalows and hostels

Most of Thailand's **budget accommodation** (❶–❸) is in **guest houses** and **bungalows**. These are small, traveller-friendly hotels whose services nearly always include an inexpensive restaurant and safe storage for valuables and left luggage, and often also run to internet access (sometimes even in-room wi-fi) and a tour desk. The difference between guest houses and bungalows is mostly in their design, with "bungalows" – which are generally found on the beach and in rural areas – mostly comprising detached or semi-detached rooms in huts, villas, chalets or indeed bungalows, and "guest houses" being either a purpose-built mini-hotel or a converted home. En-suite showers and flush toilets are common in both, but at the cheaper places you might be showering with a bowl dipped into a large water jar, and using squat toilets.

Many guest houses and bungalows offer a spread of options to cater for all budgets: their **cheapest rooms** will often be furnished with nothing more than a double bed, a blanket and a fan (window optional, private bathroom extra) and might cost anything from B150–300 for two people, depending on the location and the competition. A

Accommodation prices

Throughout this guide, guest houses, bungalows and hotels have been categorized according to the **price codes** given below. These categories represent the **minimum** you can expect to pay in the **high season** (roughly July, Aug and Nov–Feb) for a **double room**, booked via the hotel website where available; there may however be an extra "peak" supplement for the Christmas–New Year period. If travelling on your own, expect to pay between sixty and one hundred percent of the rates quoted for a double room. Where a place also offers **dormitory beds**, the price per bed is given in the text, instead of being indicated by a price code. Top-end hotels will add **seven percent tax** and **ten percent service charge** to your bill; the price codes below are based on net rates after taxes have been added.

❶ B250 and under
❷ B251–400
❸ B401–600
❹ B601–900
❺ B901–1400
❻ B1401–2000
❼ B2001–3000
❽ B3001–4500
❾ B4501 and over

Bathroom etiquette

Although modern, Western-style bathrooms are commonplace throughout Thailand, it's as well to be forewarned about local bathroom etiquette.

Sit-down **toilets** are the norm but public amenities, especially at bus and train stations, and in some homes and old-style guest houses and hotels, tend to be squat toilets. Thais traditionally don't use **paper** but wash rather than wipe themselves after going to the toilet. Modern bathrooms are fitted with a special hose for this purpose, while more primitive bathrooms just provide a **bucket of water and a dipper**. Thais always use their left hand for washing – and their right hand for eating (see p.56). As Thai plumbing is notoriously sluggish, where toilet paper is provided, it's normal to throw it in the waste basket and not down the U-bend. If a toilet is not plumbed in, you flush it yourself with water from the bucket. In really basic hotel bathrooms with no **shower** facilities, you also use the bucket and dipper for scoop-and-slosh bathing.

similar room with **en-suite** bathroom, and possibly more stylish furnishings generally comes in at B200–600, while for a room with **air-con**, and perhaps a TV and fridge as well, you're looking at B350–1500.

In the most popular tourist centres at the busiest times of year, the best-known guest houses are often full night after night. Some will take **bookings** and advance payment via their websites, but for those that don't it's usually a question of turning up and waiting for a vacancy. At most guest houses **checkout time** is either 11am or noon.

Generally you should be wary of taking accommodation advice from a **tout** or tuk-tuk driver, as they demand commission from guest-house owners, which, if not passed directly on to you via a higher room price, can have a crippling effect on the smaller guest houses. If a tout claims your intended accommodation is "full" or "no good" or has "burnt down", it's always worth phoning to check yourself. Touts can come into their own, however, on islands such as Ko Lanta where it can be a long and expensive ride to your chosen beach, and frustrating if you then discover your bungalows are full; island touts usually sweet-talk you on the boat and then transport you for free to view their accommodation, ideally with no obligation to stay.

With only 25 registered **youth hostels** in the country, bookable via ⓦwww.tyha.org, it's not worth becoming a Hostelling International member just for your trip to Thailand, especially as card-holders get only a small discount and room rates anyway work out the same as or more expensive than guest-house equivalents. In addition, hostels mostly cater for Thai students and so may not be staffed by English-speakers.

Budget hotels

Thai sales reps and other people travelling for business rather than pleasure rarely use guest houses, opting instead for **budget hotels**, which offer rooms for around B150–600. Usually run by Chinese-Thais, these functional three- or four-storey places are found in every sizeable town, often near the bus station or central market. Beds are large enough for a couple, so it's quite acceptable for two people to ask and pay for a "single" room (*hawng thiang diaw*, literally a "one-bedded room"). Though the rooms are generally clean, en suite and furnished with either a fan or air-con, there's rarely an on-site restaurant and the atmosphere is generally less convivial than at guest houses. A number of budget hotels also double as brothels, though as a farang you're unlikely to be offered this sideline, and you might not even notice the goings-on.

Advance reservations are accepted over the phone, but this is rarely necessary, as such hotels rarely fill up. The only time you may have difficulty finding a budget hotel room is during Chinese New Year (a moveable three-day period in late Jan or Feb), when many Chinese-run hotels close and others get booked up fast.

Tourist hotels

The rest of the accommodation picture is all about **tourist hotels** which, like anywhere in the world, come in all sizes and qualities and are often best booked via online discount accommodation booking services such as ⓦwww.sawadee.com. One way or another, it's a good idea to **reserve ahead** in popular tourist areas during peak season.

Rates for **middle-ranking hotels** (❹–❻) fall between B600 and B2000. For this you can expect many of the trimmings of a top-end hotel – air-con, TV and mini bar in the room, plus an on-site pool, restaurant and perhaps nightclub – but with dated and possibly faded furnishings and little of the style of the famous big names; they're often the kind of places that once stood at the top of the range, but were outclassed when the multinational luxury hotels muscled in.

Many of Thailand's **expensive hotels** (❼–❾) belong to the big international chains: Sheraton, Marriott and Sofitel all have a strong presence in the country and are closely followed by upmarket home-grown groups such as Amari, Dusit and Centara. Between them they maintain premium standards in Bangkok and major resorts at prices of B3000 (£60/US$85) and upward for a double – far less than you'd pay for equivalent accommodation in the West.

Thailand also boasts an increasing number of deliciously stylish **luxury hotels**, many of them designed as intimate, small-scale **boutique** hotels, with chic, minimalist decor, exceptional service and excellent facilities that often include private plunge pools and a spa. A night in one of these places will rarely cost you less than B6000 (£120/US$170), and may set you back more than twice as much, though they're still often outstanding value for the honeymoon-style indulgence that they offer; see accommodation listings for Bangkok, Chiang Mai, Ko Samui, Khao Lak and Phuket for some suggestions. As in the West, however, the term "boutique" is overused, and a "boutique" guest house or hotel may in practice be little more than "small". Many luxury hotels quote rates in US dollars, though you can always pay in baht.

Homestays

As guest houses have become increasingly hotel-like and commercial in their facilities and approach, many tourists looking for old-style local hospitality are choosing **homestay accommodation** instead. Homestay facilities are nearly always simple, and cheap at around B150 per person per night, with guests staying in a shared spare room and eating with the family. Homestays give an unparalleled insight into typical Thai (usually rural) life and can often be incorporated into a programme that includes experiencing village activities such as rice farming, squid fishing, rubber tapping or silk weaving. They are also a positive way of supporting small communities, as all your money will feed right back into the village. As well as listed homestays in Amphawa (see p.223), Doi Inthanon (see p.379), Mae Hong Son (see p.386 & p.394), Chiang Rai (see p.406), Ban Prasat (see p.504), Ban Khiriwong (see p.640) Pha To (see p.661), Khuraburi (see p.661), Ko Yao Noi (see p.714) and Krabi (see p.724), there are many others bookable through tour operators detailed on p.29 or via ⓦwww.homestaythai.org, though participants in the latter organization may not speak much English.

National parks and camping

Nearly all the **national parks** have accommodation facilities, usually comprising a series of simple concrete bungalows that cost at least B600 for two or more beds plus a basic bathroom. Because most of their custom comes from Thai families and student groups, park officials are sometimes loath to discount them for lone travellers, though a few parks do offer dorm-style accommodation at around B100 a bed. In most parks, advance booking is unnecessary except at weekends and national holidays.

If you do want to pre-book, you can do so up to sixty days ahead of your stay at ⓦwww.dnp.go.th/National_park.asp. As credit-card payment is not yet possible, you need to pay in cash or via bank draft within two days of booking, most conveniently at any branch of Krung Thai bank, or at designated international banks, or at the National Park headquarters in question; see the "Reservation" section of individual National Park webpages at the site given above for comprehensive details. The few national parks that accept phone bookings themselves are highlighted in the Guide chapters. If you turn up without booking, check in at the park headquarters, which is usually adjacent to the visitor centre.

In a few parks, private operators have set up low-cost guest houses on the outskirts, and these generally make more attractive and economical places to stay.

Camping

You can usually **camp** in a national park for a nominal fee of B60 per two-person tent, and some national parks also rent out fully equipped tents from B150 (bookable through a separate section on the above-listed website). Unless you're planning an extensive tour of national parks, though, there's little point in lugging a tent around Thailand: accommodation everywhere else is very inexpensive, and anyway there are no campsites inside town perimeters, though camping is allowed on nearly all islands and beaches, many of which are national parks in their own right.

Food and drink

Bangkok and Chiang Mai are the country's big culinary centres, boasting the cream of gourmet Thai restaurants and the best international cuisines. The rest of the country is by no means a gastronomic wasteland, however, and you can eat well and cheaply in even the smallest provincial towns, many of which offer the additional attraction of regional specialities. In fact you could eat more than adequately without ever entering a restaurant, as itinerant food vendors hawking hot and cold snacks materialize in even the most remote spots, as well as on trains and buses – and night markets often serve customers from dusk until dawn.

Hygiene is a consideration when eating anywhere in Thailand, but being too cautious means you'll end up spending a lot of money and missing out on some real local treats. Wean your stomach gently by avoiding excessive amounts of chillies and too much fresh fruit in the first few days.

You can be pretty sure that any noodle stall or curry shop that's permanently packed with customers is a safe bet. Furthermore, because most Thai dishes can be cooked in under five minutes, you'll rarely have to contend with stuff that's been left to smoulder and stew. Foods that are generally considered high risk include salads, ice cream, shellfish and raw or undercooked meat, fish or eggs. If you're really concerned about health standards you could stick to restaurants and food stalls displaying a **"Clean Food Good Taste"** sign, part of a food sanitation project set up by the Ministry of Public Health, TAT and the Ministry of the Interior.

Most restaurants in Thailand are open every day for lunch and dinner; we've noted exceptions throughout the Guide. In a few of the country's most expensive restaurants, mostly in Bangkok, a ten percent service charge and possibly even seven percent VAT may be added to your bill.

For those interested in **learning Thai cookery**, short courses designed for

The glorious range and flavours of **Thai cuisine** are discussed in the colour section later on in this book. For a detailed **food and drink glossary** see p.867.

Fruits of Thailand

You'll find **fruit** (*phonlamai*) offered everywhere in Thailand – neatly sliced in glass boxes on hawker carts, blended into delicious shakes and served as a dessert in restaurants. The fruits described below can be found in all parts of Thailand, though some are seasonal. The country's more familiar fruits include forty varieties of **banana** (*kluay*), dozens of different **mangoes** (*mamuang*), three types of **pineapple** (*sapparot*), **coconuts** (*maprao*), **oranges** (*som*), **lemons** (*manao*) and **watermelons** (*taeng moh*). For the lowdown on Thailand's most prized and expensive fruit, the **durian** (*thurian*), see p.174.

To avoid stomach trouble, **peel all fruit** before eating it, and use common sense if you're tempted to buy it pre-peeled on the street, avoiding anything that looks fly-blown or seems to have been sitting in the sun for hours.

Custard apple (soursop; *noina*; July–Sept). Inside the knobbly, muddy green skin is a creamy, almond-coloured blancmange-like flesh, with a strong flavour of strawberries and pears, and a hint of cinnamon, and many seeds.

Guava (*farang*; year-round). The apple of the tropics has green textured skin and sweet, crisp pink or white flesh, studded with tiny edible seeds. Has five times the vitamin C content of an orange and is sometimes eaten cut into strips and sprinkled with sugar and chilli.

Jackfruit (*khanun*; year-round). This large, pear-shaped fruit can weigh up to 20kg and has a thick, bobbly, greeny-yellow shell protecting sweet yellow flesh. Green, unripe jackfruit is sometimes cooked as a vegetable in curries.

Longan (*lamyai*; July–Oct). A close relative of the lychee, with succulent white flesh covered in thin, brittle skin.

Lychee (*linjiii*; April–May). Under rough, reddish-brown skin, the lychee has sweet, richly flavoured white flesh, rose scented and with plenty of vitamin C.

Mangosteen (*mangkut*; April–Sept). The size of a small apple, with smooth, purple skin and a fleshy inside that divides into succulent white segments that are sweet though slightly acidic.

Papaya (paw-paw; *malakaw*; year-round). Looks like an elongated watermelon, with smooth green skin and yellowy-orange flesh that's a rich source of vitamins A and C. It's a favourite in fruit salads and shakes, and sometimes appears in its green, unripe form in salads, notably *som tam*.

Pomelo (*som oh*; Oct–Dec). The largest of all the citrus fruits, it looks rather like a grapefruit, though it is slightly drier and has less flavour.

Rambutan (*ngaw*; May–Sept). The bright red rambutan's soft, spiny exterior has given it its name – *rambut* means "hair" in Malay. Usually about the size of a golf ball, it has a white, opaque flesh of delicate flavour, similar to a lychee.

Rose apple (*chomphuu*; year-round). Linked in myth with the golden fruit of immortality; small and egg-shaped, with white, rose-scented flesh.

Sapodilla (sapota; *lamut*; Sept–Dec). These small, brown, rough-skinned ovals look a bit like kiwi fruit and conceal a grainy, yellowish pulp that tastes almost honey-sweet.

Tamarind (*makhaam*; Dec–Jan). A Thai favourite and a pricey delicacy – carrying the seeds is said to make you safe from wounding by knives or bullets. Comes in rough, brown pods containing up to ten seeds, each surrounded by a sticky, dry pulp which has a sour, lemony taste.

visitors are held in Bangkok, Chiang Mai, Kanchanaburi, Ko Samui, Ko Chang, Ao Nang, Pai, Phuket and Sukhothai; see the relevant accounts for details.

Where to eat

A lot of tourists eschew the huge range of Thai **places to eat**, despite their obvious attractions, and opt instead for the much "safer" restaurants in guest houses and hotels. Almost all tourist accommodation has a kitchen, and while some are excellent, the vast majority serve up bland imitations of Western fare alongside equally pale versions of common Thai dishes. Having said that, it can be a relief to get your teeth into a processed-cheese sandwich after five days' trekking in the jungle, and guest houses do serve comfortingly familiar Western breakfasts.

Throughout the country most **inexpensive Thai restaurants** and cafés specialize in one general food type or preparation method, charging around B40–50 a dish – a "noodle shop", for example, will do fried noodles and/or noodle soups, plus maybe a basic fried rice, but they won't have curries or meat or fish dishes. Similarly, a restaurant displaying whole roast chickens and ducks in its window will offer these sliced, usually with chillies and sauces and served over rice, but their menu probably won't extend to noodles or fish, while in "curry shops" your options are limited to the vats of curries stewing away in the hot cabinet.

To get a wider array of low-cost food, it's sometimes best to head for the local **night market** (*talaat yen*), a term for the gatherings of open-air night-time kitchens found in every town. Sometimes operating from 6pm to 6am, they are typically to be found on permanent patches close to the fruit and vegetable market or the bus station, and as often as not they're the best and most entertaining places to eat, not to mention the least expensive – after a lip-smacking feast of savoury dishes, a fruit drink and a dessert you'll come away no more than B150 poorer.

A typical night market has maybe thirty-odd "specialist" pushcart kitchens (*rot khen*) jumbled together, each fronted by several sets of tables and stools. Noodle and fried-rice vendors always feature prominently, as do sweets stalls, heaped high with sticky rice cakes wrapped in banana leaves or thick with bags of tiny sweetcorn pancakes hot from the griddle – and no night market is complete without its fruit-drink stall, offering banana shakes and freshly squeezed orange, lemon and tomato juices. In the best setups you'll find a lot more besides: curries, barbecued sweetcorn, satay sticks of pork and chicken, deep-fried insects, fresh pineapple, watermelon and mango and – if the town's by a river or near the sea – heaps of fresh fish. Having decided what you want, you order from the cook (or the cook's dogsbody) and sit down at the nearest table; there is no territorialism about night markets, so it's normal to eat several dishes from separate stalls and rely on the nearest cook to sort out the bill.

Some large markets, particularly in Bangkok, have separate **food court** areas where you buy coupons first and select food and drink to their value at the stalls of your choice. This is also usually the modus operandi in the food courts found in department stores and shopping centres across the country.

For a more relaxing ambience, Bangkok and the larger towns have a range of **upmarket restaurants**, some specializing in **"royal" Thai cuisine**, which is differentiated mainly by the quality of the ingredients and the way the food is presented. Great care is taken over how individual dishes look: they are served in small portions and decorated with carved fruit and vegetables in a way that used to be the prerogative of royal cooks, but has now filtered down to the common folk. The cost of such delights is not prohibitive, either – a meal in one of these places is unlikely to cost more than B500 per person.

Vegetarians and vegans

Very few Thais are **vegetarian** (*mangsawirat*) but, if you can make yourself understood, you can often get a non-meat or fish alternative to what's on the menu; simply ask the cook to exclude meat and fish: *mai sai neua*, *mai sai plaa*. You may end up eating a lot of unexciting vegetable fried rice and *phat thai* minus the shrimps, but in better restaurants you should be able to get veggie versions of most curries; the mushroom version of chicken and coconut soup is also a good standby: ask for *tom kha hed*. Browsing food stalls also expands your options, with barbecued sweetcorn, nuts, fruit and other non-meaty goodies all common. The two ingredients that you will have to consider compromising on are the fermented **fish sauce** and **shrimp paste** that are fundamental to most Thai dishes;

only in the vegan Thai restaurants described below, and in tourist spots serving specially concocted Thai and Western veggie dishes, can you be sure of avoiding them.

If you're **vegan** (*jay*, sometimes spelt "*jeh*") you'll need to stress when you order that you don't want egg, as they get used a lot; cheese and other dairy produce, however, don't feature at all in Thai cuisine. Many towns will have one or more **vegan restaurants** (*raan ahaan jay*), which are usually run by members of a temple or Buddhist sect and operate from unadorned premises off the main streets; because strict Buddhists prefer not to eat late in the day, most of the restaurants open early, at around 6 or 7am and close by 2pm. Most of these places have a yellow and red sign, though few display an English-language name. Nor is there ever a menu: customers simply choose from the trays of veggie stir-fries and curries, nearly all of them made with soya products, that are laid out canteen-style. Most places charge around B40 for a couple of helpings served over a plate of brown rice.

How to eat

Thai food is eaten with a **fork** (left hand) and a **spoon** (right hand); there is no need for a knife as food is served in bite-sized chunks, which are forked onto the spoon and fed into the mouth. Cutlery is often delivered to the table wrapped in a perplexingly tiny pink napkin: Thais use this, not for their lap, but to give their fork, spoon and plate an extra wipe-down before they eat. Steamed **rice** (*khao*) is served with most meals, and indeed the most commonly heard phrase for "to eat" is *kin khao* (literally, "eat rice"). **Chopsticks** are provided only for noodle dishes, and north-eastern sticky-rice dishes are always eaten with the **fingers of your right hand**. Never eat with the fingers of your left hand, which is used for washing after going to the toilet.

So that complementary taste combinations can be enjoyed, the dishes in a Thai meal are served all at once, even the soup, and shared communally. The more people, the more taste and texture sensations; if there are only two of you, it's normal to order three dishes, plus your own individual plates of steamed rice, while three diners would order four dishes, and so on. Only put a serving of one dish on your rice plate each time, and then only one or two spoonfuls.

Bland food is anathema to Thais, and restaurant tables everywhere come decked out with **condiment sets** featuring the four basic flavours (salty, sour, sweet and spicy): usually fish sauce with chopped chillies; vinegar with chopped chillies; sugar; and dried chillies – and often extra bowls of ground peanuts and a bottle of chilli ketchup as well. If you do bite into a **chilli**, the way to combat the searing heat is to take a mouthful of plain rice and/or beer: swigging water just exacerbates the sensation.

Desserts

Desserts (*khanom*) don't really figure on most restaurant menus, but a few places offer bowls of *luk taan cheum*, a jellied concoction of lotus or palm seeds floating in a syrup scented with jasmine or other aromatic flowers. Coconut milk is a feature of most other desserts, notably delicious coconut ice cream, *khao niaw mamuang* (sticky rice with mango), and a royal Thai cuisine special of coconut custard (*sangkhayaa*) cooked inside a small pumpkin, whose flesh you can also eat.

Drinks

Thais don't drink water straight from the tap, and nor should you; plastic bottles of drinking **water** (*nam plao*) are sold countrywide, in even the smallest villages, for around B10 and should be used even when brushing your teeth. Cheap restaurants and hotels generally serve free jugs of boiled water, which should be fine to drink, though they are not as foolproof as the bottles.

Night markets, guest houses and restaurants do a good line in freshly squeezed **fruit juices** such as lemon (*nam manao*) and orange (*nam som*), which often come with salt and sugar already added, particularly upcountry. The same places will usually do **fruit shakes** as well, blending bananas (*nam kluay*), papayas (*nam malakaw*), pineapples (*nam sapparot*) and others with liquid sugar or condensed milk (or yoghurt, to make lassi). Fresh **coconut water** (*nam maprao*) is another great thirst-quencher – you buy the whole fruit dehusked, decapitated and chilled – as is **pandanus-leaf juice** (*bai toey*);

Thais are also very partial to freshly squeezed **sugar-cane juice** (*nam awy*), which is sickeningly sweet.

Bottled and canned brand-name **soft drinks** are sold all over the place, with a particularly wide range in the ubiquitous 7-Eleven chain stores. Soft-drink bottles are returnable, so some shops and drink stalls have an amazing system of pouring the contents into a small plastic bag (fastened with an elastic band and with a straw inserted) rather than charging you the extra for taking away the bottle. The larger restaurants keep their soft drinks refrigerated, but smaller cafés and shops add **ice** (*nam khaeng*) to glasses and bags. Most ice is produced commercially under hygienic conditions, but it might become less pure in transit so be wary (ice cubes are generally a better bet than shaved ice) – and don't take ice if you have diarrhoea. For those travelling with children, or just partial themselves to **dairy products**, UHT-preserved milk and chilled yoghurt drinks are widely available (especially at 7-Eleven stores), as are a variety of soya drinks.

Weak Chinese **tea** (*nam chaa*) makes a refreshing alternative to water and often gets served in Chinese restaurants and roadside cafés, while posher restaurants keep stronger Chinese and Western-style teas. Instant Nescafé is usually the **coffee** (*kaafae*), offered to farangs, even if freshly ground Thai-grown coffee – notably several kinds of hill-tribe coffee from the mountains of the north – is available. If you would like to try traditional Thai coffee, most commonly found at Chinese-style cafés in the south of the country or at outdoor markets, and prepared through filtering the grounds through a cloth, ask for *kaafae thung* (literally, "bag coffee"), normally served very bitter with sugar as well as sweetened condensed milk alongside a glass of black or Chinese tea to wash it down with. Fresh Western-style coffee (*kaafae sot*) in the form of Italian espresso, cappuccino and other derivatives has recently become popular among Thais, so you'll now come across espresso machines in large towns all over the country (though some of these new coffee bars, frustratingly, don't open for breakfast, as locals tend to get their fix later in the day).

Alcoholic drinks

The two most famous local **beers** (*bia*) are Singha, which has six percent alcohol content (ask for "*bia sing*"), and Chang, which delivers 6.4 percent alcohol at slightly cheaper prices: in shops around B30 for a 330ml bottle, B50 for a 660ml bottle. All manner of foreign beers are now brewed in Thailand, including Heineken and Asahi, and in the most touristy areas you'll find imported bottles from all over the world.

Wine is now found on plenty of upmarket and tourist-oriented restaurant menus, but expect to be disappointed by both quality and price, which is jacked up by heavy taxation. Thai wine is now produced at several vineyards, including at Château de Loei near Phu Reua National Park in the northeast, which produces quite tasty reds, whites including a dessert wine, a rosé and brandy (see p.541).

At about B80 for a hip-flask-sized 375ml bottle, the local **whisky** is a lot better value, and Thais think nothing of consuming a bottle a night, heavily diluted with ice and soda or Coke. The most palatable and widely available of these is Mekong, which is very pleasant once you've stopped expecting it to taste like Scotch; distilled from rice, Mekong is 35 percent proof, deep gold in colour and tastes slightly sweet. If that's not to your taste, a pricier Thai **rum** is also available, Sang Som, made from sugar cane, and even stronger than the whisky at forty percent proof. Check the menu carefully when ordering a bottle of Mekong from a bar in a tourist area, as they often ask up to five times more than you'd pay in a guest house or shop. A hugely popular way to enjoy whisky or rum at beach resorts is to pick up a bucket, containing a quarter-bottle of spirit, a mixer, Red Bull, ice and several straws, for around B200: that way you get to share with your friends and build a sandcastle afterwards.

You can **buy** beer and whisky in food stores, guest houses and most restaurants; **bars** aren't strictly an indigenous feature as Thais traditionally don't drink out without eating, but you'll find plenty of Western-style drinking holes in Bangkok and larger centres elsewhere in the country, ranging from ultra-hip haunts in the capital to basic, open-to-the-elements "**bar-beers**".

Culture and etiquette

Tourist literature has marketed Thailand as the "Land of Smiles" so successfully that a lot of farangs arrive in the country expecting to be forgiven any outrageous behaviour. This is just not the case: there are some things so universally sacred in Thailand that even a hint of disrespect will cause deep offence. TAT publishes a special leaflet on the subject, entitled Dos and Don'ts in Thailand, reproduced at ⓦwww.tourismthailand.org.

The monarchy

It is both socially unacceptable and a criminal offence to make critical or defamatory remarks about the **royal family**. Thailand's monarchy might be a constitutional one, but almost every household displays a picture of King Bhumibol and Queen Sirikit in a prominent position, and respectful crowds mass whenever either of them makes a public appearance. The second of their four children, Crown Prince Vajiralongkorn, is the heir to the throne; his younger sister, Princess Royal Maha Chakri Sirindhorn, is often on TV and in the English newspapers as she is involved in many charitable projects. When addressing or speaking about royalty, Thais use a special language full of deference, called *rajasap* (literally "royal language").

Thailand's **lèse majesté laws** are among the most strictly applied in the world, increasingly invoked as the Thai establishment becomes ever more uneasy over the erosion of traditional monarchist sentiments and the rise of critical voices, particularly on the internet (though these are generally quickly censored). Accusations of *lèse majesté* can be levelled by and against anyone, Thai national or farang, and must be investigated by the police. As a few high-profile cases involving foreigners have demonstrated, they can be raised for seemingly minor infractions, such as defacing a poster or being less than respectful in a work of fiction. Transgressions are met with jail sentences of up to 15 years.

Aside from keeping any anti-monarchy sentiments to yourself, you should be prepared to stand when the **king's anthem** is played at the beginning of every cinema programme, and to stop in your tracks if the town you're in plays the **national anthem** over its public address system – many small towns do this twice a day at 8am and again at 6pm, as do some train stations and airports. A less obvious point: as the king's head features on all Thai currency, you should never step on a coin or banknote, which is tantamount to kicking the king in the face.

Religion

Almost equally insensitive would be to disregard certain **religious** precepts. **Buddhism** plays a fundamental role in Thai culture, and Buddhist monuments should be treated with respect – which basically means wearing long trousers or knee-length skirts, covering your arms and removing your shoes whenever you visit one.

All **Buddha images** are sacred, however small, tacky or ruined, and should never be used as a backdrop for a portrait photo, clambered over, placed in a position of inferiority or treated in any manner that could be construed as disrespectful. In an attempt to prevent foreigners from committing any kind of transgression the government requires a special licence for all Buddha statues exported from the country (see p.82).

Monks come only just beneath the monarchy in the social hierarchy, and they too are addressed and discussed in a special language. If there's a monk around, he'll always get a seat on the bus, usually right at the back. Theoretically, monks are forbidden to have any close contact with women, which means, as a female, you mustn't sit or stand next to a monk, or even brush against his robes; if it's essential to pass him something, put the object down so that he can then pick it up – never hand it over directly. Nuns, however, get treated like ordinary women.

See "Contexts", p.811, for more on religious practices in Thailand.

The body

The Western liberalism embraced by the Thai sex industry is very unrepresentative of the majority Thai attitude to the body. **Clothing** – or the lack of it – is what bothers Thais most about tourist behaviour. As mentioned above, you need to dress modestly when entering temples, but the same also applies to other important buildings and all public places. Stuffy and sweaty as it sounds, you should keep short shorts and vests for the real tourist resorts, and be especially diligent about covering up and, for women, wearing bras in rural areas. Baring your flesh on beaches is very much a Western practice: when Thais go swimming they often do so fully clothed, and they find topless and nude bathing offensive.

According to ancient Hindu belief, the **head** is the most sacred part of the body and the **feet** are the most unclean. This belief, imported into Thailand, means that it's very rude to touch another person's head or to point your feet either at a human being or at a sacred image – when sitting on a temple floor, for example, you should **tuck your legs beneath you** rather than stretch them out towards the Buddha. These hierarchies also forbid people from wearing **shoes** (which are even more unclean than feet) inside temples and most private homes, and – by extension – Thais take offence when they see someone sitting on the "head", or prow, of a boat. **Putting your feet up** on a table, a chair or a pillow is also considered very uncouth, and Thais will always take their shoes off if they need to stand on a train or bus seat to get to the luggage rack, for example. On a more practical note, the **left hand** is used for washing after going to the toilet (for more on bathroom etiquette see p.51), so Thais never use it to put food in their mouth, pass things or shake hands – as a farang though, you'll be assumed to have different customs, so left-handers shouldn't worry unduly.

Social conventions

Thais never shake hands with each other, instead using the **wai** to greet and say goodbye and to acknowledge respect, gratitude or apology. A prayer-like gesture made with raised hands, the *wai* changes according to the relative status of the two people involved: Thais can instantaneously assess which *wai* to use, but as a farang your safest bet is to go for the "stranger's" *wai*, which requires that your hands be raised close to your chest and your fingertips placed just below your chin. If someone makes a *wai* at you, you should generally *wai* back, but it's safer not to initiate.

Public displays of **physical affection** in Thailand are more common between friends of the same sex than between lovers, whether hetero- or homosexual. Holding hands and hugging is as common among male friends as with females, so if you're caressed by a Thai acquaintance of the same sex, don't assume you're being propositioned.

Finally, there are three specifically Thai **concepts** you're bound to come across, which may help you comprehend a sometimes laissez-faire attitude to delayed buses and other inconveniences. The first, **jai yen**, translates literally as "cool heart" and is something everyone tries to maintain: most Thais hate raised voices, visible irritation and confrontations of any kind, so losing one's cool can have a much more inflammatory effect than in more combative cultures. Related to this is the oft-quoted response to a difficulty, **mai pen rai** – "never mind", "no problem" or "it can't be helped" – the verbal equivalent of an open-handed shoulder shrug, which has its basis in the Buddhist notion of karma (see "Religion", p.811). And then there's **sanuk**, the wide-reaching philosophy of "fun", which, crass as it sounds, Thais do their best to inject into any situation, even work. Hence the crowds of inebriated Thais who congregate at waterfalls and other beauty spots on public holidays (travelling solo is definitely not *sanuk*), the reluctance to do almost anything without high-volume musical accompaniment, and the national waterfight which takes place every April on streets right across Thailand.

Thai names

Although all Thais have a first **name** and a family name, everyone is addressed by their first name – even when meeting strangers

– prefixed by the title "**Khun**" (Mr/Ms); no one is ever addressed as Khun Surname, and even the phone book lists people by their given name. In Thailand you will often be addressed in an Anglicized version of this convention, as "Mr Paul" or "Miss Lucy" for example. Bear in mind though, that when a man is introduced to you as Khun Pirom, his wife will definitely not be Khun Pirom as well (that would be like calling them, for instance, "Mr and Mrs Paul"). Among friends and relatives, **Phii** ("older brother/sister") is often used instead of Khun when addressing older familiars (though as a tourist you're on surer ground with Khun), and **Nong** ("younger brother/sister") is used for younger ones.

Many Thai **first names** come from ancient Sanskrit and have an auspicious meaning; for example, Boon means good deeds, Porn means blessings, Siri means glory and Thawee means to increase. However, Thais of all ages are commonly known by the **nickname** given them soon after birth rather than by their official first name. This tradition arises out of a deep-rooted superstition that once a child has been officially named the spirits will begin to take an unhealthy interest in them, so a nickname is used instead to confuse the spirits. Common nicknames – which often bear no resemblance to the adult's personality or physique – include Yai (Big), Oun (Fat) and Muu (Pig); Lek or Noi (Little), Nok (Bird), Noo (Mouse) and Kung (Shrimp); and English nicknames like Apple, Joy or even Pepsi.

Family names were only introduced in 1913 (by Rama VI, who invented many of the aristocracy's surnames himself), and are used only in very formal situations, always in conjunction with the first name. It's quite usual for good friends never to know each other's surname. Ethnic Thais generally have short surnames like Somboon or Srisai, while the long, convoluted family names – such as Sonthanasumpun – usually indicate Chinese origin, not because they are phonetically Chinese but because many Chinese immigrants have chosen to adopt new Thai surnames and Thai law states that every newly created surname must be unique. Thus anyone who wants to change their surname must submit a shortlist of five unique Thai names – each to a maximum length of ten Thai characters – to be checked against a database of existing names. As more and more names are taken, Chinese family names get increasingly unwieldy, and more easily distinguishable from the pithy old Thai names.

Crime, safety and the law

As long as you keep your wits about you, you shouldn't encounter much trouble in Thailand. Theft and pickpocketing are two of the main problems – not surprising considering that a huge percentage of the local population scrape by on under US$5 per day – but the most common cause for concern is the number of con-artists who dupe gullible tourists into parting with their cash. There are various Thai laws that tourists need to be aware of, particularly regarding passports, the age of consent and smoking in public.

Theft

To **prevent theft**, most travellers prefer to carry their valuables with them at all times, but it's often possible to use a locker in a hotel or guest house – the safest are those that require your own padlock, as there are occasional reports of valuables being stolen by hotel staff. **Padlock your luggage** when leaving it in hotel or guest-house rooms, as well as when consigning it to storage or taking it on public transport. Padlocks also come in handy as extra security on your room, particularly on the doors of beachfront bamboo huts.

Theft from some long-distance **overnight buses** is also a problem, with the majority of reported incidents taking place on the temptingly cheap buses run by private companies direct from Bangkok's Thanon Khao San (as opposed to those that depart from the government bus stations) to destinations such as Chiang Mai and southern beach resorts. The best solution is to go direct from the bus stations; see p.42 for further advice.

Personal safety

On any bus, private or government, and on any train journey, never keep anything of value in luggage that is stored out of your sight and be wary of accepting food and drink from fellow passengers as it may be drugged. This might sound paranoid, but there have been enough **drug-muggings** for TAT to publish a specific warning about the problem. Drinks can also be spiked in bars and clubs; at full moon parties on Ko Pha Ngan this has led to sexual assaults against farang women, while prostitutes sometimes spike drinks so they can steal from their victim's room.

Violent crime against tourists is not common, but it does occur, and there have been several serious attacks on women travellers in recent years. However, bearing in mind that fourteen million foreigners visit Thailand every year, the statistical likelihood of becoming a victim is extremely small. **Obvious precautions** for travellers of either sex include locking accessible windows and doors at night – preferably with your own padlock (doors in many of the simpler guest houses and beach bungalows are designed for this) – and not travelling alone at night in a taxi or tuk-tuk. Nor should you risk jumping into an unlicensed taxi at the airport in Bangkok at any time of day: there have been some very violent robberies in these, so take the well-marked licensed, metered taxis instead, or one of the airport buses.

Unfortunately, it is also necessary for female tourists to think twice about spending time alone with a **monk**, as not all men of the cloth uphold the Buddhist precepts and there have been rapes and murders committed by men wearing the saffron robes of the monkhood. See p.814 for more about the changing Thai attitudes towards the monkhood.

Though unpalatable and distressing, Thailand's high-profile **sex industry** is relatively unthreatening for Western women, with its energy focused exclusively on farang men; it's also quite easily avoided, being contained within certain pockets of the capital and a couple of beach resorts.

As for **harassment** from men, it's hard to generalize, but most Western women find it less of a problem in Thailand than they do back home. Outside the main tourist spots, you're more likely to be of interest as a foreigner rather than a woman and, if travelling alone, as an object of concern rather than of sexual aggression.

Reporting a crime or emergency

In emergencies, contact the English-speaking **tourist police**, who maintain a 24-hour toll-free nationwide line (ⓣ1155) and have offices in the main tourist centres; getting in touch with the tourist police first is invariably more efficient than directly contacting the local police, ambulance or fire service. The tourist police's job is to offer advice and tell you what to do next, but they do not file crime reports, which must be done at the nearest police station.

TAT has a special department for mediating between tourists, police and accused persons (particularly shopkeepers and tour agents) called the Tourist Assistance Center, or **TAC**; it's based in the TAT office on Thanon Rajdamnoen Nok, Bangkok (daily 8.30am–4.30pm; ⓣ02 281 5051).

The British Embassy in Bangkok provides **advice** for British victims of crime in Thailand and also posts practical tips and a list of useful contacts on its website (ⓣ02 305 8333 ext 2334 or 2318, ⓦukinthailand.fco.gov.uk/en/help-for-british-nationals).

Among hazards to watch out for in the natural world, **riptides** claim a number of tourist lives every year, particularly off Phuket, Ko Chang (Trat), Hua Hin, Cha-am and Ko Samui during stormy periods of the monsoon season, so always pay attention to warning signs and red flags, and always ask locally if unsure. **Jellyfish** can be a problem on any coast, especially just after a storm (see p.39).

Regional issues

It's advisable to travel with a guide if you're going off the main roads in certain **border areas** or, if you're on a motorbike, to take advice before setting off. As these regions are generally covered in dense unmapped jungle, you shouldn't find yourself alone in the area anyway, but the main stretches to watch are the immediate vicinity of the Burmese border north of Three Pagodas Pass, between Mae Sot and Mae Sariang, around Mae Sai, and between Umphang and Sangkhlaburi – where villages, hideaways and refugee camps occasionally get shelled either by the Burmese military or by rebel Karen or Mon forces – and the border between Cambodia and southern Isaan, which is littered with unexploded mines.

Because of the **violence in the deep south**, all Western governments are currently advising against travel to or through the border provinces of Songkhla, Yala, Pattani and Narathiwat, unless essential – see p.769 for further details. For up-to-the-minute advice on current political trouble-spots, consult your government's travel advisory.

Scams

Despite the best efforts of guidebook writers, TAT and the Thai tourist police, countless travellers to Thailand get scammed every year. Nearly all **scams** are easily avoided if you're on your guard against anyone who makes an unnatural effort to befriend you. We have outlined the main scams in the relevant sections of this guide, but con-artists are nothing if not creative, so if in doubt walk away at the earliest opportunity. The worst areas for scammers are the busy tourist centres, including many parts of Bangkok and the main beach resorts.

Many **tuk-tuk drivers** earn most of their living through securing **commissions** from tourist-oriented shops; this is especially true in Bangkok, where they will do their damnedest to get you to go to a gem shop (see p.201). The most common tactic is for drivers to pretend that the Grand Palace or other major sight you intended to visit is closed for the day (they usually invent a plausible reason, such as a festival or royal occasion; see p.130), and to then offer to take you on a round-city tour instead, perhaps even for free. The tour will invariably include a visit to a gem shop. The easiest way to avoid all this is to take a **metered taxi**; if you're fixed on taking a tuk-tuk, ignore any tuk-tuk that is parked up or loitering and be firm about where you want to go.

Self-styled **tourist guides**, **touts** and anyone else who might introduce themselves as **students** or **businesspeople** and offer to take you somewhere of interest, or invite you to meet their family, are often the first piece of bait in a well-honed chain of con-artists. If you bite, chances are you'll end up either at a gem shop or in a gambling den, or, at best, at a tour operator or hotel that you had not planned to patronize. This is not to say that you should never accept an invitation from a local person, but be extremely wary of doing so following a street encounter in Bangkok or the resorts. Tourist guides' ID cards are easily faked.

For many of these characters the goal is to get you inside a dodgy **gem shop**, nearly all of which are located in Bangkok. There is a full run-down of advice on how to avoid falling for the notorious low-grade gems scam on p.201, but the bottom line is that if you are not experienced at buying and trading in valuable gems you will definitely be ripped off, possibly even to the tune of several thousand dollars. Check the 2Bangkok website's account of a typical gem scam (ⓦwww.2bangkok.com/2bangkok/Scams/Sapphire.shtml) before you shell out any cash at all.

A less common but potentially more frightening scam involves a similar cast of warm-up artists leading tourists into a **gambling** game. The scammers invite their victim home on an innocent-sounding pretext, get out a pack of cards, and then set about fleecing the incomer in any number of subtle ways. Often this can be

Governmental travel advisories

Australian Department of Foreign Affairs ⓦ www.dfat.gov.au, www.smartraveller.gov.au
British Foreign & Commonwealth Office ⓦ www.fco.gov.uk
Canadian Department of Foreign Affairs ⓦ www.international.gc.ca
Irish Department of Foreign Affairs ⓦ www.foreignaffairs.gov.ie
New Zealand Ministry of Foreign Affairs ⓦ www.mft.govt.nz
South African Department of Foreign Affairs ⓦ www.dfa.gov.za
US State Department ⓦ www.travel.state.gov

especially scary as the venue is likely to be far from hotels or recognizable landmarks. You're unlikely to get any sympathy from police, as gambling is **illegal** in Thailand.

Age restrictions and other laws

Thai law requires that tourists **carry their original passports** at all times, though sometimes it's more practical to carry a photocopy and keep the original locked in a safety deposit. The **age of consent** is 15, but the law allows anyone under the age of 18, or their parents, to file charges in retrospect even if they consented to sex at the time. It is against the law to have sex with a prostitute who is under 18. It is illegal for **under-18s** to buy cigarettes or to drive and you must be 20 or over to **buy alcohol** or be allowed into a **bar or club** (ID checks are often enforced in Bangkok). It is illegal for anyone to **gamble** in Thailand (though many do).

Smoking in public is widely prohibited. The ban covers all air-conditioned public buildings (including restaurants but usually excluding bars and clubs) and air-conditioned trains, buses and planes and even extends to parks and the street; violators are subject to a B2000 fine. Dropping cigarette butts, **littering** and spitting in public places can also earn you a B2000 fine. There are fines for **overstaying your visa** (see p.37), **working without a permit**, and **not wearing a motorcycle helmet** and violating other **traffic laws**.

Drugs

Drug-smuggling carries a maximum penalty in Thailand of death and **dealing drugs** will get you anything from four years to life in a Thai prison; penalties depend on the drug and the amount involved. Travellers caught with even the smallest amount of drugs at airports and international borders are prosecuted for trafficking, and no one charged with trafficking offences gets bail. Heroin, amphetamines, LSD and ecstasy are classed as Category 1 drugs and carry the most severe penalties: even **possession** of Category 1 drugs for personal use can result in a **life sentence**. Away from international borders, most foreigners arrested in possession of small amounts of cannabis are released on bail, then fined and deported, but the law is complex and prison sentences are possible.

Despite occasional royal pardons, don't expect special treatment as a farang: you only need to read one of the first-hand accounts by foreign former prisoners (reviewed on p.855) or read the blogs at ⓦ www.thaiprisonlife.com to get the picture. The **police** actively look for tourists doing drugs, reportedly searching people regularly and randomly on Thanon Khao San, for example. They have the power to order a urine test if they have reasonable grounds for suspicion, and even a positive result for marijuana consumption could lead to a year's imprisonment. Be wary also of **being shopped** by a farang or local dealer keen to earn a financial reward for a successful bust (there are setups at the Ko Pha Ngan full moon parties, for example), or having substances slipped into your luggage (simple enough to perpetrate unless all fastenings are secured with padlocks).

If you are arrested, ask for your embassy to be contacted immediately, which is your right under Thai law (see p.207 for phone numbers), and embassy staff will talk you through procedures; the website of the British Embassy in Thailand also posts useful information, including a list of English-speaking lawyers, at Ⓦukinthailand.fco.gov.uk/en/help-for-british-nationals. The British charity Prisoners Abroad (Ⓦwww.prisonersabroad.org.uk) carries a detailed survival guide on its website, which outlines what to expect if arrested in Thailand, from the point of apprehension through trial and conviction to life in a Thai jail; if contacted, the charity may also be able to offer direct support to a British citizen facing imprisonment in a Thai jail.

The media

To keep you abreast of world affairs, there are several English-language newspapers in Thailand, though a mild form of censorship affects the predominantly state-controlled media, even muting the English-language branches on occasion.

Newspapers and magazines

Of the hundreds of **Thai-language newspapers and magazines** published every week, the sensationalist daily tabloid *Thai Rath* attracts the widest readership, with circulation of around a million, while the moderately progressive *Matichon* is the leading quality daily, with an estimated circulation of 600,000.

Alongside these, two daily **English-language papers** – the *Bangkok Post* (Ⓦwww.bangkokpost.com) and the *Nation* (Ⓦwww.nationmultimedia.com) – are capable of adopting a fairly critical attitude to governmental goings-on and cover major domestic and international stories as well as tourist-related issues. The *Nation* has recently adopted a split personality, covering mostly business news on its main pages while carrying a lively, poppy tabloid, the *Xpress*, inside. The *Post*'s *Spectrum* supplement, which comes inside the Sunday edition, stands out for its investigative journalism. Both the *Post* and *Nation* are sold at most newsstands in the capital as well as in major provincial towns and tourist resorts; the more isolated places receive their few copies at least one day late. Details of local English-language publications are given in the relevant Guide accounts.

You can also pick up **foreign publications** such as *Newsweek*, *Time* and the *International Herald Tribune* in Bangkok, Chiang Mai, and the major resorts; from Monday to Saturday, the *IHT* now publishes a special Thai edition, though it's short on Thai news. English-language bookstores such as Bookazine and some expensive hotels carry air-freighted, or sometimes locally printed and stapled, copies of foreign national newspapers for at least B50 a copy; the latter are also sold in tourist-oriented minimarkets in the big resorts.

Television

There are six government-controlled, terrestrial **TV channels** in Thailand: channels 3, 5 (owned and operated by the army), 7 and 9 transmit a blend of news, documentaries, soaps, sports, talk and quiz shows, while the more serious-minded PBS (formerly Thaksin Shinawatra's ITV) and NBT are public-service channels, owned and operated by the government's public relations department. **Cable** networks – available in many mid-range and most upmarket hotel rooms – carry channels from all around the world, including CNN from the US, BBC World from the UK and sometimes ABC from Australia, as well as English-language movie channels, MTV and various sports and documentary channels. Both the *Bangkok Post* and the *Nation* print the daily TV and cable **schedule**.

Radio

Thailand boasts over five hundred **radio stations**, mostly music-oriented, ranging from Virgin Radio's Eazy (105.5 FM), which serves up Western pop, through *luk thung* (see p.838) on 95FM, to Fat Radio, which plays Thai indie sounds (104.5 FM). Chulalongkorn University Radio (101.5 FM) plays classical music from 9.30pm to midnight every night. Net 107 on 107 FM is one of several stations that include English-language news bulletins.

With a **shortwave radio** – or by going **online** – you can pick up the BBC World Service (ⓦwww.bbc.co.uk/worldservice), Radio Australia (ⓦwww.radioaustralia.net.au), Voice of America (ⓦwww.voanews.com), Radio Canada (ⓦwww.rcinet.ca) and other international stations right across Thailand. Times and wavelengths change regularly, so get hold of a recent schedule just before you travel or consult the websites for frequency and programme guides.

Festivals

Nearly all Thai festivals have a religious aspect. The most theatrical are generally Brahmin (Hindu) in origin, honouring elemental spirits and deities with ancient rites and ceremonial costumed parades. Buddhist celebrations usually revolve round the local temple, and while merit-making is a significant feature, a light-hearted atmosphere prevails, as the wat grounds are swamped with food and trinket vendors and makeshift stages are set up to show *likay* folk theatre, singing stars and beauty contests.

Many of the **secular festivals** (like the elephant roundups and the Bridge over the River Kwai spectacle) are outdoor local culture shows, geared specifically towards Thai and farang tourists. Others are thinly veiled but lively trade fairs held in provincial capitals to show off the local speciality, be it exquisite silk weaving or especially tasty rambutans.

Few of the **dates** for religious festivals are fixed, so check with TAT for specifics (ⓦwww.tourismthailand.org). The names of the most touristy celebrations are given here in English; the more low-key festivals are more usually known by their Thai name (*ngan* means "festival"). Some of the festivals below are designated as national holidays – see p.85.

A festival calendar

January–March

Nakhon Sawan Chinese New Year (three days between mid-Jan and late Feb). The new Chinese year is welcomed in with exuberant parades of dragons and lion dancers, Chinese opera performances, an international lion-dance competition and a fireworks display. Also celebrated in Chinatowns across the country, especially in Bangkok and Phuket.

Chiang Mai Flower Festival (usually first weekend in Feb). Enormous floral sculptures are paraded through the streets.

Nationwide Maha Puja (particularly Wat Benjamabophit in Bangkok, Wat Phra That Doi Suthep in Chiang Mai and Wat Mahathat in Nakhon Si Thammarat; Feb full-moon day). A day of merit-making marks the occasion when 1250 disciples gathered spontaneously to hear the Buddha preach, and culminates with a candlelit procession round the local temple's bot.

Phra Phutthabat, near Lopburi Ngan Phrabat (early Feb and early March). Pilgrimages to the Holy Footprint attract food and handicraft vendors and travelling players. See p.269.

Lopburi King Narai Reign Fair (Feb). Costumed processions and a *son et lumière* show at Narai's palace.

That Phanom Ngan Phra That Phanom (Feb). Thousands come to pay homage at the holiest shrine in Isaan, which houses relics of the Buddha.

Nationwide Kite fights and flying contests (particularly Sanam Luang, Bangkok; late Feb to mid-April).

Golden Triangle Elephant Polo Tournament (a week in March; ⓦ www.anantaraelephantpolo.com). Teams from around the world compete on elephant-back in this variation on the traditional game. The tournament kicks off with an elephant parade. Held at the Elephant Ground inside the *Anantara Golden Triangle Resort* north of Chiang Rai.

April and May

Mae Hong Son and Chiang Mai Poy Sang Long (early April). Young Thai Yai boys precede their ordination into monkhood by parading the streets in floral headdresses and festive garb. See p.334 and p.389.

Nationwide Songkhran (particularly Chiang Mai, and Bangkok's Thanon Khao San; usually April 13–15). The most exuberant of the national festivals welcomes the Thai New Year with massive waterfights, sandcastle building in temple compounds and the inevitable parades and "Miss Songkhran" beauty contests. See p.334.

Prasat Hin Khao Phanom Rung Ngan Phanom Rung (usually April). The three-day period when the sunrise is perfectly aligned through fifteen doorways at these magnificent eleventh-century Khmer ruins is celebrated with daytime processions and nightly *son et lumière*. See p.508.

Nationwide Visakha Puja (particularly Bangkok's Wat Benjamabophit and Nakhon Si Thammarat's Wat Mahathat; May full-moon day). The holiest day of the Buddhist year, commemorating the birth, enlightenment and death of the Buddha all in one go; the most public and photogenic part is the candlelit evening procession around the wat.

Sanam Luang, Bangkok Raek Na (early May). The royal ploughing ceremony to mark the beginning of the rice-planting season; ceremonially clad Brahmin leaders parade sacred oxen and the royal plough, and interpret omens to forecast the year's rice yield. See p.139.

Yasothon Rocket Festival (Bun Bang Fai; weekend in mid-May). Beautifully crafted, painted wooden rockets are paraded and fired to ensure plentiful rains; celebrated all over Isaan, but especially lively in Yasothon. See p.528.

June–September

Hua Hin Jazz Festival (a weekend in late June; ⓦ www.huahinjazzfest.com). Well-known musicians from Thailand and abroad play for free at various special outdoor venues throughout the beach resort.

Dan Sai, near Loei Phi Ta Khon (end June or beginning July). Masked re-enactment of the Buddha's penultimate incarnation. See p.538.

Ubon Ratchathani Candle Festival (Asanha Puja; July, three days around the full moon). This nationwide festival marking the Buddha's first sermon and the subsequent beginning of the annual Buddhist retreat period (Khao Pansa) is celebrated across the northeast with parades of enormous wax sculptures, most spectacularly in Ubon Ratchathani. See p.520.

Bangkok International Film Festival (most recently held over a week in Sept, but has also been staged in Jan & July; ⓦ www.bangkokfilm.org). An annual chance to preview new and unusual Thai films alongside features and documentaries from Southeast Asia and beyond.

Nakhon Si Thammarat Tamboon Deuan Sip (Sept or Oct). Merit-making ceremonies to honour dead relatives accompanied by a ten-day fair. See p.635.

October–December

Phuket and Trang Vegetarian Festival (Ngan Kin Jeh; Oct or Nov). Chinese devotees become vegetarian for a nine-day period and then parade through town performing acts of self-mortification such as pushing skewers through their cheeks. Celebrated in Bangkok's Chinatown by most food vendors and restaurants turning vegetarian for about a fortnight. See p.180 and p.686.

Nong Khai and around Bang Fai Phaya Nak (usually Oct). The strange appearance of pink balls of fire above the Mekong River draws sightseers from all over Thailand. See p.546.

Nationwide Tak Bat Devo and Awk Pansa (especially Ubon Ratchathani and Nakhon Phanom; Oct full-moon day). Offerings to monks and general merrymaking to celebrate the Buddha's descent to earth from Tavatimsa heaven and the end of the Khao Pansa retreat. Celebrated in Ubon with a procession of illuminated boats along the rivers, and in Nakhon Phanom with another illuminated boat procession and Thailand–Laos dragon-boat races along the Mekong.

Surat Thani Chak Phra (mid-Oct). The town's chief Buddha images are paraded on floats down the streets and on barges along the river. See p.590.

Nan, Nong Khai, Phimai and elsewhere Boat Races (Oct to mid-Nov). Longboat races and barge parades along town rivers.

Nationwide Thawt Kathin (the month between Awk Pansa and Loy Krathong, generally Oct–Nov). During the month following the end of the monks' rainy-season retreat, it's traditional for the laity to donate new robes to the monkhood and this is celebrated in most towns with parades and a festival.

Nationwide Loy Krathong (particularly Sukhothai and Chiang Mai; full moon in Nov). Baskets (*krathong*) of flowers and lighted candles are floated on any available body of water (such as ponds, rivers, lakes, canals and seashores) to honour water spirits and celebrate the end of the rainy season. Nearly every town puts on a big show, with bazaars, public entertainments, fireworks, and in Chiang Mai, the release of paper hot-air balloons; in Sukhothai it is the climax of a *son et lumière* festival that's held over several nights. See p.278, p.334 and *Loy Krathong* colour section.

Wat Saket, Bangkok **Ngan Wat Saket (first week of Nov).** Probably Thailand's biggest temple fair, held around the Golden Mount, with all the usual festival trappings.

Surin **Elephant Roundup (third weekend of Nov).** Two hundred elephants play team games, perform complex tasks and parade in battle dress. See p.515.

Kanchanaburi **River Kwai Bridge Festival (ten nights from the last week of Nov into the first week of Dec).** Spectacular *son et lumière* at the infamous bridge.

Khon Kaen **Silk and Phuk Siao Festival (Nov 29–Dec 10).** Weavers from around the province come to town to sell their lengths of silk. See p.529.

Ayutthaya **World Heritage Site Festival (mid-Dec).** Week-long celebration, including a nightly historical *son et lumière* romp, to commemorate the town's UNESCO designation. See p.255.

Nationwide **New Year's Eve Countdown (Dec 31).** Most cities and tourist destinations welcome in the new year with fireworks, often backed up by food festivals, beauty contests and outdoor performances.

Entertainment and sport

Bangkok is the best place to catch authentic performances of classical Thai dance, though more easily digestible tourist-oriented shows are staged in most of the big tourist centres as well as in Bangkok. The country's two main Thai boxing stadia are also in the capital, but you'll come across local matches in the provinces too.

Drama and dance

Drama pretty much equals **dance** in classical Thai theatre, and many of the traditional dance-dramas are based on the *Ramakien*, the Thai version of the Hindu epic the *Ramayana*, an adventure tale of good versus evil which is taught in all the schools. Not understanding the plots can be a major disadvantage, so try reading an abridged version beforehand (see p.858, or p.135 for an outline) and check out the wonderfully imaginative murals at Wat Phra Kaeo in Bangkok. There are three broad categories of traditional Thai dance-drama – *khon*, *lakhon* and *likay* – described below in descending order of refinement.

Khon

The most spectacular form of traditional Thai theatre is **khon**, a stylized drama performed in masks and elaborate costumes by a troupe of highly trained classical dancers. There's little room for individual interpretation in these dances, as all the movements follow a strict choreography that's been passed down through generations: each graceful, angular gesture depicts a precise event, action or emotion which will be familiar to educated *khon* audiences. The dancers don't speak, and the story is chanted and sung by a chorus who stand at the side of the stage, accompanied by a classical *phipat* orchestra.

A typical *khon* performance features several of the best-known **Ramakien** episodes, in which the main characters are recognized by their masks, headdresses and heavily brocaded costumes. Gods and humans don't wear masks, but the hero Rama and heroine Sita always wear tall gilded headdresses and often appear as a trio with Rama's brother Lakshaman. Monkey **masks** are wide-mouthed: monkey army chief Hanuman always wears white, and his two right-hand men – Nilanol, the god of fire, and Nilapat, the god of death – wear red and black respectively. In contrast, the demons have grim mouths, clamped shut or snarling; Totsagan, king of the demons, wears a green face in battle and a gold one during peace, but always sports a two-tier headdress carved with two rows of faces.

Khon is performed with English subtitles at Bangkok's Sala Chalermkrung (see p.192) and is also featured within the various cultural **shows** staged by tourist restaurants in Bangkok, Phuket and Pattaya. Even if you don't see a show, you're bound to come across finely crafted real and replica *khon* masks both in museums and in souvenir shops all over the country.

Lakhon

Serious and refined, **lakhon** is derived from *khon* but is used to dramatize a greater range of stories, including Buddhist *Jataka* tales, local folk dramas and of course the *Ramakien*.

The form you're most likely to come across is *lakhon chatri*, which is performed at shrines like Bangkok's Erawan and at a city's *lak muang* as entertainment for the spirits and a token of gratitude from worshippers. Usually female, the *lakhon chatri* dancers perform as an ensemble, executing sequences that, like *khon* movements, all have minute and particular symbolism. They also wear ornate costumes, but no masks, and dance to the music of a *phipat* orchestra. Unfortunately, as resident shrine troupes tend to repeat the same dances a dozen times a day, it's rarely the sublime display it's cracked up to be. Bangkok's National Theatre stages the more elegantly executed *lakhon nai*, a dance form that used to be performed at the Thai court and often re-tells the *Ramakien*.

Likay

Likay is a much more popular and dynamic derivative of *khon* – more light-hearted, with lots of comic interludes, bawdy jokes and panto-style over-the-top acting and singing. Some *likay* troupes perform *Ramakien* excerpts, but a lot of them adapt pot-boiler romances or write their own and most will ham things up with improvisations and up-to-the-minute topical satire. Costumes might be traditional as in *khon* and *lakhon*, modern and Western as in films, or a mixture of both.

Likay troupes travel around the country doing shows on makeshift outdoor stages wherever they think they'll get an audience, most commonly at temple fairs. Performances are often free and generally last for about five hours, with the audience strolling in and out of the show, cheering and joking with the cast throughout. Televised *likay* dramas get huge audiences and always follow romantic soap-opera-style plot-lines. Short *likay* dramas are also a staple of Bangkok's National Theatre but for more radical and internationally minded *likay*, look out for performances by **Makhampom** (Ⓦwww.makhampom.net), a famous, long-established troupe with bases in Bangkok and Chiang Dao that pushes *likay* in new directions to promote social causes and involve minority communities.

Nang

Nang, or shadow plays, are said to have been the earliest dramas performed in Thailand, but now are rarely seen except in the far south, where the Malaysian influence ensures an appreciative audience for *nang thalung*. Crafted from buffalo hide, the two-dimensional *nang thalung* puppets play out scenes from popular dramas against a backlit screen, while the storyline is told through songs, chants and musical interludes. An even rarer *nang* form is the *nang yai*, which uses enormous cut-outs of whole scenes rather than just individual characters, so the play becomes something like an animated film. For more on shadow puppets and puppetry, see p.638.

Film

All sizeable towns have a **cinema** or two (Bangkok has over forty; see p.193) and tickets generally start at B80. The website Ⓦwww.movieseer.com lists the weekly schedule for many cinemas around the country. In some rural areas, villagers still have to make do with the travelling cinema, or *nang klarng plaeng*, which sets up a mobile screen in wat compounds or other public spaces, and often entertains the whole village in one sitting. However makeshift the cinema, the **king's anthem** is always played before every screening, during which the audience is expected to stand up.

Fast-paced Chinese blockbusters have long dominated the programmes at Thai cinemas, serving up a low-grade cocktail of sex, spooks, violence and comedy. Not understanding the dialogue is rarely a drawback, as the storylines tend to be simple and the visuals more entertaining than the words. In the cities, **Western films** are also popular, and new releases often get subtitled rather than dubbed. They are also quickly available as pirated DVDs sold at street stalls in the main cities and resorts.

In recent years Thailand's own film industry has been enjoying a boom, and in the larger cities and resorts you may be lucky enough to come across one of the bigger Thai hits showing with English subtitles. For an introduction to Thai cinema, see p.851.

Thai boxing

Thai boxing (*muay thai*) enjoys a following similar to soccer or baseball in the West: every province has a stadium and whenever the sport is shown on TV you can be sure that large noisy crowds will gather round the sets in streetside restaurants. The best place to see Thai boxing is at one of Bangkok's two main stadia, which between them hold bouts every night of the week (see p.193), but many tourist resorts also stage regular matches.

There's a strong spiritual and **ritualistic** dimension to *muay thai*, adding grace to an otherwise brutal sport. Each boxer enters the ring to the wailing music of a three-piece *phipat* orchestra, wearing the statutory red or blue shorts and, on his head, a sacred rope headband or *mongkhon*. Tied around his biceps are *phra jiat*, pieces of cloth that are often decorated with cabalistic symbols and may contain Buddhist tablets. The fighter then bows, first in the direction of his birthplace and then to the north, south, east and west, honouring both his teachers and the spirit of the ring. Next he performs a slow dance, claiming the audience's attention and demonstrating his prowess as a performer.

Any part of the body except the head may be used as an **offensive weapon** in *muay thai*, and all parts except the groin are fair targets. Kicks to the head are the blows which cause most knockouts. As the action hots up, so the orchestra speeds up its tempo and the betting in the audience becomes more frenetic. It can be a gruesome business, but it was far bloodier before modern boxing gloves were made compulsory in the 1930s, when the Queensbury Rules were adapted for *muay* – combatants used to wrap their fists with hemp impregnated with a face-lacerating dosage of ground glass.

A number of *muay thai* gyms and camps offer training **courses** for foreigners, including several in Bangkok, listed on p.194; Fairtex Muay Thai in Pattaya (ⓦwww.fairtexbkk.com); Lanna Muay Thai in Chiang Mai (see p.332); the Thai Boxing Garden in Hua Hin (see p.576); the Muay Thai Martial Arts Academy (MTMAA) in Surat Thani (ⓦwww.muaythaitraining.com); Jungle Gym on Ko Pha Ngan (see p.620); Monsoon Gym on Ko Tao (see p.630); Suwit Gym on Phuket (ⓦwww.bestmuaythai.com); and UK–Thai-run Ko Yao Noi Gym on Ko Yao Noi (see p.713).

Takraw

Whether in Bangkok or upcountry, you're quite likely to come across some form of **takraw** game being played in a public park, a wat compound or just in a backstreet alley. Played with a very light rattan ball (or one made of plastic to look like rattan), the basic aim of the game is to keep the ball off the ground. To do this you can use any part of your body except your hands, so a well-played *takraw* game looks extremely balletic, with players leaping and arching to get a good strike.

There are at least five versions of **competitive takraw**, based on the same principles. The version featured in the Southeast Asian Games and most frequently in school tournaments is played over a volleyball net and involves two teams of three; the other most popular competitive version has a team ranged round a basketball net trying to score as many goals as possible within a limited time period before the next team replaces them and tries to outscore them.

Other *takraw* games introduce more complex rules (like kicking the ball backwards with your heels through a ring made with your arms behind your back) and many assign points according to the skill displayed by individual players rather than per goal or dropped ball. Outside of school playing fields, proper *takraw* tournaments are rare, though they do sometimes feature as entertainment at Buddhist funerals.

Spas and traditional massage

With their focus on indulgent self-pampering, spas are usually associated with high-spending tourists, but the treatments on offer at Thailand's five-star hotels are often little different from those used by traditional medical practitioners, who have long held that massage and herbs are the best way to restore physical and mental well-being.

Thai massage (*nuad paen boran*) is based on the principle that many physical and emotional problems are caused by the blocking of vital energy channels within the body. The masseur uses his or her feet, heels, knees and elbows, as well as hands, to exert a gentle pressure on these channels, supplementing this acupressure-style technique by pulling and pushing the limbs into yogic stretches. This distinguishes Thai massage from most other massage styles, which are more concerned with tissue manipulation. One is supposed to emerge from a Thai massage feeling both relaxed and energized, and it is said that regular massages produce long-term benefits in muscles as well as stimulating the circulation and aiding natural detoxification.

Thais will visit a masseur for many conditions, including fevers, colds and muscle strain, but bodies that are not sick are also considered to benefit from the restorative powers of a massage, and nearly every hotel and guest house will be able to put you in touch with a **masseur**. On the more popular beaches, it can be hard to walk a few hundred metres without being offered a massage – something Thai tourists are just as enthusiastic about as foreigners. Thai masseurs do not use oils or lotions and the client is treated on a mat or mattress; you'll often be given a pair of loose-fitting trousers and perhaps a loose top to change into. English-speaking masseurs will often ask if you have any problem areas on your body that you want them to avoid; if your masseur doesn't speak English, the simplest way to signal this is to point at the offending area while saying *mai sabai* ("not well"); if you're in pain during a massage, wincing usually does the trick, perhaps adding *jep* ("it hurts"). A session should ideally last two hours and will cost from around B300.

The **science** behind Thai massage has its roots in Indian Ayurvedic medicine, which classifies each component of the body according to one of the four elements (earth, water, fire and air), and holds that balancing these elements within the body is crucial to good health. Many of the stretches and manipulations fundamental to Thai massage are thought to have derived from yogic practices introduced to Thailand from India by Buddhist missionaries in about the second century BC; Chinese acupuncture and reflexology have also had a strong influence. In the nineteenth century, King Rama III ordered a series of murals illustrating the principles of Thai massage to be painted around the courtyard of Bangkok's Wat Pho, and they are still in place today, along with statues of ascetics depicted in typical massage poses.

Wat Pho has been the leading school of Thai massage for hundreds of years, and it is possible to take courses there as well as to receive a massage (see p.137 for details); it also runs a residential massage school and clinic in Nakhon Pathom province (Ⓦwww.watpomassage.com). Masseurs who trained at Wat Pho are considered to be the best in the country and masseurs all across Thailand advertise this as a credential, whether or not it is true. Many Thais consider blind masseurs to be especially sensitive practitioners. While Wat Pho is the most famous place to take a **course** in Thai massage, many foreigners interested in learning this ancient science head for Chiang Mai, which offers the biggest concentration of massage schools (including another satellite branch of the Wat Pho school), though you will find others all over Thailand, including in Bangkok and at southern beach resorts.

All **spas** in Thailand feature traditional Thai massage and herbal therapies in their programmes, but most also offer dozens of other international treatments, including facials, aromatherapy, Swedish massage and various body wraps. Spa centres in upmarket hotels and resorts are usually open to non-guests but generally need to be booked in advance; day- spas that are not attached to hotels are found in some of the bigger cities and resorts and some of these may not require reservations.

Thailand's most famous luxury spas include the Oriental Spa, run by the renowned five-star *Oriental Hotel* in Bangkok; the Banyan Tree spas at the hotels of the same name in Bangkok and Phuket; the spas at the *Dhara Devi* and *Four Seasons* hotels in Chiang Mai; the Six Senses spas at the *Evason* in Pak Nam Pran; and the *Sila Evason* on Ko Samui; the Prana Spa at the *Tongsai Bay* on Samui; and the dedicated wellness and detox retreat *The Spa* on Ko Chang. See the relevant accounts for details.

Meditation centres and retreats

Of the hundreds of meditation temples in Thailand, a few cater specifically for foreigners by holding meditation sessions and retreats in English. Novices as well as practised meditators are generally welcome at these wats, but absolute beginners might like to consider the regular retreats at Wat Suan Mokkh and Wat Khao Tham, which are conducted by supportive and experienced Western teachers and include talks and interviews on Buddhist teachings and practice. The meditation taught is mostly Vipassana, or "insight", which emphasizes the minute observation of internal sensations; the other main technique you'll come across is Samatha, which aims to calm the mind and develop concentration (these two techniques are not entirely separate, since you cannot have insight without some degree of concentration).

Longer **retreats** are for the serious-minded only. All the temples listed below welcome both male and female English-speakers, but strict segregation of the sexes is enforced and many places observe a vow of silence. Reading and writing are also discouraged, and you'll generally not be allowed to leave the retreat complex unless absolutely necessary, so try to bring whatever you'll need in with you. All retreats expect you to wear modest clothing, and some require you to wear white – check ahead whether there is a shop at the retreat complex or whether you are expected to bring this with you.

An average day at any one of these monasteries starts with a **wake-up call** at around 4am and includes several hours of **group meditation** and chanting, as well as time put aside for chores and personal reflection. However long their stay, visitors are usually expected to keep the eight Buddhist precepts, the most restrictive of these being the abstention from food after midday and from alcohol, tobacco, drugs and sex at all times. Most wats ask for a minimal daily **donation** (around B150) to cover the costs of the simple accommodation and food.

Further details about many of the temples listed below – including how to get there – are given in the relevant sections in the Guide chapters. Though a little out of date, *A Guide to Buddhist Monasteries and Meditation Centres in Thailand*, published by the World Fellowship of Buddhists, contains plenty of useful general information. An even more useful resource is Ⓦwww.dhammathai.org, which provides lots of general background, practical advice and details of meditation temples and centres around Thailand.

Meditation centres and retreat temples

For information on **Wat Khao Tham** on Ko Pha Ngan, see p.615; **Wat Mahathat** in Bangkok, p.140; **Wat Phra That Doi Suthep** and **Wat Ram Poeng** in Chiang Mai, p.333; and **Wat Suan Mokkh** in Chaiya, p.588, and on Ko Samui, p.611.

Dhammasukkhasatan International Vipassana Meditation Centre Don Khun Huay, near Cha-am Ⓣ02 394 5048 or 089 142 1694. Quiet, English-medium retreats that can be started on any day, for which white clothing is required. Associated with the meditation centre of Bangkok's Wat Mahathat, where you can also get further information.

House of Dhamma Insight Meditation Centre 26/9 Soi Lardprao 15, Chatuchak, Bangkok Ⓣ02 511 0439, Ⓦwww.houseofdhamma.com. Regular introductory two-day courses in Vipassana, and day, weekend and week-long retreats. Courses in reiki and other subjects available.

Thailand Vipassana Centres Ⓦwww.dhamma.org. Frequent residential courses in a Burmese Vipassana tradition for beginners (10 days) and practised meditators (1–45 days), in Khon Kaen, Phitsanulok, Prachinburi (near Bangkok) and Sangkhlaburi. Foreign students must pre-register by email (application form available on the website).

Wat Pah Nanachat Ban Bung Wai, Amphoe Warinchamrab, Ubon Ratchathani 34310, Ⓦwww.forestsangha.org/com/watnana.htm. The famous monk, Ajahn Chah, established this forest monastery, 17km west of Ubon Ratchathani, specifically to provide monastic training for non-Thais, with English the primary language. Visitors who want to practise with the resident community are welcome, but the atmosphere is serious and intense and not for beginners or curious sightseers, and accommodation for students is limited, so you should write to the monastery before visiting, allowing several weeks to receive a written response.

World Fellowship of Buddhists (WFB) 616 Benjasiri Park, Soi Medhinivet off Soi 24, Thanon Sukhumvit, Bangkok Ⓣ02 661 1284–7, Ⓦwww.wfb-hq.org. Headquarters of an influential worldwide organization of (mostly Theravada) Buddhists, founded in Sri Lanka in 1950, this is the main information centre for advice on English-speaking retreats in Thailand. Holds a Buddhist discussion group and meditation session in English on the first Sunday of every month, with dharma lectures and discussions on the second Sunday.

Outdoor activities

The vast majority of travellers' itineraries take in a few days' trekking in the northern hills and a stint snorkelling or diving off the beaches of the south. There are also plenty of national parks to explore and opportunities for rock climbing and kayaking.

Trekking is concentrated in the north, so we've covered the practicalities of trekking in that chapter (see p.315), but there are smaller, less-touristy trekking operations in Kanchanaburi (see p.236), Sangkhlaburi (see p.247) and Umphang (see p.304).

Diving and snorkelling

Clear, warm waters (averaging 28°C), prolific marine life and affordable prices make Thailand a very rewarding place for **diving** and **snorkelling**. Most islands and beach resorts have at least one dive centre that organizes trips to outlying islands, teaches novice divers and rents out equipment, and in the bigger resorts there are dozens to choose from.

Thailand's three coasts are subject to different monsoon **seasons**, so you can dive all year round; the seasons run from November to April along the Andaman coast (though there is sometimes good diving here up until late Aug), and all year round on the Gulf and east coasts. Though every diver has their favourite reef, Thailand's **premier diving destinations** are generally considered to be Ko Similan, Ko Surin, Richelieu Rock and Hin Muang and Hin Daeng – all of them off the Andaman coast and described on p.699. As an accessible base for diving, Ko Tao off the Gulf coast is hard to beat, with deep, clear inshore water and a wide variety of dive sites in very close proximity. For **snorkellers**, the spectacular shallow reefs of Ko Surin national park are incomparable.

Whether you're snorkelling or diving, try to minimize your impact on the fragile reef structures by **not touching the reefs** and by asking your boatman not to anchor in the middle of one; **don't buy coral souvenirs**, as tourist demand only encourages local entrepreneurs to dynamite reefs.

Should you scrape your skin on coral, wash the wound thoroughly with boiled water, apply antiseptic and keep protected until healed. Wearing a T-shirt is a good idea when snorkelling to stop your back from getting sunburnt.

Thailand's main dive resorts

The east coast
Ko Chang (p.474)
Pattaya (p.441)

The Andaman coast
Ao Nang (p.731)
Khao Lak (p.675)
Ko Lanta (p.756)
Ko Phi Phi (p.740)
Phuket (p.698)

The Gulf coast
Ko Pha Ngan (p.614)
Ko Samui (p.597)
Ko Tao (p.626)

The deep south
Ko Lipe (p.786)

Diving

It's usually worth having a look at several **dive centres** before committing yourself to a trip or a course. Always verify the dive instructors' PADI (Professional Association of Diving Instructors) or equivalent accreditation and check to see if the dive shop is a member of PADI's International Resorts and Retailers Association (IRRA) as this guarantees a certain level of professionalism. You can view a list of IRRAs in Thailand at Ⓦwww.padi.com.

We've highlighted IRRA dive shops that are accredited Five-Star centres, as these are considered by PADI to offer very high standards, but you should always consult other divers first if possible. Some dive operators do fake their PADI credentials. Avoid booking ahead over the internet without knowing anything else about the dive centre, and be wary of any operation offering extremely cheap courses: maintaining diving equipment is an expensive business in Thailand so any place offering unusually good rates will probably be cutting corners and compromising your safety. Ask to **meet your instructor** or dive leader, find out how many people there'll be in your group, check out the kind of instruction given (some courses are over-reliant on videos) and look over the equipment, checking the quality of the air in the tanks yourself and also ensuring there's an oxygen cylinder on board. Most divers prefer to travel to the dive site in a decent-sized **boat** equipped with a radio and emergency medical equipment rather than in a longtail. If this concerns you, ask the dive company about their boat before you sign up; firms that use longtails generally charge less.

Insurance should be included in the price of courses and introductory dives; for qualified divers, you're better off checking that your general travel insurance covers diving, though some diving shops can organize cover for you. There are **recompression chambers** in Pattaya, on Ko Samui, on Ko Tao and on Phuket and it's a good idea to check whether your dive centre is a member of one of these outfits, as recompression services are extremely expensive for anyone who's not.

For books on diving in Thailand see p.858.

Trips and courses

All dive centres run programmes of one-day **dive trips** (featuring two dives) and **night dives** for B1300–4500 plus equipment, and many of the Andaman-coast dive centres also do three- to seven-day **live-aboards** to the exceptional reefs off the remote Similan and Surin islands (from B11,800).

Renting a full set of diving **gear**, including wetsuit, from a dive centre costs about B500 per day; most dive centres also rent **underwater cameras** for about B1000–1500 per day.

All dive centres offer a range of **courses** from beginner to advanced level, with equipment rental usually included in the cost; Ko Tao is now the largest dive-training centre in Southeast Asia, with around fifty dive companies including plenty of PADI Five-Star centres. The most popular courses are the one-day **introductory** or resort dive (a pep talk and escorted shallow dive, open to anyone aged 10 or over), which costs anything from B2000 for a very local dive to B7100 for an all-inclusive day-trip to the Similan Islands; and the four-day **open-water course**, which entitles you to dive without an instructor (from B9800 including at least two dives a day). Kids' Bubblemaker courses, for children aged 8–10, cost around B2000.

Snorkelling

Boatmen and tour agents on most beaches offer **snorkelling** trips to nearby reefs and many dive operators welcome snorkellers to tag along for discounts of thirty percent or more; not all diving destinations are rewarding for snorkellers though, so check the relevant account in this book first. As far as snorkelling **equipment** goes, the most important thing is that you buy or rent a mask that fits. To check the fit, hold the mask against your face, then breathe in and remove your hands – if it falls off, it'll leak water. If you're buying equipment, you should be able to kit yourself out with a mask, snorkel and fins for about B1000, available from most dive centres. Few places rent fins, but a mask and snorkel set usually costs about B100 a day to rent, and if you're going on a snorkelling day-trip they are often included in the price.

National parks and wildlife observation

Thailand's hundred-plus **national parks**, which are administered by the National Park, Wildlife and Plant Conservation Department (Ⓣ02 562 0760, Ⓦwww.dnp.go.th/National_park.asp), are generally the best places to **observe wildlife**. Though you're highly unlikely to encounter tigers or sun bears, you have a good chance of spotting gibbons, civets, mouse deer and hornbills and may even get to see a wild elephant. A number of wetlands also host a rewarding variety of birdlife. The vast majority of visitors head for one of the parks listed opposite, as these have the best facilities and are the most accessible. All parks charge an **entrance fee**, which for foreigners is usually B200 (B100 for children), though some charge B100 and a few charge B400.

Waymarked hiking **trails** in most parks are generally limited and rarely very challenging and decent park maps are hard to come by, so for serious national-park treks you'll need to hire a guide and venture beyond the public routes. Nearly all parks provide **accommodation** and/or campsites (see p.52). Some national parks **close** for several weeks or months every year for conservation, safety or environmental reasons; dates are listed on the National Parks' website.

For a detailed guide to Thailand's wildlife and their habitats, a look at the environmental issues, and a list of Thai wildlife charities and volunteer projects, see p.826.

Rock climbing

The limestone karsts that pepper southern Thailand's Andaman coast make ideal playgrounds for **rock-climbers**, and the sport has really taken off here in the past fifteen years. Most climbing is centred round **East Railay** and **Ton Sai** beaches on Laem Phra Nang in Krabi province (see p.736), where there are dozens of routes within easy walking

Top national parks

Ang Thong (p.596). Spectacular archipelago in the Gulf of Thailand, generally visited on a day-trip from Ko Samui.

Doi Inthanon (p.378). Waterfalls, hill-tribes, orchids, around four hundred bird species and the country's highest peak.

Erawan (p.237). An exceptionally pretty, seven-tiered waterfall that extends deep into the forest. Hugely popular as a day-trip from Kanchanaburi.

Khao Sam Roi Yot (p.579). Coastal flats on the Gulf coast known for their rich birdlife plus an extensive stalactite-filled cave system.

Khao Sok (p.665). Southern Thailand's most visited park has rainforest trails and caves plus a flooded river system with eerie outcrops and raft-house accommodation.

Khao Yai (p.494). Thailand's most popular national park, three hours from Bangkok, features half a dozen upland trails plus organized treks and night safaris.

Ko Similan (p.676). Remote group of Andaman Sea islands with famously fabulous reefs and fine above-water scenery. Mostly visited by dive boat but limited national park accommodation is provided.

Ko Surin (p.664). National marine park archipelago of unsurpassed reefs and breathtakingly beautiful coastal waters in the Andaman Sea. Great snorkelling and good national park campsites.

Ko Tarutao (see p.783). Beautiful and wildly varied land- and seascapes on the main 26km-long island and fifty other smaller islands on its western side.

Phu Kradung (see p.540). Dramatic and strange 1300-metre-high plateau, probably best avoided at weekends.

distance of tourist bungalows, restaurants and beaches. **Offshore Deep Water Soloing** – climbing a rock face out at sea, with no ropes, partner or bolts and just the water to break your fall – is also huge round here. Several **climbing schools** at East Railay and Ton Sai provide instruction (from B1000 per half-day), guides and all the necessary equipment (about B2400 per day for two people). Ko Phi Phi (see p.741) also offers a few routes and a couple of climbing schools, as does the quieter and potentially more interesting Ko Yao Noi (see p.711) and Ko Lao Liang (see p.776). There are also less-developed climbing areas near Chiang Mai (see p.322) and on Ko Tao (see p.630), as well as in Lopburi (see p.265). For an introduction to climbing on Railay and elsewhere in south Thailand, see ⓦwww.railay.com.

Sea kayaking and whitewater rafting

Sea kayaking is also centred around Thailand's Andaman coast, where the limestone outcrops, sea caves, *hongs* (hidden lagoons), mangrove swamps and picturesque shorelines of Ao Phang Nga in particular (see p.714) make for rewarding paddling. Kayaking day-trips around Ao Phang Nga can be arranged from any resort in Phuket, at Khao Lak, at all Krabi beaches and islands, and on Ko Yao Noi; multi-day kayaking expeditions are also possible as are self-guided trips from Ko Yao Noi lasting up to a month. Paddle Asia (ⓦwww.paddleasia.com) offer four- to eight-day sea-kayaking trips around the Trang Islands and the Tarutao National Marine Park islands (from US$820 per person) and over on Ko Samui, Blue Stars (see p.597) organize kayaking trips around the picturesque islands of the Ang Thong National Marine Park. Many other beach resorts rent kayaks (from B150 per hr) for casual, independent coastal exploration.

You can go **river kayaking** and **white-water rafting** on several rivers in north, west and south Thailand. Some stretches of these rivers can run quite fast, particularly during the rainy season from July to November, but there are plenty of options for novices too. The best time is from October through

February; during the hot season (March–June), many rivers run too low. The most popular whitewater-rafting rivers include the Umphang and Mae Khlong rivers near Umphang (see p.304) and the Pai River near Pai (see p.398). Gentler rafting excursions take place as part of organized treks in the north, as well as on the River Kwai and its tributaries near Kanchanaburi (see p.236), on the Kok River from Tha Ton (see p.403), on the Lang Suan River near Ranong (see p.587) and at Mae Hong Son (see p.392 and Pai (see p.398). Southwest of Chiang Mai, rafts can be rented from the adjacent national park headquarters for trips in Ob Luang Gorge (see p.381).

Gay and lesbian Thailand

Buddhist tolerance and a national abhorrence of confrontation and victimization combine to make Thai society relatively tolerant of homosexuality, if not exactly positive about same-sex relationships. Most Thais are extremely private and discreet about being gay, generally pursuing a "don't ask, don't tell" understanding with their family. The majority of people are horrified by the idea of gay-bashing and generally regard it as unthinkable to spurn a child or relative for being gay.

Hardly any Thai celebrities are out, yet the predilections of several respected social, political and entertainment figures are widely known and accepted. There is no mention of homosexuality at all in Thai law, which means that the **age of consent** for gay sex is fifteen, the same as for heterosexuals. However, this also means that gay rights are not protected under Thai law.

Although excessively physical displays of affection are frowned upon for both heterosexuals and homosexuals, Western gay couples should get no hassle about being seen together in public – it's much more acceptable, and common, in fact, for friends of the same sex (gay or not) to walk hand-in-hand, than for heterosexual couples to do so.

Transvestites (known as *katoey* or "ladyboys") and **transsexuals** are also a lot more visible in Thailand than in the West. You'll find cross-dressers doing ordinary jobs, even in small upcountry towns, and there are a number of transvestites and transsexuals in the public eye too – including national volleyball stars and champion *muay thai* boxers. The government tourist office vigorously promotes the transvestite cabarets in Pattaya, Phuket and Bangkok, all of which are advertised as family entertainment. *Katoey* also regularly appear as characters in soap operas, TV comedies and films, where they are depicted as harmless figures of fun. Richard Totman's *The Third Sex* (see p.856) offers an interesting insight into Thai *katoey*, their experiences in society and public attitudes towards them.

The scene

Thailand's gay scene is mainly focused on **mainstream venues** like karaoke bars, restaurants, massage parlours, gyms, saunas and escort agencies. For the sake of discretion, gay venues are usually intermingled with straight ones. Bangkok, Phuket and Pattaya have the biggest concentrations of farang-friendly gay bars and clubs, and they all host flamboyant annual **Gay Pride festivals** as well (check the websites listed below for schedules). There's a fledgling Pride event in Chiang Mai too, as well as an established bar scene. For a detailed guide to the gay and lesbian scene throughout the country, see the *Utopia Guide to Thailand* by John Goss, which can be downloaded via Ⓦwww.utopia-asia.com.

Thai **lesbians** generally eschew the word lesbian, which in Thailand is associated with male fantasies, instead referring to themselves as either *tom* (for tomboy) or *dee* (for lady). There are hardly any dedicated *tom-dee* venues in Thailand, but we've listed established ones where possible; unless otherwise specified, gay means male throughout this guide.

The farang-oriented gay **sex industry** is a tiny but highly visible part of Thailand's gay scene. with its tawdry floor shows and host services, it bears a dispiriting resemblance to the straight sex trade, and is similarly most active in Bangkok, Pattaya, Patong (on Phuket) and Chiang Mai. Like their female counterparts in the heterosexual fleshpots, many of the boys working in the gay sex bars that dominate these districts are underage; note that anyone caught having sex with a prostitute below the age of 18 faces imprisonment. A significant number of gay prostitutes are gay by economic necessity rather than by inclination. As with the straight sex scene, we do not list commercial gay sex bars in the guide.

Information and contacts for gay travellers

Anjaree PO Box 322, Rajdamnoen PO, Bangkok 10200 Ⓔanjaree@loxinfo.com. General information on the lesbian community in Thailand.

Bangkok Lesbian Ⓦwww.bangkoklesbian.com. Organized by foreign lesbians living in Thailand, Bangkok Lesbian hosts regular parties and posts general info and listings of the capital's lesbian-friendly hangouts on its website.

Gay People in Thailand Ⓦwww.thaivisa.com/forum/Gay-People-Thailand-f27.html. Popular forum for gay expats.

Long Yang Club Ⓦwww.longyangclub.org/thailand. This international organization was founded to promote friendship between men of Western and Eastern origin and runs regular socials.

Utopia Ⓦwww.utopia-asia.com and www.utopia-asia.com/womthai.htm. Asia's best gay and lesbian website lists clubs, events, accommodation, tour operators and organizations for gays and lesbians and has useful links to other sites in Asia and the rest of the world.

Travelling with children

Despite the relative lack of child-centred attractions in Thailand, there's plenty to appeal to families, both on the beach and inland, and Thais are famously welcoming to young visitors.

Of all the **beach resorts** in the country, two of the most family friendly are the islands of Ko Samui and Ko Lanta. Both have plenty of on-the-beach accommodation for mid- and upper-range budgets, and lots of easygoing open-air shorefront restaurants so that adults can eat in relative peace while kids play within view. Both islands also offer many day-tripping activities, from elephant riding to snorkelling. Phuket is another family favourite, though shorefront accommodation here is at a premium; there are also scores of less mainstream alternatives. In many beach resorts older kids will be able to go kayaking or learn rock climbing, and many dive centres will teach the PADI children's scuba courses on request: the Bubblemaker programme is open to 8-year-olds and the Discover Scuba Diving day is designed for anyone over 10.

Inland, the many **national parks** and their waterfalls and caves are good for days out, and there are lots of opportunities to go **rafting** and **elephant riding**. Kanchanaburi is a rewarding centre for all these, with the added plus that many of the town's guest houses are set round decent-sized lawns. Chiang Mai is another great hub for all the above and also offers boat trips, an attractive, modern zoo and aquarium, the chance to watch umbrella-makers and other craftspeople at work, and, in the Mae Sa valley, many family-oriented attractions, such as the botanical gardens and **butterfly farms**. Bangkok has several child-friendly **theme parks** and activity centres (see p.192), as does the beach resort of Pattaya (see p.440).

Should you be in Thailand in January, your kids will be able to join in the free entertainments and activities staged all over the country on **National Children's Day** (Wan Dek), which is held on the second Saturday of January. They also get free entry to zoos that day, and free rides on public buses.

Practicalities

Many of the expensive **hotels** listed in this guide allow one or two under-12s to share their parents' room for free, as long as no extra bedding is required. It's often possible to cram two adults and two children into the double rooms in budget and mid-range hotels (as opposed to guest houses), as beds in these places are usually big enough for two. An increasing number of guest houses now offer three-person rooms, and may even provide special family accommodation. Decent cots are available free in the bigger hotels, and in some smaller ones (though cots in these places can be a bit grotty), and top and mid-range rooms often come with a small fridge. Many hotels can also provide a **babysitting** service.

Few museums or transport companies offer student reductions, but in some cases children get **discounts**; these vary a lot and we've cited them in the Guide only where available and relevant. One of the more bizarre provisos is the State Railway's regulation that a child aged 3 to 12 qualifies for half-fare only if under 150cm tall; some stations have a measuring scale painted onto the ticket-hall wall. Most domestic airlines charge ten percent of the full fare for under-2s, and fifty percent for under-12s.

Although most Thai babies don't wear them, **disposable nappies** (diapers) are sold at convenience stores, pharmacies and supermarkets in big resorts and sizeable towns; for stays on lonely islands, consider bringing some washable ones as back-up. A **changing mat** is another necessity as there are few public toilets in Thailand, let alone ones with baby facilities (though posh hotels are always a useful option). International brands of powdered milk are available throughout the country, and brand-name baby food is sold in big towns and resorts, though some parents find restaurant-cooked rice and bananas go down just as well. Thai women do not **breastfeed** in public.

For touring, child-carrier backpacks are ideal. Opinions are divided on whether or not it's worth bringing a **buggy** or three-wheeled **stroller**. Where they exist, Thailand's pavements are bumpy at best, and there's an almost total absence of ramps; sand is especially difficult for buggies, though less so for three-wheelers. Buggies and strollers do, however, come in handy for feeding and even bedding small children, as highchairs and cots are only provided in the more upmarket hotels. You can buy buggies fairly cheaply in most towns, but if you bring your own and then wish you hadn't, most hotels and guest houses will keep it for you until you leave. Bring an appropriately sized **mosquito net** or buy one locally in any department store; a mini **sun tent** for the beach is also useful. Taxis and car-rental companies almost never provide baby **car seats**, and even if you bring your own you'll often find there are no seatbelts to strap them in with. Most department stores have dedicated kids' sections selling everything from bottles and dummies. There are even several Mothercare outlets in Bangkok.

Even more than their parents, children need protecting from the sun, unsafe drinking water, heat and unfamiliar **food**. Consider packing a jar of a favourite spread so that you can always rely on toast if all else fails to please. As with adults, you should be careful about unwashed fruit and salads and about dishes that have been left uncovered for a long time. As diarrhoea could be dangerous for a child, rehydration solutions (see p.40) are vital if your child goes down with it. Other significant **hazards** include thundering traffic; huge waves, strong currents and jellyfish; and the **sun** – not least because many beaches offer only limited shade, if at all. Sunhats, sunblock and waterproof suntan lotions are essential, and can be bought in the major resorts. You should also make sure, if possible, that your child is aware of the dangers of **rabies**; keep children away from **animals**, especially dogs and monkeys, and ask your medical advisor about rabies jabs.

Information and advice

Nancy Chandler's Family Travel Ⓦwww.nancychandler.net/travelwkids.asp. Plenty of unusual ideas on Thai-style entertainment for kids, plus tips, links and Thailand-themed kids' books.

Thailand 4 Kids Ⓦwww.thailand4kids.com. Sells an e-book guide covering the practicalities of family holidays in Thailand.

Travel essentials

Addresses

Thai **addresses** can be immensely confusing, mainly because property is often numbered twice, first to show which real-estate lot it stands in, and then to distinguish where it is on that lot. Thus 154/7–10 Thanon Rajdamnoen means the building is on lot 154 and occupies numbers 7–10. There's an additional idiosyncrasy in the way Thai roads are sometimes named: in large cities a minor road running off a major road is often numbered as a soi ("lane" or "alley", though it may be a sizeable thoroughfare), rather than given its own street name. Thanon Sukhumvit for example – Bangkok's longest – has minor roads numbered Soi 1 to Soi 103, with odd numbers on one side of the road and even on the other; so a Thanon Sukhumvit address could read something like 27/9–11 Soi 15, Thanon Sukhumvit, which would mean the property occupies numbers 9–11 on lot 27 on minor road number 15 running off Thanon Sukhumvit.

Charities and volunteer projects

Reassured by the plethora of well-stocked shopping plazas, efficient services and apparent abundance in the rice fields, it is easy to forget that life is extremely hard for many people in Thailand. Countless **charities** work with Thailand's many poor and disadvantaged communities: listed below are a few that would welcome help in some way from visitors. The website of the *Bangkok Post* also carries an extensive list of charitable foundations and projects in Thailand at Ⓦwww.bangkokpost.com/outlookwecare. For longer-term placements, see p.83; for volunteer jobs on charitable wildlife projects, see p.833; and for organized holidays that feature volunteer activities, see p.29.

Baan Unrak, Home of Joy Sangkhlaburi Ⓦwww.baanunrak.org. Works with ethnic-minority refugee women and children from Burma. Visitors and volunteers welcome. See p.248.

Chiang Mai Disabled Centre 133/1 Thanon Ratchaphakinai, Chiang Mai Ⓣ053 231941, Ⓦwww.disabled.infothai.com. Centrally placed outlet, managed by people with disabilities, for a foundation that provides, among other things, a wheelchair workshop and a training, resource and social centre for disabled people. Skilled long-term volunteers, donations and wheelchair sponsorships are sought, or just take your custom there for laundry and massage services.

Hill Area and Community Development Foundation Chiang Rai Ⓦwww.hadf.or.th. Aiming to help hill tribes in dealing with problems such as environmental management, HIV/AIDS, child and drug abuse, the foundation has set up a community-based tourism company, Natural Focus (see p.406), to offer mountain-life tours, volunteer opportunities and study programmes.

Human Development Foundation 100/11 Kae Ha Klong Toey 4, Thanon Damrongrathhaphipat, Klong Toey, Bangkok Ⓣ02 671 5313, Ⓦwww.mercycentre.org. Since 1972, this organization has been providing education and support for Bangkok's street kids and slum-dwellers as well as caring for those with HIV/AIDS. It now runs more than thirty kindergartens in the slums. Contact the centre for information about donations and volunteering, or visit it to purchase cards and gifts. *The Slaughterhouse: Stories from Bangkok's Klong Toey Slum* (see p.856) gives an eye-opening insight into this often invisible side of Thai life.

Koh Yao Children's Community Center Ko Yao Noi Ⓦwww.koyao-ccc.com. Aims to improve the English-language and lifelong learning skills of islanders on Ko Yao Noi. Visitors welcome. See p.713.

Lifelong Learning Foundation (Thailand) 64–66 Soi 101/1 Thanon Ladprao, Bangkok Ⓣ081 894 6936, Ⓦwww.trangsea.com. Promoting nature conservation and the personal development of sea gypsies and other local people in Trang province, this nonprofit organization will accept donations, but also encourages partnerships with sympathetic overseas organizations, and especially welcomes the custom of tourists at its resorts at Ban Chao Mai (see p.775) and on Ko Mook (see p.779) and Ko Libong (see p.781), and on its award-winning tours.

Mae Tao Clinic Mae Sot Ⓦwww.maetaoclinic.org. Award-winning health centre providing free care to Burmese refugees. Visitors and volunteers welcome. See p.301.

The Mirror Art Group 106 Moo 1, Ban Huay Khom, Tambon Mae Yao, Chiang Rai ⓣ053 737412, ⓦwww.mirrorartgroup.org. NGO working with the hill tribes in Chiang Rai province to help combat such issues as drug abuse, erosion of culture and trafficking of women and children; its subsidiary, Hilltribe Tour, offers trekking and homestays (see p.406). Volunteers with IT, English and teaching skills are sought, as well as monetary and in-kind donations such as secondhand books, clothes, toys and videos for local schools.

The Students' Education Trust (SET) ⓦwww.thaistudentcharity.org. High-school and further education in Thailand is a luxury that the poorest kids cannot afford so many are sent to live in temples instead. The SET helps such kids pursue their education and escape from the poverty trap. Some of their stories are told in *Little Angels: The Real-Life Stories of Twelve Thai Novice Monks* (see p.856). SET welcomes donations and sponsorship.

Thai Child Development Foundation Pha To ⓦwww.thaichilddevelopment.org. This small Thai-Dutch-run village project in Chumphon province helps educate, feed and look after needy local children. The foundation welcomes donations of games, toys, clothes, educational materials and money, and takes on volunteers for one to three months, but you can also support it by joining one of the eco-tours organized by its sister outfit Runs 'N Roses (see p.587).

We-Train International House Bangkok ⓦwww.we-train.co.th. Hotel in northern Bangkok whose profits help provide emergency housing, a clinic, a rape crisis centre, a training centre and other support for women and children, as well as a research institute. See p.121.

Costs

Thailand can be a very cheap place to travel. At the bottom of the scale, you can manage on a **budget** of about B650 (£13/US$19) per day if you're willing to opt for basic accommodation, eat, drink and travel as the locals do, and stay away from the more expensive resorts like Phuket, Ko Samui and Ko Phi Phi – and you'd have to work hard to stick to this daily allowance in Bangkok. On this budget, you'll be spending around B200 for a dorm or shared room (more for a single room), around B200 on three meals (eating mainly at night markets and simple noodle shops, and eschewing beer), and the rest on travel (sticking to non-air-con buses and third-class trains where possible) and incidentals. With extras like air-conditioning in rooms and on long-distance buses and trains, taking the various forms of taxi rather than buses or shared songthaews for cross-town journeys, and a meal and beer in a more touristy restaurant, a day's outlay would look more like B1000 (£20/US$30). Staying in well-equipped, mid-range hotels and eating in the more exclusive restaurants, you should be able to live very comfortably for around B2000 a day (£40/US$60).

Travellers soon get so used to the low cost of living in Thailand that they start **bargaining** at every available opportunity, much as Thai people do. Although it's expected practice for a lot of commercial transactions, particularly at markets and when hiring tuk-tuks and unmetered taxis (though not in supermarkets or department stores), bargaining is a delicate art that requires humour, tact and patience. If your price is way out of line, the vendor's vehement refusal should be enough to make you increase your offer: never forget that the few pennies or cents you're making such a fuss over will go a lot further in a Thai person's hands than in your own.

It's rare that foreigners can bargain a price down as low as a Thai could, anyway, while **two-tier pricing** has been made official at government-run sights, as a kind of informal tourist tax: at national museums and historical parks, for example, foreigners often pay a B30–40 admission charge while Thais get in for B10; and at national parks, foreigners pay up to B400 entry while Thais generally pay just B20. A number of privately owned tourist attractions follow a similar two-tier system, posting an inflated price in English for foreigners and a lower price in Thai for locals.

Big-spending shoppers who are departing via Suvarnabhumi, Chiang Mai, Hat Yai, Pattaya or Phuket airports can save some money by claiming a **Value Added Tax refund** (ⓦwww.rd.go.th/vrt), though it's a bit of a palaver for seven percent (the current rate of VAT). The total amount of your purchases (gems are excluded) from participating shops needs to be at least B5000 per person, of which a minimum of B2000 per shop per day. You'll need to show your passport and fill in an application form (to which original tax invoices need to be attached) at the shop. At the relevant airport, you'll need to show your form and purchases to customs officers before checking in, then make your claim from VAT refund officers – from which fees of at least B100 are deducted.

Customs regulations

The **duty-free** allowance on entry to Thailand is 200 cigarettes (or 250g of tobacco) and a litre of spirits or wine.

To **export antiques** or newly cast **Buddha images** from Thailand, you need to have a licence granted by the Fine Arts Department (the export of antique Buddhas is forbidden). Licences can be obtained for example through the Office of Archeology and National Museums, 81/1 Thanon Si Ayutthaya (near the National Library), Bangkok (Ⓣ02 628 5032), or through the national museums in Chiang Mai or Phuket. Applications take at least three working days in Bangkok, generally more in the provinces, and need to be accompanied by the object itself, some evidence of its rightful possession, two postcard-sized colour photos of it, taken face-on and against a white background, and photocopies of the applicant's passport; furthermore, if the object is a Buddha image, the passport photocopies need to be certified by your embassy in Bangkok. Some antiques shops can organize all this for you.

Departure taxes

International and domestic **departure taxes** are included in the price of all tickets.

Electricity

Mains **electricity** is supplied at 220 volts AC and is available at all but the most remote villages and basic beach huts. Where electricity is supplied by generators and/or solar power, for example on the smaller, less populated islands, it is often rationed to evenings only. If you're packing phone and camera chargers, a hair dryer, laptop or other appliance, you'll need to take a set of travel-plug adapters with you as several plug types are commonly in use, most usually with two round pins, but also with two flat-blade pins, and sometimes with both options.

Insurance

Most visitors to Thailand will need to take out **specialist travel insurance**, though you should check exactly what's covered. Insurers will generally not cover travel in Songkhla, Yala, Pattani and Narathiwat provinces in the deep south, as Western governments are currently advising against going to these areas unless it's essential – see p.769 for further details. Policies generally also exclude so-called **dangerous sports** unless an extra premium is paid: in Thailand this can mean such things as scuba diving, white-water rafting and trekking.

Internet

Internet access is very widespread and very cheap in Thailand. You'll find traveller-oriented **internet cafés** in every touristed town and resort in the country – there are at least twenty in the Banglamphu district of Bangkok, for example – and even remote islands like Ko Mak and Ko Phayam provide internet access via satellite phones. In untouristed neighbourhoods throughout the country you can always check your email at the ubiquitous online games centres, favourite after-school haunts that are easily spotted from the piles of schoolboy pumps outside the door. Competition keeps prices low: upcountry you could expect to pay as little as B20 per hour, while rates in tourist centres average B1 per minute or B2 by satellite. Some mid-sized towns and cities in Thailand also offer a public internet service, called **Catnet**, at the government telephone office (usually located inside or adjacent to the main post office). To use the service, you need to buy a B100 card with a Catnet PIN, which should give you around three hours of internet time at any of these public terminals.

Small but increasing numbers of budget guest houses and cheap hotels, especially in Bangkok, offer **wi-fi** in all or parts of their establishment; most upmarket hotels have it, though rates are sometimes astronomical. Plenty of cafés, bars and other locations across the country provide wi-fi, but some places such as *Starbuck's* charge around B150 per hour for the privilege. For a list of hot spots nationwide, try Ⓦwww.jiwire.com; for free locations, go to Ⓦwww.stickmanweekly.com.

Laundry

Guest houses and hotels all over the country run low-cost, same-day **laundry** services. In some places you pay per item, in others you're charged by the kilo (generally from B30–50 per kg); ironing is often included in the price.

Left luggage

Most major train stations have **left luggage** facilities, where bags can be stored for up to twenty days (from B30–80 per item per day); at bus stations you can usually persuade someone official to look after your stuff for a few hours. Many guest houses and hotels also offer an inexpensive and reliable service and there's also left luggage at Bangkok, Chiang Mai and Phuket international airports (B50–100 per day).

Living in Thailand

The most common source of **employment** in Thailand is **teaching English**, and Bangkok and Chiang Mai are the most fruitful places to look for jobs. You can search for openings at schools all over Thailand on ⓦwww.ajarn.com, which also features extensive general advice on teaching and living in Thailand. Another useful resource is the excellent ⓦwww.thaivisa.com, whose scores of well-used forums focus on specific topics that range from employment in Thailand to legal issues and cultural and practical topics.

If you're a qualified **dive instructor**, you might be able to get seasonal work at one of the major resorts – in Phuket, Khao Lak and Ao Nang and on Ko Chang, Ko Phi Phi, Ko Lanta, Ko Samui and Ko Tao, for example. Guest-house noticeboards occasionally carry adverts for more unusual jobs, such as playing extras in Thai movies. A tourist visa does not entitle you to work in Thailand, so, legally, you'll need to apply for a **work permit**.

Study, work and volunteer programmes

For voluntary work at smaller grassroots projects, see p.80; for volunteer placements at wildlife charity projects, see p.833.

AFS Intercultural Programs ⓦwww.afs.org. Intercultural exchange organization with programmes in over fifty countries.

Council on International Educational Exchange (CIEE) US ⓦwww.ciee.org. Leading NGO that organizes paid year-long placements as English teachers in schools in central and northern Thailand.

Phuket English teachers ⓦwww.phukethasbeengoodtous.org. Welcomes short- and longer-term volunteers to teach and assist on its Practical English Language programme at schools on Phuket. The aim of the foundation is to improve kids' standards of English so that they can get the better-paid jobs in Phuket's tourist industry.

Reefcheck Thailand ⓦwww.thaiecolodge.com/reefcheck.php. The Thai chapter of the international marine conservation NGO welcomes interested paying volunteer divers, trainee divers and snorkellers to help survey local reefs, especially along the north Andaman coast, including the Surin and Similan islands. Based on Ko Ra (see p.662).

Starfish Ventures ⓦwww.starfishvolunteers.com. Paying volunteer and gap-year placements at environmental and social community projects in Surin, Mae Hong Son, Rayong and Phuket.

Volunteer Teaching in Thailand ⓦwww.volunteerteacherthailand.org. Continuing the good work begun by the thousands of volunteers who came to Khao Lak to help rebuild lives and homes following the 2004 tsunami, this organization teaches English to Khao Lak kids and adults to enhance their future prospects in the local tourist industry. Teaching experience is appreciated but not essential.

Volunthai ⓦwww.volunthai.com. Invites young volunteers to teach English in rural schools in northeast Thailand; minimum one-month commitment. The minimal fees cover homestay accommodation.

Thai language classes

The most popular places to **study Thai** are Chiang Mai and Bangkok, where there's plenty of choice, including private and group lessons for both tourists and expats. AUA (American University Alumni; ⓦwww.auathailand.org) has outlets in both Bangkok and Chiang Mai (see p.333). In Bangkok, there's also Jentana and Associates (ⓦwww.thai-lessons.com), and Nisa Thai Language School (ⓦwww.nisathailanguageschool.com). For more information and directories of language schools, see ⓦwww.learningthai.com.

Mail

Overseas airmail usually takes around seven days from Bangkok, a little longer from the more isolated areas (it's worth asking at the post office about their express EMS services, which can cut this down to three days and aren't prohibitively expensive). **Post offices**, many of which offer money-wiring facilities (in association with Western Union) and parcel packing, are generally open Monday to Friday 8.30am to 4.30pm, Saturday 9am to noon; some close Monday to Friday noon to 1pm and may stay open until 6pm, and a few open 9am to noon on Sundays and public holidays. Almost all main post offices across the country operate a **poste restante** service and will hold letters for one to three months. Mail should be addressed: *Name* (family name underlined or capitalized), Poste Restante, GPO, *Town or City*, Thailand. It will be filed by surname, though it's always wise to check under your first initial as well. The smaller post offices pay scant attention to who takes what, but in the busier GPOs you need to show your passport, pay B1 per letter or B2 per parcel received, and sign for them.

Post offices are the best places to buy **stamps**, though hotels and guest houses often sell them too, charging an extra B1 per stamp. An airmail letter of under 10g costs B17 to send to Europe or Australia and B19 to North America; standard-sized postcards cost B12, larger ones and aerogrammes B15, regardless of where they're going. The **surface** rate for parcels to the UK is B950 for the first kg, then B175 per kg; to the US B550 for the first kg, then B140 per kg; and to Australia B650 for the first kg, then B110 per kg; the package should reach its destination in three months. The **airmail** rate for parcels to the UK is B900 for the first kg, then B380 per kg; to the US B950 for the first kg, then B500 per kg; and to Australia B750 for the first kg, then B350 per kg; the package should reach its destination in one or two weeks.

Maps

For most major destinations, the **maps** in this book should be all you need, though you may want to supplement them with larger-scale maps of Bangkok and the whole country. Bangkok bookshops are the best source of these; where appropriate, detailed local maps and their stockists are recommended throughout the Guide. If you want to buy a map before you get there, Rough Guides' 1:1,200,000 map of Thailand is a good option – and, since it's printed on special rip-proof paper, it won't tear. Reasonable alternatives include the 1:1,500,000 maps produced by Nelles and Bartholomew.

For **drivers**, the best atlas (also in CD format) is *Thailand Deluxe Atlas* published by thinknet (Ⓦwww.thinknet.co.th): at a scale of 1:550,000 it's bilingual and regularly updated, but costs B550. It's available at most bookstores in Thailand where English-language material is sold. If you can't get hold of that, you could go for the relevant 1:300,000 maps of each province published by PN Map Centre; some of the detail on these maps is only in Thai, but they should have enough English to be useful.

Trekking maps are hard to come by, except in the most popular national parks where you can usually pick up a free handout showing the main trails.

Money and banks

Thailand's unit of currency is the **baht** (abbreviated to "B"), divided into 100 satang – which are rarely seen these days. Coins come in B1 (silver), B2 (golden), B5 (silver) and B10 (mostly golden, encircled by a silver ring) denominations, notes in B20, B50, B100, B500 and B1000 denominations, inscribed with Western as well as Thai numerals, and generally increasing in size according to value.

At the time of writing, **exchange rates** were around B35 to US$1, B45 to €1 and B50 to £1. A good site for current exchange rates is Ⓦwww.xe.com. Note that Thailand has no black market in foreign currency. Because of severe currency fluctuations in the late 1990s, a few tourist-oriented businesses now quote their prices in **US dollars**, particularly luxury hotels and dive centres.

Banking hours are Monday to Friday from 8.30am to 3.30 or 4.30pm, but exchange kiosks in the main tourist centres are always open till at least 5pm, sometimes 10pm, and upmarket hotels change money 24 hours a day. The Suvarnabhumi Airport exchange counters also operate 24 hours, while exchange kiosks at overseas airports with flights to Thailand usually keep Thai currency.

Sterling and US dollar **travellers' cheques** are accepted by banks, exchange booths and upmarket hotels in every sizeable Thai town, and most places also deal in a variety of other currencies; everyone offers better rates for cheques than for straight cash. Generally, a total of B33 in commission and duty is charged per cheque – though kiosks and hotels in isolated places may charge extra – so you'll save money if you deal in larger cheque denominations.

American Express, Visa and MasterCard **credit and debit cards** are accepted at top hotels as well as in some posh restaurants, department stores, tourist shops and travel agents, but surcharging of up to seven percent is rife, and theft and forgery are major industries – try not to let the card out of your sight, always demand any carbon copies, and never leave cards in baggage storage. With a debit or credit card and personal identification number (PIN), you can also withdraw cash from hundreds of 24-hour **ATMs** around the country. Almost every town now has at least one bank with an ATM that accepts overseas cards (all the banks marked on our maps throughout the Guide have ATMs), and there are a growing number of stand-alone ATMs in supermarkets.

Opening hours and public holidays

Most **shops** open long hours, usually Monday to Saturday from about 8am to 8pm, while department stores operate daily from around 10am to 9pm. Private office hours are generally Monday to Friday 8am to 5pm and Saturday 8am to noon, though in tourist areas these hours are longer, with weekends worked like any other day. Government offices work Monday to Friday 8.30am to noon and 1 to 4.30pm, and national museums tend to stick to these hours too, but some close on Mondays and Tuesdays rather than at weekends.

Many tourists only register **national holidays** because trains and buses suddenly get extraordinarily crowded: although banks and government offices shut on these days, most shops and tourist-oriented businesses carry on regardless, and TAT branches continue to dispense information. Some national holidays are celebrated with theatrical festivals, for a calendar of which see p.65. The only time an inconvenient number of shops, restaurants and hotels do close is during **Chinese New Year**, which, though not marked as an official national holiday, brings many businesses to a standstill for several days in late January or February. You'll notice it particularly in the south, where most service industries are Chinese-managed.

Thais use both the Western Gregorian **calendar** and a Buddhist calendar – the Buddha is said to have died (or entered Nirvana) in the year 543 BC, so Thai dates start from that point: thus 2010 AD becomes 2553 BE (Buddhist Era).

National holidays

Jan 1 Western New Year's Day
Feb (day of full moon) Maha Puja: commemorates the Buddha preaching to a spontaneously assembled crowd of 1250.
April 6 Chakri Day: the founding of the Chakri dynasty.
April (usually 13–15) Songkhran: Thai New Year
May 1 National Labour Day
May 5 Coronation Day
May (early in the month) Royal Ploughing Ceremony: marks start of rice-planting season.
May (day of full moon) Visakha Puja: the holiest of all Buddhist holidays, which celebrates the birth, enlightenment and death of the Buddha.
July (day of full moon) Khao Pansa: the start of the annual three-month Buddhist rains retreat, when new monks are ordained.
Aug 12 Queen's birthday
Oct 23 Chulalongkorn Day: the anniversary of Rama V's death.
Dec 5 King's birthday: also celebrated as national Fathers' Day.
Dec 10 Constitution Day
Dec 31 Western New Year's Eve

Phones

Local **calls within Thailand** are very cheap (as little as B1 for 3min from a coin payphone), but inter-provincial rates cost B3–12 per min; dial ☎1234 before the zero to reduce this to B0.50–2 per min. Deregulation of the Thai telecommunications industry has made **calling internationally** from Thailand a convoluted, though cheaper, business, with the state-owned companies, CAT (contact centre ⓣ1322, ⓦwww.cattelecom.com) and TOT (ⓣ1100, ⓦwww.tot.co.th), competing for business: each now offers a premium-rate service with its own **prefix** (CAT's ⓣ001 and TOT's ⓣ007), as well as a cheaper, generally lower-quality, VOIP (voice-over-internet protocol) prefix (CAT's ⓣ009 and TOT's ⓣ008). Visitors can access these prefixes variously on mobile phones or via phone cards, while many private international call offices (where your call is timed and you pay at the end) in tourist areas such as Bangkok's Thanon Khao San now use ⓣ009 or 008 to access the lower VOIP rates – plus a service charge to the customer, of course.

When **dialling** any number in Thailand, you must now always preface it with what used to be the area code, even when dialling from the same area. Where we've given several line numbers – eg ⓣ02 431 1802–9 – you can substitute the last digit, 2, with any digit between 3 and 9. For **directory enquiries** within Thailand, call ⓣ1133.

All mobile-phone numbers in Thailand have recently been changed from nine to ten digits, by adding the number "8" after the initial zero (you may still come across cards and brochures giving the old nine-digit number). Note also, however, that Thais tend to change mobile-phone providers – and therefore numbers – comparatively frequently, in search of a better deal.

One final local idiosyncrasy: Thai phone books list people by their first name, not their family name.

Phone cards

The most flexible **phone card** available is TOT's **Pin Phone 108 Card**, which allows both domestic and international calls. Equipped with a PIN number, it can be used from any payphone or fixed landline. Offering the same services, the **TOT Card** has no PIN number but can only be used in special TOT green-and-yellow payphones, not in the more commonly found stainless-steel payphones. With either of these cards, which are available in B50–500 denominations from 7-Eleven and Family Mart supermarkets, for example, calls to the UK and Australia cost B9 (ⓣ007) or B7 (ⓣ008) per minute, US and Canada B9 (ⓣ007) or B5 (ⓣ008), New Zealand B17 (ⓣ007) or B15 (ⓣ008) and South Africa B32 (ⓣ007) or B7 (ⓣ008); calls to Ireland currently cost B24 per minute with either prefix.

CAT's cards are available from most post offices and many supermarkets, but can only be used for international calls. Their Thaicard, available in B100–1000 denominations, can be used in designated purple cardphones – if you can't happen to find one, head for the nearest government telephone centre, which is usually located within or adjacent to a town's main post office. With a Thaicard, you use the ⓣ001 prefix, at rates roughly comparable with TOT's ⓣ007 phone-card charges. CAT's **Phone Net** cards, which use the ⓣ009 prefix and come in B200–500 denominations, can be used, in conjunction with a PIN number, from any payphone or fixed landline or from a mobile with international roaming. Rates are roughly comparable with TOT's ⓣ008 phone-card charges, though there's currently a long-term special promotion of B2 per minute to landlines in the UK, US and Canada, B2.5 Ireland, Australia and New Zealand, and B4 South Africa.

There's also a **private cardphone system** called **Lenso** (ⓦwww.lensophonecard.com), which operates mostly in Bangkok and tourist centres. To use Lenso's yellow phones, you either need a special Lenso phone card (available from shops such as 7-Eleven and Family Mart in B200, B300 and B500 denominations), or you can use a credit card. Rates, however, are generally higher than TOT's phone-card rates. If you're really hunting for a telephonic bargain, keep your eyes peeled for new, smaller **private phone cards**, such as Dee (ⓦwww.thookdee.com) and Hello by Hatari (ⓦwww.hatari.net), which use call-back and/or PIN number systems, and offer international calls to the most popular destinations for as little as B1 per minute.

Mobile phones

An increasing number of tourists are taking their **mobile phones** (*moe toe*) to Thailand. Visitors from the US may well need to have a dual- or tri-band phone, but GSM 900Hz and 1800Hz, and 3G, the systems most commonly found in other parts of the world, are all available in Thailand. Most foreign networks have links with Thai networks, but it's worth checking with your phone provider before you travel; it's also worth checking how much coverage there is for your network within Thailand. For a list of network types and providers in Thailand, along with coverage maps and roaming partners, go to Ⓦwww.gsmworld.com/roaming.

If you want to use your mobile a lot in Thailand, it may well be worth getting hold of a rechargeable **Thai SIM card** with a local phone number. An AIS 1-2-Call card (Ⓦwww.one-2-call.ais.co.th) will give you the widest coverage in Thailand, and top-up cards are available at 7-Eleven stores across the country. Their call rates start at B0.75 per minute within Thailand; international call rates depend on the prefix used (see above), ranging from B7 per minute to the UK, for example, on Ⓣ008 or 009, through B9 on Ⓣ007, to B18 on Ⓣ001. Texts cost B2 domestic, B9 to the UK, for example.

Your own network operator may be able to give you useful advice before you leave home about **exchanging SIM cards**, including any unlocking codes that may be necessary. Thai SIM cards are available at mobile-phone outlets all over the country, but the best place to buy a card and have any necessary technical adjustments made, including setting up voicemail, is the Mah Boon Krong Centre in Bangkok (see p.194); an AIS 1-2-Call SIM card, for example, will cost you around B300, including your first B50 worth of calls, though look out for periodic special offers that include substantial credit bonuses.

International dialling codes

Calling from abroad, the international **country code** for Thailand is **66**, after which you leave off the initial zero of the Thai number.

Calling from Thailand, you'll need the relevant country code (see above for information on prefixes):

Australia 61
Canada 1
Ireland 353
New Zealand 64
South Africa 27
UK 44
US 1

For **international directory enquiries** and operator services, call Ⓣ100.

Photography

Most towns and all resorts have at least one **camera shop** where you will be able to get your digital pictures downloaded on to a CD for B100–150; the shops all have card readers. In tourist centres many internet cafés also offer CD-burning services, though if you want to email your pictures bringing your own cable will make life easier.

Time

Thailand is in the same time zone year-round, with no daylight savings period. It's five hours ahead of South Africa, seven hours ahead of GMT, twelve hours ahead of US Eastern Standard Time, three hours behind Australian Eastern Standard Time and five hours behind New Zealand Standard Time.

Tipping

It is usual to **tip** hotel bellboys and porters B20, and to round up taxi fares to the nearest B10. Most guides, drivers, masseurs, waiters and maids also depend on tips, and although some upmarket hotels and restaurants will add an automatic ten percent service charge to your bill, this is not always shared out.

Tourist information

The **Tourism Authority of Thailand**, or **TAT** (Ⓦwww.tourismthailand.org), maintains offices in several cities abroad and has 31 branches within Thailand (all open daily 8.30am–4.30pm, though a few close noon–1pm for lunch) plus counters at Suvarnabhumi International Airport. Regional offices should have up-to-date information on local festival dates and transport schedules, but none of them offers accommodation booking, and service can be variable. You can contact the TAT tourist assistance phoneline from anywhere in the country for free on Ⓣ1672 (daily 8am–8pm). In Bangkok, the Bangkok Tourism Division is a better source of information on the capital (see p.102). In some smaller towns that don't qualify for a local TAT office, the information gap is filled by a **municipal**

tourist assistance office, though at some of these you may find it hard to locate a fluent English-speaker.

TAT offices abroad

Australia & New Zealand Suite 2002, Level 20, 56 Pitt St, Sydney, NSW 2000 ⓣ02/9247 7549, ⓦwww.thailand.net.au.
South Africa Contact the UK office.
UK & Ireland 1st Floor, 17–19 Cockspur St, London SW1Y 5BL ⓣ0870/900 2007, ⓦwww.tourismthailand.co.uk.
US & Canada 61 Broadway, Suite 2810, New York, NY 10006 ⓣ212/432-0433, ⓔinfo@tatny.com; 611 North Larchmont Blvd, 1st Floor, Los Angeles, CA 90004 ⓣ323/461-9814, ⓔtatla@tat.or.th.

Travellers with disabilities

Thailand makes few provisions for its disabled citizens and this obviously affects **travellers with disabilities**, but taxis, comfortable hotels and personal tour guides are all more affordable than in the West and most travellers with disabilities find Thais only too happy to offer assistance where they can. Hiring a local tour guide to accompany you on a day's sightseeing is particularly recommended: government tour guides can be arranged through any TAT office.

Most **wheelchair-users** end up driving on the roads because it's too hard to negotiate the uneven pavements, which are high to allow for flooding and invariably lack dropped kerbs. Crossing the road can be a trial, particularly in Bangkok and other big cities, where it's usually a question of climbing steps up to a bridge rather than taking a ramped underpass. Few buses and trains have ramps but in Bangkok some Skytrain stations and all subway stations have lifts.

Several **tour companies** in Thailand specialize in organizing trips featuring adapted facilities, accessible transport and escorts. The Bangkok-based Help and Care Travel Company (ⓣ081 375 0792, ⓦwww.wheelchairtours.com) designs **accessible holidays** in Thailand for slow walkers and wheelchair-users and its website carries a (short) list of wheelchair-accessible hotels in the main tourist centres. In Chiang Mai, *Baan Khun Daeng* (ⓣ053 242874, ⓦmembers.chello.nl/danblokker/e_home.html) is a wheelchair-accessible guest house run by a wheelchair-user who can also arrange accessible tours around north Thailand. Also in Chiang Mai, Thai Focus (ⓦwww.thaifocus.com) is used to designing trips for disabled travellers and providing carers where appropriate. Phuket-based Worldwide Dive and Sail (ⓣ076 383819, ⓦwww.worldwidediveandsail.com) specializes in **diving and sailing** live-aboard trips for deaf and hard-of-hearing people and Mermaid's Dive Centre in Pattaya (ⓣ038 232219, ⓦwww.learn-in-asia.com/handicapped_diving.htm; see p.441) runs International Association of Handicapped Divers programmes for **disabled divers** and instructors.

Guide

Guide

1 Bangkok

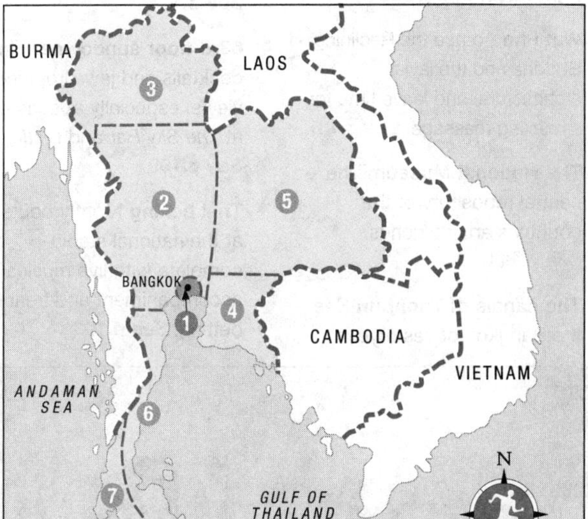
BURMA
LAOS
BANGKOK
CAMBODIA
VIETNAM
ANDAMAN SEA
GULF OF THAILAND
MALAYSIA
N
0
250 km
1
2
3
4
5
6
7
8

CHAPTER 1

Highlights

* **Thanon Khao San** Legendary hangout for Southeast Asia backpackers; the place for cheap sleeps, baggy trousers and tall tales. See p.111
* **The Grand Palace** The country's least-missable sight, incorporating its holiest and most dazzling temple, Wat Phra Kaeo. See p.130
* **Wat Pho** Admire the Reclining Buddha and the lavish architecture, and leave time for a relaxing massage. See p.137
* **The National Museum** The central repository of the country's artistic riches. See p.141
* **The canals of Thonburi** See the Bangkok of yesteryear on a touristy but memorable longtail-boat ride. See p.155
* **Jim Thompson's House** An elegant Thai design classic. See p.162
* **Chatuchak Weekend Market** Eight thousand stalls selling everything from triangular pillows to secondhand Levis. See p.171
* **63rd-floor sundowner** Fine cocktails and jaw-dropping views, especially at sunset, at *The Sky Bar* and *Distil*. See p.189
* **Thai boxing** Nightly bouts at the national stadia, complete with live musical accompaniment and frenetic betting. See p.193

▲ Restoring the murals at Wat Phra Kaeo

1

Bangkok

The headlong pace and flawed modernity of Bangkok match few people's visions of the capital of exotic Siam. Spiked with scores of high-rise buildings of concrete and glass, it's a vast flatness that holds a population of at least nine million, and feels even bigger. But under the shadow of the skyscrapers you'll find a heady mix of chaos and refinement, of frenetic markets, snail's-pace traffic jams and hushed golden temples, of dispiriting, zombie-like sex shows and early morning alms-giving ceremonies. One way or another, the place will probably get under your skin – and if you don't enjoy the challenge of taking on the "Big Mango", you can spend a couple of days on the most impressive temples and museums, have a quick shopping spree and then strike out for the provinces.

Most budget travellers head for the **Banglamphu** district, where if you're not careful you could end up watching DVDs all day long and selling your shoes when you run out of money. The district is far from having a monopoly on Bangkok accommodation, but it does have the advantage of being just a short walk from the major sights in the **Ratanakosin** area: the dazzling ostentation of the **Grand Palace** and **Wat Phra Kaeo**, lively and grandiose **Wat Pho** and the **National Museum**'s hoard of exquisite works of art. Once those cultural essentials have been seen, you can choose from a whole bevy of lesser sights, including **Wat Benjamabophit** (the "Marble Temple"), especially at festival time, and **Jim Thompson's House**, a small, personal museum of Thai design.

For livelier scenes, explore the dark alleys of **Chinatown**'s bazaars or head for the water: the great **Chao Phraya River**, which breaks up and adds zest to the city's landscape, is the backbone of a network of **canals** that remains fundamentally intact in the west-bank Thonburi district. Inevitably the waterways have earned Bangkok the title of "Venice of the East", a tag that seems all too apt when you're wading through flooded streets in the rainy season. Back on dry land, **shopping** varies from touristic outlets pushing silks, handicrafts and counterfeit watches, through home-grown boutiques selling street-wise fashions and stunning contemporary decor, to thronging local markets where half the fun is watching the crowds. Similarly, the city offers the country's most varied **entertainment**, ranging from traditional dancing and the orchestrated bedlam of Thai boxing, through hip bars and clubs playing the latest imported sounds, to the farang-only sex bars of the notorious Patpong district, a tinseltown Babylon that's the tip of a dangerous iceberg. Even if the above doesn't appeal, you'll almost certainly pass through Bangkok once, if not several times – not only is it Thailand's main port of entry, it's also the obvious place to sort out **onward travel**, with good deals on international air tickets, as well as a convenient menu of embassies for visas to neighbouring countries.

A little history

Bangkok is a relatively young capital, established in 1782 after the Burmese sacked Ayutthaya, the former capital. A temporary base was set up on the western bank of the Chao Phraya River, in what is now **Thonburi**, before work started on the more defensible east bank, where the French had built a grand, but short-lived fort in the 1660s. The first king of the new dynasty, Rama I, built his palace at **Ratanakosin**, within a defensive ring of two (later expanded to three) canals, and this remains the city's spiritual heart.

Initially, the city was largely **amphibious**: only the temples and royal palaces were built on dry land, while ordinary residences floated on thick bamboo rafts on the river and canals; even shops and warehouses were moored to the river bank. A major shift in emphasis came in the second half of the nineteenth century, first under Rama IV (1851–68), who as part of his effort to restyle the capital along European lines built Bangkok's first roads, and then under Rama V (1868–1910), who constructed a new residential palace in Dusit, north of Ratanakosin, and laid out that area's grand boulevards.

Since World War II, and especially from the mid-1960s onwards, Bangkok has seen an explosion of **modernization**, which has blown away earlier attempts at orderly planning and left the city without an obvious centre. Most of the canals have been filled in, replaced by endless rows of cheap, functional concrete shophouses, high-rises and housing estates, sprawling over a built-up area of 330 square kilometres. The benefits of Thailand's **economic boom** since the 1980s have been concentrated in Bangkok, attracting migration from all over the country and making the capital ever more dominant: the population, over half of which is under 30 years of age, is now forty times that of the second city, Chiang Mai. Every aspect of national life is centralized in the city, but the governor of Bangkok is not granted enough power to deal with the ensuing problems, notably that of **traffic** – which in Bangkok now comprises four-fifths of the nation's automobiles. The Skytrain and the subway have undoubtedly helped, but the governor was unable to get the competing systems to intersect properly or ticket jointly, and it's left to ingenious, local solutions such as the Khlong Saen Saeb canal boats and side-street motorbike taxis to keep the city moving. And there's precious little chance to escape from the pollution in green space: the city has only 0.4 square metres of public parkland per inhabitant, the lowest figure in the world, compared, for example, to London's 30.4 square metres per person.

City of angels

When Rama I was crowned in 1782, he gave his new capital a grand 43-syllable name to match his ambitious plans for the building of the city. Since then, 21 more syllables have been added. Krungthepmahanakhornbowornrattanakosinmahintarayutthaya mahadilokpopnopparatratchathaniburiromudomratchaniwetmahasathanamornpiman avatarnsathitsakkathattiyavisnukarprasit is certified by the *Guinness Book of Records* as the longest place-name in the world, roughly translating as "Great city of angels, the supreme repository of divine jewels, the great land unconquerable, the grand and prominent realm, the royal and delightful capital city full of nine noble gems, the highest royal dwelling and grand palace, the divine shelter and living place of the reincarnated spirits". Fortunately, all Thais refer to the city simply as **Krung Thep**, "City of Angels", though plenty can recite the full name at the drop of a hat. **Bangkok** – "Village of the Plum Olive" – was the name of the original village on the Thonburi side; with remarkable persistence, it has remained in use by foreigners since the time of the French garrison.

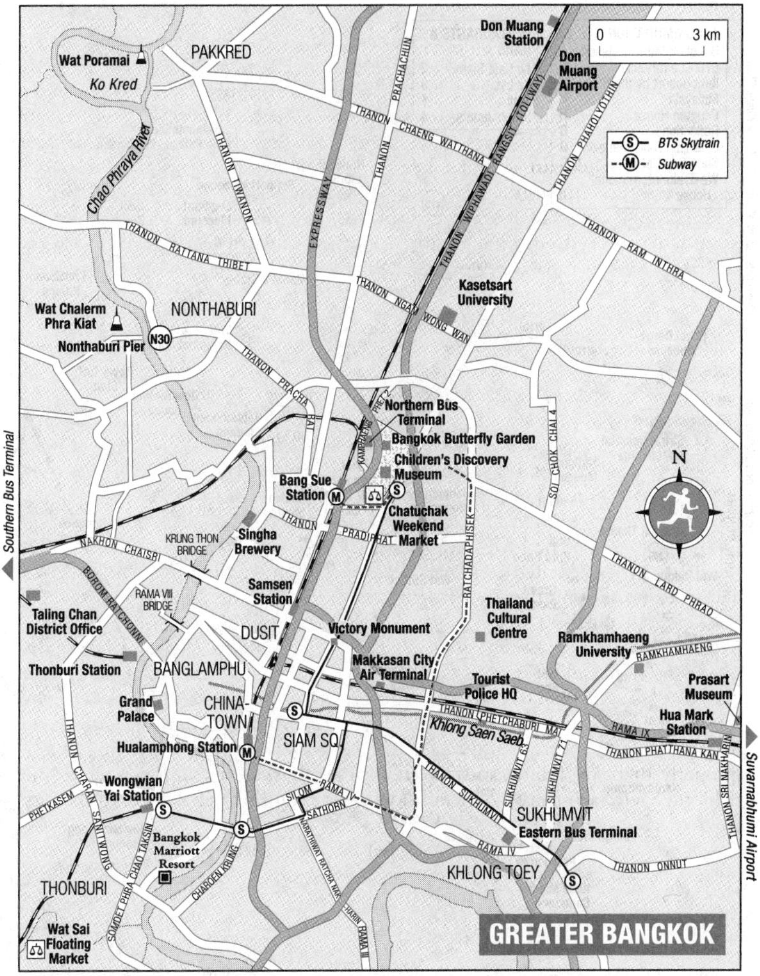

Arrival

Unless you arrive in Bangkok by train, be prepared for a long trip into the city centre. Suvarnabhumi Airport is 25km out and the three bus stations are not much closer in, though at least the Eastern Terminal is hard by a Skytrain stop.

By air

Bangkok's main airport is **Suvarnabhumi** (coded "BKK" and pronounced "soo-wanna-poom"; Ⓦ www.bangkokairportonline.com), 25km east of central Bangkok between highways 7 and 34. At the time of writing, the only scheduled flights using the old **Don Muang Airport** (coded "DMK"; Ⓦ www.donmuangairportonline.com), 25km north of the city, were Nok Air and

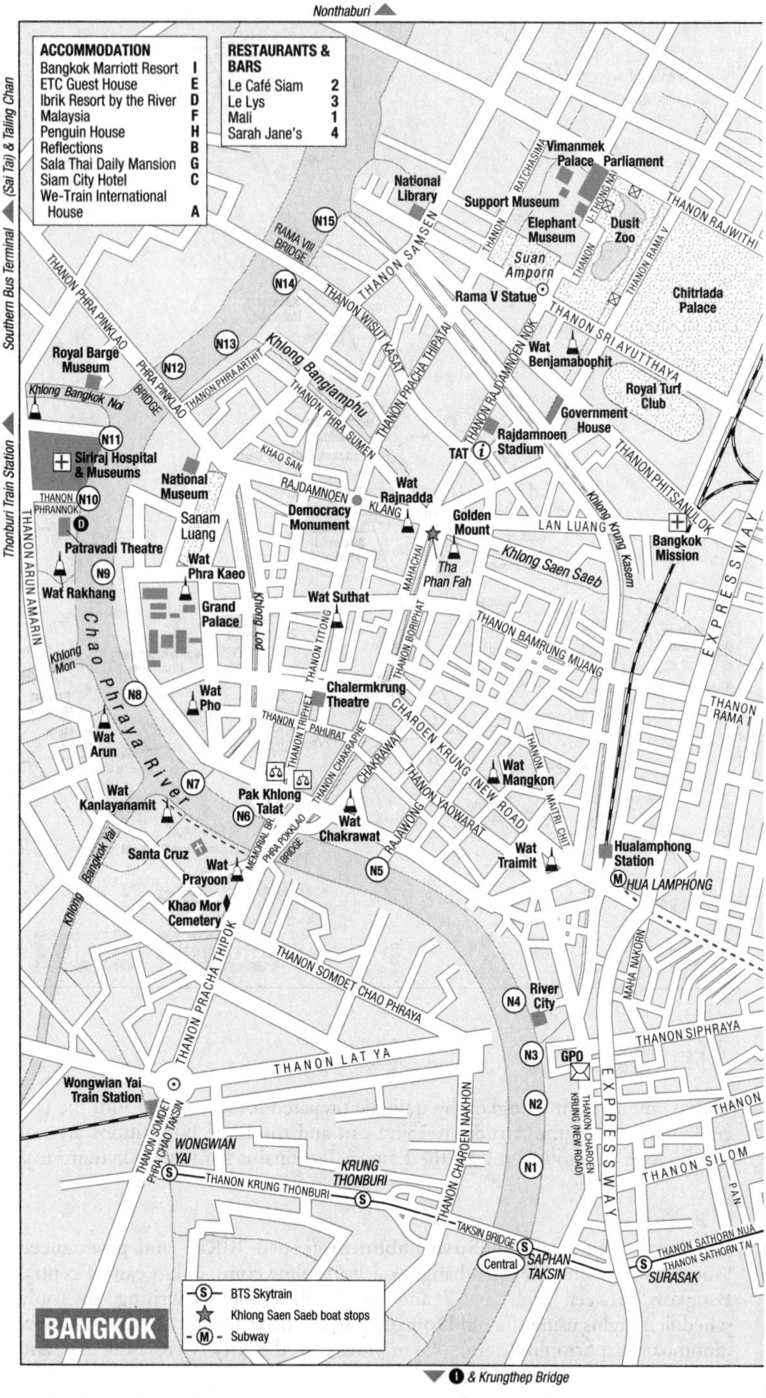
Nonthaburi
Southern Bus Terminal (Sai Tai) & Taling Chan
Thonburi Train Station
1 & Krungthep Bridge
ACCOMMODATION
Bangkok Marriott Resort I
ETC Guest House E
Ibrik Resort by the River D
Malaysia F
Penguin House H
Reflections B
Sala Thai Daily Mansion G
Siam City Hotel C
We-Train International House A
RESTAURANTS & BARS
Le Café Siam 2
Le Lys 3
Mali 1
Sarah Jane's 4
National Library
Vimanmek Palace
Parliament
Support Museum
Elephant Museum
Dusit Zoo
Suan Amporn
Rama V Statue
Chitrlada Palace
Wat Benjamabophit
Royal Turf Club
Government House
Rajdamnoen Stadium
TAT
Royal Barge Museum
Khlong Bangkok Noi
Siriraj Hospital & Museums
National Museum
Sanam Luang
Patravadi Theatre
Wat Rakhang
Wat Phra Kaeo
Grand Palace
Khlong Lod
Wat Rajnadda
Democracy Monument
Golden Mount
Tha Phan Fah
Khlong Saen Saeb
Khlong Krung Kasem
Bangkok Mission
Wat Suthat
Chalermkrung Theatre
Wat Pho
Wat Arun
Khlong Mon
Chao Phraya River
Wat Kanlayanamit
Pak Khlong Talat
Wat Chakrawat
Wat Mangkon
Wat Traimit
Hualamphong Station
HUA LAMPHONG
Santa Cruz
Wat Prayoon
Khao Mor Cemetery
Khlong Bangkok Yai
River City
GPO
Wongwian Yai Train Station
WONGWIAN YAI
KRUNG THONBURI
SAPHAN TAKSIN
Central
SURASAK
THANON PHRA PINKLAO
PHRA PINKLAO BRIDGE
RAMA VIII BRIDGE
THANON PHRA ARTHIT
Khlong Banglamphu
THANON PHRA SUMEN
THANON WISUT KASAT
THANON SAMSEN
THANON PRACHA THIPATAI
THANON RAJDAMNOEN NOK
THANON RATCHASIMA
THANON U-THONG NAI
THANON RAMA V
THANON RAJWITHI
THANON SRI AYUTTHAYA
THANON PHITSANULOK
KHAO SAN
RAJDAMNOEN KLANG
LAN LUANG
MAHACHAI
THANON PHRANNOK
THANON ARUN AMARIN
THANON TITONG
THANON BORIPHAT
THANON BAMRUNG MUANG
THANON RAMA I
THANON TRIPHET
THANON PAHURAT
THANON CHAKRAPHET
CHAKRAWAT
CHAROEN KRUNG (NEW ROAD)
THANON YAOWARAT
RAJAWONG
THANON MAITRI CHIT
MEMORIAL BR.
PHRA POKKLAO BRIDGE
THANON PRACHA THIPOK
THANON SOMDET CHAO PHRAYA
MAHA NAKORN
THANON LAT YA
THANON SIPHRAYA
THANON CHAROEN KRUNG (NEW ROAD)
THANON CHAROEN NAKHON
THANON SOMDET PHRA CHAO TAKSIN
THANON KRUNG THONBURI
TAKSIN BRIDGE
EXPRESSWAY
THANON SILOM
PAN
THANON SATHORN NUA
THANON SATHORN TAI
N1 N2 N3 N4 N5 N6 N7 N8 N9 N10 N11 N12 N13 N14 N15
BTS Skytrain
Khlong Saen Saeb boat stops
Subway
BANGKOK

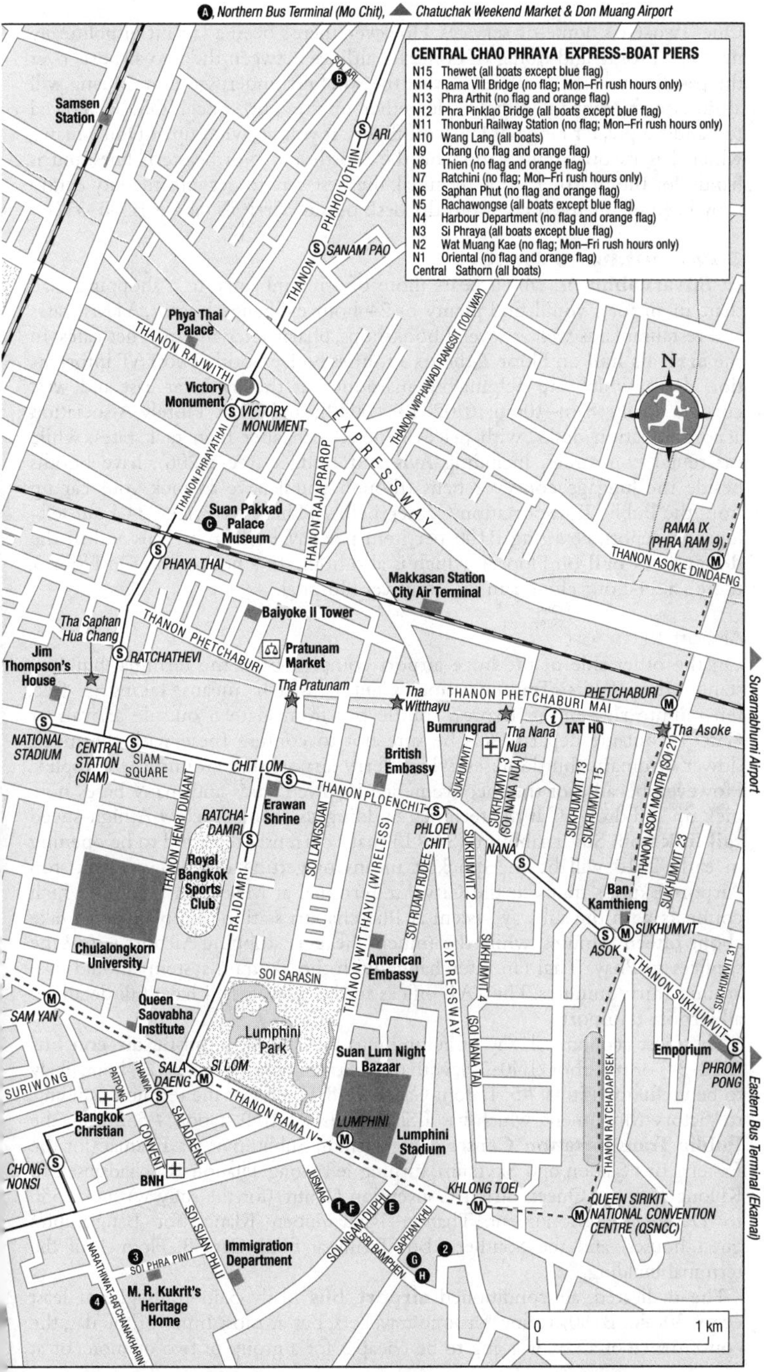
A, Northern Bus Terminal (Mo Chit), Chatuchak Weekend Market & Don Muang Airport
CENTRAL CHAO PHRAYA EXPRESS-BOAT PIERS
N15 Thewet (all boats except blue flag)
N14 Rama VIII Bridge (no flag; Mon–Fri rush hours only)
N13 Phra Arthit (no flag and orange flag)
N12 Phra Pinklao Bridge (all boats except blue flag)
N11 Thonburi Railway Station (no flag; Mon–Fri rush hours only)
N10 Wang Lang (all boats)
N9 Chang (no flag and orange flag)
N8 Thien (no flag and orange flag)
N7 Ratchini (no flag; Mon–Fri rush hours only)
N6 Saphan Phut (no flag and orange flag)
N5 Rachawongse (all boats except blue flag)
N4 Harbour Department (no flag and orange flag)
N3 Si Phraya (all boats except blue flag)
N2 Wat Muang Kae (no flag; Mon–Fri rush hours only)
N1 Oriental (no flag and orange flag)
Central Sathorn (all boats)
Samsen Station
SOI ARI
ARI
THANON PHAHOLYOTHIN
SANAM PAO
Phya Thai Palace
THANON RAJWITHI
Victory Monument
VICTORY MONUMENT
EXPRESSWAY
THANON WIPHAWADI RANGSIT (TOLLWAY)
N
THANON PHRAYATHAI
THANON RAJAPRAROP
Suan Pakkad Palace Museum
PHAYA THAI
RAMA IX (PHRA RAM 9)
THANON ASOKE DINDAENG
Makkasan Station City Air Terminal
Baiyoke II Tower
Tha Saphan Hua Chang
THANON PHETCHABURI
Pratunam Market
Jim Thompson's House
RATCHATHEVI
Tha Pratunam
Tha Witthayu
THANON PHETCHABURI MAI
PHETCHABURI
Suvarnabhumi Airport
Bumrungrad
Tha Nana Nua
TAT HQ
Tha Asoke
NATIONAL STADIUM
CENTRAL STATION (SIAM)
SIAM SQUARE
CHIT LOM
British Embassy
SUKHUMVIT 1
SUKHUMVIT 3 (SOI NANA NUA)
SUKHUMVIT 13
SUKHUMVIT 15
THANON ASOK MONTRI (SOI 21)
SUKHUMVIT 23
THANON HENRI DUNANT
THANON PLOENCHIT
Erawan Shrine
RATCHA-DAMRI
SOI LANGSUAN
THANON WITTHAYU (WIRELESS)
PHLOEN CHIT
SUKHUMVIT 2
NANA
Royal Bangkok Sports Club
RAJDAMRI
SOI RUAM RUDEE
Ban Kamthieng
SUKHUMVIT
ASOK
Chulalongkorn University
American Embassy
EXPRESSWAY
SUKHUMVIT 4 (SOI NANA TAI)
THANON SUKHUMVIT
SUKHUMVIT 31
SOI SARASIN
THANON WITTHAYU
SAM YAN
Queen Saovabha Institute
Lumphini Park
Suan Lum Night Bazaar
Emporium
PHROM PONG
Eastern Bus Terminal (Ekamai)
SURIWONG
PATPONG
THANIYA
SALA DAENG
SI LOM
THANON RAMA IV
THANON RATCHADAPISEK
Bangkok Christian
CONVENT
SALADAENG
LUMPHINI
Lumphini Stadium
CHONG NONSI
BNH
JUSMAG
SOI NGAM DUPHLI
SRI BAMPHEN
SAPHAN KHU
KHLONG TOEI
QUEEN SIRIKIT NATIONAL CONVENTION CENTRE (QSNCC)
NARATHIWAT-RATCHANAKHARIN
SOI SUAN PHLU
SOI PHRA PINIT
Immigration Department
M. R. Kukrit's Heritage Home
0
1 km

One-Two-Go's domestic services. However, there's been a fair bit of politically motivated toing and froing of domestic airlines between the two airports over the past few years: it may well be that the woefully underused Don Muang will again close to scheduled flights altogether, or it might, conceivably, be allowed to handle a greater range of low-cost flights. If you do wind up at Don Muang, which has its own train station on the North and Northeastern lines and is handy for the Northern Bus Terminal, the best way to get into the city centre is by licensed, metered taxi from the desk outside Arrivals (about B300–350).

Suvarnabhumi Airport

At **Suvarnabhumi**, which bears more of a resemblance to a shopping mall than an airport, you'll find plenty of 24-hour exchange booths, ATMs, cafés and restaurants, as well as several bookshops, pharmacies and internet cafés. In the **arrivals hall** on Floor 2, there's a tourist police booth; two TAT information desks, which are helpful but marooned at the hall's far east and west corners (daily 8am–10pm; ⓣ02 134 0040); and Thai Hotels Association accommodation desks, with prices generally cheaper than rack rates; while car-rental companies, including Avis and Budget (see p.206), have booths beside the luggage conveyor belts (though you'll have to pick your car up from the Public Transportation Center; below). There are pricey, 24-hour left-luggage depots, charging B100 per item per day, both in arrivals and in the **departures hall** on Floor 4, which is also home to a post office. On Floor 3, there's a 24-hour clinic run by Samitivej Hospital.

Airport transport

On the other side of the huge airport complex from the terminal building stands the Public Transportation Center, which means taking a free, ten-minute ride on an Express shuttle bus from Gate 5 outside arrivals or Gate 10 outside departures – be sure not to confuse these with the much slower Ordinary shuttle buses, which ferry airport staff around the complex. However, because of the inconvenience involved, taxis and many buses now pick up and drop off at the terminal building, as detailed below. A high-speed **rail link** from Suvarnabhumi (SARL) that's currently reported to be opening in early 2010 will be the quickest means of getting downtown. Non-stop Airport Express trains to the City Air Terminal at Makkasan Station (which connects with the subway system at Phetchaburi station) are planned to take about fifteen minutes, while the (much cheaper) stopping Airport City Line services to Phaya Thai (an interchange with the Skytrain system) should take around thirty minutes. The TAT offices in the arrivals hall have full details of all airport transport.

The most economical way of getting into the city is by **public air-con bus** (B22–34) or **minibus** (B40–70), with the following routes, mostly 24-hour, likely to be useful to visitors: #551, from Gate 1 or 8, Floor 1 of the terminal building, to Victory Monument, which has a Skytrain (see p.108) station; #552 from the **Public Transportation Center** along Thanon Sukhumvit via Ekamai (for the Eastern Bus Station and Skytrain), turning left along Thanon Ratchadapisek to Khlong Toey via Queen Sirikit Convention Centre (for the subway); and #556 to Democracy Monument, Thanon Rajdamnoen Klang (for Banglamphu guest houses) and the Southern Bus Terminal from Gate 8, Floor 1 of the terminal building.

The dedicated, air-conditioned **airport bus** (daily 5am–midnight; at least every 30min; B150) is fine for lone travellers, but at most times of the day, the convenience of a taxi is going to be cheaper for a group of two or more, or at least not much more expensive. These buses depart from outside Gate 8, Floor 1 of the terminal building, covering four routes: #AE1 terminates at Sala Daeng Skytrain station, via Pratunam, Thanon Rajdamri and a circuit west along Thanon Suriwong and east along Thanon Silom; #AE2 goes to Thanon Khao San in Banglamphu, via Pratunam, Thanon Phetchaburi, Democracy Monument, Sanam Luang, Thanon Phra Arthit, Thanon Phra Sumen and Thanon Chakrabongse; #AE3 runs the length of Sukhumvit and Ploenchit roads, via the Eastern Bus Terminal and Ekamai Skytrain, to the Erawan Shrine, before doubling back via Thanon Phetchaburi to Sukhumvit Soi 3; and #AE4 runs to Hualamphong Station, via Victory Monument, Siam Square, Thanon Phrayathai and Thanon Rama IV.

From the Public Transportation Center, there are also **long-distance buses** to Pattaya (a few Pattaya services each day pick up at Floor 1 of the terminal building), Rayong, Chanthaburi and Trat on the east coast, and overnight to Nong Khai, via Khorat, Khon Kaen and Udon Thani, as well as hourly buses between 8am and 9pm to the Northern Bus Terminal (Mo Chit – see p.100).

Taxis to the centre are comfortable, air-conditioned and reasonably priced, although the driving can be hairy. Walk past the pricey taxis and limousines on offer within the baggage hall and arrivals hall and ignore any tout who may offer a cheap ride in an unlicensed and unmetered vehicle, as newly arrived travellers are seen as easy prey for robbery, and the cabs are untraceable. Licensed and metered public taxis are operated from clearly signposted and well-regulated counters, outside the arrivals hall's Gates 3 and 10. Even including the B50 airport pick-up fee and around B65 tolls for the overhead expressways, a journey to Thanon Silom downtown, for example, should set you back around B300, depending on the traffic. If you find a big queue of people here, which is especially possible between 10pm and 11pm, you might want to head up to the departures level to pick up a taxi.

Airport accommodation

With time to kill and money to spare before your onward journey, you might want to rest and clean up in one of the **day-rooms** in the airport's transit area (US$80/1 person, US$87/2 people, for 4hr). Day-rooms (B4500 from 8am–6pm, or B3000 for 4hr) are also available at the airport **hotel**, the four-star *Novotel Suvarnabhumi* (Ⓣ02 131 1111, Ⓦwww.accorhotels.com; ⑨). Offering Thai, Japanese, Chinese and international restaurants, a swimming pool and fitness centre, the *Novotel* is a ten-minute walk from the terminal building – or catch the shuttle bus from outside Gate 4, Floor 2. Just outside the airport complex, to the north near Highway 7, *Queens Garden Resort* (Ⓣ02 172 6114, Ⓦwww.queensgardenresort.net; ⑤) is a more economical choice, providing hot water, air-con, mini-bar and satellite TV in all bedrooms and 24-hour pick-ups (B150).

By train

Travelling to Bangkok by **train** from Malaysia and most parts of Thailand, you arrive at **Hualamphong Station**, which is centrally located, at the southern end of the subway line (see map, p.109). The most useful of the city buses serving Hualamphong is the #159 (non-air-con), which runs west to Democracy Monument, Rajdamnoen Klang (for Banglamphu) and the Southern Bus Terminal, and east to MBK, Siam Square, Chatuchak and the Northern Bus Terminal. See box on p.106 for other bus routes via Hualamphong. The Airport Express #AE4 bus service to Suvarnabhumi departs approximately hourly from 7am to 11pm from the east side of the station on Thanon Rong Muang. Station **facilities** include an exchange booth, several ATMs, an internet centre and a makeshift **left-luggage** "office", actually just bags piled up in a corner (daily 4am–11pm; B30–80 per day, depending on size). A more economical, and possibly more secure place to store baggage is the *TT2 Guest House* (see p.118), about fifteen minutes' walk from the station (B15–20 per item per day).

One service the station does not provide is itinerant tourist assistance staff; anyone who comes up to you in or around the station concourse and offers help/information/transport or ticket-booking services is almost certainly a **con-artist**, however many official-looking ID tags are hanging round their neck. This is a well-established scam to fleece new arrivals and should be avoided at all costs (see p.62). For train-related questions, contact the 24-hour "Information" counter close by the departures board (there's more advice on buying onward rail tickets on p.202). The station area is also fertile ground for **dishonest tuk-tuk drivers**, so you'll need to be extra suspicious to avoid them – take a metered taxi or public transport instead.

Trains **from Kanchanaburi** (plus a handful from Nakhon Pathom, Hua Hin and other local trains on the Southern line) pull in at the small and very quiet **Thonburi Station**, from where it's a short ride in a red public songthaew or an 850-metre walk east to the N11 express-boat pier (Bangkok Noi; Mon–Fri rush hours only), just across the Chao Phraya River from Banglamphu and Ratanakosin; at other times you'll need to use the N10 Tha Wang Lang express-boat stop instead, which is 500m south of N11, through the Siriraj hospital compound.

By bus

Buses come to a halt at a number of far-flung spots. All services from the north and northeast terminate at the **Northern and Northeastern Bus Terminal** (**Mo Chit**) on Thanon Kamphaeng Phet 2; some east-coast buses also use Mo Chit, including several daily services from Pattaya, Rayong (for Ko Samet), Chanthaburi and Trat (for Ko Chang and the Cambodian border). The quickest way to get into the city centre from Mo Chit is to hop onto the Skytrain at Mo Chit Station, or the subway at the adjacent Chatuchak Park Station, fifteen minutes' walk from the bus terminal on Thanon Phaholyothin, and then change onto a city bus if necessary. Otherwise, it's a long bus or taxi ride into town: city buses from the Northern Bus Terminal include ordinary #159 to Siam Square, Hualamphong Station, Banglamphu and the Southern Bus Terminal; and ordinary and air-conditioned #3, and air-conditioned #509 and #512 to Banglamphu; for details of these routes, see p.106.

Most buses to and from east-coast destinations such as Pattaya, Ban Phe (for Ko Samet) and Trat (for Ko Chang) use the **Eastern Bus Terminal** (**Ekamai**; (Ⓣ02 391 2496) between sois 40 and 42 on Thanon Sukhumvit. This bus station is right beside the Ekamai Skytrain stop (see p.108), and is also served by lots of city buses, including air-conditioned #511 to and from Banglamphu and the Southern Bus Terminal (see box, p.106); alternatively, you can use the Khlong Saen Saeb canal-boat service which transports passengers to and from the edge of Banglamphu (see p.107) via a pier at Tha Ekamai, at the end of Sukhumvit Soi 63, easiest reached by taxi. There's a left-luggage booth at the bus terminal (daily 6am–6pm; B30 per day) and several places to stay quite nearby (see p.128), as well as a cineplex a few minutes' walk west, between sois 61 and 63.

The huge, airport-like **Southern Bus Terminal**, or **Sathaanii Sai Tai** (☎02 434 7192), handles transport to and from all points south of the capital, including Hua Hin, Chumphon (for Ko Tao), Surat Thani (for Ko Samui and Ko Pha Ngan), Phuket and Krabi, as well as buses for destinations west of Bangkok, such as Amphawa, Nakhon Pathom and Kanchanaburi. The terminal has recently been relocated to the junction of Thanon Borom Ratchonni and Thanon Phutthamonthon Sai 1 in Taling Chan, an interminable 11km west of the Chao Phraya River and Banglamphu, so access to and from city accommodation can take an age, even in a taxi. City buses serving Sathaanii Sai Tai include #124 for Banglamphu, #511 for Banglamphu and Thanon Sukhumvit, and #516 for Thewet and Banglamphu (see box, p.115), but note that when arriving in Bangkok most long-distance bus services make a more convenient **stop before reaching the terminus** (via a time-consuming U-turn), towards the eastern end of Thanon Borom Ratchonni, much nearer Phra Pinklao Bridge and the river; the majority of passengers get off here and it's highly recommended to do the same rather than continue to the terminal. The above-listed city buses all cross the river from this bus drop, as do many additional services, and this is also a faster and cheaper place to grab a taxi into town. The bus terminal itself has lots of facilities, including a food hall, internet access, ATMs and scores of shops. The left-luggage office is beside the *Black Canyon Coffee Shop*, near the information booth on the ticket-sales floor (5am–9pm; B20–60 per day).

Orientation

Bangkok can be a tricky place to get your bearings as it's huge and ridiculously congested, with largely featureless modern buildings and no obvious centre. The boldest line on the map is the **Chao Phraya River**, which divides the city into Bangkok proper on the east bank, and **Thonburi**, part of Greater Bangkok, on the west (see map, p.102).

The historical core of Bangkok proper, site of the original royal palace, is **Ratanakosin**, cradled in a bend in the river. Three concentric canals radiate eastwards around Ratanakosin: the southern part of the area between the canals is the old-style trading enclave of **Chinatown** and Indian **Pahurat**, connected to the old palace by Thanon Charoen Krung (aka New Road); the northern part is characterized by old temples and the **Democracy Monument**, west of which is the backpackers' ghetto of **Banglamphu**. Beyond the canals to the north, **Dusit** is the site of many government buildings and the nineteenth-century Vimanmek Palace, and is linked to Ratanakosin by the three stately avenues, Thanon Rajdamnoen Nok, Thanon Rajdamnoen Klang and Thanon Rajdamnoen Nai.

"New" Bangkok begins to the east of the canals and beyond the main rail line and Hualamphong Station, and stretches as far as the eye can see to the east and north. The main business district and most of the embassies are south of **Thanon Rama IV**, with the port of Khlong Toey at the southern edge. The diverse area north of Thanon Rama IV includes the sprawling campus of Chulalongkorn University, huge shopping centres around **Siam Square** and a variety of other businesses. A couple of blocks northeast of Siam Square stands the tallest building in Bangkok, the 84-storeyed **Baiyoke II Tower**, whose golden spire makes a good point of reference. To the east lies the swish residential quarter off **Thanon Sukhumvit**.

Information and maps

The official source of information on the capital is the **Bangkok Tourism Division**, part of the Bangkok Metropolitan Administration (BMA), whose main office is next to Phra Pinklao Bridge at 17/1 Thanon Phra Arthit in Banglamphu (daily 9am–7pm; ⓣ02 225 7612–5, ⓦwww.bangkoktourist.com). This is supported by strategically placed satellite booths around the capital (daily 9am–5pm), including in front of the Grand Palace, at the Erawan Shrine, at River City and Mah Boon Krong shopping centres, in front of Robinson Department Store on Thanon Silom, and in front of Banglamphu's Wat Chana Songkhram.

For advice on destinations further afield you need to visit the **Tourism Authority of Thailand** (**TAT**) which maintains a Tourist Service Centre within walking distance of Banglamphu, at 4 Rajdamnoen Nok (daily 8.30am–4.30pm; ⓣ02 283 1500 ext 1620; freephone tourist assistance 8am–8pm ⓣ1672, ⓦwww.tourismthailand.org), a twenty-minute stroll from Thanon Khao San, or a short ride in air-conditioned bus #503. TAT also has booths at Suvarnabhumi Airport, but its headquarters (daily 8.30am–4.30pm; ⓣ02 250 5500) is out at 1600 Thanon Phetchaburi Mai, 350m west of the junction with Sukhumvit Soi 21 and the Phetchaburi subway stop, or 150m east of the junction with Sukhumvit Soi 3 and Tha Nana Nua on the Khlong Saen Saeb canal-boat service (see map, p.109). Note, however, that the many other shops and offices across the capital displaying "TAT Tourist Information" signs or similar are **not official Tourism Authority of Thailand centres** and will not be dispensing impartial advice: the Tourism Authority of Thailand never uses the acronym TAT on its office-fronts or in its logo.

Listings magazines rise and fall with confusing rapidity in Bangkok; the best of the current publications is the attractively designed monthly *Bangkok 101*

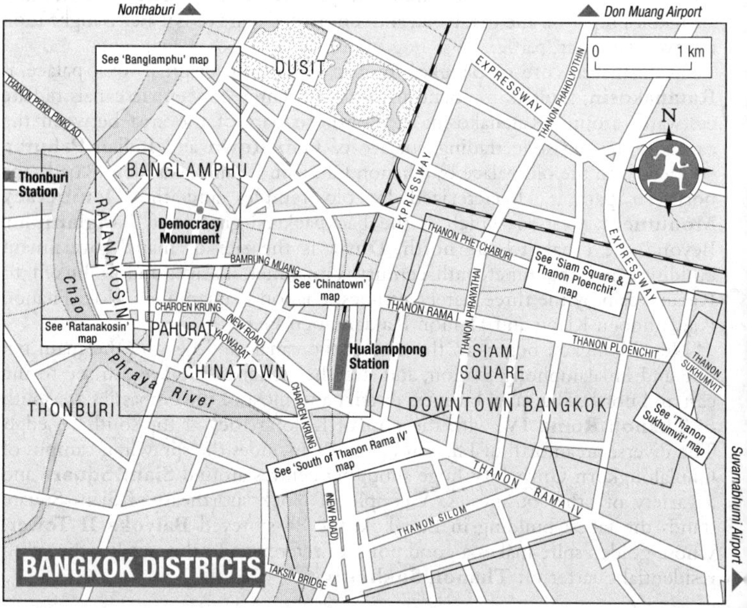

(B100), part miniature guidebook, part what's on magazine, which carries intelligent features, seasonal tips and basic sightseeing info. For monthly exhibition listings, check Ⓦwww.bangkokartmap.com.

To get around Bangkok on the cheap, you'll need to buy a **bus map**. Of the several available, the most useful and reliable is Bangkok Guide's *Bus Routes & Map*, which not only charts all major air-conditioned and non-air-conditioned bus routes but also carries detailed written itineraries of some two hundred routes. For a far more personal guide to Bangkok's most interesting shops, markets, restaurants and backstreets, look for the famously idiosyncratic hand-drawn **maps** *Nancy Chandler's Map of Bangkok* and *Nancy Chandler's Map of Khao San and Old Bangkok*. Both carry a mass of annotated recommendations, are impressively accurate and frequently reissued; they're sold in most tourist areas, and copies and interim updates are also available at Ⓦwww.nancychandler.net.

City transport

Transport can undoubtedly be a headache in a city where it's not unusual for residents to spend three hours getting to work – and these are people who know where they're going. However, the recent openings of the subway system and the elevated train network called the Bangkok Transit System, or BTS Skytrain, have radically improved movement in downtown areas of the city. Unfortunately for tourists, these systems do not stretch as far as Ratanakosin or Banglamphu, where boats still provide the best means of hopping from one sight to another.

The main form of transport in the city is **buses**, and once you've mastered the labyrinthine complexity of the route maps you'll be able to get to any part of the city, albeit slowly. Catching the various kinds of **taxi** is more expensive, and you'll still get held up by the daytime traffic jams. **Boats** are obviously more limited in their range, but they're regular and as cheap as buses, and you'll save a lot of time by using them whenever possible – a journey between Banglamphu and the GPO, for instance, will take around thirty minutes by water, half what it would usually take on land. The **Skytrain** and **subway** each have a similarly limited range but are also worth using whenever suitable for all or part of your journey; their networks roughly coincide with each other at the east end of Thanon Silom, at the corner of Soi Asoke and Thanon Sukhumvit, and on Thanon Phaholyothin by Chatuchak Park (Mo Chit), while the Skytrain joins up with the Chao Phraya River express boats at the vital hub of Sathorn/Saphan Taksin (Taksin Bridge). **Walking** might often be quicker than travelling by road, but the heat can be unbearable, pavements are poorly maintained and the engine fumes are stifling.

Buses

Bangkok is served by over four hundred bus routes, reputedly the world's largest bus network, on which operate three main types of bus service (though controversial plans, opposed by the transport unions and poorer commuters, to do away with non-air-con services are under discussion). On **ordinary** (non-air-con) buses, which are either red and white, blue and white, or small and green, fares range from B7 to B8.50; most routes operate from about 4am to 10pm, but some maintain a 24-hour service (see box, p.106). **Air-conditioned** buses are either blue, orange or white (some are articulated) and charge between B12 and B25 according to distance travelled; most stop in the late evening, but a few of the more popular routes run 24-hour services. As buses can only go as fast as

Tours of the city

The Bangkok Metropolitan Administration tourist office (see p.102) runs year-round **tours** of the city's historic centre in a "tram" (more like an open-sided bus), which covers a forty-minute circuit from the Grand Palace down to Wat Pho, up to Banglamphu, and back to the palace (daily 9am–5pm, every 45min; B30). From mid-December to mid-January, the same office has in previous years offered night-time tours by bicycle or open-topped double-decker bus, and may do so in future years, too. As part of the BMA's greening of the city, it's also possible to pick up bicycles and maps from this office, and seven other locations in and around Ratanakosin, for a self-guided tour along clearly marked cycle lanes (Aug–April Mon–Fri 10am–6pm, Sat & Sun 10am–8pm; free, passport required as deposit); unfortunately, local drivers tend to block or ignore the lanes, which makes the prospect a lot less enticing. Real Asia (Ⓣ02 665 6364, Ⓦwww.realasia.net) does full-day canal and walking tours through Thonburi and leads outings by train to the historic fishing port of Samut Sakhon (both B2000, including lunch and boat trips).

Unlikely as it sounds, there are several companies offering **cycle tours** of the city's outer neighbourhoods and beyond; these are an excellent way to gain a different perspective on Thai life and offer a unique chance to see traditional communities close up. The most popular, longest-running bicycle tours are the ABC Amazing Bangkok Cyclist Tours, which start in the Thanon Sukhumvit area and take you across the river to surprisingly rural khlong- and riverside communities; tours operate every day year-round, cover up to 30km depending on the itinerary, and need to be reserved in advance through Real Asia (see above; B1000–2000 including bicycle). Bangkok Bike Rides (Ⓣ02 712 5305, Ⓦwww.bangkokbikerides.com or www.spiceroads.com; B1000–2500 per person, minimum two people) also operates from the Sukhumvit area and runs a programme of different daily tours within Greater Bangkok, including Ko Kred, as well as to the floating markets and canalside neighbourhoods of Damnoen Saduak (see p.219). Velo Thailand runs two different bike tours out of its cycle shop at 88 Thanon Samsen Soi 2 on the edge of Banglamphu (Ⓣ02 629 1745, Ⓦwww.velothailand.com). The 1pm tour goes to Thonburi (3–4hr; B1000), while the after-dark tour (6–9pm; B1100) takes in floodlit sights including Wat Pho, Wat Arun and the Pak Khlong Talat flower market.

For details of Thonburi canal tours, see p.155; for Chao Phraya Express tourist boats, see p.106; and for dinner and cocktail cruises along the Chao Phraya River, see p.177.

the car in front, which at the moment is averaging 4km per hr, you'll probably be spending a long time on each journey, so you'd be well advised to pay the extra for cool air – and the air-conditioned buses are usually less crowded, too. It's also possible to travel certain commuter routes on yellow or pink, air-conditioned private **microbuses**, which offer the certainty of a seat (no standing allowed) and generally charge a flat fare of B30.

Some of the most useful city-bus routes are described in the box on p.106; for a comprehensive roundup of bus routes in the capital, buy a copy of Bangkok Guide's *Bus Routes & Map* (see p.103), or log onto the Bangkok Mass Transit Authority website (Ⓦwww.bmta.co.th), which gives details of all city-bus routes, bar microbuses and airport buses.

Boats

Bangkok was built as an amphibious city around a network of canals – or **khlongs** – and the first streets were constructed only in the second half of the nineteenth century. Many canals remain on the Thonburi side of the river, but most of those on the Bangkok side have been turned into roads. The Chao Phraya River itself is still a major transport route for residents and non residents alike, forming more of a link than a barrier between the two halves of the city.

Express boats

The Chao Phraya Express Boat Company operates the vital **express-boat** (*reua duan*; Ⓦ www.chaophrayaboat.co.th) services, using large water buses to plough up and down the river, between clearly signed piers (*tha*), which appear on all Bangkok maps. Tha Sathorn, which gives access to the Skytrain network at Saphan Taksin Station, has been designated "Central Pier", with piers to the south of here numbered S1, S2, etc, those to the north N1, N2 and so on – the important stops in the centre of the city are outlined in the box on p.108 and marked on our city map (see p.96). In future, express-boat services may be extended downriver to Samut Prakan.

No-flag, local-line boats call at every pier between Wat Rajsingkorn, just upriver of Krung Thep Bridge, in the south, and Nonthaburi, ninety minutes away to the north, but only operate during rush hour (Mon–Fri roughly 6–8.40am & 3–6pm, every 20min). Boats do not necessarily stop at every landing – they only pull in if people want to get on or off, and when they do stop, it's not for long – so when you want to get off, be ready at the back of the boat in good time for your pier. The only boats to run all day, every day are on the limited-stop **orange-flag** service (Nonthaburi to Wat Rajsingkorn in 1hr; roughly 6am–6.40pm, every 5–20min). Other limited-stop services run during rush hour, flying either a **yellow flag** (Nonthaburi to Tha Sathorn or Rajburana, far downriver beyond Krung Thep Bridge, in about 50min; Mon–Fri roughly 6–8.40am & 4–7pm), a **blue flag** (Nonthaburi to Tha Sathorn Mon–Fri 7–7.45am, Tha Sathorn to Nonthaburi Mon–Fri 5–6.25pm, stopping only at Wang Lang; 35min), or a **green-and-yellow flag** (Pakkred to Tha Sathorn Mon–Fri 6.15–8.05am, Tha Sathorn to Pakkred Mon–Fri 4.05–6.05pm; about 50min).

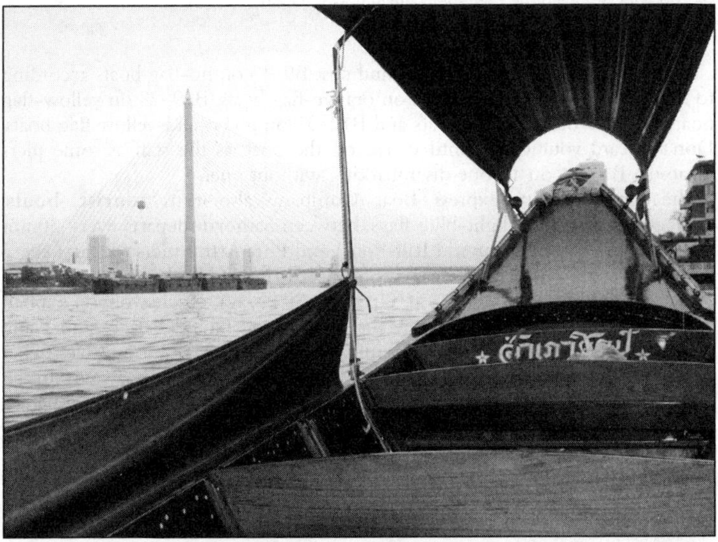

▲ Longtail boat on Chao Phraya River with Rama VIII Bridge in the background

Useful bus routes

For buses from Suvarnabhumi Airport, see p.98; for more details on Banglamphu bus stops and routes, see p.115.

#3 (ordinary and air-con, 24hr): **Northern Bus Terminal**–Chatuchak Weekend Market–Thanon Phaholyothin–Thanon Samsen–Thanon Phra Arthit (for **Banglamphu guest houses**)–Thanon Sanam Chai (for **Museum of Siam**)–Thanon Triphet–Memorial Bridge (for **Pak Khlong Talat**)–Taksin Monument (for **Wongwian Yai**) –Wat Suwan.

#15 (ordinary): Thanon Ratchadaphisek–Krung Thep Bridge–Thanon Charoen Krung–Thanon Silom–Thanon Rajdamri–**Siam Square**–Thanon Lan Luang–Sanam Luang–Thanon Phra Arthit (for **Banglamphu guest houses**).

#16 (ordinary and air-con): Thanon Srinarong–Thanon Samsen–**Thewet** (for guest houses)–Thanon Phitsanulok–Thanon Phrayathai–**Siam Square**–Thanon Suriwong.

#25 (ordinary and air-con, 24hr): Pak Nam (for **Ancient City** buses)–Thanon Sukhumvit–**Eastern Bus Terminal**–Siam Square–**Hualamphong Station**–Thanon Yaowarat (for **Chinatown**)–Pahurat–**Wat Pho**–Tha Chang (for the **Grand Palace**); some #25 buses (ordinary only) only go as far as Hualamphong Station, while during rush hours some #25 buses take the expressway, missing out Siam Square.

#53 circular (also anti clockwise; ordinary): Thewet–Thanon Krung Kasem–**Hualamphong Station**–Thanon Yaowarat (for **Chinatown**)–Pahurat–Pak Khlong Talat–Thanon Maharat (for **Wat Pho** and the **Grand Palace**)–Sanam Luang (for **National Museum**)–Thanon Phra Arthit and Thanon Samsen (for **Banglamphu guest houses**)–Thewet.

#56 circular (also clockwise; ordinary, stops at 7pm): Thanon Phra Sumen–Wat Bowoniwes–Thanon Pracha Thipatai–Thanon Ratchasima (for **Vimanmek Palace**)–Thanon Rajwithi–Krung Thon Bridge–Thonburi–Phrapokklao Bridge–Thanon Chakraphet (for **Chinatown**)–Thanon Mahachai–Democracy Monument–Thanon Tanao (for **Khao San guest houses**)–Thanon Phra Sumen.

#124 (ordinary): Sanam Luang–Thanon Rajinee, near Information Centre (for **Banglamphu guest houses**)–Phra Pinklao Bridge–**Southern Bus Terminal**–Mahidol University.

Tickets can be bought on board, and cost B9–13 on no-flag boats according to distance travelled, B14 flat rate on orange-flag boats, B19–28 on yellow-flag boats, B19–29 on blue-flag boats and B12–31 on green-and-yellow flag boats. Don't discard your ticket until you're off the boat, as the staff at some piers impose a B1 fine on anyone disembarking without one.

The Chao Phraya Express Boat Company also runs **tourist boats**, distinguished by their light-blue flags, between Sathorn (departs every 30min 9.30am–3pm on the hour and half-hour) and Phra Arthit piers (departs every 30min 10am–3.30pm on the hour and half-hour). In between (in both directions), these boats call in at Oriental, Si Phraya, Rachawongse, Saphan Phut, Thien, Maharat (near Wat Mahathat and the Grand Palace) and Wang Lang. On-board guides provide running commentaries, and a one-day ticket for unlimited trips, which also allows you to use other express boats within the same route on the same day, costs B150; one-way tickets are also available, costing, for example, B19 from Phra Arthit to Oriental.

Cross-river ferries

Smaller than express boats are the slow **cross-river ferries** (*reua kham fak*), which shuttle back and forth between the same two points. Found at or beside every express-boat stop and plenty of other piers in between, they are

#159 (ordinary): **Southern Bus Terminal**–Phra Pinklao Bridge–Democracy Monument–**Hualamphong Station**–MBK Shopping Centre–Thanon Ratchaprarop–Victory Monument–Chatuchak Weekend Market–**Northern Bus Terminal**.

#503 (air-con): Sanam Luang–Democracy Monument (for **Banglamphu guest houses**)–Thanon Rajdamnoen Nok (for **TAT** and **boxing stadium**)–Wat Benjamabophit–Thanon Sri Ayutthaya (for **Thewet guest houses**)–Victory Monument–**Chatuchak Weekend Market**–Rangsit. Note, however, that during rush hours, some #503 buses take the expressway, missing out Chatuchak Weekend Market.

#507 (air-con): **Southern Bus Terminal**–Phra Pinklao Bridge (for **Banglamphu guest houses**)–Sanam Luang–Thanon Charoen Krung (New Road)–Thanon Chakraphet–Thanon Yaowarat (for **Chinatown** and **Wat Traimit**)–**Hualamphong Station**–Thanon Rama IV–Bang Na Intersection–Pak Nam (for **Ancient City** buses).

#508 (air-con): Thanon Maharat–**Grand Palace**–Thanon Charoen Krung–Siam Square–Thanon Sukhumvit–**Eastern Bus Terminal**–Pak Nam (for **Ancient City** buses). Note, however, that during rush hours, some #508 buses take the expressway, missing out the Eastern Bus Terminal.

#509 (air-con): **Northern Bus Terminal**–Chatuchak Weekend Market–Victory Monument–Thanon Rajwithi–Thanon Sawankhalok–Thanon Phitsanulok–Thanon Rajdamnoen Nok (for **TAT** and **boxing stadium**)–Democracy Monument–Thanon Rajdamnoen Klang (for **Banglamphu guest houses**)–Phra Pinklao Bridge–Thonburi.

#511 (air-con, 24hr): **Southern Bus Terminal**–Phra Pinklao Bridge (for **Banglamphu guest houses**)–Democracy Monument–Thanon Lan Luang–Thanon Phetchaburi–Thanon Sukhumvit–**Eastern Bus Terminal**–Pak Nam (for **Ancient City** buses). Note, however, that between 4.30am and 8.30pm, some #511 buses take the expressway, missing out the Eastern Bus Terminal.

#512 (air-con): **Northern Bus Terminal**–Chatuchak Weekend Market–Thanon Phetchaburi–Thanon Lan Luang–Democracy Monument (for **Banglamphu guest houses**)–Sanam Luang–Tha Chang (for **Grand Palace**)–Pak Khlong Talat.

especially useful for exploring Thonburi. Fares are generally B3, payable at the entrance to the pier.

Canal boats

Longtail boats (*reua hang yao*) ply the **canals** of Thonburi like commuter buses, stopping at designated shelters (fares are in line with those of express boats), and are available for individual rental here and on the river (see box, p.155). On the Bangkok side, **Khlong Saen Saeb** is well served by passenger boats, which run at least every fifteen minutes during daylight hours from the Phan Fah pier at the Golden Mount (handy for Banglamphu, Ratanakosin and Chinatown), and head way out east to Wat Sribunruang, with useful stops at Thanon Phrayathai, aka Saphan Hua Chang (for Jim Thompson's House and Ratchathevi Skytrain stop); Pratunam (for the Erawan Shrine); Thanon Witthayu (Wireless Road); and Soi Nana Nua (Soi 3), Thanon Asok Montri (Soi 21, for TAT headquarters and Phetchaburi subway stop), Soi Thonglo (Soi 55) and Soi Ekamai (Soi 63), all off Thanon Sukhumvit. This is your quickest and most interesting way of getting between the west and east parts of town, if you can stand the stench of the canal. You may have trouble actually locating the piers as few are signed in English and they all look very

Central stops for the Chao Phraya express boats

N15 Thewet (all boats except blue flag) – for Thewet guest houses.

N14 Rama VIII Bridge (no flag) – for Samsen Soi 5.

N13 Phra Arthit (no flag and orange flag) – for Thanon Phra Arthit, Thanon Khao San and Banglamphu guest houses.

N12 Phra Pinklao Bridge (all boats except blue flag) – for Royal Barge Museum and Thonburi shops.

N11 Thonburi Railway Station (or Bangkok Noi; no flag) – for trains to Kanchanaburi.

N10 Wang Lang (aka Siriraj or Prannok; all boats) – for Siriraj Hospital and hospital museums.

N9 Chang (no flag and orange flag) – for the Grand Palace, Sanam Luang and the National Museum.

N8 Thien (no flag and orange flag) – for Wat Pho, and the cross-river ferry to Wat Arun.

N7 Ratchini (aka Rajinee; no flag).

N6 Saphan Phut (Memorial Bridge; no flag and orange flag) – for Pahurat, Pak Khlong Talat and Wat Prayoon.

N5 Rachawongse (aka Rajawong; all boats except blue flag) – for Chinatown.

N4 Harbour (Marine) Department (no flag and orange flag).

N3 Si Phraya (all boats except blue flag) – walk north past the *Sheraton Royal Orchid Hotel* for River City shopping complex, head south for the GPO.

N2 Wat Muang Kae (no flag) – for the GPO.

N1 Oriental (no flag and orange flag) – for Thanon Silom.

Central Sathorn (all boats) – for the Skytrain (Saphan Taksin Station) and Thanon Sathorn.

unassuming and rickety; see the map opposite for locations and keep your eyes peeled for a plain wooden jetty – most jetties serve boats running in both directions. Once on the boat, state your destination to the conductor when he collects your fare, which will be between B10 and B24. Due to the construction of some low bridges, all passengers change onto a different boat at Tha Pratunam – just follow the crowd.

The Skytrain

Although its network is limited, the **BTS Skytrain**, or *rot fai faa* (ⓦwww.bts.co.th), provides a much faster alternative to the bus, and is clean, efficient and vigorously air-conditioned. There are only two Skytrain lines, which interconnect at Siam Square (**Central Station**). Both run every few minutes from around 6am to midnight, with **fares** of B15–40 per trip depending on distance travelled. You buy tickets from machines that accept only coins, but you can change notes at staffed counters. You'd really have to be motoring to justify buying a day **pass** at B120, while the twenty-trip, thirty-trip and forty-trip cards, for B440, B600 and B800 respectively (valid for thirty days), are designed for long-distance commuters.

The **Sukhumvit Line** runs from Mo Chit (stop N8) in the northern part of the city to On Nut (Soi 77, Thanon Sukhumvit; E9) in around thirty minutes, though there are plans to extend the line eastward towards Samrong. The **Silom Line** runs from the National Stadium (W1) to Saphan Taksin (Taksin, or Sathorn, Bridge; S6), to link up with the full gamut of express boats on the Chao Phraya River, to Wongwian Yai (S8) in Thonburi (an eventual continuation to Thanon Phetkasem is planned).

The subway

Bangkok's underground rail system, the **MRT subway** (or metro; in Thai, *rot fai tai din*; Ⓦwww.bangkokmetro.co.th), has similar advantages to the Skytrain, though its current single line connects few places of interest for visitors. It runs every few minutes between around 6am and midnight from Hualamphong train station, via Silom (near Sala Daeng Skytrain station), Sukhumvit (near Asoke Skytrain) and Chatuchak Park (near Mo Chit Skytrain), to Bang Sue train station in the north of the city. Plans are afoot to continue the line westwards from Hualamphong along Thanon Charoen Krung, then across to Thonburi, finally completing a loop back to Bang Sue. Pay your **fare** of between B15 and B39 at a staffed counter or machine, where you'll receive a token to put through an entrance gate (the various day-passes and stored-value cards available are unlikely to be worthwhile for visitors).

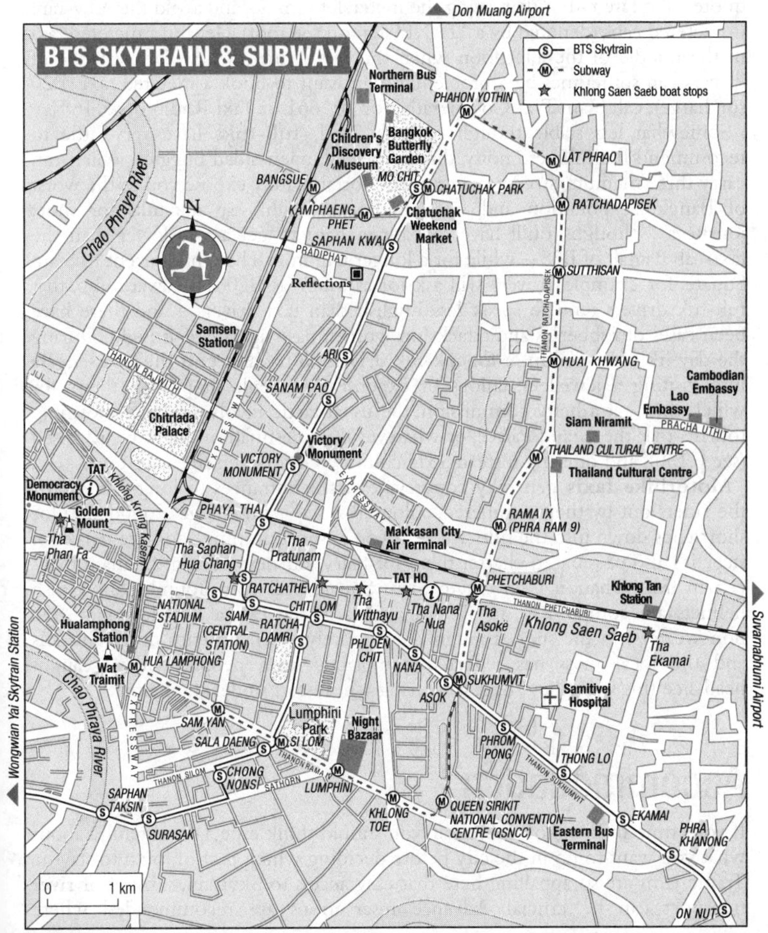

Taxis

Bangkok **taxis** come in three forms, and are so plentiful that you rarely have to wait more than a couple of minutes before spotting an empty one of any description. Neither tuk-tuks nor motorbike taxis have meters, so you should agree on a price before setting off, and expect to do a fair amount of haggling.

For nearly all journeys, the best and most comfortable option is to flag down one of Bangkok's metered, air-conditioned **taxi cabs**; look out for the "TAXI METER" sign on the roof, and a red light in the windscreen in front of the passenger seat, which means the cab is available for hire. Starting at B35, fares are displayed on a clearly visible meter that the driver should reset at the start of each trip (say "*poet meter, dai mai khrap/kha?*" to ask him to switch it on), and increase in stages on a combined distance/time formula; as an example, a medium-range journey from Thanon Ploenchit to Thanon Sathorn will cost around B50 at a quiet time of day. Try to have change with you as cabs tend not to carry a lot of money; tipping of up to ten percent is common, though occasionally a cabbie will round down the fare on the meter. If a driver tries to quote a flat fare rather than using the meter, let him go, and avoid the now-rare unmetered cabs (denoted by a "TAXI" sign on the roof). Getting a metered taxi in the middle of the afternoon when the cars return to base for a change of drivers can sometimes be a problem; if you want to book a metered taxi (B20 surcharge), call Siam Taxi Co-operative on ⓣ1661 or Taxi Radio on ⓣ1681.

Somewhat less stable though typically Thai, **tuk-tuks** have very little to recommend them. These noisy, three-wheeled, open-sided buggies, which can carry three medium-sized passengers comfortably, fully expose you to the worst of Bangkok's pollution and weather. Locals might use tuk-tuks for short journeys – though you'll have to bargain hard to get a fare lower than the taxi-cab flagfall of B35 – while for a longer trip from Thanon Convent to Siam Square, for example, drivers will ask for as much as B200. Be aware, also, that tuk-tuk drivers tend to speak less English than taxi drivers – and there have been cases of robberies and attacks on women passengers late at night. During the day it's quite common for tuk-tuk drivers to try and **con** their passengers into visiting a jewellery, tailor's or expensive souvenir shop with them, for which they get a hefty commission; the usual tactic involves falsely informing tourists that the Grand Palace, or whatever their destination might be, is closed (see p.130), and offering instead a ridiculously cheap, even free, city tour.

Motorbike taxis generally congregate at the entrances to long sois – pick the riders out by their numbered, coloured vests – and charge around B10 for short trips down into the side streets. If you're short on time and have nerves of steel, it's also possible to charter them for hairy journeys out on the main roads (a trip from Thanon Convent to Siam Square will cost around B80). Crash helmets are compulsory on all main roads in the capital (traffic police fine non-wearers on the spot), though they're rarely worn on trips down the sois and the local press has reported complaints from people who've caught head-lice this way (they suggest wearing a headscarf under the helmet).

Accommodation

If your time in Bangkok is limited, you should think especially carefully about what you want to do in the city before deciding which part of town to stay in. Traffic jams are so appalling here that easy access to Skytrain, subway or river transport can be crucial. Advance reservations are recommended where possible during high season (Nov–Feb), though some guest houses will only take cash deposits.

For ultra-cheap double rooms under B400, your widest choice lies with the no-frills guest houses on and around **Banglamphu**'s Thanon Khao San. The most inexpensive rooms here are no-frills crash-pads – small and often windowless, with thin walls and shared bathrooms – but Banglamphu also offers plenty of well-appointed mid-priced options with air-con and swimming pools. Other, far smaller and less interesting travellers' ghettoes that might be worth bearing in mind are the generally dingy **Soi Ngam Duphli**, off the south side of Thanon Rama IV, which nevertheless harbours a couple of decent shoestring options, as well as mid-range and expensive rooms; and **Soi Kasemsan I**, which is very handily placed next to Siam Square and firmly occupies the moderate range, averaging B700 for a double, though with a few rooms for B500. Otherwise, the majority of the city's moderate and expensive rooms are scattered widely across the **downtown areas**, around Siam Square and Thanon Ploenchit, to the south of Thanon Rama IV and along **Thanon Sukhumvit**, and to a lesser extent in **Chinatown**. As well as easy access to transport links and shops, the downtown views from accommodation in these areas are a real plus, especially from the deluxe hotels that are scenically sited along the banks of the Chao Phraya River.

For accommodation **near Suvarnabhumi Airport** see p.99, though the eastern Sukhumvit hotels are also worth considering.

Banglamphu

Nearly all backpackers head straight for **Banglamphu**, Bangkok's long-established travellers' ghetto, location of the cheapest accommodation and some of the best nightlife in the city, and arguably the most enjoyable area to base yourself in the city. It's within easy reach of the Grand Palace and has enough bars, restaurants and shops to keep any visitor happy for a week or more, though some people find this insularity tiresome after just a few hours.

At the heart of Banglamphu is the legendary **Thanon Khao San** (Ⓦwww.khaosanroad.com), almost a caricature of a travellers' centre, crammed with internet cafés and dodgy travel agents, the sidewalks lined with cheap backpackers' fashions, racks of bootleg PlayStation games, tattooists and hair-braiders. It's a lively, high-energy base: great for shopping and making travel arrangements (though beware the innumerable Khao San scams; see p.62), and a good place to meet other travellers. It's especially fun at night when young Thais from all over the city gather here to browse the clothes stalls, mingle with the crowds of foreigners and squash into the bars and clubs that have made Khao San *the* place to party.

The increasingly sophisticated nightlife scene has enticed more moneyed travellers into Banglamphu and a growing number of Khao San **guest houses** are reinventing themselves as good-value mini-hotels boasting chic decor, swimming pools, and even views from the windows. The cheapish sleeps are still there though, particularly immediately west of Khao San, around the neighbourhood temple **Wat Chana Songhkram**, and along riverside **Thanon Phra Arthit**, where you'll also find some upscale places offering prime views over the Chao Phraya. About ten minutes' walk north from Thanon Khao San, the handful of guest houses scattered amongst the shophouses of the **Thanon Samsen sois** enjoy a more authentically Thai environment, while the **Thewet** area, a further fifteen minutes' walk in the same direction or a seven-minute walk from the Thewet express-boat stop, is more local still. Heading south from Khao

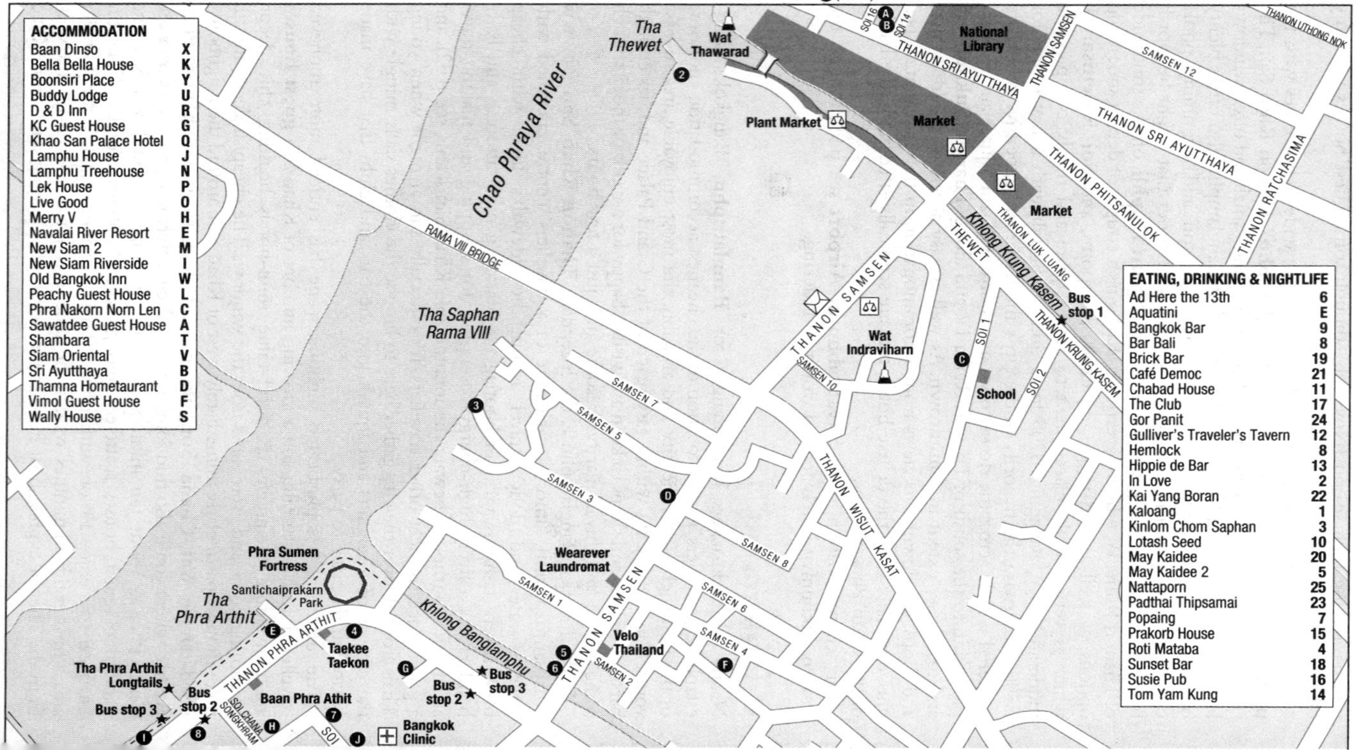
1 (100m)
ACCOMMODATION
Baan Dinso X
Bella Bella House K
Boonsiri Place Y
Buddy Lodge U
D & D Inn R
KC Guest House G
Khao San Palace Hotel Q
Lamphu House J
Lamphu Treehouse N
Lek House P
Live Good O
Merry V H
Navalai River Resort E
New Siam 2 M
New Siam Riverside I
Old Bangkok Inn W
Peachy Guest House L
Phra Nakorn Norn Len C
Sawatdee Guest House A
Shambara T
Siam Oriental V
Sri Ayutthaya B
Thamna Hometaurant D
Vimol Guest House F
Wally House S
EATING, DRINKING & NIGHTLIFE
Ad Here the 13th 6
Aquatini E
Bangkok Bar 9
Bar Bali 8
Brick Bar 19
Café Democ 21
Chabad House 11
The Club 17
Gor Panit 24
Gulliver's Traveler's Tavern 12
Hemlock 8
Hippie de Bar 13
In Love 2
Kai Yang Boran 22
Kaloang 1
Kinlom Chom Saphan 3
Lotash Seed 10
May Kaidee 20
May Kaidee 2 5
Nattaporn 25
Padthai Thipsamai 23
Popaing 7
Prakorb House 15
Roti Mataba 4
Sunset Bar 18
Susie Pub 16
Tom Yam Kung 14
Tha Thewet
Wat Thawarad
National Library
Chao Phraya River
Plant Market
Market
Thanon Sri Ayutthaya
Thanon Samsen
Samsen 12
Thanon Phitsanulok
Thanon Ratchasima
Thanon Uthong Nok
Soi 16
Soi 14
Rama VIII Bridge
Thewet
Khlong Krung Kasem
Thanon Luk Luang
Thanon Krung Kasem
Bus stop 1
Tha Saphan Rama VIII
Wat Indraviharn
Samsen 10
Soi 1
Soi 2
School
Samsen 7
Samsen 5
Samsen 3
Samsen 8
Thanon Wisut Kasat
Samsen 6
Samsen 4
Samsen 2
Samsen 1
Phra Sumen Fortress
Wearever Laundromat
Santichaiprakarn Park
Tha Phra Arthit
Velo Thailand
Khlong Banglamphu
Thanon Phra Arthit
Taekee Taekon
Tha Phra Arthit Longtails
Bus stop 3
Bus stop 2
Baan Phra Athit
Soi Chana Songkhram
Soi
Bangkok Clinic

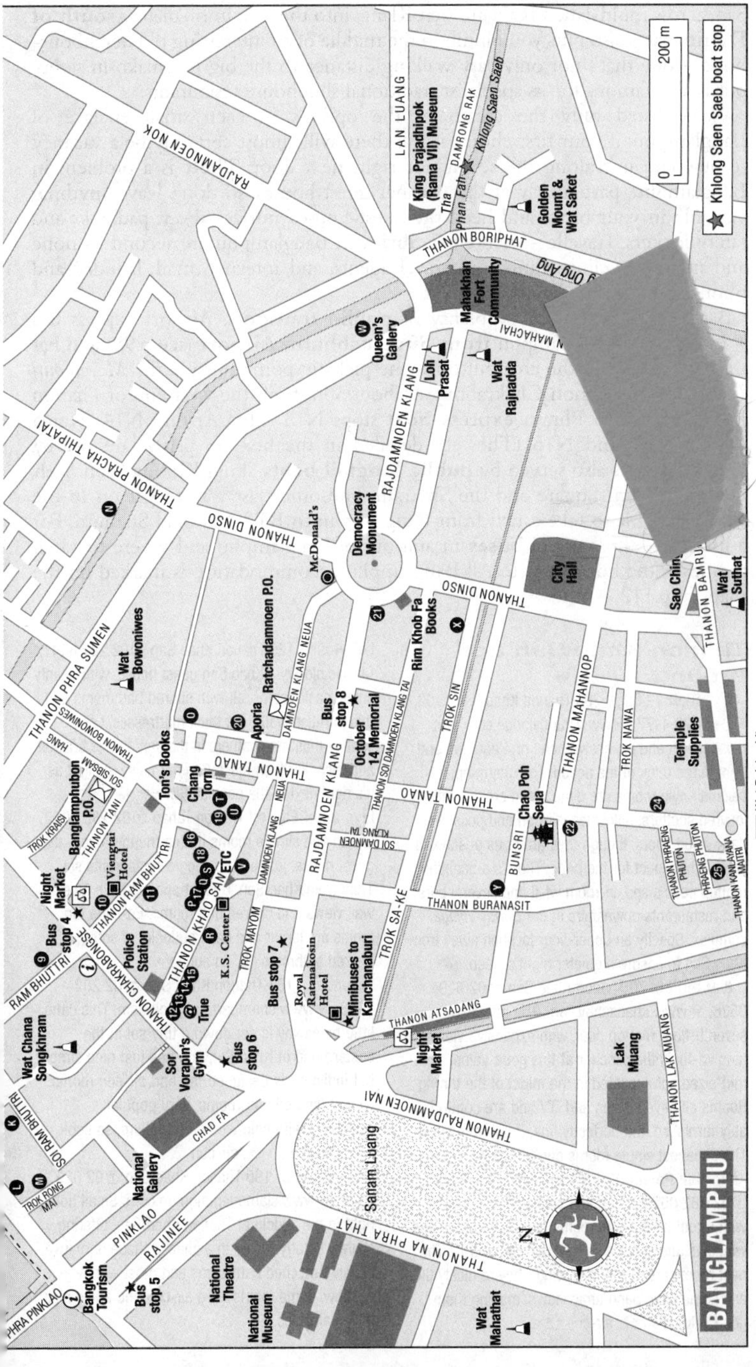
BANGLAMPHU
Sukhumvit
Wat Rajabophit
0 200 m
Khlong Saen Saeb boat stop
RAJDAMNOEN NOK
LAN LUANG
King Prajadhipok (Rama VII) Museum
DAMRONG RAK
Khlong Saen Saeb
Tha Phan Fah
Golden Mount & Wat Saket
THANON BORIPHAT
Mahakhan Fort Community
THANON MAHACHAI
Queen's Gallery
Loh Prasat
Wat Rajnadda
RAJDAMNOEN KLANG
THANON PRACHA THIPATAI
THANON DINSO
Democracy Monument
McDonald's
City Hall
Sao Ching Cha
THANON BAMRUNG MUANG
Wat Suthat
THANON PHRA SUMEN
Wat Bowoniwes
Damnoen Ratchadamnoen P.O.
DAMNOEN KLANG NEUA
Rim Khob Fa Books
TROK SIN
THANON MAHANNOP
TROK NAWA
Temple Supplies
Bus stop 8
October 14 Memorial
THANON SOI DAMNOEN KLANG TAI
THANON BOWONIWES
HANG
SOI SIBSAM
Banglamphubon P.O.
Ton's Books
Chang Torn
Aporia
THANON TANAO
SOI DAMNOEN KLANG TAI
Chao Poh Seua
BUNSRI
THANON PHRAENG PHUTON
PHRAENG PHUTON
THANON KANLAYANA MAITRI
TROK KRAISI
THANON TANI
Viengtai Hotel
Night Market
THANON RAM BHUTTRI
ETC
DAMNOEN KLANG NEUA
TROK SA-KE
THANON BURANASIT
Bus stop 4
RAM BHUTTRI
Police Station
THANON KHAO SAN
K.S. Center
TROK MAYOM
Bus stop 7
Royal Ratanakosin Hotel
Minibuses to Kanchanaburi
THANON ATSADANG
THANON CHAKRABONGSE
True
Wat Chana Songkhram
Sor Vorapin's Gym
Bus stop 6
Night Market
Lak Muang
THANON LAK MUANG
THANON RAJDAMNOEN NAI
SOI RAM BHUTTRI
CHAD FA
National Gallery
TROK RONG MAI
Sanam Luang
PINKLAO
RAJINEE
THANON NA PHRA THAT
N
PHRA PINKLAO
Bangkok Tourism
Bus stop 5
National Theatre
National Museum
Wat Mahathat

San, across multi-laned Rajdamnoen Klang, into the area immediately **south of Democracy** also puts you plumb in the middle of an interesting old neighbourhood – one that's not only easy walking distance to the big Ratanakosin sights, but is also famous for its specialist traditional shophouse restaurants.

We've listed only the cream of the options in each small enclave of Banglamphu: if your first choice is full there will almost certainly be a vacancy somewhere just along the soi, if not right next door. **Theft** is a problem in Banglamphu, particularly at the cheaper guest houses, so don't leave anything valuable in your room and heed the guest-houses' notices about padlocks and safety lockers. Traveller-oriented **facilities** in Banglamphu are second to none and include a clinic, numerous travel agents, and internet, mail, laundry and phone services; for details, see p.206.

Banglamphu is served by plenty of **public transport**. Airport express bus #AE2 runs to Banglamphu **from Suvarnabhumi Airport** (see p.98) and has many drop-offs in the area but only one pick-up point, outside the *Mayompuri Restaurant* on Thanon Chakrabongse, about 50m from the west end of Thanon Khao San. Chao Phraya **express-boat** stops N13 (Phra Arthit), N14 (Rama VIII Bridge) and N15 (Thewet), detailed in the box on p.107, are nearby. Banglamphu is also served by **public longtail boats** along Khlong Saen Saeb, useful for Siam Square and the Skytrain. The other fast way to get on to the BTS system is to take a taxi from Banglamphu to BTS National Stadium. For a list of the most useful **buses** in and out of Banglamphu and where to catch them, see the box opposite. All Banglamphu accommodation is marked on the map on p.112.

Thanon Khao San and around

Buddy Lodge 265 Thanon Khao San ⓣ02 629 4477, ⓦwww.buddylodge.com. The most stylish and expensive hotel on Khao San and right in the thick of the action. The charming, colonial-style rooms are done out in cream, with louvred shutters, balconies, air-con and polished dark-wood floors, though they aren't as pristine as you might expect for the price. There's a beautiful rooftop pool, a spa, in-room wi-fi and several bars and restaurants downstairs in the *Buddy Village* complex. Specify an upper-floor location away from Khao San to ensure a quieter night's sleep. ❼

D & D Inn 68–70 Thanon Khao San ⓣ02 629 0526, ⓦwww.khaosanby.com. The attractive seventh-floor rooftop pool, with expansive views (and wi-fi), is the clincher at this good-value, mid-sized hotel located in the midst of the throng. Rooms all have air-con and TV and are comfortably furnished and perfectly fine, if not immaculate. The cheapest single rooms don't have windows. ❹

Khao San Palace Hotel 139 Thanon Khao San ⓣ02 282 0578. Clean and well-appointed hotel with a rooftop pool. All rooms have bathrooms and windows and some also have air-con and TV. The best rooms are in the new wing; they're nicely tiled and some have panoramic views, making them good value. Fan ❸, air-con ❸–❹

Lek House 125 Thanon Khao San ⓣ02 281 8441. Classic old-style Khao San guest house, with twenty small, basic rooms, all with shared bathrooms and thin partition walls, but thick mattresses. Less shabby than many others in the same price bracket and friendlier than most. Can get noisy at night as it's right next to the popular *Silk Bar*. ❶

Live Good East off Thanon Tanao ⓣ02 282 5092. Cheap and simple rooms in this friendly, back-alley guest house, just off the veggie-restaurants soi, 1min from Khao San. Budget options have fans, wall views and shared bathrooms. En-suite fan rooms are larger and have outlooks of sorts. Shared bathroom ❶, en suite ❷

Shambara 138 Thanon Khao San ⓣ02 282 7968, ⓦwww.shambarabangkok.com. This calm little hideaway is set down a tiny soi at the eastern end of Khao San and has just nine simple but individually designed fan and air-con rooms, all with shared bathrooms. Very popular, especially with solo women travellers, so book well ahead. Fan ❸, air-con ❹

Siam Oriental 190 Thanon Khao San ⓣ02 629 0312, ⓦwww.siamorientalgroup.com. Small hotel right in the middle of Thanon Khao San, offering slightly scruffy rooms in a cheery shade of mauve, all with attached bathrooms and most with a window. Some rooms have air-con and a few also have balconies. ❷

Banglamphu's bus stops and routes

Buses running out of Banglamphu have many different pick-up points in the area: to make things simpler, we've assigned numbers to these **bus stops**, though they are not numbered on the ground. Where there are two bus stops on the same route they share a number. Bus stops are marked on the Banglamphu map on p.112. For a more detailed breakdown of Bangkok's bus routes, see p.106.

Bus stop 1: Thanon Krung Kasem, north side
#53 to Hualamphong train station (buses start from here)

Bus stop 2: Thanon Phra Arthit, south side, near *Hemlock*; and Thanon Phra Sumen, south side, near *Banglumpoo Place* hotel
#3 to the Museum of Siam, Pak Khlong Talat and Wongwian Yai train station
#9 to Wat Pho, Pak Khlong Talat
#53 to the Grand Palace and Chinatown

Bus stop 3: Thanon Phra Arthit, north side, near *New Siam Riverside*; and Thanon Phra Sumen, north side, opposite *Banglumpoo Place hotel*
#3 to Chatuchak Weekend Market and Mo Chit Northern Bus Terminal
#53 to Hualamphong train station (change at Bus Stop 1, but same ticket)
#56 (from Phra Sumen stop only) to Thanon Ratchasima for Vimanmek Palace and Dusit

Bus stop 4: Thanon Chakrabongse, near the 7-Eleven
#15, to Jim Thompson's House, Siam Square, Thanon Silom and Patpong
#30 to the Southern Bus Terminal
#32 to Wat Pho

Bus Stop 5: Thanon Rajinee (Rachini), near Bangkok Tourism Information Centre
#124 (non-air-con) to Southern Bus Terminal

Bus stop 6: Thanon Chakrabongse, outside the *Mayompuri Restaurant*
#AE2 Airport Express to Suvarnabhumi Airport

Bus stop 7: Thanon Rajdamnoen Klang, north side, outside Lottery Building
#2 to Ekamai Eastern Bus Terminal
#47 to Jim Thompson's House, Thanon Silom and Patpong
#47, #79 to Siam Square
#59, #503 (air-con; non-expressway), #509 to Chatuchak Weekend Market
#47 to Lumphini boxing stadium
#59 to Don Muang Airport
#70, #201, #503, #509 to TAT and Ratchadamnoen boxing stadium
#70 (non-expressway) to Dusit
#157 (air-con) to Mo Chit Northern Bus Terminal
#159 (non-air-con) to Hualamphong train station
#511 to Ekamai Eastern Bus Terminal and Pak Nam (for Ancient City buses)

Bus stop 8: Thanon Rajdamnoen Klang, south side
#44, #512 to Sanam Luang, the Grand Palace and Wat Pho
#60, #512 to Pak Khlong Talat
#79 to Taling Chan weekend floating market
#159 (non-air-con), # 511 and #516 to Southern Bus Terminal

Wally House 189/1–2 Thanon Khao San ⓣ02 282 7067. Small guest house behind the family restaurant, with very cheap, very small, bottom-budget fan rooms, some of them en suite. Set back from the road so quieter than many. 1–2

West: around Wat Chana Songkhram, Phra Arthit and the river

Bella Bella House Soi Ram Bhuttri ⓣ02 629 3090. The pastel-coloured rooms in this guest house are no frills but well priced, and a few boast lovely views over Wat Chana Songkhram. The cheapest share bathrooms, and the most expensive have air-con. In-room wi-fi available throughout. Fan 2–3, air-con 3

KC Guest House 64 Trok Kai Chae, off Thanon Phra Sumen ⓣ02 282 0618, ⓦwww.kcguesthouse.com. Friendly, family-run little guest house with exceptionally clean, tiled-floor rooms, with and without private bathrooms and air-con, and a terrace eating area on the soi. Fan 2, air-con 3

Lamphu House 75 Soi Ram Bhuttri ⓣ02 629 5861, ⓦwww.lamphuhouse.com. With smart bamboo beds, coconut-wood clothes rails, and elegant rattan lamps in even its cheapest rooms, this travellers' hotel set round a quiet courtyard has a calm, modern feel. Cheapest rooms share facilities and have no outside view. Wi-fi is available throughout. Fan 2, en suite 3, air-con 4

Merry V Soi Ram Bhuttri ⓣ02 282 9267. Large, efficiently run guest house offering some of the cheapest accommodation in Banglamphu. Bottom-end rooms are basic and small, many share bathrooms and it's pot luck whether you get a window or not. Better en-suites and air-con versions are also available and there's a useful noticeboard in the downstairs restaurant. Fan 1, en suite 3, air-con 3

Navalai River Resort 45/1 Thanon Phra Arthit ⓣ02 280 9955, ⓦwww.navalai.com. Style-conscious riverfront hotel, with an elegant rooftop pool, modishly furnished rooms, and river views from the most desirable. There's air-con, private balconies and wi-fi throughout and the excellent riverside *Aquatini* restaurant is at ground level (see p.178). 7–8

New Siam Riverside 21 Thanon Phra Arthit ⓣ02 629 3535, ⓦwww.newsiam.net. Occupying a prime riverside spot, this latest in the *New Siam* empire offers well-designed, good-value rooms, all with air-con, full amenities and wi-fi, and the best of them with fabulous river views from windows or private balconies. Also has a large riverside swimming pool and terrace restaurant. 6–7

New Siam 2 50 Trok Rong Mai ⓣ02 282 2795, ⓦwww.newsiam.net. Very pleasant and well run small hotel whose en-suite fan and air-con rooms stand out for their thoughtfully designed extras such as in-room safes, cable TV and drying rails on the balconies. Occupies a quiet but convenient location and has a small streetside pool. Popular with families, and triple rooms are also available. 4

Peachy Guest House 10 Thanon Phra Arthit ⓣ02 281 6471. Popular, good-value, very cheap, long-running Bangkok institution set round a small, late-night courtyard bar. Offers lots of clean, simple, wooden-floored rooms, most with shared bathrooms but some with air-con. Fan and shared bathroom 1, air-con and shared bathroom 1, air-con and bathroom 3

North: Samsen sois and Thewet

Lamphu Treehouse 155 Saphan Wanchat, Thanon Phracha Thipatai ⓣ02 282 0991, ⓦwww.lamphutreehotel.com. Named after the *lamphu* trees (as in Banglamphu, "place with *lamphu* trees") that line the adjacent canal, this attractively turned-out mid-range guest house offers smart, modish air-con rooms, all with balconies and plenty of polished teakwood fittings. There's a pool, and wi-fi in the lobby. It's in a quiet neighbourhood but just a few minutes' walk from Democracy, Khao San and the river. 5

Old Bangkok Inn 609 Thanon Phra Sumen ⓣ02 629 1787, ⓦwww.oldbangkokinn.com. This chic little boutique guest house has just ten air-con rooms, each of them individually styled in dark wood, with antique north-Thai partitions, Burmese doors, beds and ironwork lamps, plus elegant contemporary-accented bathrooms. All rooms have a PC with free broadband access, wi-fi and DVD player. Some also have a tiny private garden. A 10min walk from Khao San. 8–9

Phra Nakorn Norn Len 46 Thewet Soi 1, Thewet ⓣ02 628 8188, ⓦwww.phranakorn-nornlen.com. What was once a seedy short-time motel has been transformed into a bohemian haven with genuine eco-conscious and socially engaged sensibilities and a tangible fair-trade philosophy. Every one of the thirty comfortable, though not luxurious, rooms has been hand-painted to a different retro Thai design, and each has a platform bed, cute modern bathroom, balcony, CD player, wi-fi and air-con. The downstairs areas are filled with the owner's twentieth-century collectibles; the rooftop enjoys unrivalled views of Wat Indraviharn's huge standing Buddha and is partly given over to growing organic veg for the restaurant. 7

Sawatdee Guest House 71 Soi 16, Thanon Sri Ayutthaya, Thewet ⓣ02 281 0757. Cheap and basic, but friendlier than many in the Thewet area, this long-running old-style guest house offers basic no-frills fan rooms with partition walls, either with or without private bathroom. 2–3

Sri Ayutthaya 23/11 Soi 14, Thanon Sri Ayutthaya, Thewet ⓣ02 282 5942. The most attractive guest house in Thewet, where the good-sized rooms (choose between fan rooms with or without private bathroom and en suites with air-con) are elegantly done out with wood-panelled walls and beautiful polished wood floors. 3–4

Thamna Hometaurant 175 Thanon Samsen, between sois 3 and 5 ⓣ02 282 4979, ⓔthamnahome@yahoo.com. Upscale homestay comprising just two guest rooms on the floor above the young owners' organic veggie restaurant and below their own home. The look is simple but arty, with wooden floors, polished concrete walls and understated fabrics. Bathrooms are private but not en suite and the cheaper room has no window. Air-con and wi-fi throughout. Rates include a full veggie breakfast. 4

Vimol Guest House 358 Samsen Soi 4 ⓣ02 281 4615. Old-style, family-run guest house in a quiet but interesting neighbourhood that has just a smattering of other tourist places. The simple, cramped, hardboard-walled rooms are ultra basic and have shared bathrooms, but are possibly the cheapest in Banglamphu. 1

South: south of Democracy

Baan Dinso 113 Trok Sin, Thanon Dinso ⓣ02 622 0560, ⓦwww.baandinso.com. This tasteful, upmarket little guest house of just nine rooms occupies an elegant 1920s' Thai house all done out in cool buttermilk paintwork and polished teak floors. Prices are a little steep considering that all but the deluxe rooms have to use shared ground-floor bathrooms, but they all have air-con, TV and DVD players and there's free wi-fi. Youth Hostel members get a ten percent discount. 6

Boonsiri Place 55 Thanon Buranasart ⓣ02 622 2189, ⓦwww.boonsiriplace.com. Run by two charming sisters, this mid-range hotel is notable for its warm welcome, environmentally conscious policies and old-Bangkok neighbourhood location less than 10min walk from the Grand Palace. Each of its 48 air-con rooms is hung with a different painting commissioned from Thai traditional temple artist Chanok Chunchob, whose work is also on sale in the adjacent gallery. 6

Ratanakosin

Several small, upmarket hotels have recently opened on the west side of Ratanakosin, which put you in a peerless location, in a quiet, traditional, heavily Chinese neighbourhood of low-rise shophouses, overlooking the river and on the doorsteps of Wat Pho and the Grand Palace. Furthermore, the restaurants and nightlife of Banglamphu are within walking distance if you fancy a bit more of a buzz, while the sights of Thonburi, Chinatown, and Saphan Taksin Skytrain station are just a public boat ride away. All accommodation listed below is marked on the map on p.129.

Arun Residence 36 Soi Pratu Nokyung, Thanon Maharat ⓣ02 221 9158, ⓦwww.arunresidence.com. Stunning views of Wat Arun and charming, wooden-floored rooms that mix traditional and contemporary Thai styles. Occupying an eccentrically converted shophouse (plumbing can sometimes be a problem), the hotel also has a library with internet access, a rooftop bar and a good European and Thai restaurant, *The Deck*, where breakfast (included in the price) is served. 8

Aurum: The River Place 394/27–29 Soi Pansook, Thanon Maharat ⓣ02 622 2248, ⓦwww.aurum-bangkok.com. Modelled on a French townhouse, with wooden shutters and wrought-iron balconies, this spruce, four-storey hotel is set back slightly from the river but offers views of the water from most bedrooms. Splashed with colourful Thai fabrics and sporting heavily varnished wooden floors, the well-equipped rooms are a little on the small side, apart from those on the top floor. There's a daytime riverside café, *The Coffee Place*, where complimentary breakfast is served. 8

Chakrabongse Villas 396 Thanon Maharat ⓣ02 224 6686, ⓦwww.thaivillas.com. Riverside luxury accommodation with a difference: in the luxuriant gardens of hundred-year-old Chakrabongse House overlooking Wat Arun, four tranquil villas beautifully furnished in dark wood and silk, with polished teak floors. All have air-con and cable TV, and there's a small, attractive swimming pool and an open-sided riverfront pavilion for relaxing or dining (if ordered in advance). 9

Chinatown and Hualamphong Station area

Not far from the Ratanakosin sights, and within fifteen minutes' walk of Siam Square, **Chinatown (Sampeng)** is among the most frantic and fume-choked parts of Bangkok – and there's quite some competition. If you're in the mood however, it's got plenty of interest, sees barely any Western overnighters, and is also very handy for **Hualamphong Station**.

Hualamphong is on the **subway** system, and Chinatown is served by a number of useful **bus** routes (see box, p.106). All accommodation listed below is marked on the map on p.150.

Baan Hualamphong 336/20 Soi Chalong Krung ⓣ02 639 8054, ⓦwww.baanhualampong.com. This once strikingly stylish, now slightly faded, wooden guest house is still the most welcoming in the soi, not least for its traveller-friendly vibe. There are big, bright, double rooms plus five-person dorms at B220 per bed, but all but one room share bathrooms. Has kitchen facilities, inviting lounging areas and a small roof terrace, provides a left-luggage service and is open 24hr; 5min from Hualamphong. Fan ❸, air-con ❹

Bangkok Center 328 Thanon Rama IV ⓣ02 238 4848, ⓦwww.bangkokcentrehotel.com. The most interesting thing about this otherwise rather mediocre, old-fashioned hotel is its location, a couple of steps from the subway's exit 4 and just across the road from the train station. Rooms are air-con and adequate for the price and there's a pool, restaurant and wi-fi throughout. ❻

FF Guest House 338/10 Trok La-O, off Thanon Rama IV ⓣ02 233 4168. Tiny, family-run guest house offering ten cheap, cell-like but perfectly acceptable wooden-floored fan rooms with shared bathrooms. No other facilities, nor much English spoken. A 5min walk from the train and subway stations. ❶

Grand China Princess 215 Thanon Yaowarat ⓣ02 224 9977, ⓦwww.grandchina.com. The poshest hotel in Chinatown boasts fairly luxurious accommodation in its 27-storey tower close to the heart of the bustle, with stunning views over all the city landmarks (the best take in the river), a small rooftop swimming pool, revolving panoramic restaurant and broadband in every room. ❽

Shanghai Mansion 479 Thanon Yaowarat, next to *Scala* shark fin restaurant ⓣ02 221 2121, ⓦwww.shanghai-inn.com. The most design-conscious accommodation in Chinatown has embraced the modern Chinoiserie look with gusto. Rooms are prettily done out in silks, lacquer-look furniture and lanterns, featuring a lot of sumptuous reds and purples. There's barely any daylight in the hotel (only the noisy street-front suites have windows and views) but standard rooms are cosily isolated from the Chinatown frenzy and all have air-con, TV and free wi-fi. ❼–❽

The Train Inn 428 Thanon Rong Muang ⓣ02 215 3055, ⓦwww.thetraininn.com. Just a couple of minutes' walk from Hualamphong's side exit off platform 3, and open 24hr, this is a decent, traveller-oriented choice for weary rail passengers. Rooms – "first", "second" and "third class" – mostly share bathrooms and can be a bit scruffy, but are all air-con and the majority are a reasonable size. ❸–❹

TT2 Guest House 516 Soi Kaeo Fa (formerly Soi Sawang and known to taxi drivers as such), off Thanon Maha Nakorn ⓣ02 236 2946, ⓔttguesthouse@hotmail.com. A long-running, traveller-friendly budget place, this guest house is clean and well run, has simple singles, doubles and triples, and stores left luggage at B15–20 a day. All rooms share bathrooms. Roughly a 15min walk from either Hualamphong or the N3 Si Phraya express-boat stop; from Hualamphong, cross Thanon Rama IV, then walk left for 250m, cross Thanon Maha Nakorn and walk down it for 275m as far as Soi Kaeo Fa, where you turn left and then first right. The guest house is opposite Wat Kaeo Jam Fa. No check-in between midnight and 5.30am. ❷

Thonburi

Few tourists stay on the **Thonburi** side of the river, though many visit its canals and temples. It enjoys a nice authentic neighbourhood vibe and is surprisingly convenient, with express boats and cross-river shuttles serving Banglamphu and Ratanakosin across on the other bank. See map, p.96.

Ibrik Resort by the River 256 Soi Wat Rakang ⓣ02 848 9220, ⓦwww.ibrikresort.com. With just three rooms, this is the most bijou of boutique resorts. Each room is beautifully appointed in boho-chic style, with traditional wood floors, modernist white walls and sparkling silk accessories – and two of them have balconies right over the Chao Phraya River. It's just like staying at a trendy friend's home in a neighbourhood that sees hardly any other tourists. Located next door to *Supatra River House* restaurant and 5min walk from express-boat stop Tha Wang Lang. ⑧

Siam Square, Thanon Ploenchit and northern downtown

Siam Square – not really a square, but a low-slung grid of streetwise fashion shops, cinemas and inexpensive restaurants between Thanon Phrayathai and Thanon Henri Dunant – and nearby **Thanon Ploenchit** are as central as Bangkok gets: all the accommodation listed here is within walking distance of a Skytrain station. On hand are the city's best shopping possibilities – notably the phalanx of malls along Thanon Rama I – and a wide choice of Thai and international restaurants and food courts. There's no ultra-cheap accommodation around here, but a few scaled-up guest houses complement the expensive hotels. Concentrated in their own small "ghetto" on **Soi Kasemsan 1**, which runs north off Thanon Rama I, between the Bangkok Metropolitan Art Museum and Jim Thompson's House, these offer typical travellers' facilities and basic hotel comforts – air-conditioning and en-suite hot-water bathrooms – at moderate prices; the Khlong Saen Saeb canal-boat pier, Tha Saphan Hua Chang (easily accessed via Thanon Phrayathai), is especially handy for heading west to the Golden Mount and beyond, to Ratanakosin. All accommodation listed below is marked on the map on p.120, unless otherwise stated.

Inexpensive and moderate

A-One Inn 25/13 Soi Kasemsan 1, Thanon Rama I ⓣ02 215 3029 or 02 216 4770, ⓦwww.aoneinn.com. The original upscale guest house, and still justifiably popular, with a 24hr Internet café, wi-fi and a reliable left-luggage room. Bedrooms all have satellite TV and come in a variety of sizes, including family rooms; discounts for longer stays. ④

The Bed & Breakfast 36/42 Soi Kasemsan 1, Thanon Rama I ⓣ02 215 3004, ⓕ02 215 2493. Bright, clean and family run, though some of the rooms – carpeted and with en-suite telephones – are a bit cramped. As the name suggests, a simple breakfast – coffee, toast and fruit – is included. ④

Far East Inn 20/8–11 Soi Bangkok Bazaar, Soi Chitlom ⓣ02 255 4041–5, ⓦwww.geocities.com/fareastinn or www.tyha.org. The large rooms here are unexceptional but well-equipped – air-con, cable TV, mini-bars and baths with hot water – and the place is friendly, very central and reasonably quiet. Breakfast included in the price. Discounts for YHA members. ⑤

Golden House (VIP Guest House) 1025/5–9 Thanon Ploenchit ⓣ02 252 9535–7, ⓦwww.goldenhouses.net. Very clean and welcoming, small hotel in a peerless location. The plain but attractive, parquet-floored bedrooms are equipped with air-con, hot water, cable TV, free wi-fi and mini-bar – ask for one of the three larger front rooms with bay windows, which leave just enough space for a couple of armchairs. Breakfast included. Weekly and monthly discounts available. ⑥

Jim's Lodge 125/7 Soi Ruam Rudee, Thanon Ploenchit ⓣ02 255 3100, ⓦwww.jimslodge.com. In a relatively peaceful residential area, with friendly and helpful staff; offers international standards, including satellite TV and mini-bars, on a smaller scale and at bargain prices; no swimming pool, but there is a roof garden with outdoor jacuzzi. ⑥

Patumwan House 22 Soi Kasemsan 1, Thanon Rama I ⓣ02 612 3580–99, ⓦwww.patumwanhouse.com. Around the corner to the left at the far end of the soi, with very large, though rather bare rooms with satellite TV, fridges, wardrobes and wi-fi capability; facilities include a café and internet terminals. Discounted weekly and monthly rates. ⑤

Reno Hotel 40 Soi Kasemsan 1, Thanon Rama I ⓣ02 215 0026–7, ⓦwww.renohotel.co.th. Friendly hotel, boasting large, comfortable, en-suite rooms with air-con, hot water, baths and TV (some with

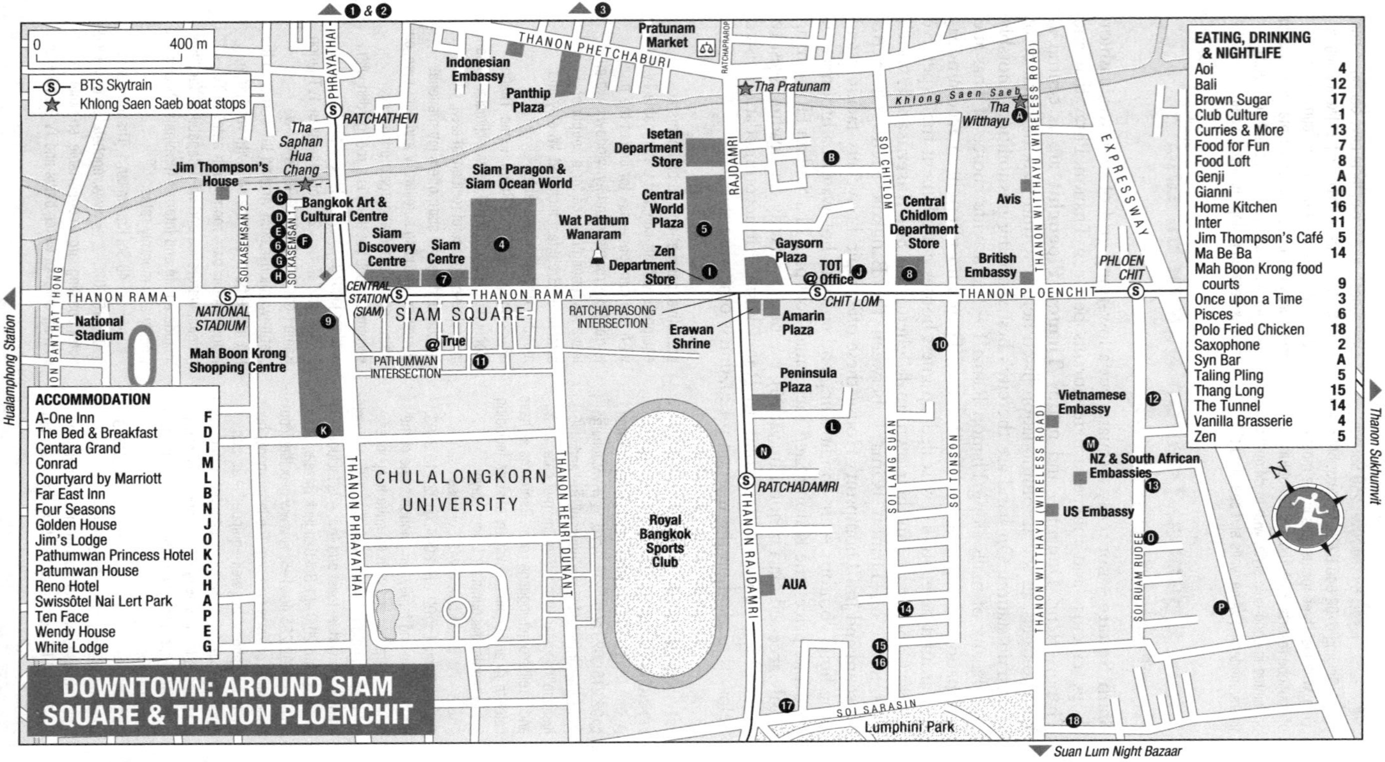
DOWNTOWN: AROUND SIAM SQUARE & THANON PLOENCHIT
0
400 m
BTS Skytrain
Khlong Saen Saeb boat stops
1 & 2
3
Hualamphong Station
Thanon Sukhumvit
Suan Lum Night Bazaar
ACCOMMODATION
A-One Inn F
The Bed & Breakfast D
Centara Grand I
Conrad M
Courtyard by Marriott L
Far East Inn B
Four Seasons N
Golden House J
Jim's Lodge O
Pathumwan Princess Hotel K
Patumwan House C
Reno Hotel H
Swissôtel Nai Lert Park A
Ten Face P
Wendy House E
White Lodge G
EATING, DRINKING & NIGHTLIFE
Aoi 4
Bali 12
Brown Sugar 17
Club Culture 1
Curries & More 13
Food for Fun 7
Food Loft 8
Genji A
Gianni 10
Home Kitchen 16
Inter 11
Jim Thompson's Café 5
Ma Be Ba 14
Mah Boon Krong food courts 9
Once upon a Time 3
Pisces 6
Polo Fried Chicken 18
Saxophone 2
Syn Bar A
Taling Pling 5
Thang Long 15
The Tunnel 14
Vanilla Brasserie 4
Zen 5
THANON PHETCHABURI
Pratunam Market
RATCHAPRAROP
Tha Pratunam
Khlong Saen Saeb
Tha Witthayu
Indonesian Embassy
Panthip Plaza
RATCHATHEVI
PHRAYATHAI
Tha Saphan Hua Chang
Jim Thompson's House
Bangkok Art & Cultural Centre
SOI KASEMSAN 2
SOI KASEMSAN 1
Siam Paragon & Siam Ocean World
Isetan Department Store
Central World Plaza
Wat Pathum Wanaram
Zen Department Store
Siam Discovery Centre
Siam Centre
RAJDAMRI
SOI CHITLOM
Central Chidlom Department Store
Avis
British Embassy
Gaysorn Plaza
TOT @ Office
THANON WITTHAYU (WIRELESS ROAD)
EXPRESSWAY
PHLOEN CHIT
THANON RAMA I
CENTRAL STATION (SIAM)
NATIONAL STADIUM
SIAM SQUARE
CHIT LOM
THANON PLOENCHIT
THANON BANTHAT THONG
National Stadium
Mah Boon Krong Shopping Centre
@True
PATHUMWAN INTERSECTION
RATCHAPRASONG INTERSECTION
Erawan Shrine
Amarin Plaza
Peninsula Plaza
Vietnamese Embassy
NZ & South African Embassies
US Embassy
SOI LANG SUAN
SOI TONSON
SOI RUAM RUDEE
RATCHADAMRI
THANON RAJDAMRI
THANON PHRAYATHAI
THANON HENRI DUNANT
CHULALONGKORN UNIVERSITY
Royal Bangkok Sports Club
AUA
SOI SARASIN
Lumphini Park
N

fridges), and a small swimming pool. Far more stylish than the bedrooms is the bar-restaurant, refurbished in contemporary Thai style, where breakfast is served (included in the price). Internet access. 5

Wendy House 36/2 Soi Kasemsan 1, Thanon Rama I ⓣ02 214 1149–50, ⓦwww.wendyguesthouse.com. Friendly and well-run guest house, with smart, clean and comfortable rooms, all with fridge, cable TV and wi-fi access. Internet terminals in the ground-floor café, where breakfast (included in the price) is served. Discounted weekly rates. Internet bookings accepted. 5

We-Train International House 3km west of Don Muang Airport (see map, p.96) ⓣ02 967 8550–4, ⓦwww.we-train.co.th. Run by the Association for the Promotion of the Status of Women, with proceeds helping disadvantaged women and children. In a peaceful setting, dorms (from B100), comfortable air-con rooms, internet access, a gym and a swimming pool. To get there by public transport, head for Don Muang train station or airport and phone for a pick-up. 3

White Lodge 36/8 Soi Kasemsan 1, Thanon Rama I ⓣ02 216 8867 or 02 215 3041, ⓕ02 216 8228. Cheapest guest house on the soi, with shining white cubicles and a lively, welcoming atmosphere – the best rooms, bright and quiet, are on the upper floors. 3

Expensive

Centara Grand at Central World 999/99 Thanon Rama 1 ⓣ02 100 1234, ⓦwww.centarahotelsresorts.com/cgcw. Occupying floors 23 to 55 atop the huge, glossy Central World Plaza mall and its fifty restaurants and fifteen cinema screens, this is a luxurious cocoon high above the hot, noisy city. The views from rooms and restaurants – particularly the appealingly laid-back, indoor-outdoor *Globe* lounge bar – are panoramic, and shared by the invitingly large swimming pool. Broadband access throughout. 8

Conrad All Seasons Place, 87 Thanon Witthayu ⓣ02 690 9999, ⓦwww.conradhotels.com. The *Conrad* places a high premium on design, aiming to add a cutting edge to traditional Thai style, and on service, including tailor-made itineraries by the concierge. Bathroom fittings include free-standing baths, glass walls and huge shower heads, and there's an enticing pool, spa, gym and two floodlit tennis courts. Restaurants include the modern Chinese *Liu* and authentic Japanese *Drinking Tea, Eating Rice*, while the *Diplomat Bar* hosts live jazz Mon–Sat eve. 9

Courtyard by Marriott 155/1 Soi Mahadlekluang 1, Thanon Rajdamri ⓣ02 690 1888, ⓦwww.courtyardbangkok.com. On a quiet, but very handy soi, this hotel offers most of the facilities of a five-star, but at more manageable prices. The modern design is seductive, gleaming white outside, candy colours and plenty of natural light inside, and there's a long, narrow, infinity pool, a fitness centre and reasonably priced massage rooms. 8

Four Seasons 155 Thanon Rajdamri ⓣ02 250 1000, ⓦwww.fourseasons.com. The stately home of Bangkok's top hotels, formerly the *Regent*. Afternoon tea is still served in the monumental lobby, which is adorned with magnificent, vibrant eighteenth-century-style murals depicting the Thai cosmology, and flanked by acclaimed Thai, Italian and Japanese restaurants and a steakhouse. Large and luxurious rooms are decorated in warm Thai colours and dark wood, and there's an excellent concierge service. 9

Pathumwan Princess Hotel 444 Thanon Phrayathai ⓣ02 216 3700, ⓦwww.pprincess. com. At the southern end of MBK Shopping Centre, affordable luxury (at the lower end of this price range) that's recently been refurbished in a crisp, modern style and is popular with families and businessmen. With Korean and Italian restaurants, a large, saltwater swimming pool with hot and cold jacuzzis, a health spa and a huge fitness club. 9

Reflections 224/2–9 (between sois 18 and 20; see map, p.109) Thanon Pradiphat ⓣ02 270 3344, ⓦwww.reflections-thai.com. Urban guerrilla meets kitsch at this idiosyncratic pop-art hotel, where every room was designed by a different artist. Browse the website to make your choice. The 36 rooms come in two sizes and all have air-con, a balcony or terrace, and in-room wi-fi, though few are luxurious. The location in an unfashionable neighbourhood is not great: it's a 10min walk south then west from BTS Saphan Kwai, but Chatuchak Weekend Market is only 20min away. There's a spa and art shop on site. 7

Siam City Hotel 477 Thanon Sri Ayutthaya (see map, p.96) ⓣ02 247 0123, ⓦwww.siamhotels.com. Elegant, welcoming luxury hotel north of downtown (next to Phaya Thai Skytrain and Suan Pakkad). Choose between an "Ayutthaya" room, done out in sharp, modern Thai style, and a larger "Siam" room with a soothing, more traditional flavour. There's a spa, health club, swimming pool and a comprehensive array of restaurants including Chinese, Japanese and Italian. At the lower end of this price code. 9

Swissôtel Nai Lert Park 2 Thanon Witthayu ⓣ02 253 0123, ⓦwww.swissotel.com. This welcoming, low-rise hotel is distinguished by its lushly beautiful gardens, overlooked by many of the chic and spacious, balconied bedrooms; set into the grounds are a landscaped swimming pool, tennis courts, squash court and popular spa and health club. Good deli-café, cool bar (see p.188) and Japanese (see p.181), French and Chinese restaurants. ⑨

Ten Face 81 Soi 2, Soi Ruam Rudee ⓣ02 695 4242, ⓦwww.tenfacebangkok.com. The name comes from Totsagan, the ten-faced demon of the *Ramakien* (see p.67), and without being gimmicky, this place ingeniously combines sleek, contemporary design with striking artworks inspired by the national myth. All the rooms are spacious suites with espresso machines, free wi-fi, SIM cards and iPods, some with small kitchens; ask for a room at the back if you're worried about noise from the nearby expressway. There's a fusion restaurant, fitness centre, long, narrow "dipping" pool and shuttle service to Ploen Chit Skytrain, plus a special concierge, who DJs in the ultra-hip *Sita Bar* and dispenses the lowdown on Bangkok parties and happenings. ⑨

Downtown: south of Thanon Rama IV

South of Thanon Rama IV, the area sometimes known as **Bangrak** contains a full cross-section of places to stay. Tucked away at its eastern edge, there are a few decent, cheap guest houses in the small travellers' ghetto of **Soi Ngam Duphli** and adjacent Soi Sri Bamphen and Soi Saphan Khu. The neighbourhood is often traffic-clogged and occasionally seedy, but is close to Lumphini Park and subway station and handy for Suvarnabhumi Airport.

Some medium-range places are scattered between Thanon Rama IV and the river, ranging from the notorious (the *Malaysia*) to the sedate (the *Bangkok Christian Guest House*). Bangrak also lays claim to the capital's biggest selection of top hotels, which are among the most opulent in the world. Traversed by the Skytrain, this area is especially good for eating and for gay and straight nightlife, mostly near the east end of **Thanon Silom** (around which several gay-friendly hotels are scattered), and has its fair share of interesting shops. Staying by the river itself in the atmospheric area around **Thanon Charoen Krung**, also known as **New Road**, has the added advantage of easy access to express boats. All accommodation listed below is marked on the maps on p.123 and p.96.

Inexpensive

ETC Guest House 5/3 Soi Ngam Duphli ⓣ02 287 1477–8, ⓦwww.etc.co.th. Above a branch of the recommended travel agent of the same name, and very handy for Thanon Rama IV, though consequently a little noisy. Helpful and very clean, catering mainly to Japanese travellers. Rooms come with fans and are further cooled by air-con in the corridors; hot-water bathrooms are either shared or en suite. Breakfast is included and free internet and wi-fi are available. ②

New Road Guest House 1216/1 Thanon Charoen Krung, between sois 34 and 36 ⓣ02 630 6994–8, ⓦwww.jysktravel.com. Thai headquarters of Danish backpacker travel agent and tour operator, Jysk, offering a wide choice of accommodation around a courtyard off New Rd, as well as interesting canal (see p.155) and Thailand (see p.209) tours. There are ten-bunk dorms (with air-con planned) and basic bunk-bedded twins sharing bathrooms, as well as free hammocks on the roof. En-suite rooms, some with air-con and cable TV, sport attractive wooden floors, mini-bars, Thai decorative touches and well-equipped, hot-water bathrooms. Guests hang out in the restaurant, the sociable bar with pool table or the DVD room; internet access and free baggage storage are available, as well as showers for guests with an evening departure. Dorms from B90, fan ②–③, air-con ⑤

Sala Thai Daily Mansion 15 Soi Saphan Khu ⓣ02 287 1436. The pick of the area, at the end of a quiet, shaded alley off Soi Saphan Khu, near Soi Sri Bamphen. A clean and efficiently run place, with bright, modern rooms with wall fans, sharing hot- and cold-water bathrooms, and a large, leafy roof garden. Good rates for single rooms. Fan ③, air-con ④

Moderate

Baan Saladaeng 69/2 Soi 3, Thanon Saladaeng ⓣ02 636 3038, ⓦwww.baansaladaeng.com. On a tiny, central alley, this chic designer guest house offers nine individually styled rooms, such as the Pop Art Mania Room and the Moroccan Suite, some with outdoor shower/bath and terrace. Air-con, rain showers, mini-bars, cable TV, comfy beds and free wi-fi throughout. No children. Continental breakfast included. ⑤–⑦

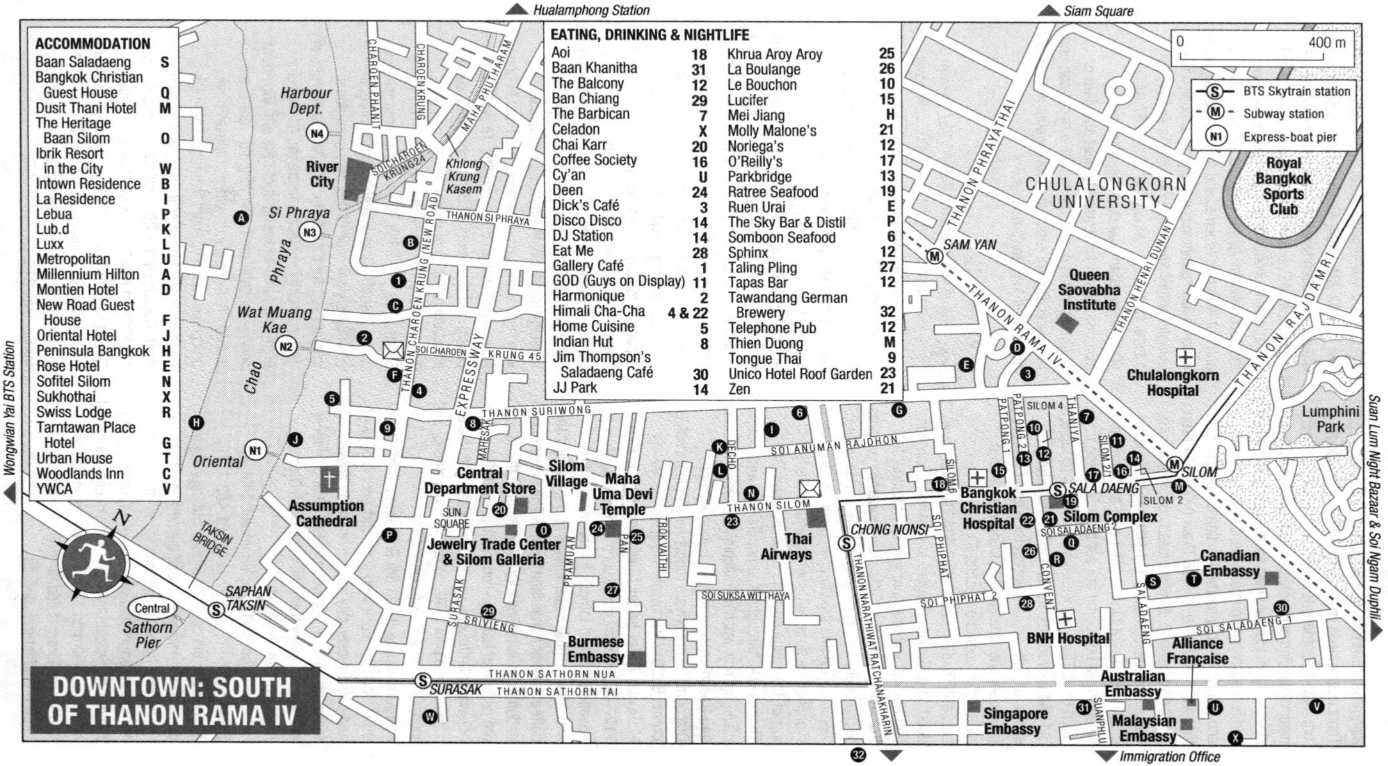
DOWNTOWN: SOUTH OF THANON RAMA IV
ACCOMMODATION
Baan Saladaeng S
Bangkok Christian Guest House Q
Dusit Thani Hotel M
The Heritage Baan Silom O
Ibrik Resort in the City W
Intown Residence B
La Residence I
Lebua P
Lub.d K
Luxx L
Metropolitan U
Millennium Hilton A
Montien Hotel D
New Road Guest House F
Oriental Hotel J
Peninsula Bangkok H
Rose Hotel E
Sofitel Silom N
Sukhothai X
Swiss Lodge R
Tarntawan Place Hotel G
Urban House T
Woodlands Inn C
YWCA V
EATING, DRINKING & NIGHTLIFE
Aoi 18
Baan Khanitha 31
The Balcony 12
Ban Chiang 29
The Barbican 7
Celadon X
Chai Karr 20
Coffee Society 16
Cy'an U
Deen 24
Dick's Café 3
Disco Disco 14
DJ Station 14
Eat Me 28
Gallery Café 1
GOD (Guys on Display) 11
Harmonique 2
Himali Cha-Cha 4 & 22
Home Cuisine 5
Indian Hut 8
Jim Thompson's Saladaeng Café 30
JJ Park 14
Khrua Aroy Aroy 25
La Boulange 26
Le Bouchon 10
Lucifer 15
Mei Jiang H
Molly Malone's 21
Noriega's 12
O'Reilly's 17
Parkbridge 13
Ratree Seafood 19
Ruen Urai E
The Sky Bar & Distil P
Somboon Seafood 6
Sphinx 12
Taling Pling 27
Tapas Bar 12
Tawandang German Brewery 32
Telephone Pub 12
Thien Duong M
Tongue Thai 9
Unico Hotel Roof Garden 23
Zen 21
0 400 m
BTS Skytrain station
Subway station
Express-boat pier
Hualamphong Station
Siam Square
Wongwian Yai BTS Station
Suan Lum Night Bazaar & Soi Ngam Duphli
Immigration Office
Harbour Dept.
River City
Khlong Krung Kasem
Si Phraya
Chao Phraya
Wat Muang Kae
Oriental
Assumption Cathedral
Central Department Store
Silom Village
Maha Uma Devi Temple
Jewelry Trade Center & Silom Galleria
Thai Airways
Burmese Embassy
Bangkok Christian Hospital
Silom Complex
BNH Hospital
Canadian Embassy
Alliance Française
Australian Embassy
Malaysian Embassy
Singapore Embassy
Chulalongkorn Hospital
Queen Saovabha Institute
CHULALONGKORN UNIVERSITY
Royal Bangkok Sports Club
Lumphini Park
Central Sathorn Pier
Taksin Bridge
Saphan Taksin
Surasak
Chong Nonsi
Sala Daeng
Silom
Sam Yan
Thanon Charoen Krung (New Road)
Thanon Si Phraya
Thanon Suriwong
Thanon Silom
Thanon Sathorn Nua
Thanon Sathorn Tai
Thanon Narathiwat Ratchanakharin
Thanon Rama IV
Thanon Phrayathai
Thanon Henri Dunant
Thanon Rajdamri
Expressway
Charoen Phanit
Charoen Krung
Maha Phutharam
Soi Charoen Krung 24
Soi Charoen Krung 45
Mahesak
Sun Square
Pramuan
Pan
Trok Vaithi
Decho
Soi Anuman Rajdhon
Soi Suksa Witthaya
Soi Phiphat
Soi Phiphat 2
Convent
Soi Saladaeng 1
Soi Saladaeng 2
Saladaeng
Suanphlu
Patpong 1
Patpong 2
Silom 2
Silom 2/1
Silom 4
Silom 6
Thaniya
Surasak
Srivieng

Bangkok Christian Guest House 123 Soi 2, Thanon Saladaeng ⓣ02 233 6303, ⓦwww.bcgh.org. Well-run, orderly missionary house in a shiny, modern building overlooking a neat garden, where plain but immaculately kept rooms come with air-con and hot-water bathrooms. Decent rates for singles, and plenty of family rooms. Breakfast included. ⑥

Intown Residence 1086/6 Thanon Charoen Krung ⓣ02 639 0960–2, ⓦwww.tarad.com/intownbkk. Clean, welcoming, rather old-fashioned and very good-value Thai-Chinese hotel with a coffee shop, where most bedrooms are set back from the noisy main road. There's a wide variety of comfortable, old and new rooms, in plain or slightly chintzy styles, all with air-con, hot-water bathrooms, mini-bars and satellite TVs. Good weekly and monthly discounts available. ④

Lub.d 4 Thanon Decho ⓣ02 634 7999, ⓦwww.lubd.com. Buzzing, upmarket hostel with air-con and hot water throughout and an industrial feel to the stylishly lit decor. This crisp modernity extends to the bedrooms, among which the dorms (some women-only) and the cheaper, bunk-bedded private rooms share large bathroom areas, while the top-of-the-range en-suite doubles boast TVs. There's wi-fi throughout, a popular bar and café, a travel agency, washing machines, storage facilities and free internet terminals, but no kitchen. Discounts in the private rooms for single travellers. Dorms B520–750 (towels extra), rooms ⑤–⑥

Malaysia Hotel 54 Soi Ngam Duphli ⓣ02 679 7127–36, ⓦwww.malaysiahotelbkk.com. Once a travellers' legend famous for its compendious noticeboard, now better known for its seedy 24hr coffee shop and massage parlour. The accommodation itself is reasonable value though: the rooms are large and have air-con, mini-bars and hot-water bathrooms; some have cable TV. There's a swimming pool (B50 per day for non-guests) and internet access. Gay-friendly. ④

Penguin House 27/23 Soi Sri Bamphen ⓣ02 679 9991. Modern block with a ground-floor café, wi-fi and large, reasonably attractive rooms above, featuring air-con, hot water, cable TV and fridges; ask for one away from the busy road. Discounted monthly rates available. ④

Urban House 35/13 Soi Yommarat, Thanon Saladaeng ⓣ02 636 3244 or 081 492 7778, ⓦwww.urbanh.com. On a quiet but very central sub-soi, this modern, cubist building is more impressive from outside than in, but the six rooms are smart, bright and well equipped, done out in browns and creams. Air-con, hot water, fridges and cable TV in all rooms, small kitchens in half of them. Free internet and wi-fi. No children under 10. Light breakfast included. ⑤

Woodlands Inn 1158/5–7 Soi 32, Thanon Charoen Krung ⓣ02 235 3894, ⓦwww.woodlandsinn.org. Simple but recently refurbished and well-run hotel next to the GPO, under Indian management, which will appeal to world travellers who are homesick for the subcontinent. All rooms have air-con, cable TV and hot-water bathrooms, and there's a good-value South Indian restaurant on the ground floor, where complimentary American breakfast is served. ④

YWCA 13 Thanon Sathorn Tai ⓣ02 287 3136, ⓦwww.ywcabangkok.com. Reliable, low-rise accommodation for women in neat standard or bright, spacious deluxe rooms, all with air-con and hot water. Decent reductions for singles and deeply discounted long-term rates. ⑤

Expensive

Bangkok Marriott Resort 257 Thanon Charoennakorn ⓣ02 476 0022, ⓦwww.marriott.com. A luxury retreat from the frenetic city centre, well to the south on the Thonburi bank, but connected to Taksin Bridge (for the Skytrain and Chao Phraya express boats), 10min away, by hotel ferries every 15min. Arrayed around a highly appealing, landscaped swimming pool, the tranquil, riverside gardens are filled with birdsong, while the stylish and spacious bedrooms come with varnished hardwood floors and balconies. There's a fitness centre, a branch of the classy Mandara Spas, and among a wide choice of eateries, a good Japanese teppanyaki house and a bakery-café. ⑨

Dusit Thani Hotel 946 Thanon Rama IV, on the corner of Thanon Silom ⓣ02 200 9000, ⓦwww.dusit.com. Elegant, centrally placed top-class hotel, geared for both business and leisure, with very high standards of service. The hotel is famous for its eight restaurants, including *Thien Duong* (see p.184) and the French *D'Sens*, which has some spectacular top-floor views. ⑨

The Heritage Baan Silom 659 Soi 19, Thanon Silom ⓣ02 236 8388, ⓦwww.theheritagehotels.com. Just off Silom in a shopping arcade, the colonial-style facade of this new hotel doesn't prepare you for the interior's striking contemporary design, mostly in black and cream. All bedrooms enjoy big-head showers, mini-bars and turn-down service; despite the name, "Studio" rooms are actually fairly spacious, while "Deluxe" have balconies and "Superior" bathtubs. There's a restaurant and free internet access, but no pool. ⑧

Ibrik Resort in the City 235/16 Thanon Sathorn Tai ⓣ02 211 3470, ⓦwww.ibrikresort.com. Downtown copy of the Thonburi boutique hotel (see p.119), also with just three rooms. Slightly off the beaten track, but near the Expressway and handy for Surasak BTS. ⑧

La Residence 173/8–9 Thanon Suriwong ⓣ02 266 5400–1, ⓦwww.laresidencebangkok.com. A small, intimate boutique hotel where the tasteful, individually decorated bedrooms – including proper single rooms at proper single rates – stretch to mini-bars, safes and cable TV. Continental breakfast included. 7

Lebua 1055 Thanon Silom ⓣ02 624 9999, ⓦwww.lebua.com. Occupying part of the landmark State Tower on the corner of Thanon Charoen Krung, *Lebua* offers extravagant suites with kitchen areas, decorated in a restrained contemporary style; it's well worth paying US$40 extra for "Riverview", for the lofty vista from the balcony, over 200m above the Chao Phraya. Staff are very solicitous and there's a gym and outdoor pool on Floor 13. Outlets include *Breeze*, for contemporary Asian seafood, and, beneath the golden, Neoclassical dome on the top floor, Italian food at *Mezzaluna* and Mediterranean *Sirocco*, the world's highest al fresco restaurant; also up here are *Sky Bar* and *Distil* (see p.189). 9

Luxx 6/11 Thanon Decho ⓣ02 635 8800, ⓦwww.staywithluxx.com. Welcoming boutique hotel offering a good dose of contemporary style at reasonable prices (with a new, larger branch with a pool, *XL*, about to open on Soi Lang Suan). Decorated in white, grey and natural teak, the rooms feature DVD players, free wi-fi and cute wooden baths surmounted by rain showers. Breakfast included. 7

Metropolitan 27 Thanon Sathorn Tai ⓣ02 625 3333, ⓦwww.metropolitan.como.bz. The height of chic, minimalist urban living, where the rooms are stylishly decorated in dark wood, creamy Portuguese limestone and lotus-themed contemporary artworks. There's a very seductive pool, a fine spa, a well-equipped fitness centre, an excellent restaurant, *Cyan* (see p.182), and a fiercely hip bar. 9

Millennium Hilton 123 Thanon Charoennakorn ⓣ02 442 2000, ⓦwww.hilton.com. Impressive new hotel with a twelve-storey lobby atrium, decorated throughout in modern Asian style. Its fourth-floor saltwater pool, fringed with white sand, is known as The Beach. There's also a secluded spa and a top-floor bar, *360*, 130m above the river with huge picture windows, while every restaurant also boasts views of the Chao Phraya: Cantonese *Yuan*, with good-value lunchtime dim sum, a steak-house and an international buffet with its own refrigerated cheese room. On the Thonburi bank, with shuttle boats across to River City shopping centre and Taksin Bridge. 9

Montien Hotel 54 Thanon Surawongse, on the corner of Rama IV ⓣ02 233 7060–9, ⓦwww.montien.com. Grand, airy and solicitous luxury hotel, long-running and with a strongly Thai character. It's had a recent face-lift but retains a quaintly old-fashioned demeanour – astrologers on the mezzanine, Latin and ballroom dancing in the nightclub and live muzak in the lobby. 9

Oriental Hotel 48 Oriental Avenue, off Thanon Charoen Krung ⓣ02 659 9000, ⓦwww.mandarinoriental.com. One of the world's best, this effortlessly stylish riverside hotel boasts immaculate standards of service. 9

Peninsula Bangkok 333 Thanon Charoennakorn ⓣ02 861 2888, ⓦwww.peninsula.com. Superb top-class hotel to rival the *Oriental* across the river. Service is flawless, the ultra-luxurious decor stylishly blends traditional Western and Asian design, and every room has a panoramic view of the Chao Phraya. The lovely riverside gardens shelter a three-tiered pool, a beautiful spa run by ESPA, a fitness centre and tennis courts. On the Thonburi bank, with shuttle boats across to a reception area by the *Shangri-La Hotel* off Thanon Charoen Krung and down to Taksin Bridge. 9

Rose Hotel 118 Thanon Suriwong ⓣ02 266 8268–72, ⓦwww.rosehotelbkk.com. Set back from the main road but very handy for the city's nightlife, this thirty-year-old hotel has been cleverly refurbished: the compact rooms (all with bathtubs) now boast a simple but stylish, retro look, in keeping with the age of the place. Suites and the ground-floor public rooms, where continental breakfast (included in the price) is served, are more elegant again, and there's a beautiful, new swimming pool at the back. Frequent discounts. 7

Sofitel Silom 188 Thanon Silom ⓣ02 238 1991, ⓦwww.sofitel.com. Towards the quieter end of Thanon Silom, a clever renovation combines contemporary Asian artworks and furnishings with understated French elegance. A wine bar and Mediterranean and rooftop Chinese restaurants, as well as a fitness club and small pool, complete the picture. 9

Sukhothai 13/3 Thanon Sathorn Tai ⓣ02 344 8888, ⓦwww.sukhothai.com. The most elegant of Bangkok's top hotels, its decor inspired by the walled city of Sukhothai: low-rise accommodation, as well as a beautiful garden spa, all coolly furnished in silks, teak and granite. Service is of the highest standard and the architecture makes the most of the views of the surrounding six acres of gardens, lotus ponds and pools dotted with statuary. Health club, 25-metre infinity pool, squash and tennis courts, and excellent restaurants including *Celadon* (see p.182). 9

Swiss Lodge 3 Thanon Convent ⓣ02 233 5345, ⓦwww.swisslodge.com. Swish, friendly, good-value, boutique hotel, with high standards of service, just off Thanon Silom and ideally placed for business and nightlife. The tiny terrace swimming pool confirms the national stereotypes of neatness and clever design, while the *Three on Convent* restaurant branches out into North Californian wine-country cuisine. ❽

Tarntawan Place Hotel 119/5–10 Thanon Suriwong ⓣ02 238 2620, ⓦwww.tarntawan.com. Set back from the main road, a pretty, flower-strewn lobby announces this gracious, well-run, gay-friendly hotel. The decent-sized, well-equipped rooms are pleasant and homely, with free wi-fi. Guests also receive free breakfast and internet access, as well as reduced-price entry to a gym and swimming pool on Soi Thaniya. Discounted fortnightly and monthly rates; in the off-season, excellent-value three-night packages. ❼

Thanon Sukhumvit

Thanon Sukhumvit is Bangkok's longest road – it keeps going east all the way to Cambodia – but for such an important artery it's way too narrow for the volume of traffic that needs to use it, and is further hemmed in by the overhead Skytrain line that runs above it. Packed with high-rise hotels and office blocks, an impressive array of specialist restaurants (from Lebanese to Lao), tailors, bookstores and stall after stall selling cheap souvenirs and T-shirts, it's a lively place that attracts a high proportion of single male tourists to its enclaves of girlie bars on Soi Nana Tai, Soi Cowboy and the Clinton Entertainment Plaza. But for the most part it's not a seedy area, and is home to many expats and middle-class Thais. The majority of overnighters are business travellers but Sukhumvit also has a couple of exceptional mid-priced guest houses. The most central accommodation is between and along sois 1 to 21; hotels further east are quite convenient for **Suvarnabhumi Airport** but far from the main shopping and eating hubs. Even in central Sukhumvit, many of the sois are refreshingly quiet, even leafy; transport down the longer sois is provided by motorbike-taxi (*mohtoesai*) drivers who wait at the soi's mouth, clad in numbered waistcoats.

Thanon Sukhumvit is well served by the **Skytrain (BTS)**, and there's an interchange with the **subway** at BTS Sukhumvit. It is however a long way from the main Ratanakosin sights, and getting there by **bus** or even **taxi** can take an hour or more, especially during rush hour (7–9am & 3–7pm). Useful buses for getting to Ratanakosin include #508 and #25; full details of bus routes are given on p.106. **Airport bus** #AE3 from Suvarnabhumi stops all the way along Thanon Sukhumvit.

A much faster way to cross town is by public **longtail boat** along Khlong Saen Saeb; this canal service begins near Democracy Monument in the west of the city and runs parallel with part of Thanon Sukhumvit. All accommodation listed below is marked on the map on opposite.

Central Sukhumvit

Amari Boulevard Hotel Soi 5 ⓣ02 255 2930, ⓦwww.amari.com. Rooms in the deluxe category and above at this long-running but modernized four-star tourist hotel enjoy fine views of the Bangkok skyline and have either wi-fi or broadband. The attractive sixth-floor rooftop swimming pool and garden terrace becomes the Thai-food restaurant *Season* in the evenings. ❽–❾

The Atlanta At the far southern end of quiet, residential Soi 2 ⓣ02 252 1650, ⓦwww.theatlantahotel.bizland.com. A Bangkok institution, this classic, five-storey budget hotel was built in 1952 around a famously photogenic Art Deco-style lobby and continues to emphasize an old-fashioned hospitality ("Bangkok's bastion of wholesome tourism"). It offers some of the cheapest accommodation on Sukhumvit: rooms are simple and some are pretty scruffy, though they are all en suite and some have air-con while others have small balconies. There's a swimming pool, wi-fi and internet access and a left-luggage facility. The hotel restaurant serves an extensive Thai menu, including lots of vegetarian dishes, and shows classic movies set in Asia. ❹

The Eugenia 267, off Soi 31 ⓣ02 259 9017, ⓦwww.theeugenia.com. This cosy little Relais & Chateaux hideaway of just twelve rooms recreates an ambience of old-fashioned Indochinese charm

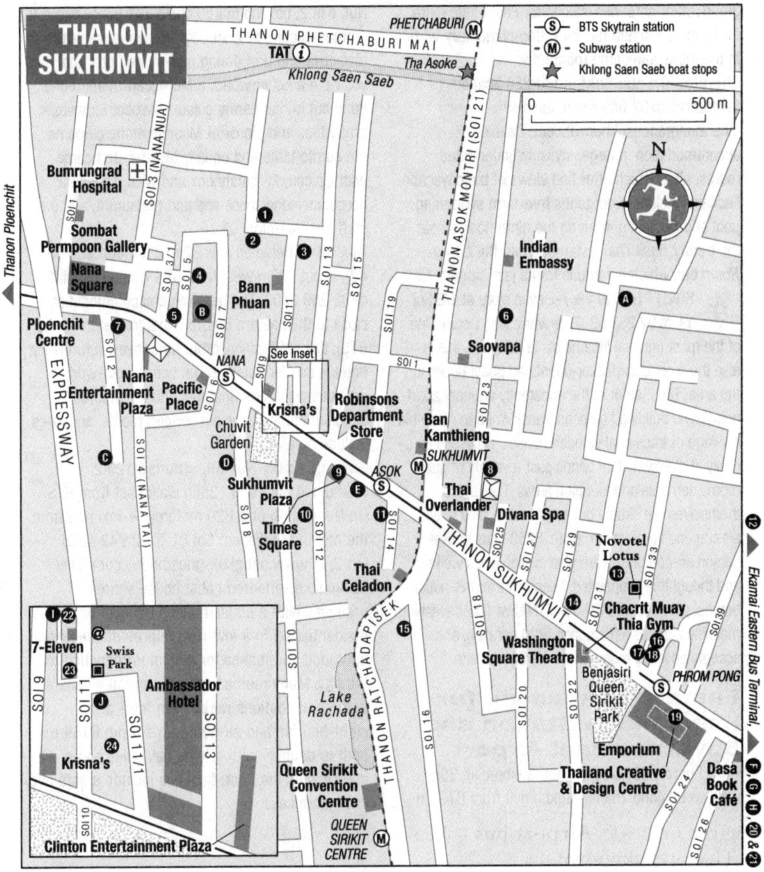

ACCOMMODATION	
Amari Boulevard Hotel	B
The Atlanta	C
The Eugenia	A
Grand Business Inn	J
Imm Fusion	G
PS Guesthouse	D
Rex Hotel	F
Sheraton Grande Sukhumvit	E
Suk 11	I
Sukhumvit On-Nut Guesthouse	H

EATING, DRINKING & NIGHTLIFE	
Al Ferdoss	5
Aoi	19
Baan Khanitha	6
The Ball in Hand	9
Bangkok Baking Company	7
Basil	E
Bed Supperclub	3
The Bull's Head	16
Cabbages and Condoms	10
Cheap Charlie's	23
Dosa King	24
Face Bangkok (La Na Thai & Hazara)	21
Gaeng Pa Lerd Rod	18
Gallery 11	22
Gulliver's Traveler's Tavern	4
Himali Cha-Cha	13
Le Dalat Indochine	8
Londoner Brew Pub	17
Long Table	15
MahaNaga	14
Nest	2
Q Bar	1
Spring Summer Winter	12
Suda Restaurant	11
Vientiane Kitchen (Khrua Vientiane)	20

with four-poster beds, freestanding copper bathtubs, mellow colour schemes and a bijou courtyard pool. It's a good 15min walk from BTS Phrom Pong but there's free hotel transport. 9

Grand Business Inn 2/4–2/11 Soi 11 ⓣ02 254 7981, ⓦwww.grandbusinessinn.net. Popular, good-value mid-range hotel offering 127 large, comfortable, standard-issue air-con rooms, all with bathtubs, cable TV and broadband access. In a very central location just a few metres from BTS Nana. Advance reservations essential. 6

PS Guesthouse 26/1 Soi 8 ⓣ02 255 2309, ⓔpsguesthouse@hotmail.com. This small, calm, friendly guesthouse offers huge, airy, very well equipped rooms, each with air-con, TV, safety box, fridge, free tea and coffee, and refreshingly green, plant-screened balconies. Pay a little extra for in-room kitchen facilities. Complimentary wi-fi in the lobby and some rooms. ⑤

Sheraton Grande Sukhumvit 250 Thanon Sukhumvit ⓣ02 649 8888, ⓦwww.sheratongrandesukhumvit.com. Deluxe accommodation in large, stylishly understated rooms, all of which offer fine views of the cityscape. Facilities include a gorgeous free-form swimming pool and tropical garden on the ninth floor, a spa, the trendy *Basil Thai* restaurant, and the *Living Room* bar, which is famous for its jazz singers. ⑨

Suk 11 Behind the 7-Eleven store at 1/3 Soi 11 ⓣ02 253 5927, ⓦwww.suk11.com. One of the most unusual little hotels in Bangkok, this is also the most backpacker-orientated guest house in the area. The interior of the apparently ordinary apartment-style building has been transformed to resemble a village of traditional wooden houses, accessed by a dimly lit plankway that winds past a variety of guest rooms, terraces and lounging areas. The rooms themselves are simple but comfortable, they're all air-con and some are en suite. B250 beds in five-person air-con dorms are also available. It's well run and thoughtfully appointed, keeps informative notice-boards, provides free breakfast, has wi-fi and washing machines, stores left luggage (B20 per day), and accepts advance reservations via the website. ④

Eastern Sukhumvit: for Ekamai Bus Station and Suvarnabhumi Airport

Imm Fusion 1594/50 Thanon Sukhumvit, 30m walk west along Thanon Sukhumvit from BTS On Nut, exit 2, beyond Soi 50 ⓣ02 331 5555, ⓦwww.immhotel.com. Step through the entrance of this attractive and welcoming mid-range hotel and you're in another world, a Moroccan-themed one done out in rich earthy colours, wrought ironwork, pretty tiles and plenty of Moorish arches. Rooms are comfortable and equally tasteful, and come with air-con, TV, safety box and wi-fi. There's a gorgeous indoor pool, spa and restaurant, and the staff are charming. ⑥

Rex Hotel Between sois 32 and 34 (opposite Soi 49), about 300m west from BTS Thong Lo, exit 2 ⓣ02 259 0106. The best-value accommodation close to the Eastern Bus Terminal (one stop on the BTS), this old-fashioned but attractively refurbished hotel is comfortable and run with an old-world graciousness. A rooftop pool and a restaurant complement the spacious air-con rooms, and rates include breakfast. ⑤

Sukhumvit On-Nut Guesthouse 125/2 Sukhumvit Soi 89, a 12min walk east from BTS On Nut (exit 3) or a B20 motorcycle-taxi ride from the mouth of adjacent Soi 81 ⓣ02 742 4525 ext 2, ⓦwww.bangkok-guesthouse.com. This backpacker-oriented guest house shares premises with a small language school on a quiet residential soi in a low-rise, unpretentious neighbourhood and makes for a calm introduction to the city. Many rooms have air-con but all share bathrooms; options range from four- and eight-bed fan and air-con dorms (from B169 per bed) to doubles with private balconies and a mattress on the floor; facilities include a café and internet access. ④

Ratanakosin

The only place to start your exploration of Bangkok is **Ratanakosin**, the royal island on the east bank of the Chao Phraya, where the city's most important and extravagant sights are. When Rama I developed Ratanakosin for his new capital in 1782, after the sacking of Ayutthaya and a temporary stay across the river in Thonburi, he paid tribute to its precursor by imitating Ayutthaya's layout and architecture – he even shipped the building materials downstream from the ruins of the old city. Like Ayutthaya, the new capital was sited for protection beside a river and turned into an artificial island by the construction of defensive canals, with a central **Grand Palace** and adjoining royal temple, **Wat Phra Kaeo**, fronted by an open cremation field, **Sanam Luang**; the Wang Na (Palace of the Second King), now the **National Museum**, was also built at this time. **Wat Pho**, which predates the capital's founding, was further embellished by Rama I's successors, who have consolidated Ratanakosin's pre-eminence by building several grand European-style palaces (now housing government institutions); Wat Mahathat, the most important centre of Buddhist learning in Southeast Asia; the National Theatre; the National Gallery; and Thammasat and Silpakorn universities.

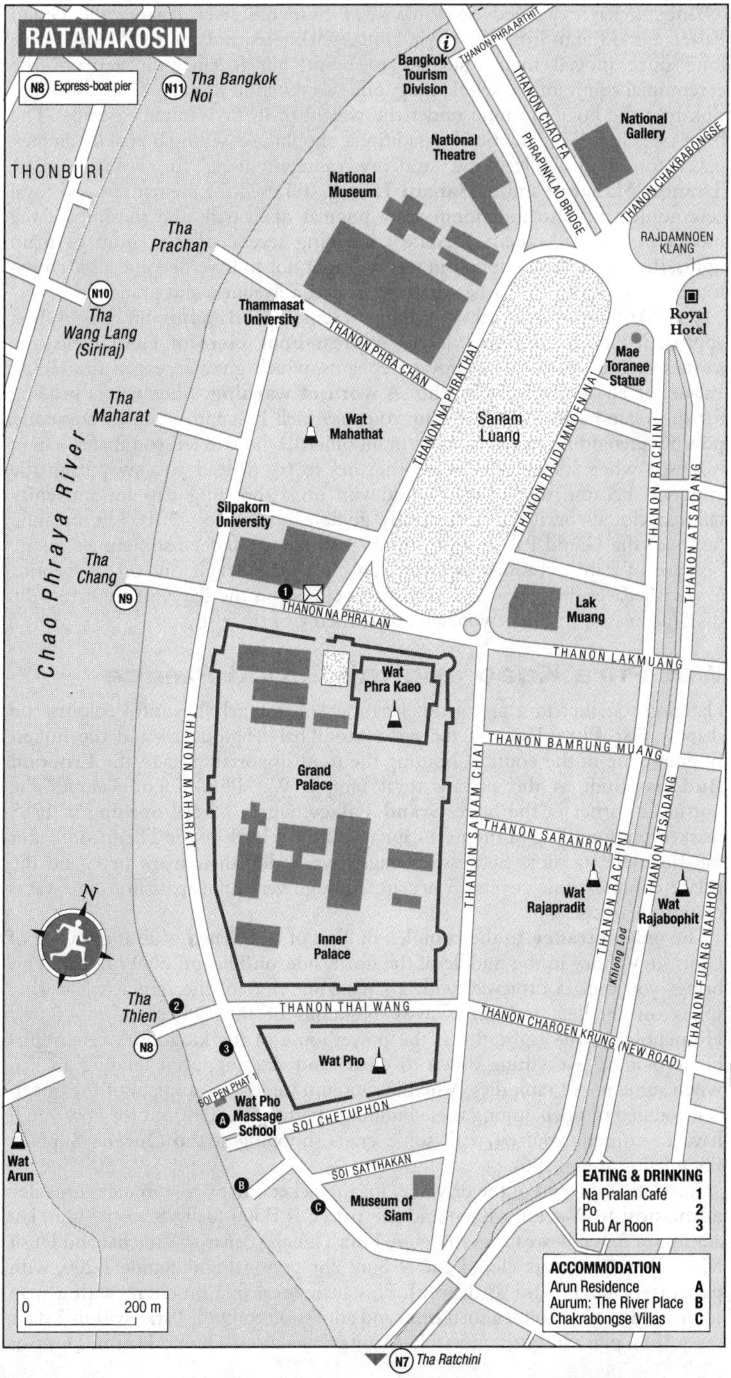
RATANAKOSIN
N8 Express-boat pier
N11 Tha Bangkok Noi
THONBURI
Bangkok Tourism Division
National Theatre
National Gallery
National Museum
THANON PHRA ARTHIT
THANON CHAO FA
PHRAPINKLAO BRIDGE
THANON CHAKRABONGSE
RAJDAMNOEN KLANG
Tha Prachan
N10 Tha Wang Lang (Siriraj)
Thammasat University
THANON PHRA CHAN
Royal Hotel
Mae Toranee Statue
Tha Maharat
Wat Mahathat
THANON NA PHRA THAT
Sanam Luang
THANON RAJDAMNOEN NAI
THANON RACHINI
THANON ATSADANG
Chao Phraya River
Silpakorn University
Tha Chang
N9
THANON NA PHRA LAN
Lak Muang
THANON LAKMUANG
Wat Phra Kaeo
THANON BAMRUNG MUANG
THANON MAHARAT
Grand Palace
THANON SANAM CHAI
THANON SARANROM
Wat Rajapradit
Wat Rajabophit
Khlong Lod
THANON FUANG NAKHON
Inner Palace
N
Tha Thien
N8
THANON THAI WANG
THANON CHAROEN KRUNG (NEW ROAD)
Wat Pho
SOI PEN PHAT 1
Wat Pho Massage School
SOI CHETUPHON
Wat Arun
SOI SATTHAKAN
Museum of Siam
EATING & DRINKING
Na Pralan Café 1
Po 2
Rub Ar Roon 3
ACCOMMODATION
Arun Residence A
Aurum: The River Place B
Chakrabongse Villas C
0 200 m
Banglamphu
Pahurat & Chinatown
N7 Tha Ratchini

Bangkok has expanded eastwards away from the river, leaving the Grand Palace a good 5km from the city's commercial heart, and the royal family have long since moved their residence to Dusit, but Ratanakosin remains the ceremonial centre of the whole kingdom – so much so that it feels as if it might sink into the boggy ground under the weight of its own mighty edifices. The heavy, stately feel is lightened by traditional shophouses selling herbal medicines, pavement amulet-sellers and studenty canteens along the riverside road, **Thanon Maharat**; and by **Sanam Luang**, still used for cremations and royal ceremonies, but also functioning as a popular open park and the hub of the modern city's bus system. Despite containing several of the country's main sights, the area is busy enough in its own right not to have become a swarming tourist zone, and strikes a neat balance between liveliness and grandeur.

Ratanakosin is within easy walking distance of Banglamphu, but is best approached from the river, via the **express-boat piers** of Tha Chang (the former bathing place of the royal elephants, which gives access to the Grand Palace) or Tha Thien (for Wat Pho). A **word of warning**: when you're heading for the Grand Palace or Wat Pho, you may well be approached by someone, possibly pretending to be a student or an official, who will tell you that the sight is closed when it's not, or some other lies to try to lead you away from the entrance, because they want to lead you on a shopping trip for souvenirs, tailored clothes or, if you seem really gullible, gems (see p.201). The opening hours of the Grand Palace – but not Wat Pho – are indeed sometimes erratic because of state occasions, but you can check the details out on its website, Ⓦwww.palaces.thai.net – and even if it's closed on the day you want to visit, that's no reason to throw yourself at the mercy of these shysters.

Wat Phra Kaeo and the Grand Palace

Hanging together in a precarious harmony of strangely beautiful colours and shapes, **Wat Phra Kaeo** is the apogee of Thai religious art and the holiest Buddhist site in the country, housing the most important image, the **Emerald Buddha**. Built as the private royal temple, Wat Phra Kaeo occupies the northeast corner of the huge **Grand Palace**, whose official opening in 1785 marked the founding of the new capital and the rebirth of the Thai nation after the Burmese invasion. Successive kings have all left their mark here, and the palace complex now covers 25 hectares, though very little apart from the wat is open to tourists.

The only **entrance** to the complex in 2km of crenellated walls is the Gate of Glorious Victory in the middle of the north side, on Thanon Na Phra Lan. This brings you onto a driveway with a tantalizing view of the temple's glittering spires on the left and the dowdy buildings of the Offices of the Royal Household on the right: this is the powerhouse of the kingdom's ceremonial life, providing everything down to chairs and catering, even lending an urn when someone of rank dies. A textile museum under the auspices of the queen is scheduled to open among these buildings, perhaps in 2009, but for now you'll have to content yourself with some crafts shopping at the Queen's Support Foundation (see p.196).

Turn left at the end of the driveway for the ticket office and entrance turnstiles: **admission** to Wat Phra Kaeo and the palace is B300 (daily 8.30am–4pm, last admission 3.30pm; weapons museum, Phra Thinang Amarin Winichai and Dusit Maha Prasat interiors closed Sat & Sun; 2hr personal audioguide B200, with passport or credit card as deposit). This includes a free brochure with a map (dispensed at the entrance turnstiles) and admission to Dusit Park (within 7 days; see p.158), plus either the missable Ananta Samakhom Throne Hall in Dusit or

Sanam Chan Palace in Nakhon Pathom (see p.219). As this is Thailand's most sacred site, you have to **dress in smart clothes**: no vests or see-through clothes; men must wear full-length trousers, women trousers or over-the-knee skirts. Suitable garments can be borrowed from the office to the right just inside the Gate of Glorious Victory (same building as the Queen's Support Foundation shop; free, deposit of B100 per item).

Wat Phra Kaeo

It makes you laugh with delight to think that anything so fantastic could exist on this sombre earth.

W. Somerset Maugham, *The Gentlemen in the Parlour*

Entering the temple is like stepping onto a lavishly detailed stage set, from the immaculate flagstones right up to the gaudy roofs. Reinforcing the sense of unreality, the whole compound is surrounded by arcaded walls, decorated with extraordinary murals of scenes from the *Ramayana*. Although it receives hundreds of foreign sightseers and at least as many Thai pilgrims every day, the temple, which has no monks in residence, maintains an unnervingly sanitized look, as if it were built only yesterday.

The approach to the bot

Inside the entrance turnstiles, you're confronted by six-metre-tall **yaksha**, gaudy demons from the *Ramayana*, who watch over the Emerald Buddha from every gate of the temple and ward off evil spirits; the king of the demons, green, ten-faced Totsagan (labelled "Tosakanth"), stands to the left of the entrance by the southwest corner of the golden Phra Si Ratana Chedi. Less threatening is

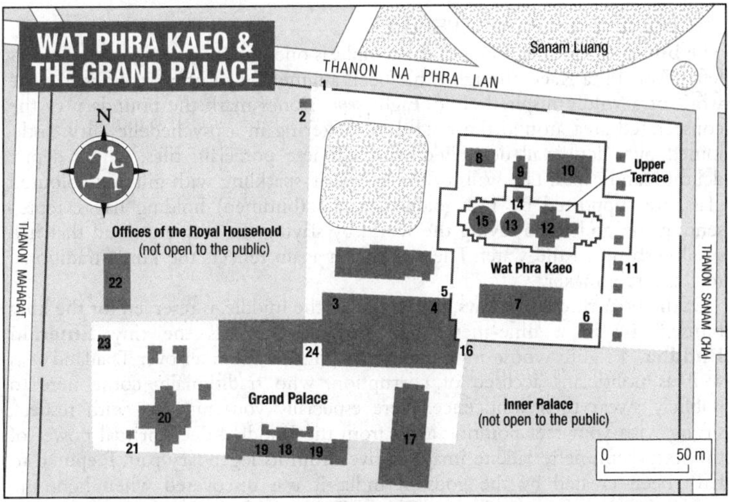

Gate of Glorious Victory	1	Porcelain viharn	9	Phra Thinang Amarin Winichai	17
Queen's Support Foundation Shop	2	Supplementary library	10	Chakri Maha Prasat	18
Ticket office	3	Prangs	11	Weapons museum	19
Royal Decorations & Coins Pavilion	4	Royal Pantheon	12	Dusit Maha Prasat	20
Entrance turnstiles to Wat Phra Kaeo	5	Phra Mondop	13	Mount Krailas model	21
Chapel of the Gandhara Buddha	6	Angkor Wat model	14	Wat Phra Kaeo museum	22
The bot and Emerald Buddha	7	Phra Si Ratana Chedi	15	Café	23
Royal mausoleum	8	Exit from Wat Phra Kaeo	16	Exit from Grand Palace	24

the toothless old codger, cast in bronze and sitting on a plinth immediately inside the turnstiles by the back wall of the bot, who represents a Hindu **hermit** credited with inventing yoga and herbal medicine. In front of him is a large grinding stone where previously herbal practitioners could come to grind their ingredients – with enhanced powers, of course. Skirting around the bot, you'll reach its **main entrance** on the eastern side, in front of which stands a cluster of grey **statues**, which have a strong Chinese feel: next to Kuan Im, the Chinese *bodhisattva* of mercy shown holding a bottle of *amritsa* (sacred elixir), are a sturdy pillar topped by a lotus flower, which Bangkok's Chinese community presented to Rama IV during his 27 years as a monk, and two handsome cows which commemorate Rama I's birth in the Year of the Cow. Worshippers make their offerings to the Emerald Buddha at two small, stand-in Buddhas here, where they can look at the main image through the open doors of the bot without messing up its pristine interior with gold leaf, candle wax and joss-stick ash.

Nearby, in the southeastern corner of the temple precinct, look out for the exquisite scenes of rice sheaves, fish and turtles painted in gold on blue glass on the doors and windows of the **Chapel of the Gandhara Buddha** (labelled "Hor Phra Kanthara Rat"). The decorations allude to the fertility of the ricefields, as this building was crucial to the old royal rainmaking ritual and is still used during the Royal Ploughing Ceremony (see p.139). Adorning the roof are thousands of nagas (serpents), symbolizing water; inside the locked chapel, among the paraphernalia used in the ritual, is kept the Gandhara Buddha, a bronze image in the gesture of calling down the rain with its right hand, while cupping the left to catch it. In times of drought the king would order a week-long rainmaking ceremony to be conducted, during which he was bathed regularly and kept away from the opposite sex while Buddhist monks and Hindu Brahmins chanted continuously.

The bot and the Emerald Buddha

The **bot**, the largest building of the temple, is one of the few original structures left at Wat Phra Kaeo, though it has been augmented so often it looks like the work of a wildly inspired child. Eight *sema* stones mark the boundary of the consecrated area around the bot, each sheltering in a psychedelic fairy castle, joined by a low wall decorated with Chinese porcelain tiles, which depict delicate landscapes. The walls of the bot itself, sparkling with gilt and coloured glass, are supported by 112 golden garudas (birdmen) holding nagas, representing the god Indra saving the world by slaying the serpent-cloud that had swallowed up all the water. The symbolism again reflects the king's traditional role as a rain maker.

Of the bot's three doorways, the largest, in the middle, is reserved for the king himself. Inside, a nine-metre-high pedestal supports the tiny **Emerald Buddha**, a figure whose mystique draws pilgrims from all over Thailand – as well as politicians accused of corruption, who traditionally come here to publicly swear their innocence. Here especially you must act with respect, sitting with your feet pointing away from the Buddha. The spiritual power of the sixty-centimetre jadeite image derives from its legendary past. Reputed to have been created by the gods in India, it was discovered when lightning cracked open an ancient chedi in Chiang Rai in the early fifteenth century. The image was then moved around the north, dispensing miracles wherever it went, before being taken to Laos for two hundred years. As it was believed to bring great fortune to its possessor, the future Rama I snatched it back when he captured Vientiane in 1779, installing it at the heart of his new capital as a talisman for king and country.

Seated in the *Dhyana Mudra* (meditation), the Emerald Buddha has three **costumes**, one for each season: the crown and ornaments of an Ayutthayan king for the hot season; a gilt monastic robe for the rainy season, when the monks retreat into the temples; this is augmented with a full-length gold shawl in the cool season. To this day it's the job of the king himself to ceremonially change the Buddha's costumes – though in recent years, due to the present king's age, the Crown Prince has conducted proceedings. The Buddha was granted a new set of these three costumes in 1997: the old set is now in the Wat Phra Kaeo Museum (see p.136) while the two costumes of the new set that are not in use are on display among the blinding glitter of crowns and jewels in the Royal Decorations and Coins Pavilion, which lies between the ticket office and the entrance to Wat Phra Kaeo.

Among the paraphernalia in front of the pedestal sits the tiny, silver Phra Chai Lang Chang (Victory Buddha), which Rama I always carried into battle on the back of his elephant for luck and which still plays an important part in coronation ceremonies. Recently covered in gold, it occupies a prestigious spot dead centre, but is modestly obscured by a fan and by the umbrella of a larger gold Buddha in front. The tallest pair of a dozen standing Buddha images, all made of bronze but encased in gold and raising both hands to dispel fear, are at the front: Rama III dedicated the one on the Emerald Buddha's left to Rama I, the one on his right to Rama II, and Rama IV enshrined relics of the Buddha in their crowns.

The upper terrace

The eastern end of the **upper terrace** is taken up with the **Prasat Phra Thep Bidorn**, known as the **Royal Pantheon**, a splendid hash of styles. The pantheon has its roots in the Khmer concept of *devaraja*, or the divinity of kings: inside are bronze and gold statues, precisely life-size, of all the kings since Bangkok became the Thai capital. Constructed by Rama IV, the building is open only on special occasions, such as Chakri Day (April 6), when the dynasty is commemorated, and Coronation Day (May 5).

From here you get the best view of the **royal mausoleum**, the **porcelain viharn** and the **supplementary library** to the north (all of which are closed to tourists, though you can sometimes glimpse Thai Buddhists worshipping in the library), and, running along the east side of the temple, a row of eight bullet-like **prangs**, each of which has a different nasty ceramic colour. Described as "monstrous vegetables" by Somerset Maugham, they represent, from north to south, the Buddha, Buddhist scripture, the monkhood, the nunhood, the Buddhas who attained enlightenment but did not preach, previous emperors, the Buddha in his previous lives and the future Buddha.

In the middle of the terrace, dressed in deep-green glass mosaics, the **Phra Mondop** was built by Rama I to house the *Tripitaka*, or Buddhist scripture, which the king had revised at Wat Mahathat in 1788, the previous version having been lost in the sack of Ayutthaya. It's famous for the mother-of-pearl cabinet and solid-silver mats inside, but is never open. Four tiny **memorials** at each corner of the mondop show the symbols of each of the nine Chakri kings, from the ancient crown representing Rama I to the present king's discus, while the bronze statues surrounding the memorials portray each king's lucky white elephants, labelled by name and pedigree. A contribution of Rama IV, on the north side of the mondop, is a **scale model of Angkor Wat**, the prodigious Cambodian temple, which during his reign (1851–68) was under Thai rule (apparently, the king had wanted to shift a whole Khmer temple to Bangkok but, fortunately, was dissuaded by his officials). At the

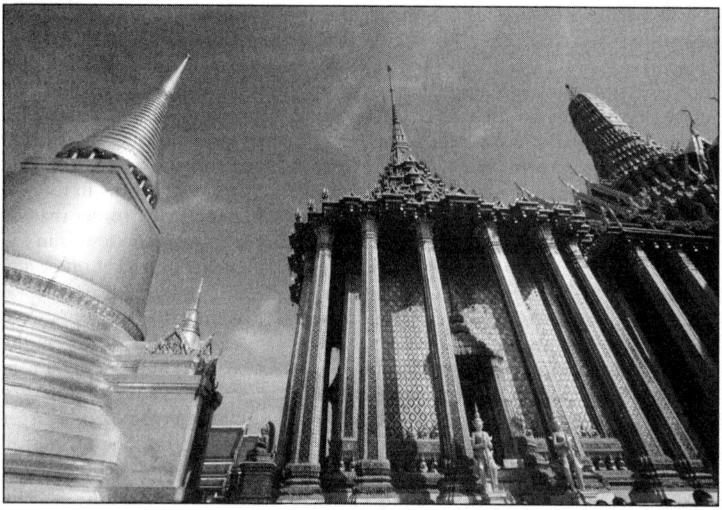

▲ Phra Si Ratana Chedi and Phra Mondop

western end of the terrace, you can't miss the golden dazzle of the **Phra Si Ratana Chedi**, which Rama IV erected, in imitation of the famous bell-shaped chedis at Ayutthaya's Wat Phra Si Sanphet, to enshrine a piece of the Buddha's breastbone.

The murals

Extending for about a kilometre in the arcades that run inside the wat walls, the **murals of the Ramayana** depict every blow of this ancient story of the triumph of good over evil, using the vibrant buildings of the temple itself as backdrops, and setting them off against the subdued colours of richly detailed landscapes. Because of the damaging humidity, none of the original work of Rama I's time survives: maintenance is a never-ending process, so you'll always find an artist working on one of the scenes. The story is told in 178 panels, labelled and numbered in Thai only, starting in the middle of the northern side opposite the porcelain viharn: in the first episode, a hermit, while out ploughing, finds the baby Sita, the heroine, floating in a gold urn on a lotus leaf and brings her to the city. Panel 109 near the gate leading to the palace buildings shows the climax of the story, when Rama, the hero, kills the ten-headed demon Totsagan (Ravana), and the ladies of the enemy city weep at the demon's death. Panel 110 depicts his elaborate funeral procession, and in 113 you can see the funeral fair, with acrobats, sword-jugglers and tightrope-walkers. In between, Sita – Rama's wife – has to walk on fire to prove that she has been faithful during her fourteen years of imprisonment by Totsagan. If you haven't the stamina for the long walk round, you could sneak a look at the end of the story, to the left of the first panel, where Rama holds a victory parade and distributes thank-you gifts.

The palace buildings

The exit in the southwest corner of Wat Phra Kaeo brings you to the palace proper, a vast area of buildings and gardens, of which only the northern edge is on show to the public. Though the king now lives in the Chitrlada Palace in

Dusit, the Grand Palace is still used for state receptions and official ceremonies, during which there is no public access to any part of the palace.

Phra Maha Monthien

Coming out of the temple compound, you'll first of all see to your right a beautiful Chinese gate covered in innumerable tiny porcelain tiles. Extending in a straight line behind the gate is the **Phra Maha Monthien**, which was the grand residential complex of earlier kings.

Only the **Phra Thinang Amarin Winichai**, the main audience hall at the front of the complex, is open to the public. The supreme court in the era of the absolute monarchy, it nowadays serves as the venue for ceremonies such as the king's birthday speech. Dominating the hall are two gleaming, intricately carved thrones that date from the reign of Rama I: a white umbrella with the full nine tiers owing to a king shelters the front seat, while the unusual *busbok* behind is topped with a spired roof and floats on a boat-shaped base. The rear buildings are still used for the most important part of the elaborate coronation ceremony, and each new king is supposed to spend a night there to show solidarity with his forefathers.

The Ramayana/Ramakien

The **Ramayana** is generally thought to have originated as an oral epic in India, where it appears in numerous dialects. The most famous version is that of the sage Valmiki, who is said to have drawn together the collection of stories as a tribute to his king over two thousand years ago. From India, the *Ramayana* spread to all the Hindu-influenced countries of South Asia and was passed down through the Khmers to Thailand, where as the **Ramakien** it has become the national epic, acting as an affirmation of the Thai monarchy and its divine Hindu links. As a source of inspiration for literature, painting, sculpture and dance-drama, it has acquired the authority of holy writ, providing Thais with moral and practical lessons, while its appearance in the form of films and comic strips shows its huge popular appeal. The version current in Thailand was composed by a committee of poets sponsored by Rama I (all previous Thai texts were lost in the sack of Ayutthaya in 1767), and runs to three thousand pages – available in an abridged English translation by M.L. Manich Jumsai (see p.858).

The central story of the *Ramayana* concerns **Rama** (in Thai, Phra Ram), son of the king of Ayodhya, and his beautiful wife **Sita**, whose hand he wins by lifting, stringing – and breaking – a magic bow. The couple's adventures begin when they are exiled to the forest, along with Rama's good brother, **Lakshaman** (Phra Lak), by the hero's father under the influence of his evil stepmother. Meanwhile, in the city of Lanka (Longka), the demon king **Ravana** (Totsagan) has conceived a passionate desire for Sita and, disguised as a hermit, sets out to kidnap her. By transforming one of his demon subjects into a beautiful deer, which Rama and Lakshaman go off to hunt, Ravana catches Sita alone and takes her back to Lanka. Rama then wages a long war against the demons of Lanka, into which are woven many battles, spy scenes and diversionary episodes, and eventually kills Ravana and rescues Sita.

The Thai version shows some characteristic differences from the Indian, emphasizing the typically Buddhist virtues of filial obedience and willing renunciation. In addition, Hanuman, the loyal monkey general, is given a much more playful role in the *Ramakien*, with the addition of many episodes which display his cunning and talent for mischief, not to mention his promiscuity. However, the major alteration comes at the end of the story, when Phra Ram doubts Sita's faithfulness after rescuing her from Totsagan. In the Indian story, this ends with Sita being swallowed up by the earth so that she doesn't have to suffer Rama's doubts any more; in the *Ramakien* the ending is a happy one, with Phra Ram and Sita living together happily ever after.

Chakri Maha Prasat and the Inner Palace

Next door you can admire the facade of the "farang with a Thai hat", as the **Chakri Maha Prasat** is nicknamed. Rama V, whose portrait you can see over its entrance, employed an English architect to design a purely Neoclassical residence, but other members of the royal family prevailed on the king to add the three Thai spires. This used to be the site of the elephant stables: the large red tethering posts are still there and the bronze elephants were installed as a reminder. The building displays the emblem of the Chakri dynasty on its gable, which has a trident (*ri*) coming out of a *chak*, a discus with a sharpened rim. The only part of the Chakri Maha Prasat open to the public is the ground-floor **weapons museum**, which houses a forgettable display of hooks, pikes and guns.

The **Inner Palace**, which used to be the king's harem (closed to the public), lies behind the gate on the left-hand side of the Chakri Maha Prasat. Vividly described in M.R. Kukrit Pramoj's *Si Phaendin* (see p.859), the harem was a town in itself, with shops, law courts and an all-female police force for the huge population: as well as the current queens, the minor wives and their children (including pre-pubescent boys) and servants, this was home to the daughters and consorts of former kings, and the daughters of the aristocracy who attended the harem's finishing school. Today, the Inner Palace houses a school of cooking, fruit-carving and other domestic sciences for well-bred young Thais.

Dusit Maha Prasat

On the western side of the courtyard, the delicately proportioned **Dusit Maha Prasat**, an audience hall built by Rama I, epitomizes traditional Thai architecture. Outside, the soaring tiers of its red, gold and green roof culminate in a gilded *mongkut*, a spire shaped like the king's crown, which symbolizes the 33 Buddhist levels of perfection. Each tier of the roof bears a typical *chofa*, a slender, stylized bird's-head finial, and several *hang hong* (swans' tails), which represent three-headed nagas. Inside, you can still see the original throne, the **Phra Ratcha Banlang Pradap Muk**, a masterpiece of mother-of-pearl inlaid work. When a senior member of the royal family dies, the hall is used for the lying-in-state: the body, embalmed and seated in a huge sealed urn, is placed in the west transept, waiting up to two years for an auspicious day to be cremated.

The Wat Phra Kaeo Museum

In the nineteenth-century Royal Mint in front of the Dusit Maha Prasat – next to a small, basic **café** and an incongruous hair salon – the **Wat Phra Kaeo**

The royal tonsure ceremony

To the right and behind the Dusit Maha Prasat rises a strange model mountain, decorated with fabulous animals and topped by a castle and prang. It represents **Mount Krailas**, the Himalayan home of the Hindu god Shiva (Phra Isuan in Thai), and was built by Rama IV as the site of the **royal tonsure ceremony**, last held here in 1932, just three months before the end of the absolute monarchy. In former times, Thai children generally had shaved heads, except for a tuft or top-knot on the crown, which, between the age of eleven and thirteen, was cut in a Hindu initiation rite to welcome adolescence. For the royal children, the rite was an elaborate ceremony that sometimes lasted seven days, culminating with the king's cutting of the hair knot, which was then floated away on the Chao Phraya River. The child was then bathed at the model Krailas, in water representing the original river of the universe flowing down the central mountain.

Museum houses a mildly interesting collection of artefacts donated to the Emerald Buddha, along with architectural elements rescued from the Grand Palace grounds during restoration in the 1980s. Highlights include the bones of various kings' white elephants, and upstairs, the Emerald Buddha's original costumes and two useful scale models of the Grand Palace, one as it is now, the other as it was when first built. Also on the first floor stands the grey stone slab of the Manangasila Seat, where Ramkhamhaeng, the great thirteenth-century king of Sukhothai, is said to have sat and taught his subjects. It was discovered in 1833 by Rama IV during his monkhood and brought to Bangkok, where Rama VI used it as the throne for his coronation.

Wat Pho (Wat Phra Chetuphon)

Where Wat Phra Kaeo may seem too perfect and shrink-wrapped for some, **Wat Pho** (daily 8am–6pm; B50; ⓦwww.watpho.com), to the south of the Grand Palace, is lively and shambolic, a complex arrangement of lavish structures which jostle with classrooms, basketball courts and a turtle pond. Busloads of tourists shuffle in and out of the **north entrance**, stopping only to gawp at the colossal Reclining Buddha, but you can avoid the worst of the crowds by using the **main entrance** on Soi Chetuphon to explore the huge compound.

Wat Pho is the oldest temple in Bangkok and older than the city itself, having been founded in the seventeenth century under the name Wat Photaram. Foreigners have stuck to the contraction of this old name, even though Rama I, after enlarging the temple, changed the name in 1801 to **Wat Phra Chetuphon**, which is how it is generally known to Thais. The temple had another major overhaul in 1832, when Rama III built the chapel of the Reclining Buddha, and turned the temple into a public centre of learning by decorating the walls and pillars with inscriptions and diagrams on subjects such as history, literature, animal husbandry and astrology. Dubbed Thailand's first university, the wat is still an important centre for traditional medicine, notably **Thai massage**, which is used against all kinds of illnesses, from backaches to

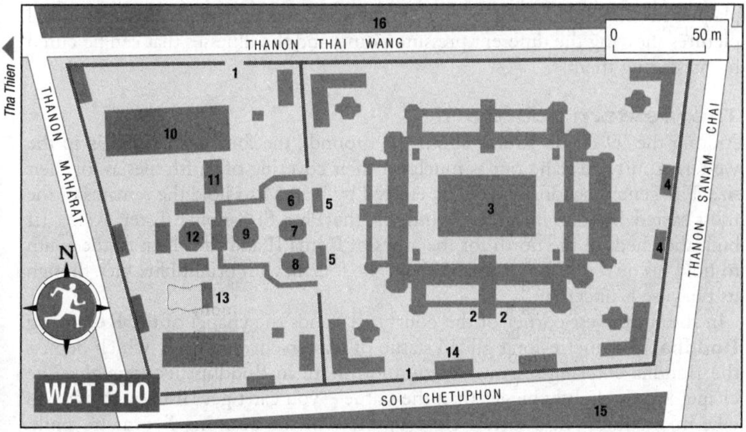

Visitors' entrances	1	Traditional Medicine Pavilions	5	Rama IV Chedi	9	European Pavilion	13
Entrances to Bot	2	Rama II Chedi	6	Chapel of the Reclining Buddha	10	Café	14
Bot	3	Phra Si Sanphet Chedi	7	Chinese Pavilion	11	Monks' Quarters	15
Massage Pavilions	4	Rama III Chedi	8	Library	12	Grand Palace	16

viruses. Excellent massages are available in the air-conditioned buildings on the east side of the main compound; allow two hours for the full works (B360 per hr; foot reflexology massage B360/45min). There are often long queues here, however, so you might be better off heading over to the massage centre's new premises just outside the temple, at 392/25–28 Soi Pen Phat 1, Thanon Maharat (Ⓣ02 622 3533 or 02 622 3551, Ⓦwww.watpomassage.com). At the latter, you can also enrol on a thirty-hour **massage training course** in English, over five days (B8500), and foot-massage courses for B6500.

The eastern courtyard

The main entrance on Soi Chetuphon is one of a series of sixteen monumental gates around the main compound, each guarded by stone **giants**, many of them comic Westerners in wide-brimmed hats – ships which exported rice to China would bring these statues back as ballast.

The entrance brings you into the eastern half of the main complex, where a courtyard of structures radiates from the bot in a disorientating symmetry. To get to the bot, the principal congregation and ordination hall, turn right and cut through the two surrounding cloisters, which are lined with hundreds of Buddha images. The elegant **bot** has beautiful teak doors decorated with mother-of-pearl, showing stories from the *Ramayana* (see p.135) in minute detail. Look out also for the stone bas-reliefs around the base of the bot, which narrate the story of the capture and rescue of Sita from the *Ramayana* in 152 action-packed panels. The plush interior has a well-proportioned altar on which ten statues of disciples frame a graceful, Ayutthayan Buddha image containing the remains of Rama I, the founder of Bangkok (Rama IV placed them there so that the public could worship him at the same time as the Buddha).

Back outside the entrance to the double cloister, keep your eyes open for a miniature mountain covered in statues of naked men in tall hats who appear to be gesturing rudely: they are *rishis* (hermits), demonstrating various positions of healing massage. Skirting the southwestern corner of the cloisters, you'll come to two pavilions between the eastern and western courtyards, which display plaques inscribed with the precepts of traditional medicine, as well as anatomical pictures showing the different pressure points and the illnesses that can be cured by massaging them.

The western courtyard

Among the 99 chedis strewn about the grounds, the four **great chedis** in the western courtyard stand out as much for their covering of garish tiles as for their size. The central chedi is the oldest, erected by Rama I to hold the remains of the most sacred Buddha image of Ayutthaya, the Phra Si Sanphet. Later, Rama III built the chedi to the north for the ashes of Rama II and the chedi to the south to hold his own remains; Rama IV built the fourth, with bright blue tiles, though its purpose is uncertain.

In the northwest corner of the courtyard stands the chapel of the **Reclining Buddha**, a 45-metre-long gilded statue of plaster-covered brick which depicts the Buddha entering Nirvana, a common motif in Buddhist iconography. The chapel is only slightly bigger than the statue – you can't get far enough away to take in anything but a surreal close-up view of the beaming five-metre smile. As for the feet, the vast black soles are beautifully inlaid with delicate mother-of-pearl showing the 108 *lakshanas*, or auspicious signs, which distinguish the true Buddha. Along one side of the statue are 108 bowls: putting a coin in each will bring you good luck and a long life.

Museum of Siam (National Discovery Museum)

The high-tech and mostly bilingual **Museum of Siam** is an excellent, new attraction that occupies the century-old, European-style, former Ministry of Commerce (Tues–Sun 10am–6pm; free; Ⓦ www.ndmi.or.th). Approached from either Thanon Maharat or Thanon Sanam Chai to the south of Wat Pho (and handy also for Ratchini express-boat pier during weekday rush hours), it looks at what it is to be Thai, with lots of humorous short films and imaginative touches such as shadow-puppet cartoons and war video games. Generally, it's great fun for adults and kids, and there's a nice little indoor-outdoor **café-restaurant** in the grounds run by the Black Canyon chain.

It all kicks off with the prehistory of Southeast Asia, or Suvarnabhumi (Land of Gold) as the Thais call it, and the arrival of Buddhism via missionaries sent by the great Indian emperor, Ashoka (Asoke). Much space is devoted to Ayutthaya, where we learn that during that kingdom's four-hundred-year history, there were no less than twenty outbreaks of war with the Burmese states, before the final annihilation in 1767. Beyond this, look out for a fascinating map of Thonburi, King Taksin's new capital between 1768 and 1782, as drawn by a Burmese spy. In the Bangkok period, there's coverage of the Chinese in Thailand and of early twentieth-century racialism, but next to nothing on the country's Muslims. Towards the end, under the banner of Westernization, visitors can wind up cartoon peep-shows and dress up in "colonial" pith helmets.

Sanam Luang

Sprawling across twelve hectares north of the Grand Palace, **Sanam Luang** is one of the last open spaces left in Bangkok, a bare field where residents of the capital gather in the early evening to meet, eat and play. The nearby pavements are the marketplace for some exotic spiritual salesmen: on the eastern side sit astrologers and palm-readers, and sellers of bizarre virility potions and contraptions; on the western side and spreading around Thammasat University and Wat Mahathat, scores of small-time hawkers sell amulets (see p.148), taking advantage of the spiritually auspicious location. In the early part of the year, especially in March, the sky is filled with kite-fighting contests (see p.140).

The field is also the venue for national ceremonies, such as **royal cremations**, when huge, intricate, wooden *meru* or *phra mane* (funeral pyres) are constructed, representing Mount Meru, the Himalayan centre of the Hindu-Buddhist universe; and the **Ploughing Ceremony**, held in May at a time selected by astrologers to bring good fortune and rain to the coming rice harvest. The elaborate Brahmin ceremony is led by an official from the Ministry of Agriculture, who stands in for the king in case the royal power were to be reduced by any failure in the ritual. At the designated time, the official cuts a series of circular furrows with a plough drawn by two white oxen, and scatters rice from the king's experimental crop station at Chitrlada Palace, which has been sprinkled with lustral water by the Brahmin priests of the court. When the ritual is over, spectators rush in to grab handfuls of the rice, which they then plant in their own paddies for good luck.

The lak muang

At 6.54am on April 21, 1782 – the astrologically determined time for the auspicious founding of Bangkok – a pillar containing the city's horoscope was ceremonially driven into the ground opposite the northeast corner of the Grand Palace. This phallic pillar, the **lak muang** – all Thai cities have one, to

Kite flying

Flying intricate and colourful **kites** is now done mostly for fun in Thailand, but it has its roots in more serious activities. Filled with gunpowder and fitted with long fuses, kites were deployed in the first Thai kingdom at Sukhothai (1240–1438) as machines of war. In the same era, special *ngao* kites, with heads in the shape of bamboo bows, were used in Brahmin rituals: the string of the bow would vibrate in the wind and make a noise to frighten away evil spirits (nowadays noisy kites are still used, though only by farmers, to scare the birds). By the height of the Ayutthayan period (1351–1767) kites had become largely decorative: royal ceremonies were enhanced by fantastically shaped kites, adorned with jingling bells and ornamental lamps.

In the nineteenth century, Rama V, by his enthusiastic lead, popularized kite flying as a wholesome and fashionable recreation. **Contests** are now held all over the country between February and April, when winds are strong enough and farmers traditionally have free time after harvesting the rice. These contests fall into two broad categories: those involving manoeuvrable flat kites, often in the shapes of animals; and those in which the beauty of static display kites is judged. The most popular contest of all, which comes under the first category, matches two teams, one flying star-shaped *chula*s, two-metre-high "male" kites, the other flying the smaller, more agile *pakpao*s, diamond-shaped "females". Each team uses its skill and teamwork to ensnare the other's kites and drag them back across a dividing line.

provide a home for their guardian spirits – was made from a four-metre tree trunk carved with a lotus-shaped crown, and is now sheltered in an elegant shrine surrounded by immaculate gardens. It shares the shrine with the taller *lak muang* of Thonburi, which was recently incorporated into Greater Bangkok. From here, mileages are calculated to the *lak muang* of every city in Thailand.

Hundreds of worshippers come every day to pray and offer flowers, particularly childless couples seeking the gift of fertility. In one corner of the gardens you can often see short performances of **classical dancing**, paid for by well-off families when they have a piece of good fortune to celebrate.

Wat Mahathat

On Sanam Luang's western side, with its main entrance on Thanon Maharat, eighteenth-century **Wat Mahathat** provides a welcome respite from the surrounding tourist hype, and a chance to engage with the eager monks studying at **Mahachulalongkorn Buddhist University** here. As the nation's centre for the Mahanikai monastic sect (where Rama IV spent 24 years as a monk before becoming king in 1851), and housing one of the two Buddhist universities in Bangkok, the wat buzzes with purpose. It's this activity, and the chance of interaction and participation, rather than any special architectural features, which make a visit so rewarding. The many university-attending monks at the wat are friendly and keen to practise their English, and are more than likely to approach you: diverting topics might range from the poetry of Dylan Thomas to English football results.

Situated in Section Five of the wat is its **Vipassana Meditation Centre**, where sitting and walking meditation practice is available in English (daily 7–10am, 1–4pm & 6–8pm; ⓣ02 222 6011 or 02 222 4981). Participants generally stay in the simple surroundings of the meditation building itself (donation requested), and must wear white clothes (available to rent at the centre) and observe the eight main Buddhist precepts (see p.813). Talks in English on meditation and Buddhism are held here every evening (8–9pm), as well as at the International Buddhist Meditation Centre (Room 106;

Ⓣ02 623 6326 or 089 220 1754, Ⓦwww.sirimangalo.org) in the Mahachulalongkorn University building on the second and fourth Saturdays of every month (3–5pm).

The National Museum

At the northwest corner of Sanam Luang, the **National Museum** (Wed–Sun 9am–4pm, some rooms may close at lunchtime; B200 including leaflet with map; Ⓦwww.thailandmuseum.com) houses a colossal hoard of Thailand's chief artistic riches, ranging from sculptural treasures in the north and south wings, through bizarre decorative objects in the older buildings, to outlandish funeral chariots and the exquisite Buddhaisawan chapel, as well as sometimes staging worthwhile temporary exhibitions. It's worth making time for the free **guided tours in English** on Wednesday and Thursday at 9.30am by the National Museum Volunteers (who also organize interesting lectures and excursions; Ⓦwww.museumvolunteersbkk.net): they're generally entertaining and their explication of the choicest exhibits provides a good introduction to Thai religion and culture. By the ticket office are a bookshop and a pleasant, air-conditioned **café**, serving drinks, sandwiches and cakes, while the **restaurant** inside the museum grounds, by the funeral chariots building, dishes up decent, inexpensive Thai food.

The first building you'll come to near the ticket office houses an informative overview of the history of Thailand, including a small archeological gem: a black stone **inscription**, credited to King Ramkhamhaeng of Sukhothai, which became the first capital of the Thai nation (c.1278–99) under his rule. Discovered in 1833 by the future Rama IV, it's the oldest extant inscription using the Thai alphabet. This, combined with the description it records of prosperity and piety in Sukhothai's Golden Age, has made the stone a symbol of Thai nationhood.

The main collection: southern building

At the back of the compound, two large modern buildings, flanking an old converted palace, house the museum's **main collection**, kicking off on the ground floor of the **southern building**. Look out here for some historic sculptures from the rest of Asia, including one of the earliest representations of the Buddha, from Gandhara in northwest India. Alexander the Great left a garrison at Gandhara, which explains why the image is in the style of Classical Greek sculpture: for example, the *ushnisha*, the supernatural bump on the top of the head, which symbolizes the Buddha's intellectual and spiritual power, is rationalized into a bun of thick, wavy hair.

Upstairs, the **prehistory** room displays axe heads and spear points from Ban Chiang in the northeast of Thailand (see p.536), one of the earliest Bronze Age cultures ever discovered. Alongside are many roughly contemporaneous metal artefacts from Kanchanaburi province, as well as some excellent examples of the developments of Ban Chiang's famous pottery. In the adjacent **Dvaravati** room (S7; sixth to eleventh centuries), the pick of the stone and terracotta Buddhas is a small head in smooth, pink clay, whose downcast eyes and faintly smiling full lips typify the serene look of this era. At the far end of the first floor, you can't miss a voluptuous Javanese statue of elephant-headed Ganesh, Hindu god of wisdom and the arts, which, being the symbol of the Fine Arts Department, is always freshly garlanded. As Ganesh is known as the clearer of obstacles, Hindus always worship him before other gods, so by tradition he has grown fat through getting first choice of the offerings – witness his trunk jammed into a bowl of food in this sculpture.

Room S9 next door contains the most famous piece of **Srivijaya** art (seventh to thirteenth centuries), a bronze Bodhisattva Avalokitesvara found at Chaiya (according to Mahayana Buddhism, a *bodhisattva* is a saint who has postponed his passage into Nirvana to help ordinary believers gain enlightenment). With its pouting face and sinuous torso, this image has become the ubiquitous emblem of southern Thailand. The rough chronological order of the collection continues back downstairs with an exhibition of **Khmer** and **Lopburi** sculpture (seventh to fourteenth centuries), most notably some dynamic bronze statuettes and stone lintels. Look out for an elaborate lintel that depicts Vishnu reclining on a dragon in the sea of eternity, dreaming up a new universe after the old one has been annihilated in the Hindu cycle of creation and destruction. Out of his navel comes a lotus, and out of this emerges four-headed Brahma, who will put the dream into practice.

The main collection: northern building

The second half of the survey, in the northern building, begins upstairs with the **Sukhothai** collection (thirteenth to fifteenth centuries), which features some typically elegant and sinuous Buddha images, as well as chunky bronzes of Hindu gods and a wide range of ceramics. The **Lanna** rooms (roughly thirteenth to sixteenth centuries) include a miniature set of golden regalia, among them tiny umbrellas and a cute pair of filigree flip-flops, which would have been enshrined in a chedi. An ungainly but serene Buddha head, carved from grainy, pink sandstone, represents the **Ayutthaya** style of sculpture (fourteenth to eighteenth centuries): the faintest incision of a moustache above the lips betrays the Khmer influences that came to Ayutthaya after its conquest of Angkor. A sumptuous scripture cabinet, showing a cityscape of old Ayutthaya, is a more unusual piece, one of a surviving handful of such carved and painted items of furniture.

Downstairs in the section on **Bangkok** or **Ratanakosin** art (eighteenth century onwards), a stiffly realistic standing bronze brings you full circle. In his zeal for Western naturalism, Rama V had the statue made in the Gandhara style of the earliest Buddha image displayed in the first room of the museum.

The funeral chariots

To the east of the northern building, beyond the café on the left, stands a large garage where the fantastically elaborate **funeral chariots** of the royal family are stored. Pre-eminent among these is the Vejayant Rajarot, built by Rama I in 1785 for carrying the urn at his own funeral. The thirteen-metre-high structure symbolizes heaven on Mount Meru, while the dragons and divinities around the sides – piled in five golden tiers to suggest the flames of the cremation – represent the mythological inhabitants of the mountain's forests. Each weighing around forty tonnes and requiring the pulling power of three hundred men, the teak chariots last had an outing in 2008, for the funeral of the present king's much-revered elder sister, Princess Galyani.

Wang Na (Palace of the Second King)

The sprawling central building of the compound was originally part of the **Wang Na**, a huge palace stretching across Sanam Luang to Khlong Lod, which housed the "second king", appointed by the reigning monarch as his heir and deputy. When Rama V did away with the office in 1887, he turned the palace into a museum, which now contains a fascinating array of Thai *objets d'art*. As you enter (room 5), the display of sumptuous rare gold pieces behind heavy iron bars includes a well-preserved armlet taken from the ruined prang of fifteenth-century Wat Ratburana in Ayutthaya. In adjacent room 6, an intricately carved ivory seat turns out, with gruesome irony, to be a *howdah*, for use on an elephant's back. Among the masks worn by *khon* actors next door (room 7), look out especially for a fierce Hanuman, the white monkey-warrior in the *Ramayana* epic, gleaming with mother-of-pearl.

The huge and varied ceramic collection in room 8 includes some sophisticated pieces from Sukhothai, while the room behind (9) holds a riot of mother-of-pearl items, whose flaming rainbow of colours comes from the shell of the turbo snail from the Gulf of Thailand. It's also worth seeking out the display of richly decorated musical instruments in room 15.

The Buddhaisawan chapel

The second holiest image in Thailand, after the Emerald Buddha, is housed in the **Buddhaisawan chapel**, the vast hall in front of the eastern entrance to the Wang Na. Inside, the fine proportions of the hall, with its ornate coffered ceiling and lacquered window shutters, are enhanced by painted rows of divinities and converted demons, all turned to face the chubby, glowing **Phra Sihing Buddha**, which according to legend was magically created in Sri Lanka and sent to Sukhothai in the thirteenth century. Like the Emerald Buddha, the image was believed to bring good luck to its owner and was frequently snatched from one northern town to another, until Rama I brought it down from Chiang Mai in 1795 and installed it here in the second king's private chapel. Two other images (in Nakhon Si Thammarat and Chiang Mai) now claim to be the authentic Phra Sihing Buddha, but all three are in fact derived from a lost original – this one is in a fifteenth-century Sukhothai style. It's still much loved by ordinary people and at Thai New Year is carried out onto Sanam Luang, where worshippers sprinkle it with water as a merit-making gesture.

The careful detail and rich, soothing colours of the surrounding two-hundred-year-old **murals** are surprisingly well preserved; the bottom row between the windows narrates the life of the Buddha, beginning in the far right-hand corner with his parents' wedding.

Tamnak Daeng

On the south side of the Buddhaisawan chapel, the sumptuous **Tamnak Daeng** (Red House) stands out, a large, airy Ayutthaya-style house made of rare golden teak, surmounted by a multi-tiered roof decorated with carved foliage and swan's-tail finials. Originally part of the private quarters of Princess Sri Sudarak, elder sister of Rama I, it was moved from the Grand Palace to the old palace in Thonburi for Queen Sri Suriyen, wife of Rama II; when her son became second king to Rama IV, he dismantled the edifice again and shipped it here to the Wang Na compound. Inside, it's furnished in the style of the early Bangkok period, with some of the beautiful objects that once belonged to Sri Suriyen, a huge, ornately carved box-bed, and the uncommon luxury of an indoor toilet and bathroom.

The National Gallery and Silpakorn University Art Centre

If the National Museum hasn't finished you off, two other lesser galleries nearby might. The **National Gallery**, across from the National Theatre on the north side of Sanam Luang at 4 Thanon Chao Fa (Wed–Sun 9am–4pm; B30; Ⓣ 02 282 0637 or 02 282 2639–40, Ⓦ www.thailandmuseum.com), displays in its upstairs gallery some rather beautiful early twentieth-century temple banners depicting

Buddhist subjects, but houses a permanent collection of largely uninspiring and derivative twentieth-century Thai art downstairs. Its temporary exhibitions can be pretty good however. The fine old wooden building that houses the gallery is also worth more than a cursory glance – it used to be the Royal Mint, and is constructed in typical early twentieth-century style, around a central courtyard.

The **Silpakorn University Art Centre** (Ⓣ02 623 6115 ext 1422, Ⓦwww.art-centre.su.ac.th) on Thanon Na Phra Lan, directly across the road from the entrance to the Grand Palace, also stages regular exhibitions, by students, teachers, artists-in-residence and national artists. The country's first art school, the university was founded in 1943, in a palace built during the reign of Rama I, by Professor Silpa Bhirasri, the much-revered, naturalized Italian sculptor; a charming, shady garden along the east wall of the art centre is dotted with his sculptures.

Banglamphu and the Democracy Monument area

Immediately north of Ratanakosin, **Banglamphu**'s most notorious attraction is **Thanon Khao San**, a tiny sliver of a road whose multiple guest houses and buzzing, budget-minded nightlife have made it an unmissable way-station for travellers through Southeast Asia. There is plenty of cultural interest too, in a medley of idiosyncratic temples within a few blocks of nearby landmark **Democracy Monument**, and in the typical Bangkok neighbourhoods that connect them, many of which still feel charmingly old-fashioned. If coming from downtown Bangkok, the fastest way to get to this area is by longtail canal boat along Khlong Saen Saeb, whose Phan Fah terminus is five minutes' walk from Democracy Monument. For details on bus and express-boat services to Banglamphu, see pp.114–115.

Around Khao San: Phra Arthit and the riverside walkway

Even if you're staying elsewhere, the **Khao San** area offers great shopping, eating and nightlife and is also a cultural curiosity in its own right, a unique and continually evolving expression of global youth culture fuelled by Thai entrepreneurship. Students from nearby Thammasat University inject an arty Thai vibe into the mix, particularly along **Thanon Phra Arthit**, which borders the Chao Phraya River. There's an attractive **riverside walkway** here too, which begins at the Bangkok Tourism Division's information centre beside Phra Pinklao Bridge and takes you past a couple of beautifully restored century-old mansions, currently occupied by Unicef and the UN's FAO; they show their most elegant faces to the river since in their heyday most visitors would have arrived by boat. The walkway terminates at the whitewashed, renovated octagonal tower of **Phra Sumen Fortress** (Phra Sumeru), one of fourteen built by Rama I in 1783 to protect the royal island of Ratanakosin. (The only other surviving tower, also renovated, is Phra Mahakhan Fortress, next to the Golden Mount.) Nowadays there's nothing to see inside the fort, but the area around it has been remodelled as grassy riverside **Santichaiprakarn Park** and retains some of the district's last remaining mangrove-like lamphu trees (*duabanga grandiflora*), after which Banglamphu "the place with lamphu trees", was named.

▲ Roti stall on Thanon Khao San

Wat Indraviharn

Though it can't match the graceful serenity of Ratanakosin's enormous Reclining Buddha, Banglamphu has its own super-sized Standing Buddha at **Wat Indraviharn** (also spelt Wat Intharawihan or Wat In), a glittering 32-metre-high mirror-plated statue of the Buddha bearing an alms bowl. Commissioned by Rama IV in the mid-nineteenth century to enshrine a Buddha relic from Sri Lanka (in the topknot), it's hardly the most elegant of images, but the foot-long toenails peep out prettily beneath offertory garlands of fragrant jasmine, and you can get reasonable views of the neighbourhood by climbing the stairways of the supporting tower; when unlocked, the doorways in the upper tower give access to the statue's hollow interior, affording vistas from shoulder level. The rest of the temple compound features the usual amalgam of architectural and spiritual styles, including a Chinese shrine and statues of Ramas IV and V.

Wat In is about twenty minutes' walk north of Khao San, on Thanon Wisut Kasat. Unfortunately, it's an established hangout for **con-artists** offering tourists a tuk-tuk tour of Bangkok for a bargain B20, which invariably features a hard-sell visit to a jewellery shop; see p.201 for more on the famous Bangkok jewellery scam and p.62 for more on con-artists. Avoid all these hassles by hailing a passing metered-taxi instead, or move on by **public transport**: Chao Phraya express-boat stops N14 and N15 are within reach, and bus #3 runs from Thanon Samsen to Thanon Phra Arthit.

Democracy Monument and the October 14 Memorial

The megalithic yellowy wings of **Democracy Monument** (*Anu Sawari Pracha Tippatai*) loom provocatively over Rajdamnoen Klang, the avenue that connects the Grand Palace and the new royal district of Dusit, and have since their erection in 1939 acted as a focus for pro-democracy rallies. Conceived as a testimony to the ideals that fuelled the 1932 revolution and the changeover to a constitutional monarchy, the monument's positioning between the royal residences is significant, as are its dimensions, which allude to June 24, 2475 BE (1932 AD), the date the system was changed. In the decades since, Thailand's leaders have promulgated numerous interim charters and constitutions, the more repressive and regressive of which have been vigorously challenged in demonstrations on these very streets.

One of the biggest and most notorious demonstrations was the fateful student-led protest of October 14, 1973, when half a million people gathered on Rajdamnoen Klang to demand an end to the autocratic regime of the so-called "Three Tyrants". It was savagely quashed and turned into a bloody riot that culminated in the death of several hundred protesters at the hands of the police and the military. After three decades of procrastination, the events of this catastrophic day were finally commemorated with the erection of the **October 14 Memorial**, a small granite amphitheatre encircling an elegant modern chedi bearing the names of some of the dead; photographs and a bilingual account of the ten-day protest fill the back wall. The memorial stands in front of the former headquarters of Colonel Narong Kittikachorn, one of the Three Tyrants, 200m west of Democracy Monument, at the corner of Rajdamnoen Klang and Thanon Tanao.

Thanon Tanao

A stroll down **Thanon Tanao** brings much-needed light relief, drawing you into some engagingly old-fashioned neighbourhoods where traditional shops still dominate. The first point of interest is **Chao Poh Seua** (Jao Paw Sua), the **Tiger God Shrine** (daily 6am–5pm), an atmospheric incense-filled Taoist shrine honouring the Chinese tiger guardian spirit and the God of the North Stars, whose image graces the centre of the main altar. It's a favourite with Chinese-Thais who come here to pray for power, prestige and successful pregnancy and offer in return pork rashers, fresh eggs, sticky rice, bottles of oil and sugar tigers.

South of the shrine, Thanon Tanao and its arterial alleys, especially the attractive Soi Phraeng Phuton, are known for their nineteenth-century wooden shophouses selling outstanding specialist **traditional Thai foods**. Many of these places have been making their specialities for generations, and there's all sorts that's fun to browse here, even if you're not inclined to taste, from beef noodles to pigs' brain soup, home-made ice-cream to sticky rice with mango. See p.179 for some recommendations, but for an exhaustive survey consult the *Good Eats Ratanakosin* map (published by Pan Siam Publishing and available in major bookstores), which is especially handy given that few of these places have English-language signs or shop numbers.

This area is also sometimes referred to as **Sao Ching Cha**, after the **Giant Swing**, which is easily reached either by following any of the east-bound lanes off Tanao to Thanon Dinso, or by browsing the Buddhist paraphernalia stalls that take you there via Thanon Bamrung Muang. Alternatively, if you continue one block south along Tanao you'll reach the lovely little temple of Wat Rajabophit.

Wat Rajabophit

One of Bangkok's prettiest temples, **Wat Rajabophit** is another example of the Chinese influence in this neighbourhood. It was built by Rama V and, typical of him, is unusual in its design, particularly the circular cloister that encloses a chedi and links the rectangular bot and viharn. Every external wall in the compound is covered in the pastel shades of Chinese *bencharong* ceramic tiles, creating a stunning overall effect, while the bot interior looks like a tiny banqueting hall, with gilded Gothic vaults and intricate mother-of-pearl doors. The wat is on Thanon Rajabophit, one block south of the Tanao/Bamrung Muang intersection, just to the east of Khlong Lod and the back of the Grand Palace compound. If you cross the canal en route to or from the Grand Palace, you'll pass a gold **statue of a pig**, erected in tribute to one of Rama V's wives, born in the Chinese Year of the Pig.

Thanon Bamrung Muang, Sao Ching Cha and Wat Suthat

Thanon Bamrung Muang, which runs east from Thanon Thanao to Sao Ching Cha and Wat Suthat, is famous as the best place in Thailand to buy **Buddhist paraphernalia**, or *sanghapan*, and is well worth a browse even for tourists. The road is lined with shops selling everything a good Buddhist might need, from household offertory tables to temple umbrellas and cellophane-wrapped Buddha images up to two metres high. They also sell special alms packs for donating to monks, which typically come in saffron-coloured plastic buckets (used by monks for washing their robes, or themselves), and include such necessities as soap, toothpaste, soap powder, toilet roll, candles and incense.

Midway along Thanon Bamrung Muang, just in front of Wat Suthat, about 700m south of Democracy Monument, you can't miss the towering, red-painted teak posts of **Sao Ching Cha**, otherwise known as the **Giant Swing**. This strange contraption was once the focal point of a Brahmin ceremony to honour the Hindu god Shiva's annual visit to earth, in which teams of young men competed to swing up to a height of 25m and grab a suspended bag of gold with their teeth. The act of swinging probably symbolized the rising and setting of the sun, though legend also has it that Shiva and his consort Uma were banned from swinging in heaven because doing so caused cataclysmic floods on earth – prompting Shiva to demand that the practice be continued on earth to ensure moderate rains and bountiful harvests. Accidents were so common with the terrestrial version that it was outlawed in the 1930s.

Were the swing still in operation, you'd get a fine view over adjacent **Wat Suthat** (daily 9am–5pm; B20) and its towering central viharn, Bangkok's tallest. This is one of Thailand's six most important temples, built in the early nineteenth century to house the eight-metre-high statue of the meditating **Phra Sri Sakyamuni Buddha**, which was brought all the way down from Sukhothai by river. It now sits on a glittering mosaic dais surrounded with surreal murals that depict the last 24 lives of the Buddha rather than the more usual ten. The encircling galleries contain 156 serenely posed Buddha images, making a nice contrast to the **Chinese statues** dotted around the temple courtyards, most of which were brought over from China during Rama I's reign, as ballast in rice boats; there are some fun character studies among them, including gormless Western sailors and pompous Chinese scholars.

Wat Rajnadda and the amulet market

Five minutes' walk east of Democracy Monument, at the point where Rajdamnoen Klang meets Thanon Mahachai, stands the assortment of religious buildings known collectively as **Wat Rajnadda** (daily 9am–5pm; free). Its most striking feature is the multi-tiered, castle-like **Loh Prasat**, or "Iron Monastery", whose 37 forbidding metal spires represent the 37 virtues necessary for attaining enlightenment. Modelled on a Sri Lankan monastery, its tiers are pierced by passageways running north–south and east–west – fifteen in each direction at ground level – with small meditation cells at each point of intersection.

In the southeast (Thanon Mahachai) corner of the temple compound, Bangkok's biggest **amulet market**, the **Wat Rajnadda Buddha Center**, comprises at least a hundred stalls selling tiny Buddha images of all designs. Alongside these miniature charms are statues of Hindu deities, dolls and carved wooden phalluses, also bought to placate or ward off disgruntled spirits, as well as love potions and CDs of sacred music.

Across the road from Wat Rajnadda, the **Phra Mahakhan Fortress community** occupies the land between the whitewashed crenellations of the renovated eighteenth-century city walls and Khlong Ong Ang. It's a historic neighbourhood and welcomes visitors with informative signboards describing some of its traditions, including massage therapy, fish bladder soup and *likay* popular theatre. Immediately south of the crenellations is a block of shops specializing in Thai and Chinese antiques.

Amulets

To invite good fortune, ward off malevolent spirits and gain protection from physical harm, Thais wear or carry at least one amulet at all times. The most popular images are copies of sacred statues from famous wats, while others show revered monks, kings (Rama V is a favourite) or healers. On the reverse side a yantra is often inscribed, a combination of letters and figures also designed to deflect evil, sometimes of a very specific nature: protecting your durian orchards from gales, for example, or your tuk-tuk from oncoming traffic. Individually hand-crafted or mass-produced, amulets can be made from bronze, clay, plaster or gold, and some even have sacred ingredients added, such as special herbs, or the ashes of burnt holy texts. But what really determines an amulet's efficacy is its history: where and by whom it was made, who or what it represents and who consecrated it. Stories of miracle cures and lucky escapes also prompt a rush on whatever amulet the survivor was wearing. Monks are often involved in the making of the images and are always called upon to consecrate them – the more charismatic the monk, the more powerful the amulet. Religious authorities take a relaxed view of the amulet industry, despite its anomalous and commercial functions, and proceeds contribute to wat funds and good causes.

The **belief in amulets** is thought to have originated in India, where tiny images were sold to pilgrims who visited the four holy sites associated with the Buddha's life. But not all amulets are Buddhist-related; there's a whole range of other enchanted objects to wear for protection, including tigers' teeth, rose quartz, tamarind seeds, coloured threads and miniature phalluses. Worn around the waist rather than the neck, the phallus amulets provide protection for the genitals as well as being associated with fertility, and are of Hindu origin.

For some people, amulets are not only a vital form of spiritual protection, but valuable **collectors' items** as well. Amulet-collecting mania is something akin to stamp collecting and there are at least half a dozen Thai magazines for collectors, which give histories of certain types, tips on distinguishing between genuine items and fakes, and personal accounts of particularly powerful amulet experiences. The most rewarding places to watch the collectors and browse the wares yourself are at Wat Rajnadda Buddha Center, probably the best place in Bangkok (see above); along "Amulet Alley" on Trok Mahathat, between Wat Mahathat (see p.140) and the river, where streetside vendors will have cheaper examples; and at Chatuchak Weekend Market (see p.171). Prices start as low as B50 and rise into the thousands.

Wat Saket and the Golden Mount

Beautifully illuminated at night, when it seems to float unsupported above the neighbourhood, the gleaming gold chedi east of Wat Rajnadda actually sits atop a structure known as the Golden Mount, within the compound of the late eighteenth-century **Wat Saket**. Being outside the capital's city walls, the wat initially served as a crematorium and then a dumping ground for sixty thousand plague victims left to the vultures because they couldn't afford funeral pyres. There's no sign of this grim episode at modern-day Wat Saket of course, which is these days a smart, buzzing hive of religious activity at the base of the golden hilltop chedi.

The **Golden Mount**, or **Phu Khao Tong** (daily 7.30am–5.30pm; B10), dates back to the early nineteenth century, when Rama III commissioned a huge chedi to be constructed here on ground that proved too soft to support it. The whole thing collapsed into a hill of rubble, but as Buddhist law states that a religious building can never be destroyed, however tumbledown, fifty years later Rama V simply crowned it with the more sensibly sized chedi we see today, in which he placed some relics, believed by some to be the Buddha's teeth. These days the old rubbly base is picturesquely planted with shrubs and shady trees and dotted with gravestones and memorials. Winding stairways take you up to the chedi terrace and a fine view over Banglamphu and Ratanakosin landmarks, including the golden spires of the Grand Palace, the finely proportioned prangs of Wat Arun across the river beyond and, further upriver, the striking superstructure of the Rama VIII Bridge.

Wat Saket hosts an enormous annual **temple fair** in the first week of November, when the mount is illuminated with lanterns and the compound seethes with funfair rides and travelling theatre shows. Easiest **access** to the Golden Mount is along Thanon Boriphat (the specialist street for custom-carved wooden doors), five minutes' walk south from the khlong bridge and Phan Fah canal-boat stop at the eastern end of Rajdamnoen Klang.

The Queen's Gallery

North across Rajdamnoen Klang from Wat Rajnadda, on the corner of Thanon Phra Sumen, the privately funded, five-storey **The Queen's Gallery** (Thurs–Tues 10am–7pm; B20; ⓦwww.queengallery.org) hosts temporary shows of contemporary Thai art, plus the occasional exhibition by foreign artists, and makes a more stimulating alternative to the rather staid National Gallery down the other end of Rajdamnoen Klang. Its bookshop sells hard-to-find Thai art books.

Chinatown and Pahurat

When the newly crowned Rama I decided to move his capital across to the east bank of the river in 1782, the Chinese community living on the proposed site of his palace was obliged to relocate downriver, to the **Sampeng** area. Two centuries on, **Chinatown** has grown into the country's largest Chinese district, a sprawl of narrow alleyways, temples and shophouses packed between Charoen Krung (New Road) and the river, separated from Ratanakosin by the Indian area of **Pahurat** – famous for its cloth and dressmakers' trimmings – and bordered to the east by **Hualamphong** train station.

The **Chinese influence** on Thai culture and commerce has been significant ever since the first Chinese merchants gained a toehold in Ayutthaya in

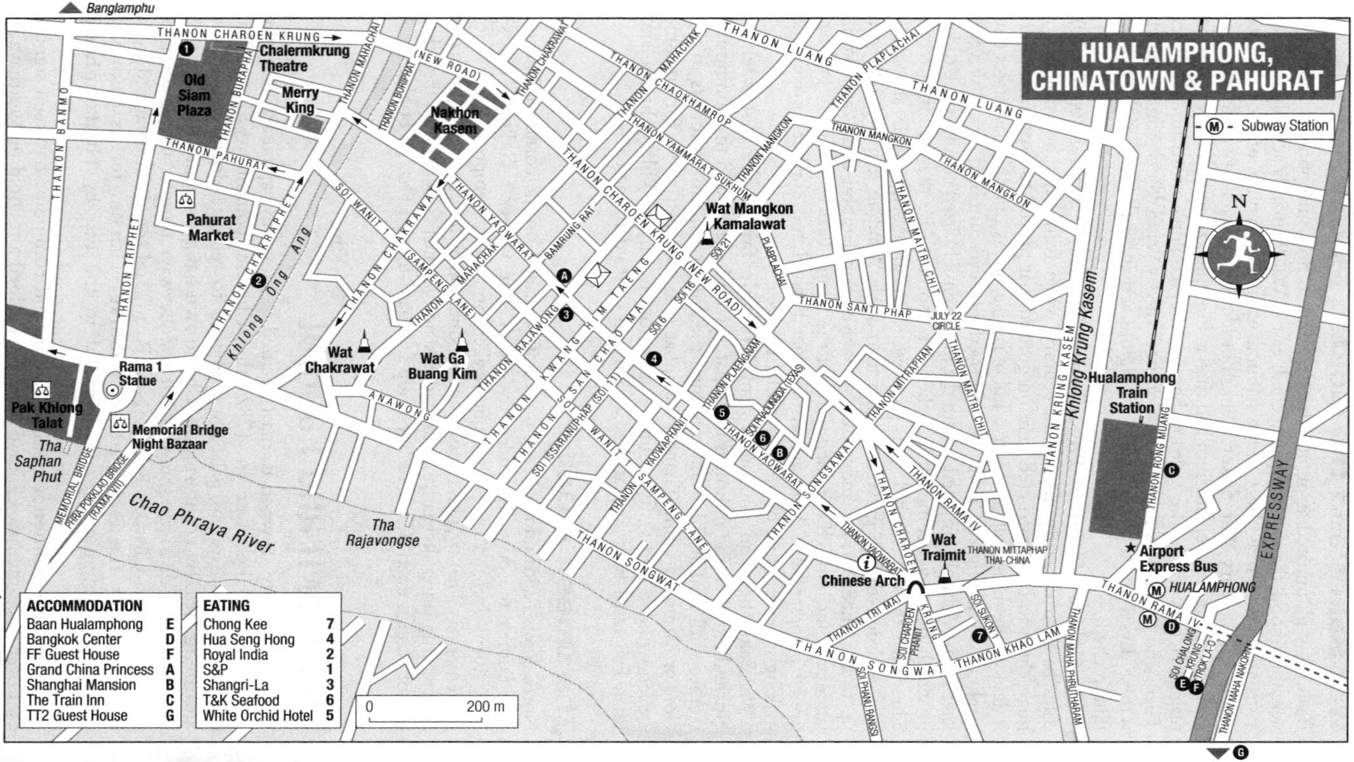
HUALAMPHONG, CHINATOWN & PAHURAT
Ⓜ - Subway Station
N
Banglamphu
Wat Prayoon
G
0 200 m
ACCOMMODATION
Baan Hualamphong E
Bangkok Center D
FF Guest House F
Grand China Princess A
Shanghai Mansion B
The Train Inn C
TT2 Guest House G
EATING
Chong Kee 7
Hua Seng Hong 4
Royal India 2
S&P 1
Shangri-La 3
T&K Seafood 6
White Orchid Hotel 5
Chalermkrung Theatre
Old Siam Plaza
Merry King
Nakhon Kasem
Pahurat Market
Wat Mangkon Kamalawat
Wat Chakrawat
Wat Ga Buang Kim
Rama 1 Statue
Pak Khlong Talat
Memorial Bridge Night Bazaar
Tha Saphan Phut
Tha Rajavongse
Chao Phraya River
Khlong Ong Ang
Khlong Krung Kasem
Hualamphong Train Station
Airport Express Bus
HUALAMPHONG
Wat Traimit
Chinese Arch
EXPRESSWAY
JULY 22 CIRCLE
THANON CHAROEN KRUNG
THANON LUANG
THANON PLAPLACHAI
THANON MANGKON
THANON MAHACHAI
THANON BURAPHA
THANON BORIPHAT
(NEW ROAD)
THANON CHAKRAWAT
THANON CHAOKHAMROP
THANON YAMMARAT SUKHUM
THANON MAHACHAK
THANON BANMO
THANON PAHURAT
THANON TRIPHET
THANON CHAKRAPHET
SOI WANIT 1
(SAMPENG LANE)
THANON YAOWARAT
BAMRUNG RAT
THANON CHAKRAWAT
THANON RAJAWONG
KWANG HIM TAENG
CHAO MAI
SOI 21
SOI 16
SOI 6
PLABPLACHAI
THANON SANTI PHAP
THANON MAITRI CHIT
THANON MITRAPHAN
THANON PLAENGNAM
SOI PHADUNGDA (TEXAS)
THANON ANAWONG
SOI SAN CHAO
SOI ISSARANUPHAP (SOI 11)
YAOWAPHANIT
THANON SONGSAWAT
THANON SONGWAT
THANON RAMA IV
THANON MITTAPHAP THAI-CHINA
THANON YAOWARAT
THANON TRI MIT
SOI CHAROEN PHANIT
SOI SUKON 1
THANON KHAO LAM
SOI PHANU RANGSI
THANON MAHA PHRUTHARAM
THANON KRUNG KASEM
THANON RONG MUANG
SOI CHALONG KRUNG
TROK LA-O
THANON MAHA NAKORN
MEMORIAL BRIDGE
PHRA POKKLAO BRIDGE
(RAMA VII)

the fourteenth century. Following centuries of immigration and intermarriage, there is now some Chinese blood in almost every Thai citizen, including the king, and Chinese-Thai business interests play an enormous role in the Thai economy. This is played out at its most frantic in Chinatown, whose real estate is said to be amongst the most valuable in the country; there are over a hundred gold and jewellery shops along Thanon Yaowarat alone.

For the tourist, Chinatown is chiefly interesting for its **markets**, shophouses, open-fronted warehouses and remnants of colonial-style architecture, though it also harbours a few noteworthy **temples**. A meander through its most interesting neighbourhoods could easily soak up a whole day, allowing for frequent breaks from the thundering traffic and choking fumes. For the most authentic Chinatown experience it's best to come during the week, as some shops and stalls shut at weekends; on weekdays they begin closing around 5pm, after which time the neighbourhood's other big draw – its **food** – takes centre stage.

Easiest access is either by **subway** to Hualamphong Station, or by Chao Phraya **express boat** to Tha Rachawongse (Rajawong; N5) at the southern end of Thanon Rajawong. This part of the city is also well served by **buses**, with Hualamphong a useful and easily recognized place to disembark (see boxes, p.106 & p.115). Be warned that buses and taxis may take an unexpectedly circuitous route due to the many and complex **one-way systems** in Chinatown.

Orientation in Chinatown can be tricky: the alleys (often known as trok rather than the more usual soi) are extremely narrow, their turn-offs and other road signs often obscured by mounds of merchandise and thronging crowds, and the longer ones can change their names several times. For a detailed tour of the alleys and markets, use *Nancy Chandler's Map of Bangkok*; alternatively, ask for help at the BMA **tourist information** booth (Mon–Sat 9am–5pm) just northwest of the Chinese Arch on Thanon Yaowarat, beside Soi 5.

Wat Traimit and the Golden Buddha

The obvious place to start a Chinatown tour is on its eastern perimeter, just west of Hualamphong train and subway stations (exit 1), with **Wat Traimit** (daily 9am–5pm) and its famous Golden Buddha, on Thanon Mittaphap Thai-China. You can see the temple mondop's golden spire from quite a distance, a fitting beacon for its gleaming treasure, the world's largest solid-gold Buddha. It's an apt attraction for a community so closely linked with the gold trade, even if the image has nothing to do with China's spiritual heritage. Over 3m tall and weighing five tonnes, the **Golden Buddha** gleams as if coated in liquid metal, seated amidst candles and surrounded with offerings of lotus buds and incense. It's a fine example of the curvaceous grace of Sukhothai art, slim-waisted and beautifully proportioned.

Cast in the thirteenth century, the image was brought to Bangkok by Rama III, completely encased in stucco – a common ruse to conceal valuable statues from would-be thieves. The disguise was so good that no one guessed what was underneath until 1955 when the image was accidentally knocked in the process of being moved to Wat Traimit, and the stucco cracked to reveal a patch of gold. The discovery launched a country-wide craze for tapping away at plaster Buddhas in search of hidden precious metals, but Wat Traimit's is still the most valuable – it's valued, by weight alone, at over US$10 million.

Sampeng Lane, Soi Issaranuphap and Wat Mangkon Kamalawat

From Wat Traimit, walk northwest from the big China Gate roundabout along Thanon Yaowarat, and make a left turn onto Thanon Songsawat, to reach **Sampeng Lane** (also signposted as Soi Wanit 1), one of Chinatown's most enjoyable shopping alleys. Stretching southeast–northwest for about 1km, it's a great place to browse, unfurling itself like a serpentine department store selling everything from Chinese silk pyjama pants to computer games at bargain-basement rates. Similar goods are more or less gathered in sections, so at the eastern end you'll find mostly cheap jewellery and hair accessories, for example, before passing through stalls specializing in ceramics, Chinese lanterns, then shoes, clothes (west of Thanon Rajawong) and, as you near Pahurat, fabrics, haberdashery and irresistibly girlie accessories.

For a rather more sensual experience, take a right about halfway down Sampeng Lane, into **Soi Issaranuphap** (also signed along its course as Yaowarat Soi 11 then Soi 6, and later Charoen Krung sois 16 and 21). Packed with people from dawn till dusk, this long, dark alleyway, which also traverses Charoen Krung, is where you come in search of ginseng roots (essential for good health), quivering fish heads, cubes of cockroach-killer chalk and a gastronome's choice of dried mushrooms and brine-pickled vegetables. Alleys branch off to florid Chinese temples and tiny squares before Soi Issaranuphap finally ends at the Thanon Plaplachai intersection amid a flurry of shops specializing in paper **funeral art**. Believing that the deceased should be well provided for in their afterlife, Chinese people buy miniature paper replicas of necessities to be burned with the body: especially popular are houses, cars, suits of clothing and, of course, money.

If Soi Issaranuphap epitomizes age-old Chinatown commerce, then **Wat Mangkon Kamalawat** (also known as **Wat Leng Nee Yee** or, in English, "Dragon Flower Temple") stands as a fine example of the community's spiritual practices. Best approached via its dramatic multi-tiered gateway 10m up Thanon Charoen Krung from the Soi Issaranuphap junction, Wat Mangkon receives a

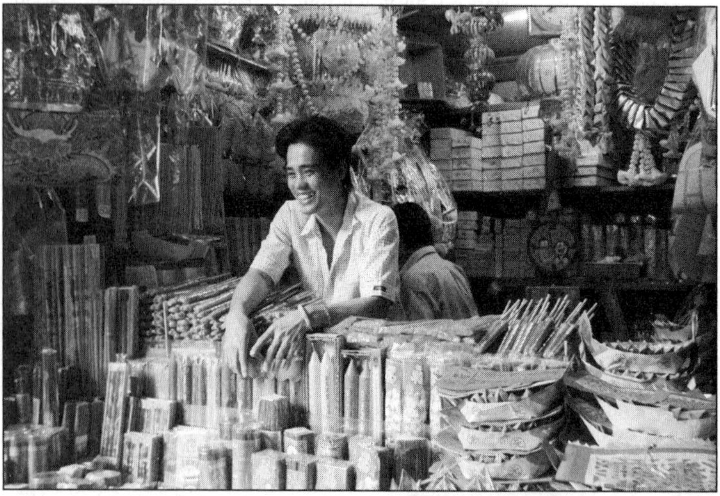

▲ Stall near Wat Mangkon Kamalawat, Chinatown

constant stream of devotees, who come to leave offerings at the altars inside this important Mahayana Buddhist temple. As with the Theravada Buddhism espoused by the Thais, Mahayana Buddhism fuses with other ancient religious beliefs, notably Confucianism and Taoism, and the statues and shrines within Wat Mangkon cover the spectrum. As you pass through the secondary gateway, under the glazed ceramic gables topped with undulating Chinese dragons, you're greeted by a set of four outsize statues of bearded and rather forbidding sages, each symbolically clasping either a parasol, a pagoda, a snake's head or a mandolin. Beyond them, a series of Buddha images swathed in saffron netting occupies the next chamber, a lovely open-sided room of gold paintwork, red-lacquered wood, lattice lanterns and pictorial wall panels inlaid with mother-of-pearl. Elsewhere in the compound are booths selling devotional paraphernalia, a Chinese medicine stall and a fortune-teller.

Wat Ga Buang Kim

Less than 100m up Thanon Charoen Krung from Wat Mangkon, a left turn into Thanon Rajawong, followed by a right turn into Thanon Anawong and a further right turn into the narrow, two-pronged Soi Krai brings you to the typical neighbourhood temple of **Wat Ga Buang Kim**, set around a tiny, enclosed courtyard. This particular wat is remarkable for its exquisitely ornamented "vegetarian hall", a one-room shrine with altar centrepiece framed by intricately carved wooden tableaux of gold-painted miniatures arranged as if in sequence, with recognizable characters reappearing in new positions and in different moods. The hall's outer wall is adorned with small tableaux, too, the area around the doorway at the top of the stairs peopled with finely crafted ceramic figurines drawn from Chinese opera stories. The other building in the wat compound is a stage used for Chinese opera performances.

Pahurat

The ethnic emphasis changes west of Khlong Ong Ang, where **Pahurat** begins, for here, in the small square south of the intersection of Chakraphet and Pahurat roads, is where the capital's sizeable Indian community congregates. Unless you're looking for *bindi* cigarettes, Punjabi sweets or Bollywood VCDs, curiosity-shopping is not as rewarding here as in Chinatown, but it's good for all sorts of **fabrics**, from shirting to curtain materials and saree lengths.

Also here, at the Charoen Krung/Thanon Triphet intersection, is the colonial-look mint-green and cream-painted **Old Siam Plaza**, whose nostalgia theme continues in part inside, with its ground-floor shopping concourse given over to stalls selling traditional, handmade Thai snacks, sweets and sticky desserts. The adjacent Sala Chalermkrung Theatre sometimes stages classical Thai drama for non-Thai speakers (see p.192).

Pak Khlong Talat and Memorial Bridge night bazaar

A browse through the 24-hour flower and vegetable market, **Pak Khlong Talat**, is a fitting way to round off a day in Chinatown, though it's also a great place to come before dawn, when market gardeners from Thonburi and beyond boat and truck their freshly picked produce across the Chao Phraya ready for sale to shopkeepers, restaurateurs and hoteliers. The market has been operating from covered halls between the southern ends of Khlong Lod, Thanon Banmo, Thanon Chakraphet and the river bank since the nineteenth century and is the biggest wholesale market in the capital. The flower stalls, selling twenty different varieties of cut orchids and countless other tropical blooms, spill onto the streets along the riverfront as well and, though prices are lowest in the early morning, you can still get some good bargains in the afternoon. The riverside end of nearby Thanon Triphet and the area around the base of **Memorial Bridge** (Saphan Phut) hosts a huge **night bazaar** (Tues–Sun 8pm–midnight) that's dominated by cheap and idiosyncratic fashions – and by throngs of teenage fashion victims.

For the most interesting **approach** to the flower market from the Old Siam Plaza, turn west across Thanon Triphet to reach Thanon Banmo, and then follow this road south down towards the Chao Phraya. As you near the river, notice the facing rows of traditional Chinese shophouses, still in use today, which retain their characteristic (peeling) pastel-painted facades, shutters and stucco curlicues. There's an entrance into the market on your right and just after sundown this southernmost stretch of Thanon Banmo fills with handcarts and vans unloading the most amazing mountains of fresh blooms. The Chao Phraya **express boat** service stops just a few metres from the market at Tha Saphan Phut (N6).

Thonburi

For fifteen years between the fall of Ayutthaya in 1767 and the founding of Bangkok in 1782, the west-bank town of **Thonburi**, across the Chao Phraya from modern-day Bangkok, stood in as the Thai capital, under the rule of General Phraya Taksin. Its time in the spotlight was too brief for the building of the fine monuments and temples that graced earlier capitals at Sukhothai and Ayutthaya, but some of its centuries-old **canals**, which once transported everyone and everything, have endured; it is these and the ways of life that depend on them that constitute Thonburi's main attractions. In some quarters, life on this side of the river still revolves around these khlongs: vendors of food and household goods paddle their boats along the canals that crisscross the residential areas, and canalside factories use them to ferry their wares to the Chao Phraya River artery. Venture onto the backroads just three or four kilometres west of the river and you find yourself surrounded by market gardens and rural homes, with no hint of the throbbing metropolis across on the other bank. The most popular way to explore these old neighbourhoods is by **boat**, but joining a bicycle tour of the older neighbourhoods is also very rewarding (see p.104). Most boat trips also encompass Thonburi's imposing riverside Temple of the Dawn, **Wat Arun**, and often the **Royal Barge Museum** as well, though both are easily visited by yourself, as are the small but historic temple of **Wat Rakhang** and the surprisingly intriguing, and child-friendly, cemetery at **Wat Prayoon**.

Getting to Thonburi is simply a matter of crossing the river. Either use Phra Pinklao or Memorial/Phra Pokklao **bridge**, take a **cross-river ferry**, or hop on the **express ferry**, which makes several stops on the Thonburi bank. Wongwian Yai is also served by the Thonburi extension of the **BTS Skytrain**, travelling west from Saphan Taksin (S6). **Getting around Thonburi** is a bit more complicated as the lack of footbridges over canals means that walking between sights often involves using the heavily trafficked Thanon Arun Amarin. A more convoluted alternative would be to leapfrog your way up or down the river by boat, using the various cross-river ferries that connect the Thonburi bank with the Chao Phraya express-boat stops on the other side.

Exploring Thonburi by boat

The most popular way to explore the sights of Thonburi is by **boat**, taking in Wat Arun and the Royal Barge Museum, then continuing along Thonburi's network of small canals. The easiest option is to take a **fixed-price trip** from one of the piers on the Bangkok side of the Chao Phraya, most conveniently from Tha Phra Arthit in Banglamphu, Tha Chang near Wat Pho or the River City pier off Thanon Charoen Krung; see below for a select list of operators. You can also charter your own longtail from these piers and others such as Tha Sathorn, and from many five-star riverside hotels, but bear the listed prices in mind when negotiating and be specific about your itinerary.

Many of the fixed-price tours include visits to one of Thonburi's two main **floating markets**, both of which are heavily touristed and rather contrived. **Wat Sai** floating market happens daily from Monday to Friday but is very commercialized, and half of it is land-based anyway, while **Taling Chan** floating market is also fairly manufactured but more fun, though it only operates on Saturdays and Sundays (approx 9am–3pm). Taling Chan market is held on Khlong Chak Phra, in front of Taling Chan District Office, a couple of kilometres west of Thonburi train station, and can also be reached by taking bus #79 from Banglamphu. For an authentic floating-market experience, consider heading out of Bangkok to Amphawa, in Samut Songkhram province (see p.220).

Arguably more photogenic, and certainly a lot more genuine, are the individual **floating vendors** who continue to paddle from house-to-house in Thonburi, touting anything from hot food to plastic buckets. You've a good chance of seeing some of them in action on almost any longtail boat tour on any day of the week, particularly in the morning.

Mitchaopaya Travel Service Tha Chang ⓣ02 623 6169. Offers trips of varying durations: in 1hr (B1000 per boat), you'll go out along Khlong Bangkok Noi and back via Khlong Mon, passing Wat Arun and the Royal Barge Museum without stopping; in 90min (B1300), you'd have time to stop at either or you could do a longer route, coming back along Khlong Bangkok Yai; while in 2hr (B1500) you'll have time to go right down the back canals on the Thonburi side and visit an orchid farm. On Sat & Sun, the 90min and 2hr trips take in Taling Chan floating market.

New Road Guest House see p.122. Recommended four-hour longtail trips with a knowledgeable, English-speaking guide that take you deep into Thonburi, passing orchards and taking in an orchid farm, with a drop-off at Wat Pho or the Grand Palace possible on the way back. B700 per person.

Real Asia ⓣ02 665 6364, ⓦwww.realasia.net. Runs guided full-day walking and boat tours of the Thonburi canals for B2000 per person.

River City pier longtails ⓣ02 237 0077 ext 180. Private longtail trips for B800/1hr per boat for two people.

Tha Phra Arthit longtails Pier in front of *The Old Phra Arthit Gastronobar*, 200m south of the N13 Tha Phra Arthit express-boat pier, Banglamphu. An enjoyable 90min loop via Khlong Bangkok Noi, Khlong Chak Phra and Khlong Bangkok Yai that takes in a variety of different khlong-side residences, temples and itinerant floating vendors, but won't include any stops. B850/1hr per boat for two people; B1300/90min per boat for two to six; B1600/2hr per boat for up to six people.

Wan Fah River City Shopping Centre pier ⓣ02 639 0704, ⓦwww.wanfahcruise.com. A 2hr cruise of the west-bank canals by a combination of longtail and converted rice barge. Daily 2.30pm; B700 per person.

Royal Barge Museum

Since the Ayutthaya era, kings of Thailand have been conveyed along their country's waterways in royal barges. For centuries these slender, exquisitely elegant, black-and-gold wooden vessels were used on all important royal outings, and even up until 1967 the current king would process down the Chao Phraya to Wat Arun in a flotilla of royal barges at least once a year, on the occasion of Kathin, the annual donation of robes by the laity to the temple at the end of the rainy season. But the hundred-year-old boats are becoming quite frail, so such an event is now rare: the last full-scale royal procession was floated for Kathin in 2007, to mark the king's 80th birthday. A **royal barge procession** along the Chao Phraya is a magnificent event, all the more spectacular because it happens so infrequently. Fifty or more barges fill the width of the river and stretch for almost 1km, drifting slowly to the measured beat of a drum and the hypnotic strains of ancient boating hymns, chanted by over two thousand oarsmen dressed in luscious brocades.

The eight beautifully crafted vessels at the heart of the ceremony are housed in the **Royal Barge Museum** on the north bank of Khlong Bangkok Noi (daily 9am–5pm; B30; Ⓦwww.thailandmuseum.com). Up to 50m long and intricately lacquered and gilded all over, they taper at the prow into imposing mythical figures after a design first used by the kings of Ayutthaya. Rama I had the boats copied and, when those fell into disrepair, Rama VI commissioned the exact reconstructions still in use today. The most important is *Sri Suphanahongse*, which bears the king and queen and is graced by a glittering five-metre-high prow representing the golden swan Hamsa, mount of the Hindu god Brahma. In front of it floats *Anantanagaraj*, fronted by a magnificent seven-headed naga and bearing a Buddha image. The newest addition to the fleet is *Narai Song Suban*, which was commissioned by the current king for his golden jubilee in 1996; it is a copy of the mid-nineteenth-century original and is crowned with a black Vishnu (Narai) astride a garuda figurehead. A display of miniaturized royal barges at the back of the museum re-creates the exact formation of a traditional procession.

The museum is a feature of most canal tours but is easily visited on your own. Just take the Chao Phraya **express boat** to Tha Phra Pinklao (N12) or, if coming from Banglamphu, take the cheaper, more frequent cross-river ferry (B4) from under Pinklao Bridge, beside the tourist information office, to Tha Phra Pinklao across the river, then walk up the road a hundred metres and take the first left down Soi Wat Dusitaram. If coming by **bus** from the Bangkok side (#507, #509 and #511 all cross the river here), get off at the first stop on the Thonburi side, which is right beside the mouth of Soi Wat Dusitaram. Signs from Soi Wat Dusitaram lead you through a jumble of walkways and stilt-houses to the museum, about ten minutes' walk away.

Wat Rakhang

The charming riverside temple of **Wat Rakhang** (Temple of the Bells) gets its name from the five large bells donated by King Rama I and is notable for the hundreds of smaller chimes that tinkle away under the eaves of the main bot and, more accessibly, in the temple courtyard, where devotees come to strike them and hope for a run of good luck. To be extra certain of having wishes granted, visitors also buy loaves of bread from the temple stalls and feed the frenzy of fat fish in the Chao Phraya River below. Behind the bot stands an attractive eighteenth-century wooden *ho trai* (scripture library) that still boasts some original murals on the wooden panels inside, as well as exquisitely renovated gold-leaf paintwork on the window shutters and pillars.

A cross-river **ferry** shuttles between Wat Rakhang's pier and the Tha Chang (Grand Palace) express-boat pier, or you can **walk** to Wat Rakhang in five minutes from the Tha Wang Lang express-boat pier: turn south (left) through the enjoyable **Phrannok pierside market**, which is good for cheap clothes and tempting home-made snacks, especially sweet ones, and continue until you reach the temple, passing the Patravadi Theatre, *Studio 9* theatre-restaurant (see p.191) and tiny *Ibrik Resort by the River* boutique hotel (see p.119) on the way.

Wat Arun

Almost directly across the river from Wat Pho rises the enormous, five-spired prang of **Wat Arun** (daily 8am–5pm; B20; Ⓦwww.watarun.org), the Temple of Dawn, probably Bangkok's most memorable landmark and familiar as the silhouette used in the TAT logo. It looks particularly impressive from the river as you head downstream from the Grand Palace towards the *Oriental Hotel*, but is ornate enough to be well worth stopping off for a closer look. All boat tours include half an hour here, but Wat Arun is also easily visited by yourself, although tour operators will try to persuade you otherwise: just take a B4 cross-river **ferry** from the pier adjacent to the Chao Phraya express-boat pier at Tha Thien.

A wat has occupied this site since the Ayutthaya period, but only in 1768 did it become known as the Temple of Dawn – when General Phraya Taksin reputedly reached his new capital at the break of day. The temple served as his royal chapel and housed the recaptured Emerald Buddha for several years until the image was moved to Wat Phra Kaeo in 1785. Despite losing its special status after the relocation, Wat Arun continued to be revered and its corncob prang was reconstructed and enlarged to its present height of 81m by Rama II and Rama III.

The prang that you see today is classic Ayutthayan style, built as a representation of Mount Meru, the home of the gods in Khmer cosmology. By climbing the two tiers of the square base that supports the **central prang**, you not only enjoy a good view of the river and beyond, but also get a chance to examine the tower's distinctive decorations. Both this main prang and the four minor ones that encircle it are studded all over with bits of broken porcelain, ceramic shards and tiny bowls that have been fashioned into an amazing array of polychromatic flowers. The statues of mythical *yaksha* demons and half-bird, half-human *kinnari* that support the different levels are similarly decorated. The crockery probably came from China, possibly from commercial shipments that were damaged at sea, and the overall effect is highly decorative and far more subtle than the dazzling glass mosaics that clad most wat buildings. On the first terrace, the mondops at each cardinal point contain statues of the Buddha at birth (north), in meditation (east), preaching his first sermon (south) and entering Nirvana (west). The second platform surrounds the base of the prang proper, whose closed entranceways are guarded by four statues of the Hindu god Indra on his three-headed elephant Erawan. In the niches of the smaller prangs stand statues of Phra Pai, the god of the wind, on horseback.

Wat Prayoon and Memorial Bridge

Just west of the Thonburi approach to Memorial Bridge, the unusual **Khao Mor cemetery** makes an unexpectedly enjoyable place to take the kids, with its miniaturized shrines and resident turtles. Its dollshouse-sized chedis and shrines are set on an artificial hillock, which was constructed by Rama III to replicate the pleasing shapes made by dripping candle wax. Wedged in among the grottoes, caverns and ledges of this uneven mass are numerous memorials to the departed, forming a not-at-all sombre gallery of different styles, from traditional Thai chedis, bots and prangs to more foreign designs like the tiny Wild West house complete with cactuses at the front door. Turtles fill the pond surrounding the mound and you can feed them with the bags of banana and papaya sold nearby. The cemetery is part of **Wat Prayoon** (officially Wat Prayurawongsawat) but located in a separate compound to the southeast side of the wat, just off Thanon Pracha Thipok, three minutes' walk from Memorial Bridge. Though it's on the Thonburi bank, it's easiest to reach from the Bangkok side, by walking over Memorial Bridge from the express ferry stop at Tha Saphan Phut (N6).

It wasn't until 1932 that Thonburi was linked to Bangkok proper by the **Memorial Bridge**, or **Saphan Phut**, built to commemorate the hundred and fiftieth anniversary of the foundation of the Chakri dynasty and of Bangkok, and dedicated to Rama I (or Phra Buddha Yodfa, to give him his official title), whose bronze statue sits at the Bangkok approach. It proved to be such a crucial river-crossing that the bridge has since been supplemented by the adjacent twin-track **Saphan Phra Pokklao**.

Dusit

Connected to Ratanakosin via the boulevards of Rajdamnoen Klang and Rajdamnoen Nok, the spacious, leafy area known as **Dusit** has been a royal district since the reign of Rama V, King Chulalongkorn (1860–1910). The first Thai monarch to visit Europe, Rama V returned with radical plans for the modernization of his capital, the fruits of which are most visible in Dusit, notably at **Vimanmek Palace** and **Wat Benjamabophit**, the so-called "Marble Temple". Even now, **Rama V** still commands a loyal following and the statue of him, helmeted and on horseback, which stands at the Thanon U-Thong Nai–Thanon Sri Ayutthaya crossroads, is presented with offerings every week and is also the focus of celebrations on Chulalongkorn Day (Oct 23). On December 2 Dusit is also the venue for the spectacular annual **Trooping the Colour**, when hundreds of magnificently uniformed Royal Guards demonstrate their allegiance to the king by parading around Suan Amporn, across the road from the Rama V statue. Across from Chitrlada Palace, **Dusit Zoo** makes a pleasant enough place to take the kids.

Today, the Dusit area retains its European feel, and much of the country's decision-making goes on behind the high fences and impressive facades along its tree-lined avenues: the building that houses the **National Parliament** is here, as is Government House (used mainly for state functions), and the king's official residence, Chitrlada Palace, occupies the eastern edge of the area. Normally a calm, stately district, in 2008 Dusit became the focus of the **mass anti-government protest** by the royalist PAD movement, whose thousands-strong mass of yellow-shirted supporters occupied Government House and part of Rajdamnoen Nok for an extraordinary three months, creating a heavily defended temporary village in this most refined of neighbourhoods.

From Banglamphu, you can get to Dusit by taking the #70 (non-expressway) **bus** from Rajdamnoen Klang and getting off outside the zoo and Elephant Museum on Thanon U-Thong Nai, or the #56 from Thanon Phra Sumen and alighting at the Thanon Ratchasima entrance to Vimanmek Palace (see box, p.115); alternatively, take the **express boat** to Tha Thewet and then walk. From downtown Bangkok, easiest access is by bus from the Skytrain and subway stops at Victory Monument; there are many services from here, including #28 and #108.

Dusit Park

Breezy, elegant **Vimanmek Palace** (daily 9.30am–4pm; compulsory free guided tours every 30min, last tour 3.15pm; B250, or free with a Grand Palace ticket, which remains valid for one week; Ⓦ www.palaces.thai.net) was built by

Rama V as a summer retreat on Ko Si Chang, from where it was transported bit by bit in 1901. The ticket price also covers entry to a dozen other specialist collections in the **Dusit Park** palace grounds, including the Support Museum and Elephant Museum. All visitors are treated to free performances of traditional Thai dance daily at 10.30am and 2pm. Note that the same **dress rules** apply here as to the Grand Palace (see p.131). The main **entrance** to the extensive Vimanmek Palace compound is on Thanon Rajwithi, but there are also ticket gates on Thanon Ratchasima, and opposite Dusit Zoo on Thanon U-Thong Nai.

Vimanmek Palace

Built almost entirely of golden teak without a single nail, the coffee-coloured, L-shaped Vimanmek Palace is encircled by delicate latticework verandas that look out onto well-kept lawns, flower gardens and lotus ponds. Not surprisingly, this "Celestial Residence" soon became Rama V's favourite palace, and he and his enormous retinue of officials, concubines and children stayed here for lengthy periods between 1902 and 1906. All of Vimanmek's 81 rooms were out of bounds to male visitors, except for the king's own apartments in the octagonal tower, which were entered by a separate staircase.

On display inside is Rama V's collection of **artefacts** from all over the world, including *bencharong* ceramics, European furniture and bejewelled Thai betel-nut sets. Considered progressive in his day, Rama V introduced many new-fangled ideas to Thailand: the country's first indoor bathroom is here, as is the earliest typewriter with Thai characters, and some of the first portrait paintings – portraiture had until then been seen as a way of stealing part of the sitter's soul.

The Support Museum

Elsewhere in the Vimanmek grounds a dozen handsome, pastel-painted royal residences have been converted into tiny, specialist-interest museums, including collections of antique textiles, photographs taken by the king, royal ceremonial paraphernalia and antique clocks. The most interesting of these is the **Support Museum Abhisek Dusit Throne Hall**, which is housed in another very pretty building, formerly used for meetings and banquets, immediately behind (to the east of) Vimanmek. The Support Museum showcases the exquisite handicrafts produced under Queen Sirikit's charity project, Support, which works to revitalize traditional Thai arts and crafts. Outstanding exhibits include a collection of handbags, baskets and pots woven from the *lipao* fern that grows wild in southern Thailand; jewellery and figurines inlaid with the iridescent wings of beetles; gold and silver nielloware; and lengths of intricately woven silk from the northeast.

Chang Ton Royal Elephant National Museum

Just behind (to the east of) the Support Museum, inside the Thanon U-Thong Nai entrance to the Vimanmek compound, stand two whitewashed buildings that once served as the stables for the king's white elephants. Now that the sacred pachyderms have been relocated, the stables have been turned into the **Royal Elephant National Museum** (Ⓦwww.thailandmuseum.com). Inside you'll find some interesting pieces of elephant paraphernalia, including sacred ropes, mahouts' amulets and magic formulae, as well as photos of the all-important ceremony in which a white elephant is granted royal status (see p.160).

Dusit Zoo (Khao Din)

Across Thanon U-Thong from the Elephant Museum is the side entrance into **Dusit Zoo**, also known as **Khao Din** (daily 8am–9pm; B100, children B50),

The royal white elephants

In Thailand the most revered of all elephants are the so-called **white elephants** – actually tawny brown albinos – which are considered so sacred that they all, whether wild or captive, belong to the king by law. Their special status originates from Buddhist mythology, which tells how the previously barren Queen Maya became pregnant with the future Buddha after dreaming one night that a white elephant had entered her womb. The thirteenth-century King Ramkhamhaeng of Sukhothai adopted the beast as a symbol of the great and the divine, decreeing that a Thai king's greatness should be measured by the number of white elephants he owns. The present king, Rama IX, has eleven, the largest royal collection to date.

Before an elephant can be granted official "white elephant" status, it has to pass a stringent assessment of its physical and behavioural **characteristics**. Key qualities include a paleness of seven crucial areas – eyes, nails, palate, hair, outer edges of the ears, tail and testicles – and an all-round genteel demeanour, manifested, for instance, in the way in which it cleans its food before eating, or in a tendency to sleep in a kneeling position. Tradition holds that an elaborate ceremony should take place every time a new white elephant is presented to the king: the animal is paraded with great pomp from its place of capture to Dusit, where it's anointed with holy water in front of an audience of priests and dignitaries, before being housed in the royal stables. Recently though, the king has called time on this exorbitantly expensive ritual, and only one of the royal white elephants is now kept inside the palace compound; the others live in less luxurious, rural accommodation.

The expression "white elephant" probably derives from the legend that the kings used to present certain enemies with one of these exotic creatures. The animal required expensive attention but, being royal, could not be put to work in order to pay for its upkeep. The recipient thus went bust trying to keep it.

which was once part of the Chitrlada Palace gardens, but is now a public park; the main entrance is on Thanon Rajwithi, and there's a third gate on Thanon Rama V, within walking distance of Wat Benjamabophit. All the usual suspects are here in the zoo, including big cats, elephants, orangutans, chimpanzees and a reptile house, but the enclosures are pretty basic. However, it's a reasonable place for kids to let off steam, with plenty of shade, a full complement of English-language signs, a lake with pedalos and lots of foodstalls.

Wat Benjamabophit

Wat Benjamabophit (aka Wat Bencha; daily 7am–5pm; B20) is an interesting fusion of classical Thai and nineteenth-century European design, with its Carrara-marble walls – hence the tourist tag "**The Marble Temple**" – complemented by the bot's unusual stained-glass windows, Victorian in style but depicting figures from Thai mythology. Inside, a fine replica of the highly revered Phra Buddha Chinnarat image of Phitsanulok presides over the small room containing Rama V's ashes. The courtyard behind the bot houses a gallery of Buddha images from all over Asia, set up by Rama V as an overview of different representations of the Buddha.

Wat Benjamabophit is one of the best temples in Bangkok to see religious **festivals** and rituals. Whereas monks elsewhere tend to go out on the streets every morning in search of alms, at the Marble Temple the ritual is reversed, and merit-makers come to them. Between about 6 and 7.30am, the monks line up on Thanon Nakhon Pathom, their bowls ready to receive donations of curry and rice, lotus buds, incense, even toilet paper and Coca-Cola; the demure row of saffron-robed monks is a sight that's well worth getting up early for. The evening candlelight processions around the bot during the Buddhist festivals of Maha Puja (in Feb) and Visakha Puja (in May) are among the most entrancing in the country.

Wat Benjamabophit is just a two-hundred-metre walk south of the zoo's Thanon Rama V entrance, or about 600m from Vimanmek's U-Thong Nai gate. Coming by bus #70 from Banglamphu, get off at the crossroads in front of the Rama V statue and walk east along Thanon Sri Ayutthaya.

Downtown Bangkok

Extending east from the main rail line and south to Thanon Sathorn, **downtown Bangkok** is central to the colossal expanse of Bangkok as a whole, but rather peripheral in a sightseer's perception of the city. This modern high-rise area is where you'll find the main financial district, around Thanon Silom, and the chief shopping centres, around Siam Square and Thanon Ploenchit, in addition to the smart hotels, restaurants and bars, the embassies and airline offices. Scattered widely across the downtown area are four attractive museums housed in traditional teak buildings: **Jim Thompson's House**, the **Ban Kamthieng**, the **Suan Pakkad Palace Museum** and **M.R. Kukrit's Heritage Home**. Downtown's other tourist highlights are far more diverse: **Siam Ocean World**, a high-tech aquarium that both kids and adults can enjoy; the noisy and glittering **Erawan Shrine**; and the wide, open spaces of Lumphini Park.

All of the sights reviewed here are within walking range of a **Skytrain** station, while Ban Kamthieng, the Snake Farm and Lumphini Park are also served by the **subway**. If you're heading downtown from Banglamphu, allow at least an hour to get to any of the places mentioned here by **bus**. Depending on the time of day, it may be quicker to take an **express boat** downriver, and then change onto the **Skytrain**. It might also be worth considering the regular **boats** on Khlong Saen Saeb.

▲ Early morning alms-giving at Wat Benjamabophit

Siam Square to Thanon Sukhumvit

Though **Siam Square** has just about everything to satisfy the Thai consumer boom – big shopping centres, Western fast-food restaurants, cinemas – don't come looking for an elegant commercial piazza: the "square" is in fact a grid of small streets to the southeast of **Pathumwan intersection** (the corner of Thanon Rama I and Thanon Phrayathai), and the name is applied freely to the surrounding area. Further east, you'll find yet more shopping malls around the Erawan Shrine, where Rama I becomes Thanon Ploenchit, an intersection sometimes known as **Ratchaprasong**. It's possible to stroll in peace here on an elevated **walkway**, beneath the Skytrain lines but above the cracked pavements, noise and fumes of Thanon Rama I, all the way from Siam Centre to the Erawan Shrine (further progress is blocked by Central and Chitlom Skytrain stations). Life becomes marginally less frenetic around **Ploenchit**, which is flanked by several grand old embassies, but picks up again once you pass under the expressway flyover and enter the shopping and entertainment quarter of **Thanon Sukhumvit**.

Jim Thompson's House

Just off Siam Square at the north end of Soi Kasemsan 2, Thanon Rama I, **Jim Thompson's House** (daily from 9am, viewing on frequent 30–40min guided tours in several languages, last tour 5pm; B100, students & under-25s B50; ⓣ02 216 7368, ⓦwww.jimthompsonhouse.org) is a kind of Ideal Home in elegant Thai style, and a peaceful refuge from downtown chaos. The house was the residence of the legendary American adventurer, entrepreneur, art collector and all-round character whose mysterious disappearance in the jungles of Malaysia in 1967 has made him even more of a legend among Thailand's farang community. National Stadium is the closest **Skytrain** station, but the house is walkable from Central Station (Siam), and a canalside path presents a shortcut from the Khlong Saen Saeb **pier** at Saphan Hua Chang.

Apart from putting together this beautiful home, Thompson's most concrete contribution was to turn traditional silk-weaving from a dying art into the highly successful international industry it is today. The complex now includes a **shop** (closes 6pm), part of the Jim Thompson Thai Silk Company chain (see p.197). Above the shop, the **Jim Thompson Center for the Arts** is a fascinating gallery that hosts both traditional and modern temporary exhibitions on textiles and the arts, such as royal maps of Siam in the nineteenth century or an interactive show that celebrated the hundredth anniversary of Thompson's birth and the vibrant evolution of Bangkok over the same period. There's also an excellent **bar-restaurant** (last food orders 4.45pm), which serves a similar menu to *Jim Thompson's Saladaeng Café* (see p.183). Ignore any con-men at the entrance to the soi looking for mugs to escort on rip-off shopping trips, who'll tell you that the house is closed when it isn't.

The grand, rambling **house** is in fact a combination of six teak houses, some from as far afield as Ayutthaya and most more than two hundred years old. Like all traditional houses, they were built in wall sections hung together without nails on a frame of wooden pillars, which made it easy to dismantle them, pile them onto a barge and float them to their new location. Although he had trained as an architect, Thompson had more difficulty in putting them back together again; in the end, he had to go back to Ayutthaya to hunt down a group of carpenters who still practised the old house-building methods. Thompson added a few unconventional touches of his own, incorporating the elaborately carved front wall of a Chinese pawnshop between the drawing room and the bedroom, and reversing the other walls in the drawing room so that their carvings faced into the room.

The legend of Jim Thompson

Thai silk-weavers, art dealers and conspiracy theorists all owe a debt to **Jim Thompson**, who even now, forty years after his disappearance, remains Thailand's most famous farang. An architect by trade, Thompson left his New York practice in 1940 to join the Office of Strategic Services (later to become the CIA), a tour of duty that was to see him involved in clandestine operations in North Africa, Europe and, in 1945, the Far East, where he was detailed to a unit preparing for the invasion of Thailand. When the mission was pre-empted by the Japanese surrender, he served for a year as OSS station chief in Bangkok, forming links that were later to provide grist for endless speculation.

After an unhappy and short-lived stint as part-owner of the *Oriental Hotel*, Thompson found his calling with the struggling **silk-weavers** of the area near the present Jim Thompson House, whose traditional product was unknown in the West and had been all but abandoned by Thais in favour of less costly imported textiles. Encouragement from society friends and an enthusiastic write-up in *Vogue* convinced him there was a foreign market for Thai silk, and by 1948 he had founded the Thai Silk Company Ltd. Success was assured when, two years later, the company was commissioned to make the costumes for the Broadway run of *The King and I*. Thompson's celebrated eye for colour combinations and his tireless promotion – in the early days, he could often be seen in the lobby of the *Oriental* with bolts of silk slung over his shoulder, waiting to pounce on any remotely curious tourist – quickly made his name synonymous with Thai silk.

Like a character in a Somerset Maugham novel, Thompson played the role of Western exile to the hilt. Though he spoke no Thai, he made it his personal mission to preserve traditional arts and architecture (at a time when most Thais were more keen to emulate the West), assembling his famous Thai house and stuffing it with all manner of Oriental *objets d'art*. At the same time he held firmly to his farang roots and society connections: no foreign gathering in Bangkok was complete without Jim Thompson, and virtually every Western luminary passing through Bangkok – from Truman Capote to Ethel Merman – dined at his table.

If Thompson's life was the stuff of legend, his disappearance and presumed death only added to the mystique. On Easter Sunday, 1967, Thompson, while staying with friends in a cottage in Malaysia's Cameron Highlands, went out for a stroll and never came back. A massive search of the area, employing local guides, tracker dogs and even shamans, turned up no clues, provoking a rash of fascinating but entirely unsubstantiated theories. The grandfather of them all, advanced by a Dutch psychic, held that Thompson had been lured into an ambush by the disgraced former prime minister of Thailand, Pridi Panyonyong, and spirited off to Cambodia for indeterminate purposes; later versions, supposing that Thompson had remained a covert CIA operative all his life, proposed that he was abducted by Vietnamese Communists and brainwashed to be displayed as a high-profile defector to Communism. More recently, an amateur sleuth claims to have found evidence that Thompson met a more mundane fate, having been killed by a careless truck driver and hastily buried.

The impeccably tasteful **interior** has been left as it was during Jim Thompson's life, even down to the place settings on the dining table – Thompson entertained guests most nights and to that end designed the house like a stage set. Complementing the fine artefacts from throughout Southeast Asia is a stunning array of Thai arts and crafts, including one of the best collections of traditional Thai paintings in the world. Thompson picked up plenty of bargains from the Thieves' Quarter (Nakhon Kasem) in Chinatown, before collecting Thai art became fashionable and expensive. Other pieces were liberated from decay and destruction in upcountry temples, while many of the Buddha images were turned over by ploughs, especially around Ayutthaya. Some of the exhibits are very rare, such as a headless but elegant seventh-century Dvaravati Buddha and a seventeenth-century Ayutthayan teak Buddha, but Thompson also bought pieces of little value and fakes simply for their looks – a shopping strategy that's all the more sensible in the jungle of today's Thai antiques trade.

After the guided tour, you're free to look again, at your leisure, at the former rice barn and gardener's and maid's houses in the small, jungly **garden**, which display some gorgeous traditional Thai paintings and drawings, as well as small-scale statues and Chinese ceramics.

Bangkok Art and Cultural Centre

A striking, white hunk of modernity, the **Bangkok Art and Cultural Centre**, overlooks the junction of Rama I and Phrayathai roads from its northwest corner (Tues–Sun 10am–9pm; ⓣ02 214 6630–1, ⓦwww.bacc.or.th). Connected by a walkway to National Stadium Skytrain station, this prestigious new centre houses several galleries on its upper floors, connected by spiralling ramps like New York's Guggenheim, as well as an auditorium and studio, and space for planned shops and restaurants. Its aim is to host temporary shows by contemporary artists from Thailand and abroad across all media, from the visual arts to music and design.

Siam Ocean World

Spreading over two spacious basement floors at the east end of the Siam Paragon shopping centre on Thanon Rama I, **Siam Ocean World** is a highly impressive, Australian-built aquarium (daily 9am–10pm, last admission 9pm; B750, children 80–120cm tall B600, under 80cm free; ⓣ02 687 2000, ⓦwww.siamoceanworld.com). Despite the relatively high admission price, it gets packed at weekends and during holidays, and can be busy with school groups on weekday afternoons – there are often long queues for the twenty-minute glass-bottomed boat rides (normally B150, though free at the time of writing, on special promotion), which give a behind-the-scenes look at the aquarium's workings. Among other outstanding features of this US$30-million development are an eight-metre-deep glass-walled tank, which displays the multicoloured variety of a coral reef drop-off to great effect, touch tanks for handling starfish, and a long, under-ocean tunnel where you can watch sharks and rays swimming over your head. In this global piscatorial display of around four hundred species, locals such as the Mekong giant catfish and the Siamese tigerfish are not forgotten, while regularly spaced touch-screen terminals provide information in English about the creatures on view. Popular daily highlights include shark feeds (currently 1pm & 4pm), and it's even possible to walk with the sharks (wearing a diving helmet; B2000 for 15min) or dive with them for thirty minutes, costing from B5300 for an experienced diver to B6600 for a first-timer (including admission price; ⓦwww.sharkdive.org). You can also watch – through 3D glasses – underwater and other nature films in "4D X-venture", where the chairs move and there are occasional sprays of water (normally B250, though free at the time of writing, on special promotion).

The Erawan Shrine

For a glimpse of the variety and ubiquity of Thai religion, drop in on the **Erawan Shrine** (*Saan Phra Prom* in Thai), at the corner of Thanon Ploenchit and Thanon Rajdamri underneath Chit Lom Skytrain station. Remarkable as much for its setting as anything else, this shrine to Brahma, the ancient Hindu creation god, and Erawan, his elephant, squeezes in on one of the busiest and noisiest intersections in modern Bangkok. And it's not the only one: half a dozen other Hindu shrines are dotted around Ratchaphrasong intersection, most notably **Trimurti**, who combines the three main gods, Brahma, Vishnu and Shiva, on the opposite corner outside Central World Plaza. Modern Bangkokians see Trimurti as a sort of Cupid figure, and those looking for love bring red offerings.

Towering over the Erawan Shrine, the *Grand Hyatt Erawan Hotel* is the reason for its existence and its name. When a string of calamities held up the building of the original hotel in the 1950s, spirit doctors were called in, who instructed the owners to build a new home for the offended local spirits: the hotel was then finished without further mishap. Ill fortune struck the shrine itself, however, in early 2006, when a young, mentally disturbed, Muslim man smashed the Brahma statue to pieces with a hammer – and was then brutally beaten to death by an angry mob. An exact replica of the statue was quickly installed, incorporating the remains of the old statue to preserve the spirit of the deity.

Be prepared for sensory overload here: the main structure shines with lurid glass of all colours and the overcrowded precinct around it is almost buried under scented garlands and incense candles. You might also catch a group of traditional dancers performing here to the strains of a small classical orchestra – worshippers hire them to give thanks for a stroke of good fortune. To increase their future chances of such good fortune, visitors buy a bird or two from the flocks incarcerated in cages here; the bird-seller transfers the requested number of captives to a tiny hand-held cage, from which the customer duly liberates the animals, thereby accruing merit. People set on less abstract rewards will invest in a lottery ticket from one of the physically disabled sellers: they're thought to be the luckiest you can buy.

Ban Kamthieng (Kamthieng House)

Another reconstructed traditional Thai residence, **Ban Kamthieng** (Tues–Sat 9am–5pm; B100; Ⓦwww.siam-society.org) was moved in the 1960s from Chiang Mai to 131 Thanon Asok Montri (Soi 21), off Thanon Sukhumvit, and set up as an ethnological museum by the Siam Society. The delightful complex of polished teak buildings makes a pleasing oasis beneath the towering glass skyscrapers that dominate the rest of Sukhumvit, and is easily reached from the Asok Skytrain and Sukhumvit subway stops. It differs from Suan Pakkad, Jim Thompson's House and M.R. Kukrit's Heritage Home in being the home of a rural family, and the objects on display give a fair insight into country life for the well-heeled in northern Thailand.

The house was built on the banks of the Ping River in the mid-nineteenth century, and the ground-level display of farming tools and fish traps evokes the upcountry practice of fishing in flooded rice paddies to supplement the supply from the rivers. Upstairs, the main display focuses on the ritual life of a typical Lanna household, explaining the role of the spirits, the practice of making offerings, and the belief in talismans, magic shirts and male tattoos. The rectangular lintel above the door is a *hum yon*, carved in floral patterns that represent testicles and designed to ward off evil spirits. Walk along the open veranda to the authentically equipped kitchen to see a video lesson in making spicy frog soup, and to the granary to find an interesting exhibition on the ritual practices associated with rice farming. Elsewhere in the Siam Society compound you'll find an esoteric bookshop (see p.200) and an antiques outlet.

Thailand Creative and Design Centre (TCDC)

Appropriately located on the sixth floor of the Emporium, one of Bangkok's most fashion-conscious shopping plazas, the **Thailand Creative and Design Centre** (Tues–Sun 10.30am–9pm; free; Ⓦwww.tcdc.or.th) seeks to celebrate, promote and inspire innovative design through exhibitions, talks, a resource centre and shop (see p.198). The concise but thought-provoking permanent bilingual display focuses on the cultural contexts of design classics from ten countries (including Spain, Japan, Finland and Brazil but sadly excluding Thailand), beginning with the Louis Vuitton trunk of 1854 and culminating with the iPod of 2001. Temporary exhibitions often focus more on Asian trends. The Emporium Shopping Centre is on Thanon Sukhumvit between sois 22 and 24, alongside BTS Phrom Pong station.

Northern downtown

The area above Thanon Phetchaburi is cut through by several major thoroughfares, including the original road to the north, Thanon Phaholyothin, which runs past the weekend market and doesn't stop until it gets to the Burmese border at Mae Sai, 900km away – though it's now more commonly known as Highway 1, at least in between towns. The start of Phaholyothin is marked by the stone obelisk of **Victory Monument** (*Anu Sawari Chaisamoraphum*, or just *Anu Sawari*), which can be seen most spectacularly from Skytrains as they snake their way round it. It was erected after the Indo-Chinese War of 1940–41, when Thailand pinched back some territory in Laos and Cambodia while the French government was otherwise occupied in World War II, but nowadays it commemorates all of Thailand's past military glories.

Suan Pakkad Palace Museum

The **Suan Pakkad Palace Museum** (daily 9am–4pm; B100; Ⓦwww.suanpakkad.com), five minutes' walk from Phaya Thai Skytrain station, at 352–4 Thanon Sri Ayutthaya, stands on what was once a cabbage patch but is now one of the finest gardens in Bangkok. Most of this private collection of beautiful Thai objects from all periods is displayed in four groups of traditional wooden houses, which were transported to Bangkok from various parts of the country. You can either take a guided tour in English (free) or explore the loosely arranged collection yourself (a leaflet and bamboo fan are handed out at the ticket office, and some of the exhibits are labelled). The attached **Marsi Gallery**, in the modern Chumbhot-Pantip Center of Arts on the east side of the garden, displays some interesting temporary exhibitions of contemporary art (Ⓣ02 246 1775–6 ext 229 for details).

The highlight of Suan Pakkad is the renovated **Lacquer Pavilion**, across the reedy pond at the back of the grounds. Set on stilts, the pavilion is actually an amalgam of two eighteenth- or late seventeenth-century temple buildings, a *ho trai* (library) and a *ho khien* (writing room), one inside the other, which were found between Ayutthaya and Bang Pa-In. The interior walls are beautifully decorated with gilt on black lacquer: the upper panels depict the life of the Buddha while the lower ones show scenes from the *Ramayana*. Look out especially for the grisly details in the tableau on the back wall, showing the earth goddess drowning the evil forces of Mara. Underneath are depicted some European dandies on horseback, probably merchants, whose presence suggests that the work was executed before the fall of Ayutthaya in 1767. The carefully observed details of daily life and nature are skilful and lively, especially considering the restraints which the lacquering technique places on the artist, who has no opportunity for corrections or touching up.

Divided between House no. 8 and the Ban Chiang Gallery in the Chumbhot-Pantip Center of Arts is a very good collection of elegant, whorled pottery and bronze jewellery, which the former owner of Suan Pakkad Palace, Princess Chumbhot, excavated from tombs at Ban Chiang, the major Bronze Age settlement in the northeast. Scattered around the rest of the museum are some attractive Thai and Khmer religious sculptures among an eclectic jumble of artefacts, including fine ceramics and some intriguing kiln-wasters, failed pots which have melted together in the kiln to form weird, almost rubbery pieces of sculpture; an extensive collection of colourful papier-mâché *khon* masks; beautiful betel-nut sets (see box, p.348); monks' elegant ceremonial fans; and some rich teak carvings, including a two-hundred-year-old temple door showing episodes from *Sang Thong*, a folk tale about a childless king and queen who discover a handsome son in a conch shell.

Southern downtown

South of Thanon Rama I, commercial development gives way to a dispersed assortment of large institutions, dominated by Thailand's most prestigious centre of higher learning, Chulalongkorn University, and the green expanse of **Lumphini Park**. Thanon Rama IV marks another change of character: downtown proper, centring around the high-rise, American-style boulevard of Thanon Silom, heart of the financial district, extends from here to the river. Alongside the smoked-glass banks and offices, the plush hotels and tourist shops, and opposite Convent Road, site of Bangkok's Carmelite nunnery, lies the dark heart of Bangkok nightlife, **Patpong**. Further west along Silom, in a still-thriving South Indian enclave, lies the colourful landmark of the Maha Uma Devi Temple (also known as Sri Mahamariamman or Wat Khaek), a gaudy, Hindu shrine built in 1895 in honour of Shiva's consort, Uma. Carrying on to the river, the strip west of Charoen Krung (New Road) reveals some of the history of Bangkok's early dealings with foreigners in the fading grandeur of the old trading quarter. Here you'll find the only place in Bangkok where you might be able to eke out an architectural walk, though it's hardly compelling. Incongruous churches and "colonial" buildings – the best being the Authors' Wing of the *Oriental Hotel*, where nostalgic afternoon teas are served – are hemmed in by the spice shops and *halal* canteens of the growing Muslim area around Thanon Charoen Krung.

The Queen Saovabha Memorial Institute (Snake Farm)

The **Queen Saovabha Memorial Institute** (*Sathan Saovabha*), at the corner of Thanon Rama IV and Thanon Henri Dunant, a ten-minute walk from Sala Daeng Skytrain station or Sam Yan or Si Lom subway stations, is a bit of a circus act, but an entertaining, informative and worthy one at that. It's often simply known as the **Snake Farm**, but takes its formal name from one of Rama V's wives, who was a notable campaigner. Run by the Thai Red Cross, the institute has a double function: to produce snake-bite serums, and to educate the public on the dangers of Thai snakes. The latter mission involves putting on live demonstrations of snake handling and feeding and venom extraction (Mon–Fri 11am & 2.30pm, Sat, Sun & hols 11am; B200, children B50; ⓣ02 252 0161–4, ⓦwww.redcross.or.th). Well presented and safe, these displays gain a perverse fascination from the knowledge that the strongest venoms of the snakes on show can kill in only three minutes. If you're still not herpetologically sated, you can look round the grounds, where a wide range of Thai snakes live in cages; some specimens are also preserved and bottled in a small snake museum.

Lumphini Park

If you're sick of cars and concrete, head for **Lumphini Park** (*Suan Lum*; daily 5am–7pm), at the east end of Thanon Silom, where the air is almost fresh and the traffic noise dies down to a low murmur. Named after the town in Nepal where the Buddha was born, it was the country's first public park, donated by Rama VI, whose statue by Silpa Bhirasri (see p.823) stands at the main, southwest entrance. The park is arrayed around two lakes, where you can join the locals in feeding the turtles and fish with bread or take out a pedalo or rowing boat, and is landscaped with a wide variety of local trees and numerous pagodas and pavilions, usually occupied by chess-players. In the early morning and at dusk, exercise freaks hit the outdoor gym on the southwest side of the park, or en masse do aerobics, balletic t'ai chi or jogging along the yellow-marked circuit, stopping for the twice-daily broadcast of the national anthem. On Sunday afternoons in the cool season, free classical concerts draw in scores of urban picnickers. To recharge your batteries, make for the inexpensive garden restaurant in the northwest corner.

Thailand's sex industry

Bangkok owes its reputation as the carnal capital of the world to a **sex industry** adept at peddling fantasies of cheap thrills on tap. More than a thousand sex-related businesses operate in the city, but the gaudy neon fleshpots of Patpong and Sukhumvit's Soi Nana and Soi Cowboy give a misleading impression of an activity that is deeply rooted in Thai culture: the overwhelming majority of Thailand's prostitutes of both sexes (estimated at anywhere between 200,000 and 700,000) work with Thai men, not farangs.

Prostitution and polygamy have long been intrinsic to the Thai way of life. Until Rama VI broke with the custom in 1910, Thai kings had always kept concubines, only a few of whom would be elevated to royal mothers. The practice was aped by the nobility and, from the early nineteenth century, by newly rich merchants keen to have lots of sons. Though the monarch is now monogamous, many men of all classes still keep **mistresses**, known as *mia noi* (minor wives); the common view is that an official wife (*mia luang*) should be treated like the temple's main Buddha image – respected and elevated upon the altar – whereas the minor wife is like an amulet, to be taken along wherever you go. For less wealthy men, prostitution is a far cheaper option: at least two-fifths of sexually active Thai men are thought to visit brothels twice a month.

The **farang sex industry** is a relatively new development, having started during the Vietnam War, when the American military set up seven bases around Thailand. The GIs' appetite for "entertainment" attracted women from surrounding rural areas to cash in on the boom, and Bangkok joined the fray in 1967. By the mid-1970s, the GIs had left, but tourists replaced them, lured by advertising that diverted most of the traffic to Bangkok and Pattaya. Sex tourism has since grown to become an established part of the Thai economy and has spread to Phuket, Hat Yai, Ko Samui and Chiang Mai.

The majority of the women who work in the country's go-go bars and "bar-beers" (outdoor hostess bars) come from the poorest rural areas of north and northeast Thailand. **Economic refugees**, they're easily drawn into an industry in which they can make in a single night what it takes a month to earn in the rice fields. In some villages, money sent home by prostitutes in Bangkok far exceeds financial aid given by the government. Many women from rural communities opt for a couple of lucrative years in the sex bars to help pay off family debts and improve the living conditions of parents stuck in the poverty trap.

Many bar girls, and male prostitutes too, are looking for longer-term **relationships** with their farang customers, bringing a temporary respite from bar work and perhaps even a ticket out. A surprising number of one-night transactions do develop into some sort of holiday romance, with the young woman accompanying her farang "boyfriend" (often twice her age) around the country and maintaining contact after he's returned home. It's a common joke that some bar girls field half a dozen mobile phones so they can juggle all their various "sponsors". An entire sub-genre of novels

Patpong

Concentrated into a small area between the eastern ends of Thanon Silom and Thanon Suriwong, the neon-lit go-go bars of the **Patpong** district loom like rides in a tawdry sexual Disneyland. In front of each bar, girls cajole passers-by with a lifeless sensuality while insistent touts proffer printed menus and photographs detailing the degradations on show. Inside, bikini-clad women gyrate to Western music and play hostess to the (almost exclusively male) spectators; upstairs, live shows feature women who, to use Spalding Gray's phrase in *Swimming to Cambodia*, "do everything with their vaginas except have babies".

Patpong was no more than a sea of mud when the capital was founded on the marshy river bank to the west, but by the 1960s it had grown into a flash district

and confessional memoirs (among them the classic *Hello, My Big Big Honey!: Letters to Bangkok Bar Girls and Their Revealing Interviews*) testifies to the role money plays in all this, and highlights the delusions common to both parties, not to mention the cross-cultural incomprehension.

Despite its ubiquity, prostitution has been **illegal** in Thailand since 1960, but sex-industry bosses easily circumvent the law by registering their establishments as clubs, karaoke bars or massage parlours, and making payoffs to the police. Sex workers, on the other hand, often endure exploitation and violence from pimps and customers rather than face fines and long rehabilitation sentences. Hardly surprising that many prefer to go freelance, working the clubs and bars in non-red-light zones such as Thanon Khao San. Life is made even more difficult because abortion is illegal in Thailand. The **anti-prostitution law** does attempt to treat sex workers as victims rather than criminals, penalizing parents who sell their children and punishing venue managers and customers with a jail sentence or heavy fine, but this is reportedly haphazardly enforced, owing to the number of influential police and politicians allegedly involved in the sex industry. A high-profile voice in the struggle to improve the **rights of sex workers** is the Empower Foundation (Ⓦwww.empowerfoundation.org), which not only organizes campaigns and runs education centres for bar workers but also manages its own bar in Chiang Mai.

Inevitably, **child prostitution** is a significant issue in Thailand, but NGOs such as EPCAT (Ⓦwww.epcat.net) say numbers have declined over the last decade, due to zero-tolerance and awareness campaigns. The government has also strengthened legislation against hiring a prostitute under the age of 18, and anyone caught having sex with an under-15 is now charged with rape. The disadvantaged are still targeted by traffickers however, who "buy" children from desperately poor hill-tribe and other minority families and keep them as bonded slaves until the debt has been repaid. Street kids and other orphans, including those displaced by the 2004 tsunami and by the ongoing conflict in the deep south, are especially vulnerable to pimps and predators.

The spectre of **AIDS** also puts the problems of the sex industry into sharp focus. UN AIDS statistics from 2004 reported that about one in twenty female sex workers in Bangkok was infected with HIV/AIDS and more than one in a hundred of the general adult Thai population. However, the rate of new HIV infections is in decline, down to 19,000 in 2003, thanks to aggressive AIDS-awareness campaigns, particularly those of the Population and Community Development Association (PDA; Ⓦwww.pda.or.th/eng), a Bangkok-based NGO, which also runs the famous *Cabbages and Condom* restaurants on Bangkok's Thanon Sukhumvit. It continues to campaign and educate the public, spurred on by fears that young Thais are too complacent about the virus, and by recent reports of a worrying rise in new infections.

of dance halls for rich Thais, owned by a Chinese millionaire godfather, educated at the London School of Economics and by the OSS (forerunner of the CIA), who gave his name to the area. In 1969, an American entrepreneur turned an existing teahouse into a luxurious nightclub to satisfy the tastes of soldiers on R&R trips from Vietnam, and so Patpong's transformation into a Western sex reservation began. At first, the area was rough and violent, but over the years it has wised up to the desires of the affluent farang, and now markets itself as a packaged concept of Oriental decadence. The centre of the skin trade lies along the interconnected sois of **Patpong 1 and 2**, where lines of go-go bars share their patch with respectable restaurants, a 24-hour supermarket and an overabundance of pharmacies. By night, it's a thumping theme-park, whose blazing neon promises tend towards self-parody, with names like *Thigh Bar* and *Chicken Divine*. Budget travellers, purposeful besuited businessmen and noisy lager louts throng the streets, and even the most demure tourists – of both sexes – turn out to do some shopping at the night market down the middle of Patpong 1, where hawkers sell fake watches, bags and designer T-shirts. By day, a relaxed hangover descends on the place. Bar-girls hang out at foodstalls and cafés in respectable dress, often recognizable by faces that are pinched and strained from the continuous use of antibiotics and heroin in an attempt to ward off venereal disease and boredom. Farang men slump at the bars on Patpong 2, drinking and watching videos, unable to find anything else to do in the whole of Bangkok.

The small dead-end alley to the east of Patpong 2, **Silom 4** (ie Soi 4, Thanon Silom), hosts some of Bangkok's hippest nightlife, its bars, clubs and pavements heaving at weekends with the capital's bright young things. There are many gay venues on Silom 4, but the focus of the scene has shifted to **Silom 2**, while in between, **Soi Thaniya**'s hostess bars and restaurants cater to Japanese tourists.

M.R. Kukrit's Heritage Home

Ten minutes' walk south of Thanon Sathorn and twenty minutes from Chong Nonsi Skytrain station, at 19 Soi Phra Pinit (Soi 7, Thanon Narathiwat Ratchanakharin), lies **M.R. Kukrit's Heritage Home**, the beautiful traditional house and gardens of one of Thailand's leading figures of the twentieth century (*Baan Mom Kukrit*; Sat, Sun & public hols 9.30am–5pm; B50; Ⓣ02 286 8185, Ⓦwww.kukritshousefund.com). M.R. (*Mom Rajawongse*, a princely title) **Kukrit Pramoj** (1911–95) was a remarkable all-rounder, descended from Rama II on his father's side and, on his mother's side, from the influential ministerial family, the Bunnags. Kukrit graduated in Philosophy, Politics and Economics from Oxford University and went on to become a university lecturer back in Thailand, but his greatest claim to fame is probably as a writer: he founded, owned and penned a daily column for *Siam Rath*, the most influential Thai-language newspaper, and wrote short stories, novels, plays and poetry. He was also a respected performer in classical dance-drama (*khon*), and he starred as an Asian prime minister, opposite Marlon Brando, in the Hollywood film, *The Ugly American*. In 1974, during an especially turbulent period for Thailand, life imitated art, when Kukrit was called on to become Thailand's prime minister at the head of a coalition of seventeen parties. However, just four hundred days into his premiership, the Thai military leadership dismissed him for being too anti-American.

The **residence**, which has been left just as it was when Kukrit was alive, reflects his complex character. In the large, open-sided *sala* (pavilion) for public functions near the entrance is an attractive display of *khon* masks, including a gold one which Kukrit wore when he played the demon king, Totsagan

(Ravana). In and around the adjoining Khmer-styled garden, keep your eyes peeled for the *mai dut*, sculpted miniature trees similar to bonsai, some of which Kukrit worked on for decades. The living quarters beyond are made up of five teak houses on stilts, assembled from various parts of central Thailand and joined by an open veranda. The bedroom, study and various sitting rooms are decked out with beautiful *objets d'art*; look out especially for the carved bed that belonged to Rama II and the very delicate, two-hundred-year-old nielloware (gold inlay) from Nakhon Si Thammarat in the formal reception room. In the small family prayer room, Kukrit Pramoj's ashes are enshrined in the base of a reproduction of the Emerald Buddha.

Chatuchak and the outskirts

The amorphous clutter of Greater Bangkok doesn't harbour many attractions, but there are a handful of places that make pleasant half-day escapes, principally **Chatuchak Weekend Market**, the cultural theme-park of **Muang Boran**, the rather more esoteric **Prasart Museum**, the upstream town of **Nonthaburi** and the tranquil artificial island of **Ko Kred**. (see map, p.95)

Chatuchak Weekend Market (JJ)

With over eight thousand open-air stalls to peruse, and wares as diverse as Lao silk, Siamese kittens and designer lamps, the enormous **Chatuchak Weekend Market**, or **JJ** as it's usually abbreviated, from "Jatu Jak" (Sat & Sun 7am–6pm), is Bangkok's most enjoyable – and exhausting – shopping experience. It occupies a huge patch of ground between the Northern Bus Terminal and Mo Chit Skytrain (N8)/Chatuchak Park subway stations, and is best reached by Skytrain or subway if you're coming from downtown areas; Kamphaeng Phet subway station is the most convenient as it exits right into the most interesting, southwestern, corner of the market. Coming from Banglamphu, you can either get a bus to the nearest Skytrain stop at National Stadium or Ratchathewi, or take the #59, #503 (non-expressway version) or #509 bus all the way from Rajdamnoen Klang (about 1hr); see p.115 for details.

Though its primary customers are Bangkok residents in search of idiosyncratic fashions and homewares, Chatuchak also has plenty of collector- and tourist-oriented **stalls**. Aside from trendy one-off clothes and accessories, best buys include antique lacquerware, unusual sarongs, traditional cotton clothing and crafts from the north, jeans, silver jewellery, and ceramics, particularly the five-coloured *bencharong*. The market is divided into 26 numbered **sections**, plus a dozen unnumbered ones, each of them more or less dedicated to a particular genre, for example household items, young fashions, plants, secondhand books, or crafts. If you have several hours to spare, it's fun just to browse at whim, but if you're looking for souvenirs, handicrafts or traditional textiles you should start with sections 22, 24, 25 and 26, which are all in a cluster at the southwest (Kamphaeng Phet subway) end of the market; sections A, B and C, behind the market's head office and information centre, are also full of interesting artefacts. *Nancy Chandler's Map of Bangkok* has a fabulously detailed and informatively annotated **map** of all the sections in the market, it's best bought before you arrive but is available at Teak House Art in Section 2, near Kamphaeng Phet subway's exit 2. Maps are also posted at various points around the market and for specific help you can also ask at the market office near Gate 1 off Thanon Kamphaeng Phet 2.

The market also contains a controversial **wildlife** section that has long doubled as a clearing house for protected and endangered species such as gibbons, palm cockatoos and Indian pied hornbills, many of them smuggled in from Laos and Cambodia and sold to private animal collectors and foreign zoos. The illegal trade goes on beneath the counter, despite occasional crackdowns, but you're bound to come across fighting cocks around the back, miniature flying squirrels being fed milk through pipettes, and iridescent red-and-blue Siamese fighting fish, kept in individual jars and shielded from each other's aggressive stares by sheets of cardboard.

There's no shortage of **foodstalls** inside the market compound, particularly at the southern end, where you'll find plenty of places serving inexpensive *phat thai* and Isaan snacks. Close by these stalls is a classy little juice bar called *Viva* where you can rest your feet while listening to the manager's jazz tapes. The biggest restaurant here is *Toh Plue*, whose main branch is on the edge of the block containing the market office and makes a good rendezvous point (there's a second branch beside Kamphaeng Phet subway station's exit 1). For veggie food, head for *Chamlong's* (also known as *Asoke*), an ultra-cheap food-court-style restaurant just outside the market on Thanon Kamphaeng Phet (across Thanon Kamphaeng Phet 2; 5min walk from Kamphaeng Phet subway's exit 1; Sat & Sun 8am–noon). You can **change money** (Sat & Sun 8am–6pm) in the market building at the south end of the market, and there are several ATMs here too. A few very small electric **trams** circulate around the market's main inner ring road, transporting weary shoppers for free, though they always seem to be full.

The Prasart Museum

Located on the far eastern edge of the city, the **Prasart Museum** at 9 Soi 4A, Soi Krungthep Kreetha, Thanon Krungthep Kreetha (Tues–Sun 10am–3pm; B1000 for 1 or 2 people; call ⓣ02 379 3601 to book the compulsory tour), is an unusual open-air exhibition of traditional Asian buildings, collected and reassembled by wealthy entrepreneur and art-lover Khun Prasart. The museum

▲ Chatuchak Weekend Market

is rarely visited by independent tourists – partly because of the intentionally limited opening hours and inflated admission price, and partly because it takes a long time to get there by public transport – but it makes a pleasant day out and is worth the effort.

Set in a gorgeously lush tropical garden, the museum comprises about a dozen beautifully crafted replicas of **traditional buildings**, including a golden teak palace inspired by the royal residence now housed at the National Museum, a Chinese temple and water garden, a Khmer shrine and a Sukhothai-era teak library set over a lotus pond. Some have been pieced together from ruined originals, while others were constructed from scratch. Many are filled with antique **artefacts**, including Burmese woodcarvings, prehistoric pottery from Ban Chiang and Lopburi-era statuettes. There's also an exquisite collection of *bencharong* ceramics. Khun Prasart also owns a ceramics workshop, which produces reproductions of famous designs; they can be bought either at the museum, or at his showroom, the Prasart Collection, on the second floor of the Peninsula Plaza shopping centre on Thanon Rajdamri.

Regular and air-con **bus** #93 runs almost to the door: pick it up near its starting point on Thanon Si Phraya near River City and the GPO, or anywhere along its route on Phetchaburi and Phetchaburi Mai roads (both the Khlong Saen Saeb canal boats and the subway have potentially useful stops at the Thanon Asok Montri/Sukhumvit Soi 21 junction with Thanon Phetchaburi Mai). The #93 terminates on Thanon Krungthep Kreetha, but you should get off a couple of stops before the terminus, at the first stop on Thanon Krungthep Kreetha, as soon as you see the sign for the Prasart Museum (about 1hr 15min by bus from Si Phraya). Follow the sign down Soi Krungthep Kreetha, go past the golf course and, after about a fifteen-minute walk, turn off down Soi 4A. To speed things up, you could instead take the Khlong Saen Saeb canal boat all the way to Tha The Mall Bangkapi (about 40min from Phan Fah, four stops after the confusingly similar Tha The Mall 3 stop), which leaves you within just a very short taxi-ride of the museum.

Nonthaburi

A trip to **NONTHABURI**, the first town beyond the northern boundary of Bangkok, is the easiest excursion you can make from the centre of the city and affords a perfect opportunity to recharge your batteries. Nonthaburi is the last stop upriver for most express boats (N30), under an hour from Central Pier (Sathorn) on an orange-flag boat. The ride itself is most of the fun, weaving round huge, crawling sand barges and tiny canoes, and the slow pace of the boat gives you plenty of time to take in the sights on the way. On the north side of Banglamphu, beyond the elegant, new Rama VIII Bridge, which shelters the Mekong whisky distillery on the west bank, you'll pass in turn, on the east bank: the Art-Nouveau Bangkhunprom Palace and the adjacent, neoclassical Devaves Palace, both former princely residences; Thewet flower market; the royal boat house in front of the National Library, where you can glimpse the minor ceremonial boats that escort the grand royal barges; the city's first Catholic church, Holy Conception, founded in the seventeenth century during King Narai of Ayutthaya's reign and rebuilt in the early nineteenth; and, beyond Krungthon Bridge, the Singha brewery. Along the route are dazzling Buddhist temples and drably painted mosques, catering for Bangkok's growing Muslim population, as well as a few remaining communities who still live in houses on stilts or houseboats – around Krungthon Bridge, for example, you'll see people living on the huge teak vessels used to carry rice, sand and charcoal.

Durians

The naturalist Alfred Russel Wallace, eulogizing the taste of the **durian**, compared it to "rich butter-like custard highly flavoured with almonds, but intermingled with wafts of flavour that call to mind cream cheese, onion sauce, brown sherry and other incongruities". He neglected to discuss the smell of the fruit's skin, which is so bad – somewhere between detergent and dog shit – that durians are barred from Thai hotels and aeroplanes. The different **varieties** bear strange names which do nothing to make them more appetizing: "frog", "golden pillow", "gibbon" and so on. However, the durian has fervent admirers, perhaps because it's such an acquired taste, and because it's considered a strong aphrodisiac. Aficionadoes discuss the varieties with as much subtlety as if they were vintage Champagnes, and treat the durian as a social fruit, to be shared around, despite a price tag of up to B3000 each. They also pour scorn on the Thai government scientists who have recently genetically developed an odourless variety, the Chanthaburi 1 durian.

Durian season is roughly April to June and the most famous durian orchards are around Nonthaburi, where the fruits are said to have an incomparably rich and nutty flavour due to the fine clay soil. To see these and other plantations such as mango, pomelo and jackfruit, your best bet is to hire a longtail from Nonthaburi pier to take you west along Khlong Om Non. If you don't smell them first, you can recognize durians by their sci-fi appearance: the shape and size of a rugby ball, but slightly deflated, they're covered in a thick, pale-green shell which is heavily armoured with short, sharp spikes (*duri* means "thorn" in Malay). By cutting along one of the faint seams with a good knife, you'll reveal a white pith in which are set a handful of yellow blobs with the texture of a wrinkled soufflé: this is what you eat. The taste is best when the smell is at its highest, about three days after the fruit has dropped. Be careful when out walking near the trees: because of its great weight and sharp spikes, a falling durian can lead to serious injury, or even an ignominious death.

Disembarking at suburban Nonthaburi, on the east bank of the river, you won't find a great deal to do, in truth. There's a market that's famous for the quality of its fruit, while the attractive, old Provincial Office across the road is covered in rickety wooden latticework. To break up your trip with a slow, scenic drink or lunch, you'll find a floating seafood restaurant, *Rim Fang*, to the right at the end of the prom.

Set in relaxing grounds about 1km north of Nonthaburi pier on the west bank of the river, elegant **Wat Chalerm Phra Kiat** injects a splash of urban refinement among a grove of breadfruit trees. You can get there from the express-boat pier by taking the ferry straight across the Chao Phraya and then catching a motorbike taxi. The beautifully proportioned temple, which has been lavishly restored, was built by Rama III in memory of his mother, whose family lived and presided over vast orchards in the area. Inside the walls of the temple compound, you feel as if you've come upon a stately folly in a secret garden, and a strong Chinese influence shows itself in the unusual ribbed roofs and elegantly curved gables, decorated with pastel ceramics. The restorers have done their best work inside: look out especially for the simple, delicate landscapes on the shutters.

Ko Kred

About 7km north of Nonthaburi, the tiny island of **KO KRED** lies in a particularly sharp bend in the Chao Phraya, cut off from the east bank by a waterway created to make the cargo route from Ayutthaya to the Gulf of Thailand just that little bit faster. Although it's been discovered by day-trippers from Bangkok, this artificial island remains something of a time capsule, a little oasis of village life completely at odds with the metropolitan chaos downriver. Roughly ten square kilometres in all, Ko Kred has no roads, just a concrete path that follows its circumference, with a few arterial walkways branching off towards the interior. Villagers, the majority of whom are Mon (see box, p.249), descendants of immigrants during the reigns of Taksin and Rama II, use a small fleet of motorbike taxis to cross their island, but as a sightseer you're much better off on a rental bicycle or just on foot: a round-island walk takes less than an hour and a half.

There are few sights as such on Ko Kred, but its lushness and comparative emptiness make it a perfect place in which to wander. You'll no doubt come across one of the island's potteries and kilns, which churn out the regionally famous earthenware flower-pots and small water-storage jars and employ a large percentage of the village workforce. The island's clay is very rich in nutrients and therefore excellent for fruit-growing, and banana trees, coconut palms, pomelo, papaya, mango and durian trees all grow in abundance on Ko Kred, fed by an intricate network of irrigation channels that crisscrosses the interior. In among the orchards, the Mons have built their wooden houses, mostly in traditional style and raised high above the marshy ground on stilts. A handful of attractive riverside wats completes the picture, most notably **Wat Paramaiyikawat** (also called **Wat Poramai**), at the main pier at the northeast tip of the island. This engagingly ramshackle eighteenth-century temple was restored by Rama V in honour of his grandmother, with a Buddha relic placed in its white, riverside chedi, which is a replica of the Mutao Pagoda in Hanthawadi, capital of the Mon kingdom in Burma. Among an open-air scattering of Burmese-style alabaster Buddha images, the tall bot shelters some fascinating nineteenth-century murals, depicting scenes from temple life at ground level and the life of the Buddha above, all set in delicate imaginary landscapes.

Practicalities

The easiest but busiest time to go to Ko Kred is on Sunday, when the Chao Phraya Express Boat Company (B300; Ⓣ02 623 6143, Ⓦwww.chaophrayaboat.co.th) and Mitchaopaya Travel Service (B300; Ⓣ02 623 6169) run **boat tours** there from central Bangkok. They both take in Wat Chalerm Phra Kiat in Nonthaburi (see opposite), and Wat Poramai and Ban Khanom Thai on Ko Kred, where you can buy traditional sweets and watch them being made. The Chao Phraya express boat departs from Tha Sathorn at 10am, calling at Tha Maharat in Ratanakosin at 10.30am, returning to the latter at 4.30pm, the former at 4.45pm. Mitchaopaya leaves Tha Chang at 9am, calling at the Royal Barge Museum (see p.155) and cruising up Khlong Bangkok Noi, returning at 4.30pm.

At other times, the main drawback of a day-trip to Ko Kred is the difficulty of **getting there**. Your best option is to take a Chao Phraya express boat to Nonthaburi, then bus #32 (ordinary and air-con, coming from Wat Pho via Banglamphu) to Pakkred or a chartered longtail boat direct to Ko Kred (about B300). There are also fast, air-con #166 buses from Victory Monument (accessible by Skytrain) to Pakkred, which are your best option for getting back as the #32 stops a fair way from Nonthaburi pier on its inbound journey. From Pakkred, the easiest way of getting across to the island is to hire a longtail boat, although shuttle boats cross at the river's narrowest point to Wat Poramai from Wat Sanam Neua, about a kilometre's walk or motorbike-taxi ride south of the Pakkred pier (getting off the bus at Tesco Lotus in Pakkred will cut down the walk to Wat Sanam Neua).

Muang Boran Ancient City

A day-trip out to the **Muang Boran Ancient City** open-air museum (daily 8am–5pm; B300, children B200; Ⓦwww.ancientcity.com), 33km southeast of Bangkok, is a great way to enjoy the best of Thailand's architectural heritage in relative peace and without much effort. Occupying a huge park shaped like Thailand itself, the museum comprises more than 116 traditional Thai buildings scattered around pleasantly landscaped grounds and is best toured by rented **bicycle** (B50; B150/tandem; B200/three-seater), though you can also make use of the circulating **tram** (B150 round trip, children B75), and doing it on foot is just about possible. Many of the buildings are copies of the country's most famous monuments, and are located in the appropriate "region" of the park, with everything from Bangkok's Grand Palace (central region) to the spectacularly sited, hilltop Khmer Khao Phra Viharn sanctuary (northeast) represented here. There are also some original structures, including a rare scripture library rescued from Samut Songkhram (south), as well as some painstaking reconstructions from contemporary documents of long-vanished gems, of which the Ayutthaya-period Sanphet Prasat Palace (central) is a particularly fine example. A sizeable team of restorers and skilled craftspeople maintains the buildings and helps keep some of the traditional techniques alive; if you come here during the week you can watch them at work.

To get to Muang Boran from Bangkok, take air-conditioned **bus** #511 to **Samut Prakan** on the edge of built-up Greater Bangkok, then change onto songthaew #36, which passes the entrance to Muang Boran. Although bus #511 runs from Banglamphu via Thanon Rama I and Thanon Sukhumvit (see p.115), the journey is likely to be much faster if you cross downtown Bangkok by Skytrain (and boat and/or subway if necessary) and pick up the #511 at the Ekamai Skytrain stop.

A couple of kilometres east of Samut Prakan, the **Crocodile Farm** (daily 7am–6pm; B300, children B200) figures on tour-group itineraries, but is a depressing place. The thirty thousand reptiles kept here are made to "perform" for their trainers in hourly shows and are subsequently turned into handbags, shoes, briefcases and wallets, a selection of which are sold on site. Songthaews run from Samut Prakan.

Eating

As you'd expect, nowhere in Thailand can compete with Bangkok's diversity when it comes to food: it boasts an astonishing fifty thousand places to eat, almost one for every hundred citizens. Although prices are generally higher here than in the provinces, it's still easy to dine well on a budget. For **Thai** food, the best gourmet restaurants in the country operate from the downtown districts around Thanon Sukhumvit and Thanon Silom, proffering wonderful royal, traditional and regional cuisines that definitely merit a visit. Over in Banglamphu, Thanon Phra Arthit is known for its idiosyncratic little restaurant-bars angled at young Thai diners. At the lower end of the price scale, one-dish meals from around the country are rustled up at the **food courts** of shopping centres and department stores, as well as at **night markets** and **street stalls**, which are so numerous in Bangkok that we can only flag the most promising areas – but wherever you're staying, you'll hardly have to walk a block in any direction before encountering something appealing.

For the non-Thai cuisines, Chinatown naturally rates as the most authentic district for pure **Chinese** food; likewise neighbouring Pahurat, the capital's

Dinner and cocktail cruises

The **Chao Phraya River** looks fabulous at night, when most of the noisy longtails have stopped terrorizing the ferries, and the riverside temples and other grand monuments – including the Grand Palace and Wat Arun – are elegantly illuminated. Joining one of the nightly **dinner cruises** along the river is a great way to appreciate it all. Call ahead to reserve a table and check departure details – some places offer free transport from hotels, and some cruises may not run during the rainy season (May to Oct). If you have other plans for dinner, it's now also possible to take a **cocktail cruise** on the *Manohra* (see below), between 6 and 7pm (B900).

Grand Pearl of Siam ⓣ02 861 0255 ext 201–4, ⓦwww.grandpearlcruise.com. A large, modern boat which departs River City at 7.30pm, returning at 9.30pm. Thai and international buffet. B1400.

Loy Nava ⓣ02 235 3108. This long-running converted rice-barge departs Si Phraya pier twice nightly, at 6pm and 8pm. Thai or seafood meal. B1300.

Maeyanang Run by the *Oriental Hotel* ⓣ02 659 9000; mid-Oct to April Tues–Sun. After cocktails in the *Oriental* gardens (7pm), this former rice-barge departs at 7.30pm, returning at 10pm. Thai set meal. B1950.

Manohra Beautiful converted rice-barge operated by the *Marriott Bangkok Resort*, south of Taksin Bridge in Thonburi ⓣ02 476 0022 ext 1416, ⓦwww.manohracruises.com. Departs hotel at 7.30pm, returning 10pm, with pick-ups at Tha Sathorn possible. Thai set dinner, accompanied by live traditional music. B1990.

Wan Fah ⓣ02 222 8679, ⓦwww.wanfahcruise.com. Departs River City at 7pm, returning at 9pm. Thai or seafood set menu. B1200.

Indian enclave, is best for unadulterated **Indian** dishes, while there's a sprinkling of Indian and (mostly southern Thai) **Muslim** restaurants around Silom's Maha Uma Devi Temple and nearby Thanon Charoen Krung. Sukhumvit's Soi 3 is a hub for **Middle Eastern** cafés, complete with hookah pipes at the outdoor tables; and good, comparatively cheap **Japanese** restaurants are concentrated on Soi Thaniya, at the east end of Thanon Silom. The place to head for inexpensive, Western, **travellers' food** – from herbal teas and hamburgers to muesli – as well as a hearty range of veggie options, is Thanon Khao San; standards vary, but there are some definite gems among the blander establishments. Meanwhile, downtown Bangkok has a good quota of **coffee shops**, including several branches of local company *Black Canyon* and the ubiquitous *Starbucks*.

In the more expensive restaurants listed below you may have to pay a ten percent **service charge** and seven percent VAT. Most restaurants in Bangkok are open every day for lunch and dinner; we've noted exceptions in the listings below.

Banglamphu and the Democracy Monument area

Copycat entrepreneurship means that Khao San is stacked full of **backpacker restaurants** serving near-identical Western and (mostly) watered-down Thai food; there's even a lane, one block east, parallel to Thanon Tanao (behind *Burger King*), that's dominated by **vegetarian** cafés, following a trend started by *May Kaidee*. Hot-food stalls selling very cheap **night-market** snacks operate until the early hours. Things are more varied down on Thanon Phra Arthit, with its arty little **café-restaurants** favoured by Thammasat University students, while the riverside places, on Phra Arthit and further north off Thanon Samsen and in Thewet, tend to be best for **seafood** with a view. For the real old-fashioned Thai taste though, browse southern Thanon Tanao and its network of sois south of Democracy and west of Sao Ching Cha (the Giant Swing), where traditional shophouses have been selling **specialist sweets and savouries** for generations; none have signs or numbers in English however. See the map on p.112 for locations of the places listed below.

Around Khao San

Chabad House 96 Thanon Ram Bhuttri ⓦwww.jewishthailand.com. A little piece of Israel, run by the Bangkok branch of the Jewish outreach Chabad-Lubavitch movement. Serves a well-priced kosher menu (B75–150) of falafels, baba ganoush, schnitzels, hummus, salads and Jewish breads in air-con calm, on the ground floor of a long-established community centre and guest house. Sun–Thurs 10am–10pm, Fri 10am–3pm.

Lotash Seed Thanon Ram Bhuttri. A tiny pocket of Buddhist calm in an increasingly frantic street, this cosy restaurant has understated lotus imagery and a menu full of delicious Thai classics and one-offs, plus cocktails and wines. The roll-your-own *miang* stuffed tea-leaf starters are a delicious opener and there are great curries, plus *yam taleh* (seafood salad) and a long vegetarian menu. Mains B80–150.

May Kaidee East off Thanon Tanao ⓦwww.maykaidee.com. Simple, neighbourhood Thai vegetarian restaurant, with two outlets on opposite sides of the soi, that still serves some of the best veggie food in Banglamphu despite having spawned a row of competitors on the same alley. Try the tasty green curry with coconut, the Vietnamese-style veggie spring rolls or the sticky black-rice pudding. May Kaidee herself also runs vegetarian cookery classes (see p.207). Most dishes B60–70.

Popaing Soi Ram Bhuttri. Popular place for cheap seafood: mussels and cockles cost just B50 per plate, squid B70, or you can get a large helping of seafood noodles for B100. Eat in the low-rent restaurant area or on the street beneath the temple wall.

Prakorb House Thanon Khao San. Archetypal travellers' haven, with only a few tables, and an emphasis on wholesome ingredients. Herbal teas, mango shakes, delicious pumpkin curry, and lots more besides (B50–90).

Sunset Bar Sunset Street, 197–201 Thanon Khao San. Follow the passageway behind *Sabai Bar* as it opens out into a tranquil, shrub-filled courtyard occupied by the *Sunset Bar* coffee shop and restaurant – the perfect place to escape the Khao San hustle with a mid-priced juice or snack. The courtyard's handsome, mango-coloured, 1907 villa is another enticement: a discreet branch of *Starbucks*, with sofas, occupies its ground floor.

Tom Yam Kung Thanon Khao San. Occasionally mouth-blastingly authentic Thai food served in the courtyard of a beautiful, early twentieth-century villa that's hidden behind Khao San's modern clutter. The menu (B115–300) includes spicy fried catfish, coconut-palm curry with tofu and shrimps in sugar cane. Well-priced cocktails, draught beer and a small wine list.

Phra Arthit area

Aquatini *Navalai River Resort*, 45/1 Thanon Phra Arthit, next to Tha Phra Arthit express-boat pier. Occupying a nice wooden deck in a perfect breezy riverfront spot beside the express-boat pier (even better after sunset when the boats stop running), this hotel restaurant does exceptionally good mid-priced Thai food. Seafood's a speciality: the deep-fried ruby fish served with cashew nuts and bell peppers is very good, and their tangy coconut-milk *tom kha kai* soup is especially delicious. Most seafood mains B200–300.

Hemlock 56 Thanon Phra Arthit ⓣ02 282 7507. Small, stylish, recommended air-con restaurant that's very popular with students and young Thai couples. Offers a long and interesting menu of unusual Thai dishes (mostly about B80), including banana-flower salad, coconut and mushroom curry, grand lotus rice and various *larb* and fish dishes. The traditional *miang* starters (shiny green wild tea leaves filled with chopped vegetables, fish and meat) are also very tasty, and there's a good vegetarian selection. Mon–Sat 5pm–midnight; worth reserving a table on Friday and Saturday nights.

Roti Mataba 136 Thanon Phra Arthit. Famous outlet for the ever-popular fried Indian breads, or *rotis*, served here in lots of sweet and savoury varieties, including with vegetable and meat curries, and with bananas and condensed milk (from B10). Mon–Sat 8.30am–10pm.

Thanon Samsen and Thewet

In Love Beside the Tha Thewet express-boat pier at 2/1 Thanon Krung Kasem. Popular place for good Thai seafood – and riverine breezes – with decent Chao Phraya views, an airy upstairs terrace, and a huge menu including baked cottonfish in mango sauce, steamed sea bass with lime and chilli, and *tom yam kung*. Most dishes B160–300.

Kaloang Beside the river at the far western end of Thanon Sri Ayutthaya. Flamboyant service and excellent seafood attracts an almost exclusively Thai clientele to this open-air riverside restaurant. Dishes well worth sampling include the fried rolled shrimps served with a sweet dip, the roast squid cooked in a piquant sauce and the steamed butter fish (mains B150–300).

Kinlom Chom Saphan Riverside end of Thanon Samsen Soi 3. This sprawling, waterside seafood restaurant boasts close-up views of the lyre-like Rama VIII Bridge and is always busy with a youngish Thai crowd. The predominantly seafood menu (B130–300) features everything from crab to grouper cooked in multiple ways, including with curry, garlic or sweet basil sauces, but never with MSG. As well as the usual complement of *tom yam* and *tom kha* soups, there are *yam* salads and meat options including stir-fried ostrich with herbs.

May Kaidee 2 33 Thanon Samsen, between the khlong and Soi 1 Ⓦwww.maykaidee.com. Air-con branch of Banglamphu's best-loved Thai veggie restaurant and cooking school; see opposite.

South: Thanon Tanao and around

Gor Panit 431–433 Thanon Tanao, on the east side, directly opposite Soi Phraeng Phuton. Outstanding take-away coconut-laced sticky rice with mango (or banana) has been sold here since 1932. No English sign, but look for the mango vendors outside, where you can choose your variety if you want. Open during the mango season only: June–Dec Mon–Sat 6.30am–8pm.

Kai Yang Boran 474–476 Thanon Tanao, immediately to the south of the Chao Poh Seua Chinese shrine (no English sign). Locally famous grilled chicken and *som tam* restaurant (with air-con). Daily 9am–8pm.

Nattaporn 94 Soi Phraeng Phuton, west off southern Thanon Tanao. This family has been specializing in its famous home-made fresh coconut ice-cream for over sixty years, topping it with classic Thai condiments like sweetcorn, red beans and taro balls. They also do chocolate, coffee and ice-tea flavours. To find it, take the first left off Soi Phraeng Phuton and follow it round until you reach Nattaporn, on the corner of the next sub-soi. Mon–Sat 9am–4pm.

Padthai Thipsamai 313 Thanon Mahachai (no English sign), near Wat Rajnadda Ⓦwww.thipsamai.com. The most famous *phat thai* in Bangkok, flash-fried by the same husband-and-wife team since 1966. The "extra" option is huge, comes with especially juicy prawns, and is wrapped in a translucent, paper-thin omelette. Best washed down with fresh coconut juice. Daily except alternate Wed, from 5.30pm.

Ratanakosin

The places reviewed below are especially handy for sightseers, but there are also plenty of street stalls around Tha Chang and a load of simple, studenty restaurants off the north end of Thanon Maharat near Thammasat University, as well as a decent restaurant at *Arun Residence* and a daytime café at *Aurum* (see p.117). See the map on p.129 for locations of the places listed below.

Na Pralan Café Thanon Na Phra Lan. This small, cheap café is ideally placed for refreshment after your tour of the Grand Palace. Popular with students, it occupies a quaint old air-con shophouse with battered, artsy decor. The menu, well thought out with some unusual twists, offers mostly Thai salads and one-dish meals with rice, and a range of ice creams, coffees, teas and beers. Mon–Sat 10.30am–10pm, Sun 10.30am–6pm.

Rub Ar Roon Opposite Wat Pho at 310–2 Thanon Maharat. Among many open-fronted, century-old shophouses on this stretch, this cosy, congenial café used to be a dispensary and still has its original teak cabinets. The Thai food is varied and very reasonably priced, and there are sandwiches, espressos, Thai herbal teas and fruit shakes. Daily 8am–6pm.

Chinatown and Pahurat

Much of the fun of Chinatown dining is in the browsing of the night-time hot-food stalls that open up all along Thanon Yaowarat, around the mouth of Soi Issaranuphap (Yaowarat Soi 11) and along Soi Phadungdao; wherever there's a crowd you'll be sure of good food. Pan Siam's *Good Eats: Chinatown* map, available from major bookshops, is also a great resource for the weirder local specialities. See the map on p.150 for locations of the places listed below.

Yellow-flag heaven for veggies

Every autumn, for nine days during the ninth lunar month (between late Sept and Nov), Thailand's Chinese community goes on a **meat-free** diet to mark the onset of the Vegetarian Festival (Ngan Kin Jeh), a sort of Taoist version of Lent. Though the Chinese citizens of Bangkok don't go in for skewering themselves like their compatriots in Trang and Phuket (see p.686), they do celebrate the Vegetarian Festival with gusto: some people choose to wear only white for the duration, all the temples throng with activity, and nearly every restaurant and foodstall in Chinatown turns vegetarian for the period, flying small yellow flags to show that they are upholding the tradition and participating in what's essentially a nightly veggie food jamboree. For vegetarian tourists this is a great time to be in town – just look for the yellow flag and you can be sure all dishes will be one hundred percent vegan. Soya substitutes are a popular feature on the vegetarian Chinese menu, so don't be surprised to find pink prawn-shaped objects floating in your noodle soup or unappetizingly realistic slices of fake duck. Many hotel restaurants also get in on the act during the Vegetarian Festival, running special veggie promotions for a week or two.

Chong Kee 84 Soi Sukon 1, near Wat Traimit. Delicious and moreishly cheap pork satay and sweet toast. Tues–Sun 9.30am–7pm, Mon 9.30am–2pm.

Hua Seng Hong 371 Thanon Yaowarat. Braised goose feet is one of the specialities here, but more familiar alternatives include wonton noodle soup and stir-fried crab noodles. Dishes from B160.

Royal India Just off Thanon Chakraphet at 392/1. Great dhal, perfect parathas and famously good North Indian curries (from B90) served in a dark little café in the heart of Bangkok's most Punjabi of neighbourhoods to an almost exclusively South Asian clientele.

S&P Next to Sala Chalermkrung Theatre and Old Siam Plaza, Thanon Triphet/Charoen Krung intersection. Moccachino frosts, blueberry smoothies (B70), iced fruit teas and various cakes all help make this chain restaurant a good place to cool down during a Chinatown circuit. It's hardly *haute cuisine*, but there's air-con and it's comfy.

Shangri-La 306 Thanon Yaowarat (corner of Thanon Rajawong). Cavernous banquet-hall serving Cantonese classics (B100–1000), including lots of seafood, and lunchtime dim sum. Very popular, especially for family gatherings.

T&K (Toi & Kid's Seafood) 49 Soi Phadungdao, just off Thanon Yaowarat. Known for their barbecued seafood, with everything from prawns (B150 a serving) to oysters (B30 each) on offer. Eat at street-side tables or inside with air-con. Daily 4.30pm–2am.

White Orchid Hotel 409–421 Thanon Yaowarat. Recommended for its dim sum, with bamboo baskets of prawn dumplings, spicy spare ribs, stuffed bean curd and the like, served in three different portion sizes at fairly high prices. Dim sum 11am–2pm & 5–10pm. All-you-can-eat lunchtime buffets also worth stopping by for.

Downtown: Around Siam Square and Thanon Ploenchit

In this area, there are also branches of *Taling Pling* (see p.184), on Floor 3, Central World Plaza (ⓣ02 613 1360–1); *Jim Thompson's Café* (see p.183), on the ground floor of Central World Plaza (ⓣ02 255 9813–4) and at Jim Thompson's House; and *Aoi* (see p.182), in the Siam Paragon shopping centre on Thanon Rama I (ⓣ02 129 4348–50). See the map on p.120 for locations of the places listed below.

Bali 15/3 Soi Ruam Rudee ⓣ02 250 0711. Top-notch, reasonably priced Indonesian food in a cosy nook, including plenty of options for veggies and authentic desserts. Blow out on the seven-course *rijstaffel* for B400 or restrain yourself with the excellent four-course version for B260. Closed Sun.

Curries & More 63/3 Soi Ruam Rudee ⓣ02 253 5408–9. And a whole lot more…this offshoot of *Baan Khanitha* (see p.184) offers something for everyone, including European-style fish, steaks and pasta, as well as curries from around the country (from B240). Try the delicious *chu chi khung nang*, deep-fried freshwater prawns with mild, Indian-style curry, or the prawn and pomelo salad. The modern, white-painted interior is hung with contemporary paintings, but the garden, surrounded by waterfalls and with water flowing over the transparent roof, is the place to be.

Food for Fun Floor 4, Siam Centre, Thanon Rama I. Highly enjoyable, inexpensive, new food court, decorated in startling primary colours. Lots of traditional Thai drinks and all manner of tasty one-dish meals – *khao man kai*, and *laab* and *som tam* from the Isaan counter – as well as pizza, pastas, Chinese and Indian food. Daily 10am–9pm.

Food Loft Floor 7, Central Chidlom, Thanon Ploenchit. Bangkok's top department store lays on a suitably upscale food court of all hues – Thai, Vietnamese, Malay, Chinese, Japanese, Indian, Italian (by *Gianni* – see below). Choose your own ingredients and watch them cooked in front of you, eat in the stylish, minimalist seating areas and then ponder whether you have room for a Thai or Western dessert. There's another, recently opened branch of *Food Loft* on Floor 7 of Zen department store in Central World Plaza.

Genji *Swissôtel Nai Lert Park*, 2 Thanon Witthayu ⓣ02 253 0123. Excellent, genteel Japanese restaurant, serving authentic food in a contemporary setting overlooking the hotel's beautiful gardens, with a sushi bar, teppanyaki grill tables and private dining rooms.

Gianni 34/1 Soi Tonson, Thanon Ploenchit ⓣ02 252 1619, ⓦwww.giannibkk.com. One of Bangkok's best independent Italian restaurants, offering a sophisticated blend of traditional and modern in both its decor and food. Offerings include a belt- (and bank-) busting tasting menu for B1290 and innovative pastas. *Gianni* also runs a couple of classy *Bar Italia* café-restaurants, on the ground floor of Gaysorn Plaza and on Floor 6 of Central World Plaza.

Home Kitchen (Khrua Nai Baan) 94 Soi Lang Suan ⓣ02 253 1888. Like an upcountry restaurant in the heart of the city, this congenial, unpretentious spot offers a choice between air-con and outdoor tables behind a huge open kitchen. On the inexpensive picture menu, you're bound to find something delicious, among dozens of soups – how about the *kaeng liang*, with shrimp, pumpkin and mixed vegetables, for B150? – six kinds of *laap* and a huge array of seafood. Success has spawned a smarter new branch, but with the same menu and just two doors away. Daily 8am–midnight.

Inter 432/1–2 Soi 9, Siam Square. Honest, efficient Thai restaurant that's popular with students and shoppers, serving good one-dish meals from B50, as well as curries, soups, salads and seafood, in a no-frills, fluorescent-lit canteen atmosphere.

Ma Be Ba 93 Soi Lang Suan ⓣ02 254 9595. Lively, spacious, late-opening Italian restaurant, extravagantly decorated with mosaics in an authentic "grotto" style, which dishes up a good variety of antipasti, excellent pastas (B375 and upwards) and pizzas (in two sizes), and traditional main courses strong on seafood. Live music, mostly pop covers, country and Latin, Mon–Sat eve. Daily noon–3pm & 6pm–midnight.

Mah Boon Krong Shopping Centre Corner of Rama I and Phrayathai roads. Two good food-courts, operating on a coupon system, at the north end of MBK: the long-running area on Floor 6 is a great introduction to Thai food, with English names and pictures of a huge variety of tasty, cheap one-dish meals from all over the country displayed at the various stalls, as well as fresh juices and a wide range of desserts; the slightly upmarket version on Floor 5 is an international affair, spanning India, Italy, Vietnam, China and Japan, plus vegetarian food at *Tamarind Café* and good home-grown cuisine at *Nara Thai*. Both daily 10am–10pm.

Once upon a Time 32 Soi 17, Thanon Phetchaburi ⓣ02 252 8629. The antique, rustic feel of this restaurant verges on the kitsch, but it's a genteel, quiet place, spread across several old wooden houses in a lush compound. And the Thai food, which includes traditional appetizers and desserts and lots of salads, is very good – try the omelette with sweet basil leaves and the pomelo salad. It's halfway down the soi directly opposite Panthip Plaza, on the right.

Pisces 36/6 Soi Kasemsan 1, Thanon Rama I. Drawing plenty of custom from the local guest houses, a friendly, family-run restaurant, neat and colourful, serving a wide variety of breakfasts and cheap, tasty Thai food, with lots of vegetarian options. Daily 8am–1pm & 5–10pm.

Polo Fried Chicken (Kai Thawt Jay Kee Soi Polo) Soi Polo, Thanon Witthayu ⓣ02 655 8489. On the access road to the snobby polo club, Bangkok's most famous purveyor of the ultimate Thai peasant dish, fried chicken. All manner of northeastern dishes, including fish, sausages and loads of salads, fill out the menu, but it would be a bit perverse to come to this basic, air-con restaurant and not have the classic combo of finger-licking chicken (B80 for a half), *som tam* and sticky rice. Daily 7am–10pm.

Thang Long 82/5 Soi Lang Suan ⓣ02 251 3504. Excellent Vietnamese food, such as lemon-grass fish (B215) in this stylish, minimalist and popular restaurant, all stone floors, ornamental plants and whitewashed walls.

Vanilla Brasserie Ground floor, Siam Paragon shopping centre ⓣ02 610 9383. Sophisticated restaurant, patisserie, crêperie, glacier and chocolatier that's a shrine to Western gourmet delights: delicious parma ham and mascarpone crêpes, salads and other main courses, spot-on desserts, and excellent teas and coffees. Their small *Vanilla Industry* café on Siam Square Soi 11 should have reopened by the time you read this. Daily 10am–11pm.

Zen Floor 6 (north end), Central World Plaza ⓣ02 255 6462; Floor 3, MBK shopping centre ⓣ02 620 9007–8; and Floor 4, Siam Centre ⓣ02 658 1183–4. Good-value Japanese restaurant with wacky and colourful modern wooden design and a sushi bar. Among a huge range of dishes, the complete meal sets (with pictures to help you choose) are filling and particularly good. Meanwhile, the recently opened, slightly upmarket *Cucina Zen*, towards the south end of Floor 3, Central World Plaza (ⓣ02 613 1580–1), promises contemporary Japanese cuisine.

Downtown: south of Thanon Rama IV

Two popular groupings of street stalls off Thanon Silom are worth noting: the top end of Thanon Convent and, away to the west opposite the Maha Uma Devi Temple, Soi 20. In this area, there are also branches of *Baan Khanitha* (see p.184) at 69 Thanon Sathorn Tai, at the corner of Soi Suan Phlu (ⓣ02 675 4200–1), and *Zen* (see above), at 1/1 Thanon Convent (ⓣ02 266 7150–1). See the maps on p.123 and p.96 for locations of the places listed below.

Aoi 132/10–11 Soi 6, Thanon Silom ⓣ02 235 2321–2. The best place in town for a Japanese blowout, justifiably popular with the expat community. Excellent authentic food and elegant decor. Good-value lunch sets (from B250) available and a superb sushi bar. *Aoi* also operates two *Ramentei* noodle restaurants in this area, at 11/1 Thanon Suriwong (ⓣ02 235 4326) and 23/8–9 Soi Thaniya (ⓣ02 234 8082).

Ban Chiang 14 Soi Srivieng, off Thanon Surasak, between Thanon Silom and Thanon Sathorn ⓣ02 236 7045. Fine, reasonably priced central and northeastern Thai cuisine in an elegant, surprisingly quiet wooden house with garden tables.

Celadon *Sukhothai Hotel*, 13/3 Thanon Sathorn Tai ⓣ02 344 8888. Consistently rated as one of the best hotel restaurants in Bangkok and a favourite with locals, serving outstanding traditional and contemporary Thai food – try the banana-flower salad and the red curry with chicken rolls and salted egg – in an elegant setting surrounded by lotus ponds.

Chai Karr 312/3 Thanon Silom, opposite *Holiday Inn* ⓣ02 233 2549. Folksy, traditional-style wooden decor is the welcoming setting for a wide variety of well-prepared, modestly priced Thai and Chinese dishes, followed by home-made coconut ice cream. Closed Sun.

Cy'an *Metropolitan Hotel*, 27 Thanon Sathorn Tai ⓣ02 625 3388. Expensive but highly inventive cooking, fusing Asian and Mediterranean (especially North African) elements to produce strong, clean flavours, with great attention to detail. Charming service to go with it, in a stylish room with the best tables on a terrace overlooking the pool.

Deen 761 Thanon Silom, almost opposite Silom Village ⓣ02 635 0441. Small, basic, air-con Muslim café (espresso coffee, but no alcohol), which offers mostly southern Thai and Malay dishes, including spicy Indian-style curries, crispy grouper fish with pepper and garlic, and *roti kaeng* (pancakes with curry).

Eat Me 1/6 Soi Phiphat 2, Thanon Convent ⓣ02 238 0931. Highly fashionable art gallery and restaurant in a striking, white, modernist building, with changing exhibitions on the walls and a temptingly relaxing balcony. The pricey, far-reaching menu is more international – with dishes such as tenderloin steak fillet with Dijon sauce – than fusion, though the lemon-grass *crème brûlée* is not to be missed. Daily 3pm–1am.

Gallery Café 86–100 Soi 30, Thanon Charoen Krung, near Si Phraya express-boat pier ⓣ02 639 5580. At this civilized all-rounder, as well as having a massage and shopping for jewellery and handbags, you can sit down at antique Chinese tables and chairs to enjoy some tasty Thai grub: a wide choice of starters and salads, such as prawn and pomelo (B180), plenty of fish and even *nam phrik*, highly traditional but hard-to-find pastes served with raw green vegetables.

Harmonique 22 Soi 34, Thanon Charoen Krung, on the lane between Wat Muang Kae express-boat pier and the GPO ⓣ02 237 8175. A relaxing, welcoming, moderately priced restaurant that's well worth a trip: tables are scattered throughout several converted shophouses, decorated with antiques and bric-a-brac, and a quiet, leafy courtyard, and the Thai food is varied and excellent – among the seafood specialities, try the crab (B160) or red shrimp (B85) curries. Closed Sun.

Himali Cha-Cha 1229/11 Soi 47/1, Thanon Charoen Krung, south of GPO ⓣ 02 235 1569. Fine, moderately priced North Indian restaurant, founded by a character who was chef to numerous Indian ambassadors, and now run by his son. Homely atmosphere, attentive service and a good vegetarian selection. There's also a branch down a short alley off the north end of Thanon Convent, opposite *Molly Malone's*.

Home Cuisine Islamic Restaurant 186 Soi 36, Thanon Charoen Krung ⓣ 02 234 7911. The short, cheap menu of Indian and southern Thai dishes here has proved popular enough to warrant a spruce refurbishment in green and white, with comfy booths, pot plants and a few outdoor tables overlooking the colonial-style French embassy. The *khao mok kai* (B60), a typical hybrid version of a chicken biryani, served with aubergine curry, is delicious. Closed Sun lunch.

Indian Hut 311/2–5 Thanon Suriwong ⓣ 02 237 8812. Bright, white-tablecloth, North Indian restaurant – look out for the *Pizza Hut*-style sign – that's fairly reasonably priced (mains from B180) and justly popular with local Indians. For carnivores, tandoori's the thing, with especially good kebabs. There's a wide selection of mostly vegetarian appetizers, as well as plenty of veggie main courses and breads, and a hard-to-resist house dahl.

Jim Thompson's Saladaeng Café 120/1 Soi 1, Thanon Saladaeng ⓣ 02 266 9167. A civilized, reasonably priced haven with tables in the elegantly informal air-con interior or out in the leafy garden. Thai food stretches to some unusual dishes such as southern *khao yam*, a refreshing salad of dried cooked rice, dried shrimps and grated coconut with a sweet sauce. There's pasta, salads and other Western dishes, plus a few stabs at fusion including linguini *tom yam kung*. The array of desserts is mouthwatering, rounded off by good coffee and a wide choice of teas. Daily 11am–11pm.

Khrua Aroy Aroy 3/1 Thanon Pan. Aptly named "Delicious, Delicious Kitchen", this simple shophouse restaurant stands out for its choice of inexpensive, tasty, well-prepared dishes from all around the kingdom, notably *khao soi*, *kaeng matsaman* and *khanom jiin*. Lunch only.

La Boulange 2–2/1 Thanon Convent ⓣ 02 631 0354. A fine choice for breakfast with great croissants and all sorts of tempting patisserie made on the premises. For savoury lunches and dinners, choose from a variety of quiches, plates of charcuterie, sandwiches, salads and simple brasserie dishes such as lamb Provençal.

Le Bouchon 37/17 Patpong 2, near Thanon Suriwong ⓣ 02 234 9109. Cosy bar-bistro that's much frequented by the city's French expats, offering French home-cooking, such as lamb shank in a white bean sauce (B580); booking is strongly recommended. Closed Sun lunchtime.

Le Café Siam 4 Soi Sri Akson, Thanon Chua Ploeng ⓣ 02 671 0030, ⓦ www.lecafesiam.com. An early twentieth-century Sino-Thai mansion in a tranquil garden that's difficult to find off the eastern end of Soi Sri Bamphen, but well worth the effort (the restaurant suggests a taxi company, ⓣ 02 611 6499; or you can download a map from their website). The French and Thai food, with main courses starting at B250, is superb, served in a relaxing ambience that subtly blends Chinese and French styles, with an especially seductive bar area upstairs. Eve only.

Le Lys 104 Soi Phra Pinit (Soi 7, Thanon Narathiwat Ratchanakharin) ⓣ 02 287 1898–9. In a large, characterful compound – with an air-con room, outdoor tables under a pergola, a bar and a petanque court – opposite M.R. Kukrit's Heritage Home, the French-Thai owners rustle up excellent, authentic Thai food, supplemented by daily bistro specials such as *assiette de rillettes*.

Mali Soi Jusmag, just off Soi Ngam Duphli ⓣ 02 679 8693. Cosy, informal, low-lit restaurant, mostly air-con with a few cramped tables out front. The Thai menu specializes in salads and northeastern food, with plenty of veggie options, while pricier Western options run as far as burgers (B180), potato salad, all-day breakfasts, delicious banana pancakes and a few Mexican dishes.

Mei Jiang *Peninsula Hotel*, 333 Thanon Charoennakorn, Klongsan ⓣ 02 861 2888. Probably Bangkok's best Chinese restaurant, with beautiful views of the hotel's riverside gardens night and day, and very attentive and graceful staff. Cantonese specialities include delicious teas, lobster rolls, smoked duck with tea and excellent lunchtime dim sum such as crystal prawn dumplings – a bargain, starting at B80 a dish.

Ratree Seafood Soi 1, Thanon Silom, opposite Soi Thaniya. Famous and popular streetside stall in the heart of the urban maelstrom, with half a dozen tables on the Silom pavement and down the soi behind. The *rot khen* (pushcart kitchen), laden with glistening seafood and even a small water tank for giant shrimp, rolls up about 6pm and barbecues away until around midnight.

Ruen Urai *Rose Hotel*, 118 Thanon Suriwong ⓣ 02 266 8268–72. Set back behind the hotel, this peaceful, hundred-year-old, traditional house, with fine balcony tables overlooking the beautiful hotel pool, comes as a welcome surprise in this full-on downtown area. And the varied Thai food is of a high quality (though you can forget the house wine): try the *tom khlong talay* (B200) and don't be misled by the name –"seafood canal soup" – it's a delicious, refined, spicy and sour soup from the northeast, with tamarind juice and herbs.

Sarah Jane's 55/21 Thanon Narathiwat Ratchanakharin, between sois 4 & 6 ⓣ02 676 3338–9. Long-standing restaurant, popular with Bangkok's Isaan population, serving excellent, simple north-eastern dishes, including a huge array of *nam tok* (B85), *laap* and *som tam*, as well as Italian food.

Somboon Seafood Thanon Suriwong, corner of Thanon Narathiwat Ratchanakharin ⓣ02 234 4499. Highly favoured, bustling seafood restaurant, known for its crab curry (B250) and soy-steamed sea bass, with simple, functional, modern decor and an array of marine life lined up in tanks outside awaiting its gastronomic fate. Daily 4–11.30pm.

Taling Pling 60 Thanon Pan ⓣ02 234 4872. One of the best Thai restaurants in the city outside of the big hotels, specializing in classic dishes from the four corners of the kingdom. The house deep-fried fish salad (B120) is delicious and refreshing, while the toothsome, deeply flavoured green beef curry with roti (B155) is recommended by the leading Thai restaurant guides. The atmosphere's convivial and relaxing, too.

Thien Duong *Dusit Thani Hotel*, corner of Silom and Rama IV roads ⓣ02 236 9999. Probably Bangkok's finest Vietnamese, a classy and expensive restaurant serving beautifully prepared dishes such as succulent *salat cua*, deep-fried soft-shell crab salad with cashew nuts and herb dressing, and zesty *goi ngo sen*, lotus-stem salad with shrimp and pork.

Tongue Thai 18–20 Soi 38, Thanon Charoen Krung ⓣ02 630 9918–9. In front of the Oriental Place shopping mall. Very high standards of food and cleanliness, with charming, unpretentious service, in a hundred-year-old shophouse elegantly decorated with Thai and Chinese antiques and contemporary art. Veggies are very well catered for with delicious dishes such as tofu in black bean sauce and deep-fried banana-flower and corn cakes, while carnivores should try the fantastic beef curry (*panaeng neua*; B170).

Thanon Sukhumvit

In this area, there are also branches of the sushi restaurant *Aoi* (see p.182), Floor 4, Emporium shopping centre (ⓣ02 664 8590), and the North Indian *Himali Cha-Cha* (see p.183), on Soi 31 (ⓣ02 259 6677). For dessert heaven take a stroll around the fifth-floor foodstalls in the Emporium, which overflows with luscious gateaux, gelati, mango surprises and other blissful sweets. For those restaurants east of sois 39 and 26 that are not shown on the map, we've given directions from the nearest Skytrain station. See the map on p.127 for locations of the places listed below.

Al Ferdoss Soi 3/1. Long-running Lebanese and Turkish restaurant in the heart of Sukhumvit's Middle Eastern soi, where you can smoke hookah pipes on the streetside terrace and choose from a menu (B80–200) that encompasses shish, hummus, tabbouleh and the rest.

Baan Khanitha 36/1 Soi 23 ⓣ02 258 4128. The big attraction at this long-running favourite haunt of Sukhumvit expats is the setting in a traditional Thai house. The food is upmarket Thai and fairly pricey, and includes lots of fiery salads (*yam*), and a good range of *tom yam* soups, green curries and seafood curries. Most mains cost B190–490.

Bangkok Baking Company Ground Floor, *JW Marriott Hotel*, between sois 2 and 4. Exceptionally delicious cakes, pastries and breads: everything from rosemary focaccia to tiramisu cheesecake (B65–120). Daily 6am–11pm.

Basil *Sheraton Grande Hotel*, between sois 12 and 14 ⓣ02 649 8888. Mouthwateringly fine traditional Thai food with a modern twist is the order of the day at this trendy, relatively informal though high-priced restaurant in the deluxe five-star *Sheraton*. Recommendations include the grilled river prawns with chilli, the *matsaman* curry (both served with red and green rice) and the surprisingly delicious durian cheesecake. Vegetarian menu on request.

Cabbages and Condoms 6–8 Soi 12 ⓦwww.pda.or.th/restaurant. The Population and Community Development Association of Thailand (PDA; see p.169) runs this restauarnt – "our food is guaranteed not to cause pregnancy" – so diners are treated to authentic Thai food in the Condom Room, and relaxed scoffing of barbecued seafood in the rainforest beer-garden. Try the spicy catfish salad (B130) or the prawns steamed in a whole coconut (B250). All proceeds go to the PDA, and there's an adjacent shop selling double-entendre T-shirts, cards, key rings and of course, condoms.

Dosa King Soi 11/1 ⓦwww.dosaking.net. Usually busy with expat Indian diners, this vegetarian Indian restaurant serves good food from both north and south, including twenty different dosa (southern pancake) dishes, tandooris and the like. It's an alcohol-free zone so you'll have to make do with sweet lassi instead. Most dishes B100–180.

Face Bangkok: La Na Thai and Hazara 29 Soi 38, about 150m walk from BTS Thong Lo Exit 4 ⓣ 02 713 6048, ⓦ www.facebars.com. Two restaurants, a bar, a bakery and a spa occupy this attractive compound of traditional, steeply gabled wooden Thai houses. Each restaurant is tastefully styled with appropriate artefacts and fabrics, and the adjacent *Face Bar* makes a chic 'n' funky place for a pre- or post-dinner drink. The very upmarket *Lan Na Thai* restaurant (daily 11.30am–2.30pm & 6.30–11.30pm) serves quality Thai food such as Chiang Mai-style pork curry and deep-fried grouper with tamarind sauce (mains from B400), while the *Hazara* (daily 6.30–11.30pm) specializes in Afghani and North -Indian tandoor cuisine, including murgh Peshawar chicken and the signature cardamom - marinated lamb (B400 and up).

Gaeng Pa Lerd Rod Soi 33/1, no English sign but it's just before the *Bull's Head*. Hugely popular outdoor restaurant whose tables are clustered under trees in a streetside yard and get packed with office workers at lunchtime. Thai curries (from B50) are the speciality here, with dishes ranging from conventional versions, like catfish and beef curries, to more adventurous offerings like fried cobra with chilli, and curried frog.

Gallery 11 Soi 11. Sharing the traffic-free sub-soi with the idiosyncratic *Suk 11* guest house, this restaurant also re-creates an atmosphere of old-fashioned village Thailand, with its wooden building, plentiful foliage, lamplight and staff dressed in late nineteenth-century fashions. The food is good, authentic, mid-priced Thai (mostly B100–200), with plenty of spicy *yam* salads, delicious chicken *larb*, tasty *phanaeng* curry plus Thai desserts, cocktails and imported wines by the glass. It all adds up to a special occasion ambience, but without the pretension or high prices of its better known competitors.

Le Dalat Indochine 14 Soi 23 ⓣ 02 661 7967. There's Indochinese romance aplenty at this delightful early twentieth-century villa decked out in homely style with plenty of photos, pot plants and eclectic curiosities. The extensive Vietnamese menu (B250–1200) features favourites such as a *goi ca* salad of aromatic herbs and shredded pork, *chao tom* shrimp sticks and *ga sa gung*, chicken curry with caramelized ginger.

MahaNaga 2 Soi 29 ⓦ www.mahanaga.com. The dining experience at this tranquil enclave is best appreciated after dark, when the fountain-courtyard tables are romantically lit and the air-con interior seduces with its burgundy velvet drapes. Cuisine is fusion fine-dining, though some east–west combos work better than others and the vegetarian selection is underwhelming. Grilled salmon in red curry is a winner, or you might brave the rack of lamb served with spicy vegetables, egg noodles and mango sauce. Set lunch B250; à la carte mains B400–600.

Spring Summer Winter 199 Soi Promsri 1, about 15min walk from BTS Phrom Pong, 700m north up Soi 39 then 350m east along Soi Promsri 1 ⓣ 02 392 2747, ⓦ www.springnsummer.com. A fashionable three-in-one experience occupying a pair of chic twentieth-century modern buildings set round a grassy lawn in a residential soi. *Spring* (daily 11.30am–2.30am & 6–11pm) serves delicious Thai and Japanese fusion cuisine – scrumptiously tangy pomelo and wingbean salad, fried rice with seared salmon and avocado (B290), snow fish with sweet tandoori sauce; *Summer* (midday–midnight) indulges chocoholics with all manner of treats from frozen forest gateaux to cheesecakes and chocolate hotpots; and *Winter* (7pm–midnight, weather permitting) sets up a bar on the lawn in between, with food from *Spring* and *Summer*, and lounging cushions.

Suda Restaurant Soi 14. Unpretentious shophouse restaurant whose formica tables and plastic chairs spill out onto the soi and are mainly patronized by budget-conscious expats and their Thai friends. The friendly proprietor serves a good, long menu of Thai favourites (mostly B50–80), including deep-fried chicken in banana leaves, battered shrimps, fried tuna with cashews and chilli, and sticky rice with mango. Mon–Sat 11am–midnight, Sun 4pm–midnight.

Vientiane Kitchen (Khrua Vientiane) 8 Soi 36, about 50m south off Thanon Sukhumvit. Just a 3min walk west then south from BTS Thong Lo (Exit 2) and you're transported into a little piece of Isaan, where the menu's stocked full of northeastern delicacies, a live band sets the mood with heart-felt folk songs, and there are even occasional performances by a troupe of upcountry dancers. The Lao- and Isaan-accented menu (B120–300) includes vegetable curry with ants' eggs, spicy-fried frog, jackfruit curry, and farm chicken with cashews, plus there's a decent range of veggie options such as meat-free *larb* and sweet and sour dishes. With its airy, barn-like interior and mixed clientele of Thais and expats, it's a very enjoyable dining experience.

Nightlife and entertainment

For many of Bangkok's male visitors, nightfall is the signal to hit the city's sex bars, most notoriously in the area off the east end of Thanon Silom known as Patpong (see p.169). Fortunately, Bangkok's **nightlife** has thoroughly grown up and left these neon sumps behind in the past ten years, offering everything from microbreweries and vertiginous, roof-top cocktail bars to fiercely chic clubs and dance bars, hosting top-class DJs: within spitting distance of the beer bellies flopped onto Patpong's bars, for example, lies Soi 4, Thanon Silom, one of the city's most happening after-dark haunts. Along with Silom 4, the high-concept clubs and bars of Sukhumvit and the lively, teeming venues of Banglamphu pull in the style-conscious cream of Thai youth and are tempting an increasing number of travellers to stuff their party gear into their rucksacks. Though Silom 4 started out as a purely **gay** area, it now offers a range of styles in gay, mixed and straight pubs, DJ bars and clubs, while the city's other main gay area is the more exclusive Silom 2 (towards Thanon Rama IV).

Most bars and clubs **open** nightly until 1am, while clubs on Silom 4 and Silom 2 can stay open until 2am. In the past few years, there have been regular "social order" clampdowns by the police, strictly enforcing these closing times, conducting occasional urine tests for drugs on bar customers, and setting up widespread ID checks to curb under-age drinking (you have to be 20 or over to drink in bars and clubs). However, at the time of writing, probably partly due to the political turmoil, things were much more chilled, with clubs staying open into the wee hours on busy nights and little sign of ID checks. It's hard to predict how the situation might develop, but you'll soon get an idea of how the wind is blowing when you arrive in Bangkok – and there's little harm in taking your passport out with you, just in case.

On the cultural front, the most accessible of the capital's performing arts are **Thai dancing**, particularly when served up in bite-size portions in tourist shows, and the graceful and humorous performances at the **Traditional Thai Puppet Theatre**. **Thai boxing** is also well worth watching: the raucous live experience at either of Bangkok's two main national stadia far outshines the TV coverage.

For something unclassifiably different, how about turbo-cool **bowling** at SF Strike Bowl, at the Rama I end of Floor 7 in the MBK Shopping Centre (Sun–Thurs 10am–1am, Fri & Sat 10am–2pm; ⓣ02 611 4555)? Designed by the same team as *Bed Supperclub* (see p.190), the alleys glow with luminous purple, blue and green and thump to the sounds of a DJ. There are pool tables, a bar and karaoke, and you can even book a VIP lounge with two lanes from just B600 per hr.

Bars and clubs

The travellers' enclave of **Banglamphu** takes on a new personality after dark, when its hub, Thanon Khao San, becomes a "walking street", closed to all traffic but open to almost any kind of makeshift stall, selling everything from fried bananas and buckets of "very strong" cocktails to share, to bargain fashions and one-off artworks. Young Thais crowd the area to browse and snack before piling in to Banglamphu's more stylish bars and indie live-music clubs, most of which are free to enter (though some ask you to show ID first).

Downtown, there's a small knot of bars popular with both foreigners and Thais on Soi Sarasin (along the north side of Lumphini Park), as well as a larger concentration around the east end of Thanon Silom. Sarasin's western end (between *Brown Sugar* and Thanon Rajdamri) supports a gaggle of good-time, gay and straight, DJ bars such as the *Seventies Bar* that heave at weekends. On Silom 4, while most of the gay venues have been around for some years now, other bars and clubs have opened and closed with bewildering speed. All the same, on a short, slow bar-crawl around this wide, traffic-free alley lined with pavement tables, it would be hard not to find somewhere to enjoy yourself. If, among all the choice of nightlife around Silom, you do end up in one of Patpong's sex shows, watch out for hyper-inflated bar bills and other cons – plenty of customers get ripped off in some way, and stories of menacing bouncers are legion. A night out on **Thanon Sukhumvit** could also be subsumed by the girlie bars and hostess-run bar-beers (open-sided drinking halls with huge circular bars) on sois Nana and Cowboy, but there's plenty of style on Sukhumvit too, especially in the rooftop bars and enjoyably trendy clubs.

During the cool season (Nov–Feb), an evening out at one of the seasonal **beer gardens** is a pleasant way of soaking up the urban atmosphere (and the traffic fumes). You'll find them in hotel forecourts or sprawled in front of dozens of shopping centres all over the city, most notably Central World Plaza.

Getting back to your lodgings should be no problem in the small hours: many bus routes run a (reduced) service throughout the night, and tuk-tuks and taxis are always at hand – though it's probably best for unaccompanied women to avoid using tuk-tuks late at night.

Banglamphu and Ratanakosin

Except where indicated, all bars listed below are marked on the map on p.112.

Ad Here the 13th 13 Thanon Samsen. Relaxed, sociable little neighbourhood live-music joint where half-a-dozen tables of Thai and expat musos congregate to listen to nightly sets from the in-house blues 'n' jazz quartet (from 10pm onwards). Well-priced beer and plenty of cocktails. Daily 6pm–midnight.

Bangkok Bar Next to *Sawasdee Inn* at 149 Soi Ram Bhuttri ⓦwww.bkkbar.com. Small, dark, tastefully furnished air-con bar-restaurant whose DJs and live indie-rock bands – including occasional big-name appearances – are popular with young Thais and can be a fun introduction to the neighbourhood live-music scene. Daily 6pm–1am.

Bar Bali 58 Thanon Phra Arthit. Typical Phra Arthit bar-restaurant, with just a handful of tables, a small menu of drinking foods and a decent selection of well-priced cocktails. Live music from student singer-songwriters (usually one rather soulful man and his guitar) most nights. Daily 6pm–1am.

Brick Bar *Buddy Village* complex, 265 Thanon Khao San ⓦwww.brickbarkhaosan.com. Massive red-brick vault of a live-music bar whose regular roster of reggae, ska and blues bands, and occasional one-off appearances, are hugely popular with Thai twenty-somethings and teens. Big, sociable tables are set right under the stage and there's food too. The biggest nights are Fridays and Saturdays when there's a B150 entry charge, which includes one free drink. Daily 7pm–1am.

Café Democ 78 Thanon Rajdamnoen Klang ⓦwww.cafe-democ.com. Fashionable, dark and dinky bar that overlooks Democracy Monument and is spread over one and a half cosy floors, with extra seating on the semi circular mezzanine. Lots of cocktails, nightly sessions from up-and-coming Thai DJs, and regular trance, techno, house and progressive nights. Tues–Sun 4pm–2am.

The Club 123 Thanon Khao San ⓦwww.theclubkhaosan.com. High ceilings, a central DJ station spinning mostly house music and an intimate dancefloor encircled by tables draw a sophisticated young Thai and international crowd. Free entry except for special events when one free drink is included in the B300–500 ticket. Daily 8pm–1am.

Gulliver's Traveler's Tavern Thanon Khao San ⓦwww.gulliverbangkok.com. Infamous, long-established tourist-oriented air-con pub with pool tables, sports TV, reasonably priced beer (happy hours often till 10pm) and a reputation for being something of a pick-up joint. Has a branch on Thanon Sukhumvit. Daily 11am–1am.

Hippie de Bar 46 Thanon Khao San. Invitingly mellow courtyard bar set away from the main fray near *Tom Yam Kung* restaurant. Attracts an indie, mostly Thai crowd, to drink cocktails (B120) and 3.5-litre towers of draft

Heineken (B500) at its wrought-iron tables and artily mismatched furniture. Cool sounds too. Daily 6pm–2am.

Po 230 Tha Thien, Thanon Maharat (see map, p.129). When the Chao Phraya express boats start to wind down around 6pm, this bar takes over the rustic wooden pier and the balcony above with their great sunset views across the river to Wat Arun. It's popular with local students and office workers, hence the loud Thai pop music; avoid the food in favour of beer and Thai whisky.

Susie Pub On the soi between Thanon Khao San and Thanon Ram Bhuttri. Big, dark, phenomenally popular pub that's often standing-room-only on weekend nights. Has a pool table, cheapish beer and DJs playing mainstream pop and generally gets a mixed crowd of farang and Thais. Daily 11am–1am; ID sometimes required.

Siam Square, Thanon Ploenchit and northern downtown

See the map on p.120 for locations of the venues listed below.

Brown Sugar 231/19–20 Soi Sarasin ⓣ02 250 1826. Tightly packed, pricey and atmospheric bar, with a certain crumpled chic, acknowledged as the capital's top jazz venue, with a popular Sunday-night jam session.

Club Culture 346/29 Thanon Sri Ayutthaya, opposite *Siam City Hotel* ⓦwww.club-culture-bkk.com. Huge, attractive former ballroom that's handy for Phaya Thai Skytrain station and trendy amongst Thais and expats. A roster of international and local DJs play house, electronica, trance, drum'n'bass, depending on the night. Tues–Sun 9pm–2am. B400 including two drinks.

Saxophone 3/8 Victory Monument (southeast corner), Thanon Phrayathai ⓣ02 246 5472, ⓦwww.saxophonepub.com. Lively, easy-going, spacious venue with decent Thai and Western food and a diverse roster of bands – mostly jazz (Mon–Thurs) and blues (Fri–Sun), plus acoustic guitar, funk, rock and reggae – which attracts a good mix of Thais and foreigners.

Syn Bar *Swissôtel Nai Lert Park*, 2 Thanon Witthayu. Hip hotel bar, popular at weekends, decorated retro style with bubble chairs and sparkling fibre-optic carpet. Excellent cocktails, including a mean Wasabi Mary, and DJs playing house and Latin.

The Tunnel Soi Lang Suan, behind *Ma Be Ba* restaurant. The after-hours club of the moment, though it suffers from sporadic police clampdowns, hence the dimly lit entrance. Like the restaurant, decor is grotto-like with a riot of mosaics; music policy is strictly electro and house. Open 10pm till 3–5am or later, depending on the constabulary, busy after 1am. Sun–Thurs free, Fri & Sat B500 including two drinks.

Southern downtown: south of Thanon Rama IV

See the map on p.123 for locations of the venues listed below.

The Barbican 9/4–5 Soi Thaniya, east end of Thanon Silom ⓣ02 233 4141–2. Stylishly modern fortress-like decor to match the name: dark woods, metal and undressed stone. With Guinness on tap and a long menu of imported beers, it could almost be a smart City of London pub – until you look out of the windows onto the soi's incongruous Japanese hostess bars. Good food, DJ sessions Tues & Fri and happy hours Mon–Fri 4–7pm.

Lucifer 76/1–3 Patpong 1. Popular dance club playing trance, techno and house in the dark heart of Patpong, largely untouched by the sleaze around it. Done out with mosaics and stalactites like a satanic grotto, with balconies to look down on the dancefloor action. Free entry on quiet nights, B150 including one drink when busy. *Radio City*, the interconnected bar downstairs, is only slightly less raucous, with jumping live bands, including famous Elvis and Tom Jones impersonators, and tables out on the sweaty pavement.

Molly Malone's 1/5 Thanon Convent, off the east end of Thanon Silom ⓣ02 266 7160. Blarney Bangkok-style: a popular Irish pub, tastefully done out in dark wood and leather and packed with expats, especially on Friday night. Guinness, Kilkenny Bitter, Hoegaarden and Leffe on tap (happy hours 4–7pm), expensive food such as Irish stew, and beef and Guinness pie, TV sports and live cover bands Mon–Sat.

Noriega's Soi 4, Thanon Silom. Unpretentious, good-time bar at the end of the alley, with nightly live bands (blues, rock or acoustic, including open mike on Thurs) or DJs. Regular salsa nights; happy hour all night Mon & Tues, till 9pm Wed–Sun.

O'Reilly's Corner of Silom and Thaniya roads. Welcoming Irish bar that's especially good for watching TV sport. Guinness and Kilkenny bitter on draught, multifarious drinks offers including 4–7pm happy hours, popular food and varied live music Tues–Sat eve.

Parkbridge Patpong 2 Ⓦwww.theparkbridge.com. An extraordinary setting in a glass-walled bridge two floors above the sleazy soi, and decor that melds imperial kitsch and urban art styles – think graffiti and silver antlers – mark out this French-run bar-disco. Throw in a 6–9pm happy hour and an imaginative menu of DJs (after 9pm) stretching from Japanese (Wed) to bring-your-own (Sun), and you might find yourself still there at closing time (currently 3am-ish weekdays, 5am weekends).

The Sky Bar & Distil Floor 63, State Tower, 1055 Thanon Silom, corner of Thanon Charoen Krung Ⓣ02 624 9555. Thrill-seekers and view addicts shouldn't miss forking out for an al fresco drink here, 275m above the city's pavements – come around 6pm to enjoy the stunning panoramas in both the light and the dark. It's standing-only at *The Sky Bar*, a circular restaurant-bar on the edge of the building with almost 360° views, but for the sunset itself, you're better off on the outside terrace of *Distil* on the other side of the building (where bookings are accepted), which has a wider choice of drinks, charming service and huge couches to recline on.

Tapas Bar Soi 4, Thanon Silom. Vaguely Spanish-oriented, pricey bar (but no tapas) with Moorish-style decor, whose outside tables are probably the best spot for checking out the comings and goings on the soi; inside, music ranges from house and hip-hop to Latin jazz and funk. Fri & Sat admission B100, Sun free, Mon–Thurs B200 including 1 drink.

Tawandang German Brewery 462/61 Thanon Rama III Ⓣ02 678 1114–6. A taxi-ride south of Thanon Sathorn down Thanon Narathiwat Ratchanakharin – and best to book a table in advance – this vast all-rounder is well worth the effort. Under a huge dome, up to 1600 revellers enjoy good food and great micro-brewed beer every night. Sunday sees cover bands, but the main attraction from Monday to Saturday is the mercurial live music and cabaret, featuring Fong Naam, led by Bruce Gaston, who blend Thai classical and popular with Western styles of music.

Unico Hotel Roof Garden Thanon Silom, opposite Thanon Decho. Budget version of Bangkok's famous roof-top bar-restaurants, at lower altitude (only the 19th floor) but with much lower prices – and with few skyscrapers in the immediate vicinity, the city panorama is still pretty special. Fairy lights, patches of lawn and occasional live music complete the picture.

Thanon Sukhumvit

Many clubs in Sukhumvit require you to show ID when you enter, to prove that you are 20 or over. See the map on p.127 for locations of the venues listed below.

▲ Views of Bangkok from *The Sky Bar*

The Ball in Hand Basement of Times Square, between sois 12 and 14. A vast and professionally managed pool hall and bar that stands out because of its high-quality imported tables, its strict no-hustle policy and its regular competitions. Daily about 1pm–1am.

Bed Supperclub 26 Soi 11 ⓣ02 651 3537, ⓦwww.bedsupperclub.com. Worth visiting for the futuristic visuals alone, this seductively curvaceous space-pod bar is still the top nightspot in this happening soi. Inside, the all-white interior is dimly lit and surprisingly cosy, with deep couches inviting drinkers to recline around the edges of the upstairs gallery, getting a good view of the downstairs bar and DJ. The vibe is always welcoming and a lot less pretentious than you might expect; some nights are themed, including a weekly gay night. The cover charge (B700 after 9pm on Wed, Fri & Sat, B600 other nights) is redeemable against two drinks. The restaurant section is starker, lit with glacial ultra-violet, and serving a Pacific Rim fusion menu 7.30–9pm (reservations essential). Bar daily 8pm–2am; ID required.

The Bull's Head Soi 33/1. A Sukhumvit institution that takes pride in being Bangkok's most authentic British pub, right down to the horse brasses, jukebox and typical pub food. Famous for its Sunday-evening "toss the boss" happy hours (5–7pm), when a flip of a coin determines whether or not you have to pay for your round. Happy hour Mon–Sat 4–7pm. Daily 11am–1.30am.

Cheap Charlie's Soi 11. Idiosyncratic, long-running, low-tech, open-air pavement bar that's famous for its cheap beer, customers' hall-of-fame gallery and lack of tables and chairs. A few lucky punters get to occupy the bar -stools but otherwise it's sidewalk standing room only. Mon–Sat 5.30pm–12.30am.

Gulliver's Traveler's Tavern 6 Soi 5 ⓦwww.gulliverbangkok.com. An offshoot of the original Khao San sports bar, this cavernous branch has tables inside and out where you can down draught Guinness (happy hour lasts from kickoff until 7pm) and nosh your way through the international menu. Shows live sporting fixtures and has table football, pool tables and internet access. Daily 10.30am–1am.

Londoner Brew Pub Mouth of Soi 33 ⓦwww.the-londoner.com. Aside from the pool table, darts board, big-screen sports TV and live music (nightly from about 9pm), it's the specially brewed pints of Londoner's Pride Cream Bitter and London Pilsner 33 that draw in the punters. Happy hour 4–7pm. Free wi-fi. Daily 11am–1am.

Long Table 25th Floor, Column Tower, 48 Soi 16. This achingly fashionable 25th-floor restaurant is named for its thirty-metre-long communal centrepiece table, which seats seventy and serves contemporary Thai cuisine. But the real attraction is the sleek, Shanghai-style open-sided balcony bar whose "long-tail" cocktails give you ample time to lounge glamorously on the leather sofas and soak up the wraparound panoramas across downtown skyscrapers. Daily midday–1am.

Nest 9th Floor, *Le Fenix* hotel, Soi 11. Whether you unfurl on a daybed, curl up in a basket - chair or recline under a hooded chaise longue at this aptly named rooftop eyrie you'll get an airy view of the condo-spiked skyline (there are covers for wet days) and a decent choice of cocktails (mostly B300) plus a few light meals. Not as slick or spectacular as the more famous downtown sky bars but very pleasant. Nightly 5pm–1am.

Q Bar 34 Soi 11 ⓦwww.qbarbangkok.com. Very dark, very trendy, New York-style bar occupying two floors and a terrace. Famous for its wide choice of chilled vodkas, and for its music, *Q Bar* appeals to a mixed crowd of fashionable people, particularly on Fri and Sat nights when the DJs fill the dancefloor. Arrive before 11pm if you want a seat, and don't turn up in shorts, singlets or sandals if you're male. Sun–Thurs B500 including two free drinks, Fri & Sat B700. Daily 8pm–1am; ID required.

Gay Bangkok

The bars, clubs and café-restaurants listed here, mostly at the east end of Thanon Silom, are the most notable of Bangkok's gay nightlife venues; *Bed Supperclub* (see above) also hosts a regular gay night. For more general background on gay life in Thailand, contacts and sources of information, most of them concentrated in Bangkok, see p.76. Don't forget **Bangkok Pride** (ⓦwww.bangkokpride.org) in November, when the capital's GLBT community struts its stuff in a week of parades, cabarets, fancy-dress shows and sports contests.

The Balcony Soi 4, Thanon Silom. Unpretentious, fun place with plenty of outdoor seats for people-watching, welcoming staff, reasonably priced drinks, karaoke and decent Thai and Western food.

Coffee Society 12/3 Thanon Silom, between sois 2 and 2/1. Gay-friendly, 24hr coffee shop and restaurant with cosy booths and free wi-fi.

Dick's Café Duangthawee Plaza, 894/7–8 Soi Pratuchai, Thanon Suriwong ⓣ02 637 0078, ⓦwww.dickscafe.com. Stylish day-and-night café-bar-restaurant (daily 10.30am–2am), hung with exhibitions by gay artists, on a traffic-free soi of go-go bars opposite the prominent Wall St Tower, ideal for drinking, eating decent Thai and Western food or just chilling out.

Disco Disco Soi 2, Thanon Silom. Small, pared-down bar-disco with a minimalist, retro feel, playing good dance music to a fun young crowd.

DJ Station Soi 2, Thanon Silom. Highly fashionable but unpretentious three-storey club, packed at weekends, attracting a mix of Thais and farangs; cabaret show nightly at 11.30pm. B100 including one drink (B200 including two drinks Fri & Sat).

GOD (Guys on Display) 60/18–21 Soi 2/1, Thanon Silom, in a small soi between Soi Thaniya and Soi 2. Large, busy club, somewhat more Thai-oriented and with later hours (till 3–6am) than *DJ Station*; occasional cabaret shows. B140 including one drink before 1am, B280 including two drinks. *Richard's* next door is a smart bar-restaurant that's open till 2am.

JJ Park 8/3 Soi 2, Thanon Silom. Classy, Thai-oriented bar, for relaxed socializing rather than raving, with nightly singers and cabaret acts, and a chill-out annexe, *Club Café*, next door.

Sphinx 98–104 Soi 4, Thanon Silom ⓣ02 234 7249. Plush decor with a vaguely Egyptian theme, terrace seating and very good Thai and Western food attract a sophisticated crowd to this ground-floor bar and restaurant; karaoke upstairs at *Pharoah's*.

Telephone Pub 114/11–13 Soi 4, Thanon Silom. Bangkok's first Western-style gay bar when it opened in 1987, this cruisey, dimly lit eating and drinking venue has a terrace on the alley, telephones on the tables inside for making new friends and karaoke upstairs.

Culture shows and performing arts

Because of the language barrier, most Thai theatre is inaccessible to foreigners and so, with a few exceptions, the best way to experience the traditional **performing arts** is at shows designed for tourists, most notably at **Siam Niramit** and the **Traditional Thai Puppet Theatre**. Many tourist restaurants offer low-tech versions of the Siam Niramit experience, in the form of nightly **culture shows** – usually a hotchpotch of Thai dancing and classical music, with a martial-arts demonstration thrown in; it's always worth calling ahead to reserve, especially if you want a vegetarian version of the set menu. You can, however, witness Thai dancing being performed for its original ritual purpose, usually several times a day, at the Lak Muang Shrine behind the Grand Palace (see p.139) and the Erawan Shrine on the corner of Thanon Ploenchit (see p.164). For background on Thai classical dance and traditional theatre, see p.67.

More glitzy and occasionally ribald entertainment is the order of the day at the capital's two **ladyboy cabaret shows**, where a bevy of luscious transvestites dons glamorous outfits and performs over-the-top song-and-dance routines: Mambo Cabaret plays at the theatre in Washington Square, between Sukhumvit sois 22 and 24 (ⓣ02 259 5715; nightly 8pm; Nov–Feb also at 10pm; B800); and New Calypso Cabaret performs inside the *Asia Hotel*, on the west side of Ratchathevi Skytrain station at 296 Thanon Phrayathai (ⓣ02 216 8937, ⓦwww.calypsocabaret.com; nightly 8.15 & 9.45pm; B1000 or half-price if booked online 5 days ahead).

National Theatre Sanam Luang, Ratanakosin ⓣ02 224 1342 or 02 222 1012. Closed for a lengthy renovation at the time of writing, but has in the past staged roughly weekly shows of music, *lakhon* (classical dance-drama) and *likay* (folk drama), monthly medley shows, plus outdoor shows of classical music and dancing at the National Museum on dry-season weekends – try the nearby Bangkok Tourism Division for the latest information (see p.102).

Patravadi Theatre 69/1 Soi Wat Rakhang, Thonburi ⓣ02 412 7287, ⓦwww.patravaditheatre.com; free shuttle-boat transport from Tha Maharaj in front of Wat Mahathat. Highly regarded, experimental, contemporary theatre company rooted in the traditional arts, who stage a dinner-theatre experience at their riverside restaurant *Studio 9* (Fri & Sat 7.30pm; à la carte menu). They also run classes in classical dance and other disciplines, some of which are accessible to non-Thai speakers.

Bangkok for kids

The following theme parks and amusement centres are all designed for kids, the main drawbacks being that many are located a long way from the city centre. Other attractions kids should enjoy include the Museum of Siam (see p.139), Siam Ocean World aquarium (see p.164), Dusit Zoo (see p.159), the Snake Farm (see p.167), cycling around Muang Boran Ancient City (see p.176), feeding the turtles at Wat Prayoon (see p.157), pedal-boating in Lumphini Park (see p.167), and the Traditional Thai Puppet Theatre (see p.193). For general tips on kids' Thailand, see p.78.

Bangkok Butterfly Garden and Insectarium In Suan Rotfai (Railway Park), just north of Chatuchak Weekend Market (Tues–Sun 8.30am–4.30pm; free; ⓣ02 272 4359). Over 500 butterflies flutter within an enormous landscaped dome. There's also a study centre, plus family-oriented cycle routes and bikes for rent in the adjacent park, which also has a kids' playpark. BTS Mo Chit or Chatuchak Park subway.

Children's Discovery Museum Opposite Chatuchak Weekend Market on Thanon Kamphaeng Phet 4 (Tues–Fri 9am–5pm, Sat & Sun 10am–6pm; B150, kids B120; ⓣ02 615 7333). Interactive and hands-on zones covering science, the environment, human and animal life. BTS Mo Chit or Chatuchak Park subway.

Dream World Ten minutes' drive north of Don Muang Airport at kilometre-stone 7 Thanon Rangsit-Ongharak (Mon–Fri 10am–5pm, Sat & Sun 10am–7pm; B120, children B95; ⓣ02 533 1152, ⓦwww.dreamworld-th.com). Theme park with different areas such as Snow Land, Dream Garden and Adventure Land. Water rides, a hanging coaster and other amusements. Non-air-con buses #39 and #59 from Rajdamnoen Klang in Banglamphu to Rangsit, then songthaew or tuk-tuk to Dream World; or bus, Skytrain or subway to Mo Chit/Chatuchak Park, then air-con bus #523.

Safari World On the northeastern outskirts at 99 Thanon Ramindra, Minburi (daily 9am–4.30pm; joint ticket to both parks B700, children B450; ⓣ02 518 1000, ⓦwww.safariworld.com). Drive-through safari park, with monkeys, lions, giraffes and zebras, and separate marine park with dolphins and sea lions. Both stage animal shows (phone for times). If you don't have your own car, you can be driven through the park in a Safari World coach. Take air-con bus #60 from Rajdamnoen Klang in Banglamphu or air-con #26 from Victory Monument, then a songthaew to Safari World.

Siam Park On the far eastern edge of town at 101 Thanon Sukhapiban 2 (daily 10am–6pm; B400, children B300; ⓣ02 919 7200, ⓦwww.siamparkcity.com). Waterslides, whirlpools and artificial surf, plus roller coasters, a small zoo and a botanical garden. Air-con bus #60 from Rajdamnoen Klang in Banglamphu or air-con #501/#1 from Hualamphong Station.

Sala Chalermkrung 66 Thanon Charoen Krung, on the intersection with Thanon Triphet in Pahurat, next to Old Siam Plaza ⓣ02 224 4499, ⓦwww.salachalermkrung.com. Mainstream traditional and contemporary theatre, plus regular *khon* performances with English subtitles (Fri & Sat 7.30pm; from B1000).

Siam Niramit Cultural Extravaganza Ratchada Theatre, 19 Thanon Tiam Ruammit, 5min walk from Thailand Cultural Centre subway, following signs for the South Korean embassy (see map, p.109) ⓣ02 649 9222, ⓦwww.siamniramit.com. Unashamedly tourist-oriented but the easiest place to get a glimpse of the variety and spectacle intrinsic to traditional Thai theatre. The 80min show presents a history of regional Thailand's culture and beliefs in a high-tech spectacular of fantastic costumes and huge chorus numbers, enlivened by acrobatics and flashy special effects. Daily 8pm; B1500; tickets can be bought on the spot or through most travel agents. The complex also includes crafts outlets and a buffet restaurant (dinner B500).

Silom Village Thanon Silom ⓣ02 234 4581, ⓦwww.silomvillage.co.th. This complex of tourist shops stages a nightly 50min show at its Ruen Thep theatre (8.30pm; B600) to accompany a set menu of Thai food (available from 7pm), as well as rather desultory free 15min shows at 7.45pm and 8.45pm at its outdoor restaurant.

Thailand Cultural Centre Thanon Ratchadapisek ⓣ02 247 0028 ext 4280, ⓦwww.thaiculturalcenter.com; BTS Thailand Cultural Centre. Mainstream classical concerts, traditional and contemporary theatre, and visiting international dance and theatre shows.

Traditional Thai Puppet Theatre Suan Lum Night Bazaar, Thanon Rama IV ⓣ02 252 9683–4, ⓦwww.thaipuppet.com; Lumphini subway. Entertaining, tourist-oriented performances that are well worth it for both adults and children, using *hun lakhon lek* (jointed stick-puppets), an art form that was developed in the early twentieth century and had all but died out before the late owner of the theatre, Sakorn Yangkeowsod (aka Joe Louis), came to its rescue in the 1980s. Each sixty-centimetre-tall puppet is manipulated by three puppeteers, who are accomplished Thai classical dancers in their own right, complementing their charges' elegant and precise gestures with graceful movements in a harmonious ensemble. Hour-long shows (B900, kids B300) are put on daily at the theatre at 8pm, preceded by a video documentary in English at 7.30pm. The puppets perform *khon*, *lakhon* and *likay* stories, accompanied by synopses in English and live traditional music of a high standard.

Cinemas

Central Bangkok has more than forty **cinemas**, many of which show recent American and European releases with their original dialogue and Thai subtitles. Most cinemas screen shows around four times a day: some programme details are advertised every day in the *Bangkok Post* but your best bet is to go to ⓦwww.movieseer.com, which allows you to search by movie or by area in Bangkok (or indeed around the country), up to a week ahead; cinema locations are printed on *Nancy Chandler's Map of Bangkok*. Whatever cinema you're in, you're expected to stand for the king's anthem, which is played before every performance. See p.66 for information about Bangkok's annual film festival.

There are half-a-dozen cinemas in Siam Square, among which the Lido on Soi 1 (ⓣ02 252 6498, ⓦwww.apexsiam-square.com) is your best bet for independent foreign films. Otherwise, head out to House, an arthouse cinema northeast of the centre in Royal City Avenue Plaza (ⓣ02 641 5177–8, ⓦwww.houserama.com; nearest subway Phetchaburi). Nearly every major downtown shopping plaza has several screens on its top floor, including Siam Paragon: on Floor 5 here, you can go for a regular auditorium (from B140), super-size to the IMAX, which shows recent Hollywood releases on a giant screen with enhanced sound (B250), or plump for the Enigma, a VIP cinema where for B3000 you get a sofa, food and drink (with waiter service) for four people. Movies at the French and German cultural centres, the Alliance Française, 29 Thanon Sathorn Tai (ⓣ02 670 4200, ⓦwww.alliance-francaise.or.th), and the Goethe Institut, 18/1 Soi Goethe, between Thanon Sathorn Tai and Soi Ngam Duphli (ⓣ02 287 0942, ⓦwww.goethe.de), are often subtitled in English, while Thammasat University's Pridi Banomyong Library in Ratanakosin hosts free weekly shows of foreign films (ⓣ02 613 3529–30 or see the *Bangkok Post*).

Thai boxing

The violence of the average **Thai boxing** match may be off-putting to some, but spending a couple of hours at one of Bangkok's two main stadia can be immensely entertaining, not least for the enthusiasm of the spectators and the ritualistic aspects of the fights. Bouts, advertised in the English-language newspapers, are held in the capital every night of the week at the **Rajdamnoen Stadium**, next to the TAT office on Rajdamnoen Nok (ⓣ02 281 4205; Mon, Wed, Sun 6pm, Thurs 5pm), and at **Lumphini Stadium** on Thanon Rama IV (ⓣ02 252 8765 or 02 251 4303, ⓦwww.muaythailumpini.com; Tues & Fri 6.30pm, Sat 4.30pm & 8.30pm; Lumphini subway). Tickets cost B1000–2000, though at Rajdamnoen the view from the B1000 seats is partially obscured. Sessions usually feature ten bouts, each consisting of five three-minute rounds with two-minute rests in between each round, so if you're not a big fan it may be worth turning up an hour late, as the better fights tend to happen later in the billing. It's more fun if you buy one of the less-expensive standing tickets, from where you can witness the frantic gesticulations of the betting aficionados at close range. For more on Thai boxing, see p.69.

To engage in a little *muay Thai* yourself, visit Sor Vorapin's Gym at 13 Trok Kasap off Thanon Chakrabongse in Banglamphu, which holds *muay Thai* **classes** twice daily (B500 per session; ⓣ02 282 3551, ⓦwww.thaiboxings.com) or Chacrit Muay Thai School, next to Washington Square Theatre on Sukhumvit, between sois 22 and 24 (Mon–Sat 9am–8pm; drop-in sessions B500; ⓣ02 260 5826, ⓦwww.chacritmuaythaischool.com). For more serious training there are a couple of well-regarded places for foreigners to train on the outskirts of the city: Jitti's Gym (ⓦwww.jittigym.com) and the Muay Thai Institute (ⓦwww.muaythai-institute.net).

Shopping

Bangkok has a good reputation for shopping, particularly for silk, gems, contemporary interior design and fashions, where the range and quality are streets ahead of other Thai cities, and antiques and handicrafts are good buys too. As always, watch out for **fakes**: cut glass masquerading as precious stones, old, damaged goods being passed off as antiques, counterfeit designer clothes and accessories, pirated CDs and DVDs, even mocked-up international driver's licences (though Thai travel agents and other organizations aren't that easily fooled). Bangkok also has the best English-language bookshops in the country. Department stores and tourist-oriented shops in the city keep late **hours**, opening daily at 10 or 11am and closing at about 9pm; many small, upmarket boutiques, for example along Thanon Charoen Krung and Thanon Silom, close on Sundays. Monday is meant to be no-street-vendor day throughout Bangkok, a chance for the pavements to get cleaned and for pedestrians to finally see where they're going, but plenty of stalls manage to flout the rule.

Downtown Bangkok is full of smart, multi-storey **shopping plazas** like Siam Paragon, Siam Centre and Emporium, which is where you'll find the majority of the city's fashion stores, as well as designer lifestyle goods and bookshops. The plazas tend to be pleasantly air-conditioned and thronging with trendy young Thais, but don't hold much interest for tourists unless you happen to be looking for a new outfit. You're more likely to find useful items in one of the city's numerous **department stores**: seven-storey Central Chidlom on Thanon Ploenchit, which boasts handy services like watch-, garment- and shoe-repair booths as well as a huge product selection (including large sizes), is probably the city's best, but the Siam Paragon department store (which also offers garment and shoe repairs), in the shopping centre of the same name on Thanon Rama I, is also good. They all have children's departments selling bottles, slings and clothes, or there are Mothercare concessions inside the Emporium (between Sukhumvit sois 22 and 24) and Siam Paragon shopping centres, and in Central Chidlom. The British chain of **pharmacies**, Boots the Chemist, has lots of branches across the city, including on Thanon Khao San, in Siam Paragon, on Patpong, in the Times Square complex between Sukhumvit sois 12 and 14, and in Emporium.

The best place to buy anything to do with **mobile phones** (see p.86) is the scores of small booths on Floor 4 of Mah Boon Krong (MBK) Shopping Centre at the Rama I/Phrayathai intersection. For **computer** hardware and genuine and pirated software, as well as digital cameras, Panthip Plaza, at 604/3 Thanon Phetchaburi (BTS Ratchathevi or canal stop Tha Pratunam) is the best place: staff are often very knowledgable and helpful, Mac-heads are catered for, including authorized resellers, and there are dozens of repair and secondhand booths, especially towards the back of the shopping centre and on the upper floors.

Markets

For travellers, spectating, not shopping, is apt to be the main draw of Bangkok's neighbourhood **markets** – notably the bazaars of Chinatown and the blooms and scents of Pak Khlong Talat, the flower and vegetable market just west of Memorial Bridge. The massive Chatuchak Weekend Market is an exception, being both a tourist attraction and a marvellous shopping experience (see p.171). With the chief exception of Chatuchak, most markets operate daily from dawn till early afternoon; early morning is often the best time to go to beat the heat and crowds.

Night-time shoppers will want to make a beeline for **Suan Lum Night Bazaar**, opposite Lumphini Park at the corner of Thanon Rama IV and Thanon Witthayu (Lumphini subway), a huge development of hundreds of booths, which is at its best between 6 and 10pm. Down the narrow alleys of tiny shops, you'll find colourful street fashions, jewellery and lots of soaps, candles and beauty products, as well as some interesting contemporary decor: lighting, paintings, ceramics and woodcarving. At the centre stands the Traditional Thai Puppet Theatre (see p.193), with a popular Thai terrace-restaurant in front, and the attractive women's clothes and furnishings, notably rugs, of the Doi Tung by Mae Fah Luang shop (see p.196), with a hip Doi Tung coffee house attached. Other options for eating and drinking are uninspiring – your best bet is probably the open-air food court and beer garden, with a stage for nightly live music, by Thanon Witthayu. The lease on the night bazaar ran out in 2007, but amidst very protracted legal wrangling and plenty of colourful rumour, it looks set to remain open for a good few years yet – though it might be worth checking with your hotel before setting out.

Handicrafts, contemporary design and textiles

Samples of nearly all regionally produced **handicrafts** end up in Bangkok, so the selection is phenomenal. Many of the shopping plazas have at least one classy handicraft outlet, and competition keeps prices in the city at upcountry levels, with the main exception of household objects – particularly wickerware and tin bowls and basins – which get palmed off relatively expensively in Bangkok. Handicraft sellers in Banglamphu tend to tout a limited range compared to the shops downtown, but several places on and around Thanon Khao San sell reasonably priced triangular "axe" pillows (*mawn khwaan*) in traditional fabrics, which make fantastic souvenirs but are heavy to post home; some places sell unstuffed versions which are simple to mail home, but a pain to fill when you return. The cheapest outlet for traditional northern and northeastern textiles – including sarongs, axe pillows and farmers' shirts – is **Chatuchak Weekend Market** (see p.171), where you'll also be able to nose out some interesting handicrafts.

Bangkok is also rapidly establishing a reputation for its **contemporary interior design**, fusing minimalist Western ideals with traditional Thai and

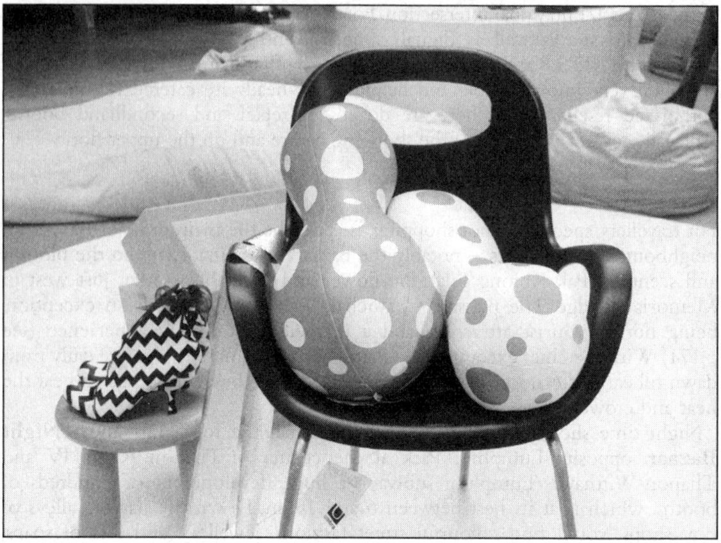

▲ Contemporary interior design store

other Asian craft elements. The best places to sample this, as detailed in the reviews below, are on Floor 4 of the Siam Discovery Centre and Floor 4 of the Siam Paragon shopping centre, both on Thanon Rama I, and Floor 3 of the Gaysorn Plaza on Thanon Ploenchit.

Noted for its thickness and sheen, **Thai silk** became internationally recognized only about fifty years ago after the efforts of American Jim Thompson (see box, p.163). Much of it comes from the northeast, but you'll find a good range of outlets in the capital. Prices are around B600 per metre for two-ply silk (suitable for thin shirts and skirts), or B800 for four-ply (for suits).

Banglamphu and Ratanakosin

Lofty Bamboo *Buddy Hotel* complex, 265 Thanon Khao San ⓦwww.loftybamboo.com. Fair-trade outlet for Thai crafts, accessories and jewellery, including silver made by Karen people from north and west Thailand, Lahu hill - tribe bags, recycled textile products from tsunami-affected communities in Phang Nga and weaving from Mae Hong Son.

Queen's Support Foundation Grand Palace (on the right just inside the Gate of Glorious Victory). Not-for-profit shop that's especially good for beautiful, top-quality *yan lipao*, traditional basketware made from delicately woven fern stems.

Taekee Taekon 118 Thanon Phra Arthit. Tasteful assortment of traditional textiles and scarves, plus a selection of Thai art cards, black-and-white photocards and Nancy Chandler greetings cards.

Downtown: around Siam Square and Thanon Ploenchit

Ayodhya Floor 4, Siam Paragon, and Floor 3, Gaysorn Plaza (also Floor 4, Emporium, Thanon Sukhumvit). With the same owners and designers as Panta (see opposite), but specializing in smaller items, such as gorgeous cushion covers, pouffes covered in dried water-hyacinth stalks, bowls, trays and mats.

Come Thai Floor 3, Amarin Plaza, Thanon Ploenchit. Wide range of unusual handwoven silk and cotton fabrics from all over Southeast Asia.

D & O Shop Floor 3, Gaysorn Plaza ⓦwww.dandoshop.com. Ten enterprising local designers have formed the Design and Objects Association to showcase their diverse contemporary, often poppy wares here: vases, lamps, tableware, jewellery, bags, stationery, even sandals.

Doi Tung by Mae Fah Luang Floor 4, Siam Discovery Centre, and Suan Lum Night Bazaar,

Thanon Rama IV Ⓦ www.doitung.org. Part of the late Princess Mother's development project based at Doi Tung, selling very striking and attractive cotton and linen in warm colours, made up into clothes, cushion covers, rugs and so on, as well as rustic ceramics.

EGG Floor 4, Siam Discovery Centre Ⓦ www.eggthai.com. The main draws here are cushion covers, table settings and boxes which tread a fine line between traditional and modern, featuring floral- and coral-inspired motifs in sumptuous colours.

Exotique Thai Floor 4, Siam Paragon. A collection of small outlets from around the city and the country – including silk-makers and clothes designers down from Chiang Mai – that makes a good, upmarket one-stop shop, much more interesting than Narai Phand (see below). There's everything from jewellery, through celadons, to beauty products, with a focus on home decor and contemporary adaptations of traditional crafts.

Gilles Caffier Floor 4, Siam Discovery Centre Ⓦ www.gillescaffier.com. From a French designer based in Nakhon Pathom, who has spent time in Japan but takes his influences from around the world, clippy leather cushions, signature brown "spaghetti" bowls, and some lovely, subtly coloured modern vases.

Lamont Contemporary Floor 3, Gaysorn Plaza Ⓦ www.lamont-design.com. Beautiful lacquerware bowls, vases and boxes, as well as bronze, glass, crystal and ceramic objects, all in imaginative contemporary styles. Lamont also have a pan-Asian antique shop opposite, and sell both contemporary and antique lines at branches in the *Sukhothai* and *Oriental* hotels.

Lofty Bamboo Floor 2, MBK, Siam Square. Branch of Banglamphu's fair-trade Thai crafts outlet.

Narai Phand Ground floor, President Tower Arcade, just east of Gaysorn Plaza, Thanon Ploenchit Ⓦ www.naraiphand.com. This souvenir centre was set up to ensure the preservation of traditional crafts and to maintain standards of quality, as a joint venture with the Ministry of Industry in the 1930s, and has a duly institutional feel, though it makes a reasonable one-stop shop for last-minute presents. It offers a huge assortment of reasonably priced goods from all over the country, including silk and cotton, *khon* masks, *bencharong*, nielloware and celadon, woodcarving, silver, basketware and beauty products.

Niwat (Aranyik) Floor 3, Gaysorn Plaza. A good place to buy that chunky, elegant Thai-style cutlery you may have been eating your dinner with in Bangkok's posher restaurants, with both traditional and contemporary handmade designs; plus lovely, handmade stainless-steel bowls.

Panta Floor 4, Siam Discovery Centre, and Floor 4, Siam Paragon Ⓦ www.pantathailand.net. Modern design store which stands out for its experimental furniture, including way-out-there items made of woven rattan and wood, and cushions covered in dried water-hyacinth stalks, string and rag clippings.

Thann Native Floor 3, Gaysorn Plaza Ⓦ www.thann.info. Striking contemporary rugs, cushion covers and furniture, plus famous spa and beauty products (with a high-concept modern spa next door).

Triphum Floor 3, Gaysorn Plaza, and Floor 4, Siam Paragon. Affordable, hand-painted reproductions of temple mural paintings, Buddhist manuscripts from Burma, repro Buddha statues in many styles, lacquerware, framed amulets and even Buddha's footprints.

Downtown: south of Thanon Rama IV

Jim Thompson's Thai Silk Company Main shop at 9 Thanon Suriwong, corner of Thanon Rama IV (including a branch of their very good café; see p.183), plus branches at the Jim Thompson House Museum and at many department stores, malls and hotels around the city; Ⓦ www.jimthompson.com. A good place to start looking for traditional Thai fabric, or at least to get an idea of what's out there. Stocks silk and cotton by the yard and ready-made items from dresses to cushion covers, which are well designed and of good quality, but pricey. They also have a home-furnishings section and a good tailoring service. A couple of hundred metres along Thanon Suriwong from the main branch, at no. 149/4–6, a Jim Thompson Factory Sales Outlet sells remnant home-furnishing fabrics and home accessories at knock-down prices (if you're really keen on a bargain, they have a much larger factory outlet way out east of the centre on Soi 93, Thanon Sukhumvit).

Khomapastr 56–58 Thanon Naret, between Suriwong and Si Phraya. Branch of the famous Hua Hin cotton shop (see p.576).

The Legend Floor 3, Thaniya Plaza, corner of Soi Thaniya and Thanon Silom. Stocks a small selection of well-made Thai handicrafts, from wood and wickerware to pretty fabrics and celadon and other ceramics, at reasonable prices. Tamnan Mingmuang, its subsidiary opposite, concentrates on basketry from all over the country: among the unusual items on offer are trays and boxes for tobacco and betel nut made from *yan lipao* (intricately woven fern vines), and bambooware sticky-rice containers, baskets and lampshades.

Silom Village 286/1 Thanon Silom. A complex of low-rise shops that attempts to create a relaxing, upcountry atmosphere as a backdrop for its diverse, pricey handicrafts.

Thanon Sukhumvit

Krisna's Just west of Soi 11. Five-floor emporium of mostly mass-produced but good quality artefacts from Thailand and beyond, especially figurines and Buddha statues in wood, lacquer and silver plus some jewellery and trinkets. Mon–Sat 10am–9pm, Sun 4–7pm.
The Shop @ TCDC Thailand Creative and Design Centre, Floor 6, Emporium, Thanon Sukhumvit, between sois 22 and 24. The retail outlet at Bangkok's design centre sells innovative products dreamt up by local creatives, mostly fairly funky stocking-fillers, bags and household items, with just a whiff of kitsch. Closed Mon.
Thai Celadon Soi 16 (Thanon Ratchadapisek). Classic celadon stoneware made without commercial dyes or clays and glazed with the archetypal blues and greens that were invented by the Chinese to emulate the colour of precious jade. Mainly dinner sets, vases and lamps, plus some figurines.

Tailored clothes

Inexpensive **tailoring shops** crowd Silom, Sukhumvit and Khao San roads, but the best single area to head for is the short stretch of Thanon Charoen Krung between the GPO and Thanon Silom (near the Chao Phraya express-boat stops at Tha Oriental and Tha Wat Muang Kae, or ten minutes' walk from Saphan Taksin Skytrain station), where most of the recommended tailors below are. It's generally advisable to avoid tailors in tourist areas such as Thanon Khao San, shopping malls and Thanon Sukhumvit's Soi Nana and Soi 11, although if you're lucky it's still possible to come up trumps here: one that stands apart is Banglamphu's well-regarded Chang Torn, located at 95 Thanon Tanao (☎02 282 9390). For cheap and reasonable shirt and dress material other than silk go for a browse around Pahurat market (see p.153), though the suit materials are mostly poor, and best avoided.

A Song Tailor 8 Trok Chartered Bank, off Thanon Charoen Krung, near the *Oriental Hotel* ☎02 630 9708. Friendly, helpful and a good first port of call if you're on a budget.
Ah Song Tailor 1203 Thanon Charoen Krung, opposite Soi 36 ☎02 233 7574. Younger brother of the above, a meticulous tailor who takes pride in his work. Men's and women's suits.
Golden Wool 1340–1342 Thanon Charoen Krung ☎02 233 0149; and **World Group** 1302–1304 Thanon Charoen Krung ☎02 234 1527, and 38 Oriental Avenue ☎02 238 3344–8. Part of the same company, they can turn around decent work in three or four days, though prices are slightly on the high side.
Marco Tailor Soi 7, Siam Square ☎02 252 0689 or 02 251 7633, and Floor 2, Amarin Plaza, Thanon Ploenchit. Long-established tailor with a good reputation, though not cheap by Bangkok standards; they require two or three weeks for a suit. Men's only.
Marzotto Tailor 3 Soi 42/1 (Soi Shangri-la Hotel), Thanon Charoen Krung ☎02 233 2880. Friendly business which makes everything from trousers to wedding outfits, and can make a suit in two days, with just one fitting, if necessary.

Fashions

Thanon Khao San is lined with stalls selling low-priced **fashions**: the tie-dyed vests, baggy cotton fisherman's trousers and embroidered blouses are all aimed at backpackers, but they're supplemented by cheap contemporary fashions that appeal to urban Thai trendies as well. The stalls of Banglamphu Market, around the edges of the abandoned New World department store, have the biggest range of inexpensive Thai fashions in this area. Downtown, the most famous area for low-cost, low-quality casual clothes is the warren-like Pratunam Market and the surrounding malls at the corner of Phetchaburi and Ratchaprarop roads, but for the best and latest trends from Thai designers, you should check out the shops in Siam Square and across the road in the more upmarket Siam Centre. Prices vary considerably; street gear in Siam Square is undoubtedly inexpensive (and look out for outlet stores such as Jaspal's in Amarin Plaza, Thanon Ploenchit), while genuine Western brand names are generally competitive but

Having clothes tailor-made

Bangkok can be an excellent place to get tailor-made suits, dresses, shirts and trousers at a fraction of the price you'd pay in the West. Tailors here can copy a sample brought from home and will also work from any photographs you can provide; most also carry a good selection of catalogues. The bad news is that many tourist-oriented tailors aren't terribly good, often attempting to get away with poor work and shoddy materials (and sometimes trying to delay delivery until just before you leave the city, so that you don't have time to complain). However, with a little effort and thought, both men and women can get some fantastic clothes made to measure.

Choosing a tailor can be tricky, and unless you're particularly knowledgeable about material, shopping around won't necessarily tell you much. However, don't make a decision wholly on prices quoted – picking a tailor simply because they're the cheapest usually leads to poor work, and cheap suits don't last. Special deals offering two suits, two shirts, two ties and a kimono for US$99 should be left well alone. Above all, ignore recommendations by anyone with a vested interest in bringing your custom to a particular shop.

Prices vary widely depending on material and the tailor's skill. As a very rough guide, for labour alone expect to pay B5000–6000 for a two-piece suit, though some tailors will charge rather more (check whether or not the price you're quoted includes the lining). For middling **material**, expect to pay about the same again, or anything up to four times as much for top-class cloth. With the exception of silk, local materials are frequently of poor quality and for suits in particular you're far better off using English or Italian cloth. Most tailors stock both imported and local fabrics, but bringing your own from home can work out significantly cheaper.

Give yourself as much **time** as possible. For suits, insist on two fittings. Most good tailors require around three days for a suit (some require ten days or more), although a few have enough staff to produce good work in a day or two. The more **detail** you can give the tailor the better. As well as deciding on the obvious features such as single- or double-breasted and number of buttons, think about the width of lapels, style of trousers, whether you want the jacket with vents or not, and so forth. Specifying factors like this will make all the difference to whether you're happy with your suit, so it's worth discussing them with the tailor; a good tailor should be able to give good advice. Finally, don't be afraid to be an awkward customer until you're completely happy with the finished product – after all, the whole point of getting clothes tailor-made is to get exactly what you want.

not breathtakingly cheaper than at home; larger sizes can be hard to find. **Shoes** and **leather goods** are good buys in Bangkok, being generally handmade from high-quality leather and quite a bargain: check out branches of the stylish, Italian-influenced Viera by Ragazze (Ⓦwww.ragazze.co.th) in the Silom Complex (Floor 2), Thanon Silom, in Central World Plaza or in the attached Isetan department store.

Central World Plaza Ratchaprasong Intersection, corner of Rama I and Rajdamri. This recently refurbished shopping centre is so huge that it defies easy classification, but you'll find plenty of Thai and international fashions on its lower floors and in the attached Zen department store at its southern end.
Emporium Thanon Sukhumvit, between sois 22 and 24. Enormous and rather glamorous shopping plaza, with a good range of fashion outlets, from exclusive designer wear to trendy high-street gear. Genuine brand-name outlets include Versace, Prada, Gucci, Chanel, Louis Vuitton – and Mango.
Gaysorn Plaza Thanon Ploenchit. The most chic of the city's shopping plazas: in amongst Burberry, Emporio Armani and Louis Vuitton, a few Thai names have made it onto the second floor, notably Fly Now, which mounts dramatic displays of women's party and formal gear, alongside more casual wear, and Myth, a gathering of six cutting-edge local designers for men and women in one store.

Mah Boon Krong (MBK) At the Rama I/Phrayathai intersection. Labyrinthine shopping centre which houses hundreds of small, mostly fairly inexpensive outlets, including plenty of high-street fashion shops.
Siam Centre Thanon Rama I. Particularly good for hip local labels, many of whom have made the step up from the booths of Siam Square across the road – look out for Baking Soda, Fly Now, Greyhound, Headquarter, Jaspal, Kloset, Senada and Theatre – as well as international names like Nike and Quiksilver.
Siam Square Worth poking around the alleys here, especially near what's styled as the area's "Centerpoint" between sois 3 and 4. All manner of inexpensive boutiques, some little more than booths, sell colourful street-gear to the capital's fashionable students and teenagers.

Books

English-language **bookstores** in Bangkok are always well stocked with everything to do with Thailand, and most carry fiction classics and popular paperbacks as well. The capital's **secondhand** bookstores are not cheap, but you can usually part-exchange your unwanted titles.

Aporia 131 Thanon Tanao, Banglamphu. This is one of Banglamphu's main outlets for new books and keeps a good stock of titles on Thai and Southeast Asian culture, a decent selection of travelogues, plus some English-language fiction. Also sells secondhand books.
Asia Books Branches on Thanon Sukhumvit between sois 15 and 19, in Landmark Plaza between sois 4 and 6, in Times Square between sois 12 and 14, and in Emporium between sois 22 and 24; in Peninsula Plaza and in the Central World Plaza, both on Thanon Rajdamri; in Siam Discovery Centre and Siam Paragon, both on Thanon Rama I; and in Thaniya Plaza on Soi Thaniya off Thanon Silom. English-language bookstore (and publishing house) that's especially recommended for its books on Asia – everything from guidebooks to cookery books, novels to art (the Sukhumvit 15–19 branch has the very best Asian selection). Also stocks bestselling novels and coffee-table books.
B2S Floors 1–3, Central World Plaza and Floor 7, Central Chidlom, Thanon Ploenchit. Decent selection of English-language books, but most notable for its huge selection of magazines, newspapers and stationery.
Bookazine Silom Complex, Thanon Silom; Soi 4, Siam Square; Gaysorn Plaza, Thanon Ploenchit; and at the mouth of Sukhumvit Soi 5. Alongside a decent selection of English-language books about Asia and novels, these shops stock a wide range of foreign newspapers and magazines.
Books Kinokuniya 3rd Floor, Emporium Shopping Centre, between sois 22 and 24 on Thanon Sukhumvit, with branches at Floor 6, Isetan, in the Central World Plaza, and Floor 3, Siam Paragon, Thanon Rama I. Huge, efficient English-language bookstore with a wide selection of books ranging from bestsellers to travel literature and from classics to sci-fi; not so hot on books about Asia though.
Dasa Book Cafe Between sois 26 and 28, Thanon Sukhumvit Ⓦ www.dasabookcafe.com. Appealingly calm secondhand bookshop that's intelligently, and alphabetically, categorized, with sections on everything from Asia to chicklit, health to gay and lesbian interest. Browse its stock online, or enjoy coffee and cakes in situ.
Orchid Books Silom Complex, Thanon Silom. Publishers' shop devoted to scholarly books, fiction and poetry, both new works and reprints, related to Asia.
Rim Khob Fa Bookshop Democracy Monument roundabout, Rajdamnoen Klang, Banglamphu. Useful outlet for the more obscure and esoteric English-language books on Thailand and Southeast Asia, as well as mainstream titles on Thai culture.
Shaman Books Thanon Khao San (3 branches), Banglamphu. Well-stocked secondhand bookshop where all books are logged on the computer. Lots of books on Asia (travel, fiction, politics and history) as well as a decent range of novels and general-interest books.
Siam Society Bookshop: Libreria
131 Sukhumvit Soi 21, inside the Ban Kamthieng compound. Extensive collection of esoteric and academic books about Thailand, including many ethnology studies published by White Lotus and by the Siam Society itself. Tues–Sat 9am–6pm, Sun noon–5pm.
Ton's Bookseller 327/5 Thanon Ram Bhuttri, Banglamphu. Exceptionally well stocked with titles about Thailand and Southeast Asia, particularly political commentary and Buddhist studies.

Jewellery and gems

Bangkok boasts the country's best **gem and jewellery** shops, and some of the finest lapidaries in the world, making this *the* place to buy cut and uncut stones such as rubies, blue sapphires and diamonds. However, countless gem-buying tourists get badly **ripped off**, so be extremely wary. Never buy anything through a tout or from any shop recommended by a "government official"/ "student"/"businessperson"/tuk-tuk driver who just happens to engage you in conversation on the street, and note that there are no government jewellery shops despite any information you may be given to the contrary. Always check that the shop is a member of the **Thai Gem and Jewelry Traders Association** by calling the association or visiting their website (ⓣ02 630 1390–7, ⓦwww.thaigemjewelry.or.th). To be doubly sure, you may want to seek out shops that also belong to the TGJTA's **Jewel Fest Club** (ⓦwww.jewelfest.com), which guarantees quality and will offer refunds; see their website for a directory of members. For independent professional advice or precious-stones certification, contact the Asian Institute of Gemological Sciences, located on the sixth floor of the Jewelry Trade Center Building, 919/1 Thanon Silom (ⓣ02 267 4325, ⓦwww.aigsthailand.com), which also runs reputable **courses**, such as a five-day (15hr) introduction to gemstones (US$250).

A common **scam** is to charge a lot more than what the gem is worth based on its carat weight. Get it tested on the spot, ask for a written guarantee and receipt. Don't even consider **buying gems in bulk** to sell at a supposedly vast profit elsewhere: many a gullible traveller has invested thousands of dollars on a handful of worthless multicoloured stones, believing the vendor's reassurance that the goods will fetch at least a hundred percent more when resold at home. Gem scams are so common in Bangkok that TAT has published a brochure about it and there are several websites on the subject, including the very informative ⓦwww.2bangkok.com/2bangkok/Scams/Sapphire.shtml, which describes the typical scam in detail and advises on what to do if you get caught out; it's also updated with details of the latest scammers. Most victims get no recompense at all, but you have more chance of doing so if you contact the website's recommended authorities while still in Thailand.The most exclusive of the reputable **gem outlets** are on Thanon Silom, notably in the Jewelry Trade Center (Silom Galleria); you can get an idea of prices at the online catalogue ⓦwww.thaigem.com. Other recommended outlets include the nearby, American-owned Lambert, Silom Shanghai Building, Soi 17, Thanon Silom (ⓣ02 236 4343, ⓦwww.lambertgems.com); the very upscale Kim's in Oriental Place in front of the *Oriental*; and Johnny's Gems at 199 Thanon Fuang Nakhon, near Wat Rajabophit (ⓣ02 224 4065). Thongtavee, Floor 2, River City, and in the Jewelry Trade Center, outlets of a famous Burmese **jade** factory in Mae Sai in northern Thailand, sells beautiful jade jewellery, as well as carved Buddha statues, chopsticks and the like. The hub of Bangkok's **gold** trade is Chinatown, specifically Thanon Yaowarat, which boasts over a hundred outlets. For cheap **silver** earrings, bracelets and necklaces, you can't beat the traveller-oriented jewellery shops along Trok Mayom in Banglamphu.

Antiques and paintings

Bangkok is the entrepôt for the finest Thai, Burmese and Cambodian **antiques**, but the market has long been sewn up, so don't expect to happen upon any undiscovered treasure. Even experts admit that they sometimes find it hard to tell real antiques from fakes, so the best policy is just to buy on the grounds of attractiveness. The **River City** shopping complex off Thanon Charoen Krung, which is near Si Phraya and Harbour Department express-boat piers and operates a shuttle boat from Saphan Taksin BTS (Ⓦwww.rivercity.co.th), devotes its third, fourth and some of its second floors to a bewildering array of pricey treasures, as well as holding an auction on the first Saturday of every month (viewing during the preceding week; Ⓣ02 237 0077 ext 459 or 461). Worth singling out here are Old Maps and Prints on Floor 4 (Ⓦwww.classicmaps.com), which has some lovely old prints of Thailand and Asia (starting at around B3000), as well as rare maps; Ingon Gallery on Floor 3, which specializes in small Chinese pieces made of jade and other precious stones, such as snuff boxes, jewellery, statuettes and amulets; and on the same floor, Beyond the Masks, which is true to its name: Asian tribal masks plus a miscellany of ornamental coconut scrapers, silver jewellery and fabrics. The other main area for antiques is the section of Charoen Krung that runs between the GPO and the bottom of Thanon Silom, and the stretch of Silom running east from here up to and including the multistorey Silom Galleria. Here you'll find a good selection of largely reputable individual businesses specializing in woodcarvings, ceramics, bronze statues and stone sculptures culled from all parts of Thailand and neighbouring countries as well. The owners of Old Maps and Prints have a second outlet, the Old Siam Trading Company in the Nailert Building at the mouth of Thanon Sukhumvit Soi 5 (Ⓦwww.oldsiamtrading.com). There are also half a dozen shops specializing in Thai and Chinese antiques on Thanon Mahachai, across the road from Wat Rajnadda in Banglamphu. Remember that most antiques require an export permit (see p.82).

Street-corner stalls all over the city sell poor-quality mass-produced traditional Thai **paintings**, but for a huge selection of Thai art, especially oil paintings, visit Sombat Permpoon Gallery at 12 Sukhumvit Soi 1 (Ⓦwww.sombatpermpoongallery.com), which carries thousands of canvases, framed and unframed, spanning the range from classical Ayutthayan-era-style village scenes to twenty-first-century abstracts. The gallery also has works by famous Thai artists like Thawan Duchanee.

Moving on from Bangkok

Bangkok is the terminus of all major highways and rail lines, and **public transport** between the capital and the provinces is inexpensive and plentiful. Bangkok is also the best place to make arrangements for onward travel from Thailand, and all the major Asian embassies are here, so getting the appropriate **visas** should be straightforward.

Travel within Thailand

As well as reliable one-way transfers, many of the Bangkok travel agents listed on p.209 offer day and overnight **excursions** to popular destinations. Prices vary quite a bit but start at B500 for a morning at Damoen Saduak floating market and B600 for a day-trip to Ayutthaya or Kanchanaburi and the River Kwai. For details of **specialist Thai tour operators** offering more distinctive cultural, cycling and trekking packages, see p.29. For information on Thailand's **domestic flight network**, see p.45.

By train

Nearly all trains depart from **Hualamphong Station**, whose 24-hour "Information" booth keeps English-language **timetables**, or you can try phoning the

Train Information Hotline on ⓣ1690; the State Railway of Thailand website (ⓦwww.railway.co.th) also carries timetables and a fare chart. For a guide to destinations and journey times from Bangkok, see "Travel details" on p.209. For details on city transport to and from Hualamphong, left-luggage facilities at the station, and a warning about **con-artists** operating at the station, see p.99. **Tickets** for overnight trains and other busy routes should be booked at least a day in advance (further ahead for travel on national holidays), and are best bought from Hualamphong, either at the clearly signed State Railway **advance booking office** at the back of the station concourse (daily 8.30am–4pm) or, outside those hours, from the main ticket counters. Train tickets can also be bought through almost any travel agent and through some hotels and guest houses for a booking fee of about B50. Hualamphong's advance booking office also sells **joint rail and boat** and **rail and bus tickets** to Ko Samui, Ko Pha Ngan, Ko Tao, Krabi and Ko Phi Phi. Sample prices include B768 for the train to Surat Thani (second-class air-con sleeper), plus either B250 for bus and boat connections to Ko Samui or B250 for bus connections to Krabi.

A few other services leave from sleepy **Thonburi Station** (sometimes still referred to by its former name, **Bangkok Noi Station**), across the river from Banglamphu in Thonburi. Chief among these is the twice-daily run to Nam Tok via Nakhon Pathom and Kanchanaburi; in addition there are a handful of commuter services (not listed on English-language timetables) to Prachuap Khiri Khan, Ratchaburi and Lang Suan. Thonburi Station is about 850m west of the Railway Station N11 express-boat pier (in use Mon–Fri rush hours only; at other times get off at N10 and walk an extra 500m to N11, through the Siriraj Hospital compound); frequent red songthaews run passengers between the N10 pier and the train station (5min), or you can walk it in about fifteen minutes by heading up the only road that runs away from the pier, passing a temple, walking alongside (under) the flyover, and turning right at the far edge of the market when you see the station sign.

The other non-Hualamphong departure is the service to Samut Sakhon, which leaves from **Wongwian Yai Station**, also in Thonburi, hidden behind market stalls on the west side of Thanon Somdet Phra Chao Taksin, just south of the Wongwian Yai roundabout with its horseback statue of General Phraya Taksin. Easiest access is by BTS Skytrain to Wongwian Yai (S8), but you can also get to the roundabout on bus #3 from Thanon Phra Arthit in Banglamphu, or by taking the cross-river ferry from River City to Khlong San and then either walking or hopping on almost any bus.

By bus

Bangkok's **three main bus terminals** are distributed around the outskirts of town and are described in full on p.100. Leave plenty of time to reach them, especially if setting off from Banglamphu, from where you should allow at least an hour and a half (outside rush hour) to get to the Eastern Bus Terminal, and a good hour to get to the Northern or Southern terminals. Seats on the most popular long-distance air-con bus services (such as to Chiang Mai, Krabi, Phuket and Surat Thani) should be **reserved** ahead of time, ideally at the relevant bus station as hotels and guest houses may book you on to one of the dodgy tourist services described on p.204.

By minibus

A faster, more convenient alternative to traipsing out to the Northern or Southern bus terminal for transport to Ayutthaya, Lopburi, Hua Hin or Kanchanaburi is to make use of the privately operated **minibus** services (*rot* *thua* or *rot waen*) that depart from central downtown locations. Unlike the tourist buses described below, these are used mainly by Thai travellers and are both fast, making few scheduled stops en route, and frequent, leaving when full (usually every 30min–1hr, approx 7am–8pm); they are generally a little pricier than the equivalent public bus service and sometimes charge extra for large luggage. Minibuses to **Ayutthaya** (1hr 30min; B80), **Lopburi** (2hr; B110) and **Hua Hin** (2hr 30min; B200) depart from the huge and hectic Victory Monument roundabout (*Anu Sawari*), most easily reached via the Victory Monument Skytrain station. The **Kanchanaburi** service (2hr; B120) leaves from outside the *Royal Hotel* at the west end of Ratchadamnoen Klang in Banglamphu.

By tourist bus

Many Bangkok tour operators sell tickets for unlicensed **budget tourist buses** to popular long-distance destinations such as Chiang Mai, Surat Thani (for Ko Samui) and Krabi (for Ko Phi Phi), and to places closer at hand such as Kanchanaburi, Ko Samet and Ko Chang. Prices can vary considerably but often work out just as cheap as air-con buses from the public bus terminals and, crucially, are more convenient as they mostly leave from the Khao San area in Banglamphu. The big drawbacks, however, are the **lack of comfort** and **poor safety**, which particularly applies to the long-distance **overnight services**. It is standard practice for budget tour operators, especially those on Thanon Khao San, to assure you that overnight transport will be in a large, luxury VIP bus despite knowing it's actually a clapped-out old banger. **Security** on overnight tourist buses is a serious problem, and because they're run by unlicensed private companies there is no insurance against loss or theft of baggage: don't keep anything of value in luggage that's stored out of sight, even if it's padlocked, as luggage gets slashed and rifled in the roomy baggage compartment. In addition, passengers often find themselves dumped on the outskirts of their destination city, at the mercy of unscrupulous touts. If you are planning a journey to Chiang Mai or Surat Thani, consider taking the train instead – the extra comfort and peace of mind are well worth the extra baht – or at the least, opt for a government bus or licensed private bus from the relevant terminal. Services to Kanchanaburi (from B140), Ko Samet (B300 including boat transfer) and Ko Chang (B380 including boat) are usually by air-con minibus; these are usually cramped and can go scarily fast but luggage is generally secure. Bear in mind that Khao San tour operators open up and go bust all the time; see p.209 for recommended travel agents and never hand over any money until you see the ticket.

Leaving Thailand

If buying onward **international air tickets**, be warned that there are many dodgy, transient travel agents in Bangkok, particularly on and around Thanon Khao San, which is known for its shady operators who display fake TAT licences, issue false tickets and flee with travellers' money overnight. The best advice is to use one of the tried and tested **agents** listed on p.209. Never hand over any money until you've called the airline to check your reservation personally (for phone numbers see p.206) and have been given the ticket; double-check that it's a return ticket if that's what you paid for.

For advice on getting to Suvarnabhumi and Don Muang airports, see the box opposite.

Getting to Suvarnabhumi and Don Muang airports

At the time of writing, all **international flights** depart from **Suvarnabhumi Airport** (coded **BKK**), about 25km east of Bangkok, as do the vast majority of **domestic flights**; however, the future role of the old **Don Muang Airport** (coded **DMK**), about 25km north of the city, remains uncertain (see p.95), and may be used for some international routes, so double-check to be absolutely sure. Currently only domestic services with Nok Air and One-Two-Go are using Don Muang.

Getting to either airport by bus, minibus or taxi can be severely hampered by traffic jams, so leave plenty of **time**. Also note that Suvarnabhumi is enormous but ill-served by travelators, so allow loads of time to get to your gate; there are also a bewildering number of (expensive) shops to engross you en route. Domestic and international **departure taxes** are included in the ticket price. In addition to the transport options described below, both airports are served by slow, crowded **city buses** (see p.98 & p.115).

For more information on **facilities** at Suvarnabhumi Airport, see p.98.

Getting to Suvarnabhumi

When the **Suvarnabhumi Airport Rail Link** finally opens for business (currently slated for early 2010), this will be the fastest way of getting to **Suvarnabhumi Airport** from downtown areas. Non-stop Airport Express trains from the City Air Terminal at Makkasan Station (which connects with the subway system at Phetchaburi station) should take about fifteen minutes to the airport, while stopping Airport City Line services from Phaya Thai (an interchange with the BTS Skytrain system) will take around thirty minutes and cost a lot less; a luggage check-in facility is also planned at Makkasan.

The Suvarnabhumi **Airport Express bus services** #AE1–AE4 that serve Silom, Banglamphu, Sukhumvit and Hualamphong, as described in detail on p.98, are less useful on the outward journey, mainly because the traffic often makes it impossible for them to stick to their schedules. The most reliable is service #AE2 **from Banglamphu**, which has a printed timetable and dedicated information and ticket sales booth at its pick-up point in front of the *Mayompuri Restaurant* at the west end of Thanon Chakrabongse (at least hourly 7am–11.15pm; B150; 1hr or 90min during rush hour 4–6pm; ⓣ02 622 3000, ⓦwww.airportexpressthai.com). For the same price most travellers opt instead for one of the private **minibus services** to Suvarnabhumi (at least every 2hr; B150; 90min) organized through guest houses and travel agents in Banglamphu and everywhere else around the city.

A **metered taxi** to Suvarnabhumi can cost anything from B160 to B350 (plus up to B75 in expressway tolls), depending on where you are and how bad the traffic is; on this route, drivers will nearly always try to leave their meters off and agree an inflated price with you – say "*poet meter, dai mai khrap/kha?*" to get them to switch the meter on. If you leave the downtown areas before 7am or after 9pm you can get to the airport in half an hour, but at other times you should set off about an hour and a half before you have to check in.

Getting to Don Muang

There are currently no scheduled airport bus or minibus services to **Don Muang**, so the fastest, most reliable option is a **metered taxi** (B150–350 plus B75 in expressway tolls). If you are coming **from the north or northeast** you can avoid going into Bangkok by alighting at Don Muang train station instead.

Getting to other Asian countries

Most travellers who choose to make their way **overland from Thailand** to Laos, Cambodia or Malaysia do so slowly, but it is possible to do the border-hop in one swoop from Bangkok, though in most cases you'll need to spend a night somewhere on the way. To get **from Bangkok to Laos**, you have to take a train or bus to the border at Chiang Khong, Nong Khai, Nakhon Phanom (which also has an airport), Mukdahan or Chong Mek. For transport **to Cambodia**, you'll need to begin by either taking a bus from Bangkok to Trat; a train or bus from Bangkok to Aranyaprathet; or a bus or train to Surin. Khao San travel agents also run direct buses to Siem Reap for as little as B350, but scams and discomfort on these services are common, for more on which see p.457. The easiest way of travelling from Bangkok **to Malaysia** is by train to the west coast of the peninsula. There is one train a day from Bangkok's Hualamphong Station to Butterworth (for Penang; 21hr), which costs about B1200 in a second-class sleeper. It's also possible to make onward train connections to Kuala Lumpur and Singapore; see p.35 for more.

All the **foreign embassies and consulates** in Bangkok are located in the downtown area (see opposite). Phone ahead to check on the opening hours (usually very limited) and documentation required. For an overview of visa requirements and travel options for Burma, Cambodia, Laos, Malaysia, Singapore and Vietnam see p.34. Some travellers prefer to avoid the hassle of trudging out to the relevant embassy by paying one of the Khao San travel agencies to get their visa for them; beware of doing this, however, as some agencies are reportedly **faking the stamps**, which causes serious problems at immigration.

Listings

Airlines Aeroflot ⓣ02 251 0617–8; Air Asia ⓣ02 515 9999; Air Canada ⓣ02 670 0400; Air France ⓣ02 635 1191; Air India ⓣ02 653 2288; Air New Zealand ⓣ02 235 8280–3; Bangkok Airways ⓣ1771 or 02 265 5555; British Airways ⓣ02 627 1701; Cathay Pacific ⓣ02 263 0606; China Airlines ⓣ02 250 9888; Druk Air ⓣ02 237 9201–3; Emirates ⓣ02 664 1040; Etihad ⓣ02 253 0099; Eva Air ⓣ02 269 6288; Finnair ⓣ02 634 0238–9; Garuda ⓣ02 679 7371–2; Gulf Air ⓣ02 254 7931–4; Japan Airlines ⓣ02 649 9500; KLM ⓣ02 635 2400; Korean Air ⓣ02 635 0465–9; Lao Airlines ⓣ02 236 9822; Lufthansa ⓣ02 264 2400; Malaysia Airlines ⓣ02 263 0565–71; Nok Air ⓣ1318 or 02 900 9955; One-Two-Go ⓣ1126; Pakistan International (PIA) ⓣ02 234 2961–5; PB Air ⓣ02 261 0222; Philippine Airlines ⓣ02 633 5713; Qantas Airways ⓣ02 627 1701; Royal Brunei ⓣ02 637 5151; SGA ⓣ02 664 6099; Singapore Airlines ⓣ02 353 6000; Sri Lankan Airlines ⓣ02 236 8450; Swiss ⓣ02 204 7744; Thai Airways ⓣ02 356 1111; United Airlines ⓣ02 353 3939; Vietnam Airlines ⓣ02 655 4137–40.

Airport enquiries Suvarnabhumi: flight information ⓣ02 132 0000, airport information counter ⓣ02 132 9324–9; Don Muang: domestic departures ⓣ02 535 1192, domestic arrivals ⓣ02 535 1253; ⓦwww.donmuangairportonline.com.

Car rental Avis ⓣ02 251 1131–2, ⓦwww.avisthailand.com: 2/12 Thanon Witthayu (Wireless Road), Suvarnabhumi and Don Muang airports. Budget ⓣ02 203 0250, ⓦwww.budget.co.th: 19/23 Building A, Royal City Avenue, Thanon Phetchaburi Mai and Suvarnabhumi Airport. National (SMT Rent-A-Car) ⓣ02 722 8487, ⓦwww.nationalcarrental.co.th: 727 Thanon Srinakharin and Suvarnabhumi Airport.

Cookery classes Nearly all the five-star hotels will arrange Thai cookery classes for guests if requested; the most famous are held at the *Oriental Hotel* (see p.125; B4500; Mon–Sat), covering four different dishes each morning, while the *Bangkok Marriott* (see p.124) offers morning classes aboard a converted rice-barge, the *Manohra* (ⓣ02 476 0022 ext 1416, ⓦwww.manohracruises.com; B2600; Mon–Fri), including a market tour to buy ingredients. In a grand, century-old building at 233 Thanon Sathorn Tai (ⓣ02 673 9353–4, ⓦwww.blueelephant.com), the *Blue Elephant* offers courses that range from B2800 for a half-day to a five-day private course for professional chefs for B68,000. Also recommended in the southern downtown area is Baipai, 150/12 Soi

Naksuwan, Thanon Nonsee, off Thanon Rama III (Ⓣ02 294 9029, Ⓦwww.baipai.com; B1600, including transfers from central hotels; closed Mon), who run thorough, morning classes in a quiet, suburban house. Banglamphu's famous vegetarian cook, May Kaidee, shares her culinary expertise at the 33 Thanon Samsen branch of her restaurant chain (Ⓣ089 137 3173, Ⓦwww.maykaidee.com) for B1200 per day. The Ministry of Education-approved courses run by Saovapa (Ⓣ02 204 1143, Ⓦwww.saovapaschool.com), on the connecting soi between Sukhumvit sois 21 and 23, cost B1600 for four classes; fruit and veg carving is also available. Set in an orchard in a rural part of Nonthaburi, *Thai House* (Ⓣ02 903 9611 or 997 5161, Ⓦwww.thaihouse.co.th) runs one- (B3500) to three-day (B16,650) cooking courses, all including transfers from downtown, the latter including vegetable and fruit-carving and home-stay accommodation in traditional wooden houses.

Couriers DHL Worldwide (Ⓣ02 345 5000, Ⓦwww.dhl.co.th) has several Bangkok depots.

Embassies and consulates See Ⓦwww.mfa.go.th/web/2694.php for a full list, with links. Australia, 37 Thanon Sathorn Tai Ⓣ02 344 6300, Ⓦwww.austembassy.or.th; Burma (Myanmar), 132 Thanon Sathorn Nua Ⓣ02 234 4789; Cambodia, 518/4 Thanon Pracha Uthit (Soi Ramkamhaeng 39) Ⓣ02 957 5851–2; Canada, 15th floor, Abdulrahim Place, 990 Thanon Rama IV Ⓣ02 636 0540, Ⓦwww.international.gc.ca/bangkok; China, 57 Thanon Rajadapisek Ⓣ02 245 7033 or 02 245 7036; India, 46 Sukhumvit Soi 23 Ⓣ02 258 0300–5, Ⓦhttp://indianembassy.gov.in/bangkok; Indonesia, 600–602 Thanon Phetchaburi Ⓣ02 252 3135–9, Ⓦwww.kbri-bangkok.com; Ireland (honorary consul), 28th Floor, Q House Lumpini Building, 1 Thanon Sathorn Tai Ⓣ02 677 7500, Ⓦwww.irelandinthailand.com; Laos, 502/1–3 Soi Sahakarnpramoon, Thanon Pracha Uthit Ⓣ02 539 6667–8 ext 106, Ⓦwww.bkklaoembassy.com; Malaysia, 35 Thanon Sathorn Tai Ⓣ02 629 6800; New Zealand, 14th Floor, M Thai Tower, All Seasons Place, 87 Thanon Witthayu Ⓣ02 254 2530; Singapore, 129 Thanon Sathorn Tai Ⓣ02 286 2111; South Africa, Floor 12A, M Thai Tower, All Seasons Place, 87 Thanon Witthayu Ⓣ02 659 2900, Ⓦwww.saembbangkok.com; UK, 14 Thanon Witthayu Ⓣ02 305 8333; US, 120 Thanon Witthayu Ⓣ02 205 4000; Vietnam, 83/1 Thanon Witthayu Ⓣ02 650 8979.

Emergencies For English-speaking help in any emergency, call either the tourist police on their free 24hr phoneline Ⓣ1155 or the Tourist Assistance Centre on Ⓣ02 281 5051. The tourist police headquarters is on the eastern edge of town at 2107 Bangkok Tower, Thanon Phetchaburi Mai (east of Phetchaburi subway station and the Wat Mai Chong Lom stop on the Saen Saeb canal-boat service; Ⓣ02 308 0333), or drop in at the more convenient Chana Songkhram Police Station at the west end of Thanon Khao San in Banglamphu (Ⓣ02 282 2323). In the evenings, you'll also find tourist police in Suan Lum Night Bazaar and at the Silom end of Patpong 1.

Exchange The Suvarnabhumi Airport exchange desks and those in the upmarket hotels are open 24hr, while many other exchange booths stay open till 8pm or later, especially along Khao San, Sukhumvit and Silom roads and in the major shopping malls. You can also withdraw cash from hundreds of ATMs around the city and at the airports.

Hospitals, clinics and dentists Most expats rate the private Bumrungrad International Hospital, 33 Sukhumvit Soi 3 (Ⓣ02 667 1000, emergency Ⓣ02 667 2999, Ⓦwww.bumrungrad.com), with its famously five-star accommodation, as the best and most comfortable in the city, followed by the BNH (Bangkok Nursing Home) Hospital, 9 Thanon Convent Ⓣ02 686 2700, emergency Ⓣ02 632 1000, Ⓦwww.bnhhospital.com; Bangkok Hospital Medical Centre, 2 Soi Soonvijai 7, Thanon Phetchaburi Mai Ⓣ02 310 3000, emergency Ⓣ17192, Ⓦwww.bangkokhospital.com; and the Samitivej Sukhumvit Hospital, 133 Sukhumvit Soi 49 Ⓣ02 711 8000, Ⓦwww.samitivej.co.th. Other recommended private hospitals include Bangkok Mission Hospital, 430 Thanon Phitsanulok, corner of Thanon Lan Luang, just east of Banglamphu Ⓣ02 282 1100, Ⓦwww.tagnet.org/mission-net, and Bangkok Christian Hospital, 124 Thanon Silom Ⓣ02 233 6981–9, Ⓦwww.bkkchristianhosp.th.com. You can get vaccinations and malaria advice, as well as rabies advice and treatment, at the Thai Red Cross Society's Queen Saovabha Memorial Institute (QSMI) and Snake Farm on the corner of Thanon Rama IV and Thanon Henri Dunant (Mon–Fri 8.30am–noon & 1–4pm, Sat 8.30am–noon; Ⓣ02 252 0161–4, Ⓦwww.redcross.or.th). Among general clinics, there's one in Banglamphu on Soi Rambuttri run by the Bangkok Hospital (Ⓣ02 629 5260; daily 8am–7pm; B300 per consultation), and Global Doctor, Ground Floor, *Holiday Inn Hotel*, 981 Thanon Silom (corner of Thanon Surasak) Ⓣ02 236 8442–4, Ⓦwww.globaldoctorclinic.com, is recommended. For dental problems, try the Bumrungrad Hospital's dental department on Ⓣ02 667 2300, or the following dental clinics (not 24hr): Dental Hospital, 88/88 Sukhumvit Soi 49 Ⓣ02 260 5000–15, Ⓦwww.dentalhospitalbangkok.com; Siam Family Dental Clinic, 292/6

Siam Square Soi 4 ⓣ02/255 6664–5, ⓦwww.siamfamilydental.com.

Immigration office About 600m down Soi Suan Phlu, off Thanon Sathorn Tai (Mon–Fri 8.30am–4.30pm; ⓣ1178, 1111 or 02 287 3101–10, ⓦwww.immigration.go.th); see p.37 for information on visa extensions. Be very wary of any Khao San tour agents who offer to organize a visa extension for you: some are reportedly faking the relevant stamps and this has caused problems at immigration.

Internet access An increasing number of hotels, guest houses and a few restaurants and bars offer wi-fi, occasionally for free, more usually for a minimal fee; *True* provide free wi-fi to the whole Siam Square area. For a list of other hot spots, try ⓦwww.jiwire.com; for free locations, go to ⓦwww.stickmanweekly.com. Banglamphu is packed with places offering internet access, in particular along Thanon Khao San, where competition keeps prices very low. To surf in style, head for *True*, housed in a beautiful early twentieth-century villa at the back of *Tom Yam Kung* restaurant at the western end of Thanon Khao San, where you also can sip coffee, recline on retro sofas and browse lifestyle mags. The Ratchadamnoen Post Office on Banglamphu's Soi Damnoen Klang Neua (Mon–Fri 8.30am–4.30pm) also has very cheap public Catnet internet booths. On Thanon Sukhumvit the Time Internet Centre on the second floor of Times Square, between sois 12 and 14 (daily 9am–midnight), is reliable. The TOT office on the north side of Thanon Ploenchit near Central Chidlom offers cheap surfing in quite a civilized atmosphere, with refreshments available, and there's a branch of *True* (see above) on Soi 3, Siam Square, that's only a little more expensive. Elsewhere in the downtown area, during the day, there are several, rather noisy, places on Floor 7 of the MBK Shopping Centre (Zone D, towards the *Pathumwan Princess Hotel*), while *Chart Gallery Café* on the ground floor of River City shopping centre offers a bit more style and tranquillity, as well as food and drink while you're online. There's a Catnet centre in the public telephone office on Thanon Charoen Krung (see below).

Laundry Nearly all guest houses and hotels offer same-day laundry services (about B35 per kg), or there are several self-service laundries on and around Thanon Khao San, including Wearever on Thanon Samsen, between sois 1 and 3, which has sofas, coffee and free wi-fi.

Left luggage At Suvarnabhumi Airport (B100 per day); Don Muang Airport (B75 per day); Ekamai Eastern Bus Terminal (B30 per day); Southern Bus Terminal (B20–60 per day); Hualamphong train station (B30–80 per day); and most hotels and guest houses.

Massage and spas Traditional Thai massage sessions and courses are held at Wat Pho (see p.137), while luxurious and indulgent spa and massage treatments are available at many posh hotels across the city, including most famously at the *Banyan Tree Hotel* on Thanon Sathorn Tai (ⓣ02 679 1054, ⓦwww.banyantreespa.com) and the *Oriental* on Thanon Charoen Krung (ⓣ02 659 9000, ⓦwww.mandarinoriental.com), and more affordably at *Buddy Lodge* on Thanon Khao San in Banglamphu (ⓣ02 629 4477). One of Banglamphu's most popular massage centres is the uninvitingly clinical looking but highly rated Pian's on Soi Susie Pub (daily 7.30am–12.30am, ⓣ02 629 0924) where a Thai massage costs B180 per hr and you can also study Thai, Swedish, herbal and foot massage (about B5000 for a 30hr course, or B250 for a 1hr introduction). In the Silom area, Ruen Nuad, 42 Thanon Convent (ⓣ02 632 2662–3; daily 10am–9pm), offers excellent Thai massages (B350 for 1hr, B600 for 2hr), as well as aromatherapy and herbal massages, in an air-con, characterful wooden house, down an alley opposite the BNH Hopsital and behind *Naj* restaurant. At the other end of Thanon Silom, in Sun Square, a small shopping arcade on the south side of the road between soi 21 and 23, Nicolie (daily 10.30am–10pm; ⓣ02 233 6957, ⓦwww.nicolie-th.com) provides superb Thai (B1600/90min) and other massages, as well as facials and scrubs, in a soothing environment decorated with Asian *objets d'art*. Recommended places on Sukhumvit include the delightful Divana Massage and Spa at 7 Soi 25 (ⓣ02 661 6784, ⓦwww.divanaspa.com; from B1150); Pimmalai, in an old wooden house 50m east of BTS On Nut, exit 1, between sois 81 and 83 (ⓣ02 742 6452, ⓦwww.pimmalai.com; 3–4hr packages B700–3400); and the Thai massage at no-frills Bann Phuan on Soi 11 (B300 per hr). For more on spa treatments, see p.70.

Post offices The GPO is at 1160 Thanon Charoen Krung (postcode 10501), near Wat Muang Kae express-boat pier and walkable from Si Phraya pier. Poste restante, which is kept for two months, can be collected here. This and most other services at the GPO are open Mon–Fri 8am–8pm, Sat & Sun 8am–1pm; the parcel-packing service, however, operates Mon–Fri 8am–5pm, Sat 9am–noon. If you're staying on or near Thanon Khao San in Banglamphu, it's more convenient to use the local postal, packing and poste restante services at either Ratchadamnoen Post Office, Soi Damnoen Klang Neua, Bangkok 10200 (Mon–Fri 8am–5pm, Sat 9am–1pm); or Banglamphubon PO, Soi Sibsam

Hang, Bangkok 10203 (daily 8am–5pm). On Thanon Sukhumvit use Nana PO, between sois 4 and 6, Thanon Sukhumvit, Bangkok 10112 (Mon–Fri 8.30am–8pm, Sat, Sun & hols 9am–5pm).

Telephones International cardphones are dotted all over the city, so there's now little call for the public telephone offices in or adjacent to post offices, though their booths do at least guarantee some peace and quiet. The largest and most convenient is the CAT office in the compound of the GPO on Thanon Charoen Krung (Mon–Fri 8am–8pm, Sat & Sun 8am–4pm) which, as well as cardphones, offers a fax and internet service, a free collect-call service and even video-conferencing (see above for location details). The Ratchadamnoen post office in Banglamphu (see above) also has international telephone offices attached, but these close at 5pm. Many entrepreneurs, particularly on Thanon Khao San, advertise very cheap international calls through the internet.

Travel agents Diethelm Travel has branches all over Indochina and is especially good for travel within Thailand and to Cambodia, China, Laos and Vietnam: 12th Floor, Kian Gwan Building II, 140/1 Thanon Witthayu ⓣ02 660 7000, ⓦwww.diethelmtravel.com; Asian Trails sells flights, does interesting Thailand tours (see p.29) and runs scheduled and private transfers to many coastal destinations from Bangkok hotels and the airport: 9th Floor, SG Tower, 161/1 Soi Mahadlek Luang 3, Thanon Rajdamri ⓣ02 626 2000, ⓦwww.asiantrails.net; Jysk at *New Road Guest House*, 1216/1 Thanon Charoen Krung, between sois 34 and 36 ⓣ02 630 6994–8, ⓦwww.jysktravel.com is a reliable agent for train, bus and air tickets, as well as their own unusual tours, including live-aboard sea safaris around Ko Kood, houseboat trips near Sangkhlaburi and home-stays near Ayutthaya. Educational Travel Centre (ETC) sells air tickets and Thailand tours and has offices inside the *Royal Hotel*, 2 Thanon Rajdamnoen Klang, Banglamphu ⓣ02 224 0043, ⓦwww.etc.co.th, at 180 Thanon Khao San, Banglamphu ⓣ02 629 1885, and at 5/3 Soi Ngam Duphli ⓣ02 286 9424; Olavi Travel sells air tickets and budget transport within Thailand and is opposite *Gulliver's Traveler's Tavern* at 53 Thanon Chakrabongse, Banglamphu ⓣ02 629 4711–3, ⓦwww.olavi.com. On Sukhumvit, the helpful Thai Overlander at #407, between sois 21 and 23, ⓣ02 258 4778-80, ⓦwww.thaioverlander.com (Mon–Fri 8.30am–5.30pm, Sat 8.30am–4pm), sells train and air tickets and day-trips. Royal Exclusive, 9 The Place, 18/2 Thanon Chan ⓣ02 676 4182–7, ⓦwww.royalexclusive.com, is good for travel to Burma, Cambodia, Laos and Vietnam, and also sells air and train tickets; and the Bangkok branch of the worldwide STA Travel is a reliable outlet for cheap international flights: 14th Floor, Wall Street Tower, 33 Thanon Suriwong ⓣ02 236 0262, ⓦwww.statravel.co.th. For Bangkok tour operators specializing in trips within Thailand, see p.29.

Travel details

Trains

Bangkok Hualamphong Station to: Aranyaprathet (2 daily; 5–6hr); Ayutthaya (23 daily; 1hr 30min–2hr); Butterworth (Malaysia; 1 daily; 21hr); Cha-am (5 daily; 3hr 10min–3hr 50min); Chiang Mai (6 daily; 12–14hr); Chumphon (12 daily; 7hr–9hr 30min); Don Muang Airport (27 daily; 50min); Hua Hin (12 daily; 4–5hr); Khon Kaen (5 daily; 7hr 30min–10hr 30min); Khorat (11 daily; 4–5hr); Lampang (6 daily; 10–12hr); Lamphun (6 daily; 12–14hr); Lopburi (15 daily; 2hr 30min–3hr); Nakhon Pathom (12 daily; 1hr 30min); Nakhon Si Thammarat (2 daily; 15–16hr); Nong Khai (3 daily; 10hr 30min–12hr 30min); Pak Chong (for Khao Yai National Park; 10 daily; 2hr 45min–3hr 30min); Pattaya (1 daily; 3hr 45min); Phetchaburi (11 daily; 2hr 45min–3hr 45min); Phitsanulok (12 daily; 5hr 15min–9hr 30min); Prachuap Khiri Khan (11 daily; 5–7hr); Pranburi (3 daily; 5hr 30min); Si Racha (1 daily; 3hr 15min); Surat Thani (10 daily; 9–12hr); Surin (10 daily; 7–10hr); Tha Naleng (near Vientiane, Laos; 1 daily; 13hr 30min); Trang (2 daily; 15–16hr); Ubon Ratchathani (7 daily; 10hr 20min–13hr 15min); Udon Thani (4 daily; 10–12hr).

Thonburi (Bangkok Noi) Station to: Hua Hin (4 daily; 4hr–4hr 30min); Kanchanaburi (2 daily; 2hr 40min); Nakhon Pathom (6 daily; 1hr 10min); Nam Tok (2 daily; 4hr 35min).

Wongwian Yai Station to: Samut Sakhon (hourly; 1hr).

Buses

Eastern Bus Terminal to: Ban Phe (for Ko Samet; 12 daily; 3hr–3hr 30min); Chanthaburi (every 30min; 4–5hr); Laem Ngop (for Ko Chang; 2 daily 5hr 15min); Pattaya (every 30min; 2hr 30min–3hr 30min); Rayong (every 40min; 2hr 30min–3hr); Si Racha (every 30min; 2–3hr); Trat (6 daily; 5–6hr).

Northern Bus Terminal to: Aranyaprathet (hourly; 4hr 30min); Ayutthaya (every 20min; 2hr); Chanthaburi (5 daily; 3–4hr); Chiang Khan (2 daily; 9hr); Chiang Khong (10 daily; 13–14hr); Chiang Mai (20 daily; 10–11hr); Chiang Rai (21 daily; 11–13hr); Chiang Saen (2 daily; 12hr 30min); Chong Mek (daily; 11hr); Kamphaeng Phet (7 daily; 6hr 30min); Kanchanaburi (9 daily; 2hr 30min); Khon Kaen (29 daily; 6–7hr); Khorat (every 30min; 2hr 30min–3hr); Kong Chiam (4 daily; 11hr); Lampang (18 daily; 8hr 30min); Loei (20 daily; 8hr); Lopburi (every 20min; 2hr 30min–3hr); Mae Hong Son (2 daily; 18hr); Mae Sai (13 daily; 13hr); Mae Sariang (2 daily; 15hr); Mae Sot (11 daily; 8hr 30min); Mukdahan (13 daily; 11hr); Nakhon Phanom (17 daily; 12hr); Nan (10 daily; 12hr); Nong Khai (24 daily; 11hr); Pak Chong (for Khao Yai National Park; every 30min; 3hr); Pattaya (every 30min; 2–3hr); Phitsanulok (up to 19 daily; 5–6hr); Phrae (11 daily; 8hr 30min); Rayong (every 30miny; 2hr 30min–3hr 30min); Si Racha (every 30min; 2hr); Sukhothai (17 daily; 6–7hr); Surin (up to 20 daily; 8–9hr); Tak (13 daily; 7hr); That Phanom (3 daily; 12hr); Trat (5 daily; 4hr 30min); Ubon Ratchathani (19 daily; 10–12hr); Udon Thani (every 30min; 9hr).

Southern Bus Terminal to: Amphawa (every 40min; 2hr); Cha-am (every 40min; 2hr 45min–3hr 15min); Chumphon (roughly hourly; 7–9hr); Damnoen Saduak (every 40min; 2hr); Hat Yai (13 daily; 12hr); Hua Hin (every 40min; 3–4hr); Kanchanaburi (every 15min; 2hr); Ko Pha Ngan (2 daily; 14hr); Ko Samui (8 daily; 13hr); Krabi (8 daily; 12–14hr); Nakhon Pathom (every 10min; 40min–1hr 20min); Nakhon Si Thammarat (19 daily; 12hr); Phang Nga (6 daily; 12hr); Phetchaburi (every 40min; 2hr 15min); Phuket (15 daily; 12hr); Prachuap Khiri Khan (every 30min; 4–5hr); Pranburi (every 40min; 3hr 30min); Ranong (6 daily; 8hr); Samut Songkhram (every 20min; 1hr 30min); Satun (5 daily; 16hr); Surat Thani (10 daily; 10–12hr); Takua Pa (10 daily; 12–13hr); Trang (11 daily; 12–14hr).

Flights

Bangkok to: Buriram (3 weekly; 1hr); Chiang Mai (25 daily; 1hr); Chiang Rai (4–5 daily; 1hr 15min); Hua Hin (2 daily; 50min); Khon Kaen (2 daily; 55min); Ko Samui (20 daily; 1hr–1hr 30min); Krabi (5 daily; 1hr 20min); Lampang (1–2 daily; 1hr); Mae Hong Son (2 weekly; 1hr 20min); Nakhon Phanom (1–2 daily; 1hr 5min); Nakhon Si Thammarat (3 daily; 1hr 5min); Nan (4 weekly; 1hr 20min); Phitsanulok (2 daily; 55min); Phuket (21 daily; 1hr 20min); Ranong (3 weekly; 1hr 5min); Roi Et (4 weekly; 1hr); Sukhothai (2 daily; 40min); Surat Thani (4 daily; 1hr 15min); Trang (2 daily; 1hr 30min); Trat (3 daily; 1hr 5min); Ubon Ratchathani (3 daily; 1hr 5min); Udon Thani (7 daily; 1hr).

2

The central plains

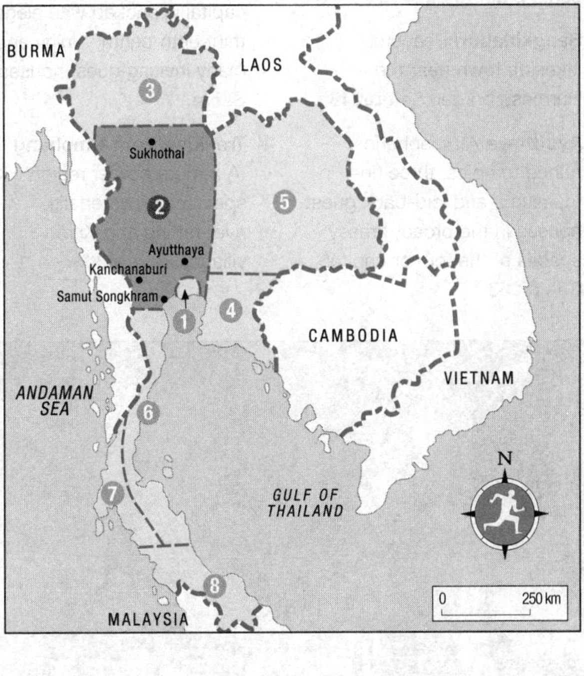

CHAPTER 2

Highlights

* **Kanchanaburi and the River Kwai** Stay in a raft house, take a scenic train ride along the Death Railway and visit some moving World War II memorials. See p.227
* **Erawan Waterfall** Seven breathtakingly beautiful crystal pools in a jungle setting. See p.237
* **Sangkhlaburi** Peaceful lakeside town near the Burmese border. See p.246
* **Ayutthaya** Atmospheric ruined temples, three fine museums and laid-back guest houses in the broad, grassy spaces of the former capital. See p.253
* **Wat Phra Phutthabat** A vibrant introduction to Thai religion at the Temple of the Buddha's Footprint. See p.269
* **Phitsanulok Folklore Museum** A fascinating look at traditional rural life. See p.275
* **Sukhothai** The nation's first capital is packed with elegant thirteenth-century ruins and many inviting guest houses. See p.277
* **Trekking from Umphang** A remote border region with spectacular waterfalls, river-rafting and Karen villages. See p.304

▲ Wat Phra Si Sanphet, Ayutthaya

2

The central plains

North and west of the capital, the unwieldy urban mass of Greater Bangkok peters out into the vast, well-watered **central plains**, a region that for centuries has grown the bulk of the nation's food and been a tantalizing temptation for neighbouring power-mongers. The most densely populated region of Thailand, with sizeable towns sprinkled among patchworks of paddy, orchards and sugar-cane fields, the plains are fundamental to Thailand's agricultural economy. Its rivers are the key to this area's fecundity, especially the Nan and the Ping, whose waters irrigate the northern plains before merging to form the Chao Phraya, which meanders slowly south through Bangkok and out into the Gulf of Thailand. Further west, the Mae Khlong River sustains the many market gardens and fills the canals that dominate the hinterlands of the estuary at **Samut Songkhram**, a centre for some of the most authentic floating markets in the country.

Sited at the confluence of the Kwai Yai and Kwai Noi rivers, the town of **Kanchanaburi** has long attracted visitors to the notorious Bridge over the River Kwai and is now well established as a travellers' hangout, mainly because of its unique raft-house accommodation. Few tourists venture much further upriver, except as passengers on the remaining stretch of the **Death Railway** – the most tangible wartime reminder of all – but the remote little hilltop town of **Sangkhlaburi** holds enough understated allure to make the extra kilometres worthwhile.

On the plains north of Bangkok, the historic heartland of the country, the major sites are the ruined ancient cities, which cover the spectrum of Thailand's art and architecture; most are conserved as historical parks and are enjoyably explored by bicycle. Closest to Bangkok, **Ayutthaya** served as the country's capital for the four hundred years prior to the 1782 foundation of Bangkok, and its ruins evoke an era of courtly sophistication. A short hop to the north, the remnants of **Lopburi** hark back to an earlier time, when the predominantly Hindu Khmers held sway over this region.

A separate nucleus of sites in the northern neck of the plains centres on **Sukhothai**, birthplace of the Thai kingdom in the thirteenth century. The buildings and sculpture produced during the Sukhothai era are the acme of Thai art, and the restored ruins of the country's first official capital are the best place to appreciate them, though two satellite cities – **Si Satchanalai** and **Kamphaeng Phet** – provide further incentives to linger in the area, and the city of **Phitsanulok** also serves as a good base. West of Sukhothai, on the Burmese border, the town of **Mae Sot** makes a refreshing change from ancient history and is the departure point for the rivers and waterfalls of **Umphang**, a remote border region that's becoming increasingly popular for trekking and rafting.

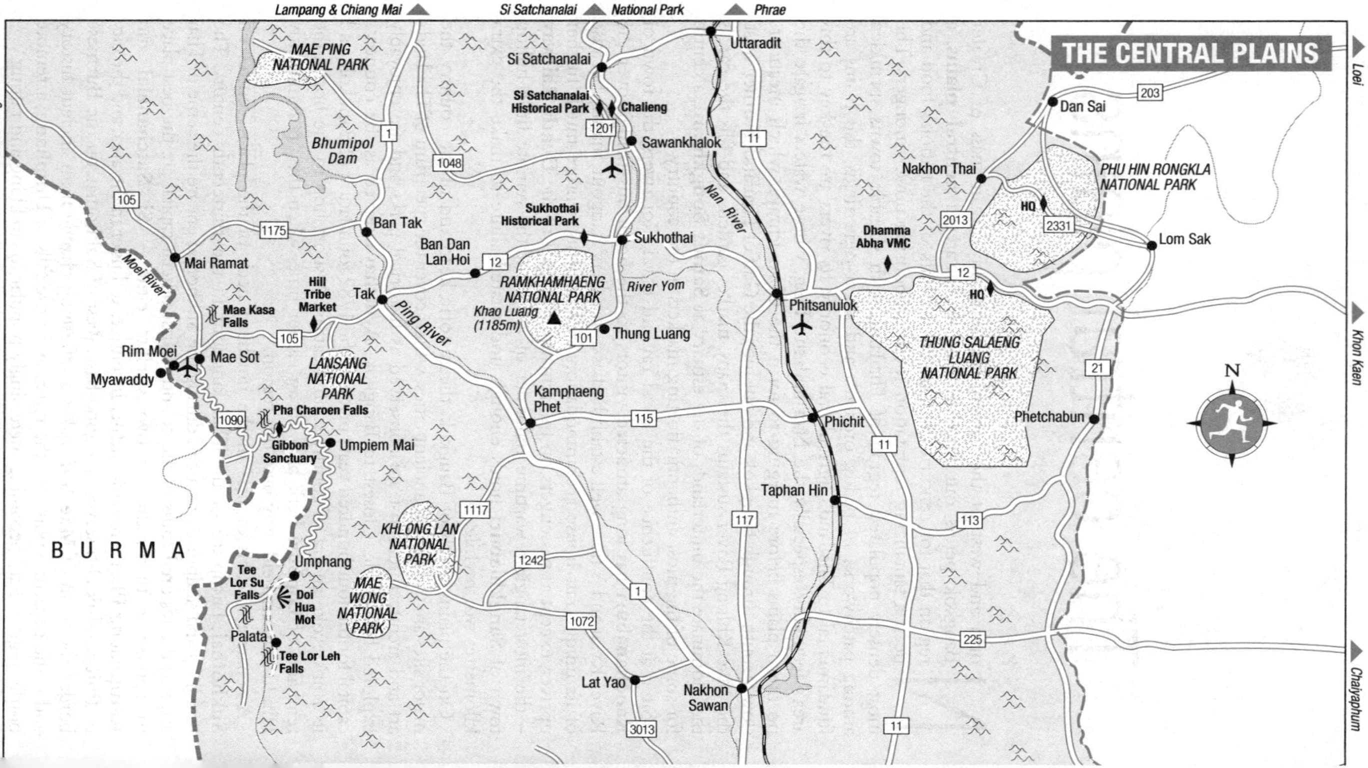
THE CENTRAL PLAINS
Lampang & Chiang Mai
Si Satchanalai
National Park
Phrae
Loei
Khon Kaen
Chaiyaphum
Mae Sariang
MAE PING NATIONAL PARK
Bhumipol Dam
Si Satchanalai
Si Satchanalai Historical Park
Chalieng
Sawankhalok
Uttaradit
Nan River
Dan Sai
Nakhon Thai
PHU HIN RONGKLA NATIONAL PARK
HQ
Lom Sak
Ban Tak
Mai Ramat
Moei River
Sukhothai Historical Park
Sukhothai
Ban Dan Lan Hoi
Hill Tribe Market
Tak
Mae Kasa Falls
RAMKHAMHAENG NATIONAL PARK
Khao Luang (1185m)
River Yom
Phitsanulok
Dhamma Abha VMC
Ping River
Thung Luang
Rim Moei
Mae Sot
Myawaddy
LANSANG NATIONAL PARK
Kamphaeng Phet
THUNG SALAENG LUANG NATIONAL PARK
Pha Charoen Falls
Gibbon Sanctuary
Umpiem Mai
Phichit
Phetchabun
N
Taphan Hin
KHLONG LAN NATIONAL PARK
BURMA
Umphang
Tee Lor Su Falls
Doi Hua Mot
MAE WONG NATIONAL PARK
Palata
Tee Lor Leh Falls
Lat Yao
Nakhon Sawan
203
105
1175
1
1048
1201
11
2013
2331
12
105
101
1090
115
21
117
113
1117
1242
1072
225
3013

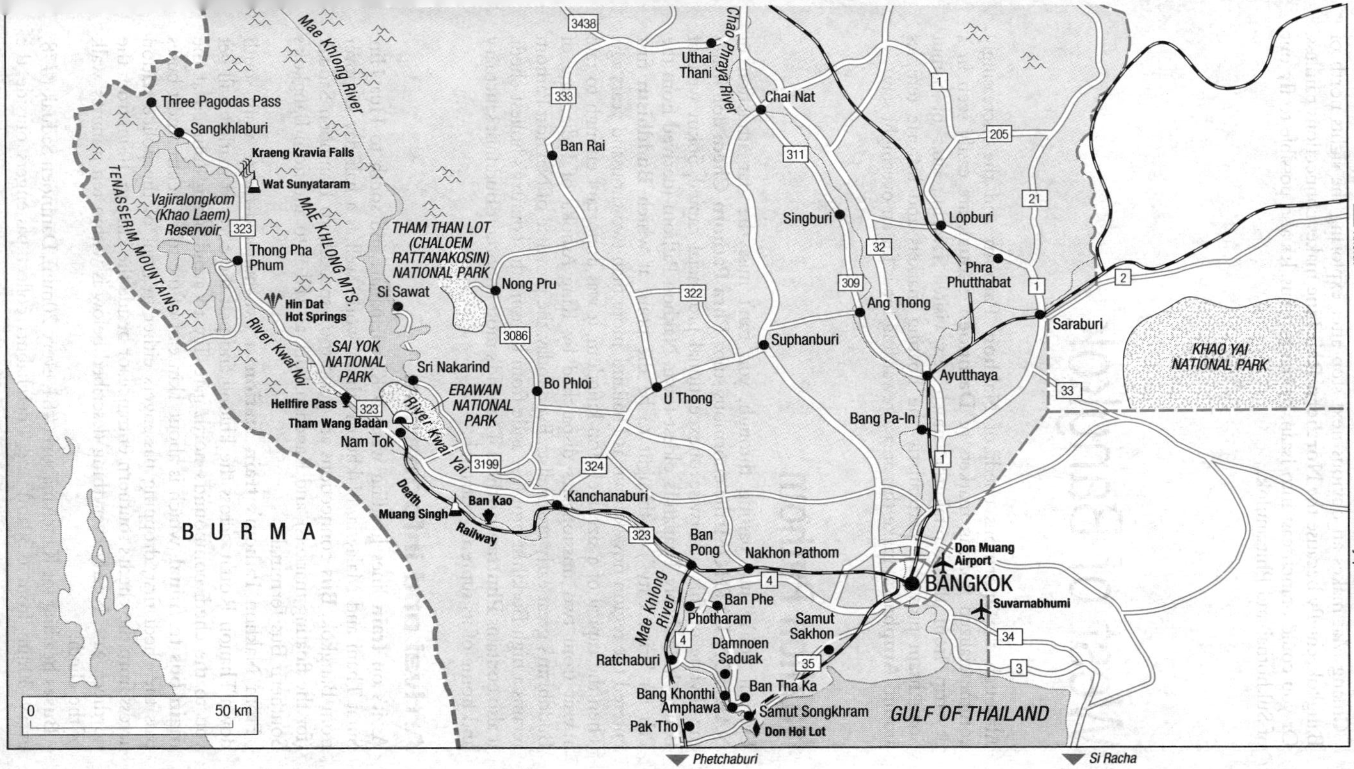

Khorat
Aranyaprathet
Phetchaburi
Si Racha
Three Pagodas Pass
Sangkhlaburi
Kraeng Kravia Falls
Wat Sunyataram
Vajiralongkom (Khao Laem) Reservoir
TENASSERIM MOUNTAINS
Thong Pha Phum
MAE KHLONG MTS.
Mae Khlong River
Hin Dat Hot Springs
River Kwai Noi
SAI YOK NATIONAL PARK
Hellfire Pass
Tham Wang Badan
Nam Tok
Si Sawat
Sri Nakarind
ERAWAN NATIONAL PARK
River Kwai Yai
THAM THAN LOT (CHALOEM RATTANAKOSIN) NATIONAL PARK
Nong Pru
Bo Phloi
Ban Rai
Uthai Thani
Chao Phraya River
Chai Nat
Singburi
Lopburi
Phra Phutthabat
Saraburi
KHAO YAI NATIONAL PARK
Ang Thong
Suphanburi
U Thong
Ayutthaya
Bang Pa-In
Death Railway
Muang Singh
Ban Kao
Kanchanaburi
BURMA
Ban Pong
Nakhon Pathom
Don Muang Airport
BANGKOK
Suvarnabhumi
Ban Phe
Photharam
Mae Khlong River
Samut Sakhon
Damnoen Saduak
Ratchaburi
Bang Khonthi
Amphawa
Ban Tha Ka
Samut Songkhram
Pak Tho
Don Hoi Lot
GULF OF THAILAND
0
50 km
3438
333
311
1
205
21
32
309
322
3086
2
33
1
323
3199
324
323
4
4
35
34
3

Chiang Mai makes an obvious next stop after exploring the sights north of Bangkok, chiefly because the **Northern Rail Line** makes connections painless. Or you could branch east into Isaan, by train or bus. It's also possible to **fly** out of Sukhothai and Phitsanulok.

West of Bangkok

Although the enormous chedi of **Nakhon Pathom** and the increasingly commercialized floating markets of **Damnoen Saduak** are easily seen in a day-trip from the capital, the much less visited riverine sites of Samut Songkhram province, particularly the floating markets and historic temples around **Amphawa**, make this area a rewarding focus for an overnight stay.

Nakhon Pathom

Even if you're just passing through, you can't miss the star attraction of **NAKHON PATHOM**: the enormous stupa **Phra Pathom Chedi** dominates the skyline of this otherwise unexceptional provincial capital, 56km west of Bangkok. Probably Thailand's oldest town, Nakhon Pathom (derived from the Pali for "First City") is thought to be the point at which **Buddhism** first entered the region now known as Thailand, more than two thousand years ago. Then the capital of a sizeable Mon kingdom, it was important enough to rate a visit from two missionaries dispatched by King Ashoka of India, one of Buddhism's great early evangelists. Even today, the province of Nakhon Pathom retains a high Buddhist profile – aside from housing the country's holiest chedi, it also contains **Phuttamonthon**, Thailand's most important Buddhist sanctuary and home of its supreme patriarch.

Arrival and information

As it's on **train** lines heading west to Kanchanaburi and south to Hua Hin, Surat Thani and Malaysia, Nakhon Pathom works well as a half-day stopover from Bangkok. **Bus** connections are good too, especially to Damnoen Saduak (for the floating markets), and Kanchanaburi, as well as to and from Bangkok's Southern Bus Terminal.

From Nakhon Pathom's **train station**, a two-hundred-metre walk south down Thanon Rotfai, across the khlong and past the covered market will get you to the chedi compound's north gate. Try to avoid being dumped at the **main bus terminal**, which is about 1km east of the town centre: most buses pass the chedi first, dropping passengers either in front of the police station across from the chedi's southern entrance, or beside the khlong, 100m from the northern gate. Nearly everything described below is within ten minutes' walk of the chedi.

Buses heading for Kanchanaburi (#81; every 20min), Damnoen Saduak (#78; every 30min from 6.30am) and Phetchaburi collect passengers outside the

The wat

Buddhist temple complexes, or wats, are central to nearly every community in Thailand and, as the main expressions of public architecture and art over the centuries, are likely to loom large in visitors' experiences of the country, too. They're much more than museum pieces, however: among Thailand's thirty thousand wats, you'll find classrooms and orphanages, massage clinics, drug rehab centres and hospitals, playgrounds and even small nature reserves. All come to life once a year for the *ngan wat* (temple fair) with food and market stalls, funfairs and other vibrant entertainment.

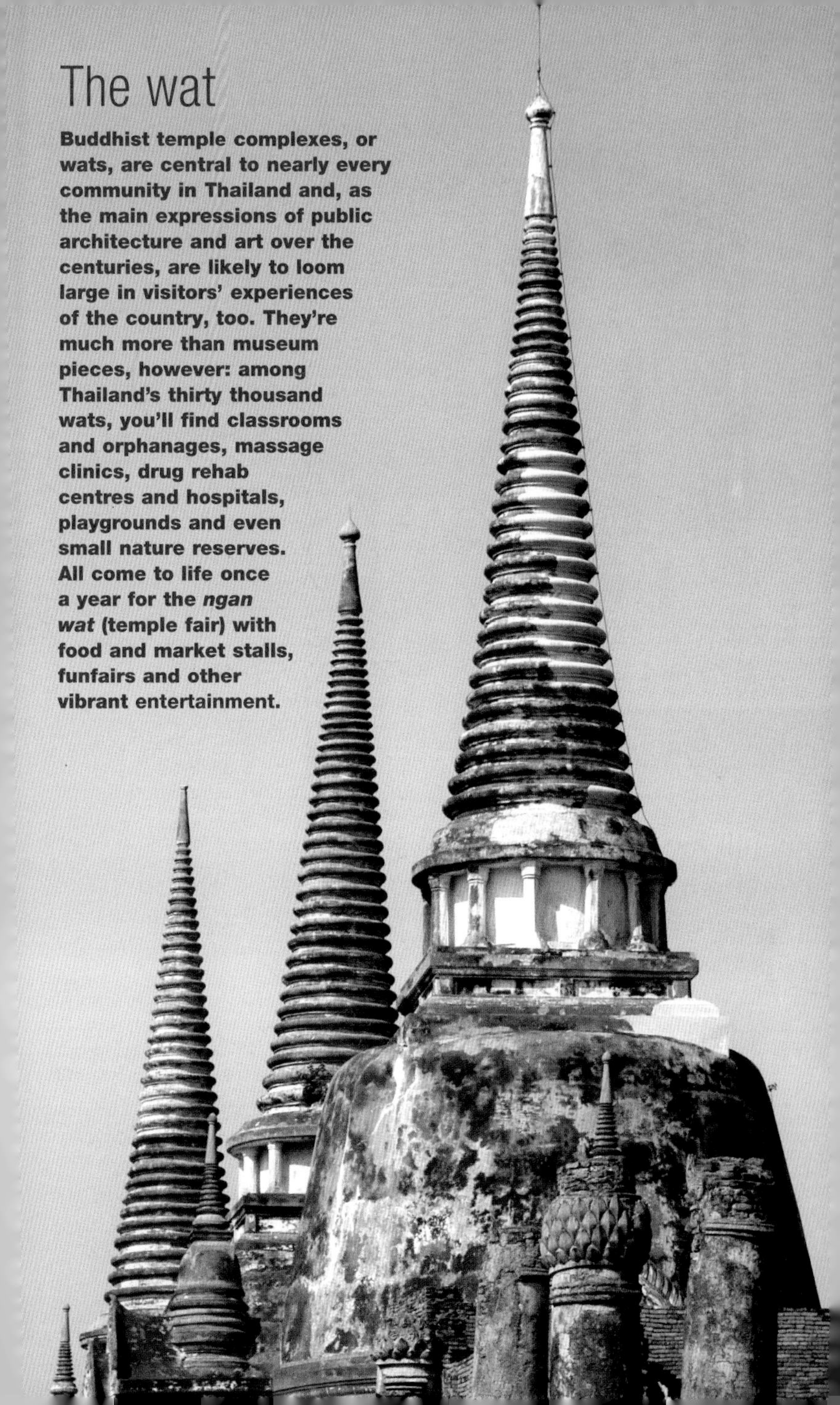

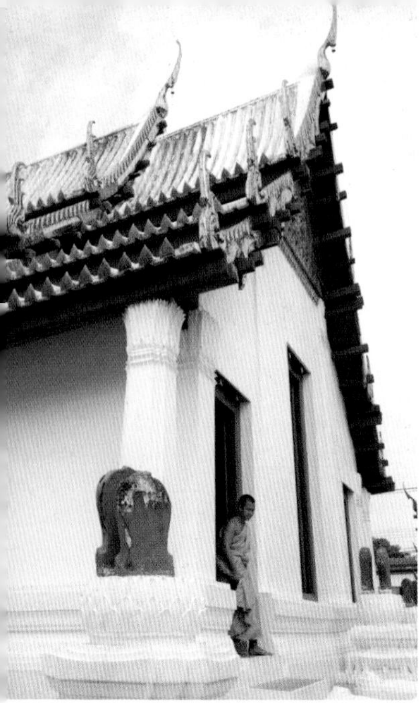

Bot with *sema* stones, Wat Yai Suwannaram, Phetchaburi ▲

Wat Phra That Doi Suthep, Chiang Mai ▼

Design

Wat architecture has evolved in ways as various as its functions, but the names and purposes of the main buildings have stayed constant in Thailand for some fifteen centuries.

Some general design features of Thai temples are also distinctive. The **Khmers**, who had ruled much of the country long before the Thais came onto the scene, built their temples to a cosmological plan, with concentric layers representing earth, oceans and heavens, rising to a central high point (Phanom Rung near Surin is a stunning example of this). Remnants of this layout persisted in Thai temples, including boundary walls – which are sometimes combined with a moat – and the multi-tiered roofs of so many wat buildings.

Furthermore, the Thais come from a tradition of building in wood rather than stone or brick, hence the leaning walls and long, curving roofs that give wats their elegant, tapering lines. On top of this, wat architects have long been preoccupied with light, the symbol of Buddhist wisdom and clarity, covering their buildings with gilt, filigree and vividly coloured glass mosaics.

The bot

The most important wat building is the **bot** (sometimes known as the *ubosot*), where monks are ordained. It usually stands at the heart of the compound, but lay people are rarely allowed inside. There's only one bot in any wat complex, and often the only way you'll be able to distinguish it from other temple buildings is by the eight **sema** or boundary stones which always surround it. Positioned at the four corners of the bot and at the cardinal points of the compass, these *sema* define the consecrated ground and usually look something like upright gravestones, though they can take many forms. They are often carved all over with symbolic Buddhist scenes or ideograms, and sometimes are even protected within miniature shrines of their own. One of the best *sema* collections is housed in the National Museum of Khon Kaen, in the northeast.

The viharn

Often almost identical in appearance to the bot, the **viharn** or assembly hall is the building you are most likely to enter, as it usually contains the wat's principal **Buddha image**, and sometimes two or three minor images as well. Large wats may have several viharns, while strict meditation wats, which don't deal with the laity, may not have one at all.

The mondop and ho trai

Less common wat buildings include the square **mondop**, usually built with a complex, cruciform roof, which houses either a Buddha statue or footprint, or holy texts. One of the most spectacular examples, with an ornate green-and-gold roof and huge doors encrusted with mother-of-pearl, shelters Thailand's holiest footprint of the Buddha, at Wat Phra Phutthabat near Lopburi.

The **ho trai**, or scripture library, is generally constructed on stilts, sometimes over a pond, to protect against termites and fire. You can see particularly good examples of traditional *ho trai* at Wat Rakhang in Bangkok, at Wat Phra Singh in Chiang Mai and at Wat Yai Suwannaram in Phetchaburi.

▲ *Ho trai*, Wat Phra Singh, Chiang Mai

▼ The *mondop*, Wat Phra Kaeo, Bangkok

▼ Buddha with garland

Reflection of Sukhothai chedi ▲

Phra Singh Buddha, Wat Phra Singh, Chiang Mai ▼

The chedi

Upon the Buddha's death, disciples from all over Asia laid claim to his **relics**, enshrining them in specially constructed towers, known as **chedis** in Thailand. In later centuries, chedis have also become repositories for the ashes of royalty or important monks – and anyone else who could afford to have one built.

Chedis are the most characteristic hallmarks of each architectural period in Thai history. The **Sukhothai** chedi (thirteenth to fifteenth centuries) is an elegant reworking of the dagoba – the version found in Sri Lanka, from where Theravada Buddhism came to Thailand. Early Sukhothai chedis are bell-shaped (symbolizing the ringing out of the Buddha's teachings), while the later, slimmer versions evoke a lotus bud. **Ayutthayan** architects (fourteenth to eighteenth centuries) owed more to the Khmers, elongating their chedis and resting them on a higher square platform. Meanwhile, the northern **Lanna** kingdom (thirteenth to sixteenth centuries) built some stupas to a squat pyramidal design that harked back to the seventh century, and other more rotund ones that drew on Burmese influences.

Contemporary chedi-builders have tended to combine historical features at will, but most still pay heed to the traditional **symbolism** of the three main components. In theory, the chedi base should be divided into three layers to represent hell, earth and heaven. Above this, the dome usually contains the cube-shaped reliquary, known as a *harmika* after the Sanskrit term for the Buddha's seat of meditation. Crowning the structure, the spire is graded into 33 rings, one for each of the 33 Buddhist heavens.

police station across Thanon Kwaa Phra from the chedi's southern gate. Buses bound for Bangkok pick up from Thanon Phaya Pan on the north bank of the khlong, across from the *Mitpaisal Hotel*.

You can **change money** at the exchange booth (open banking hours only) on Thanon Rotfai, beside the bridge over the khlong, one block south of the train station; several nearby banks also have ATMs.

Accommodation and eating

The most inviting and traveller-friendly **accommodation** in Nakhon Pathom is the conveniently located typical Chinese-Thai *Mitpaisal Hotel* (ⓣ034 242422, ⓔmitpaisal@hotmail.com; fan ❷, air-con ❸). Less than 200m from the chedi's north gateway, it has one entrance just a few metres to the right of the station exit, and another across from the north bank of the khlong (near the stop for buses to Bangkok), at 120/30 Thanon Phaya Pan. Rooms are a good size and are all en suite.

The obvious place to **eat** during the day is the hot-food stalls just outside the chedi compound's southern wall, near the museum. There are most options here, from noodle soup to grilled chicken and rice dishes. The market in front of the station serves the usual takeaway goodies, including reputedly the tastiest *khao laam* (bamboo cylinders filled with steamed rice and coconut) in Thailand. For a quality cappuccino or iced mocha, head for the air-con coffee salon *Boncafé Tongmesang* (daily 8am–9pm), beside Soi 3 on Thanon Rajdamnoen, about 300m west of the chedi's west gate; it has internet access too.

Phra Pathom Chedi

Although the Buddha never actually came to Thailand, legend held that he rested in Nakhon Pathom after wandering the country, and the original **Phra Pathom Chedi** (daily dawn–dusk; B40) may have been erected to represent this. The first structure resembled Ashoka's great stupa at Sanchi in India, with its inverted bowl shape and spire that topped 39m. Local chronicles, however,

▲ Worshippers at Phra Pathom Chedi, Nakhon Pathom

tell how the chedi was built in the sixth century as an act of atonement by the foundling Phraya Pan who murdered the tyrant Mon king before realizing that he was his father. Statues of both father and son stand inside the viharns of the present chedi.

Whatever its true origins, the first chedi fell into disrepair and was later rebuilt with a prang during the Khmer period, between the eighth and twelfth centuries. Abandoned to the jungle once more, it was rediscovered by the future Rama IV in 1853 who, mindful that all Buddhist monuments are sacred however dilapidated, set about encasing the old prang in the enormous new 120-metre-high plunger-shaped chedi, making it one of the tallest stupas in the world. Its distinctive cladding of shimmering golden-brown tiles was completed several decades later.

The present-day chedi is much revered and holds its own week-long Phra Pathom Chedi **fair**, around the time of Loy Krathong in mid-November, which attracts musicians, fortune-tellers and of course plenty of food stalls.

Around the chedi

Approaching the chedi from the main (northern) staircase, you're greeted by the eight-metre-high Sukhothai-style Buddha image known as **Phra Ruang Rojanarit**, installed in front of the north viharn. There's a viharn at each of the cardinal points and they all have an inner and an outer chamber containing tableaux of the life of the Buddha. The figures in the outer chamber of the **north viharn** depict two princesses paying homage to the newly born Prince Siddhartha (the future Buddha), while the inner one shows a monkey and an elephant offering honey and water to the Buddha at the end of a forty-day fast.

Proceeding clockwise around the chedi, as is the custom at all Buddhist monuments, you can weave between the outer promenade and the inner cloister via ornate doors that punctuate the dividing wall; the promenade is dotted with **trees**, many of which have religious significance, such as the bodhi tree (*ficus religiosa*) under one of which the Buddha was meditating when he achieved enlightenment. The wall of the **east viharn** features a diagrammatic cross-section of the chedi showing the encased original at its core, while beside the **south viharn** staircase is a three-dimensional replica of the original chedi with its Khmer prang (east side) and a model of the venerated chedi at Nakhon Si Thammarat (west side). The west viharn houses two reclining Buddhas: a sturdy, nine-metre-long figure in the outer chamber and a more delicate portrayal in the inner one. A long, golden reclining Buddha with a heart-warmingly beatific smile fills the outer chamber of the **west viharn**.

The museums

There are two, similarly named, museums within the chedi compound. The newer, more formal setup, the **Phra Pathom Chedi National Museum** (Wed–Sun 9am–noon & 1–4pm; B30; Ⓦwww.thailandmuseum.com), is just east from the bottom of the chedi's south staircase. It displays a good collection of Dvaravati-era (sixth to eleventh centuries) artefacts excavated nearby, including Wheels of Law – an emblem introduced by Theravada Buddhists before naturalistic images were permitted – and Buddha statuary with the U-shaped robe and thick facial features characteristic of Dvaravati sculpture.

For a broader, more domestic introduction to Nakhon Pathom's history, nose through the other magpie's nest of a collection, the **Phra Pathom Chedi Museum** (Wed–Sun 9am–noon & 1–4pm; free), which is halfway up the steps near the east viharn. More a curiosity shop than a museum, the small room is an Aladdin's cave of Buddhist amulets, seashells, gold and silver needles, Chinese ceramics, Thai musical instruments and ancient statues.

Sanam Chan Palace and the Contemporary Thai Art Centre

A ten-minute walk west of the chedi along Thanon Rajdamnoen brings you into a large park filled with the elegant wooden buildings of **Sanam Chandra Palace** (daily 9.30am–4pm; B50 or free if you have retained your ticket for Bangkok's Grand Palace; Ⓦwww.palaces.thai.net per day/index_sc.htm; free classical dance shows every Sat & Sun at 11am & 2pm), which was built as the country retreat of Rama VI in 1907. Sanam Chandra is located across the road from the main campus of Silpakorn University and can also be reached by following signs for the university: from the chedi's southwest corner head west along Thanon Rajvithee for about 1km and then turn right down Thanon Rajamanka Nai – a B30 ride on a motorbike taxi.

The **palace** was designed to blend Western and Eastern styles, and half a dozen of its main buildings are now open to the public. Its principal structure, the **Chaleemongkolasana Residence**, evokes a miniature Bavarian castle, complete with turrets and red-tiled roof; the **Mareerajaratabulung Residence** is a more oriental-style pavilion, built of teak and painted a deep rose colour inside and out; and the **Thub Kwan Residence** is an unadorned traditional Thai-style house of polished, unpainted golden teak. They each contain royal artefacts and memorabilia.

If you're interested in modern Thai art it's well worth seeing what's on at the **Contemporary Thai Art Centre** (Tues–Sun 9am–4pm; free; Ⓦwww.su.ac.th) just outside Sanam Chandra's southern perimeter, behind the Thub Kwan Residence on Thanon Rajamanka Nai. A purpose-built art centre set amongst outlying Sanam Chandra villas, it's the exhibition space for Bangkok's premier art school, Silpakorn University, whose satellite campus is just across the road. Their annual student show, held here every September and October, is usually very interesting.

Damnoen Saduak floating markets

To get an idea of what shopping in Bangkok used to be like before all the canals were tarmacked over, many people take an early-morning trip to the **floating markets** (*talat khlong*) of **DAMNOEN SADUAK**, 60km south of Nakhon Pathom. Vineyards and orchards here back onto a labyrinth of narrow canals, and every morning between 6 and 11am local market gardeners ply these waterways in paddle boats full of fresh fruit, vegetables and tourist-tempting soft drinks and souvenirs. Most dress in the deep-blue jacket and high-topped straw hat traditionally favoured by Thai farmers, so it all looks very picturesque, but the setup feels increasingly manufactured, and some visitors have complained of seeing more tourists than vendors, however early they arrive. For a more authentic version, consider going instead to the floating markets of Amphawa, 10km south of Damnoen Saduak (see p.223 & p.224).

The target for most tourists is the main **Talat Khlong Ton Kem**, 2km west of Damnoen Saduak's tiny town centre at the intersection of Khlong Damnoen Saduak and Khlong Thong Lang. Many of the wooden houses here have been converted into warehouse-style souvenir shops and tourist restaurants, diverting trade away from the khlong vendors and into the hands of large commercial enterprises. But, for the moment at least, a semblance of the traditional water trade continues, and the two bridges between Ton Kem and **Talat Khlong Hia Kui** (a little further south down Khlong Thong Lang) make decent vantage points. Touts invariably congregate at the Ton Kem pier to hassle you into taking a **boat trip** around the khlong network (asking an hourly rate of around B300 per person), but there are distinct disadvantages in being propelled between markets at top speed in a noisy motorized boat. For a less hectic and more sensitive look at the markets, explore via the walkways beside the canals.

Practicalities

Damnoen Saduak is 109km from Bangkok, so to reach the market in good time you have to catch one of the earliest **buses** from the capital's Southern Bus Terminal (every 40min from 5.50am; 2hr 30min). Or you could join one of the many day-trips. From Kanchanaburi, take bus #461 to Ban Phe (every 15min from 5.25am; 1hr 15min), then change to bus #78 or minibus #1733. To get to Damnoen Saduak from Phetchaburi or points further south, catch any Bangkok-bound bus and change either at Samut Songkhram or at the Photharam intersection.

Damnoen Saduak's **bus terminal** is just north of Thanarat Bridge and Khlong Damnoen Saduak, on the main Bangkok/Nakhon Pathom–Samut Songkhram road, Highway 325. Frequent yellow **songthaews** cover the 2km to Ton Kem, but walk if you've got the time: a walkway follows the canal, which you can get to from Thanarat Bridge, or you can cross the bridge and take the road to the right (west), Thanon Sukhaphiban 1, through the orchards. Drivers on the earliest buses from Bangkok sometimes do not terminate at the bus station but instead cross Thanarat Bridge and then drop tourists at a pier a few hundred metres along Thanon Sukhaphiban 1.

The best way to see the markets is to stay overnight in Damnoen Saduak and get up at dawn, well before the buses and coach tours from Bangkok arrive. There's decent budget **accommodation** at the *Little Bird Hotel*, also known as *Noknoi* (Ⓣ032 254382; fan ❶, air-con ❷), whose sign is clearly visible from the main road and Thanarat Bridge. Rooms here are good value with enormous en-suite bathrooms and air-conditioning if you want it. Staff can also arrange floating-market boat trips.

Samut Songkhram and around

Rarely visited by foreign tourists and yet within easy reach of Bangkok, the tiny estuarine province of **SAMUT SONGKHRAM** is nourished by the Mae Khlong River as it meanders through on the last leg of its route to the Gulf. Fishing is an important industry round here, and big wooden boats are still built in riverside yards near the estuary; further inland, fruit is the main source of income, particularly pomelos, lychees, guavas and coconuts. But for visitors it is the network of three hundred canals woven around the river, and the traditional way of life the waterways still support, that is most intriguing. As well as some of the most genuine floating markets in Thailand, there are chances to witness traditional cottage industries such as palm-sugar production and *bencharong* ceramic painting, plus more than a hundred historic temples to admire, a number of them dating back to the reign of Rama II, who was born in the province. The other famous sons of the region are Eng and Chang, the

Eng and Chang, the Siamese twins

Eng (In) and Chang (Chan), the "original" **Siamese twins**, were born in Samut Songkhram in 1811, when Thailand was known as Siam. The boys' bodies were joined from breastbone to navel by a short fleshy ligament, but they shared no vital organs and eventually managed to stretch their connecting tissue so that they could stand almost side by side instead of permanently facing each other.

In 1824, the boys were spotted by entrepreneurial Scottish trader Robert Hunter, who returned five years later with an American sea merchant, Captain Abel Coffin, to convince the twins' mother to let them take her sons on a world tour. Hunter and Coffin anticipated a lucrative career as producer-managers of an exotic **freak show**, and were not disappointed. They launched the twins in Boston, advertising them as "the Monster" and charging the public 50 cents to watch the boys demonstrate how they walked and ran. Though shabbily treated and poorly paid, the twins soon developed a more theatrical show, enthralling their audiences with acrobatics and feats of strength, and earning the soubriquet "the eighth wonder of the world". At the age of 21, having split from their exploitative managers, the twins became self-employed, but continued to tour with other companies across the world. Wherever they went, they would always be given a thorough examination by local **medics**, partly to counter accusations of fakery, but also because this was the first time the world and its doctors had been introduced to conjoined twins. Such was the twins' international celebrity that the term "Siamese twins" has been used ever since. Chang and Eng also sought advice from these doctors on surgical separation – an issue they returned to repeatedly right up until their deaths but never acted upon, despite plenty of gruesome suggestions.

By 1840 the twins had become quite wealthy and decided to settle down. They were granted American citizenship, assumed the family name Bunker, and became slave-owning **plantation farmers** in North Carolina. Three years later they married two local sisters, Addie and Sally Yates, and between them went on to father 21 children. The families lived in separate houses and the twins shuttled between the two, keeping to a strict timetable of three days in each household; for an intriguing imagined account of this bizarre state of affairs, read Darin Strauss's novel *Chang and Eng*, reviewed on p.860. Chang and Eng had quite different personalities, and relations between the two couples soured, leading to the division of their assets, with Chang's family getting most of the land, and Eng's most of the slaves. To support their dependents, the twins were obliged to take their show back on the road several times, on occasion working with the infamous showman P.T. Barnum. Their final tour was born out of financial desperation following the 1861–65 Civil War, which had wiped out most of the twins' riches and led to the liberation of all their slaves.

In 1874, Chang succumbed to bronchitis and died; Eng, who might have survived on his own if an operation had been performed immediately, died a few hours later, possibly of shock. They were 62. The twins are buried in White Plains in North Carolina, but there's a **memorial** to them near their birthplace in Samut Songkhram, where a statue and the small, makeshift In-Chan Museum (Mon–Fri 8.30am–4.30pm; free) have been erected 4km north of the provincial capital's centre on Thanon Ekachai (Route 3092).

"original" Siamese twins, who grew up in Samut Songkhram and are commemorated with a small museum in the town.

Despite the region's tangible charm, tourism is very much in its infancy here, so hotel options are limited. If you're dependent on public transport, your first stop will be the provincial capital of Samut Songkhram, also commonly known as Mae Khlong, after the river that cuts through it. It's a pleasant enough market town, but there's little reason to linger as the sights and most of the accommodation are out of town, mainly in the **Amphawa** district a few kilometres upriver.

If you get the chance, it's well worth venturing out onto the canals after dark to **watch the fireflies** twinkling romantically in their favourite lamphu trees like delicate strings of fairylights; any boatman will ferry you to the right spot.

Arrival

The most enjoyable way of travelling to Samut Songkhram is by **train** from Bangkok – a scenic, albeit rather convoluted route that has three stages, involves going via Samut Sakhon and could take up to three hours. It's a very unusual line, being single track and for much of its route literally squeezed in between homes, palms and mangroves, and, most memorably, between market stalls, so that at both the Samut Sakhon and Samut Songkhram termini the train really does chug to a standstill amidst the trays of seafood. Trains to Samut Sakhon leave approximately hourly from Bangkok's **Wongwian Yai station** in southern Thonburi (not to be confused with Thonburi train station further north), but for the fastest onward connections catch the 5.30am, 8.35am, 12.15pm or 3.25pm (1hr). The train pulls up right inside the wet market at **Samut Sakhon**, also known as **Mahachai**, where you need to take a ferry across the Maenam Tha Chin to get the connecting train from **Ban Laem** on the other bank. Once you've left the train, cross the track and continue in the same direction as the train was going, through a clothes market, until you emerge on to a shopping street. Cross the street to the five-storey, blue-painted *Tarua Restaurant*, right on the estuary, adjacent to the busy fishing port, where you'll find two piers. Boats from both piers will get you across the river: those departing the pier on the right of the restaurant are frequent but drop you directly across on the other bank, from where it's a twenty-minute walk to Ban Laem station (turn right and walk upriver, past a Thai temple); boats from the pier on the left of the restaurant go direct to Ban Laem station (5min), but leave infrequently, being timed to coincide with the Ban Laem trains. There are only four trains a day in each direction from **Ban Laem** to Samut Songkhram at the end of the line (1hr), a journey through marshes, lagoons, prawn farms, salt flats and mangrove and palm growth. Once again, at **Samut Songkhram**, the station is literally enveloped by the town-centre market, with traders gathering up their goods and awnings from the trackside for the arrival and departure of the service. From the station it's 50m due west to the river and the pier for cross-river ferries and taxi-boats.

The **bus** ride to Samut Songkhram from Bangkok's Southern Bus Terminal (every 20min; 1hr 30min) is faster than the train, but the views are dominated by urban sprawl until the last stretch, when Highway 35 runs through a swathe of **salt farms** whose windmills pump in the sea water via a web of canals, leaving the brine to evaporate into photogenic little pyramids of white crystals. Buses also run direct to **Amphawa** from Bangkok's Southern Bus Terminal (every 20min; 2hr). Samut Songkhram's bus station is south of the market, across from the Siam Commercial Bank off Thanon Ratchayadruksa. When returning to Bangkok, there's also a minibus service to the Northern Mo Chit bus terminal (approximately hourly; about 1hr 30min), which departs from Thanon Si Jumpa, about 100m east of the *Maeklong Hotel*.

Transport and information

Once in Samut Songkhram, you have various options for local transport, though routes don't encompass all the sights. **Songthaews** to Amphawa and

local buses to Amphawa and Damnoen Saduak, via Highway 325, leave from the north edge of the central market, and from the bus station. However, a more appealing way of exploring this area is by boat: **taxi-boats** and other chartered river transport operate from the Mae Khlong River pier, 50m west of the train station and market in the town centre, or, most rewardingly, once in Amphawa, you can take a **boat tour** from Amphawa's *Baan Tai Had Resort* or one of the nearby homestays. *Baan Tai Had* also rents out bicycles, kayaks and jet skis. Alternatively, you could join a one-day **cycling tour** of the area from Bangkok with SpiceRoads (see p.104).

All the central branches of the main banks around the edge of Samut Songkhram market offer **currency exchange**.

Accommodation and eating

If you want cheap **accommodation** then you should stay in Samut Songkhram town centre, at the welcoming and well-kept *Maeklong Hotel* (Ⓣ034 711150; ❷), which has large fan and air-con rooms about 150m due north of the train station, beyond the edge of the market, at 526/10–13 Thanon Si Jumpa. To get the most out of the area however, it's worth splashing out on the luxurious but good-value *Baan Tai Had Resort* (Ⓣ034 767220, Ⓦwww.baantaihad.com; ❺–❽), located beside the Mae Khlong River in the Amphawa district, about 6km upstream from Samut Songkhram (15min by taxi-boat from Samut Songkhram's pier). With its stylish, comfortable bungalows and rooms set around a Bali-style garden, swimming pool and restaurant, *Baan Tai Had* makes a good base, not least because of its local tour programmes and English-speaking guides. There's also a fast-growing number of canalside **homestays** in the area, catering primarily to Thai tourist groups but open to adventurous foreigners too, offering overnight packages from B800 per person: try *Baan Suan Puttaraksa* in Bang Khan Taek, 4km west of Samut Songkhram on Route 3093 (Ⓣ034 751038, Ⓦwww.puttaraksa.com) or contact Nathawut Boonpad of the homestay collective in Plai Phong Pang, 9km west of Samut Songkhram on Route 3093 (Ⓣ034 717510, Ⓦwww.thaitambon.com/SS/Ampawa1A.htm).

Seafood is the obvious regional speciality and the most famous local dish is *hoi lot pat cha*, a spicy stir-fry that centres round the tubular molluscs, known as **hoi lot** or "worm shells", that are harvested in their sackloads at low tide from a muddy sandbank known as Don Hoi Lot at the mouth of the Mae Khlong estuary. Don Hoi Lot is probably the most famous spot in the province to eat seafood, and a dozen restaurants occupy the area around the nearby pier, many offering views out over the Gulf and its bountiful sandbar; the pier is 5km south of Highway 35 and served by songthaews from Samut Songkhram market. If you're staying at *Baan Tai Had*, make use of the free taxi-boat service to the canalside *Chao Lay* restaurant whose mid-priced menu features plenty of fresh fish and seafood, usually including locally caught giant prawns (*kung yai*). In Samut Songkhram itself, the food stalls alongside the pier make a pleasant spot for a lunch of cheap seafood *phat thai*.

Tha Ka floating market and the palm-sugar centres

Unlike at the over-touristed markets of nearby Damnoen Saduak, the **floating market at Tha Ka** is still the province of local residents. Market gardeners paddle up here in their small wooden sampans, or motor along in their noisy longtails, the boats piled high either with whatever's in season, be it pomelos or betel nuts, rambutans or okra, or with perennially popular snacks like hot noodle soup and freshly cooked satay. Their main customers are canalside residents and other traders, so the atmosphere is still pleasingly but not artificially traditional. Thai tourist groups do visit, but mainly if market day happens to fall on a weekend. The Tha Ka market operates only six times a month, on a **timetable** that's dependent on the tides (for boat access) and is therefore dictated by the moon; thus market days are restricted to the second, seventh and twelfth mornings of every fifteen-day lunar cycle, from around 7 to 11am (contact any TAT office for exact dates). The market takes place on Khlong Phanla in the village of Ban Tha Ka, a half-hour **boat ride** from *Baan Tai Had Resort*, or ten to forty minutes from the homestays, and about an hour from Damnoen Saduak; it's usually incorporated into a day-trip. The boat ride to the market is half the fun, but you can also get there by **road**, following Highway 325 out of Samut Songkhram for 10km, then taking a five-kilometre access road to Ban Tha Ka.

Most boat trips to Tha Ka also make a stop at one of the nearby **palm-sugar-making centres**. The sap of the coconut palm is a crucial ingredient in many Thai sweets and the fertile soil of Samut Songkhram province supports many small-scale sugar-palm plantations. Several palm-sugar cottage industries between Amphawa and Ban Tha Ka are open to the public; they're signed off Highway 325 and if you're not on a tour you can reach them by car or by Damnoen Saduak-bound bus.

Amphawa and around

The district town of **AMPHAWA** is smaller and more atmospheric than Samut Songkhram, retaining original charm alongside modern development. Its old neighbourhoods hug the banks of the Mae Khlong River and the Khlong Amphawa tributary, the wooden homes and shops facing the water and accessed either by boat or on foot along one of the waterfront walkways. Frequent **songthaews** and local **buses** (both approximately every 30min; 15min) connect Samut Songkhram market with Amphawa market, which sets up beside the khlong, just back from its confluence with the river.

King Rama II Memorial Park, Wat Amphawan and Amphawa's floating market

King Rama II was born in Amphawa (his mother's home town) in 1767 and is honoured with a memorial park and temple erected on the site of his probable birthplace, beside the Mae Khlong River on the western edge of Amphawa town, five minutes' walk west of Amphawa market and khlong. It's accessible both by boat and by road, 6km from Samut Songkhram on the Amphawa–Bang Khonthi road.

Rama II, or Phra Buddhalertla Naphalai as he is known in Thai, was a famously cultured king and a respected poet and playwright, and the **museum** (Wed–Sun 9am–4pm; B10) at the heart of the **King Rama II Memorial Park** (daily 9am–6pm) displays lots of rather esoteric Rama II memorabilia, including a big collection of nineteenth-century musical instruments and a gallery of *khon* masks used in traditional theatre. On the edge of the park, **Wat Amphawan** is graced with a statue of the king and decorated with murals that depict scenes from his life, including a behind-the-altar panorama of nineteenth-century Bangkok, with Ratanakosin Island's Grand Palace, Wat Pho and Sanam Luang still recognizable to modern eyes. The tradition of holding a **floating market** on the canal near Wat Amphawan has recently been revived for tourists: Talat Nam Amphawa Yamyen is held here every Friday, Saturday and Sunday (4–8pm).

Wat Chulamani and Ban Pinsuwan bencharong workshop

The canalside **Wat Chulamani** was until the late 1980s the domain of the locally famous abbot Luang Pho Nuang, a man believed by many to possess special powers, and followers still come to the temple to pay respects to his body, which is preserved in a glass-sided coffin in the main viharn. The breathtakingly detailed decor inside the viharn is testament to the devotion he inspired: the intricate black-and-gold lacquered artwork that covers every surface has taken years and cost millions of baht to complete. Across the temple compound, the bot's modern, pastel-toned murals tell the story of the Buddha's life, beginning inside the door on the right with a scene showing the young Buddha emerging from a tent (his birth) and being able to walk on lilypads straightaway. The death of the Buddha and his entry into Nirvana is depicted on the wall behind the altar. Wat Chulamani is located beside Khlong Amphawa, a twenty-minute walk east of Amphawa market, or a five-minute boat ride. It is also signed off Highway 325, so any bus going to Damnoen Saduak from Samut Songkhram will drop you within reach.

A few hundred metres down the road from Wat Chulamani, and also accessible on foot, by bus and by canal, the Ban Pinsuwan **bencharong workshop** specializes in reproductions of famous antique *bencharong* ceramics, the exquisite five-coloured pottery that used to be the tableware of choice for the Thai aristocracy and is now a prized collector's item.

Kanchanaburi and the River Kwai valleys

Set in a landscape of limestone hills just 120km from Bangkok, the provincial capital of **Kanchanaburi** occupies a strategic and scenic spot at the point where the **River Kwai Noi** merges with the **River Kwai Yai** to become the Mae Khlong (though Kwai Yai is just the name that's been appropriated for the Mae Khlong as it flows through this region). The town is most famous for its World War II role as a POW camp and base for construction work on the Thailand–Burma Railway, chiefly because of the notorious Bridge over the River Kwai, which spans the river here. But there are plenty more important wartime sights in and around Kanchanaburi, and the town is also an appealing destination in its own right, with lots of riverside guest houses that make enjoyable places to unwind for a few days. The surrounding area offers numerous caves, wats and historical sites to explore, some of them easily reached by bicycle, and organized treks and rafting trips are also a major feature.

Beyond Kanchanaburi, the main area of interest is the Kwai Noi valley as this was the route followed by the **Death Railway**. Riding the train along the remaining section of this line is a popular activity and combines well with a visit to the sobering museum north of the current terminus at the aptly named **Hellfire Pass**. Following the Kwai Noi to its headwaters brings you to the

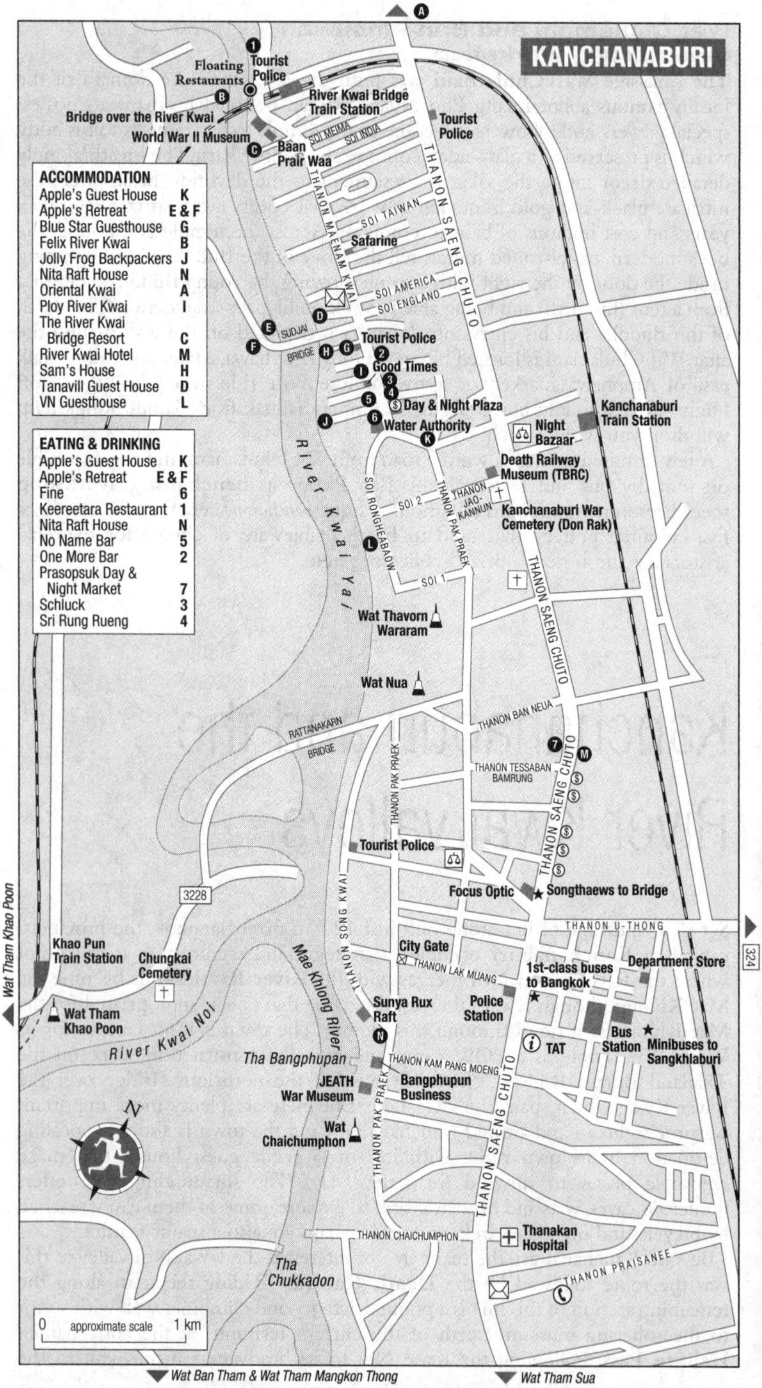
KANCHANABURI
A
ACCOMMODATION
Apple's Guest House K
Apple's Retreat E & F
Blue Star Guesthouse G
Felix River Kwai B
Jolly Frog Backpackers J
Nita Raft House N
Oriental Kwai A
Ploy River Kwai I
The River Kwai Bridge Resort C
River Kwai Hotel M
Sam's House H
Tanavill Guest House D
VN Guesthouse L
EATING & DRINKING
Apple's Guest House K
Apple's Retreat E & F
Fine 6
Keereetara Restaurant 1
Nita Raft House N
No Name Bar 5
One More Bar 2
Prasopsuk Day & Night Market 7
Schluck 3
Sri Rung Rueng 4
Floating Restaurants
Tourist Police
River Kwai Bridge Train Station
Bridge over the River Kwai
World War II Museum
Baan Prair Waa
Tourist Police
SOI MEIMA
SOI INDIA
THANON MAENAM KWAI
THANON SAENG CHUTO
SOI TAIWAN
Safarine
SOI AMERICA
SOI ENGLAND
SUDJAI
BRIDGE
Tourist Police
Good Times
Day & Night Plaza
Water Authority
Night Bazaar
Kanchanaburi Train Station
Death Railway Museum (TBRC)
Kanchanaburi War Cemetery (Don Rak)
THANON JAO-KANNUN
SOI 2
SOI RONGHEABAOW
THANON PAK PRAEK
SOI 1
River Kwai Yai
Wat Thavorn Wararam
Wat Nua
RATTANAKARN BRIDGE
THANON BAN NEUA
THANON TESSABAN BAMRUNG
THANON PAK PRAEK
Tourist Police
Focus Optic
Songthaews to Bridge
3228
THANON SONG KWAI
THANON U-THONG
324
Khao Pun Train Station
Chungkai Cemetery
Wat Tham Khao Poon
Wat Tham Khao Poon
City Gate
THANON LAK MUANG
Department Store
1st-class buses to Bangkok
Police Station
Sunya Rux Raft
Mae Khlong River
River Kwai Noi
TAT
Bus Station
Minibuses to Sangkhlaburi
Tha Bangphupan
THANON KAM PANG MOENG
Bangphupun Business
JEATH War Museum
THANON PAK PRAEK
Wat Chaichumphon
N
THANON CHAICHUMPHON
Thanakan Hospital
THANON PRAISANEE
Tha Chukkadon
0 approximate scale 1 km
Wat Ban Tham & Wat Tham Mangkon Thong
Wat Tham Sua

unhyped, ethnically mixed little lakeside town of **Sangkhlaburi**, close by the Burmese border at **Three Pagodas Pass**. Further east, the Kwai Yai valley offers fewer obvious attractions, but is the site of the much-visited **Erawan Falls**, and impressive caves at nearby **Tham Than Lot National Park**.

Kanchanaburi

With its plentiful supply of traveller-oriented accommodation and countless possibilities for easy forays into the surrounding countryside, **KANCHANABURI** makes the perfect getaway from Bangkok, a two-hour bus ride away. The big appeal here is the river: that it's the famous River Kwai is a bonus, but the more immediate attractions are the guest houses whose rooms overlook the waterway, most of them offering fine views of the serrated limestone hills beyond. The heart of this ever-expanding travellers' scene dominates the southern end of Thanon Maenam Kwai (also spelt Kwae) and is within easy reach of the train station, but the real town centre is some distance away, running north from the bus station up Kanchanaburi's main drag, Thanon Saeng Chuto.

Nearly all Kanchanaburi's official attractions relate to World War II and the building of the Thailand–Burma Railway. Day-trippers and tour groups descend in their hundreds on the infamous **Bridge over the River Kwai**, the symbol of Japanese atrocities in the region, though the town's main **war museums** and **cemeteries** are much more moving. Many veterans returning to visit the graves of their wartime comrades are understandably resentful that others have in some cases insensitively exploited the POW experience – the commercial paraphernalia surrounding the Bridge is a case in point. On the other hand, the Death Railway Museum provides shockingly instructive accounts of a period not publicly documented outside this region. The town's main war sights are located along the east bank of the Kwai Yai and Mae Khlong, but it's easy to cross the river – by road, ferry or longtail – and explore

▲ Aerial view of the River Kwai and the Bridge

some of the more tranquilly located temples along the Kwai Noi and west bank of the Mae Khlong.

The Bridge forms the dramatic centrepiece of the annual *son et lumière* **River Kwai Bridge Festival**, held over ten nights from the end of November to commemorate the first Allied bombing of the Bridge on November 28, 1944; Kanchanaburi gets packed out during this time, so book accommodation well ahead.

Arrival

Trains are the most scenic way to get to Kanchanaburi, but there are only two daily from Bangkok's Thonburi station, via Nakhon Pathom, and, gallingly, tourists are obliged to pay a flat fare of B100 in recognition of it being an attraction, though locals use the service too of course. If coming from Hua Hin, Chumphon and points further south, take the train to Ban Pong and then change to a Kanchanaburi-bound train (or bus; the bus stop is at the clock tower, about 1km from Ban Pong train station). The main **Kanchanaburi train station** (☎034 511285) is on Thanon Saeng Chuto, about 2km north of the town centre, but within walking distance of some of the Thanon Maenam Kwai accommodation. However, if you're staying at the *Felix River Kwai* or *The River Kwai Bridge Resort*, or are doing a day-trip and want to see the Bridge, get off at the **River Kwai Bridge train station** instead, five minutes further down the line, on the east bank of the river.

Faster than the train are the **buses** from Bangkok's Southern Bus Terminal (every 15min; 2hr) and Northern Bus Terminal (hourly; 2hr 30min). From Lopburi, Ayutthaya (for trains from Chiang Mai), or points further north, you'll have to return to Bangkok or change buses at Suphanburi, about 90km north of Kanchanaburi (#411; every 20min; 2hr). From Phetchaburi and Hua Hin you need to change buses at Ratchaburi for connections to Kanchanaburi (#461; every 15min; 2hr). Kanchanaburi **bus station** (☎034 511182) is at the southern edge of the town centre, a good 2km from most accommodation.

For transport by **samlor** or **tuk-tuk** from the bus or train station to Thanon Maenam Kwai accommodation, expect to pay B20–80 per person depending on the number of passengers; from the bus station you could also travel part way on the public songthaew service described below.

Moving on from Kanchanaburi

Travel agents and guest houses sell tickets for tourist minibuses to **Suvarnabhumi Airport** (5 daily; 3hr; B450); **Ayutthaya** (daily, timed to connect with the night trains to Chiang Mai; B400); and Bangkok's **Khao San** (or the nearby *Royal Ratanakosin Hotel*; hourly; 2hr; B140). Government buses run to Bangkok's Northern Mo Chit bus terminal as well as to the Southern Bus Terminal, and to all destinations described on p.308. All government buses leave from the main **bus station**; the first-class ticket office and departure point is beside the main road on the edge of the bus station, while the office for all other services is in the middle of the depot. Minibus tickets for **Sangkhlaburi** are sold from a small office at the back of the bus station.

The easiest way to get to **northern Thailand** is to go via Ayutthaya for the Northern Rail Line. For **southern Thailand**, take a train, chartered minibus or public bus #81 to Ban Pong and change to a night train headed for **Chumphon**, **Surat Thani** or beyond. Reservations for any rail journey can be made at Kanchanaburi train station, or through Good Times tour agency (see p.237) for an extra B50. Tickets for the much shorter train ride to **Bangkok** (2 daily) or **along the Death Railway** to Nam Tok (see p.240) don't need advance booking.

If you're coming from Bangkok, the fastest transport of all is to take one of the **tourist minibuses** from Thanon Khao San, which travel at breakneck speeds and take just two hours door to door (B140), though they generally only drop passengers at *Jolly Frog*, despite advertising otherwise. Locals opt instead for the minibus service that departs from outside Bangkok's *Royal Ratanakosin Hotel* on Ratchadamnoen Klang in Banglamphu, five minutes' walk from Khao San; these minibuses leave approximately hourly from 5am to 8pm and drop you wherever you want (2hr; B120).

Town transport and information

Orange public **songthaews** run along Thanon Saeng Chuto, originating from outside the Focus Optic optician's, one block north of the bus station, and travelling north via the Kanchanaburi War Cemetery (Don Rak), Death Railway Museum, train station and access road to the Bridge (#2; every 15min until 6pm; 15min to the Bridge turn-off; B10).

Guest houses and tour agencies rent out **bicycles** – ideal for exploring the main town sights and the quiet rural backroads – and many outlets supply **motorbikes** and **jeeps** for rent. Mek and Mee, next to *Jolly Frog* on Thanon Maenam Kwai (Ⓣ081 7571194), is one of the few that will provide first-class (fully comprehensive) insurance for their rental cars.

A scenic way of travelling between riverine sights is by chartered **longtail boat** from one of the small piers in the tourist areas. At the Bangphupun pier, secreted amongst the trinket shops 100m north of the JEATH Museum at 21 Thanon Pakpraek, boats operated by Bangphupun Business (Ⓣ086 3287838) cost B700 for a two-hour trip out to Khao Poon and Chungkai and back to the Bridge (maximum six people). Or you can paddle yourself down the Kwai Noi in a **kayak**, either from north of the Bridge or from further upstream at Nong Bua, available from B300 per person from several tour agencies on Maenam Kwai and from specialists Safarine (see p.236).

The **TAT** office (daily 8.30am–4.30pm; Ⓣ034 511200, Ⓔtatkan@tat.or.th) is south of the bus station on Thanon Saeng Chuto and keeps up-to-date bus and train timetables.

Accommodation

Many people choose to make the most of the inspiring scenery by staying on or near the river, in either a **raft house** (often just a rattan hut balanced on a raft of logs) or a **guest house**. The most popular area is around **Thanon Maenam Kwai**, which stretches 2km from Soi Rongheabaow to the Bridge, and is *the* backpackers' hub, crammed with bars, restaurants and tour agents; most guest houses are at the riverside end of the small sois running off this thoroughfare. Despite the tranquil views, Kwai-side accommodation can be plagued by roaring longtail engines during the day so you might want to book in for just one night until you've experienced the decibel levels for yourself. Bring mosquito repellent too, as many huts float in amongst lotus swamps.

Details of raft-house accommodation further **upstream** are given under the relevant accounts: Tham Lawa on p.243 and Sai Yok on p.245.

Apple's Guest House East off Thanon Maenam Kwai and **Apple's Retreat** Across Sudjai Bridge Ⓣ034 512017, Ⓦwww.applenoi-kanchanaburi.com. The welcoming duo who ran the original *Apple's Guest House* and cooking school for thirteen years have now moved and established new guest houses in two different locations. The new *Apple's Guest House* is between the train station and Thanon Maenam Kwai. It's set round a swimming pool and garden and has smart, modern fan and air-con rooms behind the airy two-storey restaurant. Across the river, 600m from Thanon Maenam Kwai, *Apple's Retreat* sits in a green and tranquil spot, with a lovely Kwai-side restaurant and terrace. Rooms are across the road in a two-storey building, with views across farmland to the hills beyond, plus a swimming pool and garden. There's wi-fi throughout both places and free transport between the two. Fan ❸, air-con ❹

Blue Star Guesthouse 241 Thanon Maenam Kwai ⓣ034 512161, ⓦwww.bluestar-guesthouse.com. Popular, clued-up guest house with a wide range of good-value accommodation, including very cheap, basic fan rooms in a row house; attractive, well-priced bungalows set over a lotus swamp; and cabins raised on elevated piles with downstairs bathrooms and high-level bedrooms or private upper-level terraces. The land runs down to the riverside area, though views are dominated by the overgrown islet in front. Call for free pick-up from transport terminals. Fan ❶, air-con ❷–❹

Felix River Kwai On the west bank of the Kwai Yai ⓣ034 551000, ⓦwww.felixriverkwaihotel.com. Occupying a lovely riverside spot within walking distance of the Bridge (or a 2km drive from Thanon Maenam Kwai – a little inconvenient if you don't have transport), this is one of the top hotels in the area, though it's starting to look dated and a little faded. It has over two hundred large air-con rooms, plus two swimming pools. Rates depend on whether you want a river view, and are sometimes discounted during the week; reservations are essential for weekends. ❼–❾

Jolly Frog Backpackers 28 Soi China, Thanon Maenam Kwai ⓣ034 514579, ⓦwww.jollyfrog.net. Many backpackers' first choice, this large, efficiently run complex occupies a lovely stretch of the riverfront, fronted by a grassy lawn and flowering shrubs, and has a popular restaurant (good for fresh coffee and home-made bread from 7am). Aside from some cheap single rooms and a few doubles with shared bathrooms, it mostly comprises bright and comfortable en-suite rooms in two-storey bamboo-walled blocks around the shady garden. You can swim off the jetty, though be careful of the strong current. Fan ❶, air-con ❸

Nita Raft House 271/1 Thanon Pak Praek ⓣ034 514521, ⓔnita_rafthouse@yahoo.com. Located away from the main Thanon Song Kwai fray, near the JEATH Museum, this is a genuine, old-style guest house with a very laid-back atmosphere that's been run by the same couple for years. The fourteen simple, floating rooms are among the cheapest in town and all offer some sort of river view; some are en suite and the best have air-con and a private terrace. There's a lounge for watching DVDs, and sampling the tasty guest-house food. Shared bathroom ❶, en suite ❷, air-con ❹

Oriental Kwai Off Route 3199, Ladya ⓣ034 588168, ⓦwww.orientalkwai.com. In a quiet spot beside the Kwai Yai, 15km north of town (see map, p.238), this Dutch-Thai-run little hotel offers just ten thoughtfully designed cottages in a garden with pool, pétanque, volleyball and a miniature driving range. Cottages are air-con, have wi-fi and DVD players and are tastefully decorated in modern Asian accents; some are wheelchair accessible. There's nothing to see in the immediate area but you can rent cars, motorbikes, kayaks and bicycles or join tours to all Kanchanaburi attractions. ❼

Ploy River Kwai Thanon Maenam Kwai ⓣ034 515804, ⓦwww.ploygh.com. Strikingly different in style from other guest houses on this road, this is a smart little enclave set back off the road but with distant river views only from the restaurant. The chic, sleek, contemporary-look rooms each have a platform bed and air-con, with extra charged for those with garden-style bathrooms or TVs. Good discounts if you book a week ahead. ❹–❺

The River Kwai Bridge Resort Thanon Maenam Kwai ⓣ034 514522, ⓦwww.riverkwaibridgeresort.com. Good-value simple but chic, modern cream clapboard semi-detached bungalows ranged in facing rows amidst frangipani and jasmine shrubs on a narrow strip of land that runs down to the river. All bungalows have air-con and wi-fi, there's a pool and a restaurant terrace with top views of the bridge, just a few hundred metres upriver. About 2km from restaurants on central Thanon Maenam Kwai. ❺

River Kwai Hotel 284/3–16 Thanon Saeng Chuto ⓣ034 510111, ⓦwww.riverkwai.co.th. The town centre's top hotel is nowhere near the river, but it's very good value even if it lacks the atmosphere of its riverside competitors. Rooms are of a high standard, and all have air-con and cable TV. Facilities include a pool, spa, nightclub and internet access. ❻

Sam's House Thanon Maenam Kwai ⓣ034 515956, ⓦwww.samsguesthouse.com. Choose to stay in comfortably furnished, stilted timber bungalows set among a dense tangle of riverine lotuses or on dry land in contemporary-styled white A-frame concrete bungalows. All rooms are en suite and all have the option of fan or air-con. The most expensive of the lotus rooms face onto the river, though views here are occluded by the overgrown islet directly in front. ❷–❹

Tanavill Guest House (formerly *C & C*), Soi England, off Thanon Maenam Kwai ⓣ034 518274, ⓦtanavill-guesthouse.e-monsite.com. The cheapest rooms at this motley collection of huts have by far the best outlook: they sit in a row on pontoons, with an easy chair apiece for maximum enjoyment of the excellent views, and the river as your private plunge pool. All share bathrooms and have fans and mosquito nets. The much less interesting en-suite huts are dotted around the garden further back and some have air-con. It's a very quiet spot, at the end of a winding lane. ❶–❷

VN Guesthouse 44 Soi Rongheabaow ⓣ 034 514082, ⓦ www.vnguesthouse.net. In a pretty location on a quiet stretch of the river just south of the Maenam Kwai hub, this place offers very good raft-house rooms: they're large, en suite, and come with either fan or air-con; the best have lovely outlooks and they all have terraces and wi-fi. Rooms on dry land are unexceptional. Fan ❷, air-con ❸

The Town

Strung out along the east bank of the River Kwai and its continuation, south of the Kwai Noi confluence, as the Mae Khlong, Kanchanaburi is a long, narrow ribbon of a town. The **war sights** are sandwiched between the river and the busy main drag, Thanon Saeng Chuto, with the Bridge over the River Kwai marking the northern limit, and the JEATH Museum towards the town's southern edge.

The Death Railway

Shortly after entering World War II in December 1941, Japan, fearing an Allied blockade of the Bay of Bengal, began looking for an alternative supply route to connect its newly acquired territories that stretched from Singapore to the Burma–India border. In spite of the almost impenetrable terrain, the River Kwai basin was chosen as the route for a new **Thailand–Burma Railway**, the aim being to join the existing terminals of Nong Pladuk in Thailand (51km southeast of Kanchanaburi) and Thanbuyazat in Burma – a total distance of 415km.

About 60,000 Allied POWs were shipped up from captured Southeast Asian territories to work on the link, their numbers later augmented by as many as 200,000 conscripted Asian labourers. Work began at both ends in June 1942. Three million cubic metres of rock were shifted and 14km of bridges built with little else but picks and shovels, dynamite and pulleys. By the time the line was completed, fifteen months later, it had more than earned its nickname, the **Death Railway**: an estimated 16,000 POWs and 100,000 Asian labourers died while working on it.

The appalling conditions and Japanese brutality were the consequences of the **samurai code**: Japanese soldiers abhorred the disgrace of imprisonment – to them, ritual suicide was the only honourable option open to a prisoner – and therefore considered that Allied POWs had forfeited any rights as human beings. Food rations were meagre for men forced into backbreaking eighteen-hour shifts, often followed by night-long marches to the next camp. Many suffered from beri beri, many more died of dysentery-induced starvation, but the biggest killers were cholera and malaria, particularly during the monsoon. It is said that one man died for every sleeper laid on the track.

The two lines finally met at Konkuita, just south of present-day Sangkhlaburi. But as if to underscore its tragic futility, the Thailand–Burma link saw less than two years of active service: after the Japanese surrender on August 15, 1945, the railway came under the jurisdiction of the British who, thinking it would be used to supply Karen separatists in Burma, tore up 4km of track at Three Pagodas Pass, thereby cutting the Thailand–Burma link forever. When the Thais finally gained control of the rest of the railway, they destroyed the track all the way down to Nam Tok, apparently because it was uneconomic. Recently, however, an Australian-Thai group of volunteers and former POWs has salvaged sections of track near the fearsome stretch of line known as Hellfire Pass, clearing a memorial walk at the pass and founding an excellent museum at the site (see p.244). There have been a number of books written about the Death Railway, including several by former POWs; the Death Railway Museum stocks a selection, as do the town's bookshops.

Death Railway Museum

The **Death Railway Museum** (formerly known as the Thailand–Burma Railway Centre; daily 9am–5pm; B100, kids B50; Ⓦwww.tbrconline.com) is the best place to start any tour of Kanchanaburi's World War II memorials. Located across the road from the train station, next to the Don Rak Kanchanaburi War Cemetery on Thanon Jaokannun, it was founded to provide an informed context and research centre for the thousands who visit the POW graves every week. The result is a comprehensive and sophisticated history of the entire Thailand–Burma Railway line, with plenty of original artefacts, illustrations and scale models, and particularly strong sections on the planning and construction of the railway, and on the subsequent operation, destruction and decommissioning of the line. There is more of a focus on the line itself here than at the more emotive Hellfire Pass Memorial Museum, but the human stories are well documented too, notably via some extraordinary original photographs and video footage shot by Japanese engineers, as well as through unique interviews with surviving Asian labourers on the railway.

The shop inside the entrance stocks some interesting books on the railway and also sells products made by the Women for Weaving project in Sangkhlaburi.

The Kanchanaburi War Cemetery (Don Rak)

Thirty-eight Allied POWs died for each kilometre of track laid on the Thailand–Burma Railway, and many of them are buried in Kanchanaburi's two war cemeteries. Of all the region's war sights, the cemeteries are the only places to have remained untouched by commercial enterprise. Opposite the train station on Thanon Saeng Chuto, the **Don Rak Kanchanaburi War Cemetery** (daily 8am–4pm; free) is the bigger of the two (the other cemetery, Chungkai, is described opposite), with 6982 POW graves laid out in straight lines amid immaculate lawns and flowering shrubs. It was established after the war, on a plot adjacent to the town's Chinese cemetery, as the final resting place for the remains that had been hurriedly interred at dozens of makeshift POW-camp gravesites all the way up the line. Many of the identical stone memorial slabs in Don Rak state simply, "A man who died for his country"; others, inscribed with names, dates and regiments, indicate that the overwhelming majority of the dead were under 25 years old. A commemorative service is held here, and at Hellfire Pass (see p.244), every year on April 25, Anzac Day.

The Bridge over the River Kwai

For most people, the plain steel arches of the **Bridge over the River Kwai** come as a disappointment: as a war memorial it lacks both the emotive punch of the museums and the perceptible drama of spots further up the line, and as a bridge it looks nothing out of the ordinary – certainly not as awesomely hard to construct as it appears in David Lean's famous 1957 film, *Bridge on the River Kwai* (which was in fact shot in Sri Lanka). But it is the link with the multi-Oscar-winning film, of course, that draws tour buses by the dozen, and makes the Bridge approach seethe with trinket-sellers and touts. For all the commercialization of the place, however, you can't really come to the Kwai and not see it. To get here, take any songthaew heading north up Thanon Saeng Chuto and then walk the 850m from the junction, hire a samlor, or cycle – it's 5km from the bus station. You can charter longtails from the pier beside the Bridge for trips to JEATH or out to sights along the Kwai Yai (B800 for 1hr outing).

The fording of the Kwai Yai at the point just north of Kanchanaburi known as Tha Makkham was one of the first major obstacles in the construction of the Thailand–Burma Railway. Sections of a steel bridge were brought up from Java and reassembled by POWs using only pulleys and derricks. A temporary **wooden bridge** was built alongside it, taking its first train in February 1943; three months later the steel bridge was finished. Both bridges were severely damaged by Allied bombers (rather than commando-saboteurs as in the film) in 1944 and 1945, but the steel bridge was repaired after the war and is still in use today. In fact the best way to see the Bridge is by taking the train over it: the Kanchanaburi–Nam Tok train crosses it three times a day in each direction, stopping briefly at the River Kwai Bridge station on the east bank of the river.

World War II Museum and Art Gallery

You're strongly advised to avoid the poorly designed and in some places tasteless **World War II Museum** (daily 8am–6.30pm; B40), just steps from the Bridge, and to head instead for one of the far better informed commemorations of the war at either the Death Railway Museum or Hellfire Pass. The so-called World War II Museum is actually a bizarre hotchpotch of a private collection featuring all sorts of oddities, from coins and stamps to Allied motorbikes and distasteful tableaux of dying POWs, with barely any sensible captions.

The JEATH War Museum

Founded by the chief abbot of Wat Chaichumpon in 1977 and housed within the temple grounds in a reconstructed Allied POW hut of thatched palm, the ramshackle and unashamedly low-tech **JEATH War Museum** (daily 8.30am–6pm; B30) was the town's first public repository for the photographs and memories of the POWs who worked on the Death Railway. The name JEATH is an acronym of six of the countries involved in the railway: Japan, England, Australia, America, Thailand and Holland. The museum has since been surpassed by the slicker and more informative exhibitions at the Death Railway Museum and the Hellfire Pass Memorial Museum (see p.244) and is now of most interest for its small collection of wartime photographs and for its archive of newspaper articles about and letters from former POWs who have revisited the River Kwai. The museum is located beside the Mae Khlong on Thanon Pak Praek, at the southern end of town. It's about 700m from the TAT office, or 5km from the Bridge.

Across the river

Kanchanaburi's other war cemetery, at **Chungkai**, and a handful of moderately interesting temples – including cave temples at **Wat Tham Khao Poon** and **Wat Ban Tham**, the hilltop twins of **Wat Tham Sua** and **Wat Tham Khao Noi**, and a wat featuring a rather bizarre **floating nun** – provide the focus for pleasurable trips west of the town centre, to various locations along the Kwai Noi and the Mae Khlong. All these sights are accessible by bicycle from central Kanchanaburi, and can also be reached by longtail (hired through guest houses or at one of the east-bank piers), or even by kayak (see p.229).

Chungkai Cemetery and Wat Tham Khao Poon

Scrupulously well-trimmed **Chungkai Cemetery** occupies a fairly tranquil roadside spot on the west bank of the Kwai Noi, at the site of a former POW camp. Some 1750 POWs are buried here; most of the gravestone inscriptions include a name and regimental insignia, but a number remain unnamed – at the upcountry camps, bodies were thrown onto mass funeral pyres, making identification impossible. The cemetery is a pleasant 2km cycle from Kanchanaburi's Rattanakarn Bridge, along Route 3228; much of the land in this area is sugar-cane country, for which Kanchanaburi has earned the title "sugar capital of Thailand".

Two kilometres further west along Route 3228 (4km from Rattanakarn Bridge), at the top of the road's only hill, sits the cave temple **Wat Tham Khao Poon** (daily 8am–6pm; B20). The attraction here is a nine-chambered cave connected by a labyrinth of dank stalactite-filled passages, where almost every ledge and knob of rock is filled with religious icons, the most important being the Reclining Buddha in the main chamber. Once out of the cave system, follow the track through the temple compound for 150m to reach a good vantage point over the Kwai Noi, just above the train tracks, presided over by an outsized, pot-bellied golden Buddha statue; if arriving by boat, you enter the wat compound via the cliff-side steps here.

Wat Tham Mangkon Thong (Floating Nun Temple)

The impressive scenery across on the east of the River Kwai Noi makes for an equally worthwhile bike trip, but the cave temple on this side – **Wat Tham Mangkon Thong**, otherwise known as the **Floating Nun Temple** – is fairly tacky. The draw here is a Thai nun who, clad in white robes, will get into the temple pond and float there, meditating – if tourists give her enough money to make it worth her while. It's difficult not to be cynical about such a commercial stunt, though Taiwanese visitors are said to be particularly impressed. The floating takes place on a round pond at the foot of the enormous dragon staircase that leads up to the temple embedded in the hillside behind. The temple comprises an unexceptional network of low, bat-infested limestone caves, punctuated at intervals with Buddha statues.

There's no direct access from the west to the east bank of the Kwai Noi, so to get to Wat Tham Mangkon Thong from Chungkai and Wat Tham Khao Poon you have to return to town and start again. Travelling by bicycle or motorbike, take the ferry across the Mae Khlong River at Tha Chukkadon and then follow the road on the other side for about 4km. By car, turn west off Thanon Saeng Chuto (Highway 323) about 3km south of TAT onto Route 3429, which bridges the river and takes you north then west to the temple. Alternatively, take **bus** #8191 (every 30min; 20min) from Kanchanaburi bus station; the last return bus passes the temple at about 4.15pm.

Wat Ban Tham

Because of the limestone landscape, caves are all too common around Kanchanaburi and many of them have been sanctified as shrines. **Wat Ban Tham** is yet another example, but is intriguing enough to make the twelve-kilometre trip from the town centre worthwhile. Travelling south down the Mae Khlong to get to the temple is especially pleasant by longtail or kayak, but can also be done by road: cross the river at Thanon Mae Khlong, then turn left for the six-kilometre ride along a partially unmade road or, if combining with Wat Tham Mangkon, see directions above and then head south.

Wat Ban Tham was founded around six hundred years ago but its fame rests on the seventeenth-century love story that was supposedly played out in a cave on this site. A young woman called Nang Bua Klee was forced to choose between duty to her criminal father and love for the local hero by whom she had fallen pregnant; her father eventually persuaded Bua Klee to poison her sweetheart's food, but the soldier learned of the plot and killed both his wife and their unborn son, whose souls are now said to be trapped in the cave at Wat Ban Tham. The cave is approached via an ostentatious Chinese-style dragon's mouth staircase, whose upper levels relate the legend in a gallery of brightly painted modern murals on the right-hand walls. Inside the cave, a woman-shaped stone has been painted in the image of the dead mother and is a popular object of worship for women trying to conceive: hopeful devotees bring pretty dresses and shoes for the image, which are hung in wardrobes to the side of the shrine when not in use, as well as toys for her son.

Wat Tham Sua and Wat Tham Khao Noi

If you're in the mood for more temples, continue south along the Mae Khlong from Wat Ban Tham for another 5km to reach the modern hilltop wats of Tham Sua and Tham Khao Noi, which both afford expansive views over the river valley and out to the mountains beyond. Coming by car, the quickest route is to head south out of town along Highway 323 and cross the river via the signed Mae Khlong Dam. Otherwise, take any local bus as far as Tha Muang, 12km south along Highway 323, then change to a motorbike taxi to the temples (about B40).

Designed by a Thai architect at the end of the twentieth century, **Wat Tham Sua** was conceived in typical grandiose style around a massive chedi covered with tiles similar to those used at Nakhon Pathom. Inside, a placid seated Buddha takes centre stage, his huge palms raised to show the Wheels of Law inscribed like stigmata across them; a conveyor belt transports devotees' offerings into the enormous alms bowl set into his lap. The neighbouring Chinese-designed **Wat Tham Khao Noi** was built at the same time and is a fabulously gaudy, seven-tiered Chinese pagoda within which a laughing Buddha competes for attention with a host of gesturing and grimacing statues and painted characters.

Eating and drinking

All Kanchanaburi's guest houses and raft houses have **restaurants**, and there's a cluster of floating restaurants beside the Bridge, serving good if rather pricey seafood to accompany the river views. Except where stated, all listed restaurants open daily from breakfast until late. A cheaper place to enjoy genuine local food is at the ever-reliable **night market**, which sets up alongside Thanon Saeng Chuto on the edge of the bus station. There are also a few foodstalls at the **night bazaar**, which operates in front of the train station (Thurs–Tues 6–10pm), but the focus here is mainly on cheap fashions, CDs and sarongs.

A recent influx of small, farang-managed **bars** has added a dissonant dimension to a previously very low-key nightlife and there are now some twenty tiny one-room bars competing for attention on the southern stretch of Thanon Maenam Kwai. Most of the new places offer a similar diet of loud music and cheapish beer, with bar girls and/or sports TV as an added attraction – many will not make their first birthday, but those listed here have been around long enough to last.

Restaurants

Apple's Guest House East off Thanon Maenam Kwai and **Apple's Retreat** Across Sudjai Bridge. Exceptionally delicious food at both branches of *Apple's*, prepared to traditional Thai recipes by Kanchanaburi's most famous cooking school. The extensive menu (B65–180) includes coconut- and cashew-laced *matsaman* curries – both meat and vegetarian varieties – as well as outstanding yellow curries and multi-course set dinners. Every dish is prepared to order, so service can be slow.

Fine Thanon Maenam Kwai. Cute, cheery little boho-look café with multicoloured tables and chairs and a long menu of good authentic Thai food, including delicious *tom kha* soups (B70) and veggie options available for nearly every dish.

Keereetara Restaurant Just north of the Bridge. Classy Thai food, especially seafood, contemporary styling and great views of the Bridge from the terrace make this the top place to eat near the Bridge, and a favourite haunt of celebs and movie stars filming at the nearby Promitr Studios. Most mains B100–300.

Nita Raft House Thanon Pak Praek. Home-style cooking is the thing at the kitchen attached to this raft house, especially the famous "no name" deep-fried vegetable and chicken fritters, and the authentic Japanese *okonomiyaki* (hearty savoury pancakes; B75). Seating is home-style too, on floor cushions, and there are usually DVD screenings in the evenings.

Prasopsuk Day & Night Market 277 Thanon Saeng Chuto. The streetside restaurant attached to the *Prasopsuk Hotel* is a good place for *som tam* and sticky rice, but it also serves a full menu of stir-fries, curries, seafood, rice and noodle dishes (from B45).

Schluck Thanon Maenam Kwai. Cosy air-con restaurant that entices a regular crowd of expats with its menu of pizzas, salads and steaks (from B150), plus its decent selection of authentically spicy fish and *yam* dishes. Also has a few tables outside. Daily 4pm–2am.

Sri Rung Rueng Thanon Maenam Kwai. Popular, well-priced, bamboo-roofed restaurant with a huge menu of *tom kha*, *tom yam* and curries (yellow, red, green, *phanaeng* and *matsaman*), all available in veggie and non-veggie versions (from B60), plus steaks, seafood and cocktails.

Bars

No Name Bar Thanon Maenam Kwai. Farang-run travellers' hangout that invites punters to "get shit-faced on a shoestring". Key attractions are the satellite-TV screenings of major sporting events, the pool table and the well-priced beer. Also serves British food, including roast beef and Yorkshire pudding.

One More Bar Thanon Maenam Kwai. The current backpackers' favourite is a lively, sociable place to spend an evening, not least because it has a refreshing no-bar-girls policy, hosts regular free barbecues and occasional parties, and has Nintendo Wii and DVDs in its backroom lounge.

Day-trips, rafting and trekking

All the places listed below advertise **day- and overnight trips** around the Kanchanaburi and Sangkhlaburi areas, infinite permutations of rafting, elephant-riding, Erawan Falls, Hellfire Pass and the Death Railway, sometimes with a short trek thrown in. Prices listed are per person, usually for a minimum of four. They all also do tailor-made guided tours to the war sights (often by boat or raft) and to Damnoen Saduak floating markets, and will also provide a cheap transport service – car plus driver but no guide – for the more accessible attractions.

A.S. Mixed Travel *Apple's Guest House*, east off Thanon Maenam Kwai ⓣ034 512017, ⓦwww.applenoi-kanchanaburi.com. In addition to the standard tours and treks in and around Kanchanaburi, the speciality here is village cycle tours through the rice fields and traditional rural hinterland around *Apple's Retreat* across the Sudjai Bridge.

Good Times Travel 63/1 Thanon Maenam Kwai ⓣ034 624441, ⓦwww.good-times-travel.com. Energetically run, competitively priced trips (B130–1100) that get good reviews. Especially popular for its elephant-bathing programme where tourists get to soap and shower elephants (and themselves) in the river, and for its two-day trip to a Karen area near Hin Dat hot springs, which includes four hours' trekking each day (B2100). Also offers interesting-sounding cycle tours around Thong Pha Phum and Sangkhlaburi and can arrange for joint cycle tours to Ayutthaya.

Safarine 296 Thanon Maenam Kwai ⓣ034 625567, ⓦwww.safarine.com. French-run kayaking specialist offering short, full-day and overnight kayaking trips in the Kanchanaburi area for B300–2850.

Sunya Rux Raft Thanon Song Kwai ⓣ081 856 5848, ⓔsunyaruxtravel@hotmail.com. Being tugged down the river on a floating raft "hotel" is the most popular activity for Thai holidaymakers in Kanchanaburi, but Sunya Rux is one of the only outfits to offer it to English-speaking tourists. The two-storey raft hotel, with camp beds both on the roof and under cover, is pulled by a longtail down the Mae Khlong River to the Mae Khlong Dam, making stops at various sights, with plenty of chances to swim and go inner-tubing. B2000 per person including all meals, minimum 6 people; the trip lasts 24 hours; book 24 hours ahead.

Listings

Airline tickets Domestic and international tickets from Good Times Travel, 63/1 Thanon Maenam Kwai ⓣ034 624441, ⓦwww.good-times-travel.com.
Books Several secondhand bookshops on Thanon Maenam Kwai.
Cookery classes Most famously at *Apple's Guest House*: shop at the morning market and learn how to cook the basic Thai dishes (10am–2.30pm; B1250).
Emergencies For all emergencies, call the tourist police on the free, 24hr phone line ⓣ1155, or contact them at one of their booths in town (daily 9am–6pm): right beside the Bridge ⓣ034 512795; on Thanon Song Kwai; and on Thanon Saeng Chuto (ⓣ034 512668).
Exchange There are several banks with money-changing facilities and ATMs on Thanon Saeng Chuto, immediately to the north of the Thanon U Thong junction, and around the bridge.
Hospitals The private Thanakan Hospital is at 20/20 Thanon Saeng Chuto, at the southern end of town, near the junction with Thanon Chukkadon ⓣ034 622366–75; the government-run Phahon Phonphayulasena Hospital is further south at 572/1 Thanon Saeng Chuto, near the junction with Thanon Mae Khlong ⓣ034 511507 or 034 622999.
Immigration office At 100/22 Thanon Mae Khlong ⓣ034 564265.
Mail The GPO is 1km south of the TAT office on Thanon Saeng Chuto, but there are a couple of more central postal agents on Thanon Maenam Kwai.
Massage Suan Nanachat (ⓣ081 908 0201, ⓦwww.suan-nanachaat.com) is an invitingly secluded upscale boutique-style massage centre and day-spa in green surrounds in the Nong Bua area 10km north of town on the way to Nam Tok (phone for free transport). The UK owners take a serious interest in the quality of their masseurs and visitors can choose from a range of quite pricey treatments (90min massage B500) and indulge in wholemeal sandwiches, salads and herbal teas. Reservations essential as numbers are restricted to six at a time.
Swimming pool Non-guests can use the pool at the *River Kwai Hotel* for B100 including towel (6am–8pm).
Telephones The CAT international telephone office (Mon–Fri 8.30am–4.30pm) is on a side road near the GPO, about 1.2km south of the TAT office, on Soi Praisanee/Soi 38, off Thanon Saeng Chuto. Internet cafés on Thanon Maenam Kwai have Skype.

Around Kanchanaburi

The parallel valleys of the Kwai Noi and the Kwai Yai, northwest of Kanchanaburi, are stacked full of great day-tripping opportunities, from the exceptionally beautiful **Erawan Falls** to the drama of a ride on the **Death Railway** and the pathos of the World War II museum at **Hellfire Pass**. There are Stone Age artefacts at the **Ban Kao Museum**, twelfth-century Khmer temple ruins at **Prasat Muang Singh**, the (controversial) opportunity to get up close to a tiger at the **Tiger Sanctuary Temple** and several good caves, including at **Tham Than Lot National Park**, and the riverside **Tham Lawa**.

Many of these attractions are served by public **transport**, the train being an obvious option along the Kwai Noi valley as far as its **Nam Tok** terminus, with buses useful along both valleys. But train schedules are unreliable and bus connections can be time-consuming so many people either opt instead to join one of the many mix-and-match tours offered by Kanchanaburi agents (see opposite) or rent their own wheels for a day. Distances are not large, and there's a handy connecting road between the two valleys just south of Nam Tok.

Erawan Waterfall and Srinakarind National Park

Considered by many to be the most beautiful falls in Thailand, **Erawan Waterfall** is the star attraction of **Erawan National Park** (daily 8am–4pm, tiers 1 and 2 until 5pm; B200; ⓣ034 574222). It's a great day out – so popular

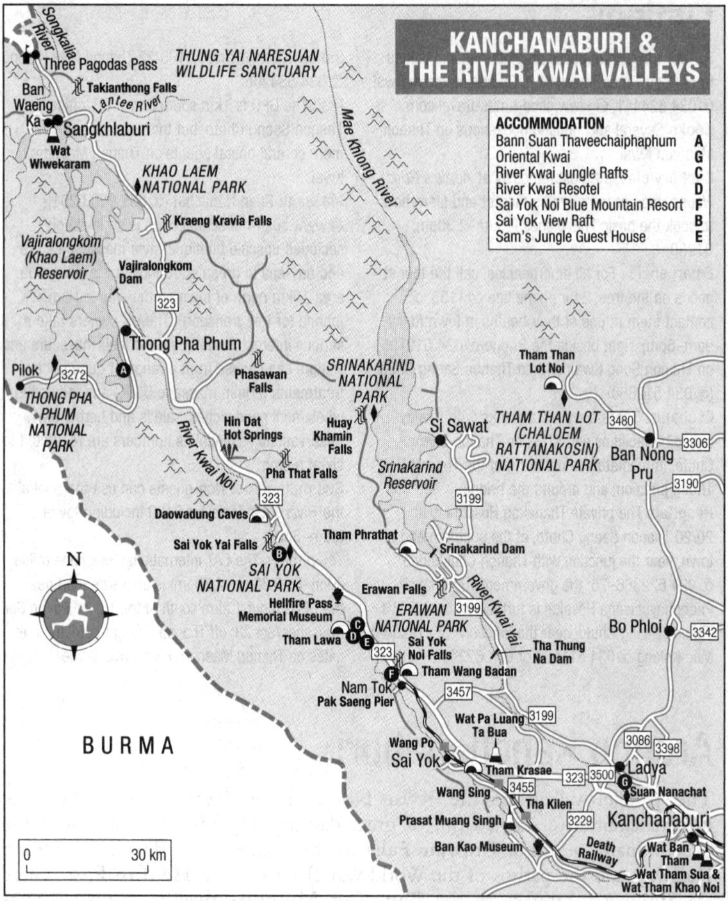

in fact that you can get a commemorative photo of yourself at the falls printed on a plate – and combines well with a ride on the Death Railway. The national park is 70km northwest of Kanchanaburi, via Route 3199 along the Kwai Yai valley, or 40km from Nam Tok.

The falls really are astonishingly lovely: the clear glacial-blue waters gush through the forest, dropping in a series of seven tiers along a route of around 2km. At each tier, cascades feed a pool shaded by bamboo, rattan and liana, and the whole course can be walked, along a riverside trail that gets increasingly tricky the further up you go. The distance between tiers, and the ascent to each, is clearly spelled out on signs in the park. It's just 720m from the visitor centre to level one, and then fairly easy going on and up to the dramatically stepped fifth stage (1800m). The route on to the sixth and seventh levels is steep and slippery and features some dilapidated bridges and ladders: wear appropriate shoes, and avoid doing the last bit alone if you can; it's about a ninety-minute hike from bottom to top. The best pools for swimming are level two (which gets the most crowded) and level seven, which is a hard slog but rarely busy, and also boasts stunning views over the jungle. The seventh tier is topped by a triple cascade and is the one that gave the falls their name: Erawan is the three-headed god of Hindu mythology.

With your own transport you might also want to visit the park's other significant feature, the two-hundred-metre-long stalactite-filled cave **Tham Phrathat** (last entry at 3pm), 12km by road from the falls, then a 500m walk. It's of particular interest to geologists for its clearly visible disjointed strata, evidence of the Sri Sawat fault line that runs under the Kwai Yai.

A few kilometres north of the turn-off to Erawan, the landscape is dominated by the scenic **Srinakarind Reservoir**, which is fed by the dammed waters of the Mae Khlong and the Kha Khaeng and gives rise to the Kwai Yai. It's a popular recreation spot and site of several resorts, all of which lie within the **Srinakarind National Park** (also known as **Khuean Srinagarindra National Park**; ⓣ034 516667). From the dam you can hire boats (about B1800) to make the two-hour journey northwest across the reservoir to **Huay Khamin Falls**, which are said to be the most powerful in the district, and reputedly get the name "Turmeric Streak" from the ochre-coloured limestone rockface. However, it's quicker and less hassle to join one of the tours from Kanchanaburi.

Practicalities

The vast majority of foreign tourists rent or charter return transport to Erawan Falls from Kanchanaburi (from B1100 per car) but you can also get a public bus from Kanchanaburi to the national park visitor centre (#8170; every 50min; 2hr; B55 each way; the last bus back to Kanchanaburi departs at 4pm). The falls are about 40km from Nam Tok so are also commonly combined with a ride on the Death Railway. If you want to stay in the park at the Erawan National Park **bungalows** (❹) or **tents** (from B150 plus B50 for bedding), you must reserve ahead via the National Parks office in Bangkok (ⓣ02 562 0760, ⓦwww.dnp.go.th/National_park.asp; see p.52); you can also pitch your own tent for B30. Several **foodstalls**, restaurants, showers and shops near the trailhead and Tiers 1 and 2 open daily until about 8pm.

Tham Than Lot (Chaloem Rattanakosin) National Park

Ninety-seven kilometres north of Kanchanaburi, off Route 3086, tiny little **Tham Than Lot National Park** (also known as **Chaloem Rattanakosin National Park**; B200; ⓣ034 519606, ⓦwww.dnp.go.th/National_park.asp; four-person bungalows B1200) covers just 59 square kilometres but boasts two very nice caves (bring a torch), a decent waterfall and an enjoyable hiking trail that links them. Four **buses** a day go all the way to the cave from Kanchanaburi bus station (#325; 6.25am, 8.10am, 12.25pm & 15.20pm; 2–3hr) but it's not a place that combines well with any other local attractions, even with your own transport.

From the visitor centre, follow the signed trail for about ten minutes to reach the first cave, **Tham Than Lot Noi**, which is 400m deep and illuminated if there are enough people (for example at weekends). A very picturesque 2.5-kilometre, two-hour trail runs on from the other side of Tham Than Lot Noi, along a stream and through a ravine to the first of three **waterfalls**, about an hour and a half's easy walk away and passing towering dipterocarps, fine jungle views and plenty of butterflies en route. The path gets more difficult after the first waterfall, and dangerously slippery in the wet season, running via another couple of waterfalls before coming to the larger of the park's two caves, the impressively deep sink-hole **Tham Than Lot Yai**, site of a small

Buddhist shrine. Another ten minutes along the trail brings you to a small forest temple, from where you'll need to retrace your steps to return to the visitor centre.

Riding the Death Railway

The two-hour journey along the notorious Thailand–Burma **Death Railway** from Kanchanaburi to **Nam Tok** is one of Thailand's most scenic, and most popular. Though the views are lovely, it's the history that makes the ride so special, so it's worth visiting the Death Railway Museum in Kanchanaburi before making the trip, as this provides a context for the enormous loss of human life and the extraordinary feat of engineering behind the line's construction (see box, p.231). Alternatively, take the bus straight up to the **Hellfire Pass Memorial Museum** (see p.244), just north of the line's current Nam Tok terminus, which provides an equally illuminating introduction to the railway's history, then return to Kanchanaburi by train.

Leaving Kanchanaburi via the Bridge over the River Kwai, the train chugs through the Kwai Noi valley, stopping frequently at country stations decked with frangipani and jasmine. The first stop of note is Tha Kilen (1hr 15min), where you can alight for Prasat Muang Singh (see opposite), and about twenty minutes later the most hair-raising section of track begins. At **Wang Sing**, also known as Arrow Hill, the train squeezes through thirty-metre-deep solid rock cuttings, dug at the cost of numerous POW lives; 6km further, it slows to a crawl at the approach to the **Wang Po viaduct**, where a three-hundred-metre-long trestle bridge clings to the cliff face as it curves with the Kwai Noi – almost every man who worked on this part of the railway died. The station at the northern end of the trestle bridge is called **Tham Krasae**, after the cave that's hollowed out of the rock face beside the bridge; you can see the cave's resident Buddha image from the train. North of Tham Krasae, the train pulls in at **Wang Po Station** before continuing alongside a particularly lovely stretch of the Kwai Noi, its banks thick with jungle and not a raft house in sight, the whole vista framed by distant tree-clad peaks. Thirty minutes later, the train reaches Nam Tok, a small town that thrives chiefly on its position at the end of the line (see p.242).

Practicalities

Three **trains** operate daily along the Death Railway in both directions, but they often run very late. At the time of writing, they're scheduled to leave Kanchanaburi at 5.57am, 10.24am and 4.19pm and to return from Nam Tok at 5.20am, 12.50pm and 3.15pm; Kanchanaburi TAT keeps up-to-date **timetables**. If you're up at the Bridge, you can join the train five minutes later. Tourists are charged an inflated flat fare of B100 from Kanchanaburi to Nam Tok or B50 if starting from Tha Kilen.

Ban Kao Museum

The **Ban Kao Museum** (daily 8.30am–4.30pm; B30) is devoted to relics from an advanced prehistoric civilization (8000 to 1000 BC) that once settled on the banks of the Kwai Noi. Items on display include unique, curiously designed pots dated to around 1770 BC that were found buried at the head and feet of fifty skeletons; polished stone tools from around 8000 BC; and inscribed bronze pots and bangles transferred from a nearby bronze-culture site, which have been placed at around 1000 BC – somewhat later than the bronze artefacts from Ban Chiang in the northeast (see p.536). The hollowed-out tree trunks in front of the museum are also unusual: they may have been used as boats or as coffins – or possibly as a metaphorical combination of the two.

The museum is 35km west of Kanchanaburi and 8km from Prasat Muang Singh. Follow Highway 323 north out of Kanchanaburi until you get to the junction with minor road 3229, then follow this road southwest for about 16km before veering on to minor road 3445 for the last couple of kilometres. There's no public transport.

Prasat Muang Singh

Eight hundred years ago, the Khmer empire extended west as far as Muang Singh (City of Lions), an outpost strategically sited on the banks of the River Kwai Noi, 43km west of present-day Kanchanaburi. Thought to have been built at the end of the twelfth century, the temple complex of **Prasat Muang Singh** (daily 8.30am–4.30pm; B40) follows Khmer religious and architectural precepts, but its origins are obscure – the City of Lions gets no mention in any of the recognized chronicles until the nineteenth century.

Prasat Muang Singh covers one-third of a square kilometre, bordered by moats and ramparts that probably had cosmological as well as defensive significance, and with an enclosed **shrine complex** at its heart. Restorations now give an idea of the crude grandeur of the original structure, which was constructed entirely from blocks of rough, russet laterite.

As with all Khmer prasats, the pivotal feature of Muang Singh is the main prang, surrounded by a series of walls and a covered gallery, with gateways marking the cardinal points. The prang faces east, towards Angkor, and is guarded by a fine sandstone statue of **Avalokitesvara**, one of the five great *bodhisattvas* of Mahayana Buddhism, would-be Buddhas who have postponed their entrance into Nirvana to help others attain enlightenment. He's depicted here in characteristic style, his eight arms and torso covered with tiny Buddha reliefs and his hair tied in a top knot. In Mahayanist mythology, Avalokitesvara represents mercy, while the other statue found in the prasat, the female figure of **Prajnaparamita**, symbolizes wisdom – when wisdom and mercy join forces, enlightenment ensues. Just visible on the inside of the north wall surrounding the prang is the only intact example of the stucco carving that once ornamented every facade. Other fragments and sculptures found at this and nearby sites are displayed beside the north gate; especially tantalizing is the single segment of what must have been a gigantic face hewn from several massive blocks of stone.

Muang Singh is 8km northwest of Ban Kao Museum, on minor road 3445. Easiest **access** from Kanchanaburi is by road: either follow directions as for Ban Kao Museum, above, or continue along Highway 323 as far as kilometre-stone 15 to take Route 3445 southwest to Muang Singh. You can also get to Muang Singh by taking the Death Railway train: get off at Tha Kilen (1hr 15min from Kanchanaburi), walk straight out of the station for 500m, turn right at the crossroads and continue for another 1km to reach the ruins.

Wat Pa Luang Ta Bua Yannasampanno: the Tiger Sanctuary Temple

Kanchanaburi's oddest and most controversial attraction is the chance to stroke a tiger at the so-called "Tiger Sanctuary Temple", **Wat Pa Luang Ta Bua Yannasampanno** (B4500 for private morning visits, or B500 1–4pm, when the temple is open to all; Ⓦwww.tigertemple.org; do not wear red clothes, which antagonize the tigers). Many tourists are seduced by the idea and join one of the numerous tours to the temple, which receives up to eight hundred visitors a day. But a lot of people return discouraged by the experience, not least because the animals are housed in small bare cages and only let out to be paraded in front of visitors in the afternoons. The temple attracts a lot of media interest and has been accused of exploiting the animals as a money-making tourist attraction. Undercover investigators sent by the British animal welfare charity Care for the Wild International (Ⓦwww.careforthewild.org) have alleged a range of **welfare problems** and other malpractices, including unauthorized trading of tigers with a breeding centre in Laos; they have also questioned the temple's safety measures.

Temples are traditionally regarded as sanctuaries for unwanted and illegally captured animals and Wat Pa Luang Ta Bua has been taking in tigers since 1999, when a distressed young tiger cub was brought to them, probably orphaned by poachers keen to tap into the lucrative trade in tiger body parts. The temple's tiger population has since grown to over seventeen animals, and the abbot is soliciting donations for the construction of an ambitious "Tigers' Island" reserve within the temple grounds.

The temple is 37km from town and signed off Highway 323 at kilometre-stone 21, a few kilometres beyond the Route 3445 turn-off to Muang Singh. It's easily combined with a ride on the train or a morning at Erawan Falls. Chartered transport arranged through Kanchanaburi tour operators costs around B120 return per person.

Nam Tok

There's not much more to **NAM TOK** than the terminus of the Death Railway line. On rainy-season weekends, Thais flock to the roadside **Sai Yok Noi Falls**, but if you're filling time between trains, you'd be better off stretching your legs on the short trek to the nearby Wang Badan cave or taking a boat trip to Tham Lawa or Sai Yok Yai Falls. It's also straightforward to get a bus on to Hellfire Pass.

Impressive stalactites, fathomless chambers and unnerving heat make **Tham Wang Badan** (daily 8.30am–4.30pm) one of the more interesting underground experiences in the region. It's easily reached by a **trail** that's signposted east off Highway 323, 600m northwest from the station road T-junction, 1.5km from the station itself. About 1km into the trail, you arrive at the park warden's office where you can rent feeble torches; it's better to bring your own or to pay the warden a nominal fee to accompany you and turn on the cave lights. From the office it's 2km of easy walking to the cave.

Practicalities

The **train station** is at the top of the town, 900m north of Highway 323, and a further 2km from the Kwai Noi; return trains to Kanchanaburi currently depart at 5.20am, 12.50pm and 3.15pm. To reach the highway from the station, walk up the station approach road, cross the tracks, turn left at the spirit-house roundabout, then first right through the small town, passing a water tower and market on your left. All Kanchanaburi–Hellfire Pass–Thong Pha Phum **buses** pass through Nam Tok, generally making a stop near the T-junction of the highway and the station road (#8203; every 30min; last bus back to Kanchanaburi at 5pm); it's about 30min to Hellfire Pass.

Longtail **boats** can be rented from the restaurant beside **Pak Saeng pier** for the forty-minute boat ride upstream to Tham Lawa and its nearby riverside accommodation (see opposite). To reach the pier from the Highway 323

T-junction, cross the road, turn southeast towards Kanchanaburi, then take the first road on your right; it's 2km from here to the river. The return journey to the cave takes roughly two hours, including half an hour there, and costs B1000 for the eight-seater boat; for B2000 you can continue to Sai Yok Yai Falls (a six-hour return trip; see p.245).

Few tourists stay in Nam Tok but should you get stuck here the best **hotel** is *Sai Yok Noi Blue Mountain Resort* (Ⓣ034 565123, Ⓦwww.saiyokebluemountain.com; ④) which has clean air-con rooms on three storeys set around a small central yard just 300m northwest up Route 323 from the station T-junction, across from the petrol station. There's an **ATM** on the station road, near the T-junction, several tourist-oriented **restaurants** at the station, and cheap hot-food stalls in the market, halfway along the station road.

Tham Lawa and around

About 10km north of Nam Tok, a side road turns off Highway 323 at kilometre-stone 54 and runs down to the river, giving access to a beautiful stretch of the Kwai Noi, the *Resotel* pier, and several pleasant places to stay. Any Kanchanaburi–Thong Pha Phum bus will drop you at the turn-off.

The most famous attraction around here is **Tham Lawa** (B200 entry), the largest stalactite cave in the area and home to three species of bat; it's a ten-minute longtail ride upriver from the pier. The river is about 50m wide at this point, embraced by sheer limestone cliffs that are artistically pitted, dramatically streaked in red and white, and grown thick with lianas and bamboos tumbling down to the water's edge – be careful when swimming as the current is very strong (hotels should have lifejackets available). There's no development along the banks apart from a few raft houses and shore-bound little hotels, and **boat** rental at the *Resotel* pier (for up to eight people, prices quoted are for return trips) to Tham Lawa cave (10min; B700), Hellfire Pass (B900 to the nearest pier, then a 4km walk), and Sai Yok Yai Falls (1hr 30min; B1800).

You might also want to visit the **Mon village** behind the *River Kwai Jungle Rafts* resort, where you're encouraged to browse the sarongs and other artefacts made and sold by the villagers, take an elephant ride, and visit the school. The Mon villagers fled here from Burma in the late 1950s but have still not been granted Thai ID papers, which means the children can't study at Thai secondary schools and adults have difficulty finding work. This village has close links with *Jungle Rafts* and many of its residents work at the hotel. For more on the Mon people, see p.249.

Accommodation

Occupying a large swathe of steep and densely grown river bank about 1km off the highway at kilometre-stone 54, *Sam's Jungle Guest House* (Ⓣ081 948 3448, Ⓦwww.samsguesthouse.com; ③) offers a range of well-priced fan and air-con **accommodation**, plus a swimming pool, in a strange and rather unstylish assortment of buildings that nonetheless enjoy an exceptionally tranquil setting; there's kayak rental too. The nearby *Resotel* pier is the departure point for two other places to stay, both owned by the same company. Located on the west bank of the river, a few metres downstream from Tham Lawa, *River Kwai Resotel* (Ⓣ081 734 5238, Ⓦwww.riverkwairesotel.net; ⑦–⑧) is the more upmarket of the two, comprising some charming thatched riverside chalets and a swimming pool. A short distance upstream, the more rustic but very popular *River Kwai Jungle Rafts* (Ⓣ02 642 5497, Ⓦwww.riverkwaijunglerafts.com; from B1850 per person full board) offers simple but tasteful floating rooms, complete with hammocks, a swimming area, canoe rental and a bar. Rooms have no electricity so there are no fans or air-con and only oil-lamps at night.

Hellfire Pass

Although the rail line north of Nam Tok was ripped up soon after the end of World War II, it casts its dreadful shadow all the way up the Kwai Noi valley into Burma. The remnants of track are most visible at **Hellfire Pass**, and many of the villages in the area are former POW sites – locals frequently stumble across burial sites, now reclaimed by the encroaching jungle. To keep the Death Railway level through the uneven course of the Kwai valley, the POWs had to build a series of embankments and trestle bridges and, at dishearteningly frequent intervals, gouge deep cuttings through solid rock. The most concentrated digging was at **Konyu**, 18km beyond Nam Tok, where seven separate cuttings were made over a 3.5-kilometre stretch. The longest and most brutal of these was Hellfire Pass, which got its name from the hellish-looking lights and shadows of the fires the POWs used when working at night. The job took three months of round-the-clock labour with the most primitive tools.

Hellfire Pass has now been turned into a memorial walk in honour of the POWs who worked and died on it, and their story is documented at the beautifully designed **Hellfire Pass Memorial Museum** (daily 9am–4pm; donation) which stands at the trailhead. This is the best and most informative of all the World War II museums in the Kanchanaburi region, using wartime relics, and POW memorabilia, photos and first-hand accounts to tell the sobering history of the construction of this stretch of the Thailand–Burma Railway. Founded by an Australian-Thai volunteer group, the museum now serves as a sort of pilgrimage site for the families and friends of Australian POWs.

The same Australian-Thai group has also cleared a four-kilometre, ninety-minute circular **memorial walk**, which begins at the museum and follows the old rail route through the eighteen-metre-deep cutting and on to Hin Tok creek along a course relaid with some of the original narrow-gauge track. The creek was originally forded by a trestle bridge so unstable that it was nicknamed the Pack of Cards Bridge, but this has long since crumbled away. The trail doubles back on itself, passing through bamboo forest and a viewpoint that gives some idea of the phenomenal depth of rock the POWs had to dig through.

Most Kanchanaburi tour-operators offer **day-trips** featuring Hellfire Pass. It's also quite easy to get to Hellfire Pass on your own, and to combine it with your own trip on the Death Railway: from Kanchanaburi or Nam Tok, take any **bus** bound for Thong Pha Phum or Sangkhlaburi and ask to be dropped off at Hellfire Pass, which is signposted on the west side of Highway 323 just after kilometre-stone 64; it's about a 75-minute journey from Kanchanaburi or twenty minutes from Nam Tok. The last return bus to Kanchanaburi passes Hellfire Pass at about 4.45pm; if you're continuing to Sangkhlaburi, the last onward bus comes past at about 1.15pm.

North to Thong Pha Phum

Expanses of impenetrable mountain wilderness characterize the Kwai Noi valley to the north of Hellfire Pass, a landscape typified by the dense monsoon forests of **Sai Yok National Park**, which stretches all the way to the Burmese border. The first significant town beyond Sai Yok is **Thong Pha Phum**

(147km from Kanchanaburi), which sits at the southern edge of the massive **Vajiralongkorn Reservoir** and features some pleasant waterside accommodation.

Sai Yok National Park, Pha That Falls and Hin Dat hot springs

The teak forests of **Sai Yok National Park** (Ⓣ034 516163; B200 entry) are best known for the much-photographed though unexceptional **Sai Yok Yai Falls** and for the eight stalactite-filled chambers of **Daowadung Caves**. It's also home to the smallest-known mammal in the world, the elusive hog-nosed or bumblebee bat, which weighs just 1.75g and has a wingspan of 1.6cm. Short trails to these attractions start from near the park's visitor centre.

Signed off the highway between kilometre-stones 80 and 81, 104km north of Kanchanaburi, the park makes a refreshing enough stopover between Nam Tok and Sangkhlaburi, particularly if you have your own transport. You can stay in the national park **bungalows** (Ⓦwww.dnp.go.th/National_park.asp; ❹ for up to four people) or the more inviting floating timber cabins at *Sai Yok View Raft* (Ⓣ081 857 2284, Ⓦsaiyokviewraft.com; ❹), one of several raft houses near the waterfall. There are plenty of hot-food stalls (daily 6am–8pm) near the visitor centre. Any of the Kanchanaburi–Thong Pha Phum **buses** will stop at the road entrance to Sai Yok, from where it's a three-kilometre walk to the **visitor centre**, trailheads and river. The last buses in both directions pass the park at about 4.30pm. Motorbike taxis sometimes hang around the road entrance, but a more scenic approach would be by longtail from Nam Tok (see p.242).

North of Sai Yok National Park, signs off Highway 323 direct you to the two long, gently sloping cascades of **Pha That Falls** (12km east of the highway's kilometre-stone 103), accessible only with your own transport or on a tour; and to **Hin Dat** (Hindad) **hot springs** (1km east off the highway's kilometre-stone 105; B20 entry), where you can immerse yourself in a big pool of soothingly warm water, and make use of the nearby showers and foodstalls. Any Thong Pha Phum bus will drop you at the Hin Dat access track.

Thong Pha Phum and around

From Sai Yok National Park, Highway 323 continues northwest, following the course of the Kwai Noi. Forty-seven kilometres on, the road skirts **THONG PHA PHUM**, a mid-sized market town with bus connections to Sangkhlaburi and Kanchanaburi and plenty of small food shops. For **accommodation**, *Som Chainuk* (Ⓣ034 599067; ❶–❸) offers fan and air-conditioned motel-style rooms around its car park on the main street, between the police station and the main market; look for the wooden "Hotel" sign (no English name).

With your own transport, a much more scenic overnight option is to drive 12km west of Thong Pha Phum market to the southeastern fringes of nearby **Vajiralongkorn Reservoir** (formerly **Khao Laem Reservoir**). This vast body of water stretches all the way to Sangkhlaburi 73km to the north and, when created in the early 1980s, flooded every village in the vicinity. **Hotels** make the most of the refreshing, almost Scandinavian, landscape of forested hills and clear, still water that's perfect for swimming. The nicest of the English-speaking options is *Bann Suan Thaveechaiphaphum* (Ⓣ034 599841, Ⓦwww.thaveechaiphaphum.com; ❹–❺) which offers stylishly decorated lakeside and garden-view fan and air-conditioned cabins and rooms, the best with private, stilted chill-out pavilions built over the water. The location is great and they can also arrange boat trips around the lake. It's about 10km from Thong Pha Phum town; follow signs for the Vajiralongkorn Dam, then instead of turning right for the dam continue along the left-hand branch of the road for another 6km. Occasional yellow songthaews travel this route from Thong Pha Phum market.

About 70km from Thong Pha Phum town, along Route 3272, **Thong Pha Phum National Park** (☎081 382 0359) is a remote and lovely place to escape to, barely visited by foreign tourists. The final 30km of road twists like a roller coaster and is slow but surfaced. The big pleasure here is waking to see the foggy jungle below; there are several trails to waterfalls and a resident toucan too. You can rent tents (B150) and there's a restaurant on site.

Sangkhlaburi and around

Beyond Thong Pha Phum the views get increasingly spectacular as Highway 323 climbs through the remaining swathes of montane rainforest, occasionally hugging the reservoir's eastern shore, until 73km later it comes to an end at **Sangkhlaburi** (often called Sangkhla for short). In the early 1980s, the old town was lost under the rising waters of the newly created Khao Laem, now Vajiralongkorn, Reservoir. Its residents were relocated to the northeastern tip

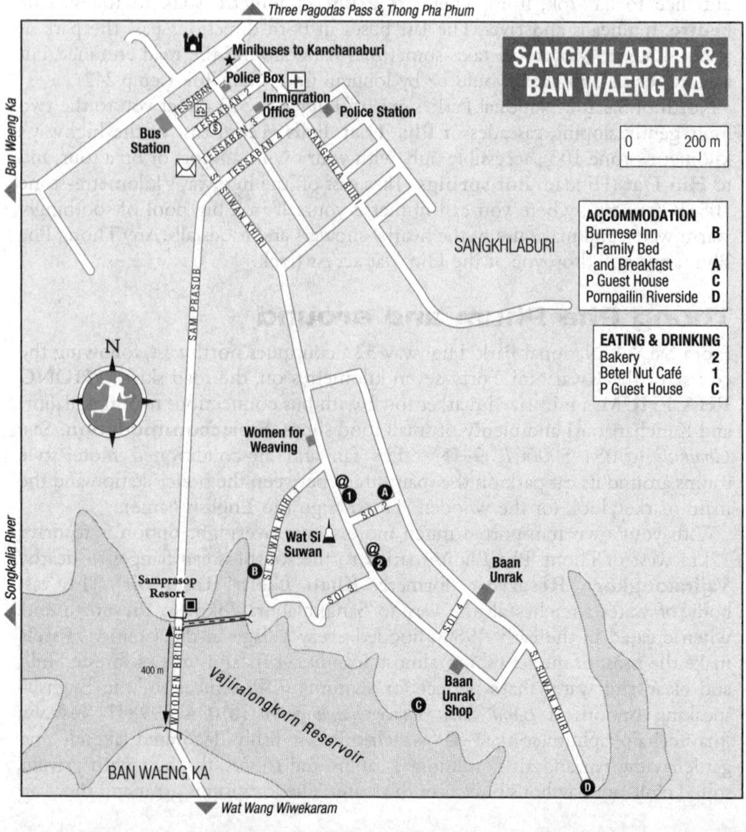

of the lake, beside the Songkalia River, where modern-day Sangkhla now enjoys an eerily beautiful view of semi-submerged trees and raft houses. It's a tiny town with no unmissable attractions, but the atmosphere is pleasantly low-key and the best of the accommodation occupies scenic lakeside spots so it's a great place to slow down for a while. Cultural interest is to be found in the villages, markets and temples of the area's Mon, Karen and Thai populations, including at **Ban Waeng Ka** across the water, and there's natural beauty in various waterfalls, whitewater rivers, and the remote Thung Yai Naresuan Wildlife Sanctuary. It sees relatively few farang tourists, but it's a popular destination for weekending Thais (come during the week for better deals on accommodation) and resident NGO volunteers add a positive vibe. Though the Burmese border is just 22km away at **Three Pagodas Pass**, at the time of writing it was closed to all visitors.

Arrival, transport and information

The fastest way to get to Sangkhla from **Kanchanaburi** is by air-conditioned **minibus** (10 daily 7.30am–4.30pm; 3hr; reserve a few hours ahead and be prepared to buy an extra seat if you have luggage); it also picks up from Thong Pha Phum. Minibuses terminate on the northern edge of Sangkhla and depart from the same spot (10 daily 6.30am–3.30pm; 3hr; reserve ahead). **Air-conditioned buses** also run from **Bangkok**'s Northern Moh Chit bus terminal via Kanchanaburi to the bus station on the western edge of Sangkhla (4 daily; 7hr). Doing it under your own steam can be tiring as the **road** is full of twists after Thong Pha Phum; the last 25km are particularly nerve-wracking for bikers because of the gravel spots in the many bends. Nonetheless, the scenery is fabulous, particularly at the lakeside **viewpoint** just north of kilometre-stone 35 (about 40km south of Sangkhlaburi).

Motorbike taxis usually charge B15 from the bus station to the guest houses and around B50 for a ride from the guest houses to Wat Wang Wiwekaram across the water. Sangkhlaburi itself is small enough to walk round in an hour; alternatively, *P Guest House* rents **motorbikes** and **bicycles**, while *Burmese Inn* should be able to arrange a pick-up **truck** and driver.

There's **internet** access at Baan Unrak's *Bakery* and the *Betel Nut Café*. Travellers' cheques and dollars can be changed at the **bank**, on the edge of the market in the town centre, which also has an ATM.

Organized trips

The two guest houses in Sangkhlaburi both run **organized trips** in the area for their guests. *P Guest House* does good-value accommodation packages featuring various combinations of elephant riding, bamboo rafting and boat trips on the lake (from B900 per person sharing). *Burmese Inn* does one-day rafting excursions on the Songkalia River (B500); two- and three-day treks in the Thung Yai Naresuan Wildlife Sanctuary, around the Karen village of Ban Sane Pong (B1800–3200); and two-day cooking classes (B500). They also keep a book of useful information on **motorbike routes** in the area, including to Takianthong waterfall and Sawan Badan cave, both accessed via the road to Three Pagodas Pass, and a back route to Erawan Waterfall.

Accommodation

The two guest houses are used by backpacking tour groups, so it's worth booking ahead; reservations are essential at all accommodation for weekends and national holidays.

Burmese Inn Soi 1 ⓣ086 168 1801, ⓦwww.sangkhlaburi.com. This rambling, traveller-oriented guest house overlooks the northeastern spur of the lake just behind the new bridge, offering easy access to the Mon village, but slightly truncated lake views. Most of the rooms and bungalows look right over the water and nearly all are en suite; the more expensive are attractively furnished and some have air-con and TV. Fan ❶–❸, air-con ❸–❺

J Family Bed and Breakfast (Kumsai Soonpoy) 17/1 Soi 2 ⓣ034 595511. A genuine homestay offering four big rooms with fan and shared bathroom in the large family home of the Mon woman, Kumsai Soonpoy, who runs the Baan Unrak shop. ❶

P Guest House West of soi 3 ⓣ034 595061, ⓦwww.pguesthouse.com. Large, popular, efficiently run, clued-up Mon-owned place that sits prettily on the banks of the lake. There's spacious, comfortable travellers' accommodation in sturdy, terraced stone-studded rooms with shared bathrooms, and en-suite rooms with air-con. Wi-fi in the restaurant. Reservations strongly advised. Fan and shared bathroom ❷, air-con ❺

Pornpailin Riverside About 2km down the hill from the bus station ⓣ034 595355, ⓦwww.ppailin.com. Resort-style place at the bottom of town whose air-con rooms nearly all offer fabulous lake views from their large glass windows and private terraces. The most interesting sit right over the water and some even have steps dropping right into the lake. ❺

The Town

Aside from crossing the famous wooden bridge over the lake to the Mon village of Ban Waeng Ka, the main pastime in Sangkhlaburi is **boating** across the reservoir in search of the **sunken temple** Wat Sam Phrasop, which was all but submerged when the valley was flooded; by the end of the dry season its upper storey usually reappears. *P Guest House* rents out two-person **canoes** for independent exploring (B150 per hr), or you can join a longtail-boat trip from either guest house.

Sangkhla's location so close to the Burmese border, along with the upheavals caused by the creation of the reservoir, mean that the town is full of displaced people, many of whom are in dire straits. Several organizations work with refugees in the area, including **Baan Unrak** (ⓣ034 595428, ⓦwww.baanunrak.org), a farang-managed programme founded by the Neo Humanist Foundation that has run an orphans' home here since 1991 and has also established a school and a weaving project for destitute women and children. To help support the project you can buy handicrafts at the Baan Unrak shop next to *P Guest House*, and visit their *Bakery* café (see p.251) to make donations of books, clothes and money, and get directions to the orphanage, which welcomes visitors and stages a yoga show every Wednesday during term-time at 6pm. Volunteer placements are also possible. Another community project worth supporting is **Women for Weaving**, set up by a group of Karen refugees in 1989. Their Hilltribe Handicrafts shop is located about 450m down the hill from the post office, or 150m up the hill from the turn-off to *Burmese Inn*, and carries a huge selection of hand-woven items, much of it in *mut mee* design and all of it made from good-quality Chiang Mai cotton, including tablecloths, sarongs, shirts and bags; for more on the Karen, see the box on p.298.

The wooden bridge, Ban Waeng Ka and Wat Wang Wiwekaram

The Mon village of **BAN WAENG KA**, across the reservoir from Sangkhlaburi, was founded in the late 1940s after the outbreak of civil war in Burma forced many to flee across the Thai border (see box opposite). The **Mon** people's homeland, Mon State, lies just west of the Tenasserim Mountains, so thousands of Mon ended up in Sangkhlaburi, illegal immigrants whose presence was permitted but not officially recognized. Most now have official

The Mon in Thailand

Dubbed by some "the Palestinians of Asia", the **Mon** people – numbering between two and four million in Burma and an estimated fifty thousand to two hundred thousand in Thailand (chiefly in the western provinces of Kanchanaburi and Ratchaburi, in the Gulf province of Samut Sakhon and in Nonthaburi and Pathum Thani just north of Bangkok) – have endured centuries of persecution, displacement and forced assimilation.

Ethnologists speculate that the Mon originated either in India or Mongolia, travelling south to settle on the western banks of the Chao Phraya valley in the first century BC. Here they founded the **Dvaravati kingdom** (sixth to eleventh centuries AD), building centres at U Thong, Lopburi and Nakhon Pathom and later consolidating a northern kingdom in Haripunchai (modern-day Lamphun). They probably introduced Theravada Buddhism to the region, and produced some of the earliest Buddhist monuments, particularly Wheels of Law and Buddha footprints.

Over on the Burmese side of the border, the Mon kingdom had established itself around the southern city of Pegu well before **the Burmese** filtered into the area in the ninth century, but by the mid-eighteenth century they'd been stripped of their homeland and were once again relocating to Thailand. The Thais welcomed them as a useful source of labour, and in 1814 the future Rama IV arrived at the Kanchanaburi border with three royal warboats and a guard of honour to chaperone the exiles. Swathes of undeveloped jungle were given over to them, many of which are still Mon-dominated today.

The **persecution** of Burmese Mon continues to this day under Burma's repressive regime, the State Peace and Development Council (SPDC; see box, p.298), and the Mon continue to struggle for the right to administer their own independent Mon State in their historical homelands opposite Kanchanaburi province in lower Burma. As one commentator has described it, while some of Burma's ethnic minority groups seek to *establish* autonomy, the Mon are attempting to *reclaim* it. Though the New Mon State Party (NMSP) entered into a ceasefire agreement with the Burmese junta in June 1995, international human-rights organizations continue to report gross violations against civilian Mon living in Burma. Thousands of Mon men, women and children have been press-ganged into unpaid labour, soldiers occupy certain Mon villages and commandeer produce and livestock, and reports of beatings and gang rapes are not uncommon. In an attempt to wipe out Mon culture, the junta has also banned the teaching of Mon language, literature and history in government schools, and outlawed the wearing of Mon national dress at official institutions.

Not surprisingly, Mon have been fleeing these atrocities in droves, the majority ending up in four **resettlement camps** in a Mon-controlled area along the Thai–Burma border, the biggest being Halockhani near Sangkhlaburi; the 9714 Mon living in these camps as of February 2009 have no right of entry into Thailand. For more information, see the website of the Human Rights Foundation of Monland (HURFOM; Ⓦwww.rehmonnya.org).

Like Thais, the Mon are a predominantly Buddhist, rice-growing people, but they also have strong animist beliefs. All Mon families have totemic **house spirits**, such as the turtle, snake, chicken or pig, which carry certain taboos; if you're of the chicken-spirit family, for example, the lungs and head of every chicken you cook have to be offered to the spirits, and although you're allowed to raise and kill chickens, you must never give one away. Guests belonging to a different spirit group from their host are not allowed to stay overnight. Mon **festivals** also differ slightly from Thai ones – at Songkhran (Thai New Year), the Mon spice up the usual water-throwing and parades with a special courtship ritual in which teams of men and women play each other at bowling, throwing flirtatious banter along with their wooden discs.

Sangkhlaburi residency, but still endure limited rights and must apply for expensive seven-day permits if they wish to travel out of the district, a system that lends itself to corruption.

Getting to the village is simply a matter of crossing the narrow northern neck of the lake, near the influx of the Songkalia River. Pedestrians can use the spider's web of a **wooden bridge** that is Sangkhla's unofficial town symbol: at almost 400m it is said to be the longest hand-built wooden bridge in the world and can be reached either by following signs from near the post office to *Samprasop Resort*, which overlooks the structure, or by using the newer connecting footbridge near the *Burmese Inn*. The concrete road bridge is several hundred metres further north. Once across the wooden bridge, turn left to get into the village – a sprawling collection of traditional wooden houses lining a network of steep tracks, with a small but lively dry-goods market at its heart.

About 2km west from the bridgehead – you might want to hail a motorbike taxi to get here – **Wat Wang Wiwekaram** (also known as **Wat Luang Pho Uttama**) is Ban Waeng Ka's most dramatic sight, its massive, golden **chedi** clearly visible from Sangkhlaburi. Built in a fusion of Thai, Indian and Burmese styles, the imposing square-sided stupa is modelled on the centrepiece of India's Bodh Gaya, the sacred site of the Buddha's enlightenment, and contains a much-prized Buddha relic (said to be a piece of his skeleton) brought to Ban Waeng Ka from Sri Lanka. It's a focal point for the Mon community on both sides of the Thai–Burma border, particularly at Mon New Year in April. There's a good **tourist market** in the covered cloisters at the chedi compound, with plenty of reasonably priced Burmese woodcarvings, checked *longyis* and jewellery. The wat is spread over two compounds, with the gleaming new bot, **viharn** and monks' quarters about 1km away from the chedi, at the end of the right-hand fork in the road. The interior of the viharn is decorated with murals showing tableaux from the five hundred lives of the Buddha, designed to be viewed in anticlockwise order.

▲ The wooden bridge, Sangkhlaburi

Three Pagodas Pass (Ban Chedi Sam Ong) and the Burmese border

All **border trade** for hundreds of kilometres north and south has to come through **Three Pagodas Pass**, 22 km north of Sangkhla and signed as **Jadee Sam Ong**, but at the time of writing the border was closed to people, and had been since 2007. Unless you're looking for heavy teak furniture or orchids, that means it's currently not worth making the trip as there's nothing more than a small market on the Thai side, in the village of **Ban Chedi Sam Ong**, plus the three eponymous little **chedis** said to have been erected in the eighteenth century by the kings of Burma and Thailand as a symbolic peace gesture. If and when the border reopens, foreigners will probably once again be allowed very limited access to the Burmese border village of **Payathonzu**, whose main attraction is the Mon temple **Wat Sao Roi Ton**, known in Burmese as **Tai Ta Ya temple**, or the Temple of One Hundred Teakwood Posts. **Songthaews** for the pass leave Sangkhlaburi bus station every forty minutes from 6am until about 5pm and take forty minutes; the last songthaew back to Sangkhla leaves at 6pm.

Eating

Day and night, the cheapest places to **eat** are at and around the market in the town centre. The large restaurant at *P Guest House* offers fine lake views from its terrace and serves good Thai, Burmese and European food, along with bottles of Kanchanaburi-made pineapple wine. The sociable *Bakery* (daily 8am–8pm), midway between the turn-offs for *Burmese Inn* and *P Guest House*, does brown-bread sandwiches, hot veggie meals, pizzas and banana cake, and is staffed by volunteers from the nearby Baan Unrak orphans' home; it has internet access too. At night, travellers and volunteers congregate at the nearby *Betel Nut Café*, which occupies the homey front yard of an expat's house, serves travellers' food and cocktails to order, shows DVDs, sells secondhand books and has internet access; the owner stages occasional Mon dance performances in the Mon village.

Ayutthaya and the Chao Phraya basin

Bisected by the country's main artery, the **Chao Phraya River**, and threaded by a network of tributaries and canals, the fertile plain to the north of the capital retains a spectrum of attractions from just about every period of the country's history. The monumental kitsch of the nineteenth-century palace at **Bang Pa-In** provides a sharp contrast with the atmospheric ruins at the former capital of **Ayutthaya**, arrayed in a grassy, riverine setting. **Lopburi**'s disparate remains, testimony to more than a millennium of continuous settlement, are less compelling, but you'll get a frenetic, noisy insight into Thai religion if you visit the nearby **Wat Phra Phutthabat** (Temple of the Buddha's Footprint), still one of Thailand's most popular pilgrimage sites after three and a half centuries.

Each of the attractions of this region can be visited on a day-trip from the capital – or, if you have more time to spare, you can slowly work your way through them before heading north or northeast. **Trains** are the most useful means of getting around, as plenty of local services run to and from Bangkok (note that the State Railway's standard English-language timetables do not list all the local services – phone the railway's hotline on ⓣ1690 for more comprehensive information). The line from the capital takes in Bang Pa-In and Ayutthaya before forking at Ban Phachi: the northern branch heads for Lopburi and goes on to Phitsanulok and Chiang Mai; the northeastern branch serves Isaan. Public **buses** between towns are regular but slow, or there are speedy minibus services between tourist hotspots.

Bang Pa-In

Little more than a roadside market, the village of **BANG PA-IN**, 60km north of Bangkok, has been put on the tourist map by its extravagant and rather surreal **Royal Palace** (daily 8.30am–5pm, ticket office closes 3.30pm; visitors are asked to dress respectfully, so no vests, shorts or sandals; B100; ⓦwww.palaces.thai.net), even though most of the buildings can be seen only from the outside. King Prasat Thong of Ayutthaya first built a palace on this site, 20km downstream from his capital, in the middle of the seventeenth century, and it remained a popular country residence for the kings of Ayutthaya. The palace was abandoned a century later when the capital was moved to Bangkok, only to be revived in the middle of the nineteenth century when the advent of steamboats shortened the journey time upriver. Rama IV (1851–68) built a modest residence here, which his son Chulalongkorn (Rama V), in his passion for Westernization, knocked down to make room for the eccentric melange of European, Thai and Chinese architectural styles visible today.

The palace

Set in manicured grounds on an island in the Chao Phraya River, and based around an ornamental lake, the palace complex is flat and compact. On the north side of the lake stand a two-storey, colonial-style residence for the royal relatives and the Italianate **Varobhas Bimarn** (**Warophat Phiman**, "Excellent and Shining Heavenly Abode"), which housed Chulalongkorn's throne hall and still contains private apartments where the present royal family sometimes stays. A covered bridge links this outer part of the palace to the **Pratu Thewarat Khanlai** ("The King of the Gods Goes Forth Gate"), the main entrance to the inner palace, which was reserved for the king and his immediate family. The high fence that encloses half of the bridge allowed the women of the harem to cross without being seen by male courtiers. You can't miss the glittering **Aisawan Thiphya-art** ("Divine Seat of Personal Freedom") in the middle of the lake: named after King Prasat Thong's original palace, it's the only example of pure Thai architecture at Bang Pa-In. The elegant tiers of the pavilion's roof shelter a bronze statue of Chulalongkorn.

In the inner palace, the **Uthayan Phumisathian** ("Garden of the Secured Land"), recently rebuilt by Queen Sirikit in grand, neocolonial style, was Chulalongkorn's favourite house. After passing the candy-striped **Ho Withun Thasana** ("Sage's Lookout Tower"), built so that the king could survey the surrounding countryside, you'll come to the main attraction of Bang Pa-In, the **Phra Thinang Wehart Chamrun Residential Hall** ("Palace of Heavenly Light"). A masterpiece of Chinese design, the mansion and its contents were shipped from China and presented as a gift to Chulalongkorn in 1889 by the Chinese Chamber of Commerce in Bangkok. The sumptuous interior gleams with fantastically intricate lacquered and gilded wooden screens, hand-painted porcelain floor tiles and ebony furniture inlaid with mother-of-pearl.

The simple marble **obelisk** behind the Uthayan Phumisathian was erected by Chulalongkorn to hold the ashes of Queen Sunandakumariratana, his favourite wife. In 1881, Sunanda, who was then 21 and expecting a child, was taking a trip on the river here when her boat capsized. She could have been rescued quite easily, but the laws concerning the sanctity of the royal family left those around her no option: "If a boat founders, the boatmen must swim away; if they remain near the boat [or] if they lay hold of him [the royal person] to rescue him, they are to be executed." Following the tragedy, King Chulalongkorn became a zealous reformer of Thai customs and strove to make the monarchy more accessible.

Practicalities

Bang Pa-In can easily be visited on a day-trip from Bangkok or Ayutthaya. The best route **from Bangkok** is by **train** from Hualamphong station, which takes just over an hour. All trains continue to Ayutthaya, with half going on to Lopburi. From Bang Pa-In station (note the separate station hall built by Chulalongkorn for the royal family) it's a two-kilometre hike to the palace, or you can take a motorbike taxi for about B30. Slow **buses** leave Bangkok's Northern Terminal roughly every half-hour and stop at **Bang Pa-In market**, about 300m southwest of the palace entrance. This is also the easiest place to catch a motorized samlor back to the train station. Many **day-tours from Bangkok** to Ayutthaya feature a stop at Bang Pa-In; see p.256.

From Ayutthaya, large songthaews leave Thanon Naresuan roughly every half hour for the forty-minute journey to Bang Pa-In market; trains are quicker (15min) and more frequent than the English-language timetable implies (most Ayutthaya guest houses keep the full Thai timetable).

There are **foodstalls** just outside the palace gates, at the back of the parking lot and at Bang Pa-In market.

Ayutthaya

In its heyday as the booming capital of the Thai kingdom, **AYUTTHAYA**, 80km north of Bangkok, was so well-endowed with temples that sunlight reflecting off their gilt decoration was said to dazzle from three miles away. Wide, grassy spaces today occupy much of the atmospheric site, which now resembles a graveyard for temples: grand, brooding red-brick ruins rise out of the fields, satisfyingly evoking the city's bygone grandeur while providing a soothing contrast to flashy modern temple architecture. A few intact buildings help form an image of what the capital must have looked like, while three fine museums flesh out the picture.

The core of the ancient capital was a four-kilometre-wide **island** at the confluence of the Lopburi, Pasak and Chao Phraya rivers, which was once encircled by a twelve-kilometre wall, crumbling parts of which can be seen at the Phom Phet fortress in the southeast corner. A grid of broad roads now crosses

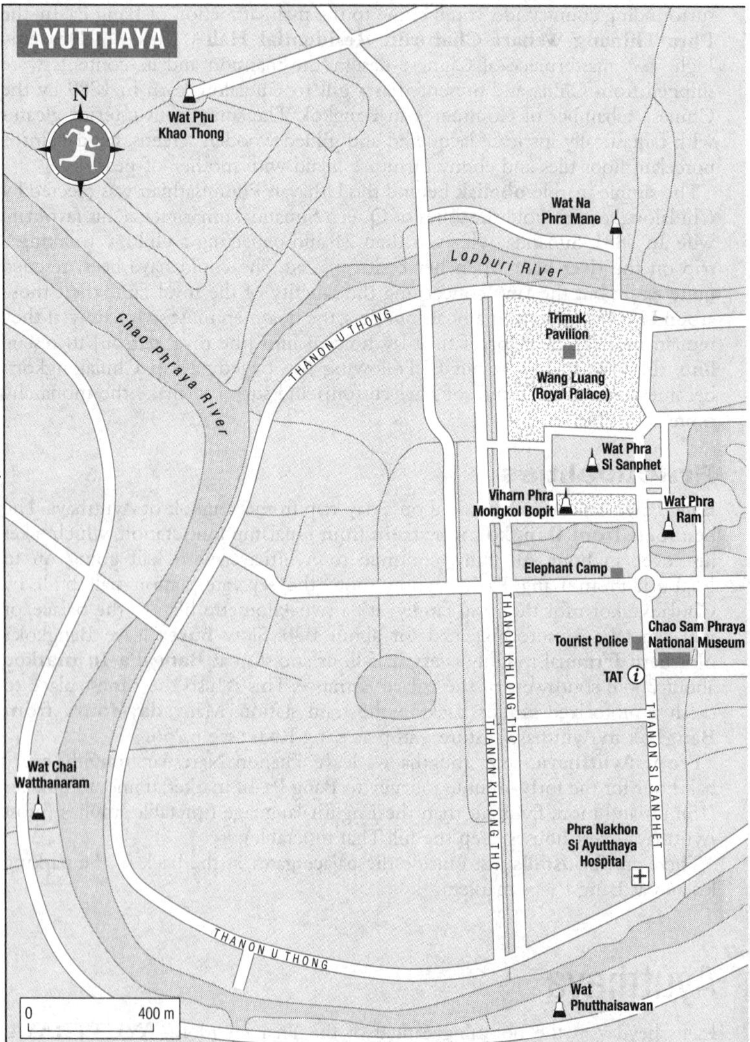

the island, known as Ko Muang: the hub of the small modern town occupies its northeast corner, around the Thanon U Thong and Thanon Naresuan junction, but the rest is mostly uncongested and ideal for exploring by bicycle.

There is also much pleasure to be had from soaking up life on and along the encircling **rivers**, either by taking a boat tour or by dining at one of the waterside restaurants. It's very much a working waterway, busy with barges carrying cement, rice and other heavy loads to and from Bangkok and the Gulf and with cross-river ferry services that compensate for the lack of bridges.

Ayutthaya comes alive each year for a week in mid-December, with a **festival** that commemorates the town's listing as a **World Heritage Site** by UNESCO

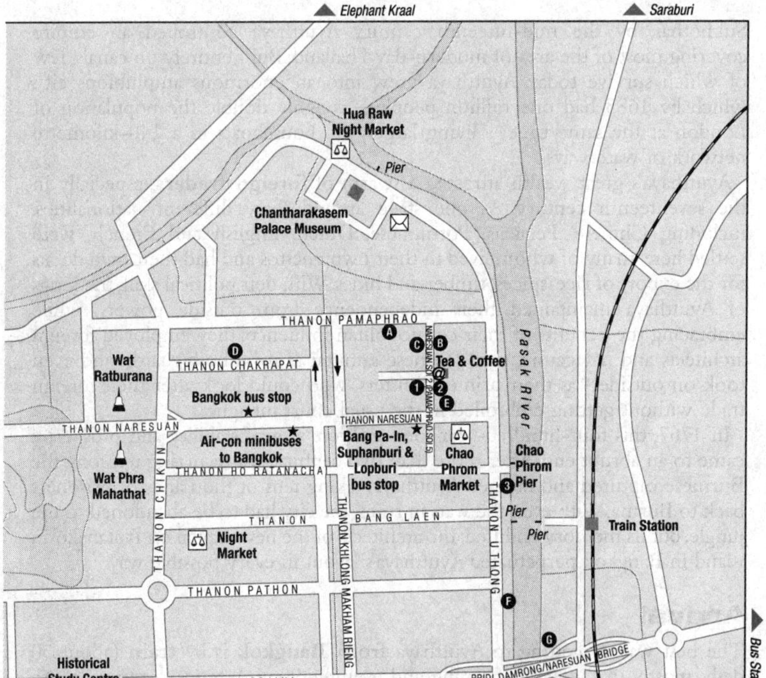

on December 13, 1991. The highlight is the nightly *son et lumière* show, featuring fireworks and elephant-back fights, staged around the ruins.

Some history

Ayutthaya takes its name from the Indian city of Ayodhya (Sanskrit for "invincible"), the legendary birthplace of Rama, hero of the *Ramayana* epic. It was founded in 1351 by U Thong – later **Ramathibodi I** – after Lopburi was ravaged by smallpox, and it rose rapidly through exploiting the expanding trade routes between India and China. Stepping into the political vacuum left by the decline of the Khmer empire at Angkor and the first Thai kingdom at

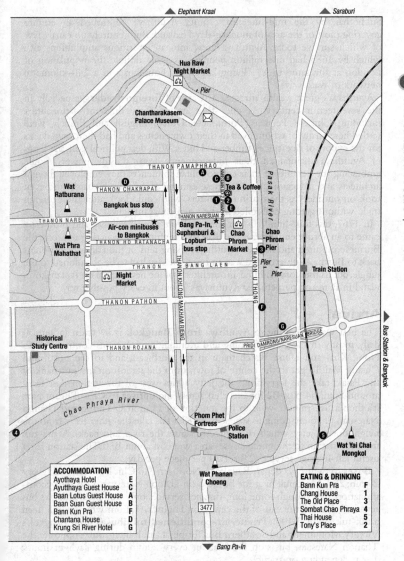

Sukhothai, by the mid-fifteenth century Ayutthaya controlled an empire covering most of the area of modern-day Thailand. Built entirely on canals, few of which survive today, Ayutthaya grew into an enormous amphibious city, which by 1685 had one million people – roughly double the population of London at the same time – living largely on houseboats in a 140-kilometre network of waterways.

Ayutthaya's great wealth attracted a swarm of **foreign traders**, especially in the seventeenth century. At one stage around forty different nationalities, including Chinese, Persians, Portuguese, Dutch, English and French, were settled here, many of whom lived in their own ghettos and had their own docks for the export of rice, spices, timber and hides. With deft political skill, the kings of Ayutthaya maintained their independence from outside powers, while embracing the benefits of their cosmopolitan influence: they employed foreign architects and navigators, used Japanese samurai as royal bodyguards, and even took on outsiders as their prime ministers, who could look after their foreign trade without getting embroiled in the usual court intrigues.

In 1767, this four-hundred-year-long **golden age** of stability and prosperity came to an abrupt end. After more than two centuries of recurring tensions, the Burmese captured and ravaged Ayutthaya, taking tens of thousands of prisoners back to Burma. With even the wats in ruins, the city had to be abandoned to the jungle, but its memory endured: the architects of the new capital on Ratanakosin island in Bangkok perpetuated Ayutthaya's layout in every possible way.

Arrival

The best way of getting to Ayutthaya **from Bangkok** is by **train** (about 30 daily, mostly in the early morning and evening; 90min); trains continue on to Nong Khai and Ubon Ratchathani in the northeast, and to the north and Chiang Mai. To get to the centre of town from the station on the east bank of the Pasak, take the ferry from the jetty 100m west of the station (last ferry around 8pm; B4 plus B2 for bicycles) across and upriver to Chao Phrom pier; it's then a five-minute walk to the junction of Thanon U Thong and Thanon Naresuan (if you're going to stay at *Bann Kun Pra*, take the other ferry from the neighbouring jetty, which runs directly across the river and back). A tuk-tuk from the station to the guest-houses area will cost about B50. The station has a useful left-luggage service (24hr; B10 per piece per day).

Buses to Ayutthaya depart Bangkok's Northern Mo Chit Bus Terminal (every 20min; 2hr). Most pull in at the bus stop on Thanon Naresuan, near the accommodation area, though some long-distance services only stop at Ayutthaya's bus terminal, 5km to the east of the centre on Highway 1, from where you'll need a tuk-tuk (about B100). Private, **air-conditioned minibuses** from Bangkok's Victory Monument and Southern Bus Terminal finish their routes opposite the Thanon Naresuan bus stop (both about every 20min during daylight hours; 1–2hr depending on traffic).

The most popular **day-trips** to Ayutthaya from Bangkok feature only the briefest whizz around the old city's three main temples, making a stop at the Bang Pa-In summer palace en route (see p.252) and rounding the day off with a three-hour river cruise back down the Chao Phraya from the northern Bangkok suburb of Nonthaburi; Grand Pearl Cruise is one of the main operators (Ⓦwww.grandpearlcruise.com; B1700, under-11s B1100). You can also cruise the river in more style, spending one or more nights on plushly converted teak rice-barges such as the *Mekhala* (Ⓦwww.asian-oasis.com) or the *Manohra* 2 (Ⓣ02 477 0770, Ⓦwww.manohracruises.com).

Moving on from Ayutthaya

Many visitors continue by **train** (see p.307) but countless **bus services** also run both from the town centre and from the public bus station 5km east on Highway 1. Any guest house can supply timetables and some will also sell you tickets, as does Sun Travel on Naresuan Soi 2 (☎035 232867). Useful services include frequent air-con buses **to Bangkok** from various locations on Thanon Naresuan: the large public air-con buses run to Mo Chit Northern Terminal while the private minibuses go to Victory Monument or Bangkok's Southern Bus Terminal. Fast but cramped tourist **minibuses** serve Suvarnabhumi Airport (2hr 30min), Bangkok's Khao San (1hr 30min), Kanchanaburi (2hr 30min) and Sukhothai (4hr 30min), and there are also connecting minibuses for Ko Samet and Ko Chang, an overnight bus service to **Chiang Mai** and another to Siem Reap in **Cambodia** (26hr).

From Kanchanaburi, it's possible to bypass the Bangkok gridlock, either by hooking up with an air-conditioned tourist minibus (2hr 30min; arranged through guest houses in Kanchanaburi) or, under your own steam, by taking a public bus to Suphanburi (every 20min; 1hr 30min), then changing to an Ayutthaya bus (every 30min; 1hr), which will drop you off on Thanon Naresuan.

Information

TAT's helpful **Ayutthaya Tourist Information Centre** (daily 8.30am–4.30pm; ☎035 322730, Ⓔtatyutya@tat.or.th) is in the former city hall on the west side of Thanon Si Sanphet, opposite the Chao Sam Phraya National Museum. It's well worth heading upstairs here to the smartly presented multi-media **exhibition** on Ayutthaya (daily except Wed 8.30am–4.30pm; free), which provides an engaging introduction to the city's history, an overview of all the sights, including a scale-model reconstruction of Wat Phra Si Sanphet, and insights into local traditional ways of life. The **tourist police** (☎035 242352 or 1155) are based just to the north of TAT on Thanon Si Sanphet and the government Phra Nakhon Si Ayutthaya **hospital** is at the southern end of Thanon Si Sanphet (☎035 241888). You can access the **internet** at several places along Naresuan Soi 2, and there's wi-fi here too (and quality coffee) at *Tea & Coffee*. There are also plenty of **ATMs** and banks with exchange services around the mouth of Naresuan Soi 2.

Transport and tours

Busloads of tourists descend on the sights during the day, but the area covered by the old capital is large enough not to feel swamped. Distances are deceptive, so it's best not to walk everywhere: **bicycles** can be rented at guest houses, around the train station and from the tourist police. Some guest houses and a few cheaper outlets in front of the station rent small **motorbikes**. Otherwise there are plenty of **tuk-tuks** around: their set routes for sharing passengers are more useful for locals than for tourists, but a typical journey in town on your own should only cost B50. **Motorbike taxis** charge around B40 for medium-range journeys.

If you're pushed for time you could hire a tuk-tuk for a whistle-stop **tour** of the old city for B200 an hour (the current going rate set by the tourist police), either from the train station or from Chao Phrom market. **Sunset tuk-tuk tours** organized by guest houses are also popular, taking in some of the illuminated ruins (the main five central ruins are lit nightly 7–9pm) and ending at the night market (about 2hr; B160 per person), or there are the guided **bicycle tours** run by Ayutthaya Boat & Travel (ⓣ081 733 5687, ⓦwww.ayutthaya-boat.com), whose itineraries include the ruins by day or night, a combination cycle and boat tour and a dinner cruise. For a serious **guided tour** of the ruins, local expert Professor Monton at Classic Tour (B1500 per day; ⓣ081 832 4849) comes highly recommended.

Circumnavigating Ayutthaya by **boat** is a very enjoyable way to take in some of the outlying temples, and possibly a few lesser-visited ones too; many of the temples were designed to be approached, and admired, from the river, and you also get a leisurely look at twenty-first-century riverine residences. All guest houses and agencies offer boat tours, typically charging B300 per person for a two-hour trip; they can also be chartered from the pier outside the Chanthara-kasem Palace museum.

It's also possible to take a brief **elephant ride** (B400 per person for 20min, B500 for 30min) past a couple of the central ruins from the roadside elephant "camp" on Thanon Pathon. The elephants and their mahouts are photogenically clad in period costume and you can buy them bananas while they wait for custom, or simply watch them return home after 6pm when they rumble across to the northeast side of town to bathe and bed down in the restored sixteenth-century kraal. Wild elephants were formerly driven to the kraal for capture and taming but these days it's the headquarters of Elephantstay (ⓦwww.elephantstay.com), an organization that runs three- to fourteen-day residential packages for visitors who want to ride, feed, water and bathe the ninety resident elephants.

Accommodation

Ayutthaya offers a good choice of **accommodation**, including a small ghetto of budget guest houses on the soi that runs north from Chao Phrom market to Thanon Pamaphrao; it's sometimes known as Soi Farang but is actually signed as Naresuan Soi 2 at the southern end and Pamaphrao Soi 5 at the northern.

Ayothaya Hotel Thanon Naresuan ⓣ035 232855. Central, good-value hotel with unexciting air-con, motel rooms in the "standard" wing behind the car park and much more salubrious superior rooms in the hotel building. All guests can use the inviting swimming pool. Nice staff and a handy location. Budget ❹, superior ❺

Ayutthaya Guest House Naresuan Soi 2 ⓣ035 232658. Large, friendly and efficiently managed establishment that's very clued up about travellers' requirements and offers bike and motorbike rental, and numerous onward transport options. Rooms are spread across two buildings and vary in size and facilities from tiny fan singles with shared bathrooms to large air-con en suites for four. Fan ❶, fan and bathroom ❷, air-con ❸

Baan Lotus Guest House Thanon Pamaphrao ⓣ035 251988. Tranquil traditional-style house with wooden floors and large plain en-suite rooms, fan and air-con, in a quiet spot at the end of a long garden with a lotus pond at the back. Keeps good local information and offers simple breakfasts. ❸

Baan Suan Guest House 23/1 Thanon Chakrapat ⓣ035 242394, ⓦwww.baansuanguesthouse.com. Choose between bright, simple fan and air-con rooms upstairs in the airy family house, sharing cold-water bathrooms, and Thai resort-style wooden bungalows in the shady little garden, with hot showers and air-con. Internet access. Also has a streetside bar. ❷–❹

Bann Kun Pra Thanon U Thong, just north of Pridi Damrong Bridge ⓣ035 241978, ⓦwww.bannkunpra.com. Airy, attractive rooms spread across two buildings: a rambling, hundred-year-old riverside teak house with a large, comfy chill-out terrace, where the nicest rooms have river-view balconies (and shared bathrooms); and a newer, noisier block near the road, where all rooms have en-suite cold-water bathrooms and some have air-con. There's also a dorm (B250) with mattresses on the teak floor and individual lockable tin trunks. Internet access, bike rental, river tours and a warm welcome. ❸–❹

Chantana House Naresuan Soi 2 ⓣ035 323200, ⓔchantanahouse@yahoo.com. At the quieter end of the travellers' soi, this low-key guest house offers large, spotlessly clean, en-suite fan and air-con rooms, though not all have outward facing windows. Friendly, but not much English spoken. Fan ❷, air-con ❸

Krung Sri River 27/2, Thanon Rojana ⓣ035 244333, ⓦwww.krungsririver.com. Ayutthaya's best hotel occupies nine storeys in a prime if noisy position beside the Pridi Damrong Bridge, with some standard and all suite rooms enjoying river views. Furnishings fall some way short of contemporary chic but there's air-con and TVs throughout, an attractive third-floor pool and a car park. Standard rooms are good value. Standard ❻, suite ❾

The City

The majority of Ayutthaya's ancient remains are spread out across the western half of the island in a patchwork of parkland: **Wat Phra Mahathat** and **Wat Ratburana** stand near the modern centre, while a broad band runs down the middle of the parkland, containing the **Royal Palace** (**Wang Luang**) and temple, the most revered Buddha image, at **Viharn Phra Mongkol Bopit**, and the two main **museums**. To the north of the island you'll find the best-preserved temple, **Wat Na Phra Mane**, and **Wat Phu Khao Thong**, the "Golden Mount"; to the west stands the Khmer-style **Wat Chai Watthanaram**, while to the southeast lie the giant chedi of **Wat Yai Chai Mongkol** and **Wat Phanan Choeng**, still a vibrant place of worship.

Wat Phra Mahathat and Wat Ratburana

Heading west out of the new town centre along Thanon Naresuan, after about 1km you'll come to the first set of ruins, a pair of temples on opposite sides of the road. The overgrown **Wat Phra Mahathat**, on the left (daily 8am–6pm; B30), is the epitome of Ayutthaya's nostalgic atmosphere of faded majesty. The name "Mahathat" (Great Relic Chedi) indicates that the temple was built to house remains of the Buddha himself: according to the royal chronicles – never renowned for historical accuracy – King Ramesuan (1388–95) was looking out of his palace one morning when ashes of the Buddha materialized out of thin air here. A gold casket containing the ashes was duly enshrined in a grand 38-metre-high prang. The prang later collapsed, but the reliquary was unearthed in the 1950s, along with a hoard of other treasures, including a gorgeous marble fish, which opened to reveal gold, amber, crystal and porcelain ornaments – all now on show in the Chao Sam Phraya National Museum (see p.261).

You can climb what remains of the prang to get a good view of the broad, grassy complex, with dozens of brick spires tilting at impossible angles and headless Buddhas scattered around like spare parts in a scrapyard; look out for the serene (and much photographed) head of a stone Buddha that has become nestled in the embrace of a bodhi tree's roots. To the west you'll see a lake, now surrounded by a popular park, and the slender prang of **Wat Phra Ram** (daily 8am–6pm; B30), built in the late fourteenth century on the site of Ramathibodi's cremation by his son and successor as king, Ramesuan.

Across the road from Wat Phra Mahathat, the towering **Wat Ratburana** (daily 8am–6pm; B30) was built in 1424 by King Boromraja II to commemorate his elder brothers, Ay and Yi, who managed to kill each other in an elephant-back duel over the succession to the throne, thus leaving it vacant for Boromraja. Here, four elegant Sri Lankan chedis lean outwards as if in deference to the main prang, on which some of the original stuccowork can still be seen, including fine statues of garudas swooping down on nagas. It's possible to descend steep steps inside the prang to the crypt, where on two levels you can make out fragmentary murals of the early Ayutthaya period.

Wat Phra Si Sanphet and the Wang Luang (Royal Palace)

Nearly a kilometre west of Wat Ratburana is **Wat Phra Si Sanphet** (daily 8am–6pm; B30), built in 1448 by King Boromatrailokanat as his private chapel. Formerly the grandest of Ayutthaya's temples, and still one of the best preserved, it took its name from one of the largest standing metal images of the Buddha ever known, the **Phra Si Sanphet**, erected here in 1503. Towering 16m high and covered in 173kg of gold, it did not survive the ravages of the Burmese, though Rama I rescued the pieces and placed them inside a chedi at Wat Pho in Bangkok. The three remaining grey chedis in the characteristic style of the old capital were built to house the ashes of three kings, and have now become the most familiar image of Ayutthaya.

The site of this royal wat was originally occupied by Ramathibodi I's wooden palace, which Boromatrailokanat replaced with the bigger **Wang Luang** (Royal Palace; same hours and ticket as Wat Phra Si Sanphet), stretching to the Lopburi River on the north side. Successive kings turned the Wang Luang into a vast complex of pavilions and halls, with an elaborate system of walls designed to isolate the inner sanctum for the king and his consorts. The palace was destroyed by the Burmese in 1767 and plundered by Rama I for its bricks, which he needed to build the new capital at Bangkok. Now you can only trace the outlines of a few walls in the grass and inspect an unimpressive wooden replica of an open pavilion – better to consult the model of the whole complex in the Historical Study Centre.

Viharn Phra Mongkol Bopit and the cremation ground

Viharn Phra Mongkol Bopit (Mon–Fri 8.30am–4.30pm, Sat & Sun 8.30am–5.30pm; free), on the south side of Wat Phra Si Sanphet, attracts tourists and Thai pilgrims in about equal measure. The pristine hall – a replica of a typical Ayutthayan viharn, with its characteristic chunky lotus-capped columns around the outside – was built in 1956, with help from the Burmese to atone for their flattening of the city two centuries earlier, in order to shelter the revered **Phra Mongkol Bopit**, one of the largest bronze Buddhas in Thailand. The powerfully austere image, with its flashing mother-of-pearl eyes, was cast in the fifteenth century, then sat exposed to the elements from the time of the Burmese invasion until its new home was built. During restoration, the hollow image was found to contain hundreds of Buddha statuettes, some of which were later buried around the shrine to protect it.

The car park in front of the viharn used to be the **cremation site** for Ayutthayan kings and high-ranking members of the royal family. Here, on a propitious date decided by astrologers, the embalmed body was placed on a towering *meru* (funeral pyre), representing Mount Meru, the centre of the Hindu-Buddhist universe. These many-gabled and -pinnacled wooden structures, which had all the appearance of permanent palaces, were a miracle of architectural technology: the *meru* constructed for King Phetracha in 1704, for example, was 103m tall and took eleven months to raise, requiring thousands of tree trunks and hundreds of thousands of bamboo poles. The task of building at such great heights was given to *yuan-hok*, a particular clan of acrobats who used to perform at the tops of long poles during special festivals. Their handiwork was not consigned to the flames: the cremation took place on a pyramid erected underneath the central spire, so as not to damage the main structure, which was later dismantled and its timber used for building temples. The cremation ground is now given over to a picnic area and a clutch of souvenir and refreshment stalls.

The museums

A ten-minute walk south of the viharn brings you to the largest of the town's three museums, the **Chao Sam Phraya National Museum** (Wed–Sun 9am–4pm, last admission 3.30pm; B30; Ⓦ www.thailandmuseum.com), where most of the moveable remains of Ayutthaya's glory – those that weren't plundered by treasure-hunters or taken to the National Museum in Bangkok – are exhibited. Apart from numerous Buddhas and some fine woodcarving, the museum is bursting with **gold treasures**, including the original relic casket from Wat Mahathat, betel-nut sets and model chedis, and a gem-encrusted fifteenth-century crouching elephant found in the crypt at Wat Ratburana.

The **Historical Study Centre** (daily 8.30am–4.30pm; B100), five minutes' walk away along Thanon Rotchana, is a more modern showpiece museum. The visitors' exhibition upstairs puts the ruins in context, dramatically presenting a broad social history of Ayutthaya through videos, sound effects and reconstructions of temple murals, along with model ships, a peasant's wooden house and a small-scale model of the Royal Palace.

In the northeast corner of the island, the **Chantharakasem Palace Museum** (Wed–Sun 8.30am–4.30pm; B30; Ⓦ www.thailandmuseum.com) was traditionally the home of the heir to the Ayutthayan throne. The Black Prince, Naresuan, built the first *wang na* (palace of the front) here in about 1577 so that he could guard the area of the city wall that was most vulnerable to enemy attack. Rama IV (1851–68) had the palace rebuilt and it now displays many of his possessions, including a throne platform overhung by a white *chat*, a ceremonial nine-tiered parasol that is a vital part of a king's insignia. The rest of the museum features beautiful ceramics and Buddha images, and a small arsenal of cannon and musketry.

Wat Na Phra Mane

Wat Na Phra Mane (daily 8am–6pm; B20), on the north bank of the Lopburi River opposite the Wang Luang, is Ayutthaya's most rewarding temple, as it's the only one from the town's golden age that survived the ravages of the Burmese.

The main **bot**, built in 1503, shows the distinctive features of Ayutthayan architecture – outside columns topped with lotus cups, and slits in the walls instead of windows to let the wind pass through. Inside, underneath a rich red-and-gold coffered ceiling that represents the stars around the moon, sits a powerful six-metre-high Buddha in the disdainful, over-decorated royal style characteristic of the later Ayutthaya period.

In sharp contrast is the dark-green **Phra Khan Thavaraj** Buddha, which dominates the tiny viharn behind to the right. Seated in the "European position", with its robe delicately pleated and its feet up on a large lotus leaf, the gentle figure conveys a reassuring serenity. It's advertised as being from Sri Lanka, the source of Thai Buddhism, but more likely is a seventh- to ninth-century Mon image from Wat Phra Mane at Nakhon Pathom.

Wat Phu Khao Thong

Head 2km northwest of Wat Na Phra Mane and you're in open country, where the fifty-metre chedi of **Wat Phu Khao Thong** rises steeply out of the fields. In 1569, after a temporary occupation of Ayutthaya, the Burmese erected a Mon-style chedi here to commemorate their victory. Forbidden by Buddhist law from pulling down a sacred monument, the Thais had to put up with this galling reminder of the enemy's success until it collapsed nearly two hundred years later, when King Borommakot promptly built a truly Ayutthayan chedi on the old Burmese base – just in time for the Burmese to return in 1767 and flatten the town. This "Golden Mount" has recently been restored and painted toothpaste-white, with a colossal equestrian statue of King Naresuan, conqueror of the Burmese, to keep it company. You can climb 25m of steps up the side of the chedi to look out over the countryside and the town, with glimpses of Wat Phra Si Sanphet and Viharn Phra Mongkok Bopit in the distance.

Wat Chai Watthanaram

It's worth the ride to reach the elegant brick-and-stucco latticework of Khmer-style stupas at **Wat Chai Watthanaram** (daily 8am–6pm; B30), across the river to the southwest of the island. These graceful ruins used to be a common stop on boat tours but because of recurrent flooding a wall now protects them from the river and access is only viable by road. Late afternoon is a popular time to visit, as the sun sinks photogenically behind the main tower.

King Prasat Thong built Wat Chai Watthanaram in 1630, possibly to commemorate a victory over Cambodia, designing it as a sort of Angkorian homage, around a towering central Khmer corncob **prang** (tower) encircled by a constellation of four minor prangs and eight tiered and tapered chedis. Most of the stucco facing has weathered away to reveal the red-brick innards in pretty contrast, but a few tantalizing fragments of stucco relief remain on the outside of the chedis, depicting episodes from the Buddha's life. Around the gallery that connects them sits a solemn phalanx of 120 headless seated Buddhas, each on its own red-brick dais but showing no trace of their original skins, which may have been done in black lacquer and gold-leaf. To the east a couple of larger seated Buddhas look out across the river from the foundations of the old bot. You can share their view by climbing the steep steps of the central prang behind them, which also gives you the chance to admire the tower's robust redented structure at close quarters.

Wat Yai Chai Mongkol

Across the Pasak River southeast of the island, you pass through Ayutthaya's new business zone and some rustic suburbia before reaching the ancient but still functioning **Wat Yai Chai Mongkol**, about 2km from the station (daily

▲ Buddhas at Wat Yai Chai Mongkol

8am–5pm; B20). If you're on a bicycle, avoid the frantic multi-laned Pridi Damrong/Naresuan Bridge and Bangkok road by taking the river ferry across to the train station and then heading south 1.5km before turning east to the temple. Surrounded by formal lawns, flowerbeds and much-photographed saffron-draped Buddhas, the wat was established by Ramathibodi I in 1357 as a meditation site for monks returning from study in Sri Lanka. King Naresuan put up the beautifully curvaceous **chedi** to mark the decisive victory over the Burmese at Suphanburi in 1593, when he himself had sent the enemy packing by slaying the Burmese crown prince in an elephant-back duel. Built on a colossal scale to outshine the Burmese Golden Mount on the opposite side of Ayutthaya, the chedi has come to symbolize the prowess and devotion of Naresuan and, by implication, his descendants right down to the present king. By the entrance, a **reclining Buddha**, now gleamingly restored in white, was also constructed by Naresuan. A huge modern glass-walled shrine to the revered king dominates the back of the temple compound.

Wat Phanan Choeng

In Ayutthaya's most prosperous period, the docks and main trading area were located near the confluence of the Chao Phraya and Pasak rivers, to the west of Wat Yai Chai Mongkol. This is where you'll find the oldest and liveliest working temple in town, **Wat Phanan Choeng** (daily 8am–5pm; B20). The main viharn is often filled with the sights, sounds and smells of an incredible variety of merit-making activities, as devotees burn huge pink Chinese incense candles, offer food and rattle fortune sticks. It's even possible to buy tiny golden statues of the Buddha to be placed in one of the hundreds of niches that line the walls, a form of votive offering peculiar to this temple. If you can get here during a festival, especially Chinese New Year, you're in for an overpowering experience.

The nineteen-metre-high Buddha, which almost fills the hall, has survived since 1324, shortly before the founding of the capital, and tears are said to have flowed from its eyes when Ayutthaya was sacked by the Burmese. However, the reason for the temple's popularity with the Chinese is to be found in the early eighteenth-century shrine by the pier, with its image of a beautiful Chinese princess who drowned herself here because of a king's infidelity: his remorse led him to build the shrine at the place where she had walked into the river.

Eating and drinking

Other than the **restaurants** listed below, the *roti* (Muslim pancake) stalls near the hospital around the southern end of Thanon Si Sanphet are good for daytime snacks and after dark there are a couple of **night markets**: beside the river at Hua Raw, about ten minutes' walk north of Naresuan Soi 2, and at the west end of Thanon Bang Laen, 150m south of Wat Phra Mahathat. Competing singers – including local boy Lek ("Little") Clapton – at the clutch of **bar-restaurants** can make Naresuan Soi 2 a bit of a battle of the bands after 9pm but it's fun and lively, and free with your beer.

Bann Kun Pra Thanon U Thong. The riverside dining terrace is just as atmospheric as the lovely guest house upstairs, and enjoys fine views. It specializes in reasonably priced fish and seafood, notably prawns, and the pork and pumpkin curry is good too. Most mains about B100.

Chang House Naresuan Soi 2. A chilled and inviting streetside travellers' restaurant that lives up to its motto: "Good food, good beer and good cheer" by serving tasty Thai standards and lots of seafood freshly cooked to authentic spiciness if requested (B70–100). Also does veggie dishes, a few Western classics and Indian curries. Imported wine, B90 cocktails and good sounds before the nightly live crooner takes over about 9pm.

The Old Place K-102 Thanon U Thong. Great Thai food and a breezy, always interesting riverside location across and up a bit from the station pier, make this place a hit with locals and tourists alike. Tables are on a wooden deck over the water, shaded by a venerable century-old kapok tree. Seafood is tip-top, especially the fish cakes and the sweet-and-sour prawns; cheap cocktails too. Mains B80–200.

Sombat Chao Phraya Thanon U Thong on the south side of town. Congenial spot where, on river-bank terraces or a moored boat with views of Wat Phutthaisawan's white prang, you can dine on such delicacies as royal tofu with wild mushrooms, crab, cashew nuts and prawns.

Thai House On the road between Wat Yai Chai Mongkol and Wat Phanan Choeng. Serves a huge variety of excellent Thai food (B100–300), including delicious deep-fried banana flowers, and a choice of Thai desserts; tables are arrayed around several stilted, wooden, traditional-style houses.

Tony's Place Naresuan Soi 2. The size of this cavernous timbered restaurant, on the ground floor of the guest house, plus its chill-out cushioned areas, blasting music and cheap internet access make this a popular travellers' meeting place; the typical travellers' food is cheap enough but nothing special.

Lopburi and around

Mention the name **LOPBURI** to a Thai and the chances are that he or she will start telling you about monkeys – the central junction in the old town of this unexceptional provincial capital, 150km due north of Bangkok, swarms with macaques. So beneficial are the beasts to the town's tourist trade that a local hotelier treats six hundred of them to a sit-down meal at Phra Prang Sam Yod temple every November, complete with menus, waiters and napkins, as a thank you for their help. In fact, the monkeys can be a real nuisance, but at least they add some life to the town's central **Khmer buildings**, which, though historically important, are rather unimpressive. More illuminating is the **Narai National Museum**, housed in a partly reconstructed seventeenth-century palace complex, and distant **Wat Phra Phutthabat**, a colourful eye-opener for non-Buddhists. Lopburi's main festival is the five-day **King Narai Reign Fair** in February, to commemorate the seventeenth-century king's birthday, featuring costumed processions, cultural performances, traditional markets and a *son et lumière* show at Phra Narai Ratchanivet.

Originally called Lavo, Lopburi is one of the longest-inhabited towns in Thailand, and was a major centre of the Mon (Dvaravati) civilization from around the sixth century. It maintained a tenuous independence in the face of the advancing Khmers until as late as the early eleventh century, when it was incorporated into the empire as the provincial capital for much of central Thailand. Increasing Thai immigration from the north soon tilted the balance against the Khmers, and Lopburi was again independent from some time early in the thirteenth century until the rise of Ayutthaya in the middle of the fourteenth. Thereafter, Lopburi was twice used as a second capital, first by King Narai of Ayutthaya in the seventeenth century, then by Rama IV of Bangkok in the nineteenth, because its remoteness from the sea made it less vulnerable to European expansionists. Rama V downgraded the town, turning the royal palace into a provincial government office and museum; Lopburi's modern role is as the site of several huge army barracks.

Arrival and information

As it's on the main line north to Chiang Mai, Lopburi is best reached by **train** from **Bangkok**'s Hualamphong Station (15 daily, mostly early morning and evening; 3hr) via **Ayutthaya** (1hr 30min). A popular option is to arrive in Lopburi in the morning, leave your bags at the conveniently central **station**

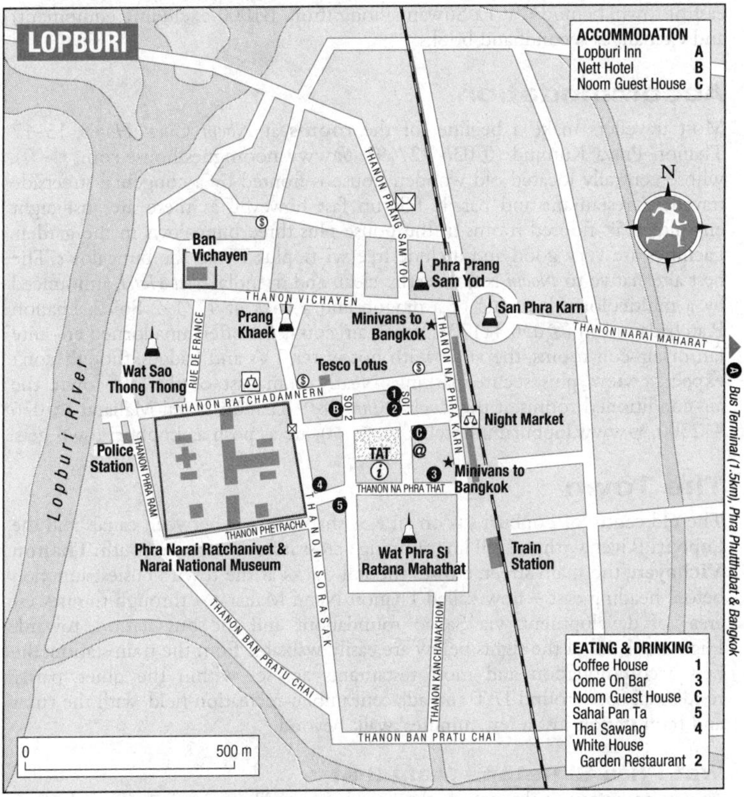

while you look around the old town, then catch one of the night trains to the north. **Buses** from Ayutthaya (every 20min) take around two hours to reach Lopburi; from Bangkok's Northern Bus Terminal (every 20min) around three hours. The long-distance **bus terminal** is on the southwest side of the huge Sakeo roundabout, 2km east of the old town: any blue city bus or red songthaew heading west on Thanon Narai Mahathat to Narai's Palace will save you the walk (B10). A couple of companies operate fast **air-conditioned minivans** between Bangkok's Victory Monument and Lopburi, which leave when full (daily from Bangkok, west side of the Monument near Ratchawithi Hospital, 5am–8pm; from Lopburi 3.30am–8pm; up to 3 per hr; 2hr; B110 or B220 with a rucksack) and terminate outside their offices on Thanon Na Phra Karn, just 200m north of the Lopburi train station. Coming **from Kanchanaburi**, it's possible to bypass Bangkok by taking a public bus to Suphanburi (every 20min; 1hr 30min), then changing to a Lopburi bus (hourly; 3hr).

TAT has an office in a restored, wooden, colonial-style building on the north side of Wat Phra Si Ratana Mahathat (daily 8.30am–4.30pm; ⓣ036 422768–9, ⓔtatlobri@tat.or.th), and **internet access** is available just around the corner on Thanon Praya Kumjud, at Connect near *Noom Guest House*, and at dozens of games centres on every other street. *Noom* rents **motorbikes**, runs tours and organizes **rock-climbing** trips to the cliff-face at Khao Chin Lae, about 20km east of town, behind Wat Pa Suwannahong (from B1000 excluding equipment) and exchanges secondhand books.

Accommodation

Most travellers make a beeline for the **rooms** at *Noom Guest House*, 15–17 Thanon Praya Kumjud (Ⓣ036 427693, Ⓦwww.noomguesthouse.com; ❶–❷), whose centrally located old wooden house is fronted by a congenial streetside travellers' restaurant and bar. It fills up fast however, as there are just eight en-suite, teak-floored rooms in the house plus three bungalows in the garden. Facilities are very good and include free wi-fi, plus TV in the bungalows. The best alternative to *Noom* is the nearby clean and friendly *Nett Hotel*, announced by a multicoloured mosaic of a dragon and a cock at 17/1–2 Soi 2, Thanon Ratchadamnern (Ⓣ036 411738; fan ❶, air-con ❸); it offers unadorned en-suite fan or air-con rooms, the latter with hot water, TVs and fridges, though don't expect a view, plus secure parking. Nearly 4km east of the old town, the air-conditioned rooms at the *Lopburi Inn*, 28/9 Thanon Narai Maharat (Ⓣ036 412300, Ⓦwww.lopburiinnhotel.com; ❺–❻), are as posh as Lopburi town gets.

The Town

The old centre of Lopburi sits on an egg-shaped island between canals and the Lopburi River, with the rail line running across it from north to south. **Thanon Vichayen**, the main street, crosses the rail tracks at the town's busiest junction before heading east – now called Thanon Narai Maharat – through the newest areas of development, via Sakeo roundabout and the bus station, towards Highway 1. All of the sights below are easily walkable from the train station: the best accommodation and most restaurants are set within the quiet, partly residential core around TAT and adjacent public-recreation field, with the ruins and train station just a few minutes' walk beyond.

Wat Phra Si Ratana Mahathat

As you come out of the station, the first thing you'll see are the sprawled grassy ruins of **Wat Phra Si Ratana Mahathat** (daily 7am–5pm; B30), where the impressive centrepiece is a laterite prang in the Khmer style of the twelfth century, decorated with finely detailed stuccowork and surrounded by a ruined cloister. Arrayed in loose formation around this central feature are several more rocket-like Khmer prangs and a number of graceful chedis in the Ayutthayan style, among them one with a bulbous peak and faded bas-reliefs of Buddhist saints. On the eastern side of the main prang, King Narai added to the mishmash of styles by building a "Gothic" viharn, now roofless, which is home to a lonely, headless stone Buddha, draped in photogenic saffron.

Phra Narai Ratchanivet (King Narai's palace)

The imposing gates and high crenellated walls of the **Phra Narai Ratchanivet**, a short walk northwest of the wat, might promise more than the complex delivers, but the museum in its central courtyard is worth a look, and the grounds are a green and relaxing spot. King Narai, with the help of French architects, built the heavily fortified palace in 1666 as a precaution against any possible confrontation with the Western powers, and for the rest of his reign he was to spend eight months of every year here, entertaining foreign envoys and indulging his love of hunting. After Narai's death, Lopburi was left forgotten until 1856, when Rama IV – worried about British and French colonialism – decided to make this his second capital and lavishly restored the central buildings of Narai's palace.

The outer courtyard

The main **entrance** to the palace complex is through the Phayakkha Gate on Thanon Sorasak (the gate is open daily 7am–5.30pm, giving access to the palace grounds, but during museum opening hours – see below – the admission fee is collected here). You'll see the unusual lancet shape of this arch again and again in the seventeenth-century doors and windows of Lopburi – just one aspect of the Western influences embraced by Narai. Around the **outer courtyard**, which occupies the eastern half of the complex, stand the walls of various gutted buildings – twelve warehouses for Narai's treasures, stables for the royal hunting elephants, and a moated reception hall for foreign envoys. With their lily ponds and manicured lawns, these well-shaded grounds are ideal for a picnic or a siesta.

The central courtyard and the Narai National Museum

Straight ahead from the Phayakkha Gate another arch leads into the **central courtyard**, where the typically Ayutthayan **Chanthara Phisan Pavilion** contains a fascinating exhibition on Narai's reign – check out the pointed white cap typical of those worn by noblemen of the time, which increased their height by no less than 50cm.

To the left is the colonial-style Phiman Mongkut Hall, now the **Somdet Phra Narai National Museum** (Wed–Sun 8.30am–4pm; B30; ⓦwww.thailandmuseum.com), whose exhibits concentrate on the period following the Khmer subjugation of Lopburi in the eleventh century. Inevitably there's a surfeit of Buddhas, most of them fine examples of the Khmer style and the distinctive **Lopburi style**, which emerged in the thirteenth and fourteenth centuries, mixing traditional Khmer elements – such as the conical *ushnisha*, or flame on the crown of the Buddha's head – with new features such as a more oval face and slender body. On the top floor is **King Mongkut's bedroom**, filled with his furniture and assorted memorabilia of his reign, including his very short and uncomfortable-looking bed and eerie painted statues of his equally vertically challenged near-contemporaries, Napoleon and Queen Victoria.

On the south side of the museum lies the shell of the **Dusit Sawan Hall**, where foreign dignitaries came to present their credentials to King Narai. Inside you can still see the niche, raised 3.5m above the main floor, where the throne was set; beneath the niche, a modern plaque showing Narai receiving the French envoy, the Chevalier de Chaumont, in 1685, is revered as an icon of the king, with offerings of gold leaf, joss sticks and garlands. The whole building is divided in two around the throne: the front half has "foreign" doors and windows with pointed arches; the rear part, from where the king would have made his grand entrance, has traditional Thai openings. The hall used to be lined with French mirrors in imitation of Versailles, with Persian carpets and a pyramidal roof of golden glazed tiles rounding off the most majestic building in the palace.

The private courtyards

King Narai's private courtyard, through whose sturdy walls only the trusted few were admitted, occupied the southwest corner of the complex. During Narai's time, hundreds of lamps were placed in niches around the walls of this courtyard by night, shedding a fairy-like light on the palace. Now there's not much more than the foundations left of his residence, the **Sutha Sawan Hall**, and its bathing ponds and artificial grotto.

Rama IV's private courtyard was built to house his harem in the northwest corner of the grounds, behind the present site of the museum. In what used to be the kitchen there's now a small folk museum of central Thai life, containing a loom and various pieces of farming and fishing equipment. In front, you can consult a crude model of the palace as it looked in Narai's time.

Wat Sao Thong Thong and Ban Vichayen

The north gate (now closed) to the palace is called the Vichayen Gate after **Constantine Phaulkon**, a Greek adventurer who came to Ayutthaya with the English East India Company in 1678 and ultimately became *ookya vichayen*, or prime minister (his story is told in *Falcon* by John Hoskins). Running directly north from here is the aptly named Rue de France, the approach to the remains of his grand residence. Halfway along this road, set back on the left, you'll pass a building whose plain terracotta roof tiles and whitewashed exterior give it a strangely Mediterranean look. This is in fact the viharn of **Wat Sao Thong Thong**, and is typical of Narai's time in its combination of Thai-style tiered roof with "Gothic" pointed windows. Erected as either a Christian chapel or a mosque for the Persian ambassador's residence, it was later used as a Buddhist viharn and has now been tastefully restored, complete with brass door-knockers and plush red carpet. Inside there's an austere Buddha image of the Ayutthaya period and, in the lamp niches, some fine Lopburi-style Buddhas.

The complex of **Ban Vichayen** (daily 7am–5pm; B30) had been built by Narai as a residence for foreign ambassadors, with a Christian chapel incongruously stuccoed with Buddhist flame and lotus-leaf motifs. Though now just a nest of empty shells, it still conjures up the atmosphere of court intrigue and dark deeds which, towards the end of Narai's reign, centred on the colourful figure of its chief resident, Phaulkon. He entered the royal service as interpreter and accountant, rapidly rising to the position of prime minister. It was chiefly due to his influence that Narai established close ties with Louis XIV of France, a move that made commercial sense but also formed part of Phaulkon's secret plan to turn Narai and his people to Christianity, with the aid of the French. (It was around this time that the word for Westerner, *farang*, entered the Thai language, from the same derivation as *français*, which the Thais render *farangset*.) In 1688, a struggle for succession broke out, and leading officials persuaded the dying Narai to appoint as regent his foster brother, Phetracha, a great rival of Phaulkon's. Phetracha promptly executed Phaulkon on charges of treason, and took the throne himself when Narai died. Under Phetracha, Narai's open-door policy towards foreigners was brought to a screeching halt and the Thai kingdom returned to traditional, smaller-scale dealings with the outside world.

Prang Khaek, Phra Prang Sam Yod and San Phra Karn

The junction of Thanon Vichayen and Thanon Sorasak is marked by an unusual traffic island, on which perch the three stubby red-brick towers of **Prang Khaek**, a well-preserved Hindu shrine, possibly to the god Shiva, and dating from as early as the eighth century. The nearby **Phra Prang Sam Yod** (daily 7am–5pm; B30), at the top of Thanon Na Phra Karn, seems also to have been a Hindu temple, later converted to Buddhism under the Khmers. The three chunky prangs, made of dark laterite with some restored stuccowork, and symbolizing the Hindu triumvirate of Brahma, Vishnu and Shiva, are Lopburi's most photographed sight, though they'll only detain you for a minute or two – at least check out some carved figures of seated hermits at the base of the door columns. The shrine's grassy knoll is a good spot for **monkey-watching**; they run amok all over this area (there's even a warning sign: "Beware Monkey Zone"), so keep an eye on your bags and pockets. Across the rail line at the modern red-and-gold shrine of **San Phra Karn**, there's even a monkey's adventure playground for the benefit of tourists, beside the base of what must have been a huge Khmer prang.

Eating

The cheap, air-conditioned café *Thai Sawang*, on Thanon Sorasak (daily 6am–8pm; most dishes B40–80), offers simple Western breakfasts, but is best known for its recommended Vietnamese **food**, especially roll-your-own fresh spring rolls stuffed with herbs, salad leaves and pork or Vietnamese sausage. Other good places for breakfasts are the quite stylish *Coffee House* on Thanon Ratchadamnern, which serves good espresso and the traveller-friendly *Noom Guest House*, where you can lounge streetside over your morning coffee and watch the low-key goings-on - in this mellow corner. *Noom* does travellers' fare throughout the day, while the classier, open-air *White House Garden Restaurant*, diagonally across on Thanon Praya Kumjud, specializes in rich Thai- and Chinese-style seafood dishes (evenings only; B50–200). The **night market**, which sets up all along the west side of the railway tracks, is a reliably cheap and varied alternative. The most popular places for a **beer**, day or night, are the sociable pavement tables at *Noom* and the petite, low-key *Come On Bar* south around the corner on Thanon Na Phra That. Nearby neon-lit *Sahai Pan Ta*, near the northwest corner of Wat Mahathat, is a dark and rowdy Wild-West-style place, with food and live music.

Wat Phra Phutthabat (Temple of the Buddha's Footprint)

Seventeen kilometres southeast of Lopburi along Highway 1 stands the most important pilgrimage site in central Thailand, **Wat Phra Phutthabat**, which is believed to house a footprint made by the Buddha. Any of the frequent **buses** to Saraburi or Bangkok from Lopburi's Sakeo roundabout will get you there in thirty minutes. The souvenir village around the temple, which is on the southern side of Highway 1, includes plenty of foodstalls for day-trippers.

The **legend** of Phra Phutthabat dates back to the beginning of the seventeenth century, when King Song Tham of Ayutthaya sent some monks to Sri Lanka to worship the famous Buddha's footprint of Sumankut. To the monks' surprise, the Sri Lankans asked them why they had bothered to travel all that way when, according to the ancient Pali scriptures, the Buddha had passed through Thailand and had left his footprint in their own backyard. As soon as Song Tham heard this he instigated a search for the footprint, which was finally discovered in 1623 by a hunter named Pram Bun, when a wounded deer disappeared into a hollow and then emerged miraculously healed. The hunter pushed aside the bushes to discover a foot-shaped trench filled with water, which immediately cured him of his terrible skin disease. A temple was built on the spot, but was destroyed by the Burmese in 1765 – the present buildings date from the Bangkok era.

A staircase flanked by nagas leads up to a marble platform, where an ornate mondop with mighty doors inlaid with mother-of-pearl houses the **footprint**, which in itself is not much to look at. Sheltered by a mirrored canopy, the stone print is nearly 2m long and obscured by layers of gold leaf presented by pilgrims; people also throw money into the footprint, some of which they take out again as a charm or merit object. The hill behind the shrine, which you can climb for a fine view over the gilded roofs of the complex to the mountains beyond, is covered in shrines.

During the dry season in January, February and March, a million pilgrims from all over the country flock to the **Ngan Phrabat** (**Phrabat Fair**), when other pilgrims are making their way to the other major religious sites at Doi Suthep, Nakhon Si Thammarat and That Phanom. During the fair, which reaches its peak in two week-long lunar periods, one usually at the beginning of February, the other at the beginning of March, stalls selling souvenirs and traditional medicines around the entrance swell to form a small town, and traditional entertainments, magic shows and a Ferris wheel are laid on. The fair is still a major religious event, but before the onset of industrialization it was the highlight of social and cultural life for all ages and classes; it was an important place of courtship, for example, especially for women at a time when their freedom was limited. Another incentive for women to attend the fair was the belief that visiting the footprint three times would ensure a place in heaven – for many women, the Phrabat Fair became the focal point of their lives, as Buddhist doctrine allowed them no other path to salvation. Up to the reign of Rama V (1868–1910) even the king used to come, performing a ritual lance dance on elephant-back to ensure a long reign.

The northern plains

Many tourists bypass the lush northern reaches of the central plains, fast asleep in an overnight train from Bangkok to Chiang Mai, yet it was here, during the thirteenth, fourteenth and fifteenth centuries, that the kingdom of Thailand first began to cohere and assume its present identity. Some of Thailand's finest buildings and sculpture were produced in **Sukhothai**, once the most powerful city in Thailand. Abandoned to the jungle by the sixteenth century, it has now been extensively restored, the resulting historical park making an attractive open-air museum. Less complete renovations have made Sukhothai's satellite cities of **Si Satchanalai** and **Kamphaeng Phet** worth visiting, both for their relative wildness and lack of visitors.

The nearest hills in which to clear the cobwebs are in **Ramkhamhaeng National Park** near Sukhothai; further west, the Burmese border town of **Mae Sot** is the departure point for the **Umphang** region, which offers excellent trekking and white-water rafting.

Phitsanulok stands at the hub of an efficient **transport** network that works well as a transit point between Bangkok, the far north and Isaan. Nearly every Bangkok–Chiang Mai train stops here, and assorted buses head east towards the Isaan towns of Loei and Khon Kaen. It's also possible to fly in and out of the northern plains via Phitsanulok and Sukhothai.

Nakhon Sawan

Heading north from Lopburi, road and rail plough through Thailand's "rice bowl", a landscape of lurid green paddies interrupted only by the unwelcoming sprawl of **Nakhon Sawan**, located at the confluence of the Ping, Wang, Yom and Nan rivers, which merge here to create the Chao Phraya.

A prosperous city of about 100,000 predominantly Chinese-Thai inhabitants, Nakhon Sawan plays a vital role as the region's main market and distribution centre for rice, but is of interest to tourists only as a place to change buses for Kamphaeng Phet or Phitsanulok. The **bus station** is in the town centre and there are a couple of passable budget hotels close by as a last resort. All Bangkok–Chiang Mai **trains** stop in Nakhon Sawan, but as the station is 10km out of town, with skeletal local transport and no station hotels, breaking your journey 130km further north at Phitsanulok makes much more sense.

The one time the city deserves a special visit is during **Chinese New Year** (between late Jan and mid-Feb), which is celebrated here with more vigour than anywhere else in the country. The place gets transformed for the three-day festival, decked out with Chinese lanterns and decorative arches, as visitors from all over Thailand gather to watch the Chinese dragons and lion-dancers snaking through the streets. Chinese opera troupes, an international lion-dance competition, fireworks and countless foodstalls complete the scene.

Phitsanulok and around

Handily located midway up the railway line between Bangkok and Chiang Mai, the likeable provincial capital of **PHITSANULOK** makes a useful and pleasant stopover with reasonable hotels and good transport connections, especially to the historical centres of Sukhothai and Kamphaeng Phet. The main sight in town is the country's second most important Buddha image, enshrined in historic Wat Mahathat and the focus of pilgrimages from all over Thailand; it is complemented by one of the best ethnology collections in Thailand, at the Folklore Museum. There are also several potentially rewarding national parks within an hour or two's drive along Highway 12, the so-called "Green Route".

Phitsanulok hosts two lively food **festivals** every year, once during the Western New Year period (Dec 25–Jan 1) and again at Songkhran, the Thai New Year (April 9–15); almost every restaurant in town participates, selling their trademark dishes from special stalls set up along the east bank of the river, and there's traditional Thai dance and other entertainments. Later in the year, on the third weekend of September, traditional longboat races are staged on the Nan River, in front of Wat Mahathat.

Arrival

Phitsanulok **train station** (ⓣ055 258005) is in the town centre and tuk-tuk rates from here to hotels and attractions are posted outside (mostly B60). The regional **bus station** (ⓣ055 242430) is 2km east on Highway 12, from where it's B60 by tuk-tuk to the centre or a ride on local bus #1 or #6 (see p.273); if coming from Sukhothai or the north you should be able to get off somewhere more central, near Topland Plaza, before the bus continues to the terminus. Phitsanulok **airport** (ⓣ055 259406) runs Thai Airways flights to Bangkok and is 7km south of town, about B150 by taxi from the centre.

If you've arrived at Phitsanulok train station and want to make an immediate **bus connection to Sukhothai**, you can either take a samlor or local bus to the regional bus station where the Sukhothai buses originate (daily 5.30am–6pm; every 30min; 1hr), or you can pick up the bus from opposite the Topland Plaza shopping centre on Thanon Singawat (B60 by samlor, or take air-con local bus #5 – non-air-con 5 goes elsewhere – to the Plaza, then cross the road).

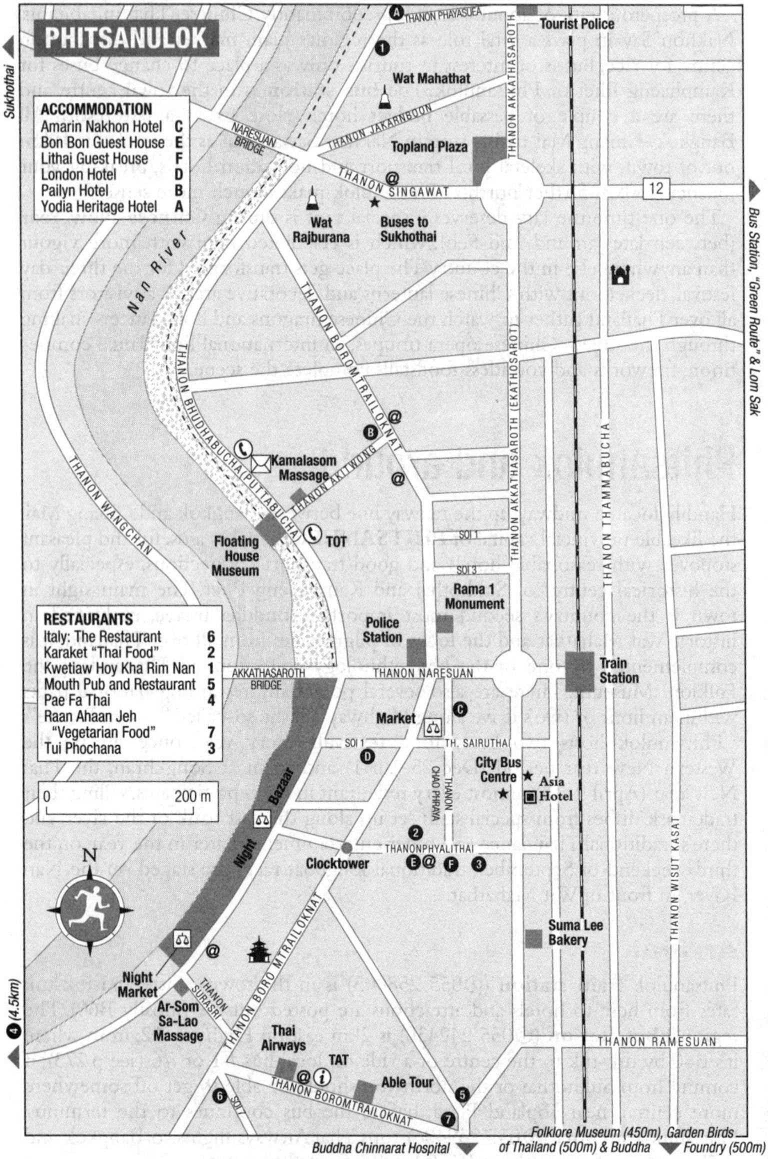

Information and transport

The helpful and well-informed **TAT** office (daily 8.30am–4.30pm; ⓣ055 252742, ⓔtatphlok@tat.or.th) is on the eastern arm of Thanon Boromtrailoknat (known to local taxi drivers as Surasi Trade Centre). There's also an **information desk** beside the river in the Floating House Museum (daily 8.30am–4.30pm).

Several local city **bus routes** (about every 30min; 5am–9pm; B8–15) criss-cross the city, most running via the city-centre bus stands on Thanon Akkathasaroth, 150m south of the train station, where southbound buses pick up outside the *Asia Hotel*, and northbound ones from across the road. The most useful routes include: #1, from the regional bus station to Wat Mahathat and the train station; #5 and #11, from the train station to Topland Plaza (for Sukhothai buses) and Wat Mahathat; #6, from the regional bus station to the *Pailyn Hotel*; and #8, from the regional bus station to the Folklore Museum, train station, Topland Plaza and Wat Mahathat.

For a cheap whizz around some of the town's main sights you could take the thirty-minute **tramway tour** that departs from in front of the tourist information booth in the car park at Wat Mahathat (departs when full from 9am–3pm, approximately every 30min on busy days; B30, kids B20). Commentary is in Thai but there's an English-language summary available and the route takes in a trio of partially excavated ruins across the river – King Naresuan's shrine and place of birth, Chandra Palace, plus the Sukhothai-era Wat Wihanthong – none of which is as yet sufficiently restored to be worth making the effort to walk to. At night a fleet of samlors twinkling with fairy lights takes tourists on an hour-long **evening tour** of Phitsanulok and its night bazaar; arrange the trip through any hotel (B250).

Accommodation

Amarin Nakhon Hotel 3/1 Thanon Chao Phraya ⓣ055 219069, ⓦwww.amarinlagoonhotel.com. Very central and good-value, tourist-oriented hotel, with compact air-con rooms, all with wi-fi and nicely tiled bathrooms; those on the uppermost of the hotel's eleven floors enjoy panoramic views of the city. In-house massage service and restaurant. ❹

Bon Bon Guest House 77 Thanon Phayalithai ⓣ055 219058. The only genuine guest house in town, this is an inviting little place set back from the road with three storeys of rooms set round a little yard. The twenty rooms are all en suite and kept very clean; some have air-con. Not as cheap as the *Lithai* next door, but friendlier and more sociable. Fan ❷, air-con ❸

Lithai Guest House 73/1–5 Thanon Phayalithai ⓣ055 219629, ⓔlithaiphs@yahoo.com. Centrally located, and sharing the Lithai Building with a travel agency and a couple of restaurants, this is a good lower- to mid-range option, used mainly by sales-people so not especially cosy and much more of a hotel than a guest house. The big, clean, bright rooms come with either fan or air-con, the cheapest sharing bathrooms; there's wi-fi here too. Fan ❶, air-con ❷

London Hotel 21–22 Soi Buddhabucha (Puttabucha) 1 ⓣ055 225145. The cheapest and most basic place in town, this converted family home – its downstairs filled with bikers' memorabilia and other curios – has just eight small, bare-bones, fan rooms upstairs, all painted to a funky mint-green-and-yellow colour scheme and all sharing bathrooms. ❶

Pailyn Hotel 38 Thanon Boromtrailoknat ⓣ055 252411, ⓦwww.phitsanuloke.com. Central, long-running three-star tourist hotel that's old-fashioned and unstylish but offers good-sized, air-con rooms with comfortable beds. Upper-floor rooms in the thirteen-storey tower enjoy expansive, long-range river views from their balconies. Has a massage centre, restaurant and nightclub and runs tours to Sukhothai. ❹–❺

Yodia Heritage Hotel Thanon Buddhabucha (Puttabucha) ⓣ055 214677, ⓦwww.yodiaheritage.com. The only boutique hotel in Phitsanulok, with just 25 upscale, contemporary-styled rooms, all with air-con, wooden floors, elegantly restrained decor, bathtubs, free wi-fi, and a balcony overlooking the small garden. Located beside the river, 250m north of Wat Mahathat. The on-site *Amore* restaurant enjoys river views, and there's also a library and free transfers from the airport. ❼–❽

The Town

Typically for a riverside town, "Phi-lok", as it's often nicknamed, is long and narrow. The heart of the city, which occupies the east bank of the Nan River, is easily walkable and still feels quite old-fashioned with its shophouses, traditional restaurants and foodstalls, particularly along Thanon Boromtrailoknat between the police station and the *Pailyn Hotel*. The two main sights, however, lie at opposite extremities: Wat Mahathat to the north, and the Folklore Museum 2.5km south.

Huge swathes of the town were destroyed by fire in 1957, but Phitsanulok's **history** harks back to a heyday in the late fourteenth and early fifteenth centuries when, with Sukhothai waning in power, it rose to prominence as the favoured home of the crumbling capital's last rulers. After supremacy was finally wrested by the emerging state of Ayutthaya in 1438, Phitsanulok was made a provincial capital, subsequently becoming a strategic army base during Ayutthaya's wars with the Burmese, and adoptive home to Ayutthayan princes. The most famous of these was **Naresuan**, a notoriously courageous warrior who was governor of Phitsanulok before he assumed the Ayutthayan crown in 1590. The ruins of Naresuan's Chandra Palace, where both he and his younger brother Akkathasaroth were born, are currently under excavation in the grounds of a former school northwest of the bridge that bears his name; the tramway tour makes a stop there.

Wat Mahathat (Wat Yai)

Officially called Wat Phra Si Ratana Mahathat (and known locally as **Wat Mahathat** or **Wat Yai**; daily 8am–6pm; B40), this fourteenth-century temple was one of the few buildings miraculously to escape Phitsanulok's great 1957 fire. Standing at the northern limit of the town on the east bank of the Nan River (and served by city buses #1, #5, #8, #12 and #13), it receives a constant stream of worshippers eager to pay homage to the highly revered Buddha image inside the viharn. Because the image is so sacred, a **dress code** is strictly enforced here, forbidding shorts and skimpy clothing.

Delicately inlaid mother-of-pearl doors mark the entrance to the viharn, opening onto the low-ceilinged interior, painted mostly in dark red and black, with gold leaf motifs, and dimly lit by narrow slits along the upper walls. In the centre of the far wall sits the much-cherished **Phra Buddha Chinnarat**: late Sukhothai in style and probably cast in the fourteenth century, this gleaming, polished-bronze Buddha is one of the finest of the period and, for Thais, second in importance only to the Emerald Buddha in Bangkok. Tales of the statue's miraculous powers have fuelled the devotion of generations of pilgrims – one legend tells how the Buddha wept tears of blood when Ayutthayan princes arrived in Phitsanulok to oust the last Sukhothai regent. The Phra Buddha Chinnarat stands out among Thai Buddha images because of its *mandorla*, the flame-like halo that symbolizes extreme radiance and frames the upper body and head like a chair-back, tapering off into nagas at the arm rests. There's an almost perfect replica of the Phitsanulok original in Bangkok's Marble Temple, commissioned by Rama V in 1901. Every February, Phitsanulok honours the Phra Buddha Chinnarat with a week-long **festival**, which features *likay* folk-theatre performances and dancing.

Behind the viharn, the gilded mosaic **prang** houses the holy relic that gives the wat its name (Mahathat means "Great Relic Stupa") – though which particular remnant lies entombed here is unclear – and the cloister surrounding both structures contains a gallery of Buddha images of different styles (Wed–Sun 9am–5.30pm; free).

Riverside stalls outside Wat Mahathat offer visitors the chance to make merit by buying their live **eels, fish and baby turtles** (kept in plastic bags) and releasing them into the Maenam Nan.

The east bank

South of Wat Mahathat and Naresuan Bridge, **the east bank** of the Nan River has been landscaped into a pleasant riverside park that runs all the way down to Akkathasaroth (Ekathosarot) Bridge. There are no exceptional attractions along its course, but you may want to make a stop at **Wat Rajburana**, just south of Naresuan Bridge and across the road from the river, which also survived the 1957 fire. Recognizable by the dilapidated brick-based chedi that stands in the compound, the wat is chiefly of interest for the *Ramakien* murals (see p.135) that cover the interior walls of the bot. Quite well preserved, they were probably painted in the mid-nineteenth century. Traditional Thai massage is available in the open-sided *sala* at the heart of the wat compound.

The most attractive feature of the riverside park is the so-called **Floating House Museum** (open all hours; free), about 500m south of Wat Rajburana and diagonally across from the post office. Understated in style and empty except for a small tourist information office, it's beautifully fashioned from teak wood and replicates a (classy) traditional river home, comprising three *sala* connected by a roofed walkway, walls of split reeds, carved window frames and elegant wood-panelled interiors. The house floats in a lily pond beside the road, high above the river.

Akkathasaroth Bridge marks the riverside park's southern boundary, beyond which the bank is dominated by the permanent stalls of the **night bazaar**, *the* place for locals and tourists to shop for bargain-priced fashions and a cheap meal.

The Folklore Museum, Buddha Foundry and Garden Birds of Thailand

Across town on Thanon Wisut Kasat, 1.3km southeast of the train station, the **Sergeant Major Thawee Folklore Museum (Jatawee Buranaket**; Tues–Sun 8.30am–4.30pm; B50) puts a different slant on the region's culture; its fascinating look at traditional rural life makes this one of the best ethnology museums in the country. Local **bus** #8 will drop you close by. The collection, which is housed in a series of wooden pavilions, belongs to former sergeant major Dr Thawee, who has pursued a lifelong personal campaign to preserve and document a way of life that's gradually disappearing. Highlights include the reconstructed kitchen, veranda and birthing room of a typical village house, known as a "tied house" because its split-bamboo walls are literally tied together with rattan cane; and an exceptionally comprehensive gallery of traps: dozens of specialized contraptions designed to ensnare everything from cockroaches to birds perched on water buffaloes' backs. There's also a display on weaving and natural dyes, a collection of traditional toys, and some fearsome-looking wooden implements for giving yourself a massage.

Cross the road from the museum and walk south about 50m for a rare chance to see Buddha images being forged at the **Buranathai Buddha Bronze-Casting Foundry**, located at 26/43 Thanon Wisut Kasat. The foundry, which also belongs to Dr Thawee, is open during working hours (usually daily 8am–5pm) and anyone can drop in to watch the stages involved in moulding and casting a Buddha image. It's a fairly lengthy procedure and best assimilated from the illustrated explanations inside the foundry. Images of all sizes are made here, from thirty-centimetre-high household icons to mega-models destined for wealthy temples. The Buddha business is quite a profitable one: worshippers can earn a great deal of merit by donating a Buddha statue, particularly a precious one, to their local wat, so demand rarely slackens. There's a gift shop on site.

Adjacent to the Buddha Foundry, and accessible from it, as well as via Soi 17, **Garden Birds of Thailand** (Suan Nok; daily 8.30am–5pm; B50) is Dr Thawee's most recent enthusiasm: a zoo containing hundreds of breathtakingly beautiful Thai birds, each one segregated and informatively described. It's an astonishing collection that offers a unique chance to admire at close range such beauties as a silver pheasant, an Asian fairy bluebird, and a rhinoceros hornbill, as well as highly endangered species such as the jambu fruit dove and the helmeted hornbill. As is often the case in such places, however, the cages are very small and few of the birds are in pairs or groups.

The Green Route

East of Phitsanulok, Highway 12 has been tagged "**the Green Route**" by TAT because it gives access to several national parks and waterfalls and provides an excuse for a pleasant day or two's excursion from the city. TAT has produced a sketch map outlining car and motorbike routes.

The first highlight is the chance to go **whitewater rafting** on the Class 1–5 rapids of the Khek River; the *Sappraiwan Resort* (Ⓣ055 293293, Ⓦwww.resort.co.th; rooms ❼), at kilometre-marker 53 on Highway 12, arranges the eight-kilometre trip (June–Oct; 2hr 30min; Mon–Fri B600, Sat & Sun B700, including return transport). Next up is **Phu Hin Rongkla National Park** (B200; Ⓣ055 233527, Ⓦwww.dnp.go.th/National_park.asp; accommodation ❷–❹), about 100km northeast of Phitsanulok: turn north off Highway 12 at kilometre-stone 68, on to Route 2013, then east on to Route 2331 to reach the visitor centre. Formerly the notorious stronghold of the insurgent Communist Party of Thailand from 1967 to 1982, the park still contains some relics from that period, though its short trails through montane forests and natural rock gardens are now its main point of interest. Or consider organizing a day's mountain-biking in **Thung Salaeng Luang National Park** (B200–400 depending on which areas you want to visit; Ⓣ055 268019, Ⓦwww.dnp.go.th/National_park.asp; bungalows ❺), 82km east of Phitsanulok (turn south off Highway 12 at kilometre-stone 79). Thung Salaeng is famous for the flowers that carpet its grasslands after the end of the rainy season (the flower meadows are only open from Oct 23–Dec) and has two designated mountain-bike trails as well as rafting opportunities.

The Dhamma Abha **Vipassana meditation centre** (Ⓣ081 646 4695, Ⓦwww.dhamma.org/schthaia.htm), which holds two ten-day meditation courses every month, is also in this area, in Ban Huayplu; turn north off Highway 12 at kilometre-stone 49.

Eating

In the evening, **night market** stalls set up within the night bazaar along the east bank of the river, south of Akkathasaroth Bridge. Fish and mussels are a speciality, but the most famous dish is "flying vegetables", in which strong-tasting morning-glory (*phak bung*) is stir-fried before being tossed flamboyantly in the air towards the plate-wielding waiter or customer.

Italy: The Restaurant Thanon Boromtrailoknat Soi 7. Huge choice of pizzas, calzones and pastas, plus wines and Thai dishes (B110–290).

Karaket "Thai Food" Thanon Phayalithai. Tasty Thai curry shop, where you make your selection from the metal trays set out on the pavement trestle, then eat in air-con comfort inside. Very popular for family takeaways and very cheap: most savouries sell for just B30 a serving. Shuts around 8.30pm.

Kwetiaw Hoy Kha Rim Nan 100m north of Wat Mahathat. The noodles here are so famously tasty they've been featured on three local TV channels. Choose from *phat thai*, Sukhothai noodles with red pork in chilli-hot broth, *tom yam* soup with noodles, or yellow noodles with pork; tofu versions are also available (B25–40). There's no English sign but it's got a brown awning, counter seating (with some river views), and is always packed. Daily 9am–4pm.

Mouth Pub and Restaurant Thanon Ramesuan. Lively indoor-outdoor corner restaurant and bar with enjoyable live music nightly and several cosy dining areas. The extensive menu covers Thai and Western cuisines, from seafood to hamburgers, pastas to stir-fried ostrich and T-bone steak. Highlights include the delicious *samlee* cottonfish with spicy mango sauce and tangy *tom kha khai* soup. Free internet access too. Cocktails from B100, mains B90–250.

Pae Fa Thai About 5km south of the night bazaar down riverside Thanon Buddhabucha (Puttabucha); near Wat Chan, just upriver from the Supanganlaya Bridge. Many locals rate this as the best of the several floating restaurants that capitalize on the romance and breeziness of Phitsanulok's river setting, though the views here, near the bridge, aren't especially gripping. The menu (mostly B100–200) naturally features lots of fish and seafood as well as curries – their *phanaeng* tofu is especially good. Daily 11am–11pm.

Raan Ahaan Jeh "Vegetarian Food" Thanon Sithamtraipidok, north around the corner from the TAT Road. Tiny, ultra-cheap vegetarian canteen where you get a plate of brown rice plus B10 servings from a selection of veggie stir-fries and curries. Daily 6am–3pm.

Tui Phochana 90 Thanon Phayalithai. One of several cheap Thai curry shops on this road, this one is famous for its curries made with jackfruit (B20–40). Shuts about 7pm.

Listings

Airline The Thai Airways office is near TAT on Thanon Boromtrailoknat ⓣ 055 242971–2; tickets also available from the tour operators listed below.

Car rental Avis (ⓣ 055 242060, ⓦ www.avisthailand.com) and Budget (ⓣ 055 301020, ⓦ www.budget.co.th) have desks at the airport.

Emergencies For all emergencies, call the tourist police on the free 24hr phoneline ⓣ 1155, or contact them at their office north of Wat Mahathat on Thanon Akkathasaroth ⓣ 055 245358.

Hospitals Rattanavej Hospital on Thanon Phra Ong Dam ⓣ 055 210819–28 is private, and Buddha Chinnarat Hospital, Thanon Sithamtraipidok ⓣ 055 219844–52 is government-run.

Left luggage At the train station (24hr; B10 per item).

Massage At many hotels. Also at two public health centres: the recommended Kamalasom on Thanon Akitwong (Mon–Sat 8.30am–4.30pm; B200/90min) and Ar-Som Sa-Lao Traditional Thai Medicine on Thanon Surasri (daily 8.30am–8.30pm; B350/90min).

Motorbike rental At PN Motor, inside the bus terminal complex on Thanon Mittraphap, then one block west ⓣ 055 303222; around B200 per day (Mon–Sat 8.30am–5.30pm).

Tour operators Able Tour and Travel (Mon–Fri 8am–6pm, Sat 8am–4pm; ⓣ 055 242206, ⓔ ablegroup@hotmail.com.com), near the TAT office on Thanon Boromtrailokanat, sells air tickets and can arrange minivans to Sukhothai or Kamphaeng Phet (B1800, plus B1200 for optional guide). Lithai Travel at 73/1–5 Thanon Phayalithai (ⓣ 055 219626) also sells air tickets.

Sukhothai

For a brief but brilliant period (1238–1376), the walled city of **SUKHOTHAI** presided as the capital of Thailand, creating the legacy of a unified nation of Thai peoples and a phenomenal artistic heritage. Now an impressive assembly of elegant ruins, the Old City, 58km northwest of Phitsanulok, has been preserved as **Sukhothai Historical Park** and is one of Thailand's most visited ancient sites.

There are several accommodation options near the historical park, but few other facilities, so many travellers stay in so-called **NEW SUKHOTHAI**, a modern market town 12km to the east, which has good travel links with the Old City and is also better for restaurants and long-distance bus connections. Straddling the Yom River, it's a small, friendly town, used to seeing tourists but by no means overrun with them. The new town also makes a peaceful and

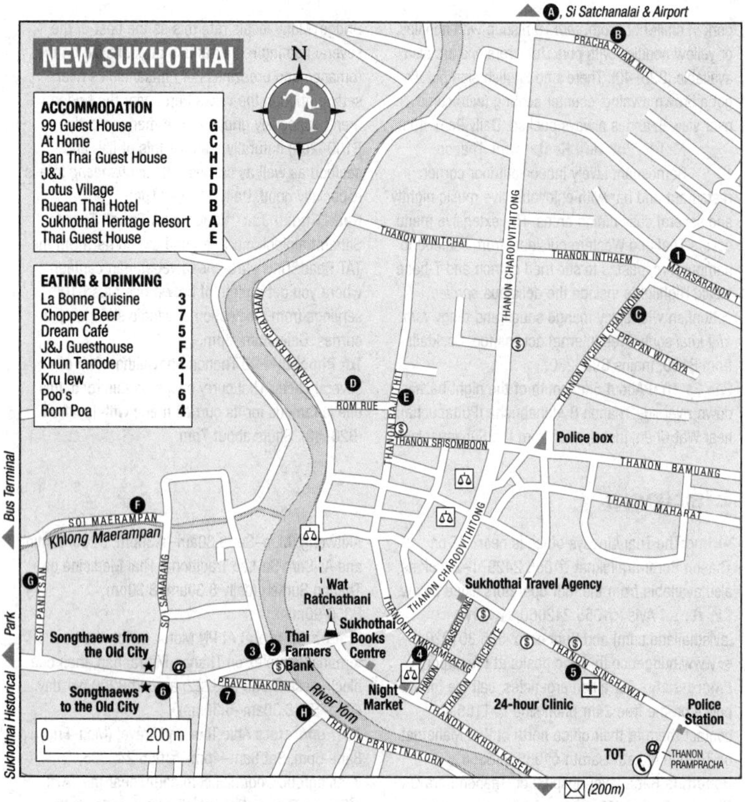

convenient base for visiting Ramkhamhaeng National Park, as well as the outlying ruins of Si Satchanalai and Kamphaeng Phet.

Sukhothai Historical Park is the most famous place in Thailand to celebrate **Loy Krathong**, the festival of light, and the ruins are the focus of a spectacular festival held over several nights around the full moon of the twelfth lunar month (Oct/Nov). The centrepiece is a charming *son et lumière* performance at Wat Mahathat, complemented by firework displays, the illumination of many Old City ruins, candles floating on many of the lotus ponds, and all sorts of parades, concerts and street-theatre shows; see the colour section for more on Loy Krathong. All accommodation gets packed out during the festival, so book ahead if possible. During the rest of the year, TAT sometime stages a **mini sound-and-light show** on the first Saturday of the month (B500); hotel staff should be able to fill you in.

Arrival and information

New Sukhothai has direct bus connections with many major provincial capitals and makes a good staging point between Chiang Mai and Bangkok. All buses use the Sukhothai **bus terminal**, located about 3km west of New Sukhothai's town centre, just off the bypass. During the dry season, when the track's not flooded, it is possible to **walk** from the bus terminal to *J&J* and *99* guest houses in New Sukhothai: see relevant guest-house accounts for details. For transport to other New Sukhothai guest houses, you can either use the public **songthaew** (B10) and get off by the river, which puts you less than ten minutes' walk from most accommodation, or you can charter a motorbike taxi, tuk-tuk or songthaew (B40–60 per vehicle); rates are posted in the bus terminal. Charters to the Old City are B120–200 per vehicle or you can catch one of the public buses that pass by the Old City (approximately hourly 6.30am–6.20pm). Note, however, that if you're arriving by bus **from Mae Sot or Tak** you will pass via the Old City anyway, before reaching New Sukhothai's bus terminal. There's a small place offering backpackers' rooms (B100) in the bus station compound.

A more comfortable, though not necessarily faster, option is to take the **train** from Bangkok, Chiang Mai or anywhere in between as far as Phitsanulok and then change onto one of the half-hourly buses to New Sukhothai (1hr; for details see p.271). This bus service also makes Sukhothai feasible as a day-trip from Phitsanulok, and vice versa.

You can also **fly** to Sukhothai from Bangkok with Bangkok Airways; the tiny, postcard-pretty airport is about 25km north of town (half way to Si Satchanalai), and shuttle buses transfer passengers to New Sukhothai hotels for B180 per person and to the Old City for B300; the return shuttle to the airport departs from the Sukhothai Travel Agency in New Sukhothai only (see p.289), and from the Old City hotels, though most New Sukhothai guest houses do their own airport transfer for about B250 per person. Private transfers to Phitsanulok airport or train station cost about B1500 per car. The local Bangkok Airways office (Ⓣ055 647224) is at the airport, though you can also buy air tickets from the more central Sukhothai Travel Agency (see p.289).

There is no reliable official **tourist information** office in town, but tour guide Naa offers free information and advice by phone or at her *99 Guest House* (Ⓣ089 858 9864). Dawn F. Rooney's lively and beautifully photographed *Ancient Sukhothai* is a great **guidebook**, not only to Sukhothai's Old City but also to those of Si Satchanalai and Kamphaeng Phet; you'll need to buy it before you arrive though (see p.860).

Accommodation

There's plenty of attractive **accommodation** in Sukhothai, just be wary of commission-hungry tuk-tuk drivers falsely claiming places are full, no good or no longer in business.

New Sukhothai

99 Guest House 234/6 Soi Panitsan (Panichsan) Ⓣ055 611315, Ⓔninetynine_gh@yahoo.com. Tiny, homely guest house run by clued-up tour guide and cooking teacher Naa. There are just five simple, good-sized and very cheap double rooms (with fan and shared bathroom) in her wood-floored house, plus a spacious, typically Thai seating area downstairs, filled with axe cushions. Guests are welcome to join the family meals and Naa also runs cooking classes (see p.289). *99* is about a 10min walk from the bus station: an indistinct track (impassable when flooded) runs from just in front of the main bus terminal building (between the spirit house and the first shop); within 100m you'll see signs for *Number 4* and 200m beyond that, having passed through a field, turn left when you reach the tarmacked road and follow signs. ❶

At Home 184/1 Thanon Wichien Chamnong Ⓣ055 610172, Ⓦwww.athomesukhothai.com. Delightful, genuinely welcoming guest house that's been converted from the fifty-year-old family home to accommodate eleven large, attractive en-suite rooms. The most atmospheric are upstairs in the teak-walled, teak-floored part of the house. The house is set back from the road in a garden with a large pond. Free internet and wi-fi. ❹

Ban Thai Guest House 38 Thanon Pravetnakorn Ⓣ055 610163, Ⓔbanthai_guesthouse@yahoo.com. On the west bank of the Yom River, this comfortable traveller-oriented budget option comprises several attractive wood-floored rooms in a single-storey house with an inviting terrace out front, plus some nice, idiosyncratic wooden bungalows with private bathroom and the option of air-con in a little garden to the back. Home-made yoghurt is a breakfast favourite, and the *matsaman* curry is popular too. Internet access and cooking courses. Shared bathroom ❶, bungalows ❷–❸

J&J Guest house 122/1 Soi Maerampan, off Soi Samarang ☎055 620095, Ⓦwww.jj-guesthouse.com. Rooms in all categories at this Belgian-Thai-run guest house are well maintained and sparklingly clean, plus there's a swimming pool and delicious home-baked bread. Choose from en-suite fan and air-con rooms in a terraced row, larger "mansion rooms" and detached air-con bungalows with TV. Within walking distance of the bus station (see *99 Guest House* for directions). Fan ❷, air-con ❹

Lotus Village 170 Thanon Ratchathani, also accessible from Thanon Rajuthit ☎055 621484, Ⓦwww.lotus-village.com. Elegantly simple, mid-priced accommodation in a traditional Thai compound of beautiful teak houses set around a mature tropical garden with lotus ponds. All but the superior rooms have polished teak floors: some are in detached bungalows, others have either fan or air-con and there's also a family house that can sleep six. There's wi-fi, internet, and a charming spa here too (see p.289). Reception shuts at 9pm. ❹–❺

Ruean Thai Hotel 181/20 Soi Praharuammit, off Thanon Charodvithitong ☎055 612444, Ⓦwww.rueanthaihotel.com. A labour of love, this idiosyncratic thirty-room hotel has been painstakingly assembled from ten century-old teak houses from the Sukhothai area. The main two-storey complex is built around a central swimming pool, its attractive facades fashioned from salvaged teak walls, windows and doors, and steeply gabled roofs; the interiors are modern, individually furnished and with good-quality contemporary bathrooms. The rooms with most character are the three large, homely doubles in a separate building above the restaurant. All rooms have air-con, fridges and wi-fi; price depends on the size. There are two restaurants, free bicycle rental, and free transfers from the bus station and around town. ❺–❽

Thai Guest House 25/4 Thanon Rajuthit ☎055 612853, Ⓔvisakkkdd@hotmail.com. Tiny, very basic, very cheap guest house run by amulet-seller and masseur Vicharee. Just five rooms with mattresses on the floor and shared bathrooms. ❶

The Old City and around

See map p.282.

Old City Guest House A few metres from the access road to the museum and central zone, on Thanon Charodvithitong ☎055 697515. Good-value guest house offering a big range of options in two-storey buildings around a yard (with parking), set back from the road. Choose between small, rather dark but very cheap rooms with shared bathrooms, attractive, well-priced, en-suite fan rooms, and large, quite plush, air-con doubles with TV. ❶–❸

Orchid Hibiscus Guest House About 1.5km southeast of the main entrance to the historical park, on Route 1272 ☎081 962 7698, Ⓔorchid_hibiscus_guest_house@hotmail.com, Ⓦwww.asiatravel.com/thailand/orchid_hibiscus/index.html. Tranquil Italian-Thai-managed garden haven within easy cycling reach of the Old City. The eight brick bungalows are furnished with four-poster beds, air-con and mosquito nets and are ranged around a pretty tropical flower garden and swimming pool. It also has a couple of more private teak bungalows plus, in a compound across the road, two four-bed family houses for rent. Email for cheapest rates and ask about their cheaper air-con rooms in nearby *PinPao Guest House*, on the Old City road. ❹–❺

Tharaburi Resort About 1.5km southeast of the main entrance to the historical park, on Route 1272 ☎055 697132, Ⓦwww.tharaburiresort.com. The most design-conscious hotel near the Old City, this little boutique hideaway has plenty of style but charges over the odds. The look is fusion chic, mixing contemporary and antique Sino-Thai styles, but deluxe rooms are small for the price. Accommodation in the attractive Baan Thai teak house is more spacious but shares bathrooms. The service gets great reviews however, and there's a pool and restaurant. Shared bathroom ❺–❻, deluxe ❾

Sukhothai Airport

Sukhothai Heritage Resort ☎055 647564, Ⓦwww.sukhothaiheritage.com. Just outside the airport compound. Calm, tastefully designed four-star hotel owned by Bangkok Airways and set in lovely rural surrounds of organic rice fields, an orchid farm and lotus ponds. The hotel garden is artfully planted with shrubs and hedges, just like the airport, and there are two pools, a restaurant and a library. Rooms are modern Thai chic with traditional accents, verandas overlooking the pool, flat-screen TVs and DVD players; there's wi-fi throughout and local cycling tours are encouraged. There's nothing else in the immediate vicinity as the hotel is approximately 40km from Sukhothai Old City in one direction and 40km from Si Satchanalai ruins in the other. ❽–❾

Sukhothai Historical Park (Muang Kao Sukhothai)

In its prime, the Old City boasted around forty separate temple complexes and covered an area of about seventy square kilometres between the Yom River and the low range of hills to the west. At its heart stood the walled royal city, protected by a series of moats and ramparts. **SUKHOTHAI HISTORICAL PARK**, or **Muang Kao Sukhothai** (daily 6am–6pm; floodlit every Sat 6–9pm; B100 per zone, or B350 inclusive, plus B10–50 per vehicle), covers all this area and is divided into five zones: all the most important temples lie within the central zone, with the Ramkhamhaeng Museum just outside it; the ruins outside the city walls are spread out over a sizeable area and divided into north, south, east and west zones.

With the help of UNESCO, the Thai government's Fine Arts Department has restored the most significant ruins and the result reveals the original town planners' keen aesthetic sense, especially their astute use of water to offset and reflect the solid monochrome contours of the stone temples. Although there is a touch of the too perfectly packaged theme-park about the central zone (and, in some critics' opinions, too liberal an interpretation of thirteenth-century design), it's a serene and rewarding site, with plenty to investigate should you want to look more closely. It does, however, take a determined imagination to visualize the ancient capital as it must once have looked, not least because houses and palaces would have filled the spaces between the wats – like their Khmer predecessors, the people of Sukhothai constructed their secular buildings from perishable materials such as wood, only using expensive, durable stone for their sacred structures.

Some history

Prior to the thirteenth century, the land now known as Thailand was divided into a collection of petty principalities, most of which owed their allegiance to the Khmer empire and its administrative centre Angkor (in present-day Cambodia). With the Khmers' power on the wane, two Thai generals joined forces in 1238 to oust the Khmers from the northern plains, founding the kingdom of **Sukhothai** ("Dawn of Happiness" in Pali) under the regency of one of the generals, Intradit. In short order they had extended their control over much of present-day Thailand, as well as parts of Burma and Laos.

The third and most important of Sukhothai's eight kings, Intradit's youngest son **Ramkhamhaeng** (c.1278–99) laid the foundations of a unique Thai identity by establishing Theravada (Hinayana) Buddhism as the common faith and introducing the forerunner of the modern Thai alphabet; of several inscriptions attributed to him, the most famous, found on what's known as Ramkhamhaeng's Stele and housed in Bangkok's National Museum (with a copy kept in Sukhothai's Ramkhamhaeng Museum), tells of a utopian land of plenty ruled by a benevolent monarch.

The Sukhothai Buddha

The classic Buddha images of Thailand were produced towards the end of the Sukhothai era. Ethereal, androgynous figures with ovoid faces and feline expressions, they depict not a Buddha meditating to achieve enlightenment – the more usual representation – but an already **enlightened Buddha**: the physical realization of an abstract, "unworldly" state. Though they produced mainly seated Buddhas, Sukhothai artists are renowned for having pioneered the **walking Buddha**, one of four postures described in ancient Pali texts but without precedent in Thailand.

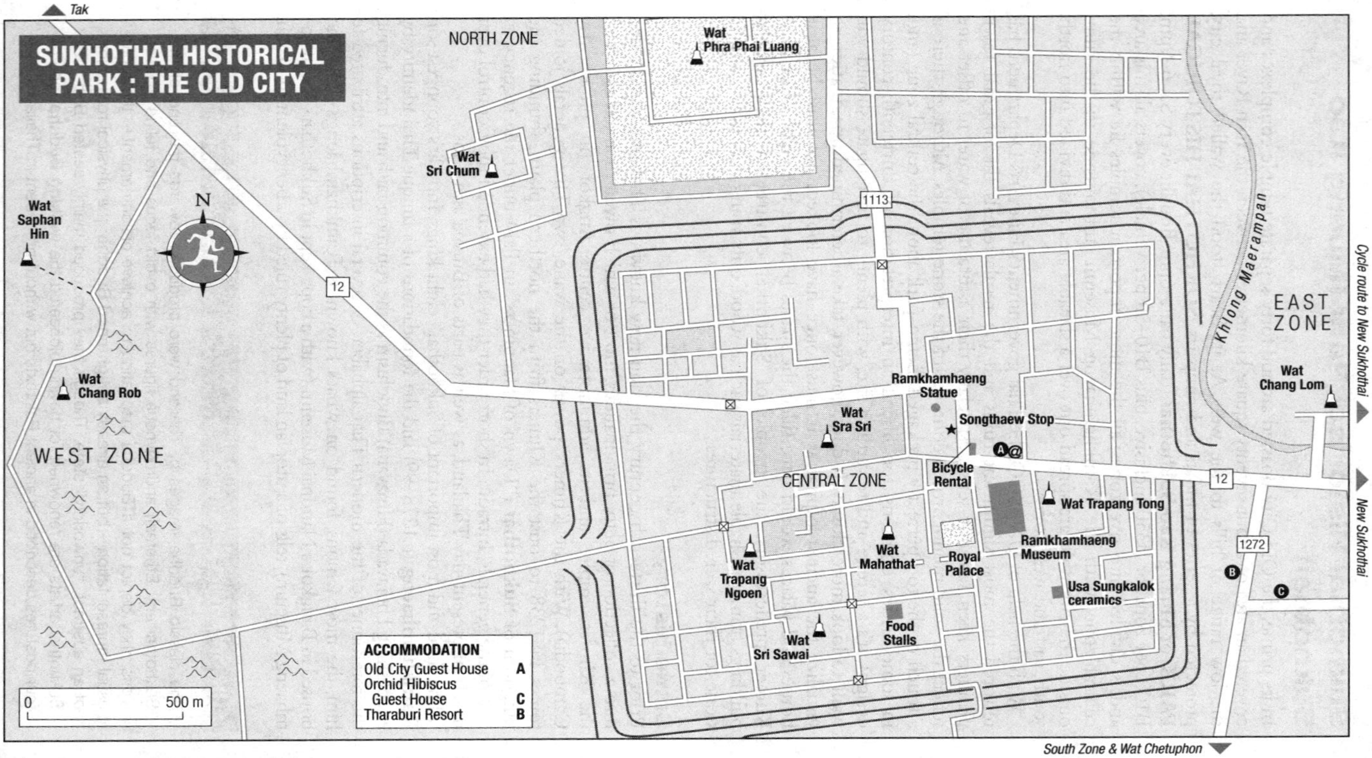
Tak
SUKHOTHAI HISTORICAL PARK : THE OLD CITY
NORTH ZONE
Wat Phra Phai Luang
Wat Sri Chum
Wat Saphan Hin
N
12
1113
WEST ZONE
Wat Chang Rob
Ramkhamhaeng Statue
Wat Sra Sri
Songthaew Stop
Bicycle Rental
CENTRAL ZONE
Wat Trapang Tong
Ramkhamhaeng Museum
Royal Palace
Wat Mahathat
Wat Trapang Ngoen
Wat Sri Sawai
Food Stalls
Usa Sungkalok ceramics
Khlong Maerampan
EAST ZONE
Wat Chang Lom
1272
Cycle route to New Sukhothai
New Sukhothai
South Zone & Wat Chetuphon
ACCOMMODATION
Old City Guest House A
Orchid Hibiscus Guest House C
Tharaburi Resort B
0
500 m

Ramkhamhaeng turned Sukhothai into a vibrant spiritual and commercial centre, inviting Theravada monks from Nakhon Si Thammarat and Sri Lanka to instruct his people in the religion that was to supplant Khmer Hinduism and Mahayana Buddhism, and encouraging the growth of a ceramics industry with the help of Chinese potters. By all accounts, Ramkhamhaeng's successors lacked his kingly qualities and so, by the second half of the fourteenth century, Sukhothai had become a vassal state of the newly emerged kingdom of Ayutthaya; finally, in 1438, it was forced to relinquish all vestiges of its independent identity.

Old City practicalities

Songthaews from New Sukhothai (every 15min; 15min; B20) terminate beside two cycle-rental outlets, about 500m northeast of the central zone entrance point. Alternatively you can **cycle from New Sukhothai** to the historical park along a peaceful canalside track. To pick up the track, start from the bridge in New Sukhothai, cycle west along the main road to the historical park for about 3km (beyond Sukhothai Hospital, just before the Big C hypermarket) until you reach a temple with an impressive gold-and-white-decorated gateway on the right-hand side. A narrow track between this temple and the adjacent little petrol station takes you via a small bridge to a track that runs along the north bank of Khlong Maerampan, nearly all the way to the Old City. It's an easy ride of about 14km, through very pleasant, and frequently shaded, traditional canalside neighbourhoods. Near the end of the ride you cross a major road to pick up the final stretch of track; then, after reaching the elephant statues at the ruins of Wat Chang Lom (see p.286), cross the bridge on your left to regain the main road into the historical park, about 1.5km away.

Even if you don't arrive at the Old City on one, it's a good idea to **rent a bicycle** there for touring the ruins: outlets near the songthaew stop rent them out for B30. Alternatively, you could hop onto the **trolley bus** that, during busy times only, starts from near the museum and takes groups round the central zone for B20 per person. Tuk-tuks at the New Sukhothai bus station and in the town offer a four-hour tour of the ruins plus return transport for about B500.

There's a **currency exchange** booth (daily 8.30am–12.30pm) next to the museum, and several ATMs on the approach road, where you'll also find plenty of small **restaurants** serving both Thai and Western food, plus internet access. Handier for Wat Mahathat are the stalls and restaurants serving hot food and fresh coffee in the lot just south of the main central zone entrance. For details of accommodation close to the historical park, see p.280. Several shops just outside the park entrance sell reproduction antique furniture and ceramics, but for a better range of **traditional-style ceramics**, especially copies of historic Sangkhalok and Sukhothai designs and glazes, visit the Usa Sungkalok Sukhothai ceramics factory, which is located outside the central zone on the narrow road that runs between the museum and Wat Trapang Tong.

Ramkhamhaeng National Museum

The well-presented **Ramkhamhaeng National Museum** (daily 9am–4pm; B100; Ⓦwww.thailandmuseum.com), located just outside the main entrance to the central zone, features several illuminating exhibitions and contains some of the finest **sculptures** and reliefs found at the temples of Sukhothai's Old City and nearby Si Satchanalai. Outstanding artefacts in the downstairs gallery of the main building include the fourteenth-century bronze statue of a walking Buddha, and the large Buddha head that was found at Wat Phra Phai Luang in the north zone of Sukhothai Historical Park. Also here is a useful guide to the many different **stucco motifs** that once decorated every Sukhothai-era temple, along with a copy of one of the finest local examples of stucco relief, depicting the Buddha being sheltered by a naga, whose original is still in situ at Si Satchanalai's Wat Chedi Jet Taew. The wide-ranging section on Ramkhamhaeng's famous **stele** features a complete translation of the inscription, plus a detailed look at the origins and evolution of the original "Tai" script. The upstairs gallery concentrates on **Sangkhalok ceramics** and provides a much more informative introduction than the kiln museum in Si Satchanalai.

The central zone

The **central zone** covers three square kilometres so a bike is recommended, though not essential. Of the eleven ruins here, Wat Mahathat is the one that should definitely not be missed. A modern **statue** of King Ramkhamhaeng sits to the right just inside the zone entrance: cast in bronze, he holds a palm-leaf book in his right hand – a reference to his role as founder of the modern Thai alphabet. Close by stands a large bronze **bell**, a replica of the one referred to on the famous stele (also reproduced here), which told how the king had the bell erected in front of his palace so that any citizen with a grievance could come by and strike it, whereupon the king himself would emerge to investigate the problem.

Wat Mahathat

First stop should be Sukhothai's most important site, the enormous **Wat Mahathat** compound, packed with the remains of scores of monuments and surrounded, like a city within a city, by a moat. This was the spiritual focus of the city, the king's temple and symbol of his power; successive regents, eager to add their own stamp, restored and expanded it so that by the time it was abandoned in the sixteenth century it numbered ten viharns, one bot, eight mondops and nearly two hundred small chedis. Looking at the wat from ground level, it's hard to distinguish the main structures from the minor ruins. Remnants of the viharns and the bot dominate the present scene, their soldierly ranks of pillars, which formerly supported wooden roofs, directing the eye to the Buddha images seated at the far western ends.

The principal chedi complex, which houses the Buddha relic, stands grandly, if a little cramped, at the heart of the compound, built on an east–west axis in an almost continuous line with two viharns. Its elegant centrepiece follows a design termed **lotus-bud chedi** (after the bulbous finial ornamenting the top of a tower), and is classic late Sukhothai in style. This lotus-bud reference is an established religious symbol: though Sukhothai architects were the first to incorporate it into building design – since when it's come to be regarded as a hallmark of the era – the lotus bud had for centuries represented the purity of the Buddha's thoughts nudging through the muddy swamp and finally bursting into flower. The chedi stands surrounded by eight smaller towers – some with their stucco decoration partially reapplied, and some with a Buddha image in one of their four alcoves – on a square platform decorated with a procession of walking Buddha-like monks, another artistic innovation of the Sukhothai school, here depicted in stucco relief. Flanking the chedi platform are two square mondops, built for the colossal standing Buddhas still inside them today.

The grassy patch across the road from Wat Mahathat marks the site of the former palace, of which nothing now remains.

Around Wat Mahathat

Three hundred metres southwest, the triple corn-cob-shaped prangs of **Wat Sri Sawai** make for an interesting architectural comparison with Wat Mahathat. Just as the lotus-bud chedi epitomizes Sukhothai aspirations, the prang represents Khmer ideals: Wat Sri Sawai was probably conceived as a Hindu shrine several centuries before the Sukhothai kingdom established itself here. The stucco reliefs decorating the prangs feature a few weatherworn figures from both Hindu and Buddhist mythology, which suggests that the shrine was later pressed into Buddhist service; the square base inside the central prang supported the Khmer Shiva lingam (phallus), while the viharn out front is a later, Buddhist addition.

Just west of Wat Mahathat, the particularly fine lotus-bud chedi of **Wat Trapang Ngoen** rises gracefully against the backdrop of distant hills. Aligned with the chedi on the symbolic east–west axis are the dilapidated viharn and, east of that, on an island in the middle of the "silver pond" after which the wat is named, the remains of the bot. Walk the connecting plank to the bot to appreciate the setting from the water. North of the chedi, notice the fluid lines of the walking Buddha mounted onto a brick wall – a classic example of Sukhothai sculpture.

Taking the water feature one step further, **Wat Sra Sri** commands a fine position on two connecting islands north of Wat Trapang Ngoen. The bell-shaped chedi with a tapering spire and square base shows a strong Sri Lankan influence, and the metallic replica of a freestanding walking Buddha is typical Sukhothai.

The outer zones

There's a much less formal feel to the ruins in the four **outer zones**, where you're as likely to find cows trampling through the remains as tourists. You'll need a bicycle or car to get around, but all sites are clearly signposted from the gates encircling the central zone. The north zone is the closest and most rewarding, followed by the east zone just off the road to New Sukhothai. If you're feeling energetic, head for the west zone, which requires a much longer bike ride and some hill climbing.

The ruins to the **south** aren't worth a special effort but you'll pass a few of them, including Wat Chetuphon, if you take the quiet, rural **back route** between the accommodation on Route 1272 and Wat Mahathat. Having passed

▲ People exercising in Sukhothai's Historical Park

the *Tharaburi Resort* on your right, take the next minor road right, just past *Sinvana* restaurant, and this will eventually get you to a T-junction in front of Wat Chetuphon (about 1km). Take the right-hand branch and continue due north for another 3km to cross the Old City's southern walls and arrive at the foodstalls near Wat Mahathat.

The north zone

Exiting the central zone north of Wat Sra Sri, the road bisects the earthen ramparts of the old city walls and enters the **north zone**. About 500m north of the walls, a footbridge (also accessible to bicycles and motorbikes) leads you across to **Wat Phra Phai Luang**, one of the ancient city's oldest structures. The three prangs, only one of which remains intact, were built by the Khmers before the Thais founded their own kingdom here and, as at the similar Wat Sri Sawai, you can still see some of the stucco reliefs showing both Hindu and Buddhist figures. Others are displayed in Ramkhamhaeng National Museum. It's thought that Wat Phra Phai Luang was at the centre of the old Khmer town and that it was as important then as Wat Mahathat later became to the Thais. When the shrine was converted into a Buddhist temple, the viharn and chedi were built to the east of the prangs: the reliefs of the (now headless and armless) seated Buddhas are still visible around the base of the chedi. Also discernible among the ruins are parts of a large reclining Buddha and a mondop containing four huge standing Buddhas in different postures.

About 750m southwest from the Wat Phra Phai Luang compound, **Wat Sri Chum** boasts Sukhothai's largest surviving Buddha image. The enormous, heavily restored brick-and-stucco seated Buddha, measuring more than 11m from knee to knee and almost 15m high, peers through the slit in its custom-built mondop. Check out the elegantly tapered fingers, complete with gold-leaf nail varnish. A passageway – rarely opened up, unfortunately – runs inside the mondop wall, taking you from ground level on the left-hand side to the Buddha's eye level and then up again to the roof, affording a bird's-eye view of the image. Legend has it that this Buddha would sometimes speak to favoured worshippers, and this staircase would have enabled tricksters to climb up and hold forth, unseen; one of the kings of Sukhothai is said to have brought his troops here to spur them on to victory with encouraging words from the Buddha.

The east zone

The only temple of interest in the **east zone**, about 1.5km east of the main entrance, is canalside **Wat Chang Lom**, beside the bicycle track to New Sukhothai and just off the road to the new city. Chang Lom means "surrounded by elephants" and the main feature here is a large Sri Lankan-style, bell-shaped chedi encircled by a frieze of elephants.

The west zone

Be prepared for a long haul out to the **west zone**, in the forested hills off the main road to Tak. Marking the western edge of the Old City, almost 5km west of the museum, the hilltop temple of **Wat Saphan Hin** should – with sufficiently powerful telescopic lenses – give a fantastic panorama of the Old City's layout, but with the naked eye conjures up only an indistinct vista of trees and stones. If you make it this far, chances are you'll share the view only with the large standing Buddha at the top. The wat is reached via a steep three-hundred-metre-long pathway of stone slabs (hence the name, which means "Stone Bridge") that starts from a track running south from the Tak road. This is the easiest approach if you're on a bike as it's completely flat; the other route, which follows a lesser, more southerly, road out of the Old City, takes you over several hills and via the elephant temple of **Wat Chang Rob**, 3km south of Saphan Hin.

Around New Sukhothai

Though the historical park is the main draw for visitors to New Sukhothai, there are enough other attractions in the area to make it worth staying on for a couple of extra days. Many of these places – such as Si Satchanalai and Kamphaeng Phet – can be fairly easily reached by public transport, but you'll need to **rent your own vehicle** for trips to Wat Thawet and Ramkhamhaeng National Park, or arrange a driver via your accommodation.

Belgian-Thai-run Cycling Sukhothai (Ⓣ085 083 1864) leads recommended sunset and half-day **bicycle tours** around local villages and countryside most afternoons from 4.30pm (B250–550 including mountain bike and transfers; bookable through most guest houses). *J&J Guest House* runs day-trips to the caves and waterfalls of Si Satchanalai National Park (as distinct from Si Satchanalai Historical Park; B1000), and half-day trips to Tham Kham Khao National Park for a swim in the lake and a chance to watch the millions of bats streaming out of a nearby cave at dusk (B500).

Sangkhalok Museum

If you have a serious interest in ceramics you'll probably enjoy the Sukhothai-era exhibits at the privately owned **Sangkhalok Museum** (Mon–Fri 8am–6pm, Sat & Sun 10am–8pm; B100, children B50; ask for one of the informative museum booklets at the ticket desk), a couple of kilometres east of New Sukhothai on Highway 101, close to the junction with Highway 12, the road to Phitsanulok. A samlor ride from central New Sukhothai should cost no more than B50.

The ground floor of the museum displays ceramic artefacts from twelfth- to sixteenth-century Sukhothai, including **water pipes** used in the city's widely admired irrigation system, and the lotus-bud **lamps** whose gracefully shaped perforations both shield the flame and diffuse its light and are still as popular in Thailand today. Some of the finest pieces are the **bowls** with scalloped rims and bluish-green patterns and the characteristically expressive **figurines**; unusually, many of these works are signed by the potter. This style of pottery has become known as Sangkhalok, after the prosperous city of Sawankhalok, near Si Satchanalai, which was part of the kingdom of Sukhothai at that time (see p.291 for a description of the Sangkhalok kilns in Si Satchanalai). Also on show are ceramics from twelfth-century Burma, China and Vietnam, all of which were found in the area and so show who the citizens of Sukhothai were trading with at that time, as well as some of the most exquisite ceramics produced in northern Thailand during the Lanna era (thirteenth to sixteenth centuries). Upstairs, the focus is on the cultural significance of certain artefacts and their recurring motifs.

Wat Thawet

Famous for its one hundred different, brightly painted, concrete statues depicting morality tales and Buddhist fables, **Wat Thawet** is quite a popular sight for Thai tourists, though farangs tend to find it a bit tacky. The temple **sculpture park** was conceived by a local monk in the 1970s, with the aim of creating a "learning garden", where visitors could learn about the Buddhist ideas of hell and karmic retribution. For example, people who have spent their lives killing animals are depicted here with the head of a buffalo, pig, cock or elephant, while those who have been greedy and materialistic stand naked and undernourished, their ribs and backbones sticking out. Then there's the alcoholic who is forced to drink boiling liquids that make his concrete guts literally explode on to the ground.

Part of the appeal of Wat Thawet is that it makes a good focus for a very pleasant **bicycle** trip from Sukhothai, a sixteen-kilometre round-trip that is almost entirely along peaceful canalside tracks. From New Sukhothai, follow riverside Thanon Ratchathani north beyond *Lotus Village* until you hit the bypass. Cross the bypass and take the concrete path from the west edge of the bridge. Stay on this calm, scenic track for the next 8km, passing typical wooden houses, several banana plantations, a wooden suspension bridge and, about 1km before the temple, going beneath a major flyover; Wat Thawet is beside the second wooden suspension bridge. Cycling Sukhothai leads bike trips here too.

Ramkhamhaeng National Park, Khao Luang and Thung Luang Pottery Village

The forested area immediately to the southwest of Sukhothai is protected as **Ramkhamhaeng National Park** (B100; Ⓣ055 619200, Ⓦwww.dnp.go.th/National_park.asp; bungalows ❸) and makes a pleasant day-trip on a motorbike, with the possibility of a challenging mountain climb at the end of it. To get to the main park entrance from New Sukhothai, follow Highway 101 towards Kamphaeng Phet for 19km, then take side road 1319, signed to Khao Luang, for the final 16km to park headquarters. Although any Kamphaeng Phet-bound bus will take you as far as the junction, you'll have trouble hitching into the park from here, so renting private transport from Sukhothai is best.

The headquarters stands at the foot of the eastern flank of the highest peak, **Khao Luang** (1185m), which can be climbed in around four hours, but only safely from November through February. Several very steep trails run up to the summit from here, but they are not very clearly marked; the first couple of kilometres are the worst, after which the incline eases up a little. From the top you should get a fine view over the Sukhothai plains. If you want to camp on the summit, simply alert the rangers at park headquarters, and they will arrange for their colleague at the summit to rent you a tent; you need to take your own food and water.

En route to or from Ramkhamhaeng National Park you could make a detour to **Thung Luang Pottery Village**, signed 16km out of New Sukhothai on Highway 101, where nearly every household is involved in the production of earthenware pots, vases and statuary. Once you've turned off the main road, you'll pass a line of roadside stalls, but to enter the heart of the pottery neighbourhoods continue for another kilometre or so, past a school and two temples.

Eating and drinking

The local speciality is a pungent bowl of **Sukhothai noodles**: thin rice noodles served in a dark, slightly sweet broth flavoured with soy sauce, coriander and chilli and spiked with chunks of pork crackling, green beans and peanuts. In New Sukhothai you should be able to find them, and many other good cheap dishes, at the **hot-food stalls** and streetside tables that set up every evening in front of Wat Ratchathani on Thanon Charodvithitong and further west near *Poo's* restaurant. There's also a permanent covered area for night market-style **restaurants** on the soi between Thanon Ramkhamhaeng and Thanon Nikhon Kasem.

Chopper Beer Thanon Pravetnakorn. Farang-oriented upstairs terrace and bar with occasional live music and a menu that runs to steak as well as seafood.

Dream Café 88/1 Thanon Singhawat. Dark and cosy, with walls and windowsills full of curios and Thai antiques, this rather cool, long-running Sukhothai institution serves great food (two courses for around B300) and is very popular. Highlights include *tom yam* with pork spare ribs and young tamarind, fresh Vietnamese-style spring rolls, and deep-fried banana-flower fritters. To complement, choose from twenty different ice-cream sundaes and a range of stamina-enhancing herbal drinks – plus gin-and-tonics.

Khun Tanode Thanon Charodvithitong. Low-key, laid-back, well-priced little riverside restaurant that's popular with locals and is prettily illuminated at night. Try the local speciality – crispy-fried chicken drumsticks in Sukhothai sauce – or mussels cooked in a herb sauce. Most mains B60–100. Daily 10am–midnight.

Kru Iew Thanon Wichien Chamnong, corner of Soi Mahasaranon 1, 50m north of *At Home* guest house; look for the "OTOP" ("One Tambon One Product") sign, signifying traditional rural produce. Award-winning, folksy lunch spot that's locally famous for its aromatic parcels of *phat thai* wrapped in thin omelette (from B20), its fresh Vietnamese-style *naim nueng* herb and pork spring rolls (B70) – and its Sukhothai noodles. Watch the white-capped cooks in their open-plan kitchens. Daily 10am–3pm.

La Bonne Cuisine Thanon Charodvithitong and **J&J Guest House** 122/1 Soi Maerampan. The two branches run by *J&J* are known for their home-made baguettes – perfect for breakfast or lunch.

Poo's Thanon Charodvithitong. Streetside travellers' bar-restaurant that serves all the standard Thai dishes plus cheap draft Chang beer, Belgian beer and B100 cocktails. Also rents motorbikes and gives Thai massages.

Rom Poa At the edge of the covered night market between Thanon Ramkhamhaeng and Thanon Nikhon Kasem. Popular place with pushy touts but a perfectly decent menu of spicy jelly-thread noodle salads (*yam wun sen*), curries, lots of seafood dishes, fruit shakes and a reasonable vegetarian selection. Most dishes B50–70, though that's still more expensive than many other stalls in the night market.

Listings

Amulets The owner of tiny *Thai Guest House* at 25/4 Thanon Rajuthit sells well-priced Buddhist amulets (mostly B10–100) at the riverside market (daily 6–8am) and from her guest house during the rest of the day.

Bicycle rental Available from a few guest houses in New Sukhothai and in great numbers at the historical park (B30).

Books A few English-language books and touring maps are available at Sukhothai Books Centre on Thanon Nikhon Kasem.

Cookery courses One- and two-day courses led by Naa at *99 Guest House* (B750 per day); shorter courses at *Ban Thai* (from B550).

Emergencies For all emergencies, call the tourist police on ⓣ1155, or go to the local police station on Thanon Singhawat.

Hospital The government-run Sukhothai Hospital (ⓣ055 611782) is a couple of kilometres west of New Sukhothai on the road to Sukhothai Historical Park; there's a more central 24hr clinic on Thanon Singhawat.

Internet access At many guest houses and some internet centres in New Sukhothai (see map, p.278 for locations).

Massage and spa treatments Most luxuriously at Baan Spa, part of *Lotus Village* (see p.280), where treatments take place in a lovely teak house and include turmeric body scrubs, herbal saunas, waxing and Thai massage (B500/60min). Many other cheaper massage places at guest houses and along Thanon Rajuthit including at *Thai Guest House* (from B150/60min).

Motorbike rental On Thanon Pravetnakorn and at nearby *Poo's* restaurant.

Shopping The *Ananda Museum Gallery Hotel* plaza, beside the Sangkhalok Museum on the bypass, sells very classy handicrafts, particularly celadon and ceramics in both traditional and modern styles. Also try Usa Sungkalok near the Old City (see p.283).

Telephones The TOT phone centre (Mon–Fri 8.30am–5pm) is on Thanon Prampracha.

Travel agent Domestic and international air tickets from Sukhothai Travel Agency, 10–12 Thanon Singhawat (Mon–Fri 8am–5pm, Sat 8am–noon; ⓣ055 613075, ⓔsukhothai_travel@hotmail.com).

Visa run *J&J Guest House* does a day-trip visa run to the Burmese border near Mae Sot (B1500 per person excluding entry into Burma).

Si Satchanalai and around

In the mid-thirteenth century, Sukhothai cemented its power by establishing several satellite towns, of which the most important was **SI SATCHANALAI**, 57km upriver from Sukhothai on the banks of the Yom. Now a UNESCO-listed historical park, the partially restored ruins of **Muang Kao Si Satchanalai** have a quieter ambience than the grander models at Sukhothai Historical Park, and the additional attractions of the riverside wat in nearby **Chalieng**, the **Sangkhalok pottery kilns** in Bang Ko Noi, and the **Sathorn Textile Museum** in New Si Satchanalai combine to make the area worth exploring.

Arrival, information and transport

Si Satchanalai works best as a day-trip from Sukhothai. The fastest way to get there is on one of the air-con **buses** bound for Chiang Rai; these depart New Sukhothai bus station at 6.40am, 9am, 10.30am and 11.30am and take just over an hour. Local buses depart about every thirty minutes, but take about one hour forty five minutes and sometimes require a change of bus in Sawankhalok. The last conveniently timed air-conditioned bus back to New Sukhothai passes Old Si Satchanalai at about 4.30pm (just flag it down from the highway); if you miss it, you'll have to wait till about 8pm. Hardly any local buses run in the afternoon. All buses drop passengers on Highway 101 at the signpost for Chalieng's Wat Phra Si Ratana Mahathat, beside a pink archway gate and a shop that does **bicycle rental**. This is the best place to rent a bike (B30) as, though it's less than 500m to Wat Mahathat from here, it's almost another 2km further to reach the next rental place, at the entry to Muang Kao Si Satchanalai proper. Pass through the pink archway and cross the Yom River via a wooden suspension bridge (open to bikes and motorbikes) to reach the first temple, Wat Phra Si Ratana Mahathat in Chalieng. Coming by car you'll need to use the road bridge about 1km further west up Highway 101. Alternatively, you could either rent a motorbike in New Sukhothai or join a tour from there.

Tickets for Chalieng, Muang Kao Si Satchanalai and the kilns are B100 each or B220 for all three, plus a B10–50 vehicle. There are **foodstalls** and small restaurants at every juncture, including at Wat Mahathat, between the road bridge and Muang Kao, and beside the Muang Kao ticket gate.

Chalieng and Wat Phra Si Ratana Mahathat

Before Sukhothai asserted control of the region and founded Si Satchanalai, the Khmers governed the area from **Chalieng**, cradled in a bend in the Yom River just over 2km to the east of Muang Kao Si Satchanalai. Just about all that now remains of Chalieng is **Wat Phra Si Ratana Mahathat** (dawn to dusk), whose compound, aligned east–west and encircled by a now sunken wall of laterite blocks, contains structures thought to date back to the Khmer era, but with later additions by Sukhothai and Ayutthayan builders. If you approach from the wooden suspension bridge you'll enter via the semi-submerged eastern gateway, passing beneath a hefty Khmer-style carved lintel that was hewn from a single block of stone. Inside, the compound is dominated by a towering corncob prang, the main shrine, which was likely remodelled during the Ayutthayan era and whose exterior has recently been renovated with all-over stucco decorations. The ruined viharn in front of the prang enshrines a large seated Buddha sculpted in typical Sukhothai style, with hand gestures symbolizing his triumph over temptation. The tall stucco relief of a walking Buddha to the left is also classic Sukhothai and is regarded as one of the finest of its genre. Immediately to the west of the prang, the remains of the octagonal laterite platform and its bell-shaped chedi are believed to date from a different era, possibly considerably earlier. A mondop containing a large standing Buddha guards one side and looks towards the River Yom; a second viharn, containing two Buddha images, occupies the other flank.

Muang Kao Si Satchanalai

From the Wat Mahathat compound it's a two-kilometre ride northwest along the quiet riverside road to the entrance point to **Muang Kao Si Satchanalai** (daily 8am–4pm). You can rent bikes here, and there are foodstalls and a trolley bus (operates during busy times only).

Most circuits begin with the most striking set of ruins, the elephant temple of **Wat Chang Lom**, whose centrepiece is a huge, Sri Lankan-style, bell-shaped chedi set on a square base studded with 39 life-sized elephant buttresses (those in Sukhothai and Kamphaeng Phet are smaller). A mahout and his elephant sometimes hang out here to prove the point. Many of the elephant reliefs are in good repair, with much of their stucco flesh still intact; others now have their bulky laterite-brick innards exposed.

Across the road from Wat Chang Lom, **Wat Chedi Jet Taew** has seven rows of small chedis thought to enshrine the ashes of Si Satchanalai's royal rulers, which makes this the ancient city's most important temple. One of the 34 chedis is an elegant scaled-down replica of the hallmark lotus-bud chedi at Sukhothai's Wat Mahathat; some of the others are copies of other important wats from the vicinity. Several have fine stucco-covered Buddha images in their alcoves, including a famously beautiful one of the Buddha sheltered by a naga (now with restored head), also reproduced in Ramkhamhaeng National Museum.

A few hundred metres along the road from Wat Chedi Jet Taew, **Wat Nang Phya** is remarkable for the original stucco reliefs on its viharn wall, which remain in fine condition; stucco is a hardy material that sets soon after being first applied, and becomes even harder when exposed to rain – hence its ability to survive seven hundred years in the open. The balustraded wall has slit windows and is entirely covered with intricate floral motifs.

About 600m north of Wat Chang Lom, the hilltop ruins of Wat Khao Phanom Pleung and Wat Khao Suan Khiri afford splendid aerial views of different quarters of the ancient city. The sole remaining intact chedi of **Wat Khao Phanom Pleung** sits on top of the lower of the hills and used to be flanked by a set of smaller chedis built to entomb the ashes of Si Satchanalai's important personages – the ones who merited some special memorial, but didn't quite make the grade for Wat Chedi Jet Taew. The temple presumably got its name, which means "mountain of sacred fire", from the cremation rituals held on the summit. **Wat Khao Suan Khiri**'s huge chedi, which graces the summit 200m northwest, has definitely seen better days, but the views from its platform – south over the main temple ruins and north towards the city walls and entrance gates – are worth the climb.

The Sangkhalok kilns

Endowed with high-quality clay, the area around Si Satchanalai – known as Sawankhalok or Sangkhalok during the Ayutthaya period – commanded an international reputation as a ceramics centre from the mid-fourteenth to the end of the fifteenth century, producing pieces still rated amongst the finest in the world. More than two hundred **kilns** have been unearthed in and around Si Satchanalai to date, and it's estimated that there could once have been a thousand in all. One of the main groups of kilns is in the village of **BAN KO NOI**, which is about 7km upstream from the park entry point and can be reached by bicycle by following the very pleasant, almost traffic-free road beside the river (not the one going into the park) through hamlets fringed with flowering shrubs and fruit trees.

At Ban Ko Noi, four excavated kilns have been roofed and turned into the **Sangkhalok Kiln Preservation Centre** (daily 9am–4.30pm), but, unfortunately, they are poorly served by almost non existent English-language captions (you'll have a much better idea of what you're looking at if you've already been to the Ramkhamhaeng National Museum in Sukhothai Historical Park). Two of the kilns are up-draught kilns and two are cross-draught kilns, the latter generating a greater and more consistent heat, which enabled the production of glazed ware. Most Sangkhalok ceramics were glazed – the grey-green celadon, probably introduced by immigrant Chinese potters, was especially popular – and typically decorated with fish or chrysanthemum motifs. A small display of **Sangkhalok ceramics** gives a hint of the pieces that were fired here: domestic items such as pots, decorated plates and lidded boxes; decorative items like figurines, temple sculptures and temple roof tiles; and items for export, particularly to Indonesia and the Philippines, where huge Sangkhalok storage jars were used as burial urns.

Several of Thailand's major museums feature collections of ceramics from both Si Satchanalai and Sukhothai under the umbrella label of Sangkhalok, and there's a dedicated collection of Sangkhalok wares just outside New Sukhothai (see p.287). Stalls across the road from the Preservation Centre sell reproduction ceramics and "antiques".

The Sathorn Textile Museum

Eleven kilometres north of the Si Satchanalai ruins, modern Si Satchanalai is worth visiting for the **Sathorn Textile Museum**, located at the northern end of the ribbon-like new town, on the east side of Highway 101. The museum houses the private collection of Khun Sathorn, who also runs the adjacent textile shop, and he or his staff open up the one-room exhibition for anyone who shows an interest. Any Sukhothai guest house can include a visit to the museum in a Si Satchanalai day-trip, or you can come here on the bus from New Sukhothai, getting off in modern Si Satchanalai rather than at the ruins.

Most of the **textiles** on show come from the nearby village of Hat Siew, whose weavers have long specialized in the art of *teen jok*, or hem embroidery, whereby the bottom panel of the sarong or *phasin* (woman's sarong) is decorated with a band of supplementary weft, usually done in exquisitely intricate patterns. Some of the textiles here are almost a hundred years old and many of the *teen jok* **motifs** have symbolic meaning showing what the cloths would have been used for – a sarong or *phasin* used for a marriage ceremony, for example, tends to have a double image, such as two birds facing each other. Elephants also feature quite a lot in Hat Siew weaving, probably a reference to the village custom in which young men who are about to become monks parade on elephants to their ordination ceremony. The tradition continues to this day and elephant parades are held at the mass ordination ceremony every year on April 7 and 8. Modern Hat Siew textiles are sold at the adjacent Sathorn shop and at other outlets further south along the main road.

Kamphaeng Phet

KAMPHAENG PHET, 77km south of Sukhothai, was probably founded in the fourteenth century by the kings of Sukhothai as a buffer city between their capital and the increasingly powerful city-state of Ayutthaya. Strategically sited 100m from the east bank of the Ping, the ruined old city has, like Sukhothai and Si Satchanalai before it, been partly restored and opened to the public as a

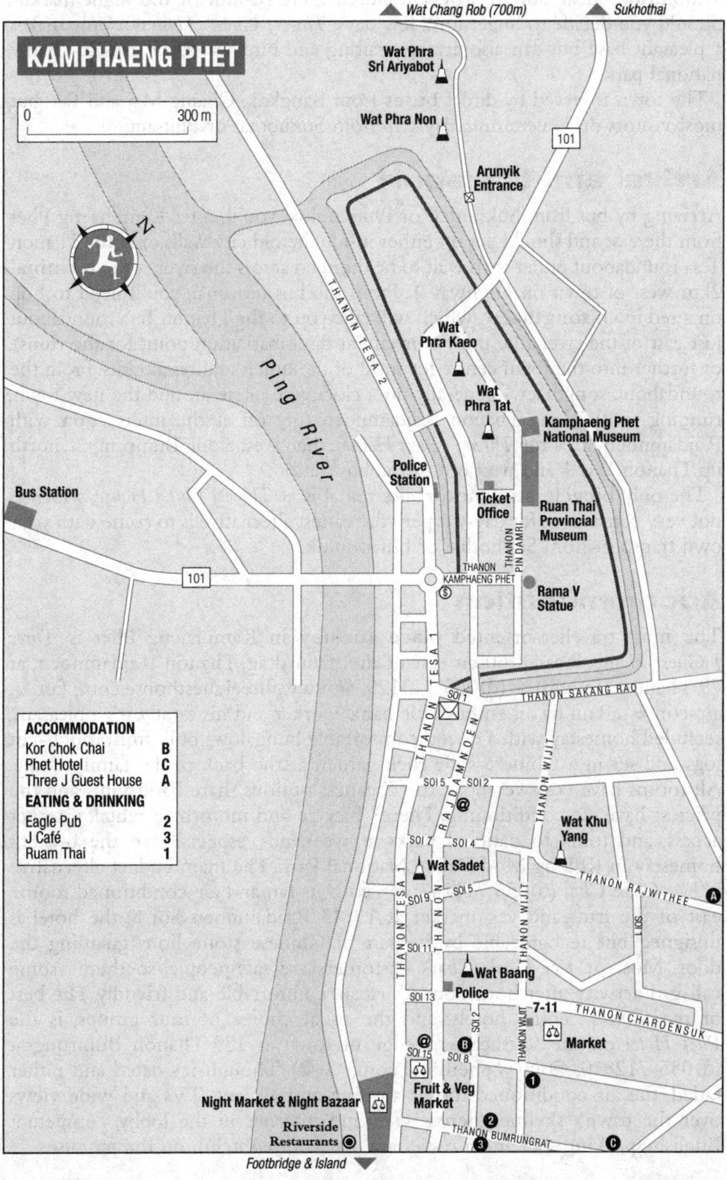

historical park and is similarly listed as a UNESCO World Heritage Site. The least visited of the three, it rivals Si Satchanalai for your attention mainly because of the untamed setting and the gracefully weathered statues of its main temple. A new city has grown up on the southeastern boundaries of the old, the usual commercial blandness offset by a riverside park, plentiful flowers and an unusual number of historic wooden houses dotted along the main thoroughfares. You can even swim off an island in the middle of the river, accessible via a footbridge near Soi 21, a few hundred metres south of the night market. Should you decide to linger for a few days, *Three J Guest House* not only makes a pleasant base but can also arrange rafting and bird-watching trips in nearby national parks.

The town is served by direct **buses** from Bangkok, Chiang Mai and Tak, but most visitors drive here on a day-trip from Sukhothai or Phitsanulok.

Arrival and transport

Arriving by bus from Sukhothai or Phitsanulok, you'll enter Kamphaeng Phet from the east and should get off either inside the old city walls or at the Thanon Tesa roundabout rather than wait to be dumped across the river at the **terminal** 2km west of town on Highway 1. From the bus terminal, you'll need to hop on a red town **songthaew**, which will take you to the Thanon Tesa roundabout just east of the river (the most convenient disembarkation point for the ruins), or further into the town centre for most of the hotels and restaurants. From the roundabout, songthaews generally do a clockwise circle around the new town, running south along Thanon Rajdamnoen (get off at the intersection with Rajdamnoen Soi 4 for *Three J Guest House*), then west along Bumrungrat, north up Thanon Tesa 1 and west out to the bus station.

The only **bicycle and motorbike** rental is at *Three J Guest House*, which is not very convenient for day-trippers; the easiest alternative is to come with your own transport from Sukhothai or Phitsanulok.

Accommodation

The most traveller-oriented **place to stay** in Kamphaeng Phet is *Three J Guest House*, located 600m east of the main drag, Thanon Rajdamnoen, at 79 Thanon Rajwithee (Ⓣ055 713129, Ⓦwww.threejguesthouse.com; fan ❷, air-con ❸). Run by an enthusiastic bank-worker and his family, it's a pleasant, secluded homestay with a dozen comfortable bungalows built from rough-cut logs and set in a Chinese-style rock garden at the back of the family home. All rooms have cosy verandas; the cheapest options share bathrooms and the priciest have air-conditioning. There's bicycle and motorbike rental, internet access, and tours to national parks at weekends, especially to the owner's homestay in Khlong Mod Daeng National Park. The main budget alternative is *Kor Chok Chai* (Ⓣ055 711247; ❷), with its fan and air-conditioned rooms, east of the fruit and veg market at 19/43 Rajdamnoen Soi 8; the hotel is unsigned but recognizable by its pair of Chinese stone lions guarding the door. Most of *Kor Chok Chai*'s customers are salespeople, so there's some call-girl activity after hours, but it's clean, comfortable and friendly. The best of the town's central hotels, and the usual choice of tour groups, is the *Phet Hotel* on the southeastern edge of town at 189 Thanon Bumrungrat (Ⓣ055 712810, Ⓦwww.phethotel.com; ❸–❹). Though it's dated and rather faded, the air-conditioned rooms are fine and all have TVs and wide views over the town's skyline; there's wi-fi and internet in the lobby, competent English-speaking staff and a restaurant, bar and nightclub on the premises.

Muang Kao Kamphaeng Phet

Ruins surround modern Kamphaeng Phet on all sides, but **Muang Kao Kamphaeng Phet** (daily 6am–7pm; B150 for both main zones or B100 for one zone, plus B10–B50 per vehicle) takes in the two most interesting areas: the oblong zone inside the old city walls, and the forested ("*arunyik*") area just north of that. A tour of both areas involves a five-kilometre round-trip, so you'll need transport. The ruins that dot the landscape across the Ping River, west of the Thanon Tesa roundabout, belong to the even older city of Nakhon Chum, but are very dilapidated.

Inside the city walls

Parts of the **city walls** that gave Kamphaeng Phet its name are still in good condition, though Highway 101 to Sukhothai now cuts through the enclosed area and a few shops have sprung up along the roadside, making it hard to visualize the fortifications as a whole. Approaching from the Thanon Tesa roundabout, you can either head up Thanon Pin Damri and start your tour at Wat Phra That and the Provincial Museum, or you enter the compound from the western gate and come in at the back end of **Wat Phra Kaeo**. Built almost entirely of laterite and adorned with laterite Buddhas, this was the city's central and most important structure, and given the name reserved for temples that have housed the kingdom's most sacred image: the Emerald Buddha, now in the wat of the same name in Bangkok, is thought to have been set down here to rest at some point. Seven centuries later, the Buddha images have been worn away into attractive abstract shadows, often aptly compared to the pitted, spidery forms of Giacometti sculptures, and the slightly unkempt feel to the place makes a perfect setting. Few tools have been unearthed at any of the Kamphaeng Phet sites, giving weight to the theory that the sculptors moulded their statues from the clay-like freshly dug laterite before leaving it to harden. Small, overgrown laterite quarry pits are still visible all over the old city. The statues would originally have been faced with stucco, and restorers have already patched up the central tableau of one reclining and two seated Buddhas. The empty niches that encircle the principal chedi were once occupied by statues of bejewelled lions.

Adjoining Wat Phra Kaeo to the east are the three chedis of **Wat Phra That**. The central bell-shaped chedi, now picturesquely wreathed in lichen and stray bits of vegetation, is typical of the Sri Lankan style and was built to house a sacred relic. Just east of Wat Phra That, **Kamphaeng Phet National Museum** (Wed–Sun 9am–4pm; B30; Ⓦ www.thailandmuseum.com) looks at the historical development of the city. The prize exhibit in its upstairs sculpture gallery is the bronze standing Shiva: cast in the sixteenth century in Khmer-Ayutthayan style, the statue has had a chequered history – including decapitation by a nineteenth-century German admirer. Also on this floor is an unusual wooden, seventeenth- or eighteenth-century Ayutthayan-style standing Buddha, whose diadem, necklace and even hems are finely carved.

While you're at the National Museum you can't miss the alluring group of recently built traditional-style teak wood *salas* in the adjacent compound. This is the **Kamphaeng Phet Ruan Thai Provincial Museum** (daily 9am–4.30pm; B10), whose exhibits and scale models introduce the history, traditions and contemporary culture of Kamphaeng Phet province.

The arunyik temples

The dozen or so ruins in the forested area north of the city walls – east 100m along Highway 101 from behind Wat Phra Kaeo, across the moat and up a road to the left – are all that remains of Kamphaeng Phet's **arunyik** (forest) temples, built here by Sukhothai-era monks in a wooded area to encourage meditation. It's an enjoyably tranquil and atmospheric area to explore if you have your own wheels, with the tumbledown structures peeking out of the thinly planted groves that line the access road; the road winds around a fair bit before eventually rejoining the Sukhothai–Kamphaeng Phet highway to the north of the walled city.

Once you're through the entrance, the first temple on the left is **Wat Phra Non**, otherwise known as the Temple of the Reclining Buddha, though you need a good imagination to conjure up the indistinct remains into the once enormous Buddha figure. Gigantic laterite pillars support the viharn that houses the statue; far more ambitious than the usual brick-constructed jobs, these pillars were cut from single slabs of stone from a nearby quarry and would have measured up to 8m in height.

Immediately to the north, the four Buddha images of **Wat Phra Sri Ariyabot** are in better condition. With cores of laterite and skins of stucco, the restored standing and walking images tower over the viharn, while the seated (south-facing) and reclining (north-facing) Buddhas have been eroded into indistinct blobs. The full-grown trees rooted firmly in the raised floor are evidence of just how old the place is.

Follow the road around the bend to reach **Wat Chang Rob**, crouched on top of a laterite hill 1km from the entrance gate. Built to the same Sri Lankan model as its sister temples of the same name in Sukhothai and Si Satchanalai, this "temple surrounded by elephants" retains only the square base of its central bell-shaped chedi. Climb one of its four steep staircases for a view out over the mountains in the west, or just for a different perspective of the 68 elephant buttresses that encircle the base. Sculpted from laterite and stucco, they're dressed in the ceremonial garb fit for such revered animals; floral reliefs can just be made out along the surfaces between neighbouring elephants – the lower level was once decorated with a stucco frieze of flying birds.

Eating and drinking

The huge range of cheap noodles, stir-fries and rice dishes served at *Ruam Thai*, south of the Charoensuk intersection on Thanon Wijit, make this very popular, unpretentious **restaurant** a reliable choice at any time of day, but from late afternoon the **night market** is the most enjoyable place to eat. It occupies a covered area in the southern part of the new town, between the river and Thanon Tesa 1 and has a mouthwateringly wide selection of specialist sweet and savoury stalls; try asking for the special local noodle dish, *kway tiaw cha kang rao*, made with cow peas and pork. For cheap Thai vegetarian food – rice plus a couple of stews, curries or stir-fries for B20–30 – head for *J Café* (daily 7am–2pm), signed just off Thanon Bumrungrat on Soi 2 at 68/3. For beer, whisky and live music (from 9pm), the *Eagle Pub*, one block south and east of *Kor Chok Chai* on Thanon Bumrungrat, is one of the livelier spots in town.

Tak and around

Highway 12 heads west from Sukhothai, crossing the westernmost reaches of the northern plains before arriving at the provincial capital of **TAK** (79km), on the east bank of the Ping River. Historically important as the birthplace of King Taksin of Thonburi (who attached the name of his hometown to the one he was born with), Tak is of little interest to tourists except as a place to change buses for continuing north to Lampang and Chiang Mai, south to Kamphaeng Phet and Bangkok, or west to Mae Sot and the Burmese border.

The one time it is worth making a special effort to visit Tak is for **Loy Krathong**, the nationwide festival of light that's held here over several nights around the full moon of the twelfth lunar month (Oct/Nov; see Loy Krathong colour section for details). The idiosyncratic Tak celebration is known as Loy Krathong Sai and involves the nightly floating of thousands of lighted coconut husks (rather than the usual banana-leaf baskets) on the Ping River.

Practicalities

Tak **bus station** is about 3km east of the town centre (B30–40 by samlor) and has internet access, fresh coffee and a B100 flophouse. **TAT** has a regional office in the town centre at 193 Thanon Taksin (daily 8.30am–4.30pm; ⓣ055 514341, ⓔtattak@tat.or.th).

If you need a **hotel** in Tak, try the very cheap, very basic fan and air-con rooms at *Mae Ping*, across the road from the fruit and veg market at 231 Thanon Mahattai Bamroong (ⓣ055 511807; ❶), or the medium-sized *Viang Tak Riverside* (ⓣ055 512507, ⓦwww.visit-mekong.com/the-viang-tak-2-hotel/; ❹–❺), one block southwest of the fruit and veg market at 236 Thanon Chumphon, which has air-con rooms, some of them with nice river views, and a swimming pool.

Around Tak

Most travellers ignore Tak, however, and go straight on to Mae Sot, via the stunning western mountain range that divides the northern plains from the Burmese border. With your own transport, there are a couple of attractions en route, beginning at kilometre-stone 12 on Highway 105, 20km west of Tak, with **Lansang National Park** (dawn to dusk; B200; ⓣ055 577207, ⓦwww.dnp.go.th/National_park.asp; bungalows ❸), which has trails and waterfalls and is reached via a three-kilometre side road off Highway 105; some Mae Sot tour operators run trips here too. This region is home to Lisu, Lahu and Maew hill tribes, many of whom live on the cool slopes of 840-metre-high Doi Muser where they grow coffee, fruit and vegetables which they trade, along with hill-tribe crafts, at the **hill-tribe market** alongside the highway between kilometre-stones 28 and 29.

Mae Sot and the border

Located just 6km from Burma, and 100km west from Tak, **MAE SOT** is very much a border town, populated by a rich ethnic mix of Burmese, Karen, Hmong and Thais (plus a lively injection of committed NGO expats), and dependent both on its thriving trade in Burmese gems and teak as well as, reportedly, on an even more lucrative cross-border black market in drugs, labourers and sex workers. For the casual visitor, however, it's a relaxed place to hang out, with a burgeoning number of good restaurants to enjoy, albeit no real sights. The short ride to the border market provides additional, if low-key, interest, and there are several caves and waterfalls within day-tripping distance.

Mae Sot's main selling point, however, is as a stopover on the way to **Umphang**, a remote village 164km further south, which is starting to get a name as a centre for interesting rafting and trekking adventures. The journey to Umphang takes at least four hours in a bumpy songthaew, so it's usually worth

Refugees from Burma: the Karen

With a population of five to seven million, the **Karen** are Burma's largest ethnic minority, but their numbers have offered no protection against persecution by the Burmese. This mistreatment has been going on for centuries, and entered a new phase after Burma won its independence from Britain in 1948. Unlike many other groups in Burma, the Karen had remained loyal to the British during World War II and were supposed to have been rewarded with autonomy when Britain pulled out; instead they were left to battle for that themselves. Fourteen years after the British withdrawal, the **Burmese army** took control, setting up an isolationist state run under a bizarre ideology compounded of militarist, socialist and Buddhist principles. In 1988, opposition to this junta peaked with a series of pro-democracy demonstrations that were suppressed by the slaughter of thousands.

In subsequent elections an overwhelming majority voted for the **National League for Democracy** (**NLD**), led by **Aung San Suu Kyi**, recipient of the 1991 Nobel Peace Prize. In response, the military placed Aung San Suu Kyi under house arrest (where she has remained on and off ever since) and declared all opposition parties illegal. The disenfranchised MPs then joined the thousands of ordinary citizens who, in the face of the savagery of the Burmese militia against the country's minorities, had fled east to jungle camps along the Thai border and beyond, into Thailand itself.

Armed wings of Burma's numerous minority groups have been fighting from their jungle bases ever since and, although many factions have reached temporary ceasefire agreements with the Burmese junta, **persecution** of minority peoples continues. The Karen, whose homeland state of Kawthulay borders northwest Thailand from Mae Sariang down to Three Pagodas Pass, have been particularly vulnerable: one of their armed factions, the Karen National Union (KNU), are the only major rebel group not to have reached a formal ceasefire agreement with the junta. (The Karen are distinct from the Karenni, or Red Karen, whose homeland is north of Kawthulay and borders Thailand's Mae Hong Song province.) Common tactics employed by the Burmese army against minority groups include the forcible razing and relocation of villages, systematic murder, rape and robbery, and the rounding-up of slave labour.

As a result, as many as one thousand Burmese are thought to flee across the Thai border every month, the majority of them Karen. Of the 135,000 registered refugees living at the ten **refugee camps** on the Thai side of the border in May 2009, 61 percent were Karen. One of the biggest camps near Mae Sot is the village-like Umpiem Mai, on the road to Umphang, which is home for about 15,000 Karen, but the largest is Mae La, near Tha Song Yang, about 60km north of Mae Sot, which houses 37,000. Following a decision in 2005 by the Thai government to finally allow

staying the night in Mae Sot; you can also organize treks to Umphang through Mae Sot tour operators. If you need to change money for the trip, you should do so in Mae Sot as there are no exchange facilities anywhere in Umphang.

Arrival and information

Mae Sot's buses and songthaews use various **transport terminals** (see map, p.300), as well as the government bus station west of town at the Thanon Indharakiri/ Highway 105 intersection. There are plenty of buses to and from Bangkok (mostly overnight), plus a few direct buses between Mae Sot and provincial capitals, but for non-Bangkok services it's often more convenient to go via Tak instead, which operates more frequent long-distance buses and runs half-hourly **minivans** to and from Mae Sot (2hr). Local services include **songthaews** to Umphang (see p.303) and to the border towns of Mae Ramat and Mae Sariang. PB Air operates flights from Bangkok (Suvarnabhumi) to Mae Sot's airport, 3km west of town.

resettlement of Burmese refugees to a third country, some of these camps are decreasing a little in size.

Registered refugees are by no means the whole story, however, as for many years **Thai government policy** has been to admit only those who are fleeing active fighting, not human-rights violations. Thailand is not a signatory to the 1951 Convention Relating to the Status of Refugees and has no legal framework for processing asylum seekers. The hundreds of thousands who have left their homeland because of politically induced economic hardship – forced labour, theft of their land and livestock, among other factors – must therefore either try to enter the refugee camps illegally, or attempt to make a living as **migrant workers**. There are an estimated 1.8 million migrants from Burma currently in Thailand. Without refugee status, these exiles are extremely vulnerable to abuse, both from corrupt officials and from exploitative employers. In Mae Sot, for example, where Burmese migrants are a mainstay of the local economy, many of them are reportedly paid as little as B70 a day (less than half Thailand's minimum wage) to work in the worst jobs available, in gem and garment factories, and as prostitutes, though recent work-permit amnesties have made it harder for police officers to further exploit the migrants. Demands for better wages and improved conditions, however, nearly always result in deportation.

Reactions in the **Thai press** to Burmese refugees are mixed, with humanitarian concerns tempered by economic hardships in Thailand and by high-profile cases of illegal Burmese workers involved in violent crimes and drug-smuggling (Burma is now one of the world's leading producers and smugglers of methamphetamines, also known as *ya baa*, or Ice, much of which finds its way into Thailand). There is often rampant negative stereotyping too, by both the press and the public. Though relations between the neighbours have been volatile ever since the Burmese razed Ayutthaya in 1767, and there are still occasional high-level political spats today, Thailand's politicians are conscious above all of Burma's potential as a lucrative trading partner. The Thai government has sometimes acted as peace broker between the junta and ethnic-minority groups, and also made a show of cracking down on Burmese dissidents and deporting thousands of migrant workers back to Burma.

For recent **news** and archive reports on the situation in Burma and on its borders, see Ⓦbnionline.net. For information on how to offer **support** to refugees from Burma, see the website of the Thai Burma Border Consortium (TBBC; Ⓦwww.tbbc.org), and further leads on p.80. A good book about the Karen struggle and the refugee situation in Mae Sot is *Restless Souls: Rebels, Refugees, Medics and Misfits* by Phil Thornton, a Mae Sot-based journalist (see p.856).

There is no TAT office here, but both *Bai Fern* and *Khrua Canadian* restaurants are good sources of local **information**, as are the guest houses.

Accommodation

Because of the many volunteers in town, most guest houses offer weekly and monthly discounts.

Bai Fern 660/ Thanon Indharakiri Ⓣ055 531349, Ⓦwww.bai-fern.com. Well-run, traveller-oriented guest house that's attached to a great restaurant. All rooms are pretty simple and share bathrooms, some have air-con: the better ones are quite large and light and are on the floor above the restaurant and in the house at the back. Wi-fi throughout. ❷

Ban Thai 740/1 Thanon Indharakiri Ⓣ055 531590, Ⓔbanthai_mth@hotmail.com. The most appealing guest house in Mae Sot occupies several traditional-style, wooden-floored houses in a peaceful garden compound (with wi-fi) at the west end of town. All rooms (fan only) are tastefully and comfortably furnished; those in the main house share bathrooms, while those in the more expensive

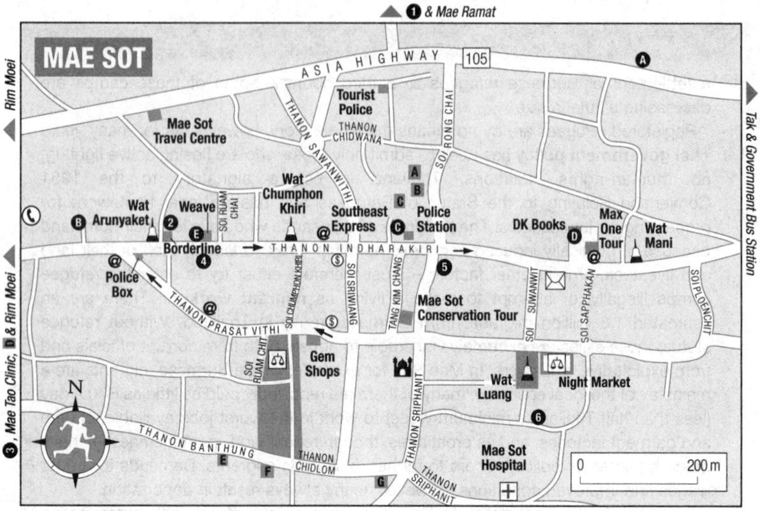

ACCOMMODATION		EATING		TRANSPORT	
Bai Fern	E	Aiya	4	Minivans to Tak	A
Ban Thai	B	Bai Fern	D	Night Buses to Bangkok	B
Centara Mae Sot Hill Resort	A	Borderline Tea Garden	2	Songthaews to Mae Sariang, Mae Ramat & Mae Salid	C
Duang Kamol (D.K.) Hotel	D	Casa Mia	3	Goverment Bus Station	D
Green Guest House	C	Khao-Mao Khao-Fang	1	Songthaews to Rim Moei	E
		Krua Canadian Restaurant	5	Songthaews to Umphang	G
		Raan Ahaan Jeh	6	Songthaews & minibuses to Pha Charoen, KM 48, Phitsanulok and Sukhothai	F

compound houses are en suite and have cable TV. Many NGO volunteers board here long-term which makes for sociable and interesting encounters in the communal garden room but also means it's a good idea to phone ahead and check for vacancies. 2–3

Centara Mae Sot Hill Resort 100 Asia Highway/ Highway 105 ⓣ055 532601, ⓦwww.centralhotelsresorts.com. The top business hotel in the area has tennis courts and a pool, though rooms are unexceptional and it's a 10min drive from the town centre. 5

Duang Kamol (D.K.) Hotel 298 Thanon Indharakiri ⓣ055 531699. The nicest and best value of the town-centre hotels is set above the bookshop of the same name, and has huge clean rooms, many of them with little balconies and some with air-con and TVs. 2–3

Green Guest House Across the stream from the Tak/Mae Sariang bus station at 460/8 Thanon Indharakiri ⓣ055 533207. Small, central, friendly little complex of ten good, clean rooms, all of them en suite. Those upstairs are nicest: large, light and with wooden floors, hot water and TV; downstairs ones are slightly cheaper and have cold water, no TV and concrete floors. Popular with long-stay NGOs. Fan 1, air-con 2

The Town

Over the last two decades the **Burmese population** of Mae Sot and its environs has swelled enormously (see box, p.298) and the Burmese influence in Mae Sot is palpable in everything from food to fashions; many of the guest houses are run by Burmese staff, who often speak good English, and the only real sights in the town are its handful of glittering Burmese-style temples.

There are currently five camps for refugees from Burma along the border to the north and south of Mae Sot, and Mae Sot itself is the headquarters for many related international **aid projects**; most of these organizations welcome donations and some are happy to receive visitors and even short-term volunteers;

ask at *Ban Thai* guest house, Borderline shop and at *Krua Canadian* and *Bai Fern* restaurants. One of the most famous organizations in Mae Sot is the **Mae Tao clinic**, which provides free medical care for around 150,000 Burmese migrants and refugees a year, focusing on those who fall outside the remit of the camps and cannot use the Thai health system. The clinic was founded in 1989 by a Karen refugee, Dr Cynthia, who has won several prestigious international awards for her work; her clinic also trains and equips "backpack teams" of mobile medics who spend months travelling through the Burmese jungle providing healthcare to internally displaced peoples. To help the clinic by giving blood or financial aid, visit the office inside the clinic compound on Thanon Indharakiri (mornings are preferable but the office opens Mon–Sat 9am–4pm; Ⓣ055 563644, Ⓦwww.maetaoclinic.org); it's about 1km west of *Ban Thai*, or 350m east of the bus station. The clinic also runs a primary and secondary school and welcomes volunteer health-workers and teachers who can commit for several months.

A number of places in town sell **Karen crafts**, including the Borderline shop (closed Mon; Ⓦwww.borderlinecollective.org) next to Wat Arunyaket on Thanon Indharakiri, which is an outlet for sarongs, bags – including ones designed for laptops and yoga mats – and other items made by Karen women living in refugee camps along the border. The nearby Weave is similar (closed Sat mornings & Sun; Ⓦwww.weave-women.org). For fashions, Burmese sarongs and daily necessities, you can't beat the well-stocked **day market** that runs south off Thanon Ruamchit. Mae Sot is most famous, however, as a good place to buy jewellery: the **gem and jade shops** on central Thanon Prasat Vithi offer a larger and less expensive selection than the stalls at the Rim Moei border market, and even if you don't intend to buy, just watching the theatrical haggling is half the fun.

Rim Moei market and the Burmese border

Frequent B15 songthaews ferry Thai traders and a meagre trickle of tourists the 6km from Mae Sot to the border at **RIM MOEI**, where a market for Burmese goods has grown up along the high street and beside the banks of the Moei River. It's a bit tacky, and not as fun to browse as Mae Sot's markets, but it's not a bad place to pick up Burmese **handicrafts**, particularly wooden artefacts like boxes and picture frames, woven Karen shoulder-bags and checked *longyis*. The best buys are chunky teak tables and chairs, most of them polished up to a fine, golden brown sheen; vendors will arrange shipping.

At the time of writing, access to the Burmese village of **Myawaddy**, across the Thailand–Burma Friendship Bridge on the opposite bank of the Moei River, is open to any foreign national for a fee of B500, payable at the bridge, though foreign visitors are allowed no further **into Burma** than this, and must return to Thailand on the same day. When coming back through Thai customs (daily 6.30am–6.30pm; last exit from Burma at 5.30pm Thai time, 5pm Burmese time, and last entry into Thailand at 6pm) you will automatically be given a new Thai visa on the spot (currently only for fifteen days; see p.36). There's nothing much to see in Myawaddy save for an awful lot of samlor drivers touting for business, a few places to eat and a number of clothes stalls and the odd lacquerware outlet. Mingalabra Tour, based at Mae Sot Travel Centre (Ⓣ081 474283, Ⓔmingalabra@yahoo.com), does trips to Myawaddy that include visits to several temples and the market (B1000 per car plus Burmese visa fee).

Around Mae Sot

There are several minor caves and waterfalls **around Mae Sot**, which are easy enough to explore if you have your own transport, though none can compare with Umphang's far mightier Thi Lor Su Falls. Borderline carries detailed route descriptions for cyclists and rents good mountain-bikes (B100).

Head north out of Mae Sot, along Highway 105 towards Mae Ramat, then take a side road at around kilometre-stone 13 for 7km to reach the three-tiered **Mae Kasa Falls** (rainy season only) and hot springs. Much further north, just after kilometre-stone 95 on Highway 105, a sign directs you the 2km off the highway to the enormous eight-hundred-metre-deep bat-cave, **Tham Mae Usu** (inaccessible July–Oct because of flooding). South out of town, off Route 1090 to Umphang, the 97 tiers of **Pha Charoen Falls** are 41km from Mae Sot. A couple of kilometres on from the falls, **Highland Farm Gibbon Sanctuary** (Ⓣ089 958 0821, Ⓦwww.highland-farm.org) cares for over forty injured and abandoned gibbons, most of whom have been rescued from abusive owners and are unable to live in the wild. The sanctuary welcomes day-trippers and homestay visitors (minimum stay three nights full-board; $25 per person per day), and also offers one-month placements ($750 all-inclusive). It's located beside the road at kilometre-stone 42.8. To get to the falls or the sanctuary (known as Baan Farang), take any songthaew bound for kilometre-stone 48 from the depot on the southern edge of Mae Sot.

Eco-conscious Mae Sot Conservation Tour (see p.305) runs **trips** to the upland jungle around Mae Lamao, home to Karen and Hmong hill tribes, about 25km east of Mae Sot off Highway 105. The jungle-craft day-trip includes a two-hour trek and whitewater - rafting (B2100, minimum four people); the overnight version adds a stay in a Karen village plus a side-trip to the gibbon sanctuary (B3900). They also do a day-trip featuring the Karen village of Mae Salao, a two-hour trek, and the Mae Kasa hot springs (B2100). Another interesting overnight adventure, unique to SP Tour at the Mae Sot Travel Centre (see p.305) takes you to the Mae Usu caves and then by longtail boat up to the Karen village of Sop Moei, south of Mae Sam Laeb (see p.383), at the confluence of the Moei and Salween rivers (B3500).

Eating and drinking

Thanon Prasat Vithi is well stocked with noodle shops and night-market stalls, there's lots of Muslim and Burmese food for sale in the market, and the NGO presence ensures a good spread of **restaurants** catering to Western palates. The NGO **bars** tend to change names and owners quite frequently, but are generally convivial places with garden seating and perhaps big-screen sports, wi-fi, regular live music, quiz nights or similar: you should find several along the stretch of Thanon Indharakiri running west from Wat Arunyaket to Thanon Don Kaew.

Aiya Thanon Indharakiri. Famous for its great Thai and Burmese food, including especially good, spiced Burmese curries (from B60), and Pennyworth chopped watercress and fried onion salad. Live music Fri & Sat evenings. Daily 4–10pm.

Bai Fern 660/2 Thanon Indharakiri. Recommended restaurant attached to the guest house of the same name, which serves some of the most imaginative food in the region. The menu (from B60–80) includes pepper steaks served with a variety of unusual sauces, salmon salad, authentic Italian carbonara (B120), traditional Thai curries and lots of vegetarian options, as well as brownies, apple pie, chocolate cake and mixed-grain bread. Daily 7am–10pm.

Borderline Tea Garden Thanon Indharakiri. In the garden at the back of their fair-trade handicrafts shop, this very relaxed café serves cheap Burmese snacks (B30) – vegetable wraps with lime sauce, potato curry with flat bread – Burmese tea, lemon-grass and other juices, sells secondhand books and runs cookery classes (see below). Tues–Fri 9am–6pm, Sat & Sun 8am–6pm.

Casa Mia Thanon Don Kaew, 5min walk past *Ban Thai* guest house. A favourite with NGOs for its twenty different home-made pastas, including an especially delicious spicy tortellini pomodoro, and another twenty pizzas. Also does a big range of Thai dishes, salads, veggie options and a daily roster of cakes and desserts – lime cheesecake, banoffee pie and the like. Most mains B30–90.

Khao-Mao Khao-Fang Out of town, 2km north towards Mae Ramat up Highway 105. A garden restaurant extraordinaire, where the artfully landscaped cascades, rivulets, rock features and mature trees make you feel as if you're sitting in a primeval forest film set, especially at night when sea-green lighting adds to the effect. A popular spot for dates and VIP lunches, it serves fairly pricey food that's nothing special, but the cocktails are fun and as one of Mae Sot's most famous attractions, it's worth the hassle to get here. During the day you could use the Mae Ramat/Mae Sariang songthaew service, but after dark you'll need your own transport.

Krua Canadian Restaurant Near the police station, just off Thanon Indharakiri. There's a great menu of delicious dishes at this NGO favourite (mostly B60–80), including local specialities such as stir-fried frog and bird curry, mango catfish salad and *matsaman* curries, plus tofu steak, imported steaks and Mexican enchiladas. Also serves several blends of local hill-tribe coffee, plus a long menu of veggie options. DVD screenings in the evening.

Raan Ahaan Jeh Off Thanon Sriphanit. Tiny vegetarian food shop serving ultra-cheap Thai veggie curries with rice (B20–30) daily until about 3pm.

Listings

Air tickets Domestic and international air tickets at SE Southeast Express internet centre and shipping agent, 522 Thanon Indharakiri ⓣ055 547048, ⓔse.southeastexpress@gmail.com.

Bicycle, car and motorbike rental Most guest houses have rental bicycles for guests. *Bai Fern* restaurant rents cars, motorbikes and bicycles and Borderline shop has good mountain-bikes. Mae Sot Travel Centre (see p.305) can arrange a car plus driver service to Umphang and back (B5000 for three days).

Cookery lessons Learn how to rustle up Shan, Karen and Burmese dishes at *Borderline Tea Garden* (8am–noon; B450–600).

Emergencies For all emergencies, call the tourist police on the free, 24hr phoneline ⓣ1155, or contact them at the police station on Thanon Indharakiri (ⓣ055 533523).

Hospitals Mae Sot Hospital is on the southeastern edge of town (ⓣ055 531970) and Pha Wawa Hospital is on the southwestern edge (ⓣ055 533912).

Immigration office At Rim Moei border crossing.

Language lessons Thai lessons through *Krua Canadian Restaurant*. Burmese lessons available through most guest houses and several restaurants.

Massage Herbal saunas (3–7pm) at Wat Mani, on Thanon Indharakiri.

Umphang

Even if you don't fancy doing a trek, consider making the spectacular trip 164km south from Mae Sot to the village of **UMPHANG**, both for the stunning mountain scenery you'll encounter along the way, and for the buzz of being in such an isolated part of Thailand. Surrounded by mountains and situated at the confluence of the Mae Khlong and Umphang rivers, Umphang itself is small and very quiet, made up of little more than a thousand or so wooden houses and a wat. It won't take long to explore the minute grid of narrow roads that bisects the village, but independent tourists are still relatively rare here, so communication could be a challenge. Bring some warm clothes as it can get pretty cool at night and in the early mornings – and the songthaew ride from Mae Sot is often windy.

Arrival and transport

Unless you've arranged a trek with a Mae Sot operator, the only access to Umphang is by **songthaew** from Mae Sot (hourly 7.30am–3.30pm; B140, or

Trekking around Umphang

Unlike treks further north around Chiang Mai, **treks around Umphang** are more about wilderness than hill-tribe villages and are far more popular with Thai tourists than farangs. The big highlight is the three-tiered, two-hundred-metre-high **Tee Lor Su Waterfall** (Nam Tok Thilawsu), star feature of the Umphang Wildlife Sanctuary (entry B200), which, unusually for Thailand, flows all year round. It's at its most thunderous just after the rainy season in November, when it can extend to a dramatic 400m across. During this period you can swim in the beautifully blue lower pool, but trails can still be muddy, which makes for tough going; trek leaders recommend wearing Wellington boots (best bought in Mae Sot, as they're hard to find in Umphang). One stretch of the route becomes so muddy during and just after the rainy season that it's impassable to human feet and needs to be done on elephant-back, a pretty uncomfortable ride of three to four hours. Nonetheless, the best **season** for trekking is November through February, even if the nights get pretty chilly. From December to April (the dry season), it's usually possible to climb to one of the waterfall's upper tiers, mud permitting. Around the falls, the vegetation is mainly montane forest, home to numerous varieties of orchid, and plenty of commonly encountered monkeys and hornbills, plus an elusive band of wild elephants.

Access to the falls is strictly controlled by national park rangers, who forbid visitors from taking food or plastic water bottles beyond the ranger station and campsite, which is 1.5km from the falls. As yet the number of visitors is reasonably small – except on public holidays, during school holidays and on some weekends, when Thai trippers flood the area. Trekkers reach Tee Lor Su Falls via a fairly challenging combination of rafting and walking, but from November 1 to May 30 the **4X4 road** to the ranger station is opened to the public, which means you only have to walk the 1.5km route to the falls; the road is currently being upgraded so from 2010 or so should be accessible all year. Some tour operators offer the car-plus-hike option as a day-trip from Umphang, usually throwing in a rafting session as well.

A **typical trek** to Tee Lor Su lasts three days and follows something like this increasingly standard itinerary. Day one: rafting down the Mae Khlong River via Tee Lor Jor Falls and some striking honeycombed cliffs; then a 9km trek (3hr) to the official campsite near Tee Lor Su Falls. Day two: morning at the falls, then a two-hour trek to a homestay at the Karen village of Khotha. Day three: a three-hour elephant ride (or trek) to Mae Lamoong junction; return to Umphang by car. Some trekkers find the three-day itinerary too baggy, with quite a lot of empty time at day's end (bring a book), so if you want a more challenging experience try to persuade your trekking agency to cover the same itinerary in two days. **Prices** start at about B2700 per person (B3200 with elephant riding) for the two-day Tee Lor Su trek (minimum two people) or B3000/3500 for three days. Add about B1000 per person for treks arranged to include transport to and from Mae Sot. Prices do vary between operators: smaller outfits can't afford to undercut the big operators and cost savings can mean lower wages – and morale – for guides. In Umphang the best time to contact **trek leaders** at the smaller outfits is often after about 4pm, when they've returned from their last trip. Guides should provide tents, bedrolls, mosquito nets and sleeping bags, plus food and drinking water; trekkers may be asked to help carry some of the gear.

Although Tee Lor Su is the most famous destination in the Umphang area, other programmes are available on request. From June through October there's **white-water rafting** from the Karen village of **Umphang Khi** via the forty-plus rapids of the

B170 if you're lucky enough to get the front seat). The drive generally takes about four hours and for the first hour proceeds in a fairly gentle fashion through the maize, cabbage and banana plantations of the Moei valley. The fun really begins when you start climbing into the mountains and the road – accurately dubbed

Umphang River, which can also include a fairly long trek and a night in the village. Alternatively, there are one- and two-day rafting trips to **Thi Lor Leh Falls**, which involve four to eight hours' rafting (depending on water levels) via a series of cataracts along the Mae Khlong River, and the possibility of a seven-hour trek on the second day. For bird-spotting, ask about trips to Thung Yai Naresuan.

Mae Sot trekking operators

Khun Om ⓣ081 785 2095, ⓦwww.geocities.com/no4guesthouse. The treks run by the taciturn Khun Om get good reviews. As well as the standard Tee Lor Su programme he does an extended five-day, four-night version featuring a hearty climb up Doi Phuwatoo (B5500) as well as – his *pièce de résistance* – a seven-day expedition all the way down to Sangkhlaburi for US$400 per person.

Mae Sot Conservation Tour 415/17 Thanon Tang Kim Chang ⓣ055 532818 (Mon–Sat 9am–5pm), ⓣ087 842 8031 (Sun), ⓔmaesotco@hotmail.com. Standard Tee Lor Su programmes.

SP Tour At the Mae Sot Travel Centre, 14/21 Asia Highway (Highway 105) ⓣ055 531409, ⓦwww.umphanghill.com. The Mae Sot branch of Umphang Hill (see below).

Umphang trekking operators

The main English-speaking trek leaders operating out of Umphang at the time of writing are listed below, but you can also arrange treks through staff at *Boonyaporn Garden Hut* (phone English-speaker Dac ⓣ089 568 5273) and *Phu Doi Campsite*. There are **no exchange facilities** in Umphang so you must bring enough cash to cover the cost of your trek.

BL Tour 1/438 Thanon Umphang-Palata ⓣ055 561021, ⓔboonlumtour_@hotmail.com. Ask for English speakers Oi or Johnny. Well-priced two- and three-day trips to Tee Lor Su; happy to do the two-day version, omitting the Khotha homestay.

Mr Boonchuay 360 Thanon Pravitpaiwan ⓣ055 561020, ⓔboonchuay_umpang@hotmail.com. Umphang-born and bred, Mr Boonchuay knows the area well and has a good reputation; his English is not perfect, but he has English-speaking guides. Offers standard Tee Lor Su programme. Trekkers can stay in the basic concrete rooms behind his office (B200 per double) or in nicer bungalows down by the river (B250 per double).

Paddle & Trek Thanon Umphang-Palata ⓣ089 958 9374, ⓔtom_trek@hotmail.com. Well-thought-out itineraries in addition to the Thi Lor Su classic include two-nighters based in the Karen village of Khotha that feature a trek to the twin lakes near Thipoji in addition to Thi Lor Su. Also does kayaking on the Bhumipol Dam reservoir north of Mae Sot and tailor-made itineraries on request.

Trekker Hill Off Thanon Pravitpaiwan ⓣ055 561090, ⓔtj_tour@hotmail.com. Mr Tee runs three- and four-day treks to Tee Lor Su and can also arrange dry-season drive-trek-and-raft tours to Tee Lor Su, one-day raft trips around Umphang Khi, and day-trips to view Doi Hua Mot mountain range (B300). Offers accommodation for trekkers in simple, en-suite double bungalows at B250 and B100 dorm beds.

Umphang Hill At *Umphang Hill Resort*, 99 Thanon Umphang-Palata ⓣ055 561063, ⓦwww.umphanghill.com. The biggest outfit in the area offers eleven itineraries and tailor-made permutations. From Dec–May, with advance notice, they can also arrange a challenging seven-day trek to Sangkhlaburi (B15,000 per person).

the "**Sky Highway**" – careers round the edges of steep-sided valleys, undulating like a fairground rollercoaster (there are said to be 1219 bends in all). The scenery is glorious, but if you're prone to car sickness, dose up on preventative tablets as the ride can be very unpleasant: the songthaews get so crammed with people and produce that there's often no possibility of distracting yourself by staring out the window. Karen, Akha, Lisu and Hmong people live in the few hamlets along the route, many growing cabbages along the cleared lower slopes with the help of government incentives (part of a national campaign to steer upland farmers away from the opium trade). The **Hmong** in particular are easily recognized by their distinctive embroidered jackets and skirts edged in bright pink, red and blue bands (see p.847). In 2000, the local **Karen** population mushroomed when three refugee camps from the Rim Moei area were relocated to the purpose-built village of Umpiem Mai alongside the Sky Highway midway between Mae Sot and Umphang (see box, p.298). As of December 2008, Umpiem Mai was home to 15,000 Karen refugees. In fact the Umphang region was inhabited by Karen hill tribes before the Thais came to settle in the area in the early twentieth century; later when the Thais began trading in earnest with their neighbours across the Burmese border, the Karen traders from Burma used to carry their identification documents into Thailand in a bamboo container which they called an "umpha" – this is believed to be the origin of the name Umphang.

There's no official **motorbike rental** in Umphang, but some guest-house owners will oblige. When it comes to public transport, Umphang is effectively a dead end, so the only way to travel on from here is to go **back to Mae Sot** first. **Songthaews** to Mae Sot leave at least hourly until noon from the top of the town, but it's usual for guest houses to phone ahead and get the songthaew to pick you up. After noon you'll probably need to charter the whole vehicle.

Accommodation

As most of the **accommodation** in Umphang is geared towards trekkers in transit, charges are usually per person rather than per room; the categories

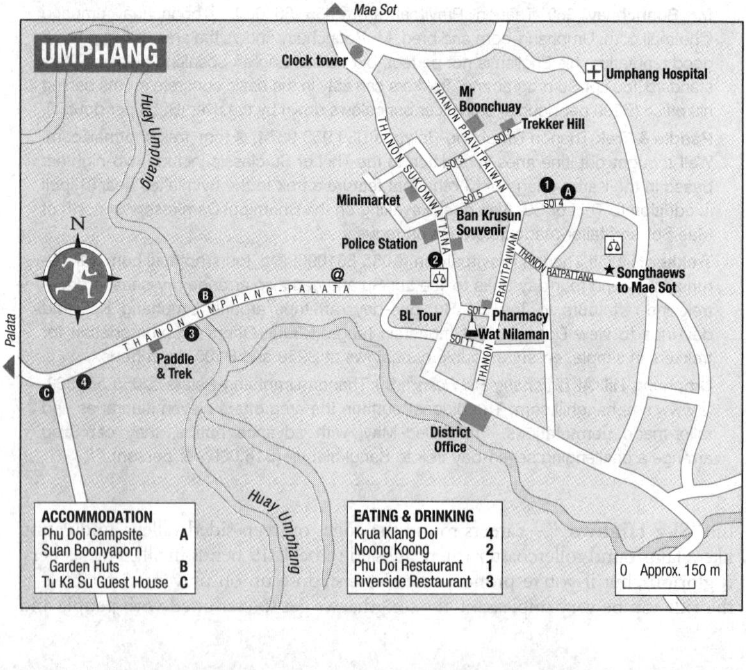

▲ Tee Lor Su Waterfall near Umphang

listed below are for two people sharing, so expect to pay half if you're on your own. Most trekking companies have their own accommodation (see p.304).

Phu Doi Campsite Prawatpriwan Soi 4 ⓣ055 561049, ⓦwww.phudoi.com. Decent set of comfortable en-suite fan rooms in a couple of wooden houses with verandas overlooking a pond, plus some rooms above the office. ③

Suan Boonyaporn Garden Huts 106 Thanon Umphang-Palata ⓣ055 561093. A spread of accommodation options, set around a pretty riverside flower garden, ranging from fairly simple wooden huts with shared facilities to quite attractive wooden bungalows with pretty basic bathrooms but fronted by decks and partial river-views. Shared bathroom ①, en suite ②–⑤

Tu Ka Su Guest House 129 Thanon Umphang-Palata ⓣ055 561295, ⓦwww.tukasu.net. In a pretty garden up the hill from the river, this quite stylish place is the most attractive in Umphang and offers nicely designed en-suite wooden cabins, with TV; some have cute, semi-garden-style bathrooms. ④

Eating

There are several **places to eat** along Thanon Umphang-Palata, including *Krua Klang Doi* just east of *Tu Ka Su*, which does good cheap Thai standards and stays open late, and the riverside restaurant opposite *Boonyaporn Garden Huts*, which is similar and a popular spot for beer. Elsewhere, Ban Krusun Souvenir Shop does cappuccinos and lattes, *Phu Doi Restaurant* has an English-language menu of curries and meat-over-rice dishes; *Noong Koong* does cheap noodles during the day; and at dusk night-time foodstalls set up close by the temple.

Travel details

Trains

Ayutthaya to: Bangkok Hualamphong Station (33 daily; 1hr 30min–2hr); Chiang Mai (6 daily; 10hr 45min–13hr 10min); Lopburi (15 daily; 45min–1hr 30min); Nong Khai (3 daily; 9hr 30min); Phitsanulok (12 daily; 4hr 30min–5hr 30min); Ubon Ratchathani (7 daily; 8hr 30min–10hr).

Bang Pa-In to: Ayutthaya (7 daily; 15min); Bangkok Hualamphong (8 daily; 1hr 30min).
Kanchanaburi to: Bangkok Thonburi (2 daily; 2hr 45min); Nakhon Pathom (2 daily; 1hr 40min); Nam Tok (3 daily; 2hr 20min).
Lopburi to: Ayutthaya (16 daily; 45min–1hr 30min); Bangkok Hualamphong Station (14 daily; 2hr 30min–3hr); Chiang Mai (6 daily; 10–12hr); Phitsanulok (12 daily; 3hr–5hr 15min).
Nakhon Pathom to: Bangkok Hualamphong (13 daily; 1hr 40min); Bangkok Thonburi (8 daily; 1hr 10min); Butterworth (Malaysia; 1 daily; 19hr 50min); Chumphon (11 daily; 5hr 45min–8hr 30min); Hat Yai (5 daily; 12hr 15min–16hr); Hua Hin (12 daily; 2hr 15min–3hr 15min); Kanchanaburi (2 daily; 1hr 35min); Nakhon Si Thammarat (2 daily; 15hr); Nam Tok (2 daily; 3hr 30min); Padang Besar (Malaysia; 1 daily; 15hr 30min); Phetchaburi (10 daily; 1hr 20min–2hr 20min); Sungai Kolok (2 daily; 18hr 30min–20hr); Surat Thani (11 daily; 8hr–11hr 30min); Trang (2 daily; 13hr 30min).
Nam Tok to: Bangkok Thonburi (2 daily; 4hr 45min).
Phitsanulok to: Ayutthaya (11 daily; 4hr 30min–5hr 30min); Bangkok Hualamphong (11 daily; 5hr 30min–8hr); Chiang Mai (6 daily; 5hr 50min–7hr 40min); Lamphun (6 daily; 5hr 40min–7hr 20min); Lopburi (11 daily; 3hr–5hr 15min).
Samut Sakhon (Mahachai) to: Bangkok Wongwian Yai (17 daily; 1hr).
Samut Songkhram (Maeklong) to: Ban Laem (4 daily; 1hr).

Buses

Ayutthaya to: Bangkok (every 20min; 2hr); Chiang Mai (14 daily; 9hr); Chiang Rai (13 daily; 12hr); Lopburi (every 20min; 2hr); Phitsanulok (10 daily; 5hr); Sukhothai (11 daily; 6hr); Suphanburi (every 30min; 1hr); Tak (2 daily; 6hr).
Bang Pa-In to: Bangkok (every 30min; 2hr).
Damnoen Saduak to: Bangkok (every 20min; 2hr).
Kamphaeng Phet to: Bangkok (7 daily; 6hr 30min); Sukhothai (hourly; 1hr–1hr 30min); Tak (hourly; 1hr).
Kanchanaburi to: Bangkok (Northern Bus Terminal; 9 daily; 2hr 30min); Bangkok (Southern Bus Terminal; every 15min; 2hr); Erawan (every 50min; 2hr); Nam Tok (every 30min; 1hr 30min); Ratchaburi (every 15min; 2hr); Sai Yok (every 30min; 2hr 30min); Sangkhlaburi (14 daily; 3–6hr); Suphanburi (every 20min; 2hr); Thong Pha Phum (every 30min; 3hr).
Lopburi to: Ayutthaya (every 20min; 2hr); Bangkok (every 20min; 2–3hr), via Wat Phra Phutthabat (30min); Chiang Mai (5 daily; 9hr); Khorat (15 daily; 3hr 30min); Phitsanulok (3 daily; 4hr); Suphanburi (hourly; 3hr).
Mae Sot to: Bangkok (13 daily; 8hr 30min); Chiang Mai (2 daily; 6hr 30min–7hr 30min); Chiang Rai (2 daily; 11hr); Mae Ramat (every 30min; 45min); Mae Sai (2 daily; 12hr); Mae Sariang (hourly 6am–noon; 5hr); Phitsanulok (9 daily; 45hr); Sukhothai (9 daily; 2hr 30min–3hr); Tak (every 30min; 2hr); Umphang (hourly 7.30am–3pm; 4–5hr).
Nakhon Pathom to: Bangkok (every 10min; 40min–1hr 20min); Damnoen Saduak (every 20min; 1hr); Kanchanaburi (every 10min; 1hr 45min).
Nam Tok to: Sangkhlaburi (4 daily; 3hr 30min).
Phitsanulok to: Bangkok (up to 40 daily; 5–6hr); Chiang Mai (up to 18 daily; 5–6hr); Chiang Rai (17 daily; 6–7hr); Kamphaeng Phet (hourly; 3hr); Khon Kaen (10 daily; 5–6hr); Khorat/Nakhon Ratchasima (21 daily; 6–7hr); Loei (15 daily; 5hr); Lomsak (hourly; 2hr); Mae Sot (7 daily; 3hr 15min–5hr); Phrae (7 daily; 2–3hr); Sukhothai (at least every 40min; 1hr 30min); Tak (every 30min; 3hr); Ubon Ratchathani (7 daily; 12hr); Udon Thani (5 daily; 7hr).
Sangkhlaburi to: Bangkok (4 daily; 7hr).
Samut Songkhram to: Bangkok (every 20min; 1hr 30min).
Sukhothai to: Ayutthaya (14 daily; 6hr); Bangkok (up to 23 daily; 6–7hr); Chiang Mai (up to 16 daily; 5–6hr); Chiang Rai (4 daily; 8–9hr); Kamphaeng Phet (14 daily; 1hr–1hr 30min); Khon Kaen (7 daily; 6–7hr); Lampang (16 daily; 4hr); Mae Sot (9 daily; 2hr 30min–3hr); Nan (2 daily; 7hr); Phitsanulok (every 30min; 1hr); Phrae (2 daily; 4hr); Si Satchanalai (every 30min; 1hr–1hr 45min); Tak (every 30min; 1hr 30min).
Tak to: Bangkok (13 daily; 7hr); Chiang Mai (8 daily; 4–6hr); Kamphaeng Phet (hourly; 1hr); Mae Sot (every 30min; 2hr); Phitsanulok (every 30min; 3hr); Sukhothai (every 30min; 1hr 30min).

Flights

Mae Sot to: Bangkok (3 weekly; 1hr 30min).
Phitsanulok to: Bangkok (2 daily; 45min).
Sukhothai to: Bangkok (2 daily; 1hr 25min).

3

The north

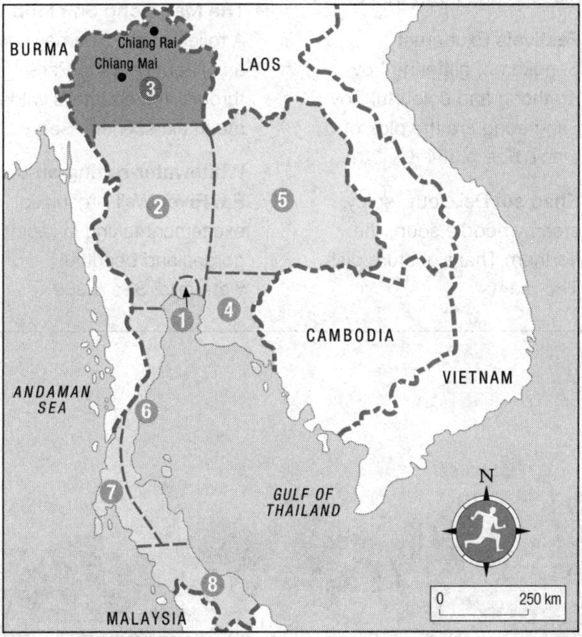
Chiang Rai
BURMA
Chiang Mai
LAOS
3
2
5
1
4
CAMBODIA
VIETNAM
ANDAMAN SEA
6
7
GULF OF THAILAND
N
8
0
250 km
MALAYSIA

CHAPTER 3

Highlights

* **Hill-tribe trekking** A chance to visit these fascinating peoples and explore the dramatic countryside. See p.315
* **Chiang Mai** Old-town temples, cookery courses, the best of Thai crafts, fine restaurants – still a great place to hang out. See p.318
* **Festivals** Exuberant Songkhran, glittering Loy Krathong and colourful Poy Sang Long are the pick of many. See p.334 & p.389
* **Khao soi** Delicious, spicy, creamy noodle soup, the northern Thai signature dish. See p.340
* **Wat Phra That Doi Suthep** Towering views from this stunning example of temple architecture. See p.351
* **Nan** An underrated all-rounder, offering beautiful temple murals, handicrafts and mountainscapes. See p.371
* **The Mae Hong Son loop** A roller-coaster journey – with a chill-out break in Pai – through the country's wildest mountain scenery. See p.377
* **Whitewater-rafting on the Pai River** Well-organized excitement taking in rapids, gorges and beautiful waterfalls. See p.389

▲ Wat Chong Kham and Wat Chong Klang, Mae Hong Son

3

The north

Travelling up by rail through the central plains, there's no mistaking when you've reached the **north** of Thailand: somewhere between Uttaradit and Den Chai, the train slows almost to a halt, as if approaching a frontier post, to meet the abruptly rising mountains that continue largely unbroken to the borders of Burma and Laos. Beyond this point the climate becomes more temperate (downright cold at night between Dec and Feb – see p.11), nurturing the fertile land which gave the old kingdom of the north the name of **Lanna**, "the land of a million rice fields". Although only one-tenth of the land can be used for rice cultivation, the valley rice fields here are three times more productive than those in the dusty northeast, and the higher land yields a great variety of fruits, as well as beans, groundnuts and tobacco.

Until the beginning of the last century, Lanna was a largely independent region. On the back of its agricultural prosperity, it developed its own styles of art and architecture, which can still be seen in its flourishing temples and distinctive handicraft traditions. The north is also set apart from the rest of the country by its exuberant festivals, a cuisine which has been heavily influenced by Burma and a dialect quite distinct from central Thai. Northerners proudly call themselves *khon muang*, "people of the principalities", and their gentle sophistication is admired by the people of Bangkok, whose wealthier citizens build their holiday homes in the clean air of the north's forested mountains.

Chiang Mai, the capital and transport centre of the north, is a great place just to hang out or to prepare for a journey into the hills. For many travellers, this means joining a trek to visit one or more of the **hill tribes**, who comprise one-tenth of the north's population and are just about clinging onto the ways of life which distinguish them from one another and the Thais around them. For those with qualms about the exploitative element of this ethnological tourism, there are plenty of other, more independent options. To the west, the trip to **Mae Hong Son** takes you through the most stunning mountain scenery in the region into a land with its roots across the border in Burma, with the option of looping back through **Pai**, a laid-back, sophisticated hill-station for travellers. Bidding to rival Chiang Mai as a base for exploring the countryside is **Chiang Rai** to the north; above Chiang Rai, the northernmost tip of Thailand is marked by the Burmese border - crossing at **Mae Sai**, and the junction of Thailand, Laos and Burma at **Sop Ruak**. Fancifully dubbed the "Golden Triangle", Sop Ruak is a must on every bus party's itinerary – you're more likely to find peace and quiet among the ruins of nearby **Chiang Saen**, set on the leafy banks of the Mekong River. Few visitors backtrack south from Chiang Mai, even though the towns of **Lamphun**, **Lampang** and **Phrae** are

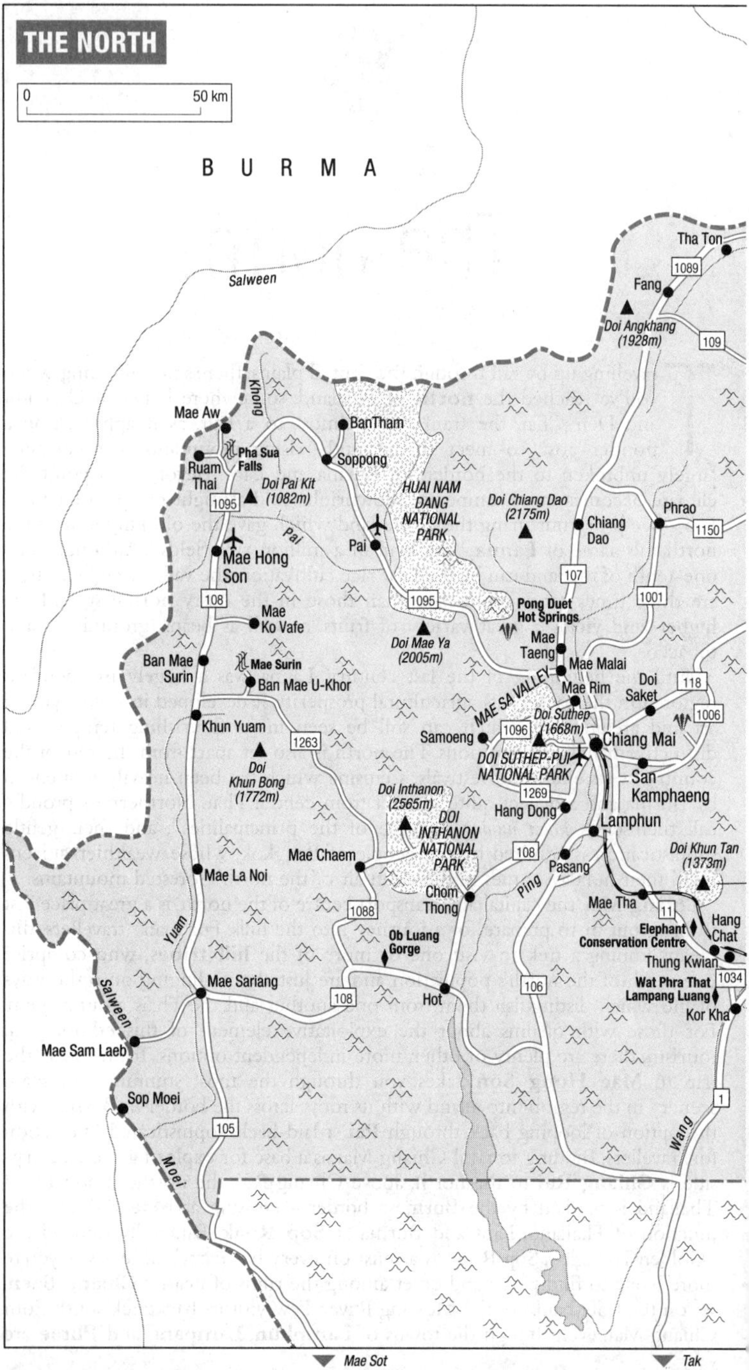
THE NORTH
0
50 km
BURMA
Salween
Tha Ton
1089
Fang
Doi Angkhang
(1928m)
109
Khong
Mae Aw
BanTham
Pha Sua
Falls
Ruam
Thai
Soppong
Doi Pai Kit
(1082m)
HUAI NAM
DANG
NATIONAL
PARK
Doi Chiang Dao
(2175m)
1095
Pai
Chiang
Dao
Phrao
1150
Mae Hong
Son
107
108
1095
1001
Pong Duet
Hot Springs
Mae
Ko Vafe
Doi Mae Ya
(2005m)
Mae
Taeng
Ban Mae
Surin
Mae Surin
Mae Malai
Ban Mae U-Khor
MAE SA VALLEY
Mae Rim
Doi
Saket
118
Khun Yuam
Doi Suthep
(1668m)
1006
1263
Samoeng
1096
Chiang Mai
Doi
Khun Bong
(1772m)
DOI SUTHEP-PUI
NATIONAL PARK
San
Kamphaeng
Doi Inthanon
(2565m)
1269
Hang Dong
Lamphun
DOI
INTHANON
NATIONAL
PARK
Mae Chaem
108
Pasang
Doi Khun Tan
(1373m)
Mae La Noi
Ping
Chom
Thong
Mae Tha
1088
11
Hang
Chat
Yuam
Elephant
Conservation Centre
Ob Luang
Gorge
Thung Kwian
Mae Sariang
Wat Phra That
Lampang Luang
1034
108
Hot
106
Kor Kha
Salween
Mae Sam Laeb
Sop Moei
1
105
Wang
Moei
Mae Sot
Tak

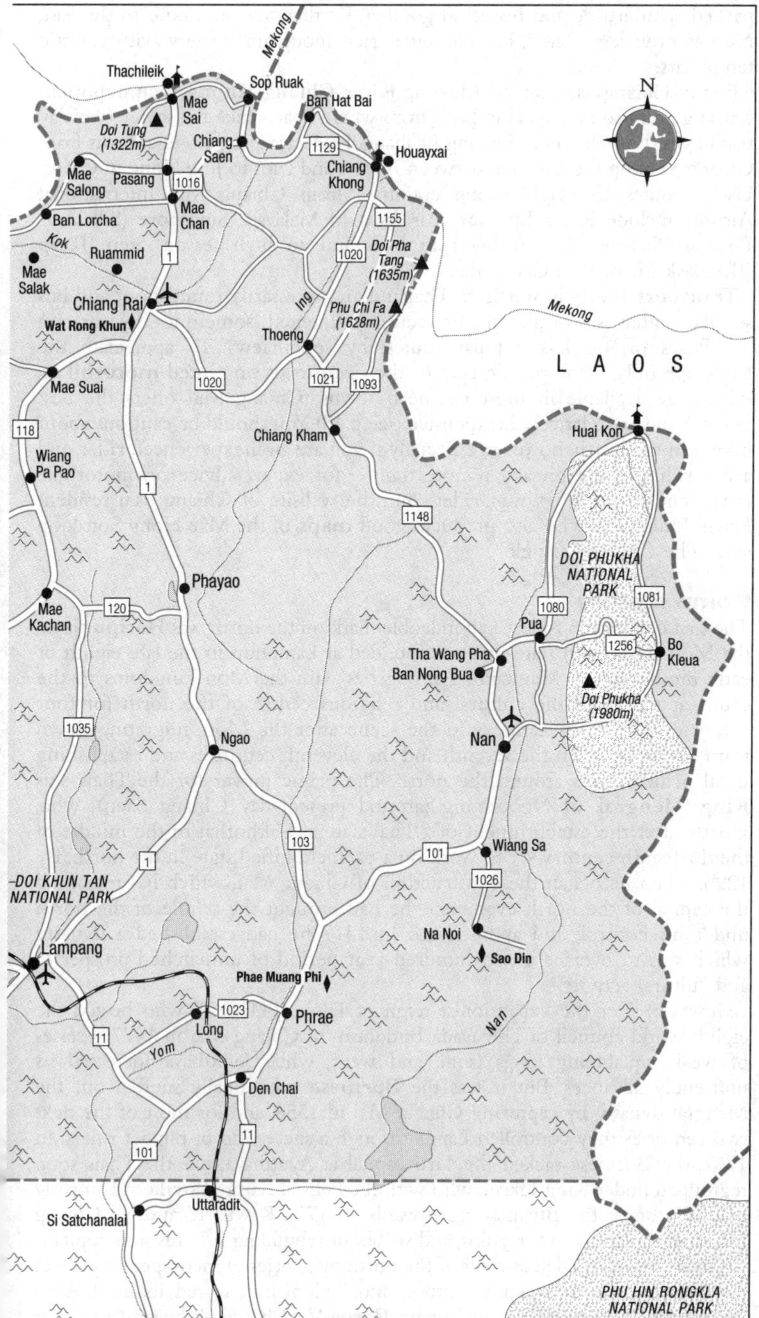
Mekong
Thachileik
Sop Ruak
Mae
Sai
Ban Hat Bai
Doi Tung
(1322m)
Chiang
Saen
1129
Houayxai
Mae
Salong
Pasang
1016
Chiang
Khong
Mae
Chan
Ban Lorcha
1155
Kok
Ruammid
1020
Doi Pha
Tang
(1635m)
Mae
Salak
1
Chiang Rai
Phu Chi Fa
(1628m)
Mekong
Ing
Wat Rong Khun
Thoeng
LAOS
Mae Suai
1020
1021
1093
118
Chiang Kham
Huai Kon
Wiang
Pa Pao
1
1148
DOI PHUKHA
NATIONAL
PARK
Phayao
1080
1081
Mae
Kachan
120
Pua
1256
Bo
Kleua
Tha Wang Pha
Ban Nong Bua
Doi Phukha
(1980m)
1035
Nan
Ngao
103
101
Wiang Sa
1
1026
DOI KHUN TAN
NATIONAL PARK
Na Noi
Lampang
Sao Din
Phae Muang Phi
1023
Phrae
Long
Nan
11
Yom
Den Chai
11
101
Uttaradit
Si Satchanalai
PHU HIN RONGKLA
NATIONAL PARK
Sukhothai
Phitsanulok

packed with artistic and historical goodies. Further out on a limb to the east, **Nan** is even less visited, but combines rich mountain scenery with eclectic temple art.

East of Chiang Saen on the Mekong River, **Chiang Khong** is an important crossing point to Houayxai in Laos, from where boats make the scenic two-day trip down the Mekong to Louang Phabang. There are also passenger boats from Chiang Saen up the Mekong between Burma and Laos to Jing Hong in China. Useful routes to neighbouring countries from Chiang Mai International Airport include Kuala Lumpur (Air Asia) in Malaysia, Singapore (Silk Air), Louang Phabang (Lao Airlines) in Laos and, in high season, Siem Reap (Bangkok Airways) in Cambodia.

Transport routes in northern Thailand are necessarily roundabout and bus services often slow, though frequent, augmented sometimes by air-con minibuses or, on less popular routes, by songthaews. To appreciate the landscape fully, many people take to the open roads on rented **motorbikes**, which are available in most northern towns (Chiang Mai offers the best choice) and are relatively inexpensive (see p.48). You should be cautious about biking in the north, however, especially if you are an inexperienced rider, and avoid riding alone on any remote trails – for expert advice on motorbike travel, check out Ⓦwww.gt-rider.com, the website of Chiang Mai resident David Unkovich, who also produces good **maps** of the Mae Hong Son loop and "The Golden Triangle".

Some history

The first civilization to leave an indelible mark on the north was **Haripunjaya**, the Mon (Dvaravati) state that was founded at Lamphun in the late eighth or early ninth century. Maintaining strong ties with the Mon kingdoms to the south, it remained the cultural and religious centre of the north for four centuries. The Thais came onto the scene after the Mon, migrating down from China between the seventh and the eleventh centuries and establishing small principalities around the north. The prime mover for the Thais was **King Mengrai** of Ngon Yang (around present-day Chiang Saen), who, shortly after the establishment of a Thai state at Sukhothai in the middle of the thirteenth century, set to work on a parallel unified state in the north. By 1296, when he began the construction of Chiang Mai, which has remained the capital of the north ever since, he had brought the whole of the north under his control, and at his death in 1317 he had established a dynasty which was to oversee a two-hundred-year period of unmatched prosperity and cultural activity.

However, after the expansionist reign of Tilok (1441–87), who hosted the eighth world council of Theravada Buddhism in Chiang Mai in 1477, a series of weak, squabbling kings came and went, while Ayutthaya increased its unfriendly advances. But it was the **Burmese** who finally snuffed out the Mengrai dynasty by capturing Chiang Mai in 1558, and for most of the next two centuries they controlled Lanna through a succession of puppet rulers. In 1767, the Burmese sacked the Thai capital at Ayutthaya, but the Thais soon regrouped under King Taksin, who with the help of **King Kawila** of Lampang gradually drove the Burmese northwards. In 1774 Kawila recaptured Chiang Mai, then deserted and in ruins, and set about rebuilding it as his new capital.

Kawila was succeeded as ruler of the north by a series of incompetent princes for much of the nineteenth century, until colonialism reared its head. After Britain took control of Upper Burma, **Rama V** of Bangkok began to take an interest in the north – where, since the Bowring Treaty of 1855, the British had established lucrative logging businesses – to prevent its annexation. He forcibly moved large numbers of ethnic Thais northwards, in order to counter the British claim of sovereignty over territory occupied by Thai Yai (Shan), who also make up a large part of the population of Upper Burma. In 1877 Rama V appointed a commissioner over Chiang Mai, Lamphun and Lampang to better integrate the region with the centre, and links were further strengthened in 1921 with the arrival of the railway from Bangkok. Since then the north has built on its agricultural richness to become relatively prosperous, though the economic booms of the last two decades have been concentrated, as elsewhere in Thailand, in the towns, due in no small part to the increase in tourism. The eighty percent of Lanna's population who live in rural areas – of which the vast majority are subsistence farmers – are finding it increasingly difficult to earn a living off the soil, due to rapid population growth and land speculation for tourism and agro-industry.

Hill-tribe treks

Trekking in the mountains of north Thailand differs from trekking in most other parts of the world in that the emphasis is not primarily on the scenery but on the region's inhabitants. Northern Thailand's **hill tribes**, now numbering over 800,000 people living in around 3500 villages, have preserved their subsistence-oriented way of life with comparatively little change over thousands of years; see p.845 for more on the tribes themselves. In recent years, the term **mountain people** (a translation of the Thai *chao khao*) is increasingly used as a less condescending way to describe them; since these groups have no chief, they are technically not tribes. While some of the villages are near enough to a main road to be reached on a day-trip from a major town, to get to the other, more traditional villages usually entails joining a guided party for a few days, roughing it in a different place each night. For most visitors, however, these hardships are far outweighed by the experience of encountering peoples of so different a culture, travelling through beautiful tropical countryside and tasting the excitement of elephant riding and river rafting.

▲ Akha woman, Mae Salong

On any trek you are necessarily confronted by the **ethics** of your role. About a hundred thousand travellers now go trekking in Thailand each year, the majority heading to certain well-trodden areas such as the Mae Taeng valley, 40km northwest of Chiang Mai, and the hills around the Kok River west of Chiang Rai. Beyond the basic level of disturbance caused by any tourism, this steady flow of trekkers creates pressures for the traditionally insular hill tribes. Foreigners unfamiliar with hill-tribe customs can easily cause grave offence, especially those who go looking for drugs. Though tourism acts as a distraction from their traditional way of life, most tribespeople are genuinely welcoming and hospitable to foreigners, appreciating the contact with Westerners and the minimal material benefits which trekking brings them. Nonetheless, to minimize disruption, it's important to take a responsible attitude when trekking. While it's possible to trek independently from one or two spots such as *Cave Lodge* near Soppong, the lone trekker will learn very little without a guide as intermediary, and is far more likely to commit an unwitting offence against the local customs, so it's best to go with a sensitive and knowledgeable **guide** who has the welfare of the local people in mind, and follow the basic guidelines on etiquette outlined in the box below. If you don't fancy an organized trek in a

Trekking etiquette

As the guests, it's up to farangs to adapt to the customs of the hill tribes and not to make a nuisance of themselves. Apart from keeping an open mind and not demanding too much of your hosts, a few **simple rules** should be observed.

- Dress modestly, in long trousers or skirt (or at least knee-length shorts if you must) and a T-shirt or shirt. Getting dressed or changing your clothes in front of villagers is also offensive.
- Loud voices and boisterous behaviour are out of place. Smiling and nodding establishes good intent. A few hill-tribe phrasebooks and dictionaries are available from bookshops and you'll be a big hit if you learn some words of the relevant language.
- If travelling with a loved one, avoid displays of public affection such as kissing, which are extremely distasteful, and disrespectful, to local people.
- Look out for taboo signs (*ta-laew*), woven bamboo strips, on the ground outside the entrance to a village, on the roof above a house entrance or on a fresh tree branch; these mean a special ceremony is taking place and that you should not enter. Be careful about what you touch; in Akha villages, keep your hands off cult structures like the entrance gates and the giant swing. Ask first before entering a house, and do not step or sit on the door sill, which is often considered the domain of the house spirits. If the house has a raised floor on stilts, take off your shoes. Most hill-tribe houses contain a religious shrine: do not touch or photograph this shrine, or sit underneath it. If you are permitted to watch a ceremony, this is not an invitation to participate unless asked. Like the villagers themselves, you'll be expected to pay a fine for any violation of local customs.
- Some villagers like to be photographed, most do not. Point at your camera and nod if you want to take a photograph. Never insist if the answer is an obvious "no". Be particularly careful with the sick and the old, and with pregnant women and babies – most tribes believe cameras affect the soul of the foetus or newborn.
- Taking gifts can be dubious practice. If you want to take something, writing materials for children and clothing are welcome, as well as sewing tools (like needles) for women – ask your guide to pass any gifts to the village headman for fair distribution. However, money, sweets and cigarettes may encourage begging and create unhealthy tastes.
- Do not ask for opium, as this will offend your hosts.

group, it's possible to hire a personal guide from an agent, at a cost of about B1000 per day.

The hill tribes are big business in northern Thailand: in **Chiang Mai** there are around two hundred agencies which between them cover just about all the trekkable areas in the north. **Chiang Rai** is the second-biggest trekking centre, and agencies can also be found in Nan, Mae Sariang, Mae Hong Son, Pai, Tha Ton and Mae Salong, which usually arrange treks only to the villages in their immediate area. Guided trekking on a smaller scale than in the north is available in Umphang (see p.304), Kanchanaburi (see p.236) and Sangkhlaburi (see p.247).

The basics

The cool, dry season from November to February is the best time for treks, which can be as short as two days or as long as ten, but are typically of three or four days' duration. The standard size of a group is between five and twelve people; being part of a small group is preferable, enabling you to strike a more informative relationship with your guides and with the villagers. Everybody in the group usually sleeps on a mattress in the village's guest hut, with a guide cooking communal meals, for which some ingredients are brought from outside and others are found locally.

Each trek usually follows a regular **itinerary** established by the agency, although they can sometimes be customized, especially for smaller groups and with agencies in the smaller towns. Some itineraries are geared towards serious hikers while others go at a much gentler pace, but on all treks much of the walking will be up and down steep forested hills, often under a burning sun, so a reasonable level of fitness is required. Many treks now include a ride on an elephant and a trip on a bamboo raft – exciting to the point of being dangerous if the river is running fast. The typical three-day, two-night trek **costs** about B2000–2500 in Chiang Mai (including transport, accommodation, food and guide), sometimes less in other towns, much less without rafting and elephant-riding.

Choosing a trek

There are several features to look out for when **choosing a trek**. If you want to trek with a small group, get an assurance from your agency that you won't be tagged onto a larger group. Make sure the trek has at least two guides – a leader and a back-marker; some trekkers have been known to get lost for days after becoming separated from the rest of the group. Check exactly when the trek starts and ends and ask about transport to and from base; most treks begin with a pick-up ride out of town, but on rare occasions the trip can entail a long public bus ride. If at all possible, meet and chat with the other trekkers, as well as the guides, who should speak reasonable English and know about hill-tribe culture, especially the details of etiquette in each village. Finally, ask what food will be eaten, check how much walking is involved per day and get a copy of the route map to gauge the terrain.

While everybody and their grandmother act as **agents**, only a few know their guides personally, so choose a reputable agent or guest house. When picking an agent, you should check whether they and their guides have licences and certificates from the Tourist Authority of Thailand, which they should be able to show you: this ensures at least a minimum level of training, and provides some comeback in case of problems. Word of mouth is often the best recommendation, so if you hear of a good outfit, try it. Each trek should be **registered** with the tourist police, stating the itinerary, the duration and the participants, in case the party encounters any trouble – it's worth checking with the agency that the trek has been registered with the tourist police before departure.

What to take

The right **clothing** is the first essential on any trek. Strong boots with ankle protection are the best footwear, although in the dry season training shoes are adequate. Wear thin, loose clothes – long trousers should be worn to protect against thorns and, in the wet season, leeches – and a hat, and cover your arms if you're prone to sunburn. Antiseptic, antihistamine cream, anti-diarrhoea **medicine** and insect repellent are essential, as is a mosquito net – check if one will be provided where you're staying. At least two changes of clothing are needed, plus a sarong or towel (women in particular should bring a sarong to wash or change underneath).

If you're going on an organized trek, **water** is usually provided by the guide, as well as a small backpack. **Blankets** or, preferably, a **sleeping bag** are also supplied, but might not be warm enough in the cool season, when night-time temperatures can dip to freezing; you should bring at least a sweater, and perhaps buy a cheap, locally made balaclava to be sure of keeping the chill off.

It's wise not to take anything valuable with you; most guest houses in trekking-oriented places like Chiang Mai have safes and left-luggage rooms, but see p.324.

Chiang Mai

Although rapid economic progress in recent years has brought problems such as pollution and traffic jams, **CHIANG MAI** still manages to preserve some of the atmosphere of an ancient village alongside its modern urban sophistication. It's the kingdom's second city, with a youthful population of about 400,000 (over 60,000 of them are students), and the contrast with the maelstrom of Bangkok is pronounced: the people here are famously easy-going and even speak more slowly than their cousins in the capital, while the moated old quarter, where new buildings are limited to a height of four storeys, has retained many of its traditional wooden houses and quiet, leafy gardens. Chiang Mai's elegant temples are the primary tourist sights, but these are no pre-packaged museum pieces – they're living community centres, where you're quite likely to be approached by monks keen to chat and practise their English. Inviting craft shops, fascinating museums, good-value accommodation, rich cuisine and riverside bars further enhance the city's allure, making Chiang Mai a place that detains many travellers longer than they expected. Several colourful festivals (see box, p.334) attract throngs of visitors here too: Chiang Mai is one of the most popular places in Thailand to see in the Thai New Year – Songkhran – in mid-April, and to celebrate Loy Krathong at the full moon in November, when thousands of candles are floated down the Ping River in lotus-leaf boats.

Founded as the capital of Lanna in 1296, on a site indicated by the miraculous presence of deer and white mice, Chiang Mai – "New City" – has remained the north's most important settlement ever since. Lanna's golden age under the Mengrai dynasty, when most of the city's notable temples were founded, lasted until the Burmese captured the city in 1558. Two hundred years passed before the Thais pushed the Burmese back beyond Chiang Mai to roughly where they are now, and the **Burmese influence** is still strong – not just in art and architecture, but also in the rich curries and soups served here. After the recapture of the city, the *chao* (princes) of Chiang Mai remained nominal rulers of the north until 1939, but, with communications rapidly improving from the beginning of the last century, Chiang Mai was brought firmly into Thailand's mainstream as the region's administrative and service centre.

The traditional tourist activities in Chiang Mai are visiting the **temples** and **shopping** for handicrafts, pursuits which many find more appealing here than in the rest of Thailand. These days, increasing numbers of travellers are taking advantage of the city's relaxed feel to indulge in a burst of self-improvement, enrolling for **courses** in **cookery**, **massage** and the like (see box, p.322). However, a pilgrimage to **Doi Suthep**, the mountain to the west of town, should not be missed, to see the sacred temple and the towering views over the valley of the Ping River, when weather permits. Beyond the city limits, a number of other day-trips can be made, such as to the ancient temples of Lamphun – and, of course, Chiang Mai is the main centre for hill-tribe **trekking** (see box, p.322).

Arrival

Central Chiang Mai divides roughly into two main parts: the **old town**, surrounded by the well-maintained moat and occasional remains of the city wall, where you'll find most of the temples, and the **new town centre**, between the moat and the Ping River to the east, for hotels, shops, banks and travel agents. The main concentration of guest houses and restaurants hangs between the two, centred on the landmark of **Tha Pae Gate** (*Pratu Tha Pae*) in the middle of the east moat. On the outskirts, the town is bounded by the Superhighway and two further huge but incomplete ring roads (none of the three meets up on the west side of town, because of the airport and Doi Suthep).

Many people arrive at the **train station** (which has a left-luggage office) on Thanon Charoen Muang, just over 2km from Tha Pae Gate on the eastern side of town (Ⓣ053 244795 or 053 245363–4), or at the **Arcade bus station** on Thanon Kaeo Nawarat (Ⓣ053 242664), 3km out to the northeast. Getting from either of these to the centre is easy by songthaew or tuk-tuk (see p.323). Services from the rest of Chiang Mai province (including Tha Ton) and Lamphun end up at the **Chang Phuak bus station** on Thanon Chotana (there are embryonic plans for a third bus station out on the Superhighway). If you insist on travelling with one of the low-cost private bus companies (see p.204) on Bangkok's Thanon Khao San, find out exactly where you'll be dropped in Chiang Mai before making a booking: many of these companies' buses stop on a remote part of the Superhighway, where they "sell" their passengers to various guest-house touts. There's no obligation to go with the touts, but if you try to duck out you'll have a hard job getting downtown and you'll certainly come in for a lot of hassle. The better guest houses – certainly including those we've listed – don't involve themselves in such shenanigans.

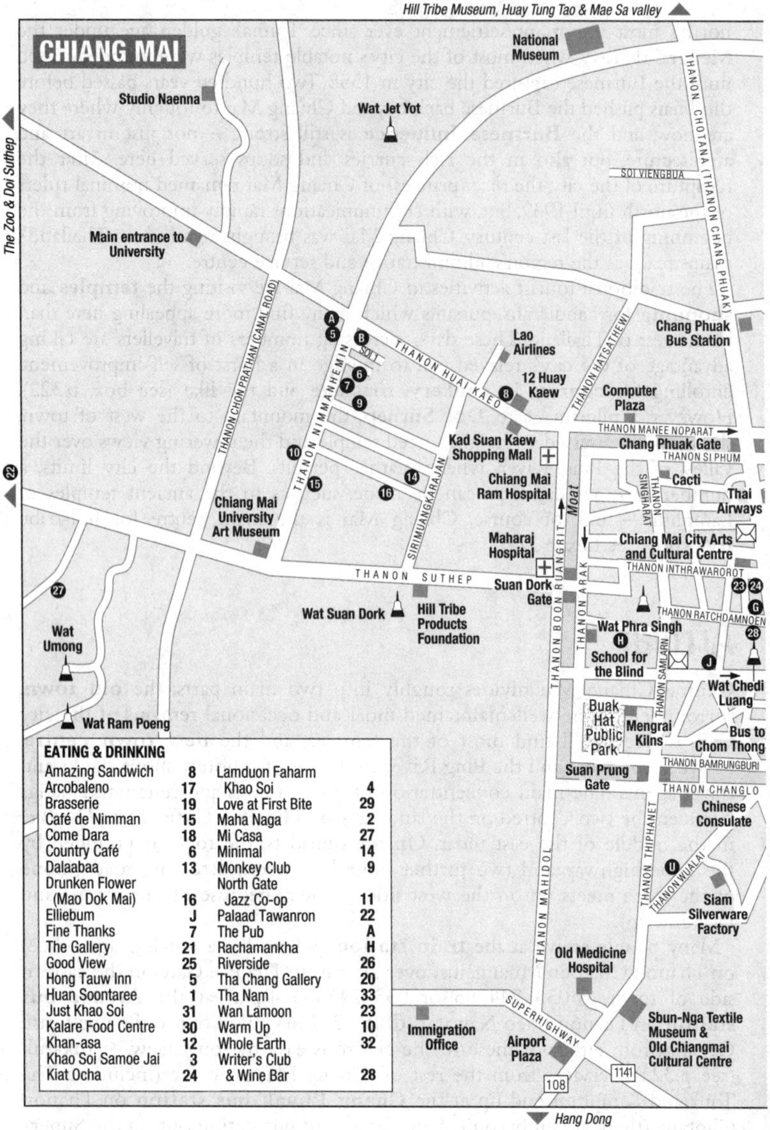

Arriving at the **airport**, 3km southwest of the centre (☎053 270222–33), you'll find in the international terminal a currency exchange booth and a post office (daily 8.30am–8pm); in the domestic terminal, an internet café, a tourist police booth, a Thai Hotels Association accommodation booking desk (☎053 280505), with prices generally cheaper than rack rates, a restaurant and a bookshop; both terminals have cafés, left-luggage facilities (B50 per day) and Avis car rental offices (☎053 201574). Metered taxis charge around B120 to take you to Tha Pae Gate in the city centre.

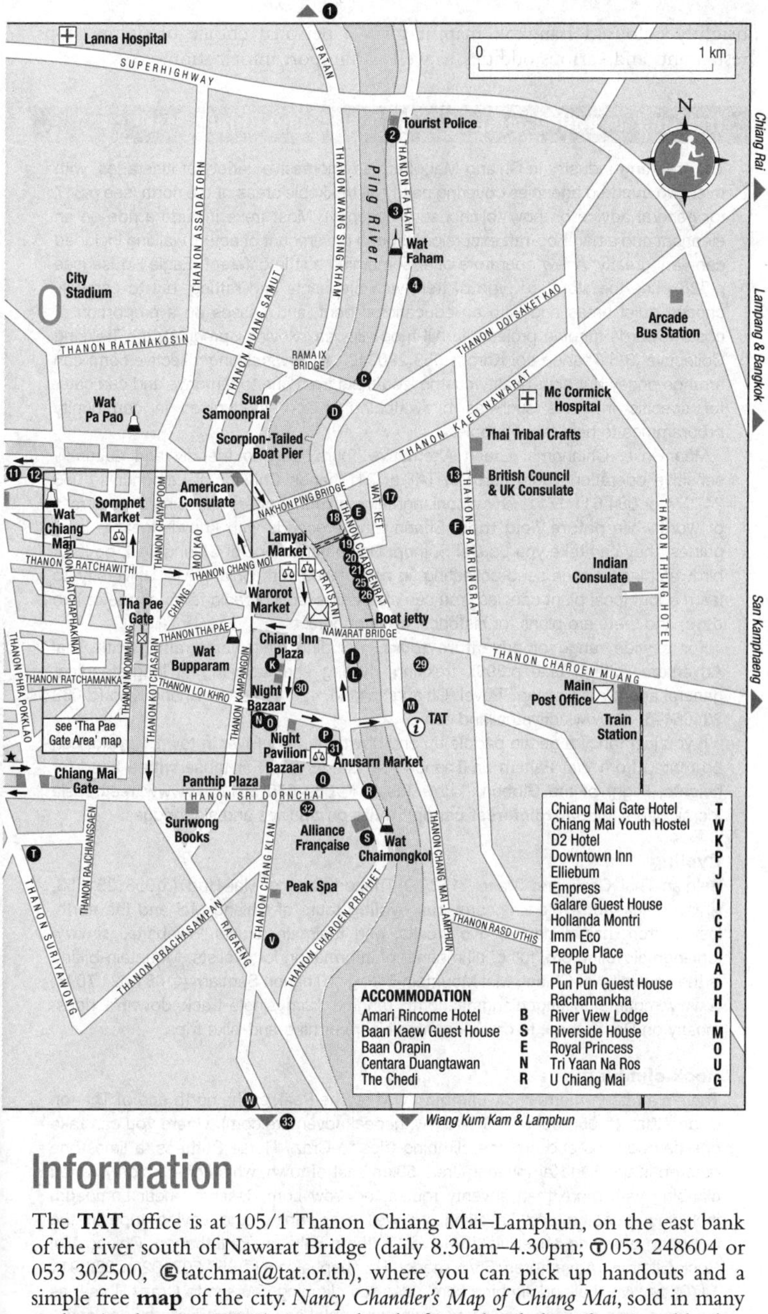

Information

The **TAT** office is at 105/1 Thanon Chiang Mai–Lamphun, on the east bank of the river south of Nawarat Bridge (daily 8.30am–4.30pm; ⓣ053 248604 or 053 302500, ⓔtatchmai@tat.or.th), where you can pick up handouts and a simple free **map** of the city. *Nancy Chandler's Map of Chiang Mai*, sold in many outlets in the city (B190), is very handy for a detailed exploration: like her brightly coloured Bangkok map, it gives a personal choice of sights, shops, restaurants and various oddities, as well as transport information.

Trekking and other outdoor activities around Chiang Mai

The **trekking** industry in Chiang Mai offers an impressive variety of itineraries, with over two hundred agencies covering nearly all trekkable areas of the north (see p.317 for general advice on how to choose an agency). Most treks include a ride on an elephant and a bamboo-raft excursion, though the amount of actual walking included can vary greatly. A few operators offer something a little different. Eagle House (see p.326) runs the standard type of trek, with elephants and rafting, but to carefully chosen quiet areas and with an educational bent, and passes on a proportion of costs towards funding projects in hill-tribe villages. Moving upmarket, the Trekking Collective (3/5 Thanon Loi Khro ⓣ053 280340, ⓦwww.trekkingcollective.com) can arrange pricey but high-quality customized treks from one to ten days and can cater for specific interests such as birdwatching; it too is involved in community programmes to help tribal people.

Meanwhile, Chiangmai Green Alternative Tours, an eco friendly and culturally sensitive operation 100m north of TAT at 31 Thanon Chiangmai–Lamphun (ⓣ053 247374 or 084 611 1711, ⓦwww.chiangmaigreen.com), offers a fascinating diversity of worthwhile **nature field trips**. Sharing the proceeds with knowledgeable local guides, they can take you up Doi Suthep, Doi Inthanon or Doi Chiang Dao, be it for birdwatching or even seed-collecting, in association with Chiang Mai University, to learn about local plant species. You can also visit a local organic farm for one or two days, and there are plans for historical cycling tours.

For a wide range of **adventure tours**, including whitewater rafting with Thai Adventure Rafting (see p.398), trekking, cycling and kayaking, a long-standing, general agency is Contact Travel, Chiangmailand, 420/3 Thanon Chang Klan (ⓣ053 204664–5, ⓦwww.activethailand.com).

If you just fancy a gentle paddle up and down the Ping River in town, **kayaks** can be rented from Wat Faham on Thanon Fa Ham (B100). For those with a head for heights, Flight of the Gibbon, 112/9 Tasala (ⓣ089 970 5511, ⓦwww.treetopasia.com), offers full-day **rainforest canopy tours** on zip lines and sky bridges.

Cycling

Belgian-Thai Click and Travel, 158/40 Thanon Chiang Mai–Hod (ⓣ053 281553, ⓦwww.clickandtravelonline.com), run **cycling** tours of Chiang Mai and the north, lasting from half a day to two weeks, and maintain a useful website, ⓦwww.chiangmaicycling.org, full of all manner of information for cyclists. Mountain-biking is the speciality of Chiang Mai Mountain Biking, 1 Thanon Samlarn (ⓣ081 024 7046, ⓦwww.mountainbikingchiangmai.com), ranging from single-track downhill rides, mostly on Doi Suthep, to cross-country leisure or hike-and-bike trips.

Rock climbing

There's a fifteen-metre **rock-climbing** wall at The Peak at the north end of Thanon Chang Klan (ⓣ053 800567–8, ⓦwww.thepeakadventure.com), where you can take one-day courses and arrange climbing trips to Crazy Horse Buttress, a limestone outcrop in the San Kamphaeng area, 50km east of town, which offers highly varied climbing with more than seventy routes, or Kiew Lom Reservoir near Lampang, including camping and kayaking, as well as climbing and caving trips in the Soppong area and abseiling down Vachiratharn Falls at Doi Inthanon. Chiang Mai Rock Climbing Adventures, 55/3 Thanon Ratchaphakinai (ⓣ053 207102 or 086 911 1470, ⓦwww.thailandclimbing.com), also run climbing courses to Crazy Horse, as well as caving courses, and offer equipment rental and sales, private guides and a partner-finding service.

▲ Chiang Mai samlor

Several free, monthly, locally published **magazines**, including *Citylife* and *Guidelines*, contain information about upcoming events in town, and articles about local culture; they're distributed in spots where tourists tend to congregate, including money-exchange booths and hotel lobbies. *Citylife* can be perused online at Ⓦwww.citylife-citylife.com and produces a fortnightly map with events listings, *City Now*. Another website loaded with information about the local area is Ⓦ1stopchiangmai.com. The *Chiang Mai Mail* **newspaper**, an affiliate of the *Pattaya Mail*, contains local news and entertainment listings, and comes out every Tuesday (B25).

City transport

Although you can comfortably walk between the most central temples, **bicycles** are the best way of getting around the old town and, with a bit of legwork, out to the attractions beyond the moat too. Sit-up-and-beg models and basic mountain bikes are available at many outlets on the roads along the eastern moat for B30–50 a day, while Cacti, 94/1 Thanon Singharat, near the corner of Si Phum (Ⓣ053 212979 or 089 757 9150), rents (B50–350 per day) and sells better-quality road and mountain bikes. If you don't fancy pedalling through the heat and pollution, consider a **motorbike** (see p.350), though these really come into their own for exploring places outside of Chiang Mai.

You'll see a few white, air-conditioned **buses** (B15) around town, but their routes are designed for commuters and their frequencies unreliable; the only services that might prove at all useful are #2 and #11, which both start at Arcade bus station (though #2 takes a very roundabout route into the centre) and head along Thanon Tha Pae (westbound; Thanon Chang Moi eastbound), before cutting across the north side of the old town. Most people use instead red **songthaews**, which act as shared taxis within the city, picking up a number of passengers headed in roughly the same direction and taking each to their specific destination. A sample fare from Tha Pae Gate to Wat Phra Singh is currently B15, but it'll naturally cost more to go somewhere off the beaten track or if the driver thinks you want to charter (*mao*) the whole vehicle.

Chiang Mai's **taxis** currently only switch on their meters when they have to, that is when leaving the airport; otherwise, they quote flat fares, typically B150 for a 2km journey (call ⓣ053 279291 for a pick-up). More prevalent are **tuk-tuks**, for which heavy bargaining is expected – allow around B50 for a short journey, say from the Night Bazaar to Tha Pae Gate. The town still has a few **samlors**, which are cheap when used by locals to haul produce home from the market, but not so cheap when chartered by groups of upmarket tourists on sightseeing tours from their hotel.

Accommodation

Chiang Mai is well stocked with all kinds of **accommodation**; usually there are plenty of beds to go around, but many places fill up from December to February and at festival time, particularly during Songkhran (April) and Loy Krathong (Nov). At these times, you need to book to stay at one of the expensive hotels, and for guest houses it's a good idea to phone ahead – even if you can't book a place, you can save yourself a journey if the place is full.

Many touts at the bus and train stations offer a free ride if you stay at a particular guest house, but you'll probably find that the price of a room is bumped up to pay for your ride – try phoning guest houses, who may pick you up for free to avoid paying commission to the touts. Conversely, some disreputable tuk-tuk and songthaew drivers will claim that the place you want to stay is full or closed, when it isn't, because they want to earn commission from a guest house that they know.

Though many guest houses offer use of their safes as a free service, some charge up to B30 per day. Be sure that you can trust the proprietor before you leave valuables in one of the safes or excess baggage in one of the left-luggage rooms while you go off trekking. Choose one of the more well-established guest houses, as they're more conscious of the need to maintain their reputation, and make a detailed inventory to be signed by both parties – the hair-raising stories of theft and credit-card abuse are often true.

For long-stay accommodation, the most economical option is usually a room with a bathroom in a guest house, which is likely to set you back around B6000 a month for an air-conditioned place (with extra charges for electricity, water, wi-fi and cable TV likely). As well as *Nice Apartment* (see p.326), good places to start looking in the centre include ⓦwww.elegantlanna.com, ⓦwww.boonthavon.com and ⓦwww.rcnguesthouse.com.

Inexpensive

The choice of **budget guest houses** is better in Chiang Mai than in Bangkok: they're generally friendlier, quieter and more atmospheric, and often have their own outdoor cafés. Most are gathered on the surprisingly quiet sois inside the old city and around the eastern side of the moat and Tha Pae Gate, which puts you in the middle of a larder of Thai and travellers' restaurants.

In nearly all of the low-cost places you can now get a hot shower – a big plus in the cool season, even if it's just in a shared bathroom – while many offer a choice between fan and air-conditioning; for much of the year there's little need for the latter in Chiang Mai, though the air-conditioned rooms tend to be more

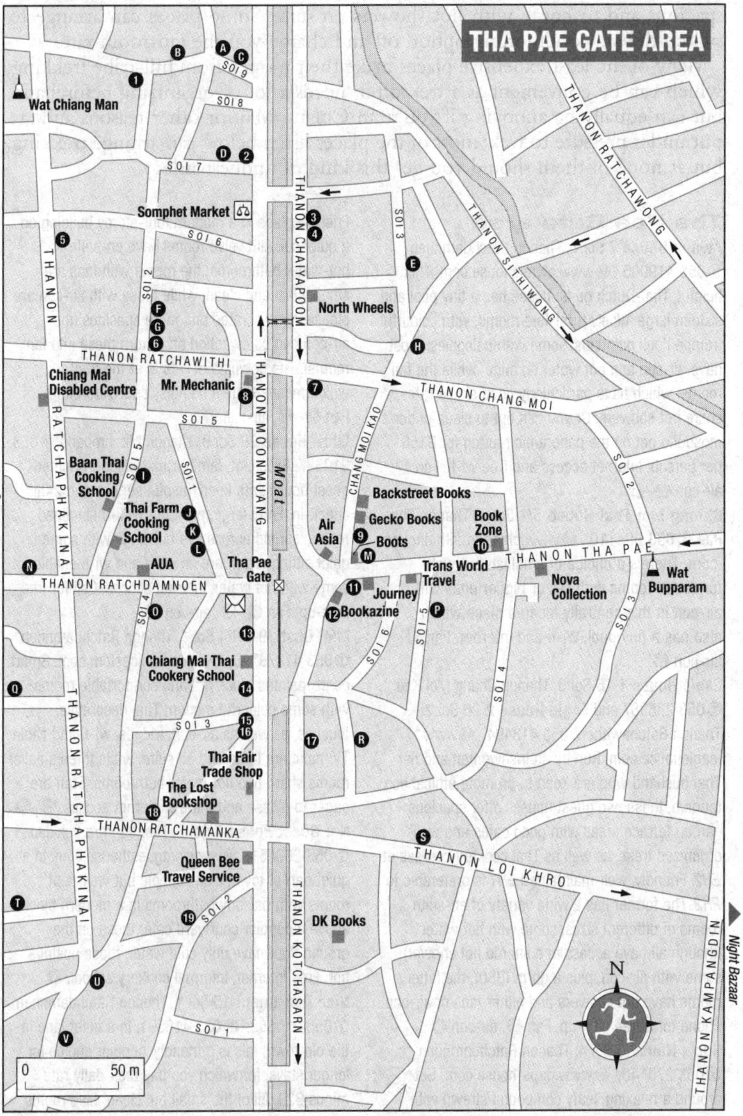

ACCOMMODATION			
3 Sis	Q	Nice Apartment	K
Awana House	L	Pha Thai House	U
Chiang Mai Thai House	P	Portico 21	R
Eagle House 1	E	Raming Lodge	S
Eagle House 2	G	Roong Ruang Hotel	M
Gap's House	O	Sabai Garden	V
Karinthip Village	H	SK House	A
Kavil Guest House	I	Sri Pat Guest House	D
Libra House	C	Supreme Guest House	B
Mini Cost	J	Tamarind Village	N
Nat Guest House	T	Your House	F

EATING & DRINKING			
Aroon Rai	17	Mike's Burgers	7
Art Café	11	Mit Mai	18
Aum Vegetarian Food	13	Pinte Blues Pub	15
Bierstube	16	Pulcinella da Stefano	9
Blue Diamond	1	Pum Pui	19
The Hemp Collective	12	Ratana's Kitchen	3 & 10
The House	2	Ruen Tamarind	N
Jerusalem Falafel	14	Spicy	4
Kafe	8	UN Irish Pub	6
May Kaidee	5		

spacious and to come with hot showers en suite. Some places can arrange to switch the air-conditioning option off and charge you the fan-room rate.

Many of the least expensive places make their money from hill-tribe trekking, which can be convenient as a trek often needs a lot of organizing beforehand, but can equally be annoying if you're in Chiang Mai for other reasons and are put under pressure to trek; most of the places listed below can arrange trekking, but at none of them should you get this kind of undue hassle.

Tha Pae Gate area

Awana House 7 Soi 1, Thanon Ratchdamnoen ⓣ053 419005, ⓦwww.awanahouse.com. This helpful, Thai-Dutch guest house has a tiny pool and sixteen large, nicely furnished rooms, with colourful trompe l'oeil paintings, some with balconies; most have air-con and hot water en suite, while the fan rooms, which have particularly good single rates, share hot showers. Or you can opt to sleep under a mosquito net on the panoramic rooftop for B150 per person. Internet access and free wi-fi. Fan ❸, air-con ❸–❺

Chiang Mai Thai House 5/1 Soi 5, Thanon Tha Pae ⓣ053 904110, ⓦwww.chiangmaithaihouse.com. There's a choice of smallish but well-furnished rooms with fan or bigger ones with air-con in this centrally located place which also has a tiny pool. Wi-fi and internet. Fan ❸, air-con ❺

Eagle House 1 16 Soi 3, Thanon Chang Moi Kao ⓣ053 235387 and **Eagle House 2** 26 Soi 2, Thanon Ratchawithi ⓣ053 418494, ⓦwww.eaglehouse.com. Run by an Irishwoman and her Thai husband who are keen to promote ethical eco tourism, these two guest houses offer spacious garden terrace areas with good cafés and well-organized treks, as well as Thai cookery courses at *EH2*. Friendly, well-maintained *EH1* is preferable to *EH2*. The former has a wide variety of en-suite rooms of different sizes, some with hot water (though all have access to a shared hot shower), some with air-con, plus a dorm (B80); the latter's rooms have hot showers and either fans or air-con. Phone for a free pick-up. Fan ❶, air-con ❷

Gap's House 3 Soi 4, Thanon Ratchdamnoen ⓣ053 278140, ⓦwww.gaps-house.com. Set around a relaxing, leafy compound strewn with antiques, is a wide variety of plush air-con rooms with hot showers. The room price includes a simple cooked breakfast, there's free internet access and wi-fi, and a vegetarian buffet is served in the evening (not Sun); one- or two-day cookery courses available. No reservations are taken, though you can call on your proposed arrival date to check availability. Decent rates for singles. ❸

Kavil Guest House 10/1 Soi 5, Thanon Ratchdamnoen ⓣ053 224740 or 089 852 1875. Friendly place in a modern four-storey building on a quiet soi. All twelve rooms have en-suite hot-water bathrooms; the rooms with fans are small, plain and clean, while those with air-con are pleasantly decorated and more spacious (the air-con can be switched off to turn these into fan rooms). The downstairs café is at the front, which means there's no noisy courtyard effect. Fan ❶–❷, air-con ❷

Libra House 28 Soi 9, Thanon Moonmuang ⓣ053 210687. Excellent, family-run, trekking-oriented guest house with keen, helpful service and 24hr check-in. Forty large, plain but well-maintained rooms, spread across five buildings with some quiet sitting areas, are en suite and wi-fi enabled, some with hot water. Internet access. Call for free pick-up. Fan ❶–❷, air-con ❷

Mini Cost 19–19/4 Soi 1, Thanon Ratchdamnoen ⓣ053 418787–8, ⓦwww.minicostcm.com. Smart ochre-painted block offering comfortable rooms with some colourful modern Thai decorative touches, as well as air-con, fridges, wi-fi and cable TV; most are large and en suite, while three smaller rooms share two hot-water bathrooms. Staff are eager to please and there's internet access. ❸–❹

Nat Guest House 7 Soi 6, Thanon Phra Pokklao ⓣ053 206851, ⓦwww.natguesthouse.com. In a quiet part of town, plain, simple but well-kept rooms with balcony bathrooms in a modern block above a popular courtyard café; those on the ground floor have only cold water, those upstairs hot. Free internet, informal cookery school. ❶

Nice Apartment 15 Soi 1, Thanon Ratchdamnoen ⓣ053 210552, ⓕ053 418591. In a quiet lane in the old town, this is a friendly, popular choice for longer stays, for which you pay their daily rate minus B20. All of the small but clean, tiled rooms have air-con, hot showers, fridges and cable TV. ❷

Pha Thai House 48/1 Thanon Ratchaphakinai ⓣ053 278013 or 081 998 6933, ⓦwww.phathai.th.gs. Wide variety of rooms, all with hot showers en suite, in a leafy, garden setting: some boast balconies, colourful decor, fridges and antique-style furniture, while plainer rooms at the front of the compound by the road are much cheaper. Family rooms and a plunge pool for the hot season are available. Fan ❷–❸, air-con ❹

Roong Ruang Hotel 398 Thanon Tha Pae ⓣ053 232017–8, ⓔroongruanghotel@yahoo.com. Tucked away off the main road, this good-value place has plain, well-kept rooms of various sizes, all with hot water, fridges and TVs, snuggled around a pretty garden courtyard. Free internet. Coffee and toast for breakfast included. Fan ③, air-con ④

Sabai Garden 36 Thanon Ratchaphakinai ⓣ053 208921, ⓔsabaigarden_vicky@yahoo.com. Homestay-style accommodation in an airy, traditional wooden house on stilts, set in a large, pretty garden where Thai food is served. Rooms sport lovely teak floorboards, old wooden furniture, cable TVs (some with DVDs) and nice touches like bathrobes and bedside books; hot showers are shared. Massages, cookery classes and bicycles are available. ③

SK House 30 Soi 9, Thanon Moonmuang ⓣ053 210690. Efficient, brick-built high-rise with a ground-floor café and internet access, a small, shaded swimming pool and a slightly institutional feel. Fan rooms come with hot-water bathrooms, while the air-con rooms are much more colourful and attractive, with cable TV. Fan ②, air-con ④

Sri Pat Guest House 16 Soi 7, Thanon Moonmuang ⓣ053 218716–7, ⓦwww.sri-patguesthouse.com. Large, attractive rooms with air-con, crisp white linen, fridges and smart, well-equipped bathrooms, or simpler fan rooms with hot water. Internet access and free wi-fi throughout. Fan ②, air-con ⑤

Supreme Guest House 44/1 Soi 9, Thanon Moonmuang ⓣ053 222480. Friendly Scottish-run guest house in a modern concrete block with a pleasant roof veranda. The rooms are comfortable and have fans and solar-heated showers. ①

Your House 8 Soi 2, Thanon Ratchawithi ⓣ053 217492, ⓦwww.yourhouseguesthouse.com. Very welcoming, old-town atmosphere (though some rooms get a bit of noise from nearby bars) and a wide choice of accommodation: in the attractive, original teak house, six airy rooms share four bathrooms (two with hot showers); the two modern annexes across the lane, both with hot water en suite, include lovely, big, new rooms with polished teak floors, small balconies, well-equipped bathrooms and internet access. Optional air-con in most rooms. The restaurant serves good Thai and French food, with buffalo steak and chips a speciality. Good for treks, day-trips and train, plane and bus tickets. Call for free pick-up. Discounts for singles. Fan ②–④, air-con ③–④

Rest of Chiang Mai

Chiang Mai Youth Hostel 54 Thanon Papraw ⓣ053 276737, ⓦwww.chiangmaiyha.org. On a side street to the west of Thanon Chang Klan about 1500m south of the night bazaar. Very clean, quiet and reliable; rooms have en-suite hot showers, cable TV and fans or air-con. Big discounts for HI members or for internet booking. Free internet access and wi-fi. Call for free pick-up (daytime). Fan ③, air-con ⑤

Hollanda Montri 365 Thanon Charoenrat ⓣ053 242450, ⓦwww.hollandamontri.com. North of the centre by the busy Rama IX Bridge, in a modern building by the river, this Dutch-Thai guest house has large, comfortable and attractive fan or air-con rooms with hot-water bathrooms and cheerful staff. A very pleasant, terraced riverside bar-restaurant offers a long menu of Thai and European dishes. Free internet and wi-fi, and free daytime bicycles. ③

The Pub 189 Thanon Huai Kaeo ⓣ053 211500, ⓦwww.thepubchiangmai.com. In the garden of this long-running watering hole sit some very good-value clapboard or brick bungalows with small terraces. They're quite tightly packed but spacious and very comfy, with air-con, fridges, cable TV, free wi-fi and big, sparkling, well-equipped bathrooms with hot water. ③

Pun Pun Guest House 321 Thanon Charoenrat ⓣ053 243362 or 053 246180, ⓔpunpungh@gmail.com. This friendly, well-informed place has some of the cheapest riverside rooms in town. Though slightly more expensive, the decent-sized rooms in a wooden house with mosquito screens and en-suite bathrooms offer better value than the small bamboo and wood huts (no mosquito nets) with shared bath. Hot water throughout, restaurant and riverside terrace. ②

Riverside House 101 Thanon Chiang Mai–Lamphun ⓣ053 241860, ⓦwww.norththaitour.com. Welcoming place with a lush garden on the east bank of the river, though just a short walk from the night bazaar, with small but clean and cosy air-con rooms with cable TV, and breakfast included. ③

Moderate

In the moderate price range – around B600 for a double and upwards – by far the best options are the upmarket guest houses and lodges, which as well as good facilities (hot water and air-con) generally offer much more appealing decor and atmosphere. Many of the inexpensive guest houses reviewed above include posher air-conditioned rooms, which often represent very good value.

Tha Pae Gate area

3 Sis 1 Soi 8, Thanon Phra Pokklao ⓣ053 273243, ⓦwww.the3sis.com. Genteel B&B opposite Wat Chedi Luang with lots of attractive open-plan public areas to loll about in. Rooms in the new building have wooden floors and tasteful furnishings that also feature a lot of dark wood, while those in the original building are equally spacious but a little less stylish; all have air-con, hot water and fridges. Free internet and wi-fi. Breakfast included. ⑥

Portico 21 7 Soi 1, Thanon Kotchasarn ⓣ053 278378, ⓦwww.portico21.com. Sleek, contemporary digs, with air-con, hot showers, TVs and fridges, centrally located behind *Aroon Rai* restaurant, but set well back from the busy roads. Free wi-fi and continental breakfast. Decent rates for singles. ⑥

Raming Lodge 17–19 Thanon Loi Kroh ⓣ053 271777, ⓦwww.raminglodge.com. Right in the heart of the downtown action, this red-brick, six-storey place offers tasteful, well-equipped air-con rooms with desks, cable TV and wi-fi. Facilities include a spa and swimming pool. ⑥

Rest of Chiang Mai

Baan Kaew Guest House 142 Thanon Charoen Prathet ⓣ053 271606, ⓦwww.baankaew-guesthouse.com. Set back from the road in a quiet, pretty garden, this attractive modern building has large, simple but well-equipped and-maintained rooms with hot water and air-con. ④

Centara Duangtawan 132 Thanon Loi Khro ⓣ053 905000, ⓦwww.centarahotelsresorts.com. This five-hundred-room, international-standard hotel by the night bazaar pulls in package groups with attractive rates (breakfast included) and an impressive range of facilities: spacious pool, well-equipped gym, spa, wi-fi and highly regarded 24th-floor Chinese restaurant with fine views of Doi Suthep. ⑥

Chiang Mai Gate Hotel 11/10 Thanon Suriyawong ⓣ053 203895–9, ⓦwww.chiangmai-online.com/cmgate/. Located just to the south of the old city, this place has well-equipped rooms with Lanna touches in the design, plus a swimming pool and helpful staff; free pick-ups. Breakfast included. ⑤

Downtown Inn 172/1–11 Thanon Loi Khro ⓣ053 270662, ⓦwww.empresshotels.com. Western-style comforts like mini-bars, TVs and a small swimming pool, without the extras of the big luxury hotels (such as its sister, the *Empress*); quiet considering its central location near the night bazaar. Rates as low as B1100 offered for internet bookings. ⑥

Elliebum 114/3–4 Thanon Ratchamanka ⓣ053 814723 or 085 018 7400, ⓦwww.elliebum.com. Sociable, homely and very helpful, a great first port-of-call in Chiang Mai. Two huge, fresh, modern rooms (big enough for a family) with air-con, hot water, TV and DVD, above a gift shop and café (see p.343), plus another eight very spruce and comfortable rooms at an affiliated guest house (ⓦwww.rachamankhaflorahouse.com) 100m away. Free wi-fi and internet, and free cooking classes if you stay five days. Wide choice of tasty breakfasts included. ⑤–⑥

Galare Guest House 7 Soi 2, Thanon Charoen Prathet ⓣ053 818887 or 053 821011, ⓦwww.galare.com. Near Narawat Bridge, a long-standing, well-run upmarket guest house that's justly popular. Air-con rooms, each with hot-water bathroom, TV, fridge and internet access, overlook a shady lawn that gives way to a riverside terrace restaurant. ⑤

Imm Eco 109 Thanon Bamrungrat ⓣ053 247111, ⓦwww.immhotel.com. This former school in huge, lush, quiet gardens has been tastefully transformed into a modern hostel-cum-hotel, with air-con and hot water throughout. Choose between well-equipped dorms or twins with smart, white bedding and shared bathrooms, and more tasteful rooms with large bathrooms in a subtle contemporary style. Lovely, 25m pool surrounded by hanging plants, stylish common rooms, washing machines, internet access and free wi-fi. At the time of writing, a new branch was about to open on Thanon Kotchasarn, opposite Tha Pae Gate. Dorms B300, rooms ④–⑤

People Place 9 Soi 8, Thanon Charoen Prathet ⓣ053 270060 or 053 282487, ⓦwww.people.infothai.com. Two compact modern buildings, just a few steps from the night bazaar, whose spacious, comfy rooms come with en-suite hot-water bathrooms, air-con, cable TV and minibars. ④

River View Lodge 25 Soi 4, Thanon Charoen Prathet ⓣ053 271109–10, ⓦwww.riverviewlodgch.com. Tasteful, well-run and good-value alternative to international-class hotels, with a beautiful riverside garden, a small swimming pool and neat decorative touches in the rooms; the most expensive have balconies overlooking the river. Breakfast included. ⑥

Expensive

There has been an explosion of top-line accommodation in Chiang Mai lately, ranging from small boutique hotels to massive projects like the Mandarin Oriental's *Dhara Devi*, most of them enhanced by traditional Lanna architectural touches. As well as those below, also worth considering at the top end of this price range is the *Four Seasons Resort*, out in the Mae Sa valley (see p.357); they'll collect you from the airport and lay on a shuttle-bus service into Chiang Mai for guests.

Tha Pae Gate area

Karinthip Village 50/2 Thanon Chang Moi Kao T 053 235414–8, W www.karinthipvillage.com. Peaceful compound located just east of the old city, with 62 rooms set around a decent-sized swimming pool, all nicely decorated in Lanna style and some with four-poster beds. Breakfast included. 7

Tamarind Village 50/1 Thanon Ratchdamnoen T 053 418896–9, W www.tamarindvillage.com. Named for a huge, two-hundred-year-old tamarind tree that shades the compound, this small, tranquil boutique resort in the heart of Chiang Mai's old city is designed in Lanna style, though the extremely comfortable rooms, which all enjoy lovely garden views, have modern touches. Good-sized pool, attractive spa and excellent restaurant (see p.341) too. 9

Rest of Chiang Mai

Amari Rincome Hotel 1 Thanon Nimmanhemin T 053 221130, W www.amari.com. Popular with tour groups, this hotel on the corner of busy Thanon Huai Kaeo has tastefully furnished rooms, a tennis court, two attractive swimming pools and a toddlers' pool, and a good Italian restaurant, *La Gritta*. Substantial discounts on their website. 8

Baan Orapin 150 Thanon Charoenrat T 053 243677, W www.baanorapin.com. Delightful compound overshadowed by tall longan trees on trendy Thanon Charoenrat, offering just fifteen big, comfy and characterful rooms with teak and rattan furnishings and wooden floors. Some rooms come with four poster beds and balconies. 7

The Chedi 123 Thanon Charoen Prathet T 053 253333, W www.ghmhotels.com. Occupying a prime riverside site on busy Charoen Prathet, this ultra-luxury place offers high-concept minimalist design in its spacious rooms, along with balconies and river views. There's a good-looking spa and swimming pool, while the renovated teak bar-restaurant – formerly the British Consulate, built in 1905 – dishes up excellent Indian, Thai and Western food. 9

D2 Hotel 100 Chang Klan T 053 999999, W www.d2hotels.com. With its muted orange theme, flat-screen TVs and helpful staff in street fashions, plus stunning lighting and minimalist furnishings, this place in the heart of the night bazaar, run by the Dusit Group, is one of the city's hippest places to stay. Two restaurants, a beer garden, a spa, fitness centre and rooftop pool are among the amenities. 9

Dhara Devi 51/4 Thanon Chiang Mai–Sankamphaeng T 053 888888, W www.mandarinoriental.com. Occupying huge grounds a few kilometres east of the city centre, the *Dhara Devi* transports its guests into another era – the heyday of the Lanna Kingdom, with traditional Lanna architecture complemented by modern touches such as air-con, dimmer switches and cable TV. The villas, suites and residences are equipped with every conceivable comfort and look out over rice fields and vegetable gardens. With its own breathtaking spa (modelled on the royal palace of Mandalay), cooking school, craft village, shopping centre, two swimming pools, tennis courts and three restaurants, guests need never leave the premises. Prices start at B20,000. 9

Empress 199 Thanon Chang Klan T 053 270240, W www.empresshotels.com. Grand international-class hotel with pool, sauna and health centre conveniently placed on the south side of town: within walking distance of the night bazaar, yet far enough removed to get some peace and quiet. 8

Rachamankha 6 Soi 9, Thanon Ratchamanka T 053 904111, W www.rachamankha.com. Looking more like a temple than a hotel, this spacious, architect-owned property with just 24 elegant rooms is hidden in the quiet backstreets of the old city. There's a lovely, large pool, an excellent restaurant (see p.342), a well-stocked library with sherry laid out for browsers, and even a small museum of lacquerware and silver. Free wi-fi and internet; breakfast included. 9

Royal Princess 111 Thanon Chang Klan T 053 253900, W www.dusit.com. Tidy, centrally located hotel close to the night bazaar, with elegant, recently refurbished rooms, a swimming pool and fitness centre, fine restaurants and impeccable service. Substantial discounts on their website. 8

Tri Yaan Na Ros 156 Thanon Wualai ⓣ053 273174, ⓦwww.triyaannaros.com. Snuggled away to the south of the old city centre, this renovated colonial building oozes atmosphere, from the four-poster beds to the photos of ancient Lanna on the walls. A small library, swimming pool, internet access and free bicycle use for guests. Breakfast included. 8

U Chiang Mai 70 Thanon Ratchdamnoen ⓣ053 327000, ⓦwww.uchiangmai.com. New hotel with lots of innovative ideas: 24hr use of room (no matter what time you check in), heritage talks and walks, breakfast (included) available in your bedroom until 5pm, free bikes and wi-fi. The reading room and spa occupy the hundred-year-old former governor's residence, while some of the rooms – decorated in contemporary Thai style, with daybeds on the balconies, rain showers and iPods – give straight onto the small, black swimming pool. 9

The City

Chiang Mai feels less claustrophobic than most cities in Thailand, being scattered over a wide plain and broken up by waterways. In addition to the moat and remnants of the defensive wall encircling the old town, the gentle Ping River brings a breath of fresh air to the eastern side of the pungent food markets above Nawarat Bridge, and the modern, hectic shopping area around Thanon Chang Klan. The most famous and fascinating **temples** in the city – Wat Phra Singh, Wat Chedi Luang and Wat Chiang Man – are clustered conveniently close to each other in the old town, though the main local place of pilgrimage, for Buddhists and tourists alike, is Wat Phra That Doi Suthep, which glitters in the sun from its perch some 1300 metres up the neighbouring mountain (see p.351). The city is also well-endowed with **museums**: the Arts and Cultural Centre in the old town for high-quality displays on Chiang Mai and Lanna culture, the National Museum to the north for the best of the region's historical artefacts, and, further north again, the Tribal Museum for a useful introduction to the hill tribes of northern Thailand.

A pleasant way to get a feel for the city and its layout is to take a **boat trip** on the Ping River. Cruises in a converted rice-barge operated by Mae Ping River Cruises (ⓣ053 274822 or 081 884 4621, ⓦwww.maepingrivercruise.com) depart from the jetty beside the *Wawee Coffee* restaurant, on the east bank just north of Nawarat Bridge, and head through lush countryside north of town; boats leave every couple of hours (currently at 9am, 11am, 1pm, 3pm & 5pm; 1hr 40min; B250). They also run two-hour private cruises – usually in a longtail boat – from Wat Chaimongkol on Thanon Charoen Prathet, sailing 8km upstream to a riverside farmhouse for a look around the fruit, herb and flower gardens, plus refreshments and fruit-tasting (B450 per person, or B550 including *khao soi* lunch; minimum two people, includes pick-up from your accommodation). Another alternative is to take a trip on a scorpion-tailed boat (currently at 9am, 11am, 1pm, 3pm and 5pm; 1hr 30min; B500 per person, minimum two people; ⓣ081 960 9398, ⓦwww.scorpiontailed.com), a reconstruction of vessels that plied the river a century ago. This cruise heads downriver from a pier on Thanon Charoenrat north of Nakhon Ping Bridge, and includes a commentary on historic places beside the river, fruit juice and a traditional Thai dessert.

Wat Phra Singh

If you see only one temple in Chiang Mai it should be **Wat Phra Singh**, perhaps the single most impressive array of buildings in the city, at the far

▲ Viharn Lai Kam, Wat Phra Singh

western end of Thanon Ratchdamnoen in the old town. Just inside the gate to the right, the wooden scripture repository is the best example of its kind in the north, inlaid with glass mosaic and set high on a base decorated with stucco angels. The largest building in the compound, a colourful modern viharn fronted by naga balustrades, hides from view a rustic wooden bot, a chedi with a typical northern octagonal base constructed in 1345 to house the ashes of King Kam Fu, and – the highlight of the whole complex – the beautiful **Viharn Lai Kam**. This wooden gem is a textbook example of Lanna architecture, with its squat, multi-tiered roof and exquisitely carved and gilded pediment: if you feel you're being watched as you approach, it's the sinuous double arch between the porch's central columns, which represents the Buddha's eyebrows.

Inside sits one of Thailand's three **Phra Singh** (or Sihing) Buddha images (see p.639), a portly, radiant and much-revered bronze in a fifteenth-century Lanna style. Its setting is enhanced by the colourful **murals** of action-packed tableaux, which give a window on life in the north a hundred years ago. The murals illustrate two different stories: on the right-hand wall is an old folk tale, the *Sang Thong*, about a childless king and queen who are miraculously given a beautiful son, the "Golden Prince", in a conch shell. The murals on the left show the story of the mythical swan Suwannahong, who forms the magnificent prow of the principal royal barge in Bangkok. Incidentally, what look like Bermuda shorts on the men are in fact Buddhist **tattoos**: in the nineteenth century, all boys in the north were tattooed from navel to kneecap, an agonizing ordeal undertaken to show their courage and to enhance their appeal to women. On one side of the wat is a high school for young yellow-sashed novices and schoolboys in blue shorts, who all noisily throng the temple compound during the day. Dally long enough and you'll be sure to have to help them with their English homework.

Courses in Chiang Mai

The most popular course on offer in Chiang Mai is how to cook Thai food (especially at the cluster of small schools on and around Soi 5, Thanon Ratchdamnoen), followed by Thai massage and meditation, but perhaps the most challenging of all, though vital for anyone planning to spend any length of time here, is the Thai language. Other skills to be tackled, besides rock-climbing (see p.322), include: **t'ai chi**, on an eight-day introductory programme at Naisuan House off Thanon Doi Saket Kao (ⓣ081 706 7406, ⓦwww.taichithailand.com); **yoga** at the Yoga Studio, 65/1 Thanon Arak (ⓦwww.yoga-chiangmai.com); **Thai boxing** at Lanna Muay Thai, 161 Soi Chang Kian, Thanon Huai Kaeo (ⓣ053 892102 or 081 951 3164, ⓦwww.lannamuaythai.com); **Thai dance** at the Thai Dance Institute, 53 Thanon Kohklong (ⓣ053 801375–6, ⓦwww.thaidanceinstitute.com); one- to five-day workshops in **jewellery making** through Nova, 201 Thanon Tha Pae (ⓣ053 273058, ⓦwww.nova-collection.com); **Lanna arts and culture** with Origin Asia (see p.29); and **crafts** such as making *sa* paper, umbrella painting and batik dyeing at the Mae Sa Crafts Village, in the Mae Sa valley northwest of town near Mae Rim (live-in accommodation, with swimming pool, also available; ⓣ053 290052, ⓔmaesa2@cm.ksc.co.th).

Cookery

Baan Thai 11 Soi 5, Thanon Ratchdamnoen ⓣ053 357339, ⓦwww.baanthaicookery.com. Offers a similar option to Thai Farm (see below), or you can learn in town (both B900), while their short evening course costs B700; all include a market tour, and vegetarians are welcome.

Chiang Mai Thai Cookery School 7/2 Thanon Moonmuang ⓣ053 206388, ⓦwww.thaicookeryschool.com. The original – and still the best – offering courses of one to five days as well as more advanced evening masterclasses. Each day begins with either an introduction to Thai ingredients, shopping in the market, making curry pastes or vegetable carving. Courses are held at the owners' house, a thirty-minute drive out of town (transport provided). B990–B4600, including a recipe book.

May Kaidee (see p.341). Dedicated vegetarian Thai cooking classes, including a market visit. B1200 per day.

Thai Farm Cooking School 2/2 Soi 5, Thanon Ratchdamnoen ⓣ081 288 5989, ⓦwww.thaifarmcooking.com. Offers something slightly different, with the chance to pick your own organic vegetables, herbs and fruits for cooking on their farm, thirty minutes' drive from town (transport provided). B900 per day; vegetarian, vegan and three-day courses also possible.

Thai massage courses

Information about having a massage is given on p.350.

Baan Hom Samunprai 9km south of town beyond Wiang Kum Kam ⓣ053 817362, ⓦwww.homprang.com. Live-in massage courses out in the countryside costing B1600–2800 per day, including accommodation in a traditional village-style, en-suite house, full board and the use of a plunge pool and bicycles; live-out courses from B4000 for 5 days.

Chetawan Thai Traditional Massage School 7/1–2 Soi Samud Lanna, Thanon Pracha Uthit ⓣ053 410360, ⓦwww.watpomassage.com. A branch of the massage school at Bangkok's Wat Pho (see p.137), which is considered to be the best place to study Thai massage in Thailand. Thirty-hour courses (6hr per day for 5 days) in traditional Thai or foot massage (B6500).

Old Medicine Hospital just off Thanon Wualai opposite the Old Chiangmai Cultural Centre ⓣ053 275085 or 053 201663, ⓦwww.thaimassageschool.ac.th. The longest-established centre in Chiang Mai, aka Shivagakomarpaj after the Indian hermit who is said to have founded the discipline over two thousand years ago. Highly respected ten-day courses in English (B5000), under the supervision of the Ministry of Education, twice a month; oil and foot massage courses also offered.

Sunshine Network ⓦwww.thaiyogamassage.infothai.com; for information in Chiang Mai, contact PM Travel at 55/1 Thanon Moonmuang ⓣ053 206614. An international group of practitioners and teachers founded by the highly respected German teacher, Harald Brust, aka Asokananda, who died in June 2005. Asokananda emphasized the spiritual aspect of what he called Thai yoga massage or Ayurvedic bodywork. Led by one of Asokananda's followers, twelve-day beginners' courses (B10,500, including basic accommodation, simple vegetarian rice meals and transportation) are held at a rural retreat in a Lahu village between Chiang Mai and Chiang Rai, often with optional yoga, t'ai chi and Vipassana meditation classes.

TMC northeast of town on the Mae Jo road, 2km beyond the Superhighway ⓣ053 854330, ⓦwww.tmcschool.com. Accredited by the Ministry of Education and highly recommended by past pupils. Three main levels of Thai massage training on offer, each taking five days, with the foundation course costing B7500. A three-day version of the foundation course is also taught (B6500), as well as reflexology (2 days; B3200) and self-stretching exercises (1 day; B3000). All courses include transportation and lunch.

Meditation

International Buddhism Centre Wat Phra That Doi Suthep ⓣ053 295012, ⓦwww.fivethousandyears.org or www.doisuthep.com (see p.352). Following a very traditional Buddhist monastic way, a variety of Vipassana retreats for beginners and advanced meditators, as well as informal dhamma talks for casual visitors (daily noon–3pm).

Mahachulalongkorn Buddhist University Wat Suan Dork ⓣ053 808411–3 ext 114 or 105, ⓦwww.monkchat.net (see p.339). Introductory courses on meditation and Buddhist culture (free, but you need to wear white clothes, available for B300). Including yoga, chanting and almsgiving, they begin at about 2pm on a Tuesday, before departure to the training centre on Doi Suthep, returning to Wat Suan Dork at 2pm the next day (in the fourth week of the month, the courses last 2 nights, returning on Thursday). As places are limited you should make contact in advance.

Northern Insight Meditation Centre Wat Ram Poeng (aka Wat Tapotaram), off Thanon Chon Prathan near Wat Umong ⓣ053 278620, ⓦwww.palikanon.com/vipassana/tapotaram/tapotaram.htm. Disciplined Vipassana courses (with a rule of silence, no food after noon and so on), taught by Thai monks with translators. The minimum stay is 10 days, with a basic course lasting 26 days, and payment is by donation.

Thai language

AUA (American University Alumni) 24 Thanon Ratchdamnoen ⓣ053 277951 or 053 278407, ⓦwww.learnthaiinchiangmai.com. The longest-established and best place to learn Thai, certified by the Ministry of Education. Several levels of classes are offered, starting with spoken Thai for beginners (60hr over about 6 weeks; B4200), with class sizes limited to 5–12 students. Individual and small-group instruction can also be arranged, starting from B290 per hr for one or two students.

Chiang Mai festivals

Chiang Mai is the best and busiest place in the country to see in the Thai New Year, **Songkhran**, which takes over the city roughly between April 12 and 15. The most obvious role of the festival is as an extended "rain dance" in the driest part of the year, when huge volumes of canal water are thrown about in a communal water-fight that spares no one a drenching. The other elements of this complex festival are not as well known but no less important. In the temple compounds, communities get together to build sandcastles in the shape of chedis, which they cover with coloured flags – this bestows merit on any ancestors who happen to find themselves in hell and may eventually release them from their torments, and also shows an intent to help renovate the wat in the year to come. Houses are given a thorough spring-clean to see out the old year, while Buddha images from the city's main temples are cleaned, polished and sprinkled with lustral water, before being ceremonially carried through the middle of the water-fight to give everyone the chance to throw water on them and receive the blessing of renewal. Finally, younger family members formally visit their elders during the festival to ask for their blessings, while pouring scented water over their hands.

Loy Krathong, on and around the night of the full moon in November, has its most showy celebration at Sukhothai, but Chiang Mai – where it is also known as **Yipeng** – is not far behind (see *Loy Krathong* colour section). While a spectacular but unnerving firework fiesta rages on the banks, thousands of candles are gently floated down the Ping River in beautiful lotus-leaf boats. As well as floating krathongs, people release **khom loy**, paper hot-air balloons that create a magical spectacle as they float heavenward, sometimes with firecrackers trailing behind. As with krathongs, they are released to carry away sins and bad luck, as well as to honour the Buddha's top knot, which he cut off when he became an ascetic (according to legend, the top knot is looked after by the Buddha's mother in heaven).

Chiang Mai's brilliantly colourful **flower festival**, centred on Buak Hat Park at the southwest corner of the old town usually on the first weekend of February, also attracts huge crowds. The highlight is a procession of floats, modelled into animals, chedis and even scenes from the *Ramayana*, and covered in flowers. In early April, the **Poy Sang Long** festival (which has its most elaborate manifestation in Thailand in Mae Hong Son; see box, p.389), centred around Wat Pa Pao near the northeast corner of the old city, is an ordination ritual for young Shan men, who are paraded round town on the shoulders of relatives. The boys are dressed in extravagant, colourful clothing with huge floral headdresses, which they symbolically cast off at the end of the festival to don a saffron robe. In late May or early June, the **Inthakin** festival, a life-prolonging ceremony for the city of Chiang Mai, using holy water from Doi Luang Chiang Dao, is focused around the city foundation pillar at Wat Chedi Luang, which throngs with locals making offerings.

Wat Chedi Luang

From Wat Phra Singh a ten-minute walk east along Thanon Ratchdamnoen brings you to **Wat Chedi Luang** on Thanon Phra Pokklao, where an enormous chedi, built to house the ashes of King Ku Na but toppled from 90m to its present 60m by an earthquake in 1545, is the temple's most striking feature. You'll need a titanic leap of the imagination, however, to picture the beautifully faded pink-brick chedi, in all its crumbling grandeur, as it was in the fifteenth century, when it was covered in bronze plates and gold leaf, and housed the Emerald Buddha (see p.132) for eighty years. Recent attempts to rebuild the entire chedi to its former glory, now abandoned, have nevertheless led to modern replacements of the elephants at the base, the nagas that line the lengthy staircases, and the Buddha images in its four niches, including an oversized replica of the

Emerald Buddha, funded by the present king for Chiang Mai's seven hundredth anniversary, in its old spot on the eastern side. In an unprepossessing modern building (which women are not allowed to enter) by the main entrance stands the city's foundation pillar, the *Sao Inthakin* (Pillar of Indra), here at the geographical centre of Chiang Mai, sheltered by a stately gum tree which, the story has it, will stand for as long as the city's fortunes prosper. On the east side of the chedi, **Monk Chat** is advertised (daily 1–6.30pm), giving you a chance to meet and talk to the monks in English. While you're in the vicinity, pop in on **Wat Pan Tao** next door on the north side, to see the recently renovated, fourteenth-century, all-teak viharn, constructed of unpolished panels, supported on enormous pillars and protected by carved wooden bars on the windows, a classic of graceful Lanna architecture.

Chiang Mai City Arts and Cultural Centre

From Wat Chedi Luang, the old town's main commercial street, Thanon Phra Pokklao, heads north past a monument to King Mengrai, the founder of Chiang Mai, set in its own small piazza on the corner of Thanon Ratchdamnoen and supposedly on the site where he was killed by lightning, aged 80. On Sunday afternoons and evenings, Thanon Ratchdamnoen and much of Phra Pokklao host a pedestrianized market with all kinds of shopping and eating, and live music (see box, p.345).

A few minutes on up Thanon Phra Pokklao, Mengrai features again in the bronze Three Kings Monument, showing him discussing the auspicious layout of his "new city", Chiang Mai, with his allies, Ramkhamhaeng of Sukhothai and Ngam Muang of Phayao. Behind the monument, the elegant 1920s former provincial office has been turned into the **Chiang Mai City Arts and Cultural Centre** (Tues–Sun 8.30am–5pm; B90; ⓣ053 217793, ⓦwww.chiangmaicitymuseum.org) by the municipality – essentially a museum with the aim of conveying the history, customs and culture of the city and the region. To this end, scale models and plenty of high-quality English-language audiovisuals are thoughtfully deployed, with some nice touches such as vivid reminiscences by Chiang Mai's older inhabitants about what the city was like in the early twentieth century. This was the site of Wat Sadeu Muang, home of the city pillar before it was moved to Wat Chedi Luang in the early nineteenth century, and the symbolic significance of this is neatly explained on a see-through display board in front of a window, through which you can see one of the wat's restored thirteenth-century Haripunjaya-style chedis outside. Upstairs, the interest tails off, though there is an engaging audiovisual and exhibit on the hill tribes. The back half of the building shelters cultural activities such as weaving demonstrations, temporary exhibitions, a souvenir shop and a small café. A new Lanna history museum is planned behind the Arts and Cultural Centre, while another colonial-style building to the east of the Three Kings Monument is slowly being converted into a museum focusing on Lanna culture.

Wat Chiang Man

Carry on up Thanon Phra Pokklao and turn right along Thanon Wiang Kaeo to reach the oldest temple in Chiang Mai, **Wat Chiang Man**, after about five minutes. Erected by Mengrai on the site where he first pitched camp, the wat is most notable for two dainty and very holy Buddha images housed in the viharn to the right of the entrance: the **Phra Sila**, a graceful marble bas-relief carved in northern India supposedly in the sixth century BC, stands in the typical *tribunga*, or hip-shot stance; its partner, the **Phra Setangamani** (or

Crystal Buddha), made four centuries later, probably in Lavo (modern Lopburi), is much revered by the inhabitants of Chiang Mai for its rainmaking powers and is carried through the streets during the Songkhran festival to help the rainy season on its way. Neither image is especially beautiful, but a powerful aura is created by making them difficult to see, high up behind two sets of iron bars.

Chiang Mai National Museum and Wat Jet Yot

In telling the history of Lanna art and culture, the **National Museum**, out on the northwestern outskirts on the Superhighway (Wed–Sun 9am–4pm; B100; Ⓦwww.thailandmuseum.com), has far fewer bells and whistles than its rival, the Chiang Mai Arts and Cultural Centre, but in terms of the quality of artefacts on display, wins hands down. Inside, the airy rooms are cool enough for a long browse, and the collection is liberally labelled in English. As you enter, you are greeted on the left by the head of a smiling bronze Buddha that is as tall as a man, but you need to go right to follow the displays, which are grouped into six sections. The first of these displays artefacts and skeletons unearthed by local archeological digs, as well as photographs of cave paintings found in the area. The second section focuses on the golden age of the Lanna kingdom, from the fourteenth to the sixteenth centuries, including some lovely ceramics from San Kamphaeng, while the third, fourth (upstairs) and fifth sections bring the history of the north up to date.

The biggest section is given over to **Thai religious art**, with a particular focus on **Lanna art**. Hundreds of Buddha images are on display, ranging from a humble, warmly smiling sandstone head of the Haripunjaya (Lamphun) era, representing the earliest northern style, to gleaming images in the Ratanakosin (Bangkok) style. In the golden age of Lanna, images were produced in two contrasting styles. One group, which resembles images from northern India, has been called the **lion-type**, after the Shakyamuni (Lion of the Shakyas) archetype at the great Buddhist temple at Bodh Gaya, the site of the Buddha's enlightenment. It's been conjectured that a delegation sent by King Tilok to Bodh Gaya in the 1450s brought back not only a plan of the temple to be used in the building of nearby Wat Jet Yot, but also a copy of the statue, which became the model for hundreds of Lanna images. These broad-shouldered, plump-bellied Buddhas are always seated with the right hand in the touching-the-earth gesture, while the face is well rounded with pursed lips and a serious, majestic demeanour. The second type is the **Thera Sumana** style named after the monk Mahathera Sumana, who came from Sukhothai in 1369 to establish his Sri Lankan sect in Lanna. The museum is well stocked with this type of image, which shows strong Sukhothai influence, with an oval face and a flame-like *ushnisha* on top of the head.

Set back from the Superhighway five minutes' walk west of the museum, the peaceful garden temple of **Wat Jet Yot** is named after the "seven spires" of its unusual chedi. The temple was built in 1455 by King Tilok, to represent the seven places around Bodh Gaya in India which the Buddha visited in the seven weeks following his enlightenment, and houses the king's ashes. Around the base of the chedi, delicate stuccos portray cross-legged deities serenely floating in the sky, a role model for all yogic fliers; their faces are said to be those of Tilok's relatives.

The Tribal Museum

One kilometre north of the Superhighway off Thanon Chotana, the **Tribal Museum** (Mon–Fri 9am–4pm; free, but various charges for audiovisuals) enjoys a superb location behind the artfully landscaped **Ratchamangkla (Rama IX) Park**. Originally established in 1965 as part of the Tribal Research Institute at Chiang Mai University, the museum was moved in 1997 to the present edifice, in the style of a Chinese pagoda. Overlooking a lake lined with trees and reconstructions of hill-tribe houses, the very pretty and peaceful setting makes a visit worthwhile, as does the opportunity to learn something about the various tribes before heading off on a trek. It's about a ten-minute walk from the park gate on Thanon Chotana to the museum entrance, but, if you are getting here by songthaew or tuk-tuk, drivers can take their vehicles round the park directly to the museum.

Set out on three floors, the museum has its main exhibition area on the ground floor, where displays about each of the main hill tribes are accompanied by concise information printed in both Thai and English. A useful wall chart shows the calendar of traditional village life, giving a month-by-month picture of the agricultural activities, ceremonies and festivals of the tribes featured; there are also photos and models of village dwellings, giving a good idea of the different styles of architecture, and a display of hill-tribe instruments accompanied by taped music. On the first Saturday of each month, there's an all-day **tribal market**, selling clothes, handicrafts and organic agricultural products, with the emphasis on a different tribe each month.

The zoo and aquarium

About 1km beyond Wat Jet Yot, the Superhighway meets Thanon Huai Kaeo, a broad avenue of posh residences and hotels that starts out from the northwest corner of the moat and ends at the foot of Doi Suthep. Heading out up Thanon Huai Kaeo, past the sprawling campus of Chiang Mai University (CMU), brings you to **Chiang Mai Zoo and Aquarium**, in an attractive park at the base of the mountain (zoo: daily 8am–6pm, last tickets 5pm; B100, children B50; aquarium: daily 9am–8pm, last tickets 7pm; B450, children B350, combined ticket B520, children B390; see below for variations and extra charges; Ⓦwww.chiangmaizoo.com).

Originally a menagerie of a missionary family's pets, the zoo now houses an impressive collection of about eight thousand animals in modern, relatively comfortable conditions. There's a children's zoo and a colourful walk-through aviary, while larger mammals include elephants, giraffes, Humboldt penguins, koalas, a rhino and the current favourites, two **giant pandas** and a baby panda, born in 2009 (B100, children B50), for whom a snow dome is planned. Despite a disorientating layout, it makes a diverting visit, especially for kids. Feeding times for animals are posted clearly, and refreshment stalls for humans are never far away. The grounds are too big to walk round, but "service cars" (small open-sided buses; B20, children B10) and a monorail (B150, children B50) are available to take you around. The zoo is better visited in the morning to avoid the afternoon heat, or in the evening, when a "**twilight zone**" features animals feeding (daily 6–9pm), and the cost of B200 for adults and B100 for children includes use of the service car and a visit to the pandas. The twilight zone has operated a little sporadically in the last few years, so it might be worth phoning Ⓣ053 221179 to check.

Towards the western side of the zoo, the new **aquarium** is the biggest in Southeast Asia, with what's said – at 130m – to be the longest underwater viewing tunnel in the world. With the aim of showing landlocked Chiang Mai some rarely seen species, the huge edifice is strictly divided in half: in the freshwater section, you can see not only the Mekong giant catfish (see p.422), but also *thae pha*, the Chao Phraya giant catfish; while the salty half displays rare white-tip reef sharks, a double-headed Maori wrasse and a giant guitarfish, which is somewhere between a ray and a shark, and a precursor of the latter. There's a saltwater touch pool, and feeding times are currently 10am and 3pm (fresh), and 11am and 3.30pm (salt).

Wat Umong

More of a park than a temple, **Wat Umong** makes an unusual, charming place for a stroll in the western suburbs. If you're driving or biking from the zoo, you'll need to get through or round (on Thanon Chon Prathan) the extensive grounds of CMU. From the centre of town, head west along Thanon Suthep for about 2km and turn left after Wang Nam Gan (a royal agricultural produce project); then follow the signs to the wat for another kilometre along a winding lane.

According to legend the wat was built by King Mengrai, but renovated in the 1380s by King Ku Na for a brilliant but deranged monk called Jan, who was prone to wandering off into the forest to meditate. Because Ku Na wanted to be able to get Jan's advice at any time, he founded this wat and decorated the **tunnels** (*umong*) beneath the chedi with paintings of trees, flowers and birds to simulate the monk's favoured habitat. Some of the old tunnels can still be explored, where obscure fragments of paintings and one or two small modern shrines can be seen. Above the tunnels, frighteningly lavish nagas guard the staircase up to the overgrown **chedi** and a grassy platform that supports a grotesque black statue of the fasting Buddha, all ribs and veins: he is depicted as he was during his six years of self-mortification, before he realized that he should avoid extremes along the Middle Path to enlightenment. Behind the chedi, the ground slopes away to a **lake** inhabited by hungry carp, where locals come to relax and feed the fish. On a tiny island here, reached by a concrete bridge, stands a statue of the late Buddhadasa Bhikkhu (see p.588), a famous southern Thai monk who re-established the monastic community here in the 1960s. Informal discussions in English on

▲ Fasting Buddha, Wat Umong

Buddhism, and some meditation practice, are normally held in the Chinese pavilion on the lake's edge here on Sunday afternoons at 3pm, with one of the farang monks who are often in residence.

Throughout the tranquil wooded grounds, the temple's diverse education-focused philosophy comes vividly alive: as you enter the compound you pass through a shady grove where signs are pinned to nearly every tree, displaying simple Buddhist maxims in Thai and English and the botanical name of the species. At certain times of the day, your stroll is accompanied by a soothing Thai voice emanating from loudspeakers, expounding on Buddhism; the subject can be explored in more depth in the library, in the centre of the temple grounds, with some books in English, and at the adjacent bookshop – and outside at tables and covered seating areas local people read, study and conduct discussions. At the entrance gate, handicrafts are sold by the community of disabled people that has a house and workshop in the wat.

Chiang Mai University Art Museum

From the turn-off to Wat Umong, Thanon Suthep heads back towards town, eventually meeting the western moat at Suan Dork Gate. A short way along on the left, entered from just around the corner on Thanon Nimmanhemin, the modern **Chiang Mai University Art Museum** (Tues–Sun 9am–5pm; free; ⓣ053 944833 or 053 218280) is not only confirmation of the city's growing importance, but also a boon to the large local artistic community. The large, purpose-built exhibition areas are well designed and lit, and the exhibitions generally change each month, giving visitors an insight into modern Thai art, as well as anything from Japanese lacquerware sculpture to Iranian carpetry art. There's a café and shop, and films and concerts are regularly put on here.

Wat Suan Dork

A little further east along Thanon Suthep stands **Wat Suan Dork**, the "Flower Garden Temple", surrounded by walls as part of Chiang Mai's fortifications. Legend says that Mahathera Sumana, when he was invited to establish his Sri Lankan sect here in 1369, brought with him a miraculous glowing relic. Ku Na, the king of Chiang Mai, ordered a huge chedi – the one you see today – to be built in his flower garden, but as the pea-sized relic was being placed inside the chedi, it split into two parts: one half was buried here, the other found its way to Doi Suthep, after further adventures (see p.351).

The brilliantly whitewashed chedi now sits next to a garden of smaller, equally dazzling chedis containing the ashes of the Chiang Mai royal family; framed by Doi Suthep to the west, this makes an impressive and photogenic sight, especially at sunset. At the back of the dusty compound, the bot is decorated with lively *Jataka* murals and enshrines a beautifully illuminated, five-hundred-year-old bronze Buddha image. Nearby signs point the way to **Monk Chat** (Mon, Wed & Fri 5–7pm; ⓦwww.monkchat.net), organized by the Mahachulalongkorn Buddhist University based at the temple, which gives you the opportunity to talk to monks about anything from Buddhism to the weather (or about the university's overnight Buddhist culture and meditation courses – see p.333), and them the chance to meet foreigners and practise their English.

Sbun-Nga Textile Museum

Anyone with at least a passing interest in textiles and the great weaving traditions of northern Thailand should make time for the **Sbun-Nga Textile**

Museum (daily except Wed 10.30am–6/6.30pm; B100; Ⓦwww.sbunnga.com) at the Old Chiangmai Cultural Centre – more famous for its *khan toke* dinners (see below) – on Thanon Wualai. Here over a thousand ancient and rare textiles are lovingly displayed and informatively labelled in English, classified according to which sub-group of Thais and which geographical area they come from. Thus you'll find among the patterns of the Thai Lue, who migrated from Sipsong Panna in southern China to various parts of northern Thailand, the brightly coloured and very intricate *lai nam lai* or "flowing water" design, signifying those who resettled by the Mekong River. Other highlights include a very beautiful royal headdress of the Thai Lao, who have migrated mainly from northeast Laos in the last two hundred years and are considered to have among the most sophisticated weaving techniques and designs in the world, and the swirling coronation dress of a Thai Yai crown prince, decorated with gems and precious metals.

Eating

The main difficulty with **eating** in Chiang Mai is knowing when to stop. All over town there are inexpensive and enticing restaurants serving typically northern food, which has been strongly influenced by Burmese cuisine, especially in curries such as the spicy *kaeng hang lay* (usually translated on menus as "Northern Thai curry"), made with pork, ginger, garlic and tamarind. At lunchtime the thing to do is to join the local workers in one of the simple, inexpensive cafés that put all their efforts into producing just one or two special dishes – the traditional meal at this time of day is *khao soi*, a thick broth of curry and coconut cream, with egg noodles and a choice of meat. The main **night markets** are at the back and front entrances to Chiang Mai University on Thanon Suthep and Thanon Huai Kaeo; along Thanon Bamrungburi by Chiang Mai Gate; plus the more touristy Anusarn Market off Thanon Chang Klan near the night bazaar and a few stalls in front of Somphet market on Thanon Moonmuang. Many of the **bars** listed below in "Drinking and nightlife" also have particularly good reputations for their food.

International food in Chiang Mai is generally more expensive than Thai, but there's plenty of it, particularly Italian-slanted, and sometimes it's hard to resist. Probably easier to refuse are the restaurants which lay on touristy **cultural shows** with *khan toke* dinners, a selection of northern dishes traditionally eaten on the floor off short-legged lacquer trays. Of these, the Old Chiangmai Cultural Centre, 185/3 Thanon Wualai (B370, including pick-up; Ⓣ053 275097, Ⓦwww.oldchiangmai.com), with its show of northern Thai and hill-tribe dancing, has the best reputation. **Dinner cruises** on the river are offered by Mae Ping River Cruises (see p.330) for B550 per person for a Thai set menu (including pick-up from your hotel at 7pm), and by *The Riverside* (see p.344). The coffee bug has hit Chiang Mai, like everywhere in Thailand: here you can sip espressos made from beans grown locally at Doi Inthanon and Doi Wawee, notably at *Wawee Coffee*, which has fourteen outlets around town, including a riverside branch on the north side of Nawarat Bridge on Thanon Charoenrat.

Thai

Tha Pae Gate area

Aroon Rai Thanon Kotchasarn. Sample all the classic Lanna dishes, such as *khao soi* and tasty *kaeng hang lay muu*, at this basic, long-standing restaurant by Tha Pae Gate, then buy their curry pastes to take home with you.

Aum Vegetarian Food 65 Thanon Moonmuang. Small and relaxing long time favourite, with air-con and lots of used books for sale. Interesting and cheap veggie dishes such as *khao soi* and Vietnamese spring rolls and Thai desserts. Daily 10am–8pm (often closes 5pm in low season).

May Kaidee 202 Thanon Ratchaphakinai ⓣ087 717 5275, ⓦwww.maykaidee.com. Small branch of Banglamphu's best-loved vegetarian restaurant (see p.178), incorporating local specialities such as *khao soi*. Daily 8am–9pm.

Ratana's Kitchen 320–322 Thanon Tha Pae ⓣ053 874173 & 82/2 Thanon Chaiyapoom ⓣ053 233459. A good-value favourite among locals and visitors both for northern specialities like *kaeng hang lay* (B70), *khao soi* (B40) and mixed hors d'oeuvres (B80), and for tasty Western breakfasts (B110 for a big one), sandwiches and steaks. Extensive vegetarian menu, wine (B70 per glass) and cocktails too. Daily 7.30am–11.30pm.

Ruen Tamarind 50/1 Thanon Ratchdamnoen. Overlooking the pool at the *Tamarind Village* hotel (see p.329), this elegant restaurant serves up excellent Thai cuisine such as *tom kha thaleh* (coconut soup with seafood; B190) and *kaeng phet linchee* (roast duck with lychees in red curry sauce; B290). Also a long vegetarian menu and a few Western dishes like chicken breast with broccoli and mushroom cream sauce (B280).

Rest of Chiang Mai

Café de Nimman Rooms Shopping Centre, 61 Thanon Nimmanhemin (south of Soi 17) ⓣ053 218405. Excellent food such as squid stuffed with pork in *phanaeng* curry at this stylish, reasonably priced bar-restaurant and terrace.

Come Dara 193 Thanon Charoenrat ⓣ053 248751–2. On a riverside terrace and balcony behind an art gallery, and to the tune of live easy-listening music, choose from a huge menu of Thai food, including lots of desserts and scores of northern specialities – try the tasty pork and puffball mushroom curry (B120). Daily 11am–midnight.

Dalaabaa 113 Thanon Bamrungrat ⓣ053 242491. A grand modernist house with mostly crimson decor and lots of orchids is the chic setting for some creative Thai cuisine, including *som tam* with fresh prawns, lots of salads and fish. Live jazz Sat. Daily 6pm–midnight.

The Gallery 25 Thanon Charoenrat ⓣ053 248601. Refined restaurant and art gallery in a nineteenth-century compound, with a stuccoed Chinese mansion at the front, a teak northern Thai house behind and soothing riverside terraces fringed with trees and flowers. Interesting selection of northern and central Thai food, including good-value *khan toke* set menus (B400 for 2 people), and live traditional northern music nightly. Daily noon–1am.

Hong Tauw Inn 95/17–18 Nantawan Arcade, Thanon Nimmanhemin ⓣ053 400039. Comfortable air-con restaurant done out in "country inn" style, with antiques, plants and old clocks, making for a relaxing environment. The reliable menu ranges from rice and noodle dishes such as *khanom jiin*, to delicious central and northern Thai main dishes, such as a *phanaeng* curry for B90, and includes a wide range of Thai desserts.

Huan Soontaree 208 Thanon Patan, 3km north of the Superhighway ⓣ053 872707–8. A convivial riverfront restaurant owned by the famous northern Thai folk-singer Soontaree Vechanont, who entertains diners from her balcony-level stage (she performs Mon–Sat, but is augmented by other good local musicians nightly). Delicious northern specialities such as fried Chiang Mai sausage with whole baby garlic. Split levels allow a choice of seating – on a leafy riverside terrace hung with paper lanterns, near the stage or on a balcony overlooking the action. Daily 4pm–midnight.

Just Khao Soi 108/2 Thanon Charoen Prathet ⓣ053 818641. If you get a taste for *khao soi*, you might like to check out this tourist-oriented spot where you can custom-build your own bowl of broth and noodles, adding condiments from a huge palette, for around B100 – aprons are provided to prevent you staining your shirt. Lots of northern Thai appetizers, too.

Kalare Night Bazaar Food Centre Thanon Chang Klan. A coupon system operates at this open-air collection of inexpensive northern and central Thai, Indian, Japanese and veggie foodstalls. Free shows of traditional music (7pm) and dancing (8.30pm) make a nice background accompaniment without being too loud or intrusive.

Khao Soi Samoe Jai Thanon Faham. Thick and tasty *khao soi* (spiced to order) and other northern specialities, plus delicious satay, *som tam* and Thai desserts, pack the locals in. No English sign – it's a wooden house with a red, white and blue awning. Daily except Wed 8am–5pm.

Kiat Ocha 41–43 Thanon Inthrawarorot, off Thanon Phra Pokklao (no English sign). Delicious and very popular satay and *khao man kai* – boiled chicken breast served with dipping sauces, broth and rice – at around B30 a dish. This and the surrounding cafés are especially handy if you're looking round the old town. Daily 5am–2.30pm.

Lamduon Faharm Khao Soi 352/22 Thanon Charoenrat. Excellent *khao soi* prepared to a secret recipe, which can be spiced according to your taste; delicious crackling with the pork version. Also satay, *khanom jiin*, *som tam* and an assortment of juices. Daily 8am–4pm.

Maha Naga 431 Thanon Charoenrat ⓣ053 261112. Enjoying one of the best riverside locations in the city, behind a hundred-year-old wooden royal palace, and with a choice of dining in elegant air-con *salas* or on a laterite terrace beneath huge banyan trees, this place offers top-quality Thai and Thai fusion dishes (main courses from B250), including a superb pomelo salad. Bus #2 from Nawarat Bridge.

Palaad Tawanron Above Chiang Mai Zoo ⓣ053 216039. Go to the end of Thanon Suthep, then turn right and follow the signs to one of Chiang Mai's most attractive restaurants, set beside a small waterfall with panoramic views of the city. Dishes like *tom yam kung* (B280) and fried sea bass in fish sauce keep the customers coming, and there's usually live music in the evening.

Rachamankha 6 Soi 9, Thanon Ratchamanka. In the grounds of the boutique hotel of the same name (see p.329), this is one of Chiang Mai's classiest places to eat, with starched linen tablecloths, elegant cutlery and live traditional music in the evening. From an unusual menu of Thai, Shan, Burmese and fusion dishes, try the Burmese-style beef curry (B390) and finish off with the mango flambé in a papaya bowl (B190).

Tha Nam 43/3 Moo 2, Thanon Chang Klan ⓣ053 275125. Restaurant on the southern edge of town serving good traditional northern and central Thai food in a ramshackle teak house, where musicians play traditional music. Eat on the huge terrace, which has a romantic atmosphere, overlooking a quiet green stretch of the river. Try the tasty and unusual *yam samoonprai pla duk foo* (crispy fried catfish with herbs) or plump for a good-value *khan toke* selection (B170).

Wan Lamoon Thanon Inthrawarorot (no English sign, but look for the pink flower on their Thai sign). Delightful spot purveying excellent, cheap lunches such as *khanom jiin*, and delicious Thai and Western desserts. One or two tables but mostly takeaway – to the square in front of the City Arts and Cultural Centre, for example. Daily 7am–5pm.

Whole Earth 88 Thanon Sri Dornchai. Mostly veggie dishes from Thailand and India, plus a big chicken and seafood selection, with main dishes costing around B150; soothing atmosphere with occasional live mood-music in a traditional Lanna house, with verandas overlooking a large garden.

International

Tha Pae Gate area

Art Café 291 Thanon Tha Pae. This Italian-run place is a popular farang hangout with a good ambience. All the café favourites, including yoghurt and muesli, American and continental breakfasts, sandwiches, soups, salads and home-made ice cream are served, as well as full meals such as pasta (from B135), pizza (from B175), Thai dishes and a big selection of vegetarian options (but avoid the Mexican menu).

Bierstube 33/6 Thanon Moonmuang. Friendly and efficient service combined with generous portions of German or Thai food at reasonable prices make this place a favourite with locals. The tables outside provide a good people-watching spot, too.

Blue Diamond Soi 9, Thanon Moonmuang. Popular vegetarian restaurant in a quiet neighbourhood of guest houses, serving very good Thai dishes, Western breakfasts (from B65), home-made bread, shakes, herbal teas and hill-tribe coffee. Mon–Sat 7am–8.30pm.

The House 199 Thanon Moonmuang ⓣ053 419011. In an imposing white mansion, this stylish, upmarket, evening-only restaurant serves very creative and successful fusion cuisine, such as ginger pork with lentils (B320). Tapas (from B90) are served here and in the attached, chic *salon de thé* (daily 10am–midnight), where the simpler menu stretches to sandwiches, pastas and Thai dishes such as pomelo salad with crispy pork.

Jerusalem Falafel 35/3 Thanon Moonmuang ⓣ053 270208. Small and friendly air-con café serving all manner of Middle Eastern food, including tasty hummus, home-made cheeses and yoghurt, and baklava; if the choices overwhelm you, go for a meze set menu (B400 for two people). Closed 2nd and 4th Mon of every month.

Kafe 127–129 Soi 5, Thanon Moonmuang. Warm and welcoming bar-restaurant, a long time favourite among locals, with tasty burgers, breakfasts, good Thai food at competitive prices and a wide range of drinks.

Mike's Burgers Corner of Thanon Chaiyapoom and Thanon Chang Moi (plus several other branches, including most usefully a relaxing venue in Anusarn market). Stools at the counter only, and the location is noisy and fumy, but that doesn't stop a steady stream of aficionados from turning up for the tasty home-made burgers (from B65) and chilli dogs (from B35). Open daily till 3am.

Mit Mai 42/2 Thanon Ratchamanka. It looks like a simple Thai eatery from the street, but in fact *Mit Mai* serves up exotic food from Yunnan Province in China, such as *fong nom thawt* (fried cheese) and white bamboo grubs, as well as dishes like Yunnanese ham stir-fried with ginger and chilli (B120).

Pulcinella da Stefano 2/1–2 Thanon Chiang Moi Kao ⓣ053 282463. One of Chiang Mai's most popular Italian restaurants, with a winning combination of tasteful decor (based on the Punch character in commedia dell'arte), efficient service and delicious, authentic food – try the home-made *tagliolini alla chitarra* (B200) or plump for a simple, good-value set menu (B230 for 3 courses). Look out also for Stefano's other Italian restaurants, *Girasole*, corner of Ratchdamnoen and Ratchaphakinai roads (ⓣ053 276388), and the more contemporary *Caffè Gourmet*, one block down on Thanon Ratchamanka (ⓣ053 283824; closed Sun).

Pum Pui 24 Soi 2, Thanon Moonmuang ⓣ053 278209. Trattoria-style, Italian-run place where you're guaranteed huge servings. The home-made pasta dishes include an excellent lasagne, and there's pizza too, lots of bruschetta and other antipasti, and a long vegetarian menu. Seating is mostly outside in a tree-filled courtyard off a quiet, fume-free lane.

Rest of Chiang Mai

Amazing Sandwich 20/2 Thanon Huai Kaeo. The place to go if you hanker for a sandwich, bagel or baguette made up to order, or fancy munching on a pie, quiche or salad. Mon–Sat 8am–8pm, Sun 8am–4pm.

Arcobaleno 60 Thanon Wat Ket ⓣ053 306254. Tasty Italian food served in and around a spacious house on a quiet lane near Nakhon Ping Bridge. Try the *spaghetti arcobaleno* (with smoked bacon, mushrooms and tomato sauce; B200) and the delicious *panna cotta* for dessert.

Country Café Soi 3, Thanon Nimmanhemin. Excellent coffee, cake, breakfast sandwiches and simple Thai dishes in an agreeable, sociable place with a small, but pretty front terrace and a mellow soundtrack. Daily 8am–8pm.

Elliebum 114/3–4 Thanon Ratchamanka (see p.328). Probably the best coffee in town, delicious fruit smoothies, top-notch breakfasts such as blueberry pancakes with maple syrup and fresh fruit, plus great *croques monsieur* and Thai dishes for lunch.

Love at First Bite 28 Soi 1, Thanon Chiang Mai–Lamphun. Head south from the east side of Nawarat Bridge, then turn into the first lane on the left to discover this relaxing haven of home-baked cakes and pies, plus delicious coffee, served in a tiny café or on a neat lawn surrounded by flower beds. Tues–Sun 10.30am–6pm.

Mi Casa Soi 4 (Soi Wat Padaeng), Thanon Suthep ⓣ053 810088. Top-notch Mediterranean cuisine by a Spanish chef in charming surroundings, whether indoors or out in the garden by the fountain. The menu features excellent tapas (B580 for six), tempting main courses (from B360), cheaper pastas and risottos and good, mostly Spanish wine. They've recently opened a tapas bar, *Su Casa*, on Soi 11, Thanon Nimmanhemin.

Drinking and nightlife

Although there's a clutch of hostess bars bordering the east moat and along Loi Khro, and several gay bars offering sex shows, Chiang Mai's **nightlife** generally avoids Bangkok's sexual excesses, but offers plenty of opportunities for a wholesome good time. The main concentrations are on the east bank of the Ping River, around Tha Pae Gate and to the west of town along Thanon Nimmanhemin, which swarms with students from nearby Chiang Mai University.

For an introduction to the city's **gay scene**, check out the small bars on Soi 1, Thanon Tha Pae, behind *D2 Hotel*, or the roads off the west side of Thanon Chotana, where there's a clutch of bars around the gay-owned *Lotus Hotel*. In the latter area, the city's main bar and club, *Adam's Apple*, 1/21–22 Soi Viengbua (ⓣ053 220381, ⓦwww.adamsappleclub.com), was just about to reopen at the time of writing after lengthy renovation.

Tha Pae Gate area

The Hemp Collective 19/4–5 Thanon Kotchasarn, opposite Tha Pae Gate. Laid-back crusty place, decorated with paper lanterns and floor cushions in the rooftop bar, where DJs play an eclectic music choice.

Pinte Blues Pub 33/6 Thanon Moonmuang. The front of this simple bar is so small that you could miss it if you blink, but it's one of the city's longest-standing venues, and an ideal spot for a chat over cheap drinks with blues in the background.

Spicy 82 Thanon Chaiyapoom. Chiang Mai's favourite late-night spot – the place to go when everywhere else is closed – is conveniently located opposite Somphet market. If it all gets too sweaty and frantic for you, repair to *Jack Van Bar* a few doors down, where you can sit at outdoor tables on a large forecourt (with a brazier for the cool season) and get drinks from a Jack Daniels-sponsored camper van.

UN Irish Pub 24/1 Thanon Ratchawithi. Though it hasn't had an Irish owner for a few years now, this is a cordial, well-run pub that serves Guinness and Heineken on tap and reasonably priced wine, as well as good, moderately priced food, including home-made bread for satisfying breakfasts and sandwiches, home-made pies, Irish stew and pizzas. Live music Wed & Fri, quiz night Thurs, and all manner of sports on TV.

Rest of Chiang Mai

Brasserie 37 Thanon Charoenrat. Decent restaurant with pretty riverside terraces, but more famous as the venue for some of the city's best live blues and rock. Warms up around 11pm.

Drunken Flower (Mao Dok Mai) Soi 17, Thanon Nimmanhemin. Laid-back and very congenial, this quirky venue is a favourite among university students and twenty-somethings, both Thai and farang. Reasonable prices for drinks and an eclectic range of background music.

Fine Thanks 119 Thanon Nimmanhemin. Popular among Thais, yet welcoming to farangs, an indoor-outdoor pub-restaurant, dimly lit and draped with plants. Thai bands play a mix of Thai and Western pop-rock.

Good View 13 Thanon Charoenrat ⓣ053 241866. An upmarket clone of the neighbouring *Riverside*, this large venue appeals to fashionable Thais with its smart staff, extensive menu of Thai, Chinese, Western and rather ropy Japanese food, and slick, competent musicians, who play anything middle of the road from country to jazz.

Khan-asa 87 Thanon Si Phum. Located inside the moat, just east of Chang Phuak Gate, this friendly bar has a cosy ambience and an eclectic range of music that make it an ideal spot for a chat with friends. Good, creative Thai food at reasonable prices, too.

Minimal 24/2 Soi 13, Thanon Nimmanhemin. Hip bar-restaurant, gallery and fashion studio run by artists, with a pleasant garden at the back.

Monkey Club 7 Soi 9, Thanon Nimmanhemin. More sophisticated than your average Chiang Mai bar-restaurant, with stylish white outdoor seating around a small pond, though none of that matters later in the evening when the crowd of twenty-something Thais starts dancing round their tables to Thai pop bands and DJs.

North Gate Jazz Co-op Thanon Si Phum. Chilled, open-fronted bar with pavement tables overlooking Chang Phuak Gate, featuring high-quality live jazz nightly.

The Pub 189 Thanon Huai Kaeo. Homely, relaxing expat hangout that's been around for forty years, with the nearest thing to an English pub atmosphere to be found in Chiang Mai. Draught beer and items like bangers and mash (B165) and Sunday roast (B250) on the menu. Quiz night Fri.

Riverside Thanon Charoenrat ⓣ053 243239. On one side of the road candlelit terraces by the water and an often heaving, lively bar for gigs, on the other a spacious complex of rooms, terraces and a stage. Various soloists and bands perform nightly on the two stages, with the tempo increasing as the night wears on. Long, reliable menu of Western and Thai food and drinks also on offer. For an extra B90, you can dine on their boat that cruises up the Ping River each evening at 8pm (boarding 7.15pm).

Tha Chang Gallery 29 Thanon Charoenrat ⓣ053 248601. Attached to *The Gallery* restaurant, this was closed for refurbishment at the time of writing but has traditionally been one of the best spots in town to catch a set of live jazz and blues, featuring some of the city's most competent musicians.

Warm Up 40 Thanon Nimmanhemin. Hugely popular venue with students and young locals, offering both live bands and local and inter national DJs spinning the latest sounds in different indoor and outdoor zones.

Writer's Club and Wine Bar 141/3 Thanon Ratchdamnoen. Welcoming bar near the centre of the old city, run by an English writer and popular among farang residents and visitors, serving a range of beers and wines, plus good Thai and Western food. Closed Sat.

Shopping

Shopping is an almost irresistible pastime in Chiang Mai, a hotbed of traditional cottage industries offering generally high standards of workmanship at low prices. Two main tourist shopping areas, the San Kamphaeng road and the night bazaar, conveniently operating at different times of the day, sell the full range of local handicrafts.

The **road to San Kamphaeng**, which extends due east from the end of Thanon Charoen Muang for 13km, is the main daytime strip, lined with every sort of shop and factory, where you can usually watch the craftsmen at work. The biggest concentrations are at **Bo Sang**, the "umbrella village", 9km from town, and at San Kamphaeng itself, once important for its kilns but now dedicated chiefly to silk weaving. It's a worthwhile trip to watch age-old crafts in process, but the main problem is getting there. Frequent white songthaews to San Kamphaeng leave Chiang Mai from the central Lamyai market, but it's difficult to decide when to get off if you don't know the area. You could sign up for a tour or hire a tuk-tuk for a few hundred baht, but the catch here is that the drivers will want to take you to the shops where they'll pick up a commission. The best way to go is by bicycle or motorbike, which allows you to stop where and when you please, but take care with the fast-moving traffic on the narrow road.

The other main shopper's playground is the **night bazaar**, sprawling around the junction of Thanon Loi Khro and Thanon Chang Klan (and into the adjacent, quieter Anusarn market). Here bumper-to-bumper street stalls and several indoor areas (including the original Chiang Mai Night Bazaar shopping centre on the west side of Thanon Chang Klan) sell just about anything produced in Chiang Mai, plus crafts from other parts of Thailand and Southeast Asia, as well as counterfeit designer goods; the action starts up at around 5pm, and there are plenty of real bargains.

During the day, bustling **Warorot market** on Thanon Chang Moi has lots of cheap and cheerful cotton, linen and ceramics for sale on the upper floors. In the heart of the market, you can watch locals buying chilli paste, sausage and sticky rice from their favourite stalls, and maybe even join the queue. There's also a pungent and colourful flower market just east of here, on Thanon Praisani by the river.

Another place worth knowing about is **Thanon Nimmanhemin**, the continuation of the western end of the Superhighway. Its northern end towards Thanon Huai Kaeo, which savvy locals sometimes tag Chiang Mai's Sukhumvit for its services to well-to-do expats, has a particular concentration of interesting boutiques and art galleries. Other fruitful hunting grounds are the **Northern Village** in the Airport Plaza shopping centre, at the corner of the Superhighway

Chiang Mai's walking streets

If you're in Chiang Mai at the weekend it's worth heading down to Thanon Wualai, just south of the old city, on a Saturday between about 5pm and 11pm, or to Thanon Ratchdamnoen and part of Thanon Phra Pokklao in the old city on a Sunday at the same time. Closed to traffic for the duration, these **walking streets** become crowded with vendors selling typical northern Thai items such as clothes, musical instruments and snacks, as musicians busk to the throngs of people. The walking streets have become almost as popular as the night bazaar, as they are ideal places to pick up a souvenir and mingle with a very mixed crowd of Thais and farangs.

and Highway 108 (free hourly songthaew shuttle from eight downtown hotels, including the *Centara Duangtawan* on the hour), for all manner of handicrafts and contemporary decorative products, including a shop selling work from the Pa-Da Cotton Textile Museum (see p.381); and **Thanon Charoenrat** on the east side of the river, which hosts several interesting outlets for clothes and interior design between Nawarat and Nakhon Ping bridges. On this stretch, at number 190, you'll also find one of the town's most interesting **art galleries**, La Luna (Tues–Sun, Mon by appointment; ⓣ053 306678, ⓦwww.lalunagallery.com), which displays and sells a striking range of paintings, posters, photos and pottery by local artists.

To make sure more of your money goes to those who make the goods, take your custom to one of the **non-profit-making shops** (usually closed Sun), which specialize in hill-tribe gear, bags, scarves and silverware and whose proceeds go to the hill tribes. These include the Hill Tribe Products Foundation (BPP and Hill Tribe), on Thanon Suthep in front of Wat Suan Dork; Thai Tribal Crafts, 208 Thanon Bamrungrat, and its partner, Thai Fair Trade Shop, 25/9 Thanon Moonmuang, near Thanon Ratchamanka.

Fabrics, clothes and contemporary interior design

The **silk** produced out towards San Kamphaeng, to the east of Chiang Mai, is richly coloured and hard-wearing, with various attractive textures. Bought off a roll, the material is generally less costly than in Bangkok, though more expensive than in the northeast – prices are around B400 a metre for two-ply (for thin shirts and skirts) and B500 a metre for four-ply (suitable for suits). Ready-made silk clothes and made-to-measure tailoring, though inexpensive, are generally staid and more suited to formal wear; for **tailoring**, Neramit, off Thanon Chang Moi at 91/2 Thanon Ratchawong (ⓣ053 234353, ⓦwww.neramit-custom-tailoring.com), has a good reputation.

In Chiang Mai you'll also find plenty of traditional, pastel-coloured **cotton**, which is nice for furnishings, most of it from the village of Pa Sang southwest of Lamphun. Outlets in the basement of the main Chiang Mai night bazaar shopping centre on Thanon Chang Klan have good, cheap selections of this sort of cloth at around B200–300 per metre, plus hand-painted and batik-printed lengths, and ready-made tablecloths and the like.

If you're interested in the whole process of traditional fabric production, particularly the use of **natural dyes**, Studio Naenna, 138/8 Soi Changkhian, Thanon Huai Kaeo (ⓦwww.studio-naenna.com), is an excellent place to begin. If you phone for an appointment (ⓣ053 226042) you can see a demonstration of dyeing, including the plants from which the dyes are extracted; you can then watch the weavers in action (Mon–Fri) and buy the finished products, which consist of top-quality, ready-made silk and cotton garments and accessories. They also have a textile art gallery with rotating exhibitions on the grounds (Wed 10am–4pm or by appointment) and an outlet for their products, Adorn, at 22 Soi 1, Thanon Nimmanhemin.

Often sharing shelf-space with upmarket fabrics, you'll also find some stunning examples of **contemporary interior design** in Chiang Mai, fusing local crafts with modern, often minimalist elements.

Classic Model 95/22 Thanon Nimmanhemin, opposite Soi 1, and Northern Village, Airport Plaza. Striking and classy ready-to-wear clothes for women, made from local fabrics by traditional northern methods.

Ga-Boutique 1/1 Thanon Kotchasarn. If you just need to replenish your backpack, try this shop opposite Tha Pae Gate, which sells ordinary casual clothes of reasonable quality at low prices.

Ginger 199 Thanon Moonmuang (in the compound of *The House* restaurant) and 6/21 Thanon Nimmanhemin. Chi-chi boutique selling striking and original women's and men's wear, accessories and contemporary home decor, especially cushion covers.

Gong Dee Soi 1, Thanon Nimmanhemin, behind the *Amari Rincome Hotel*. Stunning, contemporary wood and lacquer vases, boxes, lamps and bowls, much of it gleaming with gold and silver leaf, plus jewellery and furniture.

Nussara 66 Thanon Charoenrat. Chunky cotton clothes, mostly in muted, natural colours, as well as scarves and other fabrics.

Pa Ker Yaw 180 Thanon Loi Khro, near the *Downtown Inn*. Weather-beaten wooden shophouse stuffed with a selection of rich fabrics from Thailand, Laos and Burma, as well as hill-tribe jewellery and basketware and other crafts. Closed Sun.

Shinawatra 7km out on the San Kamphaeng road, with a shop at 18/1 Thanon Huai Kaeo. Century-old silk factory and showroom, once graced by no less a personage than Diana, Princess of Wales, that's a good place to follow the silk-making process right from the cocoon.

Sop Moei Arts 150/10 Thanon Charoenrat Ⓦwww.sopmoeiarts.com. Gorgeous fabrics – scarves, wall-hangings, bags and cushion covers – and stylish basketware, with part of the profits going back to the eponymous Karen village and nearby refugee camp near Mae Sariang, where they're made.

Vila Cini 30–34 Thanon Charoenrat. Lacquerware and sumptuously coloured silk scarves and cushion covers, plus cotton and basketware next door at Oriental Style, under the same ownership.

Woodcarving

Chiang Mai has a long tradition of **woodcarving**, which expresses itself in everything from salad bowls to half-size elephants. In the past the industry has relied on the cutting of Thailand's precious teak, but manufacturers are now beginning to use other imported hardwoods, while bemoaning their inferior quality. Carl Bock, who travelled through the region in 1882, observed a habit which is still common today: "The woodcarvers have a quaint taste for inlaying their work with odd bits of coloured glass, tinsel or other bright material: such work will not bear close inspection, but it has a remarkably striking effect when the sun shines on these glittering objects." Wooden objects are sold all over the city, but the most famous place for carving is **Ban Tawai**, a large village of shops and factories where prices are low and where you can watch the woodworkers in action. One of Thailand's most important woodcarving centres, Ban Tawai relied on rice farming until thirty years ago, but today virtually every home here has carvings for sale outside and each backyard hosts its own cottage industry. To get there, you'll need your own transport: follow Highway 108 south from Chiang Mai 13km to Hang Dong, then head east for 2km. A regularly updated, free map of Ban Tawai's outlets, which now include all manner of antiques and interior decor shops, is available around town.

Lacquerware

Lacquerware can be seen in nearly every museum in Thailand, most commonly in the form of **betel sets**, which used to be carried ceremonially by the slaves of grandees as an insignia of rank and wealth (see box, p.348). Betel sets are still produced in Chiang Mai according to the traditional technique, whereby a woven bamboo frame is covered with layers of rich red lacquer and decorated with black details. A variety of other objects, such as trays and jewellery boxes, are also produced, some decorated with gold leaf on black gloss. Lacquerware makes an ideal choice for gifts, as it is both light to carry, and at the same time typically Thai. Just about every other shop in town sells lacquerware, but few places have such an appealing selection of original designs as Living Space, 6/9–10 Thanon Nimmanhemin (closed Sun; Ⓦwww.livingspacedesigns.com).

Betel

Betel-chewing today is popular only among elderly Thais, particularly country women, but it used to be a much more widespread social custom, and a person's betel tray set was once a Thai's most prized possession and an indication of rank: royalty would have sets made in gold, the nobility's would be in silver or nielloware, and poorer folk wove theirs from rattan or carved them from wood. A set comprises at least three small covered receptacles, and sometimes a tray to hold these boxes and the knife or nutcracker used to split the fruit.

The three essential ingredients for a good chew are betel leaf, limestone ash and areca palm fruit. You chew the coarse red flesh of the narcotic fruit (best picked when small and green-skinned) first, before adding a large heart-shaped betel leaf, spread with limestone-ash paste and folded into manageable size; for a stronger kick, you can include tobacco and/or marijuana at this point. An acquired and bitter taste, betel numbs the mouth and generates a warm feeling around the ears. Less pleasantly, constant spitting is necessary: in traditional houses you spit through any hole in the floorboards, while in more elegant households a spittoon is provided. It doesn't do much for your looks either: betel-chewers are easily spotted by their rotten teeth and lips stained scarlet from the habit.

Celadon

Celadon, sometimes known as greenware, is a delicate variety of stoneware which was first made in China over two thousand years ago, and later produced in Thailand, most famously at Sukhothai and Sawankhalok. Several kilns in Chiang Mai have revived the art, the best of them being Mengrai Kilns at 79/2 Soi 6, Thanon Samlarn (Ⓦwww.mengraikilns.com). Sticking to the traditional methods, Mengrai produces beautiful and reasonably priced vases, crockery and larger items, thrown in elegant shapes and covered with transparent green and blue glazes. More contemporary pieces are sold by Aka Gallery, Soi 1, Thanon Nimmanhemin (Ⓦwww.aka-aka.com).

Umbrellas and paper

The village of **Bo Sang** bases its fame on souvenir **umbrellas** – made of silk, cotton or mulberry paper and decorated with bold, painted colours – and celebrates its craft with a colourful **umbrella fair** every January. The artists who work here can paint a small motif on your bag or camera in two minutes flat. The grainy mulberry (*sa*) **paper**, which makes beautiful writing or sketching pads, is sold almost as an afterthought in many of Bo Sang's shops; it can also be bought from a few shops in the centre of the basement of the Chiang Mai Night Bazaar building and, along with a huge range of other specialist papers, at HQ, opposite Wat Phra Singh at 3/31 Thanon Samlarn (closed Sat & Sun; Ⓦwww.hqpapermaker.com).

Silver and jewellery

Of the traditional craft quarters, only the **silversmiths**' area on Thanon Wualai remains in its original location. The oldest factory in Chiang Mai, Siam Silverware on Soi 3, a ramshackle and sulphurous compound loud with the hammering of hot metal, gives you a whiff of what this zone must have been like in its heyday. The end results are repoussé plates, bowls and cups, and attractive, chunky jewellery. If you want sterling silver, check for the stamp that shows the item is 92.5 percent pure; many items are only eighty percent pure and sell much more cheaply. A good general **jewellery** store is Nova Collection at 201 Thanon Tha Pae, which has some lovely rings and necklaces blending gold, silver and precious stones in striking and original designs.

Listings

Airlines The following maintain downtown offices: Air Asia, Thanon Chaiyapoom opposite Tha Pae Gate; Bangkok Airways, *Imperial Mae Ping Hotel*, Thanon Sri Dornchai ⓣ053 276176 ext 11, 12; Lao Airlines, Nakornping Condo, 115 Thanon Ratchapruek, off Thanon Huai Kaeo ⓣ053 223401, ⓦwww.laoairlines.com; Silk Air, *Centara Duangtawan Hotel*, 132 Thanon Loi Kroh ⓣ053 904985–7, ⓦwww.silkair.com; Thai Airways, 240 Thanon Phra Pokklao ⓣ053 920999. For further contact details, including for Nok Air and One-Two-Go, which along with Air Asia, Bangkok Airways and Thai, currently serve the Bangkok route, see p.45.

Banks and exchange Dozens of banks are dotted around Thanon Tha Pae and Thanon Chang Klan, and many exchange booths here stay open for evening shoppers.

Books Book Zone at 318 Thanon Tha Pae stocks a wide range of English-language publications, including novels, books about Thailand and maps, while Bookazine, with a branch on Thanon Kotchasarn opposite Tha Pae Gate, for example, carries magazines, newspapers and books. Two large book stores, Suriwong at 54/1 Thanon Sri Dornchai (closed Sun afternoons) and DK Books at 79/1 Thanon Kotchasarn, also have a wide selection; the former's display is the better organized, and it features newspaper and stationery sections and a *Wawee Coffee* shop downstairs. Secondhand bookshops, where you can buy or exchange books, include The Lost Bookshop, 34/3 Thanon Ratchamanka, and Backstreet Books, 2/8 Thanon Chang Moi Kao, and Gecko Books, 2/6 Thanon Chang Moi Kao (plus several other branches around town), conveniently located next to each other near Tha Pae Gate.

Car rental Many outlets in the Tha Pae Gate area rent out cars and four-wheel drives, from as little as B800 a day: reliable companies offering insurance and breakdown recovery include Journey, 283 Thanon Tha Pae ⓣ053 208787, ⓦwww.journeycnx.com; North Wheels, 70/4–8 Thanon Chaiyapoom ⓣ053 874478, ⓦwww.northwheels.com; and Queen Bee, 5 Thanon Moonmuang ⓣ053 275525, ⓦwww.queen-bee.com. The more expensive international chains include Avis (ⓦwww.avisthailand.com), Chiang Mai airport ⓣ053 201798–9, and *Royal Princess Hotel* (see p.329); and National, *Amari Rincome Hotel*, Thanon Huai Kaeo ⓣ053 210118, ⓦwww.smtrentacar.com.

Cinemas Go to ⓦwww.movieseer.com for details of which English-soundtrack or English-subtitled films are showing at the various cineplexes around town. French-language films with English subtitles are screened at the Alliance Française, 138 Thanon Charoen Prathet on Fri at 8pm (ⓣ053 275277). Popular, mostly recent, arthouse films are shown at CMU Art Museum Theatre every Sat at 7pm (see p.339; ⓣ053 974846 ext 22 or 081 175 6800).

Computers For sales and repairs, either Panthip Plaza, corner of Chang Klan and Sri Dornchai roads, or Computer Plaza, Thanon Manee Nopparat on the north side of the moat.

Consulates China, 111 Thanon Chang Lo ⓣ053 276457 or 053 280380; India, 33/1 Thanon Thung Hotel ⓣ053 243066; US, 387 Thanon Witchayanon ⓣ053 252629. Honorary consulates include Australia, 236 Thanon Chiang Mai–Doi Saket ⓣ053 492480; Canada, 151 Chiang Mai–Lampang Superhighway ⓣ053 850147; Ireland, *Eagle Guest House* (Annette Kunigagon; see p.326); and UK, 198 Thanon Bamrungrat ⓣ053 263015 (British Council).

Hospitals Lanna, at 103 Superhighway ⓣ053 999777, east of Thanon Chotana, has a 24hr emergency service and dentistry department; McCormick ⓣ053 262200–19 is cheaper, used to farangs and is nearer, on Thanon Kaeo Nawarat; Chiang Mai University's Special Medical Service Centre at Maharaj Hospital near Suan Dork Gate (ⓣ053 946900–1, after 8pm ⓣ053 946623–4, ⓦwww.cmed.cmu.ac.th) and Chiang Mai Ram at 8 Thanon Boonruangrit ⓣ053 224851–61, also have very good reputations.

Immigration office On the southern leg of the Superhighway, 300m before the airport, on the left (Mon–Fri 8.30am–4.30pm; ⓣ053 201755–6).

Internet access Most guest houses and hotels have internet access, many have wi-fi, and every second shop in town appears to be an internet café. Rates vary from as little as B20 per hr in locations near Chiang Mai University to as much as B120 in downtown areas; B1 per min is the most typical rate, charged at *Click'n'Drink*, 147 Thanon Chang Klan opposite the *Royal Princess Hotel*, which stays open until midnight and offers a range of coffees.

Laundry Most guest houses and hotels have an efficient laundry service, but it's well worth patronizing the Chiang Mai Disabled Centre, 133/1 Thanon Ratchaphakinai (Ⓣ053 231941; see p.80), who offer pick-up and delivery.

Mail The GPO is on Thanon Charoen Muang near the train station (Mon–Fri 8.30am–4.30pm, Sat & Sun 9am–noon) and offers a packing service. Poste restante should be addressed to: Chiang Mai Post and Telegraph Office, Thanon Charoen Muang, Chiang Mai 50000. There are also post offices at 43 Thanon Samlarn (Phra Singh PO), and on Thanon Phra Pokklao at the junction with Thanon Ratchawithi (Sri Phum PO), plus a small branch office on Thanon Ratchdamnoen by Tha Pae Gate, all in the old town, as well as on Thanon Wichayanon near Nawarat Bridge (Mae Ping PO), and at the airport.

Massages and spas The Old Medicine Hospital (see p.332; daily 8am–5pm) offers very good Thai (B200 for 90min), herbal and foot massages, as does Suan Samoonprai, just north of Talat Muang Mai at 8 Thanon Wang Sing Kham (B100/hr for traditional massage; also does oil massages; open daily till about 7pm, longer if you phone ahead; Ⓣ053 252716). Traditional massages by extremely competent, blind masseurs are on offer at the School for the Blind, 41 Thanon Arak (B150 for 90min; Mon–Fri 8.30am–4.30pm; Ⓣ053 278009). Out in the countryside at Baan Hom Samunprai (see p.332), two-hour massages cost B400–800. Let's Relax, Night Bazaar Pavilion, Thanon Chang Klan (Ⓣ053 818498, Ⓦwww.bloomingspa.com), lays on a few more frills, longer opening hours and a wider range of treatments (from B400 for a 1hr Thai massage). A very good mid-range choice, with service and facilities comparable to a luxury hotel, is Peak Spa & Beauty Salon, Twin Peaks Condo, 187/13 Thanon Chang Klan (from B800 for 90min Thai massage; call for pick-up; Ⓣ053 818869, Ⓦwww.peak-spa.com). Many of the top hotels now have full-service spas, and there are several upmarket stand-alones including: Ban Sabai, 17/7 Thanon Charoen Prathet in town (Ⓣ053 285204–6, Ⓦwww.ban-sabai.com), with a village branch on the north side of town (Ⓣ053 854778–9); and Chiangmai Oasis Spa, which has three branches, including at 4 Thanon Samlan, just south of Wat Phra Singh (Ⓣ053 815000, Ⓦwww.chiangmaioasis.com).

Motorbike rental Motorbikes of all shapes and sizes are available for rent around Tha Pae Gate, starting from about B130–150 per day for an 80cc step-through. Among reliable rental outlets, Queen Bee, 5 Thanon Moonmuang (Ⓣ053 275525, Ⓦwww.queen-bee.com), and Mr Mechanic, Thanon Moonmuang, near the corner of Thanon Ratchawithi (Ⓣ053 214708, Ⓦwww.mr-mechanic1994.com), who has bikes of all sizes and two branches on Thanon Ratchaphakinai, can also offer insurance. Cacti (see p.323) is also trustworthy.

Pharmacy Boots branches include Thanon Tha Pae, opposite Tha Pae Gate, and Thanon Chang Klan, in front of the Chiang Inn Plaza.

Swimming The best central venue is the big, cool, shaded pool at the City Stadium (*Sanam Kila*) off the north side of the moat, though it's only open 4–8pm daily. There's also a lovely pool at *Imm Eco* (see p.328; B100, including free wi-fi).

Tourist police Rimping Plaza, Thanon Charoenrat, near the Superhighway Ⓣ053 247318 or 1155.

Travel agents Affiliated with worldwide STA Travel, Trans World Travel, 259–261 Thanon Tha Pae Ⓣ053 272415, is reliable for plane tickets, as is Queen Bee, 5 Thanon Moonmuang Ⓣ053 275525, Ⓦwww.queen-bee.com, who also handle train tickets and all manner of minibuses and buses, including VIP services to Bangkok for B650.

Around Chiang Mai

You'll never feel cooped up in Chiang Mai, as the surrounding countryside is dotted with day-trip options in all directions. Dominating the skyline to the west, **Doi Suthep** and its eagle's-nest temple are hard to ignore, and a wander around the pastoral ruins of **Wiang Kum Kam** on the southern periphery has the feel of fresh exploration. Much further south, the quiet town of **Lamphun** offers classic sightseeing in the form of historically and religiously significant temples and a museum. To the north, the **Mae Sa valley** may be full of tour buses, but its highlight, the **Queen Sirikit Botanic Gardens**, as well as the nearby lake of **Huay Tung Tao** and **Darapirom Palace**, merit an independent jaunt. Distinctly missable, however, is the recently opened Chiang Mai **Night Safari** to the southwest of the city, which has encroached on land belonging to

Doi Suthep National Park, and even announced as an opening promotion that the meat of all the animals on display would also be available in its restaurant (though the offer has now been withdrawn) – much better to spend your money at Chiang Mai Zoo (see p.337). All the excursions described here can be done in half a day; there are also some good options for longer jaunts, notably to Doi Inthanon National Park (see p.378), to Lampang and the National Elephant Institute (see p.360) and to the Elephant Nature Park (see p.401).

Doi Suthep

A jaunt up **DOI SUTHEP**, the mountain which rises steeply at the city's western edge, is the most satisfying brief trip you can make from Chiang Mai, chiefly on account of beautiful **Wat Phra That Doi Suthep**, which dominates the hillside and gives a towering view over the goings-on in town. This is the north's holiest shrine, its pre-eminence deriving from a magic relic enshrined in its chedi and the miraculous legend of its founding. The original chedi was built by King Ku Na at the end of the fourteenth century, after the glowing relic of Wat Suan Dork had self-multiplied just before being enshrined. A place had to be found for the clone, so Ku Na put it in a travelling shrine on the back of a white elephant and waited to see where the sacred animal would lead: it eventually climbed Doi Suthep, trumpeted three times, turned

Khruba Srivijaya

Khruba Srivijaya, widely regarded as the "patron saint" of northern Thailand, was born in 1878 in a small village 100km south of Chiang Mai. His birth coincided with a supernatural thunderstorm and earthquake, after which he was given the auspicious nickname Faa Rawng (Thunder) until he joined the monkhood. Appointed abbot of his local temple by the age of 24, he came to be regarded as something of a rebel – though a hugely popular one among the people of Lanna. Despite the suspicions of the Sangha, both locally and in Bangkok, he became abbot of Lamphun's Wat Chama Thevi, which he set about restoring with gusto. This was the beginning of a tireless campaign to breathe life into Buddhist worship in the north by renovating its religious sites: over a hundred temples got the Khruba treatment, including Chiang Mai's Wat Phra Singh, Wat Phra That Haripunjaya in Lamphun and Wat Phra That Doi Tung near Mae Sai, as well as bridges, schools and government buildings. His greatest work, however, was the construction in 1935 of the paved road up to Wat Phra That Doi Suthep, which beforehand could only be reached after a climb of at least five hours. The road was constructed entirely by the voluntary labour of people from all over the north, using the most primitive tools. The project gained such fame that it attracted donations of B20 million, and on any one day as many as four thousand people were working on it. So that people didn't get in each other's way, Khruba Srivijaya declared that each village should contribute 15m of road, but as more volunteers flocked to Chiang Mai, this figure had to be reduced to 3m. The road was completed after just six months, and Khruba Srivijaya took the first ride to the temple in a donated car.

When Khruba Srivijaya died back in his native village in 1938, Rama VIII was so moved that he sponsored a royal cremation ceremony, held in 1946 (a long wait until the auspicious day for a cremation signifies high respect for the deceased). The monk's relics were divided up and are now enshrined at Wat Suan Dork in Chiang Mai, Wat Phra Kaeo Don Tao in Lampang and at many other holy places throughout the north. You'll see photos of him in temples, shops and restaurants all over the north, where Khruba amulets are still hugely popular, over seventy years after his death.

round three times, knelt down and died, thereby indicating that this was the spot. Ever since, it's been northern Thailand's most important place of pilgrimage, especially for the candlelit processions on **Maha Puja**, the anniversary of the sermon to the disciples, and **Visakha Puja**, the anniversary of the Buddha's birth, enlightenment and death.

Songthaews leave from Thanon Huai Kaeo in front of the zoo or Chiang Mai University for the sixteen-kilometre trip up to Wat Phra That (B40 to the wat, B80 return; B180 return to include Phuping Palace and Doi Pui village), but will only set off once they have a complement of six passengers. It costs around B500 and up to charter the whole vehicle, so you might be better off arranging a trip with, for example, *Your House* (see p.327), for B500 all-in. The road, although steep in places, is paved and well suited for motorbikes. At the end of Thanon Huai Kaeo, a statue of Khruba Srivijaya, the monk who organized the gargantuan effort to build the road from here to the wat, points the way to the temple.

A signpost halfway up is about the only indication that you're in **Doi Suthep-Pui National Park** (B200; Ⓦwww.dnp.go.th), which also encompasses the 1685-metre peak of Doi Pui to the northwest of Doi Suthep; however, an entry fee is not levied if you are only visiting the wat, Phuping Palace and Doi Pui village. Despite the nearness of the city, its rich mixed forests support 330 species of bird, and the area is a favoured site for nature study, second in the north only to the larger and less-disturbed Doi Inthanon National Park. On the higher slopes near the park headquarters (Ⓣ053 210244), about 1km beyond the wat, there are national park **bungalows** with hot-water bathrooms (from B400 for two people), as well as a visitor centre. Here you can get information about the park's **campsites**, for which **tents** can be rented (from B150 for two people), and trails, including a track up to Doi Pui summit beyond Phuping Palace.

About 5km from the statue of Khruba Srivijaya, a road on the right leads 3km to **Mon Tha Than Falls**, a beautiful spot, believed by some to be home to evil spirits. There's a campsite and bungalows with hot-water bathrooms (B1500 for six people) beside the pretty lower cascade, where refreshment stalls are open during the day. The higher fall is an idyllic five-metre drop into a small bathing pool, completely overhung by thick, humming jungle.

Wat Phra That Doi Suthep

Opposite a car park and souvenir village, a flight of three hundred naga-flanked steps – or the adjacent funicular – is the last leg on the way to **Wat Phra That Doi Suthep** (B30, or B50 including the funicular; Ⓦwww.doisuthep.com; see p.333 for information about meditation courses and talks). From the temple's **lower terrace**, the magnificent views of Chiang Mai and the surrounding plain, 300m below, are best in the early morning or late afternoon in the cool season, though peaceful contemplation of the view is frequently shattered by people sounding the heavy, dissonant bells around the terrace – they're supposed to bring good luck. At the northwestern corner is a two-metre-high statue of the elephant which, so the story goes, expired on this spot.

Before going to the **upper terrace** you have to remove your shoes – and if you're showing a bit of knee or shoulder, the temple provides wraps to cover your impoliteness. This terrace is possibly the most harmonious piece of temple architecture in Thailand, a dazzling combination of red, green and gold in the textures of carved wood, filigree and gleaming metal – even the tinkling of the miniature bells and the rattling of fortune sticks seem to keep the rhythm. A cloister, decorated with gaudy murals, tightly encloses the terrace, leaving room

▲ Chedi at Wat Phra That Doi Suthep

only for a couple of small minor viharns and the altars and ceremonial gold umbrellas which surround the central focus of attention, the **chedi**. This dazzling gold-plated beacon, a sixteenth-century extension of Ku Na's original, was modelled on the chedi at Wat Phra That Haripunjaya in Lamphun – which previously had been the region's most significant shrine – and has now become a venerated emblem of northern Thailand.

A small *hong*, or swan, on a wire stretching to the pinnacle is used to bless the chedi during major Buddhist festivals: a cup in the swan's beak is filled with water, and a pulley draws the swan to the spire where the water is tipped out over the sides of the chedi. Look out also for an old photograph opposite the northwestern corner of the chedi, showing a cockerel which used to peck the feet of visitors who entered with their shoes on.

Beyond the wat

Another 4km up the paved road from the wat, **Phuping Palace** (daily 8.30am–4.30pm, tickets on sale 8.30–11.30am & 1–3.30pm; B50; dress politely – no shorts or bare shoulders; Ⓦwwwbhubingpalace.org) is the residence for the royals when they come to visit their village development projects in the north (usually Jan–early March, when it is closed to the public). There is a viewpoint over the hills to the south, rose and fern gardens and some pleasant trails through the forest, but the buildings themselves are off-limits. About 3km from the palace along a side road and accessible by songthaew, **Ban Doi Pui** is a highly commercialized Hmong village, only worth visiting if you don't have time to get out into the countryside – seeing the Hmong is about all you get out of it.

Wiang Kum Kam

The well-preserved and rarely visited ruins of the ancient city of **WIANG KUM KAM** – traditionally regarded as the prototype for Chiang Mai – are hidden away in the picturesque, rural fringe of town, 5km south of the centre. According to folklore, Wiang Kum Kam was built by King Mengrai as his new capital of the north, but was soon abandoned because of inundation by the Ping River. Recent excavations, however, have put paid to that theory: Wiang Kum Kam was in fact established much earlier, as one of a cluster of fortified satellite towns that surrounded the Mon capital at Lamphun. After Mengrai had conquered Lamphun in 1281, he resided at Kum Kam for a while, raising a chedi, a viharn and several Buddha statues before moving on to build Chiang Mai. Wiang Kum Kam was abandoned sometime before 1750, probably as a result of a Burmese invasion.

About 3km square, the ancient city can be explored on a bicycle or a motorbike, though it's easy to get lost in the maze of lanes connecting the ruins. It's more enjoyable to rent a **horse and cart** for B200, which will take you on a leisurely ride round the main sites for about an hour. These are available from either Chedi Si Liam (see below) or the new **museum** (daily 8.30am–5pm; B5; ⓣ053 277322) on the southern edge of Wiang Kum Kam: if you head east on Chiang Mai's second ring road, it's just after the first permissible left turn after the river bridge. The museum, which gives a dry, basic introduction to the temples, also organizes roughly hour-long **tram rides** around ten of the temples, stopping off at three of them (B250–400 depending on the number of people) and rents out bicycles (B20). You could also arrange a **cruise** down the river with Mae Ping River Cruises (see p.330; B700 per person including pick-up, minimum two people; 2hr altogether), followed by a carriage ride to six temples and the museum. If you're happy to look around under your own steam, the best way to approach Wiang Kum Kam is from Chiang Mai's first ring road, the Superhighway; immediately to the east of the bridge over the Ping River, take the signposted turning to the south.

About half of Wiang Kum Kam's 22 known temple sites have now been uncovered, along with a stone slab (now housed in the Chiang Mai National Museum) inscribed in a unique forerunner of the Thai script. Head first for **Chedi Si Liam**, 1km south of the Superhighway, which provides a useful landmark: this Mon chedi, in the shape of a tall, squared-off pyramid with niched Buddha images was built by Mengrai in memory of his dead wife. Modelled on Wat Kukut in Lamphun, it was restored in 1908 by a wealthy Burmese Mon using Burmese artisans and is still part of a working temple.

Backtracking along the road you've travelled down from Chiang Mai, take the first right turn, turn right again and keep left through a scattered farming settlement to reach, after about 2km, **Wat Kan Thom** (aka Chang Kham), the centre of the old city and still an important place of worship. Archeologists were only able to get at the site after much of it had been levelled by bulldozers building a playground for the adjacent school, but they have managed to uncover the brick foundations of Mengrai's viharn. The modern shrine next to it is where Mengrai's soul is said to reside. Also in the grounds are a white chedi and a small viharn, both much restored, and a large new viharn displaying fine craftsmanship.

If you have your own transport, from here you can head off along the trails through the thick foliage of the longan plantations to the northwest of Wat Kan Thom, back towards Chedi Si Liam. On this route, you come across surprisingly well-preserved chedis and the red-brick walls of Wiang Kum Kam's temples in a handful of shady clearings set between rural dwellings.

Lamphun

Though capital of its own province, **LAMPHUN** lives in the shadow of the tourist attention (and baht) showered on Chiang Mai, 26km to the north. Yet for anyone interested in history, a visit to this former royal city is a must. The town's largely plain architecture is given some character by the surrounding waterways, beyond which stretch lush rice-fields and plantations of *lamyai* (longan); the sweetness of the local variety is celebrated every year in early August at the **Ngan Lamyai** (Longan Festival), when the town comes alive with processions of fruity floats, a drum-beating competition and a Miss Lamyai beauty contest. Lamphun also offers a less frantic alternative to Chiang Mai during the Songkhran and Loy Krathong festivals, the Khuang River being a far less congested place to float your *krathong* than Chiang Mai's Ping River. Though the streets of the town are usually sleepy, the ancient working **temples** of Wat Phra That Haripunjaya and Wat Kukut are lively and worth aiming for on a half-day trip from Chiang Mai.

Lamphun claims to be the oldest continuously inhabited town in Thailand, and has a history dating back to the late eighth or early ninth century when the ruler of the major Dvaravati centre at Lopburi sent his daughter, Chama Thevi, to found the Theravada Buddhist state of **Haripunjaya** here. Under the dynasty she established, Haripunjaya flourished as a link in the trade route to Yunnan in southwest China, although it eventually came under the suzerainty of the Khmers at Angkor, probably in the early eleventh century. In 1281, after a decade of scheming, King Mengrai of Chiang Mai conquered Lamphun and integrated it once and for all into the Kingdom of Lanna, which by then covered all of the north country.

The Town

Chama Thevi's planners are said to have based their design for the town on the shape of an auspicious conch shell. The rough outcome is a rectangle, narrower at the north end than the south, with the Khuang River running down its kilometre-long east side, and moats around the north, west and south sides. The main street, Thanon Inthayongyot, bisects the conch from north to south, while the road to Wat Kukut (Thanon Chama Thevi) heads out from the middle of the west moat.

One of the north's grandest and most important temples, **Wat Phra That Haripunjaya** has its rear entrance on Thanon Inthayongyot and its bot and ornamental front entrance facing the river. The earliest guess at the date of its founding is 897, when the king of Haripunjaya is said to have built a chedi to enshrine a hair of the Buddha. More certain is the date of the main rebuilding of the temple, under King Tilok of Chiang Mai in 1443, when the present ringed chedi was erected in the then-fashionable Sri Lankan style (later copied at Doi Suthep and Lampang). Clad in brilliant copper plates, it has since been raised to a height of about 50m, crowned by a gold umbrella.

The plain open courtyards around the chedi contain a compendium of religious structures in a wild mix of styles and colours. On the north side, the tiered Haripunjaya-style pyramid of **Chedi Suwanna** was built in 1418 as a replica of the chedi at nearby Wat Kukut. You get a whiff of southern Thailand in the open space beyond the Suwanna chedi, where the **Chedi Chiang Yan** owes its resemblance to a pile of flattened pumpkins to the Srivijayan style. On either side of the viharn (to the east of the main chedi) stand a dark red **bell tower**, containing what's claimed to be the world's largest bronze gong, and a weather-beaten **library** on a raised base. Just to add to the temple's mystique, an open pavilion at the southwest corner of the chedi shelters a stone indented with four overlapping **footprints**, believed by fervent worshippers to confirm an ancient legend that the Buddha once passed this way. Next to the pavilion is a small **museum** which houses bequests to the temple, including some beautiful Buddha images in the Lanna style. Finally, beside the back entrance, is the **Phra Chao Tan Jai**, a graceful standing Buddha, surrounded by graphic murals that depict a horrific version of Buddhist hell.

Across the main road from the wat's back entrance, the **Hariphunchai National Museum** (Wed–Sun 9am–4pm; B30; Ⓦ www.nationalmuseum.com) contains a well-organized but not quite compelling collection of religious finds, and occasionally stages some interesting temporary exhibitions. The terracotta and bronze Buddha images here give the best overview of the distinctive features of the Haripunjaya style: large curls above a wide, flat forehead, bulging eyes, incised moustache and enigmatic smile.

Art-history buffs will get a thrill out of **Wat Chama Thevi** (also known as Wat Kukut), where two brick chedis, dated to 1218, are the only complete examples not just of Haripunjaya architecture, but of the whole Dvaravati style. Queen Chama Thevi is supposed to have chosen the site by ordering an archer to fire an arrow from the city's western gate – to retrace his epic shot, follow the road along the National Museum's southern wall to the west gate at the city moat, and keep going for nearly 1km along Thanon Chama Thevi. The main chedi – Suwan Chang Kot – is tiered and rectangular, the smaller Ratana Chedi octagonal, and both are inset with niches sheltering beautiful, wide-browed Buddha images in stucco, typical of the Haripunjaya style. Suwan Chang Kot, believed to enshrine Chama Thevi's ashes, lost its pinnacle at some stage, giving rise to the name Wat Kukut, the temple with the "topless" chedi. On your way back to the town centre from Wat Chama Thevi, you might like to pop in at **Wat Mahawan**, famous for the Buddha image amulets on sale here and located just outside the west gate.

Practicalities

The direct (and scenic) route from Chiang Mai to Lamphun is Highway 106, for much of the way a stately avenue lined by thirty-metre-tall *yang* trees that makes for a pleasant motorbike ride. Otherwise you could catch a blue **songthaew** from the Chiang Mai–Lamphun road, just south of Narawat Bridge and opposite the TAT office, or a **bus** from Chang Puak bus station, via Lamyai market, either of which will put you off outside the back entrance of Wat Haripunjaya. It's not worth considering the train as the station is way out to the northeast of the town centre.

Among the few **restaurants** in Lamphun with an English-language menu is *Lamphun Ice*, which serves tasty Thai food at reasonable prices; it's conveniently situated at 6 Thanon Chaimongkol, the road that runs along the south wall of Wat Haripunjaya. It's unlikely you'll want to **stay** overnight in Lamphun, but the recently renovated *Lamphun Will Hotel* on Thanon Chama Thevi opposite Wat Kukut (Ⓣ 053 534865–6; ⑤, including breakfast) is a decent choice. There's a restaurant on the fourth floor, and en-suite, hot-water bathrooms, air-conditioning and wi-fi in all the bedrooms; a swimming pool is planned.

North of Chiang Mai

On the north side of Chiang Mai, Thanon Chotana turns into Highway 107, which heads off through a flat, featureless valley, past a golf course and an army camp, towards the small market town of **Mae Rim**, 16km away. With your own transport, you can head off down side roads to the west of Highway 107, either to **Huay Tung Tao** for a swim and chillout, or to the **Mae Sa valley**, which despite its theme-park atmosphere, boasts the lovely botanic gardens, as well as some pretty resorts that might even tempt you to spend a night out of Chiang Mai. Without your own vehicle, it's best to organize a tour as public transport here is at best sporadic – *Your House*, for example (see p.327), charge around B600.

Huay Tung Tao

About 10km out of Chiang Mai, look for the signpost to the left to **Huay Tung Tao**, a large man-made lake at the base of Doi Suthep, 2km west of the turn-off. A great place to cool off during the hot season, the lake is safe to swim in, with canoes and inner tubes to rent, and is also used by anglers and windsurfers. Floating bamboo shelters along the water's edge provide shade from the sun, and you can order simple food such as sticky rice, grilled chicken and *som tam*.

Darapirom Palace

In Mae Rim itself, look out for a sign on the left just before the police station to the **Darapirom Palace** (Tues–Sun 9am–5pm; B50), a gorgeous colonial-style building from the early twentieth century. The palace was once the home of Princess Dara Rasamee (1873–1933), daughter of Chao Inthanon, the lord of Lanna, who became the favourite concubine of King Chulalongkorn of Siam in the days when Lanna was still a vassal state. Extremely proud of her northern heritage – and now something of a heroine to lovers of Lanna culture – the princess had this residence built in 1914, a few years after Chulalongkorn's death, when she returned from Bangkok to live out her later years in her homeland. Chulalongkorn University has recently opened the palace as a museum, featuring period furnishings and many items that once belonged to the princess. Photographs of her show her knee-length hair – which contrasted strongly with the fashion among Siamese women of the time to sport short-cropped hair – and the various rooms of the museum display her wardrobe and personal effects including musical instruments.

The Mae Sa valley

Turn left about 1km after Mae Rim to enter the **Mae Sa valley**, where a good sealed road, Route 1096, leads up into the hills. The main road through the valley passes a menagerie of snake farms, monkey shows, elephant camps, "adventure sports" venues, and orchid and butterfly farms, as well as the unspectacular **Mae Sa Waterfall** (part of Doi Suthep-Pui National Park; B200), where you can walk up a peaceful trail passing lots of little cascades along the way. Twelve kilometres from the turn-off is the main reason for coming here, the magnificent **Queen Sirikit Botanic Gardens** (daily 8.30am–4.30pm; B40, cars B100; Ⓦwww.qsbg.org). If you are at all botanically inclined, you could easily spend the whole day here, exploring the four nature trails that link its arboretum, ornamental beds, rock garden, orchid nursery, areas of climbers and medicinal plants and a dozen glasshouses; shuttle buses (B30) run around the extensive grounds, if the heat gets too much.

Among several **resorts** in the Mae Sa valley, the pick is the *Four Seasons* (Ⓣ053 298181, Ⓦwww.fourseasons.com; ⑨), down a side road on the left just 1km after the turning into the valley from Mae Rim. The last word in Lanna luxury, the resort has superbly appointed rooms and apartments, a swimming pool and a gorgeous spa, all set around a picturesque lake and rice paddies (where you can learn to plant rice) with fine views of Doi Suthep behind. On a long menu of activities, there's a top-quality cooking school – where popular Sunday brunches are also served – and it's a good spot to stop even if you're not staying, especially in the late afternoon, to enjoy a meal or drink on the terrace. Other resorts in the valley are far simpler than the *Four Seasons*, but attractive nonetheless; among these the *Pong Yang Garden Resort* (ⓣ053 879151–3, ⓦwww.pongyangangdoi.com; ❼) stands out, located a couple of kilometres beyond the botanic gardens on the south side of the road. It boasts cosy, well-equipped bungalows as well as a restaurant with a view of an attractive waterfall.

Once you've seen all you want to in the valley, you have the option of continuing west for a scenic drive in the country: turn left on to Route 1269 before Samoeng, and follow this road as it swoops up and down over hills, skirting Doi Suthep to join Highway 108 8km south of Chiang Mai, a two-hour drive in all.

East of Chiang Mai

From Chiang Mai, visitors usually head northwest to Pai or Mae Hong Son, or north to Chiang Rai, but a trip eastwards to the ancient city-states of Lampang, Phrae and Nan can be just as rewarding, not only for the dividends of going against the usual flow, but also for the natural beauty of the region's upland ranges – seen to best effect from the well-marked trails of **Doi Khun Tan National Park** – and for its eccentric variety of Thai, Burmese and Laotian art and architecture. Congenial **Lampang** contains Thai wats to rival those of Chiang Mai for beauty – in Wat Phra That Lampang Luang the town has the finest surviving example of traditional northern architecture anywhere – and is further endowed with pure Burmese temples and some fine old city architecture, while little-visited **Phrae**, to the southeast, is a step back in time to a simpler Thailand. Further away but a more intriguing target is **Nan**, with its heady artistic mix of Thai and Laotian styles and steep ring of scenic mountains.

A couple of major **roads**, covered by regular through buses from Chiang Mai, serve the region: Highway 11 heads southeast through Lampang and the junction town of Den Chai before plummeting south to Phitsanulok; while from Den Chai, Highway 101 carries on northeast through Phrae to Nan. Winding Route 1148 between Tha Wang Pha and Chiang Kham makes it tempting to continue north from Nan to Chiang Rai or Chiang Khong, through some spectacular scenery. The **Northern Rail Line** follows a course roughly parallel with Highway 11 through this area, including a useful stop at Doi Khun Tan National Park, and although trains here are generally slower than buses, the stations at Den Chai (from where buses and songthaews run to Phrae and Nan) and Lampang are useful if you're coming up from Bangkok.

Doi Khun Tan National Park

One of three major national parks close to Chiang Mai, along with Suthep and Inthanon, **DOI KHUN TAN NATIONAL PARK** (B100; ⓣ053 546335 or 053 519216–7, ⓦwww.dnp.go.th) is easily accessible by train from Chiang Mai: a 1352-metre-long rail tunnel, the longest in Thailand, built between 1907 and 1918 by German engineers and Thai workers (of whom over a thousand died due to accidents, malaria and tigers), cuts through the mountain that gives the park its name. Despite this, and the fact that the king has famously holidayed here, the park is the least spoiled of the three, but has enough infrastructure to encourage overnighting.

Covering 255 square kilometres, the park's vegetation varies from bamboo forest at an altitude of 350m to tropical evergreen forest between 600 and 1000m; the 1373-metre summit of Doi Khun Tan is known for its wild flowers, including orchids, gingers and lilies. Most of the small mammal species in the park are squirrels, but you're more likely to see some birds, with over 182 species found here. A leaflet on the park's ecology can sometimes be obtained at the park **headquarters**, a 1300-metre walk up the summit trail from the train station.

The **trails** are clearly marked, running from short nature trails around the park headquarters (where maps are available) to three major trails that all eventually lead to the summit of **Doi Khun Tan** – with impressive views of the surrounding countryside, it's clear how it fulfilled its role as a World War II military lookout. The main 8.3-kilometre trail from the train station to the Doi Khun Tan summit, though steep, is very easy, divided into four quarters of approximately 2km each, with each quarter ending at a resting place. While you shouldn't have a problem getting to the summit and back in a day, a more rewarding option is to do the walk in two days, staying overnight in the bungalows or at one of the campsites along the trail. Alternatively, you can take a circular route to the summit and back, forsaking a large chunk of the main trail for the two subsidiary trails which curve around either side, taking in two **waterfalls**.

Practicalities

There are currently two morning and three afternoon **trains** daily from Chiang Mai to Khun Tan station (about 1hr 30min) on their way to Lampang and beyond, but there's no longer an evening train back, ruling out a day-trip by rail from the city (though it might be worth checking the latest timetables, just in case the evening service is reinstated). A **car** or motorbike can take you to the park headquarters, though no further: follow Highway 11 to the turn-off to Mae Tha and head northeast for 18km, following signs for the park.

The park is most popular on weekends, when groups of Thai schoolchildren visit, and during the cool season. Park **bungalows**, which are mostly spacious and well-appointed log cabins with hot-water bathrooms (from B1500 for six people), are located just up the main trail from the headquarters, while tents, if you don't have your own, can be hired for the **campsites** (from B150 sleeping two people). There are basic **restaurants** at headquarters and beside the bungalows.

Lampang and around

A high road pass and a train tunnel breach the narrow, steep belt of mountains between Chiang Mai and **LAMPANG**, the north's second-largest town, 100km to the southeast. Lampang is an important transport hub – Highway 11, Highway 1 and the Northern Rail Line all converge here – and given its undeniably low-key attractions, nearly all travellers sail through it on their way to the more trumpeted sights further north. But unlike most other provincial capitals, Lampang has the look of a place where history has not been completely wiped out: houses, shops and temples survive in the traditional style, and the town makes few concessions to tourism. Out of town, the beautiful complex of Wat Phra That Lampang Luang is the main attraction in these parts, but while you're in the neighbourhood you could also stop by to watch a show at the Elephant Conservation Centre, on the road from Chiang Mai.

Founded as Kelang Nakhon by the ninth-century Haripunjaya queen Chama Thevi, Lampang became important enough for one of her two sons to rule here after her death. After King Mengrai's conquest of Haripunjaya in 1281, Lampang suffered much the same ups and downs as the rest of Lanna, enjoying a burst of prosperity as a **timber** town at the end of the nineteenth century, when it supported a population of twenty thousand people and four thousand working elephants. Many of its temples are financially endowed by the waves of outsiders who have settled in Lampang: refugees from Chiang Saen (who were forcibly resettled here by Rama I at the beginning of the nineteenth century), Burmese teak-loggers and-workers, and, more recently, rich Thai pensioners attracted by the town's sedate charm.

Arrival, information and transport

The **train and bus stations** lie less than 1km to the southwest of the town centre, while Chiang Rai buses also make a stop on Thanon Phaholyothin in the centre. PB Air (see p.45) run **flights** from Bangkok once or twice a day to the airport, just south of town, and songthaews are on hand for the short ride to the centre. The small, municipal **tourist information** centre (Mon–Fri 8.30am–noon & 1–4.30pm, Sat & Sun roughly 9am–noon & 1–5pm; Ⓣ054 237229, Ⓦwww.lampangcity.go.th), just west of the clocktower and next to the fire station on Thanon Takrao Noi, can provide a map of the town and help with advice on excursions. You can access the **internet**, while sipping an espresso, at *Coffee Bus* on the ground floor of the *Pin Hotel*.

Most of the town can be covered on foot, though to get out to Wat Phra Kaew Don Tao you might want to employ the services of a **horse-drawn carriage**, which along with white chickens (see opposite) is a prevalent symbol of Lampang (in fact, Thais often refer to the city as *muang rot mah*, or "horse-cart city"). These colourfully decked-out carriages, complete with Stetson-wearing driver, can be hired towards the east end of Thanon Boonyawat or opposite the tourist office. Standard routes around town cost B150 for about fifteen minutes, B200 for around thirty minutes or B300 for one hour, which includes a visit to Wat Phra Kaew Don Tao and other points of interest. Apart from this quirky mode of transport, there are plenty of yellow-and-green **songthaews** that cruise the streets looking for custom (B20 per person within the city). **Bicycles** (B50–60 per day) can be rented at *Akhamsiri Home* and *Riverside Guest House*, **motorbikes** (B200 per day) at the latter, and cars (B1500 per day) at *Pin Hotel*.

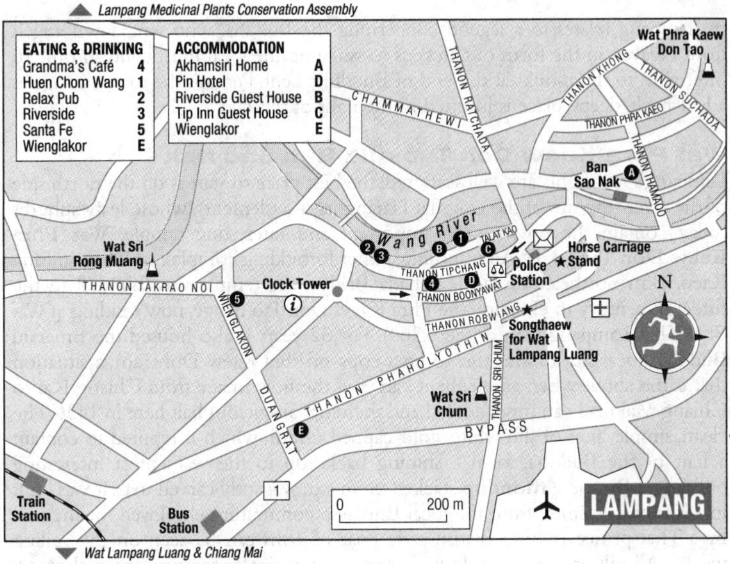

Accommodation

Lampang offers a wide variety of good-value accommodation, including an excellent guest house on the quiet southern bank of the Wang River.

Akhamsiri Home 54/1 Thanon Pamaiket ⓣ 054 228791, ⓦ www.akhamsirihome.com. In a quiet part of town, attractive, slightly cutesy rooms in modern Thai style, with balconies upstairs, small gardens downstairs; all have air-con, hot water and fridges. There's also a café with internet access. ③

Pin Hotel 8 Thanon Suandok ⓣ 054 221509, ⓔ pinhotel@yahoo.com. On a quieter side street, this place has a touch more class than other moderately priced hotels in town. The good-sized and attractively furnished rooms all have air-con, cable TV and hot water, and breakfast is included. ④

Riverside Guest House 286 Thanon Talat Kao ⓣ 054 227005, ⓦ www.theriverside-lampang.com. At the far west end of the street, a peaceful traditional compound of two teak houses with a small, attractive garden. The tasteful rooms, all with en-suite, hot-water bathrooms and a few with air-con, are more elegant in the main house, simpler in the second house; some boast balconies or terraces overlooking the river. Varied breakfasts are served in the relaxing riverside café. Local tours available. Fan ②–③, air-con ④

Tip Inn Guest House 143 Thanon Talat Kao ⓣ 054 221821. Rooms at this Thai-Chinese establishment are classic budget travellers' digs – small, cheap and without views, though all have access to hot showers, whether shared or en suite. Nice little front porch to sit back and watch the comings and goings. Internet access. Fan ①–②, air-con ②

Wienglakor 138/35 Thanon Phaholyothin ⓣ 054 316430–5, ⓦ www.wienglakor.com. Of several big and expensive hotels in town, this one has the cosiest rooms and the most tasteful decor, with coffered ceilings, parquet floors and ornamental ponds in traditional Thai style. Breakfast included. ⑥

The Town

The modern centre of Lampang sprawls along the south side of the Wang River, with its most frenetic commercial activity taking place along Thanon Boonyawat and Thanon Robwiang near Ratchada Bridge. Here, you'll find stalls and shops selling the famous local **pottery**, a kitsch combination of whites, blues and browns, made from the area's rich and durable kaolin clay. On all street signs around town, and in larger-than-life statues at key intersections, is a **white chicken**. This symbol of Lampang relates to a legend concerning the Buddha, who sent down angels from Heaven in the form of chickens to wake up the local inhabitants in time to offer alms to the monks at the end of Buddhist Lent. Perhaps the town's image as a laid-back, sleepy place is justified in the light of this tale.

Wat Phra Kaew Don Tao and Ban Sao Nak

Lampang's few sights are well scattered; the best place to start is on the north side of the river (the site of the original Haripunjaya settlement), whose leafy suburbs today contain the town's most important and interesting temple, **Wat Phra Kaew Don Tao** (B20). An imposing, rather forbidding complex on Thanon Phra Kaeo, 1km northeast of the Ratchada Bridge, the temple was founded in the fifteenth century to enshrine the Phra Kaew Don Tao image, now residing at Wat Phra That Lampang Luang (see p.364). For 32 years it also housed the Emerald Buddha (local stories aver this to be a copy of Phra Kaew Don Tao), a situation that came about when an elephant carrying the holy image from Chiang Rai to Chiang Mai made an unscheduled and therefore auspicious halt here in 1436. The clean, simple lines of the white, gold-capped **chedi**, which is reputed to contain a hair of the Buddha, form a shining backdrop to the wat's most interesting building, a Burmese **mondop** stacked up in extravagantly carved tiers; it was built in 1909 by craftsmen from the local Burmese community, employed for the task by a Thai prince (whose British-style coat of arms can be seen on the ceiling inside). All gilt and gaudy coloured glass, the interior decoration is a real fright, mixing Oriental and European influences, with some incongruously cute little cherubs on the ceiling. The mondop's boyish bronze centrepiece has the typical features of a Mandalay Buddha, with its jewelled headband, inset black and white eyes, and exaggerated, dangling ears, which denote the Buddha's supernatural ability to hear everything in the universe. In front of the Buddha is an image of Khruba Srivijaya, the north's most venerated monk (see box, p.351).

The small **museum** at the back of the compound displays some dainty china among its exhibits, but its main focus is woodcarving, a craft at which Burmese artisans excel. To see a better, though still small, display of ceramics, lacquerware and teak furnishings, make your way to **Ban Sao Nak** ("many pillar house") at 6 Thanon Ratwattana, not far from Wat Phra Kaew Don Tao (daily 10am–5pm; B50). Built in 1895 in a mixture of Burmese and Lanna styles, this sprawling wooden mansion is supported by a maze of 116 teak pillars and contains some interesting fading photographs of its former occupants, who were local notables.

Wat Sri Chum and south of the river

The Burmese who worked on Wat Phra Kaew Don Tao were brought to Lampang in the late nineteenth century when, after the British conquest of Upper Burma, timber companies expanded their operations as far as northern Thailand. Fearing that the homeless spirits of fallen trees would seek vengeance, the Burmese loggers often sponsored the building of temples, most of which still stand, to try to appease the tree spirits and gain merit. Though the spirits had to wait nearly a century, they seem to have got their revenge: due to a short circuit in some dodgy wiring, the viharn of **Wat Sri Chum**, which is the biggest Burmese temple in Thailand as well as the most important and beautiful Burmese temple in town, burnt to the ground in 1992. Now restored to its former glory, with fresh carvings and murals by Burmese craftsmen, it's sited in a small grove of bodhi trees five minutes' walk south of Thanon Robwiang. None of the remaining wats is of outstanding architectural merit, but to get more of a flavour of Burma, try hundred-year-old **Wat Sri Rong Muang**,

▲ Wat Sri Rong Muang

towards the west end of Thanon Takrao Noi, which presents a dazzling ensemble: the crazy angles of its red-and-yellow roof shelter more Mandalay Buddhas and several extravagantly carved gilt sermon-thrones, swimming in a glittering sea of coloured-glass wall tiles.

When you've had your fill of temples, **Thanon Talat Kao**, the "Old Market Street", running behind the south bank of the river, is good for a quiet stroll in the early morning. It has some very old shophouses and mansions, showing a mixture of European, Burmese and Chinese influences (it used to be known as Talat Jiin, "Chinese market"), with intricate balconies, carved gables and unusual sunburst designs carved over some of the doors. On Saturday and Sunday evenings (roughly 4.30–9.30pm), Talat Kao comes to life as a "**walking street**", similar to those in Chiang Mai, with food, silk and other crafts for sale and musicians playing.

Lampang Medicinal Plants Conservation Assembly

Though the **Lampang Medicinal Plants Conservation Assembly** (Rak Samoonprai; ⓣ054 313128, ⓦwww.herblpg.com) sounds like the kind of place where botanists might hold seminars, it is in fact a traditional health centre set in a shady compound about 3km northwest of the town centre. If you feel like pampering your body, head out here for a strong traditional massage (from B100 per hr), herbal sauna, face scrub, mud skin treatment or even a bare-footed health walk over a path of rounded pebbles designed to provide a natural foot massage. The facilities are spotless, the grounds are full of labelled herbs, and a huge range of medicinal plant products is on sale. To get there, a songthaew from the centre of Lampang costs around B60; if you're driving yourself, follow Thanon Chammathewi towards Haeng Chat for a couple of kilometres, then turn right and left, following signs for "Lampang Herbs Conservation".

Eating and drinking

Along with the riverfront, whose restaurants are reviewed below, the stretch of Thanon Takrao Noi between the clocktower and Thanon Wienglakon is a lively part of town after dark, featuring many simple restaurants and the Atsawin night market running off its side streets to the south, as well as pubs, karaoke bars and Wild West **bars** such as *Santa Fe*.

Grandma's Café Thanon Tipchang. Popular hangout for artsy young Lampangers in the evening, serving espressos and lots of noodle and rice dishes. Closed Sun.

Huen Chom Wang 276 Thanon Talat Kao. The English sign here isn't obvious – look for the alley 100m east of the *Riverside Guest House* – but this peaceful, sprawling wooden building has fine views of the river and its menu features many northern specialities.

Relax Pub Thanon Tipchang, just west of the *Riverside*. Generally livelier than its more famous neighbour, featuring live music at night and serving a range of good Thai and Western food.

Riverside 328 Thanon Tipchang. Cosy, relaxing spot on rustic wooden terraces overlooking the water, serving a wide variety of excellent Thai dishes, including northern specialities, and Western food, to the sounds of live music in the evenings. A wood-fired pizza oven is stoked up Tues, Thurs, Sat & Sun (from B110); during the daytime, *Riverside* operates as a bakery-café.

Wienglakor 138/35 Thanon Phaholyothin. The best hotel restaurant in town with a wide choice of well-prepared, good-value dishes and an inviting ambience, overlooking the landscaped gardens.

Wat Phra That Lampang Luang

A grand and well-preserved capsule of Lanna art and design, 18km southwest of Lampang, **Wat Phra That Lampang Luang** is one of the architectural highlights of northern Thailand. Blue songthaews will take you to the temple direct from Thanon Robwiang (around B40). On a motorbike (which can be rented from the *Riverside Guest House*) or other transport, head south from Lampang on Highway 1, then cross the bridge over the Wang River at Kor Kha and turn right, heading north for about 3km on Route 1034; if you're coming from Chiang Mai or the elephant centre, save yourself a roundabout trip into Lampang by turning right off Highway 11 onto Route 1034.

The wat was built early in the Haripunjaya era as a *wiang* (fortress), one of a satellite group around Lampang – you can still see remains of the threefold ramparts in the farming village around the temple. A naga staircase leads you up to a wedding cake of a gatehouse, richly decorated with stucco, which is set in the original brick boundary walls. Just inside, the oversized fifteenth-century **viharn** is open on all sides in classic Lanna fashion, and shelters a spectacular centrepiece: known as a *ku*, a feature found only in the viharns of northern Thailand, this gilded brick tower looks like a bonfire for the main Buddha image sitting inside, the Phra Chao Lan Thong. Tall visitors need to mind their heads on the panels hanging from the low eaves, which are decorated with attractive, though fading, early nineteenth-century paintings of battles, palaces and nobles in traditional Burmese gear.

This central viharn is snugly flanked by three others. In front of the murky, beautifully decorated viharn to the left, look out for a wooden *tung chai* carved with flaming, coiled nagas, used as a heraldic banner for northern princes. The battered, cosy **Viharn Nam Tame**, second back on the right, dates to the early sixteenth century. Its drooping roof configuration is archetypal: divided into three tiers, each of which is divided again into two layers, it ends up almost scraping the ground. Under the eaves you can just make out fragments of panel paintings, as old as the viharn, illustrating a story of one of the exploits of the Hindu god Indra.

The wat's huge central **chedi** enshrines a hair of the Buddha and ashes from the right side of his forehead and neck. By its northwest corner, a sign points to a drainage hole in the wat's boundary wall, once the scene of an unlikely act of derring-do: in 1736, local hero Thip Chang managed to wriggle through the tiny hole and free the *wiang* from the occupying Burmese, before going on to liberate the whole of Lampang.

To the south of the chedi, the **Haw Phra Phuttabhat** (no entry for women) is a small chamber that acts as a camera obscura. If you close the door behind you, an image of the chedi is projected through a small hole in the door onto a sheet hung on a wall. A gate in the south side of the boundary wall leads to a spreading **bodhi tree** on crutches: merit-makers have donated hundreds of supports to prop up its drooping branches. The tree, with its own small shrine standing underneath, is believed to be inhabited by spirits, and the sick are sometimes brought here in search of a cure.

Don't miss the small, unimpressive viharn to the west of the main complex (go on round beyond the bodhi tree) – it's the home of **Phra Kaew Don Tao**, the much-revered companion image to Bangkok's Emerald Buddha, and the wat's main focus of pilgrimage. Legend has it that the statuette first appeared in the form of an emerald found in a watermelon presented by a local woman to a venerated monk. The two of them tried to carve a Buddha out of the emerald, without much success, until the god Indra appeared and fashioned the marvellous image, at which point the ungrateful townsfolk accused the monk of having an affair with the woman and put her to death, thus bringing down upon the town a series of disasters which confirmed the image's awesome power. In all probability, the image was carved at the beginning of the fifteenth century, when its namesake wat in Lampang was founded. Peering through the dim light and the rows of protective bars inside the viharn, you can just make out the tiny meditating Buddha – it's actually made of jasper, not emerald – which on special occasions is publicly displayed wearing a headdress and necklace.

Cashing in on Phra Kaew Don Tao's supernatural reputation, a shop in the viharn sells amulets and Buddha images. Outside the wat, simple snacks, handicrafts and antiques can be bought from market stalls; also available are the small china cows with which devotees make merit, inscribing the models first with their name and the date in black ink and then offering them to the shrine in front of the chedi, making a curious display.

The Thai Elephant Conservation Centre

The **Thai Elephant Conservation Centre** (aka the National Elephant Institute; shows at 10am, 11am & 1.30pm; bathing at 9.45am & 1.15pm; admission B70, children B30; Ⓦwww.thailandelephant.org), 34km west of Lampang on Highway 11, is the most authentic and worthwhile place in Thailand to see elephants displaying their skills. Entertaining **shows** put the elephants through their paces, with plenty of loud trumpeting for their audience. After some photogenic bathing, they walk together in formation and go through a routine of pushing and dragging logs, then proceed to paint pictures and play custom-made instruments. You can feed them bananas and sugarcane after the show, and if you are impressed by their art or music you can buy a freshly painted picture or a CD by the Thai Elephant Orchestra, as well as souvenirs such as cards made from elephant-dung paper. Visitors are also free to look around the hospital (see p.366), but not the royal stables, where six of Rama IX's eleven white elephants are kept. **Elephant-rides** (daily 8am–3.30pm) cost from B50 per person for ten minutes, up to B800 for two people for an hour, which will give you the chance to get out into the nearby forest; overnight treks into the forest are also possible. A full-day programme,

The elephant in Thailand

To Thais the **elephant** has profound **spiritual significance**, derived from both Hindu and Buddhist mythologies. Carvings and statues of **Ganesh**, the Hindu god with an elephant's head, feature on ancient temples all over the country and, as the god of knowledge and remover of obstacles, Ganesh has been adopted as the symbol of the Fine Arts Department – and is thus depicted on all entrance tickets to historical sights. The Hindu deity Indra rarely appears without his three-headed elephant mount **Erawan**, and miniature devotional elephant effigies are sold at major Brahmin shrines, such as Bangkok's Erawan Shrine. In Buddhist legend, the future **Buddha's mother** was able to conceive only after she dreamt that a white elephant had entered her womb: that is why elephant balustrades encircle many of the Buddhist temples of Sukhothai, and why the rare white elephant is accorded royal status (see p.160) and featured on the national flag until 1917.

The **practical** role of the elephant in Thailand was once almost as great as its symbolic importance. The kings of Ayutthaya relied on elephants to take them into battle against the Burmese – one king assembled a trained elephant army of three hundred – and during the nineteenth century King Rama IV offered Abraham Lincoln a male and a female to "multiply in the forests of America" and to use in the Civil War. In times of peace, the phenomenal strength of the elephant has made it invaluable as a beast of burden: elephants hauled the stone from which the gargantuan Khmer temple complexes of the northeast were built, and for centuries they have been used to clear forests and carry timber.

The traditional cycle for domestic elephants born in captivity is to spend the first three years of their lives with their mothers (who are pregnant for 18–22 months and get five years' maternity leave), before being separated and raised with other calves in training schools. Each elephant is then assigned its own **mahout** (*kwan chang*) – a trainer, keeper and driver rolled into one – who traditionally would stay with it for the rest of its working life. Training begins gently, with mahouts taking months to earn the trust of their charge; over the next thirteen years the elephant is taught about forty different commands, from simple "stop" and "go" orders to complex instructions for

combining a show, bathing and riding with the chance to meet the staff and see the hospital, plus lunch, costs B3500. Various **homestay** and mahout training programmes are also on offer (ⓣ054 247875 or 089 755 4917), ranging up to a ten-day course that includes two nights out in the jungle (B35,000 including accommodation and meals); for more information, check out their website.

Run by the Thai government, the conservation centre was originally set up in 1969 in another nearby location as a young elephant training centre, the earliest of its kind in Thailand. However, since the ban on logging, the new centre, opened in 1992, emphasizes the preservation of the elephant in Thailand. By promoting ecotourism the centre is providing employment for the elephants and enabling Thai people to continue their historically fond relationship with these animals. Money raised from entrance fees and donations helps to finance the **elephant hospital** here, which cares for sick, abused, ageing and abandoned elephants.

Practicalities

With its entrance gates and ticket office on Highway 11, the Elephant Conservation Centre is on the bus route between Chiang Mai and Lampang: just ask the bus conductor to stop at the centre. From the gates there are regular shuttle buses into the elephant showground a couple of kilometres away. There's a simple **restaurant** on site, as well as **bungalows** with en-suite hot-water bathrooms at hooking and passing manoeuvres with the trunk. By the age of 16, elephants are ready to be put to work and are expected to carry on working until they reach 50 or 60, after which they are retired and may live for another twenty years.

Ironically, the **timber industry** was the animal's undoing. Mechanized logging destroyed the wild elephant's preferred river-valley grassland and forest habitats, forcing them into isolated upland pockets. As a result, Thailand's population of wild elephants is now thought to be under 2000, while there are around 2500 domesticated animals – down from a roughly estimated total population of 100,000 in 1900 (the Asian elephant is now officially classified as an endangered species). With the 1989 **ban on commercial logging** within Thai borders – after the 1988 catastrophe when the effects of deforestation killed a hundred people and wiped out villages in Surat Thani province, as mudslides swept down deforested slopes carrying cut timber with them – elephants and their mahouts were faced with the further problem of **unemployment**. Though a small number of elephants continue to work in the illegal teak-logging trade along the Burmese border, most mahouts struggle to find the vast amount of food needed to sustain their charges – about 125kg per beast per day. Tourism has stepped into the breach, mostly in the form of elephant shows and trekking, though it's been a mixed blessing to say the least, as the elephants are often poorly treated, overworked or downright abused. In town streets and on beaches, you'll often see mahouts charging both tourists for the experience of handfeeding their elephants bananas or sugar cane, and Thais for the chance to stoop under their trunks for good luck. At any one time, there may be up to two hundred elephants effectively begging in this way in Bangkok, which is simply not the right environment for them – they're regularly involved in road accidents, for example, despite the red reflectors that many sport on their tails; overall, it's best not to feed city elephants in this way. Demand from the tourism industry is now outstripping supply, and it's feared that captive beasts – which have a lower birth rate than elephants in the wild – may disappear in the next ten years or so, which in turn will mean that wild elephants will again be under threat (see also p.833).

the *Chang Thai Resort* (☎086 181 5445; ⑤). If you have your own vehicle, the Thung Kwian **market**, 21km from Lampang on Highway 11, offers not only a useful stop for refreshments near the elephant centre, but also a chance to view the panoply of products on sale – rabbits and birds, honeycombs, bugs and creepy crawlies of every description. This is a favourite spot for city Thais to pick up some exotic taste to take back home with them.

Phrae

From Lampang, buses to Phrae follow Highway 11 to the junction town of Den Chai (Bangkok–Chiang Mai trains also stop here), 83km to the southeast, then veer northeastwards on Highway 101 through the tobacco-rich Yom valley, dotted with distinctive brick curing-houses. Frequent songthaews and buses from Den Chai head for the small city of **PHRAE**, 20km further on, the capital of the province of the same name which is famous for woodcarving and the quality of its *seua maw hawm*, the deep-blue, collarless working shirt seen all over Thailand (produced in the village of Ban Thung Hong, 4km north of Phrae on Highway 101). If you're driving here from Lampang, turn left from Highway 11 at Mae Khaem onto Route 1023 and approach the town via **Long** and some lovely scenery.

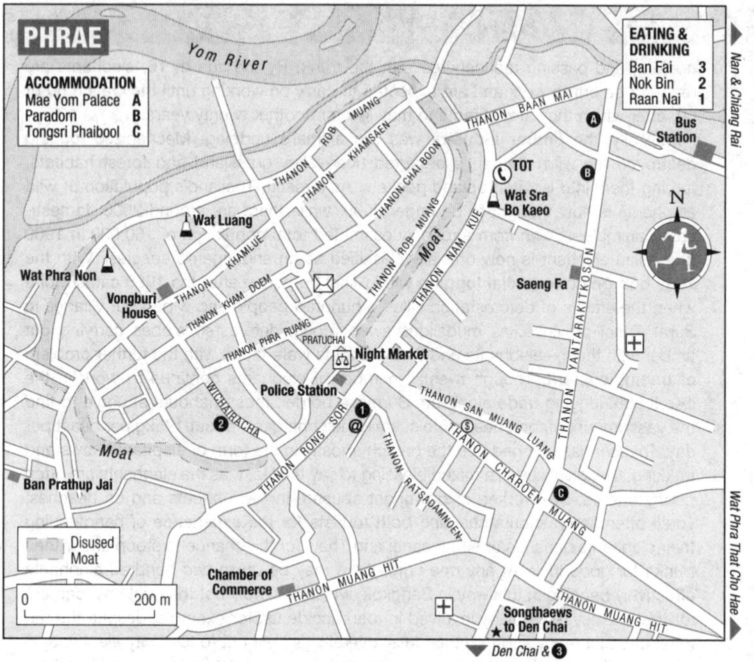

The main reason to stop in Phrae is to explore the old city, delineated by an earthen moat, with its peaceful lanes filled with temples and traditional teak houses – as in Lampang, the former logging industry attracted Burmese workers and the influence is evident – and to enjoy the old-fashioned and friendly nature of a place still virtually untouched by tourism. Out of town, 18km to the northeast off Highway 101, are the so-called ghost pillars at **Phae Muang Phi**, a geological quirk of soil and wind erosion, which are probably only worth visiting if you are going on through to Nan with your own transport.

The Town

Sited on the southeast bank of the Yom River, Phrae is clearly divided into old and new towns; an earthen wall surrounds the roughly oval-shaped old town, with a moat on its southeastern side and the new town centre beyond that. At the centre of the **old town**, a large roundabout is the main orientation point; running northwest–southeast through the roundabout, through Pratuchai (the main gate on the southeastern side of the old town), and into the new town is Thanon Charoen Muang, where several shops sell the trademark deep-indigo shirts. The main street in the new town, Thanon Yantarakitkoson, intersects Thanon Charoen Muang about 300m southeast of the old town.

Vongburi House

The white-and-pink **Vongburi House** (Baan Wongburi; daily 9am–5pm; B30) on Thanon Khamlue is a good place to begin an exploration of the old town. Built of teak between 1897 and 1907 in Thai-European style for the wife of the last lord of Phrae, it's smothered in elaborate, lace-like woodcarving, on all the eaves, gables and balconies, and around doors and windows. Inside the house, exhibits include fine silverware, antique furniture, undershirts with magic spells written on them to ward off danger, and various documents such as elephant identity papers and artefacts that shed light on the history of the family, who still live in part of the complex.

Wat Luang and Wat Phra Non

Around the corner from the Vongburi House, Phrae's oldest temple complex, **Wat Luang**, dates from the town's foundation around the twelfth century; it contains the only intact original brick entrance gate to the city, though unfortunately it has been closed up and turned into an ugly shrine to Chao Pu, an early Lanna ruler. Apart from the gate, the oldest component of the wat is the crumbling early Lanna-style **chedi** called Chang Kham after the four elephants – now mostly trunkless – which sit at its octagonal base; these alternate with four niches containing Buddha images and some haphazardly leaning, gilded bronze parasols. Architectural experts have been called in from Bangkok to plan the restoration of the chedi and the overall complex: unfortunately, over the years, Wat Luang has been added to and parts of it have been quite spoiled in a gaudy modernization process. Until recently, a dishonest monk was even taking down parts of the temple to sell. Apart from the ruined entrance gate, this meddling is most evident in the **viharn** opposite, where an ugly and very out-of-place laterite brick facade has been placed in front of the original Lanna-style sixteenth-century entrance. Opposite the chedi on the north side of the compound, a **museum** on two floors houses some real treasures, the most important being a collection of sixteenth-century bronze Buddhas and several glass cases containing old manuscripts with beautifully gilded covers, which are located upstairs.

Still within the old city, about a block west of Wat Luang along the boundary road is **Wat Phra Non**, established three centuries ago, whose name comes from the reclining Buddha in a small viharn; look out for the Lanna-style bot's finely carved wooden pediment showing scenes from the *Ramayana*.

Ban Prathup Jai

Signposted among the peaceful lanes out beyond the old town's west gate lies the massive two-storey teak house of **Ban Prathup Jai** (daily 8am–5pm; B40), constructed out of nine old houses in the mid-1980s. A visit here allows you to appreciate the beauty and strength of the wood, even if the overall effect is just too ornate: the lower floor has an impressive interior of 130 pillars of solid teak carved with jungle scenes; huge wooden elephants wander among the columns set against solid teak walls and ornately carved furniture (plus a souvenir shop where you can buy all things wooden). Upstairs has the feel of a traditional house, and the furniture and objects are those that you might find in a well-to-do Thai home: ornately carved cabinets crammed with bowls and other ordinary household objects, tables displaying framed family portraits, wall carvings and even a teak bar.

Wat Sra Bo Kaeo

Just to the east of the old town, near the northern end of Thanon Nam Khue, **Wat Sra Bo Kaeo** is set in a peaceful, shady grove of trees. Its Burmese-style viharn is of no great age, but has an intriguing, marble Buddha image and beautiful teak floorboards. The most striking aspect of the temple is the brightly painted Shan chedi with two unusually attractive guardian figures in flowing robes. Also note the intricate, decorative stuccowork on the spire of the bot to the left of the viharn.

Wat Phra That Cho Hae

Wat Phra That Cho Hae, 9km east of town (1km on from the village of Padang), is an important pilgrimage centre sited on a low hill, approached by two naga stairways through a grove of teak trees. One staircase leads to a shrine where a revered Buddha image, Phra Chao Tan Chai, is said to increase women's fertility. The small grounds also house a gilded 33-metre-high **chedi**, traditionally wrapped in the yellow satin-like cloth, *cho hae* (which gives the wat its name), in March or April, and a brightly decorated viharn with an unusual cruciform layout. To the north of the main compound, a new viharn houses a shiny Buddha and some well-crafted murals and window carvings. To get to the wat without your own transport, you'll need to charter a songthaew (about B300) from town, for example, the bus station.

Practicalities

From Lampang, air-con minibuses (16 daily; 2hr), as well as buses, run to Phrae's **bus station**, which is off Thanon Yantarakitkoson, 1km northeast of the modern centre; there are usually some **samlors** and **motorbike taxis**, the main forms of transport around town, congregating here. For information about the town, as well as **bicycle rental** (B70 per day), go and see Khun Apinya at her coffee shop, *Nok Bin*, 24 Thanon Wichairacha (Ⓣ089 433 3285). A TAT office is planned for 34/130 Thanon Muang Hit (Ⓣ054 521118, Ⓔtatphrae@tat.or.th), next to the helpful Chamber of Commerce, where limited information is currently available. **Motorbikes** can be rented for B200 per day at Saeng Fa (no English sign; Ⓣ054 521598), next to the Bank of Ayudhaya on Thanon Yantarakitkoson, **four-wheel drives** for B1200 per day at the *Maeyom Palace Hotel*. You can access the internet at a tiny, unnamed shop down a soi off Thanon Ratsadamnoen, on the north side of the *Nakhon Phrae Hotel*.

Among Phrae's budget hotels, a reasonable choice is the *Tongsri Phaibool* at 84 Thanon Yantarakitkoson (Ⓣ054 511011; fan ❶, air-con ❷), near the junction with Thanon Charoen Muang, with fairly clean, very simply furnished rooms and attached (cold-water) bathrooms, around a courtyard car park. Moving up a notch, the outlook is much brighter: "absolutely clean" proclaims the sign outside the *Paradorn* at 177 Thanon Yantarakitkoson (Ⓣ054 511177, Ⓦwww.phrae-paradorn.th.gs; fan ❷, air-con ❸) and they make a fairly good job of it, adding regular licks of sky blue and yellow paint. All rooms have hot water, wi-fi is available in the lobby and a simple breakfast is included; choose between air-conditioning on the first floor and second-floor fan rooms that get the full heat of the sun but have balconies. The city's best upmarket hotel is the *Mae Yom Palace* near the bus station at 181/6 Thanon Yantarakitkoson (Ⓣ054 521028–35, Ⓔwccphrae@hotmail.com; ❺ including breakfast), which features a large, attractive swimming pool, a restaurant with a pleasant outdoor terrace, bicycle rental and internet access among its amenities.

For **eating** in the town centre, your best bet is the lively night market by the Pratuchai gate on Thanon Charoen Muang. Otherwise, *Raan Nai*, next to the *Nakhon Phrae Hotel* on Thanon Ratsadamnoen, is a decent, air-conditioned fall-back. Phrae's best restaurant, however, is *Ban Fai*, a couple of kilometres south out of town (about B30 by motorbike taxi), at the junction of the Nan and Den Chai roads, an open-sided barn-like place serving very good Thai food including northern specialities such as *nem* (spiced pork sausages) and the typical Lanna pork curry, *kaeng hang lay*.

Nan

After leaving the Yom River, Highway 101 gently climbs through rolling hills of cotton fields and teak plantations to its highest point, framed by limestone cliffs, before descending into the high, isolated valley of the Nan River, the longest in Thailand (740km) and one of the tributaries of the Chao Phraya. Ringed by high mountains, the small but prosperous provincial capital of **NAN**, 225km northeast of Lampang, rests on the grassy west bank of the river. Few visitors make it out this far, but it's a likeable place with a thriving handicraft tradition, a good museum and some superb temple murals at **Wat Phumin**, as well as at **Wat Nong Bua** out in the countryside. The town comes alive for the **Lanna boat races**, usually held in late October or early November, when villages from around the province send teams of up to fifty oarsmen to race in long, colourfully decorated canoes with dragon prows. The lush surrounding valley is noted for its cotton-weaving, sweet oranges and the attractive grainy paper made from the bark of local *sa* (mulberry) trees.

Although it has been kicked around by Burma, Laos and Thailand, Nan province has a history of being on the fringes, distanced by the encircling barrier of mountains. Rama V brought Nan into his centralization programme at the start of the twentieth century, but left the traditional ruling house in place, making it the last province in Thailand to be administered by a local ruler (it remained so until 1931). During the troubled 1970s, communist insurgents holed up in this twilight region and proclaimed Nan the future capital of the liberated zone, which only succeeding in bringing the full might of the Thai Army down on them; the insurgency faded after the government's 1982 offer of amnesty. Today, energies are focused on development, and the province has become less isolated with the building of several new roads.

Arrival and information

The bus journey to Nan from Chiang Mai takes around six hours, so it might be worth catching one of the first-class air-con or VIP vehicles that serve this

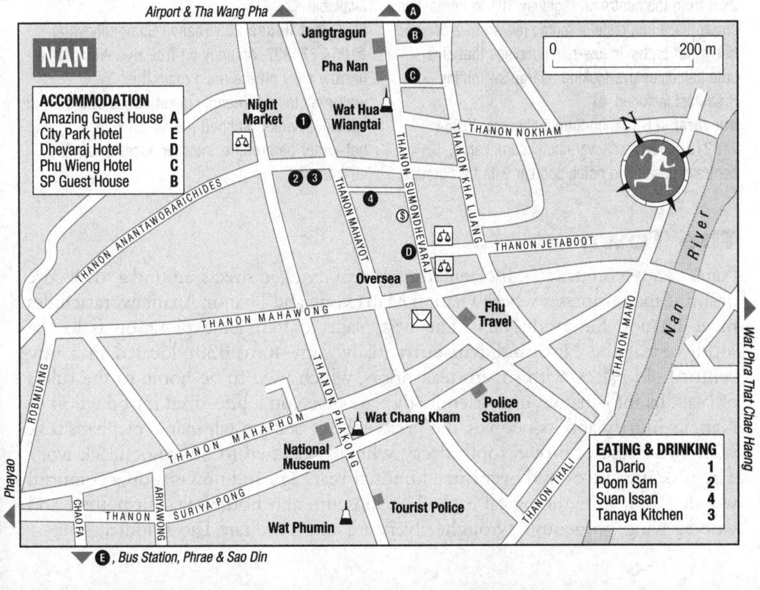

route. Meanwhile, one bus a day winds its tortuous way over the mountains from Chiang Rai, via Chiang Kham; if you're prone to motion sickness, it might be worth changing buses in Phrae instead. The main **bus station** is in the southwest corner of town, off the main road to Phrae, and songthaews to the centre cost B10. The **airport** is 2km northwest of town, served by PB Air flights from Bangkok (at the airport Ⓣ054 771729, Ⓦwww.pbair.com), as well as by air-con minibuses to the *Dhevaraj Hotel*. For **tourist information** about the town and the province, visit Fhu Travel (see p.375), while for exploring the area, Oversea, at 488 Thanon Sumondhevaraj, rents out decent **bicycles** (B80 a day) and **motorbikes** (B200). **Internet outlets** open and close frequently; locals recommend going to the *Dhevaraj Hotel*. There's a **tourist police** booth (Ⓣ054 710216 or 1155) opposite Wat Phumin, as well as a national parks information booth (Mon–Sat 8.30am–4.30pm; Ⓣ054 710216).

Accommodation

Despite being a small town with few visitors, Nan has some attractive accommodation options, ranging from family-run guest houses to clean, reasonably priced hotels. The only time of year when finding somewhere to stay might be a problem is during the Lanna boat races (late Oct or early Nov).

Amazing Guest House 25/7 Thanon Rat Amnuay Ⓣ054 710893. About 1km north of the centre, tucked away in a tiny lane to the west of Thanon Sumondhevaraj (off Thanon Prempracharat). Offers clean, simple rooms in a family-style, wooden house with shared hot-water bathroom (including good rates for singles), as well as five bungalows, all with hot water, some with air-con, in a shady garden. Bicycles and motorbikes are available for rent. Fan ❶, air-con ❷

City Park Hotel 99 Thanon Yantarakitkoson Ⓣ054 741343–52, Ⓦwww.thecityparkhotel.com. About 2km from the centre on Highway 101 to Phrae, this smart place has tasteful rooms (all with air-con and hot-water baths) in low-rise buildings that give onto balconies overlooking a large swimming pool. Breakfast included. ❹

Dhevaraj 466 Thanon Sumondhevaraj Ⓣ054 710212, Ⓦwww.dhevarajhotel.com. Large, centrally positioned hotel, popular with tour groups, that has a slightly institutional feel but is a hub of Nan social life. There's a pool, gym and a wide range of well-maintained accommodation, all with hot water, from plain fan rooms to quite plush air-con affairs with baths. Internet access. Fan ❸, air-con ❹

Fah Place 237/8 Thanon Sumondhevaraj Ⓣ054 710222. Just down a small, unnamed soi off the main road, this striking, modern, cream block contains spacious, very good-value, air-con rooms, done out with attractive tiles, tasteful wooden furniture and large hot-water bathrooms. Wi-fi available. ❷

SP Guest House 233 Thanon Sumondhevaraj Ⓣ054 774897. Actually on Trok Hua Wiangtai, a narrow alley off the main road, this well-maintained, friendly guest house offers spacious, well-equipped rooms, all with hot-water bathrooms. Internet access. Fan ❷, air-con ❸

The Town

Nan's centre comprises a disorientating grid of crooked streets, around a small core of shops and businesses where Thanon Mahawong and Thanon Anantaworarichides meet Thanon Sumondhevaraj. The best place to start an exploration is to the southwest at the **National Museum** (daily 9am–4pm; B30), located in a tidy, century-old palace with superb teak floors, which used to be home to the rulers of Nan. Its informative, user-friendly displays give you a bite-sized introduction to Nan, its history and its peoples, the prize exhibit being a talismanic elephant tusk with a bad case of brown tooth decay, which is claimed to be magic black ivory. The tusk was discovered over three hundred years ago and now sits on a colourful wooden *khut*, a mythological eagle. The museum also houses elegant pottery and woodcarving, gorgeously wrought silverware and some rare Lao Buddhas.

Nearby on Thanon Phakong, **Wat Phumin** will grab even the most over-templed traveller. Its five-hundred-year-old centrepiece is an unusual cruciform building, combining both the bot and the viharn, which balances some quirky features in a perfect symmetry. Two giant nagas pass through the base of the building, with their tails along the balustrades at the south entrance and their heads at the north, representing the sacred oceans at the base of the central mountain of the universe. The doors at the four entrances, which have been beautifully carved with a complex pattern of animals and flowers, lead straight to the four Buddha images arranged around a tall altar in the centre of the building – note the Buddhas' piercing onyx eyes and pointed ears, showing the influence of Laos, 50km away. What really sets the bot apart are the **murals**, whose bright, simple colours seem to jump off the walls. Executed in the late nineteenth century – though occasionally retouched – the paintings take you on a whirlwind tour of heaven, hell, the Buddha's previous incarnations, local legends and incidents from Nan's history, and include stacks of vivacious, sometimes bawdy, detail, which provides a valuable pictorial record of that era. Diagonally opposite Wat Phumin, **Wat Chang Kham** is also over five hundred years old, though the two viharns that stand side by side are unexceptional in design. The main feature here is a gorgeous, gold-capped chedi, supported by elephants on all sides; those on the corners are adorned with gold helmets and straps. The temple is attached to a school, a reminder that temples were once the only source of education in the country.

Wat Phra That Chae Haeng, on the opposite side of the river 2km southeast of town, is another must, as much for its setting on a hill overlooking the Nan valley as anything else. The wat was founded in 1300, at a spot determined by the Buddha himself when he passed through this way – or so local legend would have it. The nagas here outdo even Wat Phumin's: the first you see of the wat across the fields is a wide driveway flanked by monumental serpents gliding down the slope from the temple. A magnificent gnarled bodhi tree with hundreds of spreading branches and roots guards the main gate, set in high boundary walls. Inside the walls, the highlight is a slender, 55-metre-high golden chedi, surrounded by four smaller chedis and four carved and gilded umbrellas, as well as small belfries and stucco lions. Close competition comes from the viharn roof, which has no fewer than fifteen Lao-style tiers, stacked up like a house of cards and supported on finely carved *kan tuei* (wood supports) under the eaves.

Eating and drinking

Plenty of **restaurants** cluster around Thanon Anantaworarichides, while the **night market** is just around the corner on Thanon Phakong.

Da Dario Thanon Mahayot. Decent pastas, pizzas, salads and a short menu of Italian main courses, plus Thai food.

Poom Sam (Poom 3) Thanon Anantaworarichides, next to the *Sukkasem Hotel*. It may look like any other streetside restaurant, but *Poom Sam* prepare excellent Thai and Chinese food with great service at rock-bottom prices, and there's a comfy air-con room as well. Try the *tom yam kung* (B80) or the delicious green aubergines with minced pork and sweet basil. Evenings only.

Suan Issan 2/1 Thanon Anantaworarichides (actually on a narrow alley just south). Cheap and clean, hidden by lots of plants out front, this restaurant has good service, and the fiery Isaan food will have your tongue flapping.

Tanaya Kitchen Thanon Anantaworarichides. Right next door to *Poom Sam*, a tiny, homely café that serves good vegetarian food. Mon–Sat 10am–3.30pm & 5–8pm.

Crafts and shops

Loyalty to local traditions ensures the survival of several good **handicrafts shops** in Nan, most of which are found on Thanon Sumondhevaraj north of the junction with Anantaworarichides. Traditional lengths of superb **cotton** (much of it *pha sin*, used as wraparound skirts) woven in local villages are sold at Pha Nan, 21/2 Thanon Sumondhevaraj (ⓣ054 774439 or 086 923 2046), between Wat Hua Wiangtai and the Chinese temple; as the owner is a teacher, the shop has sporadic hours – best to try in the evenings. Jangtragun, at nos. 304–306, stocks all sorts of everything local, including a good selection of *seua maw hawm*, Phrae's famous blue working shirts, silk, cotton and even local foodstuffs.

A large **silverware** showroom and workshop named Chom Phu Phukha (no English sign) is situated about 2km west of Wat Phumin along the road to Phayao (Route 1091), on the right opposite a petrol station. They stock a wide range of bracelets, necklaces, bowls and trays, priced according to design and weight, and are happy for visitors to look round the workshop at the back. A small selection of local hand-woven cloth is also on sale here.

Around Nan

The remote, mountainous countryside around Nan runs a close second to the precipitous scenery of Mae Hong Son province, but its remoteness means that Nan has even worse transport – though Oversea (see p.372) rents out motorbikes – and is even more poorly mapped. This does, of course, make it an exciting region to explore, where you may encounter the province's ethnic minorities – the Thai Lue (see p.376); the **Htin**, an upland Mon-Khmer people, most of whom have migrated since the Communist takeover of Laos in 1975; the **Khamu**, skilled metalworkers who have moved to Nan over the last 150 years from southwest China and Laos; and the little-known Mrabri (see box below).

Spirits of the Yellow Leaves

Inhabiting the remote hill country west of Nan, the population of about three hundred **Mrabri** represent the last remnants of nomadic hunter-gatherers in Thailand, though their way of life is rapidly passing. Believing that spirits would be angered if the tribe settled in one place, grew crops or kept animals, the Mrabri traditionally built only temporary shelters of branches and wild banana leaves, moving on to another spot in the jungle as soon as the leaves turned yellow; thus they earned their poetic Thai name, **Phi Tong Luang** – "Spirits of the Yellow Leaves". They eked out a hard livelihood from the forest, hunting with spears, trapping birds and small mammals, digging roots and collecting nuts, seeds and honey.

In recent decades, however, deforestation by logging and slash-and-burn farming has eaten into the tribe's territory, and the Mrabri were forced to sell their labour to Hmong and Mien farmers, often under slave-like conditions. But in the last few years, salvation for many Mrabri has come in the form of weaving **hammocks**: foreign visitors noticed their skill at making string bags out of jungle vines and helped them to set up a small-scale hammock industry. The hammocks are now exported to fifteen countries, and the Mrabri weavers have the benefits of education, free healthcare and an unemployment fund. For more information, go to ⓦwww.jumbohammock.com.

With or without your own vehicle, your best option is to head for the reliable Fhu Travel, at 453/4 Thanon Sumondhevaraj (ⓣ054 710636 or 081 287 7209, ⓦwww.fhutravel.com). As well as dispensing advice about the region, Fhu and Ung, his wife, organize popular and enjoyable guided **tours** and trekking trips. One-day tours to Wat Nong Bua, including a visit to the local weavers, cost B2800 for two people or B800 per person for five people, including lunch. Two- to three-day treks (from B1600 per person, minimum five people) head west, through tough terrain of thick jungle and high mountains, visiting Mrabri, Htin, Hmong and Mien villages. As well as offering **cycling tours** around town, one- to three-day **whitewater-rafting** excursions on the Wa River near Mae Charim to the east of town, and **kayaking**, whether overnight or just paddling for half a day on the Nan River near town, Fhu can also arrange trips **to Louang Phabang** in Laos, via the border crossing at **Huai Kon** in the extreme north of Nan province, which has recently opened to foreigners.

Sao Din

One of several brief excursions from Nan possible with your own transport, **Sao Din** ("earth pillars"), 60km to the south, provides a more intriguing example of soil erosion than the better-known site at Phae Muang Phi near Phrae. Here the earth pillars cover a huge area and appear in fantastic shapes, the result of centuries of erosion by wind and rain. The site is almost impossible to reach by public transport, but if you have a motorbike or car, head south on Highway 101 to Wiang Sa, then turn left and follow Route 1026 to Na Noi; a turning on the right just after Na Noi leads into the site. If you visit, take care to wear long trousers and boots, especially in the cool season, as a thorny plant that grows in the region can cause discomfort.

Nan Riverside Art Gallery and Ban Nong Bua

The easiest and most varied day-trip out of Nan is to the north up Route 1080, which is covered by roughly hourly services from Nan bus station to the town of **Tha Wang Pha**, 40km away. After 20km, the road passes the impressive **Nan Riverside Art Gallery** (daily except Wed 9am–5pm; B20; ⓣ054 798046, ⓦwww.nanartgallery.com), founded by local artist, Winai Prabripu, in a lovely setting by the banks of the Nan River. His work – mostly local landscapes focusing on details of plants in season and paintings inspired by the Wat Phumin murals – is displayed upstairs, while the ground floor and the studio gallery host rotating exhibitions by other contemporary Thai artists.

The main focus of this journey, however, is **BAN NONG BUA**, site of a famous muralled temple of the same name – on the southern outskirts of Tha Wang Pha, signs in English point you left across the Nan River to **Wat Nong Bua**, 3km away (coming by bus, either hire a motorbike taxi in the centre of Tha Wang Pha, or walk the last 3km). The temple's beautifully gnarled viharn was built in 1862 in typical Lanna style, with low, drooping roof tiers surmounted by stucco finials – here you'll find horned nagas and tusked makaras (elephantine monsters), instead of the garuda finial which invariably crops up in central Thai temples. The viharn enshrines a pointy-eared Laotian Buddha, but its most outstanding features are the **murals** that cover all four walls. Executed between 1867 and 1888, probably by the Wat Phumin painters, they depict with much humour and vivid detail scenes from the *Chanthakhat*

Jataka (the story of one of the Buddha's previous incarnations, as a hero called Chanthakhat). This is a particularly long and complex *Jataka* (although a leaflet outlining the story in English is sometimes available, in return for a small donation to temple funds), wherein our hero gets into all kinds of scrapes, involving several wives, other sundry liaisons, some formidably nasty enemies and the god Indra transforming himself into a snake. The crux of the tale comes on the east wall (opposite the Buddha image): in the bottom left-hand corner, Chanthakhat and the love of his life, Thewathisangka, are shipwrecked and separated; distraught, Thewathisangka wanders through the jungle, diagonally up the wall, to the hermitage of an old woman, where she shaves her head and becomes a nun; Chanthakhat travels through the wilderness along the bottom of the wall, curing a wounded naga-king on the way, who out of gratitude gives him a magic crystal ball, which enables our hero to face another series of perils along the south wall, before finally rediscovering and embracing Thewathisangka in front of the old woman's hut, at the top right-hand corner of the east wall.

Ban Nong Bua and the surrounding area are largely inhabited by **Thai Lue** people, distant cousins of the Thais, who've migrated from China in the past 150 years. They produce beautiful cotton garments in richly coloured geometric patterns; walk 200m behind the wat to the west side of the village and you'll find weavers at work at the house of Khun Chansom Prompanya, who sells the opulent fabrics in her on-site shop. The quality of design and workmanship is very high here, and prices, though not cheap, are reasonable for the quality.

Doi Phukha National Park

East of Tha Wang Pha, Route 1080 curves towards the town of **Pua**, on whose southern outskirts Route 1256, the spectacular access road for **Doi Phukha National Park** (B200; ⓣ054 701000, ⓦwww.dnp.go.th), begins its journey eastwards and upwards; you can pick up a brochure with map from the national parks information booth in Nan town (see p.372). It's difficult to get into the park on public transport, and you'll usually have to stay the night. Hourly buses from Nan's main station run to Pua in two hours, from where irregular songthaews (best in the mornings, though you may find school songthaews in the late afternoon) serve the handful of villages along Route 1256 towards Bo Kleua. The trip is most exciting if tackled on a motorbike (though watch out for loose chippings on the bends). The paved road climbs up a sharp ridge, through occasional stands of elephant grass and bamboo, towards Doi Dong Ya Wai (1939m), providing one of the most jaw-droppingly scenic drives in Thailand. Across the valleys to north and south stand rows of improbably steep mountains (including the 1980-metre Doi Phukha itself, far to the south), covered in lush vegetation with scarcely a sign of human habitation.

At park headquarters, 24km up the road from Pua, **accommodation** ranges from large bungalows sleeping six or seven (B2000–2500), through rooms for four (B800), to small, basic bungalows for two (B300); there's also a **campsite** and a restaurant. Another alternative is *Bo Klua View* (ⓣ054 778140 or 081 809 6392, ⓦwww.bokluaview.com; ❻, including breakfast), about 20km beyond park headquarters towards Bo Kleua, which has a dozen stylish bungalows with large verandas set around a terraced rice field. There's a self-guided, 4km trail around headquarters but to hike up any of the park's many peaks, you'll need to hire a guide (about B200 per day).

The Mae Hong Son loop

Two main roads from Chiang Mai head over the western mountains into Mae Hong Son, Thailand's most remote province, offering the irresistible prospect of tying the highways together into a six-hundred-kilometre loop. The towns en route give a taste of Burma to the west, but the journey itself, winding over implausibly steep forested mountains and through tightly hemmed farming valleys, is what will stick in the mind.

The southern leg of the route, Highway 108, first passes **Doi Inthanon National Park**, with its lofty views over half of northern Thailand and enough waterfalls to last a lifetime; from here with your own vehicle, you could shortcut the southernmost part of the loop by taking the paved but very winding Routes 1088 and 1263 from Mae Chaem to Khun Yuam. Sticking to the main loop, however, you'll next reach **Mae Sariang**, an important town for trade across the Burmese border and a gentle, low-key base for trekking and trips on the Salween River. The provincial capital, **Mae Hong Son**, roughly at the midpoint of the loop, is a more developed hub for exploring the area's mountains, rivers and waterfalls, though it can become frantic with tour groups in the cool season, especially on November and December weekends when the sunflowers are out. The northern leg, Route 1095, heads northeast out of Mae Hong Son into an area of beautiful caves, notably **Tham Lot**, appealing accommodation and stunning scenery to trek, cycle or kayak through, around **Soppong**. Halfway back towards Chiang Mai from Mae Hong Son is **Pai**, a cosy, cosmopolitan and hugely popular hangout with plenty of activities and some gentle walking trails in the surrounding valley.

We've taken the loop in a clockwise direction here, in part because Doi Inthanon is best reached direct from Chiang Mai, but you could just as easily go the other way round. Travelling the loop is straightforward, although the mountainous roads go through plenty of bends and jolts. Either way, Mae Hong Son is about eight hours' travelling time from Chiang Mai by air-con or ordinary **bus**, although services along the shorter but even more winding northern route are now augmented by faster, hourly **air-con minibuses**, which cover the ground via Pai in about six hours. From Chiang Mai, there are also Thai Airways and SGA flights to Mae Hong Son and SGA **flights** to Pai. Above all, though, the loop is made for **motorbikes** and **jeeps**: the roads are generally quiet (but watch out for huge, speeding trucks) and you can satisfy the inevitable craving to stop every five minutes and admire the mountain scenery. A useful piece of equipment for this journey is the 1:375,000 **map** of the Mae Hong Son loop, with useful insets of Pai's and Mae Hong Son's environs, published by Golden Triangle Rider (Ⓦwww.gt-rider.com) and available in local bookshops at B175.

Highway 108: Chiang Mai to Mae Hong Son

Bus drivers on **Highway 108** are expected to have highly sharpened powers of concentration and the landlubber's version of sea legs – the road negotiates almost two thousand curves in the 349km to Mae Hong Son, so if you're at all prone to travel sickness plan to take a breather in Mae Sariang. Buses to Mae

Sariang and Mae Hong Son (about half of which are air-con) depart from Chiang Mai's Arcade bus station; blue buses to Chom Thong (for Doi Inthanon National Park) from Chang Puak bus station can be picked up at the southern end of Thanon Phra Pokklao (Chiang Mai Gate).

Doi Inthanon National Park

Covering a huge area to the southwest of Chiang Mai, **DOI INTHANON NATIONAL PARK** (Ⓦwww.dnp.go.th), with its Karen and Hmong hill-tribe villages, dramatic waterfalls and panoramas over rows of wild, green peaks to the west, gives a pleasant, if slightly sanitized, whiff of northern countryside, its attractions and concrete access roads kept in good order by the national parks department. The park, named after the highest mountain in the country and so dubbed the "Roof of Thailand", is geared mainly to wildlife conservation but also contains a hill-tribe agricultural project producing strawberries, apples and flowers for sale. Often shrouded in mist, Doi Inthanon's temperate forests shelter a huge variety of flora and fauna, which make this one of the major destinations for naturalists in Southeast Asia. The park supports about 380 bird species, the largest number of any site in Thailand – among them the ashy-throated warbler and a species of the green-tailed sunbird, both unique to Doi Inthanon – as well as, near the summit, the only red rhododendrons in Thailand and a wide variety of ground and epiphytic orchids. The waterfalls, birds and flowers are at their best in the cool season, but night-time temperatures sometimes drop below freezing, making warm clothing a must.

Access and information

The gateway to the park is **CHOM THONG**, 58km southwest of Chiang Mai on Highway 108, a market town with little to offer apart from the attractive **Wat Phra That Si Chom Thong**, whose impressive brass-plated chedi dates from the fifteenth century. The nearby bo tree has become an equally noteworthy architectural feature: dozens of Dalí-esque supports for its sagging branches have been sponsored by the devoted in the hope of earning merit. Inside the renovated sixteenth-century viharn, a towering, gilded *ku* housing a Buddha relic (supposedly from the right side of his skull) just squeezes in

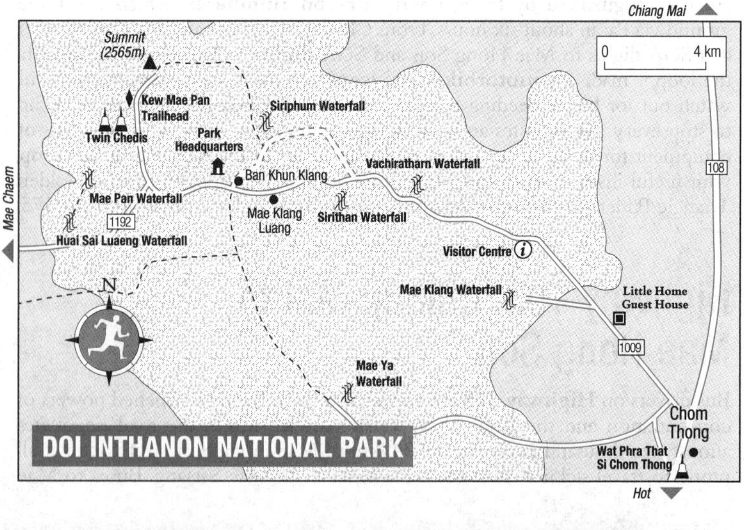

beneath the ceiling, from which hangs a huge, sumptuous red-and-green umbrella. Weaponry, gongs, umbrellas, thrones and an elephant-tusk arch carved with delicate Buddha images all add to the welcoming clutter.

The main road through the park turns west off Highway 108, 1km north of Chom Thong, winding generally northwestwards for 48km to the top of Doi Inthanon, passing the park headquarters about 30km in. A second paved road forks left 10km before the summit, affording breathtaking views as it helter-skelters down for 20km to the sleepy, riverside weaving village of **Mae Chaem**, southwest of the park. Several tour operators in Chiang Mai offer **day-trips** to the national park (around B1500 per person), or you could charter a whole songthaew or air-conditioned minibus from Chom Thong for around B1000–1500 for the day. By **motorbike** or **jeep**, you could do the park justice in a day with an early start from Chiang Mai, or treat it as the first stage of a longer trip to Mae Hong Son: from Mae Chaem, either follow Route 1088 south to pick up Highway 108 again towards Mae Sariang, 25km west of Hot; or take Route 1088 north then Route 1263 west through remote countryside, joining Highway 108 just north of Khun Yuam.

A checkpoint by Mae Klang Falls collects **entrance fees** of B200 for foreigners, plus B20 per motorbike, and B30 per car. For information on the park, stop at the **visitor centre**, 1km beyond the checkpoint, or at the **park headquarters**, a further 22km on. Two hundred metres beyond the headquarters on the left, at Uncle Daeng's **Birds Visitor Centre** (Ⓣ053 286731–2 or 081 884 8108, Ⓦwww.mrdeang.com), birdwatchers can consult a useful logbook, pick up a simple, photocopied map of birding sites, or hire a guide for B1000–3000 per day for up to five people.

Accommodation and eating

National park **accommodation** comes in the standard log-cabin or concrete varieties, with electricity, mattresses or beds and bedding. Three- to 23-berth bungalows (bookings at the park on Ⓣ053 286730, or in Bangkok, see p.52; B800–8000 per bungalow), set among dense stands of pine near the headquarters, have hot-water bathrooms, while simpler, fifteen-person bungalows at Huai Sai Luaeng Falls cost B1500 per night. Accommodation is often fully booked at weekends and national holidays, but at other times you should be all right turning up on the day. More stylish hotel-type rooms with balconies are available at the Royal Agricultural Project (Ⓣ053 286770–7, Ⓦwww.royalinthanon.com; ❼), between park headquarters and Siriphum Waterfall. At his Birds Visitor Centre, Uncle Daeng offers pleasant, colourful, tile-floored rooms with hot water and TV (see above; ❸), while simple **homestays** are available at the Karen coffee-growing village of Mae Klang Luang, 5km east of headquarters on the south side of the main road (Ⓣ081 960 8856 or 087 178 0231, Ⓦwww.cbt-i.org; B200 per person including breakfast and dinner). Elsewhere, the *Little Home Guest House and Restaurant*, 7km from Chom Thong along the main park road (Ⓣ053 267382, Ⓦwww.littlehomeinthanonresort.com; fan ❹, air-con ❹–❺), has clean, well-maintained, fan or air-conditioned bungalows and rooms with hot-water bathrooms.

Camping, an often chilly alternative, is permitted on a site about 500m from the park headquarters and another site at Huai Sai Luaeng Falls. Two- to three-person tents can be rented at headquarters for B225 per night (bedding extra).

In the daytime, **foodstalls** operate at Mae Klang, Vachiratharn and Mae Ya falls, and there's a popular canteen with a reasonable variety of food by the twin chedis. The restaurants beside park headquarters and at the Birds Visitor Centre open daytime and evening.

The park

Four sets of waterfalls provide the main roadside attractions on the way to the park headquarters: overrated **Mae Klang Falls**, 8km in, which with its picnic areas and food vendors gets overbearingly crowded at weekends; **Vachiratharn Falls**, the park's most dramatic, with a long, misty drop down a granite escarpment 11km beyond; **Sirithan Falls**, which looks like a smaller version of Vachiratharn and is just a couple of kilometres further up the hill; and finally the twin cascades of **Siriphum Falls**, backing the park headquarters a further 9km on. With your own wheels you could reach a fifth and much more beautiful cataract, **Mae Ya**, which is believed to be the highest in Thailand – the winding, fourteen-kilometre paved track to it heads west off the main park road 2km north of Highway 108. At the Karen village of **Mae Klang Luang**, 5km east of headquarters on the south side of the main road, you can hire an English-speaking guide to walk with you to Pha Dok Siew waterfall (2hr return; B300) or up Doi Huea Sua (1881m; 6hr; B500).

For the most spectacular views in the park, continue 11km beyond the headquarters along the summit road to the sleek, twin chedis looming incongruously over the misty green hillside: on a clear day you can see the mountains of Burma to the west from here. Built by the Royal Thai Air Force, the chedis commemorate the sixtieth birthdays of the Thai king and queen; the king's monument, **Napamaytanidol Chedi** (1987), is brown to the more feminine lilac of the queen's **Napapolphumsiri Chedi** (1992). Starting a short distance up the road from the chedis, the rewarding **Kew Mae Pan Trail**, a two-hour circular walk (closed June–Oct), wanders through sun-dappled forest and open savanna as it skirts the steep western edge of Doi Inthanon, where violent-red epiphytic rhododendrons (in bloom Dec–Feb) are framed against open views over the canyoned headwaters of the Pan River,

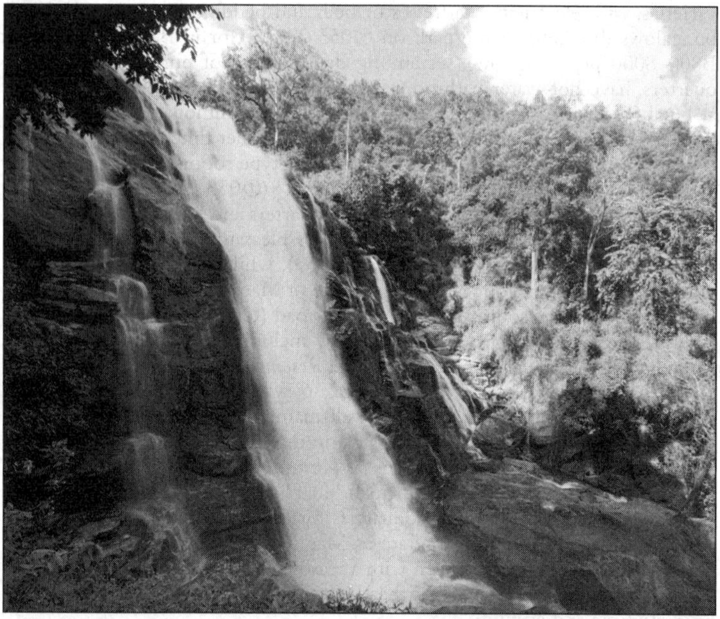

▲ Vachiratharn waterfall, Doi Inthanon National Park

when the weather allows. To do this walk, you have to hire a local Karen or Hmong guide at the trailhead (B200).

Doi Inthanon's **summit** (2565m), 6km beyond the chedis, is a big disappointment – from the car park you can see little beyond the radar installation. For many people, after a quick shiver and a snapshot in front of a board proclaiming this the highest point in Thailand, it's time to hop in the car and get back to warmer climes. A small, still-revered stupa behind this board contains the ashes of King Inthanon of Chiang Mai (after whom the mountain was renamed): at the end of the nineteenth century he was the first to recognize the importance of this watershed area in supplying the Ping River and ultimately the Chao Phraya, the queen of Thailand's rivers. One hundred metres back down the road, it's an easy stroll along a raised walkway to the bog known as **Ang Ka** (Crow's Pond), which is the highest source of these great waterways and one of the park's best birdwatching sites. The cream and brown sphagnum mosses that spread underfoot, the dense ferns that hang off the trees and the contorted branches of rhododendrons give the place a creepy, primeval atmosphere.

The paved **Mae Chaem road** skirts yet another set of waterfalls, 7km after the turning off the summit road: look for a steep road to the right, leading down to a ranger station and, just to the east, the dramatic long drop of **Huai Sai Luaeng Falls**. A 2.5km circular walking trail from the ranger station takes in **Mae Pan Falls**, a series of short cascades in a peaceful, shady setting.

West towards Mae Sariang

Among several weaving villages to the south of Chom Thong, the **Pa-Da Cotton Textile Museum** (daily except Thurs 8.30am–4.30pm; free) at Ban Rai Pai Ngarm is well worth a look; it's reached down a beautiful avenue of bamboo trees, on the east side of Highway 108 between kilometre-stones 68 and 69. The museum is dedicated to the work of Saeng-da Bansiddhi, a local woman who started a co-operative practising traditional dyeing and weaving techniques using only natural products. Saeng-da died in the late 1980s, and the museum, which displays some of her personal effects as well as looms, fabrics and plants used in dyeing, was established to honour her efforts to revive these disappearing skills. It's situated on the upper floor of a large wooden building, while on the ground floor weavers can be seen busy at work. Lovely bolts of cloth and a small range of clothes and scarves in earthy and pastel colours are on sale at reasonable prices.

Highway 108 parallels the Ping River downstream as far as **Hot**, a dusty, forgettable place 27km from Chom Thong, before bending west and weaving through pretty wooded hills up the valley of the Chaem River. Another 17km brings you to **Ob Luang Gorge National Park** (B200; ⓣ053 315302, ⓦwww.dnp.go.th), billed with wild hyperbole as "Thailand's Grand Canyon". A wooden bridge over the short, narrow channel lets you look down on the Chaem River bubbling along between sheer walls 50m below. The park is also tagged "Land of Prehistoric Human" because of the discovery of Bronze Age graves here, containing seashell bracelets and other decorative items, as well as rock paintings of elephants and human figures. Upstream from the bridge near park headquarters, you can relax at the roadside foodstalls and swim in the river when it's not too fast, and the shady river bank shelters a **campsite** (B225 to rent a two- to three-person tent). There are also a few large **bungalows** with three bedrooms and two bathrooms, sleeping eight people (B1800), in which you can usually rent a room for two for B600. At headquarters you can arrange one-hour, five-kilometre **whitewater-rafting** trips on the river (from B1400 for four people up to B1800 for eight, including guides, transport, life jackets and helmets). West of Ob Luang, the highway gradually climbs through pine forests, the road surface bad in patches and the countryside becoming steeper and wilder.

Mae Sariang and around

After its descent into the broad, smoky valley of the Yuam River, Highway 108's westward progress ends at **MAE SARIANG**, 191km from Chiang Mai, a quietly industrious market town showing a marked Burmese influence in its temples and rows of low wooden shophouses. Halfway along the southern route between Chiang Mai and Mae Hong Son, this is an obvious place for a stopover. From here you can make an intriguing day-trip to the trading post of **Mae Sam Laeb** on the border with Burma and out onto the Salween River.

Arrival and accommodation

As well as **buses** on the Chiang Mai–Mae Hong Son route, Mae Sariang is served by three daily buses from Bangkok (12hr) and by one air-con minibus a day from Wat Ubokut on Chiang Mai's Thanon Tha Pae (on the corner of Thanon Chang Klan; 4hr). Scenic Highway 105 up from Mae Sot (see p.297) is covered only by songthaews (5–7 daily; B200 per person), with a journey time of about six hours – really too much on a rattling bench seat. **Internet access** is available on Thanon Laeng Phanit at Computer House, immediately south of *River House Hotel*.

For such a tiny town, Mae Sariang has a good range of **accommodation. Homestays** in a Lawa village near Mae La Noi to the north of town, where you can learn to make jewellery, cook hill-tribe cuisine and weave, among many other activities, can be arranged through Thailand Hilltribe Holidays (Ⓣ089 956 9897, Ⓦwww.thailandhilltribeholidays.com).

Northwest Guest House 81 Thanon Laeng Phanit Ⓣ089 700 9928, Ⓦwww.northwestthai.multiply.com. Clean, friendly spot with plenty of local information and tidy, polished-wood rooms, some with their own computers with internet access; hot-water bathrooms are either shared or en suite. Reductions for singles. Fan ①, air-con ③

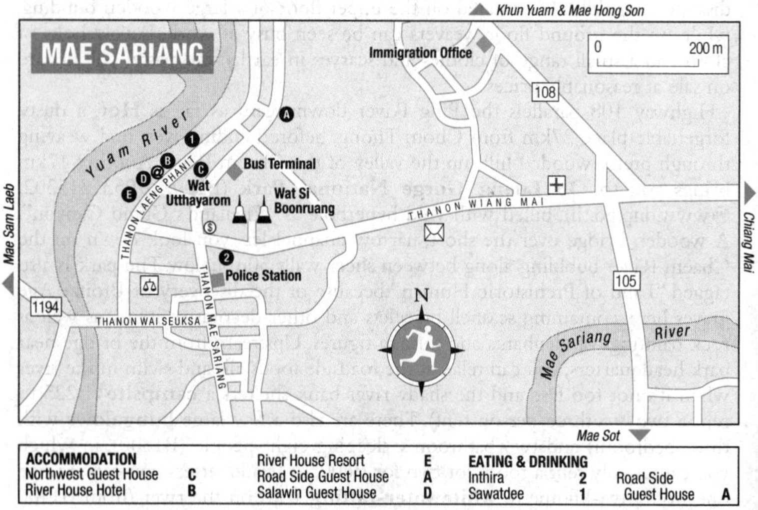

ACCOMMODATION				EATING & DRINKING			
Northwest Guest House	C	River House Resort	E	Inthira	2	Road Side Guest House	A
River House Hotel	B	Road Side Guest House	A	Sawatdee	1		
		Salawin Guest House	D				

River House Hotel 77 Thanon Laeng Phanit ⓣ053 621201, ⓦwww.riverhousehotels.com. Modern all-wood hotel in traditional open-plan style, where the rooms have simple, tasteful furnishings, fine river views, verandas, air-con and en-suite hot-water bathrooms. Internet and wi-fi. Breakfast included. ❺

River House Resort Thanon Laeng Phanit ⓣ053 683066, ⓦwww.riverhousehotels.com. Run by the owner of *River House Hotel*, this is Mae Sariang's fanciest place to stay. All rooms come with air-con, hot water and smart teak furnishings; some have river-view balconies, while the more expensive ones boast bathtubs, and there's also an attractive garden overlooking the river. Internet and wi-fi. Breakfast included. ❻

Road Side Guest House 44 Thanon Mae Sariang ⓣ053 682713 or 089 552 7616, ⓔroad-sidegh@hotmail.com. An appealing budget option, where six simple bedrooms share four attractive bathrooms with hot water (en-suite bathrooms and air-con are planned). Their enthusiastic and helpful owner, Aekkasan, is a mine of local information and has maps of the area. ❶

Salawin Guest House 2 Thanon Laeng Phanit ⓣ053 681490. Just half a dozen clean and cosy rooms with attached, hot-water bathrooms in this large house set in a small but pretty garden. Internet access. At the lower end of this price code. ❸

The Town

Soaking up the atmosphere is the main activity in this border outpost, which is regularly visited by local hill tribes and dodgy traders from Burma. If you want something more concrete to do, stroll around a couple of temples off the north side of the main street, whose Burmese features provide a glaring contrast to most Thai temples. The first, **Wat Si Boonruang**, sports a fairy-tale bot with an intricate, tiered roof piled high above. Topped with lotus buds, the unusual *sema* stones, which delineate the bot's consecrated area, look like old-fashioned street bollards. The open viharns here and next door at **Wat Utthayarom** (aka Wat Jong Sung) are mounted on stilts, with broad teak floors that are a pleasure to get your feet onto. Both wats enshrine Burmese-style Buddhas, white and hard-faced.

Motorbikes (B150–200 per day) and bicycles (B50–100) for exploring temples and Karen weaving villages in the surrounding Yuam valley can be rented from *Road Side* and *Northwest* guest houses. These two guest houses also organize local tours, such as three-day **treks** (around B3000 per person for two people, cheaper in a larger group) into the wild countryside along the Burmese border near Mae Sam Laeb, including boat trips on the Salween River; Aekkasan at *Road Side Guest House* also throws in breakfast before and dinner at the end of the trek, or can just organize a **boat trip from Mae Sam Laeb** (see p.384).

Eating and drinking

When it's time for **food**, don't be put off by the basic appearance of the *Inthira Restaurant* on Thanon Wiang Mai – it's the locals' favourite, and dishes up huge portions of excellent Thai food at give-away prices. Among traveller-oriented places, *Road Side Guest House* serves Western breakfasts, lots of milkshakes and ice cream – as befits this former dairy – and tasty Thai dishes: try the *khao klook kapii*, a delicious combination of rice fried with shrimp paste, sweet pork, omelette, pomelo, chilli and soup. Popular with local NGO workers, *Sawatdee* bar-restaurant offers mostly Thai food, as well as good coffees and breakfasts, on a terrace overlooking the river, with some low tables and axe cushions for chilling out.

Mae Sam Laeb

Some 46km southwest of Mae Sariang and accessible by hourly songthaews from the market in the morning (1hr 30min), **MAE SAM LAEB** lies on the mighty Salween (or Salawin) River, which, having descended from Tibet through Burma, forms the Thai–Burmese border for 120km here, before emptying into the Andaman Sea. The village is no more than a row of bamboo stores and restaurants, but with its Thai, Chinese, Karen and Burmese inhabitants, it has a classic frontier feel about it. The best way to soak up Mae Sam Laeb's atmosphere is to sign up for one of the highly recommended **boat trips** organized by Aekkasan at *Road Side Guest House*, which include breakfast (B600–1500 per person). The boat cruises down the Salween through idyllic countryside for an hour to the small unspoilt Karen village of Sop Moei, right on the confluence of the Moei River with the Salween, where lunch is taken before sailing back to Mae Sam Laeb.

North towards Mae Hong Son

North of Mae Sariang, wide, lush valleys alternate with tiny, steep-sided glens – some too narrow for more than a single rice paddy – turning Highway 108 into a winding roller coaster. The market town of **KHUN YUAM**, 95km from Mae Sariang, is a popular resting spot, especially for those who've taken the direct route here (Route 1263) over the mountains from Mae Chaem. There's not much here in the way of attractions, though the **World War II Museum** in the Thai–Japan Friendship Memorial Hall (daily 8am–5pm; B50), on the left of the main thoroughfare, Thanon Rajaburana, at the north end of town, has a curious collection of rusting relics from the Japanese World War II occupation – old trucks, rifles, water canisters and uniforms. Lining the walls, hundreds of black-and-white photos document this period, when after their retreat from Burma in 1944, some of the Japanese rested here with the sick and wounded for two years and longer. The *Ban Farang* **guest house** (ⓣ053 622086; fan ❸, air-con ❻), north again from the museum and well signposted just off Thanon Rajaburana, can put you up in fine style. Each of its smart, very clean rooms has duvets and a hot-water bathroom; the restaurant serves up good Thai and Western food, at reasonable prices.

Just north of Khun Yuam, Route 1263 branches off to the east over the hills towards Mae Chaem; after about 20km, a side road leads north up to the **Buatong fields** on the slopes of Doi Mae U-Khor, where Mexican sunflowers make the hillsides glow butter-yellow in November and early December. Much of the roadside elsewhere is bordered by these same flowers at this time of year, but the sheer concentration of blooms at Mae U-Khor, combined with sweeping views over endless ridges to the west, draws dozens of tour groups in air-con minibuses. Around 15km further down the same road from the Hmong village of Ban Mae U-Khor, **Mae Surin Waterfall** in Nam Tok Mae Surin National Park (B200; ⓣ053 061073, ⓦwww.dnp.go.th) is arguably the most spectacular waterfall in the whole country, the waters hurtling over a cliff and plunging almost 100m before crashing on huge boulders and foaming down a steep gorge. The kind topography of the region allows a great view of the falls from directly in front, but the best view, from below, requires a steep and at times precarious three-hour hike down and back from the well-appointed **campsite**.

Back on Highway 108, 35km north of Khun Yuam, a right turn leads up to **Mae Ko Vafe** – a Thai rendition of "microwave", referring to the transmitters that grace the mountain's peak; the paved road climbs for 10km to a Hmong village, where the fantastic view west stretches far into Burma. Around 15km beyond this turn-off Highway 108 climbs to a roadside **viewing area**, with fine vistas, this time to the east, of the sheer, wooded slopes and the Pha Bong Dam in the valley far below. Subsequently the road makes a dramatic, headlong descent towards Mae Hong Son, passing the **Ban Pha Bong** hot springs, 7km north of the viewing area (11km before Mae Hong Son). These have been turned into a small spa complex, with private rooms with hot spring-water baths, traditional masseurs and a restaurant.

Mae Hong Son and around

MAE HONG SON, capital of Thailand's northwestern-most province, sports more nicknames than a town of ten thousand people seems to deserve. In Thai, it's Muang Sam Mok, the "City of Three Mists": set deep in a mountain valley, Mae Hong Son is often swathed in mist, the quality of which differs according to the three seasons (in the hot season it's mostly composed of unpleasant smoke from burning fields). In former times, the town, which wasn't connected to the outside world by a paved road until 1968, was known as "Siberia" to the troublesome politicians and government officials who were exiled here from Bangkok. Nowadays, thanks to its mountainous surroundings, it's increasingly billed as the "Switzerland of Thailand": eighty percent of Mae Hong Son province is on a slope of more than 45 degrees.

To match the hype, Mae Hong Son has become one of the most popular tourist centres in the country, sporting, alongside dozens of backpacker guest houses, several luxury hotels and resorts for Thai and farang package tourists who like their city comforts. Most backpackers come here for **trekking** (see box, p.386) and day-hiking in the beautiful countryside, others just for the cool climate and lazy upcountry atmosphere. The town is still small enough and sleepy enough to hole up in for a quiet week, though in the high season (Nov–Feb) swarms of minibuses disgorge tour groups who hunt in packs through the souvenir stalls and fill up the restaurants.

Mae Hong Son was founded in 1831 as a training camp for elephants captured from the surrounding jungle for the princes of Chiang Mai (Jong Kham Lake, in the southeastern part of the modern town, served as the elephants' bathing spot). The hard work of hunting and rearing the royal elephants was done by the **Thai Yai** (aka Shan), who account for half the population of the province and bring a strong Burmese flavour to Mae Hong Son's temples and festivals. The other half of the province's population is made up of various hill tribes (a large number of Karen, as well as Lisu, Hmong and Lawa), with a tiny minority of Thais concentrated in the provincial capital. The latest immigrants to the province are **Burmese refugees** (see box, p.298), based in camps between Mae Hong Son and the border, who generally do not encourage visitors as they've got quite enough on their plates without having to entertain onlookers.

Arrival and information

Running north to south, Mae Hong Son's main drag, Thanon Khunlumprapas, is intersected by Thanon Singhanat Bamrung at the traffic lights in the centre of town. From the new **bus station**, south of the centre, and from the **airport** to the east (served by Thai Airways and SGA flights from Chiang Mai), motorbike taxis (B30–40) and tuk-tuks (B50) run into the centre. **TAT** have a helpful office (daily 8.30am–4.30pm; Ⓣ053 612982–3, Ⓦwww.travelmaehongson.org) opposite the post office on Khunlumprapas; in the same building is a government-sponsored shop selling some attractive fabrics (including bags and clothes), local teas and other foodstuffs. The **tourist police** are on Thanon Singhanat Bamrung (Ⓣ053 611812 or 1155).

Trekking around Mae Hong Son

There's no getting away from the fact that **trekking** up and down Mae Hong Son's steep inclines is tough, though the scenery is magnificent. Most of the hill-tribe villages here are Karen, interspersed with indigenous Thai Yai (Shan) settlements in the valleys. Heading east, where many villages are very unspoilt, having little contact with the outside world, is preferable to the more populous, less traditional west; to the southeast, you'll be able to visit Hmong and Karen, to the northeast, Lisu also. In the latter direction, if you're very hardy, you might want to consider the five- to six-day routes to Soppong or Pai, which has the best scenery of the lot.

About a dozen guest houses and travel agencies in Mae Hong Son run multi-day treks, on which guides can often build a camp of natural materials while overnighting in the forest. The somewhat mercurial Khun Tho at Mae Hong Son Travel, Thanon Khunlumprapas (Ⓣ053 620644), is an especially good guide for **birdwatchers**, while the currently independent guide, Chakaphan (Jon) Prowinchaikul (Ⓣ053 611040 or 081 951 5880, Ⓔnatural_walks@hotmail.com), specializes in flowers and insects. It might also be worth asking for Khun La at *Sunflower* bar-restaurant, who hopes to restart his recommended trekking, birdwatching and cycling tours, and is happy to give general advice about trekking. Among a wide variety of tours, Tour Merng Tai at 89 Thanon Khunlumprapas (Ⓣ053 611979, Ⓦwww.maehongson4u.com) offer several community-based tourism programmes, employing village guides and cooks and contributing part of the profits to local communities. They're mostly one-day treks, involving four or five hours' walking to Lahu, Thai Yai and Karen villages (B1100–2200 per person, including 4X4 transport where necessary, English-speaking guide and lunch), though longer treks and homestays are possible.

Accommodation

Mae Hong Son has a healthy roster of **guest houses**, most of them being good-value, rustic affairs built of bamboo or wood and set in their own quiet gardens; many are sited around Jong Kham Lake or on the northern slopes of Doi Kong Mu on the northwestern edge of town, which greatly adds to their scenic

▲ Hmong boys, near Mae Hong Son

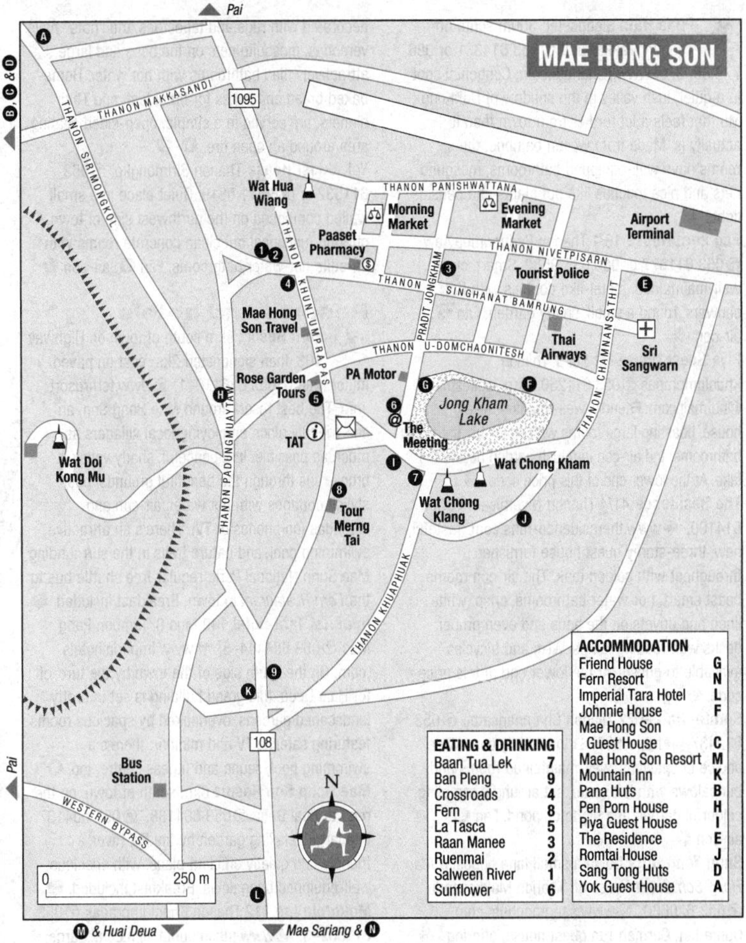

appeal. If you've got a little more money to spend, you can get out into the countryside to one of several self-contained **resorts**, though staying at one of these is not exactly a wilderness experience – they're really designed for weekending Thais travelling by car. Finally, several **luxury hotels** have latched onto the area's meteoric development, offering all the usual international-standard facilities.

Guest houses

Friend House 20 Thanon Pradit Jongkham ⓣ053 620119. Decent, clean, modern teak-and-concrete house with upstairs balcony giving views of the lake. Larger rooms have hot-water bathrooms, smaller ones share hot showers. ①–②

Johnnie House Thanon U-Domchaonitesh ⓣ053 611667. In a small compound near the lake, this clean, friendly place has airy rooms, sharing hot showers, in a nice, old, wooden house, as well as bright, concrete affairs with en-suite hot-water bathrooms. ①–②

Mae Hong Son Guest House 295 Thanon Makkasandi ⓣ053 612510, ⓔlotee@hotmail.com. Relaxing old-timer in a big, shady garden on the western outskirts of town, with a restaurant and friendly staff. Large, attractive, en-suite bungalows, and simpler, shared or en-suite rooms, all with hot water. ①–④

Pana Huts Signposted 300m south off Thanon Makkasandi ⓣ053 614331 or 086 772 8502, ⓦwww.panahuts.com. Congenial spot in a quiet, lush valley in the shadow of Doi Kong Mu that feels a lot further from town than it actually is. Made from woven bamboo, the six rooms have well-equipped bathrooms, mosquito nets and nice touches like pot plants and bedside lights. ④

Pen Porn House 16/1 Thanon Padungmuaytaw ⓣ053 611577 or 089 635 9588. Smart, clean, well-maintained, motel-like doubles with hot showers, round a small, shady garden. Fan ②, air-con ③

Piya Guest House 1/1 Soi 3, Thanon Khunlumprapas ⓣ053 611260, ⓔpiyaguesthouse@hotmail.com. Friendly, well-run, hotel-like guest house, boasting large rooms with spacious, hot-water bathrooms and air-con in a lush garden beside the lake. At the lower end of this price code. ④

The Residence 41/4 Thanon Nivetpisarn ⓣ053 614100, ⓦwww.theresidence-mhs.com. Tasteful, new, three-storey guest house furnished throughout with golden teak. The air-con rooms boast smart, hot-water bathrooms, crisp, white linen and duvets on the beds and even proper desks with reading lamps. Wi-fi and bicycles available to guests. At the lower end of this price code. ⑤

Romtai House 22 Thanon Chamnansathit ⓣ053 612437, ⓦhttp://5007311117.itfifty.com. Wide choice of spacious, well-maintained rooms and bungalows with hot water, set around a rambling, colourful garden and big lotus pond. Fan ③, air-con ④

Sang Tong Huts Down a small lane opposite *Mae Hong Son Guest House* off Thanon Makkasandi ⓣ053 620680, ⓦwww.sangtonghuts.com. Upmarket, German-run guest house, offering tasteful rustic chic on a steep, jungly slope on the edge of town, with a cute swimming pool. Roofed with traditional, thatched *tong teung* leaves, and decorated with rugs and tapestries, the "huts" have verandas, mosquito nets on the beds and large, attractively tiled bathrooms with hot water. Home-baked bread and cakes for breakfast, and Thai dinners, are served in a simple, open-sided seating area around an open fire. ③–⑥

Yok Guest House Thanon Sirimongkol ⓣ053 611532 or 086 611 5819. Quiet place in a small walled compound on the northwest side of town, offering functional but clean concrete rooms with en-suite hot-water bathrooms. Fan ②, air-con ③

Resorts and hotels

Fern Resort 6km south of town on Highway 108, then signposted 2km east on paved minor road ⓣ053 686110–1, ⓦwww.fernresort.info. The best resort around Mae Hong Son, an eco-friendly place employing local villagers as much as possible. In a peaceful, shady valley, a brook runs through the beautiful grounds, past stylish cottages with hot water, air-con and verandas (no phones or TV). There's an attractive swimming pool, and nature trails in the surrounding Mae Surin National Park; regular free shuttle bus to the *Fern Restaurant* in town. Breakfast included. ⑦

Imperial Tara Hotel 149 Moo 8, Tambon Pang Moo ⓣ053 684444–5, ⓦwww.imperialhotels.com. On the south side of the town by the turn-off for Huai Deua, this grand building is set in pretty landscaped gardens, overlooked by spacious rooms featuring satellite TV and minibar; there's a swimming pool, sauna and fitness centre, too. ⑧

Mae Hong Son Resort 6km south of town, on the road to Huai Deua ⓣ053 684138, ⓕ053 684137. In a large, relaxing garden by the Pai River, a friendly and quietly efficient place, with spacious, well-equipped bungalows. Breakfast included. ⑤

Mountain Inn 112 Thanon Khunlumprapas ⓣ053 611802–3, ⓦwww.mhsmountaininn.com. Large, neat and tasteful rooms with air-con, hot-water bathrooms, carpeting, minibars and TVs, set round a flower-strewn garden and swimming pool. ⑦

The Town

Beyond the typical concrete boxes in the centre, Mae Hong Son sprawls lazily across the valley floor and up the lower slopes of Doi Kong Mu to the west, trees and untidy vegetation poking through at every possible opportunity to remind you that open country is only a stone's throw away. Plenty of traditional Thai Yai buildings remain – wooden shophouses with balconies, shutters and corrugated-iron roof decorations, homes thatched with *tong teung* leaves and fitted with herringbone-patterned window panels – though they take a severe beating from the weather and may eventually be replaced by inexpensive, all-engulfing concrete.

Mae Hong Son's classic picture-postcard view is its twin nineteenth-century Burmese-style temples from the opposite, north shore of Jong Kham Lake

Poy Sang Long

Mae Hong Son's most famous and colourful festival is **Poy Sang Long**, held over the first weekend of April, which celebrates the ordination into the monkhood, for the duration of the schools' long vacation, of Thai Yai boys between the ages of seven and fourteen. Similar rituals take place in other northern Thai towns at this time, but the Mae Hong Son version is given a unique flavour by its Thai Yai elements. On the first day of the festival, the boys have their heads shaved and are anointed with turmeric and dressed up in the colours of a Thai Yai prince, with traditional accessories: long white socks, plenty of jewellery, a headcloth decorated with fresh flowers, a golden umbrella and heavy face make-up. They are then announced to the guardian spirit of the town and taken around the temples. The second day brings general merry-making and a spectacular parade, headed by a drummer and a richly decorated riderless horse, which is believed to carry the town's guardian spirit. The boys, still in their finery, are each carried on the shoulders of a chaperone, accompanied by musicians and bearers of traditional offerings. In the evening, the novices tuck into a sumptuous meal, waited on by their parents and relatives, before the ordination ceremony in the temple on the third day.

(Nong Jong Kham), their gleaming white and gold chedis and the multi-tiered roofs and spires of their viharns reflected in the water. In the viharn of **Wat Chong Kham** is a huge, intricately carved sermon throne, decorated with the *dharmachakra* (Wheel of Law) in coloured glass on gold; the building on the left has been built around the temple's most revered Buddha image, the benign, inscrutable Luang Pho To. Next door, **Wat Chong Klang** is famous for its paintings on glass, which are said to have been painted by artists from Mandalay over a hundred years ago; they're displayed over three walls on the left-hand side of the viharn. The first two walls behind the monks' dais (on which women are not allowed to stand) depict *Jataka* stories from the Buddha's previous incarnations in their lower sections, and the life of the Buddha himself in their upper, while the third wall is devoted entirely to the Buddha's life. A room to the left houses an unforgettable collection of **teak statues**, brought over from Burma in the middle of the nineteenth century. The dynamically expressive, often humorous figures are characters from the *Vessantara Jataka*, but the woodcarvers have taken as their models people from all levels of traditional Burmese society, including toothless emaciated peasants, butch tattooed warriors and elegant upper-class ladies.

The town's vibrant, smelly **morning market**, just south of the bus station, is worth dragging your bones up at dawn to see. People from the local hill tribes often come down to buy and sell, and the range of produce is particularly weird and wonderful, including, in season, porcupine meat, displayed with quills to prove its authenticity. Next door, the many-gabled viharn of **Wat Hua Wiang** shelters, under a lace canopy, one of the most beautiful Buddha images in northern Thailand, the **Chao Palakeng**. Copied from a famous statue in Mandalay, the strong, serene bronze has the regal clothing and dangling ears typical of Burmese Buddhas. Though the town is generally quiet during the day while visitors are out exploring the hills, the main streets come alive in the evening as **handicraft stalls** display colourful bolts of cloth, lacquerware, Burmese puppets, ceramics and jewellery.

For a godlike overview of the area, drive or climb up to **Wat Doi Kong Mu** on the steep hill to the west. From the temple's two chedis, which enshrine the ashes of respected nineteenth-century Thai Yai monks, you can look down on the town and out across the sleepy farming valley north and south. Behind the chedis, the viharn contains an unusual and highly venerated white marble image of the Buddha, surrounded in gold flames. If you've got the energy, trek up to the bot on the summit, where the view extends over the Burmese mountains to the west.

Eating and drinking

Nobody comes to Mae Hong Son just for the **food** – the available options are limited, although a few good restaurants have sprung up in order to cater specifically to visitors. There's a small, popular, takeaway-only **evening market** on Thanon Panishwattana, along from the day market, that closes around 8pm.

Baan Tua Lek South side of Jong Kham Lake. Stylish bakery with a small garden patio, serving good coffees, cakes, croissants, bagels and pies.

Ban Pleng 108/5 Thanon Khunlumprapas ⓣ053 612522. Divided in two by the main road, this restaurant with its traditional roofs of *tong teung* leaves specializes in northern Thai and local Thai Yai dishes, many of which are available in small B30 portions; try the crunchy fern salad with sesame seeds and oil or the very tasty *pla lung*, minced fish balls with tomato, garlic and ginger.

Crossroads 16 Thanon Singhanat Bamrung. Appropriately named as it is located at the junction of the town's two main roads, this welcoming bar serves up Thai and Western food, including American breakfasts (B120), great shakes, good coffee and draught Singha beer, and is a cool place to chillout in the evenings.

Fern 87 Thanon Khunlumprapas ⓣ053 611374. Large, justly popular eating place, with a nice terrace and a good reputation for its Thai food, such as spicy coconut shoot salad (B75) and river fish with spicy mango salad (B150). It also serves a few Thai Yai, northern Thai and Western dishes, and there's an espresso and cake shop at the front with internet access (10min free).

La Tasca 88/4 Thanon Khunlumprapas ⓣ053 611344. Reasonably authentic Italian restaurant with home-made pizzas and a long menu of familiar pasta dishes, including home-made gnocchi, lasagne and fettuccini (B170).

Raan Manee 9 Thanon Pradit Jongkham. Shophouse (no English sign – look for the "OTOP" sign) offering traditional Thai Yai desserts during the day, mostly made from coconut milk and sticky rice – cheap, freshly made and delicious.

Ruenmai 5 Thanon Singhanat Bamrung. Next to *Salween River*, this classic travellers' haunt serves cheap rice dishes, grilled river fish and a few Western dishes.

Salween River Thanon Singhanat Bamrung ⓣ053 612050. English- and Thai-run restaurant and bar, with wi-fi and a book exchange, dishing up a wide variety of Western favourites (B80 and up), as well as northern Thai, Thai Yai and Burmese food (mostly B50–80), including a delicious green tea salad.

Sunflower Thanon Pradit Jongkham. A good place for breakfast, lunch, dinner or just a drink, on a terrace overlooking the lake and the temples behind; in the evenings you can relax to the sounds of a live band playing Western and Thai pop and folk music. Home-made bread, cakes, pizzas and pastas, espresso coffees, and some tasty Thai dishes, including Lanna and Thai Yai specialities. Wi-fi available.

Listings

Airlines SGA, airport ⓣ053 698207; Thai Airways, 71 Thanon Singhanat Bamrung ⓣ053 612220.

Airport For flight information, call ⓣ053 612057 or 053 612097.

Exchange The airport has a bank currency exchange (daily roughly 10am–5pm). There are also several banks and exchange booths along Thanon Khunlumprapas.

Hospital Sri Sangwarn, Thanon Singhanat Bamrung ⓣ053 611378 or 053 611907.

Immigration office Thanon Khunlumprapas, north of the town centre (Mon–Fri 8.30am–4.30pm; ⓣ053 612106).

Internet access *The Meeting* bar, Thanon Pradit Jongkham.

Mail and telephones The post office is on Thanon Khunlumprapas, with cardphones outside and at the 7-Eleven supermarket across the road.

Pharmacy Paaset, Thanon Singhanat Bamrung.

Around Mae Hong Son

Once you've exhausted the few obvious sights in town, the first decision you'll have to grapple with is whether to visit one of the three villages of **"long-neck" women** around Mae Hong Son. Our advice is don't: they're effectively human zoos for snap-happy tourists, offering no opportunity to discover anything about Padaung culture. Less controversially, **boat and raft trips** on the babbling Pai River are fun, while the roaring **Pha Sua Falls** and the villages of **Mae Aw** and **Ruam Thai** to the north of town make a satisfying day out. Other feasible targets include the hot springs at Ban Pha Bong (see p.384) and, further out, Mae Surin Waterfall (see p.384) and Tham Lot (see p.393). If all that sounds too easy, Mae Hong Son is Thailand's third-largest centre for **trekking** (see p.386).

Local transport, in the form of songthaews from the north side of the morning market, is thinly spread and unreliable, so for all of these excursions it's best to rent your own vehicle or join an organized tour through your guest

"Long-neck" women

The most famous – and notorious – of the Mae Hong Son area's spectacles is its contingent of **"long-neck" women**, members of the tiny Padaung tribe of Burma who have come across to Thailand to escape Burmese repression. Though the women's necks appear to be stretched to 30cm and more by a column of brass rings, the "long-neck" tag is a technical misnomer: a *National Geographic* team once X-rayed one of the women and found that instead of stretching out her neck, the pressure of eleven pounds of brass had simply squashed her collarbones and ribs. Girls of the tribe start wearing the rings from about the age of 6, adding one or two each year up to the age of 16 or so. Once fastened, the rings are for life, for to remove a full stack may eventually cause the collapse of the neck and suffocation – in the past, removal was a punishment for adultery.

The **origin** of the ring-wearing ritual remains unclear, despite an embarrassment of plausible explanations. Padaung legend says that the mother of their tribe was a dragon with a long, beautiful neck, and that their unique custom is an imitation of her. Tour guides will tell you the practice is intended to enhance the women's beauty. In Burma, where it is now outlawed as barbaric, it's variously claimed that ring-wearing arose out of a need to protect women from tiger attacks or to deform the wearers so that the Burmese court would not kidnap them for concubines.

In spite of their handicap (they have to use straws to drink, for example), the women are able to carry out some kind of an ordinary life: they can marry and have children, and they're able to weave and sew, although these days they spend most of their time posing like circus freaks for photographs. Only half of the Padaung women now lengthen their necks; left to its own course, the custom would probably die out, but the influence of tourism may well keep it alive for some time yet. The villages in Mae Hong Son, and now also in Chiang Rai Province, where they live, are set up by Thai entrepreneurs as a money-making venture (all visitors are charged B250 to enter these villages). At least, contrary to many reports, the "long necks" are not held as slaves – they are each paid a living wage of about B1500 per month – though their plight as refugees is certainly precarious and vulnerable. Since 2005, the United Nations High Commission for Refugees has been offering permanent resettlement in third countries for about twenty Padaung. However, the authorities in Thailand, where the "long necks" bring in a huge amount of tourist dollars every year, have refused to sign the necessary paperwork on a technicality.

house or one of the many travel agents in town. As well as its community-based tourism programmes, Tour Merng Tai (see p.386) offers a wide range of half- and full-day trips (B400–2300 per person), as does Rose Garden Tours, 86/4 Thanon Khunlumprapas (Ⓣ053 611577, Ⓦwww.rosegarden-tours.com; B500–1700 per person). PA Motor on Thanon Pradit Jongkham opposite *Friend House* rents out **motorbikes** for B150–200 per day and **four-wheel drives** for B1200.

Trips on the Pai River

Scenic **boat trips** on the Pai River start from Huai Deua, 7km southwest of town near the *Mae Hong Son Resort*. Any travel agent can fix up an organized tour, but the cheapest way to do it is generally to rent a motorbike and approach the owners at Huai Deua boat station yourself. Twenty minutes downriver from Huai Deua (B600) will get you to the "long-neck" village of **Ban Nam Phiang Din**, but you're better off enjoying the river for its own sake, as it scythes its way between cliffs and forests towards the nearby Burmese border. **Elephant-rides** into the surrounding jungle, for B400–500 per hour for two people (best in the morning), can also be arranged next to the *Mae Hong Son Resort*.

A small stretch of the Pai River to the northwest of Mae Hong Son is clear enough of rocks to allow safe clearance for bamboo **rafts**. The journey takes between one and one-and-a-half-hours, as the rafts glide down the gentle river, partly hemmed in by steep wooded hills. Mae Hong Son Travel (see p.386) can fix this trip up for you, including the fifteen-minute drive from town, for B700 per raft (two passengers).

Pha Sua Falls, Mae Aw and Ban Ruam Thai

North of Mae Hong Son, a trip to Pha Sua Falls and the border villages of Mae Aw and Ruam Thai takes in some spectacular and varied countryside. Your best options are to rent a vehicle or join a tour – from B800 per person for a one-day excursion, including a visit to the highly overrated Fish Cave – as there are only occasional songthaews up to Mae Aw from the market in the morning, and no guarantees for the return journey to Mae Hong Son. Under your own steam, turn left off Route 1095 10km north of town, following signposts for Pha Sua and passing Phu Klon Country Club (Ⓣ053 282579, Ⓦwww.phuklon.co.th), more commonly known as the mud spa, where you can get a face or body mask or bathe in the hot spring water. About 20km from the turn-off you'll reach **Pha Sua Falls**, a wild, untidy affair, which crashes down in several cataracts through a dark overhang cut in the limestone. The waterfall is in full roar in October after the rainy season, but has plenty of water all year round. Take care when swimming, as several people have been swept to their deaths here.

Above the falls the paved road climbs precipitously, giving glorious, broad vistas of both Thai and Burmese mountains, before reaching the unspectacular half-Hmong, half-Thai Yai village of **Naphapak** after 11km. From here, a largely flat stretch of tarmac (built by the Thai military to help the fight against the opium trade) heads north for 7km to **MAE AW** (aka Ban Rak Thai), a settlement of Kuomintang anti-Communist Chinese refugees (see p.412), right on the Burmese border. The tight ring of hills around the village heightens the feeling of being in another country: delicate, bright-green tea bushes line the slopes, while Chinese ponies wander the streets of long, unstilted bamboo houses. In the central marketplace on the north side of the village reservoir, shops sell great bags of Oolong and Chian Chian teas, as well as dried mushrooms.

Heading 6km west from Naphapak along a fairly rough paved road, you'll come to **BAN RUAM THAI**, a Thai Yai settlement where a royal project has had a lot of success in substituting coffee for opium. On the left at the start of the village, English-speaking Mr Hilary (Ⓣ053 070589 or 083 571 6668) can take you through the process of drying, roasting and grinding coffee, and of course serve you a nice cuppa. He can also put you up in simple, en-suite **bungalows** (no electricity; ❸–❺) or tents (B300), under majestic stands of bamboo on the slope behind his basic restaurant, with pleasant views of the valley. At the other end of the village lies **Pang Oung**, a large reservoir surrounded by pine-clad slopes that's very popular with Thai tourists and has been dubbed "Switzerland in Mae Hong Son" – the locals have even put bells on their cows.

Route 1095: Mae Hong Son to Chiang Mai

Route 1095, the 243-kilometre northern route between Mae Hong Son and Chiang Mai, is every bit as wild and scenic as the southern route through Mae Sariang – if anything it has more mountains to negotiate, with a greater contrast between the sometimes straggly vegetation of the slopes and the thickly cultivated valleys. Much of the route was established by the Japanese army to move troops and supplies into Burma after its invasion of Thailand during World War II. The labour-intensive job of paving every hairpin bend was completed in the 1990s, but ongoing repair work can still give you a nasty surprise if you're riding a motorbike. Three daily **buses** and roughly hourly air-con **minibuses** run between Mae Hong Son and Chiang Mai's Arcade station via Pai.

Soppong and Tham Lot

The small market town of **SOPPONG**, 68km from Mae Hong Son in the district of Pang Ma Pha (which is sometimes used on signposts), gives access to the most famous of over two hundred known caves in the area, **Tham Lot**, 9km north in **BAN THAM**. Motorbike taxis (B70) and pick-ups (B300) run along the gentle paved forest road to the village from the bus stop in the centre of Soppong. Due to its proximity to Pai, Soppong has become popular for day-trippers, and now even supports an ATM at its far west end in front of the police station.

Turn right in Ban Tham to find the entrance to the **Tham Lot Nature Education Station** set up to look after the cave, where you'll need to hire a local Thai Yai guide with lantern for B100 per group. A short walk through the forest brings you to the entrance of Tham Lot, where the Lang River begins a 600-metre subterranean journey through the cave. Access to the various parts of the cave depends on the time of year and how much rain there has been, and may involve hiring a bamboo raft for some or all of your journey (B100–400 for up to three people): for most of the year you'll need to raft from Doll to Coffin Cave, while at the driest times it may be possible to wade, and at the highest water levels it may be necessary to walk around to the exit and get to the last part, Coffin Cave, from there. Normally two hours should allow you enough time for travelling through the broad, airy tunnel, and for the main attraction, climbing up into the sweaty caverns in the roof – be sure not to touch any of the cave formations.

The first of these, **Column Cavern**, 100m from the entrance on the right, is dominated by a twenty-metre-high cave stalagmite snaking up towards the ceiling. Another 50m on the left, bamboo ladders lead up into **Doll Cave**, which has a glistening, pure white wall and a weird red and white formation shaped like a Wurlitzer organ; deep inside, stalagmites look like dolls. Just before the vast exit from the cave, wooden ladders on the left lead up into **Coffin Cave**, named after the remains of a dozen crude log coffins discovered here, one of them preserved to its full length of 5m. Hollowed out from teak trunks about 1700 years ago, they are similar to those found in many of the region's caves: some are raised 2m off the ground by wooden supporting poles, and some still contained bones, pottery and personal effects when they were discovered. It's worth hanging round the cave's exit at sunset, when hundreds of thousands of tiny black chirruping swifts pour into the cave in an almost solid column, to find their beds for the night.

Practicalities

Cave Lodge (053 617203, www.cavelodge.com; 1–4), on the other side of **Ban Tham** from the cave, makes an excellent, friendly base for exploring the area. The owners have plenty of useful information about Tham Lot and other **caves** in the region, and organize more robust, active **guided trips**. They also offer **kayaking**, including trips through Tham Lot, plus 6km of fun rapids, in the rainy and cool seasons (B490). Maps for self-guided walking from the lodge to local Thai Yai, Karen, Lahu and Lisu villages are available, as well as local, English-speaking guides for full-on **trekking** (typically B1700 for 3 days). Other activities include learning to weave or cook, mountain-biking and birdwatching. Dorm beds here are B90–120, and the wooden rooms and bungalows, some with shared hot showers and others with their own bathrooms, are scattered over the overgrown hillside. There's also a relaxing communal area around an open fire for hanging out and eating Thai, Thai Yai and Western food, including home-baked bread.

For budget travellers, *Cave Lodge* is by far your best bet, but if you need to stay in **Soppong** itself, try *Jungle Guest House* (053 617099; 2), on the south side of the main road towards the western end of town. Accommodation is in simple huts with hot-water bathrooms, and the owner can give advice on local walks to Lisu villages or organize inexpensive trekking trips to Lisu, Lahu and Karen settlements. Moving upmarket, *Little Eden Guest House* (053 617054, www.littleeden-guesthouse.com; 3–7), a short walk east of Soppong's bus stop, has a variety of neat, attractive bungalows and rooms with their own hot-water bathrooms, in a pretty garden with a decent-sized swimming pool, sloping down to the Lang River and a relaxing riverside pavilion; plenty of services such as motorbike rental, free internet access and tours and treks are on offer, as well as Thai, Western and Thai Yai food. The pick of the bunch, however, is *Soppong River Inn* at the west end of town (053 617107, www.soppong.com; 4–5). Here on a densely foliated plot, you'll find seven diverse rooms, tastefully decorated and thoughtfully designed, many with outdoor bathrooms but all having hot showers. As well as internet access, there's a lovely, partly thatched deck over the Pai River, which here runs swiftly through a craggy, jungly defile. **Homestays** are available in the nearby Lisu village of Ban Nong Tong (089 998 4886, www.lisuhilltribe.com), where you can learn the hill tribe's crafts, music, dance and cooking, and go trekking.

Pai

Set in a broad, gentle valley 43km beyond Soppong, **PAI** was once just a small-town stopover on the tiring journey to Mae Hong Son, but in recent years has established itself as a major tourist destination in its own right. There's nothing special to see here, but you can partake of all manner of outdoor activities, courses and holistic therapies – even retail therapy at the art studios, bookstores, leather and jewellery shops – and the guest houses, out-of-town resorts and restaurants have tailored themselves to the flood of visitors who make the journey out from Chiang Mai. Westerners settle into the town's full-on traveller culture and laid-back, New-Agey feel for weeks or even months – the local tourist maps even give handy lists of tattoo studios and non-MSG restaurants. Meanwhile, Pai is now firmly on the radar of Thai tourists, so in high season, especially on weekends when the sunflowers near Mae Hong Son are out (see p.384), the narrow through-streets get clogged with air-con minibuses. It can be an odd mix, but an evening promenade along the "walking street" of Thanon Chaisongkhram, with its Thai-style galleries and gift shops in the traditional buildings at the western end and more traveller-oriented outlets to the east – plus a sprinkling of local hill-tribe people and shrouded Thai Muslims – is undoubtedly pleasant and *sanuk*.

Over ten days in November and December 2008, Pai held its first **film festival** (Ⓣ053 612982–3, Ⓦwww.paifilmfestival.com), showing Thai and international films and animations and hosting gigs by Thai pop stars, which may well be repeated in future years.

Arrival and local transport

SGA Airlines (Ⓦwww.sga.co.th) now **fly** to Pai from Chiang Mai in half an hour between one and three times a day, landing at the airstrip on the north side of town. As well as **buses**, faster, more comfortable, hourly air-con minibuses run

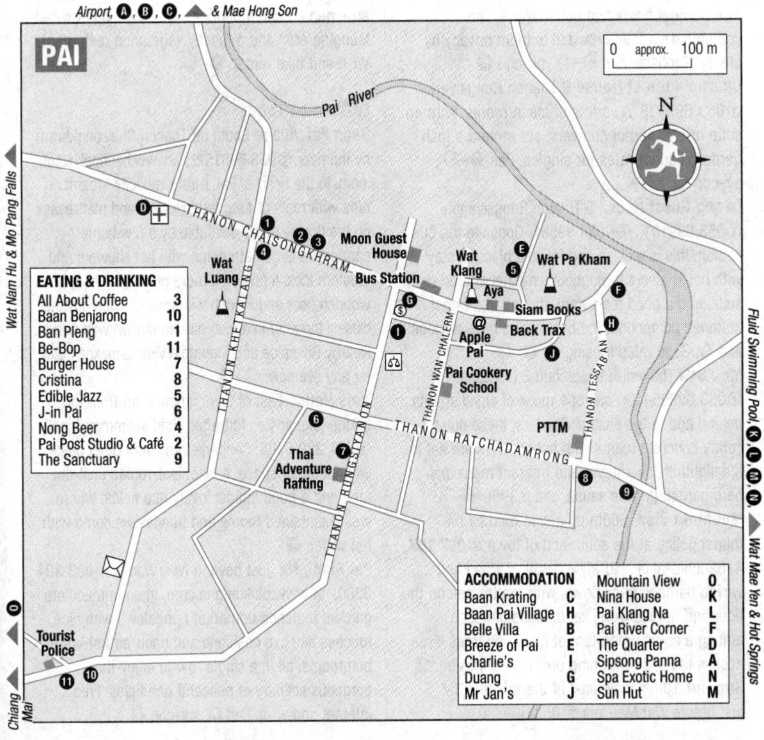

to Pai from both Chiang Mai and Mae Hong Son: Prempracha (Ⓣ053 064307) covers both routes, using the respective **bus stations**, while Aya, a travel agency on Thanon Chaisongkhram (Ⓣ053 699940 or 053 699888 in Pai, Ⓣ053 247663 in Chiang Mai; Ⓦwww.ayaservice.com), runs from Chiang Mai only, but offers pick-ups from your accommodation. Motorbike **taxis** wait on Thanon Chaisongkhram opposite the bus station, while Aya is the best place to **rent motorbikes**, charging from B80 a day, not including insurance, which is an extra B40–80, as well as pick-ups (B1200 per day). If you're driving yourself, note that the eastern part of Thanon Chaisongkhram, the north end of Rungsiyanon and Thanon Tessaban 1 are pedestrianized, at least in the tourist season. Several places in town rent out **mountain bikes**, including *Moon Guest House* (B50), down the continuation of Thanon Rungsiyanon behind the bus station.

Accommodation

Coinciding with the town's soaring popularity, **guest houses** are springing up all the time. There are now over fifty within town, as well as dozens in the countryside around Pai, useful for escaping the growing bustle downtown. Upmarket **resorts** have also proliferated, especially in the countryside, catering largely for Thai weekenders with their own transport.

Inexpensive

Breeze of Pai Just off Thanon Chaisongkhram near Wat Pa Kham Ⓣ081 998 4597. Congenial, well-maintained place with large, simple but chic, ochre bungalows and single-storey rooms with nice parquet floors and hot showers. The compound's a little crowded but lent privacy by plenty of foliage. Fan ❸–❹, air-con ❺

Charlie's Guest House 9 Thanon Rungsiyanon Ⓣ053 699039. A variety of clean rooms, with en suite or shared hot showers, set around a lush garden; decent rates for singles. Fan ❶–❷, air-con ❹

Duang Guest House 5 Thanon Rungsiyanon Ⓣ053 699101, Ⓕ053 699581. Opposite the bus station, this is a clean and reliable place to stay, with hot showers throughout, whether shared or en suite, and a good restaurant, though in a rather cramped compound; the best rooms have a fridge and TV. Good rates for singles. ❶–❹

Mr Jan's Thanon Sukhaphibun 3 (Tessaban) Ⓣ053 699554. On one of a mess of small streets behind and to the east of *Charlie's*, these quiet, comfy concrete rooms with hot showers are set in a delightfully overgrown and fragrant medicinal herb garden (for the sauna, see p.398). ❷

Mountain View 500m up a side road by the tourist police at the south end of town Ⓣ087 187 4702. Laid-back, old-style resort of wood and woven bamboo bungalows, with mattresses on the floor and hot showers, set in loads of space among a small arboretum of flowering trees. Free access to Fluid swimming pool (see opposite). ❶

Sun Hut 10min walk east of the bridge, just before Wat Mae Yen Ⓣ053 699730, Ⓦwww.thesunhut.com. In a large, grassy garden by a stream, this quiet, friendly place has lots of nice touches such as flowers and hammocks. Sturdy bungalows with hot-water bathrooms, some with nice views over the rice paddies, are arranged around a pond, a communal, open-sided lounging area and a mostly vegetarian restaurant. Wi-fi and bike rental. ❸–❺

Moderate

Baan Pai Village South off Thanon Chaisongkhram by the river Ⓣ053 698152, Ⓦwww.baanpaivillage.com. In the heart of Pai, rural simplicity – bamboo huts with roofs of *tong teung* leaves and mattresses on the floor – made palatable by a few home comforts – large bathrooms with hot showers and Western loos. A few baht more gets you a bed, a wooden floor and French windows. Clustered rather closely together in a lush garden strewn with ponds. Nearby Riverside and Mountain View annexes cater for any overspill. ❹–❺

Nina House East of town, about 2km from the bridge (signposted left after Fluid swimming pool) Ⓣ081 289 6408. Congenial and very quiet place, with plenty of space, a nice, leaf-roofed chill-out area and a pond amidst lovely rice fields, where well-maintained rooms and bungalows come with hot water. ❹

Pai Klang Na Just beyond *Nina House* Ⓣ083 304 3300, Ⓦwww.paiklangna.com. In an immaculate garden, thatched upmarket bungalows with nice touches like axe cushions and open-air hot-water bathrooms, all in a single row to enjoy the gorgeous scenery of peaceful rice fields. Free internet and wi-fi. Fan ❻, air-con ❼

Sipsong Panna Guest House On the Pai River north of town ⓣ053 698259, ⓔsipsongpanna33@hotmail.com. Head 1km north from town on the Mae Hong Son road, then turn right for another kilometre to the village of Wieng Neua and follow the signs. Airy Thai-style rooms with mosquito nets and stylish, hot-water bathrooms on the river, and a good vegetarian café. Breakfast included. ⑤

Spa Exotic Home 6km south of Wat Mae Yen, off the minor road to the hot springs ⓣ053 065722, ⓦwww.spaexotic.com. Cosy teak bungalows with bathtubs fed by hot spring-water and verandas, and a pretty restaurant and sitting area, in a shady garden by the Pai River that features an attractive, landscaped spa pool. ⑤

Expensive

Baan Krating About 1km north of town, signposted to the right off the Mae Hong Son road, just beyond *Belle Villa* ⓣ053 698255, ⓦwww.amari.com. Welcoming upmarket place with a large swimming pool and jacuzzi, set amidst green fields. Similar luxury to *Belle Villa* with a more traditional feel: bright, air-con villas with verandas, bamboo cladding and roofs covered with *tong teung* leaves. ⑦

Belle Villa About 1km north of town, signposted to the right off the Mae Hong Son road ⓣ053 698226–7, ⓦwww.bellevillaresort.com. Elegant luxury rooms and villas on stilts, all with balconies, mini-bars and safes. Traversed by a stream and decorated with rice fields, the grounds sport a stylish pool. Wi-fi, mountain bikes for rent and free transfers to town. Breakfast included. ⑦

Pai River Corner Resort By the river at the eastern end of Thanon Chaisongkhram ⓣ053 699049, ⓦwww.pairivercorner.com. Elegant, Mediterranean-style resort with beautifully furnished, balconied rooms, some of which have their own jacuzzis, set around an attractive garden and swimming pool. Wi-fi and breakfast included. ⑧

The Quarter Thanon Chaisongkhram, just west of Pai Hospital ⓣ053 699423, ⓦwww.thequarterhotel.com. Chic and welcoming luxury hotel, in a central but quiet location, with an attractive spa. Set in two-storey houses around a lovely contemporary Thai garden and a smart pool with jacuzzi, the modern minimalist rooms feature distressed concrete, dark wood and splashes of dark silk. Free internet, wi-fi and mountain bikes. Breakfast included. ⑧

Activities

Several undemanding **walks** can be made around Pai's broad, gently sloping valley. The easiest – one hour there and back – takes you across the river bridge on the east side of town and up the hill to Wat Mae Yen, which commands a great view over the whole district. On the way to the wat, you'll pass Fluid, the town's large open-air **swimming pool** (daily 9am–6pm; adults B60, kids free), with food and drink available, as well as fitness equipment, a steam room and yoga classes. To the west of town beyond Pai Hospital, the continuation of Thanon Chaisongkhram passes, after 3km, Wat Nam Hu, whose Buddha image has an unusual hinged top-knot containing holy water. Beyond, the road gradually climbs through comparatively developed Thai Yai, Kuomintang (with a Chinese Cultural Centre where you can taste tea), Lisu and Lahu villages to **Mo Pang Falls**, with a pool for swimming, about 10km west of Pai.

Pai makes a good base for **trekking**, which can be arranged through the guest houses or trekking agents, among which *Duang Guest House*, Thai Adventure Rafting (see p.398, or phone Mem on ⓣ081 028 6275) and Back Trax at 17 Thanon Chaisongkhram (ⓣ053 699739, ⓔbacktraxinpai@yahoo.com) are reliable. Thai Adventure Rafting head off to friendly, hassle-free Karen, Lisu and Lahu villages to the north of Soppong near the border, taking in Tham Lot (see p.393), some beautiful scenery and, in the rainy season, waterfalls; two days cost B1600 per person (minimum four people), three days B2300, the latter including one night in a camp you build with the guide, with a bit of jungle cooking and survival training thrown in. Their one-day treks head north of Pai (B800 per person, minimum three people). *Duang* charge B750–800 for one day (two to three people), B750 per day for two or three days (minimum four people). Both of these places can add bamboo rafting and can arrange one-way treks to Mae Hong Son (5–7 days), while *Duang* also offer sightseeing tours.

If you just fancy a bit of **bamboo-rafting** without the trekking, *Duang* and plenty of other agents can arrange transport and a two-hour trip down the Pai River for around B500 per person. Among several **elephant camps** on the minor road from Wat Mae Yen towards the hot springs, Joy, 5km from town (Ⓣ081 881 3923), charges B300 per hour per person for an elephant ride (minimum two people), which includes going into the river with the elephant and feeding it, as well as a free bathe in a hot spring pool. Horseriding is available at *Phu Pai Art Resort*, just beyond the airport (Ⓣ053 065111–2; B350 per hr).

With a little more cash to spare, you could strike up with the reliable and experienced, French-run Thai Adventure Rafting on Thanon Rungsiyanon for a **rubber-raft trip** (Ⓣ053 699111, Ⓦwww.thairafting.com; second branch planned for the east end of Thanon Chaisongkhram; not to be confused with the imitative Pai Adventure Rafting). Heading down the Pai River to Mae Hong Son, you'll pass through gorges and sixty rapids and take in waterfalls and hot springs. The full journey lasts two days, including a night at a comfortable jungle camp by the river, and costs B2500 per person, though one-day trips (B1500) are also available; the season normally runs from mid-June to the end of February, with the highest water from August to early September, and participants must be able to swim.

Accessible from the minor road south from Wat Mae Yen, 2km beyond Joy Elephant Camp, or by turning left off the main Chiang Mai road straight after the bridge over the Pai River, the **hot springs** (B200; part of Huai Nam Dang National Park – see p.400) have one or two very hot, rough pools and aren't really up to much, though there is an attractive valley campsite here. Better to go to one of the nearby **spas**, which put the piped hot water from the springs to much more productive use. *Pai Hotsprings Spa Resort* (Ⓣ053 065748–9, Ⓦwww.paihotspringssparesort.com), down a side road about 1km north of the springs, has two shady mineral pools (B50) and provides various massages (B300 per hr). They also offer rooms with spa-water bathrooms, but for accommodation you're better off going to the more congenial and attractive *Spa Exotic Home* nearby (see p.397); the latter also admits non-guests to its pool (B100) and offers massages.

Massages are also available at several spots in town, including *Mr Jan's Guest House*, famous for its Thai (B150 per hr) and Burmese/Shan massages (B200 per hr) and saunas (B60). Having trained at the Old Medicine Hospital in Chiang Mai, the staff at Pai Traditional Thai Massage (PTTM) on Thanon Tessaban 1 (Ⓣ053 699121, Ⓦwww.pttm1989.com) also have a good reputation for traditional massages (B180 per hr), as well as foot, herbal and oil massages (B250–300 per hr) and saunas (B80), and run government-approved, three-day **massage courses** (B2500). The Pai Cookery School, Thanon Wan Chalerm (Ⓣ081 706 3799; B750 per day), holds Thai **cooking courses** of one to three days, including a trip to the market to learn about ingredients, making six dishes, eating them and getting a free recipe book; vegetarians are catered for.

Eating, drinking and nightlife

As with the accommodation scene, new **cafés and restaurants** are opening practically every week, ever more sophisticated and cosmopolitan. *The Sanctuary* restaurant and several **bars** offer live music: as well as those listed below, look out for posters around town, which sometimes also announce one-off parties.

Cafés and restaurants

All About Coffee Thanon Chaisongkhram. Superb coffee in any variety you might want, in an atmospheric wooden shophouse. Also great breakfasts with home-made bread, a daily selection of home-made cakes, sandwiches and

▲ Writing postcards, Pai

teas, hot chocolate, shakes and juices. Daily 8.30am–5.30pm.

Baan Benjarong South end of town, near *Be-Bop Bar*. In a town where you can get everything from sushi to falafel, this place offers a wide variety of authentic and tasty Thai dishes – the banana-flower salad (*yam hua pree*) is especially delicious (B90). Small and often full on busy nights (no reservations).

Ban Pleng Corner of Chaisongkhram and Khetkalang (no English sign). Branch of the Mae Hong Son restaurant specializing in local food (see p.390), in a landmark two-storey house on the junction.

Burger House Thanon Rungsiyanon. Surprisingly tasty burgers in various forms using imported beef (mostly B80–135), plus breakfasts, baguettes and other Western dishes, in a good central location.

Cristina Thanon Ratchadamrong, just west of the bridge over the river. Currently the best and most authentic of Pai's few Italian restaurants, offering large, crispy pizzas (B110–230), great salads, home-made pasta and Italian wines.

J-in Pai Thanon Ratchadamrong. Chinese vegetarian and vegan garden restaurant, offering tasty buffet food such as green curry with tofu on brown rice (B25) and pricier made-to-order dishes like tempura. Follow it with excellent espresso at the hairdresser's next door. Daily 8am–8pm.

Nong Beer Corner of Chaisongkhram and Khetkalang (no English sign). One of Pai's longest-standing and most popular places for cheap eats – now self-service but with loads of tables – dishing up great *khao soi*, pork satay and a wide range of buffet stir-fries and curries.

The Sanctuary Thanon Ratchadamrong. Satellite restaurant of the Ko Pha Ngan resort (see p.620; a resort is planned in Pai, too), in a pleasant riverfront setting hard by the bridge. On offer – besides wi-fi – are organic, mostly vegetarian food such as sweet potato dal, home-baked bread and cakes, a wide range of smoothies and teas, and live music nightly in the upstairs bar.

Bars

Be-Bop South end of town, beyond the junction of Khetkalang and Rungsiyanon. Amongst a clutch of nightspots, this large, well-designed bar hosts live music every evening and is a popular spot for travellers to congregate.

Edible Jazz Just off Thanon Chaisongkhram near Wat Pa Kham. This garden café and bar on a quiet, leafy lane is a mellow spot for a drink, currently offering an acoustic set 9–10pm, followed by "fake jazz" – whatever that might be.

Pai Post Studio & Café Thanon Chaisongkhram. Super-cool, minimalist white hangout for evening drinks with a good soundtrack and live music promised every night. Inside, there's a small art gallery with regularly changing exhibitions; outside, tables on the busy, car-free street for people-watching.

Listings

Bookshop Siam Books, Thanon Chaisongkhram.
Cinema Apple Pai, an internet café on Thanon Chaisongkhram, has a selection of 500 movies that you can choose from and watch in its three comfy rooms (B75 per person). Thai and Mexican food and cocktails are also available.
Hospital Thanon Chaisongkhram ⓣ053 699211.
Internet access Several shops near the intersection of Thanon Rungsiyanon and Thanon Ratchadamrong, or Apple Pai (see "Cinema", above).
Newspaper The free, bi-monthly, English-language *Pai Post*.
Tourist police South end of town, on the road to Chiang Mai ⓣ053 611812–3 or 1155.
Travel agent Aya (see p.396) sells air, bus, boat and train tickets and organizes overnight minibuses directly to Chiang Khong (B750), arriving in time to take the morning boat to Louang Phabang.

From Pai to Chiang Mai

Once out of the Pai valley, Route 1095 climbs for 35km of hairpin bends, with beautiful views north to 2175-metre Doi Chiang Dao near the top. In the cool season, with your own transport, you can witness – if you get started from Pai an hour before dawn – one of the country's most famous views of the sun rising over a sea of mist at **Huai Nam Dang National Park** (B200). The viewpoint is signposted on the left 30km out of Pai; take this turning and go on 6km to the park headquarters. Once over the 1300-metre pass, the road steeply descends the south-facing slopes in the shadow of Doi Mae Ya (2005m), before working its way along the narrow, more populous lower valleys. After 55km (at kilometre-stone 42), a left turn leads 6.5km over some roller-coaster hills to **Pong Duet hot springs** (also part of Huai Nam Dang National Park), where scalding water leaps up to four metres into the air, generating copious quantities of steam in the cool season. A few hundred metres downstream of the springs, a series of pools allows you to soak in the temperature of your choice. The last appealing detour of the route is to **Mokfa Falls** (part of Doi Suthep-Pui National Park; B200), where a cascade tumbles about 30m into a sand-fringed pool that is ideal for swimming, making an attractive setting for a break – it's 2km south of the main road, 76km from Pai. Finally, at **Mae Malai**, turn right onto the busy Highway 107 and join the mad, speeding traffic for the last 34km across the wide plains to Chiang Mai.

Chiang Rai and the borders

The northernmost tip of Thailand, stretching from the Kok River and **Chiang Rai** to the border, is a schizophrenic place, split in two by Highway 1, Thailand's main north–south road. In the western half, rows of wild, shark's-tooth mountains jut into Burma, while to the east, low-lying rivers flow through Thailand's richest rice-farming land to the Mekong River, which forms the border with Laos here. In anticipation of Burma and Laos opening up further to tourism, the region is well connected and has been thoroughly kitted out for visitors. Chiang Rai now has thousands of hotel rooms, catering mostly to package tourists, who plough through the countryside in air-conditioned Scenicruisers in search of quaint, photogenic primitive life. What they get – fairground rides on boats and elephants, and colourfully dressed hill people performing artificial folkloric rituals – generally satisfies expectations, but has little to do with the harsh realities of life in the north.

Chiang Rai town has more to it than package hotels though, including some fascinating sights and appealing travellers' guest houses. The other highlights of this region are **Mae Salong**, the dizzying mountain perch of Chinese Nationalists, and the grassy ruined temples of **Chiang Saen** on the Mekong. If you're coming up **from Chiang Mai**, the quickest and most obvious route to Chiang Rai is Highway 118, a fast, 185-kilometre road that swoops through rolling hill country. A much more scenic approach, however, is to follow Highway 107 and Highway 1089 to the congenial village of **Tha Ton** and then complete the journey by longtail boat or bamboo raft down the **Kok River**. The best **map** of this region is *The Golden Triangle* at 1:360,000 by David Unkovich (Ⓦwww.gt-rider.com), available in local bookshops for B150.

To Chiang Rai via Tha Ton

Set aside two days if you're catching a bus from Chiang Mai, then a longtail along the **Kok River**, allowing for an overnight stay in **Tha Ton**, which boasts several appealing riverside resorts and a wide variety of outdoor activities. Four daily services between Chiang Mai's Chang Phuak bus station and Tha Ton take about four hours; it's best to leave the longtail-boat trip to Chiang Rai until the following afternoon. If you don't catch one of the direct buses, you could take one of the half-hourly buses to the ugly frontier outpost of Fang, 153km from Chiang Mai, then change onto a half-hourly songthaew to Tha Ton. With your own transport, you can give Fang a miss altogether by branching west on a bypass signposted to Mae Ai. Several worthwhile diversions, notably the admirable **Elephant Nature Park** and a couple of good guest houses that can arrange trekking in the countryside near **Chiang Dao**, may slow you down further on the journey north from Chiang Mai. From Tha Ton, it's also possible to move on to Mae Salong by songthaew or Mae Sai by bus.

The Elephant Nature Park

From Chiang Mai the route towards Tha Ton heads north along Highway 107, retracing the Mae Hong Son Loop as far as Mae Malai. About 3km after Mae Taeng, a signposted left turn leads 9km to the **Elephant Nature Park**, which is essentially a rescue centre and hospital for sick, orphaned and neglected elephants, but hands-on educational – and recreational – visits by the public are encouraged. On a daytime visit, you'll get to feed, bathe and learn about the elephants close up, but it's also possible to stay for two days or sign up as a paying volunteer for a week or longer. The park's owner, Sangduan ("Lek") Chailert, has become something of a celebrity in recent years, being featured on the BBC and in *Time* magazine for her conservation efforts. You can find out more about the park at Ⓦwww.elephantnaturepark.org, and to visit the camp, you'll need to book at 209/2 Thanon Sridornchai (Ⓣ053 818754) or one of their several other offices in Chiang Mai.

Chiang Dao

Around kilometre-stone 72 **CHIANG DAO**, an oversized market village, stretches on and on along the road as the dramatic limestone crags and forests of Thailand's third-highest peak, Doi Luang Chiang Dao (or Doi Luang, "Great Mountain"; 2240m), loom up on the left. A new ring road now sweeps round to the west of town, carrying traffic heading straight for Tha Ton.

From the town itself, a road served by yellow songthaews and motorbike taxis heads northwest for 5km, across the bypass, to an extensive complex of interconnected caverns, **Tham Chiang Dao**, with an attached monastery (the caves were given religious significance by the local legend of a hermit sage who is said to have dwelt in them for a millennium). Several of the caverns can be visited; a couple have electric light but others need the services of a guide with a lantern. Admission to the caves is B20 and guides ask around B100 to take a group of up to five people on a tour of about thirty minutes, during which they point out unusual rock formations. About 1500m further north along the road from the caves, the secluded *Malee's Nature Lovers Bungalows* (ⓣ053 456426 or 081 961 8387, ⓦwww.maleenature.com; ❷–❻) is a cosy compound delightfully set in the shadow of the mountain. Comfy rooms and bungalows of varying size, some with shared hot showers and others with en-suite bathrooms, as well as camping facilities (B80 per person), two-person tents to rent (B200) and good food, are available here. They can arrange treks, elephant trekking and bird-watching trips, or just point birders in the right direction; bicycle and motorbike rental is available. On either side of *Malee's* is a branch of *Chiang Dao Nest* (ⓣ053 456242, ⓦwww.chiangdao.com; ❹–❺), who offer similar trips, provide free internet access and wi-fi and rent out mountain bikes; both branches have half a dozen or so bungalows with attached hot-water bathrooms and balconies. The one nearer to the caves serves Thai food, while the further one – which has a small swimming pool – turns out gourmet Western dishes, with mains at around B300 each. Guided treks to the **summit of Doi Chiang Dao**, famous for its many rare alpine plants and birds, can be arranged by both *Malee's* and *Chiang Dao Nest* during the cool season, roughly from November to March. It takes two to three days to go up and down and costs from around B2300 per person in a large group.

Doi Angkhang

Back on Highway 107, the road shimmies over a rocky ridge marking the watershed between the catchment areas of the Chao Phraya River to the south and the Mekong River ahead, before descending into the flat plain around Fang and the Kok River. Branching off to the left some 60km from Chiang Dao, a steep and winding 25-kilometre road, Route 1249, leads up to **Doi Angkhang** (1928m; map of the mountain available from Chiang Mai TAT office). Besides a royal agricultural project that produces peaches, raspberries and kiwis in the cool season, the mountain is home to the eco-friendly **Angkhang Nature Resort** (ⓣ053 450110, ⓦwww.amari.com/angkhang; ❾), where the luxurious teak pavilions have balconies with great views, the restaurant uses organic produce from the royal project, and birdwatching or trekking, mule riding or mountain biking to nearby hill-tribe villages are the main activities.

Tha Ton and around

The tidy, leafy settlement of **THA TON**, nearly 180km north of Chiang Mai, huddles each side of a bridge over the Kok River, which flows out of Burma 4km to the north upstream. Life in Tha Ton revolves around the bridge – buses and boats pull up here, and most of the accommodation is clustered nearby. Among several simple restaurants opposite the boat landing, *Coffee Mug* offers good espressos and internet access, while about 200m before the bridge on the Fang road, there's an ATM at *Hotel Alilak*.

The main attractions here are longtail-boat and bamboo-raft rides downstream to Chiang Rai (see below), but on the west side of the bridge the over-the-top ornamental gardens of **Wat Tha Ton** (Ⓦwww.wat-thaton.org), endowed with colossal golden and white Buddha images and an equally huge statue of Kuan Im, the Chinese *bodhisattva* of mercy, are well worth the short climb. From any of the statues, the views up the narrow green valley towards Burma and downstream across the sun-glazed plain are heady stuff.

Accommodation

On the east bank of the river, 300m north from the bridge, *Garden Home Nature Resort* (Ⓣ053 373015, Ⓦwww.gardenhomenature.com; fan ❶–❷, air-con ❹–❺) is a very appealing option, with friendly, clued-up staff, internet access and attractive en-suite rooms and bungalows (all with hot showers) sheltering in plenty of space under an orchard of lychees. The restaurant serves Western breakfasts, espressos and a good choice of Thai food – at lovely, thatched *salas* on stilts over the river if you like – and they offer **motorbike rental**, off-road motorbike day-trips and **trekking**, from half a day, including a boat ride on the river (B950 per person), to three days (B2000 per person), as well as various journeys down the Kok River (they can even arrange for the 12.30pm boat to Chiang Rai to pick you up from the resort). About 200m beyond *Garden Home*, the *River View Resort* (Ⓣ053 373173–5, Ⓕ053 459288; ❻, breakfast included) enjoys an even better location, on a bend in the river that is hemmed in by densely forested hillsides, of which the well-equipped, air-conditioned rooms and bungalows and the excellent Thai terrace restaurant have great views. In extensive gardens about 1km east of the bridge on the right-hand side of Highway 1089, the family-friendly *Mae Kok River Village Resort* (Ⓣ053 459328, Ⓦwww.maekok-river-village-resort.com; ❽) is another good upmarket choice. Well-designed, stylish, air-conditioned rooms are set around a swimming pool, with a jacuzzi and toddlers' pool, and a huge range of outdoor activities are on offer. At this multi-dimensional resort – which encompasses a diverse educational project – visitors can also sign up for courses in Thai cooking or rock-climbing.

En route to Mae Salong: Ban Lorcha

Beyond Tha Ton, Route 1089 heads east towards Mae Chan and Highway 1; about 20km out of town, at Ban Kew Satai, an exciting roller-coaster of a side road leads north for 16km to Mae Salong (see p.412). Four direct yellow **songthaews** a day (B70) to Mae Salong leave a few hundred metres north of the bridge in Tha Ton, but it's worth breaking your journey about 1km west of Kew Satai on Route 1089 at **BAN LORCHA**. As part of a community-based tourism development project, owned and managed by the villagers, with technical assistance from the PDA in Chiang Rai (see p.409), this Akha settlement has been opened to visitors, who pay an entrance fee of B80 (income goes into a village development fund). A guide leads you on a one-kilometre walk through the village, which is strategically dotted with interesting display boards in English, and you'll get a chance to have a go on an Akha swing (not the ceremonial one), see a welcome dance and watch people weaving and tool-making, for example.

Along the Kok River

Travelling down the hundred-kilometre stretch of the **Kok River** to Chiang Rai gives you a chance to soak up a rich diversity of typical northern

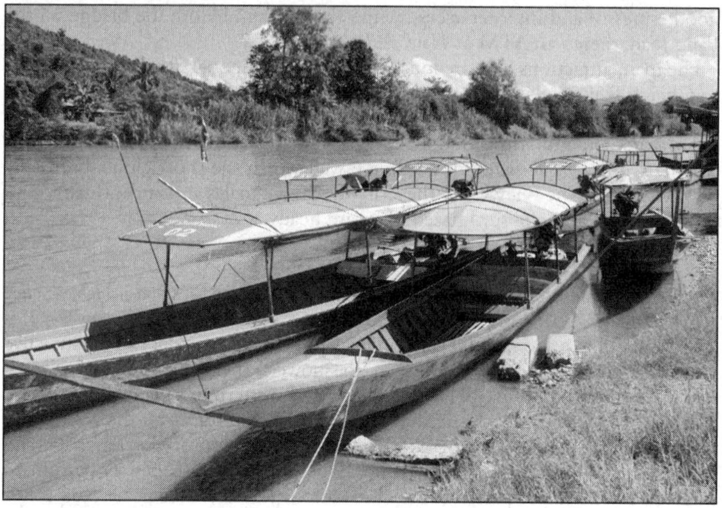

▲ Longtail boats on the Kok River

landscapes, which you never get on a speeding bus. Heading out of Tha Ton, the river traverses a flat valley of rice fields and orchards, where it's flanked by high reeds inhabited by flitting swallows. After half an hour, you pass the nine-hundred-year-old **Wat Phra That Sop Fang**, with its small hilltop chedi and a slithering naga staircase leading up from the river bank. Beyond the large village of **Mae Salak**, 20km from Tha Ton, the river starts to meander between thickly forested slopes. From among the banana trees and giant wispy ferns, kids come out to play, adults to bathe and wash clothes, and water buffalo emerge simply to enjoy the river. About two hours out of Tha Ton the hills get steeper and the banks rockier, leading up to a half-hour stretch of small but feisty rapids, where you might well get a soaking. Beyond the rapids, crowds of boats suddenly appear, ferrying tour groups from Chiang Rai to the Karen village of **Ruammid**, 20km upstream, for elephant-riding. From here on, the landscape deteriorates as the bare valley around Chiang Rai opens up.

The best time of year to make this trip is in the cool season (roughly Nov–Feb), when you'll get both lush vegetation and exciting rapids. Canopied **longtail boats** (B350 per person) leave from the south side of the bridge in Tha Ton every day at 12.30pm for the trip to Chiang Rai, which takes around four rather noisy hours. The slower, less crowded journey upriver gives an even better chance of appreciating the scenery – the longtails leave Chiang Rai at 10.30am. If you can get a group of up to six people together (up to twelve when the river's deeper in the rainy season), it's better to charter a longtail from the boat landing in Tha Ton (B2200; ⓣ053 459427), which will allow you to stop at the hill-tribe villages and hot springs en route.

If you have more time, the peaceful **bamboo rafts** which glide downriver to Chiang Rai in three days almost make you part of the scenery. Each party is accompanied by two steersmen who dismantle the rafts in Chiang Rai and bring the bamboo back to be recycled in Tha Ton. *Garden Home Nature Resort*, for example, charge B8000–12,000 per boat for two to six passengers, including soft drinks and food, staying at a Lahu village and the hot springs along the way. They also offer two-day versions, starting at Ban Pa Tai, east of Tha Ton (B6000 for two people), as well as half- and full-day trips downriver from Tha Ton, by either raft or kayak, returning by car.

Passengers departing from Tha Ton boat landing are required to sign the log book at the adjacent **tourist police** booth. A peaceful **guest house** between Mae Salak and Ruammid, from which you can go trekking (guided or self-guided), might tempt you to break your river journey. *Akha Hill House* (Ⓣ089 997 5505 or 081 460 7450, Ⓦwww.akhahill.com; ❶–❻), on the south bank of the Kok, 3km on foot from the riverside hot springs near Huai Kaeo waterfall, offers lofty views, comfortable rooms and bungalows, some with en-suite hot showers (with decent rates for singles), and free transport daily to and from Chiang Rai.

Chiang Rai

Sprawled untidily over the south bank of the Kok River, **CHIANG RAI** continues to live in the shadow of the local capital, Chiang Mai, but in the last few years has acquired several genuine sights of interest, notably **Rai Mae Fah Luang**, a beautiful storehouse of Lanna art. There's now also a good choice of guest houses and upmarket riverside hotels to lay your head down in, and from here you can set up a wide range of trekking, day-trips and other outdoor activities in the surrounding countryside. The town quietly gets on with its own business during the day, when most of its package tourists are out on manoeuvres, but at night the neon lights flash on and souvenir stalls and ersatz Western restaurants are thronged. Meanwhile, Chiang Rai keeps up its reputation as a dirty-weekend destination for Thais, a game given away by just a few motels with carports – where you drive into the garage and pay for a discreet screen to be pulled across behind you.

Chiang Rai is most famous for the things it had and lost. It was founded in 1263 by King Mengrai of Ngon Yang who, having recaptured a prize elephant he'd been chasing around the foot of Doi Tong, took this as an auspicious omen for a new city. Tradition has it that Chiang Rai then prevailed as the capital of the north for thirty years, but historians now believe Mengrai moved his court directly from Ngon Yang to the Chiang Mai area in the 1290s. Thailand's two holiest images, the Emerald Buddha (now in Bangkok) and the Phra Singh Buddha (now perhaps in Bangkok, Chiang Mai or Nakhon Si Thammarat, depending on which story you believe), also once resided here before moving on – at least replicas of these can be seen at Wat Phra Kaeo and Wat Phra Singh.

Arrival, information and transport

Chiang Rai has recently opened an unpopular new **bus station** about 6km south of the centre on Highway 1 to handle inter-provincial routes (including air-con and some non-air-con services to Lampang), while the old bus station on Thanon Phaholyothin serves Chiang Rai province (Mae Sai, Chiang Saen, Chiang Khong), plus Nan and most non-air-conditioned buses to Lampang; some services will stop at both, however, and the division of labour may change. To make the opening more palatable, fares on shared shuttles between the two bus stations are currently being kept very low: B10 by songthaew, B20 by tuk-tuk. Longtails from Tha Ton dock at the **boat station**, northwest of the centre on the north side of the Mae Fah Luang Bridge. Thai Airways (Ⓣ053 798200), Air Asia (Ⓣ02 515 9999) and One-Two-Go (Ⓣ1126 or 02 229 4100–1) **fly** from

Tours and trekking from Chiang Rai

Communities from all the hill tribes have settled around **Chiang Rai**, and the region offers the full range of terrain for **trekking**, from reasonably gentle walking trails near the Kok River to tough mountain slopes further north towards the Burmese border; elephant riding is included in most treks. However, this natural suitability has attracted too many tour and trekking agencies, and many of the hill-tribe villages, especially between Chiang Rai and Mae Salong, have become weary of the constant to-ing and fro-ing; the south side of the river to the west of town is generally a better bet. Sizes of group treks from Chiang Rai tend to be smaller than those from Chiang Mai, often with just two or three people, with a maximum of about seven in a group. Nearly all guest houses in Chiang Rai can fit you up with a trek – *Chat*, *Chian* and *Mae Hong Son* are responsible and reliable, typically charging B2500–3500 per person for three days and two nights in a group of between two and six people. One place to avoid is the Union of Hilltribe Villages, just north of Chiang Rai's airport, where people from various ethnic groups, including "long-neck" women (see p.391), are brought to live together in an artificial village for the convenience of tourists.

More expensive treks are offered by several nonprofit foundations promoting community-based tourism that are based in and around Chiang Rai. The Hill Area and Community Development Foundation has set up Natural Focus (Ⓣ053 758658 or 085 888 6869, Ⓦwww.naturalfocus-cbt.com), which offers one- to fifteen-day tours to learn about mountain life, as well as youth, workstay and volunteer skills programmes. Hilltribe Tour, part of the Mirror Art Group (see p.81), runs tours, one- to three-day treks and longer village **homestays**, on which you can learn a hill-tribe skill such as weaving or playing an instrument. The development agency PDA at the Hilltribe Museum (Ⓣ053 740088, Ⓦwww.pda.or.th/chiangrai; see p.409) offers one- or multi-day jungle treks to non-touristy areas, usually including elephant riding and a longtail-boat trip. They also lay on a wide range of **guided tours**, to their Akha project at Ban Lorcha (see p.403), Mae Salong and other places of interest. Most of the guest houses can also arrange sightseeing tours, as well as boat trips, elephant rides and motorbike trekking.

Bangkok, SGA (Ⓣ02 664 6099) from Chiang Mai, to Chiang Rai's **airport**, from where **taxis** run into town (8km south), for about B300.

TAT has a helpful office at 448/16 Thanon Singhaklai (daily 8.30am–4.30pm; Ⓣ053 717433 or 053 744674–5, Ⓔtatchrai@tat.or.th) with some useful free maps and information brochures. From here they organize the Tour of the Mekong, a one-week bike trip through Thailand, China and Laos every October. You can access the **internet** over coffee and snacks at *Connect Café*, 868/10 Thanon Phaholyothin, while Gare Garon Bookshop opposite (evenings only) has a small range of new and used books, as well as a gallery and drinks for sale. The **tourist police** (Ⓣ1155) are on Thanon Phaholyothin next to the *Golden Triangle Inn*.

Shared blue **songthaews**, which have no set routes, cost B15 for short hops, while **tuk-tuks** start at around B50. **Mountain bikes** (B80–100 per day) and **motorbikes** (B150–300) can be rented at *Mae Hong Son Guest House*, **bicycles** (B50) and motorbikes (B150–1000) at *Chat Guest House*, and bicycles at *Tourist Inn* (B60). **Car rental** is available through North Wheels – who also have motorbikes with insurance – at 591 Thanon Phaholyothin, next to the tourist police office (Ⓣ053 740585, Ⓦwww.northwheels.com) or through Avis at the airport (Ⓣ053 793827). If you're driving yourself, note that a new road north from the centre was being built at the time of writing, extending Thanon Rattanakhet across the river before joining Highway 1.

Accommodation

A wide choice of good **guest houses** are within walking distance of central Chiang Rai, while several very appealing **hotels** hug the tranquil banks of the Kok River on the town's fringes.

Inexpensive

Baan Bua Guest House 879/2 Thanon Jet Yot ⓣ053 718880, ⓦwww.baanbuaguesthouse.com. Congenial and well-run establishment arrayed around a surprisingly large, quiet and shady garden, set back off the road. The very clean and attractive concrete, single-storey rooms all come with hot showers. Fan 2–3, air-con 3

Baan Rub Aroon Guest House 65 Thanon Ngam Muang ⓣ053 711827, ⓦwww.baanrubaroon.net. In a pretty, quiet garden, this lovely early-twentieth-century mansion with polished teak floors and lots of houseplants tries to recreate the atmosphere of home. The downside is that the five bright, tasteful, air-con rooms and a dorm (B300) share two hot-water bathrooms, but there's also a very well-equipped kitchen, a nice terrace upstairs and free internet and wi-fi. Breakfast included. 3–4

Chat House 3/2 Soi Sangkaew, Thanon Trairat ⓣ053 711481, ⓦwww.chathouse32.com.

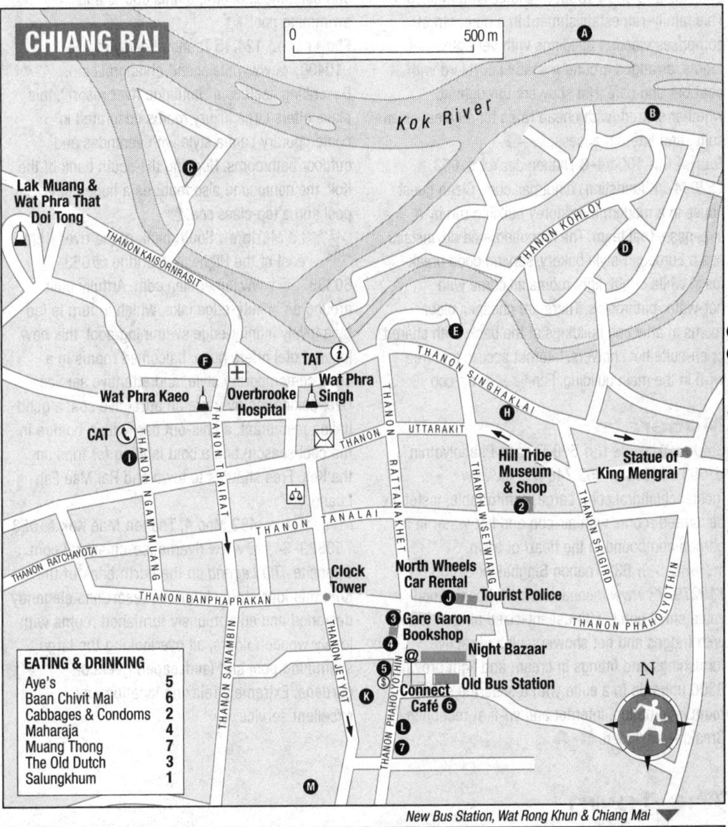

ACCOMMODATION

Baan Bua Guest House	K	Chian House	D	The Legend	B	Moon & Sun	H
Baan Rub Aroon Guest House	I	Dusit Island Resort Hotel	C	Le Meridien	G	River House	A
Chat House	F	Golden Triangle Inn	J	Mae Hong Son Guest House	E	Tourist Inn	M
						Wiang Inn	L

Located behind its own garden café on a quiet soi, this is Chiang Rai's longest-running travellers' hangout, with a laid-back, friendly atmosphere. The cheaper rooms (including a dorm and three singles for B80) are in an old, mostly wooden house with shared hot showers, while a concrete row of garden rooms have en-suite hot water, some with air-con. Internet access and free wi-fi. Fan ❶–❷, air-con ❷

Chian House 172 Thanon Kohloy ⓣ053 713388, ⓔchianguesthouse@hotmail.com. Welcoming place with internet access in a quiet compound around a small swimming pool. Pleasant, good-sized rooms and spacious, nicely furnished wooden bungalows with cool tiled floors, all with en-suite hot showers. Fan ❶–❷, air-con ❷–❸

Mae Hong Son Guest House 126 Thanon Singhaklai ⓣ053 715367, ⓔlotee@hotmail.com. This family-run establishment in a quiet street comprises wooden buildings with very pleasant rooms, arranged around a shady courtyard with neat bar and café. Hot showers throughout, whether shared (with cheap rates for singles) or en suite, and internet access. ❶–❷

Tourist Inn 1004/4–6 Thanon Jet Yot ⓣ053 752094, ⓔtouristinn1@hotmail.com. Clean guest house in a modern four-storey building run by a Japanese-Thai team. The reception area downstairs has a European-style bakery, serving good breakfasts, while bright, light rooms all come with hot-water bathrooms. There are cheaper, older rooms in attached buildings at the back, with shared or en-suite hot showers. Internet access and free wi-fi in the main building. Fan ❶–❷, air-con ❸

Moderate

Golden Triangle Inn 590 Thanon Phaholyothin ⓣ053 713918 or 053 740478, ⓦwww.goldenchiangrai.com. Large, comfortable, tastefully decorated rooms with air-con and hot water in a garden compound in the heart of town. ❺

Moon & Sun 632 Thanon Singhaklai ⓣ053 719279, ⓦwww.moonandsunhotel.com. Good-value small hotel, with decent-sized air-con rooms with fridges and hot showers, plus attractive furnishings and fittings in cream and light brown; a B300 upgrade to a suite with a separate sitting room is tempting. Internet and wi-fi at reception. Breakfast included. ❹–❺

Wiang Inn 893 Thanon Phaholyothin ⓣ053 711533, ⓦwww.wianginn.com. Set back off the main road, this 260-room hotel has a bright and spacious lobby, an attractive pool and comfortably furnished rooms equipped with all facilities and decorated with Thai murals. Breakfast included. ❻

Expensive

Dusit Island Resort Hotel 1129 Thanon Kaisornrasit ⓣ053 607999, ⓦwww.dusit.com. Set on an expansive island in the Kok River offering unbeatable views of the valley, this is one of the swankiest places to stay in town, with high standards of service. The huge rooms are lavishly furnished, with fancy bathrooms, minibars and big TVs. Hotel facilities include a rooftop restaurant and bar, fitness centre, tennis courts and swimming pool. ❾

The Legend 124/15 Thanon Kohloy ⓣ053 910400, ⓦwww.thelegend-chiangrai.com. Describing itself as a "boutique river resort", this place offers large luxury rooms decorated in contemporary Lanna style with verandas and outdoor bathrooms. Hugging the south bank of the Kok, the compound also features a huge infinity pool and a top-class spa. ❽

Le Meridien South bank of the river, 1km east of the Highway 1 bridge ⓣ053 603333, ⓦwww.lemeridien.com. Artfully built around an infinity-edge lake, which in turn is fed by a lovely infinity-edge swimming pool, this new luxury hotel offers huge, balconied rooms in a crisp contemporary style, and attentive service. Overlooking the river are an attractive spa, a good Italian restaurant, a chill-out bar (with a bonfire in the cool season) and a boat landing for trips on the Kok. Free shuttles to town and Rai Mae Fah Luang. ❾

River House 482 Moo 4, Thanon Mae Kok ⓣ053 750829–34, ⓦwww.riverhouse-chiangrai.com. Opposite *The Legend* on the north bank of the Kok, this four-storey boutique resort has elegantly designed and sumptuously furnished rooms with lovely wooden floors, all overlooking the large swimming pool and landscaped riverside gardens. Extremely relaxing location and excellent service. ❾

The Town

A walk up to **Doi Tong**, the hummock to the northwest of the centre, is the best way to get your bearings in Chiang Rai and, especially at sunset, offers a fine view up the Kok River as it emerges from the mountains to the west. On the highest part of the hill stands a kind of phallic Stonehenge centred on the town's

Loy Krathong Festival

Every year on the evening of the full moon of the twelfth lunar month (usually in November), Thais all over the country celebrate the end of the rainy season with Loy Krathong, the Festival of Light. One of Thailand's most beautiful festivals, it's held to honour the spirits of the water at a time when all the fields are flooded and the canals and rivers are overflowing their banks.

Krathong for sale ▲

Making a traditional-style *krathong* ▼

Honouring the water goddess

To thank and appease Phra Mae Khong Kha, the goddess of water, to ask forgiveness for polluting her waters, and to cast adrift any bad luck that may have accrued over the past year, nearly everyone makes or buys a **krathong** and sets it afloat (*loy*) on the nearest body of water.

These miniature basket-boats are fashioned from banana leaves that have been elegantly folded and pinned, origami style, and then filled with flowers, three sticks of incense and several lighted candles; the traditional base is a slice of banana tree trunk, but it's increasingly popular to buy your *krathong* ready-made from the market, often with an eco-unfriendly polystyrene bottom. Some people slip locks of hair and fingernail clippings between the flowers, to represent sinful deeds that will then be symbolically released along with the *krathong*; others add a coin or two to persuade the spirits to take away any bad luck that's been dogging them (swiftly raided by opportunist young boys looking for small change). Companies and civic groups commission their own outsized *krathong*, which compete for a best-in-show award, judged by local VIPs.

People release their *krathong* at around the same time and the bobbing lights of thousands of them floating on neighbourhood rivers, beachfronts, ponds, canals and even swimming pools make a fantastic spectacle. It's traditional to make a wish or a prayer as you launch your *krathong* and to watch until it disappears from view: if your candle burns strong, your wishes will be granted and you will live long. And if you launch a *krathong* with your beloved, your union will be blessed.

Nationwide celebrations

The festival is said to have originated seven hundred years ago, when the consort of a Sukhothai king, Nang Noppamas, adapted the ancient Brahmin custom of paying homage to the water goddess by placing *krathong* on the lotus ponds. The thirteenth-century temple ruins of **Sukhothai Historical Park** are now one of the most popular places to watch the Loy Krathong festivities: while its ponds shimmer beneath thousands of floating candles, the ruins host a *son-et-lumière* performance, and there are firework displays, street entertainments and a parade of charming Nang Noppamas (Miss Loy Krathong) lookalikes.

Every community designs its own celebration and the Loy Krathong festivities in **Chiang Mai** – where the

▲ Martial arts display at Loy Krathong, Lampang

▼ Loy Krathong festival entertainment, Chiang Mai

▼ Releasing a *khom loy*

Lanterns in the sky

As with the *krathong*, a **khom loy** will also carry vices and misfortunes away when it's released in the breeze. Part lantern, part hot-air balloon, *khom loy* are usually made from local mulberry paper, to various shapes and designs, but most often with the dimensions of a large sack, up to two metres high. The power to keep it aloft comes from candles or a small bowl of flaming oil hung at the base of the lantern. Some people tuck coins inside the lantern, or paste their address inside so that the finder can claim a small reward. *Khom loy* are also said to represent the Buddha's topknot, which he cut off when he renounced the life of a prince. In the past they were used as distinctly un-Buddhist weapons, designed to explode when they touched down in enemy territory. These days they're increasingly sold, year-round, on beaches after dark, to anyone who feels like launching their own sky-high lantern.

festival is also known as Yipeng – are famous nationwide. Not only does the Ping River shine with thousands of *krathong*, but the skies are also alight, speckled with hundreds of glowing giant paper lanterns, or **khom loy**, drifting in the breeze.

Outside urban centres there's often a more earthy, irreverent flavour to the celebrations, with the entire community turning up to drink a great deal of Chang beer and to heckle at the inevitable Miss Loy Krathong contest. Entrants might be under 5, over 80, male, female or transsexual, but they'll all be dancing to the jaunty strains of the **Loy Krathong song**, which fills the nation's airwaves.

Young girls in traditional dress ▲

Crowd launching *krathong* in Chiang Mai ▼

Loy Krathong song

Wan pen duan sip sawng
Nam koh nawng taem taling
Rao tanglai chai ying
Sanuk ganjing wan Loy Krathong
Loy loy krathong
Loy loy krathong

Loy krathong gan laew
Kaw choen nawng kaew
Awk maa ramwong
Ramwong wan Loy Krathong
Ramwong wan Loy Krathong
Bun ja song hai rao suk jai
Bun ja song hai rao suk jai

The full moon of the twelfth month
As water fills the banks
We all, men and women
Have really good fun on Loy Krathong day
Float, float the krathong
Float, float the krathong

And after we have floated our krathong
I invite you my dear
To come out and dance ramwong
Ramwong on Loy Krathong day
Ramwong on Loy Krathong day
Making merit will bring us happiness
Making merit will bring us happiness

new **lak muang**, representing the Buddhist layout of the universe. Historically, the erection of a *lak muang* marks the official founding of a Thai city, precisely dated to January 26, 1263 in the case of Chiang Rai; the new *lak muang* and the elaborate stone model around it were erected 725 years later to the day, as part of the celebrations of King Bhumibol's sixtieth birthday. The *lak muang* itself represents Mount Sineru (or Meru), the axis of the universe, while the series of concentric terraces, moats and pillars represent the heavens and the earth, the great oceans and rivers, and the major features of the universe. Sprinkling water onto the garlanded *lak muang* and then dabbing your head with the water after it has flowed into the basin below brings good luck. The old wooden *lak muang* can be seen in the viharn of **Wat Phra That Doi Tong**, the city's first temple, which sprawls shambolically over the eastern side of the hill.

Wat Phra Kaeo

Thailand's most important image, the Emerald Buddha, which had supposedly been sculpted by the gods in Patna, India, in 234 BC, was placed in the chedi at **Wat Phra Kaeo** on Thanon Trairat by King Mahaprom of Chiang Rai in 1390. However, lightning destroyed the chedi 44 years later, allowing the image to continue its perambulations around Southeast Asia, finally settling down in Bangkok. A beautiful replica can now be seen here in a tiny, Lanna-style pavilion, the **Hor Phra Yok**. Carved in China from milky green Canadian jade, the replica was presented by a Chinese millionaire to mark the ninetieth birthday of the Princess Mother, Mae Fah Luang, in 1990, and consecrated by King Bhumibol himself. At 47.9cm wide and 65.9cm high, it's millimetres smaller than the actual Emerald Buddha, as religious protocol dictated that it could not be an exact copy of the original. There's much else of interest in the temple complex, which has recently been renovated to a high standard, notably the **Sangkaew Hall** (daily 9am–5pm; free). Distinguished by its informative labels on Thai religious practice in English, this museum houses all sorts of Buddhist paraphernalia, including the belongings of famous monks from Chiang Rai.

The Hill Tribe Museum – and shopping

The **Hill Tribe Museum and Handicrafts Shop** at 620/25 Thanon Tanalai stocks an authentic selection of tasteful and well-made hill-tribe **handicrafts**. The shop, on the second floor, was started by the country's leading development campaigner, Meechai Viravaidya, under the auspices of the PDA (Population and Community Development Association; see p.169) and all proceeds go to village projects. The museum (Mon–Fri 9am–6pm, Sat & Sun 10am–6pm; B50) is a great place to learn about the hill tribes before going on a trek, and includes a slick, informative slide show (20min). You can donate old clothes or money for jumpers and blankets, and they also organize treks and tours themselves (see p.406). All sorts of handicrafts, some of good quality and competitively priced, are on sale at the **night bazaar** which is set up off Thanon Phaholyothin next to the old bus station, and is usually buzzing with tour groups in the evening. On Saturday evenings from around 5pm till after 10pm, Thanon Tanalai around the junction with Wisetwiang becomes a "**walking street**" similar to those in Chiang Mai, with musicians and all manner of stalls, including lots of food and local crafts and products such as coffee and macadamias.

Rai Mae Fah Luang

By far Chiang Rai's most compelling attraction is **Rai Mae Fah Luang** (Tues–Sun 8am–5.30pm; B200; www.maefahluang.org), a beautiful showcase of

Lanna art and architecture, and its influences from Burma, Laos and China. In particular, the museum displays the consummate skills of local woodcarvers, with a focus on teak, which in Thailand is associated with concepts of dignity. Set in lovely parkland, including a young teak garden that holds 43 varieties from northern Thailand, Rai Mae Fah Luang is about 5km west of the city centre in Ban Pa Ngio. To charter a songthaew will cost you about B100 one way, B200 return (including some waiting time); to get there under your own steam, head west on Thanon Tanalai for 1.7km from Thanon Trairat, turn right at the traffic lights onto Thanon Hong Lee and follow the road for 2–3km until you see the entrance on the left-hand side.

The main reason for coming here is to see the **Haw Khum**, an amazing, multi-tiered barn of a building on massive stilts. It took five years to construct in the 1980s, in honour of the Princess Mother, Mae Fah Luang, using materials from 32 old houses in Chiang Rai province. Look out especially for the *ben grit* (fish scales) roof tiles, which inevitably are also made of teak. Lit by candles, the interior's dramatic centrepiece is a huge, slender, wooden *prasat*, representing the centre of the universe, Mount Meru, set in a sunken white sandpit – which not only symbolizes the Ocean of Milk, but also soaks up moisture to protect the teak. Dozens of very fine wooden artefacts surround the *prasat*, including a beautifully serene Burmese Buddha in a delicate, many-frilled robe that looks as if it's moving. Standouts among the displays in the nearby **Haw Kaew** – which is also made entirely of teak – are some ornate *oop*, or ceremonial alms bowls, and a bed headboard and footboard that sport scary carvings of Rahoo: the monster eating the moon connotes not only eclipses, but also a good night's sleep.

Wat Rong Khun

Around 13km south of Chiang Rai on the west side of Highway 1 (catch a Phayao-bound bus from the old bus station), **Wat Rong Khun** (Ⓦwww.watrongkhun.com) almost defies description. Begun in 1997, it's the life's work of local contemporary artist, **Chalermchai Kositpipat** (see also p.824), who has rediscovered Buddhism in a big way since spending time as a monk in 1992; he is also training dozens of "disciples", as he calls them, to finish the temple long after his death. Taking traditional Buddhist elements such as nagas and lotus flowers, and Lanna features such as long, slender *tung kradan* banners, Ajarn Chalermchai has enlarged and elaborated them, adding all sort of frills, layers and tiers. Surrounded by ponds, fountains and bridges, and done all in white – to stand for the Buddha's purity – inlaid with clear glass tiles – to represent his wisdom – the end result is like a frosted wedding cake. Inside the bot, which houses an eerily lifelike waxwork of the wat's former abbot, you can watch Chalermchai's disciples at work on the golden-toned murals, to the sound of loud, piped-in Thai pop music. In the adjacent Hall of Masterwork, some of the artist's original paintings are on display, while reproductions are on sale (to raise money for the project) in the souvenir shop, along with a useful B50 booklet on the temple in English, which explains the meaning of the complex design. If you're a fan of Chalermchai's work, you'll want to check out his new **clocktower**, back in Chiang Rai at the junction of Banphaprakan and Jet Yot roads, which hosts a mini *son et lumière* for ten minutes every night at 7, 8 and 9pm.

Eating and drinking

Chiang Rai's **restaurants**, including a growing number of Western places, congregate mostly along Phaholyothin road near the night bazaar. There's a huge **food centre** at the night bazaar itself with lots of delicious Thai snacks, as well as some more substantial dishes and Japanese food, where you can catch a free performance of transvestite cabaret, local folk-singers or traditional dancers. You need never go without a good **coffee** fix in Chiang Rai: the stuff grown on the nearby mountains of Doi Wawee, Doi Chaang and Doi Mae Salong is served up at several cafés around the main Rattanakhet–Phaholyothin junction.

Aye's 479 Thanon Phaholyothin. A spacious, popular restaurant with a relaxing atmosphere and a wide menu of international and Thai dishes – try the *kaeng hang lay* (B200), a delicious, northern pork and ginger curry.

Baan Chivit Mai 172 Thanon Pra Soop Sook, opposite the old bus station. Scandinavian bakery run by a Swedish charity that helps children in Chiang Rai and Bangkok slums (see ⓦwww.baanchivitmai.com). Very clean, air-con café with internet access serving excellent sandwiches, cakes and coffees, plus pastas and simple Thai dishes. Mon–Sat 8am–9pm.

Cabbages and Condoms Hill Tribe Museum (see p.409). Proudly proclaiming "our food is guaranteed not to cause pregnancy", this restaurant covers its walls with paraphernalia devoted to family planning and HIV/AIDS prevention. The Thai food, including some traditional northern dishes and a few dishes suitable for vegetarians, is a bit hit-and-miss but it's in a good cause. Live band every night.

Maharaja 869/19–20 Thanon Phaholyothin ⓣ053 752971–2. Congenial restaurant with bright, summery decor, serving tasty Indian food including a decent dahl (B90) and lots of other vegetarian dishes.

Muang Thong 889/1–2 Thanon Phaholyothin, just south of the *Wiang Inn Hotel*. This no-frills and inexpensive place does a wide range of Thai and Chinese dishes supposedly 24hr a day, and displays a huge selection of ingredients outside its open-sided eating area. Popular with Thais and foreigners alike.

The Old Dutch 541 Moo 2, Thanon Phaholyothin. Looking like a classic European restaurant with solid furnishings and quirky memorabilia on the walls, this conveniently located place has a huge menu of international, Dutch, Indonesian and Thai dishes – with a Thai-style annexe, *Old Siam*, next door. It's a bit pricey with steaks from around B350, but the high quality makes it worth it. Draught beer on tap and a long menu of Belgian and other imported bottles as well, plus free internet.

Salungkhum 834/3 Thanon Phaholyothin, between King Mengrai's statue and the river ⓣ053 717192. Justifiably rated by locals as serving the best Thai food in town (main dishes from B80), with a garden for evening dining; try the superb banana-flower salad with fresh prawns. There's no sign in English, but look out for the Cosmo petrol station on the opposite side of the road.

North of Chiang Rai

At a push, any one of the places described in this section could be visited in a day from Chiang Rai, while hardly anyone visits **Mae Sai** on the Burmese border except on a visa-run day-trip. If you can devote two or three days, however, you'd be better off moving camp to **Mae Salong**, a mountain-top Chinese enclave, and **Chiang Saen**, whose atmospheric ruins by the banks of the Mekong contrast sharply with the ugly commercialism of nearby **Sop Ruak**. Given more time and patience, you could also stop over at the palace, temple and arboretum of **Doi Tung** to look down over Thailand, Laos and Burma, and continue beyond Chiang Saen to **Chiang Khong** on the banks of the Mekong, which is now a popular crossing point to Laos.

For hopping around the main towns here by **public transport**, the setup is straightforward enough: frequent buses to Mae Sai run due north up Highway 1; to Chiang Saen, they start off on the same road before forking right onto Highway 1016; for most other places, you have to make one change off these routes onto a songthaew.

▲ Rice fields near Chiang Rai

Mae Salong (Santikhiri)

Perched 1300m up on a ridge, with commanding views of sawtoothed hills, stands the Chinese Nationalist outpost of **MAE SALONG**. A dizzying roller coaster of a road, Route 1130, ploughs its way up here for 36km from **Ban Pasang**, 32km north of Chiang Rai on Highway 1. A few marginally interesting attractions might tempt you to stop off en route, notably the **Hill Tribe Culture Centre**, 12km from Ban Pasang, where there's a handicrafts shop, and a couple of Mien and Akha souvenir villages. At Sam Yaek, 24km from Ban Pasang, a paved side-road heads north for 13km to **Ban Therd Thai**. In its former incarnation as Ban Hin Taek, this mixed village was the opium capital of the notorious Khun Sa (see box opposite): the Thai army drove Khun Sa out after a pitched battle in 1983, and the village has now been renamed and "pacified" with the establishment of a market, school and hospital.

Mae Salong is the focal point for the area's fourteen thousand **Kuomintang**, who for two generations now have held fast to their cultural identity, if not their political cause. The ruling party of China for 21 years, the Kuomintang (Nationalists) were swept from power by the Communist revolution of 1949 and fled in two directions: one group, under party leader Chiang Kai-shek, made for Taiwan, where it founded the Republic of China; the other, led by General Li Zongren, settled in northern Thailand and Burma. The Nationalists' original plan to retake China from Mao Zedong in a two-pronged attack never came to fruition, and the remnants of the army in Thailand became major players in the heroin trade and, with the backing of the Thai government, minor protagonists in the war against communism.

In the 1980s, the Thai government began to work hard to "pacify" the Kuomintang by a mixture of force and more peaceful methods, such as crop programmes to replace opium. Around Mae Salong at least, its work seems to have been successful, as evidenced by the slopes to the south of the settlement, which are covered with a carpet of rich green tea bushes. Since its rehabilitation, Mae Salong is now officially known as **Santikhiri** (Hill of Peace).

Drugs and the Golden Triangle

Opium will always be associated with the Far East in the popular imagination, but the opium poppy actually originated in the Mediterranean. It arrived in the East, however, over twelve centuries ago, and was later brought to Thailand from China with the hill tribes who migrated from Yunnan province. Opium growing was made illegal in Thailand in 1959, but during the 1960s and 1970s rampant production and refining of the crop in the lawless region on the borders of Thailand, Burma and Laos earned the area the nickname **the Golden Triangle**. Two main "armies" operated most of the trade within this area. The 10,000-strong **Shan United Army** (SUA), set up to fight the Burmese government for an independent state for the Shan (Thai Yai) people, funded itself from the production of heroin (a more refined form of opium). Led by the notorious warlord Khun Sa, the SUA attempted to extend their influence inside Thailand during the 1960s, where they came up against the troops of the **Kuomintang** (KMT). These refugees from China, who fled after the communist takeover there, were at first befriended by the Thai and Western governments, who were pleased to have a fiercely anti-communist force patrolling this border area. The Kuomintang were thus able to develop the heroin trade, while the authorities turned a blind eye.

By the 1980s, the danger of communist incursion into Thailand had largely disappeared, and the government was able to concentrate on the elimination of the crop, putting the Kuomintang in the area around Mae Salong on a determined "pacification" programme. In 1983 the Shan United Army was pushed out of its stronghold at nearby Ban Hin Taek (now Ban Therd Thai), over the border into Burma, and in 1996, Khun Sa cut a deal with the corrupt Burmese military dictatorship. The man once dubbed the "Prince of Death", who had a $2million bounty on his head from the United States, was able to live under Burmese army protection in a comfortable villa in Rangoon until his death in 2007.

The Thai government has succeeded in reducing the size of the opium crop within its borders to an insignificant amount, but Thailand still has a vital role to play as a conduit for heroin; most of the production and refinement of opium has simply moved over the borders into Burma and Laos. And in the last few years, opium growing within northern Thailand, although still at a very low level, has apparently started to increase again, based on small patches in remote mountains and using a high-yield, weather-resistant breed supplied by the Burmese drug barons.

The destruction of huge areas of poppy fields has had far-reaching repercussions on the hill tribes. In many cases, with the raw product not available, opium addicts have turned to injecting heroin from shared needles, leading to a devastating outbreak of AIDS. The Thai government has sought to give the hill tribes an alternative livelihood through the introduction of legitimate cash crops, yet these often demand the heavy use of pesticides, which later get washed down into the lowland valleys, incurring the wrath of Thai farmers.

The dangers of the heroin trade have in recent years been eclipsed by a flood tide of **methamphetamines** or *yaa baa* ("crazy medicine"), that is infiltrating all areas of Thai society, but most worryingly the schools. Produced in vast quantities in factories just across the Burmese border, mostly by former insurgents, the United Wa State Army, *yaa baa* is the main objective of vehicle searches in border areas, with perhaps a billion tablets smuggled into Thailand each year. The government estimates that three million Thais are methamphetamine users, prompting them into a fierce crackdown in the first half of 2003 which, much to the consternation of human rights watchers, led to 2000 extra-judicial deaths and 51,000 arrests. Things have quietened down since then, but the frequent busts of *yaa baa* dealers show that the problem has not gone away.

Arrival, information and accommodation

Mae Salong straggles for several kilometres along a roughly east–west road, with a central junction near the morning market and the steps for the Princess Mother Pagoda. Just east of this is the 7-Eleven, where local **songthaews** congregate: blue ones make the ninety-minute journey when full up from Ban Pasang on Highway 1 (B60 per person); in the opposite direction, there are four direct yellow songthaews a day between Tha Ton and Mae Salong, via the interesting Akha village of Ban Lorcha (see p.403; B70). *Shin Sane Guest House* rents out **motorbikes** for B200 per day, and all the guest houses provide **internet** access. There's a Thai Military Bank **ATM** towards the west end of town.

You'll appreciate Mae Salong best if you spend the night there, after the day-trippers have left. Fortunately, the town supports a wide range of **accommodation**, including half a dozen budget guest houses clustered around the central junction.

Accommodation

Little Home Guest House Central junction ⓣ053 765389, ⓦwww.maesalonglittlehome.com. Welcoming place with a popular Yunnanese restaurant on a pleasant balcony, and rooms in the main wooden house with a touch of style and shared hot showers, or smart bungalows in a pretty garden, with nice views from their verandas and hot water en suite. Detailed local maps available. ❶–❸

Mae Salong Villa On the main road towards the eastern end of the village ⓣ053 765114–9, ⓔmaesalongvilla@yahoo.co.th. Choose between large, comfortable rooms in a two-storey block and Chinese-style bungalows with fridges and better views from their picture windows, all with hot showers. In a pretty, sloping garden – which may host a swimming pool in the future – facing the Princess Mother Pagoda and Burmese mountains. ❹–❻

Saeng Aroon Central junction ⓣ053 765029. Large, bright rooms with tiled floors and hot showers, run by a sweet old couple who have a tea shop below. Wi-fi available. ❸

Shin Sane Guest House Central junction ⓣ053 765026, ⓦwww.maesalong-shinsane.blogspot.com. Friendly place with plenty of local information, offering small bedrooms with shared hot-water bathrooms in a funky wooden building and well-kept bungalows (with hot showers) in the garden behind. Free use of washing machine. Particularly good rates for singles. ❶–❷

The Town

Though it has temples, a church and a mosque, it's the details of Chinese life in the backstreets – the low-slung bamboo houses, the pictures of Chiang Kai-shek, ping-pong tables, the sounds of Yunnanese conversation – that make the village absorbing. Mae Salong gets plenty of Thai visitors, especially at weekends, who throng the main street's souvenir shops to buy such delicacies as sorghum whisky (pickled with ginseng, deer antler and centipedes) and locally grown Chinese tea, coffee, mushrooms and herbs. Free cups of tea are offered nearly everywhere, and it's possible to visit, for example, **Mae Salong Villa**'s own estate and factory – ask at the resort for directions and tea-processing times. It might also be worth braving the dawn chill to get to the **morning market**, held in the middle of town near *Shin Sane Guest House* from around 5am to 7am, which pulls them in from the surrounding Akha, Lisu and Mien villages.

Towering above the town on top of the hill, the **Princess Mother Pagoda**, a huge, gilt-topped chedi, is so distinctive that it has quickly become the town's proud symbol. It's a long and steep climb up 718 steps to get there, but with a rented vehicle you can follow the road to the Tha Ton end of town, and branch right opposite the evening market on a road that carries you heavenward, revealing some breathtaking views on the way. At the western edge of town, the **Chinese Martyrs Memorial Museum** (daily 8am–5pm; B30) recounts the origins of the Kuomintang in Thailand, giving details of battles such as the famous one fought against Thai and Lao communists and Hmong at Phu Chi Fa near Chiang Khong, and depicting the Kuomintang as heroic protectors of the Kingdom of Thailand. The huge building encompasses a shrine to the KMT martyrs who fell in the fighting.

The Kuomintang live up to their Thai nickname – *jiin haw*, meaning "galloping Chinese" – by offering **treks on horses**, a rare sight in Thailand. Trips to Akha, Lahu and other Chinese villages can be arranged at the *Shin Sane Guest House* from B500 for four hours, but it's worth meeting your guide and checking out the itinerary and the horses before you hand over any money. Armed with a sketch map from one of the guest houses, it would be possible to **walk** to some of the same villages yourself – or better still, hire a **guide** from *Little Home Guest House* for B200 per day.

Eating and drinking

The choice of **restaurants** in Mae Salong is narrower than its hotel selection, but the terrace of *Mae Salong Villa* has great views and cooks up some of the best food in town, including delicious but expensive Chinese specialities like roast pork, *het hawm* (wild mushrooms) and *kai dam* (black chicken), which is usually served in soup with Chinese herbs (B200–250). Between here and the centre of town, *Sweet Mae Salong* hits the spot with delicious, home-baked banana cake, excellent espresso, mellow sounds, **internet** access and lovely views from the rear terraces; they'll also rustle up a green curry with *roti*, if you're more peckish. On the main road beyond *Shin Sane Guest House*, *Salema* is a functional but friendly Yunnanese Muslim restaurant that cooks up both Thai *khao soi* and Chinese noodle soup, as well as more complex and pricey dishes like black chicken with ginger (B200).

Doi Tung

Steep, wooded hills rise abruptly from the plains west of Highway 1 as it approaches the Burmese border. Crowned by a thousand-year-old wat, the central peak here, 1322-metre **DOI TUNG**, makes a worthwhile outing just for the journey. A broad, new road, Route 1149, runs up the mountainside, beginning 43km north of Chiang Rai on Highway 1, just before Ban Huai Khrai. It's best to have your own vehicle or go on a tour from Chiang Rai, though you will also find lilac songthaews (B70) just west of the junction of highways 1 and 1149 ferrying villagers up the mountain. If you're driving yourself here from Mae Salong, there's no need to drive down to Highway 1: winding, paved Route 1338 branches north off Route 1130 near the Hill Tribe Culture Centre, approaching Doi Tung's peak from the southwest.

The old road to the mountain from the centre of Ban Huai Khrai passes after a kilometre or so the **Cottage Industry Centre and Outlet**, where you can watch crafts such as paper making from the bark of the *sa* (mulberry) tree in progress. The centre was set up by the Princess Mother, who had her country seat near the summit of Doi Tung until her death in 1995 (the mother of the present king, she was never queen herself, but was affectionately known as *Mae Fah Luang*, "great mother of mankind"). The **Royal Villa**, the **Princess Mother Commemorative Hall** and **Mae Fah Luang Garden**, 12km up the main summit road past Thai Yai, Chinese, Akha and Lahu villages, then left up a side road, are well worth a visit (daily 7am–5/6pm, villa closed if royals in residence; garden B80, villa B70, commemorative hall B30, all three B150). Regular guided tours take visitors round parts of the largely Swiss-style Royal Villa, passing the

Grand Reception Hall, where constellations have been embedded in the ceiling, as well as the positions of the planets at the time of her birth in 1900, then her living room, bedroom and study, all left as when she lived there. The swanky commemorative hall is really for royal watchers, though it does include some of the intricate screens from her funeral *that* (tower). Below, the immaculate ornamental gardens throng with snap-happy day-trippers at weekends. The Princess Mother's hill-tribe project has helped to develop local villages by introducing new agricultural methods: the slopes which were formerly blackened by the fires of slash-and-burn farming and sown with opium poppies are now used to grow teak and pine, and crops such as strawberries, macadamia nuts and coffee, which, along with pottery, *sa* paper, rugs and clothes, are sold in the shops by the entrance to the gardens. There's also a **Doi Tung** coffee shop, an excellent restaurant and self-service café, and in the woods below the Royal Villa, upmarket accommodation at *Doi Tung Lodge*, with air-conditioning, hot water, balcony, TV and fridge (Ⓣ053 767015–7, Ⓦwww.doitung.org; ⑦).

Beyond the turn-off for the Royal Villa, the main summit road climbs over a precarious saddle with some minor temple buildings 2km before the top, and passes through a tuft of thick woods to **Wat Phra That Doi Tung**. Pilgrims to the wat earn themselves good fortune by clanging the rows of dissonant bells around the temple compound and by throwing coins into a well, which are collected for temple funds. For non-Buddhist travellers, the reward for getting this far is the stunning view out over the cultivated slopes and half of northern Thailand. The wat's most important structures are its twin **chedis**, erected to enshrine relics of the Buddha's collarbone in 911. When the building of the chedis was complete, King Achutaraj of Ngon Yang ordered a giant flag (*tung*), reputedly 2km long, to be flown from the peak, which gave the mountain its name.

A very steep, sometimes rough, paved **back road** runs right along the border with Burma to Mae Sai (22km), via two army checkpoints and the Akha village of Ban Pha Mee, beginning at the saddle beneath the peak. After about 4km of asphalt, you reach the delightful **arboretum** (B50) at the pinnacle of **Doi Chang Moob** (1509m), a landscaped garden planted with rhododendrons, azaleas, orchids and ferns and furnished with fantastic terrace viewpoints looking east to Chiang Saen, the Mekong and the hills of Laos beyond, and west to the mountains around Mae Salong. For the most awesome view, however, continue a short way up the Mae Sai road to the Thai military checkpoint, to gaze at the opposing Burmese camp and seemingly endless layers of Burmese mountain stacked up to the north.

Mae Sai

With its bustling border-crossing and kilometres of tacky souvenir stalls, **MAE SAI** can be an interesting place to watch the world go by, though most foreigners only come here on a quick visa-run. Thailand's most northerly town lies 61km from Chiang Rai at the dead end of Highway 1, which forms the town's single north–south street. Wide enough for an armoured battalion, this ugly boulevard still has the same name – **Thanon Phaholyothin** – as at the start of its journey north in the suburbs of Bangkok. Buses, however, are no longer allowed to complete the journey, stopping 4km short of the frontier at the **bus station**, from where frequent red songthaews shuttle into town.

Thanon Phaholyothin ends at a short pedestrianized **bridge** over the Mae Sai River, which forms the border with Burma. Here, during daylight hours, you can have the dubious pleasure of crossing over to **Thachileik**, the Burmese

▲ Mai Sai

town opposite, for yet more tacky shopping – though remember your entry fee will be going straight into the hands of the despotic Burmese government. You'll first be stamped out by **Thai immigration** at the entrance to the bridge, then on the other side of the bridge, you pay US$10, or a rip-off B500, to Burmese immigration for a one-day stay. Coming back across the bridge, you'll be given a new fifteen-day entry stamp (unless you have a multiple-entry visa or re-entry permit – see p.36) by Thai immigration.

For a lofty perspective on the comings and goings, climb up through the market stalls to the chedi of **Wat Phra That Doi Wao**, five minutes' walk from the bridge on the west side of Phaholyothin, behind the *Top North Hotel*. As well as Doi Tung to the south and the hills of Laos in the east, you get a good view up the steep-sided valley and across the river to Thachileik.

Practicalities

There's a **tourist police** booth (Ⓣ1155) hard by the frontier bridge. For getting around the local area, **motorbikes** can be rented from Pornchai, a few doors south of *Piyaporn Place* on Thanon Phaholyothin, for B150 a day. For **internet access**, head for Empower, a charity that helps Thai sex workers (Ⓦwww.empowerfoundation.org), about 150m west of the bridge on the riverside road, Thanon Sailomjai.

A handful of mostly ropey **guest houses** are strung out along the river bank west of the bridge. By far the best of these is the furthest away: *Mae Sai Guest House* (Ⓣ053 732021, Ⓔneng_xfour@hotmail.com; ❶–❸) is a relaxing place to stay, with a pretty lawn, small, well-maintained rooms sharing hot showers and cute A-frame log cabins with riverside verandas and hot water en suite. It's a fifteen-minute walk from the main road, wedged between a steep, leafy hill and the river border, which is less than 10m wide at this point. The only other guest house in Mae Sai currently worth recommending is *Chad Guest House* on Soi Tessaban 11 – look out for the signpost on the left at the big bend in Thanon Phaholyothin, 1km before the bridge – which scores low for location but is the classic travellers' rest (Ⓣ053 732054, Ⓕ053 642496; B120 per person):

in a quiet compound set well away from the main road, the family is welcoming, with free local maps for guests, the simple, wooden rooms share hot showers, and it's an easy place to meet people.

Mae Sai's best **hotel** is *Piyaporn Place* (Ⓣ053 734511–3; ❹, including breakfast), a seven-storey block on the west side of the main road about 500m south of the bridge, which has well-equipped rooms in a smart, contemporary style, with air-conditioning, hot-water bathtubs and fridges. Otherwise, try *Yee Sun* (Ⓣ053 733455; ❸), west of the bridge at 816/13 Thanon Sailomjai, which has well-maintained, carpeted rooms with air-conditioning, hot water and fridge.

A popular **eating** place is the terrace of *Rim Nam* (*Riverside*), under the western side of the bridge, which gets crowded during the day with tourists watching the border action and serves cheap one-dish meals as well as its speciality, Burmese crab with curry powder. Alternatively, head for *Nana*, on the west side of Phaholyothin, just north of the lane to *Chad Guest House* (Soi Tessaban 11): as well as selling crafts from local Thai and hill-tribe villages, this not-for-profit shop (Ⓦwww.childlifemaesai.org) serves simple Thai food, fresh coffee and burgers during the day, satay in the evening.

Sop Ruak

The "**Golden Triangle**", which was coined to denote a huge opium-producing area spreading across Burma, Laos and Thailand (see p.413), has, for the benefit of tourists, been artificially concentrated into the precise spot where the borders meet, 70km northeast of Chiang Rai. Don't come to the village of **SOP RUAK**, at the confluence of the Ruak (Mae Sai) and Mekong rivers, expecting to come across sinister drug-runners or poppy fields – instead you'll find souvenir stalls, pay-toilets, a huge, supremely tacky golden Buddha shrine, two opium museums and lots of signs saying "Golden Triangle" which pop up in a million photo albums around the world.

Under the auspices of the Mae Fah Luang Foundation based at Doi Tung (see p.415), the ambitious **Hall of Opium** at the Mae Sai end of the village (Tues–Sun 8.30am–5.30pm, last ticket sale 4pm; B300; Ⓦwww.maefahluang.org) took B400 million and nine years to research and build, with technical assistance from the People's Republic of China. It provides a well-presented, largely balanced picture, in Thai and English, of the use and abuse of opium, and its history over five thousand years, including its spread from Europe to Asia and focusing on the nineteenth-century Opium Wars between Britain and China. Dioramas, games and audiovisuals are put to imaginative use, notably in a reconstruction of a nineteenth-century Siamese opium den, playing the interactive "Find the Hidden Drugs", and, most movingly, watching the personal testimonies of former addicts and their families.

The Hall of Opium is worth the high admission fee and far preferable to the small, imitative **House of Opium** in the centre of town (daily 7am–7pm; B50), which tends more to glorify opium use. All the paraphernalia of opium growing and smoking is housed in several display cases, including beautifully carved teak storage boxes, weights cast from bronze and brass in animal shapes and opium pipes.

The meeting of the waters is undeniably monumental, but to get an unobstructed view of it you need to climb up to **Wat Phra That Phu Khao**, a 1200-year-old temple perched on a small hill above the village: to the north, beyond the puny Ruak River, the mountains of Burma march off into infinity, while eastwards across the mighty Mekong spread the hills and villages of Laos. This pastoral scene has now been transformed, however, by the appearance of a

Thai luxury hotel, which is actually over on an uninhabited strip of Burmese land immediately upstream of the confluence. The attached casino bypasses Thai laws against gambling, and the usually strict border formalities are waived for visitors coming from Thailand. For B400, you can have the thrill of stepping on Lao soil. A longtail **boat** from next to *Sriwan Restaurant*, for example, will give you a kiss-me-quick tour of the "Golden Triangle", including a stop at a souvenir market on the Lao island of Done Xao (B20 admission).

Practicalities

From Mae Sai, blue songthaews make the 45-minute trip to Sop Ruak from the Kasikorn Bank on the east side of Thanon Phaholyothin, about 300m south of the bridge (they leave when they're full). **From Chiang Saen** you can go by regular, blue songthaew from the market or rented bike (an easy 10km ride on a paved road, though not much of it runs along the river bank).

There's nowhere decent to **stay** in Sop Ruak for budget travellers, but for those willing to splurge, one of the north's finest hotels, the *Anantara* (ⓣ053 784084, ⓦwww.anantara.com; ⑨), tastefully designed in a blend of traditional and contemporary styles and set in extensive grounds, is located at the Mae Sai end of the village. The balconies of all its rooms and its swimming pool offer great views over the countryside to the Mekong, Burma and Laos. Among many amenities available to guests are a lovely spa, a northern-Thai cookery school, yoga classes and a well-run **elephant camp** that rescues street elephants (ⓦwww.helpingelephants.org), set up in conjunction with the Thai Elephant Conservation Centre in Lampang, where you can even take a basic three-day training course as a mahout. Every March, the *Anantara* hosts a week-long **elephant polo tournament**, with proceeds going to the Thai Elephant Conservation Centre. Somewhat cheaper, though more institutional rooms, with balconies, fridges, hot water and air-conditioning, are available at the *Greater Mekong Lodge* in the Golden Triangle Park, next to the Hall of Opium, either in the main hotel building or in two-room stilted chalets with better views (ⓣ053 784450, ⓦwww.greatermekonglodge.com; ⑥, including breakfast). Among the many riverfront **restaurants** in Sop Ruak, the central *Sriwan* in front of the *Imperial Golden Triangle Hotel* specializes in *tom yam pla buk* (giant catfish), but also offers cheaper dishes such as chicken fried rice (B40), as well as great views of the Mekong.

Chiang Saen

Combining dozens of tumbledown temple ruins with sweeping Mekong River scenery, **CHIANG SAEN**, 60km northeast of Chiang Rai, is a rustic haven and a good base camp for the border region east of Mae Sai. The town's focal point, where the Chiang Rai road (Thanon Phaholyothin) meets Thanon Rim Khong, the main road along the banks of the Mekong, is a lively junction thronged by buses, songthaews and longtails. Turning left at this T-junction soon brings you to Sop Ruak, and you may well share the road with the tour buses that sporadically thunder through (though most of them miss out the town itself by taking its western bypass). Very few tourists turn right in Chiang Saen, passing the port for cargo boats from Laos and China, along the road to Chiang Khong, even though this is the best way to appreciate the slow charms of the Mekong valley.

Originally known as Yonok, the region around Chiang Saen seems to have been an important Thai trading crossroads from some time after the seventh century. The city of Chiang Saen itself was founded around 1328 by the

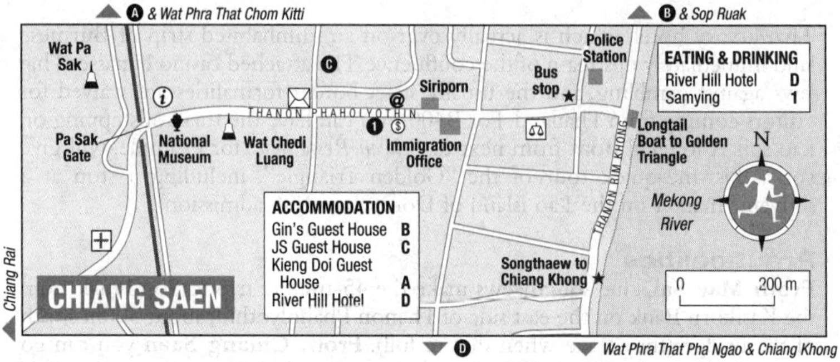

successor to the renowned King Mengrai of Chiang Mai, Saen Phu, who gave up his throne to retire here. Coveted for its strategic location guarding the Mekong, Chiang Saen passed back and forth between the kings of Burma and Thailand for nearly three hundred years until Rama I razed the place in 1804. The present village was established only in 1881, when Rama V ordered a northern prince to resettle the site with descendants of the old townspeople mustered from Lamphun, Chiang Mai and Lampang.

Arrival, information and transport

Buses from Chiang Rai and blue **songthaews** from Sop Ruak and Mae Sai stop by the market on Thanon Phaholyothin, while green songthaews from Chiang Khong stop on the river road to the south of the T-junction; **motorized samlors** wait to ferry people around town. There's a municipal **tourist office** (daily 8.30am–4.30pm; ⓣ053 777084) on Thanon Phaholyothin opposite the National Museum, which houses exhibits on the architecture and conservation of the city.

Longtail boats for tours of the "Golden Triangle" (B500 per boat one way, B600 return), including the Lao souvenir market on Done Xao island (B20 admission), and for Chiang Khong (B2000 one way, B2500 return) congregate around the T-junction. To get around the ruins and the surrounding countryside, **bicycles** (B80 per day) and **motorbikes** (B250) can be rented at *Gin's Guest House*, while *JS Guest House* has bicycles for B25. Motorbikes are also available for B200 from Siriporn on Thanon Phaholyothin, with an **internet** shop just two doors west.

Armed with a Chinese visa from Bangkok or Chiang Mai, you can catch a passenger boat from Chiang Saen up the Mekong **to Jing Hong** in China (Mon, Wed & Fri; 12–13hr; B4000). Buy tickets from Maekhong Travel on Thanon Rim Khong, just north of the T-junction near Wat Pha Khao Pan (ⓣ053 642517–9, ⓦwww.maekhongtravel.com).

Accommodation

Chiang Saen has one **hotel** and just a few **guest houses**, the best of which are listed below.

Gin's Guest House Outside the ramparts, 2km north of the T-junction ⓣ053 650847. At this attractive guest house – which also serves good food – there's a choice between large A-frame bungalows in a lychee orchard, or pricier spacious, well-furnished rooms in the main house, with polished wood floors, all en suite, most with hot showers. The owner organizes local trekking and all manner of tours, and there's internet access too. ❶–❸

JS Guest House In a lane leading north from the post office ⓣ053 777060, ⓔsureegreutmann@bluewin.ch. A cheap but reasonably clean option offering simple, box-like concrete rooms in rows in the back garden, some with en-suite hot showers. ❶–❷

Kieng Doi Guest House Western bypass, right beside Wat Phra That Chom Kitti ⓣ053 777503. No English sign, but it's hard to miss with its lilac and green bungalows overlooking a pond. The bungalows sport equally cheery decor and hot showers inside, as well as small terraces. Fan ❷, air-con ❷–❸

River Hill About 500m south of the T-junction and a block back from the river road ⓣ053 650826–7, ⓦwww.chiangsaenriverhill.net. This hotel sets a high standard in a modern four-storey building with some traditional touches. Friendly and well run, it's in a quiet rustic street; the rooms, all of which have air-con, fridges and hot-water bathrooms, are very nicely done out right down to the axe cushion seats on the floor. Swimming pool planned. Breakfast included. ❺

The Town

The layout of the old, ruined city is defined by the Mekong River running along its east flank; a tall rectangle, 2.5km from north to south, is formed by the addition of the ancient ramparts, now fetchingly overgrown, on the other three sides. The grid of leafy streets inside the ramparts is now too big for the modern town, which is generously scattered along the river road and across the middle on Thanon Phaholyothin.

The **National Museum** (Wed–Sun 8.30am–4.30pm; B30; ⓦwww.thailandmuseum.com) makes an informative starting point, housing some impressive architectural features rescued from the surrounding ruins, with good labelling in English, as well as a plethora of Buddha images – the two typical northern Thai styles of Buddha are sometimes referred to jointly as the "Chiang Saen style", though most academics instead use the more helpful term "Lanna style" (see p.336). As in many of Thailand's museums, the back end is given over to exhibits on folk culture, one of many highlights being the beautiful wooden lintel carved with *hum yon* (floral swirls representing testicles), which would have been placed above the front door of a house to ward off evil and for ventilation. **Wat Phra That Chedi Luang**, originally the city's main temple, is worth looking in on next door for its imposing octagonal chedi, said to house a relic of the Buddha's breastbone and now decorated with weeds and a huge yellow ribbon, while handicraft stalls in the grounds sell Thai Lue cloths among their wares.

Beyond the ramparts to the west, **Wat Pa Sak**'s brick buildings and laterite columns have been excavated and restored by the Fine Arts Department, making it the most accessible and impressive of Chiang Saen's many temples (daily 8.30am–4.30pm; B30). The wat's name is an allusion to the hundreds of teak trees that Saen Phu planted in the grounds when he built the chedi in 1340 to house relics of the Buddha's right ankle from India. The chedi's square base is inset with niches housing alternating Buddhas and *deva* (angels) with flowing skirts, and above rises the tower for the Buddha relic, topped by a circular spire. Beautiful carved stucco covers much of the structure, showing intricate floral scrolls and stylized lotus patterns as well as a whole zoo of mythical beasts.

The open space around modern Chiang Saen, which is dotted with trees and another 140 overgrown ruins (both inside and outside the ramparts), is great for a carefree wander. A spot worth aiming for is the gold-topped, crooked chedi of **Wat Phra That Chom Kitti**, which gives a good view of the town and the river from a small hill outside the northwest corner of the ramparts.

Another temple that justifies a short detour is **Wat Phra That Pha Ngao**, 3km southeast along the river road – look out for the tall, brick gate on the right. The temple, thought to have been built originally in the sixth century, contains a supposedly miraculous chedi perched on top of a large boulder, but the real attraction is the new chedi on the hillside above: take the one-kilometre track which starts at the back of the temple and you can't miss the gleaming, white-tiled Phra Borom That Nimit, designed by an American, with attractive modern murals and built over and around a ruined brick chedi. From here, though you have to peer through the trees, the views take in Chiang Saen, the wide plain and the slow curve of the river. To the east, the Kok River, which looks so impressive at Chiang Rai, seems like a stream as it pours into the mighty Mekong. On the way down from the chedi, have a look at the new Lao-style bot, which was inaugurated by Princess Sirindhorn in 1999 and is covered from tip to toe in beautiful woodcarving.

Eating and drinking

Food in Chiang Saen is nothing special; you could do worse than try the street-food stalls on the riverfront promenade just north of the T-junction, where you can sprawl on mats at low tables in the evening, followed by a drink at one of the small, lively bars opposite. During the day (closes around 7pm), *Samying* on Thanon Phaholyothin beside the Krung Thai Bank is popular with locals, a cheap, clean, well-run restaurant serving river fish in various preparations and a good *tom yam*. For pleasant service and surroundings, whether indoors or in the back garden, the moderate-to-expensive Thai and international restaurant at the *River Hill Hotel* is worth a try.

Chiang Khong and around

As one of the few places in Thailand where it's possible for foreigners to **cross to Laos**, **CHIANG KHONG** is constantly bustling with travellers waiting to go over the river to the Lao town of Houayxai and embark on the lovely Mekong boat journey down to Louang Phabang. On a high, steep bank above the water, Chiang Khong is strung out along a single, north–south street, Thanon Sai Klang, between the cross-river pier at Hua Wiang and the fishing port of Ban Hat Khrai. Once you've admired the elevated view of the traffic on the Mekong and glimpsed the ruined, red-brick turrets of the French-built Fort Carnot in Houayxai, there's little to do in the town itself, though several local excursions might tempt you to stay a little longer.

Giant catfish

The **Mekong giant catfish** (*pla buk*) is the largest scaleless freshwater fish in the world, measuring up to 3m and more in length and weighing in at 300kg. Chiang Khong has traditionally been the catfish capital of the north, attracting fish merchants and restaurateurs from Chiang Rai, Chiang Mai and Bangkok – the mild, tasty meat of the *pla buk* is prized for its fine, soft texture and one fish can fetch B60,000–80,000. The catfish season is officially opened at the port of Ban Hat Khrai on April 18 with much pomp, including an elaborate ceremony to appease Chao Por Pla Buk, the giant catfish god. The season's haul used to be between thirty and sixty fish all told, but recent years have been so disappointing (only two were caught in 2008) that Thailand's Fishery Department has begun an artificial spawning programme. There was more bad news for giant catfish fans recently when a B10 million museum devoted to the species at Ban Hat Khrai collapsed a week before its scheduled opening, when water was put into its aquarium. At least the planned blasting of the rapids and whirlpools between Chiang Saen and Chiang Khong – used as a spawning ground by the fish – to improve navigation for Chinese boats has been taken off the menu, after a year-long campaign by local people.

Arrival, information and transport

On public transport, the 53km trip **from Chiang Saen** to Chiang Khong by **songthaew** (B100) is best done in the morning and usually involves a change of vehicle at Ban Hat Bai. If you're driving yourself, it's best to branch off the direct Route 1129 onto the winding, scenic, paved roads that hug the northward kink in the river here. If you're coming straight to Chiang Khong **from Chiang Rai**, note that direct buses follow three different routes taking two hours, two and a half hours or three hours; be sure to ask for the quickest time, *sawng chua mohng* (hourly, from the left side of the toilet in Chiang Rai's old bus station). All buses stop on the main road at the south end of town. Because of the popularity of the border crossing at Chiang Khong, there are now direct air-conditioned minibuses **from Chiang Mai** (5hr; B250), available through guest houses and travel agents such as *Queen Bee* (see p.350), and **from Pai** (see p.400).

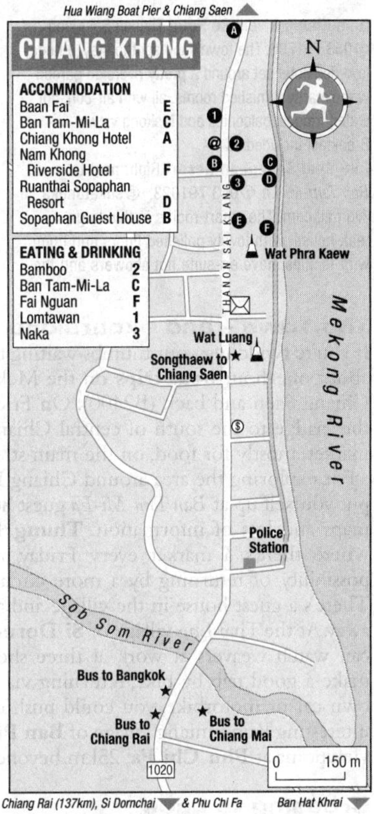

If you need to get from the bus to the ferry (or anywhere else about town), the local version of a **tuk-tuk**, a converted motorbike, should take you there for about B30. Good **mountain bikes** (B150 per day) can be rented from Khun Wat at *Ban Tam-Mi-La*, who sometimes leads afternoon cycling tours around Chiang Khong; **motorbikes** (B200 per day) can be rented through *Baan Fai* and other guest houses. **Internet** access is available opposite *Bamboo* restaurant.

Accommodation

Finding a place to stay in Chiang Khong shouldn't be difficult unless you arrive at the time of a national holiday or the catfish-season opening ceremony on April 18.

Baan Fai 27 Thanon Sai Klang ⓣ053 791394. A variety of rooms, some with shared hot showers and others with attached bathrooms, in a funky, old wooden house on a small plot of land in front of *Nam Khong Riverside Hotel* – B100 for a single is hard to argue with. Internet access. ❶

Ban Tam-Mi-La Soi 1, Thanon Sai Klang (signposted down a lane in the middle of town among a cluster of shops) ⓣ053 791234, ⓔbantammila@hotmail.com. With helpful, clued-up staff and a scenic, easy-going riverfront location, this place has tasteful, well-designed rooms and wooden bungalows on a leafy slope, with en-suite hot showers, and sells good hammocks (ⓦwww.siamhammock.com). Fan ❷–❸, air-con ❹

Chiang Khong Hotel 68/1 Thanon Sai Klang ⓣ053 791182, ⓕ053 655640. Motel-like place with large, plain, good-value rooms set back off the street with hot showers. Fan ❶, air-con ❷

Nam Khong Riverside Hotel Thanon Sai Klang ☎053 791796. The town's top spot to stay, a huge, low-rise hotel set around a pretty riverside garden with smartly furnished rooms, all with air-con, hot water, fridges, balconies and Mekong views. Breakfast included. ❹

Ruanthai Sopaphan Resort Right next to *Ban Tam-Mi-La* ☎053 791023, ©sukatungka @gmail.com. The smart rooms in this large teak house, with lovely polished floors and hung with textiles, have en-suite hot showers and the best have good views of the river. Internet access. ❷–❸

Sopaphan Guest House Thanon Sai Klang ☎053 792022, ©sukatungka@gmail.com. Under the same ownership as *Ruanthai Sopaphan* opposite, a slightly more basic guest house, but also sporting a small forest's worth of highly polished teak. The warren-like premises contain a huge variety of rooms (including three very cheap singles), with hot showers either shared or en suite. Internet access. ❶–❸

The Town – and excursions

If you're twiddling your thumbs waiting to cross to Laos, ask at your guest house about one-hour **boat trips** on the Mekong (B400) or full-day voyages up to Chiang Saen and back (B2400). On Fridays, there's a bustling **market** around the bridge to the south of central Chiang Khong, while Saturdays see a night market, mostly for food, on the main street.

For exploring the area around Chiang Khong more fully, the best option is to put yourself up at *Ban Tam-Mi-La* guest house, where Khun Wat has simple local maps and lots of information. **Thung Na Noi**, a Hmong village 8km west where there's a market every Friday, makes a good cycling trip, with the possibility of returning by a more circuitous, 12km route through the forest. There's a guest house in the village and an attractive waterfall, Huai Tong, 3km away. At the Thai Lue village of **Si Dornchai**, 14km south on Route 1020, you can watch weavers at work at three shops near the bridge – this would also make a good trip by bike, returning via back roads along the river. With your own car or motorbike, you could push on from Si Dornchai for 50km to the interesting Kuomintang village of **Ban Pha Tang** and the precipitous mountain viewpoint at **Phu Chi Fa**, 25km beyond.

Crossing to Laos

Foreigners can get thirty-day Lao **visas** on arrival in Houayxai (US$30 or B1500 and up, depending on nationality; see p.36 for information about other means of getting a Lao visa); as paying in baht is so unfavourable, gold shops (where the rates are often best), guest houses and banks in Chiang Khong sell dollars. Hua Wiang pier, at the north end of town, is the departure point for frequent passenger **ferries to Houayxai** (B30, plus B10 for a big bag, plus B20 "overtime" payment to Lao immigration after 4pm and on Sat or Sun). These cross-river ferries are likely to be phased out when the new Mekong bridge, 8km downstream from Chiang Khong, is completed in 2011 or 2012.

From Houayxai, there are buses to Louang Phabang, Vientiane, Louang Namtha and Oudomxai, but by far the most popular option is to catch a **passenger boat to Louang Phabang**. Usually departing between 10am and noon every morning, these glide down the scenic Mekong in two days, with an overnight and a change of boat at Pakbeng (B1000 per person). Cramped and noisy **speedboats**, on which passengers have to wear helmets and life jackets, cover the same stretch in six to seven hours for B1500 (minimum six people; best to be at the speedboat pier around 9–10am). From Houayxai's cross-river pier, **tuk-tuks** charge B30 to either the regular passenger-boat pier or the speedboat pier.

There's really no need to pay commission to a Thai travel agent to book any of this in advance. The passenger boats are never full – in fact, a strict queue system operates, in which boats sometimes wait for several months before they can leave for Pakbeng.

Eating and drinking

An increasing number of visitors means that eating options have improved in Chiang Khong, and with only one street in town, the restaurants and foodstalls are not difficult to find.

Bamboo Thanon Sai Klang. Small, eclectic bakery, juice bar and restaurant, with home-baked pies, good espressos, a wide choice of breakfasts and small selections of Thai and Mexican food.
Ban Tam-Mi-La 113 Thanon Sai Klang. Excellent guest-house terrace restaurant with a sweeping view of the river, making it an ideal spot to while away the time, though it closes around 6.30pm. Very good Thai food, lots of vegetarian options and a few Western dishes, plus espressos, home-baked cakes and bread, and hearty breakfasts.
Fai Nguan *Nam Khong Riverside Hotel*, Thanon Sai Klang. Well-appointed restaurant overlooking the river, with a wide range of Thai dishes, notably salads (B80–100), plus burgers (B70) and a few pizzas. Live music every night.
Lomtawan 354 Thanon Sai Klang. Congenial bar/restaurant serving Thai dishes such as spicy salads (around B80) and a few Western dishes such as spaghetti (B80) on a candlelit terrace overlooking the canal, as well as drinks at the bar inside.
Naka Thanon Sai Klang. Lively, evening-only bar-restaurant, with good music, serving Lanna dishes such as the pork curry *kaeng hang lay*, as well as steak and spaghetti.

Travel details

Trains

Chiang Mai to: Bangkok (6 daily; 12hr–14hr 30min).
Den Chai to: Bangkok (8 daily; 8–10hr); Chiang Mai (7 daily; 4–5hr).
Doi Khun Tan to: Bangkok (4 daily; 11–13hr); Chiang Mai (5 daily; 1hr 30min).
Lampang to: Bangkok (6 daily; 10–12hr); Chiang Mai (7 daily; 2hr–2hr 30min).
Lamphun to: Bangkok (6 daily; 12–14hr); Chiang Mai (6 daily; 20–30min).

Buses

Chiang Khong to: Bangkok (10 daily; 13–14hr); Chiang Mai (3 daily; 6hr); Chiang Rai (every 20min; 2–3hr).
Chiang Mai to: Bangkok (20 daily; 10–11hr); Chiang Khong (3 daily; 6hr); Chiang Rai (every 30min; 3–4hr); Chiang Saen (5 daily; 5hr); Chom Thong (11 daily; 1hr); Fang (every 30min; 3hr 30min); Khon Kaen (13 daily; 12hr); Khorat (12 daily; 12hr); Lampang (every 30min; 1hr 30min); Lamphun (every 10min; 1hr); Mae Hong Son (5 daily via Mae Sariang, 8–9hr; 3 daily via Pai, 8hr); Mae Sai (6 daily; 4–5hr); Mae Sot (4 daily; 6hr); Nan (8 daily; 6hr); Pai (5 daily; 4hr); Phitsanulok (10 daily; 6hr); Phrae (hourly; 4hr); Rayong (8 daily; 17hr); Sukhothai (12 daily; 5hr); Tha Ton (4 daily; 4hr); Ubon Ratchathani (6 daily; 17hr); Udon Thani (4 daily; 12hr).
Chiang Rai to: Bangkok (24 daily; 11–12hr); Chiang Khong (every 20min; 2–3hr); Chiang Mai (every 30min; 3–4hr); Chiang Saen (every 20min; 1hr 30min); Khon Kaen (6 daily; 12hr 30min); Khorat (6 daily; 13hr); Lampang (every 30min; 4–5hr); Mae Sai (every 20min; 1hr 30min); Mae Sot (2 daily; 10hr); Nakhon Phanom (3 daily; 19hr); Nan (1 daily; 6–7hr); Phitsanulok (1 daily; 7hr); Phrae (hourly; 4hr); Rayong (4 daily; 19hr); Sukhothai (4 daily; 7hr 30min); Udon Thani (3 daily; 13hr).
Lampang to: Bangkok (18 daily; 8hr); Chiang Mai (every 30min; 1hr 30min); Chiang Rai (every 30min; 4–5hr); Mae Sai (3 daily; 5hr); Nan (8 daily; 4hr); Phrae (hourly; 2hr 30min).
Mae Hong Son to: Bangkok (2 daily; 16hr); Chiang Mai via Mae Sariang (5 daily; 8–9hr); Chiang Mai via Pai (3 daily; 8hr).
Mae Sai to: Bangkok (13 daily; 13hr); Chiang Mai (6 daily; 4–5hr); Chiang Rai (every 20min; 1hr 30min); Fang, via Tha Ton (1 daily; 2hr 30min);

Khorat (6 daily; 14hr); Lampang (3 daily; 5hr); Mae Sot (2 daily; 12hr); Phitsanulok (1 daily; 10hr); Sukhothai (1 daily; 8hr).

Nan to: Bangkok (10 daily; 12hr); Chiang Mai (8 daily; 6hr); Chiang Rai (1 daily; 6–7hr); Den Chai (hourly; 2hr 30min); Phitsanulok (6 daily; 8hr); Phrae (hourly; 2hr).

Pai to: Chiang Mai (5 daily; 4hr); Mae Hong Son (4 daily; 4hr).

Phrae to: Bangkok (11 daily; 8hr); Chiang Mai (hourly; 4hr); Chiang Rai (hourly; 4hr); Den Chai (hourly; 30min); Nan (hourly; 2hr); Phitsanulok (hourly; 4hr).

Flights

Chiang Mai to: Bangkok (25 daily; 1hr); Chiang Rai (8 weekly; 40min); Koh Samui (daily; 2hr); Mae Hong Son (2–4 daily; 35min); Pai (1–3 daily; 30min); Phuket (daily; 2hr);

Chiang Rai to: Bangkok (5 daily; 1hr 15min); Chiang Mai (8 weekly; 40min).

Lampang to: Bangkok (1–2 daily; 1hr).

Nan to: Bangkok (4 weekly; 1hr 20min).

4

The east coast

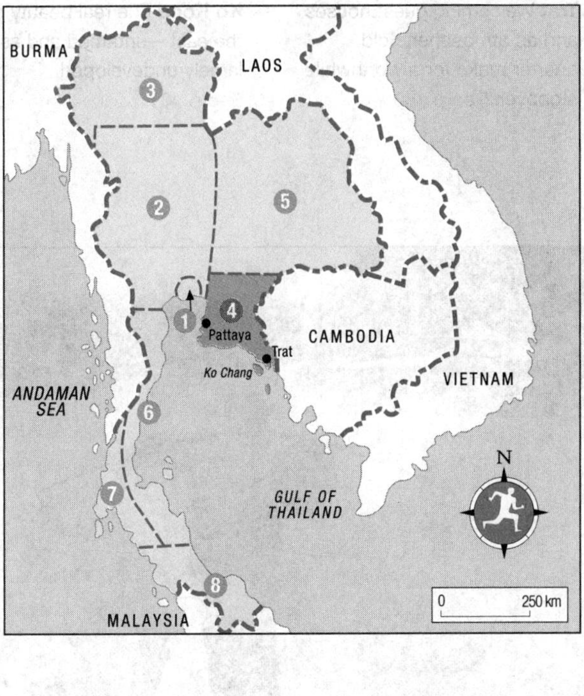

CHAPTER 4

Highlights

* **Ko Si Chang** Tiny, barely touristed island with craggy coastlines, glorious views, and an appealingly laid-back ambience. See p.431

* **Ko Samet** Pretty (and popular) little island fringed with dazzlingly white beaches. See p.446

* **Trat** Welcoming guest houses and an atmospheric old quarter make for a worthwhile stopover. See p.458

* **Ko Chang** Head for Lonely Beach if you're in the mood to party, or to Hat Khlong Phrao for a more tranquil scene. See p.463

* **Ko Mak** Lovely, lazy, palm-filled little island with peaceful white-sand beaches. See p.477

* **Ko Kood** The real beauty of the east – untamed and as yet largely undeveloped. See p.481

▲ Beach vendor on Ko Samet

4

The east coast

Located within just a few hours' drive from the capital, the **east coast** resorts and islands attract a mixed crowd of weekending Bangkokians, pleasure-seeking expats and sybaritic tourists. Transport connections are good and, for overlanders, there are several Cambodian border crossings within easy reach. Beautiful beaches are not the whole picture, however, as the westernmost stretch of the east coast is also crucial to Thailand's industrial economy, its natural gas fields and deep-sea ports having spawned massive development along the first 200km of coastline, an area often dubbed the **Eastern Seaboard**. The initial landscape of refineries and depots shouldn't deter you though, as offshore it's an entirely different story, with island sands as glorious as many of those at the more celebrated southern retreats and enough peaceful havens to make it worth packing your hammock.

The first worthwhile stop comes 100km east of Bangkok at the town of **Si Racha**, which is the point of access for tiny **Ko Si Chang**, whose dramatically rugged coastlines and low-key atmosphere make it a restful retreat. In complete contrast, nearby **Pattaya** is Thailand's number-one package-tour destination, its customers predominantly middle-aged Western and Chinese males enticed by the resort's sex-market reputation and undeterred by its lacklustre beach. Things soon look up, though, as the coast veers sharply eastwards towards Ban Phe, revealing the island of **Ko Samet**, the prettiest of all the beach resorts within comfortable bus-ride range of Bangkok.

East of Ban Phe, the landscape becomes lusher and hillier around **Chanthaburi**, the dynamo of Thailand's gem trade and one of only two eastern provincial capitals worth visiting. The other is **Trat**, 68km further along the highway, and an important hub both for transport into **Cambodia** via Hat Lek – one of this region's two main border points, the other being Aranyaprathet – and for the forty islands of the Ko Chang archipelago. The star of this island group is large, forested **Ko Chang** itself, whose long, fine beaches have made it into Thailand's latest resort destination. A host of smaller, less-developed islands fill the sea between Ko Chang and the Cambodian coast, most notably the temptingly diverse trio of **Ko Wai**, **Ko Mak** and **Ko Kood**.

Highway 3 extends almost the entire length of the east coast, beginning in Bangkok as Thanon Sukhumvit, and known as such when it cuts through towns, and hundreds of **buses** ply the route, connecting all major mainland destinations. It's also possible to travel between the east coast and the northeast and north without doubling back through the capital: the most direct routes into **Isaan** start from Pattaya, Rayong and Chanthaburi. Bangkok's Suvarnabhumi Airport is less than 50km from Si Racha, and there are two domestic **airports** along the east coast itself: at U-Tapao naval base, southeast of Pattaya,

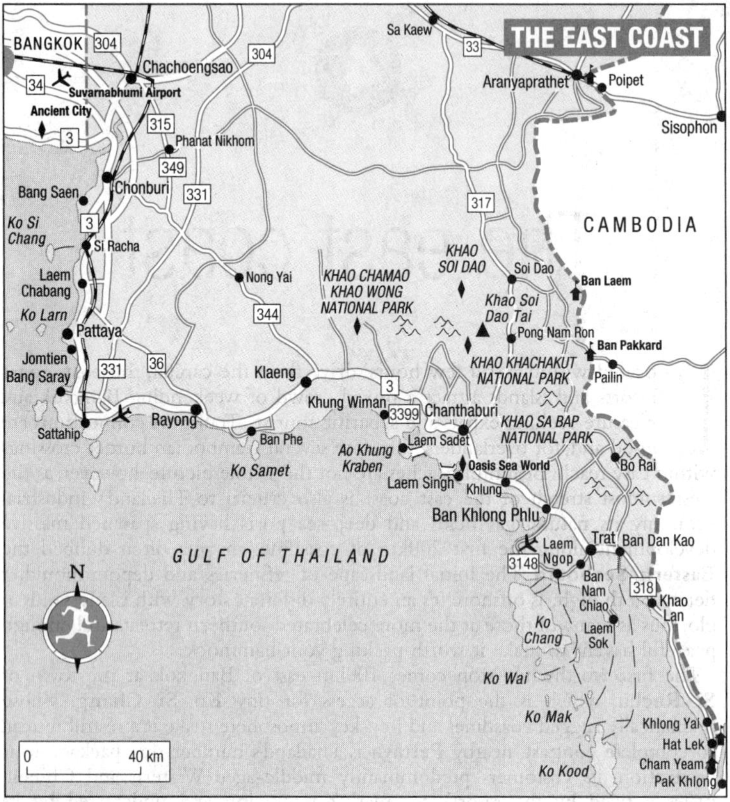

and just west of Trat. Though a rail line connects Bangkok with Si Racha and Pattaya, it is served by just one slow **train** a day in each direction; a branch line makes two journeys a day to Aranyaprathet near the Cambodian border.

Si Racha

The eastbound journey out of Bangkok is not at all scenic, dominated initially by traffic-choked suburban sprawl and then by the industrial landscape of the petrochemical and shipping industries that power Thailand's Eastern Seaboard. The first major population centre is the provincial capital of **Chonburi**, whose only notable attraction is its annual October bout of buffalo-racing. Twenty kilometres on and you reach the fast-growing town of **SI RACHA**, a prosperous residential and administrative hub for the Eastern Seaboard's industries and home to a sizeable population of expat families. The town is best known though as the source of *nam phrik Si Racha*, the chilli-laced ketchup found on every kitchen table in Thailand, and as the departure point for the island of **Ko Si Chang** (see opposite). Si Racha's only sight is the Sino–Thai "island temple" of **Wat Ko Loy**, a gaudy hexagon presided over by a statue of the Chinese Goddess of Mercy, Kuan Im, and located on an islet at the end of a 1500-metre-long causeway, adjacent to the pier for boats to Ko Si Chang.

Buses to Si Racha leave frequently from both Bangkok's Eastern (Ekamai) and Northern (Mo Chit) bus terminals, and from Pattaya, Rayong and Trat further east. They all drop passengers near the huge Robinsons/Pacific Park shopping centre on Thanon Sukhumvit in Si Racha's town centre. It's about 2.5km from here to the end of the Ko Si Chang pier, known as Tha Wat Ko Loy, which is west off the Thanon Chermchompon/Thanon Surasak junction. A motorbike taxi or tuk-tuk will drive you there for B30–40 or, if walking, take any road west towards the sea as far as Thanon Chermchompon (also spelt Jermjompol), then head north up Chermchompon until you reach the junction for the Ko Si Chang pier and Wat Ko Loy. White songthaews from Naklua, the northern suburb of Pattaya, run about twice an hour to Si Racha, dropping passengers near the clocktower, about 1km south down Thanon Chermchompon from the pier junction. The one slow **train** a day from Bangkok departs the capital at 6.55am, takes over three hours, and arrives at the train station on the far eastern edge of town, a tuk-tuk ride from the pier.

The most atmospheric of the cheap places **to stay** are the very simple, cabin-like, en-suite fan rooms of *Sri Wattana* (Ⓣ038 311037; ❶), built on a jetty jutting out over the waterfront, with a pleasant sea-view terrace; the hotel is on Soi Sri Wattana, directly across Thanon Chermchompon from Thanon Si Racha Nakhon 3, about 500m south of the pier junction. For flashier, air-con digs, head for the eleven-storey *City Hotel* (Ⓣ038 322700, Ⓦwww.citysriracha.com; ❼), 300m south of Pacific Place at 6/126 Thanon Sukhumvit, which has wi-fi and a pool. For **eating**, Thanon Si Racha Nakhon 3 is a good place to browse, lined with restaurants and night-time foodstalls, or there's an official night market by the day market and clocktower further south down Thanon Chermchompon.

Ko Si Chang

The unhurried pace and absence of consumer pressures make tiny, rocky **KO SI CHANG** an engaging place to wind down for a few days. Unlike most other east-coast destinations, it offers no real beach life – though the water can be beautifully clear and there are opportunities to dive and snorkel – and there's little to do here but explore the craggy coastline by kayak or ramble up and down its steep contours on foot or by motorbike. The island is famous as the location of one of Rama V's summer palaces, parts of which have been prettily restored, and for its rare white squirrels, who live in the wooded patches inland.

Arrival and information

Ferries to Ko Si Chang leave from Tha Wat Ko Loy in Si Racha (see opposite), departing approximately hourly from 7am to 8pm (45min; B40), and wending their way past the congestion of international cargo boats and Thai supply barges that anchor in the protected channel between the mainland and Ko Si Chang. On **arrival**, all boats dock first at Tha Lang (also signed as Tateawavong Bridge), with many then continuing to Tha Bon a short distance up the east coast. Samlor drivers meet the boats and charge B40 to most accommodation, or B80 to Hat Tham Pang; as they are paid commission by some hotels and restaurants, be wary of any opinionated remarks. The first boat back to the mainland leaves Tha Lang at 6am and the last at 6pm; the same boats depart Tha Bon about fifteen minutes earlier.

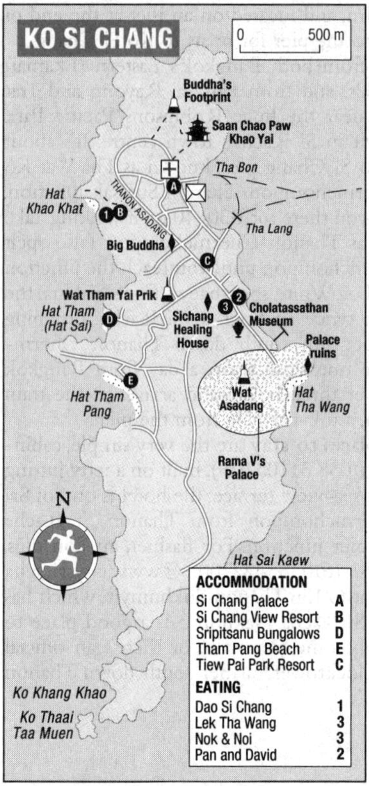

Both piers connect with Thanon Asadang, a small ring road on which you'll find the market, shops and many of the island's houses. Much of the rest of the island is accessible only by paths and tracks. In town it's easy enough to walk from place to place, but to really enjoy what Ko Si Chang has to offer you'll need to either rent a **motorbike** from the pier (B250), or charter a samlor for the day. The island's trademark **samlors** are driven by distinctive, elongated 1200cc motorbikes and virtually monopolize the roads, as there are barely any private cars on Ko Si Chang; a tour of the island will only set you back around B250.

There are **exchange facilities** and an ATM at the bank between the two piers; the hospital is also near Tha Bon. For a fee of B50, non-guests can use the **swimming pool** at *Si Chang Palace* hotel. The charming Sichang Healing House (daily except Wed 9am–5pm; ⓣ038 216467) offers Ayurvedic **massage** (from B400) and herbal treatments at its cute little garden retreat west off the road to the old palace. It also sells watercolour views of Ko Si Chang. For detailed **information** on Ko Si Chang, consult the website ⓦwww.ko-sichang.com, compiled by David at *Pan and David Restaurant*.

Ko Si Chang celebrates three particularly interesting **festivals**. **Songkhran** is marked here from April 17–19 with sandcastle-building, greasy-pole-climbing and an exorcist ritual for any islanders who have suffered unpleasant deaths over the previous year. At **Visakha Puja**, the full-moon day in May when Buddha's birth, death and enlightenment are honoured, islanders process to the old palace with hand-crafted Chinese lanterns. And on September 20, Ko Si Chang honours its royal patron **King Chulalongkorn's birthday** with a *son et lumière* in the palace grounds and a beauty contest staged entirely in costumes from the Chulalongkorn era.

Accommodation

Because water on the island has to be bought from a private desalination company at six times the price it costs on the mainland, **accommodation** on Ko Si Chang is expensive and disappointingly poor value. West-coast accommodation enjoys the best views, while Thanon Asadang and east-coast options are more convenient for restaurants and shops. Booking ahead is advisable for weekends and public holidays. For the very finest sea views, nothing can beat **camping**: the cliffs at Hat Khao Khat are a particularly popular site, though quite exposed. You can rent tents for B100 from Uncle Juk on Hat Tham Pang (☎081 822 5540), but phone ahead to reserve one for weekends.

Si Chang Palace Across from Tha Bon on Thanon Asadang ☎038 216276, Ⓦwww.sichangpalace.com. The most upmarket place on the island has good air-con rooms, the best of them enjoying fine eastward sea views. There's a pool here too. ❺

Si Chang View Resort Hat Khao Khat ☎038 216210, Ⓔjiyakiat@yahoo.com. Run by a friendly, English-speaking family, the thirteen well-maintained fan and air-con rooms occupy a couple of two-storey buildings in a nice garden set back from a prime cliffside spot (not quite visible from the rooms sadly) above Hat Khao Khat. There's wi-fi and fresh coffee in the restaurant. Fan ❹, air-con ❺

Sripitsanu Bungalows Hat Tham ☎038 216336. Remote and stunningly located place whose dozen large, plain and rather haphazardly maintained fan and air-con rooms and bungalows sit almost right at the edge of the cliff – some are actually built into the rockface. It's a gorgeous spot, with unsurpassed views and the possibility of swimming at low tide, though there's not much English spoken. Some bungalows have their own cooking facilities. From *Tiew Pai*, cross Thanon Asadang and walk a few metres to the left, then follow signs up the first right, a narrow road heading uphill; it's a 10min walk from here. Fan ❸, air-con ❹

Tham Pang Beach Hat Tham Pang ☎038 216179. The busiest west-coast accommodation, whose twenty fairly rudimentary concrete bungalows – all with bathroom, fans, verandas and partial sea views – are stacked in tiers up the cliffside behind Ko Si Chang's only real beach. There's a restaurant plus beach equipment for rent. Reservations essential for weekends. ❸

Tiew Pai Park Resort Thanon Asadang ☎038 216084, Ⓦwww.tiewpai.com. Very central and cheaper than the competition, this is most backpackers' first choice. Bungalows and rooms are crammed around a scruffy garden across the road from the restaurant and many are pretty basic; the best value are the en-suite fan bungalows (with TV and fridge) and there are also some cheap single rooms with shared bathrooms. Fan ❷–❸, air-con ❹

Around the island

The main sights on the island are **Rama V's old palace** on the southeast coast and the popular Chinese pilgrimage temple **Saan Chao Paw Khao Yai** on the northeastern tip, with west-coast **Hat Tham Pang** the main beach. **Fishing** boats with a skipper can be chartered from the two Ko Si Chang piers for B1500 per day, or *Tiew Pai Park Resort* does half-day fishing trips for B2000 per ten-person boat.

Rama V's Palace and around

The most famous sight on the island is the partially ruined Rama V's Palace, which occupies a large chunk of gently sloping land midway down the east coast, behind pebbly **Hat Tha Wang**. It's an enjoyable place to explore and can be reached on foot from *Tiew Pai Park Resort* in about half an hour. Shortly before reaching the palace grounds, you'll pass the small and less than riveting **Cholatassathan Museum** (Tues–Sun 9am–5pm; entry by donation), established by the resident Aquatic Resources Research Institute to provide an introduction to the coral and marine life around Ko Si Chang.

Built in the 1890s as a sort of health resort for sickly royals, **Rama V's Palace**, or **Phra Judhadhut Ratchathan** (daily 9am–5pm; free), formed the heart of an extensive complex comprising homes for royal advisers, chalets for convalescents, quarters for royal concubines and administrative buildings. By the turn of the twentieth century, however, Rama V (King Chulalongkorn) had lost interest in his island project and so in 1901 his golden teak palace was moved piece by piece to Bangkok, and reconstructed there as Vimanmek Palace; its foundations are still visible just south of the palace's Saphan Asadang pier. Following recent renovations, the elegant design of the palace grounds is apparent once more. They fan out around an elaborate labyrinth of fifty interlinked ponds and a

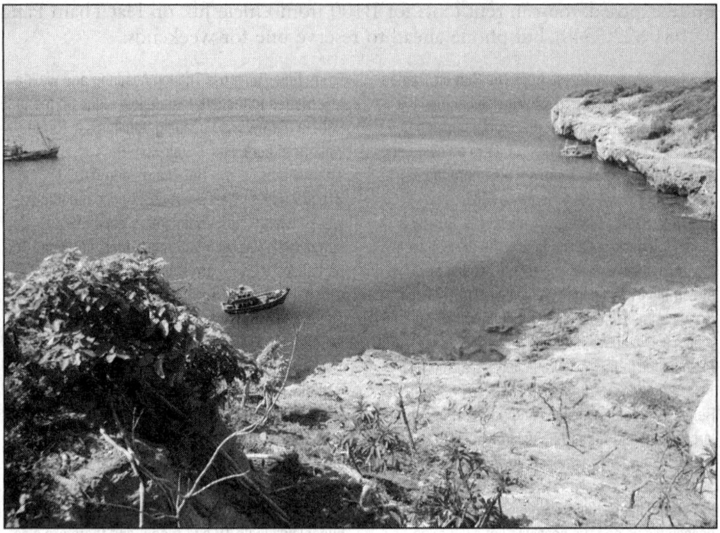

▲ Ko Si Chang's rocky coastline

maze of stone steps and balustrades that still cling to the shallow hillside. Close to the shore, four of the original Western-style **villas** have been reconstructed to house displays, of varying interest, on Chulalongkorn's relationship with Ko Si Chang; one of them also doubles as a coffee shop. Inland, signs direct you up the hillside to the palace's unusual whitewashed shrine, **Wat Asadang**, whose circular walls are punctuated with Gothic stained-glass windows and surmounted by a chedi.

Hat Tham Pang and around

The main beach on the west coast, and the most popular one on the island, is small, crowded **Hat Tham Pang**, a B80 samlor ride from either pier. Its sandy front is packed with deckchairs and beach umbrellas and you can rent snorkels, kayaks, inner tubes and fishing rods here too. The best **snorkelling** spots are further south, around the tiny islands off Ko Si Chang's southern tip, particularly off the north coast of **Ko Khang Khao**, forty minutes by kayak from Hat Tham Pang.

North of Hat Tham Pang, and also accessible via a fork off Thanon Asadang opposite *Tiew Pai* (a ten-minute walk), you'll find the **Wat Tham Yai Prik** temple and meditation centre, which is open to interested visitors and holds frequent retreats. Unusually, nuns as well as monks here wear brown (rather than white) and everyone participates in the upkeep of the monastery: you can see some of the fruits of their labour in the extensive roadside orchard. Just west of the wat, the dramatically situated *Sripitsanu Bungalows* offers glorious views over the pretty, rocky cove known as **Hat Tham** or **Hat Sai**, which is only really swimmable at low tide.

North to Saan Chao Paw Khao Yai

Back down on the ring road, if you continue in a northwesterly direction, you'll pass beneath the gaze of a huge yellow Buddha before reaching the rocky northwest headland of **Khao Khat**, a few hundred metres further on. The uninterrupted panorama of open sea makes this a classic sunset spot, and there's a path along the cliffside.

From here the road heads east to reach the showy, multi-tiered Chinese temple, **Saan Chao Paw Khao Yai** (Shrine of the Father Spirit of the Great Hill), stationed at the top of a steep flight of steps and commanding a good view of the harbour and the mainland coast. Established here long before Rama V arrived on the island, the shrine was dedicated by Chinese seamen who saw a strange light coming out of one of the **caves** behind the modern-day temple. The caves, now full of religious statues and related paraphernalia, are visited by boatloads of Chinese pilgrims, particularly over Chinese New Year. Continue on up the cliffside to reach the small pagoda built for Rama V and enshrining a **Buddha's Footprint**. Two very long, very steep flights of stairs give access to the footprint: the easternmost one starts at the main waterfront entrance to the Chinese temple and takes you past a cluster of monks' meditation cells, while the westerly one rises further west along the ring road and offers the finest lookouts.

Eating

One of the most enjoyable **places to eat** on the island is *Pan and David Restaurant* (Mon, Tues, Thurs & Fri 11am–9.30pm, Sat 8.30am–10pm, Sun 8.30am–8.30pm), 200m before the entrance to the old palace grounds, which is run by a sociable and well-informed American expat and his Thai wife. The long and delicious menu (B50–395) includes authentically fiery *som tam*, home-made fettuccine, fillet steak, Thai curries, brownies and home-made fresh strawberry ice cream, as well as good-value Italian wine. *Nok and Noi*, across the road from *Pan and David*, and the locally famous *Lek Tha Wang*, slightly further down the road towards the palace, are both well known for their seafood. *Dao Si Chang*, on the clifftop in front of *Si Chang View Resort*, also specializes in seafood and is a great spot for a sunset dinner.

Pattaya

With its streets full of high-rise hotels and hustlers on every corner, **PATTAYA** is the epitome of exploitative tourism gone mad, but most of Pattaya's two million annual visitors don't mind that the place looks like the Costa del Sol because what they are here for is sex. The city swarms with male and female **prostitutes**, spiced up by a sizeable population of transvestites (*katoey*), and plane-loads of Western men flock here to enjoy their services in the rash of hostess bar-beers, go-go clubs and massage parlours for which "Patpong-on-Sea" is notorious. The signs trumpeting "Viagra for Sale" say it all. Pattaya also has the largest **gay scene** in Thailand, with several exclusively gay hotels and an entire zone devoted to gay sex bars.

Pattaya's evolution into sin city began with the Vietnam War, when it got fat on selling sex to American servicemen. When the soldiers and sailors left in the mid-1970s, Western tourists were lured in to fill their places, and ex-servicemen soon returned to run the sort of joints they had once blown their dollars in. These days, at least half the bars and restaurants in Pattaya are Western-run. More recently, there has been an influx of criminal gangs from Germany, Russia and Japan, who reportedly find Pattaya a convenient centre for running their rackets in passport and credit-card fraud, as well as child pornography and prostitution; expat murders are a regular news item in the *Pattaya Mail*.

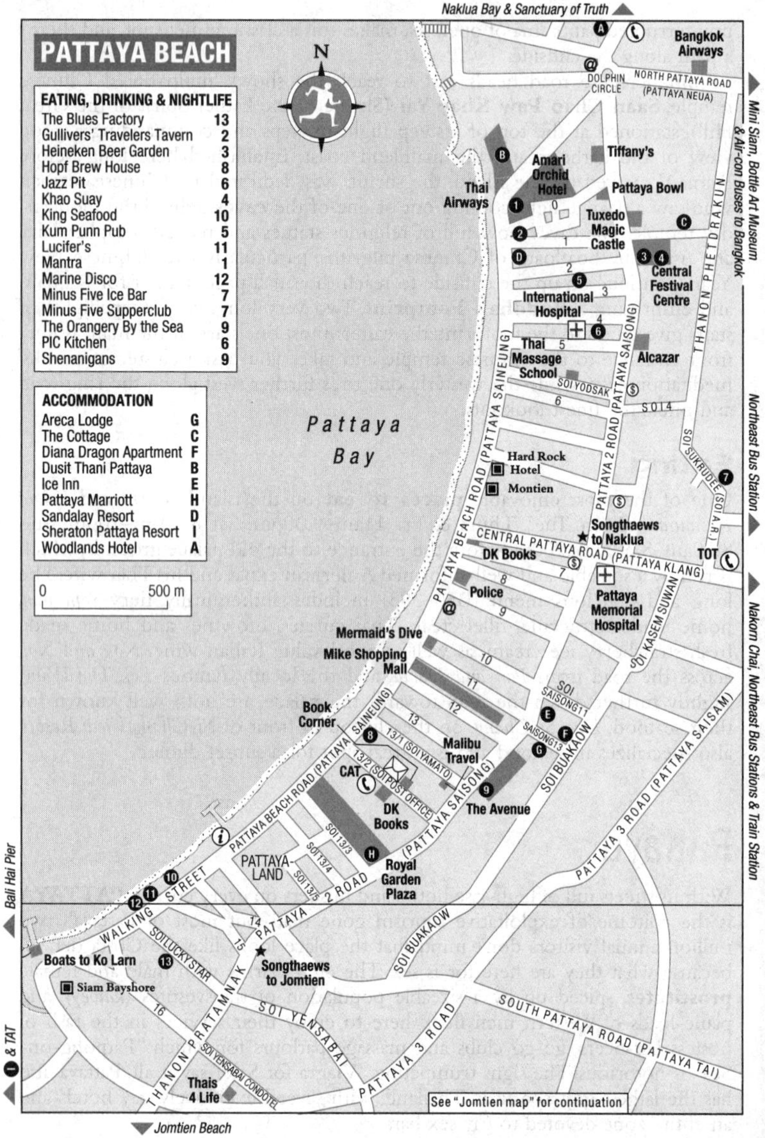

Meanwhile, local tourism authorities are trying hard to improve **Pattaya's image**, and with surprising success have begun enticing families and older couples with a catalogue of more wholesome entertainments such as theme parks, golf courses, shopping plazas and year-round diving. Russian holidaymakers seem particularly keen and Cyrillic script is now much in evidence around the resort. A recent flush of more sophisticated boutique hotels and restaurants is also starting to bring in a younger Thai crowd, which has brightened the picture a little. But in truth the beach here is far from pristine – way outshone by Ko Samet just along the coast – so after-hours "entertainment" is still the primary inducement.

Arrival and information

Dozens of air-con **buses** run from **Bangkok**'s Eastern and Northern bus terminals to Pattaya, and there's a slightly less frequent service from the Southern Bus Terminal. In addition there are up to seven buses a day from **Suvarnabhumi Airport** to Pattaya (some operate direct from Arrivals, others from the public transport terminal), and at least four in the opposite direction (Ⓣ038 231142). All Bangkok and most airport buses arrive at and depart from the bus station on North Pattaya Road (Ⓣ038 429877). Metered taxis from Suvarnabhumi cost around B1300 (90min); returning to the airport from Pattaya costs from B800 per car or B450 per person in a shared minibus arranged through any hotel.

Coming **by bus from Si Racha**, **Rayong** or **Trat** you'll probably get dropped on Thanon Sukhumvit, the resort's eastern limit, from where songthaews will ferry you into town. If heading on to these towns, you need to pick up your bus from one of the drops on Thanon Sukhumvit, but if you're going **to Ko Samet** or **Ko Chang** it's much easier and not much more expensive to use the tourist minibus services run by Samet Island Tour on Soi Yamato (Ⓣ038 427277, Ⓦwww.malibu-samet.com) and Koh Chang Travel on Soi Post Office (Ⓣ038 710145, Ⓦwww.kohchangtravel.com), both of which operate door-to-door services to the Ban Phe pier (for Ko Samet; B230), and the Ko Chang piers (B500); tickets can also be booked through most tour agents. Some airport and most **local buses** use the Baw Kaw Saw government bus station on Thanon Chaiyapruk in Jomtien.

It's also possible to get to Pattaya direct **from Isaan and the north**: Nakorn Chai buses to and from Chiang Mai, Chiang Rai, Khorat and Ubon use a terminus on Thanon Sukhumvit, across from the Central Pattaya Road intersection (Ⓣ038 424871); other bus services to the northeast use the Northeastern Bus Station on Central Pattaya Road, just east of the Pattaya 3 Road intersection.

Pattaya is on a branch line of the eastern rail line, and there's one slow **train** a day in each direction between the resort and Bangkok. Pattaya's station (Ⓣ038 429285) is on Thanon Sukhumvit, about 500m north of the Central Pattaya Road intersection. Pattaya's **U-Tapao airport** (Ⓣ038 245595) is located at the naval base near Sattahip, about 25km south of the resort, and runs Bangkok Airways flights to and from Ko Samui and Phuket.

There's a municipal **tourist service centre** (daily 8.30am–4.30pm) on the beach at the mouth of Walking Street; the **TAT** office is inconveniently located at 609 Thanon Pratamnak between South Pattaya and Jomtien (daily 8.30am–4.30pm; Ⓣ038 428750, Ⓔtatchon@tat.or.th). Alternatively, call the 24-hour Pattaya City Call Centre **information service** on Ⓣ1337. The weekly *Pattaya Mail* (Ⓦwww.pattayamail.com) is one of several **local newspapers** that fills readers in on the often lurid goings-on.

Orientation

At the heart of this ever-expanding playground is the four-kilometre-long **Pattaya Beach**, the noisiest, most unsightly zone of the resort, crowded with yachts and tour boats and fringed by a sliver of sand and a paved beachfront walkway. The densest glut of hotels, restaurants, bars, fast-food joints, souvenir shops and tour operators is halfway down Pattaya Beach Road (also signed as Pattaya Saineung), in **Central Pattaya** (Pattaya Klang), between

JOMTIEN BEACH & BUDDHA HILL

South Pattaya ▲ Train Station ▲

Bali Hai Pier ★ Songthaews to Jomtien

■ Siam Bayshore

SOUTH PATTAYA ROAD (PATTAYA TAI)

SOI YENSABAI

Tourist Police
ℹ

PATTAYA 3 ROAD

See "Pattaya map" for continuation

BUDDHA HILL
(KHAO PHRA TAMNAK
PATTAYA HILL)

TAT

Rama IX
Memorial
Park

THANON TABPHAYA

THEP PRASIT

Tesco Lotus

THANON SUKHUMVIT

PATTAYA
PARK

SOI PATTAYA PARK

● Pattaya Park Tower

❶

Mermaid Dive Centre

Underwater World

Jomtien
Complex

Ⓒ

❷

Dongtan Beach

Bookazine

Police

● KFC

Immigration

Mermaid's Dive

Ⓓ

Pattaya City
Windsurfing Club

JOMTIEN BEACH ROAD (THANON HAT JOMTIEN)

THANON WAT BOONKANJANA (WAT BUN)

Alangkarn Theatre & Ban Phe ▶

ACCOMMODATION
GI Guest House D
Rabbit Resort C
Sheraton Pattaya Resort A
Sugar Hut B

EATING & DRINKING
Bruno's 1
Sea Falcon 3
Shenanigans 2
Sugar Hut B

N

Baw Kaw Saw
Bus Station

THANON CHAIYAPRUK

0 1 km

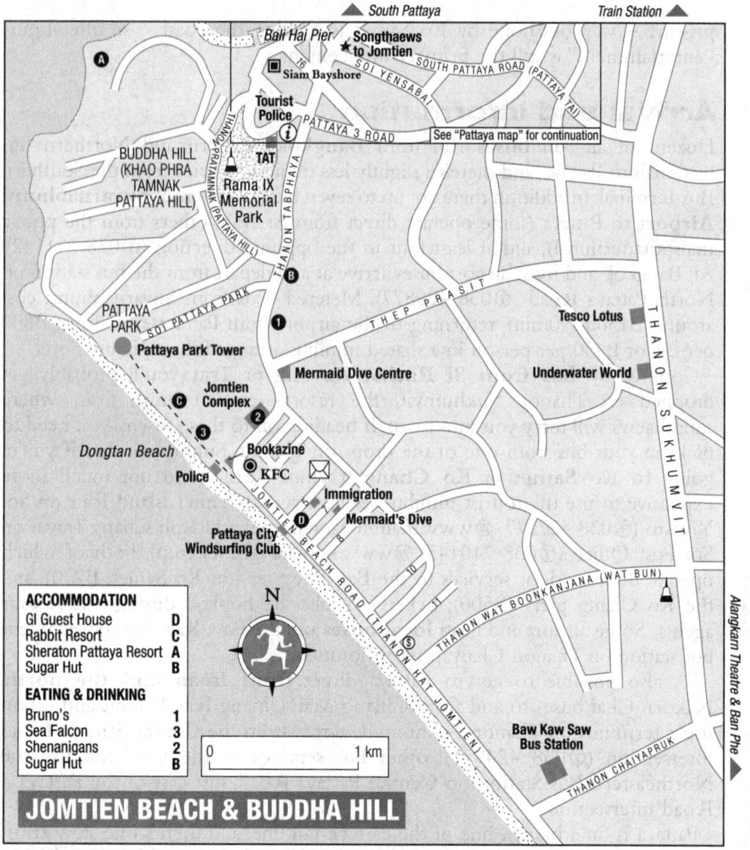

sois 6 and 13, but after dark the action moves to the neon zone south of Soi 13/2. Here, in **South Pattaya**, and specifically along ultra-sleazy **Walking Street**, sex is peddled in hundreds of go-go bars, discos, massage parlours and open-sided bar-beers. The gay district is also here, in the lanes known as **Pattayaland** sois 1, 2 and 3 (or **Boyz Town**), but actually signed as sois 13/3, 13/4 and 13/5. The quietest and least sleazy end of town to stay in is **North Pattaya**, between Central Pattaya Road and North Pattaya Road (Thanon Hat Pattaya Neua).

South around the headland from South Pattaya, **Jomtien Beach** (sometimes spelt Chom Tian) is also fronted by enormous high-rises, many of them condominiums. Though the atmosphere here is not as frantic as in Pattaya, Jomtien also flounders under an excess of bar-beers and shops flogging tacky souvenirs and, like its neighbour, is forever under construction. The nicest stretch of sand is **Dongtan Beach**, beyond the northern end of Jomtien Beach Road: shady, and car-free between 10am and 5pm, it is Pattaya's main gay beach, though used by all. The bulge of land behind Dongtan Beach, separating Jomtien from South Pattaya, is Khao Phra Tamnak, variously translated as **Pattaya Hill** or **Buddha Hill**, site of several posh hotels and the Pattaya Park waterpark and funfair.

Transport

Public **songthaews** – known locally as baht buses – circulate continuously around the resort from dawn until at least 11pm. In **Pattaya** most follow a standard anticlockwise route up Pattaya 2 Road as far as North Pattaya Road and back down Pattaya Beach Road, for a fixed fee of B10 per person; avoid jumping in a parked songthaew, however, as you'll be charged for chartering the whole vehicle. Songthaews **to Jomtien** start from the junction of Pattaya 2 Road and South Pattaya Road and cost B10 to *KFC* or up to B30 to Thanon Wat Boonkanjana. Songthaews **to Naklua**, beyond north Pattaya, head north from the junction of Pattaya 2 Road and Central Pattaya Road and cost B10 to Naklua Soi 12.

Motorbike rental is available everywhere from B200 per day, but beware of faulty vehicles, and of scams – sometimes rented bikes get stolen by touts keen to keep the customer's deposit, so you may want to use your own lock. Avis **car rental** (ⓦwww.avisthailand.com) have offices inside the *Dusit Resort* (ⓣ038 361627) and the *Hard Rock Hotel* (ⓣ038 428755) in North Pattaya; Budget (ⓣ038 710717, ⓦwww.budget.co.th) has an office in Tipp Plaza on Beach Road, between sois 10 and 11; and many of the motorbike touts also rent out jeeps for about B1200 per day.

Accommodation

There's no travellers' scene in Pattaya and **hotels** offering doubles under B450 outside low season are almost impossible to find; the cheapest alternatives are often rooms above the bars on sois 6, 13/2, 13/3 and 13/4.

Areca Lodge 198/21 Soi Saisong 13 (aka Soi Diana Inn), Central Pattaya ⓣ038 410123, ⓦwww.arecalodge.com. Unusually stylish place for Pattaya, with pleasantly furnished air-con rooms in two wings built around two swimming pools, all of them with balconies. Wi-fi in public areas. ❻

The Cottage Off Pattaya 2 Rd, North Pattaya ⓣ038 425650, ⓦwww.thecottagepattaya.com. Good-value, simply furnished semi-detached brick bungalows, all with air-con, pleasantly set among tall trees within a mature tropical garden away from the main road but opposite the Central Festival shopping centre. Facilities include two small swimming pools and wi-fi in most rooms. ❺

Diana Dragon Apartment 198/16 Soi Saisong 13 (aka Soi Diana Inn), Central Pattaya ⓣ038 423928, ⓦwww.dianapattaya.co.th. This long-running Pattaya institution has the cheapest doubles in town, and they're good value considering the competition: huge and quite light, with either fan or air-con, plus use of the pool at *Diana Inn*, 100m away. Fan ❸, air-con ❹

Dusit Thani Pattaya 240/2 Pattaya Beach Road, North Pattaya ⓣ038 425611, ⓦwww.dusit.com. In the less sleazy part of town, this upper-bracket Thai chain hotel is one of only a few Beach Rd hotels to be actually on the beach (the others are the southern end). Sea-view rooms are worth paying extra for as the impressive panoramas take in the whole bay. ❾

GI Guest House 75/14 Soi 5 (Soi Post Office), off Beach Rd, Jomtien ⓣ038 232968, ⓔgitravel@gmail.com. Bright, cheery air-con rooms with TV in a small block across the road from the GI Tour office. Sea views cost a bit extra. ❹

Ice Inn Corner of Saisong 12 and Pattaya 2 Rd, Central Pattaya ⓣ038 720671, ⓦwww.iceinnpattaya.com. Cheap fan-cooled singles and reasonably priced doubles in this small thirty-room hotel behind a handicrafts shop a few metres from the busier bar-beer sois. Rooms are simple but are all en suite; all doubles have air-con. ❸–❹

Pattaya Marriott 218 Pattaya Beach Rd, Central Pattaya ⓣ038 412120, ⓦwww.marriotthotels.com/pyxmc. Located in the heart of the resort (attached to the Royal Garden Plaza shopping centre), and across the road from the beach, this international chain hotel is both very central and refreshingly calm, not least because it's designed around a huge swimming pool and tropical garden full of palms. Not surprisingly it's the first choice for anyone in Pattaya on business. Rooms are capacious and comfortable and have either pool- or sea view. Facilities include a spa, floodlit tennis courts, mountain-bike rental and a kids' club. ❹

Rabbit Resort Dongtan beachfront, Jomtien ⓣ038 303303, ⓦwww.rabbitresort.com. Beautiful place that's the most appealing option in Jomtien, and located on the nicest stretch of beach, the predominantly but not exclusively gay Dongtan Beach. Most accommodation is in teakwood cottages that are elegantly furnished with Thai fabrics and antiques and have garden-style bathrooms; there are also some "forest rooms" in a two-storey block. All are set around a tropical garden just metres off the beach. ⑨

Sandalay Resort Between sois 1 and 2, Pattaya Beach Rd, North Pattaya ⓣ038 422660, ⓦwww.sandalayresort.com. This hundred-room hotel with swimming pool is in the quieter northern part of town just across the road from the beach. It has contemporary-styled, well-designed, though quite small, standard air-con rooms plus impressively large deluxe versions. Both options are available with sea view and tiny balcony at extra cost, but all have free wi-fi. Good discounts often available. ⑦

Sheraton Pattaya Resort 437 Thanon Pratamnak (Cliff Rd), South Pattaya ⓣ038 259888, ⓦwww.starwoodhotels.com. Pattaya's best hotel is smaller and more intimate than most in its class and offers five-star rooms in its two hotel wings as well as in private pavilions. The beautiful series of freeform swimming pools is set within lush gardens – compensating for the minuscule private beach – though it's built on a hill so be prepared for lots of steps. You'll need transport to get to the shops and restaurants of downtown Pattaya. ⑨

Sugar Hut 391/18 Thanon Tabphaya, midway between South Pattaya and Jomtien ⓣ038 251686, ⓦwww.sugar-hut.com. The most characterful accommodation in Pattaya comprises a charming collection of 33 Ayutthaya-style traditional wooden bungalows set in a fabulously profuse garden with three swimming pools. The bungalows are in tropical-chic style, with low beds, open-roofed shower rooms, mosquito nets and private verandas; the more expensive ones have a sitting room as well. You'll need your own transport as it's nowhere near the restaurants, shops or sea. ⑧

Woodlands Hotel and Resort 164 Thanon Pattaya-Naklua, North Pattaya ⓣ038 421707, ⓦwww.woodland-resort.com. A quiet, unpretentious and welcoming family-friendly garden resort 100m north of the Dolphin Circle, 400m from a scruffy but quiet thread of beach. The quite elegant, wooden-floored air-con rooms are in two storeys set round the pools and garden; the most expensive in each category have direct access to the pool from ground-floor balconies. Broadband throughout. ⑦–⑧

The resort

Many tourists in Pattaya spend the days recovering from the night before, but there's an increasing number of other resort-style attractions, including theme parks, watersports facilities, dive centres and golf courses.

Theme parks and indoor attractions

One of Pattaya's most enjoyable indoor attractions is **Ripley's Believe It Or Not** (daily 11am–11pm; B380, kids B280), on the third floor of the Royal Garden Plaza on Pattaya Beach Road. It's part of a worldwide chain of museums-of-the-bizarre inspired by the collections of American cartoonist and adventurer Robert Leroy Ripley. The Pattaya branch is good fun, featuring plenty of amusing and outlandish curios from Thailand and beyond – everything from shrunken heads and models of the world's tallest, smallest and fattest men to an exhibition on sharks.

Mini Siam (daily 8am–10pm; B300, kids B150) is just what it sounds like: the cream of Thailand's finest monuments reconstructed to 1:25 scale, plus miniature replicas of international icons such as the Sydney Opera House and the Statue of Liberty. It's just north of the North Pattaya Road/Thanon Sukhumvit intersection but you can arrange free transport if you call ⓣ038 727333. Advertised as the only one of its kind in the world, the nearby **Bottle Art Museum** (daily 9am–6.30pm; B200/100), just south of the North Pattaya Road/Thanon Sukhumvit intersection, also deals in miniatures, in this case extraordinarily tiny versions encased in bottles; among the three hundred delicately hand-crafted pieces, painstakingly assembled inside the bottles by their Dutch creator, are Dutch windmills, Thai temples, a Saudi mosque and a British coach and horses.

The hugely ambitious **Sanctuary of Truth**, or **Wang Boran** (daily 8am–5pm; B500, kids B250; ⓣ038 225407, ⓦwww.sanctuaryoftruth.com; daily dolphin shows at 11.30am & 3pm), is also a kind of replica, but on a 1:1 scale. Conceived by the man behind the Muang Boran Ancient City complex near Bangkok, it's a majestic 105-metre-high temple-palace built entirely of wood and designed to evoke the great ancient Khmer sanctuaries of Angkor. Though begun in 1981, it is still a work-in-progress, its external walls covered in a growing gallery of beautiful, symbolic woodcarvings inspired by Cambodian, Chinese, Thai and Indian mythologies. The Sanctuary occupies a dramatic seaside spot, behind imposing crenellated walls off the west end of Naklua Soi 12, close to the *Garden Sea View* hotel; from Central Pattaya, take a Naklua-bound songthaew as far as Soi 12, then a motorbike taxi.

If you've been disappointed with local reef life, the small and expensive but rather beautiful aquarium at **Underwater World** (daily 9am–6pm; B450, kids B250 or free if under 90cm tall; Ⓦwww.underwaterworldpattaya.com) might make up for it with its trio of long fibreglass tunnels that transport you through shallow rocks pools to the ocean floor; there are touch pools and masses of reef fish and you can also arrange to dive with the resident sharks and rays. It's on Thanon Sukhumvit, just south of the Thep Prasit junction, near Tesco Lotus.

Diving, snorkelling, watersports and golf

Though Pattaya's reefs are far less spectacular than those along the Andaman Coast, it can be dived year-round, and underwater visibility is consistent. Most **dive trips** focus on the group of "outer islands" about 25km from shore, which include Ko Rin, Ko Man Wichai and Ko Klung Badaan, where you have a reasonable chance of seeing barracuda, moray eels and blue-spotted stingrays. There are also three rewarding wreck dives in the Samae San/Sattahip area. Be careful when choosing a **dive operator** as there are plenty of charlatans around. One of the most reputable is the PADI Five-Star National Geographic Dive Centre Mermaid's Dive Centre, which has branches next to *Siam Bayview* hotel between sois 10 and 11 on Beach Road in Central Pattaya, and on Soi White House in Jomtien; its head office is on Thanon Tabphaya in Jomtien (Ⓣ038 303333, Ⓦwww.mermaiddive.com). It charges B2990 for two dives,

▲ Walking Street, Pattaya

with accompanying snorkellers paying B1000, and B14,000 for the four-day Openwater course.

All tour agents sell **snorkelling** trips to nearby islands, the majority of them going to the reefs and beaches of **Ko Larn**. You can also make your own way to Ko Larn by public boat from the Bali Hai pier at the far southern end of Walking Street (approximately hourly 7am–6.30pm; 45min; B20). Beachfront stalls in Pattaya and Jomtien offer **water-skiing**, **jet-skiing** and **parasailing**, but for **windsurfing** you need to go to the Pattaya City Windsurfing Club opposite Soi 6 in Jomtien (B400 per hour). The more family-oriented **Pattaya Park Water Park** (daily 11am–10pm; ⓣ038 251201, ⓦwww.pattayapark.com), whose gigantic 240-metre-high tower on Buddha Hill, at the far northern end of Jomtien, is visible from all over the resort, features water slides, a Viking ship, a 170-metre tower jump, and other funfair-style rides, as well as panoramic revolving restaurants, 52 floors up. Jomtien songthaews will drop you about 750m from the entrance.

On dry land, there are over fifteen international-standard **golf courses** within easy reach of Pattaya (ⓦwww.thaigolfer.com), some of them designed by famous golfers; visitors' green fees start at around B1000.

Eating

In among the innumerable low-grade Western cafés that dominate Pattaya's **restaurant** scene are a few much classier joints serving good, sophisticated cuisine – at top-end prices. For the cheapest, most authentic Thai food, just head for the nearest of Pattaya's myriad building sites and you'll find street stalls catering to the construction-site workers.

Bruno's 306/63 Chateau Dale Plaza, Thanon Tabphaya, Jomtien ⓦwww.brunos-pattaya.com. A local institution that's a favourite with expats celebrating special occasions. The food is upscale, expensive, European – Provençal-style rack of lamb, sirloin steak, dark-chocolate mousse – and there's a cellar of some 150 wines. Main dishes from B200. Daily noon–2.30pm & 6pm–late.

Khao Suay Ground Floor, Central Festival Centre, Pattaya 2 Rd, North Pattaya. A long menu of good modern Thai food (most mains about B110) draws Thai families to this tiny café inside the shopping centre. The varied options include prawns with long beans and chillis, fish and tamarind soup, and Isaan sausage salad.

King Seafood Opposite Soi 15, Walking St, South Pattaya. Considered to be the best of South Pattaya's three famously enormous seafront seafood restaurants, at the heart of super-seedy Walking Street. Tiger prawns, giant lobsters and the rest for B150–300. Daily 11am–1am.

Mantra *Amari Orchid* hotel, Beach Rd, North Pattaya ⓦwww.mantra-pattaya.com. Setting the standard unexpectedly high for Pattaya, this large, beautifully designed bar-restaurant creates an ambience somewhere between a contemporary Shanghai hotel and a maharaja's palace with its silken drapes, lacquered shuttering, cosy romantic booths and burnished amber glow throughout. Downstairs there's an open-plan view of the five different, equally eclectic kitchens specializing in Japanese, Chinese, Thai, Indian and Mediterranean food. A meal might begin with avocado sushi, supplemented with bite-sized Peking duck, continue with seafood linguine, and end with lemon grass and pandanus crème brulée. The walk-in wine cellar keeps over 150 imported wines. Mains B270–600. Daily 5–11pm, Sunday brunch 11am–3pm.

Minus Five Supperclub *Amari Nova Suites*, Soi Sukrudee, North Pattaya ⓣ038 489488, ⓦwww.minus5pattaya.com. A copycat version of Bangkok's ultra-trendy *Bed Supperclub*, *Minus Five* brings a welcome dash of style to Pattaya's dining scene. Here, you loll on comfy loungers in an all-white diner as you're served a three-course dinner of modern Pacific-fusion cuisine (goats cheese and pomegranate salad, steamed monkfish with bacon and cider) for B950; there's a live band until 10pm and house music until closing. The super-cool *Icebar* is in the same building. Nightly from 6pm, last orders at midnight.

The Orangery By the Sea The Avenue plaza, Pattaya 2 Rd, Central Pattaya. Like its Bangkok sister in the Siam Paragon mall, this invitingly summery conservatory of a restaurant serves several different cuisines – Thai, Chinese, Russian,

French – prepared in discrete kitchens, so a typical meal might feature shrimp spring rolls, *matsaman* curry and *crêpe suzette*. A major draw is that after 6pm you get to sit on swing seats on the plant-filled roof terrace: a great spot for sipping delicious berry smoothies and forgetting where you are. Mains B160–400.

PIC Kitchen Soi 5, North Pattaya. One of Pattaya's top traditional Thai restaurants, set in a stylish series of teak buildings with the option of Thai-style cushion seating. Elegantly presented curries, lots of different seafood platters (served grilled or fried, laced with chilli and/or coconut, or accompanied by asparagus and mushroom), spicy salads and some vegetarian dishes. Mains from B150. Daily 11am–2pm & 6–11pm.

Sea Falcon Dongtan beachfront, Jomtien. Popular, mid-priced almost-on-the beach restaurant known for its lobster and steak. There's even a three-course lobster blowout (featuring bisque and thermidor) for B600.

Sugar Hut 391/18 Thanon Tabphaya, Jomtien. Attached to the charming hotel of the same name (see p.440), this restaurant gives you the chance to soak up the ambience and enjoy the tropical gardens without shelling out for a bungalow (though the food's not cheap either). Meals are served in an open-sided *sala* and the menu is mainly classy Thai; recommendations include fried catfish in coconut milk and chilli, and chicken baked with pineapple. Set menus from B500–750.

Drinking, nightlife and entertainment

Entertainment is Pattaya's *raison d'être* and the **nightlife** is what most tourists come for, as do expats from Laem Chabang port, oilfield workers from the Arabian Gulf and shore-leave marines on R&R. Of the thousand plus bars in the resort, the vast majority are staffed by women and men whose aim is to get bought for the night. Sex makes more money than booze in Pattaya – depending on who you believe, there are between six thousand and twenty thousand Thais working in Pattaya's **sex industry**; most depressing of all is that this workforce includes children as young as 10, despite fairly frequent high-profile paedophile arrests. It is, however, just about possible to have a night out without getting entangled in sleaze, either at one of the growing number of hostess-free **bars** listed below, a few of which are surprisingly style-conscious, or at one of the **family-oriented** cabarets and cultural extravaganzas.

However you choose to spend your evening, be warned that Pattaya is notorious for its transvestite **pickpockets** who target drunk men walking home in the early hours: while one "distracts" the victim from the front, the other extracts the wallet from behind.

Bars

The vast majority of Pattaya's bars are open-air "**bar-beers**", which group themselves in neon clusters all over North, Central and South Pattaya so that there's barely a 500-metre stretch of road without its rowdy enclave. The setup is the same in all of them: from mid-afternoon the punters – usually lone males – sit on stools around a brashly lit circular bar, behind which the hostesses keep the drinks, bawdy chat and well-worn jokes flowing. Beer is generally inexpensive, the atmosphere low-key and good-humoured, and, though most of the hostesses are aiming to score for the night, couples as well as single women drinkers are almost always made welcome.

Drinks are a lot more expensive in the bouncer-guarded **go-go bars** on Walking Street in South Pattaya, where near-naked hostesses serve the beer and live sex shows keep the boozers hooked through the night. The scene follows much the same pattern as in Patpong, Nana and Soi Cowboy in Bangkok, with the women dancing on a small stage in the hope they might be bought for the night – or the week. Go-go dancers, shower shows and striptease are also the mainstays of the **gay scene**, centred on Pattayaland Soi 3 (Soi 13/5), South Pattaya.

Despite the proliferation of lonely men and business-minded working girls, there are more and more **bars** aimed at couples, families and singles who just want a fun, even sophisticated, night out, the best of which are listed here.

The Blues Factory Soi Lucky Star, Walking Street, South Pattaya ⓦwww.thebluesfactorypattaya.com. Considered to be the best live-music venue in Pattaya, with nightly sets (except Mondays) from the famously charismatic rock guitarist Lam Morrison and his band, and (except on Wed) from the house blues band as well. Happy hour 8.30–10pm.

Gulliver's Traveler's Tavern Pattaya Beach Rd, north of Soi 1, North Pattaya. Like its branches on Bangkok's Khao San and Sukhumvit roads, this is a big-screen sports pub with pool tables, wi-fi and a streetside beer-garden.

Heineken Beer Garden Central Festival Centre, Pattaya 2 Road, North Pattaya. Outdoor tables and live music nightly (from about 8pm) from Thai singers and bands, doing mostly Thai pop and country.

Hopf Brew House Pattaya Beach Rd, between sois 13/1 (Yamato) and 13/2 (Post Office), Central Pattaya. Cavernous and very popular air-con beer hall that brews its own Pilsener and wheat beer, serves generous wood-fired pizzas and stages live music nightly. Attracts a youngish crowd, including vacationing couples.

Jazz Pit Soi 5, North Pattaya. Nightly live jazz (from 8pm) from the in-house trio in the cosy lounge-bar adjacent to the *PIC Kitchen* restaurant, and occasional high-profile celeb jamming sessions.

Kum Punn Pub Soi 2, North Pattaya. Typically Thai take on a country-and-western bar (lots of wood and the occasional buffalo head) that's known for its live bands who play nightly sets of authentic Thai folk music as well as soft rock.

Minus Five Ice Bar *Amari Nova Suites*, Soi Sukrudee, North Pattaya ⓣ038 489488, ⓦwww.minus5pattaya.com. Your chance to literally chillout at this cube of a bar sculpted entirely from ice, right down to the draught beer kegs on the ice-cold counter. For B500 (or B300 before 8pm) you get lent a winter coat and mittens and are given 20min to down as many vodka shots as you can. Then it's back out into the warmth of the trendy Bangkok-style bar adjacent, or to the *Supperclub* restaurant next door (see p.442). Phone for free transport for groups of four or more. 6pm–2am.

Shenanigans The Avenue plaza, Pattaya 2 Rd, Central Pattaya; and Jomtien Complex Condotel, Thanon Tabphaya, Jomtien. Both branches of this long-established Irish pub keep Guinness, Kilkenny Bitter and John Smith, serve UK-style pub food, and show big-screen sports. Leather sofas, pool tables plus free internet and wi-fi are additional draws, not to mention the 4.30–7pm happy hour.

Cabarets

Tour groups – and families – constitute the main audience at Pattaya's **transvestite cabarets**. Glamorous and highly professional, these shows are performed three times a night at Alcazar, opposite Soi 4 on Pattaya 2 Road in North Pattaya (daily 6pm, 8pm & 9.30pm); and at Tiffany's, north of Soi 1 on Pattaya 2 Road in North Pattaya (daily 6pm, 7.30pm & 9pm). Each theatre has a troupe of sixty or more transvestites who run through twenty musical-style numbers in fishnets and crinolines, ball gowns and leathers, against ever more lavish stage sets. All glitz and no sleaze, the shows cost from B500 per person. The even more ambitious **cultural extravaganza** staged by Alangkarn in southern Jomtien (Thurs–Tues from 6pm; B1000) features a highly theatrical medley of Thai classical dance, martial arts, acrobatics and pyrotechnics, while Tuxedo Magic Castle, north of Central Festival on Pattaya 2 Road, North Pattaya, is a family-friendly show of classic **magic tricks and illusions** (shows nightly from 6.30pm; B450, kids B225). Any tour agent will organize tickets and transport to all the above shows.

Listings

Airlines Fairtex Arcade, 179/85–212, North Pattaya Rd ⓣ038 412382; Thai Airways, inside the *Dusit Resort*, North Pattaya ⓣ038 420995.

Bookshops Very good English-language selections at DK Books on Soi 13/2 and at the Beach Rd/Central Pattaya Rd junction; and at Bookazine, in

The Avenue, Central Festival and Royal Garden shopping plazas. One of Pattaya's best second-hand bookshops is Thais4Life (Mon–Sat noon–6pm; ⓦwww.thais4life.com) at 504 Soi Yensabai Condotel, off Soi 17 (Soi VC), South Pattaya; run as a charity, it sells all its books for B80 and donates profits to medical and other needy projects including Baan Jing Jai orphanage.
Cinemas Several English-language screenings a day at the multiplexes: Major Cineplex, The Avenue plaza, Pattaya 2 Rd, Central Pattaya; Central Cineplex, Central Festival Centre, Pattaya 2 Rd, North Pattaya; and Royal Garden Plaza, South Pattaya.
Emergencies For all emergencies, call the tourist police on the free, 24hr phone line ⓣ1155 or contact them at their office beside TAT on Buddha Hill, between South Pattaya and Jomtien. Pattaya's main police station is more central, on Beach Rd, between sois 8 and 9, in Central Pattaya (ⓣ038 425937).
Hospitals and dentists The best-equipped hospital is the private Bangkok-Pattaya Hospital ⓣ1719 or 038 259999 ⓦwww.bangkokpattaya hospital.com on Thanon Sukhumvit, about 400m north of the intersection with North Pattaya Rd. It also has dental services, as does the private Pattaya International Hospital on Soi 4 ⓣ038 428374, ⓦwww.pih-inter.com.
Immigration office Soi 5, off Jomtien Beach Road, Jomtien (Mon–Fri 8.30am–4.30pm; ⓣ038 252750). Many travel agents offer cheap visa-renewal day-trips to Cambodia, including Five Star Visa Runs on Soi 13, South Pattaya ⓣ038 416088.
Massage In among the full-body soaps and "full-service" massage joints you'll find the innocent Thai Massage Development School (Soi Yodsak, Central Pattaya; daily 10am–10pm; ⓣ038 414115), where you can have a proper traditional massage (B300 per 60min) and also learn Thai massage (60hr over two weeks; B5000).
Shopping The main shopping plazas – the Avenue, Pattaya 2 Rd, South Pattaya; Central Festival Centre, Pattaya 2 Rd, North Pattaya; and Royal Garden Plaza in South Pattaya – are all good for designer boutiques, international brands and smart gift and handicraft outlets.
Yoga and fitness The huge, sleek California Wow fitness centre at The Avenue, Pattaya 2 Rd, Central Pattaya (daily 6am–11pm; ⓣ038 399999, ⓦwww.californiawowx.com), issues B800 day passes covering full use of all the gym equipment plus access to the many daily yoga and fitness classes.

Rayong

Few farang travellers choose to stop for longer than they have to in the busy and rapidly expanding provincial capital of **RAYONG**, 65km southeast of Pattaya, whose main concern is the Eastern Seaboard's petrochemical and shipping industries. But it's a useful place for **bus connections**, particularly if you're travelling between the east coast and the northeast or north (see p.488 for destinations), or if you're trying to get to Ko Samet; Ban Phe, the ferry pier for Ko Samet, is about 17km east and served by frequent songthaews from Rayong bus station (every 30min; 20min).

If you get stuck in town overnight, try the basic but serviceable fan and air-con **rooms** at *Burapa Palace*, 100m east of the bus station at 69 Thanon Sukhumvit (ⓣ038 622946; ③), or the huge, upscale business-oriented *Star Hotel* (ⓣ038 614901, ⓦwww.starhotel.th.com; ⑤) just behind and to the west of the bus station, near the lively market, on Soi 4 of the Rayong Trade Centre complex.

The region's best **hospital**, the private Bangkok-Rayong Hospital (ⓣ038 921999, ⓦwww.rayonghospital.com), is on Soi Saengchan Neramit, on the southwest edge of town. The **TAT office** (ⓣ038 655420, ⓔtatryong@tat.or.th) for the Rayong region and Ko Samet is inconveniently located 7km east of Rayong town centre at 153/4 Thanon Sukhumvit (Highway 3), on the way to Ban Phe; any Ban Phe-bound bus or songthaew will drop you at its door.

Ko Samet

Blessed with the softest, squeakiest sand within weekending distance of Bangkok, the tiny island of **KO SAMET**, which measures just 6km from top to toe, is a favourite escape for Thais, expats and tourists. Its fourteen small but dazzlingly white beaches are breathtakingly beautiful, lapped by pale blue water and in places still shaded by coconut palms and the occasional cajeput (*samet*) tree that gave the island its name. But they are also crowded, developed to full capacity with over fifty sprawling, albeit low-rise bungalow developments, a disfiguring number of which pay scant attention to landscaping and rubbish disposal. It's a sobering state of affairs considering that much of the island's coastline has been protected as part of the Khao Laem Ya – Mu Ko Samet **national park** since 1981; all visitors to Ko Samet are required to pay the standard national park fee on arrival (B200, 3–14-year-olds B100), and most hoteliers also pay rent to park authorities, but there's little evidence that this income has been used to improve the island's infrastructure.

Samet's best **beaches** are along the **east coast**, where you'll find nearly all the bungalow resorts, though there's one rather exclusive beach on the otherwise largely inaccessible west coast, and the north-coast shoreline retains a pleasingly village ambience. Most islanders and many resort staff live in the **northeast**, near the island's main pier, in the ramshackle, badly drained village of **Na Dan**, which has small shops and cheap foodstalls as well as Samet's only school, health centre and wat. A few narrow tracks, mostly signed at crucial junctions, cross the island's forested central ridge to link the east and west coasts with the trans-island dirt-road, but much of the **interior** is dense jungle, home to hornbills, gibbons and spectacular butterflies. The evergreen vegetation belies the fact that there are no rivers on this unusually dry island, which gets only scant rainfall in an average year. Lack of rain is another plus point for tourists, though it means water is a precious and expensive commodity as it has to be trucked in from the mainland.

The trend across the island is upmarket and in high season you'll be hard pressed to secure an en-suite bungalow for under B700, though a few simple no-frills B300 huts do remain. The most backpacker-oriented beaches are east-coast **Ao Hin Kok**, **Ao Phai** and **Ao Tub Tim**, with Ao Hin Kok and Ao Phai both quite lively in the evenings; the travellers' vibe at nearby **Ao Nuan** is more alternative, with **Ao Thian** and north-coast **Ao Noi Na** also worth investigating. **Hat Sai Kaew** and **Ao Wong Duan** are the biggest centres on the east coast, dominated by upper scale accommodation aimed at families, package tourists and Bangkok trendies. Samet's super-deluxe accommodation is on west-coast **Ao Phrao** and southern beauty **Ao Kiu**.

All beaches get packed on **weekends** and national holidays, when booking ahead is advisable, though, unusually for Thailand, walk-in guests are often offered the best rates. Many bungalow managers raise their prices by sixty percent during peak periods and sometimes for weekenders as well: the rates quoted here are typical weekday high-season rates.

Getting to Ko Samet

The mainland departure-point for Ko Samet is the small coastal town of **BAN PHE**, 17km east of Rayong, 80km southeast of Pattaya, and about 200km from Bangkok. It's served by hourly buses **from Bangkok**'s Eastern (Ekamai) Bus Terminal, by songthaews from the nearby provincial capital of **Rayong** (which has bus connections to many towns; see p.488), and by fast but cramped tourist minibuses from Bangkok's **Thanon Khao San** (about 4hr; B250) and **Pattaya**

▲ Ban Phe

▲ Ban Phe

▲ Ban Phe

N

0 1 km

Ao Noi Na

Na Dan Pier
Taxis ★

Health Centre
7-Eleven
& ATM
Police
Taxis

National Park
Visitors' Centre

Ao Prao

★ Taxis

Hat Sai Kaew

Ao Hin Kok

Ao Phai

Ao Tub Tim

Laem Ruataek

Ao Nuan

Ao Cho

Taxis

National Park Booth

Ao Wong Duan

Ao Thian

Ao Lung Dum

Ao Wai

Ao Kiu Na Nok

Ao Kiu Na Nai

Laem Khut

Ao Pakarang

Ko Chan

ACCOMMODATION

Ao Nuan	T
Ao Phai Hut	N
Ao Prao Resort	E
Baan Pou Paan	C
Blue House	D
Blue Sky Bungalow	U
Candlelight Resort	Y
Jelly Fish Lung Dum	Z
Jep's Bungalow	M
Laemyai Hut Home	H
Le Vimarn Cottages	I
Lima Bella	F
Lima Coco	G
Lost Resort	O
Mooban Talay Resort	A
Naga Bungalows	L
Paradee Resort and Spa	bb
Pudsa Bungalows	R
Sai Kaew Beach Resort	J
Samed Resort	B
Samed Villa	Q
Sametville Resort	aa
Sang Thian Beach Resort	X
Silver Sand	P
Sinsamut	K
Ton Sak Resort	S
Tub Tim Resort	V
Vong Deuan Resort	W
Vongduern Villa	W

EATING & DRINKING

Banana Bar	3
Buzz	4
Ploy Samed Restaurant	2
Ploy Talay	5
Summer	1

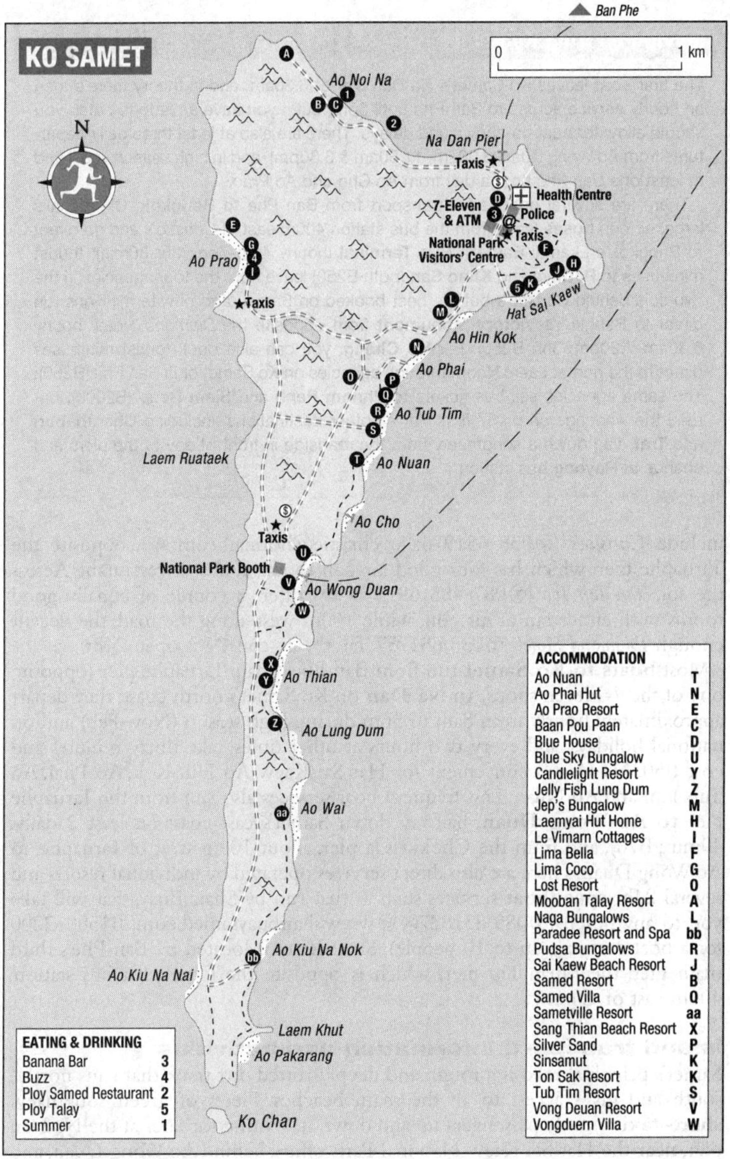

(about 90min; B230). A meter-taxi ride from **Suvarnabhumi Airport** should cost around B2000. Coming by bus from **Chanthaburi** or **Trat**, you'll most likely be dropped on Highway 3, from where a songthaew or motorbike taxi will take you the remaining 5km to the Ban Phe piers.

The area around Ban Phe's main Taruaphe pier-head has many **tour desks** selling onward bus tickets and private transfers, plus minimarkets, internet centres and the well-stocked Blue Sky second-hand bookshop. Places **to stay**

Moving on from Ko Samet

The first **boat** leaves Ko Samet's Na Dan pier at 6.30am, and in theory there's then an hourly service across to Ban Phe until 6pm, but if you have a plane to catch you should allow for boat no-shows and delays. There are also at least three daily departures from Ao Wong Duan (8.30am, 11.30am & 3.30pm), and in high season you'll find at least one Ban Phe boat a day from Ao Cho and Ao Prao.

There are several options for transport from Ban Phe **to Bangkok**. Cherdchai's large, air-con **buses** leave from the bus station 400m east of *Christie's* and go direct to Bangkok's Ekamai **Eastern Bus Terminal** (hourly 4am–7pm; 3hr 30min); tourist minibuses to **Pattaya** and **Khao San** (both B250) leave from the tour agencies in the two sois behind *Christie's* but are best booked on Samet; and private minivans run direct to Bangkok's **Victory Monument** from opposite the *Diamond Hotel* (hourly 6.30am–7.30pm; 3hr; B250). For **Ko Chang**, you can also book tourist minibuses direct to the port at Laem Ngop, through agencies on Ko Samet or in Ban Phe (B250). The same agencies sell bus tickets to **Phnom Penh** and **Siem Reap** (B2000), but read the warnings on p.457 first. For all other destinations, including **Chanthaburi** and **Trat**, flag down a songthaew from the roadside in front of any of the piers and change at **Rayong** bus station.

include *Christie's* (ⓣ038 651976; Je_christie@hotmail.com; ❸), opposite the Taruaphe pier, which has four good air-con rooms above its restaurant. Across the soi, *Tan Tan Too* (ⓣ087 485 6913 ❷–❸) offers a couple of equally good rooms with either fan or air-con, while 100m west along the road, the decent enough *Diamond Hotel* (ⓣ038 651757; fan ❷, air-con ❸) is open 24hr.

Most **boats to Ko Samet** run from Ban Phe's main Taruaphe pier (opposite one of the 7-Eleven shops) **to Na Dan** on Ko Samet's north coast; they depart approximately hourly from 8am to 5pm during high season (Nov–Feb) and on national holidays, and every two hours at other times, take thirty minutes and cost B50. Na Dan is convenient for Hat Sai Kaew, Ao Hin Kok, Ao Phai, Ao Tub Tim and Ao Nuan. Less frequent boat services also run from the Taruaphe pier **to Ao Wong Duan**, halfway down Samet's east coast (at least 2 daily; 40min; B70), and from the Chokkrisda pier, about 100m west of Taruaphe, to Ao Wong Duan. There are also direct services operated by individual resorts and several 24hr **speedboat** services such as that run by Shair Buay, that will take you to any beach (ⓣ089 8316270, ⓦwww.shairbuaysamed.com; B1500–2200 for a boat carrying up to 10 people); Shair Buay is located by Ban Phe's third main pier, the Nuan Tip pier, which is opposite the Cherdchai bus station, 400m east of *Christie's*.

Island transport, information and activities

Samet's principal road is a rough and deeply rutted dirt track that runs north–south and gives access to all the main beaches. Fleets of green songthaew **share-taxis** shuttle passengers up and down it, waiting for fares at the Na Dan pier, near the Hat Sai Kaew National Park office, behind Ao Wong Duan, and at Ao Prao; they will also pick up from accommodation if you get staff to phone them. Transfer rates are fixed and are generally charged per trip not per person, with most routes (eg Na Dan to Ao Prao or Hat Sai Kaew to Wong Duan) costing B200–B250. You need to be pretty confident to negotiate the mud and potholes on a **motorbike**, available for rent at Na Dan pier and on almost every beach (B400 per day), which is why it's become fashionable to rent a lumbering four-wheeled ATV instead, either from the Na Dan pier-head or via hotels elsewhere (from B1500 per 24hr).

Shops and stalls in Na Dan and on all the main beaches sell basic travellers' necessities. There are **ATMs** at the Na Dan pier-head, beside the Hat Sai Kaew national park office and on Ao Wong Duan; the bigger bungalows also change money. There are **internet centres** around the National Park office on the Na Dan road, a couple of which have wi-fi, and on almost every beach, and the island's **post office** is at *Naga Bungalows* on Ao Hin Kok. CP Travel on Hat Sai Kaew (ⓣ038 644136), in the beach-access arcade near the National Park office, sells domestic and international **air tickets** as well as bus and minibus tickets for onward travel. It also sells a few new books. Ko Samet's **health centre** and **police station** (ⓣ038 644111) are on the Na Dan–Hat Sai Kaew road, but for anything serious you should go to the Bangkok-Rayong hospital in Rayong (see p.445). Many bungalows have **safety deposits** and it's worth making use of them: theft is an issue on Samet and there are occasional instances of drinks being spiked by freelance bar-girls and punters waking next day without their valuables.

Samet has no decent coral reefs of its own, so you'll have to take a boat trip to the islands of Ko Kudi, Ko Thalu and Ko Mun, off the northeast coast, to get good **snorkelling** (from B500 from most beaches) or **diving**; Ploy Scuba on Hat Sai Kaew charges B2700 for two dives and B15,000 for the four-day PADI Openwater course (ⓣ038 644 212, ⓦwww.ployscuba.com). From the main beaches you can also organize **boat trips** around Samet itself (from B350), rent kayaks and jet skis and arrange banana boat rides and parasailing.

Hat Sai Kaew and Na Dan

From **NA DAN** pier, a ten-minute walk south along the road brings you to **HAT SAI KAEW**, or Diamond Beach, named for its long and extraordinarily beautiful stretch of luxuriant sand, so soft and clean it squeaks underfoot – a result, apparently, of its unusually high silicon content. Unsurprisingly, it's the busiest beach on Samet, its shorefront packed with bungalows, restaurants, beachwear stalls, deckchairs and parasols, though the northern end is slightly more peaceful.

Accommodation

Much of the **accommodation** here is crammed uncomfortably close together and prices are high. Cheap rooms are sometimes available above the shops and restaurants on the Na Dan road.

Blue House On the Na Dan Rd ⓣ086 332 5903. Budget, mostly windowless singles and simple en-suite fan and air-con options in two different locations on the Na Dan road. Fan ②, air-con ③

Laemyai Hut Home ⓣ038 644282. The fan bungalows here are the best of the cheapest options on this beach, not least because they're dotted round a shaded sandy garden in one of the prettiest spots, under the Laem Yai headland at the quieter northern end. Fan bungalows are simple, with platform beds; air-con versions are also available. Fan ④, air-con ⑤

Lima Bella ⓣ02 938 1811, ⓦwww.limabella.com. This hip but invitingly homely little garden haven occupies a quiet heliconia-filled plot with its own pretty swimming pool, about 3min walk from the beach. Its 26 architecturally striking, design-conscious air-con rooms have daybeds, DVD players and free wi-fi; some have separate mezzanine bedrooms or living areas and many have bathtubs. The ambience is more intimate and private than most hotels on Samet and it's popular with families. It's expensive, but discounts are often available on request. ⑧

Sai Kaew Beach Resort ⓣ038 644197, ⓦwww.samedresorts.com. This popular and highly efficient resort has over 150 rooms, most of them in distinctive and thoughtfully if quite simply designed blue-and-white air-con bungalows; many have their own tiny lawn, and the priciest have uninterrupted sea views. The "deluxe cottages" occupy their own grassy haven with swimming pool, in front of a separate and pretty but minute little patch of sandy shoreline; they have garden bathrooms and private decks. ⑧–⑨

Sinsamut ⓣ038 644134, ⓦwww.sinsamut-kohsamed.com. Initial appearances aren't encouraging here, with various types of rooms stuffed into cheek-by-jowl little blocks behind the restaurant midway down the beach, but most rooms are pleasant inside, with bright, contemporary decor, and some have outdoor space. The quirky fan-cooled "*katom*" bungalows, set around a grassy little roof garden, enjoy the best outlook. Fan ❹, air-con ❺

Ton Sak Resort ⓣ038 644314, ⓦwww.tonsak.com. The timbered cabins here are packed very close together, but the surrounding borders of shrubs add a little privacy, and few are more than 100m from the water. Interiors are comfortable if a little old-fashioned, and have air-con and modern bathrooms. ❼–❽

Eating and drinking

At sundown the deckchairs give way to the low tables, mats and cushions that the **restaurants** spread out along the sand. By far the most popular is *Ploy Talay*, which, like many other places on Hat Sai Kaew, serves barbecued seafood dinners, buffet style, plus à la carte choices, but livens up proceedings with nightly entertainment from its Filipino cover band and its troupe of athletic fire-jugglers, who spark up around 8.30pm. Away from the sea, the growing number of congenial little bars and restaurants on the Na Dan road tend to serve cheaper and more interesting menus; in particular, the tiny *Banana Bar*, not far from the police station, serves tastily authentic yellow, green and *matsaman* curries, as well as *tom yum* and spicy salads.

Ao Hin Kok

Separated from Hat Sai Kaew by a low promontory on which sits a mermaid statue (a reference to the early nineteenth-century poem, *Phra Abhai Mani*, by famous local poet Sunthorn Phu), **AO HIN KOK** is much smaller than its neighbour, and has more of a travellers' vibe. Just three sets of bungalows overlook the petite white-sand beach from the slope on the far side of the dirt road, and you can walk here from Na Dan in about fifteen minutes.

The long-running, consciously traveller-focussed, English-run *Naga Bungalows* (ⓣ038 644168, ⓔsuewildnaga@gmail.com; ❷–❸) has some of the cheapest **accommodation** on Ko Samet, with prices consistent year round

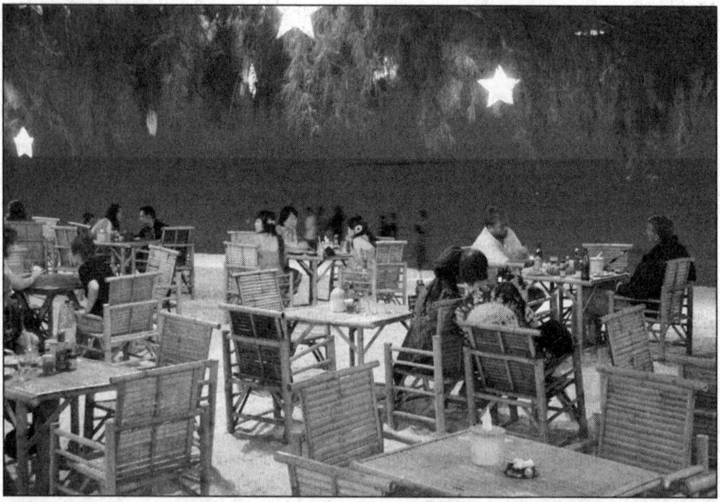

▲ Beach restaurant, Ao Hin Kok, Ko Samet

and at weekends. It offers simple bamboo and wood huts stacked in tiers up the slope, with decks, mosquito nets and shared bathrooms, as well as pricier concrete bungalows with their own adjacent bathroom. Its restaurant does lots of vegetarian dishes, and sells home-made bread, cakes and pizzas. Next door but one, *Jep's Bungalow* (ⓣ038 644112, ⓦwww.jepbungalow.com; fan ❷–❸, air ❺–❼) has a spread of options in unremarkable wooden chalets and concrete bungalows, the latter with air-con and TV and ranged up the shady, terraced, sandy-soiled garden. It has internet access and a tour desk and a **restaurant**, which serves up a great menu of authentic Thai dishes (including popular *som tam* sets), seafood, Indian curries, Japanese food, brownies and the rest at its tables on the beach, set under trees strung with fairylights and given extra atmosphere by mellow music. A nearby cappuccino stall does various fresh and liqueur coffees.

Ao Phai

Narrow but sparkling little **AO PHAI**, around the next headland, is Samet's party beach, with the shoreside *Silver Sand* bar and disco known for its late-night dance music and fire-juggling shows fuelled by cocktails and buckets of vodka Red Bull (Saturday is unofficial gay night). Not everyone has to join in though, as the bungalows on the fringes of the bay are far enough away for a good night's sleep. There's a minimarket on the beach, a dive shop, tour service and exchange facilities, and you can walk to Na Dan pier in twenty minutes.

Ao Phai Hut (ⓣ038 644075; fan ❹, air-con ❺) sits on the rocky divide between Ao Phai and Hin Kok and offers a wide range of rather variable split-bamboo and concrete **huts**, the more basic ones set in a scruffy area among the trees, the pricier options, some of them with air-con, occupying a scenic spot overlooking the rocky end of the shore. At the centre of the beach, party-hub *Silver Sand* (ⓣ038 644301, ⓦwww.silversandresort.samet.i8.com; fan ❹, air-con ❺–❻) has a spread of well-turned-out rooms, including whitewashed, air-con chalets ranged around a pretty garden; they all come with safety boxes, verandas and good modern bathrooms, and some have polished wooden floors. The huge villa-style bungalows at well-managed *Samed Villa* (ⓣ038 644094, ⓦwww.samedvilla.com; ❻–❼) are packed into a fairly small area along the rocks at the southern end of the bay (good views from the front row) and up the slope behind the restaurant. Interiors are luxurious and well furnished and especially good for families; they all have air-con and TV and free tea and coffee. Immediately behind *Sea Breeze*, on the road to Wong Duan, the two-storey block that is *Lost Resort* (ⓣ038 644041, ⓦwww.thelostresort.net; fan ❸, air-con ❺) sits peacefully in a grove of tall trees, just a couple of minutes' walk from the beach but with no sea view. The twelve rooms here can be fan or air-con and are of a good standard and well priced.

Ao Tub Tim

Also known as Ao Pudsa, **AO TUB TIM** is another cute white-sand bay sandwiched between rocky points, partly shaded with palms and backed by a wooded slope. It has just two bungalow operations and feels secluded, if a bit crowded, but is only a short stroll from Ao Phai and the other beaches further north, and a half-hour hike from Na Dan pier.

The most popular **place to stay** is the sprawling, well-run *Tub Tim Resort* (ⓣ038 644025, ⓦwww.tubtimresort.com; fan ❹–❺, air-con ❻–❼), with over sixty handsome chalet-style wooden bungalows of various sizes and designs, all with classy modern furnishings and outdoor space. Their restaurant is very good indeed, especially for Thai favourites like *haw mok* (fish curry steamed in banana leaf). At adjacent *Pudsa Bungalows* (Ⓣ038 644030; fan 4, air-con 6) you get large, sturdy huts, including some especially well located fan ones that sit on the northern rocks alongside the footpath (next to *Samet Villa*'s much pricier ones on neighbouring Ao Phai) and enjoy direct sea views.

Ao Nuan

Clamber up over the next headland (which gives you a fine panorama over Hat Sai Kaew) to reach Samet's smallest and most laid-back beach, the secluded **AO NUAN**. This is effectively the private domain of *Ao Nuan* bungalows (no phone; shared bathroom 4, en suite 6), whose octagonal veggie restaurant and simple, idiosyncratic huts hark back to a mellower, old-school island vibe, entirely removed from the commercialism of the other beaches (though room rates are definitely modern-day). The nine sturdy timber huts are each built to a slightly different design and dotted across the slope that drops down to the bay, with a few hanging right over the beach. The furnishing is spartan – the cheapest have just a platform bed and a mosquito net, and all but three share bathrooms – but they all have fans and 24-hour electricity and one has air-con. Because it's some way off the main track, the beach gets hardly any through-traffic and so feels quiet and private. Although not brilliant for swimming, the rocky shore reveals a good patch of sand when the tide withdraws; the more consistent beach at Ao Tub Tim is only five minutes' walk to the north and Ao Cho, which has some coral, is a five-minute walk south along the footpath.

Ao Wong Duan

The horseshoe bay of **AO WONG DUAN**, a ten-minute walk round the next-but-one point from Ao Nuan, is Samet's second most popular beach after Hat Sai Kaew. Though it's not as pretty and suffers even more from hordes of day-trippers, it does offer some attractive upscale accommodation; most guests are either package tourists, Pattaya overnighters, or weekending Bangkokians so shoestring travellers aren't well catered for. Although the beach is fairly long and broad, the central shorefront is almost lost under a knot of tiny bars (many with irresistibly comfy armchairs) and tourist shops, and the main stretch of beach all but disappears at high tide. Facilities include minimarkets, ATMs, money exchange and internet access. At least two direct **boats** a day should run from Ban Phe to Wong Duan (see p.448), and vice versa.

Blue Sky Bungalow (Ⓣ089 936 0842; fan 4, air-con 5) is the last remaining bastion of budget **accommodation** on Wong Duan, with just a handful of basic wooden fan bungalows plus some air-con concrete ones set up on the hill at the north, rocky, end of the bay, above the *Blue Sky Restaurant*. Ideally located in the middle of the beach, *Vong Deuan Resort* (Ⓣ038 651777, Ⓦwww.vongdeuan.com; 7–8) comprises attractive air-con bungalows in various designs set around a pretty tropical garden, including nice cottages with dark-wood exteriors, contemporary styled interiors and garden bathrooms. Service is efficient, attentive and hotel-like, which makes it a favourite with older guests. The younger, hipper crowd mostly goes for *Vongduern Villa* (Ⓣ038 644260, Ⓦwww.vongduernvilla.com; 5–8), which has character, even if it's not quite pristine. Occupying a big chunk of the bay's southern end, it features various types and standards of room, all of them design-conscious and air-con, and ranging from whitewashed timber huts built on stilts and with picture windows, decks and modern furnishings to more minimalist versions kitted out with dark-wood floors and Japanese-style platform beds. There's also an attractive restaurant deck jutting out over the water.

Ao Thian (Candlelight Beach) and Ao Lung Dum

A favourite with Thai students, who relish the natural beauty of its slightly wild setting, **AO THIAN** ("Candlelight Beach") and contiguous Ao Lung Dum display almost none of the commerce of Wong Duan, a couple of minutes' walk over the hill, though the scenic shorefront is fronted by an unbroken line of bungalows and the eponymous "candlelight" lighting is long gone. The narrow, white-sand coastline is dotted with wave-smoothed rocks and partitioned by larger outcrops that create several distinct bays; as it curves outwards to the south you get a great view of the island's east coast. To get here either take a **boat** from Ban Phe to Ao Wong Duan and then walk, or pay B250 for a place on the scheduled direct speedboats (up to 6 daily from Taruaphe pier).

Towards Ao Thian's northern end, *Sang Thian Beach Resort* (Ⓣ038 644255, Ⓦwww.sangthain.com; ❻) has very tasteful air-con timber chalets built up the cliffside on a series of decks and steps – decor is navy-and-white chic, and views, mostly encompassing the sea, are pretty; it also has much less interesting compact brick **bungalows** up the northern slope. Further down the shore, the ten very nice wooden bungalows belonging to *Candlelight Resort* (Ⓣ089 247 9597; fan ❹, air-con ❺) are strung out in a long line, with each one facing the water, making them good value considering the competition.

At its southern end, Ao Thian becomes **AO LUNG DUM**, and the various little bungalow outfits fringing the shore here are pretty similar: *Jelly Fish Lung Dum* (Ⓣ038 644331; fan ❹ air-con ❺) is just about the cheapest, and all sixteen of its bungalows are right on the rocky shore, practically overhanging the water.

Ao Wai and Ao Kiu

A fifteen-minute walk along the coast path from Lung Dum brings you to **AO WAI**, a very pretty white-sand bay, partially shaded and a good size considering it supports just one (large) **bungalow** operation, *Sametville Resort* (Ⓣ038 651681, Ⓦwww.sametvilleresort.com; fan ❺, air-con ❻–❽), which also spills across on to neighbouring little Ao Hin Kaleng. Bungalows in all categories vary in quality, but you've plenty to choose from, unless you come at a weekend when it tends to fill up with Thai groups. There's usually a morning **boat** here from Ban Phe (Mon–Sat 10am, Sun 9am; B90) plus possible extra ones on weekends, but call the resort to confirm.

Over an hour's walk south of Ao Thian, via a track that begins behind *Vong Deuan Resort* on Ao Wong Duan and can be joined at the southern end of Ao Thian, the gorgeous little twin bays of **AO KIU** – Ao Kiu Na Nok on the east coast and Ao Kiu Na Nai on the west – are separated by just a few hundred metres of land. Both beaches are the domain of Samet's most exclusive hotel, the very luxurious, five-star, butler-service villa resort *Paradee Resort and Spa* (Ⓣ038 644283, Ⓦwww.paradeeresort.com; ❾ published rates from B17,800).

Ao Prao (Paradise Bay)

Across on the upper west coast, the rugged, rocky coastline only softens into beach once, at **AO PRAO**, also known as Paradise Bay, on the northwestern stretch, some 4km north of Ao Kiu Na Nai. This is Samet's top-notch beach, dominated by two expensively elegant resorts, plus one slightly more affordable option, and nothing else to lower the tone. If you're only visiting for the day, the most direct route from the east-coast beaches is via the inland track from behind *Sea Breeze* on Ao Phai, which takes about twenty minutes on foot, though the track from the back of *Tub Tim* on Ao Tub Tim will also get you there. If staying on Ao Prao, your hotel will arrange boat transfers.

Ao Prao Resort (ⓣ038 644101, ⓦwww.samedresorts.com; ➒) boasts some of the most luxurious **accommodation** on the island, in comfortable wooden chalets set in a mature tropical garden that slopes down to the beach. All chalets have air-con, TVs and balconies looking out to sea. There's a dive centre, boat tours and kayak rental, and a picturesquely sited restaurant extending over the water. The even more indulgent *Le Vimarn Cottages* (ⓣ038 644104, ⓦwww.samedresorts.com; ➒, prices start from B10,500) is owned by the same company and comprises charming, gorgeously furnished cottages, a delightful spa and a swimming pool. Its very refined *Buzz* restaurant serves highly regarded, highly priced Thai food (mains cost up to B600) in its chic modern dining room and upstairs terrace. *Lima Coco* (ⓣ089 105 7080, ⓦwww.limacoco.com; ➐–➒) is younger, trendier and cheaper, with a Bangkok contemporary chic look and lots of white walls, brightly coloured cushions, day beds and decks. Rooms are built up the side of the hill, with the priciest enjoying front-row sea views.

Ao Noi Na

West of Na Dan, the island's north coast – known simply as **AO NOI NA** even though it's not strictly a single bay – has a refreshingly normal village feel compared to the rest of Samet. There are an increasing number of places to stay along the narrow coastal road here, offering serene views across the water to the mainland hills behind Ban Phe, and just one white-sand beach of note at the far western end. Though this beach has been hogged by the luxurious *Mooban Talay Resort*, it's not private and you can walk there from Na Dan pier in about 25 minutes. En route you'll pass several good **restaurants**, including a floating seafood restaurant, *Ploy Samed Restaurant,* where diners have to ring a bell on the shore to alert the boatman to come over and pick you up; rock lobster is a speciality, and you eat on a deck at low tables with your feet dangling above the water.

Less than fifteen minutes' walk from Na Dan, Scottish-run *Baan Pou Paan* (ⓣ081 172 4486, ⓔlizziecj@hotmail.com; ➍–➏) is a chilled-out boutique **guest house** offering three beautiful en-suite fan and air-con bungalows built on stilts in the sea, with large decks and unparalleled views, plus another three air-con rooms in the building at the water's edge; they're all furnished with cushions, lamps and lots of plants, and prices stay the same year-round and at weekends. There's a stunningly sited eating area at the end of a jetty, for diners at the hotel's *Summer* restaurant, whose speciality is modern Mediterranean (evenings only; mains B120–380). Guests can either swim off the jetty or from the tiny beaches to either side, and there's table tennis and free wi-fi. Next-door-but-one, the dozen bungalows at British-managed *Samed Resort* (ⓣ038 644334, ⓦwww.samed-resort.com; shared bathrooms ➋, fan ➌, air-con ➎) occupy a wide sandy grove just across the road from a tiny, almost private beach; though the beach is a bit scruffy it has shade, with hammocks, and good swimming. Bungalows range from old-style bamboo huts with shared bathroom to en-suite fan and air-con bungalows; interiors in all are modern and cheery. You can also rent tents here (B300 for two including bedding). The shoreside restaurant, and its lively bar, has a pool table, table tennis and free wi-fi. Ten minutes' walk further west, you reach the poshest place on Ao Noi Na – and one of the classiest on the island: *Mooban Talay Resort* (ⓣ038 644251, ⓦwww.moobantalay.com; ➒), a secluded haven at the end of the road, set under the trees on a gorgeous, quiet, white-sand beach. Accommodation is in large, attractive bungalows, all with platform beds, garden bathrooms and outdoor seating: the priciest, seafront ones have enormous decks, and there's a beachside pool.

Chanthaburi and around

For over five hundred years, the seams of rock rich in sapphires and rubies that streak the hills of eastern Thailand have drawn prospectors and traders of all nationalities to the provincial capital of **CHANTHABURI**, 80km east of Ban Phe. Many of these hopefuls established permanent homes in the town, particularly the Shans from Burma, the Chinese and the Cambodians. Though the veins of precious stones have now been all but exhausted, Chanthaburi's reputation as a gem centre has continued to thrive and this is still one of the most famous places in Thailand to trade in gems (most of them now imported from Sri Lanka and elsewhere), not least because Chanthaburi is as respected a cutting centre as Bangkok, and Thai lapidaries are considered among the most skilled – and affordable – in the world.

Chanthaburi is an exceptionally fertile province, renown for its abundance of orchards, particularly durian, rambutan and mangosteen, which are celebrated

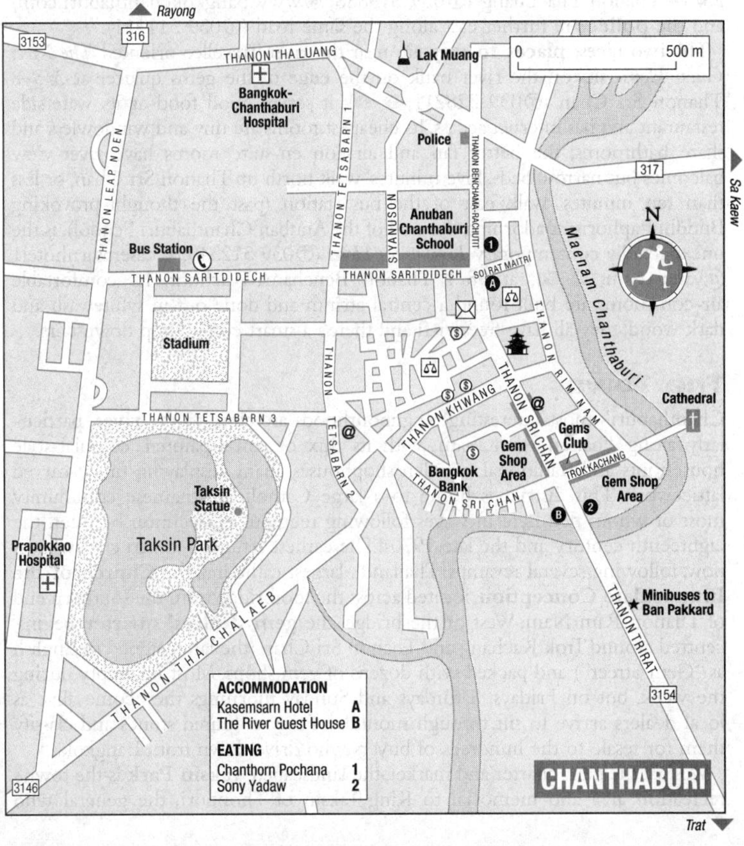

with an annual **fruit festival**, held in May or June. Its barely developed coastline is also very pretty, popular with Thai visitors for its empty beaches and shady casuarina trees that are just perfect for long seafood lunches. Though most foreign tourists passing through this province are either racing to cross the **Cambodian border** or have their sights set firmly on Ko Chang, a deviation via **the Chanthaburi coast** offers a much calmer, and very Thai, alternative.

Arrival, information and accommodation

Even if you're not planning a visit to Chanthaburi, you may find yourself stranded here for a couple of hours between **buses**, as this is a major transit point for east-coast services (including most Rayong–Trat buses) and a handy terminus for buses to and from the northeast. Eight daily buses make the scenic six-hour Chanthaburi–Sa Kaew–Khorat journey in both directions, with Sa Kaew being a useful interchange for buses to **Aranyaprathet and the Cambodian border** (see box opposite). Buses to and from all these places, as well as Bangkok's Eastern (Ekamai) and Northern (Mo Chit) stations (a few of which go via Suvarnabhumi Airport), use the Chanthaburi **bus station** (Ⓣ039 311299) on Thanon Saritdidech, about 750m northwest of the town centre and market. Chartered songthaew taxis from here to the Ko Chang piers at Laem Ngop charge B500.

The best **hospital** in town is the private Bangkok-Chanthaburi Hospital at 25/14 Thanon Tha Luang (Ⓣ039 319888, Ⓦwww.bangkokchanthaburi.com) and the **police** are further east along the same road (Ⓣ039 311111).

The two nicest **places to stay** are near the river. Traveller-oriented *The River Guest House* sits on the river bank on the edge of the gems quarter at 3/5–8 Thanon Sri Chan (Ⓣ039 328211; ❶–❷); it serves good food at its waterside restaurant and has internet access. Its cheapest rooms are tiny and windowless and share bathrooms; the better fan and air-con en-suite rooms have river-view balconies but narrow beds. Five minutes' walk north up Thanon Sri Chan, or less than ten minutes' walk east of the bus station (past the thought-provoking Buddhist aphorisms adorning the wall of the Anuban Chanthaburi School), is the unexpectedly contemporary *Kasemsarn Hotel* (Ⓣ039 312340, Ⓔkasemsarnhotel1@yahoo.com; ❹–❺), at 98/1 Thanon Benchama-Rachutit. Its comfortable air-con rooms are built round a central atrium and done out in whitewash and dark wood; they all have free wi-fi and there's a smart coffee shop downstairs.

The Town

Chanthaburi's most interesting neighbourhoods are close to the **river**, particularly along Thanon Rim Nam, with its mix of pastel-painted, colonial-style housefronts and traditional wooden shophouses, many displaying finely carved latticework. This district is home to a large Catholic Vietnamese community, most of whom fled here in waves following religious persecution between the eighteenth century and the late 1970s. The earliest refugees constructed what is now, following several revamps, Thailand's largest cathedral, the **Church of the Immaculate Conception**, located across the footbridge from the southern end of Thanon Rim Nam. West of the bridge, the **gem dealers' quarter** begins, centred around Trok Kachang and Thanon Sri Chan (the latter signed in English as "Gem Street") and packed with dozens of gem shops. Most lie empty during the week, but on Fridays, Saturdays and Sunday mornings they come alive as local dealers arrive to sift through mounds of tiny coloured stones and classify them for resale to the hundreds of buyers who drive down from Bangkok.

West of the gem quarter and market, the landscaped **Taksin Park** is the town's recreation area and memorial to King Taksin of Thonburi, the general who

Overland into Cambodia via Aranyaprathet–Poipet and Chanthaburi province

The most commonly used **overland crossing into Cambodia** is at **Poipet**, which lies just across the border from the Thai town of **Aranyaprathet**. The border here is open daily from 7am to 8pm and officials will issue thirty-day Cambodian **visas on arrival** (see p.34; ⓦwww.thaivisa.com for its visa-run forum; and ⓦwww.talesofasia.com/cambodia-overland.htm for a very detailed description of the crossing and for advice on onward transport into Cambodia). Once you're through, it's about three hours in a share-taxi or tourist bus to reach Siem Reap, 150km away. If you need a **hotel** in Aranyaprathet, try either the comfortable fan and air-con rooms at *Inter Hotel* at 108/7 Thanon Chatasingh (ⓣ037 231291, ⓦwww.ourweb.info/interhotel; fan ❷, air-con ❸), or the cheaper en-suite rooms at *Aran Garden II*, 110 Thanon Rat Uthit (fan ❶, air-con ❷).

To reach Aranyaprathet from east-coast towns, the easiest route is to take a bus **from Chanthaburi** to the town of **Sa Kaew**, 130km to the northeast, and then change to one of the frequent buses for the 55-kilometre ride east to Aranyaprathet. **From Bangkok**, you can travel to Aranyaprathet by **train** (2 daily; 6hr), though you'll need to catch the 5.55am to ensure reaching the border before 5pm; the other leaves at 1.05pm. Return trains depart Aranyaprathet at 6.35am and 1.35pm. Tuk-tuks will take you the 4km from the train station to the border post. Alternatively, take a **bus** from Bangkok's Northern (Mo Chit) Bus Terminal to Aranyaprathet (at least hourly; 4hr 30min), then a tuk-tuk from the bus station to the border. The last Aranyaprathet–Bangkok bus leaves at 7pm. It's also possible to buy a **through ticket to Siem Reap** from Trat and Ko Chang, or from Thanon Khao San in Bangkok (B200–600), but this option is dogged by **scams** (including a visa "service charge", described in detail at ⓦwww.talesofasia.com/cambodia-overland-bkksr-package.htm and on the forum at ⓦwww.thaivisa.com), can take up to ten hours longer than doing it independently, often travels via the less convenient Pailin or O'Smach border crossings instead, and nearly always uses clapped-out buses or even pick-ups on the Cambodian side, despite the promised "luxury bus".

There are also two less-used crossings in **Chanthaburi province**, giving access to the Cambodian town of **Pailin**, just east of the border. Daung Lem Border Crossing at **Ban Laem** is 88km northeast of Chanthaburi and the Phsa Prom border crossing is at **Ban Pakkard** (aka Chong Phakkat), 72km northeast of Chanthaburi. There's a minibus service in the morning from Chanthaburi (just east across the bridge from *The River Guest House*) to Ban Pakkard (1hr; B150), or you can take a songthaew from Chanthaburi to **Pong Nam Ron**, 42km north of Chanthaburi on Highway 317 (90min), then charter another to either border pass. The borders are open daily from 7am to 8pm and issue **visas on arrival**; if entering Thailand via this route you'll probably be obliged to show proof of onward travel from Thailand.

reunited Thailand between 1767 and 1782 after the sacking of Ayutthaya by the Burmese. Chanthaburi was the last Burmese bastion on the east coast – when Taksin took the town he effectively regained control of the whole country. The park's heroic bronze statue of Taksin is featured on the back of the B20 note.

Eating

A few metres up the road from the *Kasemsarn Hotel* on Thanon Benchama-Rachutit, *Chanthorn Phochana* **restaurant** at 102/5–8 Thanon Benchama-Rachutit serves a delicious range of spicy *yam* salads, Thai curries and stir-fries. Another place that's worth investigating is the tiny vegetarian Indian restaurant *Sony Yadaw*, opposite *The River Guest House*. **Foodstalls** in the market and along the riverside sois sell Vietnamese spring rolls (*cha gio*) with sweet sauce, and locally made Chanthaburi rice noodles (*sen Chan*); *sen Chan* are popularly used in *phat thai* throughout Thailand, but in Chanthaburi they're also crucial to the local noodle soup, *muu liang*, whose dark broth is flavoured with pungent herbs.

Coastal Chanthaburi

An ideal base from which to appreciate the understated charm of **coastal Chanthaburi** is the New Zealand–Thai owned *Faasai Resort* (T 039 417404, W www.faasai.com; 5–6), a fifteen-room environmentally conscious **resort** in **Khung Wiman**, just off Route 3399, about 30km southwest of Chanthaburi, or 80km east of Ban Phe. Its comfortable, family-friendly, air-con bungalows sit in a tropical garden with views to the Cardamon mountains on the Cambodian border and there's a swimming pool, wi-fi and Wat Pho-trained massage therapists on site. Very unusually, the resort also has its own private little **wetland conservation area**, where you can sit birdwatching, swim in the natural spring pool or kayak along the rivulet. The quiet, shady, bronze-sand beach of Hat Khung Wiman is ten minutes' walk away and *Faasai* rents bicycles, motorbikes and cars and organizes interesting local tours. On Khung Wiman beach itself you can also stay in one of the eight rather chic Moroccan-inspired rooms at *Al Medina Beach House* (T 085 838 1200, W www.almedinabeach.com; 8–9).

A couple of kilometres southeast of Hat Khung Wiman and you're at the lip of **AO KHUNG KRABEN**, a deep, lagoonlike scoop of a bay that's occasionally visited by dugongs and is edged by dense mangrove forest. A wide swathe of this mangrove swamp is protected under a royal conservation project and crossed by a kilometre-long boardwalk; you can also rent kayaks here (Oct–May Tues–Sun 8.30am–4pm) to follow a signed riverine trail. Access is via **LAEM SADET** on the southern curve of the bay. Across the road from the mangrove project, down on Laem Sadet's beach road, the impressively stocked **KKB Aquarium** (daily 8.30am–4.30pm; free) is another royal initiative and displays a multicoloured variety of reef fish, some seahorses and a few larger marine creatures, with informative English signage. A bridge across the next estuary at Ban Pak Nam Khaem Nu, and another one further east, means that it's now possible to continue on to **LAEM SING**, 25km southeast, via scenic coastal backroads 4002 and 6001. Hat Laem Sing is another long and lovely gold-sand beach, popular on Sundays for seafood lunches, but it's most famous for the chance to swim with Irawaddy and pink humpback **dolphins** at nearby **Oasis Sea World** (daily 9am–6pm; shows every 2hr; B180; swims B400; last swims from 3.45pm; W swimwithdolphins.information.in.th), 25km south of Chanthaburi. The dolphinarium is offered as a day-trip from Pattaya and Ko Chang, but don't expect a particularly heart-warming experience: you'll be encouraged to take "your" dolphin through a set routine of tricks and to then grab hold of its tail as it pulls you round the pool for a couple of minutes.

Trat and around

The small and pleasantly unhurried provincial capital of **TRAT**, 68km east of Chanthaburi, is the perfect place to stock up on essentials, extend your visa, or simply take a break before striking out again. Most travellers who find themselves here are heading either for Ko Chang, via the nearby port at **Laem Ngop**, for the outer islands, or for Cambodia, via the border at **Hat Lek**, 91km southeast of town. But Trat itself has its own distinctive, if understated, old-Thailand charm and there are lots of welcoming guest houses to tempt you into staying longer.

Though there are no real sights in town, the historic neighbourhood down by Khlong Trat, where you'll find most of the guest houses and traveller-oriented restaurants, is full of old wooden shophouses and narrow, atmospheric sois. The covered market in the heart of town is another fun place to wander. Out-of-town attractions that make enjoyable focuses for a leisurely cycle ride (ask at *Cool Corner* restaurant for detailed directions and other recommended routes) include the ornate seventeenth-century **Wat Buppharam**, 2km west of Trat Department Store, and the nearby lake. Slightly further afield, in the **mangrove forest** near Dan Khao, 5.5km southeast of town, a boardwalk with informative English signs takes you through the swamp; after dark it's a good place to see twinkling fireflies too. The boardwalk access is currently unsigned in English, but head for Dan Kao and after about 5.4km you'll pass dolphin statues on your left; the track to the mangroves is about 100m further on, on the right (if you get to the estuary and road's end you've gone about 500m too far).

Arrival and information

Trat is served by **buses** from Bangkok's Eastern (Ekamai) Bus Terminal (about every 2hr; 5–6hr), and Northern (Mo Chit) Bus Terminal (5 daily; 4hr 30min),

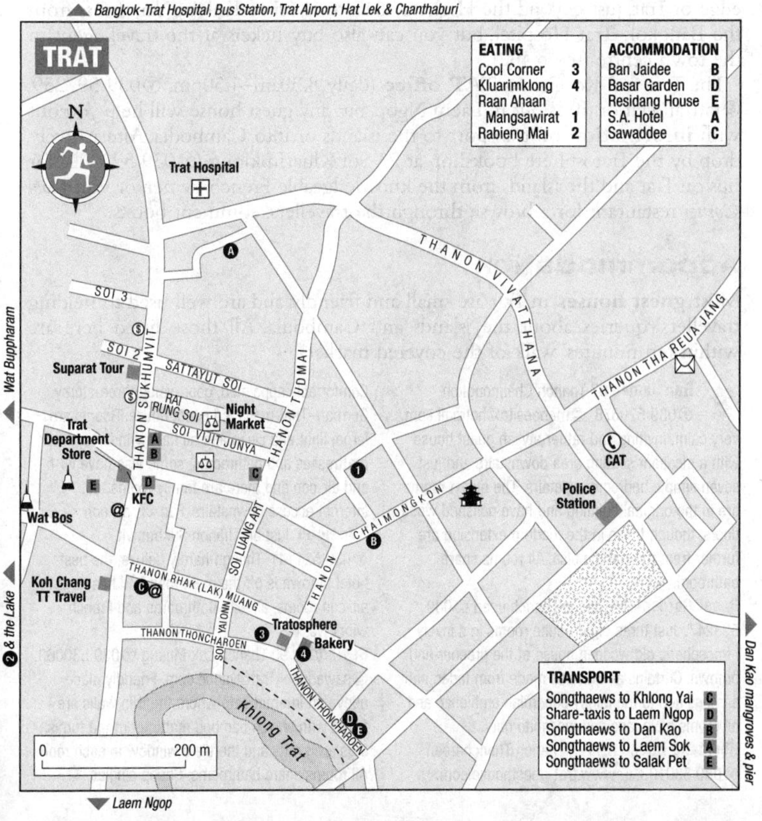

Yellow oil

Trat is famous across Thailand for the **yellow herbal oil** mixture, *yaa luang*, invented by one of its residents, Mae Ang Ki, and used by Thais to treat many ailments: sniff it for travel sickness and blocked sinuses, or rub it on to relieve mosquito and sandfly bites, ease stomach cramps, or sterilize wounds. Ingredients include camphor and aloe vera. It's well worth investing in a lip-gloss-sized bottle of the stuff before heading off to the sandfly-plagued islands; you can buy it for about B100 at Trat market and at nearby Tratosphere bookshop. There are now several imitations, but Mae Ang Ki's original product has a tree logo to signify that it's made by royal appointment.

the latter going via Suvarnabhumi Airport (4hr 10min). It also has useful bus connections with Ban Phe (for Ko Samet), Chanthaburi, Pattaya and Si Racha. All buses terminate at the bus station, 1.5km northeast of central Trat on Highway 318, from where songthaews shuttle passengers into the town centre (B20, or B60 if chartered) or on to the **departure points for the islands** (see p.462).

Tiny Trat **airport** (Ⓣ039 525767) is served by Bangkok Airways flights to and from Bangkok. The airport is about 16km from the Ko Chang piers at Laem Ngop and there's an airport shuttle direct to Ko Chang hotels for B350 per person, including ferry ticket. Trat town is a thirty-minute, B500 taxi ride from the airport. The Bangkok Airways office (Ⓣ039 525299) is on the northern edge of Trat, just beyond the Highway 317 turn-off to Khlong Yai, across from the Bangkok-Trat Hospital, but you can also buy tickets at the travel agent in the town centre (see p.462).

The Trat and Ko Chang **TAT office** (daily 8.30am–4.30pm; Ⓣ039 597259, Ⓔtattrat@tat.or.th) is out in Laem Ngop, but any guest house will help you out with **information** on transport to the islands or into Cambodia. Alternatively, drop by the Tratosphere bookshop at 23 Soi Kluarimklong (Ⓣ039 523200) for tips on Trat and the islands from the knowledgeable French owner, or visit *Cool Corner* restaurant for a browse through the travellers' comment books.

Accommodation

Most **guest houses** in Trat are small and friendly and are well used to fielding travellers' queries about the islands and Cambodia. All those listed here are within ten minutes' walk of the covered market.

Ban Jaidee 67 Thanon Chaimongkon Ⓣ039 520678, Ⓔmaneesita@hotmail.com. Very calm, inviting and rather stylish guest house with a pleasant seating area downstairs and just seven simple bedrooms upstairs. The nicest rooms are in the original building and have polished wood floors, though those in the modern extension are further from the traffic noise. All rooms share bathrooms. ❶

Basar Garden 87 Thanon Thoncharoen Ⓣ039 523247. Just three big en-suite rooms in a lovely atmospheric old wooden house at the greener end of town. Curtains and drapes made from faded batik sarongs add to the faintly bohemian ambience and all rooms have fans and mosquito nets. ❷

Residang House 87/1–2 Thanon Thoncharoen Ⓣ039 530103, Ⓦwww.trat-guesthouse.com. Comfortably appointed, good-value three-storey German–Thai-managed guest house. Rooms are large, light and clean and all have windows, thick mattresses and bathrooms; some also have wi-fi and air-con and there are family rooms too. Internet access downstairs. Fan ❷, air-con ❸

S.A. Hotel Just off Thanon Sukhumvit Ⓣ039 511141. Though hardly deluxe, the best hotel in town is off the main road and has large air-con rooms, all with bathrooms and French windows. ❸

Sawaddee 90 Thanon Lak Muang Ⓣ039 530063, Ⓔsawaddee_Trat@yahoo.com. Friendly place above an internet café where the thin walls are faced with woven bamboo matting but the furnishings are pretty and there's a window in each room. All rooms share bathrooms. Cheap singles. ❶

Overland into Cambodia via Hat Lek–Koh Kong

Many travellers use the **Hat Lek–Koh Kong border crossing** (daily 7am–8pm) for overland travel into Cambodia: **visas on arrival** are issued here (see p.34) and Koh Kong has reasonable transport connections to Sihanoukville and, via Sre Ambel, Phnom Penh. For a comprehensive guide to the crossing and to the various transport options – and scams – on both sides of the border, see Ⓦwww.talesofasia.com/cambodia-overland.htm and the Ⓦwww.thaivisa.com forum. Trat travel agents (see p.462) also do all-inclusive transport via Hat Lek to Siem Reap, Phnom Penh and Sihanoukville for B750/1000, but see the warnings on p.457.

The only way to get to **Hat Lek** is by minibus from Trat, 91km northwest. **Minibuses** leave Trat bus station approximately every 45 minutes between 6am and 5pm (1hr–1hr 30min; B120), though you can also arrange to be picked up from the Suparat Tour office (Tanakavee Transport; daily 6am–11.30pm; Ⓣ039 511481) in central Trat. In the reverse direction, the timetable is almost the same.

Hat Lek (on the Thai side) and Koh Kong (in Cambodia) are on opposite sides of the Dong Tong River estuary, but a bridge connects the two banks. Once through immigration, taxis ferry you into **Koh Kong** town for onward transport to Sihanoukville and Phnom Penh or for guest houses should you arrive too late for connections (mid-afternoon onwards). **Vans and share-taxis** to Phnom Penh take seven to eleven hours, depending on the state of the road; the trip to Sihanoukville takes around the same time but you need to change in Sre Ambel. The alternative is to take the daily **speedboat** service to Sihanoukville (departs Koh Kong pier at 8am; 4hr), or to Sre Ambel (daily at 7am; 3hr) for road connections to Phnom Penh. However, though much faster, this can be a nerve-racking, even dangerous experience, especially in rough weather, as the boats used were built for river travel not open seas.

Eating

Two of the best and cheapest **places to eat** in Trat are at the covered day market on Thanon Sukhumvit, and the night market (5–9pm), between Soi Vichidanya and Soi Kasemsan, east of Thanon Sukhumvit.

Cool Corner 49-51 Thanon Thoncharoen. Run single-handedly by a local writer/artist, this place has lots of personality, both in its cute hand-painted decor, and in its traveller-oriented menu of real coffee, Indian chai, veggie specials, quality breakfasts and great Thai curries (from B50). A good place to while away an extra hour or three, listening to the mellow music and perusing the travellers' comment books.

Kluarimklong Soi Kluarimklong. More Bangkok than Trat in its style and menu, this unexpectedly classy little place has both an indoor and a courtyard dining area and serves delicious, upmarket Thai food (dishes B50–80), including steamed *haw mok thalay* fish curry with coconut and lots of spicy *yam* salads and *tom yum* soups.

Raan Ahaan Mangsawirat No English sign, but follow the soi near *Ban Jaidee*, off Thanon Chaimongkon. Typical no-frills, very cheap Thai vegetarian place, where you choose two portions of veggie curry, stir-fry or stew from the trays laid out in the display cabinet, and pay about B30 including rice. Shuts about 2pm.

Rabieng Mai Beside the lake, south of Wat Bos, on the southwest corner of town. Mid-priced Thai seafood place – with famously good catfish curries – whose lake views make it a good focus for a hike or cycle trip out to Wat Buppharam. Mains B60–180.

Listings

Bookshops The French-Thai run Tratosphere, at 23 Soi Kluarimklong, is a cut above most second-hand bookshops and a very good source of local information; you can also buy curios from all over Thailand here, and hammocks.

Cooking course At Tratosphere bookshop (B800 per three dishes).

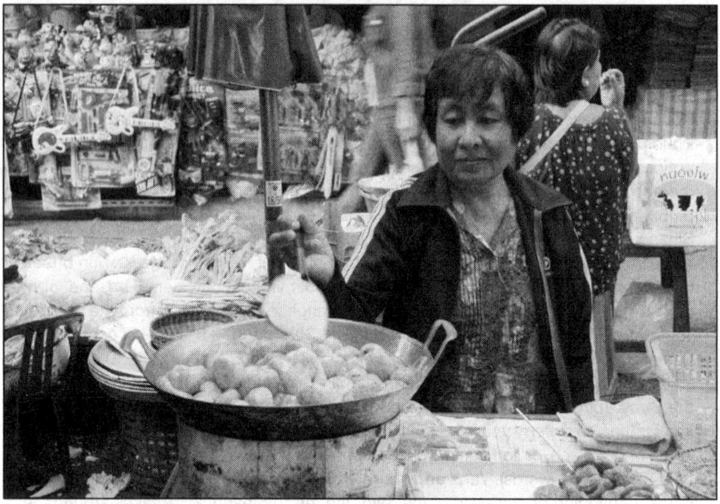

▲ Trat's night market

Emergencies For all emergencies, call the tourist police on the free, 24hr phone line ⓣ1155, or contact the local police station off Thanon Vivatthana ⓣ039 511239.

Hospital The best hospital is the private Bangkok–Trat Hospital ⓣ039 522555, ⓦwww.bangkoktrathospital.com, part of the Bangkok Hospital group, which also offers dental care services; it's on the Sukhumvit Highway, 1km north of Trat Department Store.

Immigration office Located in Laem Ngop, 100m west of the TAT office (Mon–Fri 8.30am–4.30pm; ⓣ039 597261).

Massage Available all over town and from Wat Pho-trained Pu at Tratosphere bookshop, who also teaches massage (30hr; B4500).

Travel agencies International and domestic flights from Koh Chang TT Travel on Thanon Sukhumvit ⓣ039 531420 (closed Sun); they also book accommodation on the islands (B200–5000), arrange taxis to Trat airport and transport to Cambodia, provide local information and rent motorbikes.

Moving on to the islands: Laem Ngop and nearby ports

All ferries to Ko Chang and Ko Wai and some services to Ko Mak leave from one of four different piers west along the coast from the small port town of **LAEM NGOP**, 17km southwest of Trat, which is served by songthaew share-taxis from Trat's bus station and, less frequently, from Thanon Sukhumvit in the town centre; they cost B50 (20–40min) per person or B150 if chartered (for the latter price you get collected from your guest house) and should drop you at the correct pier. Details of the different boat services are given in the relevant island accounts. Long-distance transport direct to Laem Ngop is either by **tourist minibus** from Bangkok's Thanon **Khao San**, **Pattaya** or **Ko Samet**, or by public bus from **Bangkok**'s Eastern (Ekamai) Bus Terminal (2 daily at 7.45am & 9.45am; 5hr 15min; return buses depart Laem Ngop at 12.30pm, 2pm & 4pm). All other **public transport**, including most buses from Bangkok's Eastern Bus Terminal and all buses from Bangkok's Mo Chit Northern Bus Terminal, Suvarnabhumi Airport, Pattaya, Rayong and the Cambodian border, terminates in **Trat**. If you're going to the remote **Long Beach** on Ko Chang you can take a direct songthaew to Salak Pet (B150, including car ferry) from the temple compound behind *KFC* and Trat Department Store. Some boats to Ko Mak and nearly all boats to Ko Kood depart from **Laem Sok**, 30km south of Trat; boat tickets bought in Trat should include free transfers to Laem Sok, but there's also a Laem Sok songthaew service that leaves from the town centre and takes thirty minutes (see map, p.459). A few boats to the outer islands depart from **Ban Dan Kao**, on the river estuary 6km northeast of Trat town; Dan Kao songthaews leave from the town centre and take ten minutes.

Ko Chang

Edged with a chain of long, mostly white-sand beaches and dominated by a broad central spine of jungle-clad hills, **KO CHANG** is developing fast but still feels green. It's Thailand's second largest island, after Phuket, but unlike its bigger sister has no villages or tourist facilities within its steeply contoured and densely forested interior, just a few rivers, waterfalls and hiking trails that come under the auspices of the Mu Ko Chang National Park. Some of its marine environment is also protected, as the national park extends to over forty other islands in the Ko Chang archipelago. Ko Chang's own coast, however, has seen major development over the past decade, and the island is now well established as a mainstream destination, crowded with package tourists and all the usual resort facilities, and suffering the inevitable inflated prices and inappropriate architecture. That said, it's still possible to find accommodation to suit most budgets and though the beaches may be busy they're undeniably handsome, with plenty of inviting places to swim, stroll, or snooze under a palm tree.

At 30km north to south, Ko Chang has plenty of coast to explore. The western **beaches** are the prettiest and the most congested, with **White Sand Beach** (**Hat Sai Khao**) drawing the biggest crowds to its mainly upmarket and increasingly overpriced mid-range accommodation; smaller **Hat Kai Bae** is also busy. Most backpackers opt for so-called **Lonely Beach** (officially **Hat Tha Nam**), with its roadside village of travellers' accommodation and famous beachfront party scene; those in search of quiet choose the more laid-back **Hat Khlong Phrao**, a long and lovely sweep of sand that caters to most pockets, or the jetty village of **Bang Bao**, which has bay views but no direct beach access. Every beach has **currency exchange** and most have **ATMs**, along with minimarkets, tour agents, dive shops (see p.474), internet access, clothes stalls and souvenir shops. White Sand Beach and Hat Kai Bae have the densest concentrations of facilities. During **peak season**, accommodation on every beach tends to fill up very quickly, so it's worth booking ahead. The island gets a lot quieter (and cheaper) from June to October, when heavy downpours and fierce storms can make life miserable, though sunny days are common too; be especially careful of riptides on all the beaches during the monsoon season.

Getting to Ko Chang

Access to Ko Chang **from the mainland** is by boat from the **Laem Ngop coast**, 17km southwest of Trat; details of transport to Laem Ngop are given opposite. During high season there are also boats to Ko Chang **from Ko Wai**, **Ko Mak** and **Ko Kood**; for details of these services, which all terminate at Bang Bao on Ko Chang's southwest coast, see relevant island accounts.

The main **Laem Ngop–Ko Chang boat services** are operated by two different car ferry companies from two different piers, but unless you're in your own vehicle you'll likely just get taken to the next departing service.

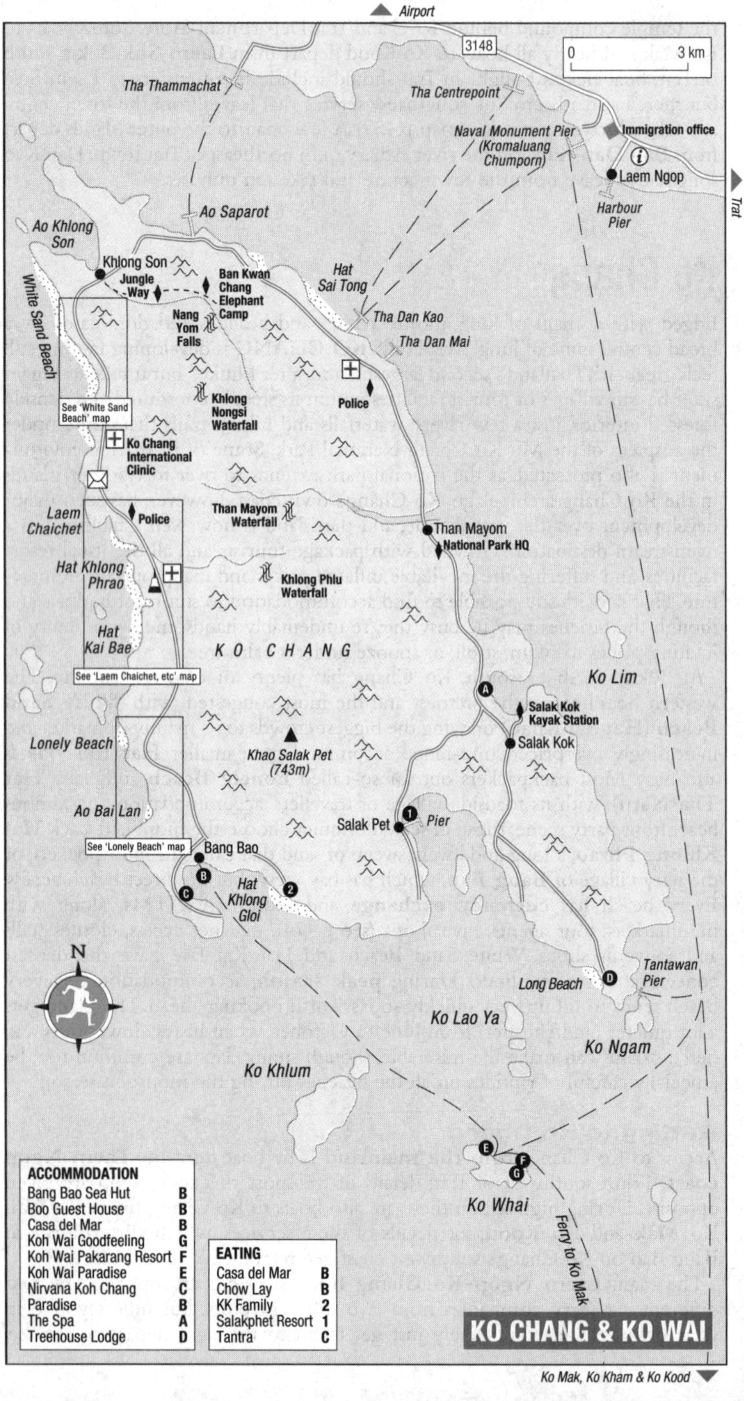
Airport
3148
0 3 km
Tha Thammachat
Tha Centrepoint
Naval Monument Pier (Kromaluang Chumporn)
Immigration office
Laem Ngop
Trat
Harbour Pier
Ao Saparot
Ao Khlong Son
Khlong Son
White Sand Beach
Jungle Way
Ban Kwan Chang Elephant Camp
Hat Sai Tong
Tha Dan Kao
Tha Dan Mai
Nang Yom Falls
Police
Khlong Nongsi Waterfall
See 'White Sand Beach' map
Ko Chang International Clinic
Laem Chaichet
Police
Than Mayom Waterfall
Than Mayom
National Park HQ
Hat Khlong Phrao
Khlong Phlu Waterfall
Hat Kai Bae
KO CHANG
See 'Laem Chaichet, etc' map
Ko Lim
Salak Kok Kayak Station
Salak Kok
Lonely Beach
Khao Salak Pet (743m)
Ao Bai Lan
Salak Pet
Pier
See 'Lonely Beach' map
Bang Bao
Hat Khlong Gloi
Tantawan Pier
Long Beach
Ko Lao Ya
Ko Ngam
Ko Khlum
N
Ko Whai
Ferry to Ko Mak
ACCOMMODATION
Bang Bao Sea Hut B
Boo Guest House B
Casa del Mar B
Koh Wai Goodfeeling G
Koh Wai Pakarang Resort F
Koh Wai Paradise E
Nirvana Koh Chang C
Paradise B
The Spa A
Treehouse Lodge D
EATING
Casa del Mar B
Chow Lay B
KK Family 2
Salakphet Resort 1
Tantra C
KO CHANG & KO WAI
Ko Mak, Ko Kham & Ko Kood

Moving on from Ko Chang

Every tour agency on Ko Chang offers transport direct from Ko Chang **to Bangkok** (big bus/minibus to Khao San Road B350/550, 5hr; minibus to Sukhumvit Road hotels B900, 5hr); **Suvarnabhumi Airport** (minibus B900, whole taxi B3900; 5hr); Ban Phe (for Ko Samet, B250); Pattaya (B500); and Cambodia (minibus to Siem Reap B750, 12hr; see warnings on p.457); and Bangkok Airways runs a shuttle bus service to Trat Airport (contact the office in central Hat Sai Khao on ⓣ039 551654; B350 per person). Prices include the ferry crossing from Ko Chang but may not include transport from your Ko Chang accommodation to the ferry pier. Share-taxis transport passengers to the ferry piers from all Ko Chang's western beaches (simply wait on the side of the road and flag one down), or you can charter your own; drivers should take you to whichever ferry is next to depart.

From November to May, car ferries to the mainland leave Ko Chang at least every 45 minutes between about 7am and 6pm, departing from Ao Saparot or Tha Dan Kao on the northeast coast and arriving at either Tha Thammachat (25min) or Tha Centrepoint (45min) near Laem Ngop. During the rest of the year boats may only run every two hours.

From September to June, Bang Bao Boat (ⓣ087 054 4300, ⓦwww.bangbaoboat.com) runs one or two daily boats from Ko Chang direct to the **outer islands** (one slow boat and sometimes one speedboat as well); timetables vary according to how busy things are, so check locally first, and see relevant island accounts for more details. Tickets are sold at every tour agency on Ko Chang, and transfers to the Bang Bao pier are sometimes included: **Ko Wai** (1hr/15min; B300/400), **Ko Mak** (2hr/1hr; B400/550), and **Ko Kood** (5hr including transfer/2hr; B700/900). Other speedboat services come and go but any tour agency will have current details.

Ferries run between 6.30am and 7pm, at least once an hour from November to May and at least once every two hours during the rest of the year. Fares are competitive and change frequently: expect to pay about B100 single or B160 return, and not much more if you have a vehicle, though deals on the latter can vary considerably. Centrepoint Ferry (ⓣ039 538196) runs from Tha Centrepoint, 3km west of Laem Ngop, to Tha Dan Kao (45min); and Ferry Ko Chang (ⓣ039 518588) runs from Tha Thammachat, 9km west of Laem Ngop, to Ao Saparot (25min).

On Ko Chang, **songthaew share-taxis** meet boats at Tha Dan Kao and Ao Saparot and transport passengers to west-coast beaches (B50 to White Sand Beach, 25min; B100 to Lonely Beach, 1hr; B150 to Bang Bao, 1hr 15min). If you're heading **to Salak Pet** or **Long Beach** on Ko Chang's southeast coast, you can make use of the bargain B150 songthaew service that departs central Trat, behind the *KFC*, and takes you all the way to Salak Pet, car-ferry passage included.

Island transport and information

A wide road runs nearly all the way round the island, served by **songthaew share-taxis** which tend to charge according to how many passengers they have as well as the distance travelled (usually B50–150 per person). You can rent **motorbikes and cars** on every beach, but the road is notoriously dangerous, with steep hills, sharp, unexpected hairpins and many reckless drivers, so think twice if you're an inexperienced motorcyclist – accidents happen every day and fatalities are all too frequent. Goodquality **mountain bikes** are available through Ko Chang Gym in the VJ Plaza complex in Laem Chaichet (ⓣ081 003 8468; B400 per 6hr).

Island activities

Tour agents on every beach will sell you tickets for the **activities** described below and prices should include return transport from your accommodation. If you're still looking for something unusual to do you might consider taking a **microlight flight** over Ko Chang (15min; B1700 per person) from the Koh Chang Flying Club; its airfield is just past the turnoff to Khlong Phlu falls in Khlong Phrao. For information on snorkelling and diving in the Ko Chang archipelago, see p.474.

Ko Chang or "Elephant Island" is named for its hilly profile rather than its indigenous pachyderms, but there are several **elephant camps** on the island that have brought in their own lumbering forest dwellers so that tourists can ride and help bathe them. The one with the best reputation is **Ban Kwan Chang Elephant Trek** (ⓣ089 815 9566), based in a forested area in the north of the island, east of Khlong Son village, near Nang Yom Waterfall. It was set up by the man behind the Asian Elephant Foundation and is staffed by ten Suay mahouts and their elephants from Ban Ta Klang village in northeast Thailand, which has for centuries been a traditional centre for working elephants (see p.516). Visitors can either do a forty-minute elephant ride through adjacent plantations (B500) or extend the ride to an hour and bathe the elephants as well (B900). Nearby Thai–British-run **Jungle Way** leads guided **treks** through the forest here as well as more strenuous hikes on the northern Chang Noi peninsular (ⓣ089 223 4795, ⓦwww.jungleway.com; from B600). If you're in the area, you could make the easy 300m walk to tiny **Nang Yom falls**, 500m beyond Ban Kwang Elephant Camp, but Khlong Phlu falls in Khlong Phrao are more satisfying (see p.469).

For a more demanding physical challenge, make an afternoon of it at **Treetop Adventure Park**, just south of the *Dusit Princess* hotel on Ao Bai Lan, south of Lonely Beach (daily 9am–5pm; B950 including transport; ⓣ084 310 7600, ⓦwww.treetopadventurepark.com), an enjoyable and professionally managed jungle activity centre where you get to swing through the trees on a series of trapezes, flying foxes, aerial skateboards, rope ladders and webs. Everyone gets a full safety harness and gloves and starts off with a training session before tackling the two adventure courses (or the special kids' one), which take around two hours in all, though there's no limit to repeat attempts.

Also at Ao Bai Lan, and the perfect place to tease out any sore muscles, is **Bailan Herbal Sauna** (daily 4–8pm; ⓣ086 252 4744). This charming, creatively designed US–Thai-run herbal steam sauna is an alternative little haven of adobe buildings with glass-bottle windows, secluded within a patch of roadside forest. Entry into the sociable communal sauna costs B200, with home-made DIY herbal treatments (kaffir lime for hair, white-mud for face and turmeric for skin) mostly just a bargain B50. Lao and herbal massage are also available (B350–700), along with fresh juices and spirulina. For more conventional **spa and detox treatments**, *The Spa* near Salak Kok on the east cost (see p.476) offers the biggest range and is an appealingly tranquil place to while away a few hours. On Hat Khlong Phrao, Baan Zen (ⓣ086 530 9345, ⓦwww.baanzen.com) runs **yoga classes** and short courses (from B900/lesson) as well as **reiki** courses. The amiable chef who runs the recommended *KaTi* restaurant in nearby Khlong Phrao teaches well-regarded **cooking classes** at her restaurant (KaTi Culinary Cooking School; 6hr B1200, for three to nine dishes; ⓣ081 903 0408, ⓔkati-culinary@hotmail.com).

The widely distributed detailed free maps and quarterly Ko Chang guides published by Whitesands Publications (ⓦwww.whitesandsthailand.com) are a handy source of **information** and advertisements, and the website provides an accommodation-booking service, but for more intelligent insights and opinionated advice, check out ⓦwww.iamkohchang.com, compiled by a Ko Chang resident.

The island's **post office** is 2km south of the southern end of White Sand Beach, across from the access road to Hat Sai Mook. The private 24hr **Ko Chang International Clinic** (℡039 551555, Ⓦwww.bangkoktrathospital .com), part of the Bangkok Hospital Group, is located between southern White Sand Beach and Hat Kai Mook, 1km south of *Plaloma Resort*; it deals with minor injuries and has a dental service, and will transfer seriously ill patients to its parent Bangkok-Trat Hospital in Trat. There's also a small clinic in Khlong Phrao. The island's main **police station** is at Dan Mai on the northeast coast (℡039 5586191), and there are police boxes on White Sand Beach and at Hat Khlong Phrao's Ko Chang Plaza.

Though mosquitoes don't seem to be much in evidence, Ko Chang is one of the few areas of Thailand that's still considered to be **malarial**, so you may want to start taking your prophylactics before you get here (see p.39). Staff at the Ko Chang International Clinic, however, say that the risk to tourists is minimal and that cases are confined to those who work and stay overnight in the island's jungle interior. **Sandflies** can be more of a problem on the southern beaches (see p.40). Watch out for **jellyfish**, which plague the west coast in April and May, and for **snakes**, including surprisingly common cobras, sunbathing on the overgrown paths into the interior. The other hazard is **theft** from rooms and bungalows: use your own padlock on bags (and doors where possible) or, better still, make use of hotel safety boxes.

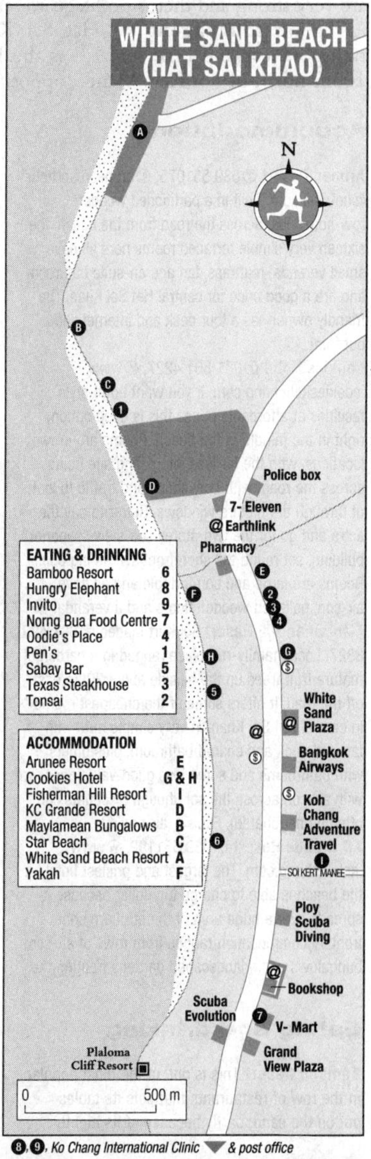

White Sand Beach (Hat Sai Khao)

Framed by a broad band of fine white sand at low tide, a fringe of casuarinas and palm trees and a backdrop of forested hills, **Hat Sai Khao**, more commonly referred to as **White Sand Beach**, is, at 2.5km long, the island's longest beach and its most commercial, with scores of mid-range and upmarket hotel and bungalow operations squashed in along the shore, plus dozens of shops, travel agents, bars and restaurants lining the inland side of the road. The vibe is much more laid-back and traveller-oriented at the far

WHITE SAND BEACH (HAT SAI KHAO)

N

Ao Saparot & Tha Dan Kao

Police box

7- Eleven
@ Earthlink
Pharmacy

EATING & DRINKING
Bamboo Resort 6
Hungry Elephant 8
Invito 9
Norng Bua Food Centre 7
Oodie's Place 4
Pen's 1
Sabay Bar 5
Texas Steakhouse 3
Tonsai 2

ACCOMMODATION
Arunee Resort E
Cookies Hotel G & H
Fisherman Hill Resort I
KC Grande Resort D
Maylamean Bungalows B
Star Beach C
White Sand Beach Resort A
Yakah F

White Sand Plaza

Bangkok Airways

Koh Chang Adventure Travel

SOI KERT MANEE

Ploy Scuba Diving

@ Bookshop

Scuba Evolution

V- Mart

Plaloma Cliff Resort

Grand View Plaza

0 500 m

8, 9, Ko Chang International Clinic ▼ & post office

quieter northern end of the beach, however, beyond *KC Grande*, and this is where you'll find the most budget-priced accommodation, some of it pleasingly characterful and nearly all of it enjoying its own sea view. An extra bonus is that the road is well out of earshot up here, and there's hardly any passing pedestrian traffic. There are some low-key beach **bars** up there too, and more along the shorefront in the central beach area – all of them quite different in feel from the rash of brash, Pattaya-style bar-beers inland from *Plaloma Cliff Resort* in southern Hat Sai Khao. Wherever you stay on Hat Sai Khao, be careful when swimming as the **currents** are very strong and there's no lifeguard service.

A good **tour agent** on Hat Sai Khao – for flights, day-trips, onward transport, car and bike rental – is the helpful Koh Chang Adventure Travel, 100m north of Soi Kert Manee, opposite *Bamboo Resort* (Ⓣ081 887 9515).

Accommodation

Arunee Resort Ⓣ039 551075, Ⓔaruneeresorttour@hotmail.com. Built in a partitioned wooden row-house just across the road from the beach, the sixteen very simple terraced rooms here all have a small veranda, mattress, fan and en-suite bathroom and are a good price for central Hat Sai Khao. The friendly owner has a tour desk and internet shop out front. ②

Cookies Hotel Ⓣ081 861 4227, Ⓦwww.cookieskohchang.com. If you want hotel-style facilities at affordable prices this is good option, right in the middle of the beach. Rooms are in two locations, with the far less interesting site being across the road, with only shops and traffic to look at through the picture windows. Better to pay the extra and go for the two-storey sea-view "superior" building, set round the shorefront swimming pool. Rooms are large and comfortable and all have air-con, polished wooden floors and a veranda. ⑦

Fisherman Hill Resort Soi Kert Manee Ⓣ081 429 3827. Local, family-run place ranged in a garden of mature fruit trees up the hillside about 200m east off the road. It offers some of the cheapest rooms in central Hat Sai Khao, in very simple huts with fan and deck and shared bathroom, plus others with bathrooms and some less good-value ones with air-con across the soi (though discounts can often be negotiated). Fan ②, air-con ⑤

KC Grande Resort Ⓣ039 551199, Ⓦwww.kckohchang.com. The largest and priciest hotel on the beach is able to charge top dollar because it spreads over a huge area of the northern shorefront. Accommodation ranges from rows of air-con bungalows set in landscaped gardens fronting the beach to deluxe sea-view rooms in the three-storey hotel block. Facilities are good and include two pools. ⑧–⑨

Maylamean Bungalows Ⓣ086 144 5865. In the cluster of funky, north-beach cliffside shanty bungalows, this one stands out both for its lilac paintwork and because its en-suite wooden huts, while also built on stilts steeply up the cliffside, are larger and a bit more private than many of its neighbours. ④

Star Beach Ⓣ087 558 4085. Ten basic, cheerily painted plywood huts squat limpet-like on the rock-face here, just above the sand on the quiet, funky northern stretch of White Sand Beach. Rooms are very simple but are all en suite and enjoy high-level sea views and breezes. ②

White Sand Beach Resort Ⓣ081 863 7737, Ⓦwww.whitesandbeachresort.net. Spread across a long, attractive stretch of uncommercialized beach at the far north end of the beach, *White Sand* offers a big range of nicely spaced huts, many of them lapping up uninterrupted sea views. Interiors are fairly simple, but have air-con, wooden floors, TVs, and a faintly contemporary style. For a proper peaceful beach vibe and a little bit of affordable comfort, within 10min walk of resort facilities, this is a good option considering the competition. If arriving by songthaew, get off at the 7-Eleven beside *KC Grande* and phone for transport. ⑤–⑥

Yakah Ⓣ039 551 1086. Just eleven teak-log bungalows in a tiny, crowded enclave right on the beach, all pretty nice inside and with air-con, TV, fridge and at least partial sea view; avoid the one next to the drainage khlong if you can. ⑥

Eating and drinking

Bamboo Resort This is one of the most popular in the row of restaurants that sets its tables out on the sand, partly because of its nightly high-season fireshows at 8.30pm. As for food, there's a fresh seafood barbecue every night, a good Thai menu and a variable Italian one (pizzas from B200). plus cheapish house wine by the glass too.

Hungry Elephant Opposite the sign for *Saffron* hotel, 2km south of southern White Sand Beach. The French and Thai food at this unassuming roadside place has a good reputation with local expats. The Thai chef trained at the Alliance Française in Bangkok and does toothsome steaks – au poivre, chateaubriand and crème cognac – mostly for about B260. Good espressos too.

Invito On the hill, about 800m south of *Plaloma Resort*. Expensive but highly rated, authentic Italian food (from B300) including wood-fired pizzas, pastas and imported wines. Daily 5–11pm.

Norng Bua Food Centre Very cheap night-market-style Thai food, including noodle soups, fried noodles and satays.

Oodie's Place One of Ko Chang's most famous live-music venues, with live blues, rock, reggae and r'n'b played most nights, plus daily movies, and a Euro-Asian menu with a French accent; most main dishes cost B60–200.

Pen's Tiny beachfront restaurant in the northern bungalow cluster that serves exceptionally good home-style Thai food at fairly cheap prices.

Sabay Bar One of Ko Chang's longest-running institutions, where you can choose to sit in the chic air-con bar and watch the nightly live sets from the in-house cover band (from 9pm), or lounge on mats and cushions on the sand and listen in via the outdoor speakers. You pay for the pleasure, however, as drinks are pricey. Also stages fire-juggling shows on the beach and full-moon parties.

Texas Steakhouse Rooftop restaurant that serves delicious ribs (from B300), plus imported steaks (from B220) and a few Thai dishes.

Tonsai The atmosphere at this mostly vegetarian restaurant is pleasingly mellow: seating is on Thai-style cushions scattered around a circular platform wedged between half a dozen trees, and the menu (B50–180) includes Thai curries, pastas, Vietnamese sausage and around fifty cocktails.

Laem Chaichet and Hat Khlong Phrao

Four kilometres south of Hat Sai Khao, the scenic, rocky cape at **LAEM CHAICHET** curves round into sweeping, casuarina-fringed **HAT KHLONG PHRAO**, one of Ko Chang's nicest beaches, not least because it has yet to see the clutter and claustrophobic development of both its neighbours. For the moment at least, most of the restaurants, bars and shops are way off the beach, along the roadside, with the shorefront left mainly to a decent spread of accommodation. Laem Chaichet protects an inlet and tiny harbour and offers beautiful views south across the bay and inland to the densely forested mountains. To the south, Hat Khlong Phrao begins with a nice kilometre-long run of beach that's interrupted by a wide khlong, whose estuary is the site of some characterful stilt homes and seafood restaurants. At low tide you can just about wade across it; more reliably, during daylight hours, you can rent your own kayak from almost anywhere along the beach, or make use of the boatman who ferries guests at *Aana Resort* to the private patch of sand behind *Panviman Resort*. (After dark, you can use your kayak to paddle upriver to see the fireflies twinkling in the khlongside *lamphu* trees.) Beyond the estuary, the long southern beach is partly shaded by casuarinas and backed in places by a huge coconut grove that screens the shore from the road; it's quite a hike to the roadside shops and restaurants from here though, at least a kilometre along a rutted track.

Upstream from Hat Khlong Phrao, the khlong that divides the beach in two tumbles into Ko Chang's most famous cascade, **Khlong Phlu Falls** (Nam Tok Khlong Phlu), a couple of kilometres east off the main road. Signs lead you inland to a car park and some hot-food stalls, where you pay your national park entry fee (B200, kids B100) and walk the final 500m to the twenty-metre-high waterfall (best in the rainy season) that plunges into an invitingly clear pool defined by a ring of smooth rocks.

Both Chaichet and Khlong Phrao have roadside tourist villages with **ATMs**, minimarkets, tour agents, dive centres, internet access, shops and restaurants. The **police** have a post at Chaichet, and in Khlong Phrao there's a **clinic,** a fuel

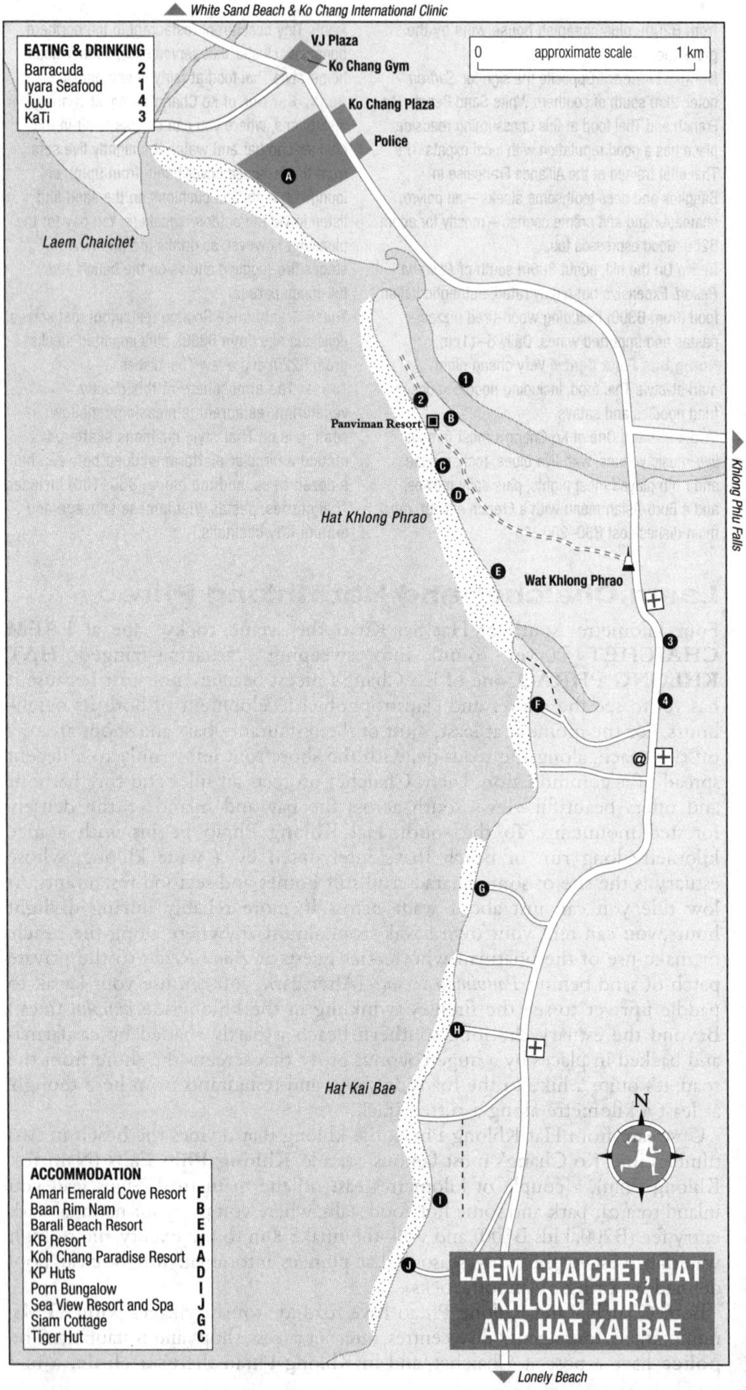
White Sand Beach & Ko Chang International Clinic
EATING & DRINKING
Barracuda 2
Iyara Seafood 1
JuJu 4
KaTi 3
VJ Plaza
Ko Chang Gym
Ko Chang Plaza
Police
0 approximate scale 1 km
Laem Chaichet
Panviman Resort
Hat Khlong Phrao
Wat Khlong Phrao
Khlong Phlu Falls
Hat Kai Bae
ACCOMMODATION
Amari Emerald Cove Resort F
Baan Rim Nam B
Barali Beach Resort E
KB Resort H
Koh Chang Paradise Resort A
KP Huts D
Porn Bungalow I
Sea View Resort and Spa J
Siam Cottage G
Tiger Hut C
N
LAEM CHAICHET, HAT KHLONG PHRAO AND HAT KAI BAE
Lonely Beach

station and a community temple, Wat Khlong Phrao. And from the southern end of Khlong Phrao it's only a few hundred metres south to the start of the Kai Bae tourist village amenities.

Accommodation

Amari Emerald Cove Resort ⓣ039 552000, ⓦwww.amari.com. Top-of-the-scale chain hotel that occupies a lovely tranquil spot on the southern beach, complete with its own palm-shaded sandy terrace and huge seafront swimming pool. Rooms are in low-rise three-storey blocks set around the pool, tropical garden and lagoons, and are typical deluxe style, with wooden floors and balconies. ⑨

Baan Rim Nam ⓣ087 005 8575, ⓦwww.iamkohchang.com. Peaceful, scenic and unusual, this converted fishing family's house is built on stilts over the wide, attractive khlong at the end of a walkway through the mangroves. Run by the British author of the best Ko Chang website, it has just three comfortable air-con rooms with good bathrooms and free wi-fi, plus a big deck for soaking up views of the khlongside village, but no restaurant. You can borrow kayaks and it's a couple of minutes' walk to the beach and *Barracuda* restaurant, or 20min to the main Khlong Phrao facilities. ⑤

Barali Beach Resort ⓣ039 557238, ⓦwww.baralikohchang.com. One of the more elegant spots on the southern beach, with forty tastefully designed, Balinese-style rooms, furnished with four-poster beds, sunken baths and lots of polished wood, and set around a beachfront tropical garden with an infinity-edge swimming pool. ⑨

Koh Chang Paradise Resort ⓣ039 551100, ⓦwww.kohchangparadise.com. The biggest and most popular place to stay on the Chaichet end of the beach occupies a huge area between the road and the shore so offers easy access to the beach as well as shops and restaurants. Its generously designed concrete bungalows have French windows and comfortable, hotel-style, air-con interiors. Some have private plunge pools and there's also a central swimming pool. ⑧–⑨

KP Huts ⓣ084 099 5100. Though the fifty timber huts here are very simple for the price, they are attractively scattered through the broad shoreside coconut grove (about 1.5km from roadside amenities) with plenty of sea views. Even some of the cheapest options (with shared bathrooms) are right on the shore, and a few are raised high on stilts for an extra-seductive panorama; en-suite huts are huge, and some are designed for families. Shared bathroom ③, en suite ④–⑤

Tiger Hut ⓣ084 109 9660. One of the few budget-minded, old-school travellers' beach bungalows left on Ko Chang, occupying a sandy beachfront garden just south of the khlong and about 2km down a track from the main road. The woven-bamboo huts have simple but fresh interiors and there's a restaurant deck and bar with pool table plus motorbike rental. Shared bathroom ②, en suite ③

Eating and drinking

Restaurants on Hat Khlong Phrao worth making a special effort for include the beachfront-shack *Barracuda*, between *Tiger Hut* and *Panviman Resort*, which serves especially good, mid-priced seafood; and, for its khlongside setting, the posh *Iyara* seafood restaurant, built on stilts over the estuary behind *Tiger Hut*. On the roadside, *KaTi* restaurant and cookery school (see p.466) serves great Thai food, including infinite permutations of red, green, yellow and southern curries, plus delicious home-made ice-creams and inventive mint, lychee and lemon smoothies. Across from the *Amari* turnoff, *JuJu* beer garden is run by a French musician and known for its **world music** band, its jam sessions and its good-quality visiting musicians.

Hat Kai Bae

Narrow, pretty little **HAT KAI BAE** (see map opposite) presents a classic picture of white sand, pale blue water and overhanging palms, but in places the shorefront is very slender indeed – and filled with bungalows – and the beach can disappear entirely at high tide. The beach is bisected by a khlong and rocky point, with most of the accommodation to the south. Seaward views from the southernmost end take in the tiny island of Ko Man Nai, whose sandy shores are easily reached by kayak, half an hour offshore from *Sea View Resort*. Kai Bae's roadside tourist village is busy and stretches a couple of kilometres. It's got plenty of shops, bars and restaurants, as well as ATMs, currency exchange, dive shops (see p.474), a second-hand bookshop and internet access.

The most famous of the dwindling number of budget **accommodation** options on the beach is *Porn Bungalow* (☎089 099 8757, ⓦwww.pornsbungalows -kohchang.com; ❷–❺), which has scores of fan bungalows in various styles, set under palm trees along a big expanse of the shorefront. The cheapest are in old-style bamboo and concrete huts; the most luxurious are spacious wooden cabins with wraparound decks. *Porn's* over-water restaurant deck does seafood barbecues nightly in high season and has a pool table and bar. Also affordably priced considering the competition, but at the northern end of Hat Kai Bae, is *Siam Cottage* (☎089 153 6664; ❸), whose 36 wooden bungalows face each other across a narrow lot that runs down to the sea. There's a restaurant and internet access here and bungalows have modern, cheerily painted interiors with a hint of style, plus fans and private decks. The best of Kai Bae's mid-priced options is the attractive shorefront *KB Resort* (☎039 557125, ⓦwww.kbresort .com; fan ❺, air-con ❼) with 49 good-quality bungalows set around a tropical garden with swimming pool. The air-con bungalows have huge windows, many of which enjoy direct sea views; fan versions stand further back. The swankiest beachfront hotel is *Sea View Resort and Spa* (☎081 830 7529, ⓦwww .seaviewkohchang.com; ❼–❾), set around a lawn and tropical flower garden towards the southern end of Hat Kai Bae. It has a swimming pool and a pretty spa and its air-con "spa" (hotel) rooms and cottages are large, light and airy.

▲ Hat Kai Bae

LONELY BEACH & AO BAI LAN

Siam Beach

Lonely Beach

Minimart

ACCOMMODATION
Bhumiyama Beach Resort	B
Nature Beach	A
Paradise Cottage	F
Siam Hut	C
The Sunflower	D
Sunset Hut	E

EATING
Coffee House	2
Saïan	3
Sign Ngam	1

❶ Ploy Scuba Diving

❷ Scuba Evolution

Motorbike Repair

@

❸

Ⓕ BB Divers

N

Ao Bai Lan

@

Dusit Princess Resort ◼
Bailan Herbal Sauna

Treetop Adventure Park

0 150 m

Bang Bao ▼

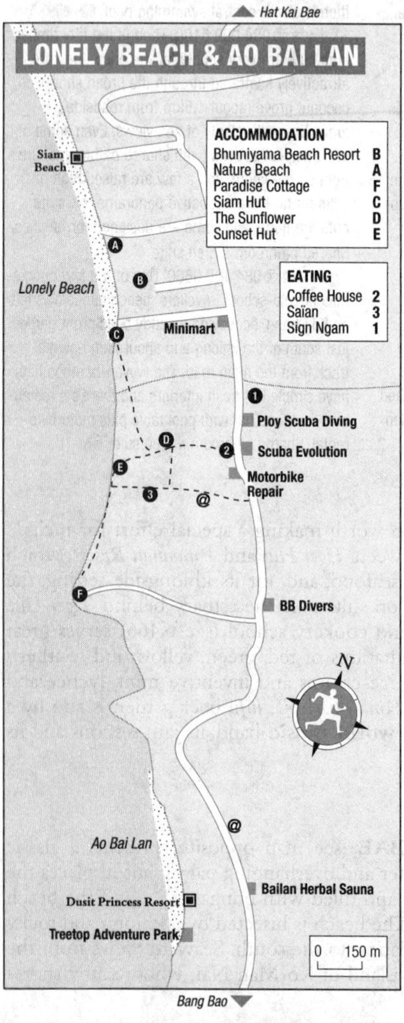

Lonely Beach (Hat Tha Nam) and Ao Bai Lan

Hat Tha Nam – dubbed **LONELY BEACH** before it became Ko Chang's top place to party – is small and lively, with a shorefront that's occupied by just four sets of increasingly expensive accommodation and a hinterland village, ten minutes' walk away, that's the most traveller-oriented on the island. It's here, overlooking the rocks immediately south of the beach, and along the sandy sois that run inland to the main road, that backpackers feel most at home, in little bungalows and guest houses squashed any old how beneath the remaining trees, with every other shop-shack offering tattoos or internet access. Despite the creeping concrete, creatively designed little wood and bamboo bar-restaurants abound, some of them offering chilled, low-key escapes from the loud dance music, all-night parties and B250 buckets of vodka Red Bull that the beachfront places are notorious for, others cranking it up just as hard and fast. The most intense partying mostly happens down on the beach, usually at *Nature Beach*, which kicks off most high-season nights with seafood barbecues, live music and fire-juggling shows.

Day and (especially) night, you should be extremely careful when swimming off Lonely Beach, especially around *Siam Beach* at the northern end, as the steep shelf and dangerous current result in a sobering number of double-figure **drownings** every year, particularly during the monsoon season; do your swimming further south and don't go out at all when the waves are high. Also be careful with your belongings – many a drunken night sees cameras, phones and wallets pilfered unnoticed. Among the roadside shops you'll find an **ATM** and a dive shop (see p.474), plus tour agents and motorbike rental and repair.

A fifteen-minute walk along the road and over the hill from the southern end of Lonely Beach village will bring you to **AO BAI LAN**, which hasn't got much of a beach to speak of, but is the site of two of Ko Chang's most interesting attractions, the **Treetop Adventure Park** and the **Bailan Herbal Sauna** (see p.466 for both).

Accommodation

Bhumiyama Beach Resort Central beach area ☎081 860 4623, www.bhumiyama.com. The poshest place on the beach has just 45 attractively furnished rooms, in deluxe two-storey bungalows and hotel wings set around grassy seafront lawns and a good-sized swimming pool. Interiors are quite chic – bungalows have four-poster beds and polished wooden floors – and all have bathtubs; only the premier rooms have sea views. 8–9

Nature Beach Central beach area ☎081 803 8933. Responsible for Lonely Beach's party reputation, this place is hugely popular and, at the time of writing, was planning to upgrade all 65 of its tasteful but simple fan and air-con bungalows. Prices have always been on the high side because it occupies a prime location in the middle of the beach and is at the heart of the action (so if you prefer a quiet night's sleep it's best to head elsewhere). There's a tour desk, internet access and massage, plus a big restaurant and bar with live music, DJs and the rest. 3–5

Paradise Cottage On the rocky shore, a 10min walk south along the rocks from the sandy beach ☎081 773 9337, loengbkk@hotmail.com. Backpacker chic is the style here, where accommodation is no frills but there's an air of Bangkok sophistication about the design, especially the communal wooden decks whose hammocks and easy chairs are perfect for lounging, horizon-gazing and sipping cocktails; there's wi-fi here too. Though the 32 en-suite wood and thatch huts are fairly simple they are also in good condition and look stylish; they all have fans and mozzie nets. The slightly more expensive ones have sea views, and the rest are enveloped by banana trees in the tropical, heliconia-filled-garden. There's no sand here, but you can swim off the rocks at high tide. 3

Siam Hut Central beach area ☎086 609 7772, www.siamhutkohchang.com. The cheapest place to stay right on the beach has rows and rows of primitive, split-bamboo huts – eighty in total – all of them en suite and with little else but plank floors, mattresses and mozzie nets. It's first come, first served for the prime seafront spots. Fan 2–3, air-con 4

The Sunflower Inland, on Soi Sunset ☎084 017 9960, www.the-sunflower.com. Run by a genial German and his Thai family, the two-dozen bungalows here are set under palm and banana trees 200m from the roadside village and equidistant from the rocky coast at *Sunset*, a 5min walk south of the sandy beach. Choose between old bamboo huts with shared bathrooms, sturdy wooden fan bungalows with open-roofed bathrooms, and concrete bungalows; all have good thick mattresses and are kept very clean. The restaurant is good and has wi-fi. Shared bathroom ❷, en suite ❸, air-con ❹

Sunset Hut 5min walk south beyond *Siam Hut*, on the rocks ⓣ081 818 7042. The good-quality concrete en-suite bungalows here have proper beds and big windows and some also have perfect, private, over-sea decks. There are also some cheaper en-suite huts at the back plus a few big air-con bungalows. The seafront deck-restaurant and bar attracts a lively crowd and holds occasional parties. Though you can only swim here at high tide, it's a short walk to the sandy beach and just 400m inland to roadside shops and restaurants. Fan ❷–❸, air-con ❹–❺

Diving and snorkelling in the Ko Chang archipelago

Because there's just one tide a day in the inner Gulf, the **reefs** of the Ko Chang archipelago are much less colourful and varied than Andaman coast dive sites, and they can get very crowded, but they're rewarding enough to make a day-trip worthwhile. The main **dive and snorkel sites** are west of Ko Mak, in the national marine park around **Ko Rang** and its satellite islets. These range from beginners' reefs with lots of hard corals and anemones at depths of 4–6m, frequented by plenty of reef fish – including a resident ten-thousand-strong shoal of yellow fusiliers – and the occasional moray eel, to the more challenging 25-metre dive at the Pinnacles. There are also some technical wreck dives of Japanese boats from World War II and even some centuries-old Chinese trading ships. The coral around Ko Yuak, off Ko Chang's Hat Kai Bae, is mostly dead, though some operators still sell trips there.

Dive shops on Ko Chang

The biggest concentration of dive shops is on Ko Chang, though there are also some on Ko Wai, Ko Mak and Ko Kood (see relevant accounts for details). Some **Ko Chang dive shops** have their main office in Bang Bao, where most boats depart, as well as a branch office or agent elsewhere on the island; those listed below are the main reputable operators. All dive shops will organize pick-ups from any beach. See p.73 for a general introduction to diving in Thailand and for advice on what to look for in a dive centre.

Waves permitting, Ko Chang dive shops run trips year round, though during the **monsoon season**, from June to September, visibility can be poor. **Prices** for local dive trips, with two tanks, average B2200–B2900, or B1000 for accompanying snorkellers. Dive courses cost about B14,500 for the four-day Openwater, and B4500 for the one-day Discover Scuba introduction.

BB Divers Lonely Beach and Bang Bao ⓣ086 155 6212, ⓦwww.bbdivers.com. Belgian-run, PADI Five-Star IDC centre which uses fishing boats (with sun decks) rather than speedboats.

Ploy Scuba Diving Hat Sai Khao, Hat Kai Bae, Lonely Beach and Bang Bao ⓣ086 155 1331, ⓦwww.ployscuba.com. Big Thai run-operation.

Scuba Dreams Hat Kai Bae ⓣ089 472 8782, ⓦwww.scuba-dreams.com.

Scuba Evolution Hat Sai Khao, Hat Kai Bae, Lonely Beach ⓣ087 926 4973, ⓦwww.scuba-evolution.com. British-run dive company that specializes in technical and wreck diving.

Snorkelling

From about November to May, several companies run dedicated **snorkelling trips** to reefs and islands around Ko Chang, Ko Wai and Ko Rang. Tickets are sold by tour agents on every beach and prices range from B600 to B1250, depending on the size of the boat (some take as many as a hundred people in high season) and the number of islands visited. In general the more islands "featured" (sailed past), the less time there is for snorkelling, though nearly all the actual snorkelling happens around **Ko Rang**.

Eating

Along the roadside you'll find some good, cheap, local Thai **restaurants**, including the Isaan specialist *Sign Ngam*, beside the khlong bridge at the north end of the village, which does several types of *som tam*, catfish curry and snakehead fish soup (B25–60). Invitingly idiosyncratic *Coffee House* (8am–3pm), on Soi Sunset, serves strong coffee and breakfasts, and *Saïan*, on parallel Soi Warapura, is run by a young French chef who serves charcuterie plates, bakes his own baguettes and croissants and does filet mignon and mushroom and pork tagliatelle. The restaurant at *The Sunflower* (open high season only) dishes up very generous set breakfasts for B150 and authentically spicy Thai curries.

Bang Bao and Hat Khlong Gloi

Almost at the end of the west-coast road, the southern harbour village of **BANG BAO**, much of it built on stilts off a central jetty, is the departure point for boat trips and transfers to the outer islands and is also an increasingly popular place to stay. Though it has no beach of its own, you're within a short motorbike ride of both undeveloped Hat Khlong Gloi, 2km to the east, and Lonely Beach, 5km up the coast. Accommodation is mostly in jetty homes and bungalows, often with exceptional bay views, and some pleasingly chilled bar-restaurants share the outlook. Bang Bao is, however, almost entirely given over to tourist facilities, and vanloads of day-trippers clog the jetty village as they linger over the trinket shops, clothes stalls and dive shops (see opposite). Seafood lunches are another attraction, most famously at the long-running *Chow Lay* restaurant.

The cushions, hammocks and swing-seats at the cool and funky Ibiza-vibe *Casa del Mar* **lounge-bar** and guest house (Ⓣ083 174 5695, Ⓦwww.casadelmarkohchang.com; ❺–❻), halfway along the jetty's east side, are an ideal place to escape the day-tripping crowds. Aside from stunning panoramas of the bay, there's good music and free wi-fi plus Thai and Western food, cocktails (happy hour 6–8pm) and Saturday evening parties; **accommodation** is in one of seven tasteful fan or air-con rooms. Other places to stay on the main jetty

▲ Jetty village, Bang Bao, Ko Chang

include the no-frills jetty huts with shared bathrooms at *Paradise* (Ⓣ089 934 8044; ❶); the jetty rooms at *Boo Guest House* (Ⓣ089 831 1874; ❸), which are very clean but have no particular view; and the very attractive *Bang Bao Sea Hut* (Ⓣ081 285 0570; ❼), whose fourteen tastefully modern, octagonal over-sea villas – with air-con and polished wood floors – overlook the harbour and are connected to the main jetty by a series of walkways.

Secluded on a narrow neck of land across the bay to the west of the village, boutique little *Nirvana Koh Chang* (Ⓣ039 558061, Ⓦwww.nirvanakohchang.com; ❾) is a relaxed and lushly landscaped retreat with private forest walks, a cliffside boardwalk, two pools and access to two swimmable coasts but no real beach. Accommodation is in fifteen rather chic, Balinese-accented villas, some with direct sea views. Even if you're not staying you could come and eat at the dramatically sited waterside *Tantra* restaurant, creatively furnished with woodcarvings from the Indonesian archipelago and serving a menu of contemporary Thai dishes and seafood; set lunches are B300 or you could book the dinner package (B1000), which includes sunset drinks, food and transport.

The nearest swimmable beach to Bang Bao and *Nirvana* is long, sandy **Hat Khlong Gloi**, 2km east of the village and not far short of the end of the tarmac. It's backed by a lagoon and a long stretch of beach-scrub and for the time being at least has nothing much more than a couple of small beach cafés, a few deckchairs, and the construction site for a ten-room resort; it can still get quite busy though. *KK Family* café (Ⓣ081 715 3940) rents tents on the beach (B250 including bedding) or you can pitch your own for B100.

The east coast

Beaches along the mangrove-fringed **east coast** are less inviting than those in the west, but this side of Ko Chang is much less developed and makes for a fun day-trip; it's about 35km from Khlong Son in the north to Salak Pet in the south.

South of the piers at Ao Saparot and Tha Dan Kao, the east-coast road runs through long swathes of rubber and palm plantations, with jungle-clad hills to the west and bronze-coloured beaches to the east, passing the national park office and bungalows at **Than Mayom**, where signs direct you inland to Than Mayom falls, a 45-minute uphill hike away. South another 6km and you come to *The Spa* (Ⓣ039 553091, Ⓦwww.thespakohchang.com; ❼–❾), a beautifully designed upscale but reasonably priced wellness and detox retreat specializing in colema treatments (coffee enemas); it also has branches on Ko Samui and in Chiang Mai. It's set in a lovely mature tropical garden that runs down to the mangrove-ringed bay of western **Ao Salak Kok** and welcomes day visitors for massage, herbal saunas and facials (from B500) as well as guests who don't want to detox. The restaurant has a good reputation and the menu includes raw-food dishes, goats' yogurt and halal meals. Fork left at the junction just south of *The Spa* to reach the southern edge of the bay and its small fishing settlement, **SALAK KOK**, site of the award-winning Salak Kok Kayak Station, a community tourism venture that runs **kayak tours** along a marked route through the mangroves (B100 per hr for kayak rental or B200 with guide) and does mangrove seafood-dinner cruises (Ⓣ081 919 3995; B1200) on a wooden catamaran too.

From Salak Kok, continue down to the tip of the southeastern headland to reach **Hat Sai Yao**, or **LONG BEACH**, the prettiest white-sand beach on this coast, which is good for swimming and has some coral close to shore. The famous *Treehouse* bungalows from Lonely Beach have relocated here under new management as *Treehouse Lodge* (Ⓣ081 847 8215, Ⓦwww.tree-house.org; ❷; closed in low season); accommodation is in simple, idiosyncratic, thatched bamboo huts and it all feels pretty remote. A daily songthaew travels here from Lonely Beach (10am; B100) but if coming from Trat, either take the 3pm Ko Wai boat from Laem Ngop, which will drop you near *Treehouse Lodge*, or use the Trat-Salak Pet songthaew service; staff from *Treehouse Lodge* should meet both the boat and the songthaew.

Most day-trippers turn right not left just after *The Spa* and head instead for the little fishing port of **SALAK PET** on the south coast. Still a fairly quiet spot, Salak Pet is best known for its excellent **seafood restaurant**, *Salakphet Resort*, whose bayside dining deck offers fine views and food that's so good people travel here all the way from Trat just for lunch; crabs are a speciality – particularly stir-fried with black pepper, or with curry powder – but it's all fresh so the possibilities are infinite.

Ko Wai

Lovely, palm-edged little **KO WAI** (or Ko Whai), 10km south of Ko Chang, is only 3km long and 1.5km wide – perfect for circumnavigating in a kayak – and is encircled by sparkling turquoise water and several reefs. It has just a few **places to stay** (Oct–May only). Of these, the ultra laid-back *Koh Wai Paradise* (Ⓣ081 762 2548; ❷) has the prettiest beach, on the northern headland, and offers forty very basic, no-frills-at-all bamboo huts in varying sizes (electricity 6–11pm only); unfortunately it serves lunch to the hordes of day-trippers from Ko Chang so it's not always peaceful. Further south, on a secluded brown-sand beach, *Koh Wai Goodfeeling* (Ⓣ081 850 3410; ❷) has its reception off the main pier and just seven simple en-suite bungalows spread across the rocky coast. To the east, a twenty-minute walk from *Paradise*, the more comfortable though less atmospheric *Koh Wai Pakarang Resort* (Ⓣ084 113 8946, Ⓦwww.kohwaipakarang.com; fan ❹–❺, air-con ❼) has 39 en-suite wood and concrete beachside bungalows, a restaurant pavilion built off the pier, plus internet access and nightly movies.

Boats from the mainland to Ko Wai depart from Laem Ngop's Tha Kromaluang Pier, 3km west of Laem Ngop and 20km southwest of Trat, once a day at 3pm (approximately Nov–May; 2hr 30min; B250). From approximately June to September, Bang Bao Boat (Ⓣ087 054 4300, Ⓦwww.bangbaoboat.com) runs one slow service and usually one speedboat as well to Ko Wai **from Ko Chang** (1–2 daily; 20min, B400; 45min, B300) and **Ko Mak** (1–2 daily; 20min, B400; 45min, B300). Several companies on Ko Chang also offer day-trips to Ko Wai.

Ko Mak

Small, slow-paced, peaceful **KO MAK** (sometimes spelt "Maak") makes an idyllically low-key alternative to Ko Chang, 20km to the northwest. Home to little more than four hundred people, many of them descended from the islands' five main clans, Ko Mak measures just sixteen square kilometres and is dominated by coconut and rubber plantations. A couple of narrow concrete roads traverse the island; elsewhere a network of red-earth tracks cuts through the trees. The island is shaped like a star, with fine white-sand beaches along the northwest coast at **Ao Suan Yai** and the southwest coast at **Ao Kao**, where most of the island's (predominantly mid-range and upper-bracket) tourist accommodation is

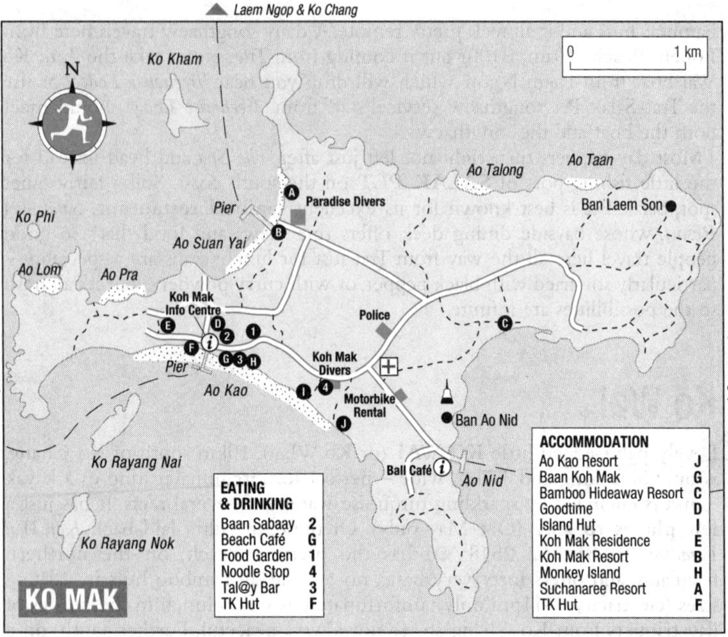

concentrated; the principal village of **Ban Ao Nid** is on the southeast coast and there's another village at **Ban Laem Son** on the east coast. The main beaches are just about within walking distance of each other, and other parts of the island are also fairly easy to explore on foot, or by mountain bike, motorbike or kayak – the best way to discover the empty undeveloped beaches hidden along the north and eastern coasts. The **reefs** of Ko Rang are also less than an hour's boat ride away so snorkelling and diving trips are quite popular.

During the **rainy season**, from early June through September, choppy seas mean that boat services to Ko Mak are much reduced. Most Ko Mak accommodation stays open – and offers tempting discounts – but the smaller places often don't bother to staff their restaurants. Islanders say that it can be very pleasant during this "green season", though you may be unlucky and hit a relentlessly wet few days.

Getting to Ko Mak

As the island gets more popular, **boat services** from the mainland and the other islands are increasing: check Ⓦwww.kohmak.com for current routes and schedules. Boats arrive at one of Ko Mak's three **piers** – at *Koh Mak Resort* on Ao Suan Yai, at the *Makathanee Resort* on Ao Kao or at Ao Nid – and are always met by a modest welcoming committee of accommodation staff offering free transport. When it comes to moving on, all hotels keep current boat schedules and can sell you a ticket; if going to Ko Chang be sure to pre-book a taxi from the arrival pier to your hotel at the same time as not all Ko Mak boats dock at the main piers.

In principle, there's at least one year-round slow boat **from the Trat mainland**, which departs from Laem Ngop Pier, in Laem Ngop, some 20km southwest of Trat (3hr; B300). From approximately October to May, up to five daily speedboat services also operate from this pier to Ko Mak (B450; 45min). In addition, there are currently three daily October to May services to Ko Mak from Laem Sok, 30km south of Trat (B300–450 including free transfer from central Trat; 40min–1hr 10min). If you stay over in Trat you can consult Trat guest houses and tour agents for the best option, and buy tickets from them; if arriving direct from Bangkok, Ko Samet or elsewhere, and bypassing Trat, you'll likely be whisked straight to Laem Ngop by waiting taxi drivers (see p.462). A taxi service all the way **from Bangkok** to Ko Mak is also available (B1100 including boat transfer; Ⓦwww.kohmak.com).

Except during the rainy season, there are also a number of boat services from nearby islands. Between September and June there's one daily Bang Bao slow boat and usually a speedboat as well (Ⓣ087 054 4300; Ⓦwww.bangbaoboat.com) **from Ko Chang** (slow boat 2hr, B400; speedboat 50min, B550) to Ko Mak, via **Ko Wai** (1hr, B300; 20min, B400). **From Ko Kood** you have the option of one daily ferry (45min; B250) and at least a couple of speedboats (35min–1hr; B350).

Island practicalities

The best one-stop shop for **information** about Ko Mak and transport to Trat and the other islands is the comprehensive website Ⓦwww.kohmak.com and its creator, who runs *Ball Café* at the Ao Nid pier-head (Nov–May daily 7am–6pm; Ⓣ086 972 4918), where you can also access the internet (and wi-fi), rent mountain bikes and quaff cappuccinos; it's a twenty-minute walk from *Island Hut* on Ao Kao or about thirty minutes from *Koh Mak Resort*. There are additional information centres and tour agents on Ao Suan Yai and Ao Kao.

The island has no public transport and virtually no traffic of any sort, so most visitors rent a **mountain bike** (B150 per day) or **motorbike** (B350 per day), either from one of the hotels, from the shop next to the *White Elephant Restaurant* on the Ao Nid road, about 300m south of the T-junction, or from the Koh Mak Information Centre in front of *Makathanee Resort* on Ao Kao. The island does have some long and potentially interesting signed **mountain-bike routes** – discreet concrete posts enigmatically carved with route numbers A1-C7 – but the explanatory map for navigating them is currently out of print: either ask about them at *Ball Café* or simply go exploring. Apparently it's possible to walk, wade and swim around the entire perimeter of the island in ten hours.

There is as yet no major commercial development on the island and **no bank or ATM**, just a few local shops in Ban Ao Nid and along its access road, and another behind *Baan Ko Mak* on the Ao Kao road. Bungalows on both beaches will **change money** and *Koh Mak Resort* on Ao Suan Yai does Visa card cash advances. For **internet access** on Ao Kao go to *Ao Kao Resort*, *Makathanee Resort* or *Baan Sabaay* restaurant (which has wi-fi too), and on Ao Suan Yai go to *Koh Mak Resort*, which is also a **postal agent**. There's a small **clinic** off the Ao Nid road, though for anything serious a speedboat will whisk you back to the mainland.

The mediocre reefs of Ko Rang (see p.474), part of the Ko Chang National Marine Park, are less than an hour's boat ride west of Ko Mak and are the island's main **diving and snorkelling** destination; they're also the main focus of Ko Chang dive and snorkel boats, so you won't be alone. Snorkelling and inland excursions to Ko Kood are also available. Island dive shops, which operate from October through May only, include the British-run Koh Mak Divers (Ⓣ083 297 7724, Ⓦwww.kohmak-divers.com), on the Ao Kao road just east of *Island Hut*, and German-run Paradise Divers at *Koh Mak Resort* on Ao Suan Yai (Ⓦwww.thailandtauchen.com). Out of season, contact British freelance dive instructor Stuart (☎089 062 5071) at his house near *Baan Chai Lay* resort towards the western end of Ao Kao. Prices average B2300 for two fun dives, and B650 for snorkellers. Most hotels can also book snorkelling trips to the nearby Ko Rayang islands.

Ao Kao

Ko Mak's longest and nicest beach is **AO KAO** on the southwest coast, a pretty arc of sand that's overhung with stooping palm trees and backed in places by mangroves. The beach is divided towards its southern end by a low rocky outcrop that's straddled by *Ao Kao Resort*, with *Sunset Resort* occupying the southern headland beyond, while the long western beach is shared by a dozen other sets of bungalows. The roadside inland from the main accommodation area is where you'll find most of the restaurants and bars: if you're walking from the southern end, by far the easiest access is via the beach, tides permitting.

Koh Mak Information Centre (Oct–May daily 7.30am–7pm; ☎081 870 6287, Ⓦwww.makathanee.com) at the upmarket *Makathanee Resort*, west of *Baan Koh Mak*, is a one-stop shop for boat and plane tickets, tour and transfer **information** (including Cambodia visa runs), day-trips, and bicycle and motorbike rental.

Accommodation

Ao Kao Resort ☎039 501001, Ⓦwww.kohmak.com. This long-running and efficiently managed set of upscale bungalows occupies an attractive garden fronting the prettiest part of the beach. Its thirty large, comfortable en-suite timber bungalows come with fan or air-con and some have direct sea views. There's massage and internet access and kayaks and motorbikes for rent. Fan ⑤, air-con ⑧

Baan Koh Mak ☎089 895 7592, Ⓦwww.baan-koh-mak.com. The eighteen cute rose-and-lime-painted bungalows here are modern and comfortable, with air-con, comfortable beds and good bathrooms, and each is enclosed within its own white picket fence. There's a very good restaurant here, plus motorbike and kayak rental and boat trips. ⑤

Goodtime ☎039 501000, Ⓦwww.goodtime-resort.com, and **Koh Mak Residence** Ⓦwww.kohmakresidence.com. Villa developments by these two companies are rented to visiting tourists by the day or week. The serviced houses are luxurious Thai and tastefully styled: most are one- and two-bed homes with a living area, deck and kitchen, plus DVD player, wi-fi and use of a pool. They're located on higher ground inland from Ao Kao's *Makathanee Resort*, around 20min walk from the beach. ⑧–⑨

Island Hut ☎087 139 5537. This family-run little place has the best value and most idyllically sited accommodation on the beach, though not always the friendliest welcome. The two-dozen en-suite rough-hewn timber huts are more artfully designed than they might appear: most have cheery stripey doors and idiosyncratic driftwood artwork; all have fans, hanging space and their own deckchairs on decks or on private sandy porches. Price depends on proximity to the narrow but pretty shore: the most expensive are at the water's edge. ①–③

Monkey Island ☎087 692 1001, Ⓦwww.monkeyislandkohmak.com. There's a big range of quality, contemporary styled bungalows here, all in timber and thatch. Top-end "Gorilla" seafront villas are huge, with air-con and the possibility of connecting villas; the large fan and air-con "Chimpanzee" bungalows are also good, while some of the small "Baboon" options share bathrooms. There's a kids' swimming pool, plus wi-fi and internet access. Fan ③–⑤, air-con ⑥

TK Hut ☎087 134 8435, Ⓦkohmak.com. One of Ko Mak's first resorts, whose old-fashioned but well-priced wood, stone and concrete bungalows are set around a shady garden of casuarinas and little hedges. Also has a seafront bar and restaurant, internet access, plus kayak and motorbike rental. Rates include buffet breakfast. Fan ④, air-con ⑤–⑥

Eating and drinking

Baan Sabaay Between *Baan Ko Mak* and *Makathanee*, inland side of the road. A congenial and lively place for a few Beer Changs and a chat with island expats. Also serves food and has internet terminals and wi-fi.

Beach Café At *Baan Ko Mak*. The kitchen here serves exceptionally delicious Thai food, including good *tom kha* soups and great *phanaeng* curries. Mains from B60.

Food Garden Opposite *Monkey Island*. A cross between a beer garden and a night market, this very popular, cheap and enjoyable outdoor restaurant comprises several concessions serving *phat thai*, yellow curry, recommended *haw mok* (steamed fish and coconut curry), chicken satay, grilled seafood, *som tam* and beer. Dishes start at B30 and there's a big screen for major sports fixtures.

Noodle Stop Between *Island Hut* and Koh Mak Divers. A good cheap place for noodle soups (B30) and the rest.

Tal@y Bar On the beach in front of *Ko Mak Cottages*. Deckchairs and lamps on the sand and great margaritas (B120) plus a long list of other cocktails. Happy hour 9–10pm.

TK Hut The thrice-weekly all-you-can-eat seafood barbecues here get lots of returnees; from 6.30pm.

Ao Suan Yai and around

Long, curvy **AO SUAN YAI** is not as pretty a beach as Ao Kao, but the sand is fine and the outlook is beautiful, with Ko Chang's hilly profile filling the horizon and Ko Kham and other islets in between. You'll need a bicycle or motorbike to access the variety of restaurants on the Ao Kao road as there's just a couple of **accommodation** options here. The biggest is the extensive *Koh Mak Resort* (ⓣ039 501013, ⓦwww.kohmakresort.com; ❻–❾), which offers various air-con bungalows, all enjoying lovely panoramas, the most interesting of which are the very modern, design-conscious, sea-view and beachfront suites – all polished concrete, stacked slate walls, huge picture windows and private little walled gardens. There's a swimming pool and similarly chic pool bar here too, plus currency exchange, Visa cash advance, internet access and a tour desk, plus postal services, a taxi service, motorbike and kayak rental, a dive shop and a pier. Neighbouring *Suchanaree Resort* (ⓣ081 983 2629, ⓔSuchanaree_Tour@hotmail.com; ❸) couldn't be more different. Comprising just half-a-dozen shoreside bungalows, it's an intimate, friendly little place and deservedly popular. The cute, good-quality, shaggy-thatched wooden bungalows all have fan, mozzie nets and bathrooms.

A couple of kilometres southeast of Ao Suan Yai, accessed via tracks through the rubber plantations, *Bamboo Hideaway Resort* (ⓣ039 501085; ⓦwww.bamboohideaway.com; ❼) is an idiosyncratic haven, built almost entirely from lengths of polished bamboo. Its eight comfortable air-con rooms all have four-poster beds and hammocks and are connected by a raised bamboo walkway. Although the south coast is just a couple of minutes' walk downhill, Ao Suan Yai has the nearest decent beach. There's a good-sized swimming pool on site, along with the *Naked Fish* restaurant, which specializes in upscale authentic Thai and northeastern food (non-guests can phone for free transport) and is presided over by a genial New Zealand host.

Ko Kood

The fourth-largest island in Thailand, forested **KO KOOD** (also spelt Ko Kut and Ko Kud) is still a wild and largely uncommercialized island. Though it's known for its sparkling white sand and exceptionally clear turquoise water, particularly along the west coast, Ko Kood is as much a nature-lover's destination as a beach-bum's. Swathes of its shoreline are fringed by scrub and

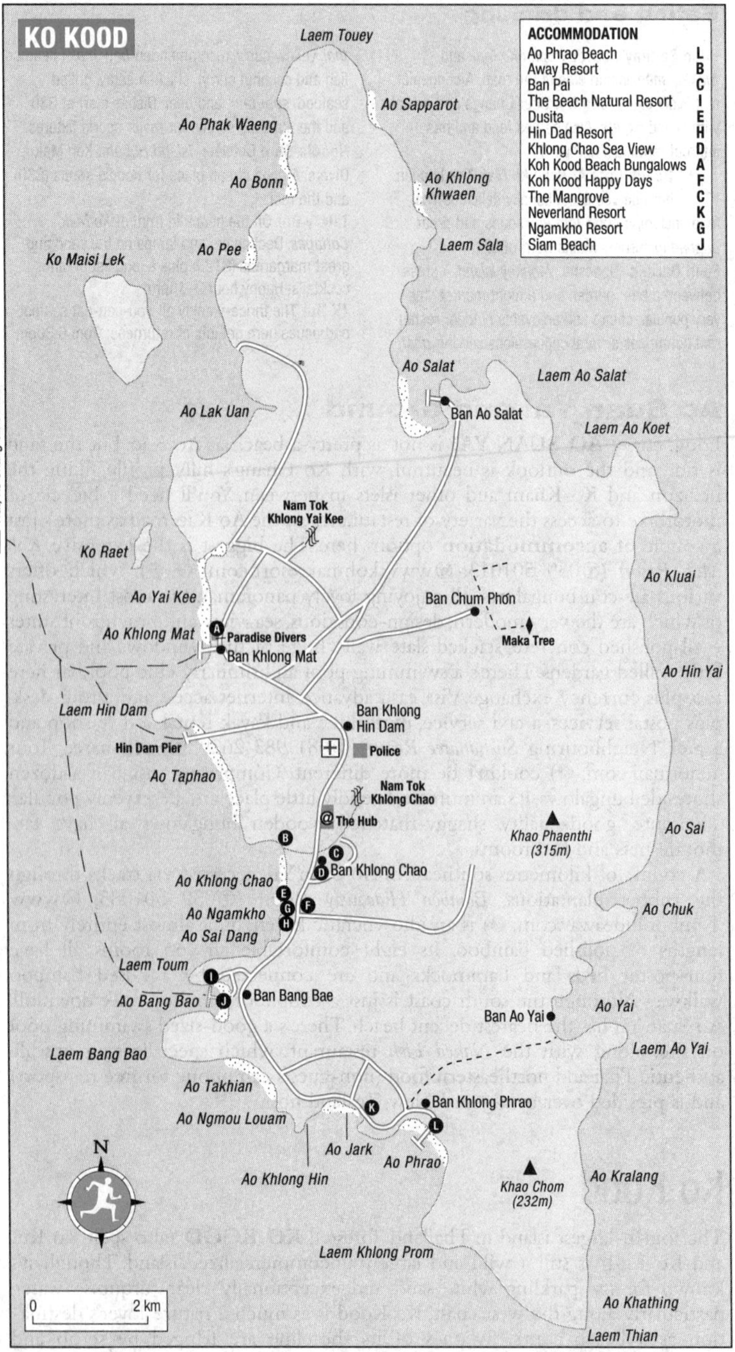
KO KOOD
ACCOMMODATION
Ao Phrao Beach L
Away Resort B
Ban Pai C
The Beach Natural Resort I
Dusita E
Hin Dad Resort H
Khlong Chao Sea View D
Koh Kood Beach Bungalows A
Koh Kood Happy Days F
The Mangrove C
Neverland Resort K
Ngamkho Resort G
Siam Beach J
Laem Touey
Ao Sapparot
Ao Phak Waeng
Ao Bonn
Ao Khlong Khwaen
Laem Sala
Ao Pee
Ko Maisi Lek
Ao Salat
Laem Ao Salat
Ban Ao Salat
Laem Ao Koet
Ao Lak Uan
Nam Tok Khlong Yai Kee
Ko Raet
Ao Kluai
Ao Yai Kee
Ban Chum Phon
Ao Khlong Mat
Paradise Divers
Maka Tree
Ban Khlong Mat
Ao Hin Yai
Laem Hin Dam
Ban Khlong Hin Dam
Hin Dam Pier
Police
Ao Taphao
Nam Tok Khlong Chao
The Hub
Khao Phaenthi (315m)
Ao Sai
Ban Khlong Chao
Ao Khlong Chao
Ao Ngamkho
Ao Chuk
Ao Sai Dang
Laem Toum
Ao Bang Bao
Ban Bang Bae
Ao Yai
Ban Ao Yai
Laem Ao Yai
Laem Bang Bao
Ao Takhian
Ban Khlong Phrao
Ao Ngmou Louam
Ao Jark
Ao Phrao
Ao Khlong Hin
Khao Chom (232m)
Ao Kralang
N
Laem Khlong Prom
Ao Khathing
Laem Thian
0
2 km

mangrove rather than broad sandy beaches and those parts of the island not still covered in virgin tropical rainforest are filled with palm groves and rubber plantations. Though the island is 25km long and 12km wide, it supports barely more than 20km of concrete road, with many areas penetrated only by the odd sandy track and, in places, by navigable khlongs, if at all. The highest point on the island, at just 315m, is Khao Phaenthi, towards the southeast. All of this makes Ko Kood a surprisingly pleasant place to explore on foot (or kayak), especially as the cool season brings refreshing breezes most days. The interior is also graced with several waterfalls, the most famous of which is Nam Tok Khlong Chao, inland from Ao Khlong Chao and the focus of occasional day-trips from Ko Chang and Ko Mak.

Because of its lack of roads, Ko Kood has to date been the almost exclusive province of package-tourists, but things are becoming much easier for independent travellers now, with a choice of scheduled boat services from the mainland, as well as from Ko Chang and Ko Mak (and even plans for a possible run to Ban Hat Lek, on the Cambodian border, from Ban Ao Salat on the northeast coast), and the emergence of some budget-minded guest houses. The island is still pretty much a **one-season destination**, however, as rough seas mean that nearly all the boat services only operate from November through May. An increasing number of places are staying open year-round, however, and offer tempting discounts to those willing to chance the rains and the off-season quiet.

Most of Kok Kood's fifteen hundred residents make their living from fishing and growing coconut palms and rubber trees. Many have Khmer blood in them as the island population mushroomed at the turn of the twentieth century when Thais and Cambodians resident in nearby Cambodian territory fled French control. The main settlements are **Ban Khlong Hin Dam**, just inland from the main Hin Dam pier; **Ban Khlong Mat**, a natural harbour-inlet a few kilometres further north up the coast; the stilted fishing village of **Ban Ao Salat** across on the northeast coast; and the fishing community of **Ban Ao Yai** on the southeast coast. On the southwest coast, several of the main beaches also have small villages. Of these, the obvious choice for budget travellers are **Ao Khlong Chao** and **Ao Ngamkho**, which both have a choice of accommodation and eating options and are within walking distance of each other; **Ao Bang Bao** also has cheapish bungalows and is the longer and arguably better beach but has no village and is more isolated. Seclusion is the thing on all the other west-coast beaches, most of which are the province of just one or two upmarket resorts: **Ao Jark** is the most heart-stoppingly gorgeous, and very private, while **Ao Khlong Mat** offers notably good value.

Getting to Ko Kood

In all but the worst weather, Ninmoungkorn (☎086 126 7860) runs a year-round **boat service** to Ko Kood from the **Trat** mainland, departing from Laem Sok, about 30km south of Trat (see p.463), and terminating at Ao Salat on the island's northeast coast during the rainy season but serving west-coast piers at Hin Dam and Bang Bao from November to May (1–2 daily; 2–3hr; B400 including transfer from Trat to the Laem Sok pier). There are also several different companies offering high-season **speedboat** services between the Trat mainland and Ko Kood's western piers and beaches; these are faster and more expensive (up to 4 daily; 1hr 10min–1hr 50min; B600) but can be wet and uncomfortable in all but the flattest seas. Schedules and mainland departure points vary (usual departure points are Laem Sok; Dan Kao, 6km northeast of central Trat; and Laem Ngop Pier, 20km southwest of Trat) and are best checked with Trat guesthouses, the TAT office in Laem Ngop, or tour agents in Trat or Laem Ngop. Some of the high-season speedboats go via **Ko Mak** (Nov–May 2–3 daily; 35min–1hr; B350), and Bang Bao Boat runs a connecting service **from Ko Chang and Ko Wai** via Ko Mak to Ko Kood (Sept–June, 1 daily slow boat with speedboat connection, 5hr, B700; 1 daily speedboat, 2hr, B900; Ⓦwww.bangbaoboat.com). Local tour operators on the islands are the best source of current timetables. As arrival points for speedboats vary, it's always worth calling ahead to your accommodation for a pick-up: there are only a few share-taxis on the island and they don't meet all arrivals. Return schedules from Ko Kood operate at the same frequency as the outbound services; all Ko Kood hotels keep current timetables and sell tickets.

Island practicalities

Getting around Ko Kood is mainly a question of walking or renting your own transport, though you should be able to charter a songthaew for the day for around B1000. You can rent **kayaks** on every beach, and **motorbikes** through *Koh Kood Happy Days* guest house on Ao Ngamkho and The Hub activity centre on Ao Khlong Chao (from B300 per day), but be warned that the west-coast road is very narrow, concrete only in parts, and dirt, stone and occasionally badly rutted in others. The number of hills may also deter you from doing it by **mountain bike**, which are available at The Hub (B200 per day) and through some resorts. Exploring the island **on foot** is both feasible and fun, and south of Ao Khlong Chao much of the route is shady. From Ao Khlong Chao to Ao Bang Bao takes about forty minutes; from Ao Bang Bao to Ao Jark is about an hour's walk, then another twenty minutes to Ao Phrao.

There's **no bank** on Ko Kood, but you can **change money** at *Happy Days* in Ao Ngamkho and at the biggest resorts. There's a postal agent in the shop next to *Happy Days* and **internet** access both at *Happy Days* and The Hub on Ao Khlong Chao. The **police** are in Ban Khlong Hin Dam (Ⓣ039 521745), as is the **hospital** (Ⓣ039 521852); the shop across from the hospital has a small **pharmacy** section and sells antihistamine tablets for sandfly bites (see p.40), which can be legion on Ko Kood. There is some **malaria** on the island so be especially assiduous with repellent and nets if you are not taking prophylactics; there's a malaria-testing station in Ban Khlong Hin Dam.

There are two **dive operators** on Ko Kood: The Hub, part of *Away Resort* in Ao Khlong Chao (Ⓣ081 835 4517, Ⓦwww.awaykohkood.com), and Paradise Divers (Ⓣ087 144 5945, Ⓦwww.thailandtauchen.com), whose headquarters are at *Ko Kood Beach Resort* at Ao Khlong Mat, with another desk at *Happy Days*. Two dives cost B3000, with snorkellers paying B900; you might prefer to opt for a local Ko Kood dive as the usual sites around Ko Rang (see p.474) are always packed with dive boats from Ko Chang and Ko Mak.

The Hub organizes guided kayak **trips** to Khlong Chao Falls and around the coast, as well as round-island boat tips, snorkelling trips and hikes.

Ao Khlong Chao and Khlong Chao Falls

About 5km south of the main Hin Dam pier, **AO KHLONG CHAO** (pronounced "Jao") is a fun place to stay because as well as a small sandy beach – no great beauty but a perfectly pleasant "village" beach – you've got the pretty two-kilometre-long mangrove-lined Khlong Chao that runs down from the famous Khlong Chao Falls. Close by the road-bridge that spans the khlong, just 300m from the palm-fringed beach, is a cluster of little guest houses, some of them built partially on stilts over the river, which offer the cheapest accommodation on the island, as well as a couple of package-tour resorts, complete with intrusive, late-night karaoke restaurants which unfortunately mar the atmosphere considerably at weekends.

Away Resort's roadside **activity centre** The Hub (Nov–May 8am–8pm) has internet access and wi-fi, runs PADI dive trips and courses, organizes snorkelling and other day trips and rents motorbikes, bicycles and kayaks.

The three-tiered **Nam Tok Khlong Chao** is a pretty if not exceptional waterfall that tumbles down into a large, refreshing pool that's perfect for a dip; it's quietest in the mornings, before the package groups arrive. It takes around twenty minutes to kayak upriver from the Khlong Chao bridge to the jetty near the falls, followed by a ten-minute walk – though you can also walk the whole thing in half an hour, or even take a car or motorbike to within 500m: just follow the signs from the bridge over the khlong in Khlong Chao. The track continues beyond the falls through jungle for another few kilometres before terminating at a rubber plantation, making for a pleasant and very quiet four-hour walk there and back, though watch out for snakes, especially cobras.

Accommodation

Away Resort ⓣ081 835 4517, ⓦwww.awayresorts.com. The most upmarket place to stay in Khlong Chao occupies a garden that drops down to a rocky chunk of the shore; though there's no beach here you can swim off the jetty, laze in the garden, or take a free kayak across to Ao Khlong Chao beach proper, just a couple of minutes' paddle away. The seaside and sea-view bungalows are large and quite stylish, with air-con, wooden floors and inviting verandas; their cheapest accommodation is in fixed safari-style tents (with fans and hot water) which aren't worth the money. ❻–❾

Ban Pai ⓣ089 931 5683. Has the cheapest rooms in Khlong Chao (with shared bathrooms), in an extended stilt house centred round a lovely breezy communal khlong-side deck. The pricier rooms and bungalows are not such good value but the home-cooked food is exceptional, especially for fish dishes. ❷–❺

Khlong Chao Sea View ⓣ087 908 3593. Away from the khlong – and the karaoke-singing weekenders on the north bank – this friendly place is set in a garden beside the road 200m beyond the bridge, from where you can indeed see the sea, 200m away, through the thinly planted palm grove. Its half-dozen bamboo bungalows each have a bathroom and a little veranda and there's good food at the popular garden restaurant too, especially the *phanaeng* curries. Fan ❸, air-con ❺

The Mangrove ⓣ081 290 7455. The best of the khlong-side options, with very nice sturdy wooden bungalows spaced around a grassy lawn, all with river views. Interiors are modern and well furnished with TV and hot water. Fan ❹, air-con ❺

Ao Ngamkho

Having climbed over the point at the south end of Ao Khlong Chao, the road dips down again to the tiny village at **AO NGAMKHO** and its beach, actually a series of pretty, miniature bays either side of a khlong and between rocky points, with quite rewarding snorkelling and plenty of fish at its southern end.

The backpacker-oriented *Koh Kood Happy Days* (ⓣ087 144 5945; ⓦwww.kohkood-happydays.com; ❸–❹) is beside the road here, 200m from the northern section of the beach, and offers ten en-suite fan and air-con **rooms** in a little guest-house block, all with wooden floors, pretty furnishings and a shared veranda. There's also motorbike rental and internet access, plus a sociable bar and restaurant and a general store next door. Directly on the shore, just south of the khlong, small, friendly *Dusita* (ⓣ081 420 4861, ⓦwww.dusitaresorts.com; ❺–❻) offers plainly outfitted fan and air-con wooden cabins that all enjoy beautiful sea views and some shade among the sparse coconut grove hung with hammocks; it's open November to May only. Also right on the beach, traveller-oriented *Ngamkho Resort* (ⓣ081 825 7076, ⓦwww.kohkood-ngamkho.com; ❹) has just nine well-designed and attractively furnished en-suite bamboo bungalows, all with fans, decks and hammocks, plus a restaurant in the secluded little shorefront garden. The twenty sturdy fan and air-con chalets of *Hin Dad Resort* (Ⓣ081 762 9519, Ⓔhindadresort@hotmail.com; 6–7; closed July–Sept) sit atop the little rocky point at the southern end of the bay, with panoramic sea views and easy access to the beach.

Ao Bang Bao

From Ao Ngamkho, follow signs for *The Beach* to reach **AO BANG BAO**, about twenty minutes' walk further south (fifteen minutes west off the main road). This is one of Ko Kood's prettiest beaches, fronted by a longish sweep of bleach-white sand and deliciously clear turquoise water, plus the inevitable fringe of coconut palms, and embraced by a pair of protective promontories. Though *The Beach Natural Resort* (Ⓣ086 009940, Ⓦwww.thebeachkohkood.com; fan 5, air-con 7) doesn't actually sit on the nicest part of the beach, but behind a rocky area towards the northern end, its 34 thatched Balinese-style **bungalows** are tastefully furnished and have garden bathrooms; they're grouped quite closely together so most only offer sea glimpses. Neighbouring *Siam Beach* (Ⓣ081 899 6200, Ⓦwww.siambeachkohkood.net; fan 4, air-con 5–6) occupies almost all of the best part of the beach, sprawling across an extensive area, and is popular with budget travellers, though it's more isolated than similarly priced options on Ao Ngamkho and Ao Khlong Chao. It offers big, rustic, no-frills timber huts on the seafront with the option of either fan or air-con, and nearly all enjoy uninterrupted bay views. Some of the newer, pricier air-con rooms are in a less idyllic spot close to a khlong and back from the shore a bit. The restaurant cooks up regular seafood barbecues and there's internet access, motorbike and kayak rental.

Ao Jark, Ao Phrao and Ao Yai

Back on the main southbound road at the Ao Bang Bao turnoff, a 35-minute walk through coconut and rubber plantations brings you to **Ao Khlong Hin**, a wild little bay that's dominated by a small coconut-processing centre and is not really great for swimming. Ten minutes further along the road, which hugs the coast so close here it gets washed by the waves at high tide, remote and breathtakingly lovely little **AO JARK** sits at the mouth of a wide, serene khlong and feels secluded and private. The only accommodation here, set among the palms between the limpid blue sea and the calm green khlong, is at *Neverland Resort* (Ⓣ081 762 6254, Ⓦwww.neverlandresort.com; 6–7), which offers fourteen comfortable air-con bungalows and fully equipped two-person tents (B450). Prices go up a little at weekends, and from June to October you need to call ahead to make sure it's open.

Continue twenty minutes further along the pretty coastal road to reach the most southerly bay, **AO PHRAO** (about 2km from Ao Jark), a long, stunning beach of white sand backed by densely planted palms and the slopes of Khao Chom. You can stay here at *Ao Phrao Beach* (Ⓣ081 429 7145, Ⓦwww.kokut.com; 8; closed June–Sept), in mainly but not exclusively package-oriented clusters of thatched and concrete air-con bungalows; facilities include internet, wi-fi and kayak rental. Behind Ao Phrao, the tiny fishing village of **Ban Khlong Phrao** occupies the mangrove-lined banks of Khlong Phrao (which extends another kilometre inland). There's a clinic here as well as a few small shops and hot-food stalls.

A five-kilometre track that's very steep and rough in places connects Ban Khlong Phrao with **Ao Yai**, the southeast coast's main if rather lacklustre fishing village, built entirely on stilts and jetties around the shoreline of a natural harbour. Its main visitors are the crews of anchored fishing boats from Thailand and Cambodia, who come here for drink, supplies, karaoke and the rest.

North, inland and east

The bays of **northern Ko Kood**, beyond Ao Khlong Chao, are even more thinly populated than the southwest coast, with just a few resorts up here open to tourists who don't come on pre-booked packages. Inland is the island's administrative centre, **Ban Khlong Hin Dam**, 3.5km north of Ao Khlong Chao, site of a few shops, the hospital, police station, school and principal island temple. Ko Kood's main pier is a couple of kilometres to the west, at **Laem Hin Dam**.

The best value of the northwest resorts is Danish-run *Koh Kood Beach Bungalows* (Ⓣ081 908 8966, Ⓦwww.jysktravel.com; 7–8), set above the small, effectively private little bay at **AO KHLONG MAT**, beside the deep natural harbour in the adjacent stilt village, about 2km north of Ban Khlong Hin Dam. The widely spaced, high-roofed Balinese-style bungalows here all have air-con, TV and garden-style bathrooms and each enjoys a sea view from its generous deck. There's a swimming pool, motorbike, bicycle and kayak rental, internet access and a dive shop on site. The company also runs interesting sounding four-day **sea-safaris**: guests sleep in special billets on the deck of a fishing boat and visit various local islands including Ko Mak.

About 5km northwest of Ban Khlong Hin Dam, the small but appealing three-tiered waterfall **Nam Tok Khlong Yai Kee** is basically a miniature version of the famous Nam Tok Khlong Chao and rushes down into a good-sized pool that's ideal for swimming. It's accessible via a five-minute path that's very steep in places, but there are ropes at the crucial points.

East off the road to the north coast, in the mature rainforest near Ban Chum Phon, is a locally famous **five-hundred-year old maka tree** (*Bridelia insulana*), known to islanders as the *dtohn maai yai*, that's an impressive 35m or more in height and drips with lianas and epiphytes. A kilometre-long path that runs through rubber trees and rainforest will get you there, but you'll need to go with a local to stay on the right track.

The road currently serves just one spot on the northeast coast and that's the tiny stilt-village and fishing community of **Ban Ao Salat**, 9km northeast of Ban Khlong Hin Dam. Several of the wooden houses strung out along the jetty-promenade serve food so this is a great place for a fresh-seafood lunch, especially crab. The rainy season boat service usually terminates here.

Travel details

Trains

Aranyaprathet to: Bangkok (2 daily; 5hr 25min–6hr).
Pattaya to: Bangkok (1 daily; 4hr); Si Racha (1 daily; 30min).
Si Racha to: Bangkok (1 daily; 3hr 30min); Pattaya (1 daily; 30min).

Buses

Aranyaprathet to: Bangkok (10 daily; 4hr 30min).
Ban Phe to: Bangkok (14 daily; 3hr); Chanthaburi (6 daily; 1hr 30min); Rayong (every 30min; 30min); Trat (6 daily; 3hr).
Chanthaburi to: Bangkok (Eastern Bus Terminal; 18 daily; 4–5hr); Bangkok (Northern Bus Terminal; 5 daily; 3–4hr); Bangkok (Suvarnabhumi Airport; 4 daily; 3hr); Khorat (8 daily; 6hr); Rayong (8 daily;

2hr); Sa Kaew (for Aranyaprathet; 8 daily; 3hr); Trat (every 1hr 30min; 1hr 30min).
Laem Ngop to: Bangkok (Eastern Bus Terminal; 2 daily; 5hr 15min).
Pattaya to: Bangkok (Eastern/Northern bus Terminals; every 30min; 2hr 30min); Bangkok (Southern Bus Terminal; 12 daily; 3hr 30min); Bangkok (Suvarnabhumi Airport; 4 daily; 2hr); Chanthaburi (6 daily; 3hr); Chiang Mai (8 daily; 12–14hr); Chiang Rai (2 daily; 15–17hr); Khorat (4 daily; 5–6hr); Nong Khai (7 daily; 12hr); Rayong (every 30min; 1hr 30min); Trat (6 daily; 4hr 30min); Ubon Ratchathani (6 daily; 10–12hr).
Rayong to: Bangkok (Eastern Bus Terminal; every 40min; 2hr 30min–3hr); Bangkok (Northern Bus Terminal; 5 daily; 3hr); Ban Phe (for Ko Samet; every 30min; 30min); Chanthaburi (every 30min; 2hr); Chiang Mai (8 daily; 15–18hr); Khorat (18 daily; 4hr); Mae Sai (4 daily; 17–20hr); Ubon Ratchathani (10 daily; 11–14hr).
Si Racha to: Bangkok (Eastern/Northern bus terminals; every 30min; 2hr); Chanthaburi (6 daily; 3hr 30min); Pattaya (every 20min; 30min); Rayong (every 30min; 2hr); Trat (6 daily; 5hr).
Trat to: Bangkok (Eastern Bus Terminal; 6 daily; 5–6hr); Bangkok (Northern Bus Terminal; 5 daily; 4hr 30min); Bangkok (Suvarnabhumi Airport; 5 daily; 4hr 10min); Chanthaburi (11 daily; 1hr 30min); Hat Lek (for the Cambodian border; every 45min; 1hr–1hr 30min); Pattaya (6 daily; 4hr 30min); Rayong (6 daily; 3hr 30min); Si Racha (6 daily; 5hr).

Boats

Ban Phe to: Ko Samet (at least 6 daily; 30min).
Ko Chang to: Ko Kood (Nov–May 1–2 daily; 2hr–5hr); Ko Mak (Sept–June 1–2 daily; 50min–2hr); Ko Wai (Sept–June 1–2 daily; 15min–1hr 15min); Trat province (at least every 2hr; 25min–45min).
Ko Kood to: Ko Chang (Nov–May daily; 2hr); Ko Mak (Nov–May 2–3 daily; 35min–1hr); Trat province (1–5 daily; 1hr 10min–4hr).
Ko Mak to: Ko Chang (Sept–June 1–2 daily; 50min–2hr); Ko Kood (Nov–May 2–3 daily; 35min–1hr); Trat province (1–9 daily; 40min–3hr).
Si Racha to: Ko Si Chang (hourly; 40min).
Trat province to: Ko Chang (at least every 2hr; 25–45min); Ko Kood (1–6 daily; 1hr 10min–4hr); Ko Mak (1–9 daily; 40min–3hr); Ko Wai (Nov–April 1 daily; 2hr 30min).

Flights

Pattaya (U-Tapao) to: Ko Samui (2 daily; 1hr); Phuket (1 daily; 1hr 35min).
Trat to: Bangkok (3 daily; 50min).

5

The northeast: Isaan

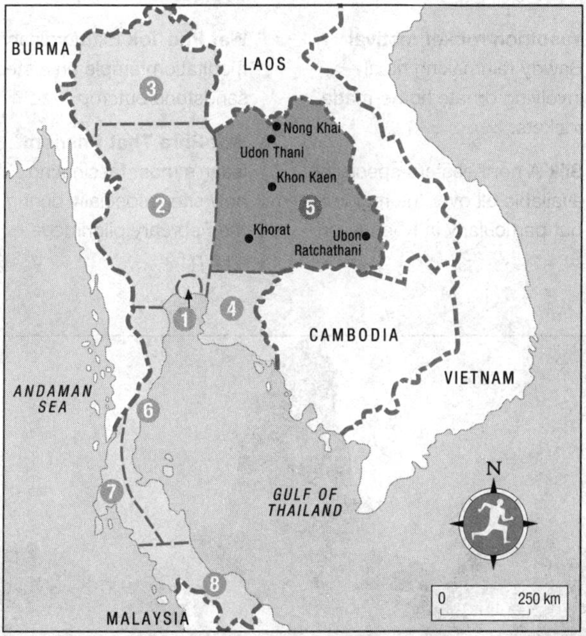

CHAPTER 5

Highlights

* **Khao Yai National Park** Easy and tough trails, lots of birds, gibbons, elephants, several waterfalls and night safaris. See p.494
* **Khmer ruins** Exquisite Angkor Wat–style temples at Phimai, Phanom Rung and Khao Phra Viharn. See p.504, p.508 & p.517
* **Yasothon rocket festival** Bawdy rainmaking ritual involving ornate home-made rockets. See p.528
* **Silk** A northeastern speciality, available all over the region but particularly in Khon Kaen. See p.533
* **Phu Kradung** Teeming table mountain, the most dramatic of the region's national parks. See p.540
* **The Mekong** The best stretch in Thailand for gentle exploration of the mighty riverscape is between Chiang Khan and Nong Khai. See p.542
* **Wat Phu Tok** Extraordinary meditation temple on a steep sandstone outcrop. See p.554
* **Wat Phra That Phanom** Isaan's most fascinating holy site, especially during the February pilgrimage. See p.556

▲ Khmer temple complex at Phimai

5

The northeast: Isaan

Bordered by Laos and Cambodia on three sides, the tableland of **northeast Thailand** – known as **Isaan**, after the Hindu god of death and the northeast – comprises a third of the country's land area and is home to nearly a third of its population. This is the least-visited region of the kingdom, and the poorest: some seventy percent of Isaan villagers earn less than the regional minimum wage of B148–170 a day. Farming is the traditional livelihood here, despite appallingly infertile soil (the friable sandstone contains few nutrients and retains little water) and long periods of drought punctuated by downpours and intermittent bouts of flooding. In the 1960s, government schemes to introduce hardier crops set in motion a debt cycle that has forced farmers into monocultural cash-cropping to repay their loans for fertilizers, seeds and machinery. For many families, there's only one way off the treadmill: of the twenty million who live in Isaan, an average of two million economic refugees leave the area every year, most of them heading for Bangkok where northeasterners now make up the majority of the capital's lowest-paid workforce. Children and elderly parents remain in the villages, increasingly dependent on the money sent back every month from the metropolis and awaiting the annual visit in May when migrant family members often return for a couple of months to help with the rice planting.

Most northeasterners speak a dialect that's more comprehensible to residents of Vientiane than Bangkok, and Isaan's historic allegiances have tied it more closely to Laos and Cambodia than to Thailand. Between the eleventh and thirteenth centuries, the all-powerful **Khmers** covered the northeast in magnificent stone temple complexes, the remains of which constitute the region's most satisfying tourist attractions. During subsequent centuries the territories along the Mekong River changed hands numerous times, until the present border with Laos was set at the end of World War II. In the 1950s and 1960s, **Communist insurgents** played on the northeast's traditional ties with Laos; a movement to align Isaan with the Marxists of Laos gathered some force, and the Communist Party of Thailand, gaining sympathy among poverty-stricken northeastern farmers, established bases in the region. At about the same time, major US air bases for the **Vietnam War** were set up in Khorat, Ubon Ratchathani and Udon Thani, fuelling a sex industry that has plagued the region ever since. When the American military moved out, northeastern women turned to the tourist-oriented Bangkok flesh-trade instead, and nowadays the majority of prostitutes in the capital come from Isaan.

Rather than the cities – which are chaotic, exhausting places, with little going for them apart from accommodation and onward transport – Isaan's prime destinations are its **Khmer ruins** and **Khao Yai National Park**. Five huge

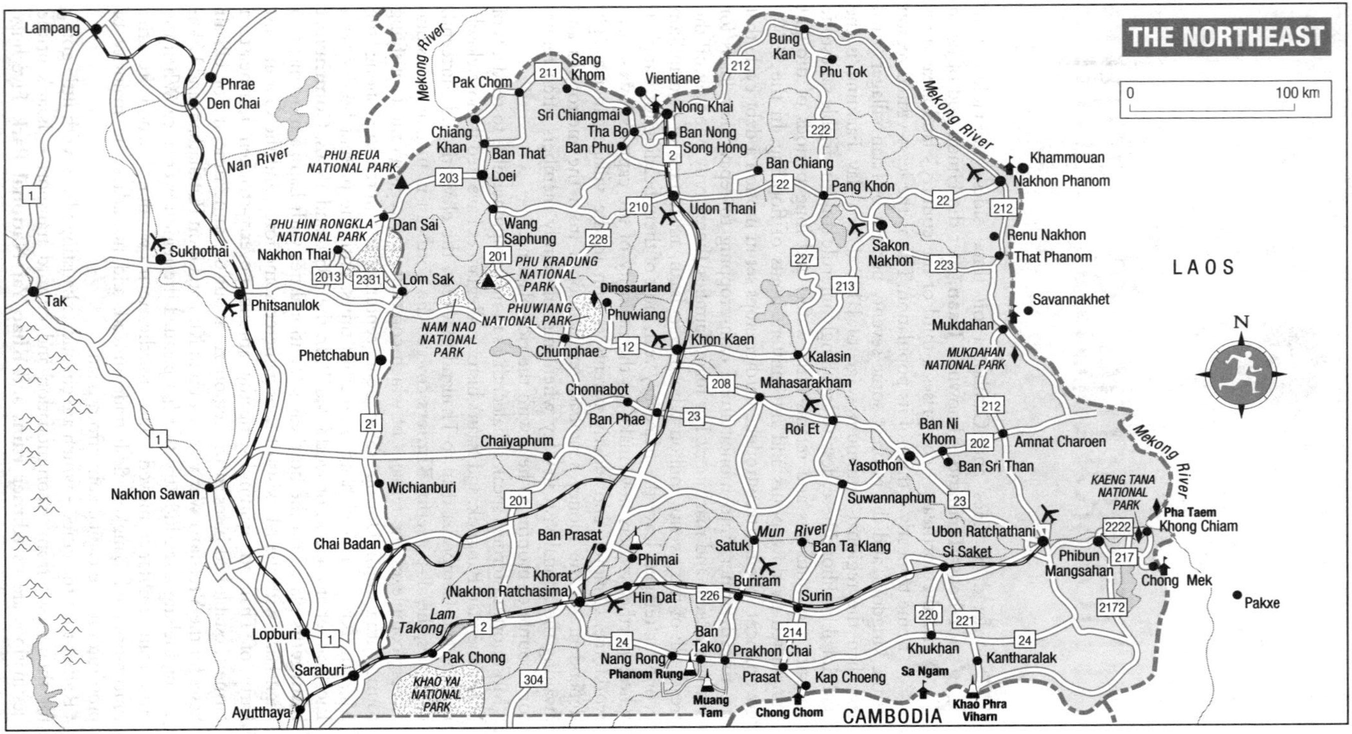
THE NORTHEAST
0
100 km
N
LAOS
CAMBODIA
Mekong River
Nan River
Mun River
Lam Takong
Lampang
Phrae
Den Chai
Sukhothai
Tak
Phitsanulok
Nakhon Thai
Phetchabun
Nakhon Sawan
Chai Badan
Lopburi
Saraburi
Ayutthaya
PHU REUA NATIONAL PARK
PHU HIN RONGKLA NATIONAL PARK
NAM NAO NATIONAL PARK
PHU KRADUNG NATIONAL PARK
PHUWIANG NATIONAL PARK
KHAO YAI NATIONAL PARK
MUKDAHAN NATIONAL PARK
KAENG TANA NATIONAL PARK
Pak Chom
Chiang Khan
Ban That
Loei
Dan Sai
Lom Sak
Wang Saphung
Sang Khom
Sri Chiangmai
Tha Bo
Ban Phu
Vientiane
Nong Khai
Ban Nong Song Hong
Udon Thani
Bung Kan
Phu Tok
Ban Chiang
Pang Khon
Sakon Nakhon
Khammouan
Nakhon Phanom
Renu Nakhon
That Phanom
Savannakhet
Mukdahan
Dinosaurland
Phuwiang
Khon Kaen
Chumphae
Kalasin
Mahasarakham
Chonnabot
Ban Phae
Roi Et
Chaiyaphum
Wichianburi
Ban Ni Khom
Ban Sri Than
Amnat Charoen
Yasothon
Suwannaphum
Ban Prasat
Phimai
Satuk
Ban Ta Klang
Ubon Ratchathani
Si Saket
Phibun Mangsahan
Pha Taem
Khong Chiam
Chong Mek
Pakxe
Khorat (Nakhon Ratchasima)
Hin Dat
Buriram
Surin
Pak Chong
Nang Rong
Phanom Rung
Ban Tako
Muang Tam
Prakhon Chai
Prasat
Kap Choeng
Chong Chom
Khukhan
Sa Ngam
Kantharalak
Khao Phra Viharn
1
2
12
21
22
23
24
201
202
203
208
210
211
212
213
214
217
220
221
222
223
226
227
228
304
2013
2172
2222
2331

northeastern **festivals** also draw massive crowds: in May, Yasothon is the focus for the bawdy rocket festival; the end of June or beginning of July sees the equally raucous rainmaking festival of Phi Ta Kon in Dan Sai near Loei; in July, Ubon Ratchathani hosts the extravagant candle festival; in October, strange, pink fireballs float out of the Mekong near Nong Khai; while the flamboyant, though inevitably touristy, "elephant round-up" is staged in Surin in November.

Isaan's only mountain range of any significance divides the uninspiring town of **Loei** from the central plains and offers some stiff walking, awesome scenery and the possibility of spotting unusual birds and flowers in the **national parks** that spread across its heights. Due north of Loei at Chiang Khan, the **Mekong River** begins its leisurely course around Isaan with a lush stretch where a sprinkling of guest houses has opened up the river countryside to travellers. Marking the eastern end of this upper stretch, the border town of **Nong Khai** is surrounded by possibly the most outlandish temples in Thailand. The grandest and most important religious site in the northeast, however, is **Wat Phra That Phanom**, way downstream beyond **Nakhon Phanom**, a town which affords some of the finest Isaan vistas.

The other big draw for travellers is Isaan's four **border crossings into Laos**, at each of which you can now get a Lao visa on arrival. The most popular of these is at Nong Khai, a route that provides easy road access to the Lao capital, Vientiane; the others are Nakhon Phanom, Mukdahan and Chong Mek (see p.35 for a full rundown on overland travel into Laos). If you need to, you can get a Lao visa in advance from the consulate in the central Isaan town of Khon Kaen, where there's also a Vietnamese consulate issuing visas for Vietnam. It's also possible to travel **overland between Isaan and Cambodia** through two different border crossings: via the Thai town of Kap Choeng, in Surin province, to O'Smach, which has transport to Anlong Veng and then on to Siem Reap; and via Sa Ngam in the Phusing district of Si Saket province to Choam in Anlong Veng. (See p.34 for a roundup of overland crossings on the Thai–Cambodia border.)

Many travellers approach Isaan from the north, either travelling directly from Chiang Mai to Loei, or going via Phitsanulok, in the northern reaches of the central plains, to Khon Kaen, but you can also take direct **buses** to Khorat from the east-coast towns of Pattaya, Rayong and Chanthaburi. All major northeastern centres have direct bus services from Bangkok. Two **rail** lines cut through Isaan, providing useful connections with Bangkok and Ayutthaya and there are also **flights** between Bangkok and several northeastern cities. All towns and cities in Isaan are connected by public transport, as are many of the larger villages, but compared to many other regions of the country, northeastern roads are fairly traffic-free, so renting your own vehicle is also a good option.

Southern Isaan

Southern Isaan more or less follows one of two branches of the northeastern rail line as it makes a beeline towards the eastern border, skirting the edge of **Khao Yai National Park** before entering Isaan proper to link the major provincial capitals of **Khorat**, **Surin** and **Ubon Ratchathani**. However, it's in the smaller towns and villages that you'll learn most about Isaan life, particularly if you head for the exceptionally welcoming **guest houses** in Surin, Nang

Rong, Phimai and Khong Chiam. For even more of an immersion into a rural community, consider booking yourself onto the **homestay** programme in the village of **Ban Prasat**.

Even if your time is limited, you shouldn't leave this part of Isaan without visiting at least one set of Khmer ruins: those at **Phimai** are the most accessible, but it's well worth making the effort to visit either **Phanom Rung** or **Khao Phra Viharn** as well, both of which occupy spectacular hilltop locations, though the latter was closed at the time of writing. Relics of an even earlier age, prehistoric cliff-paintings also draw a few tourists eastwards to the little town of **Khong Chiam**, which is prettily set between the Mekong and Mun rivers. Nearby **Chong Mek** is both a legal entry point into Laos and the site of a border market.

Khao Yai National Park

About 120km northeast of Bangkok, the cultivated lushness of the central plains gives way to the thickly forested Phanom Dangkrek mountains. A 2168-square-kilometre chunk of this sculpted limestone range has been conserved as **KHAO YAI NATIONAL PARK**, the country's first national park to be established (1962) and one of its most popular. Spanning five distinct forest types and rising to a height of 1341m, the park sustains over three hundred bird and twenty large land-mammal species – hence its UNESCO accreditation as a World Heritage Site – and offers a plethora of waterfalls and several undemanding walking trails.

During the daytime you're bound to hear some of the local wildlife, even if you don't catch sight of it. Noisiest of all are the **white-handed (lar) gibbons**, which hoot and whoop from the tops of the tallest trees, and the bubbling trills of the **pileated** (**capped**) **gibbons**. Gibbons generally avoid contact with the ground, but this is not the case with the hard-to-miss **pig-tailed macaques**, many of whom gather at favoured spots on the road through the park. **Hornbills** also create quite a racket, calling and flapping their enormous wings; Khao Yai harbours large flocks of four different hornbill species, which makes it one of the best observation sites in Southeast Asia. The great hornbill is particularly beautiful, with brilliant yellow and black undersides and a two-metre wingspan; the magnificent oriental pied hornbill boasts less striking black and white colouring, but is more commonly seen at close range because it swoops down to catch fish, rats and reptiles. You might also see red-headed trogons, orange-breasted trogons, woodpeckers and Asian fairy-bluebirds and, if you're very lucky, silver pheasants or Siamese firebacks, endemic only to Thailand and western Cambodia. From November to March Khao Yai hosts several species of **migrant birds**, including the dramatically coloured Siberian thrush and the orange-headed thrush.

A herd of about two hundred and fifty Asian **elephants** lives in the park, and its members are often seen at night – it's the only place in Thailand where you have much likelihood of spotting wild elephants. Khao Yai is also home to an ever-dwindling number of **tigers**, sightings of which are extremely rare, though not mythical. You're almost certain to spot **civets**, and you might come across a **slow loris**, while barking **deer** and sambar deer are less nervous after dark. **Wrinkle-lipped bats** assemble en masse at sunset, especially at the cave entrance next to Wat Tham Silathong, just outside the

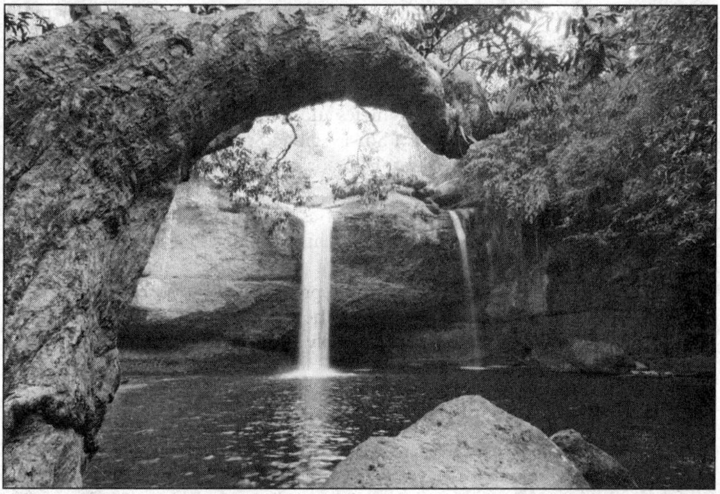

▲ Haew Suwat Falls, Khao Yai National Park

north (main) gate into the park, which every evening disgorges millions of them on their nightly forage.

For many Thais, however, especially Bangkokians, Khao Yai is not so much a place for wildlife spotting as an easy weekend escape from the fumes. Some have second homes in the area, while others come for the golf and the soft-adventure activities, especially horse riding and off-road driving in ATVs, offered by the increasingly popular "dude-ranch" resorts. The cooler climate here has also made Khao Yai one of Thailand's most productive areas for viticulture and dairy farming.

There's camping and basic accommodation in the park itself, and plenty more comfortable options both just beyond the perimeter and in the nearby town of **Pak Chong**. It's quite easy to trek the park trails by yourself, but as some of Khao Yai's best waterfalls, caves and viewpoints are as much as 20km apart, a tour is worth considering. Try to avoid visiting at weekends and holidays, but even at quiet times, don't expect it to be like a safari park; bring binoculars if you have them and some warm clothes, as it gets cool at the higher altitudes, especially at night.

Getting to and from Khao Yai

There are two access roads to the park – one from the south and another from the north, though everyone travelling by public transport approaches the park from **Pak Chong** (see p.499), about 25km north of the northern entrance. From here the cheapest way to get **to Khao Yai** is to take a public **songthaew** from outside the 7-Eleven shop, 200m west of the footbridge on the north side of the main road near Soi 21 (every 30min 6.30am–4pm, less frequently on Sun; 30min; B25). Public songthaews, however, are not allowed to enter the park itself, so you'll be dropped at the park checkpoint, about 14km short of the Khao Yai visitor centre, park headquarters and most popular trailheads. At the checkpoint (where you pay the B400 national-park entrance fee, or B200 for kids), park rangers will flag down passing cars and get them to give you a ride up to the visitor centre; this is common practice here. The whole journey from Pak Chong to Khao Yai visitor centre takes about an hour. Note that if you are not planning to stay the night inside the park but want to make two or more day-trips into the park, you'll have to pay the park entry fee every time you come through the checkpoint.

A less time-consuming but pricier option is to **charter a songthaew** from Pak Chong: these count as private vehicles and are allowed inside the park. They can be chartered from the corner of Soi 19, and cost around B1000 for the ride from Pak Chong to Haew Suwat Falls, or about B1500 for a return trip, including several hours in the park.

Coming back from the park is often easier, as day-trippers will usually give lifts all the way back to Pak Chong. Otherwise, hitch a ride as far as the checkpoint, or walk to it from the visitor centre – it's a pleasant three- to four-hour walk along the fairly shaded park road, and you'll probably spot lots of birds and some macaques, gibbons and deer as well. At the checkpoint you can pick up a songthaew to Pak Chong: the last one usually leaves here at about 5pm.

Khao Yai tours and guides

Tours of Khao Yai are reasonably priced and cater primarily for independent tourists rather than big groups. In recent years, Khao Yai has been plagued with unscrupulous tour operators, so we are recommending only three reputable outfits. These all offer customized trips as well as their own version of the popular, undemanding **one-and-a-half-day programme** (average price B1500 per person, not including the B400 park entry fee) which typically features a trip to a bat cave just outside the park at dusk, walks along one or two easy trails, a swim in Haew Suwat Falls and some after-dark wildlife spotting; it's usual, though not compulsory, to stay in the tour operator's own accommodation on the middle night. If you're on your own and your time is limited it's worth booking ahead, as prices quoted are for a minimum of two trekkers. Advance booking is essential for overnight expeditions in the park.

Wildlife Safari ⓣ044 312922, mobile ⓣ089 628 8224, ⓔwildlifekhaoyai@yahoo.co.uk Emphasizes plant-spotting and animal observation rather than hearty hikes. They are based about 2km north of Pak Chong train station at 39 Thanon Pak Chong Subsanun, Nong Kaja (call to arrange free transport from Pak Chong); their accommodation here is in comfortable rooms in the garden of the family home (fan ❸, air-con ❸).

Khao Yai Garden Lodge ⓣ044 365178, ⓦwww.khaoyai-gardenlodge.com. Large, efficient and long-established *Garden Lodge* is based at kilometre-stone 7 on the road that runs from Pak Chong into the park. It runs a variety of programmes, including half-day visits (B500), one-day outings (B1100 plus B400), and tailor-made treks. Their knowledgeable guides can lead you to some exciting wildlife sightings. For details of *Garden Lodge*'s accommodation, see opposite.

Green Leaf Guest House and Tour ⓣ044 365073, mobile ⓣ089 424 8809, ⓦwww.greenleaftour.com. At this family-run outfit treks are mostly led by owner Nine, who gets good reviews, particularly as a bird-spotter. It's based at kilometre-stone 7.5 on the park road (B20 by songthaew from Pak Chong). Accommodation is available at the family guest house (see opposite).

An alternative would be to **hire a park ranger** as your personal guide for the more remote trails, though their command of English is limited; you can arrange this at the park headquarters the night before, but will have to sort out your own transport. There's no set fee, but a fair rate would be B500 for a few hours, or around B1000 for the whole day.

It's also possible to arrange an upmarket **bicycle tour** of Khao Yai and its wineries, departing from Bangkok, through **Spice Roads** (2 days, 1 night B7750 per person all-inclusive; ⓣ02 712 5305, ⓦwww.spiceroads.com/thailand/khao_yai).

Accommodation and eating

You have several options when it comes to **accommodation** in Khao Yai, either in the park, or the road that leads up to it. Alternatively you could stay in Pak Chong (see p.499), 37km from the park's centre. If you decide to do a tour, it's usual to stay in the lodgings run by your tour guide.

In the park

If you're intending to do several days' independent exploring in the park, the most obvious places to stay are the national park lodges, dorms and tents in the heart of Khao Yai. The **lodges** (which sleep from two to thirty people; doubles ④) usually have to be booked in advance at the Royal Forestry Department office in Bangkok (Ⓣ02 562 0760, Ⓦwww.dnp.go.th/National_park.asp; see p.52) and you need to bring the receipt to the Khao Yai accommodation office, next to the visitor centre. However, you could also contact the Khao Yai accommodation office direct (daily 6am–9pm; Ⓣ08 1877 3127), as they claim that accommodation is often available to walk-ins from Sunday to Thursday. The **dorms** (35–50 beds; B50 per person) behind the visitor centre are only available to individuals if there are no groups booked in.

Advance booking is not essential for camping, but is advisable at weekends. Two-person **tents** (B150) are for rent at *Lam Takong* campsite, about 5km from the headquarters, and at *Pha Kluai Mai* campground (aka *Orchid Camp*, very good for bird-spotting), about 4km east of the park headquarters, on the road to Haew Suwat Falls. Equipment such as sleeping bags (B50) and pillows (B20) is available for rent as well. You can pitch your own tent at either site for B30.

Hot **food** is served in the cafeteria complex (6am–6pm) opposite the park headquarters, where you'll also find a small shop selling water and snacks. There are also **restaurants** at Haew Suwat Falls and both campsites.

The park road

Thanon Thanarat, the 23-kilometre road that runs from Pak Chong up to the park checkpoint, is dotted with luxurious "lodges"; most guests arrive by car, but Pak Chong transfers are usually available and the Pak Chong songthaew will also bring you here. Addresses are determined by the nearest kilometre-stone on Thanon Thanarat.

The cheapest place to stay on the park road is *Green Leaf Guest House and Tour* (Ⓣ044 365073, Ⓦwww.greenleaftour.com; ①–②), a friendly, family-run outfit 12.5km out of Pak Chong, at kilometre-stone 7.5, with fourteen en-suite rooms behind the good, cheap restaurant; it also does guided treks into the national park (see opposite). Five hundred metres south of *Green Leaf*, at kilometre-stone 7, *Khao Yai Garden Lodge* (Ⓣ044 365178, Ⓦwww.khaoyai-gardenlodge.com; shared bathroom ②, en suite ④, air-con ⑥) is a large, well-designed and popular resort set in a landscaped garden, complete with a swimming pool, ponds and an aviary. There's a restaurant and internet access, free pick-up from Pak Chong, tours of the park and day-trips to Isaan's Khmer temples. *Juldis Khao Yai Resort* (Ⓣ044 297297, Ⓦwww.khaoyai.com; ⑥–⑦; discounts on weekdays), at kilometre-stone 17, offers good-value upmarket accommodation in its large air-con rooms and has a swimming pool, tennis courts, mountain-bike rental, a restaurant and a pub.

Exploring the park

Several well-worn **trails** radiate from the area around the visitor centre and park headquarters at kilometre-stone 37, and a few more branch off from the roads that traverse the park; a few are signposted en route and some are colour-coded.

The **visitor centre** (daily 7am–6pm) provides brochures showing the more popular trails. Wear good boots, be prepared for some wading through rivers, and take a hat and plenty of water. If hiking during or just after the rainy season you will almost certainly have some unsolicited encounters with **leeches**; mosquito repellent helps deter them, as do leech socks (canvas gaiters), available from the cafeteria complex opposite the visitor centre. To get leeches off your skin either burn them with a lighted cigarette, or douse them in salt; oily suntan lotion or insect repellent can make them lose their grip and fall off.

If you don't fancy walking, you can rent **mountain bikes** from outside the visitor centre (B50 per hr) when available. Rangers discourage visitors from exploring the outer, non-waymarked reaches unguided, partly for environmental reasons, but also because of trigger-happy **sandalwood poachers**. The highly prized sandalwood oil is extracted by making cuts in a mature aloewood tree and collecting chunks of oil-saturated wood – which sells for B20,000–40,000 per kg – several months later. Sandalwood trees are indigenous to Khao Yai and though oil-collection does not usually kill the tree it does weaken it. Guides can point out trees that have been cut in this way along the trails.

The trails

It's not possible to spot much wildlife trekking alone without knowing where to look, which is one reason it makes sense to join a tour of the park, since the guides will know which trees the hornbills perch on and where gibbons go to feed. However, if you prefer to go it alone, the following trails are the most popular options.

The shortest and least taxing trail is the kilometre-long **Kong Kaew Nature Trail**, which starts just behind the visitor centre. It's paved all the way and takes just thirty minutes in each direction; if it's not too crowded, you could see gibbons, woodpeckers and kingfishers en route.

Of the more adventurous hikes that begin from the park headquarters, the most popular runs from just uphill of the visitor centre restaurant to **Nong Pak Chee observation tower** in the west of the park. This is a fairly easy walk through forest and grassland that culminates at an observation tower built next to a lake. En route you'll hear (if not see) white-handed gibbons in the tallest trees, and might spot barking deer in the savanna. If you stay at the tower long enough you could see eagles soaring or needletails dive-bombing the lake; elephants and gaurs sometimes come to drink here, too. The walk takes about two and a half hours to the observation tower (4.5km), from where it's another 900m down a dirt track which meets the main road between kilometre-stones 35 and 36. From the road, you can walk or hitch back either to the headquarters (2km) or down to the checkpoint (12km) and then travel on to Pak Chong. If you just want to spend a few hours at the observation tower and forget the main part of the walk, stop beside the main road between kilometre-stones 35 and 36 (before reaching the park headquarters) and walk the kilometre down the access track to the tower.

Another good focus for walks is the area around **Haew Suwat Falls**, east of the visitor centre. These 25-metre-high falls are a great place for an invigorating shower, and they featured in the 1999 film *The Beach*. To get to the falls from the park headquarters, either follow the trail, or walk, drive or hitch the six-kilometre road beyond the headquarters to Haew Suwat – it's a popular spot, so there should be plenty of cars. The **trail** to the falls (8km one way; 3–4hr) begins on the Nature Trail behind the visitor centre, then veers off it, along a path marked with red flashes. En route to Haew Suwat you'll pass a turn-off to *Pha Kluai/Orchid* campsite and waterfall (6.1km from the park headquarters; see below); near the end of the trail you may hear **Haew Sai Falls** in the distance, though these are easier to reach from Haew Suwat itself.

Day-trippers often do the shorter walk from Haew Suwat waterfall to **Pha Kluai/Orchid campsite**, which is paved most of the way and takes two hours at most (3.1km). You've a good chance of spotting gibbons and macaques along this route, as well as kingfishers and hornbills. The area around nearby Pha Kluai Falls is famous for its impressive variety of orchids.

Night safaris

A much-touted park attraction are the hour-long **night safaris**, or "night-lightings", which take truckloads of tourists round Khao Yai's main roads in the hope of catching some interesting wildlife in the glare of the specially fitted searchlights. Regular night-time sightings include deer and civets, and elephants are sometimes spotted as well. However, opinions differ on the quality of the night-lighting experience: some find it thrilling just to be out on the edges of the jungle after dark, others see it as rather a crass method of wildlife observation, especially at weekends when the park can feel like a town centre, with four or five trucks following each other round and round the main roads.

The night-lighting trucks leave the park headquarters every night at 7pm and 8pm (they can pick you up from the campsite if requested). All night-lightings are run by the park rangers, so tour operators sometimes join forces to hire a truck with ranger and searchlights. If you're on your own, you'll probably need to accompany one of these groups, as the trucks cost B500 to rent and can take up to ten people: book your place at the national park accommodation office, next to the visitor centre.

Pak Chong

Whether you decide to see Khao Yai on your own or as part of a tour, your first port of call is likely to be the town of **PAK CHONG**, 37km north of Khao Yai's visitor centre and major trailheads, and served by trains and buses. One of the three recommended Khao Yai tour leaders operates from Pak Chong, and there are a couple of places to stay in town too.

Pak Chong **train station** is on Soi 15 (☎044 311534), one short block north of Thanon Tesaban. The **bus station** is towards the west end of town, one block south off the main road between sois 8 and 10, but some long-distance buses also stop in the town centre, beside the footbridge; private air-con buses to Bangkok and Khorat leave from an office on Thanon Tesaban just west of Soi 18.

Thanon Tesaban cuts through central Pak Chong, and numerous small sois shoot off it: sois to the north are odd-numbered in ascending order from west to east (Soi 13–Soi 25) while those on the south side of the road have even numbers, from west to east (from Soi 8–Soi 18). The heart of the town is on the north side, between the train station on Soi 15 and the footbridge a few hundred metres further east at Soi 21, and this is where you'll find the day market. Beyond the footbridge is the **post office**, on the corner of Soi 25, and the CAT international **phone office** on the other side of Thanon Tesaban. There are several **internet centres** near the train station, along with ATMs; on the south side of the main road you'll find a supermarket, and there's a branch of the **Bangkok Hospital** (☎044 316611) at 51 Thanon Mittraphap.

The obvious drawback to basing yourself in Pak Chong is that it's about an hour's journey from the Khao Yai trailheads, but if you make an early start you can make use of the cheap public songthaew service.

Pak Chong's most acceptable budget **hotel** is the spartan and shabby but fairly clean *Phubade Hotel* (ⓣ044 314964; fan ❶, air-con ❷), 50m south down Tesaban Soi 15 from the train station. Smarter and more appealing, if a little frayed, *Rim Tarn Inn* (ⓣ044 313364; weekends ❺, weekdays ❹) is on the south side of the main road, about 300m west of the bus station; it has large, fairly comfortable air-con rooms, plus a pool, restaurant and beer garden.

The cheapest and most popular place to **eat** after dark is the night market, which sets up along the main road, between Tesaban sois 17 and 19. The *Riverside* **bar** and restaurant, signed off the southern end of Tesaban Soi 8, stages live music most nights.

Khorat (Nakhon Ratchasima) and around

Beyond Pak Chong, Highway 2 and the rail line diverge to run either side of picturesque Lam Takong Reservoir, offering a last taste of undulating, forested terrain before gaining the largely barren Khorat plateau. They rejoin at **KHORAT** (officially known as **Nakhon Ratchasima**) – literally "Frontier Country" – which is considered the gateway to the northeast.

If this is your first stop in Isaan, it's not a particularly pleasant introduction: Khorat is one of Thailand's most populous cities, its streets teem with traffic, and there's nothing here you could call a genuine tourist attraction. On the plus side, Khorat is at the centre of a good transport network and is within striking distance of the **Khmer ruins** at Phimai, Phanom Rung and Muang Tam, as well as the archeological remains of **Ban Prasat** and the pottery village at **Dan Kwian**. Aside from serving Bangkok and all the main centres within Isaan, Khorat's bus network extends south along Highway 304 to the east coast, enabling you to travel directly to Pattaya, Rayong and Chanthaburi without going through the capital.

Arrival, information and city transport

There are two bus terminals in town. **Bus Terminal 2** (ⓣ044 256006–9), situated on the far northern edge of the city on Highway 2, is the main one and is the arrival and departure point for regular and air-con buses serving regional towns such as Pak Chong (for Khao Yai), Pak Tong Chai and Phimai, as well as long-distance destinations such as Bangkok (24hr service), Ban Tako (for Phanom Rung), Chiang Mai, Khon Kaen, Nong Khai, Pattaya, Rayong (for Ko Samet) and Surin. The easiest way to get to and from Bus Terminal 2 is by tuk-tuk (B60 to the train station or nearby hotels), but city bus #15 also runs between Terminal 2 and the night bazaar area on Thanon Manat, from where city bus/songthaew #1 runs west along Thanon Chumphon to the train station and beyond. **Bus Terminal 1** (ⓣ044 268899) is more centrally located just off Thanon Suranari, and also operates both fan and air-con buses to Bangkok, via Pak Tong Chai and Pak Chong, but the service from Terminal 2 is more frequent. The **train station** on Thanon Mukkhamontri (ⓣ044 242044) is served by city bus routes #2 and #3.

The **TAT office** (daily 8.30am–4.30pm; ⓣ044 213666, ⓔtatsima@tat.or.th) on the western edge of town gives out free maps of the city and is reached from the city centre by city bus #2 or #3, as described below.

Flat-fare **songthaews** (B8) and **city buses** (B8) travel most main roads within town. The most useful routes – served by both songthaews and buses – are **#2,**

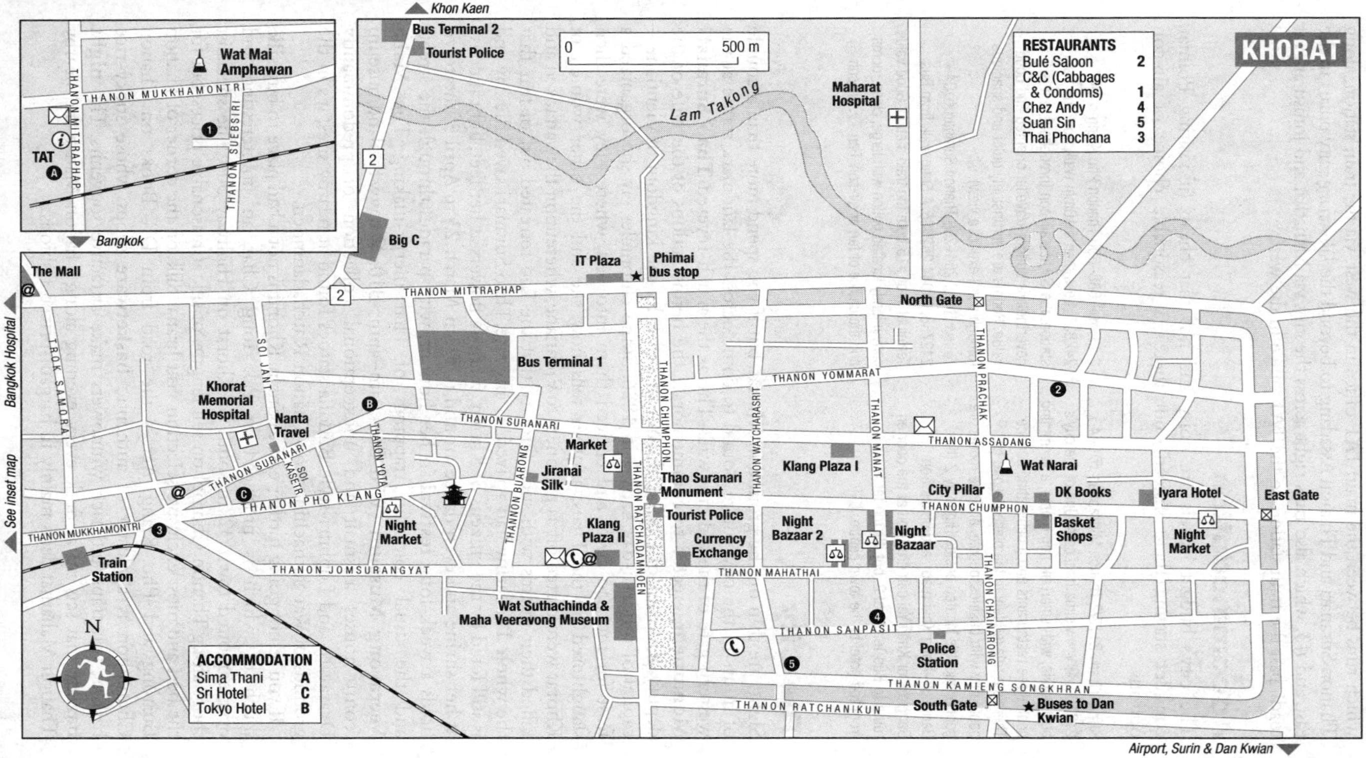
KHORAT
RESTAURANTS
Bulé Saloon 2
C&C (Cabbages & Condoms) 1
Chez Andy 4
Suan Sin 5
Thai Phochana 3
ACCOMMODATION
Sima Thani A
Sri Hotel C
Tokyo Hotel B
0 500 m
N
Khon Kaen
Bangkok
Bangkok Hospital
See inset map
Airport, Surin & Dan Kwian
Wat Mai Amphawan
THANON MUKKHAMONTRI
THANON MITTRAPHAP
THANON SUEBSIRI
TAT
Bus Terminal 2
Tourist Police
Lam Takong
Maharat Hospital
Big C
IT Plaza
Phimai bus stop
The Mall
THANON MITTRAPHAP
North Gate
Bus Terminal 1
THANON YOMMARAT
THANON PRACHAK
Khorat Memorial Hospital
Nanta Travel
SOI JANT
TROK SAMORA
THANON SURANARI
THANON ASSADANG
THANON CHUMPHON
THANON WATCHARASRIT
THANON MANAT
Market
Jiranai Silk
Thao Suranari Monument
Klang Plaza I
Wat Narai
City Pillar
DK Books
Iyara Hotel
East Gate
SOI KASETR
THANON YOTA
THANON BUARONG
THANON PHO KLANG
THANON RATCHADAMNOEN
Tourist Police
Night Market
Klang Plaza II
Currency Exchange
Night Bazaar 2
Night Bazaar
Basket Shops
Night Market
THANON MUKKHAMONTRI
Train Station
THANON JOMSURANGYAT
THANON MAHATHAI
THANON CHAINARONG
Wat Suthachinda & Maha Veeravong Museum
THANON SANPASIT
Police Station
THANON KAMIENG SONGKHRAN
THANON RATCHANIKUN
South Gate
Buses to Dan Kwian

which runs between the main TAT office in the west, via the train station, along Thanon Suranari and Thanon Assadang to beyond the *lak muang* (city pillar) in the east, and **#3**, which also runs right across the city, via Mahathai and Jomsurangyat roads, past the train station, to the TAT office in the west.

Accommodation

The city's budget **hotels** are noisy and not that cheap (if visiting Phimai, consider staying there instead), but there's a reasonable choice of air-con options.

Sima Thani 2112/2 Thanon Mittraphap ⓣ044 213100, ⓦwww.simathani.com. One of the city's best hotels, with smart air-con rooms, a swimming pool, three restaurants and a babysitting service. There's a relaxed feel to the place despite its popularity with businesspeople, and the rooms are good value. It's located beside Highway 2 (the Bangkok–Nong Khai road), and buses from Bangkok or Khao Yai can drop you at the door en route to Bus Terminal 2, but it's too far to walk from the hotel to the town centre. ⑥

Sri Hotel 688–690 Thanon Pho Klang ⓣ044 242831. Less than a 10min walk from the train station, the *Sri* has air-con throughout, but is nevertheless budget-traveller oriented and good value. Rooms are surprisingly quiet and spacious (though don't expect a view). ③

Tokyo Hotel 256–258 Thanon Suranari ⓣ044 242788, ⓕ044 252335. A 5min walk from Bus Terminal 1, or #15 from the train station. Good value, conveniently located option with large, clean rooms and the choice of fan or air-con. Fan ②, air-con ③

The City

Sights are thin on the ground in Khorat, but if you spend more than a couple of hours in the city you're bound to come across the landmark statue at the western gate of the old city walls. This is the much-revered **Thao Suranari Monument**, erected to commemorate the heroic actions of the wife of the deputy governor of Khorat, during an attack by the kingdom of Vientiane – capital of modern-day Laos – in 1826. Some chronicles say she organized a feast for the Lao army and enticed them into bed, where they were then slaughtered by the Thais; another tells how she and the other women of Khorat were carted off as prisoners to Vientiane, whereupon they attacked and killed their guards with such ferocity that the Lao retreated out of fear that the whole Thai army had arrived. At any rate, Thao Suranari saved the day and is still feted by the citizens of Khorat, who lay flowers at her feet, light incense at her shrine and even dance around it. From March 23 to April 3, the town holds a week-long **festival** in her honour, with parades through the streets and the usual colourful trappings of Thai merry-making. The **Maha Veeravong Museum** (Wed–Sun 9am–4pm; B10; ⓦwww.thailandmuseum.com) houses a small and unexceptional collection of predominantly Dvaravati- and Lopburi-style Buddha statues found at nearby sites; it's in the grounds of Wat Suthachinda, on Thanon Ratchadamnoen.

If you're not going further east to Surin, Khorat is not a bad place to buy **silk**, much of which is produced in Pak Tong Chai, an uninteresting and over-exploited town 32km south of Khorat on Highway 304. The specialist shops along Thanon Chumphon sell lengths of silk at reasonable prices, but for the best and most exclusive selection visit Jiranai Silk, on the corner of Thanon Buarong and Pho Klang. Across the road from DK Books on Thanon Chumphon is a cluster of authentic **basketware** shops whose sticky-rice baskets, fish traps and rice winnowers make attractive souvenirs. The **night bazaar** that sets up at dusk every evening along Thanon Manat and nearby Thanon Mahathai deals mainly in bargain-priced fashions.

Eating and drinking

The night bazaar on and around Thanon Manat includes a few hot-food stalls, but there's a bigger selection of **night-market**-style foodstalls, with some streetside tables, about 800m further east near the *Iyara Hotel* on Thanon Chumphon. A smaller, more convenient grouping of night-time foodstalls sets up about 400m east of *Sri Hotel* on the corner of Thanon Yota. Because of its sizeable contingent of (mostly retired) expats, Khorat also offers the chance to satisfy foreign-food cravings, with a number of cuisines on offer, from Swiss to Italian.

Bulé Saloon Thanon Yommarat. Wild West-style pub and beer garden that stages live music (mainly soft rock) every night and offers a wide selection of Thai dishes. Daily 6pm–1am.

C&C (Cabbages & Condoms) 86/1 Thanon Suebsiri. Excellent Thai food at this cosy, mid-priced restaurant (most dishes B60–B100), managed along the same lines as its sister operation in Bangkok, with all proceeds going to the Population and Community Development Association of Thailand (PDA). Daily 10am–10pm.

Chez Andy 5–7 Thanon Manat ⓦwww.chezandy.com. Swiss-run restaurant famous for its Australian steaks (around B250), but which also does some Swiss cuisine and Thai dishes. Mon–Sat 11am–midnight.

Suan Sin 163 Thanon Watcharasrit. Cheap place that's highly rated by locals for its tasty Isaan favourites, especially *som tam* and *kai yang* (from B50). Daily 10am–10pm.

Thai Phochana 1421 Thanon Jomsurangyat. Centrally located air-con restaurant known for its duck curries (*kaeng pet*) and Khorat-style noodles cooked with coconut cream (*mii khorat*). Also has several vegetarian options. Most dishes cost B50–120. Daily 7am–9pm.

Listings

Hospitals Expats favour the private Bangkok Hospital at 1308/9 Thanon Mittraphap (Highway 2), near Tesco Lotus ⓣ044 429999; the government Maharat Hospital is on the northeast edge of town ⓣ044 254990–1.

Internet access Catnet terminals in the CAT overseas phone office on Thanon Jomsurangyat (Mon–Fri 8.30am–4.30pm, Sat 8.30am–noon).

Tourist police For all emergencies, call the tourist police on the free, 24hr phone line ⓣ1155, or contact them at one of their booths in town: their main office is opposite Bus Terminal 2 on Highway 2 ⓣ044 341777–9, and there's a more central booth beside the Thao Suranari Monument on Thanon Chumphon.

Tours, transport rental and travel agents The clued-up Nanta Travel Service, located a couple of doors east of the *Sripatana Hotel* at 334 Thanon Suranari (daily 8am–5.30pm; ⓣ044 251339, ⓔnantatravel@hotmail.com), sells domestic and international air tickets, rents motorbikes (B250 per day) and cars (from B1200 per day), and offers day-trips with car and driver to local sights on request, including to Phimai and Ban Prasat (B1800), to Phanom Rung, Muang Tam and Dan Kwian (B2500), and to Khao Yai (B3000).

Dan Kwian

Some of the most popular household pottery in Thailand is produced by the potters of **DAN KWIAN**, a tiny village 15km south of Khorat on Route 224. To get there, take local bus #1307 (destination Chok Chai; every 30min; 30min) from Bus Terminal 2, or pick it up at Khorat's southern city gate; get off as soon as you see the roadside pottery stalls. The local clay, dug from the banks of the Mun River, has a high iron content, which when fired in wood-burning kilns combines with ash to create the unglazed metallic finish that is characteristic of **Dan Kwian pottery**. The geometrical latticework pattern is also typical, and is incorporated into everything from incense burners and ashtrays to vases and storage jars. Dan Kwian potters also produce ceramic tiles and large-scale religious and secular murals, a favourite in modern wats and city homes.

Ban Prasat

The quintessentially northeastern village of **BAN PRASAT** has become a source of great interest to archeologists following the discovery in the 1990s of a series of **burial grounds** within its boundaries, some of which date back three thousand years. The skeletons and attendant artefacts have been well preserved in the mud, and many are now on display; the village has made extra efforts to entice tourists with low-key craft demonstrations and a homestay programme. It's also a pleasant village in its own right, a traditional community of stilt houses set beside the Tarn Prasat River.

There are currently three **excavation pits** open to the public, each clearly signed from the centre of the village and informatively labelled. From these pits archeologists have surmized that Ban Prasat was first inhabited in around 1000 BC and that its resident rice farmers traded with coastal people. Each pit contains bones and objects from different eras, buried at different depths but also with the head pointing in different directions, suggesting a change in religious or superstitious precepts.

Signs in the village direct you to local family-run projects, such as the household of **silk-weavers**, where you should be able to see several stages of the sericulture process (see box, p.514) and buy some cloth. Other village crafts include the weaving of floor mats from locally grown bulrushes, and the making of household brooms.

Practicalities

Ban Prasat is 2km off Highway 2, 46km north of Khorat and 17km southwest of Phimai. Any Khorat–Phimai bus (#1305 from Khorat's Bus Terminal 2; every 30min; about 1hr from Khorat or 20min from Phimai) will drop you at the Highway 2 junction, from where motorbike taxis will ferry you to the village. There are no hotels or restaurants in the village, but there is a **homestay** programme (B400 per person half-board); stays should be arranged a week in advance by contacting the village headman, Khun Thiam Laongkarn, of the Eco-tourism Society, 282 Mu 7, Tambon Tarn Prasat, Amphoe Non Sung, Nakhon Ratchasima 30420 (Ⓣ044 367075). Alter-natively, staff at the Khorat TAT office may be able to help (Ⓣ044 213666, Ⓔtatsima@tat.or.th).

Phimai

Hemmed in by its old city walls and encircled by tributaries of the Mun River, the small modern town of **PHIMAI**, 60km northeast of Khorat, is dominated by the charmingly restored Khmer temple complex of **Prasat Hin Phimai**. No one knows for sure when the prasat was built or for whom, but as a religious site it probably dates back to the reign of the Khmer king Suriyavarman I (1002–49); the complex was connected by a direct road to Angkor and oriented southeast, towards the Khmer capital. Over the next couple of centuries Khmer rulers made substantial modifications, and by the end of Jayavarman VII's reign in 1220, Phimai had been officially dedicated to Mahayana Buddhism. Phimai's other claim to fame is **Sai Ngam** (Beautiful Banyan), reputedly the largest banyan tree in Thailand.

Phimai's biggest event of the year is the festival of **boat races**, held on the Mun's tributaries over a weekend in early November, in a tradition that's endured for over a century. In common with many other riverside towns,

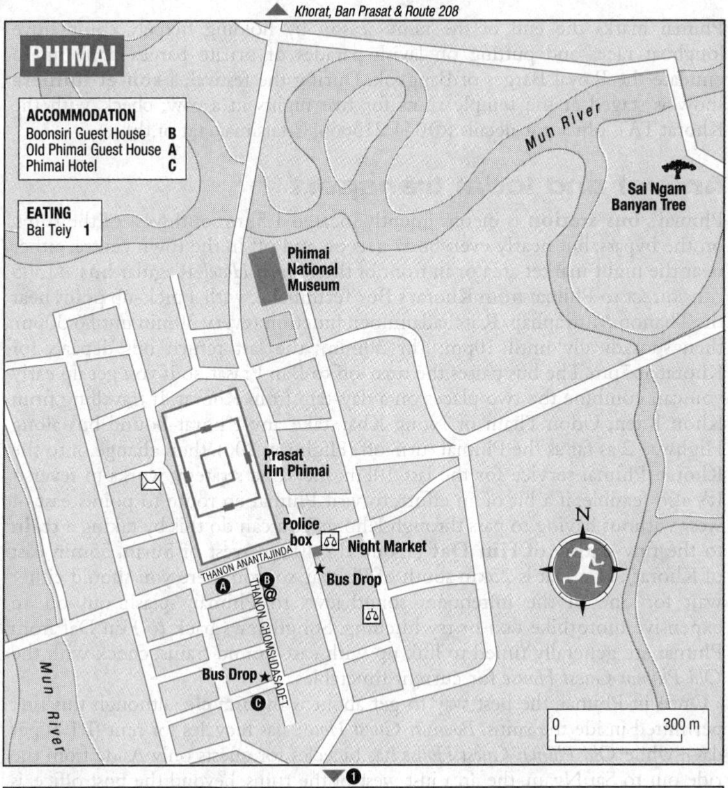

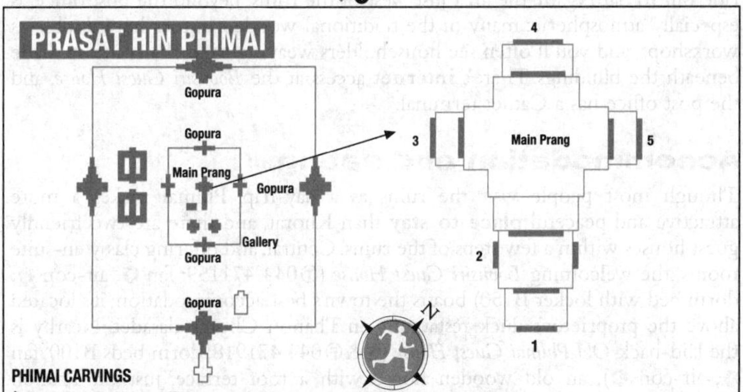

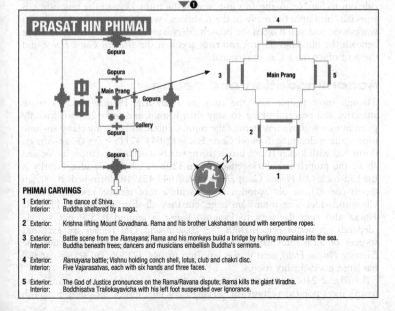

PHIMAI CARVINGS

1	Exterior:	The dance of Shiva.
	Interior:	Buddha sheltered by a naga.
2	Exterior:	Krishna lifting Mount Govadhana. Rama and his brother Lakshaman bound with serpentine ropes.
3	Exterior:	Battle scene from the *Ramayana*; Rama and his monkeys build a bridge by hurling mountains into the sea.
	Interior:	Buddha beneath trees; dancers and musicians embellish Buddha's sermons.
4	Exterior:	*Ramayana* battle; Vishnu holding conch shell, lotus, club and chakri disc.
	Interior:	Five Vajarasatvas, each with six hands and three faces.
5	Exterior:	The God of Justice pronounces on the Rama/Ravana dispute; Rama kills the giant Viradha.
	Interior:	Boddhisatva Trailokayavicha with his left foot suspended over Ignorance.

Phimai marks the end of the rainy season by holding fiercely competitive longboat races and putting on lavish parades of ornate barges done up to emulate the Royal Barges of Bangkok. During the festival, a **son et lumière** show is staged at the temple ruins for five nights in a row; check with the Khorat TAT office for details (ⓣ044 213666, ⓔtatsima@tat.or.th).

Arrival and local transport

Phimai's **bus station** is inconveniently located 1.5km southwest of the ruins, on the bypass, but nearly everybody gets on and off in the town centre, either near the night market area or in front of the *Phimai Hotel*. Regular **bus** #1305 runs direct to Phimai from Khorat's Bus Terminal 2, with a pick-up point near the Thanon Mittraphap/Ratchadamnoen junction (every 30min until 6.30pm, then sporadically until 10pm; 1hr 30min); the last return bus departs for Khorat at 7pm. The bus passes the turn-off to Ban Prasat, so if you get up early you can combine the two places on a day-trip from Khorat. If travelling from Khon Kaen, Udon Thani or Nong Khai, take any Khorat-bound bus along Highway 2 as far as the Phimai turn-off (Highway 206), then change onto the Khorat–Phimai service for the last 10km; the same strategy works in reverse. It's also feasible, if a bit of an effort, to visit Phimai en route to points east or west without having to pass through Khorat. You can do this by taking a **train** to the tiny station of **Hin Dat** (about 1hr 40min west of Surin, 55min east of Khorat). Hin Dat is 25km south of Phimai, so from here you should either wait for one of the infrequent songthaews to Phimai, splash out on an expensive motorbike taxi or try hitching. Songthaews back to Hin Dat from Phimai are generally timed to link up with east-bound trains; check with the *Old Phimai Guest House* for current timetables.

Once in Phimai, the best way to get about is by **bicycle**, although this isn't permitted inside the ruins. *Boonsiri Guest House* has bicycles for rent (B100 per day), while *Old Phimai Guest House* has bicycles for guests only. Aside from the ride out to Sai Ngam, the area just west of the ruins, beyond the post office, is especially atmospheric: many of the traditional wooden houses here double as workshops, and you'll often see householders weaving cane chairs in the shade beneath the buildings. There's **internet** access at the *Boonsiri Guest House*, and the post office has a Catnet terminal.

Accommodation and eating

Though most people visit the ruins as a day-trip, Phimai makes a more attractive and peaceful **place to stay** than Khorat, and there are two friendly guest houses within a few steps of the ruins. Central, and offering classy en-suite rooms, the welcoming *Boonsiri Guest House* (ⓣ044 471159; fan ❸, air-con ❸; dorm bed with locker B150) boasts the town's best accommodation; it's located above the proprietor's duck restaurant on Thanon Chomsudasadet. Nearby is the laid-back *Old Phimai Guest House* (ⓣ&ⓕ044 471918; dorm beds B100, fan ❶, air-con ❷), an old wooden house with a roof terrace, just off Thanon Chomsudasadet. The rooms are large, but they all share bathrooms. The *Old Phimai* also runs day-trips to Phanom Rung at around B2500 per vehicle (depends on petrol price). Both the *Boonsiri* and *Old Phimai* are excellent sources of local information. A few steps further away from the ruins, the friendly *Phimai Hotel*, next to the bus drop (ⓣ044 471306; fan ❷, air-con ❸), has large, good-quality rooms.

Bai Teiy, at 246/1 Thanon Chomsudasadet, south of the town centre, is the town's most popular **restaurant**, serving tasty Thai dishes, including fresh fish from the river. If you prefer a meal with a view, head out to the string of pricier restaurants alongside Sai Ngam. The **night market** sets up at dusk on the eastern stretch of Thanon Anantajinda, just southeast of the ruins.

The ruins

Built mainly of dusky pink and greyish white sandstone, **Prasat Hin Phimai** (daily 7.30am–6pm; B100) is a seductive sight from a distance; closer inspection reveals a mass of intricate carvings.

From the main southeastern gate, a staircase ornamented with classic naga (serpent) balustrades leads to a gopura in the **outer walls**, which are punctuated on either side by false balustraded windows – a bit of sculptural sleight-of-hand to jazz up the solid stonework without piercing the defences. A raised pathway bridges the space between these walls and the inner gallery that protects the prangs of the **inner sanctuary**. The minor prang to the right, made of laterite, is attributed to the twelfth-century Buddhist king Jayavarman VII, who engaged in a massive temple-building campaign during his reign. Enshrined within is a statue of him; it's a copy of the much more impressive original, now housed in the Phimai National Museum. The pink sandstone prang to the left, connected to a Brahmin shrine where seven stone linga were found, was probably built around the same time.

After more than twenty years of archeological detective work and painstaking reassembly, the magnificent white-sandstone **main prang** has now been restored to its original cruciform groundplan and conical shape, complete with an almost full set of carved lintels, pediments and antefixes, and capped with a stone lotus-bud. The **carvings** around the outside of the prang depict predominantly Hindu themes. Shiva the Destroyer dances above the main entrance to the southeast antechamber: his destruction dance heralds the end of the world and the creation of a new order, a supremely potent image that warranted this position over the most important doorway. Most of the other external carvings pick out momentous episodes from the *Ramayana* (see box, p.135), starring heroic Rama, his brother Lakshaman and their band of faithful monkeys in endless battles of strength, wits and magical powers against Ravana, the embodiment of evil. Inside, more sedate Buddhist scenes give evidence of the conversion from Hindu to Buddhist faith, and the prasat's most important image, the Buddha sheltered by a seven-headed naga, sits atop a base that once supported a Hindu Shiva lingam.

Phimai National Museum

Much of the ancient carved stonework discovered at Phimai but not fitted back into the renovated structure can be seen at the **Phimai National Museum** (daily 9am–4pm; B100; Ⓦwww.thailandmuseum.com), where it's easier to appreciate, being at eye-level, well labelled and put in context. The museum stands between one of the old Khmer reservoirs and the Mun River, just inside the old city walls to the northeast of the ruins. It's an easy walk from the ruins, but if you're here for the day from Khorat, you can save your legs a bit as the Khorat–Phimai bus will stop outside the museum if requested. The museum's *pièce de résistance* is the exceptionally fine sandstone statue of Jayavarman VII that was found in Phimai's laterite prang; seated and leaning slightly forward, he's lost his arms and part of his nose, but none of his grace and serenity. Elsewhere in the galleries, displays take you through the religious and cultural history of the Phimai region, featuring prehistoric items from Ban Prasat as well as some exquisite Buddha statues from more recent times.

Sai Ngam

Two kilometres northeast of the museum – get there by bicycle (see p.506) or samlor – **Sai Ngam** is a banyan tree so enormous that it's reputed to cover an area about half the size of a soccer pitch (approximately 2300 square metres). It might look like a grove of small banyans, but Sai Ngam is in fact a single *Ficus bengalensis* whose branches have dropped vertically into the ground, taken root and spawned other branches, so growing further and further out from its central trunk. Banyan trees are believed to harbour animist spirits, and you can make merit here by releasing fish into the artificial lake that surrounds Sai Ngam. The tree is a popular recreation spot, and several restaurants have sprung up alongside it.

Phanom Rung and Muang Tam

East of Khorat the bleached plains roll on, broken only by the occasional small town and, if you're travelling along Highway 24, the odd tantalizing glimpse of the smoky Phanom Dangkrek mountain range above the southern horizon. That said, it's well worth jumping off the Surin-bound bus for a detour to the fine Khmer ruins of **Prasat Hin Khao Phanom Rung** and **Prasat Muang Tam**. Built during the same period as Phimai, and for the same purpose, the temple complexes form two more links in the chain that once connected the Khmer capital with the limits of its empire. Sited dramatically atop an extinct volcano, Phanom Rung has been beautifully restored, and the more recently renovated Muang Tam lies on the plains below.

Arrival

Most people do the ruins of Phanom Rung and Muang Tam as a **day-trip** from Khorat or Surin, though it's also possible to stay closer to the sights, in **Nang Rong** or **Buriram**. There's public transport from Khorat, Surin, Nang Rong and Buriram as far as the little town of **Ban Tako**, from where you'll need to take a motorbike taxi for the final few kilometres to the ruins. Alternatively, rent your own motorbike from Nang Rong, or join a **day-tour** from Phimai or Khorat.

Served by frequent **buses** from Khorat (via Nang Rong) and Surin, the town of **BAN TAKO** is located on Highway 24 about 115km southeast of Khorat or 83km southwest of Surin. Bus #274 travels between the two provincial capitals (every 30min 24hr a day; 2hr 25min from Khorat, 1hr 45min from Surin).

From Ban Tako it's 12km south to Phanom Rung and another 8km southeast along a side road to Muang Tam, and as there's no public transport direct to the ruins most people rent an expensive **motorbike taxi** here, which usually costs B300–400 per person for the round trip to Phanom Rung, Muang Tam and back to Ban Tako. Alternatively you could try **hitching** – a time-consuming option during the week (so you should take a very early bus from Khorat or Surin), but a lot easier at weekends. The best place to hitch from is a small village south of Ban Tako called **Ban Don Nong Nae**, which you can reach from Ban Tako by taking a ten-minute ride on bus #523.

Accommodation

The nearest **accommodation** to Phanom Rung is in the town of **NANG RONG**, on the #274 and #523 bus routes, 14km west of Ban Tako on Highway 24. Here, the welcoming guest house *Honey Inn* (Ⓣ044 622825, Ⓦhoneyinn.com; fan or air-con ❷), at 8/1 Soi Sri Koon, offers motorbike rental, meals with the family and internet access. To get to *Honey Inn* from the Nang Rong bus terminal, either take a B30 samlor ride or walk north about 100m onto Highway 24, cross the highway, turn right and walk east along the highway for about 300m, passing a PTT petrol station after about 200m. Turn left at the *Honey Inn* sign and it's about 100m further on. Another appealing place is the *P. Inter California Hostel* (ⓣ044 622214, ⓦwww.nangronghomestay.com; fan ❷, air-con ❹), located at 59/11 Thanon Sangkhakrit to the east of the bus station (about B40 by samlor), which has comfortable rooms with cable TV and views over the countryside. For onward **transport to the ruins**, either take the #274 bus to Ban Tako, then a motorbike taxi as described above; hire a motorbike taxi all the way from Nang Rong (slightly pricier than from Ban Tako) or rent a car or motorbike from *Honey Inn* or *P. Inter California Hostel*.

If arriving direct from Bangkok, it may be easier to stay in the provincial capital of **BURIRAM**, 40km north of Ban Tako, which is served by all Bangkok–Ubon **trains**, and (currently) by PB Air **flights** (ⓣ044 680132, ⓦwww.pbair.com) between Bangkok and Buriram Airport, 30km from town. Buses connect Buriram with Ban Tako (about 1hr). About 200m south of Buriram train station along the main drag, Thanon Romburi, the *Thai Hotel* (ⓣ044 611112, ⓕ044 612461; fan ❷, air-con ❷), at 38/1, has decent air-con **rooms**, or there's slightly more upmarket accommodation at the *Vongthong Hotel* (ⓣ044 620860, ⓦwww.sawadee.com/hotel/isan/vongthong; ❹–❺), a few minutes' walk west of the bus terminal, off Thanon Buladmuan at 512/1 Thanon Jira, which offers large rooms with air-con and TV.

Prasat Hin Khao Phanom Rung

Prasat Hin Khao Phanom Rung (daily 6am–6pm; B100 or B150 including entrance to Muang Tam) is the finest example of Khmer architecture in Thailand, graced with innumerable exquisite carvings and with its sandstone and laterite buildings so perfectly aligned that on the morning of the fifteenth day of the waxing moon in the fifth month of the lunar calendar you can stand at the westernmost gopura and see the rising sun through all fifteen doors. This day (usually in April: check dates at ⓦwww.thailandgrandfestival.com or contact Buriram municipality on ⓣ044 613315) is celebrated with a day-long **festival** of huge parades all the way up the hill to the prasat – a tradition believed to go back eight hundred years. As at most Khmer prasats, **building** at Phanom Rung spanned several reigns, probably from the beginning of the tenth century to the early thirteenth. The heart of the temple was constructed in the mid-twelfth century, in early Angkorian style, and is attributed to local ruler Narendraditya and his son Hiranya. Narendraditya was a follower of the Shivaite cult, a sect which practised yoga and fire worship and used alcohol and sex in its rituals; carved depictions of all these practices decorate the temple.

There are three car parks and three **entrances** to the Phanom Rung complex; if you have your own transport, ignore the Gates 2 and 3 (west) entrances, signed off the access road, and carry on to the main, Gate 1 (east), entrance and car park; the drama of the site is lost if you explore it back-to-front. Motorbike taxis should take you to the main entrance. There are cheap foodstalls outside the Gate 1 entrance and in its car park area. The excellent, museum-like **Phanom Rung Tourist Information Centre** inside the Gate 1 car park (daily 9am–4.30pm; free) provides an outstanding introduction to the temple's construction, iconography and restoration. Most people visit in the morning, but in the afternoon the site is less crowded.

Exploring the temple

The approach to **the temple** is one of the most dramatic of its kind. Symbolic of the journey from earth to the heavenly palace of the gods, the ascent to the inner compound is imbued with metaphorical import: by following the 200-metre-long avenue, paved in laterite and sandstone and flanked with lotus-bud pillars, you are walking to the ends of the earth. Ahead, the main prang, representing Mount Meru, home of the gods, looms large above the gallery walls, and is accessible only via the first of three **naga bridges**, a raised cruciform structure with sixteen naga balustrades, each naga having five heads. Once across the bridge you have traversed the abyss between earth and heaven. A series of stairways ascends to the eastern entrance of the celestial home, first passing four small ponds, thought to have been used for ritual purification. A second naga bridge crosses to the **east gopura**, entrance to the inner sanctuary, which is topped by a lintel carved with Indra (god of the east) sitting on a lion throne. The gopura is the main gateway through the **gallery**, which runs right round the inner compound and has been restored in part, with arched stone roofs, small chambers inside and **false windows**; real windows wouldn't have been strong enough to support such a heavy stone roof, so false ones, which retained the delicate pilasters but backed them with stone blocks, were an aesthetically acceptable compromise.

The main prang

Phanom Rung is surprisingly compact, so the east gopura leads almost directly into the **main prang**, separated from it only by a final naga bridge. A dancing Shiva, nine of his ten arms intact, and a lintel carved with a relief of a **reclining Vishnu** preside over the eastern entrance to the prang. This depicts a common Hindu creation myth, known as "Reclining Vishnu Asleep on the Milky Sea of Eternity", in which Vishnu dreams up a new universe, and Brahma (the four-faced god perched on the lotus blossom that springs from Vishnu's navel) puts the dream into practice. On the pediment above this famous relief is a lively carving of **Shiva Nataraja**, or Shiva's Dance of Destruction, which shows him dancing on Mount Kailash in front of several other gods, including Ganesh,

▲ Detail of one of the naga bridges, Prasat Hin Khao Phanom Rung

Brahma and Vishnu. The dance brings about the total destruction of the extant world and replaces it with a new epoch. Of the other figures decorating the prang, one of the most important is the lion head of Kala, also known as Kirtimukha, symbolic of both the lunar and the solar eclipse and – because he's able to "swallow" the sun – considered far superior to other planetary gods. Inside the prang kneels an almost life-size statue of Shiva's vehicle, the bull Nandi, behind which stands the all-powerful **Shiva lingam**, for which the prang was originally built; the stone channel that runs off the lingam and out of the north side of the prang was designed to catch the lustral water with which the sacred stone was bathed.

Two rough-hewn laterite libraries stand alongside the main prang, in the northeast and southeast corners, and there are also remains of two early tenth-century brick prangs just northeast of the main prang. The unfinished **prang noi** ("Little Prang") in the southwest corner now contains a stone Buddha footprint, which has become the focus of the merit-making at the annual April festivities, thus neatly linking ancient and modern religious practices.

Prasat Muang Tam

Down on the plains 8km to the southeast of Phanom Rung and accessed via a scenic minor road that cuts through a swathe of rice fields, the small but elegant temple complex of **Prasat Muang Tam** (daily 6am–6pm; B100 or B150 including entrance to Phanom Rung) is sited behind a huge kilometre-long *baray* (Khmer reservoir), which was probably constructed at the same time as the main part of the temple, in the early eleventh century. Like Phanom Rung, Muang Tam was probably built in stages between the tenth and thirteenth centuries, and is based on the classic Khmer design of a central prang flanked by minor prangs and encircled by a gallery and four gopura. Its history is presented in brief at the **tourist information centre** (daily 9am–4.30pm; free) in the temple car park.

The ruins

The approach to Muang Tam is nothing like as grand as at Phanom Rung but, once through the main, eastern, gopura in the outside wall, it's a pretty scene, with the central gallery encircled by four **L-shaped ponds** – such important features that they are referred to in a contemporary inscription that states "this sanctuary is preserved by sacred water". The shape of the ponds gives the impression that the prasat is set within a moat that's been severed by the four entrance pathways at the cardinal points. Each pond is lined with laterite brick steps designed to enable easy access for priests drawing sacred water, and possibly also for devotees to cleanse themselves before entering the central sanctuary. The rims are constructed from sandstone blocks that form naga, the sacred water serpents.

The rectangular central **gallery** was probably roofed with timber (long since rotted away) and so could be punctuated with real windows, rather than the more load-bearing false versions that had to be used at Phanom Rung. Inside, the **five red-brick towers** of the inner sanctuary are arranged on a laterite platform, with three prangs in the front (eastern) row, and two behind. The main, central, prang has collapsed, leaving only its base, but the four other towers are merely decapitated and some have carved **lintels** intact. The lintel above the doorway of the front right tower is particularly lively in its depiction of the popular scene known as Ume Mahesvara (Uma and her consort Shiva riding the bull Nandi). There are interesting details in the temple complex, including recurrent motifs of foliage designs and Kala lion-faces, and figures of ascetics carved into the base of the doorway pillars on the eastern gopura of the outer wall.

Surin and around

Best known for its much-hyped annual elephant round-up, the provincial capital of **SURIN**, around 150km east of Khorat, is an otherwise typical northeastern town, a good place to absorb the easy-going pace of Isaan life, with the bonus of some atmospheric Khmer ruins nearby as well as a lively nightlife. The elephant tie-in comes from the local Suay people, whose prowess with pachyderms is well known and can sometimes be seen first-hand in the nearby village of **Ban Ta Klang**. Thais, Lao and Khmers make up the remainder of the population of Surin province; the Khmers have lived and worked in the region for over a thousand years, and their architectural legacy is still in evidence at the ruined temples of Ta Muean and Ban Pluang. For the twenty-first-century traveller, there's **overland access between Thailand and Cambodia** via Surin province's Chong Chom checkpoint near Kap Choeng.

Arrival and information

Several services a day make the Bangkok–Surin connection, stopping at the **train station** (Ⓣ044 511295) on the northern edge of town. The **bus terminal** (Ⓣ044 511756) off Thanon Jitbumrung runs frequent services to and from Bangkok, to major northeastern towns, and to Pattaya, Rayong, Phitsanulok, Lampang and Chiang Mai.

There's a **TAT office** (Ⓣ044 514447–8, Ⓔtatsurin@tat.or.th; daily 8.30am–4.30pm) at 355/3-6 Thanon Thetsabarn 1, just east of the town centre, and the provincial government has quite a useful website (Ⓦwww.surin.go.th), which includes booking forms for the elephant round-up.

Accommodation

Except during the elephant round-up – when room rates in Surin rocket and **accommodation** is booked out weeks in advance – you'll have no trouble finding a place to stay.

Overland into Cambodia via Chong Chom

If you're planning to cross **overland into Cambodia**, there are air-con buses (every 30min 5am–5.30pm; 1hr 30min; B60) and non-air-con buses (every 30min 8am–3pm; B40; 2hr) via Prasat to the Chong Chom border pass, 70km south of Surin; or you can arrange a taxi through *Farang Connection*, located behind Surin bus station (Ⓣ044 511509, Ⓦwww.farangconnection.com). Cambodian visas are issued on arrival at the Chong Chom–O'Smach checkpoint (daily 7am–8pm; US$20 or B1000), from where you can get transport to Anlong Veng and then on to Siem Reap, which is 150km from the border crossing. Arriving **from Cambodia**, songthaews and motorbike taxis ferry travellers from the border checkpoint to the bus stop for Prasat and Surin. For travellers' accounts of the border crossing see Ⓦwww.talesofasia.com/cambodia-overland-osm-reports.htm; for details on other overland routes into Cambodia, see p.34.

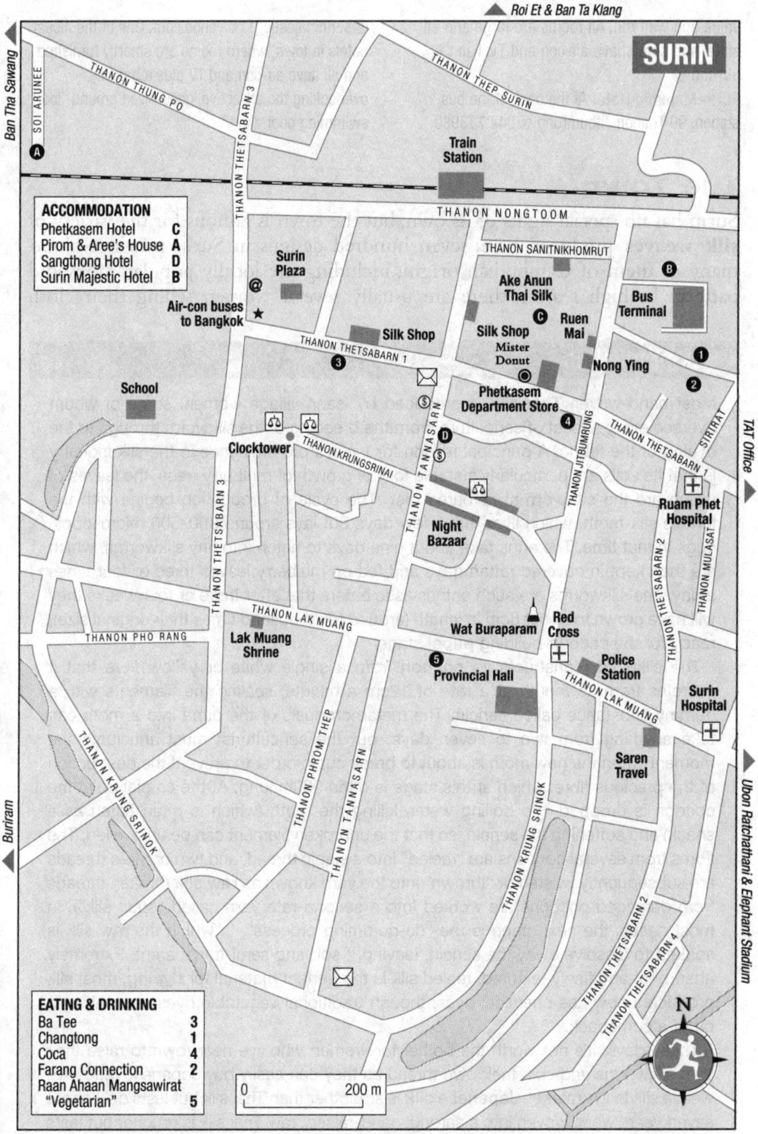

Phetkasem Hotel 104 Thanon Jitbumrung ⓣ 044 511274, ⓔ pkhotel@yahoo.com. One of Surin's better mid-range hotels, offering good-value, sizeable air-con rooms with (Thai) TV, plus there's a swimming pool, nightclub and karaoke bar. ❹

Pirom & Aree's House At the far end of Soi Arunee off Thanon Thung Po ⓣ 089 355 4140. Surin's famously long-running guest house occupies a tranquil spot overlooking rice fields about 1.5km northwest of the train station. Rooms in this modern take on a traditional home are large, simply furnished with fans and shared bathrooms, plus there are garden seating areas. ❶

Sangthong Hotel 279-281 Thanon Tannasarn ⓣ 044 512099, ⓕ 044 514329. The best of the budget hotels, this place is friendly, good value and well run. All rooms are large and en suite, and some have air-con and TV. Fan ❶, air-con ❷

Surin Majestic Hotel At the back of the bus station, 99 Thanon Jitbumrung ⓣ044 713980, ⓔsurinmajestic_11@yahoo.com. One of the nicest hotels in town, where rooms are smartly furnished and all have air-con and TV plus a balcony overlooking the attractive, good-sized ground-floor swimming pool. ❺–❻

The Town

Surin has no special sights of its own, but the town is famous for the variety of **silk weaves** produced here: seven hundred designs in Surin province alone, many of them of Cambodian origin, including the locally popular rhomboid pattern. In high season, there are usually several women selling their cloth

Silk production

Most hand-woven **Thai silk** is produced by Isaan village women, some of whom oversee every aspect of sericulture, from the breeding of the silkworm through to the dyeing of the fabric. A principal reason for Isaan's pre-eminence in the silk industry is that its soils are particularly suitable for the growth of mulberry trees, the leaves of which are the **silkworms'** favoured diet. The cycle of production begins with the female silk-moth, which lives just a few days but lays around 300–500 microscopic eggs in that time. The eggs take about nine days to hatch into tiny silkworms, which are then kept in covered rattan trays and fed on mulberry leaves three or four times a day. The silkworms are such enthusiastic eaters that after three or four weeks they will have grown to about 6cm in length (around ten thousand times their original size), ready for the cocoon-building **pupal** stage.

The silkworm constructs its **cocoon** from a single white or yellow fibre that it secretes from its mouth at a rate of 12cm a minute, sealing the filaments with a gummy substance called sericin. The metamorphosis of the pupa into a moth can take anything from two to seven days, but the sericulturist must anticipate the moment when the new moth is about to break out in order to prevent the destruction of the precious fibre, which at this stage is often 900m long. At the crucial point the cocoon is dropped into boiling water, killing the moth (which is often eaten as a snack) and softening the sericin, so that the unbroken filament can be unravelled. The fibres from several cocoons are "reeled" into a single thread, and two or three threads are subsequently twisted or "thrown" into the yarn known as **raw silk** (broken threads from damaged cocoons are worked into a second-rate yarn called "spun silk"). In most cases, the next stage is the "de-gumming process", in which the raw silk is soaked to dissolve away the sericin, leaving it soft and semi-transparent. Extremely absorbent and finely textured, reeled silk is the perfect material for **dyeing**; most silk producers now use chemical dyes, though traditional vegetable dyes are making a bit of a comeback.

These days, it's not worth the bother for women who live near town to raise their own silkworms and spin their own thread as they can easily buy Japanese ready-to-weave silk in the market. **Japanese silk** is smoother than Thai silk but lasts only about seven years when woven into a sarong; hand-raised, raw Thai silk is rougher but lasts around forty years, and so is still favoured by women living in remote villages.

Once dyed (or bought), the silk is ready for **weaving**. This is generally done during slack agricultural periods, for example just after the rice is planted and again just after it's harvested. Looms are usually set up in the space under the house, in the sheltered area between the piles, and most are designed to produce a sarong of around 1m by 2m. Isaan weavers have many different weaving techniques and can create countless patterns, ranging from the simplest single-coloured plain weave for work shirts to exquisitely complex wedding sarongs that may take up to six weeks to complete.

around the Tannasarn–Krungsrinai intersection, or you can try the Ruen Mai **shop** just outside the *Phetkasem Hotel* at 162–164 Thanon Jitbumrung; nearby Nong Ying, at 52 Thanon Jitbumrung, which has a superb selection of silks as well as ready-made silk jackets, bags and accessories, silver jewellery and axe pillows; or Ake Anun Thai Silk at 126 Sanitnikhomrut. For details on visiting local silk-weaving villages, see p.516.

Surin's **elephant round-up**, held every year on the third weekend of November, draws some forty thousand spectators to watch four hundred elephants play football, engage in tugs of war and parade in full battle garb. These shows last about three hours and give both trainers and animals the chance to practise their skills, but if you arrive early (about 7.30am) you can watch the preliminary street processions when locals set out long trestle tables filled with pineapples, bananas and sugar cane so the elephants can munch their way into town. Note that however well controlled the elephants appear, you should always approach them with caution – in the past, frightened and taunted elephants have killed tourists. Tickets cost B500–800 and can be booked through TAT, the provincial government website (ⓦwww.surin.go.th) or Saren Travel, who can also arrange accommodation and transport if you contact them three months ahead; alternatively, you could join one of the overnight packages organized by Bangkok travel agencies.

One of the best reasons for coming to Surin during the rest of the year is to take one of the excellent **local tours** (from B1400 per person) organized from *Pirom & Aree's House*. Pirom is a highly informed former social worker whose trips give tourists an unusual chance to catch glimpses of rural northeastern life as it's really lived. His village tours feature visits to local silk-weavers and basket-makers, as well as to Ban Ta Klang elephant trainers' village, and it's also possible to do overnight village trips, including one that takes in Khao Phra Viharn (when open), Khong Chiam and Pha Taem.

Eating and drinking

Aside from a reasonable range of local **restaurants**, Surin boasts a good-sized **night bazaar**, which occupies the eastern end of Thanon Krungsrinai and offers a tasty selection of local food (including roasted crickets and barbecued locusts when in season), as well as stalls selling fashions and toys. Surin also has a surprisingly sophisticated **nightlife** for such a provincial town, with a clutch of hip bars and discos that cater to a largely Thai clientele around the northern end of Thanon Sirirath and along Soi Kola, just north of the *Thong Tharin Hotel*.

Ba Tee (Pae Ti) 40–42 Thanon Thetsabarn 1 (no English sign, but enter via the shopfront with the Johnnie Walker billboard). Huge place that serves the best, and priciest, Chinese food in Surin, including lots of seafood.

Chantong At the back of the bus terminal, off Thanon Sirirat (no English sign, but it's next to *Oasis Café*). Despite its unprepossessing location, this is a rather classy air-con restaurant, serving good Thai food, including *tom yam* and various sea bass dishes, from B80.

Coca 128 Thanon Thetsabarn 1 (no English sign but it's easy to spot opposite Phetkasem Department Store). A good range of Chinese and Thai dishes such as fluffy catfish salad with mango for B80, served in a clean and welcoming setting.

Farang Connection 257/11 Thanon Jitbumrung, at the back of the bus terminal, off Thanon Sirirat. The place to come for imported beer, TV sports, internet access and the chance to meet local expats. It serves great Western breakfasts and roast dinners, as well as a good range of Thai dishes, with prices around B80–350.

Raan Ahaan Mangsawirat "Vegetarian" 641 Thanon Lak Muang (no English sign, but look for the trademark, small yellow pennant). Cheap, canteen-style pre-cooked veggie curries, spicy salads and the like, served over rice for about B30 per set. Daily 7am–6pm.

Listings

Hospitals Ruam Phet Hospital, on the eastern arm of Thanon Thetsabarn 1 ⓣ044 513638 & 044 513192; and the government-run Surin Hospital on Thanon Lak Muang ⓣ044 511006 & 044 511757.

Immigration For visa extensions you need to go to the immigration office in Kap Choeng (Mon–Fri 8.30am–4.30pm; ⓣ044 559166), the town nearest Cambodia's Chong Chom border pass, about 50km south of Surin; see p.512 for transport details.

Internet access At *Farang Connection* at the back of the bus station; and at Focus Comnet next to Surin Plaza off the north end of Thanon Thetsabarn.

Tours, transport rental and travel agents Saren Travel 202/1-4 Thanon Thetsabarn 2 (Mon–Sat 8am–6pm; ⓣ044 713828, ⓔsarentour@yahoo.com; outside office hours ⓣ089 949 1185), sells air and train tickets, does car rental with/without driver (from B1500 per day), arranges day-trips (from B800 per person), runs transfers to Champasak (Laos) and Siem Reap (Cambodia). Also an outlet for elephant-show tickets. Organizes elephant riding at the village of Ban Ta Klang, from B200–400 per person. *Farang Connection* restaurant, at 257/11 Thanon Jitbumrung (ⓣ044 511509, ⓦwww.farangconnection.com), offers car and motorcycle rental.

Ban Tha Sawang and other silk-weaving villages

Though it is possible to visit the nearby **villages** where women weave most of Surin's silk and cotton, you'll need to go with a guide to get more of a behind-the-scenes insight (see p.514); you can arrange a guide through *Pirom & Aree's House* or Saren Travel. The best months to visit are between November and June, when the women aren't required to work all day in the fields.

Some of Thailand's most exclusive silk is produced in the village of **BAN THA SAWANG**, 7km west of Surin. The Tha Sawang fabric is gold-brocade silk whose ancient designs are so intricate that it takes four weavers working simultaneously on a single loom a whole day to produce just 6cm. And while a standard everyday *mut mee* sarong might use five heddles (vertical frames of threads that determine the pattern) in its design, a Ban Tha Sawang sarong will use more than eight hundred; not surprisingly, Ban Tha Sawang sarongs cost B30,000 and must be ordered several months in advance. The Ban Tha Sawang weaving centre houses around twenty looms and visitors are welcome to observe the weavers at close quarters. There's a display area across the road, down the asphalt chipping path, where you can see some fine examples of brocade cloth. Several stalls in the village sell local silk, but not the Ban Tha Sawang brocades. It's possible to get to Ban Tha Sawang by **bus** from Surin, but as there is no English information you'll have a more rewarding experience on a tour. If doing it on your own, flag down any bus from the corner of Thanon Thung Po, just north of the railway tracks in Surin, and get off at the sign "Wat Sameka 300m"; follow the side road on the opposite side of the road from the wat sign for about 1km to reach the weaving centre.

Ban Ta Klang

Fifty-eight kilometres north of Surin, the "elephant village" of **BAN TA KLANG** is the main settlement of the Suay people and training centre for their elephants. One out of every two Ta Klang families owns its own elephant, occasionally using it as a Western farmer would a tractor, but otherwise treating it as a much-loved pet (see box on p.366 for an introduction to the role of the elephant in Thailand). Traditionally regarded as the most expert hunters and trainers of elephants in Thailand, the **Suay** tribe (also known as the Kui people) migrated to the region from Central Asia before the rise of the Khmers in the ninth century. It was the Suay who masterminded the use of elephants in the construction of the great Khmer temples, and a Suay chief who in 1760 helped recapture a runaway white elephant belonging to the king of Ayutthaya, earning the hereditary title "Lord of Surin". Surin was governed by members of the Suay tribe until Rama V's administrative reforms of 1907.

Now that elephants have been replaced almost entirely by modern machinery in the agricultural and logging industries, there's little demand for the Suay mahouts' skills as captors and trainers of wild elephants, or their traditional pre-hunting rituals involving sacred ropes, magic clothing and the keeping of certain taboos. The traditions are, however, documented, along with other elephant-related subjects, at the rather desultory **Centre for Elephant Studies** in Ban Ta Klang (daily 8.30am–4.30pm; free). To satisfy tourist curiosity, the centre also puts on **elephant shows** to coincide with the arrival of tour groups.

There are currently around sixty **elephants** registered as living in Ban Ta Klang, but because there's not much for them to do around Surin they spend a lot of the year travelling through Thailand with their mahouts, charging curious urbanites for the pleasure of feeding them or even walking under their trunk or belly for good luck (pregnant women who do this are supposedly guaranteed an easy birth). It's not unheard of for a Suay mahout to walk his elephant the 450km from Surin to Bangkok, charging around B20 per limbo en route and earning up to B20,000 a month for his troubles. This doesn't always go down well: town officials view them as a traffic menace, and animal rights' activists see it as cruel. Less controversially, a group of Suay mahouts and their elephants have established themselves as a tourist attraction on the east-coast island of Ko Chang, at the **Ban Kwan Chang Elephant Trek** (see p.466).

All of which means you're unlikely to turn up and find Ban Ta Klang teeming with elephants. Mahouts and their elephants do, however, return to Ban Ta Klang every November to help with the rice harvest and to prepare for the annual elephant show in Surin. In addition, every year on the first weekend of November, the elephants compete in **swimming races**, held further up the Mun River in the town of Satuk, 30km west of Ta Klang. A more authentic local elephant spectacle is the annual **monks' ordination ceremony**, which usually takes place in May in Ban Ta Klang as part of the preparations for the beginning of Buddhist Lent, when young men ride to the temple on ceremonially-clad elephants. At other times of the year, if you are not on a tour, you might turn up at Ban Ta Klang and not find a single elephant. Local **buses** to Ban Ta Klang depart approximately hourly from the Surin terminal and take about two hours. If driving yourself, head north along Highway 214 for 36km, turn left at the village of Ban Nong Tad and continue for 22km until you reach Ban Ta Klang.

Khao Phra Viharn, Kantharalak and Si Saket

Perched atop a 547-metre-high spur of the Dangkrek mountains right on the Thai–Cambodian border, about 140km southwest of Ubon Ratchathani and 220km southeast of Surin, the ninth-to-twelfth-century Khmer ruins of **KHAO PHRA VIHARN** (or **Preah Vihear**) surpass even the spectacularly set Phanom Rung. A magnificent avenue over 500m long rises to the clifftop sanctuary, from where you get breathtaking views over the jungle-clad hills of Cambodia. The temple buildings themselves, built of grey and yellow sandstone, retain some fine original carvings and have been sufficiently restored to give a good idea of their original structure. Constructed over a three-hundred-year period, Khao Phra Viharn was dedicated to the Hindu god Shiva and is thought to have served both as a retreat for Hindu priests – hence the isolated site – and an object of pilgrimage, with the difficulty of getting there an extra challenge. The large complex would have also been inhabited by a big cast of supporting villagers who took care of the priests and the pilgrims, and this explains the presence of several large reservoirs on the site.

Unfortunately, at the time of this update, the sanctuary had been closed for some months due to a **territorial dispute** between Thailand and Cambodia over who owns the site. However, given that it represents a lucrative source of income from tourism for both countries, there is every chance it will reopen by the time this book is on the shelves, so check the latest situation with TAT or hotel owners. The complex was only opened to visitors in 1998, following almost a century of squabbling between the two governments. The situation was complicated by Cambodia's civil war, with the Khmer Rouge taking control of the temple in 1975 and laying mines around it, making the temple far too dangerous to visit. Although the ruins have now been de-mined, there are skull-and-crossbones signs in the vicinity, which should be heeded. It's generally accepted that the central sanctuary of the Khao Phra Viharn complex stands on Cambodian land, but the temple is very difficult to reach from the Cambodian side of the border, so most visitors arrive via the northern cliffside-staircase, which starts just inside Thailand's southern border.

For the tourist, this dual ownership means having to pay both parties to get into the ruins: there's a B200 national park **entry fee** payable to the Thai authorities about 12km north of the temple car park, at the barrier near the Ban Phum Saron junction (where you have to relinquish your passport); a B5 fee for an "ID check"; and another B200 entry fee at the base of the temple steps, which goes to the Cambodians. In addition to the expense involved, Khao Phra Viharn is very difficult to get to without your own **transport**, often involving an overnight stop in either **Kantharalak** or **Si Saket** – and when you do get there you have to contend with large crowds of tourists and a big gaggle of persistent hawkers. But, if you can ignore the hassle, the ruins are worth the effort.

From the temple car park it's about 1km to the base of the temple steps or B5 on the **shuttle bus**. En route you'll pass the beginning of the path up to the **Pha Mo I Daeng viewpoint**, from where you get a good view of the temple cliff and can just about make out the Khao Phra Viharn complex on its summit. There's not much information on the temple available at the site, so consider buying a copy of the excellent *Preah Vihear* **guidebook** before you come; published by River Books, it's available from most Bangkok bookshops.

The ruins

The approach to the **temple complex** (when open, daily from 8.30am; last entry 3.30pm; total entry fee B405) begins with a steep stairway and continues up the cliff face via a series of pillared causeways, small terraces with naga balustrades and four cruciform-shaped **gopura** (pavilions), each built with doorways at the cardinal points, and decorated with carved reliefs of tales from Hindu mythology. Beyond the first gopura, you'll see to the left (east) one of the temple's biggest **reservoirs**, a large stone-lined tank sunk into the cliff and guarded by statues of lions.

As you pass through the last, southernmost, doorway of the second gopura, look back at the door to admire the pediment carving, which depicts the

Hindu creation myth, the **Churning of the Sea of Milk**, in which Vishnu appears in his tortoise incarnation and, along with a naga and a sacred mountain (here symbolized by the churning stick), helps stir the cosmic ocean and thereby create the universes, as well as the sacred nectar of immortality. The third gopura is much larger than the others and is extended by east and west wings. Its central doorways are decorated with clearly discernible carvings; a particularly eye-catching one above the outside of the northern doorway shows an episode from the Hindu epic the *Mahabarata*, in which the god Shiva fights the heroic Arjuna over who gets the credit for the killing of a wild boar – in fact the carving here looks as if they are enjoying an affectionate embrace. A causeway flanked with two naga balustrades links the third gopura to the fourth; the buildings on either side of the fourth gopura are thought to have been libraries.

The ascent of the cliff face finally reaches its climax at the **central sanctuary**, built on the summit and enclosed within a courtyard whose impressive colonnaded galleries are punctuated by windows to the east and west. Cambodian monks tend the modern Buddha image inside the sanctuary, keeping a fire burning and selling offertory garlands and incense to tourists. The pediment above the northern entrance to this shrine depicts the multi-armed **dancing Shiva**, whose ecstatic dance brings about the destruction of the existing world and the beginning of a new epoch. Climb through one of the gallery windows to walk across to the cliff edge, from where you get far-reaching views of Cambodia and can appreciate just how isolated the temple must have been. A look back at the temple complex shows that though the sanctuary's southernmost wall is punctuated by a couple of beautifully carved false doors, there are no genuine south-facing doors or windows; experts assume that this was to stop priests being distracted by the clifftop panorama.

Practicalities

Even when it is open, Khao Phra Viharn is not served by public **transport**, so by far the easiest way of getting to the ruins is to join a tour or rent a vehicle from Ubon Ratchathani, Surin or **Si Saket**. Alternatively, you could take a combination of motorbike taxi and songthaew to the temple from **Kantharalak**.

Kantharalak

The small town of **KANTHARALAK** is just off the Khao Phra Viharn–Si Saket road (Highway 221), 36km north of the temple. There's an hourly **bus** service here from Ubon Ratchathani's Warinchamrab suburb (1hr 30min), and a half-hourly bus service from Si Saket; buses arrive at Kantharalak **bus station** (Ⓣ045 661486), 50m from the market on the main street, Thanon Sinpradit.

There is no **songthaew** service from Kantharalak to the temple, but occasional songthaews do connect Kantharalak with **Ban Phum Saron**, the junction near the national-park barrier 12km north of Khao Phra Viharn, from where you can get a **motorbike taxi** to the temple; you can also get a motorbike taxi all the way from Kantharalak to Khao Phra Viharn (about B120 each way).

Kantharalak is a two-street town, with the best of the budget **hotels**, the friendly *Kantharalak Hotel* (Ⓣ045 661085; fan ❷, air-con ❷), on the main street at 131/35–36 Thanon Sinpradit, about 1km off Highway 221; its rooms, scruffy but serviceable (the better ones are upstairs), are set back off the road, all with en-suite bathrooms.

Si Saket

Though it is 98km from Khao Phra Viharn, the quiet provincial capital of **SI SAKET** is a more enjoyable place to base yourself than Kantharalak, with a better choice of hotels, a good night market and decent transport connections. Si Saket **train station** (ⓣ045 611525) is in the centre of the town; the **bus station** (ⓣ045 612500) is in the southern part of town and connects Si Saket with Ubon Ratchathani, Phibun Mangsahan, Chong Mek, Surin and Bangkok, but there are no buses from here to Khao Phra Viharn, so you have to get the orange bus to Kantharalak (hourly; 2hr) and make onward arrangements from there. You should also be able to get buses from here to **Sa Ngam** for access to the **Cambodian border crossing** to Choam (for Anlong Veng and Siem Reap).

For **hotels** within easy walking distance of the train station, try the *Phrompiman* (ⓣ045 612677, ⓕ045 612271; air-con ④), at 849/1 Thanon Lak Muang (about 200m west of the train station on the road that parallels the rail line to the south), where all rooms are big, clean and bright, if a bit characterless. Or there's the *Kessiri Hotel*, at 1102–5 Thanon Khukan (ⓣ045 614007, ⓕ045 614008; ④), which offers similar amenities and also has a restaurant; Thanon Khukan runs south from the rail line from a point some 150m east of the train station.

The best place to **eat** in town is the lip-smackingly diverse night market, which sets up around a small plaza along the southern edge of the rail line. Otherwise there are half a dozen small Thai-Chinese restaurants on Thanon Khukan, between the *Kessiri Hotel* and the rail line; along this road you'll also find several handicraft shops selling locally produced lengths of silk and triangular axe pillows.

Ubon Ratchathani

East of Si Saket, the sprawling provincial capital of **UBON RATCHATHANI** (almost always referred to simply as Ubon – not to be confused with Udon, aka Udon Thani, to the north) holds little in the way of attractions beyond a couple of wats and a decent museum. It's only really worth visiting in order to make trips out: east to Khong Chiam beside the Mekong River and the Lao border market at Chong Mek, or southwest to the Khmer ruins of Khao Phra Viharn, astride the Cambodian border, when they are open.

If you're near Ubon in early July, however, you should definitely consider coming into town for the local **Asanha Puja** festivities, an auspicious Buddhist holiday celebrated all over Thailand to mark the beginning of Khao Pansa, the annual three-month Buddhist retreat. Ubon's version is the most spectacular in the country, famous for the majestic orange beeswax sculptures created by each of its temples, which are mounted on floats around enormous candles and paraded through the town – hence the tourist name for the celebrations, the **Ubon Candle Festival**. The sculptures are judged and then returned to the temple, where the candle is usually kept burning throughout the retreat period. The end of the retreat, **Awk Pansa** (early to mid-Oct), is also exuberantly celebrated with a procession of illuminated boats, each representing one of the city's temples, along the Mun River between Wat Suphat and the night market, as well as beauty contests, parades and lots of fireworks throughout the city, and *likay* theatre shows in Thung Si Muang park. Traditional longboat races are staged on the river in the days following Awk Pansa.

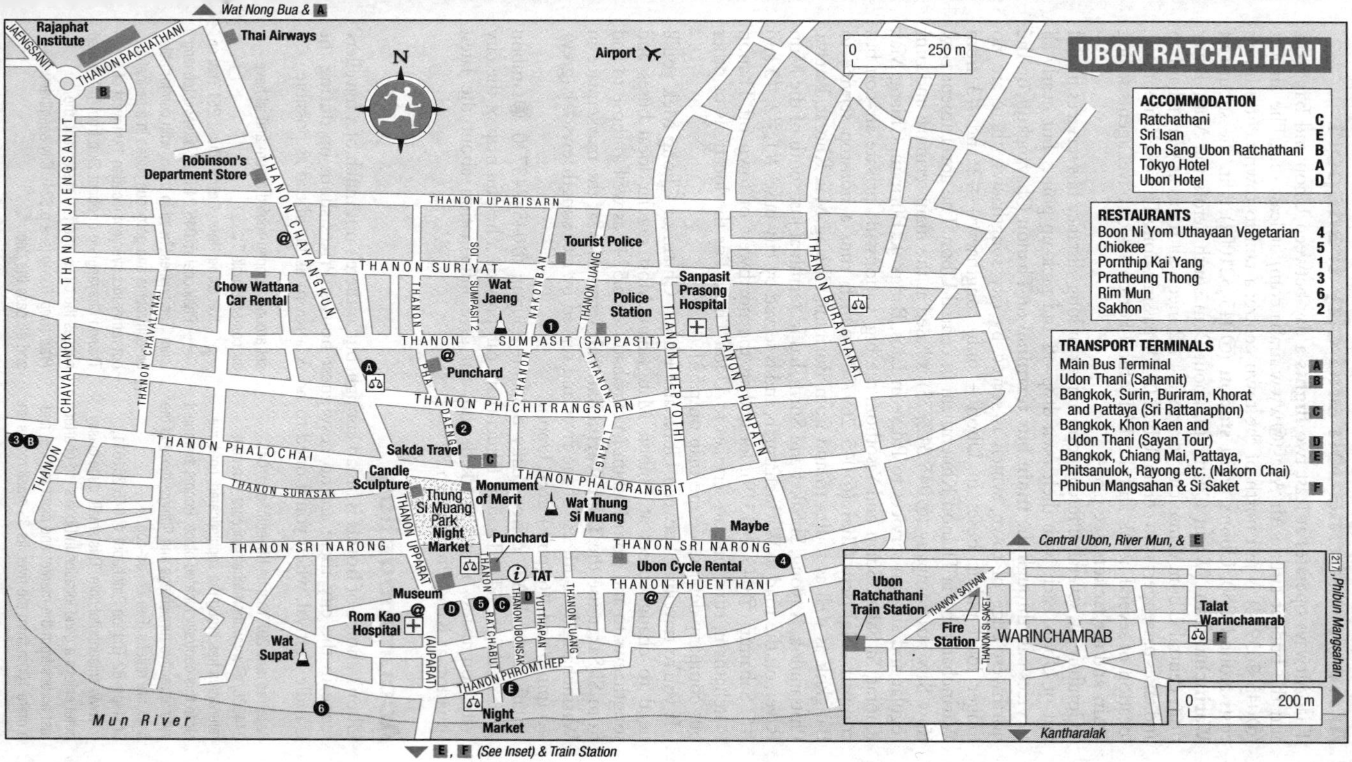

UBON RATCHATHANI
ACCOMMODATION
Ratchathani C
Sri Isan E
Toh Sang Ubon Ratchathani B
Tokyo Hotel A
Ubon Hotel D
RESTAURANTS
Boon Ni Yom Uthayaan Vegetarian 4
Chiokee 5
Pornthip Kai Yang 1
Pratheung Thong 3
Rim Mun 6
Sakhon 2
TRANSPORT TERMINALS
Main Bus Terminal A
Udon Thani (Sahamit) B
Bangkok, Surin, Buriram, Khorat and Pattaya (Sri Rattanaphon) C
Bangkok, Khon Kaen and Udon Thani (Sayan Tour) D
Bangkok, Chiang Mai, Pattaya, Phitsanulok, Rayong etc. (Nakorn Chai) E
Phibun Mangsahan & Si Saket F
Wat Nong Bua & A
Rajaphat Institute
Thai Airways
Airport
0 250 m
N
Robinson's Department Store
Chow Wattana Car Rental
Tourist Police
Police Station
Sanpasit Prasong Hospital
Wat Jaeng
Punchard
Sakda Travel
Candle Sculpture
Thung Si Muang Park Night Market
Monument of Merit
Wat Thung Si Muang
Maybe
Punchard
TAT
Ubon Cycle Rental
Museum
Rom Kao Hospital
Wat Supat
Night Market
Mun River
JAENGSANIT
THANON RACHATHANI
THANON JAENGSANIT
THANON CHAYANGKUN
THANON UPARISARN
THANON SURIYAT
SOI SUMPASIT 2
THANON NAKONBAN
THANON LUANG
THANON SUMPASIT (SAPPASIT)
THANON THEPYOTHI
THANON PHONPAEN
THANON BURAPHANAI
THANON PHA DAENG
THANON PHICHITRANGSARN
CHAVALANOK
THANON CHAVALANAI
THANON PHALOCHAI
THANON SURASAK
THANON UPPARAT
(AUPARAT)
THANON PHALORANGRIT
THANON SRI NARONG
THANON KHUENTHANI
THANON RATCHABUT
THANON UBONSAK
YUTTHAPAN
THANON LUANG
THANON PHROMTHEP
E, F (See Inset) & Train Station
Central Ubon, River Mun, & E
Kantharalak
217 Phibun Mangsahan
Ubon Ratchathani Train Station
THANON SATHANI
Fire Station
THANON SI SAKET
WARINCHAMRAB
Talat Warinchamrab
0 200 m

Arrival, information and city transport

Thai Airways operates at least two **flights** a day between Ubon and Bangkok, and the budget airline Air Asia (ⓦwww.airasia.com) at least one. The airport (ⓣ045 263916) is just north of the town centre; a taxi to town-centre hotels costs around B80. Ubon's **train station** (ⓣ045 321004) is in the suburb of **Warinchamrab** (Warin Chamrap), about 2km south across the Mun River from central Ubon. White city songthaew #2 meets all trains at Warinchamrab and takes passengers into central Ubon (B10), passing along Thanon Khuenthani, location of several hotels and the TAT office. For details of travel agents selling **train** and **air tickets**, see p.524.

Confusingly, several different companies run long-distance bus services in and out of Ubon, each with their own drop-off and pick-up points, but nearly all services pass through the **main bus terminal** on Thanon Chayangkun, on the northwest edge of town, which is served by city songthaews (there are no longer local public buses in Ubon – only songthaews) #2 and #3 from Warinchamrab via Thanon Khuenthani in central Ubon. The government Baw Kaw Saw bus company (ⓣ045 312773) is based at the main terminal and runs regular and air-con services to Pakxe in Laos, Bangkok, Buriram, Chiang Mai, Khorat, Si Saket, Surin and Yasothon; the big, nationwide private air-con bus company **Nakorn Chai** (ⓣ045 269777), which runs a nonstop service to Bangkok as well as routes to and from Buriram, Chiang Mai, Khorat, Pattaya, Phitsanulok, Rayong, Si Saket and Surin, has its terminal just south of the Mun River, on the road to Warinchamrab, and is served by city buses #1, #2, #3 and #6. Sahamit (ⓣ045 241319), located in the northwest of town off Thanon Ratchathani, runs air-con services to Udon Thani. For the locations of other bus company depots, see the map on p.521.

If you're travelling between Ubon and Khong Chiam or Chong Mek you'll need to change buses at Phibun Mangsahan. Most regular local buses and songthaews to and from Phibun Mangsahan (see p.524), as well as those to and from Si Saket, use the **Talat Warinchamrab** terminal near the marketplace in Warinchamrab, southeast of the river and served by city songthaews #1 (grey), #3 (pink) and #6 (pink) from Ubon.

Staff at the **TAT office** (daily 8.30am–4.30pm; ⓣ045 243770, ⓔtatubon@tat.or.th) at 264/1 Thanon Khuenthani can provide a helpful map of the city with songthaew routes marked, and can give information about the latest situation at Khao Phra Viharn.

Accommodation

Ubon's choice of **hotels** is broad enough, but as there's not much of a travellers' scene in the city, there are no cosy guest houses. Prices shoot up during the Candle Festival, when you'll need to book a room as far ahead as possible.

Ratchathani 297 Thanon Khuenthani ⓣ045 244388, ⓦwww.theratchathani.com. A recent renovation has brought a sophisticated, boutique air to this centrally located place. Rooms are bright with attractive furnishings and fittings; those at the back are quieter. Fan ❸, air-con ❹

Sri Isan 62 Thanon Ratchabut ⓣ045 261011, ⓦwww.sriisanhotel.com. This small, quite classy hotel enjoys a good location in Ubon's old quarter, just across from the market and night market, and a mere 100m from the river. Its 33 small rooms are set around an open-roofed atrium and all have air-con and cable TV. ❹

Toh Sang Ubon Ratchathani 251 Thanon Phalochai ⓣ045 245531, ⓦwww.tohsang.com. The poshest hotel in town, with comfortable air-con rooms and gorgeous suites in a peaceful but rather inconvenient location 1km west of Thanon Chayangkun or about 2km from TAT. It also houses the city's smartest restaurant, the *Pratheung Thong* (see p.524). City songthaews #4 and #8 pass the door. ❺

Tokyo Hotel 360 Thanon Upparat ⓣ045 241739, ⓕ045 263140. About a 5min walk north of the museum, this is most budget travellers' first choice in central Ubon. Fan and air-con rooms in the old block are a bit shabby, but those in the new wing (all air-con) are decent enough, and all come with cable. Served by city songthaew #6. Old wing ❶, new wing ❸

Ubon Hotel 333 Thanon Khuenthani ⓣ045 241045, ⓕ045 209020. Centrally located, nine-storey tower offering tatty fan rooms as well as basic air-con rooms that are reasonable value. Fan ❷, air-con ❸

The City

Ubon's centrepiece is **Thung Si Muang Park** and the unmissable 22-metre-high **Candle Sculpture**, an enormous yellow-painted replica of the wax sculptures that star in the annual Candle Festival. This particular sculpture was inspired by a story written by the king and features a boat with an enormous garuda figurehead that's ploughing past various figures who are apparently being devoured by sea monsters. In the northeast corner of the park stands a far more unassuming memorial in the shape of a three-metre-high obelisk. Known as the **Monument of Merit**, it was erected by a group of POWs who wanted to show their gratitude to the people of Ubon for their support during World War II. Despite the real threat of punishment by the Japanese occupiers, between 1941 and 1943 Ubon citizens secretly donated food and clothes to the POWs imprisoned in a nearby camp.

South from the park across Thanon Sri Narong and also accessible from Thanon Khuenthani, **Ubon Ratchathani National Museum** (Wed–Sun 9am–4pm; B100; ⓦwww.thailandmuseum.com) is airily designed around a central courtyard and offers a good overview of the history, geology and culture of southern Isaan, with well-labelled displays on everything from rock formations to folk crafts, plus a couple of very fine Khmer sculptures and examples of the star-embroidered fabric that is a speciality of Ubon.

Of the city's eight main wats, **Wat Thung Si Muang**, a few hundred metres east of Thung Si Muang Park, along Thanon Sri Narong, is the most noteworthy, mainly for its unusually well-preserved teak library (*ho trai*) which is raised on stilts over a pond to keep book-devouring insects at bay. The murals in the bot, to the left of the library, have also survived remarkably well; their lively scenes of everyday life in the nineteenth century include local merit-making dances and musicians playing *khaen* pipes, as well as conventional portraits of city activities in Bangkok.

Off Thanon Chayangkun near the main bus terminal at the northern edge of town, the much more modern **Wat Nong Bua** (city songthaew #2 or #3 via Thanon Khuenthani) is modelled on the stupa at Bodh Gaya in India, scene of the Buddha's enlightenment; the whitewashed replica is carved with scenes from the *Jataka* and contains a scaled-down version of the stupa covered in gold leaf. Of more interest, especially if you don't happen to be here during the Candle Festival, is the wax float kept in a small building behind the chedi.

Silk, cotton and silverware are all good buys in Ubon. The biggest selection of clothes made from the stripey rough **cotton** weaves peculiar to the Ubon area is at Maybe, on the eastern end of Thanon Sri Narong. You'll find cotton tableware and clothes made to local designs, as well as Ubon's best collection of **northeastern crafts**, at Punchard, which has one branch at 128–130 Thanon Ratchabut, 50m east of the museum, and another on Thanon Pha Daeng. Both shops specialize in fine-quality regional goods, like triangular axe pillows (*mawn khwaan*) and lengths of **silk**, and also deal in antique farm and household implements.

Eating

Ubon is a good place for sampling local Isaan specialities, either in air-conditioned comfort at some of the restaurants listed below, or at one of the city's night markets: behind the day market on the north bank of the Mun River; on Thanon Ratchabut (north off Thanon Khuenthani); and on the sidewalk next to the *Tokyo Hotel*.

Boon Ni Yom Uthayaan Vegetarian Restaurant and Centre Thanon Sri Narong; no English sign but its barn-like, open-sided wooden structure is unmistakeable. Famous, canteen-style veggie place that's run by members of a Buddhist organization who grow, sell and cook their own produce. All sorts of meat substitutes and tasty veg and tofu dishes are on offer here at very cheap per-plate prices (B20–30). Tues–Sun 6am–2pm.

Chiokee 307–317 Thanon Khuenthani. Café-style place serving a large menu of Thai and Western staples (B30–90). Especially popular at breakfast time, when Westerners come for the ham and eggs, local office workers for rice gruel. Daily 6am–8pm.

Pornthip Kai Yang 136 Thanon Sumpasit, just east of Wat Jaeng. This simple streetside restaurant, which also has an air-con room, is famous across town for its signature barbecued chicken (*kai yang*) and papaya salad (*som tam*), for B20–60. Daily 8am–6pm.

Pratheung Thong *Toh Sang Hotel*, 251 Thanon Phalochai. With its starched tablecloths and wide-ranging menu of Thai and Chinese dishes (B80–220), this restaurant oozes sophistication, and a pianist serenades diners in the evening. Daily 6am–11pm.

Rim Mun On the river bank near Wat Supat. Floating restaurant that makes the most of the breeze from the river and specializes in fish dishes (B60–150). Daily 10am–10pm.

Sakhon 66–70 Thanon Pha Daeng. One of Ubon's top northeastern restaurants, particularly recommended for its more unusual seasonal dishes, like *tom yam* with fish eggs and red-ant eggs. Most dishes around B60. Daily 10am–10pm.

Listings

Airline The Thai Airways office is at 364 Thanon Chayangkun ⓣ045 313340, in the north part of town.

Hospitals Sunpasit Prasong Hospital (ⓣ045 524 0074), to the northeast of the town centre, has a 24hr emergency clininc.

Immigration office In the town of Phibun Mangsahan (see below), 45km east of Ubon (Mon–Fri 8.30am–4.30pm; ⓣ045 441108).

Tourist police For all emergencies, call the tourist police on the free, 24hr phone line ⓣ1155, or contact them at their office on Thanon Suriyat ⓣ045 244941.

Transport rental and travel agents Sakda Travel World, at 234 Thanon Phalorangrit, central Ubon ⓣ045 243560, and at 150/1 Thanon Kantharalak in Warinchamrab ⓣ045 32158, sells air tickets, does guided tours around Isaan and into Laos, and offers car plus driver from B1500 per day. Bicycle rental from Ubon Cycle Rental, 115 Thanon Sri Narong, east of the post office (ⓣ045 242813; B100/24hr). Motorbikes (B200–500 per day) and cars (B1200 per day) from Chow Wattana at 269 Thanon Suriyat, opposite Nikko Massage ⓣ045 242202, and at the airport; Budget car rental at the airport (ⓣ045 240507, ⓦwww.budget.co.th).

Around Ubon

On the whole, the area **around Ubon** is a deal more interesting than the metropolitan hub, particularly if you venture eastwards towards the appealing Mekong riverside town of **Khong Chiam** and the prehistoric paintings at **Pha Taem**. There is legal entry into Laos, and a border market, southeast of Ubon at **Chong Mek**.

Phibun Mangsahan

Sited at a turbulent point of the Mun River called Kaeng Saphue (*kaeng* means rapids), the town of Phibun Mangsahan (known locally as Phibun), 45km east of Ubon, is an inevitable interchange on any eastbound journey. Buses depart Ubon's Talat Warinchamrab bus station several times an hour until 4.30pm and terminate at Phibun's town centre **bus station** behind the market, where you can change onto the songthaews that run to Chong Mek. Khong Chiam songthaews leave from **Kaeng Saphue bridge**, a short tuk-tuk ride or ten-minute walk from Phibun's bus station: exit the bus station through the market to the main road, turn right and walk the few hundred metres to the main highway (passing currency exchange and internet facilities), then turn left to reach the river and the songthaew stop.

Khong Chiam

The riverside village of **KHONG CHIAM** (pronounced Kong Jiem) is a popular destination for day-tripping Thais, who drive out here to see the somewhat fancifully named "two-coloured river" for which the village is nationally renowned. Created by the merging of the muddy brown Mun with the muddy brown Mekong at "the easternmost point of Thailand", the water is hardly an irresistible attraction, but the village has a certain tranquil appeal. Comprising little more than a collection of wooden houses and a few resorts, Khong Chiam feels like an island, with the Mun defining its southern limit and the Mekong its northern one. A paved walkway runs several hundred metres along the banks of the Mekong, lined by predictable souvenir stalls and leading to the large *sala* that's built right over the confluence and affords uninterrupted views. Behind the *sala*, **Wat Khong Chiam** is a typically charming rural Thai temple and has an old wooden bell tower in its compound. Khong Chiam's other temple, the cliffside **Wat Tham Khu Ha Sawan**, located near the point where Route 2222 turns into Khong Chiam, is a striking white colour, with natural wood sculptures festooned with orchids in its grounds, and a huge Buddha image staring down on the villagers below.

Khong Chiam's sights are thin on the ground, but you can rent motorbikes (B200 per day) or bicycles (B100 per day) from *Apple Guest House* and explore the area, or charter a **longtail boat** for a trip up the Mekong River to see the Pha Taem cliff-paintings (B1500 per boat; ask at your hotel). Otherwise you could charter a songthaew to **Pha Taem** from Khong Chiam (round trip about B500); ask at the bus station. Even though Laos is just a few hundred metres away from Khong Chiam, on the other bank of the Mekong, foreigners are not supposed to cross the border here, though you can usually persuade boatmen to take you there and back for B350 per boat, with a quick stop at the bankside village of Ban Mai; the official border crossing is further downstream at Chong Mek.

Arrival and information

Khong Chiam is 30km northeast of Phibun, along Route 2222, or 75km from Ubon. Khong Chiam-bound **songthaews** leave Phibun Mangsahan's Kaeng Saphue bridge every half-hour throughout the morning and then hourly until 4.30pm (1hr 30min). Four daily buses run between Khong Chiam and Bangkok in both directions. Songthaews and buses terminate at the Khong Chiam **bus station** at the west end of Thanon Kaewpradit, Khong Chiam's main drag. If you have your own transport, Khong Chiam combines well with visits to Chong Mek (just 27km away) and Kaeng Tana National Park. There's a small **minimarket** and a **pharmacy** on Thanon Kaewpradit, along with a bank that has an **exchange** facility and an ATM.

Accommodation

Khong Chiam has a nice range of reasonably priced guest houses and resorts.

Apple Guest House Opposite the post office on Thanon Kaewpradit, but also accessible from Thanon Phukamchai, about a 5min walk from the bus station and the Mekong ⓣ045 351160. The most traveller-oriented place in Khong Chiam, this is a convivial setup with decent en-suite rooms around a yard. Fan ❶, air-con ❷

Araya Resort This resort has two properties, both located near the eastern end of Thanon Phukamchai, a 10min walk from the bus station ⓣ045 351191 (old), ⓣ045 351385 (new). The old resort consists of steeply roofed, whitewashed, chalet-style bungalows, built around a garden with several ponds (❸–❹); the new resort features smartly furnished rooms with balconies in two-storey buildings that flank an attractive pool, with a few bungalows enjoying excellent river views (❺–❻).

Ban Rim Khong Resort 37 Thanon Kaewpradit ⓣ045 351101. Also has another entrance one block north on the road in front of the Mekong River, between the district office and the wat. Great-looking little resort with half a dozen timbered chalets wreathed in bougainvillea and ranged round a lawn, plus a couple of fabulous riverside ones (#1 and #2, worth phoning ahead to reserve) with huge verandas overlooking the Mekong. The interiors are nothing special but all are spacious and have air-con, TVs and fridges, and there are discounts for stays of more than one night. ❹–❺

Toh Sang Khong Chiam On the south bank of the Mun ⓣ045 351174, ⓦwww.tohsang.com. Romantically located, upmarket resort where all rooms have balconies overlooking the river and are very comfortably, if a little kitschly, furnished. There's a swimming pool, table-tennis room, spa, internet access, bicycle and kayak rental, plus a couple of restaurants and boat trips to Pha Taem and other riverside sights. Check out their website for spa/resort package offers. It's about 3km from Khong Chiam; with your own wheels, follow Highway 2134 south past Khong Chiam bus station, cross the river, take the first left and follow the signs. ❽

Eating

The most popular places to eat are the two **floating restaurants**, *Araya* and *Chonlada*, moored on the Mekong in front of the district office. Neither is signed in English, but there's little to choose between them as both serve fairly pricey menus of Thai-Chinese dishes and, of course, plenty of fish. Among the string of cheaper, less flashy little restaurants nearby, try the friendly *Rim Khong*, next to the two riverside *Rim Khong* bungalows. Away from the river, about 10m east of the bus station on Thanon Kaewpradit, the (unsigned) restaurant-shack *Tuk Tik Tham Mua* serves up good local dishes at good cheap prices: spicy *som tam*, green bean salads (*yam thua fak yao*), grilled fish (*ping plaa*) and chicken (*ping kai*), all served with individual baskets of sticky rice.

The Pha Taem cliff-paintings

Contained within Pha Taem National Park (daily 5am–6pm; B200, kids B100), the **Pha Taem cliff-paintings** cover a 170-metre stretch of cliff face 18km up the Mekong from Khong Chiam. Clear proof of the antiquity of the fertile Mekong valley, these bold, childlike paintings are believed to be between three thousand and four thousand years old, the work of rice-cultivating settlers who lived in huts rather than caves. Protected from the elements by an overhang, the clearly discernible red-painted images (daubed from a mixture of soil, tree gum and fat) include human forms, handprints and geometric designs as well as massive depictions of animals and enormous fish – possibly the prized catfish still occasionally caught in the Mekong.

Pha Taem ("Taem Cliff") is clearly signposted from Khong Chiam. Try to avoid coming here on a weekend when the place gets swamped with tour buses. It's an especially popular spot at sunrise, this being the first place in Thailand to see the sun in the morning – a full eighteen minutes ahead of Phuket, the westernmost point. Just after the checkpoint, the road passes a group of weird, mushroom-shaped sandstone rock formations known as **Sao Chaliang** before reaching the Pha Taem car park, site of a restaurant and the visitor centre, on top of the cliff. From the car park, follow the path to the left of the visitor centre, which runs down the cliff face and along the shelf in the rock to the paintings. If you continue along the path past the paintings, you'll eventually climb back up to the top of the cliff again, via the **viewpoint** at Pha Mon, taking in fine views of the fertile Mekong valley floor and glimpses of hilly western Laos. It's about 1700m from Pha Mon back to the car park, along a signed trail across the rocky scrub. Should you feel inclined to stay and catch the sunrise, you can rent national park **bungalows** (fan B1200 for up to six people, air-con B2000 for up to five people) and large two-person tents (B150) near the national park checkpoint at Sao Chaliang, about 2km before the car park; these must be booked in advance through the Pha Taem office (ⓣ045 246332, ⓔphataem_3@hotmail.com, or via ⓦwww.dnp.go.th/National_park.asp).

Chong Mek and the Lao border

The village of **CHONG MEK**, 44km east of Phibun Mangsahan at the Thai–Lao border, hosts a busy Thai-Lao market and is one of the legal border crossings for foreigners, with onward transport to Pakxe. Buses run twice a day (9.30am & 3.30pm) from Ubon Ratchathani's main bus station to Pakxe, the smoothest way to do the trip. Alternatively, large pale-blue **songthaews** run to Chong Mek from Phibun Mangsahan bus station (approximately hourly 7am–3.30pm; 1hr 30min) and there is a daily **bus** between Chong Mek and Bangkok, departing Chong Mek market at 4pm, arriving at Mo Chit Northern Bus Terminal about eleven hours later.

It is possible to get a Lao **visa** on arrival at Chong Mek **border crossing**; you'll be charged US$30 and will receive a thirty-day visa; you'll also need two passport photos. If you get an advance visa from Khon Kaen or elsewhere, it must specify Chong Mek as the entry point (see p.35 for more information). Whichever option you choose, once at Chong Mek you first need to get the Thai exit stamp from the office hidden behind the market on the Thai side (daily 8.30am–noon & 1–4.30pm; ⓣ045 485107); once you have crossed over to the Lao side of the market, Vangtao, you pass via the Lao immigration office (official hours Mon–Fri 8am–4pm; "surcharge" hours Mon–Fri 4–6pm, Sat, Sun & hols 8.30am–6pm), where you need to pay US$1 if you arrive during "surcharge" hours and an extra B20 (B50 during "surcharge" hours) for an entry stamp. A songthaew service runs from Vangtao to the city of Pakxe, 40km away (until about 5pm). In reverse, you simply pay the Lao exit tax (B20/50) and get your Thai visa on arrival for free (but note the shorter hours on the Thai side).

Even if you're not planning to cross into Laos, the **border market** at Chong Mek is good for a browse, especially at weekends when it's at its liveliest. The market on the Thai side of the border is full of Bangkok fashions, jeans and sarongs, but you'll also find traditional herbalists flogging bits of dried vegetable and animal matter, lots of basketware sellers and plenty of restaurant shacks serving both Thai and Lao dishes. Foreign shoppers can cross over to the Lao-side market in Vangtao simply by paying B5 at the checkpoint across from the duty-free shop (no visa required). Descend into the market area beside the café selling fresh Lao coffee for a huge selection of sarongs, as well as cheap VCDs and foreign whisky.

Yasothon and Ban Sri Than

By the beginning of May, Isaan is desperate for rain; there may not have been a significant downpour for six months and the rice crops need to be planted. In northeastern folklore, rain is the fruit of sexual encounters between the gods, so at this time villagers all over Isaan hold the bawdy, merit-making **Bun Bang Fai rocket festival** to encourage the gods to get on with it. The largest and most public of these festivals takes place in the provincial capital of **YASOTHON**, 98km northwest of Ubon, on a weekend in mid-May (check with TAT for dates). Not only are the fireworks spectacular, but the rockets built to launch them are superbly crafted machines in themselves, beautifully decorated and carried proudly through the streets before blast-off. Up to 25kg of gunpowder may be packed into the nine-metre-long rockets and, in keeping with the fertility theme, performance is everything. Sexual innuendo, general flirtation and dirty jokes are essential components of Bun Bang Fai; rocket-builders compete to shoot their rockets the highest, and anyone whose missile fails to leave the ground gets coated in mud as a punishment. At other times of the year, Yasothon has little to tempt tourists other than a handful of unremarkable wats and a few evocative old colonial-style shopfronts near **Wat Singh Tha** at the west end of Thanon Srisonthoon.

The most interesting attraction in the surrounding area is the village of **BAN SRI THAN**, 21km east of Yasothon, where nearly every household is employed in the making of the famous *mawn khwaan* triangular **axe pillows**. However, the scenes of sewing machines surrounded by heaps of cloth are not exactly photo contest winners, so it's really only worth a visit if you plan to buy the product. These pillows (*mawn*), so named because their shape supposedly resembles an axe-head (*khwaan*), have been used in traditional Thai homes for centuries, where it's normal to sit on the floor and lean against a densely stuffed *mawn khwaan*. It's possible to buy the cushions unstuffed so you can actually fit them in your luggage. The price depends on the number of triangular pods that make up the pillow: in Ban Sri Than, a stand-alone ten-triangle pillow costs B120, or B370 with three attached cushions – about half of what it'll cost in Bangkok or Chiang Mai. If you're driving to Ban Sri Than from Yasothon, follow Route 202 northeast towards Amnat Charoen as far as kilometre-stone 18.5km, then turn south (right) off the highway for 3km to reach the village. Coming by public transport, take a **songthaew** (half-hourly until noon) or **bus** (approximately hourly throughout the day) from Yasothon bus station to **Ban Ni Khom** on Route 202, then a motorbike taxi to cover the last 3km to the village.

Practicalities

All Khon Kaen-bound **buses** from Ubon stop in Yasothon, at the bus station on Thanon Rattanakhet. The nearest airports are near Roi Et (85km northwest) and in Ubon Ratchathani. If you want to stay here during festival time, book your **hotel** well in advance and be prepared to pay double the normal prices quoted here. *Orchid Garden Hotel*, at 219 Thanon Prachasamphan, just east of the town centre (Ⓣ045 721000, Ⓕ045 721020; ③), has big, clean, air-con rooms and friendly, helpful staff. The fanciest hotel in town is the comfortable *JP Emerald*, which has large, attractive air-con rooms close to the provincial hall on the far west perimeter at 36 Thanon Pha Pa (Ⓣ045 724848, Ⓕ045 724655; ④). The most rewarding place to **eat** is at the covered **night bazaar**, which runs east off the central section of Thanon Chaeng Sanit; some of the stalls here also open during the day, including a vegetarian one (6am–2pm only). Thanon Chaeng Sanit is where you'll find all the main **banks**, with ATMs and currency exchange, plus the **post office**, a couple of blocks west of the night bazaar. The **travel agent** inside the *JP Emerald* hotel sells domestic and international air tickets.

Central Isaan

The more northerly branch of the northeastern rail line bypasses Khorat, heading straight up through **central Isaan** to the Lao border town of Nong Khai via Khon Kaen and Udon Thani, paralleling Highway 2 most of the way. West of these arteries, the smaller Highway 201 is shadowed by the thickly wooded Phetchabun hills and Dong Phaya Yen mountain range, the westernmost limits of Isaan, chunks of which have been turned into the **national parks** of Thung Salaeng Luang, Phu Hin Rongkla (for both see p.276), Phu Kradung and Phu Reua. But hills play only a minor part in central Isaan's landscape, most of which suffers from poor-quality soil that sustains little in the way of profitable crops and, quite apart from what it does to the farmers who work it, makes for drab views from the bus or train window.

Nevertheless, there are a handful of towns worth stopping off at: **Khon Kaen**, for its museum of local history, its textiles and its handicraft shops; **Udon Thani**, a departure point for the Bronze Age settlement of **Ban Chiang**; and **Loei**, for its access to the mountainous national parks. Trains connect only the larger towns, but **buses** link all the above centres, also conveniently serving the town of Phitsanulok – the springboard for a tour of the ruins of Sukhothai and a junction for onward travel to Chiang Mai – via a spectacularly hilly route through the rounded contours of Phetchabun province.

Khon Kaen and around

Geographically at the virtual centre of Isaan, **KHON KAEN** is the wealthiest and most sophisticated city in the northeast, seat of a highly respected university as well as Channel 5 and Channel 11 television studios. There's a noticeably upbeat feel to the place, underlined by its apparently harmonious combination of traditional Isaan culture – huge markets and hordes of street vendors – and flashy shopping plazas and a world-class hotel. Its location, 188km northeast of Khorat on the Bangkok–Nong Khai rail line and Highway 2, makes it a convenient resting point, even though a startling modern temple and the provincial museum are just about the only sights in town; municipal authorities do, however, make a big deal of the province's prehistoric credentials – the **dinosaur graveyard** at Phuwiang is within day-tripping distance of the city, so you can hardly round a street corner without coming across a cute statue of a tyrannosaurus. Local silk is another draw, available year-round at outlets across the city, it gets special focus during the annual **Silk and Phuk Siao Festival** (usually Nov 29–Dec 10; check with TAT) when weavers from across the province congregate at the City Hall on Thanon Na Soon Rachakarn to display and sell their fabrics; this is also the chance to witness the moving *phuk siao* ceremony, a traditional friendship-deepening ritual involving the exchange of symbolic wrist strings. During the rest of the year, the foreigners staying in the city tend to be expat husbands of local women, businesspeople or university teachers rather than tourists, though an increasing number of travellers are stopping here for **Lao and Vietnamese visas**, now that both nations have consulates in Khon Kaen.

Arrival, information and city transport

Khon Kaen is well served as a transport hub: the **train station** (Ⓣ043 221112) is on the southwestern edge of town, about fifteen minutes' walk from the main hotel area; the non-air-con **bus station** (Ⓣ043 237472) is a five-minute walk northwest of the Thanon Klang Muang hotels; and the air-con bus terminal (Ⓣ043 239910) is right in the town centre. Khon Kaen **airport** (Ⓣ043 227708), 10km northwest of the city centre, runs daily Thai Airways **flights** to and from Bangkok; hotel minibuses meet all flights and while some hotels provide this service for free, others charge B70–90. The **TAT** office (daily 8.30am–4.30pm; Ⓣ043 244498, Ⓔtatkhkn@tat.or.th) is at 15/5 Thanon Prachasamoson, about five minutes' walk east of the non-air-con bus station. For information about the city and attractions in the surrounding area, Ⓦwww.khonkaen.com is a useful resource.

Local songthaews ply Khon Kaen's streets from 5am to 8pm, charging a fixed fare of B10–15. Unfortunately, route numbers change regularly, so it's best to ask staff at your hotel for advice. A short **tuk-tuk** ride within the city should cost you B50, while the minimum fare in a **samlor** is B20. For **car and motorbike rental** outlets, see p.534.

Accommodation

Accommodation in Khon Kaen is plentiful and reasonably priced, particularly in the mid-price range.

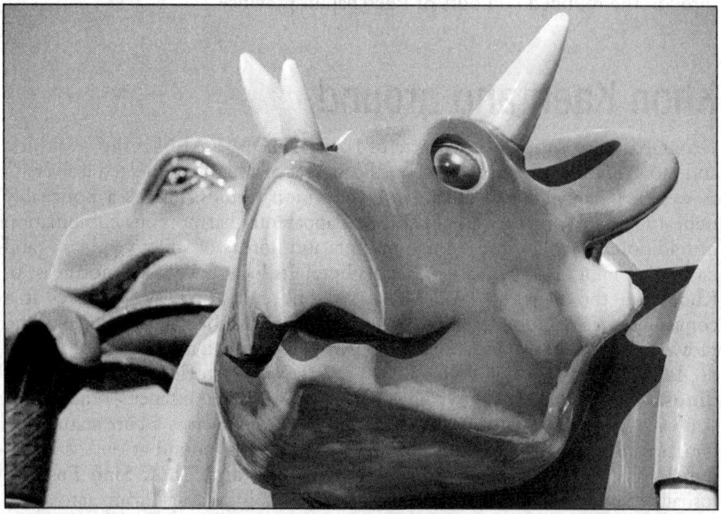

▲ Dinosaur statue in Khon Kaen

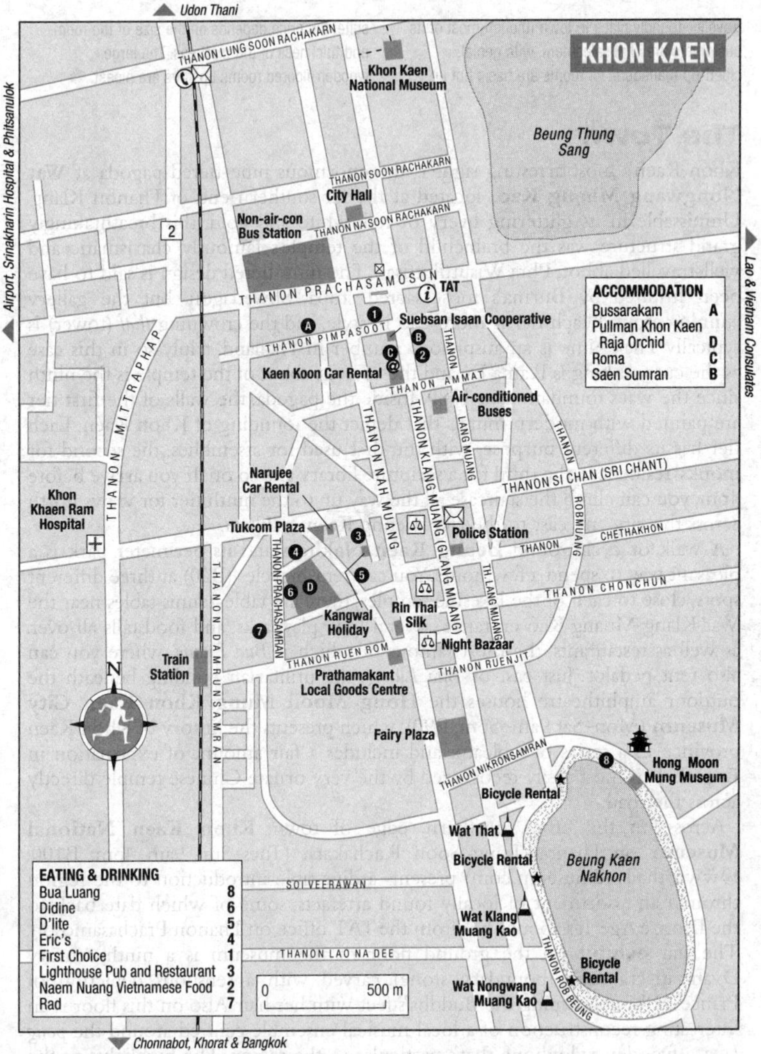

Bussarakam 68 Thanon Pimpasoot ⓣ 043 333666, ⓔ bussarakamhotel@yahoo.com. Smart, six-storey, mid-range option, with smart, tiled superior rooms and comfier, carpeted deluxe rooms with air-con and cable TV. ❺

Pullman Khon Kaen Raja Orchid 9/9 Thanon Prachasamran ⓣ 043 322155, ⓦ www.pullmanhotels.com. Quite simply the nicest hotel in the northeast, this gorgeously appointed, luxury high-rise hotel has extremely comfortable rooms, a swimming pool and spa, and plenty of bars and restaurants. It's shaped in the form of a giant *khaen*, the bamboo pan-pipes played in northeastern folk music. Significant discounts are often available, which makes it well worth splashing out on. ❼–❽

Roma 50/2 Thanon Klang Muang ⓣ 043 334444, ⓕ 043 237711. All rooms in this old, sizeable hotel are fairly basic, but if you're after cheap air-con then it's worth considering, and they also have cable TV. Fan ❶, air-con ❸

Saen Sumran 55 Thanon Klang Muang ⓣ 043 239611, ⓔ saensamran@gmail.com. One of the oldest hotels in Khon Kaen, this is also the most traveller-friendly place in town (though most of its customers are Thai salesmen), with genial, clued-up managers. All rooms are basic but en suite: the price depends on the size of the room and thickness of the mattress. The large, wooden-floored rooms upstairs are nicest. ❶

The Town

Khon Kaen's most arresting sight is the enormous nine-tiered pagoda at **Wat Nongwang Muang Kao**, located at the far southern end of Thanon Klang. Unmissable in its glittering livery of red, white and gold, this breathtakingly grand structure was the brainchild of the temple's famously charismatic and well-travelled abbot, Phra Wisuttikittisan. The nine-tiered design is said to have been inspired by Burma's most sacred stupa, Shwedagon, but the gallery running around each tier is more Lao in style, and the crowning *that* (tower) is typically Thai. Nine is an auspicious number in Thailand, triply so in this case as the current king is Rama IX and the current abbot of the temple is the ninth since the wat's foundation in 1789. Inside the pagoda, the walls of the first tier are painted with modern murals that depict the founding of Khon Kaen. Each tier has its different purpose, with the first used for assemblies, the second for monks' residences, the third for a scripture library and so on. If you arrive before 4pm, you can climb the staircase all the way up to the ninth tier for views north across the city and east to the lake, Beung Kaen Nakhon.

A walk or cycle round **Beung Kaen Nakhon** and its perimeter park is a pleasant way to spend a few hours. You can rent bicycles (B20) at three different spots, close to each of the lakeside temples, there are table-tennis tables near the Wat Klang Muang Kao entrance, several kids' playparks, and foodstalls all over, as well as restaurants, the most famous of which is *Bua Luang*, where you can also rent pedalos. Just east of *Bua Luang*, the utilitarian building beneath the outdoor amphitheatre houses the **Hong Moon Mung Khon Kaen City Museum** (Mon–Sat 9am–5pm; B90), which presents the history of Khon Kaen province in a series of tableaux and includes a fair amount of explanation in English. It is most easily recognized by the very ornate Chinese temple directly across the road.

Across on the other, northern, edge of town, **Khon Kaen National Museum** on Thanon Lung Soon Rachakarn (Tues–Sun 9am–4pm; B100; Ⓦwww.thailandmuseum.com) presents a digestible introduction to the region through an assortment of locally found artefacts, some of which date back to the Bronze Age. It's about 1km from the TAT office on Thanon Prachasamoson. The star **exhibit** on the ground floor of the museum is a ninth-century Dvaravati-era *sema* (boundary stone) carved with a sensuous depiction of Princess Bhimba wiping the Buddha's feet with her hair. Also on this floor is an interesting reconstruction of a local musical ensemble centred around the *pong lang*, a wooden xylophone that's particular to the region. The highlights of the upstairs gallery are some exquisite little Khmer-influenced Lopburi-style bronze Buddha images.

Eating, drinking and entertainment

Khon Kaen has a reputation for very **spicy food**, particularly sausages, *sai krog isaan*, which are served with cubes of raw ginger, onion, lime and plenty of chilli sauce at stalls along Thanon Klang Muang to the north of the *Roma Hotel*. These and other local favourites – such as pigs' trotters, roast duck and shellfish – can also be sampled at the stalls along the northern edge of lake Bueng Kaen Nakhon. Foodstalls pop up all over other parts of town at dusk, with a particular concentration at the **night bazaar** on the eastern end of Thanon Ruen Rom.

Nightlife in Khon Kaen is mainly focused along Thanon Prachasamran, to the west of the *Pullman Hotel*.

Bua Luang North shore of Beung Kaen Nakhon, off Thanon Rob Beung. The largest and most popular of the lakeside restaurants, where you can choose to dine right on a terrace over the water. The cuisine is classy Thai, with plenty of seafood (B80–180).

Didine Thanon Prachasamran. Run by a Franco-Thai couple, this welcoming place attracts an eclectic crowd with 150 European dishes, seventy Thai dishes, well-priced drinks and free pool table. Try the chicken fillet with tarragon sauce and garlic potatoes (B159). Daily 4pm–late.

D'lite On the lane immediately east of the *Pullman Hotel*. Smooth, live jazz serenades diners and drinkers every evening at this convivial al fresco venue serving Thai food. 6pm–late.

Eric's Across from the *Pullman Hotel* driveway, off Thanon Prachasamran. Popular expat-run and expat-oriented bar-restaurant; one of several in the area.

First Choice 18/8 Thanon Pimpasoot. Tourist-friendly restaurant, featuring an English-language menu offering Thai, Western and Japanese options (B60–120), plus a sizeable vegetarian selection and decent breakfasts. Daily 7.30am–10pm.

Lighthouse Pub and Restaurant In the car park of *Charoen Thani Princess* hotel, just off Thanon Si Chan. A favourite with Thais and expats for its cheap eats (*phat thai* for B35), spicy Shanghai *hai fun* noodles and American breakfasts. You can choose to dine out front or in the air-con interior, and there are copies of the *Bangkok Post* to keep you occupied between mouthfuls.

Naem Nuang Vietnamese Food Next door but one to the *Saen Sumran* hotel at 87/14–15 Thanon Klang Muang. Very popular air-con place that serves mainly Vietnamese food plus some north-eastern standards. Their eponymous speciality is *naem nuang*, Vietnamese spring rolls made with barbecued fermented pork sausage, which you assemble yourself from half a dozen or more ingredients of your choice, including lots of fresh coriander, mint, ginger, lemon rind, thin noodles and beansprouts. Spring-roll sets from B70 and all-you-can-eat lunch buffets from B119. Daily 6am–9.30pm.

Rad Thanon Prachasamran. This one-stop entertainment complex has it all – restaurant and coffee shop, raucous rock and easy listening live music venues, plus girls dancing on the bar. Daily 6pm–late.

Shopping

Khon Kaen's shops carry a wide range of regional **arts and crafts**, particularly high-quality Isaan **silk** of all designs and weaves. One of the best outlets is the cavernous Prathamakant Local Goods Centre (Mon–Sat 9am–8pm), about 500m south from the *Kosa Hotel*, at 81 Thanon Ruen Rom. The selection here is quite phenomenal (much better than the disappointing government-sanctioned OTOP (One Tambon One Product) shop beside the *Kosa Hotel* on Soi Kosa), with hundreds of gorgeous *mut mee* cotton and silk weaves, as well as clothes, furnishings, triangular axe pillows (B400 for an unstuffed three-seater), *khaen* pipes and silver jewellery. Though it feels touristy, locals buy their home furnishings and dress fabrics here too. Rin Thai Silk at 410–412 Thanon Nah Muang stocks a smaller range of Isaan silk, but will tailor clothes too. Itinerant vendors, who wander the main streets with panniers stuffed full of silk and cotton lengths, also offer competitive prices, and you can be sure most of the money will go to the weavers; they often gather around the *Roma Hotel* and along the stretch of Thanon Klang Muang just north of the hotel. Another fair-trade outlet for local craftspeople is the Suebsan Isaan Cooperative shop at 16 Thanon Klang Muang, which sells textiles fabricated from bamboo fibre and water hyacinth, as well as more usual *mut mee* silks and cottons, basketware, herbal cosmetics and other traditional products. Nearby on this stretch of Thanon Klang Muang, just north of *Roma Hotel*, Naem Lap Lae is the place to buy local food specialities such as spicy sausages, sugar-coated beans and other Khon Kaen delicacies.

For everything else you should either head to the huge, modern Fairy Plaza, between Nah Muang and Klang Muang, which has the usual clothes, accessories and mobiles concessions, plus *Pizza Co*, *McDonald's* and *Swensen's* and a cinema, or to the smaller, more central Tukcom Plaza in front of the *Kosa Hotel*.

Listings

Airline The Thai Airways office is inside the *Pullman Hotel* on Thanon Prachasamran ⓣ043 227701 (Mon–Fri 8am–5pm).

Car and motorbike rental Avis ⓣ043 344313, ⓦwww.avis.com, and Budget ⓣ043 345460, ⓦwww.budget.co.th, both have desks at the airport. Cars, with or without driver (B1500/1700), and motorbikes (B250) are also available from: Narujee Car Rent, next to Tukcom Plaza department store at 178 Soi Kosa off Thanon Si Chan ⓣ043 224220; cars only from Kaen Koon Car Rental at 54/1–2 Thanon Klang Muang ⓣ043 239458.

Cinema Fairy Cineplex inside Fairy Plaza, between southern Thanon Nah Muang and Klang Muang (B80–120).

Consulates The Lao consulate is located some way east of TAT at 171/102-103 Thanon Prachasamoson (Mon–Fri 8am–noon & 1–4pm; ⓣ043 242856–8). Thirty-day visas usually take three working days to process or can be done in 15min for an extra fee; see ⓦwww.bkklaoembassy.com. For more details on travel into Laos, see p.35. There's also a Vietnamese consulate in Khon Kaen (Mon–Fri 8–11.30am & 1.30–4.30pm; ⓣ043 242190 and 043 241586), south of the Lao consulate and about 1.5km from the TAT office, off Thanon Prachasamoson at 65/6 Thanon Chataphadung; see ⓦwww.vietnamembassy.or.th for details.

Hospitals Khon Kaen Ram Hospital, on the far western end of Thanon Si Chan, is the main private hospital in town ⓣ043 333900–3, or there's the government Srinakarin Hospital, attached to Khon Kaen University, north of town on Highway 2 ⓣ043 348360–9.

Internet access There are several internet/computer games centres around the *Roma Hotel* on Thanon Klang Muang.

Tourist police For all emergencies, call the tourist police on the free, 24hr phone line ⓣ1155, or contact them at the TAT office on Thanon Prachasamoson ⓣ043 236937.

Travel agents Domestic and international air tickets are available from Kaen Koon Car Rent at 54/1–2 Thanon Klang Muang ⓣ043 239458, ⓔkaenkoontravel@yahoo.co.uk; and Kangwal Holiday, on the *Charoen Thani* approach road on Thanon Si Chan ⓣ043 227777, ⓦwww.kangwal.com.

Around Khon Kaen

The outer reaches of Khon Kaen province hold a couple of places that are worth exploring on **day-trips**. If you're looking for other things to occupy yourself, don't be duped by the TAT brochure on the "tortoise village" in the village of Ban Kok, about 5km west of Chonnabot, which is both duller and more depressing than the tourist literature implies.

Chonnabot

Khon Kaen makes a reasonable base from which to explore the local silk-weaving centre of **CHONNABOT**, about 54km southwest of the city. Traditionally a cottage industry, this small town's **silk production** has become centralized over the last few years, and weavers now gather in small workshops in town, each specializing in just one aspect of the process. You can walk in and watch the women (it's still exclusively women's work) at their wheels, looms or dye vats, and then buy from the vendors in the street out front. For more details on silk-weaving processes, see the box on p.514. To get to Chonnabot from Khon Kaen, take any ordinary Khorat-bound bus to **Ban Phae** (every 30min), then a songthaew for the final 10km to Chonnabot.

Phuwiang National Park

Khon Kaen hit the international headlines in 1996 when the oldest-ever fossil of a tyrannosaur **dinosaur** was unearthed in Phuwiang, about 90km northwest of Khon Kaen, which has since been made into a national park. Estimated to be 120 million years old, it measures just 6m from nose to tail and has been named *Siamotyrannus isanensis* – Siam for Thailand, and Isaan after the northeastern region of Thailand. Before this find at Phuwiang, the oldest tyrannosaur fossils were the sixty-five-million- to eighty-million-year-old specimens from China, Mongolia and North America. These younger fossils are twice the size of the *Siamotyrannus*; the latter's age and size have therefore established the *Siamotyrannus* as the ancestor of the *Tyrannosaurus rex*, and confirmed Asia as the place of origin of the tyrannosaur genus, which later evolved into various different species.

The fossil of this extraordinary dinosaur – together with eight moderately interesting paleontological finds – is on show to the public at Dinosaurland in **Phuwiang National Park** (daily 8.30am–6pm; B200; ⓣ085 852 1771, ⓦwww.dnp.go.th/National_park.asp). The main attractions here, apart from waterfalls and nature trails, are nine dig sites and a **museum** (Tues–Sun 9am–5pm; free), which is located just before the park entrance. There's one room for rent that can accommodate fifteen people (B1500; must be booked through the website) and two-person tents for rent at B250 a day.

The *Siamotyrannus isanensis* is displayed at **Site 9**, which is accessible via the 1.5-kilometre track that starts across the road from the visitor centre; from the car park at the end of the track, it's a five-hundred-metre climb to the quarry. The fossil is an impressive sight for paleontologists, with large sections of the rib cage almost completely intact, but many visitors will wonder what all the fuss is about. **Site 1**, 900m south along a track from Site 9, contains the cream of the other finds, including two previously undiscovered species. The theropod *Siamosaurus sutheethorni* (named after the paleontologist Warawut Suteehorn) is set apart from the other, carnivorous, theropods by its teeth, which seem as if they are unable to tear flesh; the fifteen- to twenty-metre-long *Phuwiangosaurus sirindhornae* (named in honour of Thailand's Princess Royal) is thought to be a new species of sauropod.

Though it's possible to take a non-air-con **bus** from Khon Kaen to Phuwiang town (every 30min; about 1hr), you then need to hire a motorbike taxi to continue to Dinosaurland and back (about B150 return), so it's easier to rent your own wheels in Khon Kaen. To **get to the park**, head west out of Khon Kaen on Highway 12, following the signs for Chumpae as far as kilometre-stone 48, marked by a dinosaur statue. Turn right off the main road here, and continue for another 38km along Highway 2038, passing through the small town of Phuwiang and following signs for the national park. About halfway between Phuwiang and the national park, there is a park to the left of the road containing many life-size statues of many species of dinosaur. There's a **food** and drink stall at the car park in front of Quarry #3, which is about 1km north of the visitor centre.

Udon Thani and Ban Chiang

Economically important but charmless, **UDON THANI** looms for most travellers as a misty, early morning sprawl of grey cement seen from the window of the overnight train to Nong Khai. The capital of an arid sugar-cane and rice-growing province, 137km north of Khon Kaen, Udon was given an economic shot in the arm during the Vietnam War with the siting of a huge American military base nearby, and despite the American withdrawal in 1976, the town has maintained its rapid industrial and commercial development. The only conceivable reason to alight here would be to satisfy a lust for archeology at the excavated Bronze Age settlement of **BAN CHIANG**, 50km to the east in sleepy farming country, though plenty of travellers avoid spending time in Udon by visiting Ban Chiang on a day-trip from the much preferable base of Nong Khai (see p.546) or by staying in the village itself.

Listed as a UNESCO World Heritage Site in 1992, the village of Ban Chiang is unremarkable nowadays, although its fertile setting is attractive and the villagers, who still weave (and sell) especially rich and intricate lengths of silk and cotton *mut mee*, are noticeably friendly to visitors. It achieved worldwide fame in 1966, when a rich seam of archeological remains was accidentally discovered: clay pots, uncovered in human graves alongside sophisticated **bronze** objects, were eventually dated to around 2000 BC, implying the same date for the bronze pieces. Ban Chiang has been hailed as the Southeast Asian vanguard of the Bronze Age, about three hundred years after Mesopotamia's discovery of the metal.

The present village's fine **National Museum** (Wed–Sun 9am–4pm; B30) has managed to retain some of the choicest Bronze Age finds, which it fleshes out with a fascinating and thoughtful rundown of Ban Chiang culture, including its agriculture, pathology and burial rites. It also houses the country's best collection of characteristic late-period Ban Chiang clay pots, with their red whorled patterns on a buff background, which were used as funeral offerings – although not of prime historical significance, these pots have become an attractive emblem of Ban Chiang, and are freely adapted by local souvenir producers. In the grounds of **Wat Pho Si Nai**, on the east side of the village, part of an early dig has been covered over and opened to the public (daily 8.30am–6pm; same ticket as the museum). A large burial pit has been left exposed to show how and where artefacts were found.

Arrival, information and local transport

Udon's **train station** is on the east side of the centre, while **buses** pull in at a variety of locations, depending on where they've come from: Loei, Phitsanulok

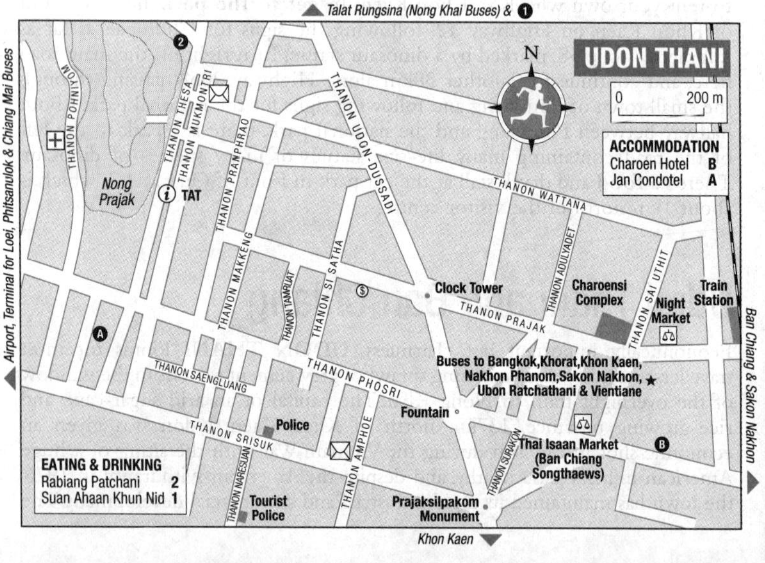

and Chiang Mai services use the terminal on the town's western bypass; Nong Khai buses are stationed at Talat Rungsina (Rungsina market, also used by Ban Phu buses) on the north side of town; and Bangkok, Khorat, Khon Kaen, Nakhon Phanom and Ubon Ratchathani services use the other main terminal on Thanon Sai Uthit, which also has a new service direct to Vientiane (B100), across the border in Laos, for those who already have a Lao visa. Thai Airways, Air Asia and Nok Air all operate several **flights** a day from Bangkok to Udon Thani, while Thai currently runs a daily service from Chiang Mai and Lao Airlines fly twice a week from Louang Phabang; air-con minibuses meet incoming flights at the airport, 3km southwest of the centre, charging B80 per person to drop off anywhere in town. Alternatively, Avis (ⓣ042 244770, ⓦwww.avisthailand.com) has a **car-rental** desk at the airport.

Udon's **TAT office** (daily 8.30am–4.30pm; ⓣ042 325406–7, ⓔtatudon@tat.or.th) is at 16/5 Thanon Mukmontri on the south side of Nong Prajak, a landscaped lake and park to the northwest of the centre. Numbered **songthaews** ply set routes around town for B10 per person (a rough map is available from TAT); among the more useful routes, #7 connects the Thanon Sai Uthit bus terminal with the terminal on the western bypass, while #6, supplemented by a white bus, runs the length of Thanon Udon-Dussadi to Talat Rungsina (the #6 songthaew then continues to the Chiang Mai bus station on the western bypass). Alternatively, there are plenty of **skylabs**, Udon's version of tuk-tuks, for hire (about B50 for a medium-length journey). There are dozens of **internet** places in and around the Charoensi Complex shopping centre on Thanon Prajak.

To **get to Ban Chiang** from Udon, either take one of the direct but irregular songthaews (big, multicoloured truck versions) from the morning market, Talat Thai Isaan (Mon–Fri until about noon, sometimes on Sat & Sun also), or catch a Sakon Nakhon–bound bus from the Thanon Sai Uthit terminal (every 20min) to Ban Palu and then a motorized samlor (B50 per person) for the last 5km or so from the main road to the village. Heading back to Udon the same day by songthaew is not possible as the service runs only until about 9am, so you'll have to make do with a samlor-and-bus combination.

Accommodation and eating

For budget travellers, far preferable to Udon's grim flophouses is **Ban Chiang**'s very own **guest house**, the excellent *Lakeside Sunrise* (ⓣ087 220 7769 or 042 208167, ⓦwww.banchianglakeside.com; ❶), just a few minutes' walk from the museum: facing the museum, head left then turn right at the first intersection and look for a large Western-style wooden two-storey house overlooking an artificial lake. Guests here sleep in clean first-floor rooms with fans, mosquito screens and shared hot showers and can relax on a huge balcony, equipped with a small library, and access the internet; the friendly owner, Tong, will cook Thai meals if you order in advance (otherwise, there are half a dozen simple restaurants in the village). Bicycles are available for exploring the surrounding countryside, or Tong can sometimes arrange motorbike rental; there's a bird and animal sanctuary 6km away, and a couple of interesting forest wats closer to the village, all marked on a useful hand-drawn map of the area.

Among **Udon**'s more upmarket **accommodation** options, *Jan Condotel* at 102/17 Soi Sansuk, a narrow, quiet soi off Thanon Phosri opposite the unedifying Udon Thani Museum (ⓣ042 329223–7, ⓔjan_condo2005@hotmail.com; ❸), offers excellent value: in a well-appointed condo, rooms are equipped with air-con, hot water, cable TV, fridges and duvets; some also have broadband, or there's internet access downstairs. Moving up the scale again, the smart, well-run *Charoen Hotel*, 549 Thanon Phosri (Ⓣ042 248155, Ⓔcharoenhotel@hotmail.com; ④), has 250 air-con rooms with hot showers, fridges and satellite TV, plus an attractive swimming pool in the garden, wi-fi and internet access.

In Udon the main **night market** offers a wide variety of low-priced comestibles – Thai, Chinese and Vietnamese – on the west side of the train station. Along Thanon Thesa, a good spot to catch the sunset over Nong Prajak, several simple bar-restaurants set out low-slung tables in the evening, alongside paint-your-own-pottery and massage stalls. One of Udon's most popular restaurants is the *Rabiang Phatchani* (no English sign; Ⓣ042 241515), around the corner on Thanon Supakitjunya, with a wide choice of Isaan food – plus probably the biggest selection of Thai salads in the country – and outdoor seating on a leafy terrace overlooking the lake. For a real culinary treat, head out into the northern suburbs to the very clean and friendly *Suan Ahaan Khun Nid*, which is famous among Thai gourmets for its carefully prepared Isaan food, such as spiced, salted and grilled snakehead fish, deep-fried land crab, deep-fried sun-dried beef and a wide variety of northeastern salads. It's on Soi 9 (Soi Nonniwate), Thanon Udon-Dussadi (Ⓣ042 246128): to get there, take a skylab or catch songthaew #6 or the white bus up Udon-Dussadi, then walk ten minutes west along the soi past the temple and it's on the left at the end of a short alley (no English sign).

Loei and around

Most people carry on from Udon Thani due north to Nong Khai, but making a detour via **LOEI**, 147km to the west, takes you within range of several towering national parks and sets you up for a lazy tour along the Mekong River. The capital of a province renowned for the unusual shapes of its stark, craggy mountains, Loei is, more significantly, the crossroads of one of Thailand's least-tamed border regions, with all manner of illegal goods coming across from Laos. This trade may be reined in – or perhaps spurred on – by the recent opening of a 3km-long bridge across the Heuang River,

Phi Ta Kon

One reason to make a special trip to Loei province is to attend the unique rain-making **festival of Phi Ta Kon**, or Bun Phra Wet, held over three days either at the end of June or the beginning of July in the small town of **Dan Sai**, 80km southwest of the provincial capital. In order to encourage the heavens to open, townsfolk dress up as spirits in colourful patchwork rags and fierce, brightly painted masks (made from coconut palm fronds and the baskets used for steaming sticky rice), then rowdily parade the town's most sacred Buddha image round the streets while making fun of as many onlookers as they can, waving wooden phalluses about and generally having themselves a whale of a time. Top folk and country musicians from around Isaan are attracted to perform in the evenings during Phi Ta Kon; the afternoon of the second day of the festival sees the firing off of dozens of bamboo rockets, while the third day is a much more solemn affair, with Buddhist sermons and a purification ceremony at Wat Phon Chai. The carnival can be visited in a day from Loei, though rooms are hard to come by at this time. Or contact Dan Sai's library (*hawng samut*; Ⓣ042 891094), about 1km up the town's high street, Thanon Kaew Asa, from the main through-road (R2013), if you fancy immersing yourself in a local **homestay**.

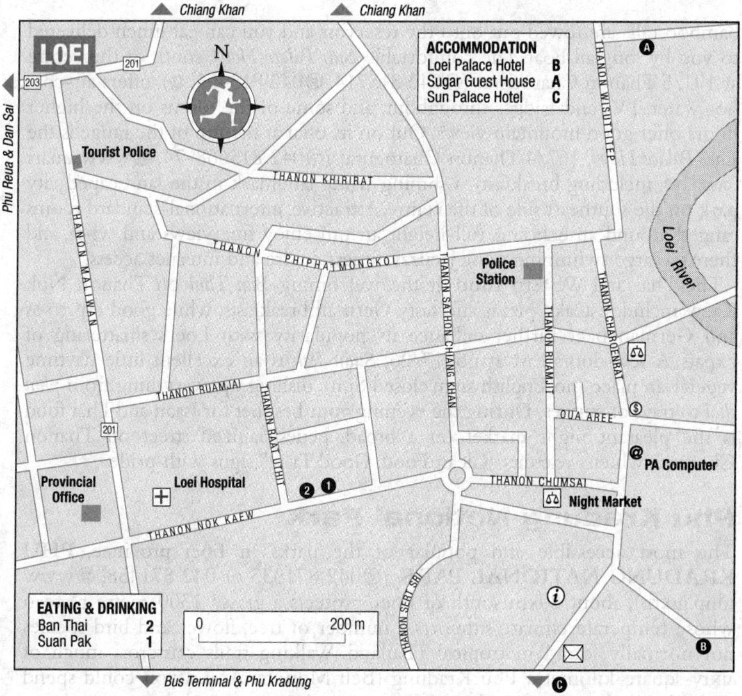

80km northwest of Loei, to Xainyabouli province in Laos (the crossing is open to foreigners, but there's no public transport on either side). Despite its frontier feel, the town, lying along the west bank of the small Loei River, is friendly and offers legitimate products of its own, such as sweet tamarind paste and pork sausages, which are for sale along Thanon Charoenrat, Loei's main street, and the adjacent Thanon Oua Aree.

Practicalities

Beyond its meagre attractions, Loei is really only useful as a transport hub and a base for the nearby national parks. The **bus terminal** is on Thanon Maliwan, the main through north–south road (Highway 201), about 2.5km south of the centre. The TAT **tourist office**, in the old district office on Thanon Charoenrat (daily 8.30am–4.30pm; ⓣ042 812812, ⓔtatloei@tat.or.th), has information about the region's many national parks, including Phu Luang Wildlife Sanctuary to the west and Nam Nao to the southwest, while the **tourist police** have an office on Thanon Maliwan (ⓣ042 861164 or 1155). For **internet access**, PA Computer is a little nearer the centre at 139 Thanon Charoenrat.

Unless it's festival time, finding a decent **place to stay** in Loei shouldn't be a problem. In a quiet residential area, five minutes' walk from the top of Thanon Charoenrat on the north side of the centre, lies *Sugar Guest House*, 4/1 Soi 2, Thanon Wisuttitep (ⓣ042 812982; ❷). Bright, colourful rooms are either fan-cooled with shared hot-water bathrooms, or air-con with cable TV and en-suite hot-water bathrooms. **Bicycles** (B50) and **motorbikes** (B250) can be rented, and the owners can arrange **day-trips** in a car with driver to, for example, Phu Reua (B1600) or the relaxing Huay Krating (B500), where bamboo rafts are towed out onto the reservoir and you can eat lunch delivered to you by longtail boat. The comfortable *Sun Palace Hotel*, south of the centre at 191/5 Thanon Charoenrat (Ⓣ042 815714, Ⓕ042 815453; ③), offers air-con, hot water, TVs and fridges throughout, and some of the rooms on the higher floors offer good mountain views. Out on its own at the top of the range is the *Loei Palace Hotel*, 167/4 Thanon Charoenrat (Ⓣ042 815668–74, Ⓦwww.amari.com; ⑥, including breakfast), a shining white landmark in the landscaped city park on the southeast side of the centre. Attractive, international-standard rooms ranged around an echoing, full-height atrium enjoy fine views and wi-fi, and there's a large swimming pool, jacuzzi, fitness centre and internet access.

The Thai and Western **food** at the welcoming *Ban Thai* on Thanon Nok Kaew includes steaks, pizzas and tasty German breakfasts, while good espressos and German beer further enhance its popularity with Loei's smattering of expats. A few doors east at no. 17/26, *Suan Pak* is an excellent little daytime vegetarian place (no English sign; closed Sun), dishing up everything from *phat thai* to trays of curries. During the evening your best bet for Isaan and Thai food is the pleasant night market on a broad, pedestrianized street off Thanon Chumsai, which wears its "Clean Food, Good Taste" signs with pride.

Phu Kradung National Park

The most accessible and popular of the parks in Loei province, **PHU KRADUNG NATIONAL PARK** (Ⓣ042 871333 or 042 871458, Ⓦwww.dnp.go.th), about 80km south of Loei, protects a grassy 1300-metre plateau whose temperate climate supports a number of tree, flower and bird species not normally found in tropical Thailand. Walking trails crisscross much of sixty-square-kilometre Phu Kradung (Bell Mountain), and you could spend three days here exploring them fully – at a minimum you have to spend one night, as the trip from Loei to the top of the plateau and back can't be done comfortably in a day. The park is closed during the rainy season (June–Sept), owing to the increased risk of mud-slides and land-slips, and is at its busiest during weekends in December and January, when the summit headquarters is surrounded by a sea of tents.

The park

This popular national park supports two visitor centres, Wang Kwang at headquarters up on the plateau, and Sri Taan down at ground level. The challenging main **trail** leads from Sri Taan 5.5km up the eastern side of Phu Kradung, passing occasional refreshment stalls, and becoming steeper and rockier on the last 1km, with wooden steps over the most difficult parts; most people take at least three hours, including rest stops. The main trail is occasionally closed for maintenance, when a parallel 4.5-kilometre trail is opened up in its place. At the end of the climb, the unbelievable view as your head peeps over the rim more than rewards the effort: flat as a playing field, the broad plateau is dotted with odd clumps of pine trees thinned by periodic lightning fires, which give it the appearance of a country park. Several feeder trails fan out from here, including a 9.5-kilometre path along the precipitous southern edge that offers sweeping views of Dong Phaya Yen, the untidy range of mountains to the southwest that forms the unofficial border between the northeast and the central plains. Another trail heads along the eastern rim for 2.5km to Pha Nok An – also reached by a two-kilometre path east from the Wang Kwang Visitor Centre – which looks down on neat rice fields and matchbox-like houses in the valley below, an outlook that's especially breathtaking at sunrise.

The attractions of the mountain come and go with the **seasons**. October is muddy after the rains, but the waterfalls that tumble off the northwestern edge of the plateau are in full cascade and the main trail is green and shady. December brings out the maple leaves; by February the waterfalls have disappeared and the vegetation on the lower slopes has been burnt away. April is good for rhododendrons and wild roses, which in Thailand are only found at such high altitudes as this.

Among the park's **wildlife**, mammals such as elephants, sambar deer and gibbons can be seen very occasionally, but they generally confine themselves to the evergreen forest on the northern part of the plateau, which is out of bounds to visitors. In the temperate pines, oaks and beeches that dot the rest of the plateau you're more likely to spot resident **birds** such as jays, sultan tits and snowy-browed flycatchers if you're out walking in the early morning and evening.

Practicalities

To get to the park, take any **bus** between Loei and Khon Kaen and get off at the village of Phu Kradung (1hr 30min), then hop on a **songthaew** for the remaining 5km to the well-organized **Sri Taan Visitor Centre** (Oct–May daily 8.30am–4.30pm) at the base of the plateau, where you can pick up a trail map and pay the B400 admission fee. You can also leave your gear at the visitor centre, or hire a porter to tote it to the top for you. Four national park **bungalows** at Sri Taan (B1200, sleeping four people), with the added bonus of hot water, take the overflow when accommodation on the mountain itself is full. Up on the plateau at the **Wang Kwang Visitor Centre**, 8km from the Sri Taan Visitor Centre, there are over twenty **bungalows** and **rooms** sleeping four to twelve people (B900–4000), most with hot-water bathrooms; at busy times it's best to reserve in advance through the Parks Department in Bangkok (see p.52). There are also fully equipped tents for rent (from B270 for two people). Simple **restaurants** at Wang Kwang rustle up inexpensive, tasty food from limited ingredients, so there's no need to bring your own provisions. On the plain beneath the plateau (2–3km from the Sri Taan Visitor Centre towards Phu Kradung village), *Phu Kradung Resort* has en-suite bungalows, with either fan and cold water or air-con and hot water, and a restaurant (Ⓣ042 871076; fan ❸, air-con ❹).

Phu Reua National Park

About 50km west of Loei, the 120-square-kilometre **PHU REUA NATIONAL PARK** gets the name "Boat Mountain" from its resemblance to an upturned sampan, with the sharp ridge of its hull running southeast to northwest. The highest point of the ridge, Yod Phu Reua (1365m), offers one of the most spectacular panoramas in Thailand: the land drops away sharply on the Laos side, allowing views over toy-town villages and the Heuang and Mekong rivers to countless green-ridged mountains spreading towards Louang Phabang. To the northwest rises Phu Soai Dao (2102m) on Laos' western border; to the south are the Phetchabun mountains. If you happen to be driving yourself here from the west along Highway 203, it might be worth breaking your journey 10km from the Phu Reua turn-off at the **Château de Loei vineyard**, for the novelty value if nothing else: you can drive for 6km around the vast, seemingly incongruous fields of vines and taste a variety of wines and brandy, as well as getting something to eat at the simple restaurant and perusing a dizzying array of local foodstuffs in the attached shop.

In the park itself, a day's worth of well-marked trails fan out over the mountain's meadows and pine and broad-leaved evergreen forests, taking in gardens of strange rock formations, orchids that flower year-round, the best sunrise viewpoint, Loan Noi, and, during and just after the rainy season, several waterfalls. The most spectacular **viewpoint**, Yod Phu Reua (Phu Reua Peak), is an easy one-kilometre stroll from the top of the summit road. The park's population of barking deer, wild pigs and pheasants has declined over recent years, but you may be lucky enough to spot one of 26 bird species, which include the crested serpent-eagle, green-billed malkoha, greater coucal, Asian fairy-bluebird, rufescent prinia and white-rumped munia, as well as several species of babbler, barbet, bulbul and drongo.

Practicalities

The nine-kilometre paved road north from the village of Ban Phu Reua on Highway 203 to the summit means the park can get crowded at weekends, though during the week you'll probably have the place to yourself. The snag is that there's no organized **public transport** up the steep summit road – regular Lom Sak and Phitsanulok buses from Loei can drop you at the turn-off to the park on Highway 203, but then you'll have to walk/hitch or charter a songthaew (B400–700, depending on how far up the mountain you want to be taken). The easiest option would be to **rent a motorbike** at the *Sugar Guest House* in Loei (see p.539). Once on the summit road, you have to pay B200 admission at a checkpoint, before reaching the **headquarters** and **visitor centre 1** (Ⓣ042 801716 or 042 807625, Ⓦwww.dnp.go.th) after 4km, which has a trail map, a simple restaurant, and, in the pretty, pine-shaded grounds, six four- to six-berth national park **bungalows** with hot showers (B2000–3000 per bungalow). **Visitor centre 2** (Phuson), a three-kilometre walk or 5.5-kilometre drive further up the mountain near Hin Sam Chan waterfall, boasts several restaurants and is at the heart of the mountain's network of paths. At both visitor centres, a variety of fully equipped **tents** can be rented, costing from B270 for two people. Warm clothes are essential on cool-season nights – the lowest temperature in Thailand (-4°C) was recorded here in 1981 – and even by day the mountain is usually cool and breezy.

There are also plenty of **private accommodation** options, both on Highway 203 around Ban Phu Reua and on the summit road itself. *Chatchada Resort* (Ⓣ042 899399 or 081 841 4111; fan ❸, air-con ❻), at the east end of the village, 1km towards Loei from the turn-off to the national park, offers decent, spacious chalets, all with hot water, around a spacious lawn, or you could stay 800m up the summit road at the small, friendly *Phupet Hill Resort* (Ⓣ042 899157 or 081 320 2874; ❸), in one of their large, attractive rooms or chalets with hot water, air-con and TV.

Along the Mekong

The **Mekong** is the one of the great rivers of the world and the third longest in Asia, after the Yangtse and the Yellow rivers. From its source 4920m up on the east Tibetan plateau it roars down through China's Yunnan province – where it's known as Lancang Jiang, the "Turbulent River" – before snaking its way a little more peaceably between Burma and Laos, and then, by way of the so-called "Golden Triangle", as the border between Thailand and Laos. After a brief shimmy into rural Laos via Louang Phabang, the river reappears in Isaan to form 750km of the border between Thailand and Laos. From Laos it crosses Cambodia and continues south to Vietnam, where it splinters into the many arms of the Mekong Delta before flowing into the South China Sea, 4184km from where its journey began.

This dramatic stretch around Isaan is one of the more accessible places to observe the mighty river, and as Laos opens further border crossings to visitors, the Mekong is slowly becoming more of a transport link and less of a forbidding barrier. The guest houses along the upper part of this stretch, in **Chiang Khan** and **Sang Khom**, are geared towards relaxation and gentle exploration of the rural way of life along the river bank. **Nong Khai**, on the rail line from Bangkok and the principal jumping-off point for trips to the Lao capital of Vientiane, is the pivotal town on the river, and retains most of its restful charm despite the building of the massive Thai-Australian Friendship Bridge and the ensuing increase in cross-border trade. East of Nong Khai you're into wild country; here the unique natural beauty of **Wat Phu Tok** is well worth the hefty detour, and your Mekong journey wouldn't be complete without seeing **Wat Phra That Phanom**, a place of pilgrimage for 2500 years. Sights get sparse beyond that, although by continuing south through **Mukdahan** you can join up with the southern Isaan route at Ubon Ratchathani (see p.520).

A road, served by slow **buses** and **songthaews**, runs parallel to – rarely beside – the river as far as Mukdahan. If you've got the time (allow at least a week to do it any sort of justice) you could make the entire marathon journey described in this section; on a shorter trip, it's best to concentrate on the stretch of tarmac between Chiang Khan and Nong Khai, which offers more frequent views of the Mekong. **Motorbike rental**, available in Chiang Khan, Sang Khom and Nong Khai, may provide a further incentive to concentrate on this stretch; the roads are quiet and easy to negotiate, though they're sometimes in a state of disrepair and you'll need to watch out for occasional but massive timber trucks. There's no official long-distance **boat** transport on the river, at least from the Thai side, though several interesting river trips are available from Chiang Khan.

Chiang Khan to Nong Khai

Rustic "backpackers' resorts" – and the travelling between them – are the chief draw along the reach of the Mekong from **Chiang Khan**, via **Sang Khom**, to Nong Khai, which is paralleled all the way by Highway 211.

Chiang Khan

The Mekong route starts promisingly at **CHIANG KHAN**, a friendly town, 55km north of Loei, that happily hasn't been entirely converted to concrete yet. Rows of shuttered wooden shophouses stretch out in a two-kilometre ribbon parallel to the river, which for much of the year runs red with what locals call "the blood of the trees": rampant deforestation on the Lao side causes the rust-coloured topsoil to erode into the river. The town has only two streets – the main through-route (Highway 211), also known as **Thanon Sri Chiang Khan**, and the quieter **Thanon Chai Khong** on the waterfront – with a line of sois connecting them, numbered from west to east.

Arguably the most enjoyable thing you can do here is to hitch up with other travellers for a **boat trip** on the river, organized through one of the guest houses. If you opt to go **upstream**, you'll head west towards the lofty mountains of Khao Laem and Khao Ngu on the Thai side and Phu Lane and Phu Hat Song in Laos, gliding round a long, slow bend in the Mekong to the mouth of the Heuang River tributary, 20km from Chiang Khan, which forms the border to the west of this point; stops can be arranged to share the fine views with Phra Yai, a twenty-metre-tall golden Buddha standing on a hilltop at the confluence, and at Hat Sai Kaew, a sandy beach for swimming, fishing and picnicking. Upstream trips, costing B1500 per boat, take three hours or so and are best undertaken in the afternoon, returning at sunset. A ride **downstream to Pak Chom** and back will take you through some of the most beautiful scenery on the Thai Mekong: hills and cliffs of all shapes and sizes advance and recede around the winding flow, and outside the rainy season, the rapids are dramatic without being dangerous (best between Dec and April), and the shores and islands are enlivened by neat grids of market gardens. This jaunt costs around B3000 for the boat, and takes around six hours. Most guest houses also offer a one-hour **sunset on the Mekong** cruise for B750 per boat and a trip to Kaeng Kut Khu (see below; B1000 per boat).

About 2km east of town along the main highway, a left turn back towards the river will bring you to **Wat Tha Khaek**, a formerly ramshackle forest temple which, on the back of millions of bahts' worth of donations from Thai tourists, has embarked on an ambitious but slow-moving building programme in a bizarre mix of traditional and modern styles. One kilometre further along this side road lies the reason for the influx of visitors: at this point, the river runs over rocks at a wide bend to form the modest rapids of **Kaeng Kut Khu**. Set against the forested hillside of imaginatively named Phu Yai (Big Mountain), it's a pretty enough spot, with small restaurants and souvenir shops shaded by trees on the river bank. If you're feeling brave, try the local speciality *kung ten*, or "dancing shrimp" – fresh shrimp served live with a lime juice and chilli sauce. Boats can be hired at Kaeng Kut Khu, costing from B400 for a half-hour pootle around the rapids. With your own transport you could continue your explorations to **Phu Thok**, an isolated hill topped by a communications mast to the south of here. On Highway 211 just east of the turn-off to Wat Tha Khaek and Kaeng Kut Khu, a small signpost will point you down 3km of rough paved road, before you fork right and climb steeply for nearly 2km to the summit. From there, you'll be rewarded with splendid views of Chiang Khan, the Mekong and the striking patchwork of fields in the broad valley to the south, especially at sunset.

Practicalities

Big, slow **songthaews** (roughly every 30min) and **buses** from Loei (roughly hourly) stop at the west end of town near the main junction of Highway 201 (the road from Loei) and Highway 211. There's **internet access** at *Sang Thong* pub on Thanon Chai Khong near Soi 12, and a **bank** with ATM near the main junction. Most of Chiang Khan's guest houses rent out **bicycles** (B50–100 per day) and **motorbikes** (B200–250 per day), and can arrange herbal steam baths and traditional massages.

For **accommodation**, there are several appealing guest houses strung out along the riverside Thanon Chai Khong, as listed below. The **night market** is on Thanon Chiang Khan, between sois 17 and 18, while the best **restaurant** in town, with peaceful water views and inexpensive Chinese and Thai dishes, is *Rabieng* next to *Tonkhong Guest House*.

Chiang Khan Guesthouse Thanon Chai Khong, near Soi 19 ⓣ042 821691, ⓦwww.thailandunplugged.com. Friendly, Thai-Dutch place in a characterful and well-kept old wooden house with a riverside balcony upstairs. Mosquito nets and shared hot-water bathrooms. ❷

Chiang Khan Hill Resort at Kaeng Kut Khu ⓣ042 821285, ⓦwww.chiangkhanhill.com. Upmarket resort with a swimming pool and a variety of air-con rooms and bungalows, all with hot-water bathrooms, TVs and fridges, in a pretty garden overlooking the river. ❹

Loogmai Guesthouse 112 Thanon Chai Khong, near Soi 5 ⓣ042 822334 or 086 234 0011. Spacious, colonial-style, white mansion, adorned with green shutters and hung with modern art. Most of the lovely, airy rooms share hot showers (one large room is en suite), and there's a pretty garden terrace overlooking the river. ❷–❸

Mekong Villas 35km east on Highway 211 (5km west of Pak Chom) ⓣ02 224 6686, ⓦwww.thaivillas.com. Three luxurious riverside villas of varying sizes (one- to three-bedroom) with a swimming pool, under the same ownership as Bangkok's *Chakrabongse Villas* (see p.117). ❾

Rimkong Pub and Guesthouse 294 Thanon Chai Khong, opposite Soi 8 ⓣ042 821125, ⓦrimkhong.free.fr. There's a wide variety of recently refurbished wooden rooms here (some riverside), with mosquito screens and hot-water bathrooms, as well as French bread and filter coffee for breakfast. The helpful Thai-French owners, who have lived in Chiang Khan for over ten years, are a good source of information on the area. ❶

Tonkhong Guest House 299/3 Thanon Chai Khong, between sois 9 and 10 ⓣ042 821879, ⓔben_jama@hotmail.com. Easy-going, friendly place with slightly scrappy but clean rooms, some en suite (with shared hot showers), some with air-con. The popular Thai restaurant provides veggie options and Western breakfasts, as well as a choice between streetside seating downstairs and river-view tables on the first-floor terrace. Extras on offer include occasional local day-trips, cooking courses and plenty of information including maps of the town. Fan ❶–❷, air-con ❸

Sang Khom and on towards Nong Khai

The route from Chiang Khan to the otherwise forgettable town of Pak Chom, 41km downriver, is beautiful and winding but unfortunately isn't covered by **public transport**. Two or three small, green buses a day run from Loei to Pak Chom, Sang Khom and Nong Khai (as long as there are enough takers, and sometimes terminating at Pak Chom in the afternoon). But to continue eastwards from Chiang Khan, you need to take a bus or songthaew 20km south down Highway 201 to Ban That, where you can pick up one of these buses towards Nong Khai.

Beyond Pak Chom, the road through the Mekong valley becomes a little flatter and straighter. After 50km, a sign in English points down a side road to **Than Tip Falls**, 3km south, which is well worth seeking out. The ten-metre-high waterfall splashes down into a rock pool overhung by jungle on three sides; higher up, a bigger waterfall has a good pool for swimming, and if you can face the climb you can explore three higher levels.

Staying in **SANG KHOM**, which straggles along the tree-shaded south bank of the Mekong about 60km east of Pak Chom (and which now supports a bank and two ATMs), puts you in the heart of an especially lush stretch of the river within easy striking distance of several backroad villages and temples. *Bouy Guest House* (ⓣ042 441065, ⓔtoy_bgh@hotmail.com; ❶) is the best of the accommodation here, enjoying a particularly choice location: decent bamboo huts, with beautiful views out over the river, are set in a spacious, flower-strewn compound on a spit of land that's reached by a wooden bridge over a small tributary. The welcoming owners can arrange day-trips to Ban Phu (see p.552), or if that sounds too strenuous, you can settle for a massage or just relax in the hammocks strung from the veranda of each hut. Good Thai and Western food is available on a deck overlooking the stream (most of it also in vegetarian versions), and you can access the **internet**, make international phone calls and rent **motorbikes** (B200 per day). On the Pak Chom side of town, just west of the bridge, the tidy, concrete bungalows of friendly *Bungalow Cake Resort* shelter in a small, shady garden, with a large, attractive riverside terrace (Ⓣ042 441440 or 087 219 9184; fan ❶, air-con ❸); some have air-con, hot water and TVs, but the best of them, with fans and cold-water bathrooms, overlook the Mekong.

Another 19km east on Route 211, overlooking a narrow section of the Mekong, **Wat Hin Maak Peng** is a famous meditation temple, popular with Thai pilgrims and rich donors. The long white boundary wall, huge modern buildings and immaculate riverside gardens are evidence of the temple's prosperity, but its reputation is in fact based on the asceticism of the monks of the Thammayut sect, who keep themselves in strict poverty and allow only one meal a day to interrupt their meditation. The flood of merit-makers, however, proved too distracting for the founder of the wat, Luang Phu Thet, who before his death in 1994 decamped to the peace and quiet of Wat Tham Kham near Sakon Nakhon. Further east, between Tha Bo and Ban Nong Song Hong, the main route to Nong Khai passes Wat Phra That Bang Phuan (see p.552).

Nong Khai and around

The major border town in these parts is **NONG KHAI**, which is still a relative backwater but was given a huge shot in the arm with the construction of the **Thai-Australian Friendship Bridge** over the Mekong on the west side of town in 1994. Occupying a strategic position at the end of Highway 2 and the northeastern rail line, and just 24km from Vientiane, Nong Khai acts as a conduit for goods bought and sold by Thais and Lao, who are allowed to pass between the two cities freely for day-trips. Consequently, the souvenir market that sprawls to the east of the main pier, **Tha Sadet**, carries Lao silver, wood and cane items, as well as goods from as far afield as China, Korea and Russia, plus local basketware and silk.

As with most of the towns along this part of the Mekong, the thing to do in Nong Khai is just to take it easy, enjoying the riverside atmosphere and the

Naga fireballs

Nong Khai celebrates the generic Thai and Isaan festivals with due gusto, but in recent years a peculiarity of this stretch of the Mekong River has been attracting thousands of celebrants from Bangkok and beyond. Every year on the full-moon night in October, silent and vapourless **naga fireballs** appear from the river, small, pink spheres that float vertically up to heights of as much as 300m, then disappear; in some years, several thousand appear, in others, just a handful. A tentative scientific theory proposes that the balls are a combination of methane and nitrogen from decomposed matter on the bottom of the river, which reach a certain temperature at that time of the year and are released, self-combusting in the presence of oxygen when they break the water's surface; romantics will prefer the local belief that the nagas or naks (serpents) of the river breathe out the fireballs to call the Buddha to return to earth at the end of Buddhist Lent. This strange occurrence has now been consolidated into the two-day festival of **Bang Fai Phaya Nak**, which coincides with Awk Phansa and the end of the longboat racing season on the river. The fireballs have appeared as far afield as Sang Khom and Bung Khan, but are generally most numerous at Phon Phisai, 40km east of Nong Khai; if you make the trek out there, take great care on the way back when the road is thronged with drunk drivers.

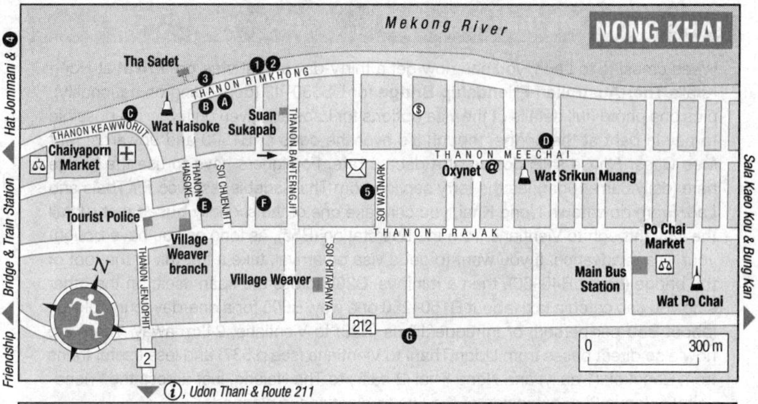

ACCOMMODATION				EATING & DRINKING			
Janhom Apartment	F	Nongkhai Grand Thani Hotel	G	Daeng Namnuang	2	Vegetarian Food	5
Khiang Khong Guest House	B	Pantawee Hotel	E	Mut Mee Guest House	C	Zodiac	4
Mut Mee Guest House	C	Ruan Thai Guest House	A	Nam Tok Rim Khong	1		
		Sawasdee Guest House	D	Rotsading	3		

peaceful settings of its guest houses, which offer good value. Before you lapse into a relaxation-induced coma though, try joining an evening river-tour, or make a day-trip out to see the impressive sculptures and rock formations in the surrounding countryside.

Arrival, information and transport

From Bangkok, you'll most likely be coming to Nong Khai by night **train**, arriving just after dawn at the station 3km southwest of the centre near the Friendship Bridge. Day **buses** from all points in Isaan and night buses from further afield pull in at the bus station on the east side of town off Thanon Prajak; Udon Thani buses make an extra stop at the corner of highways 2 and 212. There are also **air-con minibuses** from Udon Thani airport (B120–150), which meet incoming flights from Bangkok and drop passengers at their hotels.

The **TAT office**, 1.5km south of the centre on the west side of Highway 2 (daily 8.30am–4.30pm; ⓣ042 421326, ⓔtat_nongkhai@yahoo.com), has information about local homestays. The **tourist police** are based on Thanon Prajak (ⓣ 042 460186 or 1155). There are plenty of places offering **internet access**, including Oxynet, 569/2 Thanon Meechai, and the Hornbill Bookshop, which stocks an excellent selection of new and secondhand **books** in English, on the funky little lane leading to *Mut Mee Guest House*. Good, strong **massages** and foot massages can be had at Suan Sukapab, 623 Thanon Banterngjit (ⓣ042 423323).

As everything in Nong Khai is so spread out, you might want to consider hopping on a **tuk-tuk** for getting around (around B25–30 for a short journey such as bus station–Tha Sadet, up to B60 for bus station–train station). To get around under your own steam, **bicycles** (B30 per day) and **motorbikes** (around B200 per day) can be rented on Thanon Keawworut in front of the *Mut Mee Guest House*; bicycles are also available at *Ruan Thai*, *Khiang Khong* and *Sawasdee* guest houses.

Crossing to Laos from Nong Khai

When crossing to Laos, you can now get a thirty-day tourist **visa on arrival** at Nong Khai's **Thai-Australian Friendship Bridge** for US$30–42 (depending on nationality), plus one photo (full details of the visa options for Laos are given on p.35). It's possible to pay in baht at the bridge, though it's over the odds at B1500 and upwards; *Mut Mee Guest House* sells dollars at a decent rate. Foreigners have to use the bridge here (daily 6am–10pm), as the ferry service from Tha Sadet is reserved for Thais and Lao. From downtown Nong Khai, you can take one of the six daily **buses** that run all the way through to Vientiane from the bus station (B55), as long as you have bought your visa in advance. If you want to get a visa on arrival, take a tuk-tuk to the foot of the bridge (about B40–60), then a minibus (B20) across the span itself; on the other side you can catch a taxi (about B150–250 one way, B600 for a one-day tour), tuk-tuk (about B50 per person) or infrequent bus (B20) to Vientiane, 24km away. There are now also direct buses from Udon Thani to Vientiane (see p.537) and less useful trains from Bangkok (1 daily) and Nong Khai (2 daily) to Tha Naleng, just across the Friendship Bridge; a 9km extension of the line to Vientiane is planned.

Accommodation

Nong Khai has an excellent choice of inexpensive **guest houses**, as well as several more upmarket places that cater largely to expats on visa runs.

Janhom Apartment 479 Soi Srichumchuen, Thanon Prajak ⓣ042 460293, ⓕ042 460415. A modern, lime-green block on a quiet soi, set against the wall of Wat Sri Chum Chuen and with a pleasant, shady sitting area at the front. Not really apartments, though they are available by the month, with substantial discounts, but large, clean, air-con rooms with armchairs, fridges, TVs and hot-water bathrooms. Internet access. ❸

Khiang Khong Guest House 541 Thanon Rimkhong ⓣ042 422870 or 081 832 3925. In a spruce, cream, modern block next door to *Ruan Thai*, spacious rooms with TVs and tiled, hot-water bathrooms that are on the small side. Fan ❷, air-con ❸

Mut Mee Guest House 1111 Thanon Keawworut ⓣ042 460717, ⓦwww.mutmee.com. A magnet for travellers, where well-kept rooms sprawl around an attractive riverside terrace restaurant. Bathrooms with cold or hot water are either shared or en suite, and three-bed dorms are available (dorm bed B90). With helpful, well-informed staff, it also offers yoga (ⓦwww.pantrix.net), meditation and massage sessions, as well as local information about bicycle and motorbike tours and homestays. Fan ❶–❸, air-con ❹

Nongkhai Grand Thani Hotel 589 Moo 5, Nongkhai–Phonpisai road ⓣ042 420033, ⓦwww.nongkhaigrand.com. On the southern bypass but handy for the centre, this luxury hotel has high standards of service, a small swimming pool (under long-term renovation at the time of writing) and a rooftop terrace restaurant offering panoramic views over Nong Khai and Laos. Breakfast included. ❺

Pantawee Hotel 1049 Thanon Haisoke ⓣ042 411568, ⓦwww.pantawee.com. A comfortable, efficiently run, though rather brash mid-range choice, festooned with neon and filled with muzak. Clean air-con rooms come with hot-water bathrooms, TVs, DVD players, fridges, computers and free wi-fi. There's also a small jacuzzi pool, a beer garden and a 24hr restaurant. Breakfast included. ❹

Ruan Thai Guest House 1126 Thanon Rimkhong ⓣ042 412519. Renovated wooden houses in a quiet, welcoming garden compound with attractive, well-maintained rooms, which range from keenly priced singles with shared hot-water bathrooms, through standard rooms with hot-water en suites, to family rooms. Internet access available. Fan ❷, air-con ❸

Sawasdee Guest House 402 Thanon Meechai ⓣ042 412502, ⓔsawasdee_gh@hotmail.com. A well-restored, grand old wooden shophouse round a pleasant courtyard, with helpful and meticulous management: free luggage storage and showers available for those catching a night train or bus. Fan-cooled rooms sharing bathrooms (try to avoid those overlooking the noisy main road), with hot showers available, and air-con rooms with en-suite hot-water bathrooms. Massages, internet access and wi-fi also available. Fan ❶, air-con ❸

The Town

Nong Khai lays itself out along the south bank of the Mekong in a four-kilometre band which is never more than 500m deep. Running from east to west, Thanon Meechai dominates activity: the main shops and businesses are plumb in the middle around the post office and Tha Sadet. Although most of the old buildings have been replaced by concrete boxes, one or two weather-beaten wooden houses remain, their attractive balconies, porticoes and slatted shutters showing the influence of colonial architecture, which was imported from across the river before the French were forced out of Laos in 1954.

The most pleasant place for a stroll is the riverside area. There's a pedestrianized promenade in the centre to the east of Tha Sadet, while things become more rustic and leafy around the fringes, which are often busy with people bathing, washing their clothes and fishing, especially in the early morning and evening. If you're lucky, you might also catch sight of a sunken chedi at the far eastern end of town, **Phra That Nong Khai**, which slipped into the river during floods in 1847 and has since subsided so far that it's only visible in the dry season (though a replica has been constructed on the adjacent bank); this is thought to be a good spot to see naga fireballs (see above), said to be produced by the serpent that guards the relic of the Buddha's right foot in the chedi. To catch the best of life on the river, take a **boat trip** on the *Nagarina*, which sets out from the *Mut Mee Guest House* every evening at around 5.30pm (B100) and runs up and down the length of Nong Khai for ninety minutes or so, sticking to the Thai side. Drinks are available and food (see p.550) can be ordered before the boat leaves. There's no stunning scenery, but plenty of activity on both river banks as the sun sets behind the Friendship Bridge. If you're toiling around Nong Khai in the dog days of the hot season, you might want to cool off at **Hat Jommani**, the so-called "Pattaya of Isaan", 2km west of the centre beyond the Friendship Bridge: this riverine beach can stretch for up to 200m when the river is at its lowest in April.

The main temple of the region is **Wat Po Chai** off the east end of Thanon Prajak. The cruciform viharn, with its complex and elegant array of Lao tiers, shelters a venerated golden image, the Phra Sai Buddha, which is paraded around town and blessed with water during Songkhran. Prince Chakri, the future Rama I, is said to have looted the image from Vientiane, along with the Emerald Buddha, but the boat which was bringing back the Phra Sai overturned and sank in the Mekong. Later, the statue miraculously rose to the surface and the grateful people of Nong Khai built this great hangar of a viharn to house it, decorating the walls with murals of its miraculous journey; the present king, Chakri's descendant, still comes every year to pay his respects. It's worth a visit for the Buddha's stagy setting, in front of a steep, flame-covered altar, dazzlingly lit from above and below. The solid gold head is so highly polished that you have to peer carefully to make out the Sukhothai influence in its haughty expression and beaked nose.

Fifteen minutes' walk west of Wat Po Chai at 1151 Soi Chitapanya, just off Thanon Prajak, **Village Weaver Handicrafts** (Mon–Sat 8am–5pm; ⓣ042 411236, ⓦwww.villageweaver.net) specializes in **mut mee** (literally "tied strings"), the northeastern method of tie-dyeing bundles of cotton thread before hand-weaving, which produces geometrical patterns on a coloured base; Village Weaver also sells silk at a branch shop (daily 9am–7pm) slightly nearer the centre at 1020–1020/1 Thanon Prajak, on the corner of Thanon Haisoke. The work is produced in nearby villages through a self-help project initiated in 1982 to help rural women earn cash. White on indigo is the simplest, most traditional form of *mut mee*, but the shops also carry a wide range of more richly patterned lengths of silk and cotton (tailoring available), as well as ready-made clothes, wall hangings, bags and axe pillows; they offer a very reasonable and professional posting and packing service back to your home country, and it's also possible to order through the website. You're welcome to visit the **Village Vocational Training Centre**, 7km south of Nong Khai on the road to Udon Thani, to see the weavers at work (Mon–Sat 8am–noon & 1–4.30pm).

Eating and drinking

Nong Khai is a great place to sample Isaan cuisine, as well as Vietnamese at *Daeng Namnuang*, the town's most famous restaurant. If you're counting the baht, head for the night-time stalls on Thanon Prajak, near the corner of Banterngjit, which include a good *phat thai* place on the north side of the road.

Daeng Namnuang Thanon Rimkong. Delicious, inexpensive Vietnamese food at this immaculately clean and popular place, with an air-con room and a lovely riverside terrace. Specialities include *nam nuang* (Vietnamese sausages), fresh spring rolls and deep-fried prawns on sugar-cane skewers. Closes at 8pm.
Mut Mee Guest House 1111 Thanon Keawworut. You're spoilt for choice at this traveller's favourite. As well as evening boat trips (see p.549), there's the *Nagarina* floating restaurant, which specializes in seafood and Isaan dishes – try the squid with preserved eggs and the *som tam* with Chinese crispy bacon; the cosy, attached *Gaia* bar hosts singer-songwriters on Sunday night. Meanwhile, under bamboo shelters back on dry land, the main guest-house restaurant is inexpensive and relaxing: good Thai and Isaan dishes, particularly vegetarian versions, vie with tasty Western efforts including home-made apple pie.
Nam Tok Rim Khong Thanon Rimkhong (no English sign). Simple but popular and cheap restaurant in an old wooden building with an attractive terrace overlooking the river, specializing in *nam tok*, spicy hot beef salad, as well as other Isaan delicacies such as *som tam*, dried beef and sausages. Closes at 8.30pm.
Rotsading Thanon Rimkhong. Cheap, clean restaurant with nice views of the river, where the speciality is fish stuffed with lemon-grass and grilled. Also various flavours of *som tam*, *kai yang*, *nam tok muu* and Isaan sausages. No English sign but easy to spot, a lime-green, open-sided place just east of Tha Sadet. Daily 7am–6pm.
Vegetarian Food Soi Watnark, Thanon Meechai. Cheap, tasty veggie buffet, plus *phat thai*, *som tam* and fresh juices. Daily around 8am–4pm.
Zodiac (*Phae 12 Rasii*) Thanon Keawworut, about 1km west of *Mut Mee Guest House*. Go through the grounds of Wat Meechaitha on the north side of Thanon Keawworut and descend the steps to this very good floating restaurant, which catches any breezes going on the river. The menu features Isaan specialities, including a taster plate of local appetizers (B150), as well as plenty of fish and vegetarian dishes.

Around Nong Khai

By far the easiest and most popular day-trip out of Nong Khai takes in **Sala Kaeo Kou**, with its surreal sculptures, a short hop to the east. To the southwest of town and also fairly easy to get to, **Wat Phra That Bang Phuan** offers classic temple sightseeing, while the natural rock formations at **Ban Phu** require much more effort and a full day out. The scenic riverside route upstream to Chiang Khan (see p.543), as well as Wat Phu Tok (see p.554), are also within day-tripping distance, and it's quite possible to get to **Ban Chiang** (see p.536) and back in a day, changing buses at Udon Thani.

Sala Kaeo Kou

Just off the main highway 5km east of Nong Khai, and about B120 return in a tuk-tuk, **Sala Kaeo Kou** (aka Wat Khaek; daily 6am–6pm; B20) is best known for its bizarre sculpture garden, which looks like the work of a giant artist on acid. The temple was founded by the late **Luang Phu Boonlua Surirat**, an unconventional Thai holy man who studied under a Hindu guru in Vietnam and preached in Laos until he was thrown out by the Communists in the 1970s. His charisma – those who drank water offered by him would, it was rumoured, give up all they owned to the temple – and heavy emphasis on morality attracted many followers among the farmers of Nong Khai. Luang Phu's popularity suffered, however, after his eleven-month spell in prison for insulting King Bhumibol, a crime alleged by jealous neighbours and probably without foundation; he died aged 72 in August 1996, a year after his release.

Arrayed with pretty flowers and plants, the **sculpture garden** bristles with Buddhist, Hindu and secular figures, all executed in concrete with imaginative abandon by unskilled followers under Luang Phu's direction. The religious statues, in particular, are radically modern. Characteristics that marked the Buddha out as a supernatural being – tight curls and a bump on the crown of the head called the *ushnisha* – are here transformed into beehives, and the *rashmis* on top (flames depicting the Buddha's fiery intellect) are depicted as long, sharp spikes. The largest statue in the garden shows the familiar story of the kindly naga king, Muchalinda, sheltering the Buddha, who is lost in meditation, from the heavy rain and floods: here the Buddha has shrunk in significance and the seven-headed snake has grown to 25m, with fierce, gaping fangs and long tongues.

Many of the statues illustrate **Thai proverbs**. Near the entrance, an elephant surrounded by a pack of dogs symbolizes integrity, "as the elephant is indifferent to the barking dogs". The nearby serpent-tailed monster with the moon in his mouth – Rahoo, the cause of eclipses – serves as an injunction to oppose all obstacles, just as the people of Isaan and Laos used to ward off eclipses by banging drums and firing guns. In the corner furthest from the entrance, you enter the complex Circle of Life through a huge mouth representing the womb, inside which a hermit, a policeman, a monk, a rich man and a beggar, among others, represent different paths in life (for a detailed map of the Circle of Life sculpture, go to Ⓦwww.mutmee.com). A man with two wives is shown beating the older one because he is ensnared by the wishes of the younger one, and an

▲ Sculpture garden at Sala Kaeo Kou

old couple who have made the mistake of not having children now find they have only each other for comfort.

The disturbingly vacant, smiling faces of the garden Buddhas bear more than a passing resemblance to Luang Phu himself, photos of whom adorn the **temple building**, a huge white edifice with mosque-like domes. On the second floor, his corpse is preserved on a domed palanquin, which is decorated with fairy lights and a virtual fish-tank. If you're heading over to Laos, the **Xiang Khouan** sculpture garden – Sala Kaeo Kou's precursor, 25km from downtown Vientiane on the Mekong River – shouldn't be missed; Luang Phu spent twenty years working on the sculptures there before his expulsion.

Wat Phra That Bang Phuan

More famous as the site of a now concealed two-thousand-year-old Indian chedi than for its modern replacement, rural **Wat Phra That Bang Phuan** remains a highly revered place of pilgrimage. The wat is in the hamlet of **Ban Bang Phuan**, southwest of Nong Khai on Highway 211; buses from Nong Khai to Pak Chom and Loei pass this way (though not buses to Tha Bo, which use the minor road west along the river bank from Nong Khai), or it might be quicker to take an Udon-bound service 12km down Highway 2 to Ban Nong Song Hong, then change onto an Udon–Sri Chiangmai bus for the remaining 12km. On the way to or from Wat Phra That Bang Phuan, it might be worth breaking your journey at the Village Vocational Training Centre, between Nong Khai and Ban Nong Song Hong on Highway 2 (see p.550).

The original **chedi** is supposed to have been built by disciples of the Buddha to hold 29 relics – pieces of breastbone – brought from India. A sixteenth-century king of Vientiane piously earned himself merit by building a tall Lao-style chedi over the top of the previous stupa; rain damage toppled this in 1970, but it was restored in 1977 to the fine, gleaming white edifice seen today. The unkempt compound also contains a small museum, crumbling brick chedis and some large open-air Buddhas.

Ban Phu

Deep in the countryside 61km southwest of Nong Khai, the wooded slopes around **BAN PHU** are dotted with strangely eroded sandstone formations, which have long exerted a mystical hold over people in the surrounding area. Local wisdom has it that the outcrops, many of which were converted into small temples from around the ninth century onwards, are either meteorites – believed to account for their burnt appearance – or, more likely, were caused by glacial erosion. Together with a stupa enshrining a Buddha footprint that is now an important pilgrimage site, especially during its annual festival in March, the rock formations have been linked up under the auspices of fifty-square-kilometre **Phu Phra Bat Historical Park** (daily dawn–dusk; B30). The **information centre** (daily 8.30am–4.30pm) by the park entrance contains fairly interesting displays on the red prehistoric paintings of animals, humans, hands and geometric patterns that are found on the rock formations, and on the tale of Ussa and Barot (see opposite). Around the information centre, a well-signposted network of **paths** has been cleared from the thin forest to connect 25 of the outcrops, each of which has a helpful English-language information board attached. It would take a good five hours to explore the whole park, but the most popular circuit, covering all the sights listed below, can be completed in an ambling two hours.

Among the most interesting of the outcrops are **Tham Wua** and **Tham Khon**, two natural shelters whose paintings of oxen and human stick figures suggest that the area was first settled by hunter-gatherers two to three thousand years ago. A legend that's well known in this part of Thailand and Laos accounts for the name of nearby **Kok Ma Thao Barot** (Prince Barot's Stable), a broad platform overhung by a huge slab of sandstone. A certain Princess Ussa, banished by her father to these slopes to be educated by a hermit, sent out an SOS that was answered by a dashing prince, Barot. The two fell in love and were married against the wishes of Ussa's father, prompting the king to challenge Barot to a distinctly oriental sort of duel: each would build a temple, and the last to finish would be beheaded. The king lost. Kok Ma Thao Barot is celebrated as the place where Barot kept his horse when he visited Ussa.

The furthest point of the circuit is the viewpoint at **Pha Sadej**, where the cliff drops away to give a lovely view across the green fields and forests of the Mekong valley to the distant mountains. More spectacular is **Hor Nang Ussa** (Ussa's Tower), a mushroom formed by a flat slab capping a five-metre-high rock pillar. Under the cap of the mushroom, a shelter has been carved out and walled in on two sides. The *sema* found scattered around the site, and the square holes in which others would have been embedded, indicate that this was a shrine, probably during the ninth to eleventh centuries in the Dvaravati period. Nearby, a huge rock on a flimsy pivot miraculously balances itself against a tree at **Wat Por Ta** (the Father-in-Law's Temple); the walls and floor have been evenly carved out to form a vaguely rectangular shrine, with Dvaravati Buddha images dotted around.

The left fork shortly before the park entrance leads to **Wat Phra Bat Bua Bok**: a crude *that* built in imitation of Wat Phra That Phanom (see p.556), it's decorated with naive bas-reliefs of divinities and boggle-eyed monsters, which add to the atmosphere of simple, rustic piety. In a gloomy chamber in the tower's base, the only visible markings on the sandstone **Buddha footprint** show the Wheel of Law. Legend has it that the Buddha made the footprint here for a serpent that had asked to be ordained as a monk, but had been refused because it was not human. Higher up the slope, a smaller *that* perches on a hanging rock that seems to defy gravity.

On **public transport**, the easiest way of getting there from Nong Khai is to take the 7.15am bus to Ban Phu; if you leave any later you won't have time to see the park properly, as the whole journey takes at least a couple of hours and the last bus back to Nong Khai leaves at around 3.30pm. From Ban Phu, it's another 14km west to the historical park; take a songthaew for the first 10km to the Ban Tiu intersection; from here a motorbike taxi will bring you the final 4km up to the main park entrance and information centre. If you are coming from Udon Thani, it's best to catch a bus from Talat Rungsina towards either Nam Som or Na Yung, which will drop you off at Ban Tiu.

Downstream to Mukdahan

East of Nong Khai, the land on the Thai side of the Mekong becomes gradually more arid, while jagged forest-covered mountains loom on the Laos side. Not many visitors make it this far, to the northeast's northeast, though the few attractions are surprisingly varied, ranging from the strange natural beauty of **Wat Phu Tok**, through painterly riverscapes, to Isaan's major religious site, **Wat Phra That Phanom**. **Transport** along Highway 212 out of Nong Khai is fairly straightforward: hourly buses from Nong Khai run to Bung Kan, 137km away, of which seven daily continue to the frontier town of **Nakhon Phanom**, where you have to change onto one of the roughly hourly buses to get to That Phanom and **Mukdahan**, which derives most of its significance – and income – from its bridge across to Savannakhet in Laos.

Wat Phu Tok

The most compelling destination in the area to the east of Nong Khai is the extraordinary hilltop retreat of **Wat Phu Tok**. One of two sandstone outcrops that jut steeply out of the plain 35km southeast of Bung Kan, Phu Tok has been transformed into a meditation wat, its fifty or so monks building their scattered huts on perches high above breathtaking cliffs. The outcrop comes into sight long before you get there, its sheer red face sandwiched between green vegetation on the lower slopes and tufts of trees on the narrow plateau above. As you get closer, the horizontal white lines across the cliffs reveal themselves to be painted wooden walkways, built to give the temple seven levels to represent the seven stages of enlightenment.

In an ornamental garden at the base, reflected in a small lake, an elegant, modern marble chedi commemorates **Phra Ajaan Juen**, the famous meditation master who founded the wat in 1968 and died in a plane crash ten years later while on his way to Bangkok to celebrate the queen's birthday. Within the chedi, the monk's books and other belongings, and diamond-like fragments of his bones, are preserved in a small shrine.

The first part of the ascent of the outcrop takes you to the third level up a series of long, sometimes slippery, wooden staircases, the first of many for which you'll need something more sturdy than flip-flops on your feet. A choice of two routes – the left fork is more interesting – leads to the fifth and most important level, where the **Sala Yai** houses the temple's main Buddha image in an airy, dimly lit cavern. The artificial ledges that cut across the northeast face are not for the fainthearted, but they are one way of getting to the dramatic northwest tip here on level five: on the other side of a deep crevice spanned by a wooden bridge, the monks have built an open-sided Buddha viharn under a huge anvil rock (though the gate to the viharn is usually locked). This spot affords stunning **views** over a broad sweep of countryside and across to the second, uninhabited outcrop. The flat top of the hill forms the seventh level, where you can wander along overgrown paths through thick forest.

Practicalities

Getting to Wat Phu Tok isn't easy – the location was chosen for its isolation, after all – but the journey out gives you a slice of life in remote countryside. The best option is to hire a motorbike in Nong Khai, as it's a real slog by public transport, which begins with catching a bus to Bung Kan; once there, you might be lucky enough to coincide with one of the occasional songthaews to Phu Tok via **Ban Siwilai**, 25km south on Route 222; otherwise, take one of the hourly buses to Siwilai and charter a motorized samlor (B200–250) for the last 20km east to Phu Tok. It's possible to **stay** in simple lodgings at the base of the temple, while the attached village sports a collection of simple **restaurants** and foodstalls.

Nakhon Phanom

Beyond Bung Kan, the river road rounds the hilly northeastern tip of Thailand before heading south through remote country where you're apt to find yourself stopping for water buffalo as often as for vehicles. The Mekong can only be glimpsed occasionally until you reach **NAKHON PHANOM** ("City of Mountains"), 313km from Nong Khai, a clean and prosperous town, which affords the finest view of the river in northern Isaan, framed against the giant ant-hills of the Lao mountains opposite.

The town makes a pleasant place to hang out, its quiet broad streets lined with some grand old public buildings, colonial-style houses and creaking wooden shophouses. A new bridge is being built across the Mekong, but for now you'll have to make do with the passenger **ferry** from the main pier across to **Khammouan** (Tha Khaek) in Laos (daily 8.30am–noon & 1–6pm; usually every half-hour or so, depending on demand; B60 one way), and thirty-day **Lao visas** can be bought on arrival for US$30–42 (see p.35). If you're not crossing the border, you can still appreciate the beautiful riverscape by joining one of the daily **boat trips** that depart from just south of the main pier at 5pm (B50; drinks available). Walking around town, you'll see several lit-up boat shapes around the place, a reminder of Nakhon Phanom's best-known festival, the **illuminated boat procession**, which is held on the river every year at the end of the rainy season, usually in late October. Around fifty boats of up to ten metres in length, adorned with elaborate lights and carrying offerings of food and flowers, are launched on the river in a spectacular display. The week-long celebrations – marking the end of the annual three-month Buddhist Rains Retreat – also feature colourful dragon-boat races along the Mekong, pitting Thai and Lao teams against each other.

Practicalities

The main **bus station** is about 1km west of the centre off the north side of Highway 22. You can fly to Nakhon Phanom from Bangkok with PB Air, who have an office by the bus terminal (ⓣ042 516300, ⓦwww.pbair.com); taxis from the **airport** 15km west of town cost B100 per person. **TAT** has an office in an impressive old mansion at 184/1 Thanon Suntorn Vichit, corner of Thanon Salaklang (daily 8.30am–4.30pm; ⓣ042 513490–1, ⓔtatphnom@tat.or.th), 500m north of the pier for Laos; they also cover Mukdahan province. Ask here for directions if you're interested in visiting the house where the Vietnamese national hero, Ho Chi Minh, lived in the late 1920s, when he was forced to go underground during the struggle for independence from France. Around 5km away on the southwestern edge of Nakhon Phanom at Ban Na Joke, the Vietnamese-style wooden house – terracotta roof tiles and no stilts – has recently been reconstructed, but is really only for Uncle Ho devotees; homestays at Ban Na Joke can be arranged through TAT. There's a **tourist police** office on the riverfront just north of the *Nakhonphanom River View Hotel* (ⓣ1155) and cheap **internet access** at Crab Technology opposite the *Grand Hotel* on Thanon Sri Thep.

The best of Nakhon Phanom's budget **hotels** is the friendly four-storey *Grand Hotel* at 210 Thanon Sri Thep (ⓣ042 511526, ⓕ042 511283; fan ❶, air-con ❷), a block back from the river just south of the passenger ferry, which has bright, clean rooms, all with hot water en suite. Top of the range is the eight-storey *Nakhonphanom River View* hotel (ⓣ042 522333–40, ⓦwww.nakhonphanomriverviewhotel.com; ❺, including breakfast), on Highway 212 towards the southern edge of town, with an outdoor swimming pool, internet access and smart, tasteful riverside rooms that boast facilities ranging from wi-fi to bathtubs.

Among several riverside **restaurants**, friendly *Satang*, a few hundred metres north of the *Nakhonphanom River View Hotel*, stands out, though it has no English menu: here you can sit at the pleasant tables out front or on an open balcony, tucking into specialities such as *thawt man kung* (deep-fried prawn cakes), *hor mok* (seafood curry soufflé) and *gataa rawn* (a sizzling hot plate of seafood). Otherwise, Thanon Fueng Nakhon, which runs west from the clocktower just north of the pier, has a choice of several simple places to eat and is a lively spot at night.

That Phanom

Fifty kilometres south of Nakhon Phanom, **THAT PHANOM**, a riverside village of weather-beaten wooden buildings, sprawls around Isaan's most important shrine. Popularly held to be one of the four sacred pillars of Thai religion (the other three are Chiang Mai's Wat Phra That Doi Suthep, Wat Mahathat in Nakhon Si Thammarat, and Wat Phra Phutthabat near Lopburi), **Wat Phra That Phanom** is a fascinating place of pilgrimage, especially at the time of the ten-day Phra That Phanom festival, usually in February, when thousands of people come to pay homage and enjoy themselves in the traditional holiday between harvesting and sowing; pilgrims believe that they must make the trip seven times during a full moon before they die.

This far-northeastern corner of Thailand may seem like a strange location for one of the country's holiest sites, but the wat was built to serve both Thais and Lao, as evidenced by the ample boat-landing in the village. Plenty of Lao still come across the river for the fascinating Monday and Thursday morning waterfront **market**, bringing for sale such items as wild animal skins, black pigs and herbal medicines, alongside the usual fruit and veg. The temple reputedly dates back to the eighth year after the death of the Buddha (535 BC), when five local princes built a simple brick chedi to house bits of his breastbone. It's been restored or rebuilt seven times, most recently after it collapsed during a rainstorm in 1975; the latest incarnation is in the form of a Lao *that*, 57m high, modelled on the That Luang in Vientiane.

From the river pier, a short ceremonial way leads under a Disneyesque victory arch erected by the Lao, past a stubby, brick replica of the original chedi on an island in a pond, then through the temple gates to the present **chedi**, which, as is the custom, faces water and the rising sun. A brick-and-plaster structure covered with white paint and gold floral decorations, the chedi looks like nothing so much as a giant, ornate table-leg turned upside down. From each of the four sides, an eye forming part of the traditional flame pattern stares down, and the whole thing is surmounted by an umbrella made of 16kg of gold, with precious gems and gold rings embedded in each tier. The chedi sits on a gleaming white marble platform, on which pilgrims say their prayers and leave every imaginable kind of offering to the relics. Look out for the brick reliefs in the shape of four-leaf clovers above three of the doorways in the base: on the northern side, Vishnu mounted on a garuda; on the western side, the four guardians of the earth putting offerings in the Buddha's alms bowl; and above the south door, a carving of the Buddha entering nirvana. At the corners of the chedi, brick plaques, carved in the tenth century but now heavily restored, tell the stories of the wat's princely founders.

Practicalities

The **bus station** has been unpopularly moved out to the western bypass, but all services from Nakhon Phanom and Mukdahan also stop in front of the temple; the Nakhon Phanom route is also covered by frequent songthaews, which gather to the north of the wat.

That Phanom's outstanding **accommodation** choice is the welcoming *Niyana Guest House* on Soi Weethee Sawrachon, which runs between the river-front road and Thanon Phanom Phanarak, a block north of the victory arch and the pier (ⓣ042 540880; ❶).The effusive owner, Niyana, is a fund of information and has bicycles for local exploration: popular routes are to Renu Nakhon, a weaving village with its own crude imitation of the Phra That Phanom, 15km northwest, and south down the backroads along the river.The pleasant rooms in her quiet, two-storey house are decorated with her own paintings and share hot-water bathrooms. Slightly upmarket and about 200m north along the river bank from *Niyana* is *Kritsada Resort* (ⓣ042 540038, ⓦwww.ksdresort.com; ❸), a compound of bright, well-kept rooms with air-con and hot water, some with fridges and small kitchen areas.

For somewhere to **eat**, there are several riverside restaurants to the north of *Niyana*'s and a night market just north of the temple. Otherwise, try *That Phanom Pochana* on the north side of the victory arch, a simple, clean, airy place which is good for a *phat thai* or a choice of Isaan, Thai and Chinese dishes. There are several **banks** with ATMs on Thanon Chayangkun near the wat, and a few **internet** places scattered around town, including one by the victory arch.

Mukdahan and around

Fifty kilometres downriver of That Phanom, **MUKDAHAN** is the last stop on the Mekong trail before Highway 212 heads off inland to Ubon Ratchathani, 170km to the south. You may feel as if you're in the Wild East out here, but this is one of the fastest-developing Thai provinces, owing to increasing friendship between Laos and Thailand and the proximity of **Savannakhet**, the second-biggest Lao city, just across the water. Very few farang visitors make it this far, though Mukdahan–Savannakhet is an officially sanctioned crossing to Laos, via the new bridge 7km north of town.

In the heart of town by the main river **pier**, the promenade overlooking Savannakhet is swamped by the daily **Indochina Market**, which is especially busy at weekends. On sale here are household goods and inexpensive ornaments, such as Vietnamese mother-of-pearl and Chinese ceramics, brought over from Laos; the market is also good for local fabrics like lengths of coarsely woven cotton in lovely muted colours, and expensive but very classy silks. At the southern edge of town rises the 65-metre-high **Mukdahan Tower** (*Ho Kaeo Mukdahan*; daily 8am–6pm; B20), a modern white edifice that looks somewhat out of place in the low-rise outskirts. Built in 1996 to commemorate the fiftieth anniversary of the king's accession to the throne, the tower houses an interesting array of historic artefacts from the Mukdahan area, including traditional Isaan costumes, pottery, coins, amulets, vicious-looking weaponry and fossils. The highlight, however, is the expansive view from the sixth floor – 50m high to reflect fifty years of Rama IX – over Mukdahan and the Mekong into Laos. On the smaller floor above is a much-revered, Sukhothai-style silver Buddha image, the Phra Phuttha Nawaming Mongkhon Mukdahan, fronted by the bone relics of famous monks in small glass containers.

Practicalities

Hourly buses from That Phanom and Ubon Ratchathani stop at the **bus terminal** about 2km northwest of the centre on Highway 212. This is also where you have to come if you're **going into Laos**: twelve buses a day (B45–50) cross the bridge to Savannakhet, though thirty-day visas on arrival (US$30–42; see p.35 for further details) are currently only available from Monday to Friday before noon. **Songthaews** shuttle between the bus station and Mukdahan Tower via the corner of Thanom Pitakpanomkhet, the main east–west street, and Thanon Samut Sakdarak, the main north–south street (B10–15 per person).

Mukdahan boasts an excellent budget **hotel**, the friendly, well-run *Huanum*, 36 Thanon Samut Sakdarak at the corner of Thanon Song Nang Sathit, a block back from the pier (Ⓣ042 611137, Ⓔpueeainbkk@hotmail.com; fan ❶, air-con ❷). Choose between simple, cheap rooms with shared cold-water bathrooms and smarter, quieter affairs overlooking the internal courtyard with air-con, en-suite hot showers and TVs. The lobby shelters a modern café, serving Western breakfasts, sandwiches and great espressos; wi-fi and **internet** access and **mountain bike** (B100 per day) and **motorbike rental** (B250 per day) are also available. West of the centre at 40 Thanon Pitakpanomkhet, *Ploy Palace Hotel* (Ⓣ042 631111, Ⓦwww.ploypalace.com; ❺, including breakfast), a grand pink edifice with a marbled lobby and tasteful bedrooms, is the best of Mukdahan's upmarket options, with good service, a rooftop restaurant with fine views and an outdoor swimming pool on the third floor.

Of the **restaurants** that dot the riverside promenade, Thanon Somranchaikhong, the best – and priciest – is the popular *Riverside*, 1km south of the pier, which serves excellent food on a pretty bougainvillea-covered terrace built out over the Mekong. En route you'll pass the friendly *Wine, Wild, Why*, a small restaurant-bar in a cute wooden house, with a terrace overlooking the river and a good range of Thai meals, notably salads. There's also a lively, popular night market, where you'll find deep-fried insects and plenty of other Isaan specialities, four blocks back from the pier along Thanon Song Nang Sathit. If you fancy a drink, don't be misled by the *Kingdom Country Club*'s name, opposite Mukdahan Tower: it's actually a good-time country-and-western-style bar with live Thai pop and folk music nightly.

Mukdahan National Park

If you're tired of concrete Isaan towns, stretch your legs exploring the strange rock formations and beautiful waterfalls of **Mukdahan National Park** (aka Phu Pha Terp; Ⓣ042 601753; B100), down a minor road (R2034) along the Mekong southeast of Mukdahan. Regular songthaews towards Don Tan pass the turning for the park 14km out of town, and from there it's just over a one-kilometre walk uphill to the park headquarters (you may be able to persuade the songthaew driver to make the detour). Just above the headquarters is a hillside of bizarre rocks, eroded into the shapes of toadstools, camels and crocodiles, which is great for scrambling around. The hillside also bears two remnants of the area's prehistory: the red finger-painting under one of the sandstone slabs is reckoned to be four thousand years old, while a small cage on the ground protects a 75-million-year-old fossil. Further up, the bare sandstone ridge seems to have been cut out of the surrounding forest by a giant lawnmower, but from October to December it's brought to life with a covering of grasses and wildflowers. A series of ladders leads up a cliff to the highest point, on a ridge at the western end of the park (a two-kilometre walk from the park headquarters), which affords a sweeping view over the rocks to the forests and paddies of Laos. Nearby, at least from July to November, is the park's most spectacular waterfall, a thirty-metre drop through thick vegetation, and a cave in which villagers have enshrined scores of Buddha images.

The park has just one standard-issue **bungalow** (sleeps six; B1800), and you can camp with your own gear. The simple **foodstalls** near headquarters will keep you going with fried rice and noodles.

Travel details

Trains

Buriram to: Ayutthaya (10 daily; 4hr 30min–7hr 45min); Bangkok (10 daily; 6hr–9hr 30min); Khorat (10 daily; 1hr 30min–2hr 40min); Pak Chong (10 daily; 2hr 30min–5hr); Si Saket (8 daily; 1hr 45min–3hr 20min); Surin (10 daily; 35–65min); Ubon Ratchathani (7 daily; 2hr 30min–4hr 15min).

Khon Kaen to: Ayutthaya (4 daily; 6hr–8hr 20min); Bangkok (4 daily; 7hr 30min–10hr 20min); Khorat (1 daily; 2hr 30min); Nong Khai (3 daily; 2hr 25min–3hr); Udon Thani (4 daily; 1hr 35min–2hr 15min).

Khorat (Nakhon Ratchasima) to: Ayutthaya (11 daily; 3hr 30min); Bangkok (11 daily; 4–5hr); Khon Kaen (1 daily; 3hr 20min); Pak Chong (11 daily; 1hr 30min–2hr); Si Saket (8 daily; 4hr–5hr 30min); Surin (10 daily; 2hr 5min–3hr 40min); Ubon Ratchathani (7 daily; 5hr–6hr 40min); Udon Thani (1 daily; 3hr 20min).

Nong Khai to: Ayutthaya (3 daily; 9hr 30min–11hr); Bangkok (3 daily; 11–13hr); Khon Kaen (4 daily; 2hr 45min); Khorat (1 daily; 6hr); Tha Naleng (Laos; 2 daily; 15min); Udon Thani (4 daily; 1hr).

Pak Chong (for Khao Yai) to: Ayutthaya (11 daily; 2hr–2hr 45min); Bangkok (11 daily; 3hr 30min–4hr 45min); Khorat (11 daily; 1hr 30min–2hr); Si Saket (8 daily; 4hr 20min–7hr 30min); Surin (10 daily; 3hr 10min–5hr 15min); Ubon Ratchathani (7 daily; 6hr 50min–8hr 40min); Udon Thani (1 daily; 6hr 40min).

Surin to: Ayutthaya (10 daily; 5hr 10min–9hr); Bangkok (10 daily; 7–10hr); Buriram (10 daily; 35–65min); Khorat (10 daily; 2hr–3hr 15min); Pak Chong (10 daily; 3hr 30min–5hr 30min); Si Saket (8 daily; 1hr 35min–2hr 10min); Ubon Ratchathani (7 daily; 2hr 30min–3hr 30min).

Ubon Ratchathani to: Ayutthaya (7 daily; 7–12hr); Bangkok (7 daily; 8hr 30min–14hr); Buriram (7 daily; 2hr 30min–4hr 15min); Khorat (7 daily; 5hr–6hr 40min); Si Saket (7 daily; 1hr 10min); Surin (7 daily; 2hr 30min–3hr 30min).

Udon Thani to: Ayutthaya (4 daily; 8–10hr); Bangkok (4 daily; 10–12hr); Khon Kaen (6 daily; 1hr 35min–2hr 15min); Khorat (3 daily; 4hr 30min–5hr 30min); Nong Khai (4 daily; 1hr).

Buses

Chiang Khan to: Bangkok (2 daily; 9–11hr); Khorat (hourly; 7hr); Loei (hourly, plus frequent songthaews; 45min–1hr).

Chong Mek to: Bangkok (1 daily; 11hr); Phibun Mangsahan (every 30min; 90min).

Khong Chiam to: Bangkok (4 daily; 11hr).

Khon Kaen to: Bangkok (26 daily; 6–7hr); Chiang Mai (9 daily; 11–12hr); Khorat (hourly; 2hr 30min–3hr); Loei (every 30min; 4hr); Nong Khai (10 daily; 2–3hr); Phitsanulok (6 daily; 5–6hr); Rayong (13 daily; 10–12hr); Surin (hourly; 4hr 30min–6hr); Ubon Ratchathani (9 daily; 4–6hr); Udon Thani (every 30min; 1hr 30min–2hr).

Khorat to: Bangkok (every 20min; 4–5hr); Ban Tako (for Phanom Rung; every 30min; 2hr); Buriram (every 30min; 3hr); Chanthaburi (8 daily; 6–8hr); Chiang Mai (9 daily; 12–14hr); Chiang Rai (5 daily; 14–16hr); Dan Kwian (every 30min; 30min); Khon Kaen (hourly; 2hr 30min–3hr); Lopburi (12 daily; 3hr 30min); Nakhon Phanom (3 daily; 8hr); Nong Khai (11 daily; 6–8hr); Pattaya (8 daily; 6–8hr); Phimai (every 30min; 1hr–1hr 30min); Phitsanulok (9 daily; 7–9hr); Rayong (for Ko Samet; 8 daily; 6–8hr); Si Racha (7 daily; 5hr); Surin (every 30min; 4–5hr); Ubon Ratchathani (10 daily; 5–7hr); Udon Thani (11 daily; 3hr 30min–5hr).

Loei to: Bangkok (20 daily; 10hr); Chiang Khan (hourly, plus frequent songthaews; 1hr); Chiang Mai (6 daily; 9–11hr); Chiang Rai (4 daily; 9–12hr); Khon Kaen (every 30min; 4hr); Nong Khai (2–3 daily via Pak Chom; 6–7hr); Phitsanulok (3 daily; 4hr); Sang Khom (2–3 daily; 3hr); Udon Thani (every 30min; 3–4hr).

Mukdahan to: Bangkok (20 daily; 11hr); Khon Kaen (every 30min; 4hr); Khorat (20 daily; 6hr); Nakhon Phanom (hourly; 2hr); That Phanom (hourly; 1hr 20min); Ubon Ratchathani (roughly hourly; 2–3hr); Udon Thani (5 daily; 4hr–4hr 30min).

Nakhon Phanom to: Bangkok (17 daily; 12hr); Khon Kaen (5 daily; 5hr 30min); Mukdahan (hourly; 2hr); Nong Khai (7 daily; 6hr); That Phanom (hourly; 1hr); Ubon Ratchathani (roughly hourly; 5hr); Udon Thani (14 daily; 5hr).

Nong Khai to: Bangkok (20 daily; 11hr); Bung Kan (hourly; 2hr); Khon Kaen (20 daily; 3hr 30min); Khorat (20 daily; 6hr 30min); Loei (2–3 daily via Pak Chom; 7hr); Nakhon Phanom (7 daily; 6hr); Rayong (19 daily; 12hr); Sang Khom (2–3 daily; 3–4hr); Udon Thani (every 30min; 1hr); Vientiane; (Laos; 6 daily; 1hr).

Sang Khom to: Bangkok (2 daily; 10hr); Loei (2–3 daily via Pak Chom; 3hr); Nong Khai (2–3 daily; 3–4hr).

That Phanom to: Bangkok (4 daily; 12hr); Mukdahan (hourly; 1hr 20min); Nakhon Phanom (hourly; 1hr); Ubon Ratchathani (hourly; 3–4hr); Udon Thani (4 daily; 4–5 hr).

Ubon Ratchathani to: Bangkok (hourly; 10–12hr); Chiang Mai (6 daily; 17–18hr); Kantharalak (every 15min; 1hr 30min); Khon Kaen (19 daily; 4–6hr); Khorat (hourly; 5–7hr); Mukdahan (every 30min; 2–3hr); Pattaya (10 daily; 12hr–13hr 30min); Phibun Mangsahan (every 25min; 1hr); Rayong (10 daily; 14hr); Si Saket (every 45min; 45min–1hr); Surin (at least 7 daily; 2hr 30min–3hr); Udon Thani (19 daily; 5–7hr); Yasothon (19 daily; 1hr 30min–2hr).

Udon Thani to: Bangkok (every 30min; 9hr); Chiang Mai (4 daily; 11–13hr); Chiang Rai (4 daily; 12–14hr); Khon Kaen (every 30min; 1hr 30min–2hr); Khorat (hourly; 3hr 30min–5hr); Loei (every 30min; 3–4hr); Mukdahan (5 daily; 4hr–4hr 30min); Nakhon Phanom (14 daily; 5hr); Nong Khai (every 30min; 1hr); Phitsanulok (5 daily; 7hr); Rayong (7 daily; 12hr); Sakon Nakhon (every 20min; 3hr); That Phanom (4 daily; 4–5hr); Ubon Ratchathani (9 daily; 6hr); Vientiane, (Laos; 6 daily; 1hr 30min).

Yasothon to: Khon Kaen (hourly; 3hr–3hr 30min).

Flights

Buriram to: Bangkok (3 weekly; 55min).

Khon Kaen to: Bangkok (3 daily; 55min).

Nakhon Phanom to: Bangkok (1–2 daily; 1hr 5min).

Roi Et to: Bangkok (daily; 1hr).

Ubon Ratchathani to: Bangkok (5 daily; 1hr 5min).

Udon Thani to: Bangkok (7 daily; 1hr); Chiang Mai (daily; 1hr); Louang Phabang (Laos; 2 weekly; 1hr).

6

Southern Thailand: the Gulf coast

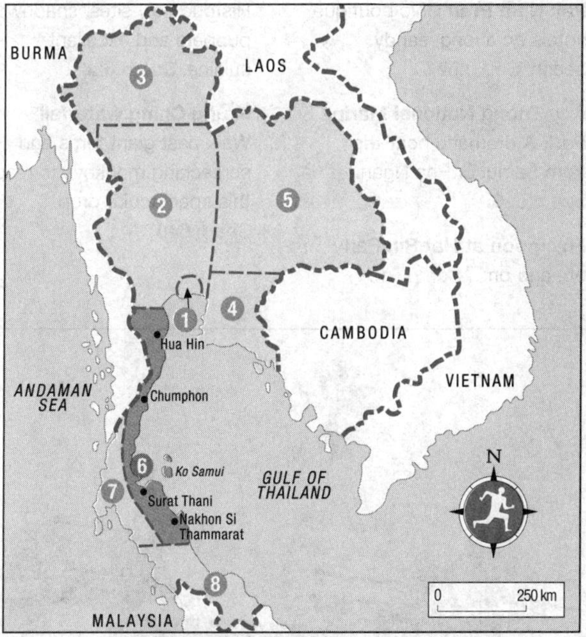

CHAPTER 6

Highlights

* **Phetchaburi** Charming historic town, boasting several fine old working temples. See p.565
* **Leisurely seafood lunches** At the squid-pier restaurants in Hua Hin or under the trees at Ban Krud. See p.576 & p.584
* **Pak Nam Pran** Chic boutique hotels on a long, sandy beach. See p.577
* **Ang Thong National Marine Park** A dramatic boat-trip from Samui or Pha Ngan. See p.596
* **Full moon at Hat Rin** Party on, and on... See p.615
* **Ao Thong Nai Pan on Ko Pha Ngan** Beautiful, secluded bay with good accommodation. See p.621
* **A boat-trip round Ko Tao** Satisfying exploration and great snorkelling. See p.628
* **Nakhon Si Thammarat** Historic holy sites, shadow puppets and excellent cuisine. See p.634
* **Krung Ching waterfall** Walk past giant ferns and screeching monkeys to reach this spectacular drop. See p.640

▲ Wat Yai Suwannaram, Phetchaburi

6

Southern Thailand: the Gulf coast

Southern Thailand's gently undulating **Gulf coast** is famed above all for the Samui archipelago, three small idyllic islands lying off the most prominent hump of the coastline. This is the country's most popular seaside venue for independent travellers, and a lazy stay in a Samui beachfront bungalow is so seductive a prospect that most people overlook the attractions of the mainland, where the sheltered sandy beaches and warm clear water rival the top sunspots in most countries. Added to that you'll find scenery dominated by forested mountains that rise abruptly behind the coastal strip, especially impressive in **Khao Sam Roi Yot National Park**, and a sprinkling of historic sights – notably the crumbling temples of ancient **Phetchaburi**. Though not a patch on the islands further south, the stretch of coast around **Cha-am** and **Hua Hin** is popular with weekending Thais escaping the capital and is crammed with condos, high-rise hotels and bars, not to mention a large population of foreign tourists. Far quieter and preferable are the sophisticated little beach resort of **Pak Nam Pran**, just a short distance further south, the welcoming town of **Prachuap Khiri Khan**, fronted by a lovely bay and flanked by an equally appealing beach, and laid-back, lightly developed **Ban Krud**.

Of the islands, **Ko Samui** is by far the most naturally beautiful, with its long white-sand beaches and arching fringes of palm trees. The island's beauty has not gone unnoticed by tourist developers of course, and its varied spread of accommodation these days draws as many package tourists and second-homers as backpackers. In recent years the next island out, **Ko Pha Ngan**, has drawn increasing numbers of backpackers away from its neighbour: its bungalows are generally simpler and cost less than Ko Samui's, and it offers a few stunning beaches with a more laid-back atmosphere. The island's southeastern headland, **Hat Rin**, has no less than three white-sand beaches to choose from, but now provides all the amenities the demanding traveller could want, not to mention its notorious full moon parties. The furthest inhabited island of the archipelago, **Ko Tao**, has taken off as a **scuba-diving** centre, but despite a growing nightlife and restaurant scene, still has the feel of a small, rugged and isolated outcrop.

Tucked away beneath the islands, **Nakhon Si Thammarat**, the cultural capital of the south, is well worth a short detour from the main routes through the centre of the peninsula – it's a sophisticated city of grand old temples,

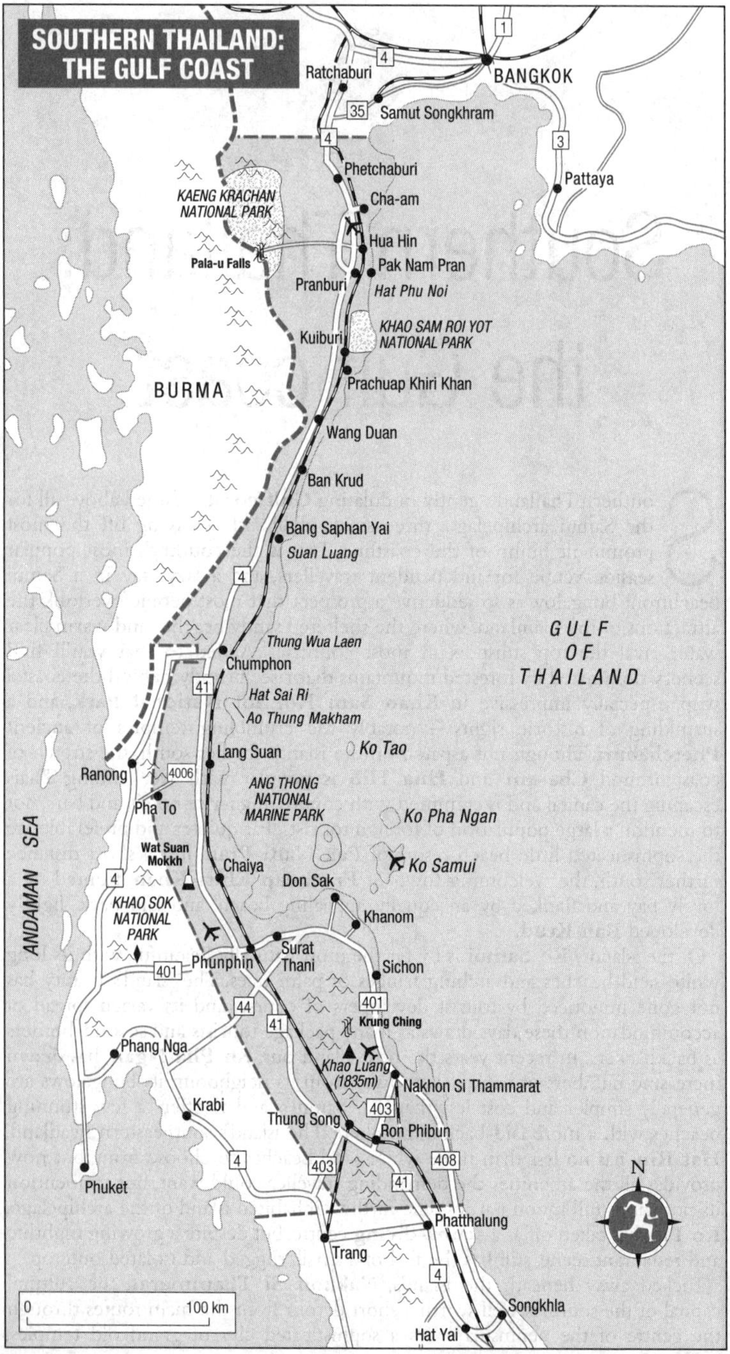
SOUTHERN THAILAND:
THE GULF COAST
BANGKOK
Ratchaburi
Samut Songkhram
Pattaya
Phetchaburi
Cha-am
KAENG KRACHAN
NATIONAL PARK
Hua Hin
Pak Nam Pran
Pala-u Falls
Pranburi
Hat Phu Noi
KHAO SAM ROI YOT
NATIONAL PARK
Kuiburi
BURMA
Prachuap Khiri Khan
Wang Duan
Ban Krud
Bang Saphan Yai
Suan Luang
GULF
OF
THAILAND
Thung Wua Laen
Chumphon
Hat Sai Ri
Ao Thung Makham
Lang Suan
Ko Tao
Ranong
ANG THONG
NATIONAL
MARINE PARK
Pha To
Ko Pha Ngan
ANDAMAN SEA
Wat Suan
Mokkh
Ko Samui
Chaiya
Don Sak
KHAO SOK
NATIONAL
PARK
Khanom
Surat
Thani
Phunphin
Sichon
Krung Ching
Phang Nga
Khao Luang
(1835m)
Nakhon Si Thammarat
Krabi
Thung Song
Ron Phibun
Phuket
N
Phatthalung
Trang
Songkhla
Hat Yai
0
100 km
1
4
35
3
41
4006
401
44
403
408

delicious cuisine and distinctive handicrafts. With its small but significant Muslim population, and machine-gun dialect, Nakhon begins the transition into Thailand's deep south.

The **railway** from Bangkok connects all the mainland towns, including a branch line to Nakhon; nearly all services depart from Hualamphong Station, but a few slow trains (not shown on the English-language timetable) use Thonburi Station. You can also head south from Kanchanaburi by train, changing at Ban Pong (not listed on English-language timetables) or Nakhon Pathom. **Bus** services, along highways 4 (also known as the Phetkasem Highway, or usually Thanon Phetkasem when passing through towns) and 41, are generally faster and more frequent than the trains. From Bangkok, Thai Airways and Air Asia **fly** to Surat Thani, Nok Air to Nakhon Si Thammarat, while Bangkok Airways operates a variety of popular routes to Ko Samui's airport, which is now also served by Thai Airways from the capital. Daily boats run to the islands from two jumping-off points: **Surat Thani**, 650km from Bangkok, has a better choice of routes, but the faster alternatives from **Chumphon**, 200km nearer the capital, take you straight to the tranquillity of Ko Tao.

The Gulf coast has a slightly different **climate** from the Andaman coast and much of the rest of Thailand, being hit heavily by the northeast monsoon's rains, especially in November, when it's best to avoid this part of the country altogether. Most times during the rest of the year should see pleasant, if changeable, weather, with some effects of the southwest monsoon felt on the islands between May and October. Late December to April is the driest period, and is therefore the region's high season, which also includes July and August.

Phetchaburi

Straddling the Phet River about 120km south of Bangkok, the provincial capital of **PHETCHABURI** (sometimes "Phetburi") has been settled ever since the eleventh century, when the Khmers ruled the region, but only really got going six hundred years later, when it flourished as a trading post between the Andaman Sea ports and Burma and Ayutthaya. Despite periodic incursions from the Burmese, the town gained a reputation as a cultural centre – as the ornamentation of its older temples testifies – and after the new capital was established in Bangkok it became a favourite country retreat of Rama IV, who had a hilltop palace built here in the 1850s. Modern Phetchaburi's main claim to fame is as one of Thailand's finest sweet-making centres, the essential ingredient for its assortment of *khanom* being the sugar extracted from the sweet-sapped palms that cover the province. This being very much a cottage industry, today's downtown Phetchaburi has lost relatively little of the ambience that so attracted Rama IV: the central riverside area is hemmed in by historic wats in varying states of disrepair, along with plenty of traditional wooden shophouses.

Despite the attractions of its old quarter, Phetchaburi gets few overnight visitors as most people see it on a day-trip from Bangkok, Hua Hin or Cha-am. It's also possible to combine a day in Phetchaburi with an early-morning expedition from Bangkok to the floating markets of Damnoen Saduak, 40km north; budget tour operators in Bangkok's Thanon Khao San area offer this option as a day-trip package for about B600 per person. The town sees more overnighters during the **Phra Nakhon Khiri Fair**, spread over at least five days in February; it features parades in historic costumes, cooking demonstrations and traditional entertainments such as *likay* and *lakhon*.

Arrival, information and transport

Arriving by **bus**, you may be dropped in one of four places. Through-buses on Highway 4 will set you down at the corner of Thanon Banda-It on the western edge of town. Non-air-con buses to and from Cha-am and Hua Hin use the small terminal in the town centre, less than ten minutes' walk from Chomrut Bridge. The **terminal** for Phetchaburi–Bangkok **air-con buses** is also about ten minutes' walk from Chomrut Bridge, just off Thanon Rajwithi. If you're coming here from Kanchanaburi, you can avoid Bangkok by heading for Ratchaburi, where you can catch an air-con bus that'll put you off at a terminal on the west side of Khao Wang. Phetchaburi **train station** is on the northern outskirts of town.

There's no TAT office in town, but *Rabieng Rimnum Guest House* is a good source of local **information**. **Internet access** is available, for example, at an unnamed shop on Thanon Phongsuriya, five minutes' walk east of Chomrut Bridge. To see the major temples in a day and have sufficient energy left for climbing Khao Wang, you might want to hire a **samlor** for a couple of hours, at about B100 per hour. Alternatively make use of the public **songthaews** that circulate round the town, or **rent** a **bicycle** or **motorbike** from *Rabieng Rimnum Guest House.*

Accommodation

Most travellers **stay** at the *Rabieng Rimnum (Rim Nam) Guest House*, centrally located at 1 Thanon Chisa-in, on the southwest corner of Chomrut Bridge (Ⓣ032 425707 or 089 919 7446, Ⓔrabieng@hotmail.com, Ⓦwww.rabiengrimnum.com; ❶). Occupying a century-old house next to the Phet River and, less appealingly, a noisy main road, the guest house offers nine simple rooms with shared bathrooms, lots of local information and the best restaurant

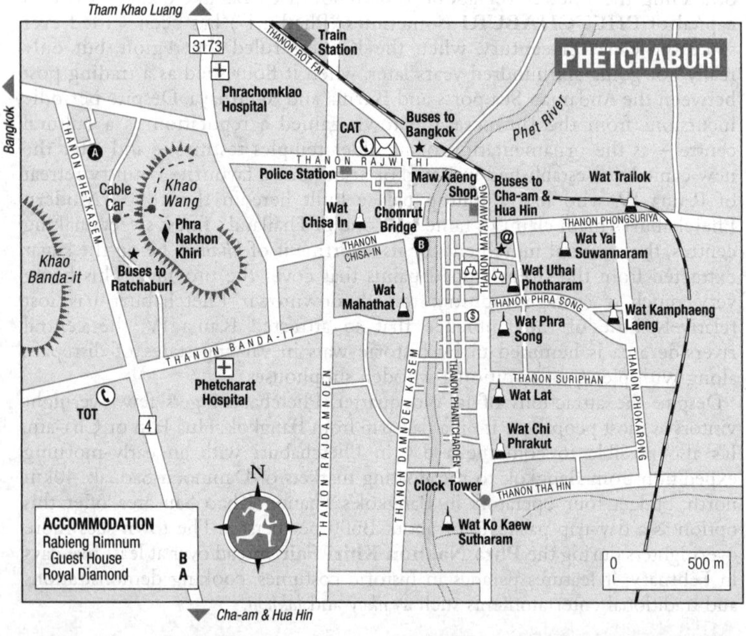

in town; it also organizes day-trips and overnight visits to Kaeng Krachan National Park for birdwatching and hiking. If *Rabieng Rimnum* is full, ask the owners about the sporadically open *Ban Thai Guest House* about 1km south just off Thanon Damnoen Kasem. West of Khao Wang, on the outskirts of town, is Phetchaburi's most upmarket option, the *Royal Diamond* (ⓣ032 411061, ⓦwww.royaldiamondhotel.com; ⑤), which has comfortable air-con rooms with hot water, TVs and fridges and is located on Soi Sam Chao Phet, just off the Phetkasem Highway.

The Town

The pinnacles and rooftops of the town's thirty-odd **wats** are visible in every direction, but only a few are worth stopping off to investigate; the following description takes in the top three, which can be seen on a leisurely two-hour circular walk beginning from Chomrut Bridge. Phetchaburi's other significant sight, the palace-museum at Phra Nakhon Khiri, is on a hill about 1km west of the bridge.

Wat Yai Suwannaram

Of all Phetchaburi's temples, the most attractive is the still-functioning seventeenth-century **Wat Yai Suwannaram** on Thanon Phongsuriya, about 700m east of Chomrut Bridge. The temple's fine old teak **sala** has elaborately carved doors, bearing a gash reputedly inflicted by the Burmese in 1760 as they plundered their way towards Ayutthaya. Across from the *sala* and hidden behind high, whitewashed walls stands the windowless Ayutthaya-style bot. The bot compound overlooks a pond, in the middle of which stands a small but well-preserved scripture library, or **ho trai**: such structures were built on stilts over water to prevent ants and other insects destroying the precious documents. Enter the walled compound from the south and make a clockwise tour of the cloisters filled with Buddha statues before entering the bot itself via the eastern doorway (if the door is locked, one of the monks will get the key for you). The **bot** is supported by intricately patterned red and gold pillars and contains a remarkable, if rather faded, set of murals, depicting Indra, Brahma and other lower-ranking divinities ranged in five rows of ascending importance. Once you've admired the interior, walk to the back of the bot, passing behind the central cluster of Buddha images, to find another Buddha image seated against the back wall: climb the steps in front of this image to get a close-up of the left foot, which for some reason was cast with six toes.

Wat Kamphaeng Laeng

Fifteen minutes' walk east and then south of Wat Yai, the five tumbledown prangs of **Wat Kamphaeng Laeng** on Thanon Phra Song mark out Phetchaburi as the probable southernmost outpost of the Khmer empire. Built to enshrine Hindu deities and set out in a cruciform arrangement facing east, the laterite corncob-style prangs were later adapted for Buddhist use, as can be seen from the two that now house Buddha images. There has been some attempt to restore a few of the carvings and false balustraded windows, but these days worshippers congregate in the modern whitewashed wat behind these shrines, leaving the atmospheric and appealingly quaint collection of decaying prangs and casuarina topiary to chickens, stray dogs and the occasional tourist.

Wat Mahathat

Heading west along Thanon Phra Song from Wat Kamphaeng Laeng, across the river you can see the prangs of Phetchaburi's most fully restored and important temple, **Wat Mahathat**, long before you reach them. Boasting the "Mahathat" title only since 1954 – when the requisite Buddha relics were donated by the king – it was probably founded in the fourteenth century, but suffered badly at the hands of the Burmese. The five landmark prangs at its heart are adorned with stucco figures of mythical creatures, though these are nothing compared with those on the roofs of the main viharn and the bot. Instead of tapering off into the usual serpentine *chofa*, the gables are studded with miniature *thep* and *deva* figures (angels and gods), which add an almost mischievous vitality to the place. In a similar vein, a couple of gold-embossed crocodiles snarl above the entrance to the bot, and a caricature carving of a bespectacled man rubs shoulders with mythical giants in a relief around the base of the gold Buddha, housed in a separate mondop nearby.

Khao Wang

Dominating Phetchaburi's western outskirts stands Rama IV's palace, a stew of mid-nineteenth-century Thai and European styles scattered over the crest of the hill known as **Khao Wang** ("Palace Hill"). During his day, the royal entourage would struggle its way up the steep brick path to the summit, but now there's a **cable car** (daily 8.30am–4.30pm; B70 return, including admission to Phra Nakhon Khiri), which starts from the western flank of the hill off Highway 4; there's also a path up the eastern flank, starting near Thanon Rajwithi. If you do walk up the hill, be warned that hundreds of quite aggressive monkeys hang out at its base and on the path to the top.

Up top, the wooded hill is littered with wats, prangs, chedis, whitewashed gazebos and lots more, in an ill-assorted combination of architectural idioms – the prang-topped viharn, washed all over in burnt sienna, is particularly ungainly. Whenever the king came on an excursion here, he stayed in the airy summer house, **Phra Nakhon Khiri** (daily 9am–4pm; B40; Ⓦwww.thailandmuseum.com), with its Mediterranean-style shutters and verandas. Now a museum, it houses a moderately interesting collection of ceramics, furniture and other artefacts given to the royal family by foreign friends. Besides being cool and breezy, Khao Wang also proved to be a good star-gazing spot, so Rama IV, a keen astronomer (see also p.583), had an open-sided, glass-domed observatory built close to his sleeping quarters.

Eating

Phetchaburi's best **restaurant** is the *Rabieng Rimnum* (daily 8.30am–1am), an airy, wooden house with riverside tables attached to the guest house of the same name. It offers a long and interesting menu of inexpensive Thai dishes, from banana-blossom salad to tasty sugar-palm fruit curry with prawns, and is deservedly popular with local diners.

Almost half the shops in the town centre stock Phetchaburi's famous **sweet snacks** (*khanom*), as do many of the souvenir stalls crowding the base of Khao Wang and vendors at the day market on Thanon Matayawong. The most well known local speciality is *maw kaeng* (best sampled from a shop on the west side of Thanon Matayawong just north of Phongsuriya), a baked sweet egg custard made with mung beans and coconut and sometimes flavoured with lotus seeds, durian or taro. Other Phetchaburi classics to look out for include *khanom taan*, small, steamed, saffron-coloured cakes made with local palm sugar, coconut and rice flour, and wrapped in banana-leaf cases; and *thong yot*, orange balls of palm sugar and baked egg-yolk. The town is also known for **khao jae**: originally a Mon dish, it consists of rice in chilled, flower-scented water served with delicate, fried side dishes, such as shredded Chinese radish and balls of shrimp paste, dried fish and palm sugar. It's available at the day market until sold out, usually around 3pm.

Cha-am and around

Forever in the shadow of its more famous neighbour, Hua Hin, 25km to the south, the resort of **CHA-AM** is nevertheless very popular with Thais on short breaks, and it sports a few package-holiday high-rises and Western-style restaurants for Europeans, too. Mostly, though, it's weekending families and partying student groups from Bangkok who eat and drink at the rows of umbrella-shaded tables and deckchairs on the sand, or brave the sea on banana boats or rubber tyres. The long, straight beach here is pleasantly shaded, though rather gritty and very narrow at high tide, and the water is perfectly swimmable, if not pristine. During the week the pace of life in Cha-am is slow, and it's easy to find a solitary spot under the thick canopy of casuarinas, particularly at the northerly end of the beach, but that's rarely possible at weekends, when prices shoot up and traffic thickens considerably.

Arrival and information

Through-**buses** and local services to and from Hua Hin and Phetchaburi stop on Thanon Phetkasem (Highway 4), close to the junction with Thanon Narathip, the main access road to the beach, 1km to the east. Bangkok–Cha-am air-con buses use the depot at the little plaza off the beachfront Thanon Ruamchit, just south of Thanon Narathip. If you're heading for Bangkok, you could also phone for the Hua Hin–Victory Monument air-con minibus to pick you up (see p.572). The **train station**, a few blocks west of the main Phetkasem–Narathip junction, is not included on the State Railways' English-language timetables but a handful of services a day, from either Hualamphong or Thonburi stations in Bangkok, stop there.

Cha-am has a functional pocket of development around the Phetkasem bus stop, but Thanon Ruamchit's three-kilometre seaside promenade is where you'll find most of the hotels, restaurants and a few other tourist-oriented businesses; Thanon Ruamchit's sois are numbered according to whether they're north or south of Thanon Narathip. There are **internet** terminals inside the CAT **phone office**, which is 200m west along Thanon Narathip from the seafront, and at several shops along Thanon Ruamchit – notably the photo shop sandwiched between the 7-Eleven at the Thanon Narathip junction and Siam Commercial Bank. A number of shops along the beachfront rent **motorbikes** as well as **bicycles**, tandems and even three-person bikes. The local **TAT** office (daily 8.30am–4.30pm; Ⓣ032 471005, Ⓔtatphet@tat.or.th), which theoretically provides information about Phetchaburi and Prachuap Khiri Khan provinces (including Hua Hin), is on Highway 4, about 1km south of the centre.

Accommodation

There are no obvious backpacker-oriented guest houses in Cha-am; instead you'll find mainly small, mid-range hotels, concentrated on Thanon Ruamchit and the adjoining sois, and upmarket, out-of-town resorts. Many Cha-am hotels give a fifteen- to thirty-percent discount from Sunday to Thursday.

Alila Cha-am 6km north of central Cha-am ⓣ032 709555, ⓦwww.alilahotels.com. Sleek, eco-friendly hideaway, featuring a triumphal, white-marble staircase up to the lobby and a huge reflective pool as its centrepiece. The accommodation blocks have a striking cubic design but are very comfortable for all that, while creative, beautifully presented food is served at the breezy restaurant, *Clouds Loft*. There are two swimming pools (plus seven villas with private pools), a spa and an events centre offering cooking classes, kite flying and bicycles. 9

Dusit Resort Hua Hin 14km south of Cha-am and 9km north of Hua Hin at 1349 Thanon Phetkasem ⓣ032 520009, ⓦhuahin.dusit.com. One of the most luxurious spots on this stretch of coast, with 300 large, elegant rooms set around a tropical garden and lotus-filled lagoon. Facilities include four restaurants, a huge pool and children's pool, a spa, fitness centre, watersports, horse-riding, tennis and squash courts and an Avis car rental desk. 9

Golden Beach Cha-am Hotel Just south of Soi Cha-am North 8 at 208/14 Thanon Ruamchit ⓣ032 433833, ⓦwww.goldenbeachchaam.com. Good-value 20-storey hotel with a full-height atrium, a swimming pool, gym and internet access, set back from the promenade. The nicely appointed rooms have air-con, hot water, minibars and TVs, as well as balconies, most with sea-views. Breakfast included. 6

Kaenchan Beach Hotel North of Soi Cha-am North 7 at 241/4 Thanon Ruamchit ⓣ032 470777–9. Stylish mid-sized hotel, with a papaya-coloured facade, a sixth-floor swimming pool and appealing, sleekly furnished rooms, all with air-con, TV, fridge and hot water, some with sea view. Also has some cheaper terraced bungalows in the garden behind. 4–5

Nirandorn 3 Just south of the Narathip junction on Thanon Ruamchit ⓣ032 470300, ⓕ032 470303. Clean, well-maintained hotel rooms and a few tightly packed, motel-style bungalows, mostly decorated in crisp, modern whites and browns, with air-con, TVs, fridges and hot water; all rooms in the hotel block are sea-facing, sporting balconies and deckchairs. 4

Eating and drinking

The choice of **restaurants** in Cha-am is not a patch on the range you get in Hua Hin, but for a change from hotel food you might want to drop by *Poom*, north of Soi Cha-am North 6 at 274/1 Thanon Ruamchit, which serves a good selection of Thai-style seafood dishes (mostly B100–250) on its sea-view terrace – try the shrimps with garlic. Further north beyond Soi 7, *O-Zone* is a welcoming and popular bar-restaurant; attractions here include mellow live music early evening, followed by bands playing Thai and Western pop until midnight, and a menu that encompasses a few Western dishes such as spaghetti with meat sauce, one-plate Thai dishes and more complex offerings such as crispy fried catfish salad. On Thanon Chao Lay (which parallels Thanon Ruamchit), south of Narathip and the Bangkok bus depot, look out for the ornate garden of *Crawford's Irish Bar* (or call ⓣ032 471774 for a free pick-up); here you can eat Irish stew, steak and kidney pie and Thai food, play pool or watch big-screen sports, and in high season listen to a live band playing Sixties and Seventies covers and Irish ballads.

Phra Ratchaniwet Marukhathaiyawan

Ten kilometres south of Cha-am, on the way to Hua Hin, stands the lustrous seaside palace of Rama VI, **Phra Ratchaniwet Marukhathaiyawan** (aka Mrigadayavan Palace; daily except Wed 8.30am–4.30pm; B30), a rarely visited place, despite the easy access; the half-hourly Cha-am–Hua Hin buses stop within a couple of kilometres' walk of the palace at the sign for Rama VI Camp – just follow the road through the army compound.

Designed by the king himself in a Victorianized Thai style, but completed by an Italian architect in 1923, the complex of sixteen golden teak pavilions stands on over a thousand concrete columns to keep out ants. It's often referred to as "the palace of love and hope" as Rama VI first visited with his pregnant consort, who later miscarried, but it was abandoned to the corrosive sea air after the king's death in 1925. Restoration work began in the 1970s, and today most of the structure looks as it once did, a stylish composition of verandas and latticework painted in pastel shades of beige and blue, with an emphasis on cool simplicity. The spacious open hall in the north wing, hung with chandeliers and encircled by a first-floor balcony, was once used as a theatre, and the upstairs rooms, now furnished only with a few black-and-white portraits from the royal family photo album, were given over to royal attendants. The king stayed in the centre room, with the best sea view and access to the promenade, while the south wing contained the queen's apartments.

Hua Hin

Thailand's oldest beach resort, **HUA HIN** used to be little more than an overgrown fishing village with one exceptionally grand hotel, but the arrival of mass tourism, high-rise hotels and farang-managed hostess bars has made a serious dent in its once idiosyncratic charm. With the far superior beaches of Ko Samui, Krabi and Ko Samet so close at hand, there's little to draw the dedicated sunseeker here. The town's most distinctive attractions are its squid-pier restaurants and guest houses on Thanon Naretdamri, characterful spots to stay or enjoy fine seafood (though in recent years plans have been mooted to knock them down and build a shopping plaza), while at the other end of the scale the former *Railway Hotel* provides all the atmosphere you can afford. In addition, the town makes a convenient base for day-trips to Khao Sam Roi Yot National Park to the south and Pala-u Falls in Kaeng Krachan National Park to the west. If none of that appeals, you might consider stopping by for Hua Hin's well-respected **jazz festival** in June (Ⓦ www.huahinjazzfest.com).

The **royal family** were Hua Hin's main visitors at the start of the twentieth century, but the place became more widely popular in the 1920s, when the

▲ Jetty restaurants, Hua Hin

opening of the Bangkok–Malaysia rail line made short excursions to the beach much more viable. The Victorian-style *Railway Hotel* was opened in 1922, originally as a necessary overnight stop on the three-day journey to Malaysia. At the same time Rama VI commissioned the nine-hole Royal Hua Hin Golf Course (now 18 holes; ⓣ032 512475) to the west of the station, and in 1926 Rama VII had his own summer palace, Klai Klangwon (Far from Worries), erected at the northern end of the beach. It was here, ironically, that Rama VII was staying in 1932 when the coup was launched in Bangkok against the system of absolute monarchy. The current king lives here most of the time now, apparently preferring the sea breezes to the traffic fumes of the capital, which means that the navy is on constant guard duty in the resort and the police are also on their best behaviour; consequently both Thais and expats consider Hua Hin an especially safe place to live and do business – hence the number of farang-oriented real estate agencies in the area.

Arrival and information

All services to the south from Bangkok stop at photogenic Hua Hin **train station**, which has changed little since it was built in the 1920s. It's a ten-minute walk east to the seafront from here, or hop on a motorbike taxi, samlor, tuk-tuk or songthaew. Tiny Hua Hin **airport** (ⓣ032 522300–1) is 6km north of town, beside the Phetkasem Highway, and is currently served only by little SGA Cessna planes (ⓦwww.sga.co.th or www.nokair.com; 2 daily; 50min; B2300) to and from Bangkok's Suvarnabhumi Airport. Green songthaews run to Thanon Sa Song in town from the airport every twenty minutes.

Most government and many private **buses** use the main Baw Khaw Saw terminal, which is well to the south of the centre, between Thanon Phetkasem sois 96 and 98. These include second-class air-con services to and from Bangkok's Southern Bus Terminal, but much faster, first-class air-con buses to the same place, stopping only at Phetchaburi, leave from beside the *Sri Phetkasem* hotel on Thanon Sa Song; nearby, you'll find non-air-con buses to Pranburi (for a faster, air-con service, head for the Baw Khaw Saw). Non-air-con Cha-am and Phetchaburi buses from the Baw Khaw Saw also pick up at a spot just north of the junction of Thanon Phetkasem and Thanon Chomsin, while private **air-con minibuses** to and from Bangkok's Victory Monument are down a soi just behind (departing when full, usually around every 30min; 2hr 30min; B200; ⓣ086 992 7422). **Lomprayah** (ⓣ032 553739, ⓦwww.lomprayah.com; book at their office on Soi Kanjanomai or through most travel agents) runs a twice-daily bus and catamaran service, beginning in Bangkok and picking up at Hua Hin's clocktower (daily at 8.30am and midnight) to Ko Tao (B850), Ko Pha Ngan (B1200) and Ko Samui (B1400) via Chumphon; you could catch one of their buses in the reverse direction to Banglamphu at 4.45pm or 9.45pm (B400).

There's a **tourist information** office (Mon–Fri 8.30am–8pm, Sat & Sun 9am–5pm; ⓣ032 511047, ext 100) in the local government buildings on the corner of Thanon Damnern Kasem and Thanon Phetkasem, with a satellite office just up Phetkasem at the clocktower (same times). TAT (ⓦwww.tourismthailand.org) also plan to open an information office in Hua Hin. Among Hua Hin's many English-language **publications** and maps, the *Hua Hin Pocket Guide*, a free, monthly booklet, is worth looking out for, while ⓦwww.huahinafterdark.com is a useful **website**.

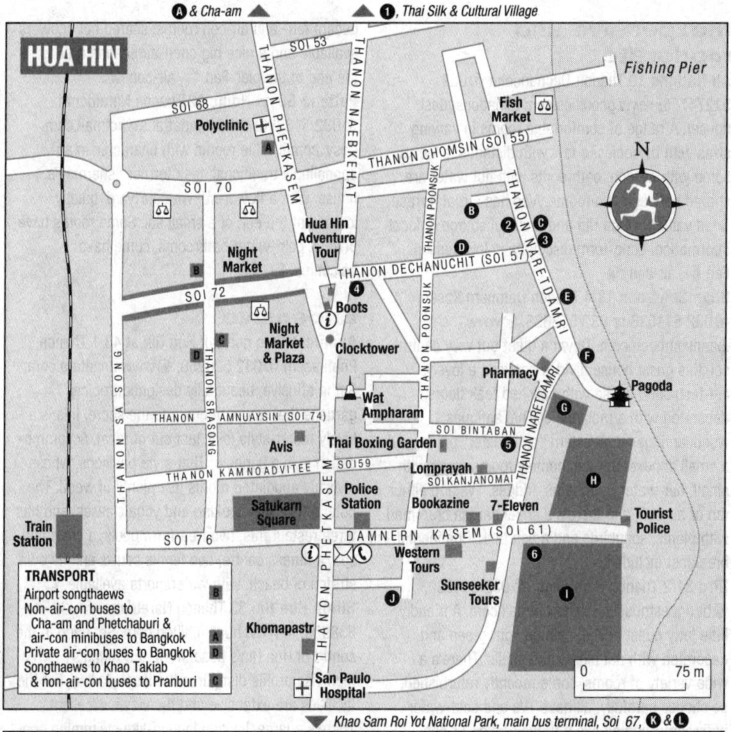

ACCOMMODATION				EATING & DRINKING	
All Nations	D	Jinning Beach Guest House	L	Chao Lay	3
Anantara Resort & Spa	A	Karoon Hut	C	Hagi	6
Baan Somboon	J	Pattana Guest Home	B	Monsoon	2
Bird	F	Sofitel Centara Grand	H & I	Som Moo Joom	4
Fu-Lay Guest House & Hotel	E	Veranda Lodge	K	Takeang Bar	5
Hilton Hua Hin	G			Youyen	1

Accommodation

A night or two at the former *Railway Hotel* (now the *Sofitel*) is reason in itself to visit Hua Hin, but there are plenty of other **places to stay**. The most unusual guest houses are those built on the squid piers, with rooms strung out along wooden jetties so you can hear, feel – and smell, especially at low tide – the sea beneath you, even if you can't afford a room with an actual sea view. Room rates at many places can drop significantly from Mondays to Thursdays, so don't be afraid to ask for a discount.

About 15 minutes' walk south down the beach from the *Sofitel*, or 2km by road down Thanon Phetkasem, there's a little knot of accommodation on **Soi 67**. Here, facing each other across the short, narrow soi about 200m back from the beach, are a dozen little guest houses, mainly Scandinavian-Thai run, which share a swimming pool; none comprise more than twenty rooms and most charge about B900. They're very popular with older European couples, many of whom return for several months every winter, so booking is essential. **Resorts** beyond the northern fringes of Hua Hin, on the stretch of coast between Hua Hin and Cha-am, are described on p.570.

Inexpensive and moderate

All Nations 10 Thanon Dechanuchit ⓣ032 512747, ⓦwww.geocities.com/allnationsguesthouse/. A range of comfortable rooms in varying sizes with balconies, a few with distant sea views, some with air-con; bathrooms with hot water are shared between two rooms. Also has a roof terrace. Good value for Hua Hin and a useful source of local information. Long-term discounts in low season. Fan 3, air-con 4

Baan Somboon 13/4 Thanon Damnern Kasem ⓣ032 511538 or 032 553638, ⓦwww.baansomboon.com. Down a quiet but very central soi, this guest house divides between a lovely, old-fashioned house with polished teak floors, decorated with a melange of Thai antiques, woodcarvings and Western "old master" prints, and a small annexe. Spruce, homely rooms come with small, hot-water bathrooms, fridges, TVs and either fan or air-con, and there's a small garden crammed with plants, songbirds and a fish tank. Continental breakfast included. 5

Bird 31/2 Thanon Naretdamri ⓣ032 511630, ⓔbirdguesthousehuahin@hotmail.com. A friendly little jetty guest house, painted light green and decorated with pot plants and shells. There's a wide variety of rooms, some recently refurbished, so choose carefully: all have TVs and cold-water bathrooms, some have a fridge and/or air-con, while the best fan room occupies the prime end-of-pier position. There's a nice, broad, breezy sea-view terrace at the end. Reserve ahead as it's very popular. Fan 2–3, air-con 4

Fu-Lay Guest House and Hotel 110/1 Thanon Naretdamri, guest house ⓣ032 513145, hotel ⓣ032 513670, ⓦfulay-huahin.com. *Fu-Lay* is in two halves, with guest house rooms strung along a jetty and hotel accommodation in a low-rise block across the street. The jetty guest house is the most stylish of its kind in Hua Hin, offering attractively appointed air-con rooms with nice hot-water bathrooms and TV, plus some cheap en-suite fan rooms (some with hot water) and a breezy seating area set right over the water. Air-con rooms in the hotel are similar, with some on the upper floors offering sea views from their shared verandas. Fan 2–3, air-con 4–5

Jinning Beach Guest House East end of Soi 67, off Thanon Phetkasem ⓣ032 532597, ⓦwww.jinningbeachguesthouse.com. Typical Soi 67 guest house under welcoming Danish-Thai management, with seventeen mostly good-sized air-con rooms, some with verandas, and all with TV and fridge. 5

Karoon Hut 80 Thanon Naretdamri ⓣ032 530242, ⓕ032 530737. Friendly jetty guest house, with decent fan- and air-con rooms, shared hot showers available and a nice big open-air seating area at the end of the pier. Fan 3, air-con 4

Pattana Guest Home 52 Thanon Naretdamri ⓣ032 513393, ⓔhuahinpattana@hotmail.com. Cosy, comfortable rooms with character, in an appealingly traditional, teak former fisherman's house, with a flower-strewn courtyard, quietly located at the end of a small soi. Some rooms have private, cold-water bathrooms, some have balconies. 2–3

Expensive

Anantara 5km north of Hua Hin at 43/1 Thanon Phetkasem ⓣ032 520250, ⓦwww.anantara.com. Set in effusive, beautifully designed tropical gardens that run right down to the shore, this is a lovely resort-style idyll, just out of town. Accommodation is in a series of Thai-style pavilions, whose stylishly appointed rooms use plenty of wood. The hotel offers Thai cooking and yoga classes, and has three restaurants, two free-form pools, a charming spa, a fitness centre, two tennis courts and its own stretch of beach, with watersports available. 9

Hilton Hua Hin 33 Thanon Naretdamri ⓣ032 538999, ⓦwww.huahin.hilton.com. Set bang in the centre of Hua Hin's beachfront, the *Hilton's* high-rise profile disfigures the local skyline, but the facilities are extensive and the views excellent. There's a large, inviting lagoon-like swimming pool right on the seafront, a spa, a kids' club, a panoramic rooftop Chinese restaurant and an impressive indoor-outdoor water garden in the lobby. All three hundred rooms are large and comfortable and have sea-view balconies. 9

Sofitel Centara Grand 1 Thanon Damnern Kasem ⓣ032 512021–38, ⓦwww.sofitel.com. The original Thai "destination hotel", the main building is a classic of colonial-style architecture, boasting high ceilings, polished wood panelling, period furniture, wide sea-view balconies and a huge, landscaped garden full of topiary animals. Across the road, lush gardens shelter gorgeous, all-white clapboard villas, most with their own marble pools with resistance machines, some with large outdoor jacuzzis. With a total of four swimming pools, a spa, tennis courts, a kids' club, canoeing and a giant chessboard, you need never leave the grounds. You can even tuck into a high tea buffet at *The Museum*, the original lobby, which now displays hotel memorabilia. 9

Veranda Lodge Beachfront end of Soi 67, off Thanon Phetkasem ⓣ032 533678, ⓦwww.verandalodge.com. Chic 18-room boutique hotel set a little apart from the Soi 67 guest houses in its own beachfront garden. Deluxe rooms have a contemporary look (lime green, pink or china-blue walls) and petite balconies; suites have separate living rooms, small kitchen areas and sea-view balconies. All rooms have air-con and cable TV, and there's a small pool fed by a waterfall and a seafront terrace restaurant. 8

The resort

The prettiest part of Hua Hin's five-kilometre-long **beach** is the patch in front of and to the south of the *Sofitel*, where the sand is at its softest and whitest. North of here the shore is crowded with tables and chairs belonging to a string of small restaurant shacks, beyond which the beach ends at a Chinese temple atop a flight of steps running down to Thanon Naretdamri. The coast to the north of the pagoda is dominated by the jetties and terraces of the squid-pier guest houses and seafood restaurants, the hub of the original fishing village, which dates back to the early nineteenth century.

South of the *Sofitel*, holiday homes and high-rise condos overshadow nearly the whole run of beach down to the promontory known as Khao Takiab (Chopstick Hill), 6km further south, but during the week it's fairly quiet along here, with just a few widely spaced food stalls along the broad, squeakily soft beach. Kiteboarding Asia (Ⓣ081 591 4592–3, Ⓦwww.kiteboardingasia.com) offers **kiteboarding** courses and rental from a spot off the end of Soi 75/1, about 2.5km south of the *Sofitel* (B4000 for a 1-day course, B11,000 for 3 days; best conditions from March to May). **Khao Takiab** itself is a wooded outcrop surmounted by a temple and home to a troupe of monkeys; the road to the top is guarded by a tall, golden, standing Buddha and affords good coastal views. Green songthaews run to Khao Takiab every twenty minutes from Thanon Sa Song.

Excursions from Hua Hin

Hua Hin is well placed for **excursions** (see p.577 for tour operators) to Khao Sam Roi Yot National Park, Phetchaburi and Damnoen Saduak floating markets, as well as to the old summer palace of Phra Ratchaniwet Marukhathaiyawan just to the north (see p.570). Another popular day-trip from Hua Hin is 63km west to the fifteen-tiered **Pala-u Waterfall**, situated close to the Burmese border and within **Kaeng Krachan National Park** (B200; Ⓦwww.dnp.go.th). Though the falls themselves are hardly exceptional, the route there takes you through lush, hilly landscape and past innumerable pineapple plantations. There's no public transport to the falls, but every tour operator features them in its programme (about B1300 per person). To get there under your own steam, follow the signs from the west end of Thanon Chomsin along Highway 3218. Once inside the park you'll see hundreds of butterflies and may also catch sight of monitor lizards and six species of hornbills. A slippery and occasionally steep path follows the river through the fairly dense jungle up to the falls, passing the (numbered) tiers en route to the remote fifteenth level, though most people opt to stop at the third level, which has the first pool of any decent depth (full of fish but not that clear) and is a half-hour walk from the car park.

Also worth singling out is the trip south to the **Pran River** run by eco-friendly Mermaid Cruises (Ⓣ032 632223 or 084 800 7400, Ⓦwww.huahincruises.com; B1950 per person, minimum 2 people). The company uses quiet electric-powered longtails – solar-powered boats are planned – that allow you to get close to the wildlife, including three-metre monitor lizards, egrets, ospreys, wild peacocks and six species of kingfisher. The tour includes a stroll on a walkway through the mangrove swamps of the Pranburi Forest Park, lunch and transfers, and kayaking can be worked into the day if you're feeling energetic. Mermaid also run full-day **sea cruises** on a big boat down to Khao Sam Roi Yot, with the opportunity to see dolphins and to fish for squid (same price).

Eating, drinking and entertainment

Hua Hin is renowned for its **seafood**, and some of the best places to enjoy the local catch are the seafront and squid-pier restaurants along Thanon Naretdamri. Fish also features heavily at the large and lively **night market**, which sets up at sunset along Soi 72 (the western end of Thanon Dechanuchit). The biggest concentration of **bars** is in the network of sois between the *Hilton Hotel* and Wat Hua Hin, particularly along Soi Bintaban, Soi Kanjanomai and Thanon Poonsuk; many of these places are so-called "bar-beers", with lots of seating round the bar and hostesses dispensing beer and flirtation through the night.

The **Sasi Garden Theatre**, near the *Hyatt Regency*, about 4km south of the *Sofitel*, stages a performance of classical Thai **dance**, plus traditional fighting and contemporary ballet, with dinner nightly at 7pm (vegetarians catered for); book through any travel agent (B750 including set dinner and transfer; ⓣ032 512488 or 081 880 4004, ⓦwww.sasirestaurant.com). Tuesdays and Saturdays are fight nights at the **Thai Boxing Garden** off Thanon Poonsuk (ⓣ032 515269), with programmes starting at 9pm and featuring five different fights (B350–500); it's owned by local *muay Thai* champion Khun Chop, who also runs Thai boxing classes every day at 5pm (B300 per hr).

Chao Lay 15 Thanon Naretdamri. Hua Hin's most famous jetty restaurant is deservedly popular, serving up high-quality seafood, including rock lobster, blue crab, scallops, cottonfish, mixed seafood hot plates and specialities such as mackerel curry soufflé (*haw mok*). Most main dishes cost B150–200. Daily 10am–10pm.

Hagi *Sofitel*, corner of Damnern Kasem and Naretdamri roads ⓣ032 512021–38. Tasty, authentic sushi, including delicious, hand-rolled *temaki* with crispy salmon skin and cucumber, tempura and *teppanyaki* grills at this elegant and welcoming Japanese restaurant. Pick your spot in the Zen-style garden, adorned with black slate, bamboo plants and a rocky pond, or in the air-con section with its sushi counter. Not too pricy, especially if you go for local, rather than imported seafood. Daily 3–11pm.

Monsoon 62 Thanon Naretdamri ⓣ032 531062. Atmospheric teakwood house, with brass fans, mellow lighting and a garden patio, that serves Thai and Vietnamese food, including Vietnamese *pho* (noodle soup), fresh spring rolls and *luc lac* (warm beef and watercress salad; B250), as well as duck curry and seafood. Also serves afternoon tea, tapas and a vegetarian menu. Daily from 3pm.

Som Moo Joom (Jek Pia) 51/6 Thanon Dechanuchit (corner of Thanon Naebkehat); no English sign. Exceptionally good seafood at very cheap prices has made this bare-bones evening restaurant (6–9pm) extremely popular with Thai holidaymakers. The trademark dish, *moo joom*, is a clear soup with vegetables and pork (or shrimp/squid), but the menu also covers the range of standard seafood dishes. At lunchtime, several popular stalls take over the space, offering seafood, satay and noodle soup with seafood.

Takeang Bar Soi Bintaban. Rustic bar, furnished every inch in wood, down to the wagon wheel lights, that makes a welcome change from the surrounding hostess bars. Live bands play country, rock and pop covers 9pm–2am nightly.

Youyen (Hua Hin Balcony) Thanon Naebkehat, near Soi 51 ⓣ032 531191–2. The works: lovely terrace seating by the sea, as well as air-con or open-air seating in a big, old house; keen service; and an excellent variety of authentic Thai food – try the delicious stir-fried shrimp with green sauce, green peppercorns, crispy garlic and sweet basil (B280).

Shopping

Hua Hin is famous for *pha khomapastr* (or *pha kiaw*), brightly coloured, hand-printed **cotton** with lovely, swirling *kannok* patterns, usually with strong elements of gold. At Khomapastr, 218 Thanon Phetkasem, just north of the hospital, you can buy it by the piece or yard, or made up into skirts or shirts, for example; it's particularly nice for triangular (or axe) cushion covers and bags. **Silk** and other handicrafts are available at the Thai Silk and Cultural Village (daily 9am–6pm; ⓣ032 531155–6, ⓦwww.mikeandcotailor.com) at 18 Thanon

Naebkehat, about ten minutes' walk north from the town-centre clocktower, or phone for a free pick-up. Every visitor to the "village" (actually a series of open-air workshop pavilions and an air-conditioned shop) is given a free and well-explained guided tour of the entire silk production process, after which you are encouraged to pop in to the attached tailors' shop and get yourself suited up.

Listings

Banks and exchange There are currency-exchange counters all over the resort, especially on Thanon Damnern Kasem and Thanon Naretdamri; most of the main bank branches with ATMs are on Thanon Phetkasem.
Books Bookazine, on the corner of Damnern Kasem and Naretdamri roads. Second-hand bought and sold at BB Books, Satukarn Square, Thanon Damnern Kasem.
Car and motorbike rental Avis (ⓣ032 531238, ⓦwww.avisthailand.com) is based at the *Thanavit Hotel*, on a soi near the corner of Amnuaysin and Phetkasem roads; several Hua Hin tour agencies also act as agents for Budget (ⓣ02 203 0250, ⓦwww.budget.co.th). Among the transport touts who rent out mopeds for around B150 and more per day on Thanon Damnern Kasem, try Khun Dennapa (ⓣ081 942 5615, or Khun Nui on ⓣ081 306 9179, ⓦwww.den-carrental.com), who also offers cars with or without driver – find them on the pavement in front of the *Sirin Hotel*, near 7-Eleven.
Emergencies For all emergencies, call the tourist police on the free, 24hr phoneline (ⓣ1155), or contact them at their office opposite the *Sofitel* at the beachfront end of Thanon Damnern Kasem (ⓣ032 515995).
Hospital San Paulo, 222 Thanon Phetkasem (ⓣ032 532576–80), south of the tourist office.
Mountain biking Sea Hill Mountain Biking, based on Soi 126, Thanon Phetkasem ⓣ081 173 4469, ⓦwww.huahin.tourdeasia.org, offers a variety of guided day rides for B1600 and up, including transfers and lunch, as well as rental for B400 per day.
Pharmacy Several in the resort, including the helpful and well-stocked Medihouse (daily 9.30am–11pm) opposite the *Hilton* on Thanon Naretdamri.
Tour operators Western Tours, 11 Thanon Damnern Kasem (ⓣ032 533303–4, ⓦwww.westerntourshuahin.com), sells air tickets and certain bus tickets, and has a weekly roster of day-trips to Khao Sam Roi Yot National Park (B1600 per person, kayaking on Khao Daeng canal B500 extra), Pala-u Falls (B1600), Phetchaburi (B1300) and Damnoen Saduak Floating Market (B1800). Hua Hin Adventure Tour, 69/8 Thanon Phetkasem (ⓣ032 530313, ⓦwww.huahinadventuretour.com), does trips to the same places, plus Prachuap Khiri Khan (from B1700), a boat trip in Kaeng Krachan National Park (from B2200) and snorkelling (B2200). Sunseeker Tours, 166 Thanon Naretdamri (ⓣ032 533666, ⓦwww.sunseekertours.com), offers cruises to local beaches on its motor yacht for around B1500 per person (minimum 4 people), as well as a sunset cruise around Khao Takiab and snorkelling trips.

Pak Nam Pran

The stretch of coast between Hua Hin and Chumphon barely registers on most foreign tourists' radar, but many better-off Bangkokians have favourite beaches in this area, the nicest of which is sophisticated **PAK NAM PRAN**. Just 30km or so south of Hua Hin, Pak Nam Pran used to cater only for families who owned beach villas here, but in the past few years the shorefront homes have been joined by a growing number of enticing, if pricey, boutique hotels, and signs are there's more development to come. For now, facilities consist of just a few minimarkets, car-rental outlets and independent restaurants, plus the possibility of organizing day-trips to nearby Khao Sam Roi Yot National Park through hotel staff. As along much of the Gulf coast, the beach itself is not exceptional (it has hardly any shade and is suffering from erosion in parts), but it is long, with fine sand, and nearly always empty, and you're quite likely to see dolphins playing within sight of the shore. The **beach** (also known as Hat Naresuan) stretches south from Pak Nam Pran town at the mouth of the Pran

River – which is known for its colourful fishing boats, specializing in squid – for around 5km to Khao Kalok headland and the tiny Thao Kosa Forest Park.

Practicalities

Easiest **access** is via the town of **PRANBURI**, which straddles Highway 4 and the Southern Rail Line some 23km south of Hua Hin and is served by air-con buses from Bangkok's Southern Bus Terminal as well as local buses from Hua Hin (see p.572), which drop passengers close by the town centre's main intersection. There's no public transport from Pranburi to Pak Nam Pran beach, 10km away, but hotels can arrange transfers and any Pranburi songthaew driver will taxi you there. If making your own way, the easiest route is to turn east off Highway 4 at Pranburi's town-centre traffic lights and then take minor road 3168 down to the sea, picking up the relevant sign for your hotel.

Accommodation

Pak Nam Pran's charming **accommodation** is its biggest draw: for once, "boutique" is the appropriate term, as many of the hotels here offer a dozen or fewer rooms, and the style tends to be more arty than five-star, though you will certainly be comfortable. Some hotels aren't suitable for kids owing to their multiple levels and unfenced flights of steps. Breakfast is generally included in the price of the room. During weekends in high season (Nov–May) you'll need to book ahead; conversely, many places offer weekday discounts.

The following are spread over a two-kilometre stretch of the beachfront road, starting about 4km south of Pak Nam Pran town.

Aleenta Central Pak Nam Pran beach ⓣ032 618333, ⓦwww.aleenta.com. This stunningly designed hotel, divided between the Main Wing and the newer Frangipani Wing, 500m down the beach, is the resort's sleekest outfit, offering gorgeous circular, thatch-roofed bungalows and very tasteful villa-style rooms, most with uninterrupted sea views, decks and personal plunge pools. The feel is modernist chic, with elegantly understated local furnishings and huge glass windows, and iPods and wi-fi capability rather than TVs in every room. There's a small rooftop pool, a spa and restaurant; yoga and Thai cooking classes are available. ⑨

Baan Panali Southern Pak Nam Pran beach, 200m south of *Huaplee* ⓣ086 051 2333 or 081 844 2484, ⓦwww.baan-panali.com. Not as striking as some of the beach's other offerings, but much cheaper and stylish enough: a cream-painted, adobe-style block with large, colourful, tiled rooms and a cute little swimming pool on its beachfront terrace. All but one room face the sea with a terrace or balcony, and all have air-con, hot showers, TVs and fridges; free bicycles. ⑦

Huaplee Lazy Beach Central Pak Nam Pran beach ⓣ032 630554–5, ⓦwww.huapleelazybeach.com. This exceptionally cute collection of eight idiosyncratic white-cube beachfront rooms around a pretty lawn is the work of the architect-interior designer owners. It's a characterful place of whimsical, marine-themed interiors done out with white-painted wood floors, blue-and-white colour schemes and funky shell and driftwood decor. The rooms are airy and bright but all have air-con, as well as fridges and TVs (no hot water); some have fantastic sea-view terraces. ⑧

Jamsawang Resort Northern Pak Nam Pran beach ⓣ032 570050, ⓦwww.jamsawang.com. One of the cheapest places to stay in the area, run by a friendly family. Dotted around a neatly trimmed garden across the road from the beach, all bungalows have air-con, hot water, fridge and TV; a few ("Thai-style") are comfortable if not especially sophisticated pale-blue concrete affairs, but most are pricier, more stylishly furnished, yellow-painted "Bali-style" bungalows, with garden bathrooms. ⑥–⑦

Pran Havana Central Pak Nam Pran beach ⓣ032 570077, ⓦwww.pranhavana.net. More white-cube architecture right next to *Huaplee* at this slightly bigger but equally charming beachfront accommodation, where the warren of individually furnished rooms is accessed by a series of whitewashed steps, wooden walkways and sea-view terraces. Interiors are idiosyncratic seaside-chic, personalized with hand-crafted furnishings and artworks. The price depends on the view; discounts offered for stays of two nights or more (except around Christmas and bank holidays) and on weekdays. ⑧–⑨

Eating

The simple shorefront **restaurant** *Krua Sawatdikan Khao Kalok* (unsigned in English), by the headland at the far southern end of Pak Nam Pran beach, about 1km from *Baan Panali*, has an extensive menu of very good seafood dishes; mosquitoes are a problem here though, so take repellent. On the edge of Pak Nam Pran town, about 2km north of the *Evason*, seafront *Krua Jaew* (also unsigned in English) offers an enormous, mid-priced menu of 120 mostly fish and seafood dishes, including very good crab curry, seafood curry soufflé (*haw mok thalay*) and pork with garlic.

Khao Sam Roi Yot National Park

With a name that translates as "The Mountain with Three Hundred Peaks", **KHAO SAM ROI YOT NATIONAL PARK** (B200; ⓣ032 619078, ⓦwww.dnp.go.th), with its northern entrance 28km south of Pak Nam Pran beach or 63km from Hua Hin, encompasses a small but varied, mosquito-ridden, coastal zone of just 98 square kilometres. The dramatic limestone crags after which it is named are the dominant feature, looming 600m above the Gulf waters and the forested interior, but perhaps more significant are the mud flats and freshwater marsh which attract and provide a breeding ground for thousands of migratory birds. **Birdwatching** at Thung Khao Sam Roi Yot swamp is a major draw, but the famously photogenic Phraya Nakhon Khiri cave is the focus of most day-trips, while a few decent trails and a couple of secluded beaches provide added interest.

Orientation in the park is fairly straightforward. One main inland road runs roughly north–south through it from the R3168 (the road from Pranburi's main junction to Pak Nam Pran), passing in order the turn-off for **Hat Phu Noi**, a quiet, golden-sand beach that offers several resort alternatives to the park's accommodation; the northern park checkpoint; the turn-offs for Ban Bang Pu (the jumping-off point for Tham Phraya Nakhon), Ban Khung Tanot (for Tham Sai) and Hat Sam Phraya (all to the east); then going over Khao Daeng canal; before looping westwards around the main massif, past park headquarters and the southern checkpoint (14km from the northern checkpoint), to Highway 4 at kilometre-stone 286.5. A park brochure with a **map** is available at headquarters.

The park

Khao Sam Roi Yot's most visited attraction is the **Tham Phraya Nakhon** cave system, hidden high up on a cliffside above **Hat Laem Sala**, an unremarkable sandy bay that's inaccessible to vehicles. The usual way to get to Hat Laem Sala is by a five-minute boat ride from the knot of food stalls behind Wat Bang Pu on the edge of **Ban Bang Pu** fishing village (6km from the northern checkpoint); prices are fixed at B300 per boat for the round trip. It's also possible to walk over the headland from behind Wat Bang Pu to Hat Laem Sala, along a signed, but at times steep, 500-metre trail. From Hat Laem Sala, another taxing though shaded trail runs up the hillside to Tham Phraya Nakhon in around thirty minutes.

The huge twin **caves** are filled with stalactites and stalagmites and wreathed in lianas and gnarly trees, but their most dramatic features are the partially collapsed roofs, which allow the sunlight to stream in and illuminate the interiors, in particular beaming down on the famous royal pavilion, Phra Thi Nang Khua Kharunhad, which was built in the second cave in 1890 in honour of Rama V. A three-hour trek south from Tham Phraya Nakhon brings you to

Tham Sai, a thoroughly dark and dank limestone cave, complete with stalactites, stalagmites and petrified waterfalls; lamps are available here for B40. The trek offers some fine coastal views, but a shorter alternative is the twenty-minute trail from **Ban Khung Tanot** village (accessible by road, 8km on from the Ban Bang Pu turn-off).

The next turning off the main road will take you down to **Hat Sam Phraya**, a quiet, kilometre-long beach, while a little further on the road crosses mangrove-fringed **Khao Daeng canal**. From beside Wat Khao Daeng, on the west side of the main road here, you can charter a boat (B400 for up to six people) for a one-hour cruise that's best in the early morning or the late afternoon. Kayaks are available at the same spot for B300 per person (ⓣ089 903 1619), or for B400 from Horizon, across the main road on the beach (ⓣ089 504 3694). A couple of kilometres on, you can scramble up **Khao Daeng** itself, a 157-metre-high outcrop that offers good summit views over the coast, via a thirty-minute trail that begins near the park headquarters. The park's two official **nature trails** also start from close by HQ – the 30-minute "Horseshoe Trail" takes in the forest habitats of monkeys, squirrels and songbirds, while the 45-minute "Mangrove Trail" leads through the swampy domiciles of monitor lizards and egrets, with the chance of encountering long-tailed (crab-eating) macaques.

The park hosts up to three hundred species of **birds** and between September and November the mud flats are thick with migratory flocks from Siberia, China and northern Europe. To the west of Khao Sam Roi Yot lies Thailand's largest freshwater marsh, **Thung Khao Sam Roi Yot**, near the village of Rong Jai (Rong Che). It's accessed not from the main park road, but by turning east off Highway 4, 200m north of kilometre-stone 276, and continuing for 9km (the wetlands are outside the park boundary and not subject to the park entry fee). This is an excellent place for observing waders and songbirds, and is one of only two places in the country where the **purple heron** breeds; punts are available here for one-hour bird-watching excursions (B200 per person).

Practicalities

Like most of Thailand's national parks, Khao Sam Roi Yot is hard to explore without your own **transport**, and its sights are spread too far apart to walk between. The only public transport is an hourly **songthaew** service in the morning from Pranburi to Ban Bang Phu. Otherwise, you could charter a songthaew or motorbike taxi (around B200–300) from Pranburi, or hook up with Khun Lamai Thongsuk (ⓣ089 533 8664), park information officer and local fixer, who offers a **taxi** service, for example, to headquarters from Pranburi (B700) or from the closer bus drop to the south at Kuiburi (B500); you could then rent a **bicycle** from him at HQ. The easiest options are to join a one-day **tour** from Hua Hin or Pak Nam Pran, or to rent your own transport from Hua Hin. As well as at HQ, there are national park **visitor centres** at Hat Laem Sala and Hat Sam Phraya.

Park accommodation is at headquarters, at Hat Sam Phraya, a beach between Khao Daeng canal and Ban Khung Tanot, and at Hat Laem Sala; all three sites have **restaurants**. At Hat Laem Sala it's a choice between camping, at B150–225 per tent, or staying in one of the national park bungalows (B1600–2200 for 6–9 people); at Sam Phraya it's camping only and at the headquarters it's bungalows only (B1200–1400 for 5–7 people). Bungalows must be booked ahead through the National Parks office in Bangkok (see p.52). It's also possible to stay at *Kasemsuk Bungalows* in Ban Khung Tanot near Tham Sai, which have fridges, TVs and cold-water en-suite bathrooms and belong to Khun Lamai (see above; fan ❸, air-con for up to 8 people ❼).

Hat Phu Noi

Given the limitations of the park accommodation, many people prefer to stay a few kilometres to the north at the long, pleasingly shaded beach of **HAT PHU NOI**, where dolphins are a daily sight from October to March – you may even spot the very rare, pink Indo-Pacific humpback dolphin. Hat Phu Noi is signed off the main road into the park, 4km before the northern checkpoint, and is at the end of a two-kilometre side road. Your best bet for a moderately priced **hotel** here is the long-running, eco-conscious and family-friendly *Dolphin Bay* (Ⓣ032 559333 or 032 559360, Ⓦwww.dolphinbayresort.com; ⑥), towards the northern end of the beach. The resort offers about fifty comfortable air-con rooms and bungalows with fridges, hot water and TVs, large children's and adults' pools set in an attractive, palm-fringed lawn, plus a big restaurant with a bar, kids' playground and internet access and wi-fi. Pick-ups from Pranburi (B250–350) can be arranged and there's no shortage of things to do once you're here: songthaews into the park (about B250), boat trips for dolphin-watching, snorkelling or night-time squid-fishing, plus kayak, motorbike and bicycle rental. At the bottom end of Hat Phu Noi but the top of the price range is *Brassiere Beach* (Ⓣ032 630554–5, Ⓦwww.brassierebeach.com; ⑨), under the same architect-designer owners as *Huaplee* at Pak Nam Pran (see p.578). It gets its name from the two conical Nom Sao ("Breast") islands offshore and the mainland spirit house where fishermen leave bras for good luck, and contains rooms with playful monikers like "La Perla". That may sound a bit naff to some, but the hotel itself is the height of quirky chic, airy and light-filled, with elegant tiled floors and a mostly white- and-blue colour scheme. All the spacious rooms have air-con and hot water, some have their own small jacuzzi and pool or an outdoor bathroom, and kayaks and bicycles are available.

South to Chumphon

Most foreign tourists zip through the region immediately south of Khao Sam Roi Yot en route to the more obvious delights of the Ko Samui archipelago, but the unexpectedly charming seaside town of **Prachuap Khiri Khan** and the small beach resort at **Ban Krud** are worth investigating if you're happy to substitute good seafood and laid-back Thai hospitality for full-on resort facilities. Twenty-two kilometres south of Prachuap, Highway 4 passes through Wang Duan, where a sign announces the fact that this is the narrowest part of Thailand: just 10.96km of Thai land separates the Gulf of Thailand from the Burmese border at this point.

Prachuap Khiri Khan and around

Despite lacking any must-see attractions, the tiny, unfrequented provincial capital of **PRACHUAP KHIRI KHAN**, 67km south of Pranburi, makes a pleasant place to break any journey up or down the coast. Its greatest asset is its setting, a huge, palm-fringed, half-moon bay, dotted with colourful fishing boats and tipped by a rocky outcrop at the north end and by a small group of jungly islands to the south – the waterfront promenade in the town centre is great for a seafood lunch with a view. There's a lovely **beach** in the next bay to the south, Ao Manao, and generally Prachuap is a fine spot to settle into small-town Thai life.

The town is contained in a small grid of streets that runs just 250m east to west, between the sea and the train station – with Highway 4 beyond the railway tracks – and around 1km north to south, from the Khao Chong Krajok hill at the northern end to the Wing 5 air-force base in the south. **Orientation** couldn't be simpler: the major road across from the station to the pier is Thanon Kongkiat, and there are four main north–south roads: Thanon Phitak Chat near the station, Thanon Salacheep, Thanon Susuek and the seafront road, Thanon Chai Thalay.

Arrival and information

Nearly all services on the Southern Line from Bangkok stop at the **train station** at the western end of Thanon Kongkiat. The **non-air-con bus stop** for Chumphon (on departure, roughly hourly in the morning) is nearby on Thanon Kongkiat, while that for Pranburi and Hua Hin is one block east of the station and one block north, on east–west Thanon Thetsaban Bamrung; at the same spot stop second-class **air-con buses** from Bangkok (every 30min), via Pranburi, Hua Hin and Phetchaburi. First-class bus services **from Bangkok** (hourly), via Pranburi and Phetchaburi but bypassing Hua Hin, are based just south of Thanon Kongkiat, on Thanon Phitak Chat. On departure, for the fastest service to Chumphon and Surat Thani you need to wait on Highway 4 at the Highway Police office, about 1km north of the access road into town, for the air-con buses that whizz down from Bangkok; several southbound services pick up passengers here between 8.30am and 11.30am (and many more around midnight).

There's a small, clued-up **tourist information** office (daily 8.30am–4.30pm, occasionally closing noon–1pm for lunch; ⓣ032 611491), where town maps are available, at the far northern end of town in a compound of provincial offices; it's on the ground floor of a modern, white building facing the beachfront road. The **post office** is directly behind the *Hadthong Hotel* on Thanon Susuek (Mon–Fri 8.30am–4.30pm, Sat & Sun 9am–noon), and there's an **internet** place one block west and around the corner to the left on Thanon Salacheep. There are ATMs and **currency exchange** on Thanon Salacheep and Thanon Phitak Chat, notably on the latter at Krung Thai Bank, which opens daily. **Motorbikes** can be rented from *Sun Beach Guesthouse*, **bicycles** from the *Hadthong Hotel*, **kayaks** from Kayak Adventures, on the seafront next to *Hadthong*.

Accommodation

Prachuap doesn't get enough visitors to support a wide choice of accommodation, but it does have one outstanding option, the *Sun Beach Guest House*.

Akan Ti Pak Sawatdikan Ao Manao ⓣ032 661088–90. If you don't mind cosying up to the Thai military, this spruce, wi-fi-enabled air-force hotel on the Wing 5 base puts you right on the beach. All rooms have sea-view balconies, air-con, hot water, TV and fridge. Ten-percent discount on weekdays. No English sign. ❺

Hadthong Hotel 21 Thanon Susuek, but also with an entrance just south of the pier on the beachfront road ⓣ032 601050–6, ⓦwww.hadthong.com. Well-run spot with comfortable rooms, many sporting balconies and great sea views, most with fridges, and air-con, hot water and TVs all round – plus a 15m swimming pool and snooker club. The cheapest options are in the basement. ❸–❹

Prachuapsuk Hotel 69 Thanon Susuek ⓣ032 611019. One of the cheapest places in town, popular with travelling salesmen, this friendly enough place has simple, slightly battered but large en-suite rooms with parquet floors. It's 50m south of the post office or about 300m southeast of the train station. Fan ❶, air-con ❷

Sun Beach Guesthouse 160 Thanon Chai Thalay, 500m or so down the promenade from the pier ⓣ032 604770, ⓦwww.sunbeach-guesthouse.com. Run by a welcoming and helpful Thai-German couple, this palatial guest house is done out like a Mediterranean villa, with Corinthian columns and smart tiling everywhere. The bright, comfortable, sky-blue rooms come with air-con, hot water, fridges, TVs and balconies, with prices varying according to the quality of the sea view. There's a seductive pool and whirlpool, and free internet access. ❹–❺

The Town

Monkey-infested **Khao Chong Krajok** is Prachuap's main sight: if you climb the 417 steps from Thanon Salacheep to the golden-spired chedi at the summit you get a great perspective on the scalloped coast below and west to the mountainous Burmese border, just 12km away. At the far southern end of town, the long sandy beach at **Ao Manao** is the best place in the area for swimming and sunbathing. The bay is inside the air-force base, so you usually need to sign in at the checkpoint 2km north of the beach itself. To get there, just head south down Thanon Salacheep (or down the promenade and turn right) until you get to the base sign and checkpoint; a tuk-tuk to the beach should cost around B60. On weekdays you're likely to have the sand almost to yourself, but it's a very popular spot with Thai families on weekends when the stalls at the beachfront food centre do a roaring trade in the locally famous *som tam puu* (spicy papaya salad with fresh crab), which you can eat at the deckchairs and tables under the trees on the beach. You can walk to the north end of the bay to the base of an outcrop known as Khao Lommuak, where a memorial commemorates the battle that took place here between Thai and Japanese forces in World War II.

King Mongkut Memorial Park

About 12km south of town, on the beach at Wa Ko (Waghor), the main feature of the **King Mongkut Memorial Park of Science and Technology** (also signed as Phra Chomklao Science Park; daily 9am–5pm) is the extensive and well-stocked **Waghor Aquarium** (B20; ⓣ032 661726). Highlights include an underwater tunnel, touch pools and fish-feeding at 11am and 2pm (subject to change, so worth phoning in advance to check), and there are display boards and labels for most of the fish in English. It's nothing like as slick as Siam Ocean World in Bangkok, but then again it's less than a tenth of the price. About 500m south along the beach road, the park also contains an astronomy museum that's decidedly low-tech but with enough labels in English to maintain interest. To reach the park, the easiest way is to turn east off Highway 4 at kilometre-stone 335, or you can get there through Ao Manao air-force base, bearing left along the coast all the way.

The park marks the spot where **Rama IV**, known as the father of Thai science, came to observe a solar eclipse on August 18, 1868. Having predicted the eclipse's exact course, King Mongkut decided to publicize science among his subjects by mounting a large expedition, aiming specifically to quash their centuries-old fear that the sun was periodically swallowed by the dragon Rahoo. To this end, he invited scientists all the way from France and the British governor of Singapore, and himself turned up with fifty elephants and all his court, including the astrologers – who, as the leader of the French expedition noted, "could hardly be blamed if they did not display much enthusiasm for the whole project". Unfortunately, both the king and his 15-year-old son contracted malaria at Waghor; Mongkut passed away in Bangkok on October 1, but Chulalongkorn survived to become Thailand's most venerated king, Rama V.

Eating and drinking

Prachuap's famously good seafood is most cheaply sampled at the town's lively and varied main **night market**, which sets up shop in the empty lot around the junction of Thanon Kongkiat and Thanon Phitak Chat. *Plern Smud*, south of the pier on Thanon Chai Thalay, alongside the *Hadthong Hotel*, is probably the town's best **restaurant**, serving delicious pan-fried oysters on its seafood-dominated menu (English-sign at the Thanon Suseuk entrance only, not on the beachfront road). Try not to let the awful muzak put you off at *Ma-prow*, an otherwise mellow, rustic, airy restaurant a little further down the front – it serves tasty crispy fish with green mango salad, as well as a few Western dishes such as fish'n'chips. The sounds improve markedly at *Rome Bar (MC Club)* just to the south, an excellent spot for a waterside **drink**, hung with motorcycle memorabilia and home to some of the friendliest bikers you're ever likely to meet.

Ban Krud

Graced with a tranquil, five-kilometre sweep of white sand, pale-blue sea and swaying casuarinas, **BAN KRUD**, 70km south of Prachuap, supports a dozen or so fairly upmarket bungalow outfits and seafood restaurants along the central stretch of its beachfront road. At the beach's northern end are a colourful fishing village, which hosts a Thursday afternoon market, and a panoramic headland beyond, **Khao Thongchai**, that's dominated by the fourteen-metre-high Phra Phut Kitti Sirichai Buddha image and its sparkling modern temple, Wat Phra Mahathat Phraphat. Crowned with nine golden chedis, the temple displays an impressive fusion of traditional and contemporary features, including a series of charming modern stained-glass windows depicting Buddhist stories; reach it via a 1500-metre-long road that spirals up from the beachfront. Other than a visit to the temple and possibly a snorkelling trip to Ko Thalu (B400 per person), the main pastime in Ban Krud is sitting under the trees and enjoying a long seafood lunch or dinner.

Practicalities

Most southbound **buses** drop passengers on Highway 4, from where motorbike taxis (with sidecars) cover the 8km down to the beach; just two Bangkok–Bang Saphan air-con buses a day stop at Ban Krud itself. Near Ban Krud **train** station, about 1km from the beach, are a couple of **ATMs** but no bank as yet. About 1km north of the central beachfront T-junction is friendly *Sala Thai* (Ⓣ032 695181, Ⓦwww.salathaibeachresort.com; ❸–❺, including breakfast; discounts for long stays), whose cutesy wooden **bungalows** with air-con, hot water and TV are spread around a pretty garden just across the road from the beach; it also has a restaurant and a popular burger bar. North of the headland and the ramshackle youth hostel, 4km from *Sala Thai* on Hat Tangsai, *Bayview* is a very welcoming and relaxed spot with a swimming pool, a kids' pool and a lovely area for deckchairs under the beachside casuarinas (Ⓣ032 695566–7, Ⓦwww.bayviewbeachresort.com; ❻ breakfast included). All the well-spaced bungalows boast air-con and hot water, and there's an excellent restaurant, internet access and wi-fi, free bicycles, and kayaks and motorbikes to rent. A surprisingly urban feel pervades *Lumra Resort*, 2km further on (Ⓣ032 602714, Ⓦwww.reflections-thai.com; ❻ breakfast included), which often hosts holistic healing courses (Ⓦwww.naturalhealing.co.th). Sister resort to Bangkok's *Reflections Hotel* (see p.121), the concrete rooms, running back in two rows from the beach, have a similarly colourful, modern style. All feature air-con and hot water, but the pick of the bunch are the two beachside affairs, one of which sports an outside wooden bath. Internet access and free pick-ups from the train or bus are available.

Chumphon and around

South Thailand officially starts at **CHUMPHON**, where the main highway splits into west- and east-coast branches, and inevitably the provincial capital saddles itself with the title "gateway to the south". Most tourists take this tag literally and use the town as nothing more than a transport interchange between the Bangkok train and **boats to Ko Tao**, so the town is well equipped to serve these passers-through, offering clued-up travel agents, efficient transport links and plenty of internet cafés. In truth, there's little call for exploring the fairly average beaches, islands and reefs around town when the varied and attractive strands of Ko Tao are just a short hop away, while the Chumphon National Museum is little short of pitiful. The most rewarding direction for day-trippers is inland, through Chumphon province's famously abundant fruit orchards to **Pha To** for some **rafting** on the Lang Suan River.

Arrival and information

Chumphon **train station** is on the northwest edge of town, less than ten minutes' walk from most guest houses and hotels. The government **bus station** is 11km south of town on Highway 4, connected to the centre by songthaews (B50 per person), though if they have enough customers, long-distance services will sometimes drop in town. There are also several private **air-con bus and minibus** services that depart from other parts of town (see map for locations), including minibuses to Ranong (in theory hourly, but will leave early if full); Rungkit buses to Phuket, via Ranong and Khao Lak (4 daily; ☎077 812324), and Chokeanan Tour buses to Bangkok (3 daily; ☎077 511757).

The best **fixer** in town, offering a personal, unbiased service, is Suda at her eponymous guest house, who, as well as tickets to Ko Tao, can arrange bus and train tickets, including hourly air-con minibuses to Surat Thani; twice-daily visa runs via Ranong to Burma (from B650, excluding B500 visa); **motorbike** (B200 per day) and **car rental** (B1000–1300 per day); and jungle treks and rafting on the Lang Suan river (see p.587). Among the bigger multi-purpose **travel agents**, avoid if you can busy Farang Bar, which resembles a human meat-processing factory, in favour of Fame, which offers the same transport

E, Tha Yang, Pak Nam & Ao Thung Makham ▶

EATING & DRINKING

Ahaan Jeh	2
Boom	5
Fame	B
Green Kitchen	3
Kozo Sushi	4
Papa 2000	1

ACCOMMODATION

Chumphon Guest House	A
Fame	B
Novotel	E
Paradorn Inn	C
Suda Guest House	D

CHUMPHON

Highway 4, bus station & TAT office ▼

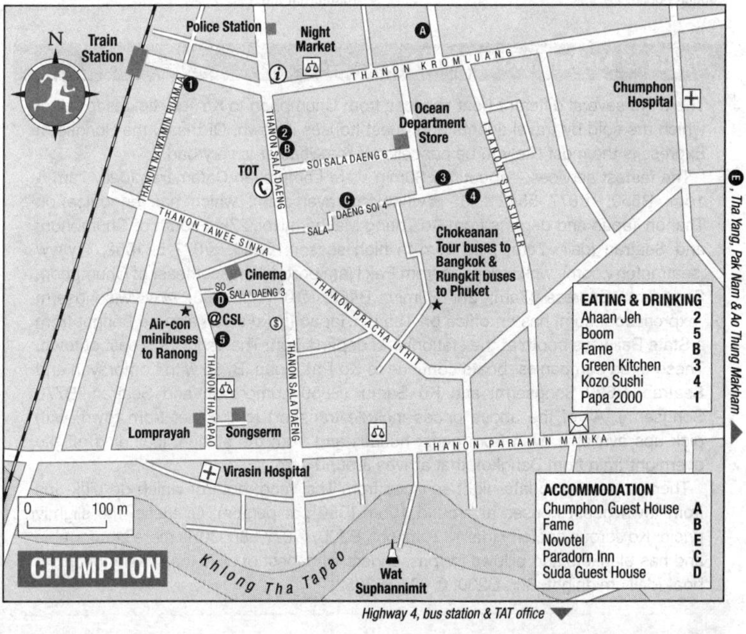

services as Suda, as well as a guest house and restaurant, snorkelling trips, airline tickets and twice-daily air-con minibuses to Krabi and Ko Lanta that coincide with boats from Ko Tao.

The provincial **tourist information** centre, at the junction of Thanon Kromluang and Thanon Sala Daeng (Mon–Fri 8.30am–4.30pm; ⓣ077 504833), can do little more than hand out brochures, while the TAT office covering Chumphon and Ranong (ⓣ077 556191, ⓦwww.tourismthailand.org) is currently 16km south on Highway 4, though planning a move closer to the centre.

Accommodation

Chumphon's **guest houses** are well used to accommodating Ko Tao-bound travellers, so most are happy to store luggage until the night boat leaves and offer shower services to non-guests.

Fame 188/20–21 Thanon Sala Daeng ⓣ077 571077, ⓦwww.chumphon-kohtao.com. Above the restaurant and tour agency of the same name, this place has good-sized and very clean rooms with mattresses on the floor, fans and hot water in either shared or en-suite bathrooms; internet access. ❶

Chumphon Guest House (Kae House) Soi 1, Thanon Kromluang ⓣ077 502900. Sociable place with 24hr check-in, hosted by the effervescent Kae, on a quiet, residential soi with a pleasant outdoor bar-restaurant. Motorcycle rental, boat tickets, internet and informal cooking classes and day-trips around Chumphon. Accommodation ranges from small rooms out front with mattresses on the floor to en-suites with beds in the main wooden house. ❶–❷

Novotel 15km southeast near Pak Nam ⓣ077 529529, ⓦwww.novotel-chumphon.com. This new, low-rise luxury hotel on Paradornpab beach, done out in an unobtrusive Thai contemporary style, features spacious rooms with balconies and lots of dark wood, two restaurants (Mediterranean and Thai/international), two swimming pools, a spa, fitness centre, golf course and kids' club. Substantial discounts online. ❽

Paradorn Inn 180/12 Thanon Sala Daeng ⓣ077 511598 or 077 511500, ⓦwww.chumphon-paradorn.com. The best value of the town's mid-range hotels, though not particularly welcoming, a shining, white block where all rooms have air-con, hot water and TV. There's a restaurant too. ❷

Boats to Ko Tao and beyond

There are several different boat services from Chumphon to Ko Tao, tickets for all of which are sold by travel agents and guest houses in town. Of these, the Songserm Express is the most likely to be cancelled if the weather is very bad.

The fastest services – about 1hr 30min – are Lomprayah Catamaran (daily 7am & 1pm; B550; ⓣ077 558212–3, ⓦwww.lomprayah.com), which has an office on Thanon Tapao and departs from Ao Thung Makham Noi, 27km south of Chumphon; and Seatran (daily 7am, plus 1pm in high season; B550; ⓣ077 521052, ⓦwww.seatranferry.com), which departs from Pak Nam port, 14km southeast of Chumphon. Songserm Express (7am; 2hr 30min; B450; ⓣ077 506205, ⓦwww.songserm-expressboat.com) has an office on Thanon Tapao (tickets can also be bought from a State Railways booth at the station) and departs from Tha Yang, 7km east of town. These three companies' boats continue to Ko Pha Ngan (B750 with Lomprayah and Seatran, B620 Songserm) and Ko Samui (B850 Lomprayah and Seatran, B770 Songserm). All of the above prices include transport to the pier from town, with pick-ups available even from guest houses and from the station, including off the overnight train from Bangkok that arrives around 4am.

There are also two late-night services from Tha Yang, both of which do pick-ups from town guest houses at around 10pm (B50 per person). Of these, the slightly pricier Ko Jaroen car ferry (daily 11pm; 6hr; B300; ⓣ077 580030) is more comfortable and has blankets and pillows for passengers; cheapest of all is the smaller midnight boat (daily midnight; 6hr; B200; ⓣ077 553052).

Suda Guest House Thanon Sala Daeng Soi 3 (aka Soi Bangkok Bank), 30m off Thanon Tha Tapao ⓣ077 504366 or 085 571 2229. Chumphon's most genuine and welcoming home-stay, offering seven clean and well-maintained fan or air-con rooms, most with shared hot-water bathrooms, one en-suite, in the owner's own modern house. Plenty of information available, B20 showers for passers-through and much more (see p.585). Phone for free transport from train or bus station. Fan ❶–❸, air-con ❷–❸

Eating and drinking

The cheapest place to eat is the **night market**, which sets up along both sides of Thanon Kromluang and is an enjoyable place to munch your way through a selection of fried noodles, barbecued chicken and sticky, coconut-laced sweets. *CSL* on Thanon Sala Daeng is a friendly, informative **internet café** (which also offers drinks, sandwiches and egg breakfasts).

Ahaan Jeh Right next to *Fame* on Thanon Sala Daeng. Tiny place offering a ready-cooked buffet of Thai-Chinese vegetarian food at B20 per serving. Daily 7am to about 5pm, though most dishes will be finished long before then.

Boom (The Bakery Café) Thanon Tha Tapao. Good espressos, tasty brownies and other Western and Thai cakes. Mon–Sat 7.30am–8pm.

Fame 188/20-21 Thanon Sala Daeng. Travellers' restaurant specializing in Italian food, including pizzas available whole or by the slice, as well as plenty of other home-baked goods, Indian dhal, loads of sandwiches, and huge American and veggie breakfasts (B100–120). Daily 4.30am–midnight.

Green Kitchen Behind *Jansom Chumphon Hotel*, between Thanon Suksumer and Thanon Sala Daeng. Good, authentic Vietnamese cuisine such as grilled beef in betel leaves and fresh spring rolls, plus Thai food and some European dishes.

Kozo Sushi Off Thanon Suksumer opposite *Green Kitchen* ⓣ077 512239. Great Japanese restaurant offering a huge range of dishes on a picture menu – big portions, reasonable prices. Closed Mon.

Papa 2000 Across from the train station on Thanon Kromluang. One of the liveliest places to eat dinner is this huge restaurant, open air with an air-con room, which has an extensive menu of fresh seafood and salads, plenty of Western and Chinese standards – and live music every evening, as well as an attached nightclub.

Inland to Pha To

Chumphon's reputation as a major **fruit-growing** region is well established, and a great way to appreciate this is to head inland for some **rafting** on the pretty if not spectacular Lang Suan River near **PHA TO**. Beginning 71km down Highway 41 from the provincial capital, Highway 4006 winds its exceptionally scenic way westwards for 26km to Pha To, passing through endless plantations of papayas, mangosteens, durians, bananas, rambutans, pomelos and coconuts, plus the occasional *robusta* coffee field as well (over fifty percent of Thailand's *robusta* coffee crop is grown in Chumphon).

Travel agencies and guest houses in town offer either whitewater rafting in an inflatable or a more gentle float on a PVC punt from around B1000 per person, depending on the size of the group, including transport and lunch. Whitewater rafting is also offered by the Thai-Dutch eco-tourism outfit Runs 'N Roses (ⓣ086 172 1090, ⓦwww.runsnroses.com), based near Pak Song village in Pha To municipality (see the website on how to get there). In addition, they have **accommodation** in their lodge or bungalows (❺ for two people including all meals) and many more **trips and activities**, including trekking, mountain-bike rental, horse-riding, yoga, Thai cooking, cultural and language workshops and plenty for kids to do. Profits support the **Thai Child Development Foundation**, which welcomes donations and volunteers – see p.80 for more details.

Chaiya and around

About 140km south of Chumphon, **CHAIYA** was the capital of southern Thailand under the Srivijayan empire, which fanned out from Sumatra between the eighth and thirteenth centuries. Today there's little to mark the passing of the Srivijayan civilization, but this small, sleepy town has gained new fame as the site of **Wat Suan Mokkh**, a progressively minded temple whose meditation retreats account for the bulk of Chaiya's foreign visitors (most Thais only stop to buy the famous local salted eggs). Unless you're interested in one of the retreats, the town is best visited on a day-trip, either as a break in the journey south, or as an excursion from Surat Thani.

Chaiya is 3km east of Highway 41, the main road down this section of the Gulf coast: **buses** running between Chumphon and Surat Thani will drop you off on the highway, from where you can catch a motorbike taxi or walk into town; from Surat Thani's Talat Kaset II bus station, hourly air-con minibuses and more frequent but slower songthaews take around an hour to reach Chaiya. The town also lies on the main Southern Rail Line, served by nine, mostly overnight **trains** from Bangkok (8–11hr).

The Town

The main sight in Chaiya is **Wat Phra Boromathat** on the western side of town, where the ninth-century chedi – one of very few surviving examples of Srivijayan architecture – is said to contain relics of the Buddha himself. Hidden away behind the viharn in a pretty, red-tiled cloister, the chedi looks like an oversized wedding cake surrounded by an ornamental moat. Its unusual square tiers are spiked with smaller chedis and decorated with gilt, in a style similar to the temples of central Java.

The **National Museum** (Wed–Sun 8am–4pm; B30; Ⓦwww.thailandmuseum.com), on the eastern side of the temple, is a bit of a disappointment. Although the Srivijaya period produced some of Thailand's finest sculpture, much of it discovered at Chaiya, the best pieces have been carted off to the National Museum in Bangkok. Replicas have been left in their stead, which are shown alongside fragments of some original statues, two intricately worked 2000-year-old bronze drums, found at Chaiya and Ko Samui, and various examples of Thai handicrafts. The best remaining pieces are a calm and elegant sixth- to seventh-century stone image of the Buddha meditating from Wat Phra Boromathat, and an equally serene head of a Buddha image, Ayutthayan-style in pink sandstone, from **Wat Kaeo**, an imposing ninth- or tenth-century brick chedi on the south side of town. Heading towards the centre from Wat Phra Boromathat, you can reach this chedi by taking the first paved road on the right, which brings you first to the restored base of the chedi at Wat Long, and then after 1km to Wat Kaeo, enclosed by a thick ring of trees. Here you can poke around the murky antechambers of the chedi, three of which house images of the Buddha subduing Mara.

Wat Suan Mokkh

The forest temple of **Wat Suan Mokkh** (Garden of Liberation), 6km south of Chaiya on Highway 41, was founded by the abbot of Wat Phra Boromathat, **Buddhadasa Bhikkhu**, southern Thailand's most revered monk until his death in 1993 at the age of 87. His radical, back-to-basics philosophy, encompassing Christian, Zen and Taoist influences, lives on and continues to draw Thais from all over the country to the temple, as well as hundreds of foreigners. It's not necessary to sign up for one of the wat's retreats to enjoy the temple, however

– all buses from Surat Thani to Chaiya and Chumphon pass the wat, so it's easy to drop by for a quiet stroll through the wooded grounds.

The layout of the wat is centred on the Golden Hill: scrambling up between trees and monks' huts, past the cremation site of Buddhadasa Bhikkhu, you'll reach a hushed clearing on top of the hill, which is the temple's holiest meeting-place, a simple open-air platform decorated with images of Buddha and the Wheel of Law. At the base of the hill, the outer walls of the Spiritual Theatre are lined with bas-reliefs, replicas of originals in India, which depict scenes from the life of the Buddha. Inside, every centimetre is covered with colourful didactic painting, executed by resident monks and visitors in a jumble of realistic and surrealistic styles.

Meditation retreats

Meditation retreats are led by Western and Thai teachers over the first ten days of every month at the International Dharma Heritage, a purpose-built compound 1km from the main temple at Wat Suan Mokkh. Large numbers of foreign travellers, both novices and experienced meditators, turn up for the retreats, which are intended as a challenging exercise in mental development – it's not an opportunity to relax and live at low cost for a few days. Conditions imitate the rigorous lifestyle of a *bhikkhu* (monk) as far as possible, each day beginning before dawn with meditation according to the Anapanasati method, which aims to achieve mindfulness by focusing on the breathing process. Although talks are given on Dharma (the doctrines of the Buddha – as interpreted by Buddhadasa Bhikkhu) and meditation technique, most of each day is spent practising Anapanasati in solitude. To aid concentration, participants maintain a rule of silence, broken only by daily chanting sessions, although supervisors are available for individual interviews if there are any questions or problems. Men and women are segregated into separate dormitory blocks and, like monks, are expected to help out with chores.

Each course has space for about one hundred people – turn up at the information desk in Wat Suan Mokkh as early as possible on the last day of the month to enrol. The fee is B1500 per person, which includes two vegetarian meals a day and accommodation in simple cells. Bring a flashlight (or buy one outside the temple gates) and any other supplies you'll need for the ten days – participants are encouraged not to leave the premises during the retreat. For further information, go to Ⓦwww.suanmokkh.org or telephone Ⓣ077 531552 or 077 431597.

Surat Thani

Uninspiring **SURAT THANI** ("City of the Good People"), 60km south of Chaiya, is generally worth visiting only as the jumping-off point for the Samui archipelago. Strung along the south bank of the Tapi River, with a busy port for rubber and coconuts near the river mouth, the town is experiencing rapid economic growth and paralysing traffic jams. It might be worth a stay, however, when the Chak Phra Festival (see box, p.590) is on, or as a base for seeing the nearby historic town of Chaiya.

Arrival and information

Buses arrive at three different locations, two of which are on Thanon Taladmai in the centre of town: Talat Kaset I on the north side of the road (Phunphin,

The Chak Phra Festival

At the start of the eleventh lunar month (usually in October) the people of Surat Thani celebrate the end of Buddhist Lent with the **Chak Phra Festival** (Pulling the Buddha), which symbolizes the Buddha's return to earth after a monsoon season spent preaching to his mother in heaven. On the Tapi River, tugboats pull the town's principal Buddha image on a raft decorated with huge nagas, while on land sleigh-like floats bearing Buddha images and colourful flags and parasols are hauled across the countryside and through the streets. As the monks have been confined to their monasteries for three months, the end of Lent is also the time to give them generous offerings in the *kathin* ceremony, of which Surat Thani has its own version, called Thot Pha Pa, when the offerings are hung on tree branches planted in front of the houses before dawn. Longboat races, between teams from all over the south, are also held during the festival.

Chumphon, non-air-con Nakhon Si Thammarat and Ranong services, and other local buses) and opposite at Talat Kaset II (many long-distance buses, including those from Krabi, Phang Nga, Phuket, Hat Yai, and Ranong and Nakhon Si Thammarat air-con services). The Baw Khaw Saw terminal, 2km southwest of the centre on the road towards Phunphin, handles mostly services from Bangkok. If you're coming from points south by **air-conditioned minibus** or **share-taxi**, you should be deposited at the door of your destination.

Arriving by **train** means arriving at **Phunphin**, 13km to the west, from where buses run into Surat Thani, via the Baw Khaw Saw bus terminal, every ten minutes or so between around 5.30am and 7.30pm, while share-taxis (based in Surat at Talat Kaset II) charge B140 to charter the whole car into town. It's also possible to buy through-tickets to Ko Samui and Ko Pha Ngan from the train station for the same price as they would be from Surat Thani town, including a connecting bus to the relevant pier. There's a basic **hotel**, *Queen* (Ⓣ077 311125; ❶), in Phunphin if you get really stuck.

Arriving by **air**, you can take a B100 Phantip minibus for the 27km journey south from the airport (Ⓣ077 441230–1) into Surat Thani, or a combination ticket to Ko Samui (B350) or Ko Pha Ngan (B550). Budget (Ⓣ077 441166) have an outlet at the airport for **car rental**.

TAT's helpful office is at the western end of town at 5 Thanon Taladmai (daily 8.30am–noon & 1–4.30pm; Ⓣ077 288817–9 or 077 282352, Ⓔtatsurat@tat.or.th), while the **tourist police** (Ⓣ1155 or 077 405575) are based out on the southern bypass near the junction with Thanon Srivichai, the westward continuation of Thanon Taladmai. Small **share-songthaews** buzz around town, charging around B15–20 per person. There's **internet access**, as well as good coffee, snacks and breakfast, at *Tukta Capuccino* on Thanon Taladmai in front of Talat Kaset II. Surat's best **travel agency** is the helpful and reliable Phantip, in front of Talat Kaset I at 293/6–8 Thanon Taladmai (Ⓣ077 272230 or 077 272906), where among many other things you can book train and plane tickets. Thai Airways have an office at 3/27–28 Thanon Karoonrat, off Thanon Chonkasem (Ⓣ077 272610).

Accommodation

Most budget **accommodation** in Surat Thani is noisy, grotty and overpriced – you may consider yourself better off on a night boat to one of the islands. If you do get stuck here, head for the *Ban Don Hotel*, above a restaurant at 268/2 Thanon Namuang (Ⓣ077 272167; fan ❷, air-con ❸), where most of the very clean rooms with en-suite cold-water bathrooms and fans or air-con and TV

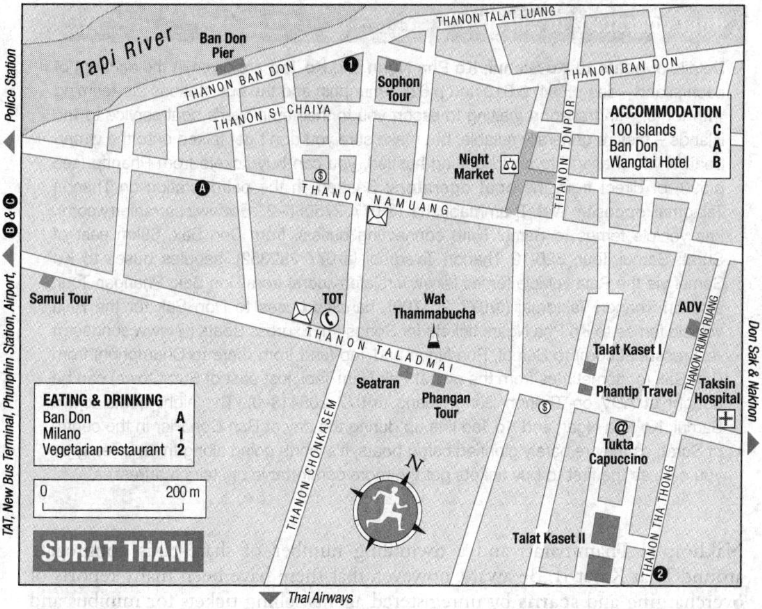

are set back from the noise of the main road. In the moderate range, *100 Islands* (*Roi Koh*; ⓣ077 201150–8, ⓦwww.roikoh.com; ④ including breakfast) offers attractive, comfortable rooms with air-con and hot water, a small spa and a decent-sized pool set in a lush garden with a waterfall. However, it's right out on the southern bypass near the tourist police and opposite Tesco Lotus. On the western side of the centre by the TAT office, *Wangtai Hotel*, 1 Thanon Taladmai (ⓣ077 283020–39, ⓦwww.wangtaisurat.com; ⑤), is Surat Thani's best upmarket option, and surprisingly good value, with over two hundred large, smart rooms around a swimming pool and several good restaurants.

Eating

For large portions of tasty, inexpensive Thai and Chinese **food**, head for the restaurant on the ground floor of the *Ban Don Hotel*. The **night market** between Thanon Si Chaiya and Thanon Ban Don displays an eye-catching range of dishes; a smaller offshoot by Ban Don pier offers less choice but is handy if you're taking a night boat. Also near the night-boat piers on Thanon Ban Don, *Milano* has an authentic oven turning out very tasty and reasonably priced pizza, and serves panini, home-made pasta and a few Italian fish and meat main courses; you can augment these with *som tam* from the popular stall that parks outside in the afternoons. During the day, an unnamed vegetarian restaurant, one block east of Talat Kaset II bus station on Thanon Tha Thong, offers a wide selection of cheap and delicious tray food or fried noodles, (look for the yellow flags outside and a sign saying "vegetarian food"; closes 4pm).

Moving on

For **moving on** to the rest of the mainland, air-con minibuses (to Chumphon, Ranong, Ratchabrapa Dam, Khao Sok, Phang Nga, Phuket, Krabi, Trang and

Boat operators in Surat

Details of **boats to Ko Samui**, **Ko Pha Ngan** and **Ko Tao** are given in the account of each island – see p.594, p.613 and p.625. Phunphin and the bus stations are teeming with touts, with transport waiting to escort you to their employer's boat service to the islands – they're generally reliable, but make sure you don't get talked onto the wrong boat. If you manage to avoid getting hustled, you can buy tickets from Phantip (see p.590) or direct from the **boat operators**: Seatran, in the petrol station on Thanon Taladmai opposite Wat Thammabucha (ⓣ077 275060–2, ⓦwww.seatranferry.com), has vehicle ferries to Samui (with connecting buses), from Don Sak, 68km east of Surat; Samui Tour, 326/12 Thanon Taladmai (ⓣ077 282352), handles buses to Ko Samui via the Raja vehicle ferries (ⓦwww.rajaferry.com) from Don Sak; Phangan Tour, also on Thanon Taladmai (ⓣ077 205799), handles buses to Don Sak for the Raja vehicle ferries to Ko Pha Ngan; tickets for Songserm Express Boats (ⓦwww.songserm-expressboat.com) to Samui, Pha Ngan and Tao (and from there to Chumphon) from Don Sak (or sometimes from the pier at Pak Nam Tapi, just east of Surat town) can be bought at ADV on Thanon Rung Ruang (ⓣ077 205418–9). The night boats to Ko Samui, Ko Pha Ngan and Ko Tao line up during the day at Ban Don Pier in the centre of Surat; as they're barely glorified cargo boats, it's worth going along there as early as you can, as the first to buy tickets get the more comfortable upstairs mattresses.

Nakhon Si Thammarat) and a dwindling number of share-taxis congregate around Talat Kaset II. Be aware, however, that there have been many reports of overcharging and **scams** by unregistered agents selling tickets for minibus and bus services out of Surat, especially involving any kind of combination ticket, including those heading for Khao Sok National Park (see p.665), Phuket, Krabi and Malaysia. To avoid this, either go direct to the relevant air-con minibus office rather than let yourself be hustled by a tout at Talat Kaset II bus station (local offices are generally on the west side of the station, long-distance ones on the east side, and they all have to be authorized by the provincial office); or walk the short distance to the reliable Phantip Travel (see p.590); or buy a bus ticket direct from the station. If you're heading for Krabi, as well as air-con minibuses, there are roughly hourly non-air-con buses from Talat Kaset II and faster hourly air-con buses through Phantip. For Bangkok, choose between second-class, first-class and VIP buses from the Baw Khaw Saw, and a cheaper VIP service from Sophon Tour, near the corner of Talat Luang and Ban Don roads (ⓣ077 420275). Buses heading out of Surat to Phang Nga, Phuket and Hat Yai also make a stop at Phunphin train station, which might save you a journey into town and out again. If you're flying out of Surat, you can catch the **airport minibus** from town at the Phantip office (B100; see p.590).

Ko Samui

A million visitors a year, ranging from globetrotting backpackers to suitcase-toting fortnighters, come to southern Thailand just for the beautiful beaches of **KO SAMUI**, 80km from Surat. At 15km across and down, Samui is generally large enough to cope with this diversity – except during the rush at Christmas and New Year – and the paradisal sands and clear blue seas have to a surprising extent kept their good looks, enhanced by a thick fringe of palm trees that gives a harvest of more than two million coconuts each month. However, development behind the beaches – which has brought the islanders far greater prosperity than the crop could ever provide – speeds along in a messy, haphazard fashion with little concern for the environment. At least there's a local bye-law limiting new construction to the height of a coconut palm (usually about three storeys), though this has not deterred either the luxury hotel groups or the real-estate developers who have recently been throwing up estates of second homes for Thais and foreigners.

The island's most appealing beach, **Chaweng**, has seen the heaviest, most crowded development and is now the most expensive place to stay, though it does offer by far the best range of amenities and nightlife, ranging from tawdry bar-beers to hip nightclubs. Its slightly smaller neighbour, **Lamai**, lags a little behind in terms of looks and top-end development, but retains large pockets of backpacker bungalow resorts. The other favourite for backpackers is **Maenam**, which though less attractive again, is markedly quiet, with plenty of room to breathe between the beach and the round-island road. Adjacent **Bophut** is similar in appearance, but generally more sophisticated, with a cluster of boutique resorts, fine restaurants and a distinct Mediterranean feel in its congenial beachfront village. **Choeng Mon**, set apart in Samui's northeast corner, offers something different again: the small, part-sandy, part-rocky bay is tranquil and pretty, the seafront between the handful of upmarket hotels is comparatively undeveloped, and Chaweng's nightlife is within easy striking distance.

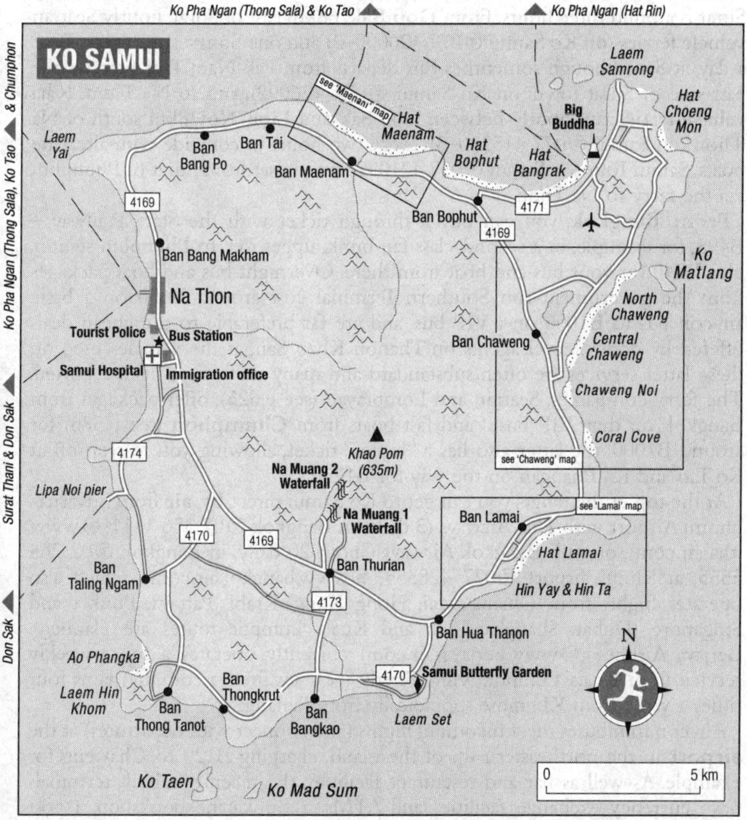

No particular **season** is best for coming to Ko Samui (see also p.11). The northeast monsoon blows heaviest in November, but can bring rain at any time between October and January, and sometimes causes high waves and strong currents, especially on the east coast. January is often breezy, March and April are very hot, and between May and October the southwest monsoon blows onto Samui's west coast and causes some rain. At the lower end of Samui's **accommodation** scale, there are very few bungalows left for under B400, while at the most upmarket places you can pay well over B4000 for the highest international standards. The prices listed are based on high-season rates, but out of season (roughly April–June, Oct & Nov) dramatic reductions are possible.

Getting to the island

The most obvious way of getting to Ko Samui is on a **boat** from the **Surat Thani** area; for contact details of **transport companies** in Surat, see p.592. Services may fluctuate according to demand, but the longest-established ferry is the night boat that leaves **Ban Don** pier in Surat Thani itself for **Na Thon** – the main port on Samui – at 11pm every night (6hr); tickets (B200) are sold at the pier on the day of departure.

All the following operators charge B240 to get to Samui, including a connecting bus from Surat or Phunphin train station; total journey time from Surat is around three hours. From **Don Sak**, 68km east of Surat, hourly Seatran vehicle ferries (on Ko Samui ⓣ077 426000–2) and one Songserm Express Boat a day, at 8am (though sometimes this departs from Pak Nam Tapi pier, on the east side of Surat town; on Ko Samui ⓣ077 426092), run to Na Thon. Raja vehicle ferries run hourly between Don Sak and **Lipa Noi**, 8km south of Na Thon (on Samui ⓣ077 415230–3); every two hours to coincide with alternate boats, Samui Tour (on Samui ⓣ077 421092) runs buses from Surat or Phunphin via the ferry to Na Thon.

From Bangkok, you can buy a through ticket with the State Railway – B498, for example, in a second-class fan bunk, upper tier, to Phunphin station, plus B240 for your bus and boat from there. Overnight bus and boat packages from the government-run Southern Terminal cost around B650 on a basic air-con bus to B1000 on a VIP bus, and are far preferable to the cheap deals offered by dodgy travel agents on Thanon Khao San, as the vehicles used on these latter services are often substandard and many thefts have been reported. The ferry companies, Seatran and Lomprayah (see p.625), offer packages from Bangkok on their VIP buses and fast boats from **Chumphon** (see p.586) for around B1000; the latter also has a "buffet" ticket, allowing you to stop off at Ko Tao and Ko Phangan on the way for B1250.

At the top of the range, you can get to Ko Samui direct **by air** from Suvarnabhumi Airport with Thai Airways (3 daily; in Bangkok ⓣ02 356 1111, ⓦwww.thaiair.com), or with Bangkok Airways (about 20 daily; in Bangkok ⓣ02 265 5555, at Samui airport ⓣ077 428555, ⓦwww.bangkokair.com), which also operates flights from Chiang Mai, Hong Kong, Krabi, Pattaya, Phuket and Singapore (Dubai, Shanghai, Bali and Kuala Lumpur routes are planned). Berjaya Airlines (ⓦwww.berjaya-air.com) currently operates a twice-weekly service from Kuala Lumpur, while Firefly (ⓦwww.fireflyz.com.my) runs four times a week from KL, more sporadically from Penang.

Air-con minibuses meet incoming flights (and connect with departures) at the **airport** in the northeastern tip of the island, charging B120 to Chaweng for example. As well as bar and restaurant facilities, the recently rebuilt terminals have currency-exchange facilities and ATMs, a Bookazine bookshop, a post office with international telephones and several car rental outlets including Avis (Ⓣ084 700 8161, Ⓦwww.avisthailand.com).

For information about boats from Ko Samui to **Ko Pha Ngan** see p.613, and to **Ko Tao** see p.625; all offer the same service in the return direction.

Information and island transport

TAT runs a small but helpful office (daily 8.30am–noon & 1–4.30pm; Ⓣ077 420504 or 077 420720–2, Ⓔtatsamui@tat.or.th), tucked away on an unnamed side road in Na Thon (north of the pier and inland from the post office). Another useful source of **information** is Ⓦsamui.sawadee.com, a website set up by a German based at Lamai, which handles, among other things, direct bookings at a range of local hotels.

Songthaews, which congregate at the car park near the southerly pier in Na Thon, cover a variety of set routes during the daytime, either heading off clockwise or anti-clockwise on Route 4169, to serve all the beaches; destinations are marked in English and fares range from B40 to Maenam to B60 to Chaweng or Lamai. In the evening, they tend to operate more like taxis and you'll have to negotiate a fare to get them to take you exactly where you want to go. Ko Samui now also sports dozens of **air-con taxis**. By law, they're required to use their meters (flag fall B50, on top of which they're allowed to add a B90 service charge), but at the moment you'd be wasting your breath trying to persuade any driver to do so (though this may change); you might be lucky enough to settle on a flat fare of B300 from Maenam to Chaweng, for example, after some hard bargaining. You'll also see some **motorbike taxis** buzzing about the island, which charge from B30 for a local drop, up to B250 from Na Thon to Chaweng. You can **rent a motorbike** from around B150 in Na Thon and on the main beaches. Dozens are killed on Samui's roads each year, so proceed with great caution, and wear a helmet – apart from any other consideration, you can be landed with an on-the-spot B500 fine by police for not wearing one. In addition, thieves have been snatching bags from the front baskets of moving motorbikes on Samui, so keep yours on your person – or think about upgrading to a **four-wheel drive**, for around B800 a day.

▲ Ko Wua Talab, Ang Thong National Marine Park

Ang Thong National Marine Park

Even if you don't get your buns off the beach for the rest of your stay, it's worth taking at least a day out to visit the beautiful **Ang Thong National Marine Park**, a lush, dense group of 42 small islands strewn like dragon's teeth over the deep-blue Gulf of Thailand, 31km west of Samui. Once a haven for pirate junks, then a Royal Thai Navy training base, the islands and their coral reefs, white-sand beaches and virgin rainforest are now preserved under the aegis of the National Parks Department. Erosion of the soft limestone has dug caves and chiselled out fantastic shapes that are variously said to resemble seals, a rhinoceros, a Buddha image and even the temple complex at Angkor.

The surrounding waters are home to dolphins, wary of humans because local fishermen catch them for their meat, and *pla thu* (short-bodied mackerel), part of the national staple diet, which gather in huge numbers between February and April to spawn around the islands. On land, long-tailed macaques, leopard cats, common wild pig, sea otters, squirrels, monitor lizards and pythons are found, as well as dusky langurs, which, because they have no natural enemies here, are unusually friendly and easy to spot. Around forty bird species have had confirmed sightings, including the white-rumped shama, noted for its singing, the brahminy kite, black baza, little heron, Eurasian woodcock, several species of pigeon, kingfisher and wagtail, as well as common and hill mynah; island caves shelter swiftlets, whose homes are stolen for bird's nest soup (see box, p.746). The largest land mass in the group is **Ko Wua Talab** (Sleeping Cow Island) where the park headquarters shelter in a hollow behind the small beach. From there it's a steep 430-metre climb (about 1hr return; bring walking sandals or shoes) to the island's peak to gawp at the panorama, which is especially fine at sunrise and sunset: in the distance, Ko Samui, Ko Pha Ngan and the mainland; nearer at hand, the jagged edges of the surrounding archipelago; and below the peak, a secret cove on the western side and an almost sheer drop to the clear blue sea to the east. Another climb from the beach, only 200m but even harder going (allow 40min return), leads to Tham Buabok, a cave set high in the cliff-face. Some of the stalactites and stalagmites are said to resemble lotuses, hence the cave's appellation, "Waving Lotus". If you're visiting in September, look out for the white, violet-dotted petals of **lady's slipper orchids**, which grow on the rocks and cliffs.

The park's name Ang Thong, "Golden Bowl", comes from a landlocked saltwater lake, 250m in diameter, on **Ko Mae Ko** to the north of Ko Wua Talab, which was the inspiration for the setting of bestselling novel and film, *The Beach*. A well-made path (allow 30min return) leads from the beach through natural rock tunnels to the rim of the cliff wall that encircles the lake, affording another stunning view of the archipelago

Island activities

For most visitors, the days are spent indulging in a few watersports or just lying on the beach waiting for the next drinks' seller, hair-braider or masseur to come along; some make it to one of Samui's many **spas**, whether independent or attached to one of the posh hotels, for further pampering. For something more active, you should not miss the almost supernatural beauty of the **Ang Thong National Marine Park** (see above), which comprises many of the eighty islands in the Samui archipelago. (Speedboat day-trips to Ko Tao are also available, but they cost a lot of money – around B2000 – for a matter of hours on the island.) A day-trip by rented car or motorbike on the fifty-kilometre round-island road, perhaps making time for a visit to the **Butterfly Garden** and a meal at *Ban Hua Thanon Seafood*, both on the south coast, will throw up plenty more fine beaches. Otherwise you could hook up with a **round-island tour**, whether on land with Mr Ung's Magical Safari Tours (bookable through travel agents or your accommodation or contact and the shallow, blue-green water far below, which is connected to the sea by a natural underground tunnel.

Practicalities

There are no scheduled **boats to Ang Thong**, only organized day-trips, which can be easily booked through your accommodation or a travel agent. The main operator is Highway, near *Coffee Island* on Thanon Chonwithi (Ⓣ077 421290, Ⓦwww.highseatour.com), whose big boats leave Na Thon every day at 8.30am, returning at around 5pm. In between, there's a two-hour stop to explore Ko Wua Talab (just enough time to visit the viewpoint, the cave and have a quick swim, so don't dally), lunch, some cruising through the archipelago, a visit to the viewpoint over the lake on Ko Mae Ko and a snorkelling stop. Tickets cost B1300 per person (or B1800 with kayaking), including pick-up from your accommodation and the B200 national park fee. Several companies in Maenam, Bangrak and Bophut on Samui do speedboat day-trips to Ang Thong (around B1500–1800), and the luxury yacht *Seatran Discovery* does the trip three times a week for B2700, including hotel pick-up, national park fee and kayaking (Ⓣ077 426000–2, Ⓦwww.seatrandiscovery.com). Similar trips run from Ko Pha Ngan (see p.614) and less frequently from Ko Tao; *Seaflower* on Ko Pha Ngan does three-day "treks" (see p.623).

If you want to make the most of the park's beautiful scenery of strange rock formations and hidden caves, take a dedicated **kayaking** trip with Blue Stars, based at Gallery Lafayette near the *Green Mango* nightclub on Chaweng (Ⓣ077 413231, Ⓦwww.bluestars.info). For a one-day trip, taking in the lake at Ko Mae Ko and kayaking and snorkelling among the islands in the northern part of the park, they charge B2200, including pick-up from your accommodation and boat over to the park, buffet lunch, snorkelling gear and national-park entrance fee; ask about overnight trips, which were suspended at the time of writing.

It's also possible to **stay** at the headquarters on **Ko Wua Talab**, where the National Parks Department maintains simple two- to eight-berth bungalows (B500–1400) and a restaurant. To book accommodation contact the Ang Thong National Marine Park Headquarters (Ⓣ077 280222 or 077 286025, Ⓦwww.dnp.go.th), or the Parks Department in Bangkok (see p.52). Camping is also possible in specified areas, and two-person tents can be rented for around B200 a night. If you do want to stay, you can go over on a boat-trip ticket – it's valid for a return on a later day. For getting around the archipelago from Ko Wua Talab, it's possible to charter a motorboat from the fishermen who live in the park; the best snorkelling is off Ko Thai Plao.

Ⓣ077 230114 or 081 895 5657; from B1200), which will take you up the rough tracks of the mountainous interior to some spectacular viewpoints; or by boat with Samui Evasion, who sail from Bangrak, via lunch and snorkelling on Ko Taen, and the bird's-nest islands of Ko Si Ko Ha, to Nathon (Mon, Wed & Sat; B1700 per person; Ⓣ077 230159, Ⓦwww.samuievasion.com).

Ko Samui has around a dozen **scuba-diving** companies, offering trips for qualified divers and a wide variety of courses throughout the year, and there's a **recompression chamber** at Bangrak (Ⓣ077 427427, Ⓦwww.sssnetwork.com). Most trips for experienced divers, however, head for the waters around Ko Tao (see p.626), which contain the best sites in the region; a day's outing costs around B3500, but of course if you can make your own way to Ko Tao, you'll save money and have more time in the water. Established and reliable PADI Five-Star dive centres, each with several branches around the island, include Samui International Diving School (Ⓦwww.planet-scuba.net), which has its head office at the *Malibu Resort* towards the north end of Central

Chaweng (☎077 422386); and Easy Divers (ⓦwww.easydivers-thailand.com), which has its head office opposite *Sandsea Resort*, towards the north end of Lamai (☎077 231190).

Other worthwhile **activities**, such as treetop cable rides on Maenam, go-karting on Bophut, Thai cookery courses on Chaweng and Lamai, meditation courses near Lamai, and boat trips to Ko Taen and Ko Madsum off the south coast, are detailed in the relevant accounts below.

Na Thon

The island capital, **NA THON**, at the top of the long western coast, is a frenetic half-built town which most travellers use only as a service station before hitting the sand: although most of the main beaches now have post offices, currency-exchange facilities, ATMs, supermarkets, travel agents and clinics, the biggest and best concentration of amenities is here. The town's layout is simple: the three piers come to land at the promenade, Thanon Chonvithi, which is paralleled first by narrow Thanon Ang Thong, then by Thanon Taweeratpakdee, aka Route 4169, the round-island road; the main cross-street is Thanon Na Amphoe, by the central pier.

Accommodation and eating

If you really need a **place to stay** in Na Thon, your best bet is the *Nathon Residence* (☎077 236081, ☎&Ⓕ077 236058; ❸), on Thanon Taweeratpakdee next to Siam City Bank and near the market, a well-run place with a café downstairs and large, plain but spotless tiled rooms with air-con, cable TV and en-suite bathrooms, some with hot water and fridge, upstairs.

Several stalls and small cafés purvey inexpensive Thai **food** around the market on Thanon Taweeratpakdee and on Thanon Chonvithi (including a lively night market by the piers), and there are plenty of Western-orientated places around the piers. Justifiably popular, especially for breakfast, is cheerful and inexpensive *RT (Roung Thong) Bakery*, with one branch on Thanon Taweeratpakdee, another opposite the southerly pier and a landmark sister operation, a little to the north on the corner of Thanon Na Amphoe, *Coffee Island*: all serve sandwiches, pancakes and pizzas, as well as Thai food and a wide variety of coffees.

Listings

Bookshop Nathon Book Store, Thanon Na Amphoe (☎077 420332; may close Sun in the future), is a good, helpful second-hand place, with some new titles and a café.

Buses The Baw Khaw Saw government bus station, about 1km south of town off Route 4169, handles a variety of through buses to Bangkok. Phantip travel agent (see below) runs through buses to Krabi, Phang Nga, Phuket and Hat Yai from Na Thon.

Hospital The state hospital (☎077 421230–2) is 3km south of town off Route 4169.

Immigration office 2km south of town down Route 4169 (Mon–Fri 8.30am–4.30pm; ☎077 421069).

Massage The Garden Home Health Center, 2km north along Route 4169 in Ban Bang Makham, dispenses good traditional Thai massages during the day (B350 per hr; booking advisable on ☎077 421311).

Post office and internet Towards the northern end of the promenade, just north of the central pier (Mon–Fri 8.30am–4.30pm, Sat & Sun 9am–noon), with poste restante and packing services. International telephones and Catnet internet access upstairs (Mon–Fri 8.30am–4pm).

Tourist police 1km south of the town centre on Route 4169 ☎1155, 077 421281 or 077 421360.

Travel agent The reliable Phantip is on Thanon Taweeratpakdee (north of Thanon Na Amphoe; ☎077 421221–2).

Laem Yai and Maenam

LAEM YAI, the steep, tree-covered headland at the island's northwest tip, shelters one exceptional top-end resort, while in contrast, **MAENAM**, 13km from Na Thon in the middle of the north coast, is Samui's most popular beach for budget travellers. Its exposed four-kilometre bay is not the island's prettiest, being more of a broad dent in the coastline, and the sloping, white-sand beach is relatively narrow and slightly coarse by Samui's high standards. But Maenam features many of the cheapest bungalows on the island, unspoilt views of fishing boats and Ko Pha Ngan, and good swimming. Despite the recent opening of some upmarket developments on the shoreline and a golf course in the hills behind, this is still the quietest and most laid-back of the major beaches, with little in the way of nightlife. Though now heavily built up with multi-storey concrete shophouses, the main road is set back far from the sea, connected to the beachside bungalows by an intricate maze of minor roads through the trees. At the midpoint of the bay, **Ban Maenam** is centred on a low-key road down to the fishing pier, which is flanked by several cafés, internet shops, travel agents and small boutiques.

You might be tempted off the beach for a couple of hours of fun with Canopy Adventures (ⓣ077 414150–1 or 087 046 7307, ⓦwww.canopyadventuresthailand.com; B1750, including transfers), who offer **cable rides** between treehouses and past waterfalls in the hills 4km above Maenam. At the far west end of the beach, beyond Wat Na Phra Larn, KSK (ⓣ086 267 1169, ⓦwww.kohsamuikiteboarding.com) runs **kiteboarding** courses, starting from B4200 for half a day. Other **watersports** such as wakeboarding and kayaking are available at *Moonhut* (see below). For **car rental** on Maenam, contact the helpful Petch Travel (ⓣ077 425276 or 081 797 0699; from around B900 per day), who offer free delivery.

Accommodation

As well as several luxury resorts, Maenam has around thirty inexpensive and moderately priced bungalow complexes, most offering a spread of accommodation; the cheapest of these are at the far eastern end of the bay.

Four Seasons Resort Laem Yai ⓣ077 243000, ⓦwww.fourseasons.com. Ultra-luxury spot, with its own small beach, enjoying lovely views of Ko Pha Ngan and the setting sun. Each of the large, beautiful villas, designed for indoor-outdoor living in a subtle, modern but natural style, using brown and marine colours, has its own infinity-edge swimming pool; the resort lays on a wide range of other activities, from spa treatments to sailing and Thai boxing classes. ❾

Harry's At the far western end, near Wat Na Phra Larn ⓣ077 425447, ⓦwww.harrys-samui.com. Popular, well-run place, set back about 100m from the beach amidst a secluded and shady tropical garden. The public areas feature strong elements of traditional Thai architecture, though not the bungalows, which are nevertheless clean and spacious, with air-con and hot water. Internet access and a decent-sized swimming pool and jacuzzi. ❺

Lolita On the east side of *Santiburi Resort* ⓣ077 425134, ⓔlolitakohsamui@yahoo.com. Quiet, friendly and efficiently run resort in a colourful, grassy garden on a long stretch of beach. Large, wooden, fan-cooled bungalows, some with hot water, and much smarter air-con rooms cluster around a kitsch, circular bar-restaurant adorned with pink Corinthian columns. Fan ❹, air-con ❻

Maenam Resort 500m west of the village, just beyond *Santiburi Resort* ⓣ077 247287, ⓦwww.maenamresort.com. A welcoming, tranquil resort (no TVs) in tidy, shady grounds, with an especially long stretch of beach. The rooms and large bungalows, with verandas, hot water and fans or air-con, offer good-value comfort. Internet access. Fan ❺, air-con ❻

Maenam Villa At the far eastern end of the bay, next to *SR* ⓣ077 425501, ⓔmaenamvilla@hotmail.com. Friendly spot on a spacious triangular plot with kayaks available. Choose between clean, bright, older bungalows with verandas and large, concrete, open-plan villas with air-con, hot water and small terraces. ❸

Moonhut On the east side of the village ⓣ077 425247, ⓦwww.moonhutsamui.com. Welcoming

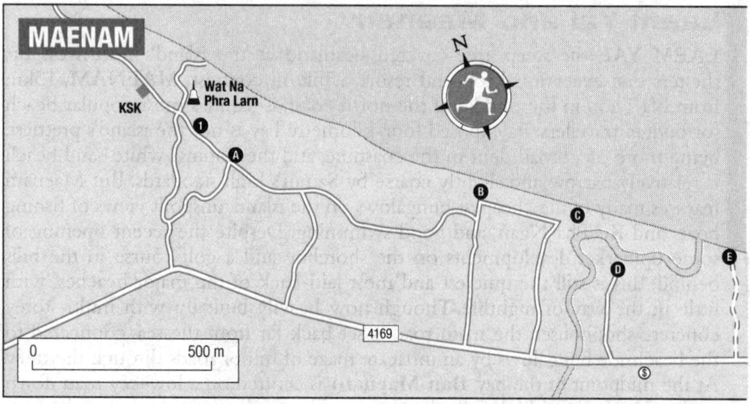

English-run place on a large, sandy, shady plot, with a lively restaurant and beach bar and colourful, substantial and very clean bungalows; all have verandas, mosquito screens, wall fans and en-suite bathrooms, some have hot water and air-con. Fan ③, air-con ⑤

Santiburi Resort 500m west of the village ⓣ077 425031–8, ⓦwww.santiburi.com. Luxury hotel in beautifully landscaped grounds spread around a huge freshwater swimming pool and stream. Accommodation is mostly in Thai-style villas, inspired by Rama IV's summer palace at Phetchaburi, each with a large bathroom and separate sitting area, furnished in luxurious traditional design; some also have a private outdoor plunge pool. Facilities include watersports on the private stretch of beach, tennis courts, squash court and golf course, a spa, car rental, and an excellent "royal" cuisine restaurant, the *Sala Thai*. ⑨

Shangrilah West of *Maenam Resort*, served by the same access road ⓣ077 425189, ⓦwww.geocities.com/pk_shangrilah. Sprawling onto the nicest, widest stretch of sand along Maenam, a flower-strewn compound of smart, well-maintained though tightly packed, en-suite bungalows with verandas, ceiling fans and decent furniture; some boast air-con and hot water, and there are some rather ugly luxury villas with fridges and cable TV. The restaurant serves good Thai food. Fan ④, air-con ⑤–⑦

SR At the far eastern end of the bay ⓣ077 427524–30, ⓔsr_bungalow@hotmail.com. A quiet, welcoming, good-value place, set in a narrow flower garden, with a very good restaurant. Accommodation is in large, smart, concrete bungalows with bathrooms (some with hot water), verandas and chairs. At the moment only those in pole position on the beachfront have air-con, though the owners may install it throughout. Fan ③, air-con ④

Eating

Most visitors to Maenam **eat** in their hotel or resort restaurant, though a couple of other places stand out. At the west end of the bay, signposted on a lane that runs east from Wat Na Phra Larn, *Sunshine Gourmet* does a bit of everything, from cappuccino and home-made yoghurt for all-day breakfast, through own-baked pies, sandwiches and cakes, to international, especially German, main courses, seafood and other Thai dishes. *Angela's Bakery*, opposite the police station on the main through-road to the east of the pier, is a popular, daytime-only expat hangout, offering great breakfasts and a wide choice of sandwiches, salads, soups and Western main courses, as well as cakes, pies and home-made chocolates.

Bophut

The next bay east is **BOPHUT**, which has a similar look to Maenam but shows a marked difference in atmosphere and facilities, with a noticeable French influence. The quiet, two-kilometre beach attracts a mix of young and old travellers, as well as families, and **Ban Bophut**, now tagged "**Fisherman's Village**", at the east end of the bay, is well geared to meet their needs, with a sprinkling of

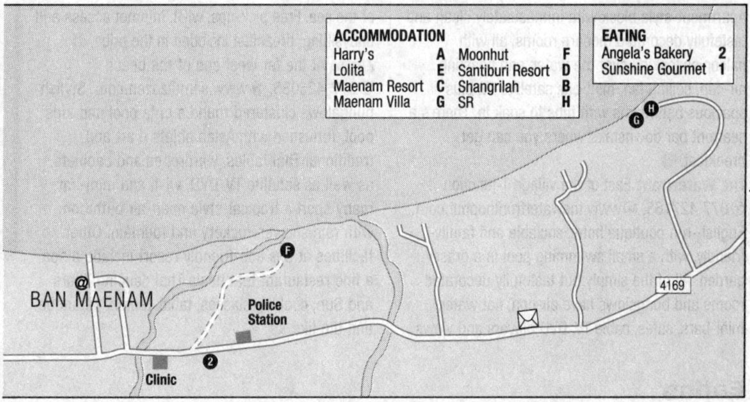

boutique hotels, and a bank, ATMs, scuba-diving outlets, travel agents, internet cafés, supermarkets and a small bookstore, Book World, at the start of Route 4171, for magazines and bestsellers. While through traffic sticks to Route 4169 to Chaweng and Route 4171 towards the airport, development of the village has been reasonably sensitive, preserving many of its old wooden shophouses on the two narrow, largely car-free streets that meet at a T-junction by the pier. At night, in sharp contrast to Chaweng's frenetic beach road, it's a fine place for a promenade, with a concentration of good upmarket restaurants and low-key farang-run bars. The nicest part of the beach itself is at the west end of the bay, towards *Zazen* resort, but again the sand is slightly coarse by Samui's standards.

Samui Go-kart, a **go-karting** track (daily 9am–8/9pm; ⓣ077 425097; from B500 for 10min) on the main road 1km west of the village, offers everyone the chance to let off steam without becoming another accident statistic on the roads of Samui. **Watersports** are also catered for, with kayaks, sailing and windsurfing available near the centre of the beach at The Dive Academy, next to *Anantara*. On the main road near the centre of the beach, Peace Tropical Spa (ⓣ077 430199, ⓦwww.peacetropicalspa.com) offers half a dozen types of **massage**, as well as body and facial treatments, at prices noticeably lower than the luxury hotel spas.

Accommodation

There's very little inexpensive accommodation left among Bophut's twenty or so resorts. Most establishments are well spaced out along the length of the beach, though a handful of small, comfortable hotels cluster together in Ban Bophut.

Anantara West of the village on the main road ⓣ077 428300–9, ⓦwww.anantara.com. Luxury hotel with attentive service in the style of an opulent oriental palace. Blocks of balconied rooms are arrayed round lush gardens, ponds, an attractive swimming pool and a central bar and restaurant, offering contemporary Italian cuisine with Asian influences. There's also a very attractive spa and a huge range of activities, from yoga and traditional crafts classes to tennis and watersports. ❾

Cactus Towards the west end of the beach ⓣ077 245565, ⓔcactusbung@hotmail.com. Welcoming place where ochre cottages with attractive bed platforms, small verandas and well-equipped bathrooms stand in two leafy rows running down to the stylish beachside bar-restaurant; the cheapest make do with fans and cold water, while the various air-con bungalows have hot water and TV. Pool table, internet access. Fan ❹, air-con ❺

Juzz'a Pizza 2 East of the village T-junction ⓣ077 245662–3, ⓦwww.juzzapizza.com. Above a good restaurant (see p.602), four small but smart rooms, well equipped with comfy beds, air-con, hot showers, fridges and cable TV. Two rooms look onto the road, while the other two have beachside terraces with great views. ❻

The Lodge Towards the western end of the village ⓣ077 425337, ⓦwww.lodgesamui.com.

Apartment-style block with immaculately clean and tastefully decorated modern rooms, all with balconies looking over the water, and boasting air-con, ceiling fan, mini-bar, satellite TV, plus spacious bathrooms with tubs to soak in. There's a seafront bar downstairs where you can get breakfast. ⑦

The Waterfront East of the village T-junction ⓣ077 427165, ⓦwww.thewaterfrontbophut.com. English-run boutique hotel, sociable and family-friendly, with a small swimming pool in a grassy garden. All of the simply but tastefully decorated rooms and bungalows have air-con, hot water, mini-bars, safes, cable TV, DVD players and views of the sea. Free pick-ups, wi-fi, internet access and babysitting; breakfast included in the price. ⑦

Zazen At the far west end of the beach ⓣ077 425085, ⓦwww.samuizazen.com. Stylish bungalows clustered round a cute pool and kids' pool, furnished with Asian objets d'art and traditional Thai tables, wardrobes and cabinets, as well as satellite TV, DVD, wi-fi and mini-bar; many sport a tropical-style open-air bathroom with rain shower, rockery and fountain. Other facilities at this eco-friendly resort include a spa, a fine restaurant that hosts Thai dancing Thurs and Sun, cooking classes, table-tennis, pétanque and the like. ⑨

Eating

A stroll through the village will turn up a wide choice of good restaurants for dinner, though it's best to book in advance at a couple of the smaller places recommended.

Happy Elephant West of the village T-junction. Good choice of mostly Thai food, including a few unusual dishes and reasonably priced seafood, and friendly service. There's an attractive beachside terrace and a contemporary-style annexe, *On the Beach*, next door.

Juzz'a Pizza 2 200m south of the village T-junction towards R4169 ⓣ077 245662–3. Friendly, small, elegant restaurant with a beachside terrace, serving excellent, authentic pizzas, with vegetarian and seafood options and a wide choice of extra toppings, as well as pastas and Thai and Western main courses. Closed Mon.

Samui French Bakery East of the village T-junction. The real deal: delicious, inexpensive croissants, breads, quiches, pizzas and patisserie. Also offers simple, reasonably priced main courses such as chicken breast with ham and cheese, sandwiches and salads. Daily 8am–8pm.

The Shack Grill West of the village T-junction ⓣ077 246041 or 087 264994. Small, pricey spot, run by an ebullient New Yorker, and focused on the large, open grill at the front of the restaurant: here all manner of local seafood and imported meats, such as Australian beef and New Zealand lamb, are cooked to your liking. Delicious apple pie and decent house wine.

Bangrak

Beyond the sharp headland with its sweep of coral reefs lies **BANGRAK**, sometimes called **Big Buddha Beach** after the colossus that gazes sternly down on the sun worshippers from its island in the bay. The beach is no great shakes, especially during the northeast monsoon, when the sea retreats and leaves a slippery mud flat, but Bangrak still manages to attract the watersports crowd, and every Sunday locals and expats descend for the family-friendly **Secret Garden Party**, with barbecues, drink and live music from around 4 to 10pm.

The **Big Buddha** (*Phra Yai*) is certainly big and works hard at being a tourist attraction, but is no beauty. A short causeway at the eastern end of the bay leads across to a messy clump of souvenir shops and foodstalls in front of the temple, catering to day-tripping Thais as well as foreigners. Here you can at least get a decent cup of coffee or tea, or a sandwich at *Big Buddha Café*. Ceremonial dragon-steps then bring you up to the covered terrace around the Big Buddha, from where there's a fine view of the sweeping north coast. Look out for the B10 rice-dispensing machine, which allows you symbolically to give alms to the monks at any time of the day.

Bangrak's **bungalows** are squeezed together in a narrow, noisy strip between busy Route 4171 and the shore, underneath the airport flight path. Best of a generally disappointing bunch is *Shambala* (ⓣ077 425330, ⓦwww.samui-shambala.com; ④), an English-run place that's well spread out in a lush garden, with chill-out areas and books to borrow; the large, smart bungalows all have verandas, en-suite bathrooms and fans, and most have hot water; massages and good Thai and Western food are also on offer as well as, diving, snorkelling, kayaking and other activities through in-house dive shop One Hundred Degrees East (ⓣ077 245936–7, ⓦwww.100degreeseast.com).

Choeng Mon

After Bangrak comes the high-kicking boot of Samui's **northeastern cape**, with its small, rocky coves overlooking Ko Pha Ngan and connected by sandy lanes. Songthaews run along Route 4171 to the largest and most beautiful bay, **Choeng Mon**, whose white sandy beach is lined with casuarina trees that provide shade for the bungalows and upmarket resorts. Choeng Mon is now popular enough to support small supermarkets, travel agents and a bank, but on the whole it remains relatively uncommercialized and laid-back.

Accommodation

Boat House Hotel Central Choeng Mon ⓣ077 425041–52, ⓦwww.imperialhotels.com. Run by the reliable Imperial group, *Boat House* is named after the two-storey rice barges that have been converted into suites in the grounds. It also offers good-value luxury rooms with balconies in more prosaic modern buildings, often filled by package tours. As well as a beachside boat-shaped pool, there's a spa and fitness room. ⑨

Island View Tucked in on the east side of the *Boat House Hotel* ⓣ077 245031, ⓕ077 425583. Smart, good-value chalets with air-con, hot water, TV and fridge, in a lively compound that crams in a supermarket, a dive shop offering kayaks and snorkelling, a small bookshop and a beachfront bar. ⑤

Kirati Resort (PP) 200m east of *Island View* ⓣ077 245360, ⓔkirati_family@hotmail.com. Spacious wooden chalets with a few nice decorative touches, fridges and large hot-water bathrooms, in a large, jungly garden. Fan ④, air-con ⑤

Ô Soleil West of the *Boat House Hotel* ⓣ077 425232, ⓔbuisseretjean@yahoo.fr. A lovely, orderly, Belgian-run place in a pretty, tranquil garden dotted with ponds. The good-value, well-built, clean bungalows all have TVs and some have hot water, fridges and air-con. Fan ③, air-con ④

The Tongsai Bay Cottages and Hotel North side of Choeng Mon ⓣ077 245480, ⓦwww.tongsaibay.co.th. The island's finest hotel, an easy-going, environmentally aware establishment with the unhurried air of a country club, and with excellent service. The luxurious rooms, red-tiled cottages and palatial villas (some with their own pool) command beautiful views over the spacious, picturesque grounds, the private beach (with plenty of non-motorized watersports), a freshwater and a vast saltwater swimming pool and the whole bay. They all also sport second bathtubs on their secluded open-air terraces, so you don't miss out on the scenery while splashing about. There's an array of very fine restaurants and a delightful health spa, as well as a tennis court, gym and an Avis car-rental desk. ⑨

Chaweng

For looks alone, none of the other beaches can match **CHAWENG**, with its broad, gently sloping strip of white sand sandwiched between the limpid blue sea and a line of palm trees. Such beauty has not escaped attention of course, which means, on the plus side, that Chaweng can provide just about anything the active beach bum demands, from thumping nightlife to ubiquitous and diverse watersports. The negative angle is that the new developments are ever more cramped and expensive, while building work behind the palm trees and repairs to the over-commercialized main beach road are always in progress.

The six-kilometre bay is framed between the small island of Ko Matlang at the north end and the 300-metre-high headland above Coral Cove in the south. From

Ko Matlang, where the waters provide some decent snorkelling, an often exposed coral reef slices southwest across to the mainland, marking out a shallow lagoon and **North Chaweng**. This S-shaped part of the beach is comparatively peaceful, though it has some ugly pockets of development; at low tide it becomes a wide, inviting playground, and from October to January the reef shelters it from the worst of the northeast winds. South of the reef, the idyllic shoreline of **Central Chaweng** stretches for 2km in a dead-straight line, the ugly, traffic-clogged and seemingly endless strip of amenities on the parallel main drag largely concealed behind the treeline and the resorts. Around a low promontory is **Chaweng Noi**, a little curving beach in a rocky bay, which is comparatively quiet in its northern part, away from the road. Well inland of Central Chaweng, the round-island road, Route 4169, passes through the original village of **Ban Chaweng**.

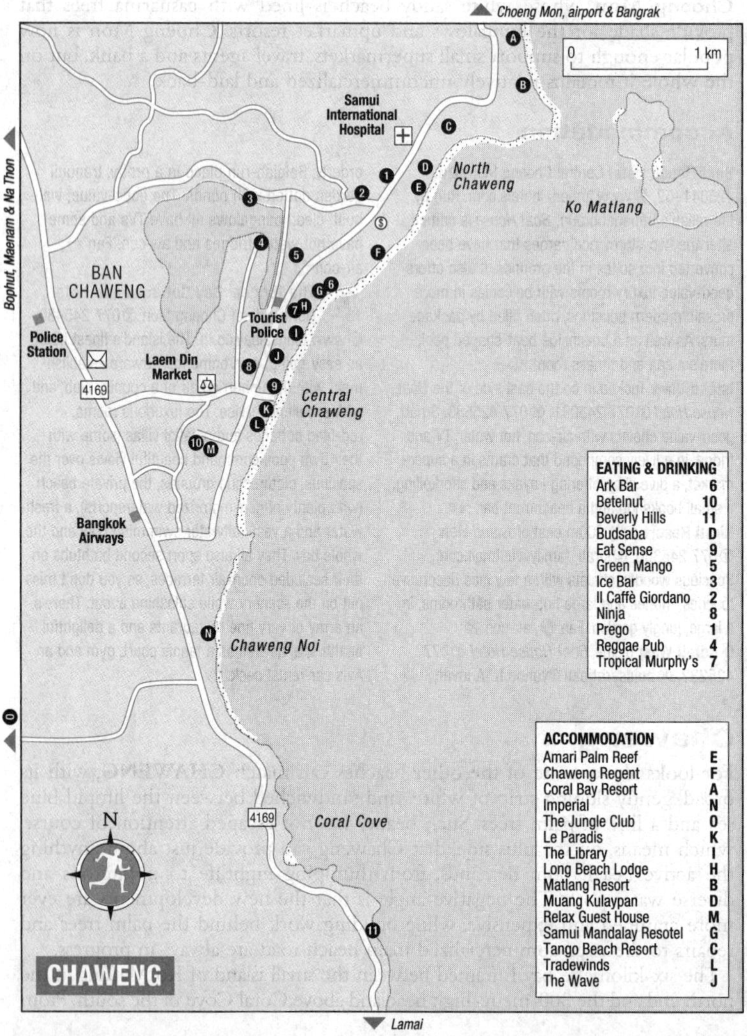

South of Chaweng, the road climbs past **Coral Cove**, a tiny, isolated beach of coarse sand hemmed in by high rocks, with some good coral for snorkelling. It's well worth making the trip to the *Beverly Hills Café*, towards the tip of the headland dividing Chaweng from Lamai, for a jaw-dropping view over Chaweng and Choeng Mon to the peaks of Ko Pha Ngan (and for some good, moderately priced food, notably seafood).

Accommodation

Over fifty **bungalow resorts** and **hotels** at Chaweng are squeezed into thin strips running back from the beachfront at right angles. The cheapest digs here are generally little more than functional, while more and more expensive places are sprouting up all the time, offering sumptuous accommodation at top-whack prices.

Inexpensive and moderate

The Jungle Club 2km up a steep, partly paved road from Chaweng Noi ⓣ081 894 2327, ⓦwww.jungleclubsamui.com. Breezy, French-Thai antidote to Chaweng's commercial clutter: a huge, grassy, shady plot with a small but attractive pool on the edge of the slope to catch the towering views of Ko Pha Ngan and beyond. A chic, open-sided bar-restaurant has been built into the rocks, while some of the smart, varied, en-suite bungalows come with hot water. Free pick-ups twice a day; long-stay discounts. ④–⑦

Long Beach Lodge Towards the north end of Central Chaweng ⓣ077 422162, ⓕ077 422372. An unusually spacious and shady, sandy compound. All the orderly, clean bungalows and rooms are a decent size and have hot water, fridge, TV and air-con. Service is friendly, and breakfast is included in the price. ⑤–⑦

Matlang Resort At the far north end of North Chaweng ⓣ077 230468–9. Tranquil, friendly place facing a broad stretch of beach with nice views of Ko Matlang. The en-suite wooden bungalows, all with verandas and mosquito screens, some with air-con and hot water, are a little bit battered, but are spread around a very pleasant, shady flower garden. Fan ③, air-con ⑤

Relax Guest House Soi Colibri, Central Chaweng, next to *Betelnut* restaurant ⓣ077 413836. Functional crashpad, but clean and well maintained by a pleasant family, and good value for the facilities: air-con, hot water and TV. ③

Samui Mandalay Resotel Central Chaweng, next to *Ark Bar* ⓣ077 422340, ⓕ077 422280. Friendly spot offering a wide variety of colourful, rather eccentrically designed bungalows in a narrow strip and rooms in the main building. Clean and well equipped, with air-con, hot water, TV and fridge. ④–⑤

The Wave Central Chaweng ⓣ077 230803, ⓦwww.thewavesamui.com. One of the cheapest guest houses on Chaweng, this helpful, English-run place is not on the beach, but above a very popular bar-restaurant on the main road. The pick of the rooms, most of which have fans and share cold-water bathrooms, is the top-floor duplex with air-con, hot water and a rooftop terrace. All kinds of advice and tours available, as well as internet access and a huge library. Fan ③–④, air-con ⑥

Expensive

Amari Palm Reef North Chaweng ⓣ077 422015–8, ⓦwww.amari.com. Congenial, eco-friendly luxury hotel that's unpretentious and good value. Spacious accommodation, stretching back across the road from the beach, includes family-friendly duplexes, and there are two elegant restaurants, including *Prego* (see p.606), a full-service spa, two swimming pools and a kids' pool. Various discounts and packages available on their website. ⑨

Chaweng Regent At the bottom end of North Chaweng ⓣ077 230391–400, ⓦwww.chawengregent.com. Reliable, well-run, luxury place offering elegant bungalows and low-rise rooms with private terraces and all mod cons, around lotus ponds, two pools, a fitness centre, sauna and spa. ⑨

Coral Bay Resort At the far north end of North Chaweng ⓣ077 234555, ⓦwww.coralbay.net. A charming, eco-friendly vision of how Chaweng might have developed – if only there'd been more space. In quiet, delightful, ten-acre gardens with over 500 species of plants, the huge, thatched villas have been thoughtfully and tastefully designed with local woods, bamboo and coconut; all have extensive verandas, waterfall showers and DVD players (movies available from the library). There's an attractive pool, a spa and a recommended beachside bar-restaurant; kayaks and snorkels available. ⑨

Imperial Chaweng Noi ⓣ077 422020–36, ⓦwww.imperialhotels.com. The longest-established luxury hotel on Samui is a grand but lively establishment with a Mediterranean feel, set in sloping, landscaped gardens; features include two pools (one sea water, one fresh with a jacuzzi), a spa, tennis court, all kinds of watersports and classes such as Thai cookery. 9

Le Paradis Central Chaweng ⓣ077 239041–3, ⓦwww.leparadisresort.com. Set in lush, spacious gardens, twelve luxurious traditional Ayutthaya-style houses on stilts, with living areas underneath and verandas, as well as fourteen stylish contemporary villas with open-air bathrooms. Attractive beachside swimming pool, gym and health spa. 9

The Library Central Chaweng ⓣ077 422767–8, ⓦwww.thelibrary.name. High-concept design hotel, based around a library of books, DVDs and CDs with computer terminals. The idea is continued in the rooms, which all sport iMacs and have a sleek, cubic theme; they're divided into suites (downstairs) and studios with balconies (upstairs). There's a blood-red swimming pool, a spa, a fitness centre and a beachfront terrace restaurant, *The Page*. Rack rates from B16,500. 9

Muang Kulaypan North Chaweng ⓣ077 230036, ⓦwww.kulaypan.com. Original, stylish boutique hotel arrayed around a large, immaculate garden with a black-tiled swimming pool and an excellent beachside restaurant (see below). Rooms – each with their own private balcony or garden – combine contemporary design with traditional Thai-style comforts. 9

Tango Beach Resort North Chaweng ⓣ077 422470, ⓦwww.tangobeachsamui.com. This helpful and welcoming place has a modern Thai style that sets it apart from most of Samui's farang-oriented hotels: a variety of cutesy, colourful, well-equipped rooms are separated by a small, shady pool and a wooden boardwalk that runs down to *Lazy Wave* bar-restaurant. Breakfast included. 7

Tradewinds Central Chaweng ⓣ077 414294, ⓦwww.tradewinds-samui.com. A cheerful, well-run place of characterful bungalows and rooms (all with air-con, hot water, mini-bar, cable TV and balcony) with plenty of room to breathe in colourful tropical gardens. The resort specializes in sailing, with its own catamarans (instruction available), as well as offering kayaks and croquet. Breakfast included. 8

Eating

Chaweng offers all manner of foreign **cuisines**, from French to Russian, much of it of dubious quality. Amongst all this, it's quite hard to find good, reasonably priced Thai food – as well as the places recommended below, it's worth exploring the cheap and cheerful night-time foodstalls at **Laem Din market**, which are popular with local workers, on the middle road between Central Chaweng and Highway 4169. The fame of *Betelnut* has attracted several other well-regarded restaurants to **Soi Colibri**, including Italian, Japanese and Chinese. *The Jungle Club* (see p.605; book the day before) offers **barbecues** for B750, including transfers, a cocktail and a swim.

Betelnut Soi Colibri, a small lane at the south end of Central Chaweng opposite the landmark *Centara Grand Resort* ⓣ077 413370. By far Samui's best restaurant, serving pricey but exceptional Californian-Thai fusion food. Few tables, so reservations highly recommended.

Budsaba Restaurant At the *Muang Kulaypan Hotel* ⓣ077 230850. This charming, upmarket beachfront restaurant fully justifies the journey up to North Chaweng: you get to recline in your own seaside *sala* or open-sided hut on stilts while tucking into unusual and excellent Thai dishes such as banana-flower and shrimp salad. Live traditional music and dance Tues, Thurs, Sat & Sun eve.

Eat Sense Central Chaweng, next to *Charlie's Huts* ⓣ077 414242. Spacious, relaxing, mostly open-air restaurant on the beachfront, serving expensive but delicious Thai food – try the deep-fried prawns with cashew nuts and tamarind sauce.

Il Caffè Giordano North Chaweng, at the start of the Ban Chaweng road. Trim café-bar run by a congenial Florentine. Good coffees of course, plus tiramisu, pizza by the slice, sandwiches and simple pastas; free internet for customers. Daily 8.30am–7pm, sometimes till 10.30pm in high season.

Ninja Near *Charlie's Huts* in Central Chaweng. Popular, well-run, very basic and cheap restaurant, serving simple Thai favourites such as *tom yam*, *som tam* and *phat thai*, as well as crêpes, breakfasts and other Western food. Open 24hr.

Prego *Amari Palm Reef*, North Chaweng ⓣ077 422015–8. Excellent, chic, open-sided restaurant that would stand on its own two feet in Milan, the head chef's home town. The varied menu of contemporary Italian dishes includes good *antipasti*, pizzas and top-notch risottos, and there's a very good selection of wines. Booking advised in high season.

Drinking and nightlife

Avoiding the raucous hostess bars and English theme pubs on the main through road, the best place to **drink** is on the beach: at night dozens of resorts and dedicated bars lay out candlelit tables with axe cushions for reclining on the sand, especially towards the north end of Central Chaweng and on North Chaweng – if you want somewhere specific to aim for, try *Lazy Wave* at *Tango Beach Resort* or *Jack Bar*, a little further down, for reggae. Meanwhile inland, overlooking the lake from its north shore, *Q Bar* was closed for refurbishment at the time of writing, but has garnered quite a reputation for its cutting-edge music from local and international DJs and its sleek decor.

Ark Bar North end of Central Chaweng. Hosts a very popular beach party, with house and funk DJs and a free barbecue, Wed from 3pm until well into the night.

Green Mango North end of Central Chaweng. Long-standing dance venue, in a huge shed that combines an industrial look with that of a tropical greenhouse. Now with its own alley, Soi Green Mango, lined with other vibrant bars and clubs, including *Sweet Soul Café*, which always seems to be rammed with dancing farangs and Thais.

Ice Bar North side of the lake ⓦwww.icebarsamui.com. Been out in the midday sun with mad dogs and Englishmen? Maybe what you need is a spell at -5°C in this sculpted ice bar – and a vodka. B375, furs included.

Reggae Pub Inland from Central Chaweng across the lake. Chaweng's oldest nightclub, a venerable Samui institution with a memorabilia shop to prove it. It does time now as an unpretentious, good-time, party venue, with plenty of drinking games, pool tables, big-screen sports and live bands most nights in high season.

Tropical Murphy's Opposite *McDonald's* in Central Chaweng. One theme pub that is worth singling out: with draught Guinness and Kilkenny, big-screen sports, quiz nights, live music and decent food, *Murphy's* has turned itself into a popular landmark and meeting place.

Listings

Airline Bangkok Airways, south end of Ban Chaweng on Route 4169 ⓣ077 422512.

Bookshop Bookazine, selling English-language books, newspapers and magazines, has several branches, most conveniently next to *Tropical Murphy's* in Central Chaweng. Saai, North Chaweng at the T-junction of the beach road and the Ban Chaweng road, is good for second-hand, and some new, books.

Cookery courses The highly recommended Samui Institute of Thai Culinary Arts (SITCA; closed Sun; ⓣ077 413172, ⓦwww.sitca.net), on Soi Colibri opposite *Betelnut* restaurant, runs two-and-a-half-hour classes in the morning and afternoon (B1950), and you get to eat what you've cooked with a friend afterwards. They also have a culinary shop selling Thai cooking accessories, ingredients and cookbooks.

Hospital The private Samui International Hospital in North Chaweng (ⓣ077 230781–2, ⓦwww.sih.co.th) provides 24hr emergency services, house calls, a dental clinic and travel inoculations.

Internet Dozens of outlets, including at travel agent Travel Solutions (see below).

Pharmacy Boots has a convenient branch in the middle of Central Chaweng, just up the road from *Tropical Murphy's* pub.

Spas Among stand-alone spas, which are generally cheaper than the luxury hotel versions, Living Senses, above *McDonald's* in the Living Square shopping plaza in Central Chaweng (ⓣ077 230917, ⓦwww.livingsensesspa.com), has a good reputation for its massages, reflexology, body wraps and scrubs; on a waterfall- and flower-splashed hillside with a plunge pool at the far north end of Chaweng, Eranda offers a wider range of treatments and a little more style, at higher prices (ⓣ077 422666, ⓦwww.erandaspa.co.th).

Tourist police Behind *McDonald's* overlooking the lake in Central Chaweng ⓣ1155 or 077 414198.

Travel agent English-run Travel Solutions, just off the main road opposite *Tropical Murphy's* (ⓣ077 239007–8, ⓦwww.travelsolutionsthailand.com), is a reliable and knowledgeable agent, for train and bus tickets among many other things.

Watersports Samui Ocean Sports, on the beach by the *Chaweng Regent* at the bottom end of North Chaweng, and south of *Long Beach Lodge* on Central Chaweng (ⓣ081 940 1999, ⓦwww.sailing-in-samui.com), rents windsurfers and kayaks, as well as offering sailing lessons, trips and charters.

Lamai

LAMAI is like a second city to Chaweng's capital, not quite as developed and much less frenetic, while lacking the latter's range of chic hotels, restaurants and nightclubs. Development is concentrated into a farang toytown of open-air hostess bars and Western restaurants that has grown up behind the centre of the beach, interspersed with supermarkets, clinics, banks, ATMs, dive shops and travel agents. Running roughly north to south for 4km, the white, palm-fringed beach itself is still a picture, and generally quieter than Chaweng, with far less in the way of watersports – it's quite easy to get away from it all by staying at the peaceful extremities of the bay, where the backpackers' resorts are preferable to Chaweng's functional guest houses. At the northern end, the spur of land that hooks eastward into the sea is perhaps the prettiest spot, though it's beginning to attract some upmarket development: it has more rocks than sand, but the shallow sea behind the coral reef is protected from the high seas of November, December and January.

The original village of **Ban Lamai**, set well back on Route 4169, remains surprisingly aloof, and its wat contains a small museum of ceramics, agricultural tools and other everyday objects. Most visitors get more of a buzz from **Hin Yay** (Grandmother Rock) and **Hin Ta** (Grandfather Rock), small rock formations on the bay's southern promontory, which never fail to raise a giggle with their resemblance to the male and female sexual organs.

Lamai boasts two of Samui's longer-standing and better **spas**. The oldest, *The Spa Resort* (ⓣ077 230855, ⓦwww.thesparesorts.net; ❺–❾; minimum three-night stay), covers everything from Thai massage (B300 per hr) and herbal saunas (B300 per hr) for guests and non-guests, to in-house fasting programmes (US$300 per week). Also on offer are a wide range of other massages, body and facial wraps, and yoga, meditation, massage and raw-food culinary classes. *The Spa* now has two main locations, the original one at the far north end of the beach, the other, more upmarket branch 3km away in the hills above Lamai (connected by shuttle buses), each with a swimming pool and a wide variety of accommodation; there's also a small complex of beachside villas with private saltwater pools, 600m north of the original branch. With less of an emphasis on clean living, and more on pampering, *Tamarind Springs* (ⓣ077 230571 or 077 424436, ⓦwww.tamarindsprings.com) is set in a beautiful, secluded coconut grove just north of *Spa Resort* off the main road. Here a session in their unique herbal steam room, set between two boulders by a waterfall-fed plunge pool, and a two-hour Thai massage, for example, costs B2600. Facials and other massages, such as head, foot and back, are also available, and there's a café and juice bar, as well as luxury villas on the site to rent (minimum three nights; ❾).

Accommodation

Lamai's **accommodation** is generally less cramped and slightly better value than Chaweng's, though it presents far fewer choices at the top end of the market. The far southern end of the bay towards the Grandparent Rocks has the tightest concentration of budget bungalows.

Bay View Resort On the bay's northern headland ⓣ077 418429, ⓦwww.bayviewsamui.com. Neat, stylish bungalows with verandas, minibars and hot-water bathrooms in an extensive, flower-bedecked compound; the poshest come with air-con and cable TV. Offers a friendly, German-Thai welcome, internet access and great sunset views of the beach from the attractive restaurant. ❺

Bill Resort At the far southern end of the bay ⓣ077 424403, ⓦwww.billresortsamui.com. A friendly, efficient and orderly setup, crammed into a fragrant, overgrown garden with a decent-sized pool and Jacuzzi, on a pleasant stretch of beach

▲ Coral Cove & Chaweng

LAMAI

N

4169

IT Complex @

A

B

C

Tamarind Springs ◆

E D

F

Police Box ■

2 1

Wat Lamai ⚓

🎵 **Market**

BAN LAMAI

G

Siam Kitchen

4169

Bookazine

3 $

4

5 H

@

Mr Samui

✉

I

J K

L

Hin Yay & Hin Ta (Grandmother & Grandfather Rocks)

4169

Wat Sila Ngu ⛪

ACCOMMODATION	
Bay View Resort	B
Bill Resort	I
Flower Paradise	A
Green Villa	J
Lamai-Wanta	H
Renaissance	C
The Spa Resort	E
Sunrise	L
Surat Palm Resort	F
Utopia	G
Weekender Villa	D
White Sand	K

EATING & DRINKING	
Bauhaus	4
Coast	H
Continental Bakery	2
Eldorado	5
Feinkost Deli	2
Ninja Crêpes	1
Radiance	E
Shamrock	3

0 500 m

▼ Ban Hua Thanon & Na Thon

SOUTHERN THAILAND: THE GULF COAST | Ko Samui

6

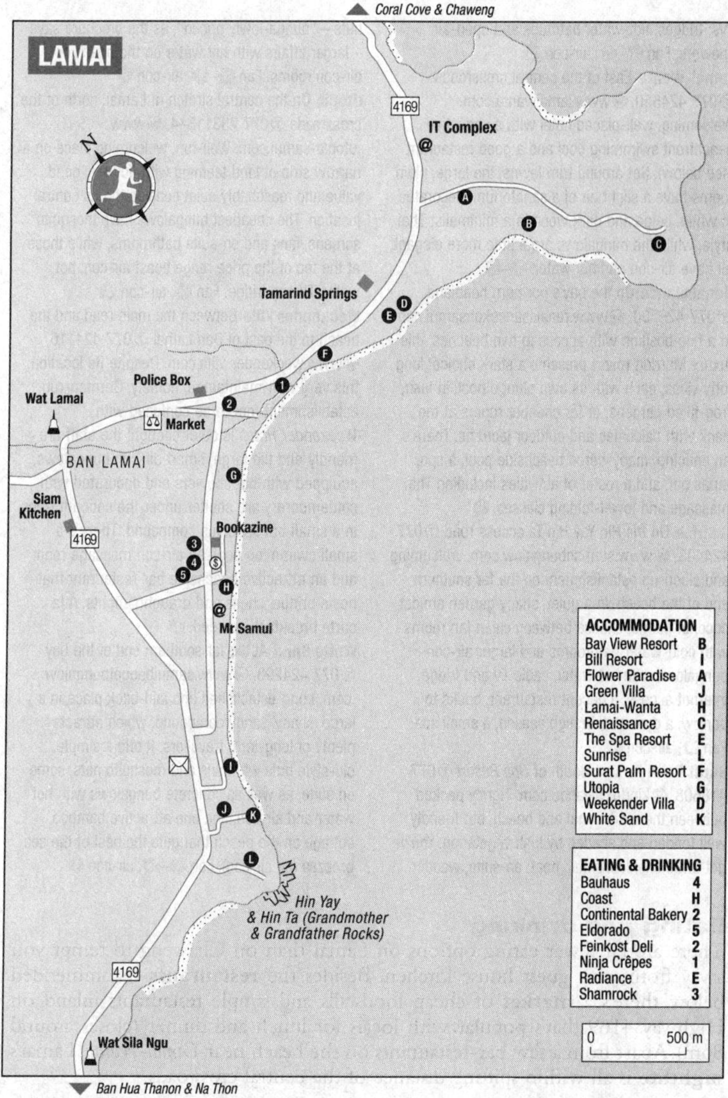

and up the hill behind. Its widely varied, clean, rooms and bungalows, most with air-con and hot water, offer good value if you don't need much elbow room. Fan ❸, air-con ❺–❾

Flower Paradise On the bay's northern headland ☎077 418059 or 089 288 8326, ⊛www .samuiroestiland.com. Just a short walk from the beach, a friendly, well-run German-Swiss place in a small but beautiful garden. All the attractive, well-tended bungalows of varying sizes have mosquito

nets and hot water, and there's a good restaurant, *Röstiland* (closed Mon), specializing in the eponymous hash browns. Fan ❸–❹, air-con ❹

Green Villa On the access road to *White Sand*, at the far southern end of the bay ☎077 424296, ⓔresagreenvilla@hotmail.com. Quiet, French-run operation set back from the beach in a spacious garden among palm trees, with a small swimming pool, clean, simple, en-suite bungalows with fans (some with hot water) and grand, air-con villas with

TVs, fridges, hot-water bathtubs and open-air showers. Fan ❷–❸, air-con ❻

Lamai-Wanta East of the central crossroads ⓣ077 424550, ⓦwww.lamaiwanta.com. Welcoming, well-placed hotel with a seductive beachfront swimming pool and a good restaurant (see below). Set around trim lawns, the large, plain rooms have a slight air of a sanatorium, decorated in white, beige and dark wood in a minimalist Thai style, while the bungalows are a little more elegant; all have air-con and hot water. ❻–❼

Renaissance On the bay's northern headland ⓣ077 429300, ⓦwww.renaissancekohsamui.com. In a fine position with access to two beaches, this luxury Marriott resort presents a stark choice: long, lofty villas, each with its own plunge pool, in lush, frog-filled gardens, or far cheaper rooms at the back with balconies and outdoor jacuzzis. There's an enticing, many-tiered beachside pool, a spa, tapas bar, and a roster of activities including Thai massage and towel-folding classes. ❾

Sunrise On the Hin Yay Hin Ta access road ⓣ077 424433, ⓦwww.sunrisebungalow.com. Welcoming and clued-up establishment on the far southern end of the beach. In a quiet, shady garden amidst coconut palms, choose between clean fan rooms with cold-water bathrooms and larger air-con bungalows with hot water, cable TV and fridge. Internet access, a decent restaurant, books to borrow, a gym and, in high season, a small spa. Fan ❸, air-con ❻

Surat Palm Resort South of *Spa Resort* ⓣ077 418608, ⓔkjorlux@yahoo.com. Tightly packed between the road, canal and beach, but friendly, well tended and shaded by lush vegetation. You've got three choices: small, neat, en-suite, wooden huts – "bunga-lowly priced", as the brochure says – larger affairs with hot water on the beach or air-con rooms. Fan ❸–❺, air-con ❻

Utopia On the central stretch of Lamai, north of the crossroads ⓣ077 233113–4, ⓦwww.utopia-samui.com. Well-run, welcoming place on a narrow strip of land teeming with flowers, good value and reasonably quiet considering its central location. The cheapest bungalows have mosquito screens, fans and en-suite bathrooms, while those at the top of the price range boast air-con, hot water, TV and fridge. Fan ❹, air-con ❻

Weekender Villa Between the main road and the beach to the east of Ban Lamai ⓣ077 424116, ⓦwww.weekender-villa.com. Despite its location, this very well-maintained, homely, German-run establishment (not to be confused with *Weekender Hotel*) is quiet enough; the staff are friendly and the large, smart air-con bungalows, equipped with hot showers and decorated with contemporary art, shelter under the coconut trees in a small but spacious compound. There's a small swimming pool, an air-con massage room and an attractive beachside bar-restaurant that hosts bridge, chess and draughts nights. À la carte breakfast included. ❻

White Sand At the far southern end of the bay ⓣ077 424298, ⓦwww.samuibudgetbungalow.com. Long-established and laid-back place in a large, shady, sandy compound, which attracts plenty of long-term travellers. It offers simple, old-style huts with fans and mosquito nets, some en suite, as well as concrete bungalows with hot water and air-con, and one attractive bamboo cottage on the beach that gets the best of the sea breezes (no air-con). Fan ❶–❺, air-con ❹

Eating and drinking

There are far fewer eating options on Lamai than on Chaweng to tempt you away from your guest house kitchen. Besides the **restaurants** recommended below, there's a **market** of cheap foodstalls and simple restaurants inland on Highway 4169 that's popular with locals for lunch and dinner (closes around 8pm). Apart from a few bar-restaurants on the beach near *Lamai-Wanta*, Lamai's **nightlife** is all within spitting distance of the central crossroads.

Bauhaus North of the central crossroads. Barn-like complex sporting a bistro and a dance floor, with entertainment provided by big-screen TVs, pool tables and foam parties (Mon & Fri).

Coast *Lamai-Wanta*, east of the central crossroads ⓣ077 424550. Hip, open-sided restaurant by the hotel pool and beach, minimalist but mellow, with a menu that's half Thai, including tasty *kaeng matsaman kai* (B160), and half international fusion.

Continental Bakery North of the central crossroads, near Highway 4169. Friendly, Swiss-run place serving good breads, cakes, burgers, sandwiches and espressos, as well as all-day breakfasts ranging from French and American to Belgian (with pork steak, apparently). Daily 8am–8pm.

Eldorado Just west of the central crossroads. Highly recommended, good-value Swedish restaurant, serving a few Thai favourites, salads, steaks, pizzas and other international main courses, plus one or two indigenous specialities such as Swedish meatballs. All-you-can-eat barbecue on Wed evenings for B260.

Feinkost Deli next to *Continental Bakery*. Deli for meats, cheeses and own-baked breads, plus café-bar serving a wide selection of Western, mostly German food, including plenty of sausages, schnitzels and good pizzas, with German beer to wash it all down and apple strudel to finish you off.
Ninja Crêpes On Highway 4169, east of Ban Lamai. A branch of Chaweng's backpacker hotspot, a dependable, simple, cheap, 24hr café, with internet booths, serving basic Thai favourites, as well as crêpes and other Western food.
Radiance *The Spa Resort*, at the far north end of the beach. Excellent, casual, moderately priced beachside restaurant, serving a huge range of mostly vegetarian Thai and international (including Mexican) dishes, plus raw and vegan food, as well as plenty of meat and marine offerings. The veggie "ginger nuts" stir-fry and *som tam* with spicy Thai sausage are excellent. A long menu of juices, smoothies and shakes includes a delicious lime juice with honey.
Shamrock North of the central crossroads. Popular Irish bar with pool tables and TV sports, which hosts lively cover bands and keeps Guinness and Kilkenny bitter on draught.

Listings

Bookshop Bookazine, selling English-language books, newspapers and magazines, on the main beachside drag.
Cookery classes Learn Thai cooking, take a market tour and eat your own-cooked lunch or dinner, on two- to four-person classes at Siam Kitchen on R4169 (3hr; B1200 including Lamai pick-ups; ⓣ086 109 1915, ⓦwww.siamkitchen.net).
Internet Among dozens of options on Lamai, a couple stand out. Mr Samui's art gallery and café, just south of the central crossroads, is a congenial choice offering good espresso coffee, or you could head for the unmissable, shiny IT Complex at the north end of the bay, headquarters of website Sawadee, which offers fast internet and fierce air-con.
Meditation retreats Wat Suan Mokkh (see p.588) has recently branched out to offer five-day retreats at Dipabhavan, a hermitage in the hills above Lamai (ⓦwww.dipabhavan.com). Helped by farang co-ordinators, Suan Mokkh's abbot, Ajarn Poh, leads the retreats himself, which take place in English from the 22nd to the 27th of each month; pick-ups are laid on from *The Spa Resort*, *Utopia* and Wat Sila Ngu on the 21st for registration. For more information, contact Khun Siriwan at *Utopia* or on ⓣ081 892 3457.

The south and west coasts

Lacking the long, attractive beaches of the more famous resorts, the **south and west coasts** rely on a few charming, isolated spots with peaceful accommodation. Heading south from Lamai, you come first to the Muslim fishing village of **Ban Hua Thanon** and *Ban Hua Thanon Seafood*, a justly famous **restaurant** on Highway 4169, recommended in all the Thai food guides. A world away from Samui's slick resort restaurants, this rustic wooden shophouse with lovely outdoor tables on the water keeps its reasonably priced fish in tanks at the front. Recommended dishes include baked green mussels with lemon grass and excellent crispy, shredded prawn with mango salad. On Route 4170 a couple of kilometres down the coast, Kiteboarding Asia (ⓣ081 591 4592–3, ⓦwww.kiteboardingasia.com; B4000 for one day, B11,000 for three), based at *Samui Orchid Resort*, offers instruction in **kiteboarding**, which is at its best here between December and February, as well as rentals. Don't be tempted by the pitiful aquarium at the same resort, where the tanks are barely bigger than the fish.

A kilometre further on is one of the island's most secluded hotels: founded as a private club on a quiet south-facing promontory, the *Laem Set Inn* (ⓣ077 424393, ⓦwww.laemset.com; fan ❺, air-con ❽) now offers a wide range of elegant rooms and suites – some of them reassembled village houses, some with their own plunge pool – as well as an excellent restaurant, cookery courses, a spa, wi-fi, plenty of watersports and a scenically positioned swimming pool. The access road to the *Laem Set Inn* takes you past the nearby **Samui Butterfly Garden** (daily 8.30am–5.30pm; B170, children B120), opposite *Centara Villas*.

Here you can wander among artificial waterfalls and lush vegetation, on a net-covered, rocky hillside overlooking the sea, surrounded by dozens of brilliantly coloured lepidopterans.

The gentle but unspectacular coast beyond is lined with a good reef for snorkelling, which can be explored most easily from the fishing village of **Ban Bangkao**. There's also good snorkelling around **Ko Taen**, a short way offshore to the south: a five-hour boat trip from, for example, TK Tour (Ⓣ077 334052–3, Ⓦwww.tktoursamui.com) in the next village to the west, **Ban Thongkrut**, including pick-up from your accommodation, snorkelling equipment and lunch on the long beach of the neighbouring island, Ko Mad Sum, will set you back B1100 per person (B1300 with kayaking).

About 5km inland, near **Ban Thurian**, the **Na Muang Falls** make a popular outing as they're not far off the round-island road (each of the two main falls has its own signposted kilometre-long paved access road off Route 4169). The lower fall splashes and sprays down a twenty-metre wall of rock into a large pool, while Na Muang 2, upstream, is a more spectacular, shaded cascade that requires a bit of foot-slogging from the car park (about 15min uphill).

On the west coast, the flat beaches are unexceptional but make a calm alternative when the northeast winds hit the other side of the island. At **Ban Taling Ngam**, the *Five Islands Gallery Café* lays on half-day **boat trips** to **Ko Si Ko Ha**, the heavily guarded islands just offshore where sea gypsies gather swifts' nests for bird's-nest soup (see p.746). Rounded off by a varied Thai lunch or dinner at its beachside restaurant, the package costs from B6050 for two people, including transfers.

Ko Pha Ngan

In recent years, backpackers have tended to move over to Ko Samui's fun-loving little sibling, **KO PHA NGAN**, 20km to the north, but the island still has a relatively simple atmosphere, mostly because the lousy road system is an impediment to the developers. With a dense jungle covering its inland mountains and rugged granite outcrops along the coast, Pha Ngan lacks the huge, gently sweeping beaches for which Samui is famous, but it does have plenty of coral to explore and some beautiful, sheltered bays: if you're seeking total isolation, trek out to **Hat Khuat** (**Bottle Beach**) on the north coast or the half-dozen pristine beaches on the east coast; **Thong Nai Pan** at the top of the east coast is not quite as remote, and offers a decent range of amenities and accommodation; while on the long neck of land at the southeast corner, **Hat Rin**, a pilgrimage site for ravers, is a thoroughly commercialized backpackers' resort in a gorgeous setting. Much of Pha Ngan's development has plonked itself on the south and west sides along the only coastal roads on the island, which fan out from **Thong Sala**, the capital; the unattractive south coast is hard to recommend, but the west coast offers several handsome sandy bays with great sunset views, notably **Hat Yao** and **Hat Salad**.

Pha Ngan's **bungalows** all have running water and electricity (on the remotest beaches, only in the evenings and from individual generators), and nearly all come with en-suite bathrooms. There are only a handful of luxury resorts, though plenty of places now offer air-con, especially on Hat Rin. The three hundred or so resorts generally have more space to spread out than on Ko Samui, and the cost of living is lower. The prices given on the following pages are standard for most of the year (though on Hat Rin they tend to vary with the phases of the moon), but in slack periods you'll be offered discounts (possible, roughly, in May, June, Oct & Nov), and at the very busiest times (especially Dec & Jan) Pha Ngan's bungalow owners are canny enough to raise the stakes. **Nightlife** is concentrated at Hat Rin, climaxing every month in a wild **full moon party** on the beach; a couple of smaller outdoor **parties** have now got in on the act, the Half Moon Festival (twice monthly, about a week before and after the full moon; Ⓦ www.halfmoonfestival.com) and the monthly Black Moon Party (Ⓦ www.fullmoon.phangan.info), both at Ban Tai.

There's no TAT office on Ko Pha Ngan, but a couple of free, widely available booklets provide regularly updated **information** about the island: *Phangan Info* (which has a particularly good website, on which you can book accommodation, at Ⓦ www.phangan.info) and *Phangan Explorer* (Ⓦ www.phanganexplorer.com).

Getting to Ko Pha Ngan

The most obvious way of getting to Ko Pha Ngan is on a **boat** from the **Surat Thani** area (but see also p.586 for boats from Chumphon); for contact details of **transport companies** in Surat, see p.592. Boat services fluctuate according to demand, but the longest-established ferry is the night boat from Ban Don pier in Surat Thani to Thong Sala, which leaves at 11pm every night (Ⓣ 077 284928 or 081 326 8973; 6hr; B300); tickets are available from the pier on the day of

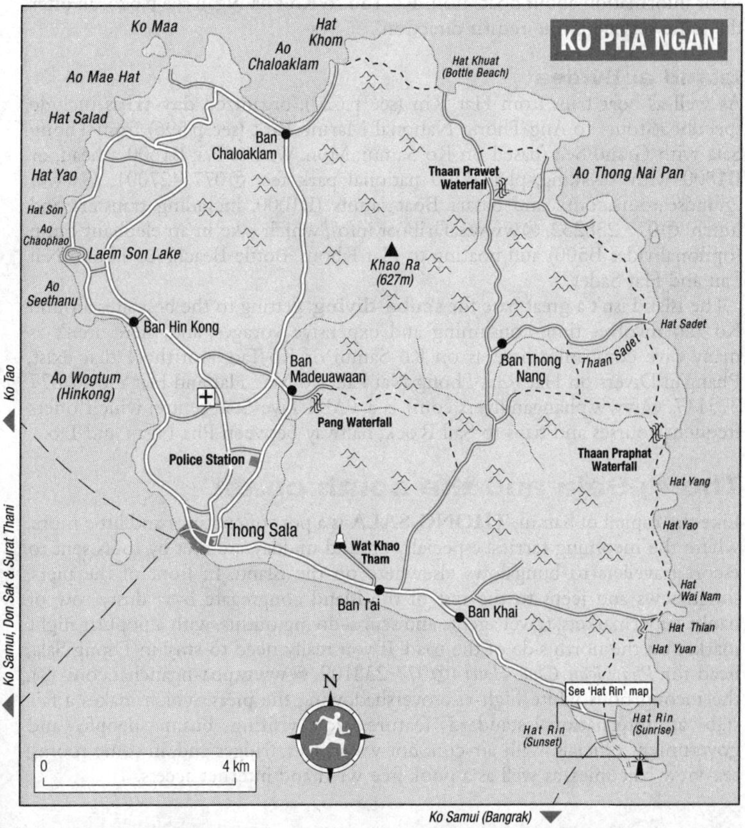

departure. From Don Sak to Thong Sala, there are six Raja vehicle ferries a day (on Pha Ngan ⓣ077 377452–3) and one Songserm Express Boat service a day (8am; on Pha Ngan ⓣ077 377704). Both the above charge B400, including bus transport to the pier from Surat Thani, with a total journey time of around four hours. **From Bangkok**, bus and train packages similar to those for getting to Ko Samui are available (see p.594), notably government buses from the Southern Terminal (first-class air-con 1 daily B750; VIP 1 daily B1050).

Two Songserm Express Boats a day do the 45-minute trip from Na Thon on **Ko Samui** to Thong Sala (B200). Two Seatran Discovery boats a day from the east end of Bangrak (on Samui ⓣ077 246086–8, Pha Ngan ⓣ077 238679, ⓦwww.seatranferry.com) and three Lomprayah catamarans from Maenam (Samui ⓣ077 427765–6, Pha Ngan ⓣ077 238412, ⓦwww.lomprayah.com) call in at Thong Sala after thirty minutes (B250), on their way to Ko Tao and Chumphon. From the centre of Bangrak, the *Haad Rin Queen* crosses four times a day to Hat Rin in under an hour (times have remained fairly constant over the years: 10.30am, 1pm, 4pm & 6.30pm; B200, or B250 including pick-up from Samui hotels; ⓣ077 484668 or 077 231069). If there are enough takers and the weather's good enough – generally reliable between roughly January and September – one small boat a day crosses from the pier in Ban Maenam at noon to Hat Rin (B150), before sailing up Ko Pha Ngan's east coast, via Hat Sadet and anywhere else upon demand, to Thong Nai Pan (B350).

For information about boats from **Ko Tao** to Ko Pha Ngan see p.625; all offer the same service in the return direction.

Island activities

As well as boat trips from Hat Rin (see p.620), organized **day-trips** include speedboat tours to Ang Thong National Marine Park (see p.596) from Thong Sala with Grand Sea (based on Ko Samui; Mon, Wed & Fri; B1600 a head, or B1800 with kayaking, plus B200 national park fee; ⓣ077 427001, ⓦwww.grandseatours.com); and Safari Boat jaunts (B1000, including transfers and lunch; ⓣ077 238232, ⓦwww.safariboat.info), which take in an elephant camp (optional rides B500) and boating to Hat Khom, Bottle Beach, Ao Thong Nai Pan and Hat Sadet.

The island isn't a great base for **scuba-diving**: getting to the best sites around Ko Tao involves time-consuming and expensive voyages, and there aren't as many dive companies here as on Ko Samui or Ko Tao – of those that exist, Phangan Divers on Hat Rin, Thong Nai Pan, Ao Mae Hat and Hat Yao (ⓣ077 375117, ⓦwww.phangandivers.com) is a PADI Five-Star centre, which offers frequent courses and trips to Sail Rock, halfway between Pha Ngan and Tao.

Thong Sala and the south coast

Like the capital of Samui, **THONG SALA** is a port of entrance and little more, where the incoming ferries, especially around midday, are met by touts sent to escort travellers to bungalows elsewhere on the island. In front of the piers, songthaews and jeeps to the rest of the island congregate by a dusty row of banks, supermarkets, travel agents and scuba-diving outfits, with a popular night market on the north side of the road. If you really need to **stay** in Thong Sala, head for *Pha Ngan Chai Hotel* (ⓣ077 238109, ⓦwww.pha-nganchai.com; ❹), the incongruous white high-rise overshadowing the piers, which makes a fair stab at international-standard features for visiting businesspeople and government officials, with air-con, hot water, TVs, fridges and, in some rooms, sea-view balconies, as well as a pool, free wi-fi and internet access.

Among many travellers' **restaurants** here, *Yellow Café*, on the corner in front of the main pier, a few doors up from *Pha Ngan Chai Hotel*, is a good, friendly choice with free wi-fi, serving tasty coffee, baguettes, baked potatoes and other Western meals; and there's a branch of *Nira's* (see p.619; daily 7am–6pm) south along the waterfront opposite the Seatran pier, offering bakery goods, deli sandwiches and Thai and Western main courses. The other Thong Sala restaurant that's worth knowing about is *Boat Ahoy* (Ⓣ077 238759), about 2km from the pier on the Hat Rin road, a complex of outdoor and air-con tables (and karaoke) specializing in seafood and salads, with plenty of vegetarian options; under the same management, *Somtum Inter* next door dishes up popular northeastern Thai food.

From Thong Sala, there's an easy excursion to the grandiosely termed Than Sadet–Ko Pha Ngan National Park (admission free), which contains **Pang (Phaeng) Waterfall**, Pha Ngan's biggest drop. The park headquarters and a simple canteen lie 4km northeast of Thong Sala off the road to Chaloaklam – if you don't have a bike, take a Chaloaklam-bound songthaew as far as Ban Madeuawaan, and then it's a one-kilometre-plus signposted walk east. The main fall – bouncing down in stages over the hard, grey stone – is a steep 250m walk up a forest path. The trail then continues for 300m to a stunning viewpoint overlooking the south and west of the island.

The long, straight **south coast** is well served by songthaews from Thong Sala, and is lined with bungalows, especially around **Ban Khai**, to take the overspill from nearby Hat Rin. It's hard to recommend staying here, however: the beaches are mediocre by Thai standards, and the coral reef that hugs the length of the shoreline gets in the way of swimming.

On a quiet hillside above **Ban Tai**, 4km from Thong Sala, **Wat Khao Tham** holds ten-day **meditation retreats** most months of the year (B4500 per person to cover food); the American and Australian teachers emphasize compassionate understanding as the basis of mental development. Space is limited (retreats are especially heavily subscribed Dec–March), so it's best to pre-register either in person or in writing; go to Ⓦwww.watkowtahm.org for full details of rules and requirements and the schedule of retreats.

Thong Sala listings

Bookshop English-language books, magazines and newspapers at Bookazine on the south side of the main road to the pier.
Hospital The island's basic main hospital (Ⓣ077 377034 or 077 375103) lies 3km north of town, on the inland road towards Mae Hat. There's also a 24hr emergency rescue service, staffed by volunteers (Ⓣ077 377500, 077 377194 or 081 698 9493).
Internet Phangan Batik, set back on the west side of the old main street (turn south off the main pier road).
Police station 2km up the Ban Chaloaklam road Ⓣ077 377114.
Post office About 500m from the pier on the old main street (Mon–Fri 8.30am–noon & 1–4.30pm, Sat 9am–noon).
Vehicle rental Motorbikes (B150–200 per day) and jeeps (B800–1000) from many places on the main road to the pier.

Hat Rin

HAT RIN is now firmly established as the major party venue in Southeast Asia, especially in the peak seasons of August, December and January, but every month of the year people flock in for the **full moon party** – something like *Apocalypse Now* without the war. The atmosphere created by thousands of folk mashing it up on a beautiful, moon-bathed beach, lit up by fireworks and fire-jugglers, ought to be enough of a buzz in itself, but unfortunately drug-related horror stories are common currency here, and many of them are true: dodgy Ecstasy, *ya baa* (Burmese-manufactured methamphetamines) and all manner of other concoctions put an average of two farangs a month into hospital for psychiatric treatment. The local authorities have started clamping down on the trade in earnest, setting up a permanent police box at Hat Rin, instigating regular roadblocks and bungalow searches, paying bungalow and restaurant owners to inform on travellers whom they've sold drugs to, and drafting in scores of police (both uniformed and plain-clothes) on full moon nights. It doesn't seem to have dampened the fun, only made travellers a lot more circumspect. Other **tips** for surviving the full moon are mostly common sense: leave your valuables in your resort's safe – it's a bad night for bungalow break-ins – and don't take a bag out with you; keep an eye on your drink to make sure it's not spiked; watch out for broken bottles on the beach; and do not go swimming while under the influence – there have been several deaths by drowning at previous full moon parties. In 2008, there were also several reports of unprovoked, late-night gang attacks in Hat Rin, especially around full moon night. Note that when the full moon coincides with an important **Buddhist festival**, the party is moved one night away to avoid a clash; check out ⓦwww.fullmoon.phangan.info for details.

Hat Rin occupies the flat neck of Pha Ngan's southeast headland, which is so narrow that the resort comprises two back-to-back beaches, joined by transverse roads at the north and south ends. The eastern beach, usually referred to as **Sunrise**, or Hat Rin Nok (Outer Hat Rin), is what originally drew visitors here, a classic curve of fine white sand between two rocky slopes; there's still some coral off the southern slope to explore, though the water is far from limpid these days. This beach is the centre of Hat Rin's action, with a solid line of bars, restaurants and bungalows tucked under the palm trees. **Sunset** beach, or Hat Rin Nai (Inner Hat Rin), which for much of the year is littered with flotsam, looks ordinary by comparison but has plenty of quieter accommodation. Unfortunately, development between the beaches does no justice to the setting: it's ugly, cramped and chaotic, with new low-rise concrete shophouses thrown up at any old angle. Businesses here, concentrated around what's known as **Chicken Corner**, where the southern transverse road meets

▲ Longtail boats on Sunrise Beach, Hat Rin, Ko Pha Ngan

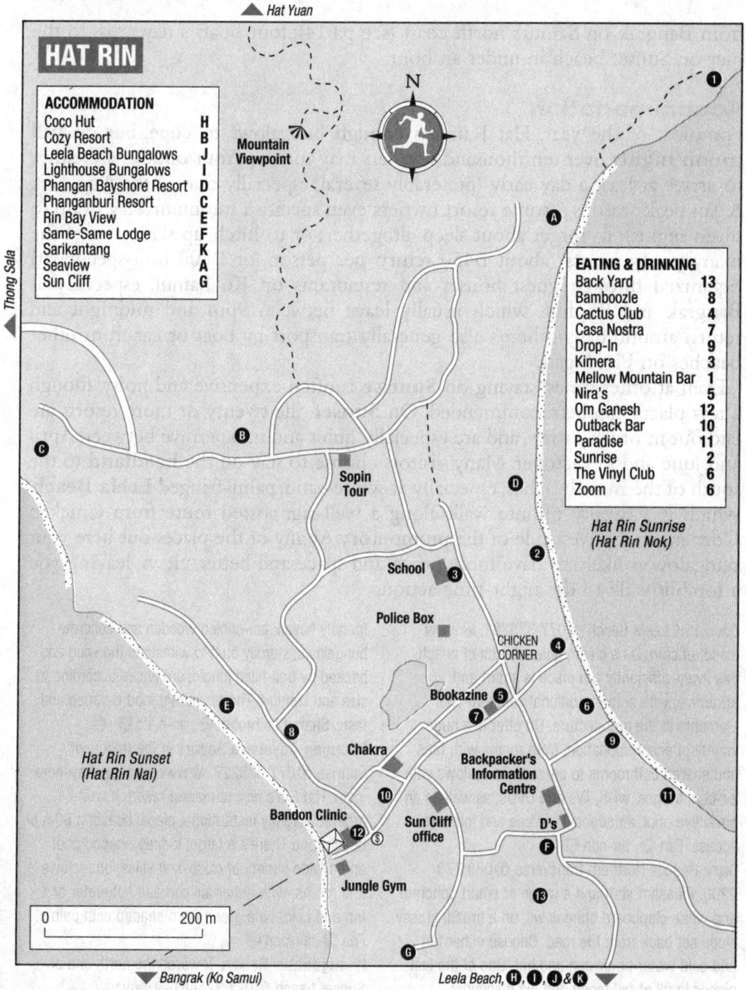

the road along the back of Sunrise, include supermarkets, overseas phone facilities, dozens of internet outlets, plenty of ATMs and bank currency-exchange booths, as well as outlets for more outré services such as bikini waxing and Playstation rental. Half-hearted attempts to tart up the large body of water in the middle of the headland with a few park benches and lights have been undermined by all-too-accurate signposts pointing to "Hat Rin Swamp".

Arrival

The awkwardness of **getting to Hat Rin** in the past helped to maintain its individuality, but this has changed now that the road in from Ban Khai has been paved. All the same, it's a winding, precipitous roller coaster of a route, covered by songthaews (B100) and air-con minibuses (B120–150) from Thong Sala – take care if you're driving a motorbike. The easiest approach of all, however, if you're coming from Ko Samui, or even Surat Thani, is on the *Haad Rin Queen* from Bangrak on Samui's north coast (see p.614): four boats a day cross to the pier on Sunset beach in under an hour.

Accommodation

For most of the year, Hat Rin has enough bungalows to cope, but on **full moon nights** over ten thousand revellers may turn up. Your options are either to arrive at least a day early (preferably several, especially during the Aug, Dec & Jan peak seasons – some resort owners even specify a minimum stay of up to seven nights); to forget about sleep altogether; or to hitch up with one of the many **party boats** (about B450 return per person, or B700 in a speedboat) organized through guest houses and restaurants on Ko Samui, especially at Bangrak and Bophut, which usually leave between 9pm and midnight and return around dawn; there's also generally transport by boat or car from other beaches on Pha Ngan.

Even at other times, staying on **Sunrise** is often expensive and noisy, though a few places can be recommended. On **Sunset**, the twenty or more resorts are laid out in orderly rows, and are especially quiet and inexpensive between April and June and in October. Many visitors choose to stay on the **headland** to the south of the main beaches, especially at white-sand, palm-fringed **Leela Beach**, which is a twenty-minute walk along a well-signposted route from Chicken Corner, on the west side of the promontory. At any of the places out here your bungalow is likely to have more peace and space and better views, leaving you a torchlit walk to the night-time action.

Coco Hut Leela Beach ⓣ077 375368, ⓦwww.cocohut.com. On a clean, quiet stretch of beach, this lively, efficiently run place is smart and attractive, with some traditional southern Thai elements in the architecture. On offer is a huge variety of accommodation, from rooms with fans and shared bathrooms to en-suite bungalows with air-con, fridges, wi-fi, TVs and DVDs, as well as an attractive pool, an adobe-style spa and internet access. Fan ❹, air-con ❽

Cozy Resort Northern transverse ⓣ089 770 2290. Pleasant staff and a range of smart concrete and white clapboard bungalows, on a broad, grassy slope set back from the road. Choose either fan and cold water or air-con and hot. One of the last places to fill at full moon and big discounts possible at other times. Fan ❹, air-con ❻

Leela Beach Bungalows Leela Beach ⓣ077 375094 or 081 995 1304, ⓦwww.leelabeach.com. A good, friendly and reliable budget choice with plenty of space under the palm trees and almost half of the white-sand beach to itself. Sturdy, well-built bungalows with mosquito nets and either cold or hot showers, or larger air-con cottages with hot water. Fan ❷–❹, air-con ❻

Lighthouse Bungalows On the far southwestern tip of the headland ⓣ077 375075, ⓦwww.lighthousebungalows.com. Phone for a boat pick-up from Sunset pier or Thong Sala, or do the 30min walk from Chicken Corner, the last section along a wooden walkway over the rocky shoreline. At this friendly haven, fan-cooled wooden and concrete bungalows, sturdily built to withstand the wind and backed by trail-filled jungle, are priced according to size and comfort. The restaurant food is varied and tasty. Shared bathroom ❷, en-suite ❹–❺

Phangan Bayshore Resort In the middle of Sunrise ⓣ077 375227, ⓦwww.phanganbayshore.com. Hat Rin's first upmarket resort, a well-ordered, slightly institutional place, boasting 80m of beachfront. There's a large, kidney-shaped pool and a wide variety of close-knit villas, bungalows and rooms, with either air-con and hot water or fan and cold, on a green lawn shaded with palms. Fan ❹, air-con ❺

Phanganburi Resort Towards the north end of Sunset beach ⓣ077 375481–9, ⓦwww.phanganburiresort.net. Welcoming, luxury complex that encompasses three hotel blocks, dozens of bungalows, a spa and two very attractive pools in its extensive, beachside grounds. Decorated in a simple but smart Thai style, all the rooms have air-con, hot water, fridge, safety box and satellite TV. Substantial discounts on their website. ❽

Rin Bay View Near the pier on Sunset ⓣ077 375188. A good-value, friendly option in a central location, occupying a narrow strip of land – though not too tightly squeezed – and ornamented with flowers and trees. The air-con bungalows and rooms with mosquito screens, hot showers and balconies are a decent size and generally well maintained and clean. ❹

Same-Same Lodge Above Sunrise at the start of the road to Leela Beach ⓣ077 375200, ⓦwww.same-same.com. Well-run, welcoming and sociable Thai-Scandinavian spot. Above a popular bar-restaurant, clean, well-maintained and decent-sized rooms come with fan and cold showers or air-con and hot water. Fan ❸, air-con ❹

Sarikantang Leela Beach ⓣ077 375055–6, ⓦwww.sarikantang.com. Boutique resort with a swimming pool, a beachside spa and a good measure of style. Accommodation includes rooms with fans, verandas and hot-water bathrooms as well as chic, white-painted "deluxe" options with air-con, TVs, DVDs and separate outdoor sunken baths. ❺

Seaview At the quieter northern end of Sunrise ⓣ077 375160. Not to be confused with a copycat *Sea View* way out on the rocks beyond *Paradise*. On a big plot of shady land, this clean, orderly old-timer with a good restaurant offers air-con at the back, fans beachside, and en-suite bathrooms (with plans to install hot showers) throughout. Fan ❹, air-con ❺

Sun Cliff High up on the tree-lined slope above the south end of Sunset ⓣ077 375134 or 077 375463. Friendly place with great views of the south coast and Ko Samui, and a wide range of bright, well-maintained bungalows, some with large balconies, fridges, hot water and air-con. Fan ❷, air-con ❹

Eating

As well as good simple Thai food at some of the bungalows, Hat Rin sports an unnerving choice of **world cuisines** for somewhere so remote, and vegetarians are unusually well provided for.

Bamboozle Off the southern transverse, near Sunset pier. Among a wide variety of tasty Mexican food here, the chicken fajitas with all the trimmings (available as a good-value combo for two people, with margaritas) are especially good; plus pizzas and a short menu of tapas.

Casa Nostra On the southern transverse, opposite 7-Eleven. Excellent, tiny, Italian café-restaurant which prepares great pasta dishes – try the spaghetti bolognese – pizzas (whole or by the slice), espresso coffee, salads and plenty of other dishes for vegetarians, such as home-made cannelloni with ricotta and spinach, and a chocolate mousse to die for. Daily 2pm–midnight.

Kimera North of Chicken Corner. Italian-run restaurant offering everything from espresso and chocolate *crostata* for breakfast, through sandwiches and antipasti, to a tasty *fritto misto* of deep-fried squid and prawns.

Nira's Near Chicken Corner. Justly popular restaurant and 24hr bakery. Around the clock it offers great croissants – sweet and savoury – cakes, quiches, sandwiches and coffees; from around 8am to 8pm, it operates like a food court in a Bangkok shopping centre, with different open kitchens rustling up burgers, hot dogs, pizzas and fish'n'chips, while more substantial Thai and Western main courses are available à la carte.

Om Ganesh On the southern transverse near the pier. Excellent, relaxing Indian restaurant with good thalis, biryanis, plenty of veggie dishes and breads, and cheerful service.

Nightlife

Nightlife normally begins at the south end of Sunrise at open-air dance halls such as the *Cactus Club* and *Drop-In*, which pump out mostly radio-friendly dance music onto low-slung candlelit tables and mats on the beach. Inland on the southern transverse, British-run *Outback Bar* is a lively meeting place with pool tables, big-screen sports, free wi-fi and well-received steak pies and the like. For somewhere to chill, head for *Mellow Mountain Bar*, which occupies a great position up in the rocks on the north side of Sunrise, with peerless views of the beach.

On **full moon night**, *Paradise* at the very southern end of Sunrise is the main party host, sometimes bringing in big-name international DJs. However, the mayhem spreads along most of Sunrise, fuelled by hastily erected drinks stalls and around a dozen major sound systems – listen out for psy-trance and driving techno at *Zoom* and *The Vinyl Club*, and house and drum'n'bass at *Sunrise* further up the beach. Next day, as the beach party winds down, *Back Yard* kicks off its afterparty at around eleven in the morning, with the best of the previous night's DJs; it's up the hill behind the south end of Sunrise off the path to Leela Beach.

Listings

Boat trips Several places on Hat Rin, such as Reggae Magic at *Cactus Club* (☎081 788 9143) and Sopin Tour on the northern transverse (☎077 375092), organize day-trips up the east coast and back, typically charging B700 (including simple lunch and snorkelling equipment) and taking in Mae Hat, Thong Nai Pan, Bottle Beach and Thaan Sadet.

Bookshops Bookazine, on the southern transverse, carries a decent line of new fiction and travel books, as well as magazines and newspapers. D's, next to the Backpackers Information Centre, is good for second-hand books.

Clinic Bandon International Hospital, a large private hospital on Ko Samui, runs a clinic on the southern transverse near the pier (☎077 375471–2).

Cookery courses *Same-Same Lodge* (see p.619) runs afternoon Thai cooking classes, including a market visit, lasting one (B900), three (B2500) or five (B4200) days.

Gym Jungle Gym (☎077 375115, Ⓦwww.junglegym.co.th), near the pier, offers Thai boxing classes, a steam room, yoga and a juice bar.

Massages Chakra, in an alley off the southern transverse (☎077 375401, Ⓦwww.islandwebs.com/thailand/chakra.htm), does the best massages in Hat Rin, and also runs massage courses.

Travel agent The excellent, English-Thai Backpackers Information Centre, based to the south of Chicken Corner (☎077 375535 or 089 471 7419, Ⓦwww.backpackersthailand.com), is a very reliable and clued-up full-service travel agency – with a useful website – which can make bookings and give advice on local tours and travel throughout Thailand and Asia. Also acts as agents for Ko Pha Ngan's Lotus Diving and Ko Tao's Crystal Diving (with special deals available).

Vehicle rental Plenty of places on Hat Rin rent jeeps (B1000 per day) and motorbikes (from B150 per day). There have been lots of reports, however, of travellers being charged exorbitant amounts if they bring the vehicle back with even the most minor damage – at the very least, check the vehicle over very carefully before renting. *Sun Cliff* (see p.619), who have an office just off the southern transverse, is a reliable place for motorbikes, and won't try this scam.

The east coast

North of Hat Rin, the rocky, exposed **east coast** stretches as far as Ao Thong Nai Pan, the only substantial centre of development. No roads run along this coast, only a rough, steep, fifteen-kilometre trail, which starts from Hat Rin's northern transverse road (near *Thai House Bungalows*, partially waymarked with green painted dots as far as Hat Yuan) and runs reasonably close to the shore, occasionally dipping down into pristine sandy coves with a smattering of bungalows. From roughly January to September, one small boat a day runs via the east coast beaches from Hat Rin to Thong Nai Pan, having started its voyage across at Maenam on Ko Samui (see p.614). Otherwise there are ample longtails at Hat Rin that will take you up the coast – around B150 per person to Hat Thian, for example. See above for information about organized day-trips by boat up this coast from Hat Rin.

Hat Yuan and Hat Thian

About ninety minutes up the trail, the adjoining small, sandy bays of Hat Yuan and Hat Thian have established a reputation as a quieter alternative to Hat Rin. A rough road has recently been bulldozed from Ban Kai, and the bays now sport about a dozen bungalow outfits between them. On **HAT YUAN**, *Barcelona* (☎077 375113; shared bathrooms ❶, en-suite ❸–❹) is a good budget choice, with plenty of space, great views and well-built accommodation either in clean, old-style huts or white bungalows with large verandas. The main operation on **HAT THIAN** is the *Sanctuary* (☎081 271 3614, Ⓦwww.thesanctuarythailand.com; ❷–❾), which offers a huge range of basic and luxury en-suite bungalows and family houses, as well as dorm accommodation (B120), kayaking and good vegetarian meals, seafood and home-made bread and cakes. It also hosts courses in yoga, meditation and the like, has a branch of Jungle Gym (see above) and provides two kinds of treatment: the spa does massage, facials and beauty treatments, while the wellness centre goes in for fasting and cleansing.

Hat Sadet

Steep, remote **HAT SADET**, 12km up the trail from Hat Rin, has a handful of bungalow operations, sited here because of their proximity to **Thaan Sadet**, a boulder-strewn brook that runs out into the sea. The spot was popularized by various kings of Thailand – Rama V visited no less than fourteen times – who came here to walk, swim and vandalize the huge boulders by carving their initials on them; the river water is now considered sacred and is transported to Bangkok for important royal ceremonies. A rough track has been bulldozed through the woods above and parallel to Thaan Sadet to connect with the unpaved road from Thong Sala to Ao Thong Nai Pan. Best of the bungalows is the welcoming *Mai Pen Rai* (ⓣ077 445090, ⓦwww.thansadet.com; ❸–❹), which has a variety of attractive, characterful accommodation with airy bathrooms (some with big upstairs terraces), either on the beach at the stream mouth or scattered around the rocks for good views; a jeep taxi leaves Thong Sala pier for the resort every day at 1pm (B150).

Ao Thong Nai Pan

AO THONG NAI PAN is a beautiful, semicircular bay backed by steep, green hills, which looks as if it's been bitten out of the island's northeast corner by a gap-toothed giant, leaving a tall hump of land dividing the bay into two parts, **Thong Nai Pan Noi** to the north, **Thong Nai Pan Yai** to the south. For non-guests it's worth making the climb up to *Panviman Resort* on the central outcrop, for the view from the restaurant perched over the cliff edge. With lovely, fine, white sand, the longer, more indented Thong Nai Pan Yai has marginally the better beach, but both halves of the bay are sheltered and deep enough for swimming. Thong Nai Pan is now developed enough for tourism to support a few internet shops, travel agents, dive outfits, bars, stand-alone restaurants, ATMs and a post office (on Thong Nai Pan Yai). A bumpy nightmare of a road, only partly paved, winds its way for 13km over the steep mountains from Ban Tai on the south coast to Thong Nai Pan: jeeps (B150 per person) connect with incoming and outgoing boats at Thong Sala every day. **Boat trips**, taking in Ao Mae Hat, Hat Khuat and Thaan Sadet, can be arranged through *White Sand*, for example (B700 per person, minimum ten people).

Accommodation

Dolphin At the quieter southern end of Thong Nai Pan Yai ⓣ077 238968, ⓔkimgiet@hotmail.com. Popular, tranquil spot, overgrown with lush vegetation and with lots of comfortable salas to recline in. The large, very clean bungalows come with fans and en-suite bathrooms (the owners may upgrade some to air-con and hot water), and the beachfront restaurant, which serves good mostly Western breakfasts and lunches and great coffee, turns into a mellow tapas bar at night. The same family run the less atmospheric *Thai House* next door (ⓣ077 445045), with smart wood and concrete, en-suite, fan-cooled bungalows set among flowers, at the same rates. ❸

Santhiya Thong Nai Pan Noi ⓣ077 428999, ⓦwww.santhiya.com. Extravagant, new, top-end resort on a lush, hilly plot, where many guests arrive by speedboat transfer from Samui. Tons of golden teak have gone into the building of the villas and rooms, which are in a traditional Thai, occasionally kitsch style, with *bencharong* lamps, colourful paintings and fabrics; some boast outdoor bathrooms and their own large, infinity-edge pools with fine views. There's an impressive pool fed by a huge artificial waterfall beside a small private beach, divided by boulders from the main part of Thong Nai Pan Noi. Rates from B10,800. ❾

Star Huts Thong Nai Pan Noi ⓣ077 445085, ⓔstar_hut@hotmail.com. Probably the best budget choice on the northern beach: very clean, well-maintained wooden bungalows, with spacious, furnished balconies and air-con and hot water or fan and cold. The friendly owners dish up good food and offer internet access. Fan ④, air-con ⑤

White Sand Next door to *Dolphin* ⓣ077 445123. Friendly establishment in a colourful garden with a decent restaurant and smart, comfortable, concrete bungalows with en-suite bathrooms; the older, cheaper ones are by the beach. ③

The north coast

The village of **BAN CHALOAKLAM**, on Ao Chaloaklam, the largest bay on the **north coast**, has long been a famous R&R spot for fishermen from all over the Gulf of Thailand, with sometimes as many as a hundred trawlers littering the broad and sheltered bay. As a tourist destination, it has little to recommend it save that it can easily be reached from Thong Sala, 10km away, by songthaew (B100) along a paved road. A handy, congenial spot for **lunch** on a round-island tour is *L'Oasi*, 1km south of the village on the main road (closed Sat). As well as burgers and barbecues, it serves up tasty Italian specialities and decent wine by the glass, in a pretty garden setting with a kids' playground.

Hat Khom has more to offer than Chaloaklam, a tiny cove dramatically tucked in under the headland to the east, with a secluded strip of white sand and good coral for snorkelling. Run by Thai rastas here, friendly *Coral Bay* (ⓣ077 374245, ⓦwww.coral-bay-haad-khom.blogspot.com; ①–③) has plenty of space and great views on the grassy, flower-strewn promontory dividing Hat Khom from Ao Chaloaklam. The sturdy bungalows range from simple affairs with shared bathrooms and no fans to large pads with funky bathrooms built into the rock and fans (electricity evenings only); snorkelling equipment can be rented to make the most of Hat Khom's reef.

If the sea is not too rough, longtail boats run several times a day for most of the year from Ban Chaloaklam (east of the fishing pier; B100 per person or B400 per boat) to isolated **HAT KHUAT (BOTTLE BEACH)**, the best of the beaches on the north coast, sitting between steep, jungle-clad hills in a perfect cup of a bay; you could also walk there along a testing trail from Hat Khom in around ninety minutes. Among a handful of resorts here, the best is *Smile Resort* (ⓣ081 956 3133; ③), which has a pleasant, quiet setting for its en-suite, fan-cooled bungalows, on a pretty flower-strewn hillside at the western end of the beach, and serves good Thai, Western and vegetarian food.

The west coast

Pha Ngan's **west coast** has attracted about the same amount of development as the forgettable south coast, but the landscape here is more attractive and varied, broken up into a series of long sandy inlets with good sunset views over the islands of the Ang Thong National Marine Park to the west; most of the bays, however, are sheltered by reefs which can keep the sea too shallow for a decent swim, especially between May and October. There's a paved coastal road up as far as Hat Salad, where it loops inland to meet the main inland road from Thong Sala via the hospital to Ao Mae Hat.

The first bay north of Thong Sala, Ao Wogtum (aka Hinkong), yawns wide across a featureless expanse that turns into a mud flat when the sea retreats behind the reef barrier at low tide. The nondescript bay of **AO SEETHANU** beyond is home to the excellent *Loy Fa* (ⓣ077 377319, ⓔloyfabungalow@yahoo.com; fan ③, air-con ⑥), a well-run, flower-strewn place that commands good views from its perch on top of Seethanu's steep southern cape, and offers decent snorkelling and swimming from its private beach below; bungalows are either on the hilltop or down on the beach, and come with fan and cold showers or air-con, hot water and minibar (some with TV); internet access and wi-fi are available.

Ao Chaophao

Continuing north, there's a surprise in store in the shape of **Laem Son Lake**, a tranquil stretch of clear water cordoned by pines; however, you should avoid swimming here, as the lake, site of a former tin mine, is considered toxic. Beyond, on the small, pretty bay of **AO CHAOPHAO**, *Seaflower* (ⓣ077 349090, ⓕ077 349091; ❶–❹) is a quiet and congenial spot, set in a well-tended garden, with excellent veggie and non-veggie food. En-suite bungalows with their own bathrooms vary in price according to their size and age: the newer ones – more like cottages – have marble open-air bathrooms and big balcony seating areas. If you're feeling adventurous, ask the owner about the occasional three-day, two-night boat treks to Ang Thong National Marine Park (see p.596), which involve snorkelling, caving, catching your own seafood, and sleeping in tents or hammocks on the beach (B3500 per person, including food and soft drinks; minimum eight people). On a patch of grass behind *Seaflower*, the English-run *Village Green* pub-restaurant keeps the punters happy with a wide variety of breakfasts, great sandwiches (including the raid-the-pantry DIY option), and Thai and international (including Mexican) main courses, washed down with a big choice of drinks and cocktails; it also has a few well-equipped bungalows (ⓣ077 349217, ⓦwww.villagegreen.phangan.info; fan ❸, air-con & hot water ❺).

Hat Yao

North of Chaophao, the long, gently curved, fine-sand beach of **HAT YAO** is gradually and justifiably becoming busier and more popular, with several stand-alone bars and restaurants, diving outfits, supermarkets, a bank currency-exchange booth, ATMs and jeep and bike rental. Among a nonstop line of bungalows here, a good budget bet is *Ibiza* (ⓣ077 349121, ⓦwww.ibizaphangan.com; fan ❹, air-con ❺), a lively, central spot in a spacious garden with airy bungalows that run the full gamut, whether you're happy with a fan and cold water by the beach or want air-con and hot water. There's also internet access and an ATM, and they can arrange **boat trips** to Hat Salad, Mae Hat and Bottle Beach (B600 per person, including snorkels). On a broad, grassy bank behind the north end of the beach, English-run *Shiralea* has recently set up shop (ⓣ080 719 9256, ⓦwww.shiralea.com; ❹). Spacious, very attractive thatched bungalows here come with hot water and fans; a pool and dive school are planned, as well as some air-conditioned and some cheaper (cold water) bungalows. Hat Yao's nicest upmarket spot is *Long Bay Resort*, with a long stretch of beach and spacious gardens towards the north end of the bay (ⓣ077 349057–9, ⓦwww.longbay-resort.com; ❺–❾ including breakfast). Choose between small but smart bungalows and a range of large cottages, all with air-con and hot water. There's an attractive swimming pool, kayaks to rent and pricey internet access.

Hat Salad and Ao Mae Hat

To the north of Hat Yao, **HAT SALAD** is another pretty bay, sheltered and sandy, with good snorkelling off the northern tip. On the access road behind the beach is a rather untidy service village of shops, travel agents, bike and jeep rental outlets and internet offices. Among the dozen or so bungalow outfits, the congenial, family-friendly and well-run old-timer, *Salad Hut*, stands out (ⓣ077 349246, ⓦwww.saladhut.com; fan ❻, air-con ❼). Parallel to the beachfront behind a swimming pool, in a shady, colourful garden, are ten stylish bungalows done out in dark woods and white, with rattan furniture, day beds with axe cushions and large verandas. All come with hot water, minibar and TV, and a cooked breakfast at the chic bar-restaurant is included.

On the island's northwest corner, **AO MAE HAT** is good for swimming and snorkelling among the coral that lines the causeway to the tiny islet of Ko Maa. The broad, coarse-sand bay supports several bungalow resorts, notably the popular, friendly *Wang Sai Resort* by a shady stream at its south end (Ⓣ077 374238; ❷–❺). On a huge plot of land, most of the en-suite bungalows are set back from the beach and are generally priced according to size – the cheapest are up the slope behind, with great sunset views, while the most expensive are on the beach, with air-conditioning.

Ko Tao

KO TAO (Turtle Island) is so named because its outline resembles a turtle nose-diving towards Ko Pha Ngan, 40km to the south. The rugged shell of the turtle, to the east, is crenellated with secluded coves where one or two bungalows hide among the rocks. On the western side, the turtle's underbelly is a long curve of classic beach, **Hat Sai Ree**, facing **Ko Nang Yuan**, a beautiful Y-shaped group of islands offshore, also known as Ko Hang Tao (Turtle's Tail Island). The 21 square kilometres of granite in between is topped by dense forest on the higher slopes and dotted with huge boulders that look as if they await some Easter Island sculptor. It's fun to spend a couple of days exploring the network of rough trails, after which you'll probably know all 1100 of the island's inhabitants. Ko Tao is now best known as a venue for **scuba-diving**, with a wide variety of dive sites in close proximity; see the box on pp.626–627 for further details.

The island is the last and most remote of the archipelago that continues the line of Surat Thani's mountains into the sea. It served as a gaol for political prisoners from 1933 to 1947, then was settled by a family from Ko Pha Ngan. Now, there are around 120 sets of **bungalows** for visitors, just about enough to cope during the peak seasons of December to March and August, concentrated along the west and south sides; they include a small but rapidly growing number of upmarket resorts with such luxuries as air-con, hot water and swimming pools. There's a limited government supply of electricity, so some of it still comes from private generators – usually evenings only on the remotest beaches.

If you're just arriving and want to stay on one of the less accessible beaches, it might be a good idea to go with one of the touts who meet the ferries at Mae Hat, with pick-up or boat on hand, since at least you'll know their bungalows aren't full; otherwise call ahead, as even the remotest bungalows now have landlines or mobile phones and most owners come to market once a day (pick-ups are either free or B50–150 per person). Some resorts with attached scuba-diving operations have been known to refuse guests who don't sign up for diving trips or courses; on the other hand, many of the dive companies now have their own lodgings, available at a discounted price to divers. With a year-round customer base of divers – and resident dive instructors – more and more sophisticated Western **restaurants** and **bars** are springing up all the time, notably in Mae Hat and on Hat Sai Ree. For nightlife, your best bet is to watch out for posters advertising weekly and monthly parties around the island, which keep the crowds rotating.

The **weather** is much the same as on Pha Ngan and Samui (see p.12), but being that bit further off the mainland, Ko Tao feels the effect of the southwest monsoon more: June to October can have strong winds and rain, with a lot of debris blown onto the windward coasts.

Getting to Ko Tao

For details of boats **from Chumphon**, which is connected to Bangkok by train and bus, see p.586. The three main Chumphon–Ko Tao boat companies all offer through tickets from **Bangkok**; with Lomprayah (on Ko Tao ☎077 456176, ⓦ www.lomprayah.com), for example, this costs B850, including a VIP bus from Thanon Ram Bhuttri (☎02 629 2569–70), via **Hua Hin** (see p.572). It's better to buy a Bangkok–Tao through ticket direct from the boat company's office in

KO TAO

Ko Nang Yuan

Causeways

Ao Mamuang

Lighthouse

Ao Kluay Tuen

ACCOMMODATION

Ao Leuk Bungalows	S
Blue Wind	G
Family	Q
Freedom Beach Bungalows	X
Hin Wong Bungalows	F
Jamahkiri	V
Koh Tao Cabana	D
Koh Tao Coral Grand Resort	E
Laem Thian	N
Mango Bay Grand Resort	A
Mr J's Bungalows	M
Nangyuan Island Dive Resort	B
New Heaven Huts	W
New Heaven Resort	Y
Sai Ree Cottages	L
Sai Thong Resort	R
Save Bungalows	O
Seashell Resort	K
Sensi Paradise Resort	P
Silver Sands	J
Simple Life	I
Sunsetburi Resort	H
Tao Thong Villa	T
Thipwimarn Resort	C
Viewpoint Bungalows	U

Chumphon

Ao Hinwong

Hat Sai Ree

Ban Hat Sai Ree

Ao Mao

Laem Thian

Police station

Ban Mae Hat

Ao Ta Note

Ko Pha Ngan, Ko Samui & Surat Thani

Ban Chaloke Ban Kao

Ao Leuk

N

Ao Chaloke Ban Kao

Jon-Suwan Mountain Viewpoint

Ao Thian Ok

Hat Sai Daeng

Shark Island

Laem Tato

0 1 km

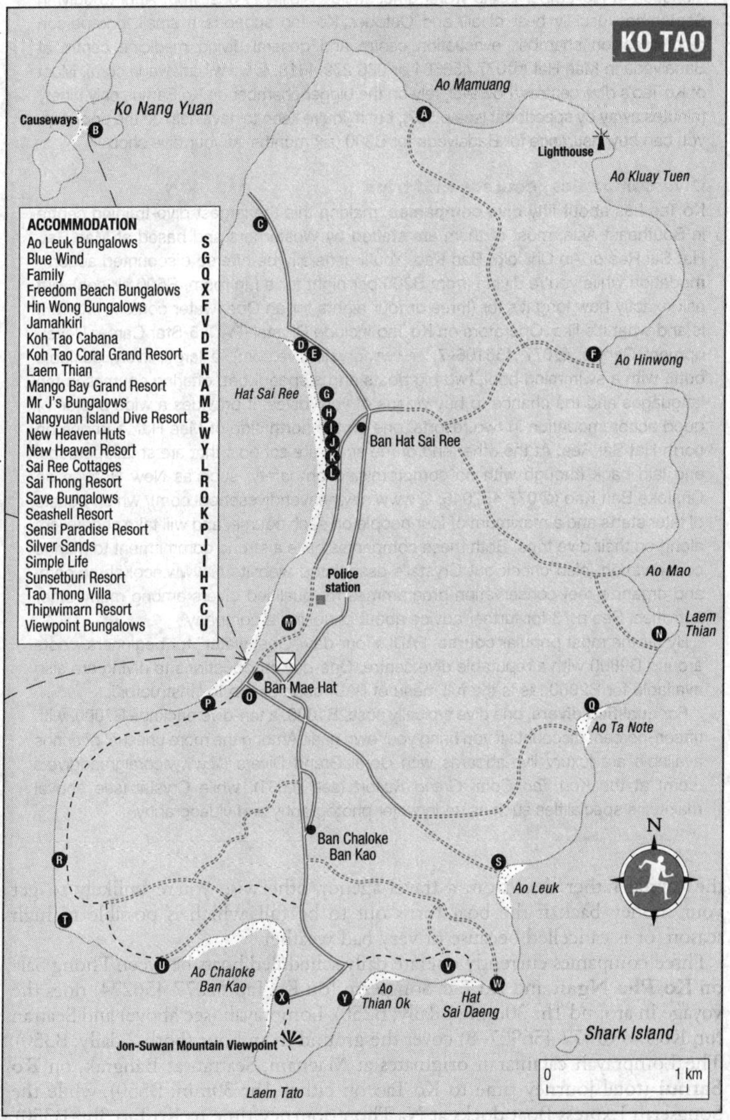

Scuba-diving off Ko Tao

Some of the best **dive sites** in Thailand are found off Ko Tao, which is blessed with outstandingly clear (visibility up to 35m), safe and relatively deep water close in to shore. On top of that, there's a kaleidoscopic array of coral species and other marine life, and you may be lucky enough to encounter whale sharks, barracudas, leatherback turtles and pilot whales. Diving is possible at any time of the year, with sheltered sites on one or other side of the island in any season – the changeover from southwest to northeast monsoon in November is the worst time, while visibility is best from April to July, in September (usually best of all) and October. Ko Tao supports a small, one-person recompression chamber, evacuation centre and general diving medicine centre at Badalveda in Mae Hat (Ⓣ077 456664 or 086 272 4618, Ⓦwww.badalveda.com). Most of Ko Tao's dive centres, however, rely on the bigger chamber on Ko Samui, only ninety minutes away by speedboat (see p.597), but if you're keen to have help on the doorstep, you can buy insurance for Badalveda for B300 (six months) at your dive shop.

Dive companies, courses and trips

Ko Tao has about fifty **dive companies**, making this the largest dive-training centre in Southeast Asia; most of them are staffed by Westerners and based at Mae Hat, Hat Sai Ree or Ao Chaloke Ban Kao. You'll generally be offered discounted accommodation while you're diving (from B200 per night for a fan room, B500 air-con), but ask exactly how long it's for (three or four nights for an Openwater course), where it is and what it's like. Operators on Ko Tao include Crystal (PADI 5-Star Career Development Centre; Ⓣ077 456106–7, Ⓦwww.crystaldive.com), a large, lively, sociable outfit with a swimming pool, two big boats and a speedboat, offering courses in ten languages and the chance to buy videos of your dives; it provides a wide choice of good accommodation in two resorts, one on the north side of Mae Hat, and one on north Hat Sai Ree. At the other end of the scale are schools that are small, personal and laid-back (though with no compromising on safety) such as New Heaven on Chaloke Ban Kao (Ⓣ077 457045, Ⓦwww.newheavendiveschool.com), which boasts of later starts and a maximum of four people on each course, and will take snorkellers along on their dive trips. Both these companies have a strong commitment to marine conservation (also check out Crystal's associated website Ⓦwww.ecokohtao.com) and organize reef conservation programmes for qualified divers among many other activities. See p.73 for further advice about choosing a company.

By far the most popular **course**, PADI's four-day "Openwater" for beginners, costs around B9800 with a reputable dive centre. One-day introductions to diving are also available for B2000, as is the full menu of PADI courses, up to "Instructor".

For **qualified divers**, one dive typically costs B1000, a ten-dive package B7000, with fifteen-percent discounts if you bring your own gear. Among the more unusual offerings available are luxury live-aboards with Coral Grand Divers (Ⓦwww.coralgranddivers.com) at the *Koh Tao Coral Grand Resort* (see p.631), while Crystal (see above) maintains specialities such as underwater photography and videography.

the capital rather than from a travel agency, otherwise you're unlikely to get your money back if the boat turns out to be full, which is possible in high season, or is cancelled because of very bad weather.

Three companies currently operate daily scheduled boats between Thong Sala on **Ko Pha Ngan** and Ko Tao. Songserm (on Ko Tao Ⓣ077 456274) does the voyage in around 1hr 30min (1 daily; B250). Lomprayah (see above) and Seatran (on Ko Tao Ⓣ077 456907–8) cover the ground in an hour (both 2 daily; B350). The Lomprayah catamaran originates at Maenam, Seatran at Bangrak, on **Ko Samui** (total journey time to Ko Tao on either 1hr 30min; B550), while the Songserm Express Boat docks at Na Thon (journey time to Ko Tao 3hr; B350).

Main dive sites

Ko Nang Yuan Surrounded by a variety of sites, with assorted hard and soft corals and an abundance of fish: the **Nang Yuan Pinnacle**, a granite pinnacle with boulder swim-throughs, morays and reef sharks; **Green Rock**, a maze of boulder swim-throughs, caves and canyons, featuring stingrays and occasional reef sharks; **Twins**, two rock formations covered in corals and sponges, with a colourful coral garden as a backdrop; and the **Japanese Gardens**, on the east side of the sand causeway, which get their name from the hundreds of hard and soft coral formations here and are good for beginners and popular among snorkellers.

White Rock (Hin Khao) Between Hat Sai Ree and Ko Nang Yuan, where sarcophyton leather coral turns the granite boulders white when seen from the surface; also wire, antipatharian and colourful soft corals, and gorgonian sea fans. Plenty of fish, including titan triggerfish, butterfly fish, angelfish, clown fish and morays.

Shark Island Large granite boulders with acropora, wire and bushy antipatharian corals, sea whips, gorgonian sea fans and barrel sponges. Reef fish include angelfish, triggerfish and barracuda; there's a resident turtle, and leopard and reef sharks may be found as well as occasional whale sharks.

Hinwong Pinnacle At Ao Hinwong; generally for experienced divers, often with strong currents. Similar scenery to White Rock, over a larger area, with beautiful soft coral at 30m depth. A wide range of fish, including blue-spotted fantail stingrays, sweetlips pufferfish and boxfish, as well as hawksbill turtles.

Chumphon or **Northwest Pinnacle** A granite pinnacle for experienced divers, starting 14m underwater and dropping off to over 36m, its top covered in anemones; surrounded by several smaller formations and offering the possibility of exceptional visibility. Barrel sponges, tree and antipatharian corals at deeper levels; a wide variety of fish, in large numbers, attract local fishermen; barracudas, batfish, whale sharks (seasonal) and huge groupers.

Southwest Pinnacle One of the top sites in terms of visibility, scenery and marine life for experienced divers. A huge pyramid-like pinnacle rising to 6m below the surface, its upper part covered in anemones, with smaller pinnacles around; at lower levels, granite boulders, barrel sponges, sea whips, bushy antipatharian and tree corals. Big groupers, snappers and barracudas; occasionally, large rays, leopard and sand sharks, swordfish, finback whales and whale sharks.

Sail Rock (Hin Bai) Midway between Ko Tao and Ko Pha Ngan, emerging from the sand at a depth of 40m and rising 15m above the sea's surface. Visibility of up to 30m, and an amazing 10m underwater chimney (vertical swim-through). Antipatharian corals, both bushes and whips, and carpets of anemones. Large groupers, snappers and fusiliers, blue-ringed angelfish, batfish, kingfish, juvenile clown sweetlips and barracuda; a possible spot for sighting whale sharks and mantas.

This Songserm boat originates at Don Sak, near **Surat Thani** (6hr to Ko Tao; B550); there's also a night boat from Surat Thani, departing at 11pm (Ⓣ077 284928 or 081 326 8973; 8hr; B550).

These services fluctuate according to demand, and in high season extra boats may appear. Voyages to and from Ko Tao may also be at the mercy of the weather at any time between June and January. Boat ticket prices fluctuate, too – for example, with so much competition between operators and routes, you'll currently find that leaving the island is a lot cheaper than the prices quoted above for getting there.

Information and island transport

There isn't a TAT office on Ko Tao, but the regularly updated and widely available free booklet, *Koh Tao Info*, is a useful source of **information**, along with its associated **website**, Ⓦwww.kohtaoonline.com, which allows online accommodation booking.

You can **get around** easily enough on foot, but there are roads of sorts now to most of the resorts, though many are still very rough tracks, suitable for four-wheel drive only; motorbike **taxis** (from B60) and pick-ups (from B100 per vehicle plus B50 per person; rates go up at night, or for a 4WD to somewhere more remote) are available in Mae Hat. There are also **rental** mopeds (from B150 per day) and even a few jeeps (around B1400 per day). If you can, resist the temptation to rent a quad bike, or **ATV** – not only do they have a disproportionate number of accidents, but they're also very polluting. As on Ko Phangan, there have been lots of reports of travellers being charged exorbitant amounts if they bring the vehicle back with even the most minor damage – avoid the outfits in front of the main pier in Mae Hat, and rent from your bungalow or someone reliable like Mr J (motorbikes) or Save Shop (motorbikes and jeeps); for both see opposite.

Longtail-boat taxis are available at Mae Hat or through your bungalow, as are **round-island boat tours**, with stops for snorkelling and swimming (B550 per person in a longtail, B650 in a bigger boat, including lunch and pick-ups, or from around B1500 to hire your own boat for the day, for example through New Heaven dive school; see p.626); these take in snorkelling in the Japanese Gardens off Ko Nang Yuan, but you'll have to pay the B100 entrance fee if you set foot on the island to climb up to the viewpoint. Recommended operators include *AC Resort* on Hat Sai Ree (B650; ⓣ077 456197), who provide an informative and ecologically aware guide.

Eco Tao

With so many divers and other visitors coming to this tiny island, the pressures on the environment, both above and below the waterline, are immense. To minimize your impact, look out for the work of a community group, **Save Koh Tao**, which has been formed among concerned locals and resident Westerners, with a sub-group devoted to marine conservation (Ⓦwww.marineconservationkohtao.com). Projects include a turtle-release programme, a campaign for septic tanks to stop waste water being run straight into the sea, and a bio-rock pilot project, an artificial reef, generated by passing an electric current through coral fragments, at Ao Thian Ok. Their monthly land and underwater clean-ups are given a big splash once a year, during the one- or two-day **Underwater Festival** in February or March, which involves mass beach-cleaning and fund-raising. At Mae Hat and on the main beaches, recycling bins are planned, as well as billboards listing businesses on the island that are involved with Save Koh Tao. Look out also for **Sabai Jai**, a free quarterly eco-travel magazine produced by the owner of Yakuzen Japanese Bath Village.

Much of what visitors can do to help is common sense: avoiding littering, recycling where possible and turning down plastic bags when you're shopping. The island suffers from a scarcity of water, with occasional droughts during the hot season after a poor rainy season, so conserve water whenever possible. In the sea, the main rule is not to touch the coral, which may mean avoiding snorkelling when the water is low from April to September – if in doubt, ask locally for advice, be careful and go out at high tide. Don't take away dead shells, and don't buy coral or shell jewellery. If you're feeling really keen, check whether your bungalow resort has a septic tank. And most dive schools have a Save Koh Tao donation box.

Mae Hat and around

All boats to Ko Tao dock at **MAE HAT**, a small, lively village in a pleasant, beachfront setting, which boasts the lion's share of the island's amenities. A paved high street heads straight up the hill from the main pier (eventually ending up in Ao Chaloke Ban Kao), with a narrower front street running at right angles, parallel to the seafront. Three of the ferry companies each have their own pier, Lomprayah and Songserm to the south of the main one, Seatran to the north.

Up a small hill on the southeast side of the village, inland from the Songserm pier, the delightful, eco-friendly **Yakuzen Japanese Bath Village** (daily except Wed 6–11pm, last admission 10pm; B700 1hr, B1000 1hr 30min; ⓣ084 837 3385) is highly recommended. Under the stars and the coconut palms here, you can relax in five landscaped bathing pools among the boulders, each set at a different temperature and made with different textures of rock and wood, and massage yourself with herbal compresses. There's also a tea lounge, an organic herb and fruit garden and a very good restaurant (see below).

Accommodation

The most characterful **accommodation** near Mae Hat is spread along the coast to the south.

Mr J's Bungalows Behind Mr J's supermarket, 5min walk north of Mae Hat ⓣ077 456066–7; and **Save Bungalows** near the Save Shop supermarket on the village's front street just south of the piers ⓣ077 456347. If you just want functional, reliable, good-value accommodation, head for either of these very similar places, owned by the same family (see p.630). Large, clean, en-suite rooms (*Mr J's*) or bungalows (*Save*), with hot showers in some of the air-con offerings. Fan ❷, air-con ❺

Sai Thong Resort 40min walk south of Mae Hat (about B100 per person in a taxi-boat) ⓣ077 456868, ⓦwww.saithong-resort.com. In shady grounds spread between its own, private Sai Nual beach and the next small bay to the south, and popular with families, this resort provides a wide variety of en-suite bungalows – those by the beach are overpriced, but the "seaview" and "hillside" versions offer good value. Attractive, relaxing restaurant serving Thai, Western and Burmese food, and internet, massages, kayaks and snorkels are available. Fan ❸–❻, air-con ❼

Sensi Paradise On the lower slopes of the headland just south of the village ⓣ077 456244, ⓦwww.kohtaoparadise.com. Charming resort in flower-covered grounds, offering a pretty beachside restaurant, free snorkelling equipment and some of the best upmarket accommodation on the island: well-designed wooden Thai-style cottages and villas with mini-bars, some with air-con and some with large terraces and open-air bathrooms. ❽

Tao Thong Villa 50min walk south of Mae Hat (about B100 per person in a taxi-boat) ⓣ077 456078. Sturdy, en-suite bungalows dotted around a rocky outcrop and the slope behind, with a breezy restaurant on the tiny, sandy isthmus in between. Plenty of shady seclusion and good snorkelling and swimming. Fan ❷, air-con ❺

Eating and drinking

Cappuccino 100m from the pier up the high street. French-run café that does a mean pain au chocolat and coffee, plus gourmet sandwiches, burgers and salads.

Dirty Nelly's Off the north side of the high street near the main pier. Helpful, Irish-managed pub, which has decent Guinness on tap, a pool table, big-screen sports, a varied menu of very good food and occasional live bands.

Kakureya Yakuzen Japanese Bath Village (see above) ⓣ087 936 2160 or 084 837 3385. Small, relaxing and thoroughly authentic Japanese restaurant, serving the best food on the island. Don't miss the excellent tasting set as a starter, which you might follow with delicious, lightly grilled tuna and seaweed salad. If you're a fan of *ramen* noodles, get there early – the chef only makes two servings a day. Daily except Wed 6–10pm.

La Matta High street, beyond *Cappuccino*. Delicious pizzas in scores of varieties, tasty home-made pastas, *panini* and a few Italian meat and fish dishes, as well as espresso coffees and home-made limoncello.

Tukta about 2km out on the Chaloke Ban Kao road. Relaxing, cheap restaurant – open-sided with a few garden tables – serving a wide choice of tasty Thai food, including a good *kaeng matsaman* with chicken.

Whitening 200m south of the main pier down the front street. Congenial, mellow and chic bar-restaurant, with a great deck and relaxing beach tables overlooking the bay. It dishes up some very tasty and creative Thai and Western food, as well as mean cocktails.

Listings

Banks Siam City Bank, up the high street on the left, with an ATM and Western Union facilities; and at the crossroads hard by the main pier, a Krung Thai Bank currency-exchange booth with an ATM.

Books B-Books up the high street on the right sells second-hand and new books and international newspapers.

Health Mae Hat has a small government health centre (halfway up the high street, turn right) plus several private clinics and pharmacies.

Internet Prasit Service, up the high street on the left, has a good reputation both as a travel agent and for internet access.

Police station 5min walk north of Mat Hat, on the narrow road towards Hat Sai Ree (☎077 456631).

Post office At the top of the village (turn left), near the start of the main paved road to Ban Hat Sai Ree, with poste restante facilities.

Supermarket and travel agency 5min walk north of Mae Hat, at the top of a small rise opposite the primary school, you'll find the head office of Ko Tao's all-purpose fixer, all-round character, Mr J. Here you can rent motorbikes, recycle batteries, buy and sell second-hand books, even borrow money. Mr J's family runs another supermarket and travel agency in Mae Hat, Save Shop, south of the Songserm pier.

Watersports MV Watersports (☎077 456065 or 087 264 2633, Ⓦwww.kohtaowatersports.com), south of the piers on the front street opposite *Save Bungalows*, is one of several places on the island that rents kayaks (B100 per hr, two-person B150 per hr), as well as offering sailing rental and tuition, windsurfer rental and tuition, wakeboarding and water-skiing.

Hat Sai Ree

To the north of Mae Hat, beyond a small promontory, you'll find **Hat Sai Ree**, Ko Tao's only long beach. The strip of white sand stretches for 2km in a gentle curve, backed by a smattering of coconut palms and around twenty bungalow resorts. A narrow, mostly paved track runs along the back of the beach to the village of Ban Hat Sai Ree, paralleled by the main road further inland. **Rock climbing** and bouldering, including courses for beginners, are offered by Goodtime Adventures, based at the *Narakaan Hotel* on the southern half of the beach (☎087 275 3604, Ⓦwww.gtadventures.com); they also organize abseiling, hiking and mountain biking, as well as pub crawls and booze cruises.

Around the northerly end of the beach spreads **BAN HAT SAI REE**, a burgeoning village of supermarkets, clinics, pharmacies, travel agents, internet outlets, a Siam City Bank currency-exchange booth with an ATM, restaurants and bars. **Yoga** classes are held twice a day at *Blue Wind Bungalows* (not Sun; B300; ☎084 440 6755, Ⓔshambhalayogaa@yahoo.co.nz), with reiki massages available on request. Inland, there's a branch of B-Books (see above) in Sairee Plaza on the main road from Mae Hat, while at the east end of the village, on the road towards Ao Hinwong, is Monsoon **gym** (☎089 866 4511), which offers *muay thai* classes.

Accommodation

Blue Wind Two doors north of *Sunsetburi Resort* ⓣ077 456116, ⓔbluewindwadear@hotmail.com. Good restaurant (see below) and a variety of smart, well-kept, en-suite rooms and bungalows, some with hot water and a few with air-con and TV, scattered about a shady compound. Fan ❷, air-con ❻

Koh Tao Cabana Far north end of beach ⓣ077 456504–5, ⓦwww.kohtaocabana.com. Welcoming, rustic-chic luxury resort on a long beach frontage, backed by pleasant lawns that are dotted with elegant day beds. All the thatched, air-con rooms (at the lower end of this price range) feature open-air bathrooms with hot water: choose between round, adobe-style villas up the slope behind the beach and stilted cottages on the headland, some with fantastic views. A spa, swimming pool, pool villas and wi-fi are planned. ❾

Koh Tao Coral Grand Resort North of Ban Hat Sai Ree ⓣ077 456431–4, ⓦwww.kohtaocoral.com. Welcoming luxury beachfront development with a dive school, where the sandstone-pink octagonal cottages with polished coconut-wood floors and large, attractive bathrooms gather – some a little tightly – around a pretty, Y-shaped pool; all have hot water, TV and air-con. Breakfast included. ❽

Sai Ree Cottages Towards the midpoint of the beach, 20min walk from Mae Hat ⓣ077 456126, ⓕ077 456558. In a large, beautiful, flower-strewn garden, the full spectrum of digs, all en suite and well maintained, from primitive huts to sturdy bungalows, many with hot water, some with air-con. Kayaks for rent and excellent grub. Fan ❷–❺, air-con ❺–❻

Seashell Resort Next door to *Sai Ree Cottages* ⓣ077 456271, ⓦwww.diveseashell.com. In a spacious, tidy compound, a friendly, well-run place with a dive school and a popular seafood restaurant (a swimming pool is planned); it offers traditional massage and massage courses, as well as very smart, sturdy, en-suite bungalows, either with fans or with air-con, hot water, fridge and TV. Fan ❹, air-con ❻

Silver Sands Ban Hat Sai Ree ⓣ077 456603–6, ⓦwww.silver-sands-resort.com. Congenial resort on a narrow but lush and shady strip of land, where the bungalows are clean and well kept. The cheapest are simple wooden affairs well off the beach, while the beachside air-con cottages with hot water command top dollar (some of the fan rooms also have hot showers). Internet access and snorkels to rent. Chic, new air-con rooms done out in black and primary colours are on the drawing board. Fan ❷–❹, air-con ❻

Simple Life Ban Hat Sai Ree ⓣ077 456142, ⓦwww.simplelifedivers.com. Good beachfront choice with a dive school, offering comfortable, en-suite, fan-cooled bungalows, great food, notably fresh, barbecued fish, and a lively beach bar. ❸

Sunsetburi Resort Ban Hat Sai Ree, next door to *Simple Life* ⓣ077 456266, ⓕ077 456101. On a narrow but tree-lined strip of land with a beachside swimming pool, modern, concrete cottages with TVs and minibars, many with air-con and some with the luxury of hot water. Fan ❹, air-con ❺–❽

Thipwimarn Resort North of Hat Sai Ree, opposite Ko Nang Yuan ⓣ077 456409, ⓦwww.thipwimarnresort.com. Stylish, eco-friendly upscale spot with a spa, which tumbles down a steep slope, past an elevated, infinity-edge swimming pool, to its own small beach. Dotted around the hillside, smart, thatched, whitewashed villas, most with hot water, enjoy a fair measure of seclusion, satellite TV, minibars and fine sunset views; in one or two, you have the option of keeping the air-con off, at a cheaper rate. ❽

Eating and drinking

Blue Wind Two doors north of *Sunsetburi Resort* (see above). Very good beachside restaurant serving up home-made breads, cakes, croissants, and fruit shakes, as well as Indian and Thai food, home-made pasta and other Western meals.

Lotus Bar On the beach near *Papa's Tapas*. Raucous, very popular late-night haunt for drinking and dancing,

New Heaven Deli & Bakery On the beach road on the south side of the village. Stylish spot offering great home-baked breads and cakes, as well as sandwiches, salads, ice cream and booster juices. Daily 7.30am–8pm.

Papa's Tapas On the beach road on the south side of the village ⓣ077 457020. The Swedish chefs here, one of Tao's few attempts at a gourmet restaurant, can be a bit hit-and-miss, though their tuna sashimi with vegetable tempura is very good. Contemporary tapas and good house wine are also available, and there's a mellow lounge with sheesha pipes. Daily 6–11pm.

Ko Nang Yuan

One kilometre off the northwest of Ko Tao, **KO NANG YUAN**, a close-knit group of three tiny islands, provides the most spectacular beach scenery in these parts, thanks to the causeway of fine white sand that joins up the islands. You can easily swim off the east side of the causeway to snorkel over the Japanese Gardens, which feature hundreds of hard and soft coral formations. Boats from the Lomprayah pier in Mae Hat, just south of the main pier, run back and forth twice a day (B150 return), but note that rules to protect the environment here include banning visitors from bringing cans, plastic bottles and fins with them, and day-trippers are charged B100 to land on the island; alternatively, it's B550 for an all-in day-trip, including boat transfers, buffet lunch and island fee (snorkels B50 extra). Transfers from and to Mae Hat are free for people staying at the *Nangyuan Island Dive Resort* (Ⓣ077 456088–93, Ⓦwww.nangyuan.com; fan ❻, air-con ❼–❾), which makes the most of its beautiful location, its bungalows, all with en-suite bathrooms and fridges, some with hot water, spreading over all three islands.

The north and east coasts

The lone bay on the north coast, **Ao Mamuang** (Mango Bay), is a beautiful, tree-clad bowl, whose shallow reef is a popular stop on snorkelling day-trips, though there's little in the way of a beach. The attractive bar-restaurant of *Mango Bay Grand Resort* spreads its large deck over the rocks here (Ⓣ077 456948–9, Ⓦwww.mangobaykohtao.com; fan ❻, air-con ❼–❽; breakfast and transfer included). Its well-appointed, colourful, heavily varnished wooden bungalows on stilts all come with hot water, and some have air-con and TV.

The sheltered inlets of the east coast, most of them containing one or two sets of bungalows, can be reached by boat, pick-up or four-wheel-drive. The most northerly inhabitation here is at **Ao Hinwong**, a deeply recessed, limpid bay strewn with large boulders and great coral reefs, which has a particularly remote, almost desolate air. Nevertheless, the bay's most spacious resort, *Hin Wong Bungalows* (Ⓣ077 456006 or 081 229 4810; ❷), is welcoming and provides good, en-suite accommodation on a steep, grassy slope above the rocks, in wooden bungalows with mosquito nets and large bathrooms. It has a nice waterside deck in front of its restaurant and rents out kayaks and snorkels. In the middle of the coast, the dramatic tiered promontory of **Laem Thian** shelters a tiny beach and a colourful reef on its south side. With the headland to itself, *Laem Thian* (Ⓣ077 456477 or 081 083 5186, Ⓔpingpong_laemthian@hotmail.com; fan ❷–❹, air-con ❺) has a secluded, castaway feel, offering comfy wooden bungalows, some with open-air bathrooms, and rooms in an incongruous hotel-style block; the layout of the resort isn't particularly appealing, but it's friendly and well maintained. The food's decent, and kayaks, snorkels and round-island boat trips (B650 per person, minimum four people) are on offer.

Laem Thian's coral reef stretches down towards **Ao Ta Note**, a horseshoe inlet sprinkled with boulders and plenty of coarse sand, with excellent snorkelling just north of the bay's mouth. The pick of the half-dozen resorts here is *Family* (*Ta Note Bay Dive Resort*; Ⓣ077 456757–8; fan ❹, air-con ❼), with a dive centre and plenty of well-designed, en-suite wooden bungalows with solar-powered hot water, set among thick bougainvillea, some enjoying large verandas and views out towards Ko Pha Ngan and Ko Samui. Snorkelling equipment is available at the resort, while the *Black Tip Dive Resort* (Ⓣ077 456488, Ⓦwww.blacktipdiving.com) offers kayaking, wakeboarding and snorkelling trips. The last bay carved out of the turtle's shell, **Ao Leuk**, has a well-recessed beach and

▲ View of Ao Chaloke Ban Kao, Ko Tao

water that's deep enough for good swimming and snorkelling, featuring hard and soft coral gardens. It's home to the en-suite wooden bungalows and large family rooms at *Ao Leuk Bungalows* (Ⓣ077 456692; ❸–❻), which enjoy plenty of space and shade, either in the palm grove behind the beach or up the hill to the south. If there happens to be no room here, don't worry – the same friendly family own the bay's other two resorts, its taxis and the beachfront bar, where snorkels and kayaks are available.

The south coast

The southeast corner of the island sticks out in a long, thin mole of land, which points towards Shark Island, a colourful diving and snorkelling site just offshore; the headland shelters the sandy beach of **Hat Sai Daeng** on one side if the wind's coming from the northeast, or the rocky cove on the other side if it's blowing from the southwest. Straddling the headland is *New Heaven Huts* (Ⓣ087 933 1329, Ⓔnewheavenhut@yahoo.com; ❸–❹), a laid-back, well-equipped place with a good kitchen and snorkelling equipment, whose pleasantly idiosyncratic en-suite bungalows enjoy plenty of elbow room and good views. Overlooking **Ao Thian Ok**, the next bay along on the south coast, is the same family's *New Heaven Resort* (Ⓣ077 456462, Ⓦwww.newheavenkohtao.com; fan ❻, air-con ❼–❽), with a scenic restaurant and attractive bungalows. On a beautiful deck perched high on the eastern flank of the Laem Tato headland, classic Thai dishes, including seafood specialities, are dished up in the evening, simpler fare at lunch-time; the bungalows, on a tree-covered slope running down to a private sandy beach, feature large bathrooms and verandas with great views, and include family and air-con rooms. The remote, rocky coastline between Hat Sai Daeng and Ao Thian Ok provides the spectacular location for a luxurious **spa resort**, *Jamahkiri* (call Ⓣ077 456400–1 for reservation and pick-up; free hourly shuttle from their Mae Hat office, next to *Café del Sol* on Mae Hat Square; Ⓦwww.jamahkiri.com; from B8000, including breakfast; ❾), which offers saunas, body wraps, massages, facials and other beauty treatments. There's also a panoramic bar-restaurant, a dive centre, a tiered swimming pool and a fitness centre, as well as opulent, secluded rooms, in a chic mix of Thai and Western design, with red silk furnishings, air-con, hot water, satellite TVs and mini-bars.

The deep indent of **Ao Chaloke Ban Kao** is protected from the worst of both monsoons, and consequently has seen a fair amount of development, with several dive resorts taking advantage of the large, sheltered, shallow bay. Behind the beach are clinics, ATMs, bike rental shops, bars and restaurants. Among them is *Koppee*, a lovely little **bakery-café** on the main road near the centre of the beach (daily 7.30am–7pm), with books and magazines to browse and reasonably priced **internet** access. It rustles up tasty gourmet sandwiches on a choice of breads, salads, all-day breakfasts, as well as a good choice of drinks and sweet treats. Opposite, at New Heaven dive school, run by the same family, drop-in **yoga** classes are held daily between 5.30 and 7pm (B200).

Two **accommodation** options stand out from the crowd here. Run by a friendly bunch, *Viewpoint Bungalows* (ⓣ077 456666 or 077 456777, ⓦwww.kohtaoviewpoint.com; ⑤–⑥) sprawl along the western side of the bay and around the headland beyond, with great sunset views; architect-designed in chic Balinese style, they boast rock bathrooms, lovely polished hardwood floors, mosquito nets and attractive verandas. There are also a couple of tasty air-con villas with their own infinity-edge pools (⑨; B10,000 per night), as well as kayaks and snorkels to explore the reef just offshore.

On the east side of the bay, *Freedom Beach Bungalows* (ⓣ077 456596; fan ③–④, air-con ⑥) offers a mix of old-style, blue-painted, en-suite huts with sturdy corrugated roofs and small verandas, and smart, new bungalows with fan or air-con and hot water; they dot a spacious slope that leads down to a lovely decked bar on the idyllic white sand of **Freedom Beach**, a secluded palm-lined spot carved out of the Laem Tato headland. Rough signposts will lead you beyond the bungalows for a fifteen-minute walk, the last stretch up a steep hillside to **Jon-Suwan Mountain Viewpoint**, which affords fantastic views, especially at sunset, over the neighbouring bays of Chaloke Ban Kao and Thian Ok and across to Ko Pha Ngan and Ko Samui.

Nakhon Si Thammarat and around

NAKHON SI THAMMARAT, the south's second-largest town, occupies a blind spot in the eyes of most tourists, whose focus is fixed on Ko Samui, 100km to the north. Nakhon's neglect is unfortunate, for it's an absorbing place: the south's major pilgrimage site and home to a huge military base, it's relaxed, self-confident and sophisticated, well known for its excellent cuisine and traditional handicrafts. The stores on Thanon Thachang are especially good for local nielloware (*kruang tom*), household items and jewellery, elegantly patterned in gold or silver often on black, and *yan lipao*, sturdy basketware made from intricately woven fern stems of different colours. Nakhon is also the best place in the country to see how Thai shadow plays work, at Suchart Subsin's workshop, and the main jumping-off point for towering **Khao Luang National Park** and its beautiful waterfall, **Krung Ching**.

The town is recorded under the name of Ligor (or Lakhon), the capital of the kingdom of Lankasuka, as early as the second century, and classical dance-drama, *lakhon*, is supposed to have been developed here. Well placed for trade with China and southern India (via an overland route from the port of Trang, on the Andaman Sea), Nakhon was the point through which the Theravada form of Buddhism was imported from Sri Lanka and spread to Sukhothai, the capital of the new Thai state, in the thirteenth century.

Known as *muang phra*, the "city of monks", Nakhon is still the religious capital of the south, and the main centre for **festivals**. The most important of these are the **Tamboon Deuan Sip**, held during the waning of the moon in the tenth lunar month (either Sept or Oct), and the **Hae Pha Khun That**, which is held several times a year, but most importantly on Maha Puja (February full moon; see also p.65) and on Visakha Puja (May full moon; see p.66). The purpose of Tamboon Deuan Sip is to pay homage to dead relatives and friends; it is believed that during this fifteen-day period all *pret* – ancestors who have been damned to hell – are allowed out to visit the world, and so their relatives perform a merit-making ceremony in the temples, presenting offerings from the first harvest to ease their suffering. A huge ten-day fair takes place at Thung Talaat park on the north side of town at this time, as well as processions, shadow plays and other theatrical performances. The Hae Pha Khun That also attracts people from all over the south, to pay homage to the relics of the Buddha at Wat Mahathat. The centrepiece of this ceremony is the Pha Phra Bot, a strip of yellow cloth many hundreds of metres long, which is carried in a spectacular procession around the chedi.

Arrival and information

Nakhon's **bus terminal** and **train station** are both fairly centrally placed, though the **airport** (ⓣ075 369546), served daily by Nok Air (ⓣ1318 or 02 900 9955, ⓦwww.nokair.com), is about 20km northwest of the city off the Surat Thani road; air-con minibuses (B80 per person) or taxis (B300) meet arriving flights to ferry passengers to the centre of town (on departure, you can catch a minibus to the airport at the *Thai Hotel*). **Air-con minibus** offices around town include one for Ko Samui (via the Don Sak ferry) about 1km north of the centre on the right-hand side of Thanon Ratchadamnoen near Wat Pradu; others are marked on our map. For getting around Nakhon, small blue **share-songthaews** ply up and down Thanon Ratchadamnoen for B12 a ride.

TAT has an office in a restored 1920s government officers' club on Sanam Na Muang (daily 8.30am–4.30pm; ⓣ075 346515–6, ⓔtatnksri@tat.or.th). Klickzone in Bovorn Bazaar on Thanon Ratchadamnoen is a good place for **internet** access. Decent, cheap **massages** are available at Wat Sala Meechai, a traditional medicine centre out beyond the National Museum on Thanon Ratchadamnoen (ⓣ075 446136; B120 per hr).

Accommodation

Nakhon has no guest houses or traveller-oriented **accommodation**, but the best of its hotels offer very good value in all price ranges.

Bue Loung (Bua Luang) Hotel 1487/19 Soi Luang Muang, Thanon Chamroenwithi ⓣ075 341518, ⓕ075 342977. Friendly and central but reasonably quiet; gets the thumbs-up from visiting sales reps, with a choice of fan and cold water or air-con and hot water in basic double or twin rooms, most with cable TV. Fan ❶, air-con ❷

Grand Park Hotel 1204/79 Thanon Pak Nakhon ⓣ075 317666–75, ⓦwww.grandparknakhon.com. If you're looking for something more upmarket in the centre of town, this place, set back a little from the busy road, is worth considering – it's large, stylish and bright, with air-con, hot water, TV and minibar in every room, and staff are cheery and attentive. ❹

Nakorn Garden Inn 1/4 Thanon Pak Nakhon ⓣ075 313333, ⓕ075 342926. A rustic but sophisticated haven in a three-storey, red-brick building overlooking a tree-shaded courtyard. Large, attractive rooms come with air-con, hot water, cable TV and mini-bars. ❸

Thai Hotel 1375 Thanon Ratchadamnoen ⓣ075 341509, ⓦwww.thaihotel-nakorn.com. Formerly top of the range in Nakhon – and still boasting some of the trappings, such as liveried doorman – this large institutional high-rise is now offering good value on its clean, reliable rooms, with fans and cold water or air-con and cold or hot water, all with cable TV. ❷

Twin Lotus About 3km southeast of the centre at 97/8 Thanon Patanakarn Kukwang ⓣ075 323777, ⓦwww.twinlotushotel.net. Gets pride of place in Nakhon – though not for its location; sports five bars and restaurants, a large, attractive outdoor swimming pool, a spa and a health club. ❻

The Town

The **town plan** is simple, but puzzling at first sight: it runs in a straight line for 7km from north to south and is rarely more than a few hundred metres wide, a layout originally dictated by the availability of fresh water. The modern centre for businesses and shops sits at the north end around the landmark **Tha Wang intersection**, where Thanon Neramit meets Thanon Ratchadamnoen. To the south, centred on the elegant, traditional mosque on Thanon Karom, lies the old Muslim quarter; south again is the start of the old city walls, of which few remains can be seen, and the historic centre, with the town's main places of interest now set in a leafy residential area.

Wat Mahathat

Missing out **Wat Mahathat** would be like going to Rome and not visiting St Peter's, for the Buddha relics in the vast chedi make this the south's most important shrine. In the courtyard inside the temple cloisters, which have their main entrance facing Thanon Ratchadamnoen, about 2km south of the modern centre, row upon row of smaller chedis, spiked like bayonets, surround the main chedi, the sixty-metre-tall **Phra Boromathat**. This huge, stubby Sri Lankan bell supports a slender, ringed spire, which is in turn topped by a shiny pinnacle said to be covered in 600kg of gold leaf. According to the chronicles, relics of the Buddha were brought here from Sri Lanka two thousand years ago by an Indian prince and princess and enshrined in a chedi. It's undergone plenty of face-lifts

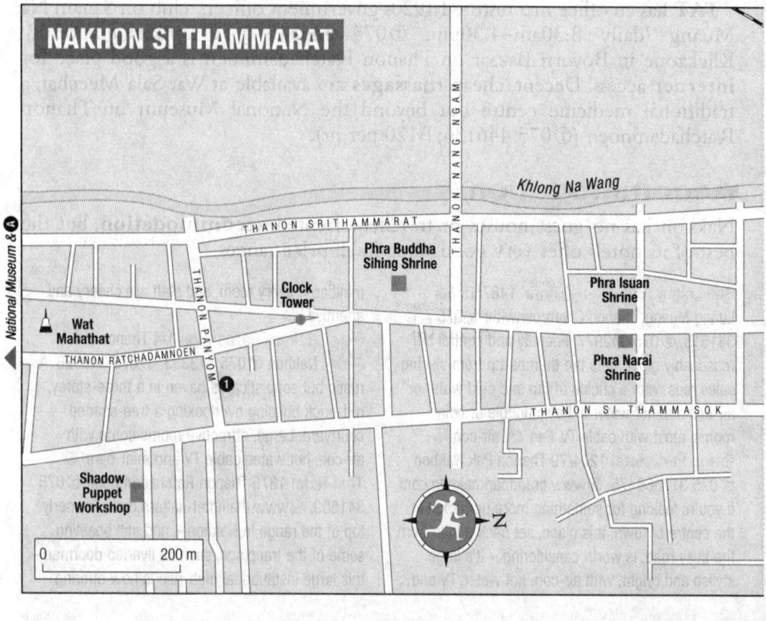

since: an earlier Srivijayan version, a model of which stands at one corner, is encased in the present twelfth-century chedi. The most recent restoration work, funded by donations from all over Thailand, rescued it from collapse, although it still seems to be leaning dangerously to the southeast. Worshippers head for the north side's vast enclosed stairway, framed by lions and giants, which they liberally decorate with gold leaf to add to the shrine's radiance and gain some merit.

The **Viharn Phra Kien Museum** (hours irregular, but usually daily 9am–5pm; free), which extends north from the chedi, is an Aladdin's cave of bric-a-brac, said to house fifty thousand artefacts donated by worshippers, ranging from ships made out of seashells to gold and silver models of the Bodhi Tree. At the entrance to the museum, you'll pass the Phra Puay, an image of the Buddha giving a gesture of reassurance. Women pray to the image when they want to have children, and the lucky ones return to give thanks and to leave photos of their chubby progeny.

Outside the cloister to the south is the eighteenth-century **Viharn Luang**, raised on elegant slanting columns, a beautiful example of Ayutthayan architecture. The interior is austere at ground level, but the red coffered ceiling shines with carved and gilded stars and lotus blooms. In the spacious grounds on the viharn's south side, cheerful, inexpensive stalls peddle local handicrafts such as shadow puppets, bronzeware and basketware.

The National Museum

Ten minutes' walk south again from Wat Mahathat, the **National Museum** (Wed–Sun 9am–noon & 1–4pm; B30; Ⓦ www.thailandmuseum.com) houses a small but diverse collection, mostly of artefacts from southern Thailand. In the prehistory room downstairs, look out for the two impressive ceremonial bronze kettledrums dating from the fifth century BC, one of them topped with chunky frogs (the local frogs are said to be the biggest in Thailand and a prized delicacy).

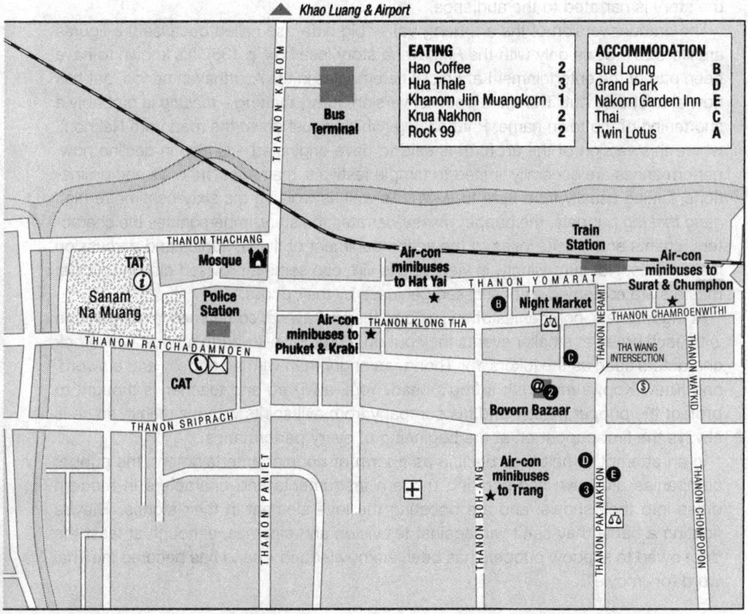

Also on the ground floor are some interesting Hindu finds, including several stone lingams from the seventh to ninth centuries AD and later bronze statues of Ganesh, the elephant-headed god of wisdom and the arts. Look out especially for a vivacious, well-preserved bronze of Shiva here, dancing within a ring of fire on the body of a dwarf demon, who holds a cobra symbolizing stupidity. Among the collections of ceramics upstairs, you can't miss the seat panel from Rama V's barge, a dazzling example of the nielloware for which Nakhon is famous – the delicate animals and landscapes have been etched onto a layer of gold which covers the silver base, and then picked out by inlaying a black alloy into the background. The nearby exhibition on local wisdom includes interesting displays on Buddhist ordinations and weddings, and on *manohra*, the southern Thai dramatic dance form.

The shadow puppet workshop

The best possible introduction to *nang thalung*, southern Thailand's **shadow puppet theatre**, is to head for Ban Nang Thalung Suchart Subsin, 110/18 Soi 3, Thanon Si Thammasok, ten minutes' walk east of Wat Mahathat (Ⓣ075 346394). In this atmospheric compound, Suchart Subsin, one of the south's leading exponents of *nang thalung*, and his son, Wathee, have opened up their

Shadow puppets

Found throughout southern Asia, **shadow puppets** are one of the oldest forms of theatre, featuring in Buddhist literature as early as 400 BC. The art form seems to have come from India, via Java, to Thailand, where it's called *nang*, meaning "hide": the puppets are made from the skins of water buffalo or cows, which are softened in water, then pounded until almost transparent, before being carved and painted to represent the characters of the play. The puppets are then manipulated on bamboo rods in front of a bright light, to project their image onto a large white screen, while the story is narrated to the audience.

The grander version of the art, **nang yai** – "big hide", so called because the figures are life-size – deals only with the *Ramayana* story (see box, p.135). It's known to have been part of the entertainment at official ceremonies in the Ayutthayan period, but has now almost died out. The more populist version, **nang thalung** – *thalung* is probably a shortening of the town name, Phatthalung (which is just down the road from Nakhon), where this version of the art form is said to have originated – is also in decline now: performances are generally limited to temple festivals, marriages, funerals and ordinations, lasting usually from 9pm to dawn. As well as working the sixty-centimetre-high *nang thalung* puppets, the puppet master narrates the story, impersonates the characters, chants and cracks jokes to the accompaniment of flutes, fiddles and percussion instruments. Not surprisingly, in view of this virtuoso semi-improvised display, puppet masters are esteemed as possessed geniuses by their public.

At big festivals, companies often perform the *Ramayana*, sometimes in competition with each other; at smaller events they put on more down-to-earth stories, with stock characters such as the jokers Yor Thong, an angry man with a pot belly and a sword, and Kaew Kop, a man with a frog's head. Yogi, a wizard and teacher, is thought to protect the puppet master and his company from evil spirits with his magic, so he is always the first puppet on at the beginning of every performance.

In an attempt to halt their decline as a form of popular entertainment, the puppet companies are now incorporating modern instruments and characters in modern dress into their shows, and are boosting the love element in their stories. They're fighting a battle they can't win against television and cinemas, although at least the debt owed to shadow puppets has been acknowledged – *nang* has become the Thai word for "movie".

workshop to the public, including a small museum of puppets dating back as far as the eighteenth century, and, for a small fee (around B100 per person), they'll usually be able to show you a few scenes from a shadow play in the small open-air theatre. You can also see the intricate process of making the leather puppets and can buy the finished products as souvenirs: puppets sold here are of much better quality and design than those usually found on southern Thailand's souvenir stalls.

The Phra Buddha Sihing shrine

In the chapel of the provincial administration complex on Thanon Ratchadamnoen sits the **Phra Buddha Sihing** statue (Mon–Fri 8.30am–noon & 1–4.30pm), which according to legend was magically created in Sri Lanka in the second century. In the thirteenth century it was sent by ship to the king of Sukhothai, but the vessel sank and the image miraculously floated on a plank to Nakhon. Two other images, one in the National Museum in Bangkok, one in Wat Phra Singh in Chiang Mai, claim to be the authentic Phra Buddha Sihing, but none of the three is in the Sri Lankan style, so they are all probably derived from a lost original. Although similar to the other two in size and shape, the image in Nakhon has a style unique to this area, distinguished by the heavily pleated flap of its robe over the left shoulder, a beaky nose and harsh features, which sit uneasily on the short, corpulent body. The image's plumpness has given the style the name *khanom tom* – "banana and rice pudding".

Eating and drinking

Nakhon is a great place for inexpensive **food**, not least at the busy, colourful night market on Thanon Chamroenwithi near the *Bue Loung Hotel*.

Hao Coffee In the Bovorn Bazaar, Thanon Ratchadamnoen. Popular place modelled on an old Chinese-style coffee shop, packed full of ageing lamps, clocks and other antiques. Offers a wide selection of inexpensive Thai dishes, cakes, teas and coffees, including Thai filter coffee and delicious iced cappuccinos. Daytime only.

Hua Thale Thanon Pak Nakhon, opposite the *Nakorn Garden Inn* (no English sign). The town's best restaurant, renowned among locals for its excellent, varied and inexpensive seafood, and almost reason in itself to come to Nakhon. Plain and very clean, with an open kitchen and the day's catch displayed out front, and relaxing patio tables and an air-con room at the back. Recommended dishes include a superb *yam plaa duk foo*, shredded and deep-fried catfish with a mango salad dip, whole baked fish and king prawns, and *hoy maleang poo op mordin*, large green mussels in a delicious herb soup containing lemon grass, basil and mint. Daily 3.30–9.30pm.

Khanom Jiin Muangkorn Thanon Panyom, near Wat Mahathat. Justly famous, inexpensive outdoor restaurant dishing up one of the local specialities, *khanom jiin*, noodles topped with hot, sweet or fishy sauce served with *pak ruam*, a platter of crispy raw vegetables. Lunchtimes only.

Krua Nakhon (Krour Nakorn) In the Bovorn Bazaar, Thanon Ratchadamnoen. A great place to sample southern food, buffet-style in a big, rustic pavilion, with good *khanom jiin* and other very cheap local dishes: *kaeng som*, a mild yellow curry; *kaeng tai plaa*, fish stomach curry; *khao yam*, a delicious southern salad of rice and vegetables; and various *khanom wan*, coconut milk puddings. Breakfast and lunch only.

Rock 99 Bovorn Bazaar. Bar-restaurant with live bands on Wed, Fri & Sat and outdoor tables.

Khao Luang National Park

Rising to the west of Nakhon Si Thammarat and temptingly visible from all over town is 1835-metre-high **Khao Luang**, southern Thailand's highest mountain. A huge **national park** (B200), with its headquarters to the south of the summit near Karom Waterfall (Ⓣ075 391240 or 075 391218, Ⓦwww.dnp.go.th), encompasses Khao Luang's jagged green peaks, beautiful streams with numerous waterfalls, tropical rainforest and fruit orchards. The mountain is also the source of the Tapi River, one of the peninsula's main waterways, which flows into the Gulf of Thailand at Surat Thani. **Fauna** here include macaques, musk deer, civets, binturongs, as well as more difficult to see Malayan tapirs, serows, tigers, panthers and clouded leopards, plus over two hundred bird species. There's an astonishing diversity of **flora** too, notably rhododendrons and begonias, dense mosses, ferns and lichens, plus more than three hundred species of both ground-growing and epiphytic orchids, some of which are unique to the park. The best time to visit is after the rainy season, from January onwards, when there should still be a decent flow in the waterfalls, but the trails will be dry and the leeches not so bad. However, the park's most distinguishing feature for visitors is probably its difficulty of access: main roads run around the 570-square-kilometre park with spurs into some of the waterfalls, but there are no roads across the park and very sparse public transport along the spur roads. Only **Krung Ching Waterfall**, one of Thailand's most spectacular, really justifies the hassle of getting there.

Before heading off to Khao Luang, be sure to drop into Nakhon's TAT office for a useful park **brochure**, with a sketch map and sketchy details of the walking routes to Krung Ching waterfall and to the peak itself. For the latter, which begins at Ban Khiriwong on the southeast side of the park and involves two nights camping on the mountain, contact the Ban Khiriwong Ecotourism Club (ⓣ075 533113), who can arrange a trek to the peak, including meals and guides, between January and June, as well as homestays in the village. Irregular **songthaews** on the main roads around the park and to Ban Khiriwong congregate on Thanon Klong Tha south of the *Bue Loung Hotel* in Nakhon. Air-conditioned **minibuses with drivers** are available from Noi Tub Tim Tours on Thanon Paniet (ⓣ075 345371; B1500 per day plus petrol).

Krung Ching

A trip to **Krung Ching**, a nine-tier waterfall on the north side of the park, makes for a highly satisfying day out, with a mostly paved nature trail taking you through dense, steamy jungle to the most beautiful, third tier. The easiest way to **get there** from Nakhon with your own transport is to head north on Highway 401 towards Surat Thani, turning west at Tha Sala on to Highway 4140, then north again at Ban Nopphitam on to Highway 4186, before heading south from Ban Huai Phan on Highway 4188, the spur road to Ban Phitham and the Krung Ching park office, a total journey of about 70km. Public songthaews run from Nakhon to Ban Huai Phan in about an hour, but you'd then have to do a deal with the driver to take you the extra 13km to the park office. Two- to forty-person **bungalows**, most with hot water, are available at the park office (B600–4000); camping is free if you bring your own tent. There's also a **campsite** and a canteen, where food needs to be ordered in advance.

The shady four-kilometre **trail** to the dramatic main fall is very steep in parts, so you should allow four hours at least there and back. On the way you'll pass giant ferns, including a variety known as *maha sadam*, the largest fern in the world, gnarled banyan trees, forests of mangosteen and beautiful, thick stands of bamboo. You're bound to see colourful birds and insects, but you may well only hear macaques and other mammals. At the end, a long, stepped descent brings you to a perfectly positioned wooden platform with fantastic views of the forty-metre fall; here you can see how, shrouded in thick spray, it earns its Thai name, Fon Saen Ha, meaning "thousands of rainfalls".

Travel details

Trains

All through trains stop at Surat Thani, Chumphon, Hua Hin and Nakhon Pathom.

Ban Krud to: Bangkok (3 daily; 5hr 30min–7hr 30min); Chumphon (6 daily; 2hr); Hat Yai (2 daily; 8hr 30min–10hr 30min); Nakhon Si Thammarat (1 daily; 10hr); Surat Thani (5 daily; 4hr–5hr 30min); Trang (1 daily; 10hr).
Cha-am to: Bangkok (5 daily; 3hr 10min–3hr 50min); Chumphon (3 daily; 5–7hr); Hat Yai (1 daily; 13hr 30min); Hua Hin (5 daily; 30min); Prachuap Khiri Khan (3 daily; 2hr).
Chumphon to: Bangkok (12 daily; 7hr–9hr 30min); Butterworth (Malaysia; 1 daily; 14hr); Hat Yai (6 daily; 7hr–8hr 30min); Nakhon Si Thammarat (2 daily; 7hr); Surat Thani (11 daily; 2hr 5min–4hr); Trang (2 daily; 7hr).
Hua Hin to: Bangkok (12 daily; 4–5hr); Butterworth (Malaysia; 1 daily; 17hr 30min); Chumphon (13 daily; 3hr 30min–5hr 20min); Hat Yai (5 daily; 10hr 30min–12hr 30min); Nakhon Si Thammarat (2 daily; 12hr); Prachuap Khiri Khan (11 daily; 1hr 30min); Surat Thani (11 daily; 5hr 40min–8hr); Trang (2 daily; 12hr).
Nakhon Si Thammarat to: Bangkok (2 daily; 15–16hr); Hat Yai (2 daily; 4–5hr).
Phetchaburi to: Bangkok (11 daily; 2hr 45min–3hr 45min); Chumphon (10 daily; 4hr–6hr 30min); Hat Yai (4 daily; 11hr 30min–13hr 30min); Hua Hin (12 daily; 1hr); Nakhon Si Thammarat (2 daily; 12–13hr); Prachuap Khiri Khan (11 daily; 2–3hr); Surat Thani (8 daily; 6hr 45min–9hr); Trang (1 daily; 13hr).
Prachuap Khiri Khan to: Bangkok (11 daily; 5–7hr); Chumphon (11 daily; 2hr–3hr 30min); Hat Yai (4 daily; 9–11hr); Nakhon Si Thammarat (2 daily; 10hr 30min); Surat Thani (8 daily; 4hr 30min–6hr); Trang (1 daily; 11hr).
Pranburi to: Bangkok (3 daily; 5hr 30min); Chumphon (2 daily; 4hr 30min); Hat Yai (1 daily; 12hr 30min); Prachuap Khiri Khan (3 daily; 1hr).
Surat Thani (Phunphin) to: Bangkok (10 daily; 9–12hr); Butterworth (Malaysia; 1 daily; 11hr 15min); Hat Yai (7 daily; 4hr 30min–6hr); Nakhon Si Thammarat (2 daily; 4hr 30min); Trang (2 daily; 4hr 30min).

Buses

Cha-am to: Bangkok (every 40min; 2hr 45min–3hr 15min); Hua Hin (every 20–30min; 35min); Phetchaburi (every 20–30min; 50min).
Chumphon to: Bangkok (roughly hourly; 7–9hr); Hat Yai (4 daily; 7hr 30min); Hua Hin (hourly; 3hr 30min–4hr 30min); Phuket (4 daily; 7hr); Prachuap Khiri Khan (6 daily; 2–3hr); Ranong (roughly hourly; 2hr); Surat Thani (roughly hourly; 3hr 30min).
Hua Hin to: Bangkok (from Baw Khaw Saw: at least hourly; 4hr; from Thanon Srasong: every 40min; 3hr); Cha-am (every 20–30min; 35min); Chumphon (hourly in the morning, fewer in the afternoon; 3hr 30min–4hr 30min); Hat Yai (4 daily; 10hr); Krabi (3 daily; 9hr); Phetchaburi (every 20–30min; 1hr 30min); Phuket (7 daily; 9hr); Prachuap Khiri Khan (every 30min; 1hr 30min–2hr); Pranburi (from Thanon Srasong: every 20min; 40min; from Baw Khaw Saw hourly; 30min); Surat Thani (4 daily; 7hr).
Ko Pha Ngan to: Bangkok (Southern Terminal; 2 daily; 14hr).
Ko Samui to: Bangkok (Southern Terminal; 8 daily; 13hr); Hat Yai (2 daily; 7hr); Krabi (3 daily; 7hr); Nakhon Si Thammarat (2 daily; 4hr); Phuket (1 daily; 8hr).
Nakhon Si Thammarat to: Bangkok (Southern Terminal; 19 daily; 12hr); Hat Yai (16 daily; 3hr 30min); Ko Samui (2 daily; 4hr); Krabi (2 daily; 4hr); Phatthalung (7 daily; 2hr); Phuket (7 daily; 6hr); Ranong (1 daily; 6hr); Surat Thani (21 daily; 2hr 30min).
Phetchaburi to: Bangkok (every 40min; 2hr 15min); Cha-am (every 20–30min; 50min); Hua Hin (every 20–30min; 1hr 30min).
Prachuap Khiri Khan to: Bangkok (every 30min; 4–5hr); Chumphon (6 daily; 2–3hr); Hua Hin (every 30min; 1hr 30min–2hr); Phetchaburi (every 30min; 3hr–3hr 30min); Pranburi (every 30min; 1hr–1hr 30min).
Pranburi to: Bangkok (every 40min; 3hr 30min); Hua Hin (every 20min; 30–40min).
Surat Thani to: Bangkok (Southern Terminal; 10 daily; 10–12hr); Chumphon (roughly hourly; 3hr 30min); Hat Yai (10 daily; 5hr); Khao Sok (11 daily; 2hr 30min); Krabi (23 daily; 3–4hr); Nakhon Si Thammarat (21 daily; 2hr 30min); Phang Nga (10 daily; 3hr 30min); Phatthalung (10 daily; 5hr); Phuket (14 daily; 5–6hr); Phunphin (every 10min; 40min); Ranong (10 daily; 4–5hr).

Flights

Hua Hin to: Bangkok (2 daily; 50min).
Ko Samui to: Bangkok (20 daily; 1hr–1hr 30min); Chiang Mai (2 weekly; 2hr 30min); Hong Kong (5 weekly; 3hr); Krabi (3 weekly; 50min); Kuala Lumpur, Malaysia (2 weekly; 2hr); Pattaya (1 daily;

1hr); Phuket (2 daily; 50min); Singapore (1 daily; 1hr 45min).

Nakhon Si Thammarat to: Bangkok 3 daily; 1hr 5min).

Surat Thani to: Bangkok (daily 1hr 15min).

7

Southern Thailand: the Andaman coast

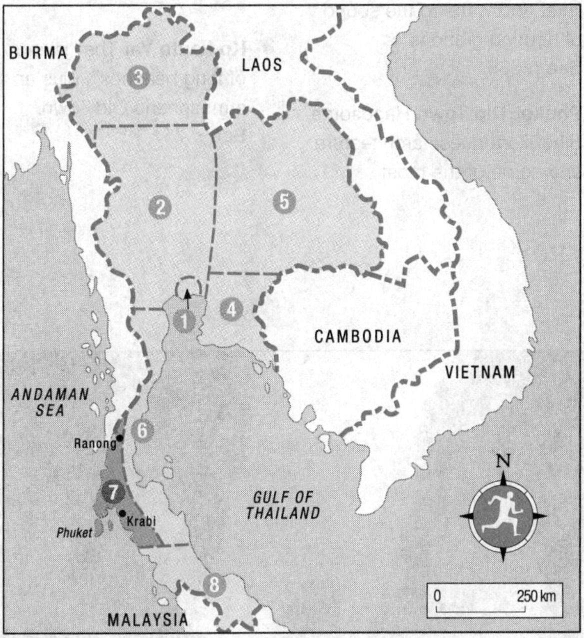

CHAPTER 7 # Highlights

* **Island idylls** Tranquillity rules on the uncommercial islands of Ko Phayam, Ko Ra, Ko Yao Noi and Ko Jum. See p.656, p.662, p.708 & p.747

* **Ko Surin and Ko Similan** Remote island chains offering the finest snorkelling and diving. See p.664 & p.676

* **Khao Sok National Park** Sleep in a treehouse or on a lake, and wake to the sound of hooting gibbons. See p.665

* **Phuket Old Town** Handsome Sino-Portuguese architecture and some of the most interesting dining on the island. See p.681

* **Sea-canoeing in Ao Phang Nga** The perfect way to explore the limestone karsts and hidden lagoons of this spectacular bay. See p.714

* **Rock-climbing** Even novices can get a bird's-eye view of the Railay peninsula's fabulous coastal scenery. See p.736

* **Ko Lanta Yai** The "island of long beaches", plus an atmospheric Old Town. See p.751

▲ Ao Phang Nga

7

Southern Thailand: the Andaman coast

As Highway 4 switches from the east flank of the Thailand peninsula to the **Andaman coast** it enters a markedly different country: nourished by rain nearly all the year round, the vegetation down here is lushly tropical, with forests reaching up to 80m in height, and massive rubber, palm-oil and coconut plantations replacing the rice and sugar-cane fields of central Thailand. Sheer limestone crags spike every horizon and the translucent Andaman Sea laps the most dazzlingly beautiful islands in the country, not to mention its finest **coral reefs**. This is of course the same sea whose terrifyingly powerful **tsunami** waves battered the coastline in December 2004, killing thousands and changing countless lives and communities forever. The legacies of that horrific day are widespread, for more on which see p.672, but all the affected holiday resorts have been re-built, with the tourist dollar now arguably more crucial to the region's well-being than ever before.

The **cultural mix** along the Andaman coast is also different. Many southern Thais are Muslim, with a heritage that connects them to Malaysia and beyond. This is also the traditional province of nomadic *chao ley*, or sea gypsies, many of whom have now settled but still work as boat captains and fishermen. The commercial fishing industry, on the other hand, is mostly staffed by immigrants – legal and not – from neighbouring Burma, just a few kilometres away along the northern Andaman coast.

The attractions of the northern Andaman coast are often ignored in the race down to the high-profile honeypots around Phuket and Krabi, but there are many quiet gems up here, beginning with the low-key little sister islands of **Ko Chang** (quite different from its larger, more famous East Coast namesake) and **Ko Phayam**, where the hammocks and paraffin lamps offer an old-style travellers' vibe that's harder to find further south. Awesome, world-class reefs draw snorkellers and divers to the remote National Park island chains of **Ko Surin** and **Ko Similan**, with many choosing to base themselves at the mainland beach resort of **Khao Lak**, though homestay programmes around **Khuraburi** offer an interesting alternative. Inland, it's all about the jungle – with twenty-first-century amenities – at the enjoyable **Khao Sok National Park**, where accommodation is on rafts on the lake and treehouses beneath the limestone crags.

Tourism begins in earnest on **Phuket**, Thailand's largest island and the region's major resort destination for families, package tourists and novice divers; its

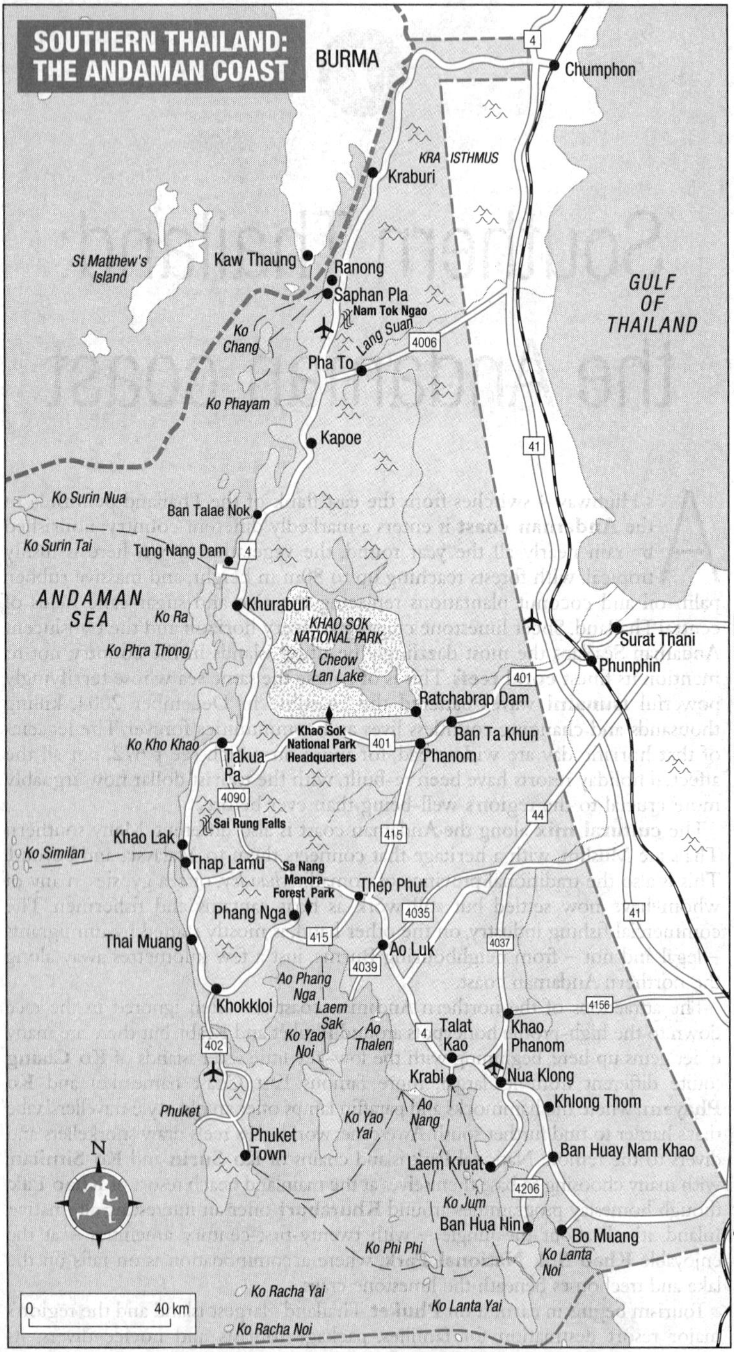
SOUTHERN THAILAND: THE ANDAMAN COAST
BURMA
Chumphon
KRA ISTHMUS
Kraburi
St Matthew's Island
Kaw Thaung
Ranong
Saphan Pla
Nam Tok Ngao
Ko Chang
Lang Suan
4006
Pha To
Ko Phayam
GULF OF THAILAND
Kapoe
41
Ko Surin Nua
Ban Talae Nok
Ko Surin Tai
Tung Nang Dam
4
ANDAMAN SEA
Ko Ra
Khuraburi
KHAO SOK NATIONAL PARK
Cheow Lan Lake
Ko Phra Thong
Surat Thani
Phunphin
Nakhon Si Thammarat
401
Ratchabrap Dam
Ban Ta Khun
Ko Kho Khao
Khao Sok National Park Headquarters
Takua Pa
Phanom
4090
Sai Rung Falls
44
415
Khao Lak
Ko Similan
Thap Lamu
Sa Nang Manora Forest Park
Thep Phut
Phang Nga
4035
Thai Muang
Ao Luk
4037
Ao Phang Nga
4039
Khokkloi
Laem Sak
4156
Ko Yao Noi
Ao Thalen
Talat Kao
Khao Phanom
402
Krabi
Nua Klong
Phuket
Khlong Thom
Ko Yao Yai
Ao Nang
Phuket Town
Laem Kruat
Ban Huay Nam Khao
4206
N
Ko Jum
Trang
Ban Hua Hin
Bo Muang
Ko Phi Phi
Ko Lanta Noi
Ko Racha Yai
0
40 km
Ko Lanta Yai
Ko Racha Noi

shopping and entertainment facilities are second to none, but the high-rises and hectic consumerism dilute the Thai-ness of the experience. There's Thai life in spades across on the quiet rural island of **Ko Yao Noi**, scenically located within spectacular **Ao Phang Nga**, whose scattered karst islets are one of the country's top natural wonders, best appreciated from a sea-canoe. The Andaman coast's second hub is **Krabi** province, rightly famous for its turquoise seas and dramatic islands. Flashiest of these is the flawed but still handsome **Ko Phi Phi**, with its great diving, gorgeous beaches and high-octane nightlife. Mainland and mainstream, **Ao Nang** can't really compete, but is at least close to the majestic cliffs and superb rock-climbing of the **Railay** peninsula at **Laem Phra Nang**. Offshore again, there's horizon-gazing aplenty at mellow, barely developed **Ko Jum** and the choice of half a dozen luxuriously long beaches, and plentiful resort facilities, at **Ko Lanta Yai**.

Unlike the Gulf coast, the Andaman coast is hit by the **southwest monsoon**, which usually generally lasts from the end of May until at least the middle of October. During this period heavy rain and high seas render some of the outer islands inaccessible, but conditions aren't usually severe enough to ruin a holiday on the other islands, or on the mainland, and you'll get tempting discounts on accommodation. Some bungalows at the smaller resorts shut down entirely during low season (highlighted in the text), but most beaches keep at least one place open, and some dive shops lead expeditions year-round.

There is no rail line down the Andaman coast, but many travellers take the **train** from Bangkok to the Gulf coast and then nip across by bus; most direct **buses** from the capital travel south overnight. The faster option is to arrive by plane: both Phuket and Krabi have international **airports**, and there are domestic airports at Trang, not far from Ko Lanta in the deep south and Ranong.

Ranong and around

Thailand's Andaman coast begins at **Kraburi**, where, at kilometre-stone 545 (the distance from Bangkok), a signpost welcomes you to the **Kra Isthmus**, the narrowest part of peninsular Thailand. Just 44km separates the Gulf of Thailand from the Andaman Sea's Chan River estuary, and Burmese border, here. Though a seemingly obvious shortcut for shipping traffic between the Indian Ocean and the South China Sea, avoiding the 1500-kilometre detour via the Strait of Malacca, the much-discussed **Kra Canal** project has yet to be realized, despite being on the table for over three hundred years.

Seventy kilometres south of the isthmus, the channel widens out at the provincial capital of **Ranong**, which thrives on its proximity to Burma. Thai tourists have been coming here for years, to savour the health-giving properties of the local spring water, but foreign travellers have only quite recently discovered it as a useful departure-point for the alluring nearby little islands of **Ko Chang** and **Ko Phayam**. The other reason to stop off in Ranong is to make a visa-run to the Burmese town of **Kaw Thaung**.

Ranong is the capital of Thailand's wettest province, which soaks up over 5000mm of rain every year – a fact you'll undoubtedly experience first hand if you linger in the region. The landscape to the south of Ranong town is particularly lush, and any journey along Highway 4 will whizz you between waterfall-streaked hills to the east and mangrove swamps, rubber plantations and casuarina groves to the west; much of this coastal strip is preserved as **Laem Son National Park**.

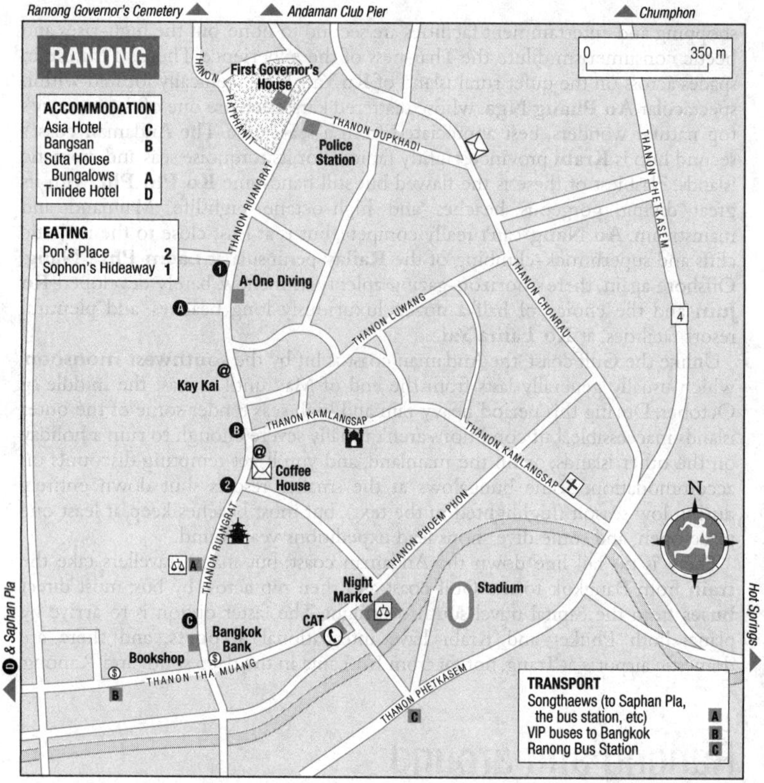

Ranong Town

Despite being the soggiest town in the country, **RANONG** has a pleasing buzz about it, fuelled by the mix of Burmese, Thai, Chinese and Malay inhabitants. It's a prosperous town, the lucrative nineteenth-century tin-mining concessions now replaced by a thriving fishing industry centred around the port of Saphan Pla, 5km southwest of town, and its scores of fishing boats and fish-processing factories staffed mainly by notoriously poorly treated Burmese workers. As with most border areas, there's also said to be a flourishing illegal trade in amphetamines, guns and labour, not to mention the inevitable tensions over international fishing rights, which sometimes end in shoot-outs, though the closest encounter you're likely to have will be in the pages of the *Bangkok Post*.

A stroll along the town centre's main road, **Thanon Ruangrat**, brings its history and geography to mind. The handsome, if faded, shopfront architecture bears many of the hallmarks of nineteenth-century Sino-Portuguese design (see p.684), with its arched "five-foot" walkways shading sidewalk pedestrians, pastel paintwork and shuttered windows. Chinese goods fill many of the shops – this is a good place to stock up on cheap clothes too – and many signs are written in the town's three main languages: Thai, Chinese and curly Burmese script.

Arrival and transport

All Andaman-coast **buses** travelling between Bangkok or Chumphon and Khuraburi, Takua Pa, Phuket or Krabi stop briefly at Ranong's **bus station** on Highway 4 (Thanon Phetkasem; ⓣ077 811548), 1500m southeast of the central market. If coming from Khao Sok or Surat Thani, you'll usually need to change buses at Takua Pa, though there is also a private minibus service from and to **Surat Thani** (hourly 7am–3pm; 3hr; B190). There is a direct government bus service from **Chumphon** (2–3hr), as well as a faster private minibus service (hourly 6am–5pm; 2hr; B120), so **from Bangkok** it's often more comfortable to take a night **train** to Chumphon and then change on to a bus or minibus. Alternatively, Air Asia currently operates Bangkok **flights** in and out of Ranong airport, which is 20km south of Ranong on Highway 4; taxis between the airport and town cost B150 per person or B200 from the Saphan Pla piers.

City songthaews shuttle across and around Ranong, most of them starting from the Thanon Ruangrat market, close to town-centre hotels. Many have their destinations written in English on the side, and most charge B10–15 per ride. Several songthaews pass Ranong bus station, including the # 2 (red), which runs to the Thanon Ruangrat hotels and day market, and the #6, which beetles between the bus station and the port area at Saphan Pla, 5km to the southwest (for boats to Ko Chang, Ko Phayam and Kaw Thaung); another songthaew runs direct from the market on Thanon Ruangrat to the Saphan Pla port area.

Information

The best source of **tourist information** in town is the ever helpful Pon at *Pon's Place* restaurant and tour agency, 129 Thanon Ruangrat (daily 7.30am–9pm; ⓣ081 597 4549, ⓦwww.ponplace-ranong.com), where you can also organize a visa run to Burma and back, arrange tours of the local area, book accommodation on Ko Chang and Ko Phayam, rent bicycles, motorbikes and cars, and buy air, bus and (Chumphon) train tickets. Should you want to fix a **diving** trip before heading out to the islands, Ko Phayam's A-One Diving has its main office in town at 256 Thanon Ruangrat (ⓣ077 832984, ⓦwww.a-one-diving.com; see p.658) and runs liveaboards to the Surin islands from the end of October to the end of April.

Coffee House at 116 Thanon Ruangrat is a **postal agent** (Mon–Fri 7am–1pm & 3–7pm, Sat & Sun 7am–6pm); the **Ranong Hospital** is at 11 Thanon Kamlangsap (ⓣ077 812630); the police station is on Thanon Dupkhadi (ⓣ077 811173); and the **immigration office**, for visa extensions, is out at Saphan Pla (see p.653), across the road from the Thai Farmers Bank (daily 8.30am–6pm).

Accommodation

Most travellers stop over in Ranong for just one night, but there's a reasonable spread of **accommodation** to choose from. At the bottom of the ladder is *Bangsan* (no phone; 100–130) whose eight thin-walled cubicles are very bare bones, share bathrooms and mostly have no windows; it's above the retro, Sixties-styled *TV Bar* at 225 Thanon Ruangrat. Some of the en-suite fan rooms at the typical Chinese–Thai *Asia Hotel* (ⓣ077 811113; fan ❶–❷, air-con ❸) only cost a bit more but are large, airy and spruce for the price and there's air-con if you want it; the hotel is painted pale blue inside and out and is just south of the market at 39/9 Thanon Ruangrat. Set 100m off the same road, the very popular *Suta House Bungalows* (ⓣ077 832707; ❸) is an unusual find in a city, with its row of small but well-maintained air-con bungalows, all of them with clean tiled floors, built-in beds and cable TV and wi-fi. They're set round a small yard, with car parking, a little bar-coffee shop and a restaurant. The top digs in town are at the modern, good-value high-rise *Tinidee Hotel @ Ranong*, a ten-minute walk from the market at 41/144 Thanon Tha Muang (Ⓣ077 835240, Ⓦwww.tinidee-ranong.com; ⑥). Its air-con rooms all come with bathtubs fed by the local mineral water and there's also a spa and swimming pool.

Around the town

Though there's little in Ranong to warrant a sightseeing tour, it can be fun to follow the crowds of domestic tourists in their quest for the medicinal and stress-relieving properties of Ranong's famously pure **geothermal springs** (daily 8am–5pm). They're the focus of forested Raksawarin Park, about 3km east of the Thanon Ruangrat market and accessible on songthaew #2 or by motorbike taxi. At the park you can sip the potable 65°C water, or paddle in one of the three mineral spa pools, but for a more leisurely soak, cross the road to the Jacuzzis at the Siam Hot Spa Ranong (daily 6.30am–10pm; Ⓣ077 813551), which also offers inexpensive spa, massage and steam treatments (from B200, reservations advisable).

Ranong's history is closely associated with its most famous son, Khaw Soo Cheang, a poor Hokkien Chinese emigrant turned tin baron who became the first governor of Ranong province in 1854; he is still so esteemed that politicians continue to pay public homage at his grave, and his descendants bear the respected aristocratic surname "na Ranong" ("of Ranong"). Little now remains of Khaw Soo Cheang's house, but in its grounds, west off Thanon Ruangrat on the northern edge of town, stands a Khaw clan shrine and small museum, the **First Governor's House** (Nai Khai Ranong; daily 9am–4.30pm; free). Follow either road running north from near the First Governor's House, in the direction of the Andaman Club pier, for about 4km to reach his burial site at the **Ranong Governor's Cemetery**, where Chinese-style horseshoe-shaped graves and a series of symbolic stone statues stand proud at the foot of the grassy hill; songthaews from the Thanon Ruangrat market should get you there in about fifteen minutes.

If you haven't had enough of water features, you could make a trip out of town to the impressive **Nam Tok Ngao**, an enormous waterfall 12km south of Ranong, which cascades almost all the way down the eastern hillside in full view of Highway 4. It's part of Nam Tok Ngao National Park (Ⓦwww.dnp.go.th/National_park.asp; B100). Any south-bound bus will drop you there. Another enjoyable day out would be to head into the interior for a day's organized rafting at **Pha To**, 51km east of Ranong, off Route 4006 to Chumphon (see p.587); Runs n' Roses tours and accommodation at Pha To (Ⓦwww.runsnroses.com) can be booked through Ranong tour agencies.

Eating and drinking

Ranong's ethnic diversity ensures a tasty range of **eating** options, and a stroll up Thanon Ruangrat takes you past Muslim foodstalls and Chinese pastry shops as well as a small but typically Thai night market. A bigger night market convenes at dusk just east of the CAT phone office off Thanon Phoem Phon. *Pon's Place* at 129 Thanon Ruangrat opens at 7.30am and is the obvious place for farang-style breakfast, free wi-fi and as much local information as you care to gather. A lively and enjoyable venue for dinner is *Sophon's Hideaway* at Thanon Ruangrat, where Thai families and expats congregate for the wide-ranging menu, which includes sour 'n spicy fish curry, fried pork spare ribs and ostrich steaks (mostly B90–150); the cheapish beer and friendly staff are also a plus and there's international sports on the TV, a pool table and free wi-fi. This

Into Burma: visa runs and Kaw Thaung (Ko Song)

The southernmost tip of Burma – known as **Kaw Thaung** in Burmese, Ko Song in Thai, and Victoria Point when it was a British colony – lies just a few kilometres west of Ranong across the Chan River estuary, and is easily reached by longtail boat from Saphan Pla fishing port just outside Ranong town centre. It's quite straightforward for foreign tourists to **enter Burma** at this point, and come back with a new fifteen-day Thai visa, though it does mean you're giving your money to the Burmese military regime. You can either do it independently, as described below, or you can make use of one of the all-inclusive **"visa run" services** advertised all over town, including at *Pon's Place* (B850 including visa). Most visa-run operators use the Saphan Pla route, but a more luxurious alternative takes you on the fast **Andaman Club boat** (15 daily 7am–11.50pm; 20min; B850 return including visa, but you must have at least three days remaining on your current Thai visa; ⓣ077 830461), which departs from the Andaman Club pier 5km north of Ranong's town centre and travels to and from the swanky *Andaman Club* hotel (ⓣ081 894 2583, ⓦwww.andamanclub.com; ⑨), casino and duty-free complex, located on a tiny island in Burmese waters just south of Kaw Thaung. Phone ahead for *Andaman Club* transport from Ranong town to the pier (B200 per person), or take a songthaew there from the Thanon Ruangrat market (B20).

Boats to Kaw Thaung leave from the so-called Burmese Pier in the port of Saphan Pla, 5km southwest of town and served by songthaews from Ranong market (red, #3; 20min; B15) and bus station (#6; 20min; B15). Thai exit formalities are done at the pier (daily 8am–6pm), after which longtail boats take you to Kaw Thaung (B400 per boat; 30min) via **Burmese immigration** on tiny Snake Island. Here you pay US$10 (or B500) for a pass that should entitle you to stay in Kaw Thaung for a fortnight but forbids travel further than 8km inland. Note that Burma time is thirty minutes behind Thailand time, and that to get back into Thailand you'll have to be at the immigration office in Saphan Pla before it closes at 6pm. Thai money is perfectly acceptable in Kaw Thaung.

There's nothing much to do in **Kaw Thaung** itself, but it has quite a different vibe to Thai towns. As you arrive at the quay, the market, immigration office and tiny town centre lie before you, while over to your right, about twenty minutes' walk away, you can't miss the hilltop **Pyi Taw Aye Pagoda**, surmounted by a huge reclining Buddha and a ring of smaller ones. Once you've explored the covered market behind the quay and picked your way through the piles of tin trunks and sacks of rice that crowd the surrounding streets, all that remains is to take a coffee break in one of the quayside pastry shops.

stretch of Thanon Ruangrat, down to the Thanon Luwang junction, is also abuzz after dark with urbane little local **bars** that keep reinventing themselves.

Ko Chang

Not to be confused with the much larger Ko Chang off Thailand's east coast (see p.463), Ranong's **KO CHANG** is a forested little island about 5km offshore, whose car-free, ultra laid-back, roll-your-own vibe more than compensates for the less than perfect beaches. The pace of life here is very slow, and for the relatively small number of tourists who make it to the island the emphasis is strongly on kicking back and chilling out – bring your own hammock and you'll fit right in. Those in search of (slightly) livelier scenes head across the water to sister-island Ko Phayam. Most islanders make their living from fishing and from the rubber, palm and cashew nut plantations that

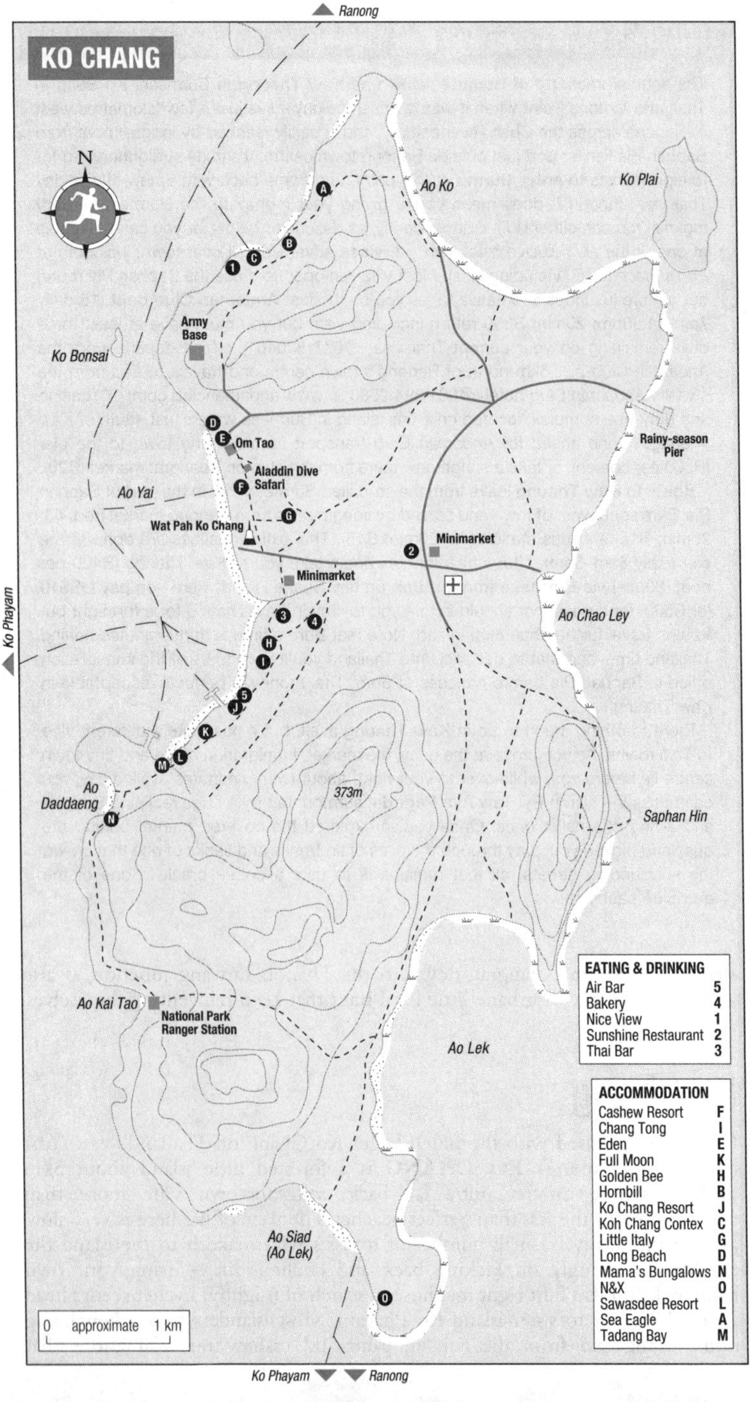
KO CHANG
Ranong
Ko Phayam
Ko Phayam
Ranong
Ko Plai
Ao Ko
Army Base
Ko Bonsai
Om Tao
Aladdin Dive Safari
Ao Yai
Wat Pah Ko Chang
Minimarket
Minimarket
Rainy-season Pier
Ao Chao Ley
Ao Daddaeng
373m
Saphan Hin
Ao Kai Tao
National Park Ranger Station
Ao Lek
Ao Siad (Ao Lek)
0 approximate 1 km
EATING & DRINKING
Air Bar 5
Bakery 4
Nice View 1
Sunshine Restaurant 2
Thai Bar 3
ACCOMMODATION
Cashew Resort F
Chang Tong I
Eden E
Full Moon K
Golden Bee H
Hornbill B
Ko Chang Resort J
Koh Chang Contex C
Little Italy G
Long Beach D
Mama's Bungalows N
N&X O
Sawasdee Resort L
Sea Eagle A
Tadang Bay M

dominate the flatter patches of the interior. The beaches are connected by tracks through the trees and there are only sporadic, self-generated supplies of electricity for a few hours each evening.

The best of Ko Chang's beaches are on the west coast, and of these the longest, nicest and most popular is **Ao Yai**. The tiny bays to the north and south mostly hold just one set of bungalows each and are good for getting away from it all, though access to Ao Yai is easy enough if you don't mind the hike. About halfway between the west and east coasts, a crossroads bisects Ko Chang's only **village**, a tiny settlement that is home to most of the islanders and holds just a few shops, restaurants and a clinic. Signs at the *Sunshine Restaurant* direct you south to Saphan Hin (3km) and Ao Lek (5km); follow the unsigned northern route for a concrete path to the northern pier (used by boats during the wet season).

Nearly all the bungalows on Ko Chang **close** down from about mid-May until mid- or late October, when the island is subjected to very heavy rain, the beaches fill with flotsam, paths become dangerously slippery and food supplies dwindle with no ice available to keep things fresh. Many bungalow staff relocate to the mainland for this period, so you should phone ahead to check first.

Getting to Ko Chang

Boats to Ko Chang leave from the Islands Pier in **Saphan Pla**, 5km south of Ranong's town centre and accessed by **songthaews** from the Thanon Ruangrat market (red; #3; 20min; B15) and the bus station (#6; 20min; B15). The songthaews drop you on the main road through Saphan Pla, from where it's about 500m to the pier and its minimarket and dive shop. Alternatively, *Pon's Place* charges B50 per person for transfers from the town centre to the pier itself.

From about mid-October to mid-May there are three daily **boat departures** to Ko Chang's Ao Yai beach (currently 9.30am, noon & 2pm; 1hr; B150), but ask at Ranong information centres for the latest schedules. You'll be dropped as close as possible to your intended bungalow, which for the little bays north of Ao Yai usually means *Contex*. If heading for Saphan Hin or Ao Siad, you'll probably be put on the Ko Phayam boat (see p.658) instead. The easiest and cheapest option **from Ko Phayam** is to use the thrice weekly daytrippers' boat run by *Ko Chang Resort*, which returns from Ko Phayam village pier around 2pm (currently Mon, Wed & Fri; B150); a charter from Ko Phayam costs about B1500 per boat. During the **rainy months** of June through October there are only three boats a week from Ranong to Ko Chang (currently Mon, Wed & Sat from Ranong, returning from Ko Chang on Mon, Wed & Fri), and they only travel as far as the island's east coast, a three-kilometre walk from Ao Yai.

During the tourist season, there's at least one morning boat from Ko Chang **back to Saphan Pla**, generally about 7.30am, and another one at about 1.30pm; ask at your bungalows the day before. Taxis meet the boats at Saphan Pla and charge B50 per person to town or the bus station; songthaews charge just B15 but you have to walk 500m to the main road to flag them down.

Island practicalities

Most of the **bungalow** operations are simple wooden-plank or woven bamboo constructions, comprising just a dozen huts and a small restaurant each. Though they nearly all have their own generators (which usually only operate in the evenings), some stick to candles and paraffin lamps so you might appreciate having a torch. None have fans. As internet access is limited on the island, few bungalow owners check their email more than once a fortnight during high season. For general **information** on the island see Ⓦ www.kohchang-ranong.com.

Part of Ko Chang's charm is its lack of commercial activity. There are, however, tiny **minimarkets** selling basic necessities at *Cashew Resort*, *Golden Bee* and behind the khlong on Ao Yai; and at *Sunshine Restaurant*, beside the crossroads in the heart of the island. The crossroads is also where you'll find the island **clinic**. *Cashew* and *Ko Chang Resort* can both do **overseas phone calls** and **internet access**, and *Cashew Resort* can also arrange bus tickets, Ranong–Bangkok flights, and speedboat charters to Ranong.

The German-Dutch-run **dive shop** Aladdin Dive Safari (ⓣ077 820472, and at the Islands Pier in Saphan Pla ⓣ077 813698, ⓦwww.aladdindivesafari.com) is based at *Cashew Resort* and from late October through mid-May teaches PADI dive courses and runs liveaboards that take in all the top local dive sites: Ko Surin, Ko Bon, Ko Tachai, Ko Similan, and Richelieu Rock (from B18,900 for four days excluding equipment and national park fees). *Air Bar* at *Ko Chang Resort* is one of several places that run **fishing**, **snorkelling and camping trips** to local islands including Ko Kham, which is famed for its beautiful beaches and reefs. Om Tao on Ao Yai holds morning Hatha **yoga** classes and afternoon qigong.

Ao Yai (Long Beach) and Ao Daddaeng

Effectively divided in two by a khlong, the main cross-island track, and the stumps of a long wooden pier, **Ao Yai**, or **Long Beach**, enjoys a fine view of the brooding silhouette of Burma's St Matthew's Island, which dominates the western horizon. The 800–metre-long stretch of Ao Yai that runs north from the khlong is the most attractive on the island, nice and wide even at high tide, and especially good for kids. South of the khlong, the beach is very narrow at high tide, but when the water goes out you have to walk a longish distance to find any depth. Further south still, around a rocky headland, tiny secluded gold-sand **Ao Daddaeng** (Tadang) is sandwiched between massive boulders and holds just a few bungalows: reach it via a five-minute footpath from behind *Tadang Bay Bungalows*.

A narrow concrete road connects central Ao Yai with the mangrove-filled little harbour on the east coast, a distance of around 1700m that can be walked in under half an hour. The western end of the road begins beside the island's only temple, **Wat Pah Ko Chang**, whose bot and monks' quarters are partially hidden amongst the trees beside the beach, with a sign that asks tourists to dress modestly when in the area and not to swim or sunbathe in front of it.

Accommodation

Cashew Resort ⓣ077 820116, ⓔcashew_resort@hotmail.com. The longest-running accommodation on the island, and also the largest, *Cashew* feels like a tiny village, with its forty en-suite bungalows spread among the cashew trees along 700m of prime beachfront, and returnees personalizing their bungalows like mini homes. It's exceptionally good value: all bungalows enjoy both a sea view and some privacy, they're well maintained, built from either wood or brick, and some have big glass windows. The resort offers the most facilities on the island, including wi-fi, internet access, foreign exchange, Visa and MasterCard capability, an overseas phone service, and a pool table. ❶–❸

Chang Tong ⓣ084 846 1198, ⓦwww.kohchang-ranong.com. The cheapest wood and bamboo bungalows at this friendly spot are very basic, though they're all en suite and are well spaced beneath the shoreside trees; pay a bit more for newer, slightly better appointed ones. ❶–❷

Full Moon ⓣ077 820130, ⓔfamilymoon99@hotmail.com. Though simple, the attractive wooden en-suite bungalows here are well designed and a cut above many others on Ao Yai. Prettily painted and with cute stencilwork on doors and bathrooms, they are comfortable, modern and have an inviting personality. ❶–❸

Ko Chang Resort ⓣ081 896 1839, ⓦwww.kohchangandaman.com. Occupying a fabulous spot high on the rocks right over the water, the best of the en-suite wooden bungalows here have fine sea views from their balconies; the bamboo ones are set further back beside the path. Interiors are very rudimentary but the decks are huge. Also has a big, more luxurious family bungalow. You can swim below the rocks at low tide, or the more reliable beach is just a couple of minutes' scramble to south or north. There's internet on site, plus a tattoo parlour and the very chilled *Air Bar*. ❶–❺

Little Italy ⓣ084 851 2760, ⓔdaniel060863@yahoo.it. This tiny Italian–Thai-run outfit has just two attractive bungalows set in a secluded garden of paperbark trees 100m inland from *Cashew Resort*, behind their recommended Italian garden restaurant. Bungalows are two storey, with exceptionally clean, smartly tiled papaya-coloured bathrooms downstairs and Thai-style bamboo-walled sleeping quarters upstairs, with varnished wood floors and big decks. One of the few places to keep both its bungalows and restaurant open all year. ❷–❸

Long Beach ⓣ087 280 8213, ⓔlongbeachbungalowkohchang@yahoo.co.th. At the far northern end of Ao Yai, this popular spot offers a choice of en-suite bungalows, the best of which are the large, robust wooden ones on the seafront; the smaller, cheaper, older ones are just one row behind. Open all year. ❷–❸

Mama's Bungalows 5min walk south over the headland from Ao Yai, on Ao Daddaeng ⓣ077 820180, ⓔmamasbungalows@yahoo.com. The ten attractive, well-maintained wooden bungalows here come in two sizes, all of them with decent bathrooms. They're built in a pretty flower garden staggered up the hillside; a couple are on the beach and the uppermost ones overlook the bay from the edge of a rubber plantation. Lighting is by paraffin lamps. The restaurant serves generous portions of good food, including many German specialities. Very popular, so book ahead. ❶–❷

Sawasdee Resort ⓣ081 803 0946, ⓔsawasdeekohchang@yahoo.com. This welcoming place at the far southern end of Ao Yai is a little pricier than many but more style conscious too and tends to attract slightly older, less hammock-bound guests. The nine thoughtfully designed wooden bungalows are not fancy but all have exceptionally good bathrooms (tiled floors, colour-washed walls, sinks and showers). The food is recommended too. Because of wave erosion a sea wall has been built around the garden, which mars the view a little, though the water is still just a couple of steps away. ❷–❸

Eating and drinking

Bungalow **restaurants** that stand out include *Cashew Resort* for its fresh bread; *Sawasdee* for its fish with tamarind sauce and its *matsaman* curries; and *Mama's* for its huge breakfasts and home-cooked south-German specialities. Italian-run *Little Italy* makes deliciously authentic sauces for its pasta – Sicilian-style succo, carbonara, arrabbiata (B100–230) – and serves them year-round in its peaceful garden 100m inland from *Cashew* (see above). There's also the very charming *Bakery*, in a tiny forest clearing about 300m inland from *Golden Bee*, where you sit at low tables under the trees and sample the home-made bread, cakes, yoghurt, sandwiches and teas.

A couple of low-key but funky little beach **bars** tempt the slightly more active beachbums out of their hammocks: *Thai Bar*, between the khlong and *Golden Bee*, puts on occasional parties, while fairy-lit *Air Bar*, in a scenic position on the rocks alongside *Ko Chang Resort*, plays cool music and stirs cheap cocktails and is a prime spot for hornbill-spotting at sunset.

The rest of the island

North of Ao Yai, the crenellated coast reveals a series of tiny bays occupied by just one set of bungalows apiece. The gritty gold-sand beaches are secluded and feel quite remote, accessible only via a track through forest and rubber plantations. Even if you don't want to base yourself up here, you can do an enjoyable **loop** around the northern bays in well under three hours from Ao Yai. Alternatively, you could make use of the Ranong boats, which charge about B50 for any hop up or down the west coast.

Following **the track** inland from *Eden*, a ten-minute walk north brings you to the top of the first of several hills (a reliable place to get a mobile phone signal) and the barbed-wire perimeters of a military camp, established here to monitor activity along the (maritime) Thai-Burma border. Ten minutes further on, *Nice View* restaurant and bungalows are aptly named: perched atop an outcrop with glorious panoramas over the unfolding little bays and islets beyond, it's a perfect spot to break for lunch or a drink. It's another twenty minutes to *Sea Eagle* (you need to go via the beach at *Hornbill* before returning inland), the last of the northern bay bungalows, beyond which a ten-minute walk up and over the next hill takes you to the edge of the northeast-facing fishing village, an unprepossessing place complete with incongruous Christian church. This is **Ao Ko**, which is linked by road to the east coast's rainy season pier, and also to Ao Yai.

Ao Siad, at the southern end of the island, is even more isolated, though there are several bungalow outfits fronting the sandy shore here. It's sometimes known as Ao Lek, though the real **Ao Lek** is the mangrove-lined bay fifteen minutes' walk to the northeast, on the other coast. The Ranong–Ko Phayam boat service makes a stop off Ao Siad (Ranong–Ko Chang boats do not), but to get anywhere else you'll need to negotiate a ride in a longtail if staying here. The alternative is to walk, either from Ao Daddaeng or from the village. From Ao Daddaeng, a clear path takes you south, in about an hour, to **Ao Kai Tao**, a pretty beach and site of the national park ranger station. From Ao Kai Tao the route then follows an indistinct path across the saddle between two hills and along a creek bed to reach east coast Ao Lek (this takes another hour), after which it's fifteen minutes south to Ao Siad. Coming **from the village**, you follow the signed track from the *Sunshine Restaurant* crossroads south to Ao Lek and then on to Ao Siad; it's 5km and should take about two hours.

Accommodation

Hornbill North around two headlands from Ao Yai, about 35min walk ⓣ077 870240, 66_hornbill@hotmail.com. Set amongst the trees fronting their own little gold-sand bay, the ten unobtrusive en-suite bungalows here are constructed to different designs, some of them extremely comfortable, and all enjoy sea views. The food here has a good reputation and the owner is very welcoming. It lives up to its name, as majestic black-and-white hornbills are a common sight. Opens earlier than many, in September, and has internet access and boat trips. ❶–❷

Koh Chang Contex 25min walk from northern Ao Yai ⓣ087 827 2874. Located in its own peaceful little bay, which is good for snorkelling and fine for swimming except at low tide, this place has seventeen wood, bamboo and concrete huts, some of them very large and all with generous decks and their own bathrooms. Some occupy elevated spots on the rocks, others are scattered around a garden just above the beach. ❶–❸

N&X 10min walk south of Ao Siad and at least a 2hr walk from either Ao Daddaeng or from the inland village. Occupying its own tiny bay, isolated even from remote Ao Siad, this place offers ten good en-suite bungalows ranged up the shorefront hillside. ❶–❸

Sea Eagle About 40min walk from Ao Yai ⓣ082 289 0683, ⓦwww.seaeaglebangkalo.com. The sole occupants of the longest and widest of the northern bays, which is graced by an attractive band of gold sand, the seven green-painted, en-suite bamboo bungalows here are set among trees just back from shore. They have comfy deck furniture for soaking up the sea views and there are kayaks for rent and a beach volleyball net. ❷

Ko Phayam

The diminutive kangaroo-shaped island of **KO PHAYAM** offers fine white-sand beaches and coral reefs and is home to around five hundred people, most of whom either make their living from prawn, squid and crab fishing, or from growing cashew nuts, *sator* beans, coconut palms and rubber trees. Many

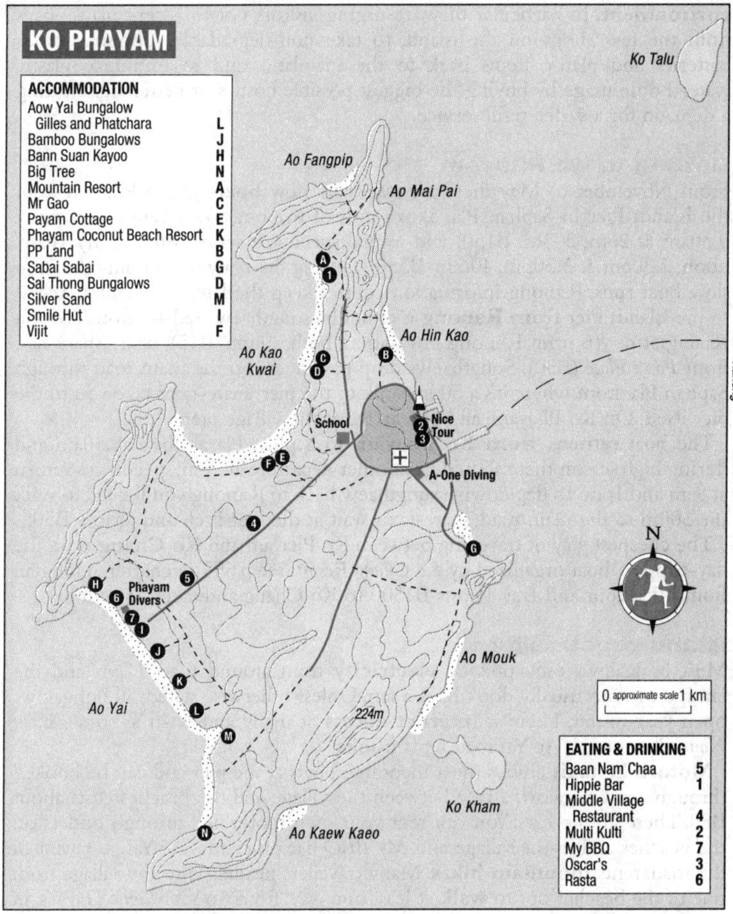

islanders live in Ko Phayam's only **village**, behind the pier on the northeast coast, which connects to other corners of the island by a network of concrete roads and rutted tracks. The bays either side of the village have a couple of nice places to stay, but the main beaches and accommodation centres are on the west coast, at **Ao Yai** and **Ao Kao Kwai**. A motorbike taxi service covers all routes, but no journey is very great as the island measures just five by eight kilometres at its widest points.

Because of the roads, Ko Phayam has a livelier and slightly more developed feel than neighbouring Ko Chang, underlined by a low-key beach-bar scene – all hand-painted signs and driftwood sculptures – and the presence of a significant number of foreigners who choose to spend six or more months here every year. Some expats even take up the **rainy-season** challenge, staying on through the downpours and rough seas that lash the island from June to October, but a number of bungalows close down during this time and staff take refuge in Ranong. As the island gets more popular, residents and expats are beginning to try and forestall the inevitable negative impact on the island's

environment. In particular they are urging visitors not to accept plastic bags from the few shops on the island, to take non-degradable rubbish such as batteries and plastic items back to the mainland, and to minimize plastic water-bottle usage by buying the biggest possible bottles or better still creating a demand for a water-refill service.

Getting to Ko Phayam

From November to May there are two daily slow **boats** to Ko Phayam from the Islands Pier in Saphan Pla, 5km south of Ranong town centre (currently 9.30am & 2pm; 2–3hr; B150) and several speedboat services (currently 10am, noon, 2.30pm & 5.30pm; 40min; B350). During the rainy season only the 2pm slow boat runs; Ranong information centres keep the latest timetables. Access to the Islands Pier **from Ranong** is either by songthaew (red #3 from Thanon Ruangrat or #6 from Ranong bus station; both 20min, B15), or by share-taxi from *Pon's Place* (B50). Songthaews drop passengers on the main road through Saphan Pla, from where it's a 500m walk to the pier; share-taxis take you to the pier itself. On Ko Phayam, all boats arrive at the village pier.

The boat **returns from Ko Phayam** to Saphan Pla at about 8.30am and during high season there should be another departure at 2pm; speedboats return at 9am and 1pm. To flag down a songthaew back to Ranong you'll need to walk the 500m to the main road; share-taxis wait at the pier itself and charge B50.

The cheapest way of travelling between Ko Phayam and **Ko Chang** is on the day-trippers' boat organized by *Ko Chang Resort* (see p.653); a chartered longtail from Nice Tour and Travel costs B1500 to Ko Chang and takes 45 minutes.

Island practicalities

Most bungalows only provide **electricity** from around 6 to 11pm and the cheapest rooms usually don't have a fan. Unless otherwise stated, all bungalows open year-round. There is **internet access** at many and wi-fi at some. *Baan Nam Chaa* on the Ao Yai road rents **books**.

Motorbike taxis always meet incoming boats at the pier and can be booked through any bungalow; a ride between the village and the beaches costs about B80. There are no cars. You can rent your own motorbike through outlets on the beaches and in the village and *My BBQ* bar on central Ao Yai, just west of the road, rents **mountain bikes**. Many travellers heading into the village from one of the beaches opt to **walk** at least one way: from Ao Yai's *Smile Hut* it's an enjoyable seven-kilometre stroll along the narrow concrete road than cuts through the cashew plantations, with the possibility of stopping for a breather at the aptly named *Middle Village Restaurant*. From southern Ao Kao Kwai to the village takes less than an hour.

A-One Diving (Ⓣ077 824303, Ⓦwww.a-one-diving.com), based in the village, teaches PADI **dive** courses and runs liveaboards to Ko Surin, Richelieu Rock and Ko Similan (from B13,900 for three days) and to Burma Banks and the Mergui archipelago. On Ao Yai, Phayam Divers at *Phayam Lodge* offers a similar deal (Ⓣ084 849 9766, Ⓦwww.phayamlodge.com). *Mr Gao* on Ao Kao Kwai (Ⓣ077 870222, Ⓦwww.mr-gao-phayam.com) runs two-day **snorkelling** trips to Ko Surin at B4000 per person including accommodation in national park tents. Most bungalows can arrange fishing and snorkelling day-trips for B1500 per boat.

The village and around

The tiny cluster of homes and shops that constitute Ko Phayam's only **village** are within a few minutes' walk of the pier. There are a few little general stores here, plus a 24-hour minimarket, several restaurants and a **clinic**. North a little way up the shoreline stands the island **temple**, with its circular viharn resting on a huge concrete lotus flower at the end of its own pier.

Oscar's bar (daily 7am–late, ⓣ084 842 5070), just north of the pier-head, is a good source of island **information**, rents motorbikes, sells speedboat tickets, charters speedboats to Ranong airport and other islands, and takes people wakeboarding in the village bay. It serves breakfasts and Thai and European standards but is most famous for its partially open-air **bar**, which is the focal point of the expat social scene (customers who can't make it home are invited to crash out at the adjacent *Hangover Hut*). Nearby *Multi Kulti* is the place to go for multi-grain sandwiches, and there are some cheap Thai *som tam* places too. **Tour agent** Nice Tour and Travel (ⓣ089 651 5177, ⓦwww.kohphayamisland.com) **changes money** and does Visa cash advance, sells bus, train, airline and speedboat tickets, can arrange boat hire and fishing tours, and offers **internet** access and an **international phone service**; it also sells creative Nepalese clothing and handicrafts.

Accommodation

Most people choose to **stay** at the west-coast beach centres, but there are a couple of nice little hideaways within easy reach of the village and its facilities. On their own little beach five minutes' walk south, *Sabai Sabai* (ⓣ087 895 4653, ⓔsabaisabai_thailand@yahoo.com; ❶–❷) has five wooden, solar-powered bungalows, all with 24-hour electricity and all but one en suite; cute, stylish touches give them a modern look. There's a cool lounge area, regular movie nights and other events, plus internet access and Nintendo Wii. Fronting a small beach about ten minutes' walk north from the village, *PP Land* (ⓣ081 678 4310, ⓦppland.cabanova.de; ❸) is a cut above many places to stay on the island, with its tasteful, green-painted shaggy thatched bungalows, pretty furnishings, polished wood floors inside and out, nice bathrooms, and big comfy decks. There's internet, wi-fi and homemade ice cream too, plus 24-hour electricity, safety boxes in the rooms and bicycles and motorbikes for rent.

Ao Yai

Ko Phayam's main beach is the three-kilometre-long **Ao Yai** on the southwest coast, a wide and handsome sweep of silvery white sand that curves quite deeply at its northern and southern ends into rocky outcrops that offer some snorkelling possibilities. The shore is pounded by decent waves that are fun for boogie-boarding and pretty safe; the sunsets are quite spectacular too. For the moment Ao Yai's bungalow operations are mostly widely spaced along the shoreline, and much of the forest behind the beach is still intact. You're more than likely to see – and hear – some of the resident black-and-white hornbills at dawn and dusk, along with many white-bellied sea eagles, and sightings of crab-eating macaques are also common.

Accommodation and eating

When it comes to **eating**, *Silver Sand* bungalows does famously tasty yellow seafood curries and *Bamboo* makes authentic spaghetti pesto. The invitingly hippyish *Ban Nam Chaa* on the Ao Yai road (Mon–Sat 8am–5pm) makes its own bread and cakes, dreams up unusual salads, Indian and Burmese curries, and stocks plenty of weird teas. Many bungalow operations on Ao Yai, including the long-running *Rasta*, also host laid-back little **beach-bar shacks** which put on fireshows and occasional parties.

Aow Yai Bungalow Gilles and Phatchara Ⓣ075 870216, Ⓔgilles_phatchara@hotmail.com. Established by a French-Thai couple, this was the first set of bungalows on the island and remains one of the most popular, especially with return guests. The 22 good-quality bungalows are dotted around an extensive garden of flowers, fruit trees and palms and come in various styles, with price depending on size. There's wi-fi and internet access, snorkels for rent and bus tickets for sale. ❷–❹

Bamboo Bungalows Ⓣ077 820012, Ⓦwww.bamboo-bungalows.com. Ao Yai's liveliest accommodation is Israeli-Thai managed and very traveller savvy, with internet access and free wi-fi, plus kayak, motorbike and boogie-board rental, currency exchange and overseas phone services. Its 39 bungalows and handful of tents (with proper mattresses) are set under the trees in a well-tended flower garden and range from luxuriously large chalets with 24hr electricity and pretty furnishings to characterful shell-studded concrete bungalows and a choice of bamboo and wood huts. Tents ❶, bungalows ❷–❻

Bann Suan Kayoo Ⓣ089 819 8782, Ⓦwww.gopayam.com. There's a genuinely warm welcome from the island-family owners here and the peaceful location at the far northern end of the bay appeals particularly to solo travellers looking for quiet. Choose between simple thatched bamboo huts nicely spaced along the shoreline and with decent beds and en-suite bathrooms, or slightly sturdier ones with tin roofs and bigger decks, the latter set within a grassy shorefront garden with floral hedges. Closed May–Oct. ❶–❸

Big Tree Ⓣ087 893 7075. Another lovely quiet spot, removed from the main action at the far southern end of the bay, and set near the eponymous tree and above a rocky point that offers some snorkelling. The thirteen bamboo, wood and concrete bungalows are a good size, with price depending on size and location, though nearly all of them have a direct sea view and some have commanding panoramas from atop a small rise. Closed during the rainy season. ❶–❹

Phayam Coconut Beach Resort Ⓣ089 920 8145, Ⓦwww.koh-phayam.com. Occupying a great spot in the centre of the bay and run by a Ko Phayam family, the 25 good-value bungalows here are of a high standard, each set in its own tiny garden. Choose between small bamboo en-suite huts through larger wood or bamboo versions to big concrete bungalows at the top end. Also rents kayaks. ❷–❹

Smile Hut Ⓣ081 810 7252, Ⓦwww.smilehutthai.com. Like *Bamboo*, this is very popular with travellers. The 35 split-bamboo huts are simple but en suite and are spread among the shorefront trees, with the slightly cheaper versions set one row behind. Has internet access. ❷–❸

Ao Kao Kwai and around

The northwest coast is scalloped into **AO KAO KWAI**, a name that's pronounced locally as **Ao Kao Fai** and translates as **Buffalo Bay**; from the cliffside midway along the bay you can see how the two halves of the beach curve out into buffalo-like horns. The southern half of Ao Kao Kwai is subject to both very low and very high tides, which makes it unreliable for swimming, but the northern stretch, from *Sai Thong* and *Mr Gao* bungalows onwards, is exceptionally pretty, secluded between outcrops with decent swimming at any tide, and none of the big waves that characterize Ao Yai. Ao Kao Kwai is particularly popular both with long-stay guests and returnees, so you might want to book your accommodation in advance. Both *Sai Thong* and *Mr Gao* have reputations for very good Thai **food**, and *Hippie Bar* has occasional parties.

North of *Mountain Resort* at the northern end of Ao Kao Kwai, a thirty-minute walk brings you to the pretty little sandy beach at **Ao Fangpip** (also spelt Ao Kwang Pib), which is the best spot on the island for snorkelling. There's also some snorkellable reef at **Ao Hin Kao** on the northeast coast.

Accommodation

Mountain Resort Ⓣ086 144 7208. Managed by a welcoming family, the five bungalows here vary in size but they're comfortable, en suite and have screened doors. They're set in a lovely grassy garden at the peaceful, northernmost end of the beach, under palms and among bougainvillea and hibiscus. The concrete road ends about 1km before *Mountain Resort*, so the last stretch is via a potholed dirt track (or you can walk via the beach instead). ❸

Mr Gao ⓣ077 870222, ⓦwww.mr-gao-phayam.com. Located on the best stretch of the beach, this is one of the most famous and popular spots, a well-established operation com-prising just ten well-designed bungalows, in assorted sizes and luxury, set in a lovingly tended garden of shrubs and bamboos. All have good bathrooms and generous decks and most have polished wood floors, screened windows and thoughtfully furnished interiors. There is internet access here and free wi-fi, and it's open all year. ❷–❸

Payam Cottage ⓣ085 222 1847, ⓦwww.payamcottage.com. More resort-like in style and facilities than others on Ko Phayam, with 24hr electricity, the option of air-con, a kids' play area, and a swimming pool in the pipeline. Bungalows are tastefully furnished and built in angled rows across a central garden to give each one some sort of sea view. Internet access and free wi-fi. Fan ❺, air-con ❻

Sai Thong Bungalows ⓣ080 141 1231, ⓔsaithong_ranongth@yahoo.com. Friendly, local setup that shares the same pretty stretch of beach with *Mr Gao* and has just five good-quality rattan huts, each furnished with a thick mattress, a mosquito net and its own well-appointed bathroom. ❷

Vijit ⓣ077 834082, ⓦwww.kohpayam-vijit.com. This long-running outfit is very popular. Some of the 26 bungalows are designed for families and they're all reasonably spacious. Has currency exchange, kayak, motorbike and bicycle rental. ❷–❸

Khuraburi and Ko Surin

The small town of **Khuraburi**, 110km south of Ranong on Highway 4, is the main departure point for the magnificent national park island chain of **Ko Surin**, a group of five small islands around 60km offshore, just inside Thai waters. Much closer to Khuraburi are the islands of **Ko Ra** and **Ko Phra Thong**, which offer empty beaches and decent snorkelling and birdwatching, or there's the chance to participate in typical village life at **homestays** in mainland coastal communities.

Khuraburi

Most travellers use the town of **KHURABURI** as a staging post en route to or from the Surin islands: the main pier for boats to the islands is just 7.5km away, and Khuraburi's tour agents sell boat tickets and offer transport to the pier, plus there is accommodation in town. Though lacking in famous attractions, the local area is nonetheless scenic, both offshore and inland: with an afternoon or more to spare, you could either rent a motorbike, mountain bike or kayak to explore it independently, or charter a motorbike taxi or longtail boat.

Khuraburi is also the headquarters of the community-based tourism initiative Andaman Discoveries (ⓣ087 917 7165, ⓦwww.andamandiscoveries.com), which runs a recommended **homestay programme** in several local villages. It was established after the tsunami to help the area's many devastated fishing communities get back on their feet and has since developed a range of stimulating packages featuring all sort of village jobs and activities, from soap-making and batik design to rubber-tapping and roof-thatching; a typical, all-inclusive three-day stay costs from B5400 per person. The office is just east off the highway, up the soi beside the police box, across from Tom & Am Tour.

Practicalities

The commercial heart of Khuraburi is a 500-metre strip of shops and businesses either side of Highway 4 and most **buses** travelling along Highway 4 between Bangkok/Chumphon/Ranong and Takua Pa/Khao Lak/Phuket stop here. Bus passengers are usually met by staff from Tom & Am Tour (ⓣ086 272 0588, ⓔtom_am01@yahoo.co.th), which runs boats to Ko Surin and rents **tents** (B100 per day), bedding sets (B30 per day) and snorkel sets (B50 per day) for

Ko Surin (all cheaper than National Park prices) as well as bicycles and motorbikes. Nearby Sabina Tour (ⓣ081 737 5801, ⓦwww.sabinatour.com) is a good operator of boats to Ko Surin and has two offices in central Khuraburi and another at the pier. For details of transport to Ko Surin see p.664. *Boon Piya Resort* (see below) rents kayaks and motorbikes and can arrange snorkelling trips to Ko Ra and Ko Phra Thong; and Indian Ocean Adventures (ⓦwww.diverichelieurock.com) runs twice-weekly liveaboard **dive trips** out of Khuraburi to Ko Tachai, Ko Surin and Richelieu Rock (three days; B12,450).

Set alongside the river at the northern end of town, about 250m north of the bus drop, *Tararin* (ⓣ076 491789; fan ❷, air-con ❸) is a cute, rustic-style place with just a handful of simple but appealing en-suite wooden and concrete **bungalows** overlooking the water, plus an attractive riverside restaurant and eating deck. The pristine concrete bungalows at the motel-style *Boon Piya Resort* (ⓣ081 752 5457; ❸–❹), 150m north of the bus drop, are better appointed, if rather tightly packed, and all have fan or air-con and powerful showers; they're the usual choice of sales reps and NGOs. The poshest accommodation in the area are the attractive wooden chalets at *Khuraburi Greenview Resort* (ⓣ076 401400, ⓦwww.kuraburigreenview.co.th; ❻–❼), 12km south of Khuraburi, beneath a range of forested hills alongside Highway 4, at kilometre-stone 739. Rooms are air-conditioned and there's wi-fi, a swimming pool and spa; the hotel also does (expensive) speedboat day-trips and transfers to Ko Surin.

At night, many people **eat** at one of the night markets near the bus drop, where the roti stall is a particular favourite, flipping out a constant pile of sizzling *roti mataba* (chicken) and *roti kluay* (banana), and *Krua Pakarang* does excellent-value seafood from 4pm. The morning market (daily from 5am) across from *Boon Piya* is the place to stock up on food for the Surin islands, but the best place for fresh coffee is next door but one to *Boon Piya* at the *Friends de Sea* **internet** café (daily 8am–9pm). Popular *Cucina Andaburi*, beside the bridge and *Tararin*, is a welcoming spot for farang food and a favourite hangout of resident NGOs.

Ko Ra and Ko Phra Thong

Chief among Khuraburi's local maritime attractions are the **islands** of Ko Ra and Ko Phra Thong, both of them accessible by chartered longtail from the Khuraburi pier (B2500 per day including snorkel gear and transfers from town). Hilly, forested **Ko Ra** (measuring about 10km north to south and 3km across) sits just off Khuraburi pier's mangrove-lined estuary and is graced with intact rainforest full of towering trees, hornbills and wild, empty beaches. The island is home to some two dozen Moken and *Mai Thai* people (see opposite) plus just one place to stay, the rather special American-Thai run *Ko Ra Ecolodge* (ⓣ089 867 5288, ⓦwww.thaiecolodge.com; ❺). The *Ecolodge* fronts a curve of bronze sand on the north coast, with magnificent views to the Khuraburi hills, but its star feature is its wild, forty-acre, forest garden. Filled with screw palms, red-barked *samet daeng* trees, dipterocarps and over seventeen epiphytic orchids, the private forest is crossed by trails and home both to a rich bird life, especially sunbirds and oriental pied hornbills, and to monitor lizards, crab-eating macaques and dusky langurs. Accommodation is in eighteen plain but spacious rooms in split-bamboo longhouses just back from the shore, communal meals are taken in the beach-side *sala* and there's a genuine focus on community and environmental projects; the *Ecolodge* also runs the Thai arm of Reef Check NGO (see p.83). There are kayak rental and trips, plus hiking, snorkelling and diving, in particular to the nearby Surin islands (B4900 for two dives) and Richelieu Rock. A longtail transfer to the *Ecolodge* from Khuraburi costs B250 per person (20min).

The chao ley: Moken and Urak Lawoy

Sometimes called sea gypsies, the **chao ley** or *chao nam* ("people of the sea" or "water people") have been living off the seas around the west coast of the Malay peninsula for hundreds of years. Some still pursue a traditional nomadic existence, living in self-contained houseboats known as **kabang**, but many have now made permanent homes in Andaman coast settlements in Thailand, Burma and Malaysia. Dark-skinned and sometimes with an auburn tinge to their hair, the *chao ley* of the Andaman Sea are thought to number around five thousand, divided into five groups, with distinct lifestyles and dialects.

Of the different groups, the **Urak Lawoy**, who have settled on the islands of Ko Lanta, Ko Jum, Ko Phi Phi, Phuket and Ko Lipe, are the most integrated into Thai society. They came north to Thailand from Malaysia around two hundred years ago (having possibly migrated from the Nicobar Islands in the Indian Ocean some two centuries prior) and are known as *Mai Thai*, or "New Thai". Thailand's Urak Lawoy have been recognized as Thai citizens since the 1960s, when the late Queen Mother granted them five family names, thereby enabling them to possess ID cards and go to school. Many work on coconut plantations or as fishermen, while others continue in the more traditional *chao ley* **occupations** of hunting for pearls and seashells on the ocean floor, attaching stones to their waists to dive to depths of 60m with only an air-hose connecting them to the surface; sometimes they fish in this way too, taking down enormous nets into which they herd the fish as they walk along the sea bed. Their agility and courage make them good bird's-nesters as well (see box, p.746).

The **Moken** of Thailand's Ko Surin islands and Burma's Mergui archipelago probably came originally from Burma and are the most traditional of the *chao ley* communities. Some still lead remote, itinerant lives, and most are unregistered as Thai citizens, and own no land or property, but are dependent on fresh water and beaches to collect shells and sea slugs to sell to Thai traders. They have extensive knowledge of the plants that grow in the remaining jungles on Thailand's west-coast islands, using eighty different species for food alone, and thirty for medicinal purposes.

The *chao ley* are **animists**, with a strong connection both to the natural spirits of island and sea and to their own ancestral spirits. On some beaches they set up totem poles as a contact point between the spirits, their ancestors and their shaman. The sea gypsies have a rich **musical heritage** too. The Moken do not use any instruments as such, making do with found objects for percussion; the Urak Lawoy, on the other hand, due to their closer proximity to the Thai and Malay cultures, are excellent violin- and drum-players. During community entertainments, such as the Urak Lawoy's twice-yearly full-moon **festivals** on Ko Lanta (see p.765), the male musicians form a semicircle around the old women, who dance and sing about the sea, the jungle and their families.

Building a new boat is the ultimate expression of what it is to be a *chao ley*, and tradition holds that every newly married couple has a *kabang* built for them. But the complex art of constructing a seaworthy home from a single tree trunk, and the way of life it represents, is disappearing. In Thailand, where **assimilation** is actively promoted by the government, the truly nomadic flotillas have become increasingly marginalized, and the number of undeveloped islands they can visit unhindered gets smaller year by year. The 2004 tsunami further threatened their cultural integrity: when the waves destroyed the Moken's boats and homes on Ko Surin, they were obliged to take refuge on the mainland, where some were encouraged by missionaries to convert from their animist religion. Though the Moken have since returned to the Surin islands, inappropriate donations and the merging of two villages have exacerbated family rivalries and caused divisions that may prove lethal to their traditional way of life.

Immediately to the south of Ko Ra, about one kilometre off the Khuraburi coast, **KO PHRA THONG** (Golden Buddha Island) also has some lovely beaches, the nicest of which, on the west coast, is 10km long and blessed with fine gold sand. This is the site of the *Golden Buddha Beach Resort* (Ⓣ081 892 2208, Ⓦwww.goldenbuddharesort.com; ❽–❾), a tasteful complex of 25 individually styled wooden Thai-style homes, sleeping two to six. The resort is ninety minutes' boat ride from the pier and offers kayaking, diving and occasional yoga retreats plus a spa and clubhouse.

Ko Surin

Spectacularly varied and unusually shallow reefs, a palette of awesomely clear turquoise waters and dazzling white sands, and dense forests of lofty diptero-carps combine to make the islands of Mu **Ko Surin** National Park (open Nov 16–May 15; B400/200 entry fee for a week; Ⓦwww.dnp.go.th/National_park.asp) one of the must-visit destinations in south Thailand. It's very much an outdoors experience, with the bulk of accommodation in national park tents, no commerce on the islands at all, and twice-daily snorkelling the main activity. Many tour operators run snorkelling and diving day-trips from Khuraburi and Ranong, and there are diving live-aboards too, but independent travel is also recommended.

The most beautiful and easily explored of the reefs are those off the two main islands in the group, Ko Surin Nua (north) and Ko Surin Tai (south), which are separated only by a narrow channel. **Surin Nua**, slightly the larger at about 5km across, holds the national park headquarters, visitor centre and park accommodation. Across the channel, **Surin Tai** is the long-established home of a community of **Moken** *chao ley* (see p.663), who these days mostly make their living as longtail boatmen for snorkellers staying on Surin Nua. Their recent history has been an unhappy one: not only were their settlements destroyed in the 2004 tsunami, but the aid and outside intervention that followed has changed the community forever, amalgamating two villages, building new homes too close together and introducing various modern-day vices. Some tour companies take visitors on a walk around the village on Ao Bon and up the hill behind it, but unless you are able to hire an English-speaking Moken guide it's a dispiriting experience; if you do visit, you'll at least be making a positive contribution if you buy one of the woven-pandanus-leaf souvenirs the villagers make. One of the Moken traditions that does persist is the new year celebration that's held every April, during Songkhran, when *chao ley* from nearby islands (including those in Burmese waters) congregate here and, among other rites, release several hundred turtles into the sea, a symbol of longevity.

Practicalities

Because the islands are so far out at sea, Ko Surin is closed to visitors from mid-May to mid-November, when monsoon weather renders the sixty-kilometre trip a potentially suicidal undertaking. During the rest of the year, most visitors either do **snorkelling day-trips** to the islands from Khuraburi or Ko Ra (around B2500), join a multi-day snorkel trip from *Mr Gao* on Ko Phayam, or opt for live-aboard **dive trips** out of Khao Lak, Phuket, Ranong, Ko Chang or Ko Phayam, the majority of which also take in nearby Richelieu Rock, considered to be Thailand's top dive site (see p.699).

Independent travel to Ko Surin is highly recommended however, as this gives you the chance to base yourself on the islands and explore the countless different reefs over several days. During the season, **boats** to Ko Surin depart from Khuraburi pier, 7.5km northwest of Khuraburi town; agencies in the town sell tickets and provide free transfers to the pier. The national park's slow boat departs the pier daily at 9am and returns from Ko Surin at 1pm (2–3hr; B1200 return); private speedboats depart at 9am and leave Ko Surin about 2.30pm (1hr 15min; B1600 return). Once on the islands, there's an efficient system of **boat hire** for access to the reefs: longtails depart twice a day from the campsites to four different reefs and charge B80 per person for about two hours. You can also charter your own for B2000. Snorkel sets cost B80 per day and there's kayak rental too.

All island **accommodation** is on Surin Nua and is provided by the national park. On the beach at **Ao Chong Khad**, near the park headquarters and pier, you have the choice between expensive en-suite national park bungalows (7) and either renting a national park tent (B300–450 per day) or pitching your own (available for rent in Khuraburi) for B80 per day; bedding sets cost B60 per day. The nicer campsite, with tents and pitches but no bungalows, is at **Ao Mai Ngam**, reached via a two-kilometre trail from headquarters or by longtail. Both campsites have bathrooms, lockers (B30 per day) and dining rooms where meals are served at fixed times three times a day (B80–200); many people take their own supplies from Khuraburi instead. Bungalows need to be booked in advance either through the National Parks website (W www.dnp.go.th/National_park.asp) or at the Khuraburi pier office (T 076 491378), but tents should be available on spec except during public holidays and long weekends.

Khao Sok National Park

Most of the Andaman coast's highlights are, unsurprisingly, along the shoreline, but the stunning jungle-clad karsts of **KHAO SOK NATIONAL PARK** (W www.dnp.go.th/National_park.asp) are well worth heading inland for. Located about halfway between the southern peninsula's two coasts and easily accessible from Khao Lak, Phuket and Surat Thani, the park has become a popular stop on the travellers' route, offering a number of easy trails, a bit of amateur spelunking and some scenic rafthouse accommodation on **Cheow Lan Lake**. Much of the park, which protects the watershed of the Sok River and rises to a peak of nearly 1000m, is carpeted in impenetrable rainforest, home to gaurs, leopard cats and tigers among others – and up to 155 species of bird. The limestone crags that dominate almost every vista both on and away from the lake are breathtaking, never more so than in the early morning: waking up to the sound of hooting gibbons and the sight of thick white mist curling around the karst formations is an experience not quickly forgotten.

The park has two centres: the **tourist village** that has grown up around the park visitor centre and trailheads, and the dam, 65km further east, at the head of **Cheow Lan Lake**. Most visitors stay in the tourist village and organize their lake trips from there, but it's also feasible to do one or more nights at the lake first.

Arrival and information

Khao Sok, its tourist village and Cheow Lan Lake are all north off Highway 401, which is served by frequent **buses**: all services between the junction town of **Takua Pa**, 40km south of Khuraburi, and Surat Thani come this way, as do some Surat Thani services to and from Khao Lak and Phuket as well. Coming from Bangkok, Hua Hin or Chumphon, take a Surat Thani-bound bus as far as the Highway 401 junction, about 20km before Surat Thani, and change onto one for Takua Pa. If coming direct from Surat Thani, note that there have been complaints about the tourist **minibus** services to Khao Sok that leave at or after

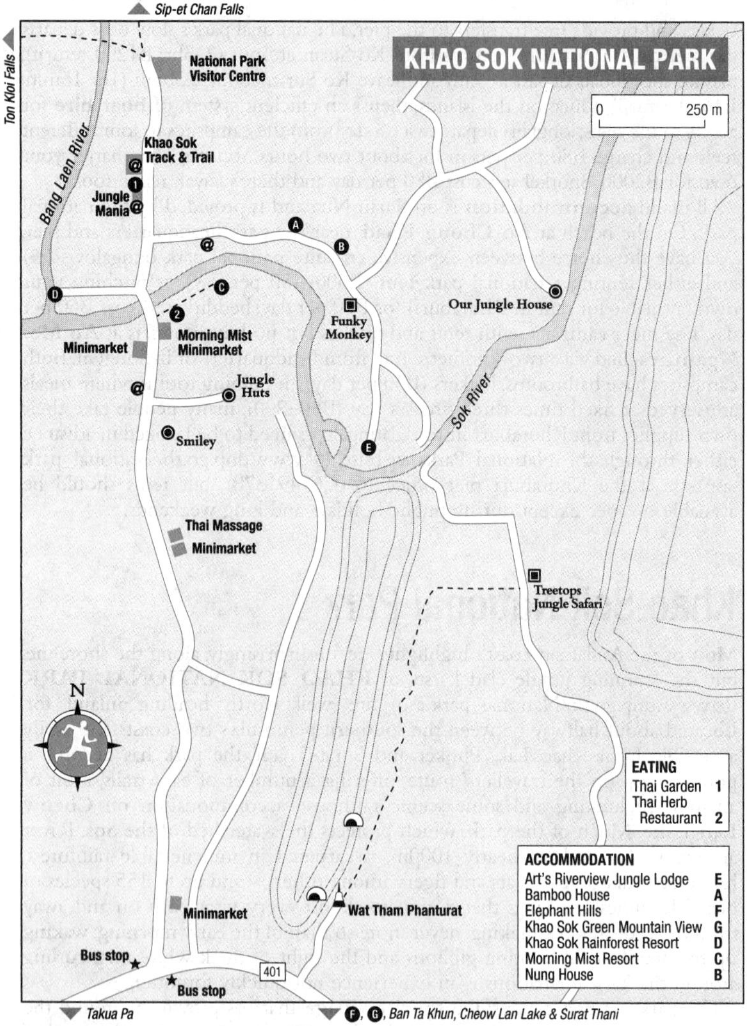

3pm: despite advertising a door-to-door service, they reputedly dump their passengers at an affiliated guest house on the Khao Sok access road, delaying their arrival until after dark. See p.670 for transport services from Surat Thani train station direct to the lake.

The access road to the tourist village and trailheads is at kilometre-stone 109 on Highway 401, where guest-house staff meet all passengers and **offer free lifts** to their accommodation, the furthest of which is 3km from the main road.

The tourist village offers all essential services – minimarkets, **internet**, laundry, massage and **motorbike rental** – but there's **no ATM** here. Khao Sok Track & Trail does currency exchange, has overseas phone services and sells bus, boat, plane and train tickets.

Moving on from Khao Sok

Onward bus connections from Khao Sok are frequent (see p.766), or you can make use of the minibus services organized by Track & Trail, including to Krabi (2hr; B300), Surat Thani train station at Phunphin (1hr 45min; B250), Ko Samui (3hr; B500), Trang (4hr 30min; B520) and Penang (12hr; B750). Jungle Mania sells tickets on the overnight VIP government bus to Bangkok's Southern Bus Terminal (12hr; B1000).

Accommodation and eating

The bulk of the budget **accommodation** is scenically sited beneath the karsts near the park visitors' centre, but despite the edge-of-the rainforest location, it can get noisy of an evening, with the sound systems at some backpacker bars pitched against the chattering of the cicadas. There are quieter, more remote alternatives further east, including the deluxe tented camp run by *Elephant Hills* as part of a package booked from southern beach resorts (Ⓣ076 381703, Ⓦwww.elephant-hills.com), and rafthouses on the lake (see p.670). Some guest houses (not listed here) can make life difficult for guests who choose not to book park trips through them. For **food**, *Thai Herb Restaurant* at *Morning Mist Resort* serves exceptionally tasty and inventive spicy *yam* salads and other Thai classics plus fresh sapodilla and tamarind juices; staff grow much of their own produce and run popular cooking classes (from B800). *Thai Garden* also does great Thai food, including vegan and gluten-free dishes, set dinners (from B240), very good stir-fried red curry with chilli, basil and pork, and delicious fresh coconut shakes.

Art's Riverview Jungle Lodge Ⓣ086 479 3234, Ⓦkrabidir.com/artsriverviewlodge/index.htm. Popular place, with 35 bungalows nicely located away from the main fray, surrounded by jungle and mostly enjoying pretty river views. The cheaper bungalows are spacious, tastefully designed wooden affairs, with shutters and a deck; the deluxe versions are bigger still and attractively furnished, and there are treehouse-style bungalows and family ones too. All rooms have fans and mosquito nets. ❹–❻

Bamboo House Ⓣ081 787 7484, Ⓦkrabidir.com/bamboohouse/index.htm. One of the first guest houses in the park and run by members of the park warden's family. The simple, en-suite, bamboo huts here are the cheapest in this part of the park and there are also stilted wooden huts, concrete versions, and a couple of treehouses. Also has a swimming platform in the river. ❶–❹

Khao Sok Green Mountain View 1500m north from km 106.5 Ⓣ087 263 2481, Ⓔgreen_mountain_view@yahoo.co.th. In a very quiet spot far from almost everyone else, this is a great budget option if you want a remote location. The seven good-quality bamboo and wood bungalows are all en suite and have some nice touches, with pretty open-roofed bathrooms, fans, mosquito nets, decks and hammocks. They sit on the edge of a rubber plantation on the other side of the karsts from the main accommodation area. There's free transport to the park village or you can walk to *Our Jungle House* across the river in 15min and on to the park headquarters in another 25. ❷–❸

Khao Sok Rainforest Resort Ⓣ077 395135, Ⓦkhaosokrainforest.com. This welcoming place has five spectacularly sited "mountain view" bungalows – set high on a jungle slope and affording unsurpassed karst views – plus seven others at ground level, overlooking the river. Interiors are decent enough if a bit faded and all rooms are en suite. ❸

Morning Mist Resort Ⓣ089 971 8794, Ⓦkhaosokmorningmistresort.com. Built within a profuse riverside garden that's filled with carefully tended tropical blooms and a big herb garden that supplies the excellent restaurant and cooking school, this well-run place offers ten large, immaculate rooms in variously styled bungalows, all with hot water and either river, mountain or garden view. It's nicely set up for families, with some rooms sleeping up to four, plus lots of space for kids to play in. ❸–❺

Nung House Ⓣ077 395147, Ⓦwww.nunghouse.com. Friendly place run by the park warden's son and his family, with fourteen very good huts set around an attractive grassy garden full of rambutan trees. Choose between simple bamboo constructions with en-suite facilities, brick and concrete bungalows, and treehouses. ❷–❸

The park: trails and tours

The B200 national park **entrance fee** (B100 for kids or with a student card) is payable at the checkpoint (6am–6pm) close to the visitor centre and is valid for 24 hours; you'll have to pay again at the lake if you arrive more than 24 hours later. The checkpoint office and **visitor centre** (daily 8am–6pm; ⓣ077 395155) both supply a small sketch map of the park and trails, and the latter also has a small display about flora and fauna, but the best introduction to Khao Sok is the **guidebook** *Waterfalls and Gibbon Calls* by Thom Henley (see p.860), which is available at some Khao Sok minimarkets and bungalows. Take plenty of water as Khao Sok is notoriously humid.

The trails

Seven of the park's nine **trails** branch off the clearly signed route that runs west of the park headquarters and visitor centre, along the Sok River. The first 3.5km constitute the **interpretative trail** described in *Waterfalls and Gibbon Calls*, an unexceptional ninety-minute one-way trail along a broad, road-like track. Most people continue to **Ton Kloi waterfall**, 7km from headquarters (allow 3hr each way), which flows year-round and tumbles into a pool that's good for swimming. En route, signs point to **Bang Liap Nam waterfall** (4.5km from headquarters), which is a straightforward hike; and **Tan Sawan waterfall** (6km from headquarters), which involves wading along the river bed for the final kilometre and should not be attempted during the rainy season. The trail to the rather spectacular eleven-tiered **Sip-et Chan waterfall**, which shoots off north from the park headquarters and follows the course of the Bang Laen River, is no longer much used and can be quite indistinct. Though the falls are only 4km from headquarters, there's a fair bit of climbing on the way, plus half a dozen river crossings, so you should allow three hours each way.

Guided treks and tours

The vast majority of visitors choose to join a **guided trek** at some point during their stay in the park. Though the trails are waymarked and easy to navigate alone, the guided experience alerts you to details you'd certainly miss on your own – the claw marks left by a sun-bear scaling a tree in search of honey, for example, or the medicinal plants used for malarial fevers and stomach upsets – and is both fun and inexpensive; prices are fixed but exclude the national park entrance fee. The usual **day trek (**B750–900) goes to Ton Kloi waterfall, and from December to March there's also a special route that takes in the blooming of the world's second-biggest flower, the **rafflesia kerrii**, a rather unprepossessing brown, cabbage-like plant whose enormous russet-coloured petals unfurl to a diameter of up to 80cm. Short after-dinner **night safaris** along the main park trails (B600 for 2hr) are also popular, not least because they're good for spotting civets, mouse deer and slow loris and, if you're exceptionally lucky, elephants and clouded leopards as well. You get to stay out in the jungle on the **overnight camping trips** (B2000), usually around Tan Sawan falls; for details of day and overnight trips to Cheow Lan Lake, see p.670. The most reputable and long-serving **guides** are those booked through *Bamboo House*, *Nung House* and *Khao Sok Rainforest Resort* and at Jungle Mania (ⓣ087 270 0938, ⓔkhaosokjunglemania@gmail.com).

Any guest houses can also arrange **elephant-rides** (2hr; B850) and fix you up with equipment and transfers for **tubing** and **canoeing** trips along the Sok River (B375/B750).

Cheow Lan Lake

Dubbed Thailand's Guilin because of its photogenic karst islands, forested inlets and mist-clad mountains encircling jade-coloured waters, the vast 28-kilometre-long **Cheow Lan Lake** (also known as **Ratchabrapa Dam** reservoir; B200 national park entry fee) is Khao Sok's most famous feature and the most popular destination for guided tours. It was created in the 1980s when the Khlong Saeng river was dammed to power a new hydro-electricity plant, and its forested shores and hundred-plus islands now harbour abundant birdlife, as well as some primates, most easily spotted in the very early morning. Tours generally combine a trip on the lake with a wade through the nearby flooded cave system and a night on a floating rafthouse. The lake is 65km from Khao Sok's accommodation area, and can only be explored by longtail boat tour, arranged either from Khao Sok or from Ratchabrapa Dam.

For many people, the highlight of their lake excursion is the adventurous three-hour trek to and through the 800-metre-long horseshoe-shaped **Nam Talu cave**, a five-minute boat ride from the national park rafthouses, or about an hour's boat ride from the dam. The **trek** is not for everyone, however, as the cave section entails an hour-long wade through the river that hollowed out this tunnel: it's slippery underfoot and pitch black and there will be at least one twenty-metre section where you have to swim. When the river level is high there will be longer swims. Never attempt the cave without an authorized park guide and heed any closure signs posted because of high water levels and strong currents; in October 2007 a flash flood caused nine fatalities here and the park authorities are now stricter. Wear sandals with decent grip and request (or take) your own torch.

Lake practicalities

Access to the lake is via the town of **Ban Ta Khun**, 50km east of Khao Sok on the Takua Pa–Surat Thani bus route, Route 401, from where it's 12km north to the dam. Many travellers book their tour of the lake from their Khao Sok

▲ Raft houses on Cheow Lan Lake

accommodation, in which case all transport is included, but if coming from Surat Thani or Phang Nga, you could do the lake first. There's a regular **minibus service** from Surat Thani's Phunphin train station to and from the dam (every 2hr; 1hr) or you could take the normal Surat Thani–Takua Pa bus service (see p.665), alight at Ban Ta Khun and get a motorbike taxi to the dam. The Australian-Thai-run Limestone Lake Rainforest Tours (Ⓣ078 954476, Ⓦwww.limestonelaketours.com) offers a big range of **lake-based tours**, including a two-hour trip (B1800 per boat) and a full-day trip with optional overnight in a rafthouse (from B2500/3500 per person for up to three people, excluding park entry fee, or cheaper with larger groups). Khao Sok guest houses charge B1500 for a day-trip and B2500 for overnighters. It's also possible to simply turn up at the dam and hire a boat for around B2000.

On overnight trips to the lake, **accommodation** is either in tents in the jungle or at rafthouses on the lake. There are both private and national park rafthouses moored at various scenic spots around the lake shore, mostly around an hour's boat ride from the dam. All rafthouse huts are rudimentary bamboo structures with nets and mattresses, offering fabulous lake views from your pillow. If you've arranged your own boat transport, you can fix accommodation at any of the lake's rafthouses for B500 per person including three meals. Jungle Yoga runs yoga retreats at the remote *500 Rai Lake* rafthouses from November to April (Ⓦwww.jungleyoga.com). Part of the appeal of a night in a rafthouse is the **dawn safari** the next morning, when you've a good chance of seeing langurs, macaques and gibbons on the lakeshore; some tours include this option, or you can usually borrow a kayak from your accommodation and paddle around the shore yourself.

Khao Lak

Handily located just an hour north of Phuket International Airport, and some 30km south of Takua Pa, **KHAO LAK** has established itself as a thriving, mid-market beach resort with plentiful opportunities for diving and snorkelling, easy access to the supreme national park reefs of Ko Similan, and a style that is determinedly unseedy. It lacks sophistication, and is mostly a bit pricey for backpackers, but is ideal for families and extremely popular with Scandinavian tourists. High season here runs from November to April, when the weather and the swimming are at their best and the Similan Islands are open to the public; during the rest of the year, Khao Lak quietens down a lot – and becomes much cheaper too.

The area usually referred to as Khao Lak is in fact a string of beaches west off Highway 4. **Khao Lak** proper is the southernmost and least developed, 5km from the most commercial part of the resort, **Nang Thong**, which throngs with shops, restaurants, dive centres and countless places to stay, both on the beachfront and inland from Highway 4. North again about 3km (5min by taxi or a 45min walk up the beach) is lower-key, slightly more youthful **Bang Niang**, a lovely long stretch of golden sand that's backed by a developing tourist village whose network of sois is away from the highway and feels more enticing than its neighbour. Removed from all this commerce, **Laem Pakarang**, 12km further up the coast, is where you find the area's most exclusive accommodation.

There is, thankfully, little obvious evidence these days of the area's devastating experience during the December 2004 **tsunami**, when the undersea earthquake off Sumatra sent a series of murderous waves on to Khao Lak's

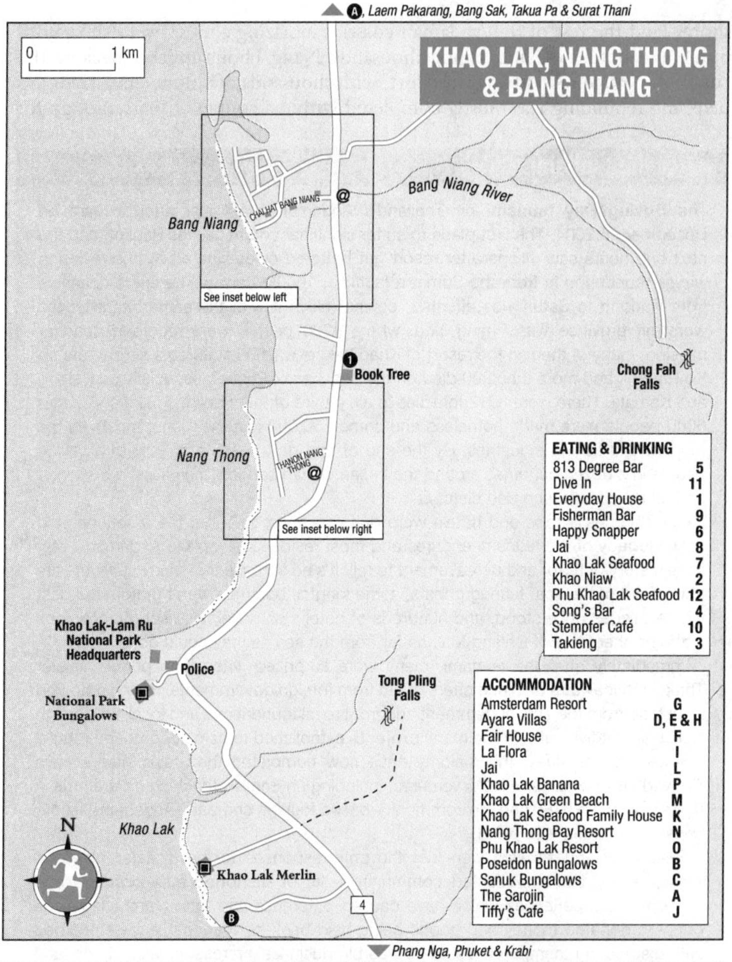

KHAO LAK, NANG THONG & BANG NIANG
A, Laem Pakarang, Bang Sak, Takua Pa & Surat Thani
0 1 km
Bang Niang River
Bang Niang
CHAI HAT BANG NIANG
See inset below left
Book Tree
Chong Fah Falls
Nang Thong
THANON NANG THONG
See inset below right
EATING & DRINKING
813 Degree Bar 5
Dive In 11
Everyday House 1
Fisherman Bar 9
Happy Snapper 6
Jai 8
Khao Lak Seafood 7
Khao Niaw 2
Phu Khao Lak Seafood 12
Song's Bar 4
Stempfer Café 10
Takieng 3
Khao Lak-Lam Ru National Park Headquarters
Police
National Park Bungalows
Tong Pling Falls
ACCOMMODATION
Amsterdam Resort G
Ayara Villas D, E & H
Fair House F
La Flora I
Jai L
Khao Lak Banana P
Khao Lak Green Beach M
Khao Lak Seafood Family House K
Nang Thong Bay Resort N
Phu Khao Lak Resort O
Poseidon Bungalows B
Sanuk Bungalows C
The Sarojin A
Tiffy's Cafe J
N
Khao Lak
Khao Lak Merlin
4
Phang Nga, Phuket & Krabi

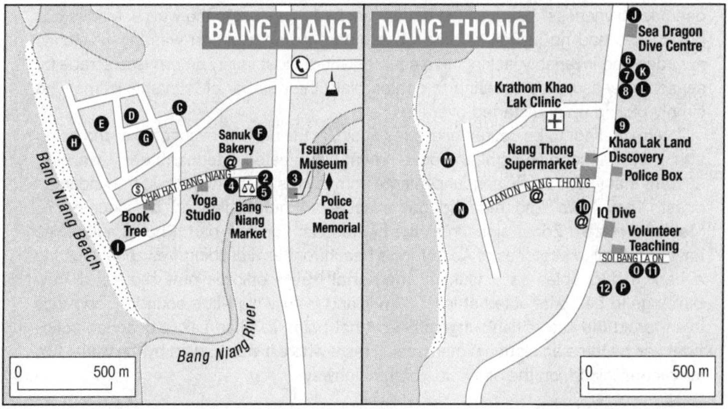

BANG NIANG
Sanuk Bakery
Tsunami Museum
CHAI HAT BANG NIANG
Yoga Studio
Bang Niang Market
Police Boat Memorial
Book Tree
Bang Niang Beach
Bang Niang River
0 500 m
NANG THONG
Sea Dragon Dive Centre
Krathom Khao Lak Clinic
Nang Thong Supermarket
Khao Lak Land Discovery
Police Box
THANON NANG THONG
IQ Dive
Volunteer Teaching
SOI BANG LA ON
0 500 m

shores (and the rest of the Andaman coast), vaporizing almost every shorefront home and hotel here and killing thousands. Nang Thong quickly became the centre of a huge reconstruction effort, with thousands of volunteers arriving to help, and rebuilding was mostly completed within a couple of years, though for

After the tsunami

The **Boxing Day tsunami** hit Thailand's Andaman coast just after 9.30am on December 26 2004. The first place to suffer significant damage was Phuket, and the next two hours saw village after resort get battered or decimated by the towering waves thundering in from the Sumatra faultline, 1000km away. The entire coastline from Ranong to Satun was affected, but not all of it with the same intensity: the worst-hit province was Phang Nga, where 4200 people were recorded dead or missing, many of them in the resort of Khao Lak; over 2000 suffered a similar fate on Ko Phi Phi; and more than 900 died on the beaches of Phuket, especially on Patong and Kamala. There were 8212 fatalities in all, a third of them holidaymakers. Another 6000 people were made homeless and some 150,000 lost their jobs, mostly in the tourism and fishing industries. By the end of that day, nearly a quarter of a million people in a dozen countries around the Indian Ocean had lost their lives in the worst natural disaster in recorded history.

Many homes, shops and hotels were quite swiftly rebuilt, but the emotional and social **legacy** of the tsunami endures and most residents along the Andaman coast have a story of terror and bereavement to tell. It's no surprise that many survivors are now afraid of the sea: fearing ghosts, some longtail boatmen won't motor solo past where villages once stood, and hundreds of hotel staff have since sought new jobs in the northern city of Chiang Mai, as far from the sea as they could go.

Immediately after the tsunami, many were surprised when then prime minister Thaksin Shinawatra declined offers of **aid** from foreign governments. But help poured in instead from the Thai government and from royal foundations and local and foreign NGOs and individuals. Of the many **projects** established to help support and rebuild affected communities, the majority have now completed their task; others have evolved into longer-term NGO ventures, including an English-teaching programme in Khao Lak (see p.676), and the community-based tourism company Andaman Discoveries in Khuraburi (see p.661).

Generosity and altruism were not the only responses to the disaster, however. Almost every tsunami-affected community talks of **dishonourable practice** and **corruption**, experiences which have caused bitterness and rifts. Many allegations concern donated money and goods being held back by the local leaders charged with distributing them, and in some cases big business interests muscled in on land deemed "ownerless" because the paperwork had been lost to the waves. Most small businesses had no insurance, and government **compensation** was inconsistently awarded and invariably lacking. In a country where most family enterprises scrape by season to season, it's sobering to contemplate the number of tsunami victims who simply picked up and started over.

Determined not to be caught unawares again, in the unlikely event of Thailand being struck by a second tsunami, the government has created a **tsunami early-warning system** that relays public announcements from towers all the way down the Andaman coast. They have also mapped out evacuation routes, flagged by innumerable "Tsunami Hazard Zone" signs in all the big resorts. For their part, Phuket authorities have remodelled stretches of Ao Patong's beachfront as a building-free zone, creating a park that doubles as a tsunami **memorial**. Krabi officials now require all new buildings to be constructed at least 30m inland from a high-tide boundary, and they even forbid the use of sunloungers below that point. In Khao Lak, a beached police boat has become an eloquent memorial: it rests where it was hurtled by the wave, two kilometres inland, on the other side of the highway.

many survivors recovery will probably take a lifetime. Inland from the highway at Bang Niang, a **beached police boat** has become a memorial to the extraordinary power of the tsunami waves – it was propelled up here, 2km inland, while patrolling the waters in front of *La Flora* resort. A tiny Tsunami Museum (daily 9am–6.30pm; donation) occupies a nearby shop but merely presents a rather dry summary of the facts; for the human story you need to read Erich Krauss' *Wave of Destruction* (see p.856).

Arrival, transport and information

Khao Lak is just 70km north of **Phuket airport** (1hr, B1700–2200 by taxi; see p.680). All **buses** running from Phuket to Takua Pa and Ranong (and vice versa), as well as some of its Surat Thani services, pass through Khao Lak and can drop you anywhere along Highway 4; coming from Krabi or Phang Nga you may need to change buses in **Khokkloi**. When it comes to moving on, the VIP overnight bus to Bangkok costs B1000 and takes twelve hours. There's also an **air-con tourist minivan** service that runs at least daily to Krabi/Ao Nang (2hr 30min; B370), with boat connections to Ko Lanta and Ko Phi Phi; to Trang (5hr; B650); and to Penang (12hr; B950).

In the Khao Lak area, a few public **songthaews** shuttle between Nang Thong and Bang Niang, charging B10–20, but mostly they act as private **taxis** instead and charge B100 or more. Many hotels can rent **motorbikes**, and rental **cars** are available through tour operators; Budget also has an agent on the soi down to *Nang Thong Resort* (Ⓣ076 443454, Ⓦwww.budget.co.th). *Khao Lak Seafood* rents **bicycles**.

Nang Thong offers plenty of **shopping**, mainly for clothes, souvenirs and handicrafts, with countless tailors and opticians too. Book Tree, in far northern Nang Thong, stocks new and second-hand books plus magazines, newspapers and art cards, and also serves coffee; it has a small branch on Chai Hat Bang Niang too. The **Bang Niang market** convenes beside the highway (Mon, Wed & Sat pm) and is a fun spot for a browse through stalls selling everything from hot food and fresh vegetables to clothes and household items. There's **internet** access, ATMs and tour agents aplenty in both Nang Thong and Bang Niang, as well as several clinics.

Accommodation

There's no really cheap accommodation in Khao Lak, but plenty of options from ❹ and up.

Laem Pakarang

The Sarojin 12km north of Khao Lak Ⓣ076 427905, Ⓦwww.thesarojin.com. With a staff-to-guest ratio of two to one and a style and attitude that exude understated, unpretentious class, this is the top place to stay around Khao Lak. The 56 sleek, tastefully simple rooms are discreetly sited around the wide beachfront garden and stunning square turquoise swimming pool. It's an obvious honeymoon choice, with a policy of no under-12s, a range of excursions designed for two, and private candlelit tables on the beach. There are complimentary Hobie Cats (sailing catamarans), kayaks and mountain bikes, and a spa. Published rates from $429 but discount packages always available. ❾

Bang Niang

Amsterdam Resort Soi 3 Ⓣ081 857 5881, Ⓦwww.khaolak-resorts.com. Just 200m inland from the beach, this Dutch-run little complex of red-brick bungalows and rooms offers some of the cheapest accommodation in Bang Niang. Bungalows vary in size and have either fans or air-con; some have hot water. Also has internet and wi-fi, cycle rental and a tour desk. ❸–❺

Ayara Villas Ⓣ076 486 4788, Ⓦwww.ayara-villas.com. An attractive upper-mid range option, spread over three different compounds. At the top end are beachfront villas right on the sand; many others are terraced bungalows just a few metres from the sea, and the rest are in a three-storey building overlooking the pool, with ground-floor rooms enjoying direct pool access. Interiors are air-con and nicely furnished with dark wood in contemporary style and all have kitchenettes. 8–9

Fair House ⓣ089 473 7985. Currently one of the cheapest place to stay in Bang Niang, with its handful of neat, fan-cooled concrete bungalows and rooms widely spaced around a garden set back from the highway, about 1km walk from the beach. 3

La Flora ⓣ076 428000, ⓦwww.lafloraresort.com. The 138 rooms at this upscale beachfront hotel are all furnished in elegant contemporary Asian style, with day beds, stylish bathrooms and balconies. The cheaper ones are in three-storey hotel wings, some with direct access to the freeform swimming pool; you pay extra for stand-alone villas, many of which enjoy direct sea views. There's also an infinity pool and a kids' pool, pus a spa, mountain bike and kayak rental and wi-fi. 9

Sanuk Bungalows ⓣ076 486800, ⓦwww.sanukresort.com. Dinky little group of five comfortable and spacious brick bungalows in a small garden with its own tiny pool, just 100m from the beach. Bungalows come with either fan or air-con and all have fridges and kitchenettes but there are no staff or other facilities on site. Check in via the office next to the Sanuk Bakery on the main access road from the highway. 5

Nang Thong

Jai ⓣ076 485390, ⓔjai_bungalow@hotmail.com. A busy, family-run place that fills up fast not least because it offers some of the cheapest accommodation in Khao Lak. The fifteen good-quality en–suite concrete bungalows are fan cooled and are dotted around a scruffy little yard behind the excellent restaurant, quite close to the highway and about 600m from the beach. 3

Khao Lak Banana Soi Bang La On ⓣ076 485889, ⓦwww.khaolakbanana.com. Dozens of thoughtfully designed banana-coloured, fan and air-con bungalows packed into a garden of banana trees and tropical flowers. All have a safety box, TV, wi-fi and fridge and there's a tiny swimming pool. 5

Khao Lak Green Beach ⓣ076 485845, ⓦwww.greenbeach.de. The attractive design and shorefront location of the bungalows here make this a good-value option, and the staff are great too. The forty cream-painted chalet-style bungalows have air-con, polished wood floors, pretty furnishings, nice bathrooms and a fridge. Price mainly depends on location: some are right on the shore and none are more than a few metres away. 6

Khao Lak Seafood Family House Soi Noen Thong ⓣ076 485318, ⓦwww.khaolakseafood.com. The large, good-quality bungalows here are set well back from the road in a garden behind the eponymous restaurant. The fan ones are especially good value for Khao Lak: roomy and nicely designed with good bathrooms; air-con rooms in a couple of two-storey blocks are also available. It's a family business and very popular with returning guests and long stayers. Fan 4, air-con 5

Nang Thong Bay Resort ⓣ076 485088, ⓦwww.nangthong.com. Well priced considering its on-the-beach location, this popular, long-established place offers smartly maintained air-con bungalows that are well spaced around the shorefront garden and mostly enjoy sea views, plus some hotel-style rooms. There's a sea-view swimming pool and restaurant as well. Prices drop by fifty percent May–Oct. 6–7

Phu Khao Lak Resort ⓣ076 485141, ⓦwww.phukhaolak.com. There is a luxurious amount of space at this well-run place, where the thirty large, spotlessly clean bungalows sit prettily amid a grassy lawned park-style coconut plantation. Fan rooms have tiled floors and hot-water bathrooms; air-con ones have picture windows and quite stylish interiors. There's a swimming pool, good restaurant and wi-fi in the lounge-library. About 500m walk from the beach. Fan 4, air-con 6

Tiffy's Cafe ⓣ084 051 4138. The cheapest beds in the area are the bunks in the six-person dorm here, behind the restaurant. B80 per person.

Khao Lak

Poseidon Bungalows ⓣ076 443258, ⓦwww.similantour.com. Seven kilometres south of central Nang Thong, surrounded by rubber plantations and set above a sandy shore of wave-smoothed rocks just north of the Thai navy's private beach, this Swedish–Thai-run guest house is both a quiet place to hang out for a few days and a long-established organizer of snorkelling expeditions to the Similan islands (see opposite). All fifteen bungalows are en suite and fan cooled, with generous amounts of space and balconies, some enjoying sea views; also has internet access and motorbike rental. Get off the bus at the *Poseidon* sign between kilometre-stones 53 and 54, then phone for a pick-up or walk 1km. Closed May–Oct. 5

Day-trips and other activities

Aside from diving and snorkelling trips to Ko Similan (see box below), there are several other attractions within day-tripping distance of Khao Lak, including a number of local **waterfalls**. Of these, Sai Rung (Rainbow Falls) about 16km north of Nang Thong in Bang Sak, is the most satisfying. Others include Tong Pling, across from the *Merlin* resort in Khao Lak; Nam Tok Lumphi, about 20km south of Khao Lak; and Chong Fah Falls, located less than 5km east of Bang Niang, but subject to a B100 entry fee because it's part of Khao Lak–Lam Ru National Park (Ⓦwww.dnp.go.th/National_park.asp), whose headquarters is on the headland between Nang Thong and Khao Lak beaches.

One of the best, though not the cheapest, local **tour operators** is the reputable Khao Lak Land Discovery (Ⓣ076 485411, Ⓦwww.khaolakland discovery.com), whose excursions include elephant riding (from B1600), kayaking around Ao Phang Nga (B3200) and trekking, canoeing and elephant-riding in Khao Sok National Park (B2800). The Green Biking Club in Bang Niang runs interesting **guided mountain-bike trips** around rural and coastal Khao Lak (from B1850; Ⓣ076 443211, Ⓦwww.greenbikingclub.com) and rents mountain bikes for B150 per day.

Everyday House restaurant at the north end of Nang Thong teaches morning **cooking courses** (B1000), there's Hatha **yoga** at The Yoga Studio on the Bang Niang beach access road (Mon–Sat 11am) and **Thai boxing** courses and bouts

Diving and snorkelling around Khao Lak

Khao Lak is the closest and most convenient departure point for **diving and snorkelling trips** to the awesome national park islands of **Ko Similan** (see p.676), which can be reached in three to four hours on a live-aboard or other large boat or in two hours in a much less comfortable speedboat. The islands are currently only open from approximately November through April and all divers have to pay a one-off national park fee of B400 plus a B200 a day diving fee, usually on top of dive-trip prices. **Local Khao Lak dives** are generally possible year round, especially the highly rated **wreck** of a tin-mining boat near Bang Sak, which is especially rich in marine life such as ghost pipefish, moray eels, scorpion fish, nudibranchs and yellow-tail barracuda. All Khao Lak dive shops also teach PADI **dive courses**, with the last two days of the Openwater course often done on location in the Similans; for advice on choosing a dive shop see p.73.

IQ Dive Nang Thong Ⓣ076 485614, Ⓦwww.iq-dive.com. Swiss–Thai-run PADI Five-Star Instructor Development Centre that specializes in one-day dive trips to the Similans, on a big dive boat (B4500 plus equipment; B2700 for snorkellers). Their Openwater courses costs B18,700 with two days spent diving the Similans.

Poseidon At *Poseidon Bungalows*, 7km south of central Nang Thong, in Khao Lak Ⓣ076 443258, Ⓦwww.similantour.com. Highly recommended three-day live-aboard snorkelling trips to the Similans (B7900). Current departures are twice weekly on Tuesdays and Fridays, from the end of October to the end of April.

Sea Dragon Dive Center Nang Thong Ⓣ076 485420, Ⓦwww.seadragondivecenter .com. Highly recommended PADI Five-Star IDC dive centre which has three live-aboard boats – including budget and deluxe options – running frequent three-day trips to the Similans and Ko Bon (from B11,800 including equipment), and four-day trips to the Similans, Surin islands, Ko Bon, Ko Tachai and Richelieu Rock (from B21,200). Snorkellers get one-third off. Also offers local wreck and other dives (B2200) that operate year-round, as do most of their PADI dive courses: the one-day Discover Scuba costs B2000 (or B7100 at the Similans), and the four-day Openwater is B9800 or B22,400 on a live-aboard.

at the Khao Lak Boxing Stadium just north of Bang Niang (Ⓣ089 589 3108, Ⓦwww.khaolakboxing.com).

The organization **Volunteer Teaching in Thailand** (Ⓦwww.volunteerteacherthailand.org; see also p.83) is based on Soi Bang La On and welcomes willing visitors to help teach English to local kids and adults, a need that's especially pressing given that an estimated eighty percent of Khao Lak's English speakers died in the tsunami.

Eating and drinking

Though farang food dominates the **restaurant** scene, there's good, cheap, authentic Thai cuisine here too. The **nightlife** scene is mellow, convivial and much influenced by dive-staff regulars. Several places host live music nights, given more of a Thai accent in Bang Niang.

Bang Niang

813 Degree Bar With its wooden tables and rustic, Thai-country vibe, this cheap, welcoming and enjoyably local bar-restaurant is a fun place to listen to live Thai music, mostly rock, at its liveliest after 10pm.

Khao Niaw Very good northeastern Thai food at deliciously cheap prices (from B50).

Song's Bar Another country-style Thai pub, with wooden tables, candles in bottles and plenty of foliage, this is Bang Niang's most famous nightlife venue and a favourite with dive staff. There's live music nightly but the biggest draw is the twice-weekly *kathoey* cabaret, a glamorously and hilariously camp production (Tues & Fri eve).

Takieng Authentic Thai food, including good *tom yum kung* and exceptional seafood hotplates, at reasonably authentic Thai prices (B60–180).

Nang Thong

Dive In Soi Bang La On. Owner and chef Sunny cooks up a storm here and is a favourite with expats, locals and returning tourists. She does all sorts of Thai food (B60–320), and her highlights include a deliciously aromatic *matsaman* curry, *khanom jiin* Phuket-style noodles with fish and red curry, deep-fried fish topped with mango, roast duck with orange sauce and rotis with yellow chicken curry.

Fisherman Bar Lively and genial watering hole that serves cocktails very cheaply during its extended happy hour (midday–8pm), holds regular barbecues and sometimes has live music.

Happy Snapper Khao Lak's most famous dive-staff hangout is chilled and pleasant, with a folksy lounge ambience, live reggae, pop and blues most nights from 10.30pm – plus the occasional open-mike session – and a drinks menu that runs to over a hundred cocktails. Daily 8.30pm–1am.

Jai Deservedly popular for its many different curries (from B60), including *kaeng phanaeng* and *matsaman*, its seafood and its *tom yam kung*.

Khao Lak Seafood Very popular, unpretentious place to sample the local catch; most dishes B60–200.

Phu Khao Lak Seafood Well-known and good-value restaurant attached to the bungalows of the same name serving exceptionally good Thai food from a menu that stretches to over a hundred dishes. Everything from red, yellow and green curries (B80–200) to seafood platters.

Stempfer Café European-run café serving eight different set breakfasts, fresh coffees, hot chocolate, lots of cakes and bread, plus salads and a few hot dishes.

Ko Similan

Rated as one of the world's best spots for both above-water and underwater beauty, the eleven islands at the heart of the Mu **KO SIMILAN** National Park (Ⓦwww.dnp.go.th/National_park.asp; B400/200; closed approximately mid-May to mid-Nov) are among the most exciting **diving** destinations in Thailand. Massive granite boulders set magnificently against turquoise waters give the islands their distinctive character, but it's the thirty-metre visibility that draws the divers. The underwater scenery is nothing short of overwhelming here: the reefs teem with coral fish, and you'll also see turtles, manta rays, moray eels, jacks, reef sharks, sea snakes, red grouper and quite possibly white-tip sharks, barracuda, giant lobster and enormous tuna.

The **islands** lie 64km off the mainland and include the eponymous Ko Similan chain of nine islands as well as two more northerly islands, Ko Bon and Ko Tachai, which are both favoured haunts of manta rays and whale sharks and are halfway between the Similan chain and the islands of Ko Surin. The Similans are numbered north–south from nine to one and are often referred to by number: Ko Ba Ngu (number nine), Ko Similan, Ko Hin Posar (aka Hin Huwagralok), Ko Payoo, Ko Ha, Ko Miang (number four), Ko Pahyan, Ko Pahyang and Ko Hu Yong. The national park headquarters and accommodation is on Ko Miang and there's also a campsite and restaurant on Ko Similan. Ko Similan is the largest island in the chain, blessed with a beautiful, fine white-sand bay and impressive boulders; Ko Miang has two pretty beaches, twenty minutes' walk apart; Ko Hu Yong has an exceptionally long white-sand bay and is used by **turtles** for egg-laying from November to February.

Such beauty has not gone unnoticed and the islands are extremely popular with day-trippers from Phuket and Khao Lak, as well as with divers and snorkellers on longer live-aboard trips. This has caused the inevitable congestion and environmental problems and the Similan reefs have been damaged in places by anchors and by the local practice of using dynamite in fishing. National parks authorities have responded by banning fishermen and enforcing strict regulations for tourist boats, including **closing the islands** during the monsoon season, from mid-May to mid-November, though there is talk of a shorter closure in future.

Practicalities

Most travel agents in Khao Lak, Phuket and Phang Nga sell snorkelling **packages** to Ko Similan, both day-trips (from B2900/1450) and overnight (from B3900/1950), featuring at least four island stops. The majority of these trips carry quite large groups and use fast boats that depart from **Thap Lamu pier**, about 8km south of central Khao Lak, 90km north of Phuket town, at about 8am and get to their first island stop, Ko Ba Ngu, in under two hours. They depart the islands at around 3pm. Independent travellers wanting to stay on the island for a few days can usually use these **boats** for transfers, with the chance of a discount if joining the boat at Thap Lamu pier rather than being picked up from one of the resorts. Companies offering this service include Medseye Travel and Tours (Ⓣ076 486796, Ⓦwww.similanthailand.com) and Jack Similan (Ⓣ076 443205, Ⓦwww.jacksimilan.com), both of which have offices at the Thap Lamu pier. If travelling independently, you'll need to use Ko Similan longtail boats to travel **between the islands** and to explore different reefs: prices are fixed and cost B150–300 per person, depending on the distance.

Limited **accommodation** is available on Ko Miang, in the shape of national park bungalows (❺–❻) and tents (❸), and there's a campsite on Ko Similan too; both islands also have a restaurant. Accommodation should be booked ahead, either at the national parks office near Thap Lamu pier (Ⓣ076 595045) or online (Ⓦwww.dnp.go.th/National_park.asp), as facilities can get crowded with tour groups, especially on weekends and holidays.

Overcrowding is a growing problem at the Similans and the best way to escape this is to join a small-scale **live-aboard** diving or snorkelling trip to the islands; they usually last two to five days and cost from B11,800 inclusive for divers, or from B8000 for snorkellers. The best and cheapest live-aboard trips run out of Khao Lak, the closest mainland resort to the Similans (see p.675);

Phuket is another popular springboard, and you can also do them from Ko Chang and Ko Phayam.

Phuket

Thailand's largest island and a province in its own right, **PHUKET** (pronounced "Poo-ket") has been a prosperous region since the nineteenth century, when Chinese merchants got in on its tin-mining and sea-borne trade, before turning to the rubber industry. It remains the wealthiest province in Thailand, with the highest per-capita income, but what mints the money nowadays is **tourism**: with an annual influx of visitors that tops five million, Phuket ranks second in popularity only to Pattaya, and the package-tour traffic has wrought its usual transformations. Thoughtless tourist developments have scarred much of the island, and the trend is upmarket, with very few budget possibilities (expect to shell out up to twice what you'd pay on the mainland for accommodation, food and transport), but many of the beaches are still strikingly handsome, resort facilities are second to none, and the offshore snorkelling and diving is exceptional. Away from the tourist hubs, many inland neighbourhoods are clustered round the local mosque – 35 percent of Phuketians are **Muslim**, and there are said to be more mosques on the island than Buddhist temples; though the atmosphere is generally as easy-going as elsewhere in Thailand, it's especially important to dress with some modesty outside the main resorts, and to not sunbathe topless on any of the beaches.

Phuket's capital, Muang Phuket or **Phuket town**, is on the southeast coast, 42km south of the Sarasin Bridge causeway to the mainland. Though it's the most culturally stimulating place on Phuket, most visitors pass straight through the town on their way to the **west coast**, where three resorts corner the bulk of the trade: high-rise **Ao Patong**, the most developed and expensive, with an increasingly seedy nightlife; the slightly nicer, if unexceptional, **Ao Karon**; and adjacent **Ao Kata**, the smallest of the trio. If you're after a more peaceful spot, aim for the seventeen-kilometre-long national park beach of **Hat Mai Khao**, its more developed neighbour **Hat Nai Yang**, or one of the smaller alternatives at **Hat Nai Thon** or **Hat Kamala**. Most of the other west-coast beaches are dominated by just a few upmarket hotels, specifically **Hat Nai Harn**, **Ao Pansea** and **Ao Bang Tao**; the southern and eastern beaches are better for seafood than swimming but also run boats to other islands such as **Ko Racha Yai**.

As with the rest of the Andaman coast, the sea around Phuket is at its least inviting during the **monsoon**, from June to October, when the west-coast beaches in particular become quite rough and windswept. At any time of year, beware the strong **undertow** and heed any red warning flags; in the first nine months of 2008 there were twenty fatalities in the water and over a hundred rescues by helpful bystanders: there is currently no official lifeguard service on the island. Some stretches of Phuket's coast were very badly damaged by the December 2004 **tsunami** (see box, p.672), which caused significant loss of life and destroyed a lot of property. Reconstruction was swift, however, and a first-time visitor to the island is now unlikely to notice any major post-tsunami effect.

There's a wide-ranging **website** about Phuket, Ⓦwww.phuket.com, which is particularly good for discounted accommodation; for a detailed historical and cultural **guide** to the island, it's hard to better Oliver Hargreave's impressive *Exploring Phuket & Phi Phi* (Within Books).

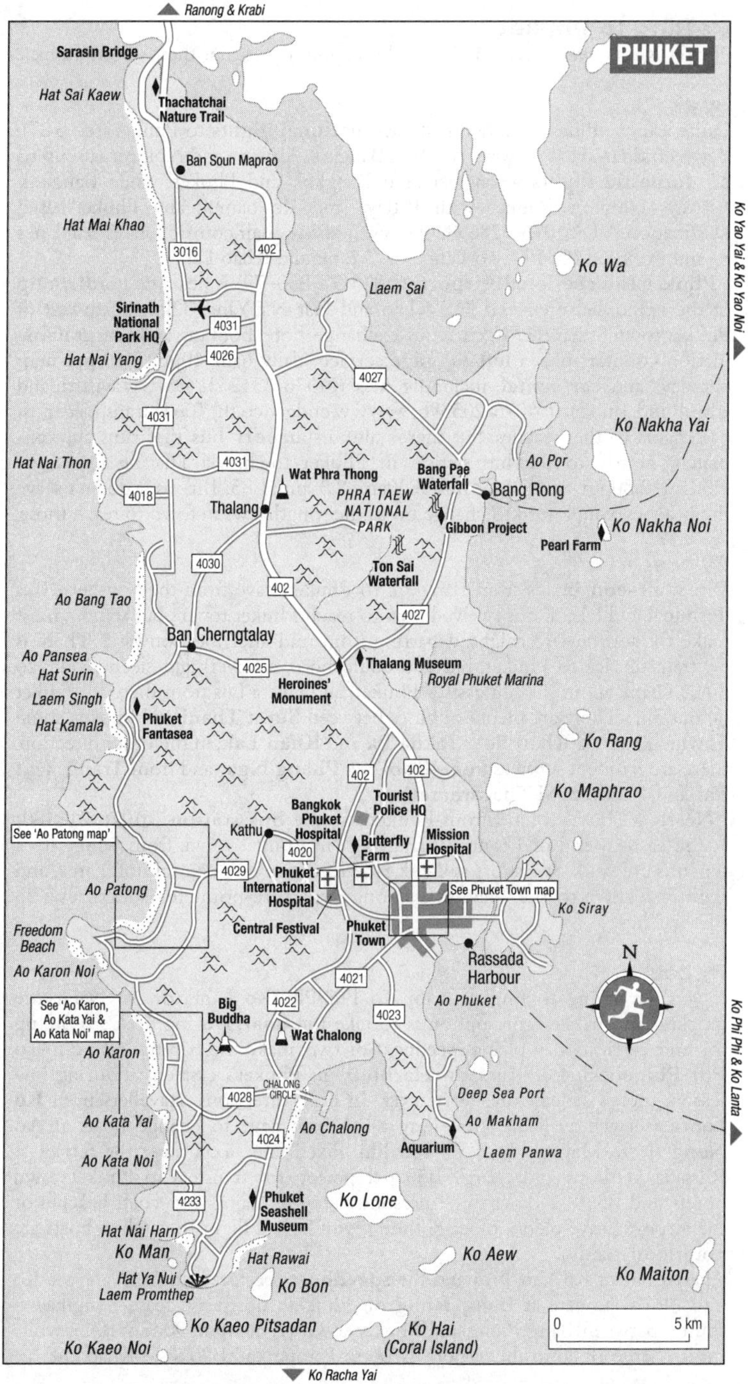
PHUKET
Ranong & Krabi
Ko Yao Yai & Ko Yao Noi
Ko Phi Phi & Ko Lanta
Ko Racha Yai
Sarasin Bridge
Hat Sai Kaew
Thachatchai Nature Trail
Ban Soun Maprao
Hat Mai Khao
3016
402
Laem Sai
Ko Wa
Sirinath National Park HQ
4031
4026
Hat Nai Yang
4027
4031
Ko Nakha Yai
Hat Nai Thon
4031
Wat Phra Thong
Bang Pae Waterfall
Ao Por
Bang Rong
4018
Thalang
PHRA TAEW NATIONAL PARK
Gibbon Project
Ko Nakha Noi
Pearl Farm
4030
Ton Sai Waterfall
402
Ao Bang Tao
4027
Ban Cherngtalay
Ao Pansea
Hat Surin
4025
Thalang Museum
Royal Phuket Marina
Heroines' Monument
Laem Singh
Hat Kamala
Phuket Fantasea
Ko Rang
402
402
Ko Maphrao
Tourist Police HQ
Bangkok Phuket Hospital
See 'Ao Patong map'
Kathu
Butterfly Farm
Mission Hospital
4020
4029
Phuket International Hospital
Ao Patong
See Phuket Town map
Ko Siray
Central Festival
Phuket Town
Freedom Beach
Rassada Harbour
Ao Karon Noi
4021
N
See 'Ao Karon, Ao Kata Yai & Ao Kata Noi' map
4022
Big Buddha
4023
Ao Phuket
Wat Chalong
Ao Karon
CHALONG CIRCLE
4028
Deep Sea Port
Ao Kata Yai
Ao Chalong
Ao Makham
4024
Aquarium
Laem Panwa
Ao Kata Noi
4233
Phuket Seashell Museum
Ko Lone
Hat Nai Harn
Ko Man
Ko Aew
Hat Rawai
Hat Ya Nui
Laem Promthep
Ko Bon
Ko Maiton
Ko Kaeo Pitsadan
Ko Hai (Coral Island)
Ko Kaeo Noi
0
5 km

Getting to Phuket

Phuket is very well served by flights, buses and ferries, but there's no rail link.

By air

Quite a few airlines operate direct **international flights** to Phuket (see p.27). Between them, Thai Airways, Air Asia, Bangkok Airways and Nok Air run up to 27 **domestic flights** a day between Bangkok and Phuket, while Bangkok Airways connects Phuket with Pattaya and Ko Samui, and Phuket-based Destination Air (ⓣ076 328638, ⓦwww.destinationair.com) operates seaplanes to and from Ko Phi Phi, Ko Lanta, Ko Mook and Khao Lak.

Phuket International Airport (ⓣ076 327230–79) is near the northern tip of the island, between Hat Mai Khao and Hat Nai Yang, 32km northwest of Phuket town. It has ATMs, currency exchange, hotel booking and tourist information counters plus a **left-luggage** service (daily 6am–10pm; B60 per item per day) and **car rental**, including Avis (ⓣ076 351243, ⓦwww.avisthailand.com) and Budget (ⓣ076 205396, ⓦwww.budget.co.th). Taxis transport most passengers to the beaches, but there's also an **airport bus** that runs approximately hourly to the bus station in Phuket town, via Thalang (Mon–Fri 6.30am–8.30pm, Sat, Sun & hols 8.30am–8.30pm; B85; 1hr); as it doesn't serve the beaches, you'll need to change on to the songthaews in town to reach those.

By bus

Direct **air-con buses** from Bangkok to Phuket leave from the Southern Bus Terminal and take about twelve hours to reach Phuket town's bus station; most make the journey overnight, departing from mid-afternoon onwards. There is no train service to Phuket, but you could book an overnight sleeper train to Surat Thani, about 290km east of Phuket, and take a bus from there to Phuket (about 5hr). There are plenty of buses between **Surat Thani** and Phuket, some of which run via **Khao Sok**, **Takua Pa** and **Khao Lak**; in the other direction, there are frequent services from **Krabi**, via **Phang Nga**, and from **Trang**, **Hat Yai** and **Nakhon Si Thammarat**.

Nearly all buses to and from Phuket use the **bus station** (ⓣ076 211480) at the eastern end of Thanon Phang Nga in Phuket town, from where it's a ten-minute walk or a short tuk-tuk ride to the town's central hotel area, and slightly further to the Thanon Ranong departure-point for songthaews to the beaches.

By boat

If you're coming to Phuket from Ko Phi Phi, Ko Lanta or Ao Nang, the quickest and most scenic option is to take the **boat**. During peak season, up to three ferries a day, plus a speedboat or two, make the trip to and from **Ko Phi Phi**, docking at **Rassada Harbour** on Phuket's east coast; during low season, there's at least one ferry a day in both directions. Travellers from **Ko Lanta** (service available Nov–May only) may have to change boats at **Ao Nang** (Nov–May only) or Ko Phi Phi. Fixed-fare **taxis** meet the ferries at Rassada Harbour and charge B50 per person for transfers to Phuket town hotels, and B500–600 per three-person car to the major west-coast beaches or the airport (leave plenty of extra time if you have a flight to catch as boats are notoriously tardy).

Ferries from **Ko Yao Noi** and the **speedboat** service from Ao Nang via Ko Yao Noi terminate at **Bang Rong** on Phuket's northeast coast. Songthaews shuttle between Bang Rong and Phuket town (7am–4pm; 90min; B35), while **taxis** charge B500 to the airport, B700 to Patong and B2000 to Khao Lak.

Moving on from Phuket

For durations and frequencies on all major routes, see Travel details, p.766.

By air

The cheapest way for solo travellers to **get to the airport** is by the airport bus from Phuket town bus station (at least every 90min Mon–Fri 5.30am–6.30pm, Sat & Sun 7am–6.30pm; 1hr; B85; ☎076 232371). From the beaches, most people use taxis organized by their hotel instead – about B500 for the hour's ride from Patong or Karon. See p.687 for **airline offices** on Phuket.

By bus

The TAT office in Phuket town keeps up-to-date bus timetables. In addition to the government bus services (see p.766), there are fast private minibus services **to Surat Thani** from outside the *Montri Hotel* on Thanon Montri in Phuket town (every 2hr 7am–5pm; 4hr 30min; B180) and to **Nakhon Si Thammarat** from opposite *Baan Suwantawe* on Thanon Dibuk (hourly 6am–4pm; 7hr; B300). Some hotels can also arrange minibus transport to **Butterworth** in Malaysia (B1200).

By boat

Ferries to **Ko Phi Phi, Ao Nang** and **Ko Lanta** depart from Rassada Harbour (see opposite). Tickets bought in advance should include transfers from your hotel. Ferries to **Ko Yao Noi** leave from Bang Rong (see p.706); the **speedboat** service to Ao Nang via Ko Yao Noi also leaves from Bang Rong.

Island transport

Although the west-coast beaches are connected by road, to get from one beach to another by **public transport** you nearly always have to go back into Phuket town; songthaews run regularly throughout the day from Thanon Ranong in the town centre to the coast and cost B25–40. **Tuk-tuks and taxis** do travel directly between major beaches, but are notoriously overpriced (there are almost no metered taxis on the island), charging around B100 from Kata to Karon or B250 between Patong and Karon; Phuket TAT issues a list of price guidelines but you'll likely end up paying at least twenty percent on top of that. For transport within resorts, the cheapest option is to make use of the public songthaews where possible, or to hail a **motorbike taxis** where available (from B20). Many tourists rent their own **motorbike** or moped, which are widely available, but be warned that there are a very sobering average of 10,000 motorbike injuries a year on Phuket, and about a hundred fatalities; it makes sense to obey the compulsory helmet law, which is anyway strictly enforced in most areas of Phuket, with flouters subject to a B500 fine.

Phuket town

Though it has plenty of hotels and restaurants, **PHUKET TOWN** (Muang Phuket) stands distinct from the tailor-made tourist settlements along the beaches as a place of tangible history and culture. Most visitors hang about just long enough to jump on a beach-bound songthaew, but you may find yourself returning for a welcome dose of real life; there's plenty to engage you in a stroll through the small but atmospherically restored heart of the Old Town, along with many idiosyncratic cafés and art shops, several notable restaurants and some of the best sarong and handicraft shops on the island. If you're on a tight budget, the town can make a more affordable base than the beaches, and certainly works well as an overnight transit point between the islands and the bus station or airport.

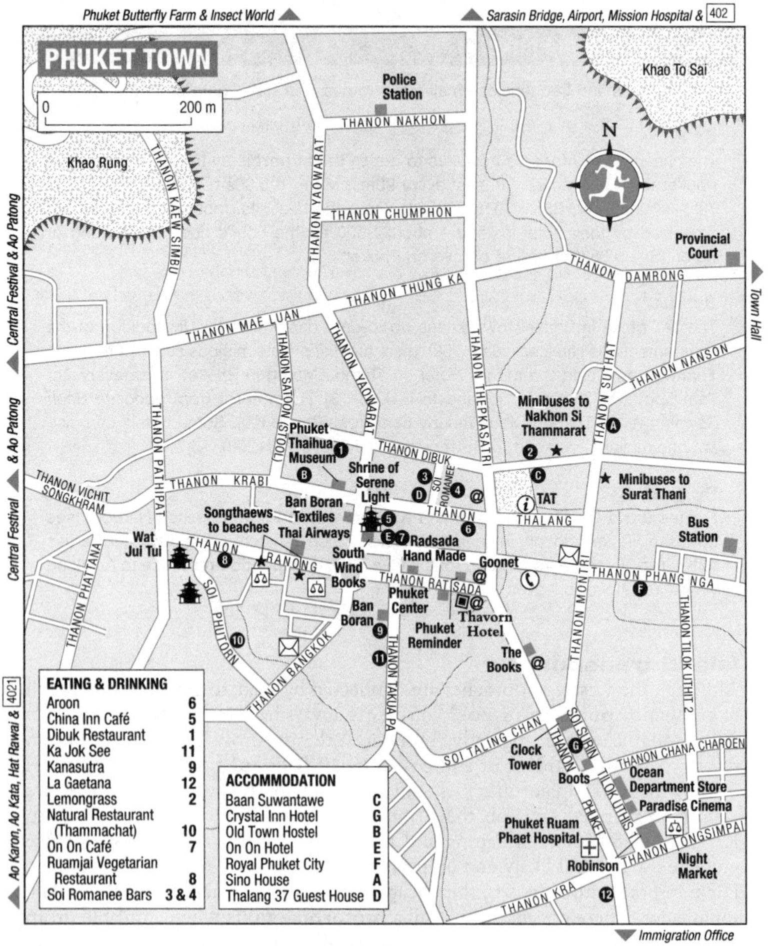

Accommodation

As befits this heritage town, there are some interesting places to stay, and more opportunities to meet other (solo) travellers than at the beaches.

Baan Suwantawe 1/10 Thanon Dibuk ⓣ076 212879, ⓦwww.baansuwantawe.co.th. Offering four-star rooms at two-star prices, this apartment-style hotel is designed with long-stay residents in mind but is also exceptionally comfortable for tourists. The huge, pleasantly decorated air-con rooms all have a balcony overlooking the small swimming pool and come with TV, broadband, fridge and kettle. There's no restaurant or hotel services but the front desk is helpful and the location very handy for TAT and the Old Town. ❺

Crystal Inn Hotel 2/1–10 Soi Surin, Thanon Montri ⓣ076 256789, ⓦwww.phuketcrystalinn.com. Surprisingly stylish and contemporary cream- and dark-wood decor makes this small, 54-room downtown hotel an inviting and good-value option. All rooms have air-con and there's internet downstairs. Good discounts if you forego breakfast. ❺

On On Hotel 19 Thanon Phang Nga ⓣ076 211154. This attractive, colonial-style 1920s building is a long-running travellers' favourite, mainly because the rooms are so cheap. They're pretty basic, with very thin walls, holes in the floorboards and ancient plumbing, but they're adequate and there are lots of them; the cheapest share bathrooms, the most expensive have air-con.

There's internet access and a tour agent in the lobby. Shared bathroom ❶, en suite ❷, air-con ❷

Royal Phuket City 154 Thanon Phang Nga ⓣ076 233333, ⓦwww.royalphuketcity.com. Large, high-rise business hotel, with swimming pool, spa, gym, business centre and light, bright, comfortable air-con rooms, most of them with fine views over the city and all with broadband. ❼

Sino House 1 Thanon Montri ⓣ076 232494, ⓦwww.sinohousephuket.com. Beautifully styled with Chinoiserie artefacts and elegant flourishes, the apartment-style rooms in this striking Art Deco building are huge and light and all come with air-con, complimentary wi-fi, coffee-making facilities and breakfast. There's a restaurant and the Raintree Spa on site, plus some tour services, but no pool. ❼

Thalang 37 Guest House 37 Thanon Thalang ⓣ076 214225, ⓔthalang37@gmail.com, ⓦwww.thalangguesthouse.com. Housed in a 1940s, Sino-Portuguese, wood-floored former shophouse in one of the Old Town's most attractive streets, this place is fairly simple but full of character, traveller-friendly and good value. The thirteen fan and air-con rooms are large and en suite – the best of them are up on the rooftop, affording unusual panoramic views. It's very popular, so phone or email to book ahead (website reservations don't work); if it's full the owner has slightly cheaper overspill rooms at the less interesting *Old Town Hostel* (ⓣ076 258272, ⓔothostel@gmail.com; ❷–❸), nearby at 42 Thanon Krabi, which mostly have no window or private bathroom. Rates at both include breakfast. ❷–❸

The Old Town

Phuket town's most interesting features are clustered together in the **Old Town** conservation zone (ⓦwww.lestariheritage.net/Phuket), a grid of streets between Thanon Dibuk and Thanon Rat Sada whose historic colonial-style **Sino-Portuguese shophouses** date back to the nineteenth century, the former homes of emigrant Chinese merchants from Penang, Singapore and Melaka. Modern-day residents have put a lot of effort into restoring these handsome old neighbourhoods and there's an engagingly bohemian style to a number of the businesses here. The Phuket Old Town Foundation publishes the excellent free **Phuket Town Treasure Map**, available all over the Old Town, and also stages the **Old Town Festival** just before Chinese New Year (sometime between Jan & March). For more on Sino-Portuguese architecture, see the box on p.684.

Some of the Old Town's most elegant buildings line the western arm of **Thanon Thalang**, where a dozen signboards – including at *Thalang Guest House* at no. 37 (see above), and outside the *China Inn Café* at no. 20 (see p.685) – highlight the special features worth an upward or sideways glance: pastel-coloured doors and shutters, elaborate stucco mouldings, ornate wooden doors, and the distinctively arched "five-foot walkways" that link them. Further east along Thanon Thalang there's more of an Islamic emphasis, with many old-style shops selling fabric and dressmaking accessories, including lots of good-value sarongs from Malaysia and Indonesia, and *roti* restaurants such as *Aroon* (see p.685). The road's former red-light alley, **Soi Romanee**, has also been given a major multi-coloured facelift and these days buzzes come sundown with arty little bars, while on nearby **Thanon Dibuk** the doors and window shutters of *Dibuk Restaurant* at no. 69 display intricate wooden and gold-leaf fretwork. You'll find other renovated Sino-Portuguese buildings on **Thanon Yaowarat**, and on **Thanon Ranong** (where the Thai Airways office occupies a fine old mansion), **Thanon Phang Nga** (especially the *On On Hotel*) and **Thanon Damrong**, whose town hall, just east of the Provincial Court, stood in for Phnom Penh's US embassy in the film *The Killing Fields*.

West across Yaowarat from Thanon Thalang at 28 Thanon Krabi, the 1930s' Neo classical-style former school – complete with grand columns, stucco decoration, shuttered windows and central light well – has been turned into the **Phuket Thaihua Museum** (Tues–Fri 1–8pm, Sat & Sun 9am–8pm; free).

Some of the old school desks are still in situ, and the pedagogic tradition continues through the Mandarin Language School upstairs, but the focus of the museum's excellent displays, videos and historic photos is on the role and traditions of Phuket's main immigrant groups, namely the Chinese and mixed-race Baba (Malay–Chinese) communities who arrived to work in the island's burgeoning tin-mining industry.

There's a much quainter, mustier whiff of the past contained within the wood-panelled lobby of Thanon Rat Sada's *Thavorn Hotel*, whose museum-like reception area and adjacent rooms, signed as the **Phuket History Corner**, are filled with faded photos of historic Phuket, plus a jumble of posters, typewriters and other everyday objects dating from the late nineteenth and early twentieth centuries, most of it amassed by the Thavorn family. Entry is free and non-guests are welcome to admire the eclectic collection, some of which also spills over into the hotel's streetside *Collector Pub*.

Old Town Sino-Portuguese architecture

As Chinese immigrant merchants got rich on tin-mining profits so they started building homes. Though the very richest commissioned enormous mansions, a number of which survive in Phuket town today, the vast majority bought themselves eminently practical terraced **shophouses** at the heart of the merchant district. Phuket's Old Town retains south Thailand's finest examples, some of which are open to the public, but there are also intact, if less well-conserved shophouse neighbourhoods in many other southern cities, including Ranong and Takua Pa.

Shophouse design followed a standard prototype favoured by the mixed-race Chinese–Malay ("Baba", or "Straits Chinese") immigrants from Melaka and other parts of the Malay Peninsula. It's a style now widely dubbed **Sino-Portuguese** because Melakan architecture of the time was itself strongly influenced by the territory's Portuguese former colonists, though it also incorporates traits from Dutch and Anglo-Indian colonial architecture. Although some features have evolved with changing fashions the basic look is still recognizably mid-nineteenth century.

Because streetside space was at a premium, shophouses were always long and thin, with narrow frontages, recessed entrances and connecting porches that linked up all the way down the block to make shady, arched colonnades known as **five-foot walkways**, ideal for pedestrians and shoppers. The front room was (and often still is) the business premises, leaving the rest of the two-or three-storey building for living. A light-well behind the front room encouraged natural ventilation and sometimes fed a small courtyard garden at its base, and the household shrine would always occupy a prominent and auspicious position. Outside, the hallmark features that make the neighbourhoods so striking today include pastel-painted **louvred windows** that might be arched or rectangular and perhaps topped by a pretty glass fantail, lacquered and inlaid wooden doors, fancy gold-leaf fretwork, detailed **stucco mouldings** and perhaps Neoclassical pilasters.

▲ Sino-Portuguese doorway, Phuket Town

The spiritual heritage of Phuket's Chinese immigrants is kept very much alive by their descendants who maintain many shrines around town, including **Saeng Tham**, the tiny **Shrine of Serene Light** (daily 8.30am–noon & 1.30–5.30pm), which is accessed via a soi through the narrow archway next to South Wind Books on Thanon Phang Nga, and whose roof is decorated with intensely coloured ceramic figurines of dragons, carp and sages in bright blues, greens and reds. The extraordinary spectacle of the annual Vegetarian Festival (see p.686) is the most public expression of the community's religious beliefs.

Phuket Butterfly Garden

Kids usually enjoy the **Phuket Butterfly Garden and Insect World** (daily 9am–5pm; B300, kids B150; ⓣ076 210861, ⓦwww.phuketbutterfly.com), located a couple of kilometres beyond the northern end of Thanon Yaowarat at 71/6 Soi Paneang in Ban Sam Kong, whose thousands of butterflies of some twenty indigenous species flit around the prettily landscaped grounds; there's also a silk museum documenting the amazingly industrious short life of the silkworm, plus scorpions, tarantulas and other notorious creepies. There's no public **transport** to the butterfly farm, but a tuk-tuk from the town centre should cost around B150 return; if you reserve ahead by phone or internet you can get transport between town or beach hotels and the Butterfly Garden for an extra B50–150 per person.

Eating and drinking

Phuket town has much the largest concentration of good Thai **food** on the island, well worth making the trip for. Unlike Thais in most other parts of the country, Phuketians like to breakfast on **noodles** rather than rice; spindly white *khanom jiin* noodles, made with rice-flour and ladled over with one of several different fiery, soupy curry sauces, are a local speciality and served at some of the restaurants listed below.

Aroon Thanon Thalang. Very popular cheap Muslim café that serves *roti* (chapatti-style pancakes) with egg, curry or *martabak* (mutton) plus several unusual southern Thai dishes from Pattani, including *khao yam Pattani*, a steamed rice dish mixed with shredded greens, roasted coconut and fish. Dishes B12–40. Mon–Sat 7am–6pm, Sun 7am–2pm.

China Inn Café 20 Thanon Thalang. This beautifully renovated heritage house and courtyard garden would be reason enough to stop by for a meal, but the menu (B120–250) is also enticing, both for its classy Thai and Mediterranean dishes, including delicious mozzarella salad, its spicy Thai salads, and its tamarind and rambutan juice. Streetside, the gallery shop displays Asian antiques, textiles and one-off artefacts. Mon–Wed 11am–6pm, Thurs–Sat 11am–11pm.

Ka Jok See 26 Thanon Takuapa ⓣ076 217903. A Phuket institution, housed in a charmingly restored traditional shophouse (unsigned), next to *Kanasutra*, this place serves fabulous Thai food and fosters a fun, sociable atmosphere. Mains are sophisticated and beautifully presented – their *goong sarong*, individual shrimps bound in a crisp-noodle wrap, is famous island-wide. Dishes are pricey at around B300, but always come with a free starter and dessert. By about 10pm there is jiving between courses as staff take the lead and encourage locals and expats to have a boogie. Reservations are essential. Tues–Sun 6pm–1am.

Kanasutra 18 Thanon Takuapa. Contemporary Indian restaurant with a tandoori oven, serving everything from sheesh kebab to prawn vindaloo (mostly B160–360). Mon–Sat 11am–3pm & 6–11pm, Sun 6–11pm.

La Gaetana 352 Thanon Phuket ⓣ076 250523. Inviting Italian-Thai restaurant whose menu includes home-made pasta with some great sauces, a special house fish stew, outstanding home-made ice creams (the durian ice cream is an acquired taste but worth the plunge) and good-value wine by the glass. Most mains cost around B220. Mon, Tues & Fri noon–2pm & 6pm–late, Thurs, Sat & Sun 6pm–late.

Lemongrass 2/9 Thanon Dibuk. Good, authentic, mid-priced Thai food (mostly B80) is the hallmark of this popular, unpretentious, al fresco restaurant that's especially recommended for its fish dishes, numerous curries, and mountain-fern, wing bean and banana-flower salads. Daily 5pm–1am.

Natural Restaurant (Thammachat) 62/5 Soi Putorn ⓦwww.naturalrestaurant-phuket.com. There are plenty of reasons to linger over dinner at this rambling, informal, hugely popular, plant-wreathed restaurant, not least the two hundred different choices on the menu, and the affordable prices (B80–120). Highlights include fried sea bass with chilli paste, fried chicken with Muslim herbs, soft-shelled crab with garlic and pepper, and spicy Phuket bean salad. Tues–Sun 10.30am–11.30pm.

On On Café Thanon Phang Nga. Sociable spot for cheap farang-style meals, especially breakfasts, including good banana pancakes, fry-ups and fresh coffee. Mon–Sat 7am–8pm.

Ruamjai Vegetarian Restaurant 219 Thanon Ranong. Cheap and simple vegan canteen where for B25 or B30 you get two main-course servings from the trays of stir-fries and curries plus a plate of brown rice. Daily 7am to about 8pm.

Soi Romanee This artfully restored soi connecting Dibuk and Thalang roads shows off its handsome new pastel paintwork and stuccoed Old Town facades with half a dozen little café-bars whose seating spills out on to the pavement for ultimate architectural appreciation. From November to April, there's free live jazz on the street on the last Sunday evening of the month.

Shopping

Unless otherwise stated all listed Phuket Town **shops** are closed on Sundays. The Books (daily 9am–9pm) on Thanon Phuket is the best source of new English-language **books** on the island; South Wind Books on Thanon Phang Nga (Mon–Sat 9am–7pm, Sun 10am–3pm) has a big range of second-hand books and Bo(ok)hemia at 61 Thanon Thalang (1–10pm) has a small, eclectic stock, plus second-hand DVDs, coffee, wi-fi and occasional film screenings. Ban Boran Textiles, at 51 Thanon Yaowarat, specializes in **clothes** made from the handspun cotton of north and northeast Thailand, and the shops on eastern Thanon Thalang keep a phenomenal range of well-priced sarongs mostly of Burmese, Malaysian and Indonesian designs. For high-street fashions, there's Robinson department store on Thanon Tilok Uthis 1, and Ocean Department

Ngan Kin Jeh: the Vegetarian Festival

For nine days every October or November, at the start of the ninth lunar month (see ⓦwww.phuketvegetarian.com for exact dates), the celebrations for **Ngan Kin Jeh** – the Vegetarian Festival – set the streets of Phuket buzzing with processions, theatre shows and food stalls, culminating in the unnerving spectacle of men and women parading about with steel rods through their cheeks and tongues. The festival marks the beginning of **Taoist Lent**, a month-long period of purification observed by devout Chinese all over the world, but celebrated most ostentatiously in Phuket, by devotees of the island's five Chinese temples. After six days' abstention from meat (hence the festival's name), alcohol and sex, the white-clad worshippers flock to their local temple, where drum rhythms help induce a trance state in which they become possessed by spirits. As proof of their new-found transcendence of the physical world they skewer themselves with any available sharp instrument – fishing rods and car wing-mirrors have done service in the past – before walking over red-hot coals or up ladders of swords as further testament to their otherworldliness. In the meantime there's singing and dancing and almost continuous firework displays, with the grandest festivities held at Wat Jui Tui on Thanon Ranong in Phuket town.

The ceremony dates back to the mid-nineteenth century, when a travelling Chinese opera company turned up on the island to entertain emigrant Chinese working in the tin mines. They had been there almost a year when suddenly the whole troupe – together with a number of the miners – came down with a life-endangering fever. Realizing that they'd neglected their gods, the actors performed elaborate rites, and most were soon cured. The festival has been held ever since, though the self-mortification rites are a later modification, possibly of Hindu origin.

Store nearby, but for the biggest brand names, including Esprit, Lacoste and Jim Thompson silk, you need to head out to the glitzy **Central Festival shopping plaza** on the bypass at the western edge of town, at the big intersection of roads to Phuket town, Ao Patong, and Ao Chalong; there's a free shuttle bus from *Royal Phuket City* hotel, or Patong- and Chalong-bound songthaews can drop you close by. Downtown, the two most fruitful shopping roads for **handicrafts** and **antiques** are Thanon Yaowarat and Thanon Rat Sada. On Thanon Rat Sada, Radsada Hand Made at no. 29 sells textiles, carved wooden textile hangers, mango-wood vases and silver jewellery, while Soul of Asia at no. 37 specializes in quality Southeast Asian antiques, fine art and furniture. Ocean Department Store's more mass-market souvenir stalls are also worth a browse.

Listings

Airlines Bangkok Airways ⓣ076 225033; Dragon Air ⓣ1800 700707 toll free from Phuket, or 02 2630367 from elsewhere; Firefly ⓣ076 239980; Korean Air ⓣ076 328540; Malaysia Airlines ⓣ076 213749; Nok Air ⓣ076 351464; Silk Air ⓣ076 304018–20; Thai Airways ⓣ076 360444.

Cinemas English-language blockbusters are shown throughout the day and evening at the Paradise Multiplex next to Ocean Department Store on Thanon Tilok Uthis 1 and the SF Coliseum inside the Central Festival shopping plaza on the bypass road.

Dentists At Phuket International Hospital and Bangkok Hospital Phuket; see "Hospitals", below.

Hospitals Phuket International Hospital (ⓣ076 249400, emergencies ⓣ076 210935, ⓦwww.phuketinternationalhospital.com), north of Central Festival shopping centre on Highway 402, just west of Phuket town, is considered to have Phuket's best facilities, including an emergency department, an ambulance service and private rooms. Reputable alternatives include Bangkok Hospital Phuket, on the northwestern edge of town just off Thanon Yaowarat at 2/1 Thanon Hongyok Uthis ⓣ1719 or 076 245425, ⓦwww.phukethospital.com, and the Mission Hospital (aka Phuket Adventist Hospital), on the northern outskirts at 4/1 Thanon Thepkasatri ⓣ076 237220–5, emergencies ⓣ076 237227, ⓦwww.missionhospitalphuket.com. See map, p.679 for locations.

Immigration office At the southern end of Thanon Phuket, in the suburb of Saphan Hin ⓣ076 221905; Mon–Fri 8.30am–4.30pm, Sat 8.30–noon.

TAT 191 Thanon Thalang (daily 8.30am–4.30pm ⓣ076 212213, ⓔtatphket@tat.or.th).

Telephones For international calls use the CAT phone office on Thanon Phang Nga (daily 8am–8pm).

Tourist police For all emergencies, call the tourist police on the free, 24hr phone line ⓣ1155, or visit them during office hours at their office just north of Tesco Lotus on the northwest edge of town, on Route 402.

Hat Mai Khao

Phuket's longest and quietest beach, the seventeen-kilometre **HAT MAI KHAO**, unfurls along the island's upper northwest coast, beginning some 3km south of the Sarasin Bridge causeway and ending just north of the airport (34km from Phuket town). It's a beautiful piece of casuarina- and palm-shaded coastline, minimally developed and protected in part as **Sirinath National Park** (ⓦwww.dnp.go.th/National_park.asp) because of the few giant marine turtles that lay their eggs here between October and February. Also within the national park is the **Thachatchai Nature Trail**.

Accommodation on Hat Mai Khao is predominantly five star: an enclave of half a dozen luxury hotels is elegantly spaced behind the sloping shoreline towards the north end of the beach, accessed by an all-but private road served by electric buggies, with guests welcome to use any neighbouring facilities. All the resorts have several swimming pools as the undertow here can be fierce and unpredictable: the *JW Marriott Phuket Resort and Spa* (ⓣ076 338000, ⓦwww.jwmarriottphuket.com; ⑨) has three, plus a water slide, a well-equipped children's pavilion, good sports facilities and extensive landscaped lawns that all help make it a favourite with families. In contrast, the sharp, Sino-modern architecture of the villa compounds at *Sala Phuket* (Ⓣ076 338888, Ⓦwww.salaphuket.com; published rates from $490; ❾) – all done out in cool creams and silver, with colour-coordinated planting and the occasional lacquered screen – attract mainly couples, especially honeymooners, who enjoy the style and privacy, especially of the pool villas. There's an enticing open-air seafront lounging area here too, with deliciously squishy sofas, plus a rooftop terrace. Though the trend on Hat Mai Khao is indisputably upmarket, it is still possible to enjoy this glorious beach on a smaller budget, at *Mai Khao Beach Bungalows* (Ⓣ081 895 1233, Ⓦmaikhaobeach.wordpress.com; ❹, tents ❶; closed May–Oct), whose four simple en-suite fan bungalows, and four tents, sit just behind the shore beneath thinly planted coconut palms hung with hammocks, some 3km south down the beach from *Sala Phuket*. There's a restaurant and motorbike rental here too, but not much else. Easiest access to *Mai Khao Beach Bungalows* is by long-distance bus to or from Phuket town: ask to be dropped in Ban Soun Maprao, a road junction just north of kilometre-stone 37 on Highway 402, from where you can phone the bungalows for a pick-up, 2km west.

Thachatchai Nature Trail

Snaking through the mangroves at Phuket's northern tip, 700m south of the Sarasin Bridge exit to the mainland, the **Thachatchai Nature Trail** (dawn to dusk; free) aims to introduce visitors to life in a mangrove swamp (see p.725). It's run by the Sirinath National Park and is located east off Highway 402; any bus travelling between Phuket town and the mainland should drop you at the sign. The six-hundred-metre **trail** follows a raised wooden walkway that loops through a patch of coastal mangrove swamp. Informative English-language boards describe the flora and fauna: you can't fail to spot the swarms of fiddler crabs scuttling around the muddy roots, and the "bok-bok" sound that you can hear above the roar of the distant highway is the noise the mangrove-dwelling shrimps make when they snap their pincers as they feed – they're the ones that give the distinctive taste to the green papaya salad, *som tam*.

Hat Nai Yang

The long curved sweep of **HAT NAI YANG**, 5km south of Hat Mai Khao and 30km north of Phuket town, is partly under the protection of Sirinath National Park and has only fairly low-key development, with plentiful shade from the feathery casuarinas and cajeput trees that run half the length of the bay, a dozen seafood restaurant shacks, and a tiny, low-rise tourist village of transport rental outlets, a few accommodation options, an ATM, a massage pavilion, and the inevitable tailors' shops. The beach is clean and good for swimming at the southern end, and there's a reasonable, shallow **reef** about 1km offshore (10min by longtail boat) from the Sirinath National Park headquarters, which are a fifteen-minute walk north of the tourist village. From May to September there's also kiteboarding here, care of Kiteboarding Asia (Ⓦwww.kiteboardingasia.com). The Thachatchai Nature Trail is quite nearby (see above).

Hat Nai Yang is just 2km south of the **airport**, B150 by taxi. An infrequent **songthaew** service (B35; 1hr 45min) runs between Phuket town and Hat Nai Yang via the airport.

Accommodation

Accommodation is pleasingly limited on Hat Nai Yang, though not aimed at budget travellers. Best of the lot is the luxurious *Indigo Pearl* (Ⓣ076 327006, Ⓦwww.indigo-pearl.com; ❾), whose rooms and villas look on to attractively landscaped plantation-style gardens that run down to the southern end of the beachfront road; facilities include a meandering lagoon-like salt-water swimming pool, a dive shop, an inventively programmed activities centre, a spa and kids' playground. Interiors are designed to evoke Phuket's tin-mining history, with metallic colour schemes, polished cement floors and a penchant for industrial art, but the look is softened by very comfortable furniture, generous balconies and plenty of greenery. Nearby *Nai Yang Beach Resort* (☎076 328300, ⓦwww.naiyangbeachresort.com; ❽–❾) is a good upper-mid-range alternative, its cosy, modern, whitewashed air-con rooms fitted with attractive dark-wood furniture and ranged in two- and three-storey wings around pretty tropical gardens; there are three swimming pools, and wi-fi throughout.

Eating and drinking

Nai Yang is locally famous for its shorefront **restaurant**-shacks that serve mostly barbecued seafood (and the odd wood-fired pizza), both on mats under the trees during the daytime and at tables on the sand, candlelit and exceptionally tranquil at night; *Mama Mia* is a favourite and gets consistently good reviews. For a really top-notch romantic dinner, however, you can't top the intimate, black-painted *sala* at ★ *Black Ginger*, inside the *Indigo Pearl* hotel (reservations advisable on ☎076 327006). Highlights from the very classy menu here include the Phuket lobster with red coconut curry, supremely creamy *phanaeng* curries (from B290), fresh Vietnamese-style rice-flour pancakes stuffed with shrimps, coriander and herbs, and indulgent set meals of four or more courses (from B1500 for two). Of the several little beach **bars**, *The Beach Club*, at the southern end of the bay, makes a cool, relaxed place for a drink in its low-slung track-side chairs or on one of its day beds with triangular cushions on the beach.

Hat Nai Thon

The next bay south down the coast from Hat Nai Yang is the small but perfectly formed five hundred-metre-long gold-sand **HAT NAI THON**, with good snorkelling at reefs a brief longtail ride offshore. Shops, hotels and restaurants line the inland side of its narrow little shorefront road, but there's still a low-key, village-like atmosphere here; most visitors rent their own transport as songthaews don't make the detour from the highway and taxis are thin on the ground. The cheapest rooms are upstairs above *Tienseng* restaurant (☎081 535 0512; fan ❹, air-con ❺), with some sea views. *Naithonburi Beach Resort* (☎076 318700, ⓦwww.naithonburi.com; ❽–❾) is huge, with 229 posh air-con rooms in a U-shaped complex enclosing an enormous pool, some of them with direct pool access, but it doesn't dominate. About 2km south over the southern headland, occupying secluded cliffside land that runs down to its own gorgeous little bay of white sand and turquoise water, *Andaman White Beach Resort* (☎076 316300, ⓦwww.andamanwhitebeach.com; ❾) offers luxurious rooms and villas with unsurpassed views, including some designed for families, plus a swimming pool.

Ao Bang Tao

Relandscaped from a former tin-mining concession, complete with lagoons, parkland, an outdoor sports centre, an eighteen-hole golf course and an impressive eight-kilometre shorefront, **AO BANG TAO** is dominated by the vast, upscale *Laguna Phuket*, a gated "integrated resort" of six luxury hotels and their all-encompassing facilities. It's a world away from the thrust and hustle of Patong and a popular choice for families, with no need to leave the *Laguna* village, though beware of the undertow off the coast here, which confines many guests to the hotel pools. There's free transport between the hotels, and (for a minimal fee) day pass access to all hotel facilities, which include thirty restaurants and five spas plus a shopping centre, tennis and badminton courts, riding stables, watersports, and abseiling and rock-climbing at the Camp Laguna kids' activity centre.

All *Laguna Phuket* **hotels** are in the top price bracket but try Ⓦwww.lagunaphuket.com for discounted rates. The family-oriented *Allamanda Laguna* (Ⓣ076 362700, Ⓦwww.allamanda.com; ⑨) comprises 150 apartment-style suites with kitchenette and separate living area; while the exclusive *Banyan Tree Phuket* (Ⓣ076 324374, Ⓦwww.banyantree.com; ⑨) offers villas in private gardens and the gloriously indulgent, award-winning, Banyan Tree spa.

Half-hourly **songthaews** (B25; 1hr 15min) cover the 24km from Phuket town to Ao Bang Tao, or there are resort shuttle buses and on-site car rental.

Hat Surin and Ao Pansea

South around Laem Son headland from Ao Bang Tao, handsome little **HAT SURIN** is a favourite weekend getaway for sophisticated Phuketians and a big draw for expats, who inhabit the ever expanding forest of condo developments inland from the small, pretty beach. The shorefront gets very crowded, however, packed with sunloungers and beach restaurants, so it can be hard to appreciate the setting. Eating and shopping facilities cater to the upmarket clientele and beachfront dining and drinking is the main pastime. Things are much quieter on Hat Surin's northern bay, **AO PANSEA**, which is divided from the main beach by a rocky promontory. **Songthaews** travel the 24km between Phuket town and Hat Surin, via Hat Kamala, approximately every half-hour and cost B25. Taxis to and from Patong charge B500.

Accommodation on Hat Surin is no bargain, but just across the small park from the beach you'll find large, attractive and stylish rooms at both *Surin Bay Inn*, above a restaurant at 106 Thanon Hat Surin (Ⓣ076 271601, Ⓦwww.surinbayinn.com; ⑦), and *Benyada Lodge*, at nearby no. 103 (Ⓣ076 271261, Ⓦwww.benyadalodge-phuket.com; ⑦–⑧); both have in-room air-con, wi-fi, TV and fridge, and *Benyada* has a rooftop terrace and bar. North around the rocks, **Ao Pansea** is secluded from the riff-raff and is a favourite haunt of royalty and Hollywood stars, who stay in the butler-staffed pavilions at the *Amanpuri* (Ⓣ076 324333, Ⓦwww.amanresorts.com; ⑨; rates start at US$700). Sharing this effectively private white-sand hideaway is the delightful, and slightly more reasonably priced *The Chedi Phuket* (Ⓣ076 324017, Ⓦwww.ghmhotels.com; ⑨; rates from B17,000 but specials often available), whose 108 generously proportioned, Bali-style thatched villas are set within a lushly planted hillside palm grove that drops down to the shore.

Among the many restaurants on and behind Hat Surin proper, sophisticated seafront *Taste* (Tues–Sun midday till late; Ⓦwww.tastesurinbeach.com) serves great seafood – steamed red snapper with lobster-dill white wine sauce; *moules marinières* (B195–395) – while the beachside lounge bar at *The Catch Beach Club* is the fashionable place to go after sundown, with its illuminated palm trees, resident DJs and very well-stocked bar; though it's open during the day, the food is very pricey and you have to pay an exorbitant B1500 rental for a sunlounger if you're not a guest at *Twinpalms Resort*. Inland, inside the Surin Plaza shopping complex, expats dining out for a special occasion come to famously elegant *Silk* (Ⓣ076 271702, Ⓦwww.silkphuket.com), which specializes in top-of-the range Thai cuisine (B195–450) such as rose-apple salad with poached prawns, *goong sarong* (prawns wrapped in Phuket-style noodles) and pan-fried snow fish with lemon grass.

Phuket day-trips and other activities

Bookings for all the following **Phuket day-trips and activities** can be made through any tour agent and should include return transport from your hotel. For details of dive operators in Phuket, see p.698. Other **sights** worth checking out, especially for kids, include the Phuket Butterfly Garden and Insect World in Phuket town (see p.685), the Aquarium on Laem Panwa (p.705), the Shell Museum in Rawai (p.704), the Big Buddha near Chalong (p.705), the Dino Park on Karon (p.699) and the Gibbon Rehabilitation Project near Thalang (p.707). Avoid any tour that features Ko Siray (Ko Sireh), the island across the narrow channel from Phuket town, which merely encourages tour-bus passengers to gawp at Phuket's largest and longest-established indigenous *chao ley* community; for more on the *chao ley* see p.663.

Activities and days out

Bicycle touring Full- and half-day guided mountain-bike rides into Phuket's rural hinterlands with Action Holidays Phuket (ⓣ076 263575, ⓦwww.biketoursthailand.com; full day from B2400/kids B2200).

Deep-sea fishing Day-trips and overnight charters with Andaman Hooker (ⓣ076 282036, ⓦwww.phuket.com/fishing/andaman.htm); and Harry's Fishing Adventures (ⓣ076 340418, ⓦwww.harrysfishing-phuket.com).

Elephant trekking Award-winning, conservation-conscious Siam Safari runs Four-in-One tours featuring their hillside elephant camp plus rubber tapping, buffalo-cart racing and a sail on a Burmese junk (from B2250, kids B1550; ⓣ076 280116, ⓦwww.siamsafari.com).

Harley-Davidson Tours Famous local HD nut Nicky, owner of Patong's *Nicky's Handlebar* Harley bar and shop (see p.697), leads riders on a 330km ride around adjacent Phang Nga province. B7500 or B10,500 for rider plus pillion, including bike rental, lunch and dinner (ⓣ076 345770).

Sea-canoeing Sunset, one- and two-day expeditions in sea kayaks around the spectacular limestone karsts of Ao Phang Nga, or in Khao Sok National Park, for around B3000–3500 per person per day. There are dozens of companies but two with the best reputations are John Gray's Sea Canoe (ⓣ076 254505, ⓦwww.johngray-seacanoe.com) and Paddle Asia (ⓣ076 240952, ⓦpaddleasia.com).

Thai cookery courses Different daily classes at Phuket Thai Cookery School east of Phuket town on Ko Siray (B2500; ⓣ076 252354, ⓦwww.phuket-thaicookeryschool.com); and at many hotels, including, most famously, every Saturday and Sunday at *Mom Tri's Boathouse* hotel on Ao Kata Yai (B2200 for one day, or B3500 for both days; ⓣ076 330015, ⓦwww.boathousephuket.com).

Thai culture and wildlife tours Full-day "Thai Life" tours that include market and temple visits, Buddhist merit-making, a cooking class and craft and rubber production. Can be combined with the Gibbon Rehabilitation project (see p.707). B1500 with Plan to Phuket (ⓣ081/691 1955).

Nights out

Phuket FantaSea ⓣ076 385111, ⓦwww.phuket-fantasea.com. Enjoyable, hi-tech mega-spectacular staged at the enormous FantaSea entertainments complex in Kamala and featuring high-wire trapeze acts, acrobatics, pyrotechnics, illusionists, comedy and traditional dance – plus a depressing baby elephant circus. Fri–Wed 9pm; B1500 for adults and kids or B1900/1700 including the unexciting pre-show dinner.

Phuket Simon Cabaret ⓣ076 342011, ⓦwww.phuket-simoncabaret.com. Famously flamboyant extravaganza starring a troupe of outré transvestites. It's all very Hollywood – a little bit risqué but not at all sleazy – and popular with tour groups and families. Nightly 7.30pm & 9.30pm at the Simon Theatre just south of Patong; B700/500.

Hat Kamala and Laem Singh

With its cheerfully painted houses and absence of high-rises, the small, village-like tourist development at **HAT KAMALA** is low-key and mid-market, sandwiched between the beach and the predominantly Muslim town of Ban Kamala, about 300m west of the main Patong-Surin road, 6km north of Patong and 26km northwest of Phuket town. Accommodation, shops, restaurants and other tourist services are mostly clustered either side of shoreside Thanon Rim Had (also spelt Rim Hat) which, despite its limited choice, is a much pleasanter place to browse than the big resorts. The beach gets prettier and quieter the further north you go, away from Thanon Rim Had, with restaurant shacks renting sunloungers along most of its course. A stretch of this area is backed by the Muslim cemetery, so it's particularly important to respect local sensibilities and avoid going topless.

Kamala was very badly hit by the 2004 **tsunami**, which killed many residents and wiped out the beachfront school, the temple and countless homes and businesses. Though extensive rebuilding has extinguished most of the physical scars, a copper sculpture in the park opposite *Print Kamala* bears witness to the devastation, and a volunteer English-teaching programme at the school (see p.83), aims to help rebuild some of the young lives affected.

The Phuket FantaSea entertainments complex (see box, p.691) is about 1km northeast of Hat Kamala on the main Patong-Surin road. Just beyond, a couple of steep paths lead west off the main road and down to **Laem Singh** cape, a pretty little sandy cove whose picturesque combination of turquoise water and smooth granite boulders makes it one of Phuket's finest. It's good for swimming and very secluded, plus there's a decent patch of shade throughout the day.

The cheapest way to get to Hat Kamala is by **songthaew** from Phuket town (every 30min, 1hr 15min; B30). Tuk-tuks charge B300 from Patong.

Accommodation

Hat Kamala is popular with long-stay tourists, and several **hotels** offer rooms with kitchenettes; there's also a preponderance of small-scale places.

Benjamin Resort 83 Thanon Rim Had, opposite the school at the southerly end of the beachfront road ⓣ076 385147, ⓦwww.phuketdir.com/benjaminresort. Set right on the beach and about the best and friendliest deal in Kamala, this block of 37 air-con rooms lacks character but couldn't be closer to the sea. Although views are obstructed from all but the most expensive rooms, the spacious interiors are almost identical and all have fridge, TV, hot water and breakfast included, plus use of sunloungers out front. ❸–❻

Coconut Garden Soi Police Station ⓣ081 477 3331, ⓦwww.coconutgarden.se. The best thing about the dozen good-sized but unexceptional concrete air-con bungalows here are their location on the nicer northerly stretch of the central beach. ❼

Kamala Dreams 74/1 Thanon Rim Had ⓣ076 279131, ⓦwww.kamaladreams.net. Epitomizing all the best things about Kamala, this is a really nice, small hotel set right on the shore, in the middle of the tourist village. Its eighteen rooms are large and furnished in contemporary style, and all have air-con, TVs, a kitchenette and a large balcony overlooking the pool and the sea. ❼

Malinee House 75/4 Thanon Rim Had ⓣ076 385094, ⓦwww.malineehouse.com. Very friendly, traveller-oriented guest house in the middle of the tourist village, with internet access and the Jackie Lee travel agency downstairs, and jut eight large, comfortably furnished and cheerfully painted air-con rooms upstairs, all of them with balconies. ❺

Print Kamala Resort 74/8 Thanon Rim Had ⓣ076 385396, ⓦwww.printkamalaresort.net. The best accommodation here is in a village-like complex of very generously sized bungalows, connected via stilted walkways around a tropical Bali-style garden. The bungalows all have prettily furnished air-con bedrooms plus separate living rooms, and capacious, shaded decks. The pricier ones are detached. The hotel also has some less interesting, but more expensive, rooms in a hotel wing, and a large pool. ❽–❾

Eating and drinking

The most famous **restaurant** in Kamala is Australian-run *Rockfish* at the *Kamala Beach Estate* hotel (ⓣ076 279732, ⓦwww.rockfishrestaurant.com), which enjoys an island-wide reputation for great food, mostly Asian fusion and seafood dishes such as tiger prawns in tamarind sauce, blue crab and mango salad and lemon grass pannacotta (B200–700); you also get lovely views from its southern headland location. Otherwise, most people eat on the beach, especially at the restaurant shacks that pretty much line the shore all the way north from opposite *Print Kamala*; seafood is the big seller here, and you can bury your feet in the sand. For a seaside **drink** with a reggae vibe try *Yellow Bar*, just before the cemetery, done out with Rasta colour schemes and driftwood decor.

Ao Patong

The busiest and most popular of all Phuket's beaches, **AO PATONG** – 5km south of Ao Kamala and 15km west of Phuket town – is vastly over-developed and hard to recommend. A congestion of high-rise hotels, tour agents and souvenir shops disfigures the beachfront road, tireless touts are everywhere, and hostess bars and strip joints dominate the nightlife, attracting an increasing number of single Western men to the most active scene between Bangkok and Hat Yai. On the plus side, the broad, three-kilometre-long beach offers good sand and plenty of shade beneath the parasols and there are hundreds of shops and bars plus a surprising number of good restaurants to keep you busy after dark.

Transport

For transport from and to the **airport** and the **ferry ports**, see p.680. **Songthaews** from Phuket town (every 15min from 6am–6pm; 20min; B20) approach Patong from the northeast, driving south along one-way Thanon Raja Uthit Song Roi Phi (Thanon Raja Uthit 200) then circling back north along beachfront Thanon Thavee Wong (also one-way) via the *Patong Merlin*, where they wait to pick up passengers for the return trip. A **tuk-tuk** or **taxi** from Patong to Ao Karon will set you back at least B200.

National/SMT **car rental** (ⓣ076 340608, ⓦwww.nationalcarrental.co.th) has a desk inside the *Holiday Inn*, the local Budget agent is at the nearby *Patong Merlin* (ⓣ076 292389, ⓦwww.budget.co.th), or you can rent jeeps and motorbikes from any transport tout on Thanon Thavee Wong.

Information

Most of the **tour agents** and **dive operators** have offices on the southern stretch of Thanon Thavee Wong: see the box on p.691 for a roundup of available day-trips and activities, and the box on p.698 for diving details.

There are **post offices** on Thanon Thavee Wong (daily 11am–7pm) and Thanon Raja Uthit Song Roi Phi (Mon–Fri 8.30am–4.30pm, Sat & Sun 9.30am–noon) and the Patong branch of Phuket's **Immigration** office (for visa extensions; Mon–Fri 10am–noon & 1–3pm; ⓣ076 340477) is next to *Sala Bua* restaurant on Thanon Thavee Wong.

Accommodation

It's hard to find much **accommodation** under ❺ in Patong, and there are no backpacker places, but upper-end hotels are reasonable value and all have excellent facilities.

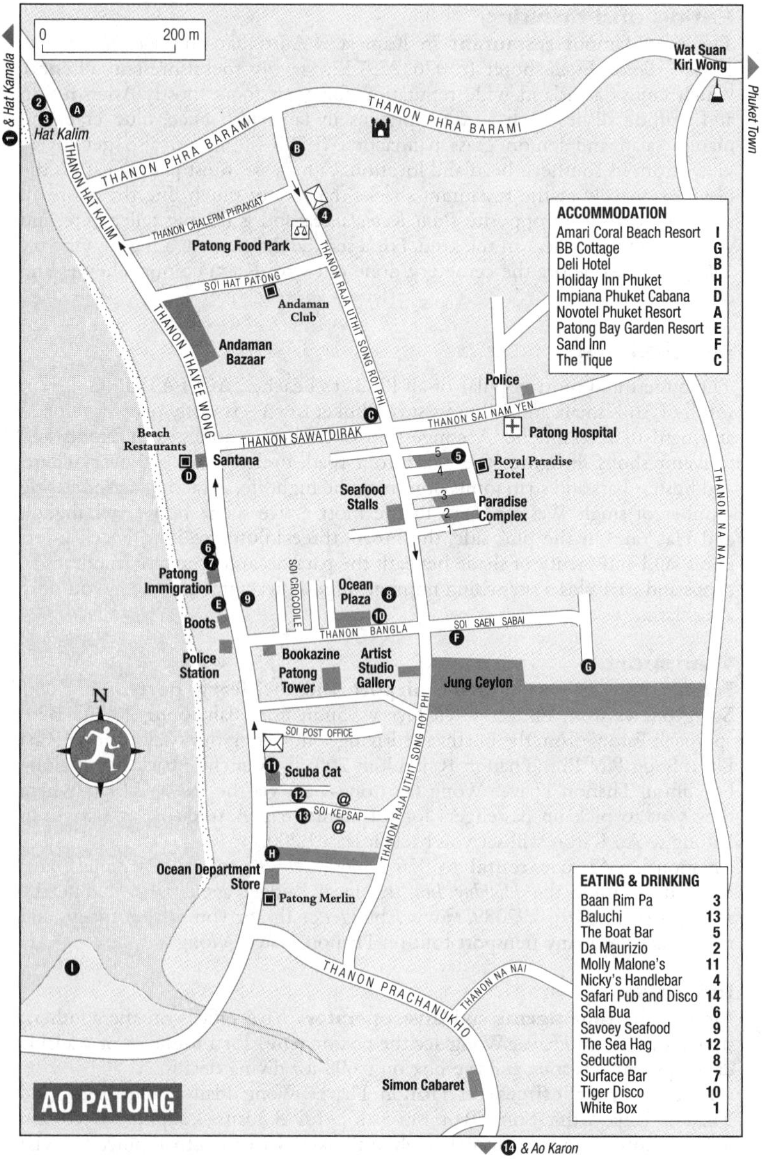

Amari Coral Beach Resort 104 Thanon Traitrang ⓣ076 340106, ⓦwww.amari.com. Occupying its own secluded little beach on a headland at the southernmost end of the bay, this upmarket Thai chain hotel offers contemporary-chic rooms with generous sea-view balconies, plus two swimming pools, romantic spa facilities, tennis courts and several restaurants. The views are exceptional and the location peaceful but convenient; as it's ranged up a slope it's not ideal for guests with mobility problems. ⑨

BB Cottage 17/21 Soi Saen Sabai ⓣ076 342948, ⓔpppropt@loxinfo.co.th. A rare thing indeed in Patong: 29 lowish-budget bungalows dotted around a peaceful green oasis of a garden, beneath the shadow of the sprawling Jung Ceylon centre and hotel. Admittedly, interiors are plain – though they are large, have TVs and fridges, and some have kitchenettes – and there are no verandas, but they're kept very clean, there's a sense of space and you're close to the nightlife yet a little bit secluded. Staff are friendly and guests can also use a nearby swimming pool. Fan 5, air-con 5–6

Deli Hotel (formerly Shamrock Park Inn) 31 Thanon Raja Uthit Song Roi Phi ⓣ076 340991. Friendly, good-value three-storey hotel at the northern end of the resort with 28 pleasant, well-maintained and cheerily painted air-con rooms, half of them with balconies and all with TVs, fridges, wi-fi and safety box. Unlike many places it doesn't raise its rates for Christmas and New Year. 4

Holiday Inn Phuket 86/11 Thanon Thavee Wong ⓣ076 340608, ⓦwww.phuket.holiday-inn.com. Reliable, upmarket chain hotel that offers smart, contemporary rooms just across the road from the beach, in two differently styled wings, and fosters an informal, unpretentious atmosphere. The poshest Busakorn villa rooms have their own inter-connected plunge-pools and there are also large pools for each wing, plus several restaurants and an interesting programme of daily activities. The hotel makes a big effort to be family-friendly, with special "kidsuites" for children, an all-day kids' club and a teens' club and two children's pools. Also offers wheelchair-accessible rooms. 9

Impiana Phuket Cabana 94 Thanon Thavee Wong ⓣ076 340138, ⓦwww.impiana.com. Located right on the beach and in the heart of the resort, the very tastefully designed air-con cabanas here are set around a garden and smallish swimming pool; also has a kids' pool and a spa. 9

Novotel Phuket Resort Thanon Phra Barami/Thanon Hat Kalim ⓣ076 342777, ⓦwww.novotelphuket.com. Luxurious and relaxing chain hotel built on the hillside above Kalim Bay, the quieter, northern end of the resort, a 10min walk or a free shuttle ride to Patong's main beach and shops, but very close to some of the best restaurants. Occupying sloping landscaped tropical gardens and offering exceptional high-level sea views, it's especially popular with families as it offers heaps of activities as well as a kids' club plus a multi-level swimming pool. 9

Patong Bay Garden Resort 33/1 Thanon Thavee Wong ⓣ076 340297, ⓦwww.patongbaygarden.com. Lively, mid-sized 71-room hotel set right on the beach, with the top "studio" rooms having uninterrupted sea views, quite unusual in central Patong. Other rooms look out on the small shore-front pool or have no view at all. Rooms are quite elegantly furnished and all have air-con and TV. 9

Sand Inn 171 Soi Saen Sabai ⓣ076 340275, ⓦwww.sandinnphuket.com. Thirty well-appointed air-con rooms, a little on the compact side, but maintained to a good standard in the ideal location for nightlife, just east off bar-packed Thanon Bangla. There's TV in all rooms, a *Euro Café* bakery downstairs, and use of a small swimming pool just a few metres up the soi. 5–6

The Tique 29 Thanon Sawatdirak ⓣ076 297023, ⓦwww.thetique.com. Tiny urban-chic boutique inn, where the 22 air-con rooms are cleverly designed in retro-neutral, bachelor-pad colour schemes and all have flatscreen TVs, wi-fi, and a petite balcony. There's a small jacuzzi pool on the fourth-floor roof terrace and rates include breakfast, high-tea, and a weekend glass of wine at cocktail hour. 7–8

Eating

Much of the **food** on Patong is dire, but in among the disastrous little cafés advertising everything from Hungarian to Swedish "home cooking" you'll find a few genuinely reputable, long-running favourites. Phone numbers are given where reservations are advisable. For cheapish food on the beach, head for the half dozen little restaurants under the shorefront trees just north of the *Impiana* hotel. For well-priced Thai fast food, there are the regional speciality stalls at the *Food Haven* foodcentre in Jung Ceylon, the *Patong Food Park* night market that sets up around 5pm towards the northern end of Thanon Raja Uthit Song Roi Phi, and the row of seafood stall-restaurants further south, opposite the *Royal Paradise Hotel* complex.

Baan Rim Pa Across from the *Novotel* on Thanon Hat Kalim ⓣ076 340789, ⓦwww.baanrimpa.com. One of Phuket's most famous fine-dining restaurants, this is an elegant spot that's beautifully set in a teak building on a clifftop overlooking the bay, with tables also on its sea-view terrace. Known for its classic "Royal Thai" cuisine (mains B250–500), including banana blossom salad, creamy duck curry and fried tiger prawns with tamarind sauce, as well as for its cellar of more than 270 wines. Live jazz in the *Piano Bar*.

Baluchi Inside the *Horizon Beach Hotel* on Soi Kepsap. One of Patong's better Indian restaurants, specializing in North Indian cuisine and tandoori dishes – Rogan josh kashmiri lamb, tandoori prawns – with most mains costing B200–400.

Da Maurizio Across from the *Novotel* on Thanon Hat Kalim ⓣ076 344079, ⓦwww.damaurizio.com. Superior Italian restaurant in a stunning location set over the rocks beside the sea. Serves authentic home-made pasta and antipasti (capellini with scallops, prosciutto-wrapped goat's cheese), fabulous seafood (Phuket lobsters, local kingfish with wild mushroom sauté), and a good wine list. Main dishes from B450.

Sala Bua 41 Thanon Thavee Wong ⓣ076 340138, ⓦwww.sala-bua.com. Fabulously stylish, breezy, beach-view restaurant attached to the *Impiana Phuket Cabana* hotel. The innovative, pricey, Pacific Rim menu (B300–1900) includes Cajun-style red snapper, local rock-lobster lasagne, Australian tenderloin steaks and sweet sushi rolls filled with green mango, sticky rice and orange sauce.

Savoey Seafood 136 Thanon Thavee Wong. Cavernous and unatmospheric but very popular for its huge selection of locally caught fish and seafood (dishes from B180), particularly Phuket lobster, cooked to Thai, Chinese and Western recipes.

The Sea Hag inland from *Zen* Japanese restaurant on Soi Dr Wattana. The same chef has been cooking great seafood here for over a decade and this is where expat hoteliers come for a good Patong feed. Fish and seafood cooked any number of Thai-style ways for B180–380.

White Box Thanon Hat Kalim, 1.5km north of the *Novotel* ⓣ076 346271, ⓦwww.whiteboxphuket.com. This chic, sophisticated waterside restaurant and bar, strikingly designed as a modernist cube with panoramic picture windows, is a magnet for visiting celebs and style-conscious expats. The very expensive menu (B320–1350) mixes Thai and Mediterranean flavours – grilled Phuket lobster with mint and ginger, beef carpaccio, red curry with roasted duck – and the rooftop sofas are ideal for a pre- or post dinner drink. Daily 5pm–1am.

Nightlife and entertainment

After dark, everyone heads to pedestrianized Thanon Bangla for their own taste of Patong's notorious **nightlife** and the road teems with a cross-section of Phuket tourists, from elderly couples and young parents with strollers, to glammed-up girlfriends and groups of lads. The big draw for the more innocent onlookers is Thanon Bangla's Soi Crocodile, better known as Soi Katoey, or "Trannie Alley", where pouting, barely clad transvestites jiggle their implants on podiums at the mouth of the soi and pose for photos with giggling tourists (B200 a shot). But the real action happens further down the many bar-filled sois shooting off Thanon Bangla, where open-air bar-beers and neon-lit go-go clubs

▲ Ao Patong, Phuket

packed with strippers and goggle-eyed punters pulsate through the night. The pick-up trade pervades most bars in Patong, and though many of these joints are welcoming enough to couples and female tourists, there are a few alternatives, listed below, for anyone not in that kind of mood.

The **gay** entertainment district is concentrated around the Paradise Complex, a network of small sois and dozens of bar-beers in front of *Royal Paradise Hotel* on Thanon Raja Uthit Song Roi Phi: see Ⓦgaypatong.com for events listings, including dates for the regular local street parties plus details of the Gay Pride festival, which is usually held in early February.

If you're looking for something else to do with yourself (or your kids) in the evening, check out the nearby transvestite Simon Cabaret, or the spectacular show at Phuket FantaSea (see box, p.691).

The Boat Bar Soi 5, Paradise Complex, off Thanon Raja Uthit Song Roi Phi. Long-running, very popular gay bar and disco, with two cabaret shows nightly after midnight. Daily from 9pm.

Molly Malone's 94/1 Thanon Thavee Wong. Genial Thai-Irish pub chain that serves draught Guinness and Kilkenny, shows international sports TV, stages live music from 9pm Mon–Sat and has a small beer garden and no overt hostess presence. Daily from 10am.

Nicky's Handlebar Thanon Raja Uthit Song Roi Phi. Harley Davidson themed bar, headquarters and rental outlet run by the man who organizes famous Harley tours from Phuket (see p.691). Daily 10am–1am.

Safari Pub and Disco Just beyond the southern edge of Patong, between Simon Cabaret and the *Le Meridien* hotel at 28 Thanon Sirirat. Decked out as a jungle theme park, complete with waterfalls and five different bars, this is a fun and hugely popular late-night party place. Two bands play nightly from around 9pm, and DJs spin everything from 80s disco to current techno, but it only really gets going once most other venues have shut at about 2am.

Seduction Soi Happy, off Soi Bangla. Currently the favourite venue for partying couples and others not looking for freelance company, this two-storey bar and disco has fairly classy lounge areas, a decent-sized dance floor, hi-tech lighting and a catholic music policy. Free until midnight, after which the B300 entry includes two drinks. Nightly from 10pm.

Surface Bar Top floor, *La Flora Resort Patong*, 39 Thanon Thavee Wong. The perfect place for a sophisticated sundowner, enjoyed from the comfort of enormous sofas on the hotel's wide rooftop terrace. Expansive ocean views and a sea breeze as well. Daily 4–11pm.

Tiger Disco 49 Thanon Bangla. By midnight, the upstairs disco in this unashamedly kitsch complex of bar-beers and go-go bars is packed with a mixed crowd of tourists, freelancers and punters. You can't miss the entrance, with its huge moulded jungle trees and rocks, plus the trademark larger-than-life tiger sculptures. It's just as unsubtle inside, where the pole dancers wear tiger outfits. B250 entry includes two drinks. Nightly from 9pm.

Shopping

Though you can't move for **shops** in downtown Patong, by far the best, and least hectic, place to browse is the enormous **Jung Ceylon** shopping centre on Thanon Raja Uthit Song Roi Phi, whose refreshingly tasteful and spacious design includes fountains and plaza seating plus countless shops and restaurants. Brand-name concessions include an Apple reseller and Sports World, plus there are branches of Robinsons Department Store and South Wind second-hand books, the That's Siam Thai handicrafts emporium in the basement, close by a massage centre, and a seven-screen **cinema** as well. Bookazine on Thanon Bangla carries a good range of English-language **books** and magazines, and the cavernous The Artist Studio Gallery on Thanon Raja Uthit Song Roi Phi, with another branch on Thanon Thavee Wong (Ⓦphuketdir.com/theartiststudio) is as good a place as any on Phuket to buy **paintings**.

Ao Karon

AO KARON, Phuket's second resort, after Patong, is very much a middle-of-the-road destination. Far less lively, or congested, than Patong, but more commercial and less individual than the smaller beaches, it's the domain of affordable guest houses and package-tour hotels and appeals chiefly to mid-budget tourists, many of them from Scandinavia. The 2.5-kilometre-long **beach** is graced with squeaky soft golden sand and is completely free of developments, though there's very little natural shade; an embankment screens most of the southern half of the beach from the road running alongside, but north of the *Hilton* the road is more often in view and parts of the shore back on to lagoons and wasteland. The **undertow** off Ao Karon is treacherously strong

Diving and snorkelling off Phuket

The reefs and islands within sailing distance of Phuket rate among the most spectacular in the world, and **diving and snorkelling** trips are both good value and hugely popular. Many trips operate year-round, though some of the more remote islands and reefs become too dangerous to reach during part or all of the monsoon season, roughly June to October.

Dive shops and trips

All the dive **shops** listed below are established and accredited PADI Five-Star Instructor Development Centres; they teach courses, organize dive trips and rent equipment. See also p.73 for general advice on choosing a dive shop and other general diving information. Prices range from an average B3300 for a one-day introductory **diving course** to B12,000–15,000 for the four-day Openwater course, including equipment. **Day-trips** to the closest of the dive sites listed below, including at least two dives, cost B3100–3900, while multi-day **live-aboard** cruises to the more distant top-rated reefs of Ko Similan and Ko Surin, Hin Daeng and Hin Muang, and the Mergui archipelago cost around B33,000 for four days, including sixteen dives and full board but excluding equipment and national park fees.

There are **recompression chambers** at Phuket International Hospital and Bangkok Hospital Phuket, both in Phuket town and detailed on p.687, and at Wachira Hospital, Soi Wachira, Thanon Yaowarat, Phuket town (Ⓣ076 211114).

Dive Asia 24 Thanon Karon, Kata/Karon headland, Ao Karon Ⓣ076 330598, and 623 Thanon Patak, Karon Circle, Ao Karon Ⓣ076 396199, Ⓦwww.diveasia.com.

Marina Divers Next to *Marina Phuket Resort* at 45 Thanon Karon, Ao Karon Ⓣ076 330272, Ⓦwww.marinadivers.com.

Santana 49 Thanon Thavee Wong, Ao Patong Ⓣ076 294220, Ⓦwww.santanaphuket.com.

Scuba Cat 94 Thanon Thavee Wong, Ao Patong Ⓣ076 293120, Ⓦwww.scubacat.com.

Snorkelling trips

The most popular snorkelling destination from Phuket is **Ko Phi Phi** (see p.740). All travel agents sell mass-market day-trips there, on huge ferries with capacities of a hundred plus; prices average B1500, or B1200 for children and include snorkelling stops at Phi Phi Leh and Phi Phi Don, snorkel rental and a seafood lunch. Smaller speedboat trips to Ko Phi Phi are usually worth the extra money to avoid the big groups; those run by Offspray Leisure (B2950/2250; Ⓣ076 281375, Ⓦwww.offsprayleisure.com) get good reviews. Speedboat snorkel trips to **Ko Racha Yai** are also widely sold (B2000/1400; see p.706), while day-trips to the remote but beautiful **Ko Similan** islands start from B2900/1450 (see p.676). Many of the dive companies listed welcome snorkellers on board their day-trips, and sometimes on the live-aboards too, for a discount of about thirty percent.

during the monsoon season from June to October, so you should heed the warning signs and flags and ask for local advice – fatalities are not uncommon. The tiny bay just north of Ao Karon – known as **Karon Noi** or Relax Bay – is almost exclusively patronized by guests of the *Le Meridien* hotel, but non-guests are quite welcome to swim and sunbathe here.

For inland entertainment, there's the Dino Park **mini-golf** (daily 10am–midnight; B240, kids B180, or B120/90 without the golf), next to *Marina Phuket Resort* on the Kata/Karon headland, which is part of a pseudo-prehistoric theme

Andaman coast dive and snorkel sites

Anemone Reef About 22km east of Phuket. Submerged reef of soft coral and sea anemones starting about 5m deep. Lots of fish, including leopard sharks, tuna and barracuda. Usually combined with a dive at nearby Shark Point. Unsuitable for snorkellers.

Burma Banks About 250km northwest of Phuket; only accessible on live-aboards from Khao Lak and Phuket. A series of submerged "banks", well away from any land mass and very close to the Burmese border. Only worth the trip for its sharks. Visibility up to 25m.

Hin Daeng and **Hin Muang** 56km southwest of Ko Lanta (see box, p.756). Hin Daeng is an exceptional reef wall, named after the red soft corals that covered the rocks, with visibility up to 30m. One hundred metres away, Hin Muang also drops to 50m and is good for stingrays, manta rays, whale sharks and silvertip sharks. Visibility up to 50m. Because of the depth and the current, both places are considered too risky for novice divers who have logged fewer than twenty dives. Unsuitable for snorkellers.

King Cruiser Near Shark Point, between Phuket and Ko Phi Phi. Dubbed the *Thai Tanic*, this became a wreck dive in May 1997, when a tourist ferry sank on its way to Ko Phi Phi. Visibility up to 20m, but hopeless for snorkellers because of the depth and collapsed sections make it dangerous for any but the most experienced divers.

Ko Phi Phi 48km east of Phuket's Ao Chalong. Visibility up to 30m. The most popular destination for Phuket divers and snorkellers. Spectacular drop-offs; good chance of seeing whale sharks. See p.740.

Ko Racha Noi and **Ko Racha Yai** About 33km and 28km south of Phuket's Ao Chalong respectively. Visibility up to 40m. Racha Yai is good for beginners and for snorkellers; at the more challenging Racha Noi there's a good chance of seeing manta rays, eagle rays and whale sharks. See p.706.

Ko Rok Nok and **Ko Rok Nai** 100km southeast of Phuket, south of Ko Lanta (see box, p.756). Visibility up to 18m. Shallow reefs that are excellent for snorkelling.

Ko Similan 96km northwest of Phuket; easiest access from Khao Lak. One of the world's top diving spots. Visibility up to 30m. Leopard sharks, whale sharks and manta rays, plus caves and gorges. Usually closed approximately mid-May to mid-Nov. See p.676.

Ko Surin 174km northwest of Phuket; easiest access from Khuraburi, or from Ko Chang and Ko Phayam. Spectacular and varied shallow reefs of soft and hard corals that are particularly good for snorkelling. Closed mid-May to mid-Nov. See p.664.

Richelieu Rock Just east of Ko Surin (see p.664), close to Burmese waters. A sunken pinnacle that's famous for its whale sharks. Considered by many to be Thailand's top dive spot.

Shark Point (Hin Mu Sang) 24km east of Phuket's Laem Panwa. Protected as a marine sanctuary. Visibility up to 10m. Notable for soft corals, sea fans and leopard sharks. Often combined with the *King Cruiser* dive and/or Anemone Reef; unrewarding for snorkellers.

park comprising a dinosaur restaurant and an erupting "volcano". For day-trip attractions elsewhere on Phuket see the box on p.691.

Transport and orientation

Ao Karon is 5km south of Patong and 20km southwest of Phuket town. For transport to and from the **airport** and **ferry ports** see p.680. **Songthaews** from Phuket town (every 20min; 30min; B25) arrive in Karon via Thanon Patak, hitting the beach at the northern end of Ao Karon and then driving south along beachfront Thanon Karon, continuing over the headland as far as *Kata Beach Resort* on Ao Kata Yai. To catch a songthaew back into town, just stand on the other side of the road and flag one down. Transport touts throughout the resort rent motorbikes and jeeps.

Karon's main **shopping and eating areas**, with all the usual resort facilities, are grouped around the *Centara Hotel* on the northern curve of Thanon Patak; along and around Thanon Luang Pho Chuain, location of the Kata Plaza enclave of accommodation, restaurants and bars; and along Thanon Taina (sometimes referred to as Kata Centre). The local branch of Bookazine, for new books and foreign newspapers, is across from the Thanon Taina junction on the Kata-Karon headland.

Accommodation

Like Patong, Karon does little to attract budget travellers, but there's a bit more space here and a decent selection of inviting **accommodation** in the mid-range and upper brackets.

Casa Brazil 9 Soi 1, Thanon Luang Pho Chuain ⓣ076 396317, ⓦwww.phuket.com/casa-brazil. Appealingly arty little hotel, designed in Santa Fe style, with adobe-look walls, earth-toned paintwork, and funky decor and furnishings. The 21 rooms are comfortable and nearly all have air-con. Choose rooms at the back for a rare green and peaceful view of Karon's hilly backdrop, best enjoyed from the French windows and private balconies. Rates include breakfast and there's wi-fi. ❻

Le Meridien on Ao Karon Noi (also known as Relax Bay), north of Ao Karon ⓣ076 370100, ⓦwww.lemeridien.com. This huge hotel complex has the tiny bay all to itself and boasts an amazing breadth of facilities, including nine restaurants, two lagoon-style swimming pools (with islands), a spa, squash and tennis courts, a climbing wall and private woods. It's a good choice for kids, with reliable babysitting services, a kids' club and lessons in everything from windsurfing and water polo to Thai cookery. ❾

Lucky Guest House 110/44–45 Thanon Taina, Kata Centre ⓣ076 330572, ⓔluckyguesthousekata@hotmail.com. Reasonable value place offering unusually large, bright en-suite rooms in a low-rise block (the best have balconies) and some rather plain but very clean semi-detached bungalows on land further back; there's a refreshing sense of space here that's at a premium on this road packed with shops, bars and restaurants. Fan ❸, air-con ❹

Marina Phuket Resort 47 Thanon Karon, far southern end of Ao Karon, on the Karon/Kata headland ⓣ076 330625, ⓦwww.marinaphuket.com. Enjoying both a very central location, backing on to the beach and just steps from restaurants and shops, and a luxuriously spacious and secluded tropical garden, this is a good upper-end choice. Accommodation is in air-con cottages – Garden View options are old-fashioned and plain, but Jungle View versions are very appealing – and there's a pool, wi-fi and the prettily located *On the Rock* restaurant. ❾

The Old Phuket Soi Aroona Karon, 192/36 Thanon Karon ⓣ076 396353, ⓦwww.theoldphuket.com. The Sino Wing at this attractive, peacefully secluded heritage-conscious hotel is designed to evoke Sino-Portuguese shophouse architecture. Its rooms are both pretty and modern, with coloured glass window panels and East Indies-style wooden doors; the "terrace deluxe rooms" have garden shower rooms and their own little front garden. Furnishings in the Serene Wing are much more contemporary and minimalist and many of its rooms have direct access to the lagoon-like pool. Also has a gym, a large grassy lawn and wi-fi throughout. ❾

Pineapple Guesthouse Karon Plaza, off Patak and Luang Pho Chuain roads ⓣ076 396223, ⓦwww.pineapplephuket.com. Good-value British–Thai-run guest house offering seventeen sprucely kept, tiled-floor rooms, all with air-con, fridges, wi-fi and hot water, plus a ten-bed mixed dorm at B200 a bed, with lockers and several fans. The downstairs restaurant serves full English breakfasts and the guest house is surrounded by other expat bars and restaurants in the enclave known as Karon Plaza (not to be confused with the Karon Plaza market stalls at the north end of Karon beachfront). Discounts sometimes available to walk-in guests. ④–⑤

Prayoon Bungalows Behind the stadium, off Thanon Karon; access via *Andaman Seaview* ⓣ 076 396196. Long-established family-run place with just seven large, comfortable, old-style fan bungalows, all with verandas and good bathrooms, widely spaced under the trees around a big, sloping garden just 150m or so off the beach. ④

Eating and drinking

Karon's choice of **restaurants** is underwhelming, lacking either the big-name restaurants of Patong or the authenticity of Phuket town.

Most of the Thanon Taina **bars** are small places: *Blue Fin* is typical, and hosts happy hours 3–6.30pm daily. Though go-go bars haven't arrived yet, clusters of outdoor bar-beers with hostess service are popping up at a depressing rate.

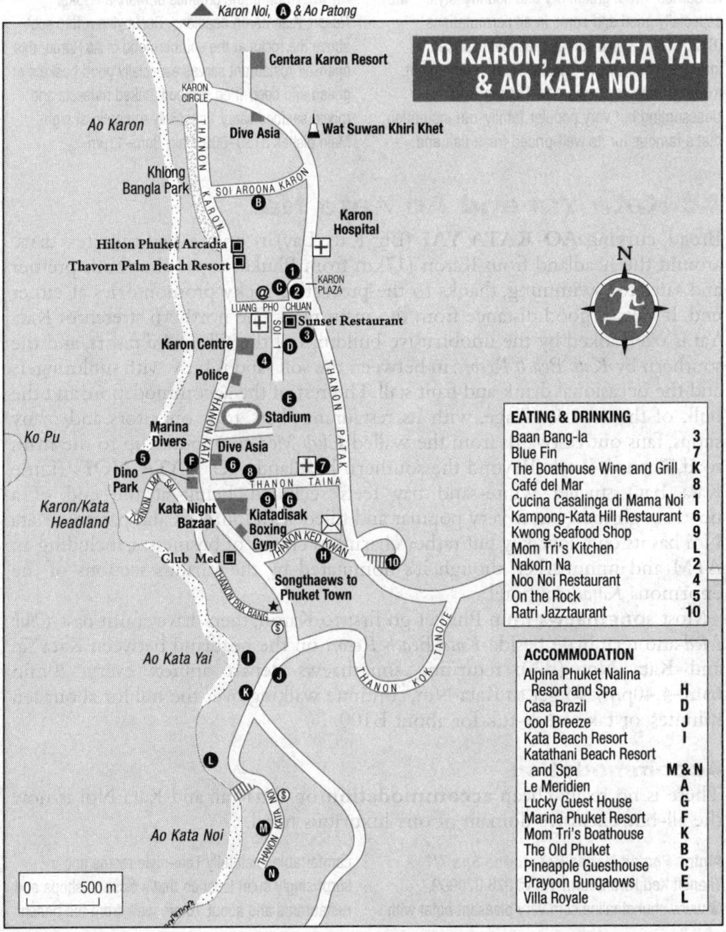

Baan Bang-la 6 Soi Patak, off Thanon Patak. The seafood here has a good reputation and there are also pizzas, pasta dishes and Thai cuisine on the menu too. Dining is mostly al fresco in Thai *salas* set around a pretty little garden. Mains B180–300.

Café del Mar Thanon Taina. An inviting, hip little bar serving margaritas, daiquiris and the rest.

Cucina Casalinga di Mama Noi Karon Plaza off Thanon Patak and Thanon Luang Pho Chuain. Expats, dive staff and Italian tourists fill this place at lunch and dinnertime, savouring the home-from-home taste of the excellent, mid-priced, pizzas and pasta.

Kampong-Kata Hill Restaurant Access via a steep ramp off Thanon Karon. Quality Thai and seafood dishes and fancy Thai-style decor set this place apart and ensure it always gets a good crowd. Its curries – red, green, dry and country-style – are especially good and come in all permutations (B120–180). It also serves reasonably priced imported wine by the glass. Daily 5pm–midnight.

Kwong Seafood Shop 114 Thanon Taina. Unassuming but very popular family-run institution that's famous for its well-priced fresh fish and seafood cooked to order; most dishes B120. Daily 11am–11pm.

Nakorn Na Karon Plaza off Thanon Patak/Thanon Luang Pho Chuain. In among the sports bars, bar-beers and rooms for rent in Karon Plaza are a couple of "art bars" run by cool local creative types, including this invitingly bohemian little place, all driftwood and found objects, with live music nightly from 9pm and a dreadlocked, reggae vibe. Nightly from 7pm.

Noo Noi Restaurant Soi 1, Thanon Luang Pho Chuain. Small, simple, family-run café, in front of the family home, that deserves a mention for determinedly continuing to dish out Thai standards (mainly fried rice and noodle dishes, from B35) at exceptionally cheap prices, despite the inflated rates charged by most other similar places. Daily 8am–10pm.

On the Rock In the grounds of *Marina Phuket Resort*, Kata/Karon headland. Occupying a fine spot above the rocks at the southern end of Ao Karon, this open-air restaurant serves especially good baskets of grilled and deep-fried seafood, baked mussels and mixed seafood satay. Especially romantic at night. Main dishes B150–600. Daily 8am–11pm.

Ao Kata Yai and Ao Kata Noi

Broad, curving **AO KATA YAI** (Big Kata Bay) is only a few minutes' drive around the headland from Karon (17km from Phuket town), but both prettier and safer for swimming, thanks to the protective rocky promontories at either end. It's also a good distance from the main road. The northern stretch of Kata Yai is overlooked by the unobtrusive buildings of the *Club Med* resort, and the southern by *Kata Beach Resort*: in between the soft sand is busy with sunloungers and the occasional drink and fruit stall. The rest of the accommodation, and the bulk of the tourist village, with its restaurants, bars, tour operators and many shops, fans out eastwards from the walled *Club Med* compound, up to the main road, Thanon Patak. Beyond the southern headland, **AO KATA NOI**'s (Little Kata Bay) smaller white-sand bay feels secluded, being at the end of a no-through road, but is very popular and filled with loungers and parasols. Kata Noi has its own low-key but rather charmless cluster of businesses, including an ATM and minimarket, though it's dominated by the various sections of the enormous *Katathani* hotel.

Most **songthaews** from Phuket go first to Karon, then drive south past *Club Med* and terminate beside *Kata Beach Resort* on the headland between Kata Yai and Kata Noi (B30; returning songthaews depart approx every 20min 6am–4.40pm). To get to Kata Noi, continue walking over the hill for about ten minutes, or take a tuk-tuk for about B100.

Accommodation

There is no really cheap **accommodation** on Kata Yai, and Kata Noi is now the all-but-exclusive domain of one luxurious hotel.

Alpina Phuket Nalina Resort and Spa 7/1 Thanon Ked Kwan, **Kata Yai** ⓣ076 370999, ⓦwww.phuketnalina.com. Very pleasant hotel with comfortable, tastefully Thai-style rooms and a surprisingly quiet location that's close to shops and restaurants and about 10min walk from the beach.

A free shuttle also runs guests to the hotel's private beach club in front of *Club Med*. Rooms have generous balconies overlooking the freeform pool and the hills beyond, with some enjoying direct pool access; suites and private pool villas are enormous. Also has a spa, several restaurants and wi-fi throughout. 9

Cool Breeze 225 Thanon Kok Tanode, **Kata Yai** ⓣ076 330484, ⓦwww.phuketindex.com/coolbreezebungalows. Though one of the cheapest places in Kata, for your money you get a spacious private bungalow, plus a view of sorts from the terrace (either of the distant sea or of the hilltop Big Buddha in profile), the sixteen bungalows being ranged steeply up the hillside, in a grassy palm- and shrub-filled garden. Interiors are nothing fancy but good value and are sufficiently far above the narrow, noisy road. Fan 4, air-con 5

Kata Beach Resort Thanon Kata, **Kata Yai** ⓣ076 330530, ⓦwww.katagroup.com. This huge 275-room, four-storey hotel occupies a great spot right on the edge of the southern end of Kata Yai's white-sand beach. It has a big, shorefront swimming pool and restaurant, a palm-shaded seaside garden, a kids' pool and lots of watersports facilities, so it's popular with families; some rooms also have direct pool access, and some have sea views Also runs Thai cooking and fruit-carving classes. 9

Katathani Beach Resort and Spa 14 Thanon **Kata Noi** ⓣ076 330124, ⓦwww.katathani.com. The various wings and offshoots of the enormous and luxurious *Katathani* now occupy almost the entire shoreline of small, secluded Kata Noi. The beachfront all-suite Thani wing has the prime position, with the narrow lawn dropping seamlessly onto the white sand; all rooms here have sea-view balconies. Across the effectively private, no-through road, the garden-view Bhuri wing has a distinctively contemporary look and its rooms too are very deluxe. There's broadband throughout and a shuttle service to town and to Patong. The hotel has six restaurants, six swimming pools and a spa, plus tennis courts, a games room, a dive shop and a kids' playground. 9

Mom Tri's Boathouse Thanon Kok Tanode, **Kata Yai** ⓣ076 330015, ⓦwww.boathousephuket.com. Exclusive beachfront boutique hotel, designed by the architect owner in graceful, understated classical Thai style, with just 38 elegantly furnished sea-front rooms, a reputation for classy service, and a famously top-notch restaurant. All rooms have free wi-fi, there's a pool and weekend cooking classes. Also has some even more luxurious suites and studios at *Villa Royale*, a "gourmet hotel" set in landscaped tropical gardens above Kata Noi. Advance booking essential. 9

Eating

Kata Yai's *The Boathouse Wine and Grill* (ⓣ076 330015, ⓦwww.boathousephuket.com) is one of the best-known **restaurants** on Phuket, not least for its famously extensive, award-winning wine list. Its French-Thai menu is also highly rated, offering, among many other interesting choices, pan-roasted beef with *tom yam* sauce and seared sea scallops on risotto with black truffle sauce (mains B410–1900, degustation menus from B1650). The beachside terrace and dining room, attached to the boutique hotel of the same name, enjoy fine views and there are Thai cooking classes here every weekend (see above). Sister restaurant *Mom Tri's Kitchen*, part of the *Villa Royale* hotel complex above Kata Noi, is also well regarded, specializing in Thai-European fusion fine dining. Also worth making the effort for is *Ratri Jazztaurant*, reached by a vertiginous but short climb (or by road) east off Thanon Patak (daily from 5.30pm). This rather sophisticated eyrie makes a panoramic spot for cocktails at sundown, with high-level views across Kata, plenty of squishy sofas to sink into and a good if pricey menu of Thai food (B220–500), including *matsaman* and Indian-Thai curries, and blue-shell crab stuffed with pork and served with plum sauce. The in-house jazz band plays nightly from about 8.30pm and is worth lingering for.

Hat Nai Harn, Hat Ya Nui and Laem Promthep

The favourite beach of the many expats who live in nearby Rawai, **HAT NAI HARN**, 18km southwest of Phuket town, is an exceptionally beautiful curved bay of white sand backed by a stand of casuarinas and plenty of foodstalls but only minimal development. It does get crowded with parasols and loungers, however, and during the monsoon the waves here are huge. The beach is dominated by a luxurious **hotel**, *The Royal Phuket Yacht Club* (Ⓣ076 380200, Ⓦwww.pura-varna.com; ⑨), whose rooms are raked up the hill and all have living-room sized balconies to make the most of the fine sea views. There's slightly cheaper accommodation next door at the well-sited though architecturally unexciting *All Seasons Naiharn Phuket* (Ⓣ076 289327, Ⓦwww.allseasons-naiharn-phuket.com; ⑧–⑨), which offers contemporary styled concrete row rooms with ocean or garden view and a decent-sized pool just over the narrow road from the shore.

Follow the coastal road 2km south around the lumpy headland and you reach the tiny roadside beach of **Hat Ya Nui**, which gets a surprising number of visitors despite being so small and right next to the admittedly quiet road. There are coral reefs very close to shore, though the currents are strong, and kayaks and sunloungers for rent. Two hundred metres uphill from the beach the friendly and very pleasant *Nai Ya Beach Bungalow* (Ⓣ076 238179; ⑤; closed May–Oct) has attractive, en-suite, fan-cooled bamboo bungalows in a garden that's nicely shaded by cashew nut trees and enjoys high-level sea views.

The rugged, wind-blasted, grassy flanked headland of **Laem Promthep**, 1km beyond Hat Ya Nui, marks Phuket's southernmost tip, jutting dramatically – and photogenically – into the deep blue of the Andaman Sea. The cape is one of the island's top beauty spots and at sunset, busloads of tour groups get shipped in to admire the spectacle; Thais pay their respects at the Hindu shrine here, offering elephant figurines in honour of the enshrined four-headed god Brahma and his elephant mount, Erawan. You can escape the crowds by following the trail along the ridge and down to the rocks just above the water.

Songthaews from Phuket town (every 30min; 45min; B40) go to Nai Harn, via Rawai, but for Hat Ya Nui and Laem Promthep you have to do the lengthy climb round the promontory on foot. Taxis from Patong cost about B500.

Hat Rawai

Phuket's southernmost beach, **HAT RAWAI**, was the first to be exploited for tourist purposes, but, half a century on, the hoteliers have moved to the far more appealing sands of Kata and Karon, leaving Rawai to its former inhabitants, the Urak Lawoy *chao ley* ("sea gypsies"; see p.663), and to an expanding expat population. Most visitors are here for the many al fresco **seafood restaurants** along Thanon Viset's beachside promenade, the best and most famous of which is *Salaloy* (daily 10am–10pm), towards the northern end, whose highlights include inexpensive fried fish with turmeric, and omelette topped with baby oysters. Nearby *Nikita's* (daily 10am till late) is a standout among the many expat-favoured café-bars in the area, not least for the horizon-gazing potential from its peaceful tables on the sand (candle-lit at night) and for the well-priced cocktails, wines by the glass and fresh coffees.

Aside from its seafront restaurants, Rawai's chief attraction is the **Phuket Seashell Museum** (daily 8am–6pm; B100), 1500m north of the beach on Highway 4024, which displays some two thousand species of shell, including 380 million-year-old fossils, giant clams, and a 140-carat gold pearl.

Songthaews from Phuket town pass through Rawai (35min; B30) on their way to and from Nai Harn.

Ao Chalong, the Big Buddha and Phuket Aquarium

North of Rawai, the sizeable offshore island of Ko Lone protects the broad sweep of **AO CHALONG**, where many a Chinese fortune was made from the huge quantities of tin mined in the bay. These days, Ao Chalong is the main departure point for dive excursions and fishing trips, and for speedboats to other islands, including Ko Racha Yai, which leave from Chalong Pier, east of the roundabout known as Chalong Circle, or Chalong Ha Yaek. **Songthaews** from Phuket town charge B25.

For islanders, Chalong is important as the site of **Wat Chalong** (8km southwest of Phuket town, on Thanon Chao Fa Nok, aka Route 4022; the Phuket–Karon songthaew passes the entrance), Phuket's loveliest and most famous temple, which enshrines the statue of revered monk Luang Pho Saem, who helped resolve a violent rebellion by migrant Chinese tin-miners in 1876. Elsewhere in the temple compound, the Phra Mahathat chedi is believed to contain a relic of the Buddha.

With your own transport, a visit to Wat Chalong combines well with an uphill pilgrimage to the newly erected **Big Buddha of Phuket**, officially Phra Buddha Mingmongkol Eaknakakeeree (daily dawn to dusk; free; Ⓦwww.mingmongkolphuket.com), a towering 45-metre statue atop Khao Nakkerd that dominates many island vistas, including from Kata Yai to the southwest, and is easily spotted from aeroplane windows. Made of concrete but faced with glistening white-marble tiles, the eastward-looking Buddha boasts enormous proportions: he sits on a lotus flower that's nearly 25m across and even his individual hair curls measure almost a metre each. Views from the base of the statue extend east over Ao Chalong to hilly Ko Lone beyond, while western panoramas take in Kata Noi; it's a popular sunset-viewing spot. **Access** to the Big Buddha is via the very steep and winding six-kilometre Soi Jao Fa 51, signed west off Thanon Chao Fa Nok (West), a couple of kilometres south of Wat Chalong, or 1km north of Chalong Circle. Taxis from Kata, a thirty-minute drive away, charge B800 for the return trip.

Ao Chalong tapers off eastwards into **Laem Panwa**, at the tip of which you'll find the **Phuket Aquarium** (daily 8.30am–4.30pm; B100, kids B50), 10km south of Phuket town and accessible by frequent songthaews from the market (B25). Run by the island's Marine Research Centre, it's not a bad primer for what you might see on a reef and has walk-through tunnels, a touch pool where you can interact with sea cucumbers and sea stars and a feeding show (Sat & Sun 11am).

Accommodation and eating

Though there's no special reason to **stay** in this part of the island, you might make an exception for alternative, traveller-oriented *Shanti Lodge* (Ⓣ076 280233, Ⓦwww.shantilodge.com; ❹–❺), 1500m south down Thanon Chao Fa Nok from Wat Chalong (or 500m north of the Big Buddha turn-off) on Soi Bangrae; the Phuket-Karon songthaew can drop you close by. It's set in a relaxing garden, with salt-water swimming pool and predominantly vegetarian restaurant, and has fan and air-con doubles with or without private bathrooms, some of them wheelchair accessible, and family rooms.

A good reason to dawdle on your way to or from the islands is the prospect of a blowout seafood meal at the classy, long-running *Kan Eang @ Pier* (daily 10.30am–11pm), one of Phuket's most famous **restaurants**, which is handily, and scenically, sited at the mouth of Chalong Pier. The big draw here is of course the seafood, the best of it barbecued old-style on burning coconut husks (from B1200 per kg of crabs, oysters, prawns, cuttlefish and the rest); deep-fried seaweed with shrimps and chill sauce is also good and the *haw mok* (fish curry steamed in a banana leaf) is exceptional. Sister restaurant *Kan Eang 2*, north up the beach, enjoys a similarly good reputation.

Ko Racha Yai

Graced with a couple of awesome white-sand beaches, crystal-clear turquoise water and several well-stocked reefs, the tiny island of **KO RACHA YAI** (**Ko Raya Yai**), 23km south off Ao Chalong, is a popular day-tripping destination (B2000/1400 including hotel transfers, lunch and snorkelling equipment) but is also an enjoyable place to stay for a night or two. Easiest independent access, from November through April, is to join the morning day-trippers' **speedboats** which depart Chalong Pier at 9am and return from the island at about 3pm (45min; B1000 per person one way or B1400 return including Phuket hotel transfers). Longtails from Hat Rawai (1hr 30min) cost about B2500 to charter.

The island measures just 3km by 3km and its beaches are small, so can get crowded with day-trippers. Handsome, deep-cut **Ao Batok** (Patok) is the main docking point, while two minutes' walk over the hill from beside *Bungalow Raya Resort*, north-facing **Ao Siam** is the longest and prettiest bay on the island and still largely backed by coconut palms; it's only really good for swimming at high tide, however. About fifteen minutes' walk due east of Ao Batok, **Ao Ter** has good snorkelling both on the shoreline, where the reef is uninteresting but the fish quite spectacular in range and number, and about 100m offshore, where there are two dive sites, including a small wreck. Further down the east coast, there's even less of a beach at **Ao Kon Kare**, though you can swim here, and its reefs are rewarding for snorkelling and diving. Exploring the interior is also fun; tracks crisscross through palm groves and a couple of hamlets, with plenty of wilderness still in evidence and occasional stands of cashew and jackfruit, mango and tamarind trees, even a few water buffaloes and some resident metre-long iguanas.

Accommodation and eating

Cheapest **accommodation** is at *Raya Seaview Bungalow* (T081 397 5141; 5; closed May–Oct), up on Ao Siam's western cliff, which has pretty en-suite bamboo bungalows, all with fans, mosquito nets and some sort of view. The *Jungle Bar* at the eastern end of the beach does barbecues and occasional live music. On Ao Batok, there are en-suite, fan-cooled bamboo bungalows at *Bungalow Raya Resort* (T076 383136, W rayaresort.net; 6), a couple of which offer unbeatable views over the sparkling sea, plus an attractively sited, if pricey, restaurant. Neighbouring *The Racha* (T076 355455, W www.theracha.com; 9) occupies the main section of the beach with its elegant white-cube and slate-roof buildings, its ultra-luxurious villas and its infinity pool, spa and restaurants.

Northeast Phuket

There's not a great deal for tourists along Phuket's northeast coast. The swanky new **Phuket Royal Marina** caters to yachties and those who can afford the waterfront condo lifestyle, while the mangrove-fringed natural harbour at **Bang Rong** is the departure point for boats to Ko Yao Noi and a speedboat service to Ao Nang, plus chartered longtail tours around the karst islands of western Ao Phang Nga (B3000–5000; see p.716). Inland, there's cultural interest at the museum in **Thalang**, and **rescued gibbons** to visit in **Khao Phra Taew Forest Reserve**.

Thalang and around

As the only official introduction to Phuket's rich and intriguing history, **Thalang National Museum** (daily 9am–4pm; B30; Ⓦwww.thailandmuseum.com) doesn't really match up to the task, but taken in conjunction with the privately funded Thaihua Museum in Phuket town, the picture starts to flesh out. Displays include some interesting exhibits on the local tin and rubber industries, accounts of some of the more colourful folkloric traditions and photos of the masochistic feats of the Vegetarian Festival (see box, p.686). The museum is on Route 4027, 200m east of the landmark **Heroines' Monument**, which stands in the centre of the Tha Rua junction, 12km north of Phuket town on Highway 402. The monument commemorates the repulse of the Burmese army by the widow of the governor of Phuket and her sister in 1785; together they rallied the island's womenfolk who, legend has it, frightened the Burmese away by cutting their hair short and rolling up banana leaves to look like musket barrels – a victory that's celebrated every March 13–15 with a monks' ordination ceremony and processions. All mainland-bound traffic and all **songthaews** between Phuket and Hat Surin and Hat Nai Yang pass the monument.

Eight kilometres north of the Heroines' Monument, just beyond the crossroads in the district town of **THALANG**, stands **Wat Phra Thong**, one of Phuket's most revered temples on account of the power of the Buddha statue it enshrines. The solid gold image is half-buried and no one dares dig it up for fear of a curse that has struck down excavators in the past. After the wat was built around the statue, the image was encased in plaster to deter would-be robbers.

Khao Phra Taew Forest Reserve and the Gibbon Project

The minor road east of the Thalang intersection takes you to the visitor centre of **KHAO PHRA TAEW WILDLIFE PARK AND FOREST RESERVE**, 3km away. Several paths cross this small hilly enclave, leading you through the forest habitat of macaques and wild boar, but the most popular features of the park are the Gibbon Rehabilitation Project and the Ton Sai and Bang Pae waterfalls, which combine well as a day-trip (or on a tour, see p.691). The Gibbon Project is located about 10km northeast of the Heroines' Monument, off Route 4027. **Songthaews** from Phuket town, more frequent in the morning, will take you most of the way: ask to be dropped off at Bang Pae (a 40min drive from town) and then follow the signed track for about 1km to get to the project centre. You can get drinks and snacks at the foodstall next to the Rehabilitation Centre, and the route to the waterfalls is signed from here.

The Gibbon Rehabilitation Project

Phuket's forests used to resound with the whooping calls of indigenous white-handed lar gibbons, but they make such charismatic pets that they were poached to extinction on the island by the mid-1980s. The lar is now an endangered species, and in 1992 it became illegal in Thailand to keep them as pets, to sell them or to kill them. Despite this, you'll come across a depressing number of pet gibbons on Phuket, kept in chains by bar and hotel owners as entertainment for their customers. The **Gibbon Rehabilitation Centre** (daily 9am–4pm, last tour at 3.15pm; national park entry B200, kids 100; Ⓦwww.gibbonproject.org) aims to reverse this state of affairs, first by rescuing as many pet gibbons as they can, and then by resocializing and re-educating them for the wild before finally releasing them back into the forests. It is apparently not unusual for gibbons to be severely traumatized by their experience as pets: not only will they have been taken forcibly from their mothers, but they may also have been abused by their owners.

Visitors are welcome at the project, which is centred in the forests of Khao Phra Taew Reserve, protected as a "non-hunting area", close to Bang Pae waterfall, but because the whole point of the rehab project is to minimize the gibbons' contact with humans, you can only admire the creatures from afar. There's a small exhibition here on the aims of the project, and the well-informed volunteer guides will fill you in on the details of each case and on the idiosyncratic habits of the lar gibbon (see p.828 for more about Thailand's primates). Should you want to become a **project volunteer** yourself, adopt a gibbon, or make a donation, you can email the project centre.

Bang Pae and Ton Sai waterfalls

If you follow the track along the river from the Gibbon Project, you'll soon arrive at **Bang Pae Falls**, a popular picnic and bathing spot, ten to fifteen minutes' walk away. Continue on the track for another 2.8km (about 1hr 30min on foot) and you should reach **Ton Sai Falls**: though not a difficult climb, the route is unsigned and indistinct, is steep in places and rough underfoot. There are plenty of opportunities for cool dips in the river en route. Once at Ton Sai you can either walk back down to the Khao Phra Taew Reserve access road and try to hitch a ride back home, or return the way you came.

Ko Yao Noi

Located in an idyllic spot on the edge of Phang Nga bay, almost equidistant from Phuket, Phang Nga and Krabi, the island of **KO YAO NOI** enjoys magnificent maritime views from almost every angle and makes a refreshingly tranquil getaway. Measuring about 12km at its longest point, it's home to some four thousand islanders, the vast majority of them Muslim, who earn their living from rubber and coconut plantations, fishing and shrimp-farming. Tourism here is low key, not least because the beaches lack the wow factor of more sparkling nearby sands, and visitors are drawn instead by the rural ambience and lack of commercial pressures. Nonetheless, there's decent swimming off the east coast at high tide, and at low tide too in a few places, and plenty of potential for kayaking and rock-climbing. Most tourists stay on the east side, which has the bulk of the accommodation, at **Hat Tha Khao**, **Hat Klong Jaak** (**Long Beach**), **Hat Pasai** and **Laem Sai**. Exploring the interior is a particular pleasure, either via the barely trafficked round-island road as it runs through tiny villages and the island's diminutive town, **Ban Tha Khai**, or via the trails that crisscross the forested interior, where you've a good chance of encountering monkeys as well as cobras and even pythons, not to mention plenty of birds, including majestic oriental pied hornbills.

Getting to Ko Yao Noi

There are three mainland departure points for **boats** to Ko Yao Noi – from Phuket, Krabi's Ao Thalen, and Phang Nga – plus a speedboat service from Ao Nang. Ko Yao Noi **taxis** meet all arriving boats and charge B70–100 per person for transfers to accommodation.

The most common route is **from Bang Rong** on Phuket's northeast coast (approximately hourly 7.30am–5pm; 1hr 10min; B120), which is served,

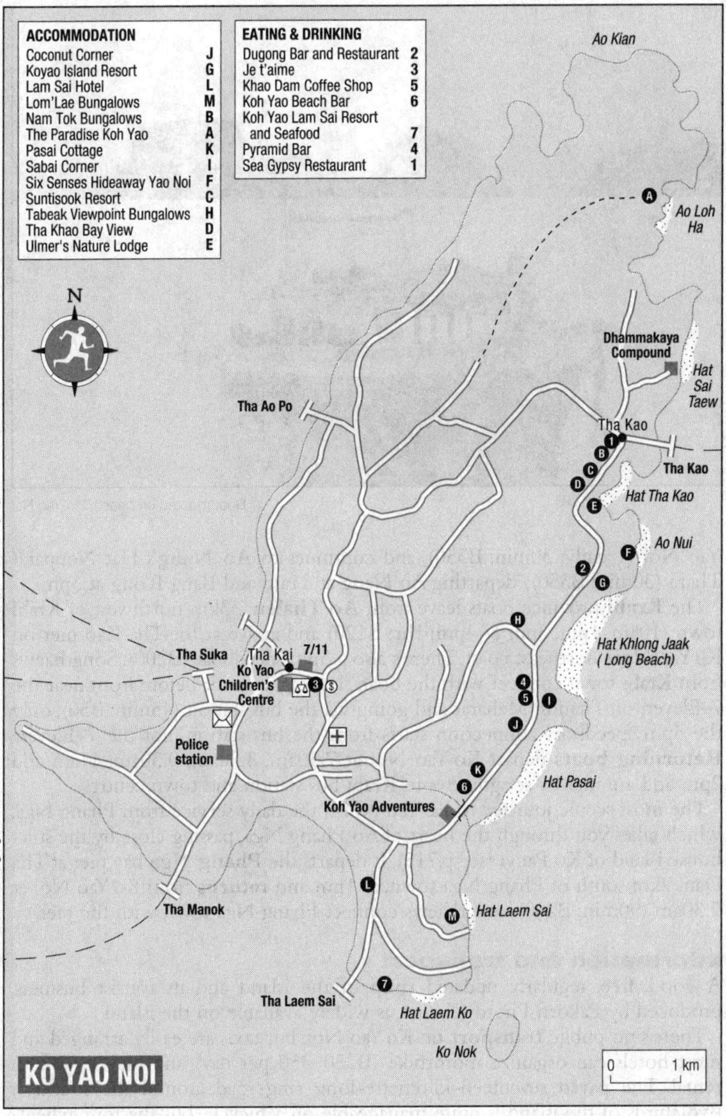

mornings only, by songthaews from Phuket town's Thanon Ranong market (8.30–11am; 90min; B35); a taxi to Bang Rong from town or the main beaches costs about B500. Bang Rong boats dock at Tha Manok or Tha Suka on Ko Yao Noi's southwest coast, depending on the tide. Returning **to Bang Rong**, boats depart Tha Manok every one to two hours from 7.15am to 4.40pm; songthaews meet incoming boats for transfers to Phuket town, or the taxi service charges B500 to Phuket airport, B700 to Patong and B2000 to Khao Lak. The Green Planet **speedboat** service also connects Bang Rong with Ko

▲ Boat moored on beach, Ko Yao Noi

Yao Noi (1 daily; 30min; B350), and continues to **Ao Nang**'s Hat Nopparat Thara (30min; B350), departing Ao Nang at 11am and Bang Rong at 3pm.

The **Krabi** province boats leave from **Ao Thalen**, 33km northwest of Krabi town (10am, 1pm, 3pm & 4pm; 1hr; B120) and arrive at the Tha Kao pier on Ko Yao Noi's northeast coast. There's also a 5pm speedboat (B200). Songthaews from Krabi town connect with the boats, leaving an hour before from near the 7-Eleven on Thanon Maharat and going via the bus station (45min; B50); only the 5pm speedboat connection starts from the bus station, not the 7–Eleven. **Returning boats** depart Ko Yao Noi at 7.30am, 8.30am, 9.30am, 11am and 2pm and are met by songthaews to Krabi bus station and town centre.

The most scenic journey to Ko Yao Noi is the daily service from Phang Nga, which takes you through the heart of Ao Phang Nga, passing close by the stilt-house island of Ko Panyi (see p.715). It departs the **Phang Nga** bay pier at Tha Dan, 9km south of Phang Nga town, at 1pm and **returns** from Ko Yao Noi at 7.30am (90min; B200); songthaews connect Phang Nga town with the pier.

Information and transport

A good, free, regularly updated **map** of the island and its tourist business, produced by Pakorn Photo Classics, is widely available on the island.

There's no public **transport** on Ko Yao Noi, but taxis are easily arranged and most hotels can organize motorbike (B250–350 per day) and bicycle (B200) rental. The paved seventeen-kilometre-long ring road around the southern two-thirds of the island is quite manageable on a bicycle, but the four-wheel-drive track up to *Paradise* on the northeast coast is notoriously challenging, especially for motorbikes. Koh Yao Adventures on Pasai (Ⓣ076 597553, Ⓦwww.kohyaoadventures.com) leads **bicycle tours** around neighbouring big-sister island Ko Yao Yai (B2500); they can also book **buses to Bangkok** via Phuket or Krabi and transport to Ko Samui.

Activities and day-trips

Kayaking around the coast is a very enjoyable pastime, and the dozens of tiny islands visible from eastern shorelines make enticing destinations for experienced paddlers; kayaks can be rented through Ko Yao Noi hotels for about B150 per hour and guided kayaking trips around Ao Phang Nga cost B2700–3500. For a really special kayaking experience, contact Koh Kayak Expeditions at *Coconut Corner* on Hat Pasai (ⓣ0879 294320, ⓦwww.kayakthailand.com), who rent out their good-quality kayaks fully equipped for self-guided overnight expeditions that can last anything from 24 hours to a month (B1200 per single or B1800 per tandem per 24hr, including camping equipment plus an itinerary and maps).

Every hotel sells **snorkelling** trips to Ko Hong and other islands in Ao Phang Nga (B2300), but **diving** trips and courses are the speciality of Koh Yao Dive and Marine Sports (ⓦwww.kohyaodiver.com), based at *Lom'Lae* and with branches in Laem Sai, at *Paradise* and at *Dugong Bar and Restaurant*. Dives to the reefs around Phuket and Phi Phi cost B3600–4600 and the Openwater course is B16,800.

Ko Yao Noi is fast becoming a respected destination for **rock-climbers**, who appreciate the fresh sites and uncrowded routes compared to the hectic scene at nearby Ton Sai and Railay. There are over a hundred bolted routes on the island, from beginner level to advanced (5 to 8A), established by the American and Thai climbers who run The Mountain Shop at *Sea Gypsy Restaurant* in Ban Tha Khao (ⓣ083 969 2023, ⓦwww.themountainshop.org). Many routes are over water and accessible only by boat, or at the least via a hike off the dirt track to *Paradise* hotel. There's also a climbing wall at *Paradise*, along with a branch office and equipment rental; on Long Beach, ask at *Khao Dam Coffee Shop*. Prices range from B2500 for a half-day's climb to B10,000 for a three-day skills' course; climbing is possible year-round but from May to October operates only out of *Paradise*.

There's also guided **birdwatching** with Thailand Bird Watching (ⓦwww.thailandbirdwatching.com; B3500 per half day) based at *Ulmer's Nature Lodge* on Hat Tha Khao – Ko Yao Noi has some 150 resident species – and **yoga and meditation**, also at *Ulmer's* (B100 per class or B3000 for an all-inclusive three-day retreat).

Hat Tha Khao and Hat Sai Taew

The most northerly of the main eastern beaches is **HAT THA KHAO**, site of a small village, **BAN THA KHAO**, with a couple of shops and restaurants, the pier for boats to and from Krabi, and the cheapest and most backpacker-oriented bungalows on the island. It's also the closest point to Ko Yao's nicest beach, so-called **Temple Beach** or **Hat Sai Taew**, 2km away, whose pretty, gold-sand shore is great for swimming at any tide. However, it's backed by private land that belongs to the Dhammakaya Foundation, a popular Buddhist sect, and is unsigned and a bit tricky to find. From Tha Khao pier, head inland and take the first right behind the shops, walk alongside the khlong and its sheltered marina, over the bridge, then via the faint trail over the hill to the beach. Or just kayak there from the pier.

Accommodation and eating

All the **bungalows** have **restaurants**, but for a change of scene there's also *Sea Gypsy Restaurant* (Nov–April only), near the pier, which has a small bar and serves à la carte Thai food as well as family-style dinners nightly for anyone who books earlier in the day.

Nam Tok Bungalows ⓣ087 292 1102. Set back from the beach, beside a khlong, a 5min walk south from the Tha Khao ferry pier, this ultra laid-back set of bungalows is one of the cheapest places to stay on the island. The budget options are spacious and comfortable wooden huts, with cute garden bathrooms and hammocks on the deck, encircling a small garden full of flowers and a fishpond; the more luxurious ones have hot water. *Nam Tok*'s manager, Danny, takes guests on camping trips to Ko Pak Bia (B5000 per boat) and also arranges massage and healing sessions with locally famous masseur Bao. 3–5

Suntisook Resort ⓣ089 781 6456, ⓦwww.suntisookkohyao.com. Run by a couple of former teachers and their genial son E, *Suntisook*'s nine bungalows are nicely spaced around a garden and mostly come with TVs, fridges and good bathrooms. They're all a bit different but each has a deck and a hammock and some have air-con and three beds. Discounts often available. 4–7

Tha Khao Bay View ⓣ086 942 0812. You have to climb a fair few steps up the cliffside to reach the simple but comfortably appointed en-suite bungalows here but the bay views from the hammocks on their decks are well worth it, and the restaurant enjoys the same panoramic outlook. 3–4

Ulmer's Nature Lodge ⓣ084 848 5112, ⓦwww.thailandbirdwatching.com. Occupying a peaceful spot on the edge of the mangroves, down a track at the far southern end of the bay, *Ulmer's Nature Lodge* is establishing itself as a centre for birdwatching and yoga, though of course anyone is welcome to stay at its five shoreside bungalows, all of which are en suite. 3

Hat Klong Jaak (Long Beach) and Hat Pasai

A couple of kilometres south of Hat Tha Khao, **HAT KLONG JAAK**, more commonly referred to as **Long Beach**, is the site of the longest-running and best-known tourist accommodation and the liveliest places to eat and drink. The beach is indeed long, around 1500m from the northern end to *Sabai Corner* on the southern headland. Much of it is rocky and all but unswimmable at low tide, except in front of *Koyao Island Resort*, the smoothest stretch. The seaward views are glorious from every angle, however, taking in the many lovely islets of eastern Ao Phang Nga. A minute's walk south from *Sabai Corner* and you're on **HAT PASAI**, a rather pretty little beach, with some shade, plus several bungalows, restaurant-bars and a tiny shop.

Accommodation

Coconut Corner ⓣ076 454221, ⓦwww.kohyaotravel.com. Offering some of the cheapest and most traveller-friendly accommodation on the island, in simple en-suite bungalows set around a small garden just across the road from the northern end of Hat Pasai beach. It's just a few minutes' walk from *Pyramid Bar* on Long Beach and has internet access, bicycle and motorbike rental. 3

Koyao Island Resort ⓣ076 597474, ⓦwww.koyao.com. This lovely, stylish resort occupies the best part of the beach and comprises just fifteen chic, thatched, fan-cooled cottage compounds, all of them with separate living areas, huge bathrooms, and sliding doors that give access to the spacious garden and its fine bay views. There's a swimming pool and spa, internet access and a restaurant serving expensive European food. 9

Pasai Cottage ⓣ076 597064, ⓦwww.kohyaotravel.com. The ten bamboo cottages here, just across from Pasai's beach but away from the road, have unexpectedly tasteful interiors, folding glass doors and prettily tiled bathrooms. 4

Sabai Corner ⓣ081 892 1827, ⓦwww.sabaicornerbungalows.com. Occupying Long Beach's rocky southern point, this long-established, Italian-Thai, laid-back little outfit has ten thoughtfully designed wooden bungalows, all with fans, nets and rustic bathrooms, plus decks and hammocks. They're dotted along a rise between the road and the beach, under cashew and jackfruit trees. Internet access, bicycle and a good restaurant on site. 4–6

Six Senses Hideaway Yao Noi ⓣ076 418500, ⓦwww.sixsenses.com. Extraordinarily luxurious and expensive retreat, hidden in its own little bay and accessed by a private road. The huge villas are designed in natural-chic style, mostly wood and thatch, but all come with private pool, expansive sun deck and personal staff. Rates from B45,500. 9

Tabeak Viewpoint Bungalows ⓣ089 590 4182, ⓦwww.kohyaotravel.com. Two hundred metres inland, on a cross-island track, this Japanese-Thai-run place has large, well-outfitted, fan-cooled, wood and bamboo bungalows, all with polished wood floors and French windows and balconies that give commanding views of the islands. The Thai owner is a community policeman and enthusiastic fisherman and an excellent source of island information. 5

Eating and drinking

Island expats congregate at the tiny Swiss–Thai café, the *Khao Dam Coffee Shop* (daily 8am–6pm; Nov–April only), about 200m north of *Sabai Corner*, drawn both by its invitingly chilled vibe and by the fresh coffees, delicious banana-chocolate muffins, home-made bread, sandwiches and salads. You can ask here about rock-climbing and can also buy le cloth bags painted by the kids at Children's Centre in Thai Khai. Next door, *Pyramid Bar* is another famous island meeting place, with its pool tabl sports TV and extensive **bar** menu; it's at its liveliest on Friday nights when lf the island turns up for the very enjoyable weekly sets by island musicians 30pm till late). *Koh Yao Beach Bar*, at the southern end of Hat Pasai, also pu n live music nights in high season, and serves good seafood through the ek. North up Long Beach, opposite *Koyao Island Resort*, *Dugong Bar and taurant* occupies a beautiful barn-like structure built from recycled woo y its batik artist and dive instructor owner and serves good Thai food, c ails and the rest.

Laem Sai

Beyond Hat Pasai, tiny **HAT LAEM SAI** ften known simply as **Hat Lom'Lae**, after the appealing Thai-Canad *Lom'Lae Bungalows* (ⓣ076 597486, ⓦwww.lomlae.com; ❼, family hous closed May–Sept) which sits on the shore. It's a beautiful, secluded haven ked by ricefields and rubber plantations and enjoying stunning bay views n its palm-fringed beach and grassy garden. The eight attractive, wooden, cooled bungalows are widely spaced and have sliding doors, decks and har cks to capitalize on the vistas. Some have additional upstairs loft beds, an ere are two-bedroom family houses as well. Kayaks, bikes and motorbikes available for rent and there's a dive shop and cooking classes.

A few hundred metres west from the *Lom* turn-off, about 3km from Tha Kai, another side-road takes you down toward **em Sai pier**, along a coast that has no real beach but is scenically dotted wi ouses on stilts, fishing platforms, dozens of longtails and some inviting views Ko Yao Noi's larger twin, Ko Yao Yai, just across the channel. A British father-daughter team run the *Lam Sai Hotel* here, a two-storey block of just eight g -quality tiled rooms, all with TVs and balconies and use of the swimmin pool (ⓣ0847 463861, ⓦwww.lamsaihotel.com; fan ❹, air-con ❻). What r lly sets them apart is that both are **muay thai boxers**; they run training sessio at their sea-view Ko Yao Noi Gym here (B250 for a two-hour drop-in class c B2000 for a week of classes) and during high season stage monthly fights open to the public (ⓦwww.phuket-krabi-muaythai.com). About 1.5km further down the road, beyond where the paving stops, *Koh Yao Lam Sai Resort and Seafood* is a great place for a **seafood lunch**, and there's a nice little beach 300m east further around the rocks.

Ban Tha Kai and north

The island's commercial and administrative centre is **BAN THA KAI**, inland from the main piers on the southwest coast. This is where you'll find the post office, bank with **exchange** counter, hospital, police station (ⓣ089 590 4182), obligatory 7-Eleven shop with **ATM** (which sometimes runs out of money), as well as a couple of **internet** centres, the main market and several roti stalls; at the crossroads, the welcoming *Je t'aime* **restaurant** is especially good for locally caught fish and seafood and has occasional live music.

Visitors are very much encouraged to drop by the **Ko Yao Children's Community Centre** (Mon–Wed 4.30–6.30pm, Sat & Sun 8.30am–4.30pm;

ⓦwww.koyao-ccc.com), at the western end of town, an NGO that aims to help improve the English-language and computer skills of island children and adults; the kids also paint and sell cloth shopping bags to support environmental projects on Ko Yao Noi. You can also experience a little of island family life for yourself in Ban Tha Kai, which runs a **homestay** community-based tourism project involving twenty local families (from B2000 per person for an all-inclusive two-day programme; ⓣ06 942 7999, ⓦwww.kohyao-cbt.com).

The road running **north fro Tha Kai**'s 7-Eleven is particularly scenic, taking you through several hamlets w their mosques and latex-pressing mangles, and past ricefields and their reside buffaloes, framed by mangroves in the middle distance, sea eagles hovering oead, and the rounded hills of nearby islands in the background. At a junction ut 3km from Thai Khai, the northbound road soon turns into a horrible tracding to Ao Loh Ha, while veering right will take you over the hill and dow Tha Khao on the east coast, about 4km away.

Within a couple of kilometre northbound road to **AO LOH HA**, Ko Yao Noi's northernmost beachs into rough, four-wheel-drive-only track which finally ends at the deluxtched rooms and villas of *The Paradise Koh Yao* (ⓣ081 892 4878, ⓦwwwradise.biz; ⓞ). The beach here is a picture, and there's a huge pool, an ouspa and a climbing wall.

Ao Phang Nga

Protected from the ravages of Andaman Sea by Phuket, **AO PHANG NGA** has a seascape both bizad beautiful. Covering some four hundred square kilometres of coast betwehuket and Krabi, the mangrove-edged bay is spiked with limestone karst foons up to 300m in height, jungle-clad and craggily profiled. This is Thailanwn version of Vietnam's world-famous Ha Long bay, reminiscent too of Gu scenery in China, and much of it is now preserved as **national park** (entr00; ⓦwww.dnp.go.th/National_park.asp). The bay is thought to have been fled about twelve thousand years ago when a dramatic rise in sea level floodee summits of mountain ranges, which over millions of years had been eroded an acidic mixture of atmospheric carbon dioxide and rainwater. Some of the karst islands have been further eroded in such a way that they are now holw, hiding secret lagoons or *hongs* that can only be accessed at certain tides an only by kayak. The main *hong* islands are in the **western** and **eastern** bay reas – to the west or east of Ko Yao Noi, which sits roughly mid-way between Phuket and Krabi. But the most famous scenery is in the **central bay** area, which boasts the biggest concentration of karst islands, and the weirdest rock formations.

Exploring the bay

There are several **departure points** for tours of the bay and several ways of seeing its many attractions. The most rewarding, and generally the most expensive option is to join a **sea-canoeing** trip (either guided or self-paddle), which enables you both to explore inside the *hongs* and to see at close quarters the extraordinary ecosystems around and inside the karst islands. Most sea-canoeing tours use large support boats carrying groups of up to thirty people; they can be arranged from any resort in Phuket, at Khao Lak, at all Krabi beaches and islands, and on Ko Yao Noi (see relevant resort accounts for details and prices), but the itinerary is usually determined by your departure point, with Phuket trips focusing on the western bay and Krabi tours concentrating on the eastern half. Most tours of the central bay are either in large **tour boats** booked out of Phuket or Krabi, which generally feature snorkelling and beach stops rather than kayaking, or in inexpensive, small-group **longtail boats** that depart from Phang Nga town, Phuket and Ko Yao Noi. All the main areas of the bay are extremely popular so don't expect a solitary experience.

The central bay

On tours of the **central bay**, the standard itinerary follows a circular or figure-of-eight route, passing extraordinary karst silhouettes that change character with the shifting light – in the eerie glow of an early morning mist it can be a breathtaking experience. Some of the formations have nicknames suggested by their weird outlines – like **Khao Machu** (**Marju**), which translates as "Pekinese Rock". Others have titles derived from other attributes – **Tham Nak** (or Nark, meaning Naga Cave) gets its name from the serpentine stalagmites inside; **Ko Thalu** (Pierced Cave) has a tunnel through it; and a close inspection of **Khao Kien** (Painting Rock) reveals a cliff wall decorated with paintings of elephants, monkeys, fish, crabs and hunting weapons, believed to be between three thousand and five thousand years old.

Ao Phang Nga's most celebrated features, however, earned their tag from a movie: the cleft **Khao Ping Gan** (Leaning Rock) and its tapered outcrop **Khao Tapu** (Nail Rock) are better known as **James Bond Island**, having starred as Scaramanga's hideaway in *The Man With the Golden Gun*. Every boat stops off here so tourists can pose in front of the iconic rock – whose narrowing base is a good example of how wave action is shaping the bay – and the island crawls with seashell and trinket vendors.

The central bay's other major attraction is **Ko Panyi**, a Muslim village built almost entirely on stilts around the rock that supports the mosque. Nearly all boat tours stop here for lunch, so you're best off avoiding the pricey seafood restaurants around the jetty, and heading instead towards the islanders' foodstalls near the mosque. You can enjoy a more tranquil Ko Panyi experience by joining one of the overnight tours from Phang Nga town (see p.718), which include an evening meal and guest-house accommodation on the island – and the chance

▲ Ao Phang Nga

The hongs

Hongs are the *pièce de résistance* of Ao Phang Nga: invisible to any passing vessel, these secret tidal lagoons are enclosed within the core of seemingly impenetrable limestone outcrops, accessible via murky tunnels that can only be navigated at certain tides in kayaks small enough to slip beneath and between low-lying rocky overhangs. Like the karsts themselves, the *hongs* have taken millions of years to form, with the softer limestone hollowed out from above by the wind and the rain, and from the side by the pounding waves. Eventually, when the two hollows met, the heart of the karst was able to fill with water via the wave-eroded passageway at sea level, creating a lagoon. The world inside these roofless hollows is an extraordinary one, protected from the open bay by a ring of cliff faces hung with vertiginous prehistoric-looking gardens of upside-down cycads, twisted bonsai palms and tangled ferns. And as the tide withdraws, the *hong's* resident creatures emerge to forage on the muddy floor, among them fiddler crabs, mudskippers, dusky langurs and crab-eating macaques, with white-bellied sea eagles often hovering overhead.

to watch the sun set and rise over the bay; you can also rent a kayak from the jetty and go exploring yourself.

At some point on your central bay tour you should pass several small brick **kilns** on the edge of a mangrove swamp, which were once used for producing charcoal from mangrove wood. You'll also be ferried beneath **Tham Lod**, a photogenic archway roofed with stalactites that opens onto spectacular limestone and mangrove vistas.

The western bay: Ko Panak and Ko Hong

The main attraction of **the western bay** is **Ko Panak**, whose limestone cliffs hide secret tunnels to no less than five different **hongs** within its hollowed heart. These are probably Ao Phang Nga's most spectacular hidden worlds, the pitch-black tunnel approaches infested by bats and the bright, roofless *hongs* an entire other world, draped in hanging gardens of lianas and miniature screw pines and busy with cicadas and the occasional family of crab-eating macaques. Western-bay tours also usually take in nearby **Ko Hong** (different from the Ko Hong in the eastern bay), whose exterior walls are coated with red, yellow and orange encrusting sponges, oyster shells and chitons (560 million-year-old slipper-shaped shells), which all make good camouflage for the scuttling red, blue and black crabs. Ko Hong's interior passageways light up with bioluminescent plankton in the dark and lead to a series of cave-lagoons.

The eastern bay: Ko Hong, Ao Thalen and Ao Luk

The principal *hong* island in the **eastern bay**, known both as **Ko Hong** and **Ko Lao Bileh**, lies about mid-way between Krabi's Hat Klong Muang beach and the southeast coast of Ko Yao Noi. The island is fringed by white-sand beaches and exceptionally clear aquamarine waters that make it a popular snorkelling destination. The island's actual *hong* lacks the drama of Ao Phang Nga's best *hongs* because it's not fully enclosed or accessed via dark tunnels as at Ko Panak, but it is pretty, full of starfish, and tidal, so can only be explored at certain times.

The eastern bay's other big attractions are the mangrove-fringed inlets along the mainland coast between Krabi and Phang Nga, particularly around **Ao Luk** and **Ao Thalen** (sometimes Ao Talin or Talane), though the latter can get very crowded with tour groups. Trips around here take you through complex networks of channels that weave through the mangrove swamps, between fissures in the limestone cliffs, beneath karst outcrops and into the occasional cave. Many of these passageways are *hongs*, isolated havens that might be up to 2km long, all but cut off from the main bay and accessible only at certain tides. The **Ban Bor Tor** (or Ban Bho Tho) area of Ao Luk bay is especially known for **Tham Lod**, a long tunnel hung with stalagmites and stalactites whose entrance is obscured by vines, and for nearby **Tham Phi Hua Toe**, whose walls display around a hundred prehistoric cave-paintings, as well as some interestingly twisted stalactite formations.

Phang Nga town and around

Friendly if unexciting little **PHANG NGA TOWN**, beautifully located under looming limestone cliffs edged with palm groves mid-way between Phuket and Krabi, serves mainly as a point from which to organize budget longtail trips around the spectacular karst islands of Ao Phang Nga. But there are also several caves and waterfalls nearby, accessible either on cheap tours run by every Phang Nga tour operator, or by motorbike, and you can also arrange trips to Ko Similan and Ko Surin.

Arrival and information

Phang Nga has good **bus** connections: all Krabi-bound services from Phuket and Takua Pa make a stop at the bus station (Ⓣ076 412014) on Thanon Phetkasem, located towards the northern end of this long, thin town; if you're heading to or from Khao Sok, it's usually fastest to change buses in Takua Pa. There are also useful services from Phang Nga to Surat Thani, with the 10.30am bus going direct to Ko Samui, and to Trang. Taxis from Phang Nga to **Phuket airport** cost B1100, to Khao Lak B1200 and to Khao Sok B1600. The pier for **boats** around Ao Phang Nga, and to Ko Yao Noi, is at Tha Dan, 9km south of town and served by songthaews that pass the bus station (B25).

There's no official **tourist information**, but the several tour operators inside the bus station compound are helpful and will store your baggage for a few hours; they also sell bus and boat tickets.

If you turn right (north) out of the bus station onto Thanon Phetkasem, you'll find **banks**, with exchange counters and ATMs and several **internet** centres. Most other municipal facilities are further south down Thanon Phetkasem: the **police station** (Ⓣ076 430390) and immigration office (Ⓣ076 412011) are about 500m south of the bus station, off Soi Thungchedi, the **telephone office** is another 100m south of them, and Phang Nga Hospital (Ⓣ076 412034) and the **post office** are over 2km south of the bus station.

Accommodation

Phang Nga's best budget **hotels** are within 250m of the bus station, on the bus station side of Thanon Phetkasem. First up, on the right-hand side as you turn right out of the bus station, is *Phang Nga Guest House* at no. 99/1 (Ⓣ076 411358; fan ❷, air-con ❸–❹), which has clean and comfortable en-suite rooms, though few have anything but a brick-wall view. The old-style, fastidiously maintained *Thawisuk Hotel* at no. 77 (Ⓣ076 412100; fan ❶, air-con ❸) has very clean and bright fan rooms, a couple of huge air-con options, and a rooftop terrace. The best accommodation in town is at *Phang Nga Inn* (Ⓣ076 411963, Ⓔphang-ngainn@hotmail.com; ❸–❹), a converted family home that's clearly signed to the left of the bus station, about 250m away, at 2/2 Soi Lohakji, just off Thanon Phetkasem. Its fourteen rooms have beautiful polished wood floors and attractive furnishings and are equipped with air-con, hot water, wi-fi and TVs; a couple have no windows, however.

Tours of Ao Phang Nga

The most popular budget tours of Ao Phang Nga are the **longtail-boat trips** run by tour operators based inside Phang Nga bus station. Competition between these outfits is fierce and the itineraries they offer are almost identical (see p.714), so it's best to get recommendations from other tourists fresh from a bay trip, especially as reputations fluctuate with every change of staff. To date the one that's remained most constant is Mr Kean Tour (Ⓣ076 430619); next door but one is Sayan Tour (Ⓣ076 430348, Ⓦwww.sayantour.com). Both offer half-day tours of the bay (daily at about 8.30am & 2pm; 3–4hr) costing B500 per person (minimum four people), as well as full-day extensions, which last until 4pm and cost B800, including lunch; take the 8.30am tour to avoid seeing the bay at its most crowded. All tours include a chance to swim in the bay, and most offer the option of an hour's canoeing around Ko Thalu as well, for an extra B300.

All tour operators also offer the chance to **stay** overnight at their own guest house on **Ko Panyi**. This can be tacked onto the half- or full-day tour for an extra B250 (departures at 8am, 2pm & 4pm); dinner, accommodation, and morning coffee are included in the price. In 2010 Mr Kean will also offer an interesting-sounding alternative overnight programme on his home island of **Ban Mai Phai**, a much less commercial version of Ko Panyi; the B1200 fee should include food and accommodation, plus cycle and kayak use and the chance to trek and go rock-climbing.

Around Phang Nga town

One of the most famous caves near Phang Nga town is **Tham Phung Chang**, or **Elephant Belly Cave**, a natural 1200-metre-long tunnel through the massive 800-metre-high wooded cliff that towers over the Provincial Hall, about 4km west of the town centre. With a bit of imagination, the cliff's outline resembles a kneeling elephant, and the hollow interior is, of course, its belly. It's possible to travel through the elephant's belly to the other side of the cliff and back on organized two-hour excursions that involve wading, rafting and canoeing along the freshwater stream, Khlong Tham, that has eroded the channel. Any Phang Nga tour operator can arrange this for you, or you can organize it yourself at the desk in the car park in front of the cliff (afternoons are quieter) for B500. To get to the cave entrance yourself, exit Phang Nga along the Phuket–Krabi highway and watch for signs – and a large statue of an elephant – on the north side of the road, before the highway forks right for Phuket and left for Krabi.

Another quite popular local attraction is **Sa Nang Manora Forest Park** (free entry), 9km north of the bus station, with a hiking trail plus several waterfalls with swimmable pools. Tour agencies will take you there for about B350; with your own transport, continue north through town along Thanon Phetkasem for about 5km, until you pick up signs for the park.

Eating

For **eating**, locals rate *Duang* as the best Thai food in town; it's been going thirty years and serves especially good *kaeng som* (sour and very spicy fish curry) from its tiny premises (unsigned in English) across the road from the bus station, between the Kaisorn (Thai Farmers) and Bangkok banks. *Bismilla* (Sat–Thurs 8.30am–10pm), left about 100m from the bus station at no. 247, has an English menu and does a reasonable if pricey range of beef, chicken and shrimp dishes (B80–120) as well as Western breakfasts. There's also a basic Thai vegetarian canteen (*raan ahaan jeh*; daily 6.30am until about 2pm), about 50m further on. For a great Thai breakfast, go left 20m from the bus station and cross the road to find the corner coffee shop *Kafeh* (no English sign but look for the picture of a coffee cup; daily 6am–8pm) at 180/2 Thanon Phetkasem, across from Soi Langkai. Fill your tray with assorted Thai *khanom* at B5 apiece – banana-leaf parcels of sticky rice laced with sweet coconut milk and stuffed with banana, mango or other delights – then order from the selection of hot and cold coffees and watch Thai breakfast TV with everyone else.

Krabi town and around

The estuarine town of **KRABI** is both provincial capital and major hub for onward travel to some of the region's most popular islands and beaches, including

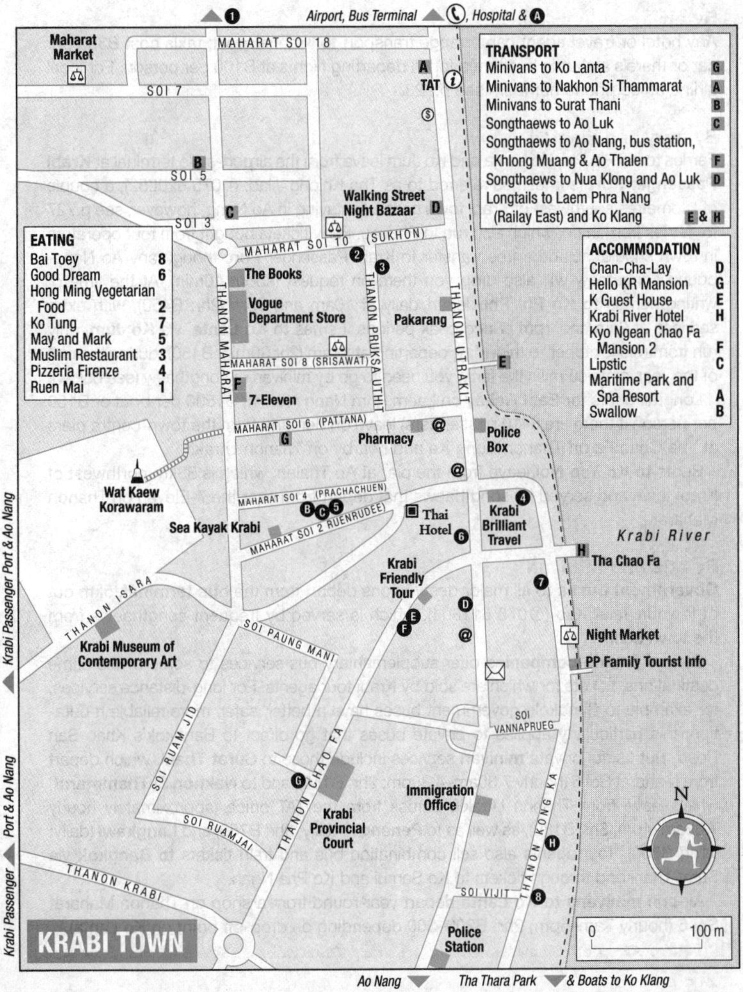

Ko Phi Phi, Ko Lanta, Ao Nang, Klong Muang and Laem Phra Nang (Railay). So efficient are the transport links that you don't really need to stop here, but it also makes an appealing base, strung out along the west bank of the Krabi estuary, with mangrove-lined shorelines to the east, craggy limestone outcrops on every horizon, and plenty of guest houses. The beaches of **Ao Nang** (p.726) and **Railay** (p.733) are both within 45 minutes of town, and other nearby attractions include the **mangrove swamps** and **Ko Klang** peninsula across the estuary, the dramatically sited Tiger Cave Temple at **Wat Tham Seua** and **Khao**

Moving on from Krabi

Onward tickets are best bought through Krabi town tour agents, who keep current timetables. For details of songthaew transport to local beaches and nearby attractions, see opposite.

By air

Any hotel or travel agent can arrange transport to Krabi **airport**: taxis cost B350 per car or there's a shuttle bus timed for all departing flights at B100 per person. For local airline office phone numbers see p.723.

By ferry and longtail

Ferries to Ko Phi Phi, Ko Lanta and Ko Jum leave from the airport-style terminal at **Krabi Passenger Port** (sometimes referred to as Tha Khlong Jilad; ⓣ075 620052), a couple of kilometres southwest of Krabi town centre (if staying in Ao Nang, however, see p.727 for ferries from there, which also run to Phuket). Ferry tickets bought from tour operators in town should include a free transfer to Krabi Passenger Port, though any Ao Nang-bound songthaew will also drop you there on request (about 10min). At the time of writing, ferries **to Ko Phi Phi** depart daily at 10am and 3pm (2hr; B450), with extra services at 9am and 1pm during peak periods. Ferries **to Ko Lanta**, via **Ko Jum**, only run from mid-October to mid-May, departing at 11am (2hr 30min; B450); during the rest of the year, or if you miss the ferry, you need to go by minivan or songthaew (see below).

Longtail boats for **East Railay** on Laem Phra Nang (45min; B1500 per boat or B150 per person if there are 8–10 passengers) leave on demand from the town-centre piers at Tha Chao Fa on Thanon Kong Ka and nearby on Thanon Utrakit.

Boats **to Ko Yao Noi** leave from the pier at Ao Thalen, which is 33km northwest of Krabi town and served by songthaews that depart from near the 7-Eleven on Thanon Maharat.

By bus and minivan

Government buses to all major destinations depart from the **bus terminal**, 5km out of town in Talat Kao (ⓣ075 611804), which is served by frequent songthaews from the town centre.

Several **private companies** offer supplementary bus services to some of the same destinations, tickets for which are sold by Krabi tour agents. For long-distance services, for example to Bangkok, government buses have a better, safer, more reliable reputation; this particularly applies to private buses that go direct to Bangkok's Khao San Road. But useful private **minivan** services include those to **Surat Thani**, which depart from Maharat Soi 5 (hourly 7.30am–4.30pm; 2hr; B150), and to **Nakhon Si Thammarat**, which leave from Thanon Utrakit, across from the TAT office (approximately hourly 7.30am–4pm; 3hr; B180), as well as to **Penang** (2 daily; 9hr; B750) and **Langkawi** (daily; 11hr; B800). Tour agents also sell combination bus and train tickets **to Bangkok** via Surat Thani and through tickets to Ko Samui and Ko Pha Ngan.

Air-con **minivans to Ko Lanta** depart year-round from a shop on Thanon Maharat Soi 6 (hourly 7am–5pm; 2hr; B200–300 depending on drop-off point on Ko Lanta).

Phanom Bencha National Park. For details of organized **day-trips in the Krabi area**, including snorkelling and kayaking excursions, see the box on p.728.

Krabi is at its busiest during high season, from November to February, a period that officially begins with the annual **Krabi Berk Fah Andaman festival**, a week of festivities featuring parades and outdoor concerts, and climaxes at Loy Krathong, the nationwide festival celebrated in late October or early November.

Arrival

Krabi International **airport** (ⓣ075 636541-2) is just off Highway 4, 18km east of Krabi town, 35km from Ao Nang, and served by international Air Asia **flights** from Kuala Lumpur and by domestic flights from Bangkok with Thai Airways and Air Asia, and from Ko Samui with Bangkok Airways. An airport **shuttle bus** runs to Krabi town at B100 per person and Ao Nang for B150, or there are fixed-price taxis at B350 per car to Krabi town and port and B600–900 to Ao Nang (30min) and Klong Muang. For car rental see p.723.

Numerous long-distance buses run to Krabi's **bus terminal**, which is 5km north of the town centre in the suburb of Talat Khao, beside Highway 4. A frequent songthaew service shuttles between the bus station and Thanon Maharat in the town centre, or a motorbike taxi will cost you B50. Air-con and VIP **buses** from Bangkok depart from the capital's Southern Bus Terminal, mainly in the late afternoon or evening, and take about twelve hours to reach Krabi; see p.204 for warnings about the private buses direct from Thanon Khao San. A more comfortable alternative is to take the overnight **train** from Bangkok to Surat Thani and then change on to one of the frequent air-con buses or minivans to Krabi (hourly; 2hr). There are also frequent bus services from Phuket, Phang Nga, Takua Pa (for Khao Sok) and Trang.

Information

Krabi's **TAT office** (daily 8.30am–4.30pm; ⓣ075 622163, ⓔtatkrabi@tat.or.th) is beside the river on Thanon Utrakit at the northern edge of the town centre. Don't confuse this with the tourist information office run by the ferry operator PP Family, which is down on Thanon Kong Ka; you can get information here, but it may be partisan. Any of the town's numerous **tour agents** will fill you in on the many organized day-trip options (see p.728), sell you bus, boat, train and air tickets, and fix you up with a room on one of the beaches – a service that's worth considering for your first night or two, particularly during the notoriously oversubscribed Christmas–New Year period. Recommended agents include Krabi Friendly Tour & Travel, currently at 13/6 Thanon Chao Fa but likely to relocate to larger premises nearby (ⓣ075 612558, ⓦwww.krabicarhire.com), and Krabi Brilliant Travel at 2/1 Thanon Kong Ka (ⓣ075 620819, ⓔorawan16@hotmail.com).

If you're spending some time in this region, it's worth buying a copy of *Krabi: Caught in the Spell – A Guide to Thailand's Enchanted Province*, expat environmentalist Thom Henley's lively and opinionated **book** about Krabi people, islands and traditions (see p.860).

Local transport

Most of the public **songthaew** services to local beaches, towns and attractions leave from outside the 7-Eleven just south of the Soi 8 intersection on Thanon Maharat (see map, p.719); they usually circulate around town and along Thanon Utrakit before heading out. Unless otherwise stated, most run at least twice an hour from dawn till noon, and then less frequently until dusk. Useful destinations include **Ao Nang**, via Krabi Passenger Port on request, and **Klong Muang**; and, via the bus station, **Ao Thalen** (5 daily), **Nua Klong** and **Ao Luk**.

Accommodation

During the busiest season, from December to February, it's worth reserving **accommodation** ahead if you can.

Chan-Cha-Lay 55 Thanon Utrakit ⓣ075 620952, ⓦwww.chanchalay.com. With its stylish blue-and-white theme throughout, funky bathrooms, white-painted wooden furniture and blue shutters, this is the most charming and arty place to stay in Krabi. The en suites in the garden come with fan or air-con and are by far the nicest option; rooms in the main building share bathrooms and some don't have windows. Shared bathroom ②, en suite fan ③, air-con ④

Hello KR Mansion 52/1 Thanon Chao Fa ⓣ075 612761, ⓔchaina_ans@hotmail.com. There are lots of rooms at this traveller-oriented five-storey hotel so it's a good place to try during busy periods. Choose between pretty decent fan and air-con rooms, with or without private bathroom; the uppermost ones have panoramic views. Also has a rooftop bar, internet access and wi-fi downstairs, and motorbike rental. Fan ①, en suite ②, air-con ③

K Guest House 15–25 Thanon Chao Fa ⓣ075 623166, ⓦwww.krabidir.com per kguesthouse. Deservedly popular and well run, in a peaceful but central spot, this long, timber-clad row house has attractive upstairs rooms with wooden floors, panelled walls and streetside balconies. Also offers some cheaper rooms with shared bathroom downstairs and at the back. Shared bathroom ②, en suite ③, air-con ④

Krabi River Hotel 73/1 Thanon Kong Ka ⓣ075 612321, ⓦwww.krabiriverhotel.com. Occupying a scenic spot beside the estuary on the southern edge of Krabi town, a few minutes' walk south of Tha Chao Fa pier, this place offers high-standard air-con rooms, the best of which have big river-view balconies; the smaller, cheaper ones look onto the wall of the adjacent hotel. There's riverside eating area too. ④, river view ⑤

Kyo Ngean ("Nern") Chao Fa Mansion 2 25/1 Thanon Chao Fa, ⓣ075 621111, ⓔkyo-ngean@hotmail.com. Great-value little mansion-style hotel with very clean and well-appointed rooms, all of them with air-con, TVs, free wi-fi, fridge, duvets, hot water and balconies; some on the upper floors have long-range river views. Staff are friendly but don't speak much English. ④

Lipstic 20–22 Soi 2, Thanon Maharat ⓣ075 612392, ⓔkayanchalee@hotmail.com. Good budget option above an Italian restaurant but tucked away off the street. Rooms are simple but well priced; some have windows and others have private bathrooms, but only the air-con ones have both. Fan ①, air-con ③

Maritime Park and **Spa Resort** 2km north of town off Thanon Utrakit ⓣ075 620028, ⓦwww .maritimeparkandspa.com. Beautifully located upper-end hotel, set beside the limestone karsts and mangroves of the Krabi River. Rooms are a little old fashioned but have fine views over the extensive landscape grounds and lake. Has a big pool and a spa, and shuttles into Krabi town and Ao Nang. ⑧⑨

Swallow 31 Soi 4, Thanon Maharat ⓣ075 612464. Tiny six-roomed guest house that's kept spotlessly clean and is a good budget option. All rooms have windows and fans; the cheapest share bathrooms. No advance booking. Shared bathroom ①, en suite ②

The Town

Krabi town has no unmissable sights, but is small enough for a pleasant stroll around its main landmarks. Its chief attraction is its setting and a good way to appreciate this is to follow the paved **riverside walkway** down to the fishing port, about 800m south of Tha Chao Fa; several hotels capitalize on the views here, across to mangrove-ringed Ko Klang, and towards the southern end the walkway borders the municipal Thara Park.

Inland, in the centre of town, you can't fail to notice the bizarre sculptures of hulking **anthropoid apes** clutching two sets of traffic lights apiece at the Thanon Maharat/Soi 10 crossroads. They are meant to represent Krabi's most famous ancestors, the tailless *Siamopithecus oceanus*, whose forty-million-year-old remains were found in a lignite mine in the south of the province and are believed by scientists to be among the earliest examples worldwide of the ape- to-human evolutionary process.

It's also hard to miss the striking white walls of the minimalist new bot at the town-centre temple, **Wat Kaew Korawaram** (Grovaram), approached via a grand naga staircase west off Thanon Maharat, opposite Soi 6. The interior murals depict traditional scenes, including Jataka episodes from the lives of the Buddha, but are spiced up with some modern twists – including warring hairy foreigners on either side of the door.

Just across Thanon Isara from Wat Kaew Korawaram's extensive compound, **Krabi Museum of Contemporary Art** (Tues–Sat 10am–1pm & 2–5pm, Sun 11am–1pm & 2–4.30pm; free) stages changing exhibitions of modern paintings by artists from the Krabi area and beyond.

Eating

Krabi has plenty of traveller-oriented **restaurants**, but there's also inexpensive al fresco dining at the **night markets** on riverside Thanon Kong Ka and on Maharat Soi 10. The **Walking Street night bazaar** on Soi 8 (Fri, Sat & Sun 5–10pm) also brims with excellent foodstalls, as well as an entertainments stage and trinket and craft stalls.

Bai Toey Next to *Thara Guesthouse* on Thanon Kong Ka. Good place for a sundowner with pleasing river views and great seafood, especially spicy mussels salad. Most dishes B60–180.

Good Dream 83 Thanon Utrakit. A great place for breakfast: mega fry-ups (B170), continental sets, muesli and fruit and a great deal more, all served with fresh coffee. There's free wi-fi and internet access for customers too.

Hong Ming Vegetarian Food Thanon Pruksa Uthit. Typical unpretentious Chinese-Thai veggie café serving meat-substitute curries and stir-fries at B25–30 for two servings over rice. Mon–Sat 9am–5pm.

Ko Tung 36 Thanon Kong Ka. Though it looks nothing much, this little Thai restaurant is always packed with locals and tourists savouring the excellent, good-value, southern-style seafood. Special highlights include the sweet mussels (*hawy wan*), baked crab, and mushroom, long bean and shrimp *yam* salads. Most dishes B60–80.

May and Mark Soi 2 Thanon Maharat. Early hours, home-baked bread, fresh coffee and full-English fry-ups make this a popular spot for breakfast. Also does tacos, sandwiches, cheese and tuna melts (B160) and pizzas. Daily 6.30am–9.30pm.

Muslim Restaurant Thanon Pruksa Uthit. Filling rotis (flat fried breads) served with a choice of curry sauces, from B15. Daily 7am–7pm.

Pizzeria Firenze Thanon Kong Ka. Authentic Italian dishes, including twenty different thin-crust pizzas (from B150), pastas, ice creams, tiramisu and imported wines. Daily 11am–10pm.

Ruen Mai About 2km north of the town centre at 315/5 Thanon Maharat. Popular with locals and well regarded, this inviting, artfully planted garden restaurant is well worth making the effort to get to. Among the many highlights of its mostly Thai menu (B60–180), standouts include the perfectly spiced *tom yam kung* with satisfyingly large prawns, juicy deep-fried ribs, and fried butterfish with tamarind and ginger. Daily 11am–9pm.

Listings

Airlines Local offices are all based at the airport: Air Asia ⓣ075 701 5514; Bangkok Airways ⓣ075 701608–9; Thai Airways ⓣ075 701591–3.

Bookshops The Books, next to Vogue Department Store on Thanon Maharat, is good for new English-language books, and the well-stocked Pakarang on Thanon Utrakit buys and sells second-hand books.

Car rental Budget (ⓣ075 636171, ⓦwww.budget.co.th) and Avis (ⓣ075 691941, ⓦavisthailand.com) have desks at the airport, or try Krabi Friendly in town (ⓣ075 612558, ⓦwww.krabicarhire.com; see p.721).

Hospitals Krabi Hospital is about 1km north of the town centre at 325 Thanon Utrakit (ⓣ075 611202) and also has dental facilities, but the better hospital is considered to be the private Muslim hospital, Jariyatham Ruam Phet Hospital (ⓣ075 611223), which is about 3km north of

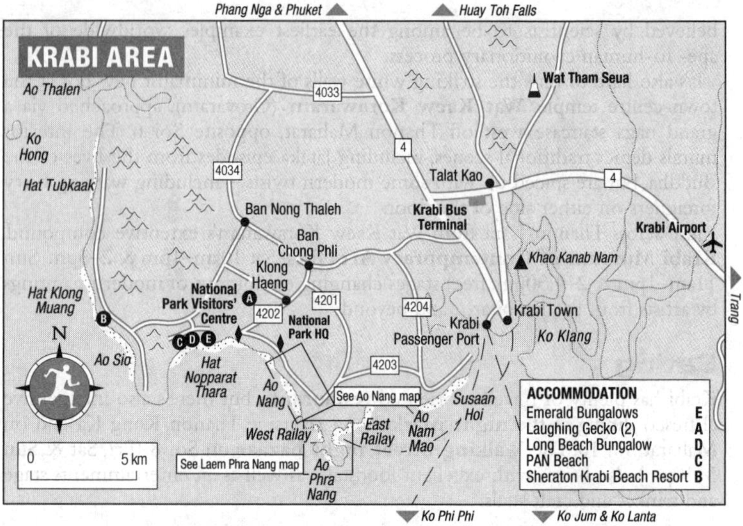

town at 514 Thanon Utrakit and has English-speaking staff.

Immigration office Currently on Thanon Utrakit (Mon–Fri 8.30am–4.30pm; ⓣ075 611097) but may move to Krabi Passenger Port.

Police For all emergencies, call the tourist police on the free, 24hr phone line ⓣ1155, or contact the local branch of the tourist police in Ao Nang on ⓣ075 637208. Krabi police station is at the southern end of Thanon Utrakit ⓣ075 611222.

Telephones The CAT phone office is about 2km north of the town centre on Thanon Utrakit (Mon–Fri 8am–8pm, Sat & Sun 8.30am–4.30pm).

Mangrove tours and Ko Klang

A boat trip through the eerily scenic **mangrove**-lined channels of the Krabi estuary is a fun way to gain a different perspective on the area. As well as a close-up view of the weird creatures that inhabit the swamps (see box opposite), you'll get to visit a riverside cave or two and can choose whether or not to stop on the Ko Klang peninsula. **Tours** are best organized directly with the longtail boatmen who hang around Krabi's two piers (B500 per boat per hr), but can also be arranged through most tour agents.

The estuary's most famous features are the twin limestone outcrops known as **Khao Kanab Nam**, which rise a hundred metres above the water from opposite sides of the Krabi River near the *Maritime Park and Spa Resort* and are so distinctive that they've become the symbol of Krabi. One of the twin karsts hides caves, which can be explored – many skeletons have been found here over the centuries, thought to be those of immigrants who got stranded by a flood before reaching the mainland.

Ko Klang

Most of Krabi's longtail boatmen come from **Ko Klang**, the mangrove-encircled peninsula just across the channel from Tha Chao Fa and Tha Thara Park. On a two-hour mangrove tour you can choose to stop off on the peninsula for a visit, or you can go there yourself, on one of the public longtail **boats** that shuttle across throughout the day, both from Tha Chao Fa (B20; 10min) and Tha Thara Park (B20; 3min). You can also stay there in Ban Ko Klang as part of a **homestay** programme, which features batik-making, rice-farming and trips to local islands, and can be booked locally through the English-speaking co-ordinator Khun Supranee (Ⓣ089 475 0495) or in advance as part of a package with Tell Tale Travel (Ⓦwww.telltaletravel.co.uk).

The predominantly Muslim peninsula is home to three small **villages** housing a total of around four thousand people, most of whom earn their living from tourism and fishing. The island is no great beauty but therein lies its charm, offering the chance to experience a little of typical southern-Thai life. The homestays have bicycles and motorbikes for rent or you can take your own over on the Tha Thara Park longtail; there's about 12km of paved road on the island. You can swim off Ko Klang's long, wild southwestern **beach**, from where you also get an excellent view of the distinctive profiles of all the famous local **islands** – Laem Phra Nang (30min boat ride away), Ko Poda (45min), Bamboo Island, Ko Phi Phi (2hr) and Ko Jum; any Ko Klang boatman will take you out there for the same price as from Krabi town.

Wat Tham Seua and Khao Phanom Bencha

Spectacularly situated amid limestone cliffs within a tropical forest, **Wat Tham Seua** (Tiger Cave Temple) is a famous meditation temple of caves, wooded trails and panoramic viewpoints, about 10km northeast of Krabi town. Infrequent **songthaews** from Krabi town go as far as Nua Klong (20min; B20), from where you'll need to either take a motorbike taxi or walk the final 2km. Bear in mind that as Wat Tham Seua is a working monastery, visitors are required to wear respectable dress (no shorts or sleeveless tops for men or women).

Wat Tham Seua's abbot is a renowned teacher of Vipassana meditation, and some of his educational tools are displayed in the main **bot**, on the left under the cliff overhang, in the main temple compound. Though these close-up photos of human entrails and internal organs may seem shockingly unorthodox, they are there as reminders of the impermanence of the body, a

Life in a mangrove swamp

Mangrove swamps are at their creepiest at low tide, when their aerial roots are fully exposed to form gnarled and knotted archways above the muddy banks. Not only are these roots essential parts of the tree's breathing apparatus, they also reclaim land for future mangroves, trapping and accumulating water-borne debris into which the metre-long mangrove seedlings can fall. In this way, mangrove swamps also fulfil a vital ecological function: stabilizing shifting mud and protecting coastlines from erosion and the impact of tropical storms.

Mangrove swamp mud harbours some interesting creatures too, like the instantly recognizable **fiddler crab**, named after the male's single outsized reddish claw, which it brandishes for communication and defence purposes; the claw is so powerful it could open a can of baked beans. If you keep your eyes peeled you should be able to make out a few **mudskippers**. These specially adapted fish can absorb atmospheric oxygen through their skins as long as they keep their outsides damp, which is why they spend so much time slithering around in the sludge; they move in tiny hops by flicking their tails, aided by their extra-strong pectoral fins. You might well also come across **kingfishers** and white-bellied **sea eagles**, or even a **crab-eating macaque**.

Though the Krabi mangroves have not escaped the **environmentally damaging** attentions of invasive industry, or the cutting down of the bigger trees to make commercial charcoal, around fifteen percent of the Andaman coastline is still fringed with mangrove forest, the healthiest concentration of this rich, complex ecosystem in Thailand.

fundamental tenet of Buddhist philosophy; the human skulls and skeletons dotted around the rest of the compound serve the same purpose. Beyond the bot, follow the path past the nuns' quarters to reach the pair of steep **staircases** that scale the 600-metre-high cliffside. The first staircase is long (1272 steps) and very steep, and takes about an hour to climb, but the vista from the summit is quite spectacular, affording fabulous views over the limestone outcrops and out to the islands beyond. There's a large seated Buddha image and chedi at the top, and a few monks' cells hidden among the trees. The second staircase, next to the large statue of the Chinese Goddess of Mercy, Kuan Im, takes you on a less arduous route down into a deep dell encircled by high limestone walls. Here the monks have built themselves self-sufficient meditation cells (*kuti*) in and around the rocky crannies, linked by paths through the lush ravine: if you continue along the main path you'll eventually find yourself back where you began, at the foot of the staircase. The valley is home to squirrels and monkeys as well as a pair of remarkable trees with overground **buttress roots** over 10m high.

With your own transport, you could combine a visit to Wat Tham Seua with a meander around the scenic backroads and a plunge into **Huay Toh Falls**, a five-tiered cascade that lies within **Khao Phanom Bencha National Park** (dawn till dusk; B200; Ⓦwww.dnp.go.th/National_park.asp), 25km north of Krabi. You can also **stay** in the Phanom Bencha area, about 10km north of Wat Tham Seua, in the tranquil garden cabins and fully equipped tents of *Phanom Bencha Mountain Resort* (Ⓣ075 660501, Ⓦwww.phanombenchamountainresort.com; cabins ④, tents B300), whose grounds border the national park.

Ao Nang and around

AO NANG (sometimes confusingly signed as Ao Phra Nang), 22km west of Krabi town, is a busy, continually expanding, rather faceless mainland resort that

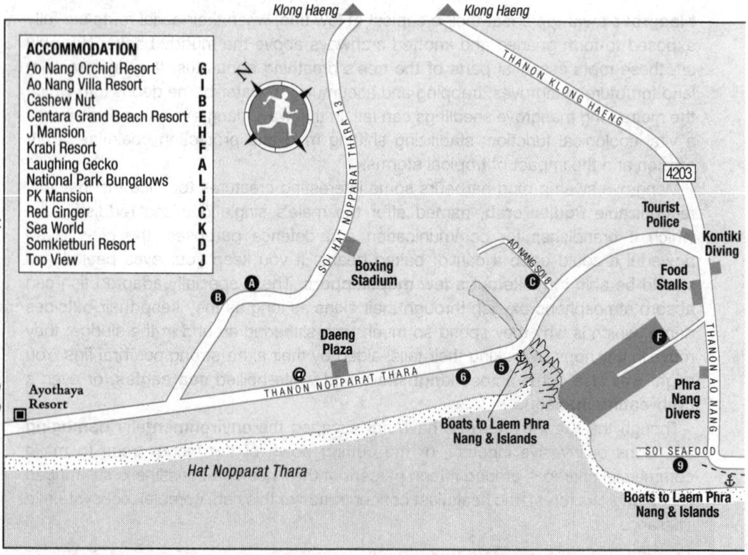

mainly caters for mid-budget and package-holiday tourists. Although it lacks the fine beaches of the nearby Railay peninsula (an easy 10min boat-ride away), it is less claustrophobic, and has a much greater choice of restaurants and bars, masses of shopping (mostly beachwear, DVDs and souvenirs), plus a wealth of dive shops, day-tripping and snorkelling possibilities and other typical resort facilities. Adjacent **Hat Nopparat Thara**, part of which comes under the protection of a national marine park, is prettier, and divided into two separate beaches by a khlong. The uncrowded, two-kilometre-long **eastern beach** is effectively linked to Ao Nang by a conurbation of accommodation and shops, but the **western beach**, sometimes known as **Hat Ton Son,** across the khlong, is an altogether quieter and more beautiful little enclave, accessible only via longtail or a circuitous back road. Fifteen kilometres drive west of Ao Nang, **Hat Klong Muang** is no great shakes as a beach but does have some attractive four- and five-star accommodation.

Arrival, transport and information

Ao Nang has no proper transport terminals of its own so most long-distance journeys entail going **via Krabi town** (see p.721). The cheapest onward connection **to Ao Nang** is by **songthaews**, which run regularly throughout the day from Krabi town centre, ferry port and bus station (every 10min; 45min; B50) and pass eastern Nopparat Thara en route. Alight at the Nopparat Thara national park T-Junction and car park for longtails across the narrow khlong **to the western beach** (B20–50) or, with your own transport, follow the Klong Muang road until signs direct you off it. There's also a songthaew service from Krabi town **to Klong Muang**. Taxis charge about B500 from Krabi to Ao Nang.

Frequent longtail boats shuttle back and forth from Ao Nang's central beachfront to West Railay and Ao Ton Sai on **Laem Phra Nang**, departing when full (10min; B80, or B100 plus after dark), while from November to May there's a daily ferry service from Tha Nopparat Thara, near the national park visitors' centre, to **Ko Phi Phi Don** (2hr 30min), **Ko Lanta** (2hr 30min) and **Phuket**

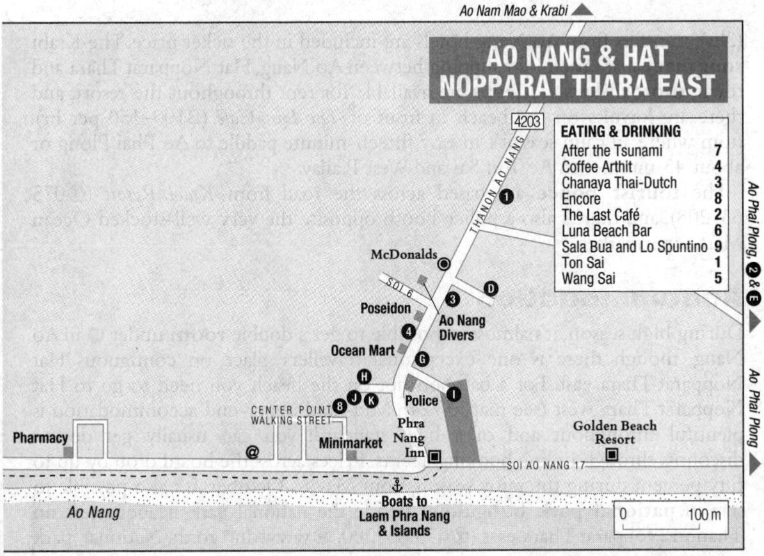

Snorkelling and other day-trips around Krabi

Any tour agent in Krabi town, Ao Nang, Klong Muang or Railay can set you up on these **snorkelling** and other **day-trips**; prices usually include transport from your accommodation.

Multi-island snorkelling trips

By far the most popular organized outings from Krabi, Ao Nang and Laem Phra Nang are the **snorkelling trips** to nearby islands. The main **islands** in question are Ko Poda, Ko Tub and Chicken Island, all of them less than half an hour's longtail ride from Ao Nang or Railay. There are various permutations, offered by numerous companies, including the number of islands you visit (usually three, four or five) and whether you go in a longtail boat or speedboat, but in all cases you should be prepared to share the experience with dozens, even hundreds of others, because pretty much everyone congregates at the same spots. It's a lot more fun than it sounds though – so long as you're not expecting a solitary experience.

One of the best and cheapest **tours** is the four-island longtail trip run by Green Planet (☎075 637488); it's professionally run, uses 22-person boats, and is a bargain at B450 including national park entry fee, packed lunch and snorkel set. The more private alternative is to organize your own boat trip with the **longtail boatmen** on Ao Nang waterfront. Their prices are fixed, but don't include snorkelling equipment, lunch or the B100 national park fee: for the return trip to either Ko Poda, Ko Tub or Chicken Island (8am–4pm), they charge B300 per person, minimum six people; for Ko Hong (see p.716) or Bamboo Island (near Ko Phi Phi; see p.740) it's B1700/3800 per boat per half/full day. Krabi town is quite a bit further from the islands so its boatmen charge B500 per hour per boat.

From some angles, one of the pinnacles on **Chicken Island** does indeed look like the scrawny neck and beaky head of a chicken. There's decent snorkelling off its coast, with a fair range of reef fish and quite a lot of giant clams, though most of the reef is either bleached or dead. Its dazzlingly white-sand northeastern shore, which has a food stall, toilets and kayak rental, is connected to the islets of **Ko Tup** by a sandbank, which is walkable at low tide – quite a striking sight as you arrive to see

(3hr); transfers from Ao Nang hotels are included in the ticket price. The Krabi **songthaews** are useful for nipping between Ao Nang, Hat Nopparat Thara and town; **motorbikes** and **jeeps** are available for rent throughout the resort; and there are **kayaks** on the beach in front of *The Last Café* (B100–150 per hr), from where, in calm seas, it's an easy fifteen-minute paddle to Ao Phai Plong or about 45 minutes to Ao Ton Sai and West Railay.

The **tourist police** are based across the road from *Krabi Resort* (☎075 637208), and there's also a police booth opposite the very well-stocked Ocean Mart supermarket.

Accommodation

During high season, it's almost impossible to get a double **room** under ❹ in Ao Nang, though there is one exceptional travellers' place on contiguous Hat Nopparat Thara east. For a bamboo hut on the beach you need to go to Hat Nopparat Thara west (see map, p.724). Mid- and upper-end accommodation is plentiful throughout and of a high standard; you can usually get decent discounts through online booking agents. Prices across the board drop by up to fifty percent during the rainy season, from May to October. It's also possible to stay in **national park bungalows** beside the national park headquarters on Thanon Nopparat Thara east (☎075 637200, Ⓦwww.dnp.go.th/National_park

other visitors seemingly walking on water. Nearby **Ko Poda**, which sits directly in front of the Ao Nang beachfront, is encircled by lovely white-sand beaches and clear turquoise water. There's a restaurant here and plenty of shade under the casuarina trees, so this is the typical lunch stop; sandwich-selling boats dock here too. Though you might get three hundred people lunching on the shore here at any one time, it's big enough to cope. Some itineraries also feature **Ao Phra Nang** and its cave, on the Laem Phra Nang (Railay) peninsula (see p.736), and this is the one to avoid unless you enjoy scrambling for your metre of sand on this overrun little bay.

Activities and day-trips

Cycle rides Half- and full-day rides into the Krabi countryside, or to Khao Phanom Bencha falls or Khlong Tom's Emerald Pool. With Krabi Eco Cycle (Ⓣ081 607 4162, Ⓦwww.krabiecocycle.com), from B1000, kids B800 inclusive.

Elephant trekking Nosey Parker's Elephant Trekking (Ⓣ075 612258, Ⓦwww.krabidir.com/noseyparkers), 7km north of Ao Nang, has a good reputation. From B800, kids B400 for an hour's trek along the river and elephant bathing.

Horse-riding Beach rides from B750/hr (kids B500), lessons from B450/hr and trips into the countryside from B1800 with Swiss-Thai run Krabi Nature Horse Riding (Ⓣ081 085 9627, Ⓦwww.krabi-horse-riding.com) east of Ao Nang at Ao Nam Mao.

Rock-climbing On Ao Ton Sai and Laem Phra Nang (see p.736).

Sea canoeing Guided and self-paddle trips around the spectacular karst islands and secret lagoons of Ao Phang Nga, usually focusing on Ao Luk, Ao Thalen and Ko Hong in the eastern bay (see p.716); B900–2100. Dozens of companies offer this, including the local branch of south Thailand's most famous kayaking outfit, John Gray's Sea Canoe (Ⓣ076 528839, Ⓦwww.seacanoe.net), and Sea Kayak Krabi (Ⓣ075 630270, Ⓦwww.seakayak-krabi.com).

Thai cookery lessons Krabi Thai Cookery School runs morning and afternoon courses (daily 9am–1pm & 2–6pm; B1300/1000 including transport; Ⓣ081 979 0677, Ⓦwww.thaicookeryschool.net).

.asp; bungalows B1000), which is 2km from Ao Nang's main facilities but just across the (quite busy) road from a nice stretch of beach and a five-minute walk from the seafood restaurants near the visitors' centre.

Ao Nang and Hat Nopparat Thara east

Inexpensive and moderate

Cashew Nut Soi Hat Nopparat Thara 13 Ⓣ075 637560. Twenty-two good, sturdy en-suite brick and concrete bungalows with fan or air-con ranged around a peaceful garden full of cashew trees 5min walk from Hat Nopparat Thara east. Family-run and peaceful. Price depends on the size. Fan ④, air-con ⑤

J Mansion Off Thanon Ao Nang Ⓣ075 695128, Ⓦwww.jmansionaonang.com. The best-known and most popular of the mini-hotels in Ao Nang's travellers' enclave, this place has large, very good, fan and air-con rooms, all with satellite TVs, safety boxes and wi-fi. Most have high-level views, some of which extend to the green-clad cliffs behind. The rooftop terrace also has a panoramic outlook. ④–⑤

Laughing Gecko Soi Hat Nopparat Thara 13 Ⓣ081 270 5028, Ⓦwww.laughinggeckothailand.com. Perhaps the last of the old-style bungalows left in the Ao Nang area, this is an easy-going and exceptionally traveller-friendly haven run by a Thai-Canadian couple. Choose from a range of simple bamboo huts set around a garden dotted with cashew trees: the cheapest beds are in a nine-person dorm (B150), or there are private rooms with shared bathrooms, en-suite huts and three-room bamboo houses for five. Also has internet access and nightly all-you-can-eat Thai buffets (B150), with live music. The owners are opening a second guest house in the same style – with swimming pool – under the same name, closer to the national park visitors' centre at Hat Nopparat Thara Soi 4. Shared bathroom ②, en suite ③, family house ⑤

PK Mansion and **Top View** Off Thanon Ao Nang ☎075 637431, Ⓦkrabidir.com/pkmansion. Offering rates similar to its budget-oriented neighbours, *PK Mansion* and its adjacent, slightly pricier, sister hotel, *Top View*, have a range of mostly very good quality rooms, with hot-water bathrooms, fan or air-con, wide balconies (with green or partial sea views), TVs and fridges. Reservations advisable. Fan ④–⑤, air-con ⑤–⑥

Sea World Off Thanon Ao Nang ☎075 637388, Ⓔseaworld999@hotmail.com. Sometimes offered at rates slightly cheaper than its neighbours on the backpackers' soi, rooms here have good facilities but can be shabbier than the competition. Most have safety boxes and the choice of fan or air-con; some also enjoy good views, mostly green ones to the karsts inland, though a few look towards the sea. Fan ③–④, air-con ④–⑥

Expensive

Ao Nang Orchid Resort 141 Thanon Ao Nang ☎075 638445, Ⓦwww.aonangorchid-resort.com. This medium-sized but well-appointed hotel is good value for Ao Nang. Choose from rooms in the hotel wing, where the nicest overlook the pool and karst mountains beyond (rather than those with "city" views), or go for stand-alone villas with direct access to the lagoon pool. Interiors are chic and attractive, rooms and bungalows all have decks and safes, many have hardwood floors. Wi-fi in some areas. ⑧–⑨

Ao Nang Villa Resort 113 Thanon Ao Nang ☎075 637270, Ⓦwww.aonangvilla.com. A very popular hotel whose grounds run down to the beachfront walkway. The 157 upscale, air-con rooms are contained within several low-rise wings, a few of them enjoying a sea view, but most overlooking the garden or the bigger of the resort's two pools. ⑧–⑨

Centara Grand Beach Resort and Villas Krabi Ao Phai Plong ☎075 637789, Ⓦwww.centarahotelsresorts.com. Ao Nang's top hotel has the secluded sandy bay of Ao Phai Plong all to itself, but is just a 20min walk (up and over the cliff) from the resort's shops and restaurants or a few minutes by longtail boat. Designed to sit almost seamlessly against the forested crags behind, there's a lovely green feel here and seaward vistas are also beautiful. Nearly all rooms in the four-storeyed hotel buildings and detached villas have sea views. Interiors are modern and generous with sun-balconies and shaded outdoor daybeds; all have bathtubs, TVs and wi-fi. There's a big pool, a dive centre, gym and spa. ⑨

Krabi Resort Ao Nang ☎075 637030, Ⓦwww.krabiresort.net. Set in a vast tropical garden that runs right down to the western end of Ao Nang beach, this is the oldest resort in Ao Nang, and one of the more old-fashioned. Air-con bungalows are staggered in rows back from the shoreline and are comfortable if not especially contemporary considering the price, though it's about the only place in central Ao Nang where you have the sea right on your doorstep. It also has more modern luxury villas and rooms in a main, low-rise building. ⑧–⑨

Red Ginger Ao Nang Soi 8 ☎075 637999, Ⓦwww.redgingerkrabi.com. Located between the two beaches and a short walk from central Ao Nang shops, this contemporary Sino-Thai hotel has jut 63 rooms, some of them duplexes, set round a saltwater pool. Lines are clean and simple with modern Chinese styling and it all feels bright and upbeat. ⑧–⑨

Somkietburi Resort Thanon Ao Nang ☎075 637990, Ⓦwww.somkietburi.com. Guests here enjoy one of the most delightful settings in Ao Nang, with the 26 rooms and swimming pools surrounded by a feral, jungle-style garden that's full of hanging vines and lotus ponds. Rooms are perfectly pleasant but nothing special; all have air-con and TV, and there's a spa. ⑦–⑧

Hat Nopparat Thara west

Emerald Bungalows ☎081 956 2566. There's some very comfortable accommodation here, in forty big, brightly painted and stylishly furnished en-suite wooden bungalows, widely spaced around a shady shorefront garden and all with at least partial sea views, huge decks, and either fan or air-con. Also has a good restaurant and a bar. Usually closed May–Aug, but phone to check. Fan ⑤, air-con ⑦

Long Beach Bungalow 600m west from khlong ☎089 777 5853, Ⓔampoeiing@gmail.com. Most of the accommodation at this small place is in very simple bamboo huts set round a grassy lawn, with nothing more than a platform bed and a mosquito net (no fans), though some are en suite. Also has a couple more solid seafront rooms. Nightly family-style dinners, cooking classes, snorkelling trips and motorbike rental. ②–③

PAN Beach At the westernmost end of the beach, about 700m walk from the khlong ☎089 866 4373, Ⓦwww.panbeachkrabi.com. Fifteen sturdy, simply furnished wooden bungalows in two sizes and styles, each with screened windows, fans and bathrooms, set just back from the shore around a lawn. Also has motorbikes for rent and organizes local boat trips. ④

Hat Klong Muang

Sheraton Krabi Beach Resort ⓣ075 628000, ⓦwww.sheraton.com/krabi. Unusually for a top-notch beachfront hotel, the *Sheraton* Krabi does not boast of its sea views because the entire low-rise resort has been built amongst the mangroves and alongside a khlong; the result is refreshingly green and cool – and full of birdsong. The sandy shore – the nicest in Klong Muang – is anyway just a few steps away, accessed via a series of wooden walkways, and there's a seafront lawn for lounging. Rooms are large, sleek and very comfortable; there's a big pool, a spa and watersports centre, plus, weather permitting, nightly films on the outdoor movie screen. ⑨

The beaches

Ao Nang's central beach is unexceptional and busy with longtail traffic; the nicer stretch is east beyond *Phra Nang Inn*, accessed by the sidewalk that takes you all the way along the shore to the appropriately named *The Last Café*, a very pleasant spot for a shady drink. En route you'll pass a crowd of two-dozen **massage** huts set out under the trees, charging a standard B300 per hour. Follow the wooden walkway from beyond *The Last Café* and scale the steps up and over the headland to reach, in about ten minutes, the beach at diminutive **Ao Phai Plong**, which is the sole province of the luxurious *Centara Grand* hotel.

Immediately west of Ao Nang, beyond the headland occupied by *Krabi Resort* but reached by simply following the road (on foot or in one of the frequent Krabi-bound songthaews), **Hat Nopparat Thara east** is long and pretty, though the road runs unscreened alongside it. Its eastern hinterland is developing fast with hotels and restaurants, but the other end, close to the T-junction with Route 4202, is the site of the Hat Nopparat Thara – Mu Ko Phi Phi **national park headquarters** and accommodation. Here too is the **tsunami memorial**, *Hold Me Close* by Louise Bourgeois (2005), a broken, roofless, wood-slatted corncob structure enclosing two pairs of hands, joined, prayer like and pleading, extending from a lumpy sea. At low tide it's almost impossible to swim on this beach, but the sands come alive with thousands of starfish and hermit crabs, and the view out towards the islands is glorious; you can walk to the nearest outcrop at low water. The **national park visitor centre** is across Route 4202, beside the khlong and its sheltered marina and jetty, Tha Nopparat Thara, which is the departure point for Ao Nang ferry services to Phuket, Phi Phi and Ko Lanta, as well as for longtails to the western beach. The visitor centre's car park is famous for its **seafood restaurants**, and Krabi residents also like to picnic under the shorefront casuarina trees here.

Hat Nopparat Thara west has a quite different atmosphere from its eastern counterpart: just a handful of small bungalow hotels and a few private residences share its long swathe of peaceful casuarina- and palm-shaded shoreline, making it a great place to escape the crowds and commerce of other Krabi beaches. The views of the karst islands are magnificent, though swimming here is also tide-dependent. Without your own transport you can only get here by longtail across the narrow but deep khlong beside the national park visitor's centre, but with a car or bike you can arrive via the very quiet back road that snakes through the mangroves from the Klong Muang road to the edge of the bungalow properties.

Diving

Ao Nang is Krabi's main centre for **dive shops**, with a dozen or more outlets, the most reputable of which include Kon-Tiki (ⓣ075 637826, ⓦwww.kontiki-thailand.com), Phra Nang Divers (ⓣ075 637064, ⓦwww.phranangdivers.com), and Poseidon (ⓣ075 637263, ⓦwww.poseidon-diving.com), all of whom have a price agreement and mostly offer the same programmes. Diving with Ao Nang operators is possible year-round, with some dive staff claiming that off-season diving is more rewarding, not least because the sites are much less crowded. Most one-day **dive trips** head for the area round Ko Phi Phi and include dives at Shark Point and the "King Cruiser" wreck dive (see p.699) for B3400 including two tanks; the Ko Ha island group, near Ko Lanta, is also popular and costs about the same (see p.756). Two dives in the Ao Nang area – at Ko Poda and Ko Yawasam – average B2700 (B1500 for snorkellers). PADI dive courses start at B5500 for the introductory Discover Scuba day, or B14,900 for the Openwater. The nearest recompression chambers are on Phuket (see p.698); check to see that your dive operator is insured to use one of them. See Basics, p.73 for general information on diving in Thailand.

Eating, drinking and entertainment

Eating and drinking options in Ao Nang are not sophisticated and there are few places that stand out from the crowd. At weekends, locals flock to the **seafood restaurants** in the national park visitors' centre car park on Hat Nopparat Thara, or buy fried chicken from nearby stalls and picnic on mats under the shorefront trees. In central Ao Nang, there are cheap hot-food stalls on the road outside *Krabi Resort*, and handcarts selling Muslim **roti** pancakes (filled with milk, banana or chocolate) pitch up all over the resort. The **bar** scene is mainly focused around Ao Nang Center Point Walking Street, a U-shaped passageway behind the beachfront shops that's packed with makeshift little bars and their flirty staff.

The *muay thai* **boxing** stadium, 2km west out of Ao Nang, near the *Laughing Gecko* guest house on Soi Nopparat Thara 13, stages heavily promoted twice-weekly bouts in high season (Mon & Fri 9pm; B1000).

After the Tsunami National park visitors' centre car park, Hat Nopparat Thara. Hugely popular with locals, expats and visiting Thais for its reasonably priced fresh seafood and shellfish (B60–180). Daily 11am–9pm.

Coffee Arthit Thanon Ao Nang. A really good place for breakfast, with its big menu of set breakfasts including vegetarian full English, a range of breads, croissants and fresh coffees. Daily from 7.30am.

Chanaya Thai-Dutch Thanon Ao Nang. With its fairy lights, trailing plants and wooden tables, this invitingly atmospheric place always gets a good crowd. The menu is mostly European – T-bone steaks done various ways, ostrich steaks, asparagus, ham and cheese bake – and there are tempting set dinners rounded off with Dutch apple pie and cream. Most mains B180; sets from B600.

Encore Ao Nang Centerpoint Walking Street. Nightly live music from 10pm – and a pool table – draws decent-sized crowds to this bar decorated with pictures of rock stars. 4pm–1am.

The Last Café Soi Ao Nang 17. Set under the cliffs on the sand at the far easternmost end of the beach, this is an especially nice spot for a beer at sunset.

Luna Beach Bar Beachside, eastern end of Hat Nopparat Thara. Beach bar with live music and several small bar-beers within the same compound whose main attraction is its late hours: it generally keeps going well after the central Ao Nang bars have shut.

Sala Bua and Lo Spuntino Soi Seafood. Enjoying great sea views especially at sunset, this is a two-in-one restaurant with two chefs. One does the Thai dishes under *Sala Bua*, including excellent *phanaeng* curries and seafood (mostly B120–150), while the other cooks authentic Italian – pizzas from B200, plus tiramisu and sambuca liquors to follow – for *Lo Spuntino*.

Ton Sai 150m north of *McDonalds* on Thanon Ao Nang. Home-style Thai cooking is the calling card at this bamboo-shack family-run restaurant. The curries are delicious, there's plenty of seafood and you can get almost any dish cooked to order. Most mains B60–80.

Wang Sai Beside the bridge at the eastern end of Thanon Nopparat Thara. Large, long-running seafood place right on the beach. Mains B80–200.

Laem Phra Nang: Railay and Ton Sai

Seen from the close quarters of a longtail boat, the combination of sheer limestone cliffs, pure white sand and emerald waters around the **LAEM PHRA NANG** peninsula is spectacular – and would be even more so without the hundreds of other admirers gathered on its four beaches. The peninsula (often known simply as **Railay**) is effectively a tiny island, embraced by impenetrable limestone massifs that make road access impossible – but do offer excellent, world-famous **rock-climbing**; transport is by boat only, from Krabi town or, most commonly, from nearby Ao Nang. It has four beaches within ten minutes' walk of each other: **Ao Phra Nang** graces the southwestern edge, and is flanked by **East and West Railay**, just 500m apart; **Ao Ton Sai** is beyond West Railay, on the other side of a rocky promontory. Almost every patch of buildable land fronting East and West Railay has been taken over by bungalow resorts, and development is creeping up the cliffsides and into the forest behind. But at least high-rises don't feature, and much of the construction is hidden among trees or set amid prettily landscaped gardens. Accommodation is at a premium and not cheap, so the scene on West and East Railay, and Ao Phra Nang, is predominantly holidaymakers on short breaks

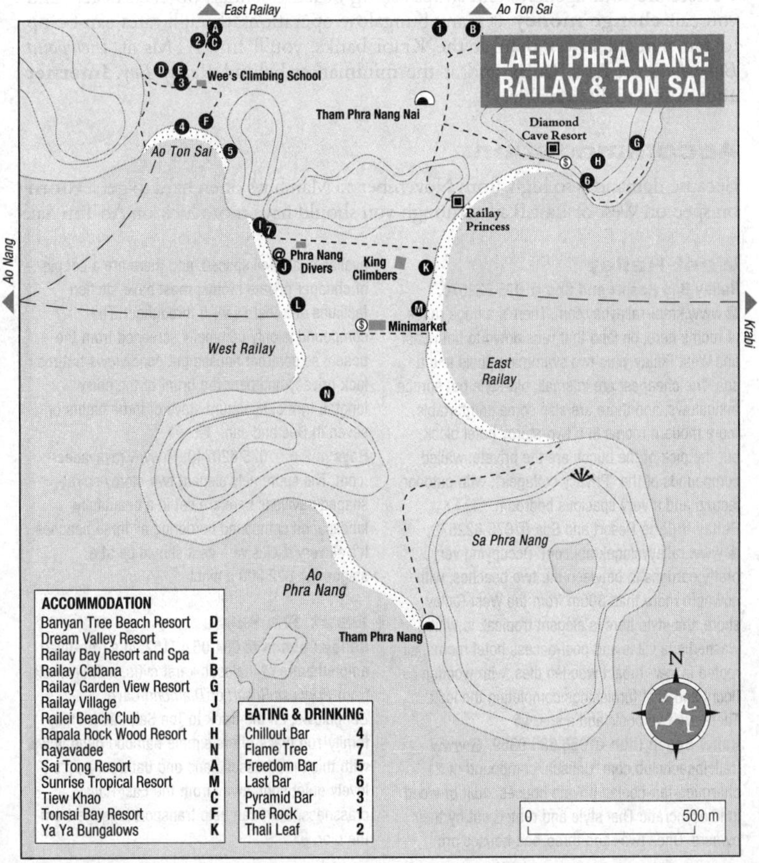

rather than backpackers. The opposite is true on adjacent Ao Ton Sai, Krabi's main travellers' hub and the heart of the rock-climbing scene.

Arrival and information

Laem Phra Nang is only accessible by **boat** from Krabi town, Ao Nam Mao, Ao Nang and Ko Phi Phi. Longtail boats to Laem Phra Nang depart from the **Krabi** riverfront (45min; B150 per person, minimum 8 people, or B1500 when chartered), leaving throughout the day as soon as they fill up. Depending on the tide, all Krabi boats land on or off East Railay, so you may have to wade; they do run during the rainy season, but the waves make it a nerve-wracking experience, so you're advised to go via Ao Nang instead. Coming back there are at least five scheduled boats between 9.30am and 5.30pm, and others on demand. **Ao Nang** is much closer to Laem Phra Nang, and longtails run from the beachfront here to West Railay and Ao Ton Sai (10min; B80, or B100 after 6pm) all year round. Boats between Ao Ton Sai and West Railay cost B50. During high season there should also be daily ferries from Ao Nang via West Railay to **Ko Phi Phi** (2hr 30min), **Ko Lanta** (2hr 30min) and **Phuket** (3hr); if not, you'll need to transfer to Ao Nang yourself.

There are tour agencies and shops selling beach essentials on each beach, and you can **change money** at many bungalow operations, though rates can be up to ten percent lower than at the Krabi banks; you'll find ATMs at *Viewpoint Bungalows* on East Railay and at the minimarket behind *Railay Bay*. **Internet access** is widely available.

Accommodation

Because demand is so high, from November to March it's often hard to get a **room** on spec on West or East Railay, though you should have more luck on Ao Ton Sai.

West Railay

Railay Bay Resort and Spa ⓣ075 622570, ⓦwww.krabi-railaybay.com. There's a huge range of rooms here, on land that runs down to both East and West Railay, plus two swimming pools and a spa. The cheapest are in small, old-style but spruce bungalows, and there are also some comfortable, more modern rooms in a two-storey hotel block, but the pick of the bunch are the private, walled compounds of the "Privacy cottages", with outdoor jacuzzi and a very spacious bedroom. ❽–❾

Railay Village Resort and Spa ⓣ075 622578, ⓦwww.railayvillagekrabi.com. Occupying very pretty gardens in between the two beaches, with nowhere more than 300m from the West Railay shore, the style here is elegant tropical, in white-washed spa villas and pool-access hotel rooms, all roofed in low-impact wooden tiles, with wooden floors and Thai furnishings completing the look. There are two pools and a spa. ❾

Railei Beach Club ⓣ086 685 9359, ⓦwww.raileibeachclub.com. Unusual compound of 21 charming fan-cooled private houses, built of wood in idiosyncratic Thai style and rented out by their owners. One- two- and three-bed houses are available, all well spaced, and there are a couple of cheaper private rooms; most have kitchen facilities and there's wi-fi throughout. The compound is only minimally screened from the beach, so seafront houses get good views but may lack privacy and bear the brunt of the noisy longtail traffic. Minimum stays of three nights or seven in Dec and Jan. ❼–❾

Rayavadee ⓣ075 620740, ⓦwww.rayavadee.com. The supremely elegant two-storey spiral-shaped pavilions here are set in a beautifully landscaped compound bordering all three beaches. It's all very exclusive – as it should be at a staggering B22,300 a night. ❾

East Railay

Railay Cabana ⓣ084 057 7167. In a tree-filled amphitheatre of majestic karst cliffs, a 5min walk from *Princess Resort* or *Diamond Cave Bungalows*, on the track to Ton Sai, this friendly family-run place offers simple bamboo bungalows with thick mattresses, fans and bathrooms. It's a lovely quiet spot, away from the East Railay crassness. Staff can help transport luggage from the pier. ❸

Railay Garden View Resort ⓣ085 888 5143, ⓦwww.railaygardenview.com. This place really stands out for it simple rustic-chic style, great high-level views over the mangroves and sea beyond, and green surrounds in a garden of jackfruit, banana and papaya trees. The twenty fan-cooled bungalows, built from good-quality split–bamboo, are widely spaced and on stilts, with colour-washed cold-water bathrooms, wooden floored bedrooms and decks, and plenty of triangular cushions for lounging. The drawback is that it's up a steep stairway beyond the far north end of East Railay, accessed via a short walkway beyond *The Last Bar*, about 15min walk from West Railay. 5–6

Rapala Rock Wood Resort ⓣ075 622586. Climb a steep flight of stairs to reach the 31 rough-hewn timber huts here, which are among the cheapest on Railay, set in rows around a scruffy garden high above the beach, with some enjoying dramatic karst views from their verandas. The very cheapest rooms are in the handful of basic terraced bamboo huts with shared facilities, but most are in simple bungalows with decent private bathrooms. There's also a nice communal deck among the treetops, and a restaurant that serves Indian food. 3–4

Sunrise Tropical Resort ⓣ075 622599, ⓦwww.sunrisetropical.com. The most stylish of the affordable hotels on the cape offers just forty rooms, most in elegantly designed air-con bungalows, and some in a couple of two-storey buildings, all with Thai furnishings and generously spacious living areas, set around a landscaped tropical garden with a small pool. Wi-fi throughout. 7–8

Ya Ya Bungalows ⓣ075 622593, ⓦyaya-resort.com. This idiosyncratic place has some of the cheapest accommodation on Railay and is built almost entirely of wood, with most of the 86 fan and air-con rooms contained in a series of sturdy, quite well-designed, three-storey wooden buildings. They all have verandas and en-suite bathrooms, but soundproofing is not great and most rooms are quite dark. Fan 4–5, air-con 7

Ao Ton Sai

Banyan Tree Beach Resort ⓣ089 470 8532. Built in a line under the trees, the 36 bungalows here come in two types: standard bamboo and wooden versions with mosquito nets and bathrooms, or nicer mint-green clapboard chalets with comfortable beds and good bathrooms. 2–4

Dream Valley Resort ⓣ089 589 2230, ⓦwww.dreamvalleyresortkrabi.com. The 85 bungalows here are ranged discreetly amongst the trees running far back towards the cliff-face, offering a range of good-quality accommodation in various categories, from split-bamboo huts with fans and bathrooms through to air-con villas, the best of which are the premier accommodation on Ao Ton Sai. Fan 4–5, air-con 6–7

Sai Tong Resort 400m along the track to East Railay ⓣ081 079 6583. This friendly, good-value little place offers cheap, woven-bamboo huts with nets, fans and bathrooms beside the track, and bigger, more comfy, cute-looking split bamboo ones, also en suite and with nets, fans and proper beds. 2

Tiew Khao 250m along the track to East Railay. The rudimentary bamboo huts here are ranged up the hillside beside the track, with the uppermost ones enjoying fine high-level views of the karst wall beyond. They're the cheapest on Ao Ton Sai: all of them share bathrooms and facilities comprise nothing more than a mattress and a veranda. 1

Tonsai Bay Resort ⓣ075 660511, ⓦwww.tonsaibay.co.th. With its large, widely spaced and plain but comfortable air-con bungalows, each one boasting huge glass windows and a big deck from which to soak up the pretty location in a grove of trees about 200m back from the shore, this is one of the top places to stay on Ao Ton Sai. The fan options nearer the beach are overpriced and within earshot of the all-night *Freedom Bar*. Fan 5, air-con 7

The beaches

The loveliest and most popular beach on the cape is **WEST RAILAY**, with its gorgeous white sand, crystal-clear water and impressive karst scenery at every turn. The best of the peninsula's bungalow hotels front this shoreline, and longtail boats from Ao Nang pull in here too, so it gets crowded. Follow any of the tracks inland, through the resort developments, and within a few minutes you reach **EAST RAILAY** on the other coast, whose mangrove swamps and muddy shore make it unsuitable for swimming; boats from Krabi town dock here. Accommodation on this side is a bit cheaper, and there's more variety in price too, though – aside from a couple of gems – it's mostly an uncomfortable mix of uninspired, low-grade developments and unsubtle bars with names like *Skunk* and *Stone*. Depressingly, much of East Railay's hinterland is despoiled by trash and building rubble, but inland it's another story, with a majestic amphitheatre of forested karst turrets just ten minutes' walk away, on the back route to Ao Ton Sai.

Continue south along East Railay's shoreline, past *Sunrise Tropical Resort*, to pick up the walkway to the diminutive, cliff-bound beach at **AO PHRA NANG** (also called **Hat Tham Phra Nang**). Though exceptionally pretty, the bay can be hard to appreciate beneath the trinket sellers and crowds of day-trippers who are deposited here in their hundreds, by boats that pollute the coastal waters. Better to visit before 10am or after 4pm if you can. The walkway from East Railay winds between the super-lux *Rayavadee* hotel and the lip of a massive karst before emerging at the beach beside **Tham Phra Nang**, or **Princess Cave**. The beach and cave, and indeed the peninsula, are named for this princess (*phra nang* means "revered lady"), whom the local fisherfolk believe lives here and controls the fertility of the sea. To encourage large catches, red-tipped wooden phalluses are left as offerings to her at the cave entrance. Buried deep inside the same cliff is **Sa Phra Nang** (**Princess Lagoon**), which is accessible only via a steep 45-minute descent that starts halfway along the walkway. You'll need proper shoes for it, as slippery descents and sharp rocks make it hard in flip-flops or bare feet. After an initial ten-minute clamber, negotiated with the help of ropes, the path forks: go left for a panoramic view over East and West Railay, or right for the lagoon. (For the strong-armed, there's the third option of hauling yourself up ropes to the top of the cliff for a bird's-eye view.) Taking the right-hand fork, you'll pass through the tropical dell dubbed "big tree valley" before eventually descending to the murky lagoon.

The beach at **AO TON SAI**, north across the oyster rocks from West Railay, is not the prettiest, prone to murk and littered with rocks that make it impossible to swim at low tide. But its orange-and-ochre-striped cliffs are magnificently scenic, dripping with curlicues and turrets that tower over a central tree-filled bowl and host scores of challenging rock climbs. Most of the accommodation here is aimed at climbers and travellers, and is well hidden several hundred metres back from the shore, scattered within the remains of a forest and along the track that, beyond *Sai Tong*, takes you to East Railay in about twenty minutes. The vibe here is green and comradely, with climbers doing their thing during the day and partying at the several chilled bars after dark. At low tide you can pick your way over the razor-sharp rocks from West Railay, while at high tide you either need to swim or get a longtail, or walk over the hill from East Railay.

Climbing and kayaking

Ton Sai and Railay are Thailand's biggest **rock-climbing** centres, attracting thousands of experienced and novice climbers every year to the peninsula's seven hundred bolted routes, which range in difficulty from 5a to 8c (see Ⓦwww.railay.com for a full rundown). Of the many climbing **schools** that rent out equipment and lead guided climbs, the most established include King Climbers (Ⓣ075 662096, Ⓦwww.railay.com/railay/climbing/climbing_king_climbers.shtml), at *Ya Ya* on East Railay, and Wee's Climbing School (Ⓦwww.weesclimbingschool.com) on Ton Sai. A typical half-day introduction costs B1000, or B1800 for a full day, and equipment is B2400 per day for two people. If you don't need instruction, King Climbers' *Route Guide* gives you all the route information you need. Unaided over-water climbing on cliffs and outcrops out at sea, known as **deep-water soloing**, with no ropes, bolts or partner, is also becoming a big thing around here and can be arranged through most climbing schools for about B1000.

Kayaking around this area is also very rewarding – you can get to Ao Nang in less than an hour; kayaks cost B200 per hour to rent. For details of kayaking trips around spectacular Ao Phang Nga, and **snorkelling** trips to nearby islands, including Ko Poda and Chicken Island, see the box on p.728. For **diving**, contact the branch of Phra Nang Divers in Flame Tree Plaza on West Railay (Ⓦ www.phranangdivers.com) and see p.699 for information on nearby sites.

Eating and drinking

It's hard to get excited about most of the unexceptional **restaurants** on East and West **Railay**, but *Flame Tree*, on the seafront at West Railay, has a slightly more varied menu than many – including cashew nut salad and mushroom steak – and does a tempting "Thai tapas" set for four (B395 per person) featuring, among other dishes, *tom yam*, fishcakes, *matsaman* curry and bananas in coconut milk. Located in the middle of the spectacular cliff-lined basin on the track to Ton Sai, ten minutes' walk from both East and West Railay, *The Rock* is worth a visit for its views alone, but luckily its food is also good, mostly seafood and Thai curries, and in the reasonable B80–120 range. There's no shortage of traveller-style **bars,** especially on East Railay, with their fire-juggling and chillums; *Last Bar*, at the far end, has a pretty deck jutting out over the water.

On **Ton Sai**, *Pyramid Bar* is busy day and night with climbers scoffing the fresh coffees, tuna and cheese melts, salads and ciabatta sandwiches; it also hosts occasional DJ parties. In the evenings, *Thali Leaf*, opposite *Tiew Khao* on the East Railay track, serves Indian curries and lassies on sumptuous silky cushions. Beachfront *Freedom Bar* and *Chillout Bar* both hold regular all-nighters and full-moon parties.

Ko Phi Phi Don

About 40km south of Krabi, the island of **KO PHI PHI DON** looks breathtakingly handsome as you approach from the sea, its classic arcs of pure white sand framed by dramatic cliffs and lapped by water that's a mouthwatering shade of turquoise. A flat sandy isthmus connects the hilly east and west halves of the island, scalloped into the much photographed symmetrical double bays of Ao Ton Sai and

▲ Twin bays of Ao Loh Dalum and Ao Ton Sai, Ko Phi Phi Don

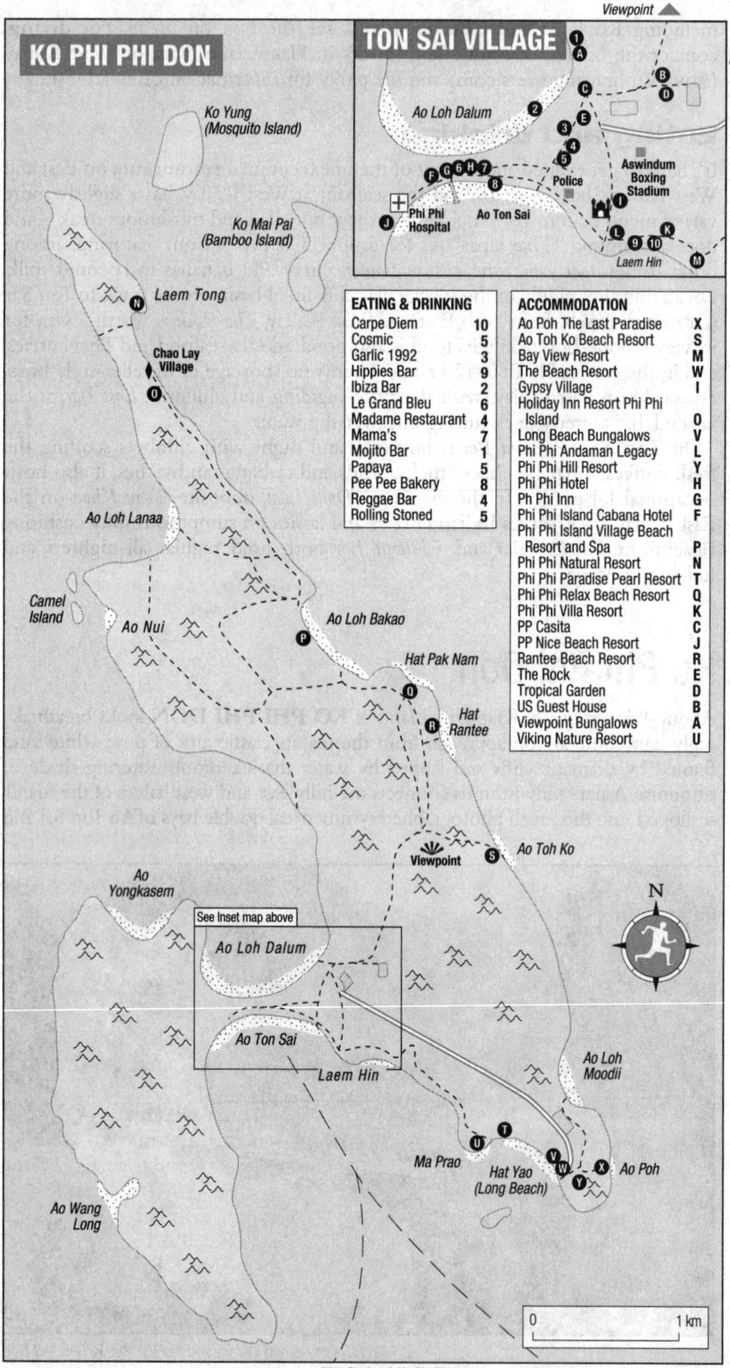
KO PHI PHI DON
TON SAI VILLAGE
Viewpoint
Long Beach
Ao Loh Dalum
Police
Aswindum Boxing Stadium
Phi Phi Hospital
Ao Ton Sai
Laem Hin
Ko Yung (Mosquito Island)
Ko Mai Pai (Bamboo Island)
Laem Tong
Chao Lay Village
Ao Loh Lanaa
Camel Island
Ao Nui
Ao Loh Bakao
Hat Pak Nam
Hat Rantee
Viewpoint
Ao Toh Ko
Ao Yongkasem
See Inset map above
Ao Loh Dalum
Ao Ton Sai
Laem Hin
Ao Loh Moodii
Ma Prao
Hat Yao (Long Beach)
Ao Poh
Ao Wang Long
N
0
1 km
Phuket & Ko Phi Phi Leh
Krabi
EATING & DRINKING
Carpe Diem 10
Cosmic 5
Garlic 1992 3
Hippies Bar 9
Ibiza Bar 2
Le Grand Bleu 6
Madame Restaurant 4
Mama's 7
Mojito Bar 1
Papaya 5
Pee Pee Bakery 8
Reggae Bar 4
Rolling Stoned 5
ACCOMMODATION
Ao Poh The Last Paradise X
Ao Toh Ko Beach Resort S
Bay View Resort M
The Beach Resort W
Gypsy Village I
Holiday Inn Resort Phi Phi Island O
Long Beach Bungalows V
Phi Phi Andaman Legacy L
Phi Phi Hill Resort Y
Phi Phi Hotel H
Ph Phi Inn G
Phi Phi Island Cabana Hotel F
Phi Phi Island Village Beach Resort and Spa P
Phi Phi Natural Resort N
Phi Phi Paradise Pearl Resort T
Phi Phi Relax Beach Resort Q
Phi Phi Villa Resort K
PP Casita C
PP Nice Beach Resort J
Rantee Beach Resort R
The Rock E
Tropical Garden D
US Guest House B
Viewpoint Bungalows A
Viking Nature Resort U

Ao Loh Dalum. The vast majority of the tourist accommodation is squashed in here, as is the island's kicking nightlife, with just a few alternatives scattered along eastern coasts. Phi Phi's few indigenous islanders mostly live in the northeast.

Such beauty, however, belies the island's turbulent recent history. By the early 1990s, Phi Phi's reputation as a tropical idyll was bringing huge crowds of backpackers to its shores, and the beaches began to lose their looks under the weight of unrestricted development and non-existent infrastructure. The problem worsened after uninhabited little sister island **Ko Phi Phi Leh** – under national marine park protection on account of its lucrative bird's-nest business (see box, p.746) – gained worldwide attention as the location for the movie *The Beach* in 1999, adding day-trippers, package-tourists and big hotels to the mix on Phi Phi Don. Then, in December 2004, the **tsunami** struck (see p.672). As a five-metre-high wave crashed in from the north, over the hotels, restaurants and hundreds of sunbathers on Ao Loh Dalum, a three-metre-high wave from the south hurtled in across the ferry dock and tourist village at Ao Ton Sai. The waves met in the middle, obliterating seventy percent of all buildings on the sandy flats, uprooting scores of trees, and killing two thousand. The rest of the island was barely affected.

Volunteers and donations poured in to help the island back on its feet, and though the rebuild was dogged by much political wrangling, the Phi Phi of today thrives much as it ever did, firmly re-established as the must-see destination on almost any trip to southern Thailand. Unfortunately, few of the pre-tsunami **problems** have been properly resolved – in part because tsunami survivors were desperate to make a new start as fast as they could. The island is now once again floundering under unregulated, unsightly and unsustainable development, with inadequate rubbish disposal and a plague of overpriced accommodation, at its most acute around the Ton Sai–Loh Dalum hub. The noise pollution from the untrammelled outdoor bars and clubs is an additional turn-off for some – though it is a fun place to party, and there are enough more remote escapes for a peaceful stay too.

All boats dock in **Ao Ton Sai**, from where it's a short walk to the main accommodation centres – in **Ton Sai village**, at **Laem Hin**, the next little stretch of sand to the east, and on **Ao Loh Dalum**, the still gorgeous, deeply curved bay across the isthmus. **Hat Yao**, another fine beach just a short boat ride away, is also very popular. To escape the crowds you need to aim for one of the smaller bays further north: **Ao Poh**, **Hat Toh Ko** and **Ao Rantee** are all good for budget breakaways, while **Hat Pak Nam**, **Ao Loh Bakao** and **Laem Tong** are pricier and more luxurious.

Getting to Ko Phi Phi Don

Ferries to Ko Phi Phi Don run year-round from **Krabi** (at least twice daily; currently 10am & 3pm, returning from Phi Phi at 9am & 2pm; 2hr; B450) and **Phuket** (currently 8.30am & 2.30pm, returning from Phi Phi at 9am & 2.30pm; 1hr 30min–2hr 30min; B450–600). Extra services are put on during peak periods, and there's also a high-season speedboat service from Phi Phi to Phuket (5pm; 45min; B800). From November to May, you can also reach Phi Phi by daily ferries from **Ao Nang**, via **West Railay** (departing Ao Nang at 9am, returning from Phi Phi at 3.30pm; 2hr 30min; B400), and from **Ko Lanta Yai** (departing Ko Lanta at 11am and returning from Phi Phi at 9am; 1hr 30min; B450). Tour agents in Phuket, Ao Nang, Krabi town and Ko Lanta all organize snorkelling day-trips to Phi Phi Don and Phi Phi Leh. For longer, overland journeys from Ko Phi Phi, any tour agent in Ton Sai can sell you bus tickets, usually via Krabi town, or train tickets, via Krabi and Surat Thani.

Touts and bungalow staff always meet the ferries; if you've pre-booked **accommodation** your luggage will be transported in a handcart. As demand frequently

Snorkelling, diving and rock-climbing off Ko Phi Phi

Ko Phi Phi and nearby islets have famously varied reefs, which make for excellent and very popular **diving and snorkelling**. There's decent **rock-climbing** here too, though it doesn't compare to Railay.

Snorkelling

There's some great **snorkelling** around Phi Phi's shallow fringing reefs, most rewardingly at strikingly beautiful, uninhabited **Ko Mai Pai** (**Bamboo Island**), off Phi Phi Don's northeast coast, where much of the reef lies close to the surface, and at nearby **Ko Yung** (**Mosquito Island**), with its spectacular, steep-sided drop. Phi Phi Don has its own worthwhile reefs too, including at west-coast **Ao Yongkasem**, within kayaking distance of Ao Loh Dalum, but the tranquil waters of **Ao Maya** (Maya Bay, *The Beach* beach) on Phi Phi Leh are more famous, and a lot more crowded (see p.746).

Outings to these and other reefs are easily arranged as part of an **organized tour** (B450–800 including equipment) or by **hiring your own longtail** boatman at the pier (B1500/3000 per boat per half/ full-day), the latter far preferable to the largest tour boats, whose groups of forty-plus trippers inundate the reefs. **Overnight camping trips** to Bamboo Island or Maya Bay are a neat way of avoiding the big crowds, offering late-afternoon snorkelling and kayaking rounded off with a barbecue on the beach; they usually depart Phi Phi about 4pm and return the next day at 10am, charging B1900.

Diving

Offering visibility touching 30m, a great diversity of healthy hard and soft corals, and potential encounters with white-tip sharks, moray eels and stingrays, the diving around Ko Phi Phi is the best in the region and the usual destination of dive boats from Ao Nang and Phuket, as well as, of course, from Phi Phi itself. Highlights include the gorgonian sea fans, barracudas, manta rays and even whale sharks at **Ko Bidah Nok** and **Ko Bidah Nai**, the mass of leopard sharks at **Hin Bidah**, and the *King Cruiser* **wreck** (see p.699).

outstrips supply on Phi Phi, if you haven't made a reservation, it's worth using the agents' booking service at the pier head, where pictures and – genuine – room prices for hotels in all categories are posted for easy browsing; staff then call ahead to secure your room, and might even carry your bag there. Be warned though that rooms are very expensive on Phi Phi, and often poorly maintained. We've quoted rates for high season, which runs from November to April, but most places slap on a thirty- to fifty-percent surcharge during Christmas and New Year and, conversely, will discount up to fifty percent in quiet periods between May and October.

Island practicalities

From Ao Ton Sai you can catch a **longtail** to any of the other beaches, or use the **paths** across the steep and at times rugged interior. There are only a few short motorbike tracks and one **road**, from the back of Ton Sai village to *The Beach* on Long Beach, which takes around forty minutes on foot. You could also get about by **kayak** (B200 per hr), which is the perfect way to explore the limestone cliffs and secluded bays, without the roar of an accompanying longtail or cruise ship.

Ton Sai village has all the essential services, including **ATMs** and **exchange** counters run by national banks (daily 7am–10pm), scores of **internet** centres, and bicycle rental (B100 per 3hr). The island's only health centre, **Phi Phi Hospital** (ⓣ081 270 4481), is at the western end of Ao Ton Sai, and there's a **police** box (ⓣ081 536 2427) next to the Apache Bar on the track to Laem Hin.

There are at least twenty dive shops on Phi Phi, the majority of them in Ton Sai, and though they all stick to a price agreement there are variations in professionalism. It's important to check credentials and equipment (see p.73) and to ask about the dive boat: some places use longtails rather than the much more comfortable, better-equipped proper dive boats. Also note that it is considered risky for a novice diver with fewer than twenty dives under their belt to dive at distant Hin Daeng and Hin Muang (see p.699), due to the depth and the current; the most reputable dive shops will only take Advanced Divers there. Recommended Ton Sai dive shops include Visa Diving (Ⓣ075 601157, Ⓦwww.visadiving.com) and Moskito (Ⓣ075 601154, Ⓦwww.moskitodiving.com), both on the main track to the pier, and Viking Divers, on the cross-island soi inland from *Chao Koh Phi Phi Lodge* (Ⓣ081 719 3375, Ⓦwww.vikingdiversthailand.com). There are also small dive centres on Hat Yao, Ao Loh Bakao and Laem Tong.

Prices for **day-trips** including two tanks, equipment and lunch start at B2500. **Dive courses** cost B3400 for the introductory Discover Scuba day, B12,900 for the certificated four-day Openwater course, and B10,400 for a two-day Advanced course. The nearest recompression chambers are on Phuket (see p.698); check to see that your dive operator is insured to use one of them.

Rock-climbing

Phi Phi's topography is a gift for **rock-climbers** and both Cat's (Ⓣ081 787 5101) and Spidermonkey (Ⓣ075 819384, Ⓦwww.spidermonkeyclimbing.com) in the village offer climbing instruction and equipment rental. Prices average B10000/1500 for a half-/full-day's instruction. The main climbing area is just to the west of Ao Ton Sai, and includes the Ton Sai Tower and the Drinking Wall, with thirty routes from grades 5 to 7a. A newer attraction is **cliff-jumping**, offered by several tour agencies and featuring jumps of up to 18m off a Phi Phi Don cliff.

Ton Sai village, Ao Loh Dalum and Laem Hin

Ton Sai village is a hectic warren of a place, both strangely old-fashioned with its alley traffic of bicycles and push carts, its tidy fresh market tucked away in the middle and its squalid shanty town and stinky sewers hidden along the edges, and of course bang up to date, the narrow lanes bursting with state-of-the-art dive shops, raucous bars and trendy boutiques.

West of the pier, **Ao Ton Sai** beach is an attractive little retreat under the limestone karsts, though it gets busy for a couple of hours around lunchtime and you're not far from the longtail moorings. Most people simply head for **Ao Loh Dalum** instead, less than 300m north across the narrow isthmus, which looks astonishingly pretty at high tide, with its glorious curve of powder-white sand beautifully set off by pale blue water; it's a different story at low-water, however, as the tide goes out for miles. Sun-loungers and parasols line the shore here and you can try parasailing and waterskiing in the bay. There's a small Tsunami Memorial Park of carefully tended shrubs, epitaphs and photos at the eastern end.

The **viewpoint** that overlooks eastern Ao Loh Dalum affords a magnificent panorama over the twin bays and every evening a stream of people makes the steep fifteen-minute climb up the steps for sunset shots; early morning is also photogenic, and the shop at the "Topview" summit, set within a pretty tropical garden, serves coffee as well as cold drinks. From the viewpoint you can descend the rocky and at times almost sheer paths to the trio of little east-coast bays at Ao Toh Ko, Ao Rantee (Lanti), and Hat Pak Nam, each of which takes about thirty minutes.

East along the coast from the Ton Sai pier, about ten minutes' walk down the main lane, is the promontory known as **Laem Hin**, beyond which lies a small beach and bungalows that enjoy a little more space. Inland, there are island homes and a mosque.

Accommodation

Ton Sai **hotels** are the least good value on the island and almost none, however expensive, is out of earshot of the thumping all-night beats cranked up by the various bars and clubs; bring some heavy-duty earplugs if you're not planning to party every night.

Ton Sai village and Ao Loh Dalum

Phi Phi Hotel ⓣ075 60023, ⓦgeocities.com/pphotel. One of the biggest hotels in Ton Sai, with a range of mid-market air-con rooms in low-rise buildings just inland from the pier. At the top-end you get some sort of sea view, either over Ton Sai or Loh Dalum, while the cheapest have no window at all. There's a small pool on site. ❻–❼

Phi Phi Inn ⓣ081 797 2088, ⓔphiphi_inn@hotmail.com. Small, sparklingly clean, all-air-con little hotel right next to *Phi Phi Hotel*, where all fifteen rooms have TVs, safety boxes and balconies, though only the upstairs ones have the chance of a view and also enjoy more privacy. ❻

Phi Phi Island Cabana Hotel ⓣ075 601170, ⓦwww.phiphi-cabana.com. The views from the contemporary rooms at this large, imposing hotel are breathtakingly lovely. Most look out across the scoop of Ao Loh Dalum and its framing cliffs, and ground-floor ones have direct access to the sand. There's a huge pool too. On the minus side, the hotel lacks atmosphere, has a cavernous restaurant and some rooms are affected by late-night club noise. Reception is west of the pier on Ton Sai. ❾

PP Casita ⓣ075 601214, ⓦgeocities.com/pphotel. Just inland from Ao Loh Dalum, this place is designed as its own little village, comprising eighty dinky buttermilk clapboard cabanas built on stilts and connected by wooden walkways that sit above a tropical garden. Interiors are on the small side but good, with air-con, platform beds, TV, wi-fi and nice tiled bathrooms. The drawback is that the cabanas are tightly packed and outdoor seating is on the walkway, making it a sociable place, but not very private or quiet. Noise from the nearby *Ibiza Bar* can also be a problem. Also has more spacious rooms in a hotel block and a pool. ❼

PP Nice Beach Resort ⓣ081 894 5164. The location here is rather lovely, almost at the westernmost end of Ton Sai, under the shadow of the cliff wall just beyond the harbour area; the sand is gorgeously white and the sea a pretty blue, though you may feel inundated by day-trippers at lunchtime. It's family run and has fairly simple fan bungalows and better quality air-con ones made from bamboo and wood. Fan ❻, air-con ❼

The Rock ⓣ081 607 897. Traveller-oriented hangout offering the cheapest beds on the island, in two mixed-sex fourteen- and sixteen-bed dorms (B250 per bed); bunk beds are crammed in, but there are fans and lockers. Also has a few singles and doubles with shared bathrooms. ❹

Tropical Garden ⓣ081 968 1436, ⓦwww.thailandphiphitravel.com. The good-sized rough-timber fan and air-con huts here are mostly built on stilts up the side of an outcrop, beyond the turn-off for the path to the viewpoint. The better ones have a breezy veranda (though not much of a view) and there's a refreshing amount of greenery around, plus a tiny pool, despite being surrounded by other accommodation. Also has some cheap rooms in the main wooden building above the restaurant; their walls are thin but all have a window and pleasant decor. ❹–❻

US Guest House ⓣ087 278 7906, ⓔjo_uspp@hotmail.com. This two-storey block of sixteen functional en-suite fan rooms has the look and feel of an urban guest house, and offers some of the cheaper rooms in the area. Interiors aren't bad at all and there's a long shared deck with seating beside the narrow lane. It's close by the base of the viewpoint access steps. ❹

Viewpoint Bungalows ⓣ075 601200, ⓦwww.phiphiviewpoint.com. Strung out across and up the cliffside at the far eastern end of Ao Loh Dalum, these fifty bungalows enjoy great views out over the bay, though interiors tend towards the cheap and flimsy and the all-night *Ibiza Bar* is too near to ignore. Facilities include a scenically sited restaurant, a couple of bars, a tour desk and a small, idyllically situated bayview pool and *Mojito Bar*. Fan ❻, air-con ❼–❾

Laem Hin

Bay View Resort Yao ⓣ075 601127, ⓦwww.phiphibayview.com. The draw at the seventy large, air-con bungalows here is their prime location: they're set high on the cliffside at the far eastern end of Laem Hin beach, strung out along the ridge almost as far as Hat Yao. All have massive windows and decks to enjoy the great views and there's a pool here too. Be prepared for lots of steps though. 8–9

Gypsy Village ⓣ075 601045, ⓦwww.ppgypsyvillage.com. The 25 plain and pretty shabby pink-painted concrete bungalows here are relatively cheap, but they're all en suite and are set round a big dry lawn about 150m down the track between the mosque and *Phi Phi Andaman Legacy*. 4

Phi Phi Andaman Legacy ⓣ075 601106, ⓦwww.phiphiandamanlegacy.com. Set in a secluded enclosure just a few metres back from the beach, the rather old-fashioned bungalows here are arranged in a square around a large lawn and small central swimming pool, while the 36 more modern rooms occupy a three-storey hotel building at the back. All rooms are air-con and come with TVs, hot water and safety boxes. 7–8

Phi Phi Villa Resort ⓣ075 601100, ⓦwww.phiphivillaresort.com. The best of the many options at this outfit are the huge air-con family cottages occupying the front section of the prettily landscaped garden, near the small pool. Also available are smaller air-con bungalows. Just a few steps from *Carpe Diem* so handy for on-the-doorstep drinks and fireshows. 8–9

Eating

Ton Sai is the best place to eat on the island, offering everything from bakery cafés to seafood **restaurants**, as well as cheap Thai curry-and-rice stalls.

Cosmic Well-priced home-made pasta (B130) and pizzas at two locations.

Garlic 1992 Cheap Thai food, especially curries and soups served with extra coconut milk straight from the fresh coconut. Mostly B70.

Le Grand Bleu Classy place close to *Phi Phi Hotel* serving a French-inspired menu (B270–350) that includes lots of fresh seafood, duck fillet with mango, sirloin steak and changing dishes of the day. Daily from 6pm.

Madame Restaurant Deservedly popular for its curries – *kaeng phanaeng*, *matsaman* green and red – mostly B80. Also does thin-crust pizzas and a decent vegetarian selection, and shows nightly movies.

Mama's Indulge yourself from the cabinet of tempting cakes, and make use of the free wi-fi at the same time or come for a leisurely seafood dinner of mackerel steak with mash or prawns in peanut sauce. Daily 11am–3pm & 6–11pm.

Papaya One of the best of several village-style kitchens whose authentic and reasonably cheap Thai standards, including noodle soups, *phat thai* (B60), fried rice dishes and fiery curries, makes it very popular with locals and dive staff.

Pee Pee Bakery The obvious place for breakfast, with its different blends of real coffee, set breakfasts (from B80) and piles of freshly baked croissants, Danish pastries, home-made breads, cakes and cookies. Has two branches. Daily 7am–8pm.

Drinking and entertainment

Ton Sai **nightlife** is young and drunken, involving endless buckets of Sansom and red bull, dance music played until dawn, and fire-juggling shows on the beach. Most of the bars offer a pretty similar formula, so it's often the one-off events and happy hours that make the difference.

The **Aswindum Thai Boxing Stadium** and training camp (ⓦphiphiaswindumresort.com), inland on the track between Laem Hin's mosque and *The Rock*, stages regular bouts of *muay thai* (Mon, Tues & Fri 9.30pm; B700–1000).

Carpe Diem Opposite *PP Villa* at Laem Hin. There's cushion seating on the upper terrace here, nightly fire shows from around 10pm and dancing on the beach. Also serves food from morning till late.

Hippies Bar Across from *PP Andaman* on Laem Hin. Hugely popular place with a chilled-out sea-view and on-the-beach bar and restaurant that shows nightly movies at 8pm, followed by fire shows some time after 10pm, and hosts regular half-moon parties. You can learn fire-juggling here yourself every afternoon.

Ibiza Bar On the beach at Loh Dalum. Very loud and very late on-the-sand bar that keeps punters entertained almost till sunrise with its booming sound system, DJs spinning mostly house and techno, fire shows and the rest.

Mojito Bar Poolside at *Viewpoint Bungalows* on Ao Loh Dalum. The best place for a cocktail or three in Ton Sai, with unsurpassed sea and sunset views, good music, very genial hosts and an especially irresistible mango daiquiri. Daily 2–10pm.

Reggae Bar In the heart of the village, on the soi that runs north beside *Chao Koh Phi Phi Lodge.* A Phi Phi institution that's been running for years in various incarnations. These days it arranges regular amateur *muay thai* bouts in its boxing ring – "beat up your friend and win free buckets" – and has pool tables and a bar around the sides. Even has reggae karaoke.

Rolling Stoned Centre of the village. Lively bar with nightly gigs from the in-house Thai cover band.

Long Beach (Hat Yao) and Ao Por

With its deluxe sand and large reefs packed with polychromatic marine life just 20m offshore, **HAT YAO** (Long Beach) is considered the best of Phi Phi's main beaches, but it's lined with hotels so gets very busy. For food you've only got hotel restaurants, but there's also the beachside *Buddha Bar*, which has fireshows and keeps serving till about 2am. The tiny bays to either side, within ten minutes' walk of Hat Yao, are much quieter and support just one set of bungalows apiece.

UK-run Long Beach Divers (ⓦwww.longbeachdivers.com) at *Long Beach* runs all the same **dive** trips and courses as shops in the village and offers discounted stays at *Long Beach Bungalows* for dive students.

Longtail **boats** do the ten-minute shuttle between Hat Yao and Ao Ton Sai (B100 per person, or B150 after dark), but at low tide it's also possible to **walk** between the two in half an hour, via the coast in front of *Bay View Resort* on Laem Hin and then via *Viking*. The island's single **road** follows an inland route to *The Beach* from *The Rock* junction in the village, passing the post-tsunami housing project and Water Hill reservoir en route; it's a hot, hilly and unshaded forty-minute walk.

Accommodation

Ao Poh The Last Paradise ⓣ084 861 7630, ⓔao_poh_resort@hotmail.com. A 10min walk over the forested headland from behind *The Beach* and *Phi Phi Hill*, the pretty little white-sand bay of Ao Poh has just a dozen rudimentary bamboo bungalows. The cheapest have neither fan nor private bathroom, the most expensive are en suite. ❸–❹

The Beach Resort ⓣ075 618268, ⓦwww.phiphithebeach.com. Currently the poshest option on Hat Yao, this place has a throng of large, timber-clad chalets built on stilts up the hillside, with the tallest, most deluxe ones enjoying commanding views of Phi Phi Leh. Interiors are fairly upscale, with air-con and liberal use of wood for flooring and wall panels. There's wi-fi and a small beach-front pool. ❽–❾

Long Beach Bungalows ⓣ086 470 8984, ⓔlongbeach@gmail.com. The first choice of most budget travellers, this fairly cheap, well-located and long-running option has dozens of tightly packed huts for rent. At the bottom end you get ultra-simple bamboo huts, many of which contain nothing more than a bed, a fan and a mosquito net, though some also have their own bathrooms. The slightly better ones are sturdier wooden huts and many of these are right on the shorefront. Shared bathroom ❸, en suite ❹, beachfront ❺

Phi Phi Hill Resort ⓣ075 618203, ⓦwww.phiphihill.com. The fifty mint-green wooden cabins here occupy a glorious spot high above the beach, overlooking the far eastern end of Hat Yao. With fine sunrise or sunset views, depending on your location, and plenty of breeze, the only off-putting factor here is the one hundred steps that connect the resort with the beach below (though there is a pulley system for luggage). Rooms are simply furnished and come with fan or air-con. Fan ❹, air-con ❺–❻

Phi Phi Paradise Pearl Resort ⓣ075 601246, ⓦwww.phiphiparadisepearl.com. The 25 bungalows at this efficiently run place are fairly well spaced along the western half of the beach, with none more than a few steps from the shore. Interiors are unremarkable but perfectly comfortable and all have air-con. There's internet access here, plus a tour counter and book exchange. ❼–❽

Viking Nature Resort ⓣ075 819399, ⓦwww.vikingnatureresort.com. Tucked away on and above two private little coves just west of Hat Yao, with easy access via a rocky path, this is a very stylish take on classic Thai beach-bungalow architecture. It's nearly all wood and bamboo here, with no air-con or hot water and in some cases no private bathroom either, but interiors that are styled with Asian boho-chic artefacts. The most

Thai cuisine

Thai food is now hugely popular in the West, but nothing, of course, beats coming to Thailand to experience the full range of subtle and fiery flavours, constructed from the freshest ingredients. Four fundamental tastes are identified in Thai cuisine – spiciness, sourness, saltiness and sweetness – and diners aim to share a variety of dishes that impart a balance of these flavours, along with complementary textures. Lemon grass, basil, coriander, galangal, chilli, garlic, lime juice, coconut milk and fermented fish sauce are just some of the distinctive components that bring these tastes to life.

Vats of curry ▲

Green and red chillies ▼

Bottles of fish sauce ▼

Curries, soups and salads

Thai **curries** (*kaeng*) have a variety of curry pastes as their foundation: elaborate blends of herbs, spices, garlic, shallots and chilli peppers ground together with pestle and mortar. The use of some of these spices, as well as coconut cream, was imported from India long ago; curries that don't use coconut cream are naturally less sweet and thinner, with the consistency of soups.

While some curries, such as *kaeng karii* (mild and yellow) and *kaeng matsaman* ("Muslim curry", with potatoes, peanuts and usually beef), still show their roots, others have been adapted into quintessentially Thai dishes, notably *kaeng khiaw wan* (sweet and green), *kaeng phet* (red and hot) and *kaeng phanaeng* (thick and savoury, with peanuts). *Kaeng som* generally contains fish and takes its distinctive sourness from the addition of tamarind or, in the northeast, okra leaves. Traditionally eaten during the cool season, *kaeng liang* uses up bland vegetables, but is made aromatic with hot peppercorns.

Eaten simultaneously with other dishes, not as a starter, Thai **soups** often have the tang of lemon grass, kaffir lime leaves and galangal, and are sometimes made extremely spicy with chillies. Two favourites are *tom kha kai*, a creamy coconut chicken soup; and *tom yam kung*, a hot and sour prawn soup without coconut milk. *Khao tom*, a starchy rice soup that's generally eaten for breakfast, meets the approval of few Westerners, except as a traditional hangover cure.

One of the lesser-known delights of Thai cuisine is the *yam* or **salad**, which imparts all four fundamental flavours in an unusual and refreshing harmony.

Yam come in many permutations – with noodles, meat, seafood or vegetables – but at the heart of every variety is a liberal squirt of lime juice and a fiery sprinkling of chillies. Salads to look out for include *yam som oh* (pomelo), *yam hua plee* (banana flowers) and *yam plaa duk foo* (fluffy deep-fried catfish).

Noodle and rice dishes

Sold on street stalls everywhere, **noodles** come in assorted varieties – including *kway tiaw* (made with rice flour) and *ba mii* (egg noodles) – and get boiled up as soups (*nam*), doused in gravy (*rat na*) or stir-fried (*haeng*, "dry", or *phat*, "fried"). Most famous of all is *phat thai* ("Thai fry-up"), a delicious combination of noodles (usually *kway tiaw*), egg, tofu and spring onions, sprinkled with ground peanuts and lime, and often spiked with tiny dried shrimps. Other faithful standbys include fried **rice** (*khao phat*) and cheap, one-dish meals served on a bed of steamed rice, notably *khao kaeng* (with curry).

▲ Seafood barbecuing at a market stall

▼ People eating at a night market

Regional dishes

Many of the specialities of **northern Thailand** originated in Burma, including *khao soi*, featuring both boiled and crispy egg noodles plus beef, chicken or pork in a curried coconut soup; and *kaeng hang lay*, a pork curry with ginger, turmeric and tamarind. Also look out for spicy dipping sauces such as *nam phrik ong*, made with minced pork, roast tomatoes and lemon grass, and served with crisp cucumber slices.

▼ Aubergines

The crop most suited to the infertile lands of **Isaan** is sticky rice (*khao niaw*), which replaces the standard grain as the staple for northeasterners. Served in a rattan basket, it's usually eaten with the

Making *som tam* ▲

Sticky rice ▼

fingers, rolled up into small balls and dipped into chilli sauces. It's perfect with such spicy local delicacies as *som tam*, a green-papaya salad with raw chillies, green beans, tomatoes, peanuts and dried shrimps (or fresh crab). Although you'll find basted barbecued chicken on a stick (*kai yaang*) all over Thailand, it originated in Isaan and is especially tasty in its home region. Raw minced pork, beef or chicken is the basis of another popular Isaan and northern dish, *laap*, a salad that's subtly flavoured with mint and lime. A similar northeastern salad is *nam tok*, featuring grilled beef or pork and roasted rice powder, which takes its name, "waterfall", from its refreshing blend of complex tastes.

Aside from putting a greater emphasis on seafood, **southern Thai** cuisine displays a marked Malaysian and Muslim aspect as you near the border, notably in *khao mok kai*, the local version of a biryani: chicken and rice cooked with turmeric and other Indian spices, and served with chicken soup. Southern markets often serve *khao yam* for breakfast or lunch, a delicious salad of dried cooked rice, dried shrimp and grated coconut served with a sweet sauce. You'll also find many types of *roti*, a pancake sold from pushcart griddles and, in its plain form, rolled with condensed milk. Other versions include savoury *mataba*, with minced chicken or beef, and *roti kaeing*, served with curry sauce for breakfast. A huge variety of curries are also dished up in the south, many substituting shrimp paste for fish sauce. Two of the most distinctive are *kaeng luang*, "yellow curry", featuring fish, turmeric, pineapple, squash, beans and green papaya; and *kaeng tai plaa*, a powerful combination of fish stomach with potatoes, beans, pickled bamboo shoots and turmeric.

glamorous accommodation is in the enormous, high-level, two- to four-bedroom "Makmai" tree houses, with their massive living-room decks overlooking the bay. Cheaper alternatives range from smaller en-suite tree houses to simple huts with shared facilities. There's a stylish lounge and dining area on the beach, with wi-fi. Shared bathroom ④, en suite ⑥–⑦ Makmai ⑨

Ao Toh Ko, Hat Rantee and Hat Pak Nam

Travellers wanting to escape the crowds around Ton Sai and Hat Yao without spending a fortune head for the trio of little bays midway along the east coast: Ao Toh Ko, Hat Rantee (Lanti) and Hat Pak Nam. Longtail transfers cost about B100 per person from Ao Ton Sai, or you can reach the bays inland, via steep forest trails that run from the Viewpoint above Ao Loh Dalum (see p.741) and take half an hour to walk. At **AO TOH KO**, it's the exceptionally welcoming family who run *Ao Toh Ko Beach Resort* (ⓣ081 537 0528, ⓔtohkobeach@gmail.com; ③–④, family ⑦) who keep people staying and returning – and they're great cooks too. The 32 bungalows here have the beach all to themselves and some sit right over the sea on the rocks to the south. They come in a range of styles, but are all good and comfortable. with fans and private bathrooms. At low tide you can walk to **HAT RANTEE** in five minutes, where *Rantee Beach Resort* (ⓣ087 472 8192; ④) has simple en-suite bamboo huts in the middle of the palm- and casuarina-fringed white-sand bay; there's great snorkelling at the reef right off the beach too. *Phi Phi Relax Beach Resort* (ⓣ089 725 4411, ⓦphiphirelaxbeach.com; ⑥–⑧) on **HAT PAK NAM** offers the most comfortable, and expensive, though still rustic, accommodation, in fifteen attractive, en-suite thatched bamboo bungalows in among the beachfront trees.

Ao Loh Bakao and Laem Tong

Far removed from the hustle of Ao Ton Sai and its environs, the beautiful, secluded northern beaches at Ao Loh Bakao and Laem Tong are the domain of just a few upscale resorts. Access is usually by hotel boat from Ao Ton Sai (generally B150–200 per person on arrival but as much as B2000 per boat thereafter) or by chartering your own longtail (about B800 per boat); it's forty minutes to Ao Loh Bakao and a further fifteen minutes north to Laem Tong.

The plush, air-conditioned chalets at *Phi Phi Island Village Beach Resort and Spa* (ⓣ075 628999, ⓦwww.ppisland.com; ⑨) have the gorgeous eight-hundred-metre-long white-sand beach and turquoise waters of **AO LOH BAKAO** all to themselves. It's a popular honeymoon spot, and a lovely location for anyone looking for a quiet, comfortable break. The thatched, split-bamboo bungalows are designed in traditional Thai style and furnished with character and elegance. There's a good-sized pool and spa centre in the prettily landscaped tropical gardens, as well as a dive centre and kayak rental. If you tire of these sands, and the hotel restaurants, there's a cluster of reasonably priced local restaurants behind the resort, and you can walk to the long, semi-circular beach at **Ao Loh Lanaa**, across on the west coast, in ten minutes, or to Laem Tong in half an hour.

Almost right at Phi Phi's northernmost tip, **LAEM TONG** is busier and more commercial than Loh Bakao, with several upmarket resorts along its white-sand shores, and views across to nearby Bamboo and Mosquito islands. The beach is home to a group of Urak Lawoy *chao ley* "sea gypsies" (see p.663), whose village is next to the *Holiday Inn*; all longtail boat tours and transfers are run by Laem Tong's *chao ley* co-operative. At the southern end of the beach, *Holiday Inn Resort Phi Phi Island* (ⓣ075 627300, ⓦwww.phiphi-palmbeach.com; ⑨) offers 76 air-conditioned bungalows set in graceful gardens of tidy lawns and flowering shrubs plus a swimming pool, dive centre and spa. Up at the northern

Bird's-nesting

Prized for its aphrodisiac and energizing qualities, **bird's-nest soup** is such a delicacy in Taiwan, Singapore and Hong Kong that ludicrous sums of money change hands for a dish whose basic ingredients are tiny twigs glued together with bird's spit. Collecting these nests is a lucrative but life-endangering business: sea swifts (known as edible-nest swiftlets) build their nests in rock crevices hundreds of metres above sea level, often on sheer cliff-faces or in cavernous hollowed-out karst. **Nest-building** begins in January and the harvesting season usually lasts from February to May, during which time the female swiftlet builds three nests on the same spot, none of them more than 12cm across, by secreting an unbroken thread of saliva, which she winds round as if making a coil pot. **Gatherers** will only steal the first two nests made by each bird, prising them off the cave walls with special metal forks. This in theory allows the bird to build a final nest and raise her chicks in peace. Gathering the nests demands faultless agility and balance, skills that seem to come naturally to the *chao ley*, whose six-man teams bring about four hundred nests down the perilous bamboo scaffolds each day, weighing about 4kg in total. At a market rate of up to $2000 per kilo, so much money is at stake that a government franchise must be granted before any collecting commences, and armed guards often protect the sites at night. The *chao ley* seek spiritual protection from the dangers of the job by making offerings to the spirits of the cliff or cave at the beginning of the season; in the Viking Cave, they place buffalo flesh, horns and tails at the foot of one of the stalagmites.

In recent years, entrepreneurs in Ban Laem, near Phetchaburi, across on south Thailand's Gulf Coast, have started competing with the *chao lay* – by constructing **sea swift condominiums** and trying to attract the swiftlets that frequent the attic of the nearby temple. The theory is that by constructing windowless concrete towers they can mimic the Andaman Sea caves – complete with cool dark interiors, droppings-smeared walls and swiftlet soundtracks on continuous replay – entice the birds in to build their nests, and harvest them with ease. To date, the main beneficiary seems to have been the company that builds these ugly towers, as the local swiftlet population suddenly has an awful lot of new accommodation to choose from.

end, the cheaper, old-style air-con rooms and wooden chalets at *Phi Phi Natural Resort* (ⓣ075 613010, ⓦwww.phiphinatural.com; ❽–❾) are scattered around an extensive tropical shorefront garden, with pool, that stretches along the coast to the next tiny uninhabited bay.

Ko Phi Phi Leh

More rugged than its twin, Ko Phi Phi Don, and a quarter the size, **KO PHI PHI LEH** is the number-one day-tripping destination from Phi Phi Don, twenty minutes' north, and a feature of all snorkelling tours out of Phuket and Ao Nang. It is very scenic indeed, and world famous, following its starring role in the film *The Beach,* so expect huge crowds, a plethora of discarded polystyrene lunch boxes, and a fair bit of damage to the reefs from the carelessly dropped anchors of tourist and fishing boats. The best way to appreciate the island is probably on one of the overnight camping and snorkelling trips from Phi Phi Don (see p.740).

Most idyllic of all the island's bays is **Ao Maya** on the southwest coast, where the water is still and very clear and the coral extremely varied; **Ao Phi Leh**, an almost completely enclosed east-coast lagoon of breathtakingly turquoise water, is also beautiful. Nearby, the **Viking Cave** gets its misleading name from the scratchy wall-paintings of Chinese junks inside, but more interesting than this 400-year-old graffiti is the **bird's-nesting** that goes on here: rickety bamboo scaffolding extends hundreds of metres up to the roof of the cave, where intrepid *chao ley* harvesters spend the day scraping the unfeasibly valuable nests made by tiny sea-swifts off the rockface for export to specialist Chinese restaurants all over the world.

Ko Jum

Situated halfway between Krabi and Ko Lanta Yai, **KO JUM** (whose northern half is also known as **Ko Pu**) is the sort of laid-back spot that people come to for a couple of days, then can't bring themselves to leave. Though there's plenty of accommodation on the island, there's nothing more than a handful of beach bars for evening entertainment, and little to do during the day except try out the half-dozen west-coast beaches and read your book under a tree. The beaches may not be pristine, and are in some places unswimmably rocky at low tide, but they're mostly long and wild, and all but empty of people. Nights are also low key: it's paraffin lamps and starlight after about 11pm at those places that are off the main grid, and many don't even provide fans as island breezes are sufficiently cooling.

The island is home to around three thousand people, the majority of them Muslim, though there are also communities of *chao ley* sea gypsies on Ko Jum (see p.663), as well as Buddhists. The main village is **Ban Ko Jum,** on the island's southeastern tip, comprising a few local shops and small restaurants, one of the island's three piers for boats to and from Laem Kruat on the mainland, and a beachfront school. It's about 1km from the village to the southern end of the island's most popular beach, the appropriately named **Long Beach**. Long Beach is connected to **Golden Pearl Beach**, which sits just south of **Ban Ting Rai**, the middle-island village that's about halfway down the west coast. North of Ban Ting Rai, a trio of smaller, increasingly remote beaches at **Ao Si**, **Ao Ting Rai**, and **Ao Luboa** complete the picture. The island's third village, **Ban Ko Pu,** occupies the northeastern tip, about 5km beyond Ban Ting Rai, and has another Laem Kruat ferry pier. Many islanders refer to the north of the island, from Ban Ting Rai upwards, as Ko Pu, and define only the south as Ko Jum. Much of the north is made inaccessible by the breastbone of forested hills, whose highest peak (422m) is Khao Ko Pu.

Very high winds and heavy seas mean that Ko Jum becomes an acquired taste from May through October, so most tourist accommodation **closes** for that period: exceptions are highlighted in the text.

Getting to Ko Jum

During high season, usual access to Ko Jum is via the Krabi–Ko Lanta **ferries** (1hr 30min–2hr from Krabi, or about 45min from Ko Lanta; B400; see p.720 for times). Ko Jum bungalows send longtails out to meet the ferries as they make two stops off the west coast: coming from Krabi, stop one is for the *Ko Pu* bungalows (on Ao Ting Rai and Ao Luboa) and the second, "Ko Jum", stop is for *Ao Si*, *Golden Pearl* and *Long Beach* bungalows. When it comes to moving on, you can also charter a longtail from Ko Jum direct to Ko Phi Phi for about B2000: the trip takes a couple of hours.

In the **rainy season** you have to travel to Ko Jum **overland**, and an increasing number of visitors now use this route year-round; some bungalow operators, for example, offer transfers from Krabi airport using this route (about B600 per car to Laem Kruat). Coming from Krabi town, you first need to take a **songthaew** to **Nua Klong**, and then another one to **Laem Kruat** (allow two hours in total, though it's only about 40km). **Boats** run from Laem Kruat to all three east-coast "village" piers on Ko Jum, from where a motorbike taxi with sidecar

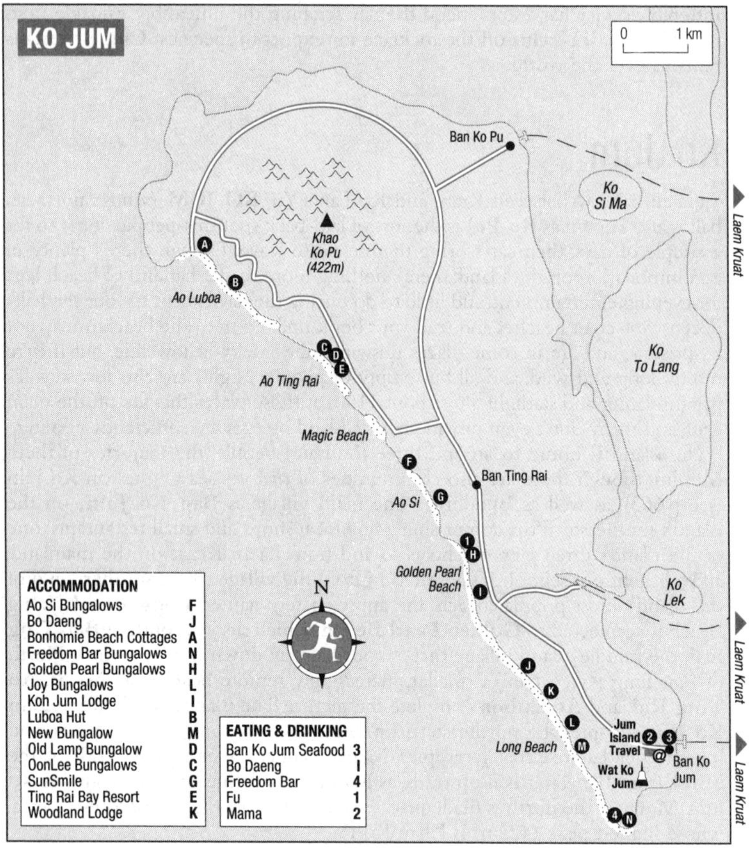

should transfer you to your bungalow for B50 per person. Timetables are a little vague: boats **to Ban Ko Jum** depart Laem Kruat between 1pm and 3pm, and return from Ko Jum about 7.30am (1hr; B70); boats to **Mu 2, east of Ban Ting Rai**, depart Laem Kruat in the afternoon until 5pm, and return from Ko Jum at 7.30am & 1.30pm (50min; B60); boats to **Ban Ko Pu** depart Laem Kruat about every two hours between 9am and 5.30pm, and return from Ban Ko Pu between 7am and 8.30am (45min; B50).

Island practicalities

Most bungalows can arrange **kayak** and **motorbike** rental. They will also organize **day-trips**, as will tour agencies in Ban Ko Jum, for example to Ko Phi Phi, Bamboo Island and Mosquito Island (B800–1500 per person or about B4000 per boat), or around Ko Jum (B1500 per boat). Many offer guided hikes up Khao Ko Pu (B500 per half day, or more from southern accommodation), and *OonLee* does a trip to Khlong Thom hot spring on the mainland (B1500 per person). Blue Juice Dive (Ⓣ086 997 9197, Ⓔbluejuicedivers@gmail.com; also has branch in Krabi town) at *Woodland Lodge* on Long Beach runs **diving trips** to Phi Phi (B3900) and diving courses (Discover Scuba B4900; Openwater B14,900).

There's no ATM on the island, but you can **change money** at Jum Island Travel next to the pier in Ban Ko Jum and *Koh Jum Lodge* on Long Beach does Visa cash advances. There's **internet** access in Ban Ko Jum and, evenings only, at one or more of the hotels on almost every beach. Ban Ko Jum also has a couple of shops selling beachwear and basic necessities. The island **medical centre** is on the road just south of *Golden Pearl* bungalows, beyond the southern edge of Ban Ting Rai. For a comprehensive **guide** to life on the island and pictures of all the bungalow operations, see Ⓦwww.kohjumonline.com.

Long Beach, Golden Pearl Beach and Ban Ko Jum

LONG BEACH (sometimes known as **Andaman Beach**) is the main backpackers' beach and is indeed long – at around 2.5km – with large chunks of the shoreline still uncultivated, backed with trees and wilderness, and well beyond sight of the island road. From *New Bungalow* towards the southern end it's a twenty-minute walk into Ban Ko Jum village.

At its northern end, Long Beach segues into **GOLDEN PEARL BEACH**, which is about 750m/fifteen minutes' walk north up the beach from *Bo Daeng*, 5km by road from Ban Ko Jum and 1km south of Ban Ting Rai. Like Long Beach, it also has only a few bungalow outfits along its curving shoreline, though these are close by the island road.

Accommodation

Accommodation on Long Beach is in three clusters, each about fifteen minutes' walk apart.

Long Beach

Bo Daeng Ⓣ081 494 8760. This funky, ultra cheap and ultra basic travellers' classic is run by a famously welcoming charismatic island *chao ley* family and has legendary food. The rudimentary bamboo huts come with or without private bathrooms – the latter are among the very cheapest on the island, but all have nets and electricity during the evening. Open all year. ❶

Freedom Bar Bungalows Ⓣ085 792 8130. Just a handful of rustic-contemporary bamboo bungalows way off on their own at the southernmost point, occupying an unparalleled spot on a tiny rocky promontory, with awesome 360-degree sea views and as yet no neighbours. The bungalows are enormous and beautifully simple, with loads of space for hammocks and chairs on the deck, plus nice partly al-fresco bathrooms. There are no real hotel facilities, just the staff at its sister outfit, the ultra laid-back *Freedom Bar* itself. ❻

Joy Bungalows Ⓣ075 618199, Ⓦwww.kohjum-joybungalow.com. This is the longest running and most famous place to stay on the island, though not necessarily the friendliest. It has a big spread of accommodation set in a grove of trees behind the shorefront, the majority of them smart wooden bungalows in various sizes and proximity to the sea, plus some cheap bamboo ones and a two-bedroom house. None has electricity, so it's paraffin lamps all round at night. ❸–❼

New Bungalow Ⓣ075 618116, Ⓔnbkohjum@hotmail.com. The two-dozen differently styled bungalows at this friendly, long-established place include a few cheapie bamboo ones with and without private bathrooms, a couple of treehouses with idyllic sea views and shared bathrooms, plus some plain, en-suite wooden huts. ❶–❹

Woodland Lodge Ⓣ081 893 5330, Ⓦwww.woodland-koh-jum.tk. Welcoming, peaceful spot owned by a UK-Thai couple and one of the few places on the island to stay open year round. Its large, attractive bungalows are widely set beneath the trees of its shorefront garden and all have good bathrooms; the doubles have platform beds, varnished wooden floors and deep shady decks, while the bigger ones are designed for families. Nearly all of them enjoy sea views between the trees. ❸–❺

Golden Pearl Beach

Golden Pearl Bungalows Ⓣ075 618131. The nineteen simple woven-bamboo huts here are set within a coconut grove across the road from the shore; the budget ones are the cheapest on the island and have neither fans nor private bathrooms, but the en-suite versions are also a very good price. ❶–❸

Koh Jum Lodge ⓣ089 921 1621, ⓦwww.kohjumlodge.com. French run, and one of the most upscale places on the island, with just sixteen thatched wooden chalets designed in charming rustic-chic style. Thoughtfully constructed to make the most of the island breezes, they have doors onto the veranda to avoid the need for air-con, low beds and elegantly simple furniture. All the bungalows can sleep up to five small kids as well as two adults. The resort has a small pool, internet access, a TV and DVD area, a massage service and a restaurant. Minimum stay one week. ⑨

Eating and drinking

All the bungalows do **food**, but for a really outstanding Thai meal, at some of the cheapest prices on the island, you should join the (often lengthy) queue at *Bo Daeng* on **Long Beach**, whose highlights include baked fish, vegetable tempura, curries and coconut shakes. *Joy* does pizzas and fresh coffee, *Woodland* makes delicious curries, and *New* has newspapers to read while you wait for your meal. **Ban Ko Jum** is good for cheap village food, including Thai breakfasts from 5am at *Mama*, but the big name here is the very popular and very good *Ban Ko Jum Seafood* (Nov–May daily 10am–10pm), whose tables occupy a scenically sited jetty near the pier, and enjoy fine view across the mangrove channel. Among its big menu of fresh seafood cooked any number of ways, the juicy fat prawns barbecued with honey are a standout, and their crab and lobster dishes are famous too.

Many people round off the night with a **drink** around the camp fire at easy-going *Freedom Bar*, right down the bottom end of Long Beach. The *Fu* beach bar on Golden Pearl holds occasional full-moon parties.

Ao Si

Around the rocky headland from Golden Pearl Beach, accessible in ten minutes at low tide or quite a bit further by road, long and beautifully uncluttered **AO SI** is good for swimming. In about the middle of the beach sits *SunSmile* (ⓣ086 280 4811; ③), whose eleven blue-roofed concrete bungalows all enjoy sea views and are kept very clean, with tiled floors, good beds, fans and decent bathrooms. Ao Si's northern headland is the sole province of Scottish-run *Ao Si Bungalows* (ⓣ081 747 2664, ⓔreena.aosi@hotmail.com; ③–④); its eight woven-bamboo, en-suite bungalows are built on piles up the side of the cliff and have wrap-around verandas for soaking up the commanding views of the bay and the southern half of the island. A big troupe of monkeys makes its home here too. A ten-minute walk through the rubber trees from the uppermost of *Ao Si*'s bungalows brings you to Magic Beach, just south of Ao Ting Rai.

Ban Ting Rai, Khao Ko Pu and Ao Ting Rai

The road begins to climb as soon as you leave Golden Pearl Beach, taking you up through the ribbon-like village of **Ban Ting Rai**, pretty with bougainvillea and wooden houses, and location of a few small restaurants and noodle shops. **Khao Ko Pu** which rises in the distance is, at 422m, the island's highest mountain and home to macaques who sometimes come down to forage on the rocks around the northern beaches; guided treks up the eastern flank to the summit take about an hour and reward you with fine 360-degree panoramas encompassing the entire island, the mainland and the outer islands.

The little bay of **AO TING RAI**, sometimes known as **Hat Kidon**, has some nice places to stay, and good snorkelling off its shore, with reef to explore and plenty of fish. At low tide it's too rocky for swimming though, when you'll need either to pick your way over the rocks, rent a kayak, or walk south 500m along the coastal road, to get to the little sandy crescent known as **Magic Beach**, which is swimmable at any tide. You can walk to Ao Ting Rai from Ao Si in about twenty minutes along the coast road.

The southernmost **accommodation** on Ao Ting Rai is at the very popular *Ting Rai Bay Resort* (ⓣ087 277 7379; ⓦwww.tingrai.com; ❸–❺), where sixteen nicely designed wooden bungalows are ranged up the sloping shorefront on stilts, most offering fine views from capacious decks (especially the "honeymoon" ones). Interiors have fans, four-poster style beds, and plenty of attention to detail. The food here is also good and there's internet access and onward transport tickets. Next door, *Old Lamp Bungalow* (ⓣ089 876 8572, ⓦwww.oldlampbungalows.com; ❸) has a dozen surprisingly spacious bungalows made from coconut wood, secreted among the trees, and designed with thoughtful, practical touches; most have nice garden bathrooms and all of them have big wooden beds. There's fresh wholewheat bread baked daily too. North again, French-Thai *OonLee Bungalows* (ⓣ087 200 8053, ⓦwww.koh-jum-resort.com; ❸–❺; phone ahead for a pick-up from your landing point; open all year) is a small, enthusiastically run and well-liked place with nine bungalows in various styles, plus a four-bed family bungalow. The wooden bungalows have plenty of storage, appealing bathrooms and sea-view verandas. Bungalows are stacked up the cliffside here, so there are quite a lot of steps; there's a stylish upper-level lounge area and restaurant, and a bar and massage area at beach level, plus free kayaks, bicycles and snorkels for guests. *OonLee* offers lots of organized **activities** and tours, including guided treks up Khao Ko Pu, fishing trips, day-trips to Ko Lola off Long Beach, round-island tours and trips to Ko Phi Phi.

Ao Luboa

Ko Jum's peaceful northernmost beach, **AO LUBOA**, feels remote. It's accessed chiefly by a loop in the main island road that circles the northeastern slopes of Khao Ko Pu and terminates at the north end of the bay, though the steeply undulating coast road from Ao Ting Rai can also be walked (in about 45min from *OonLee*) or ridden on a motorbike with good brakes. Like Ao Ting Rai, Ao Luboa's shorefront reef gets exposed at low tide, making it impossible to swim, though at high water things are fine and it's anyway a supremely quiet, laid-back beach with just a few **bungalows**. The friendly *Luboa Hut* (ⓣ081 959 4576, ⓦwww.luboahut2008.com; ❷–❹) has nine en-suite bamboo and wooden bungalows with sea view and electricity (but no fans) in a well shaded spot under shoreside trees; many of them are roomy and good quality, some have extra beds or sofas and all have mosquito nets. The owners do kayak and motorbike rental and have internet. At the far northern end of the beach, *Bonhomie Beach Cottages* (ⓣ086 788 7585, ⓦwww.bonhomiebeach.com; ❸–❹) has ten very large, attractively designed en-suite wooden chalets, many with sea view; price depends on proximity to the sea.

Ko Lanta Yai

Although **KO LANTA YAI** can't compete with Phi Phi's stupendous scenery, the thickly forested 25-kilometre-long island has the longest beaches in the Krabi area – and plenty of them. There's decent snorkelling and diving nearby, plus caves to explore, elephant trekking and kayaking, so many tourists base themselves here for their entire holiday fortnight. The island is especially popular with families, in part because of the local laws that have so far prevented jet-skis, beachfront parasols and girlie bars from turning it into another Phuket,

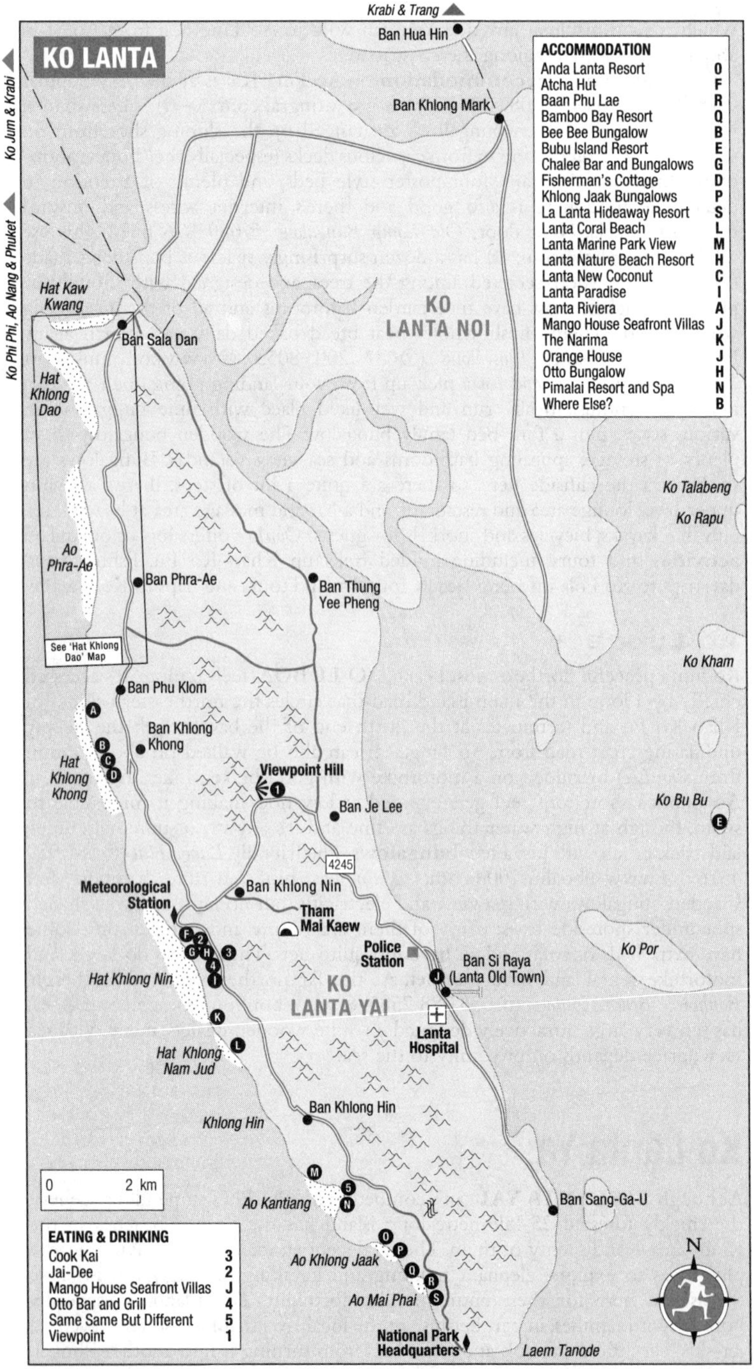
KO LANTA
Krabi & Trang
Ban Hua Hin
Ban Khlong Mark
Ko Jum & Krabi
Ko Phi Phi, Ao Nang & Phuket
ACCOMMODATION
Anda Lanta Resort O
Atcha Hut F
Baan Phu Lae R
Bamboo Bay Resort Q
Bee Bee Bungalow B
Bubu Island Resort E
Chalee Bar and Bungalows G
Fisherman's Cottage D
Khlong Jaak Bungalows P
La Lanta Hideaway Resort S
Lanta Coral Beach L
Lanta Marine Park View M
Lanta Nature Beach Resort H
Lanta New Coconut C
Lanta Paradise I
Lanta Riviera A
Mango House Seafront Villas J
The Narima K
Orange House J
Otto Bungalow H
Pimalai Resort and Spa N
Where Else? B
Hat Kaw Kwang
Ban Sala Dan
KO LANTA NOI
Hat Khlong Dao
Ao Phra-Ae
Ban Phra-Ae
Ban Thung Yee Pheng
See 'Hat Khlong Dao' Map
Ko Talabeng
Ko Rapu
Ko Kham
Ban Phu Klom
Ban Khlong Khong
Hat Khlong Khong
Viewpoint Hill
Ban Je Lee
Ko Bu Bu
4245
Meteorological Station
Ban Khlong Nin
Tham Mai Kaew
Police Station
Ban Si Raya (Lanta Old Town)
Ko Por
Hat Khlong Nin
KO LANTA YAI
Lanta Hospital
Hat Khlong Nam Jud
Ban Khlong Hin
Khlong Hin
0 2 km
Ao Kantiang
Ban Sang-Ga-U
EATING & DRINKING
Cook Kai 3
Jai-Dee 2
Mango House Seafront Villas J
Otto Bar and Grill 4
Same Same But Different 5
Viewpoint 1
Ao Khlong Jaak
Ao Mai Phai
National Park Headquarters
Laem Tanode
N

though resort facilities are expanding fast. Lanta is also rapidly being colonized by Scandinavian expats, with villa homes and associated businesses popping up all over the place, at a pace that not all islanders are happy about. The majority of Ko Lanta Yai's ten thousand indigenous residents are mixed-blood descendants of Muslim Chinese-Malay or animist *chao ley* ("sea gypsy") peoples, most of whom supported themselves by fishing and cultivating the land before the tourist boom brought new jobs, and challenges.

One of those challenges is that the **tourist season** is quite short, with the weather and seas at their calmest and safest from November to April; the main ferries don't run outside that period, and some hotels close, though most do stay open and offer huge discounts. The short money-making window, however, means that accommodation prices on Ko Lanta fluctuate more wildly than many other south Thailand destinations.

The local *chao ley* name for Ko Lanta Yai is *Pulao Satak*, "Island of Long Beaches", an apt description of the string of beaches along the **west coast**, each separated by rocky points and strung out at quite wide intervals. Broadly speaking, the busiest and most mainstream beaches are in the north, within easy reach of the port at **Ban Sala Dan**: **Hat Khlong Dao** is the family beach and **Ao Phra-Ae** the longer and more beautiful. The middle section has variable sands but some interesting places to stay, at **Hat Khlong Khong**, **Hat Khlong Nin** and **Hat Khlong Nam Jud**. Southerly **Ao Kantiang** is reliable for swimming year-round and marks the end of the made road; beyond here **Ao Khlong Jaak** and **Ao Mai Phai** are a little harder to get to and so feel more remote. Lanta Yai's mangrove-fringed **east coast** has no real tourist development but is both good for kayaking and culturally interesting because of the traditional homes in **Lanta Old Town**. North across the narrow channel from the port at Ban Sala Dan, Lanta Yai's sister island of **Ko Lanta Noi** has Ko Lanta's administrative offices and several small villages but no tourist accommodation. The rest of the Ko Lanta archipelago, which comprises over fifty little islands, is mostly uninhabited.

Every March Ko Lanta Yai celebrates its rich ethnic heritage at the **Laanta Lanta Festival**, which is held over three days in Lanta Old Town and features both traditional and modern music and dance, countless specialist foodstalls and crafts for sale (check Ⓦlantaoldtown.com for dates and specifics). Traditional *chao ley* rituals are celebrated on Ko Lanta twice a year, on the full moons of the sixth and eleventh lunar months (usually June and Oct/Nov; see p.764).

Moving on from Ko Lanta Yai

From mid-October to mid-May, there are **ferries** at least once a day, more during peak periods, to **Krabi** via **Ko Jum**; to **Ao Nang** via **West Railay**; to **Ko Phi Phi**; and to **Phuket**. See p.754 for durations and fares.

There are also daily boats in high season **to Ko Hai, Ko Mook**, **Ban Chao Mai** and **Ko Lipe** (B1500; 5hr 30min), with a mooted extension to Langkawi in Malaysia (6hr 30min), all with Tigerline (Ⓣ081 092 8800, Ⓦwww.tigerlinetravel.com); and a faster service with Satun Pakbara Speedboat (Ⓣ074 783 643, Ⓦwww.tarutaolipeisland.com), which gets to Lipe in three hours (B1900) and also makes a stop on Ko Bulon Lae. You can also make use of the day-trippers' snorkelling boats operated by Garden Hill (Ⓣ075 684042, Ⓦwww.lantaislandtours.com) and Petpailin (Ⓣ075 667033) for transfers to Ko Hai, Ko Mook and **Ko Kradan**. See p.775 for details on all these boats.

Most Ko Lanta tour agents can fix you up with an onward bus or air ticket **to Bangkok** or elsewhere and some can also organize train tickets, though this will take several days and cost quite a bit extra. Several also offer **visa-run** day-trips by minivan to Satun for about B1200.

▲ Jetty restaurants, Ban Sala Dan, Ko Lanta Yai

Getting to Ko Lanta Yai

The principal mainland gateways to Ko Lanta are Krabi, Phuket and Trang, all of which have good long-distance bus services, and **airports**; Trang also has a train station. See relevant accounts for travel information.

From approximately mid-October to mid-May there are **ferries** at least once a day, more during peak periods, to Ko Lanta Yai **from Krabi** (2hr 30min; B450), via **Ko Jum** (about 1hr; B450); from **Ko Phi Phi** (1hr 30min; B300), with connections from **Phuket** (4hr 30min; B750); and from **Ao Nang** (2hr 30min; B450) via West **Railay** (2hr; B450). In high season there are also services to Ko Lanta from the islands of **Ko Hai**, **Ko Mook**, **Ko Kradan**, **Ko Lipe** and **Ko Bulon Lae**, for details of which, see p.775. All ferries dock at Ban Sala Dan and are met by bungalow touts who usually transport you to the beach of your choice for free. If you need to use the motorbike sidecar taxi service instead, be warned that drivers will try and charge arrivals way over the normal fares quoted on opposite; walk 250m from the pier head to the main road to get a ride at more reasonable rates.

The alternative to the ferries is the **overland route** to Ko Lanta Yai – essential during the **rainy season** but increasingly popular at any time of year. This is the route used by minivans from **Krabi town** (hourly; 2hr; B200–300 depending on which beach you get dropped at); by taxis from **Krabi airport** (about B2500 per car); by minivans from **Trang** (4 daily; 3hr); and by anyone bringing their **own vehicle**. Access is via Ban Hua Hin on the mainland, 75km east of Krabi, from where a small ferry crosses to Ban Khlong Mark on Ko Lanta Noi, after which there's a seven-kilometre drive across to Lanta Noi's southwest tip, then another ferry over the narrow channel to the car-ferry port on Ko Lanta Yai's northeastern coast; both ferries run approximately every twenty minutes from about 7am to 10pm.

Island practicalities

There's no public **transport** on the island, but motorbikes are widely available for rent and there are jeeps too. A fleet of **motorbike sidecar taxis**, with drivers in numbered vests, operates out of Ban Sala Dan and will go pretty much anywhere on the island, though they usually need to be phoned (by staff at hotels or restaurants) for pick-ups from anywhere outside Sala Dan. Lanta has its share of scamming taxi-drivers, so bear in mind the following approximate rates for rides out of Sala Dan: B40 to Hat Khlong Dao, B60 to Ao Phra-Ae, B80 to Hat Khlong Kong, or about B50 between the above.

Most bungalows will **change money**, though you'll get the best rates at the bank in Ban Sala Dan, where there are also a couple of **ATMs**; there are also ATMs beside the road at most of the beaches. Many bungalows offer international telephone services for guests, and there's **internet** access on every beach. The post office is in Lanta Old Town. Nearly every beach has a clinic, there's a larger **health centre** in Ban Sala Dan (Mon–Fri 4.30–8.30pm, Sat & Sun 8.30am–4.30pm) and the rather basic island hospital is in Lanta Old Town (ⓣ075 697017), though for anything serious you'll need to go to Phuket. There's a **police** box in Sala Dan (ⓣ075 684657) but the police station is in Lanta Old Town (ⓣ075 697085).

For details on **snorkelling**, **diving**, **kayaking** and **day-trips** on Ko Lanta, see the box on p.756. During high-season there are **yoga** classes in Ban Sala Dan and at *Cha Ba* bungalows on Khlong Dao, but the most famous teacher is at *Relax Bay* on Ao Phra-Ae (B400/90min).

Ko Lanta Yai is extremely popular during high season (Nov–Feb), when it's worth either booking your first night's **accommodation** in advance or taking up the suggestions of the bungalow touts who ride the boats from the mainland. A confirmed booking also means you should get free transport from the port to your hotel. Accommodation **pricing** on Ko Lanta is disconcertingly flexible and alters according to the number of tourists on the island: bungalow rates can triple between mid-December and mid-January, while during the rainy season between May and October rates are vastly discounted. The rates we've quoted are for the beginning and end of high season (generally Nov to early Dec & late Jan to April).

Ban Sala Dan

During high season, direct boats from Krabi and Phi Phi arrive at the T-shaped fishing port and tourist village of **BAN SALA DAN**, on the northernmost tip of Ko Lanta Yai. Pretty much everything you'll need is here, from beachwear shops and minimarkets to banks with currency **exchange** and ATMs, tour agents and dive shops. The weekly Sunday market sets up south of the Health Centre and sells cheap clothes, household goods and hot food.

The old part of the village, strung out along the waterside, facing sister island Ko Lanta Yai across the narrow channel, retains its charming old wooden houses built on piles over the water. Many of these have been turned into attractive jetty **restaurants**, perfect for whiling away a breezy hour with views of marine activity. *Ko Lanta Seafood* on the left-hand arm of the T is the oldest restaurant in town and the most highly rated – its seafood is great, worth braving the service which is lackadaisical at best. Also near here is *Baan Café* (Sat–Thurs 7am–5pm) which does home-baked breads, rolls and cakes. Along the right-hand arm of the T, *Bai Fern* does inexpensive Thai food, while *Catfish* also sells art cards and has the best selection of **second-hand books** on Ko Lanta, including Thai novels in translation and Thai dictionaries and language books. Though it doesn't share the atmospheric location, *Kocha* opposite Lanta Diver on the main road is popular with locals for its excellent taste and cheap prices, especially beef in oyster sauce and *mii krop* (crispy noodles) with crispy pork (B50–60).

Diving, snorkelling, kayaking and day-trips on Ko Lanta

Any Lanta tour agent can sort you out with **day-trips** and activities.

Snorkelling trips

The best and most popular **snorkelling** is at the islands of **Ko Rok Nai** and **Ko Rok Nok**, 47km south of Ko Lanta; these forested twins are graced with stunning white-sand beaches and accessible waterfalls and separated by a narrow channel full of fabulous shallow reefs. Also hugely popular is the "**four island**" snorkelling trip that takes in the much nearer islands off Trang – the enclosed emerald lagoon on **Ko Mook** (Ko Muk), plus nearby **Ko Hai** (Ko Ngai), **Ko Cheuak** (Ko Chuk) and **Ko Kradan** (see p.775 for island descriptions) – but these sites get very crowded. Another option is the day-trip to **Phi Phi Don**, Phi Phi Leh and Bamboo Island (see p.740). The trips are typically on large **speedboats** which hold about thirty people, and cost B1800 for adults or B900 for kids under 12, including lunch, snorkel mask, and national park entry fee. One of the main operators is Lanta Garden Hill Speed Boat (ⓣ075 684042, ⓦwww.lantaislandtours.com), and their trips can be booked through any agent on Ko Lanta. For a smaller, much more personal experience, contact Sun Island Tours (ⓣ087 891 6619, ⓦwww.lantalongtail.com), whose various **longtail trips**, to the four islands, around Ko Lanta, and to Lanta's eastern islands (including an overnight camping option), come very highly rated and cost B1500.

Diving

The **reefs** around Ko Lanta are quieter and in some cases more pristine than those round Phi Phi and Phuket, and excellent for seeing whale sharks. The **diving season** runs from November to April, though a few dive shops continue to run successful trips from May to August. All dive boats depart from Ban Sala Dan, and nearly all dive courses are taught either in Sala Dan or on Hat Khlong Dao, though there are dive shops on every beach.

Some of Lanta's best **dive sites** are located between Ko Lanta and Ko Phi Phi, including the soft coral at **Ko Bidah**, where you get lots of leopard sharks, barracuda and tuna. West and south of Lanta, the **Ko Ha** island group offers four different dives on each of its five islands, including steep drop-offs and an "underwater cathedral"

Hat Khlong Dao

Long and gently curving **HAT KHLONG DAO** is known as "the family beach", both for its plentiful mid-range accommodation, and for its generous sweep of flat sandy shoreline that's safe for swimming and embraced by protective headlands. Despite being developed to capacity, it's broad enough never to feel overcrowded, the sunsets can be magnificent, and the whole is framed by a dramatic hilly backdrop. It's also the nearest resort to the facilities and ferries of Ban Sala Dan, about half an hour's walk away, or 2–3km by road. The beach also has its own minimarkets and transport outlets, shoreside and along the main road.

Accommodation

There are a couple of budget-oriented places to stay on Hat Khlong Dao, but the emphasis is on accommodation for families and others looking for air-conditioned comfort. See map, p.758.

Cha-Ba Bungalows ⓣ075 684118, ⓦwww.krabidir.com/chababungalows/index.htm. There's plenty of kitsch creativity at this idiosyncratic complex of bungalows, restaurant and art gallery, set among bright blue Flintstone walls and archways and oversized concrete sculptures. The fifteen en-suite fan and air-con bungalows are simple and flimsy, but cute, decorated with loud retro-look fabrics and wallpapers. Air-con ones come with TVs, fridges, safety boxes and hot water. Fan ③–⑤, air-con ⑥ and other caves; visibility is often very good. Much further south, about 56km from Ko Lanta, there's a fifty-metre wall at spectacular **Hin Daeng** and **Hin Muang**, plus a good chance of seeing tuna, jacks, silvertip sharks, manta rays and even whale sharks. See the descriptions of Andaman coast dive sites on p.699 for more on some of these reefs.

Ko Lanta's best **dive shops** include the German-run Ko Lanta Diving Centre, on the main road into Ban Sala Dan, with a branch office at *Lanta Island* hotel on central Hat Khlong Dao (Ⓣ075 668065, Ⓦwww.kolantadivingcenter.com); and the Swedish-owned, PADI Five-star Instructor Development Centre, Lanta Diver, also on the main road into Ban Sala Dan, and with branch offices at *Relax Bay* near Hat Khlong Dao and at *Ozone Bar* on Ao Phra-Ae (Ⓣ087 891 4141, Ⓦwww.lantadiver.com). They charge B2600–3100 for **two dives**, excluding equipment, and B1500 for accompanying snorkellers, with discounts if you do three consecutive days. Diving **courses** average out at B13,500 for the four-day Openwater course, or B10,500 for the two-day Advanced course. The nearest recompression chambers are located on Phuket (see p.698); check to see that your dive operator is insured to use one of them, and see Basics, p.73, for more information on diving in Thailand.

Kayaking

There are several rewarding **kayaking** destinations, rich in mangroves and caves, around Ko Lanta Yai's east coast and around Ko Lanta Noi and its eastern islands, including **Ko Talabeng** and **Ko Bubu**; a few companies also offer kayak-snorkel trips to the four islands described above. Trips can be arranged through tour operators in Ban Sala Dan, and on most beaches, for B750–1200 per person (kids B550–600).

Day-trips inland

Ko Lanta's biggest inland attraction is the **Tham Mai Kaew caves** (see p.763). Though it's not much more than a trickle, the **waterfall** inland from Ao Khlong Jaak is another fairly popular spot, and can be reached from the bay by walking along the course of the stream for about two hours. Alternatively join one of the tours that combine visits to the caves and the waterfall with an **elephant-ride** (from B700/500).

Costa Lanta Ⓣ075 684630, Ⓦwww.costalanta.com. You're either going to love or hate this ultra-brutal minimalist grouping of 22 polished-grey concrete boxes, each module containing an unadorned bedroom all in grey and white and a similarly styled bathroom. The setting is less than magnificent – a dry, plain garden bisected by greenish khlongs – but there's a biggish pool, a striking bar-restaurant and DVD players in every room. ⑨

Hans Ⓣ075 684152, Ⓦwww.krabidir.com/hansrestaurant. By far the cheapest place on this beach, with fifteen huts ranged along a narrow strip of garden behind the shorefront restaurant in the heart of the beach. Choose between very simple, rickety bamboo bungalows with mosquito nets and bathrooms, and better-furnished wooden versions with screened windows. All bungalows are wi-fi accessible. Closed from early April to Oct. ③–④

Kaw Kwang Beach Resort At the northernmost end of Khlong Dao Ⓣ081 979 6959, Ⓦwww.lanta-kawkwangresort.com. Welcoming, family-run outfit of 61 good-value (for Lanta) rooms occupying a huge area of beachfront land between the headland's two shores. There are many options here, from cheap, decent, old-style en-suite wood and concrete huts among the trees above the shore, through bigger, beachside air-con bungalows, family bungalows and hotel-style rooms. Has a pool and wi-fi in some rooms. Open all year with fifty-percent discounts from June to Oct. Fan ③–④, air-con ⑥–⑧

The Noble House Ⓣ075 668096, Ⓦwww.lantanoblehouse.com. Appealingly small-scale, Swiss-run place where the 23 inviting fan and air-con bungalows have big glass windows and bathtubs. They're set in facing rows, in a pretty shrub-filled garden, mostly around the little swimming pool. Also has a few rooms in a couple of small two-storey bocks. Fan ⑤, air-con ⑦

Southern Lanta Resort Ⓣ075 684175, Ⓦwww.southernlanta.com. One of the biggest hotels on the beach, offering dozens of very spacious air-con bungalows set at decent intervals around a garden of shrubs, clipped hedges and shady trees. There's a good-sized swimming pool too and wi-fi throughout. Popular with families and package tourists. ❼

Eating and drinking

Restaurant tables fill the shoreline in the evening, illuminated with fairy lights and lanterns, which lends a nice mellow atmosphere. The formula is very similar at most of them, with fresh seafood barbecues the main attraction during the season. *Costa Lanta*'s sea-view daybeds and plump bolsters are the most sophisticated venue, and a good reason to linger over the pricey but very good menu, especially its lemon grass martinis and the sea bass steamed in banana leaves. Down at the far southern end of the beach, *Slow Down* is all about keeping the family happy, with its special kids' menu (and quite limited but reasonably priced Thai-European adult version), enormous ice creams, cushion seating in a converted longtail boat and, most importantly, its volleyball net within sight of adult dining areas.

Clusters of little beach **bars** serve cocktails on deckchairs and cushions, often with a campfire to gather round and chill-out music. One of the most genial is *Indian Bar*, next to *Cha-Ba Bungalows*, where the host, easily spotted by his trademark Sioux-style feather headdress, makes a mean cocktail and does good fire-juggling shows.

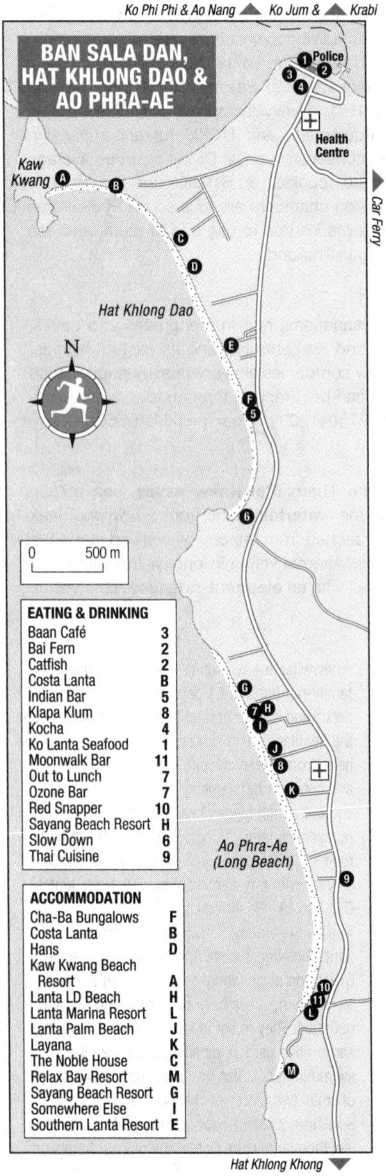

Ao Phra-Ae (Long Beach)

With its lovely long parade of soft, white sand, calm and crystal-clear water that's good for swimming and shady fringe of casuarina trees, **AO PHRA-AE** (also known as **Long Beach**) is strikingly beautiful and the best of Lanta's many long beaches. There's a little more variety and character among the accommodation options here than at Khlong Dao, a couple of kilometres to the north, and quite a development of shops, with ATM, restaurants and

Ko Phi Phi & Ao Nang ▲ *Ko Jum &* ▲ *Krabi*

BAN SALA DAN, HAT KHLONG DAO & AO PHRA-AE

Police

Health Centre

Car Ferry

Kaw Kwang

Ⓐ Ⓑ

Ⓒ

Ⓓ

Hat Khlong Dao

Ⓔ

N

Ⓕ
❺

❻

Ⓖ
❼ Ⓗ
Ⓘ

Ⓙ
❽

Ⓚ

Ao Phra-Ae (Long Beach)

❾

0 500 m

❿
⓫
Ⓛ

Ⓜ

EATING & DRINKING	
Baan Café	3
Bai Fern	2
Catfish	2
Costa Lanta	B
Indian Bar	5
Klapa Klum	8
Kocha	4
Ko Lanta Seafood	1
Moonwalk Bar	11
Out to Lunch	7
Ozone Bar	7
Red Snapper	10
Sayang Beach Resort	H
Slow Down	6
Thai Cuisine	9

ACCOMMODATION	
Cha-Ba Bungalows	F
Costa Lanta	B
Hans	D
Kaw Kwang Beach Resort	A
Lanta LD Beach	H
Lanta Marina Resort	L
Lanta Palm Beach	J
Layana	K
The Noble House	C
Relax Bay Resort	M
Sayang Beach Resort	G
Somewhere Else	I
Southern Lanta Resort	E

Hat Khlong Khong ▼

tour agents along the main road. The main stretch of the beach is divided from the southern rocky extremity by a shallow, easily wadeable khlong; *Lanta Marina Resort* marks the southern reaches of the beach and is about half an hour's walk along the beach from *Sayang* at the northern end. Phra Ae's budget enclave clusters along a network of sandy tracks behind the *Ozone Bar*.

Accommodation

Accommodation is marked on the map opposite.

Lanta LD Beach (formerly Sandy Beach) ⓣ075 684548, ⓦwww.sandybeachlanta.com. In a grassy lot just behind *Somewhere Else* and the beach bars, 100m from the sea, this place offers cheapish en-suite bamboo bungalows with fans and mosquito nets, plus more robust concrete alternatives with either fans or air-con, TVs and hot water. ④–⑤

Lanta Marina Resort ⓣ075 684168, ⓔlanta_marina_resort@yahoo.com. At the far southern end of Ao Phra-Ae, inland from a rocky point, this friendly little place has just thirteen shaggily thatched wood-and-split-bamboo bungalows angled towards the sea, connected by a wooden walkway that circles a small lawn. Huts vary in size but all have nice beds, well-designed bathrooms, high palm-leaf rooves, fans and wi-fi access. ④

Lanta Palm Beach ⓣ075 684406, ⓦwww.lantapalmbeachresort.com. A busy, central and popular spot that has a range of different bungalows within stumbling distance of several beach bars. Cheapest are the handful of bamboo huts with bathrooms, good beds and mosquito nets that enjoy a full view of the sea. The forty pricier concrete bungalows sit back from the shore, within a garden of neat clipped hedges, and come with fan or air-con and in varying degrees of luxury. Has internet access. Fan ③, air-con ④–⑥

Layana ⓣ075 607100, ⓦwww.layanaresort.com. Located plumb in the middle of the beautiful beach, this is currently the top spot on Ao Phra-Ae and one of the best and most liked on the whole island, not least for its calm ambience (the hotel has a no-under-18s policy) and attentive service. Its fifty air-con rooms occupy chunky, two-storey villas designed in modern-Thai style and set around a tidy beachfront garden of lawns and mature shrubs; the priciest have sea views. There's a gorgeous shorefront salt-water infinity pool, a spa, dive centre and plenty of day-trip activities, plus wi-fi throughout. ⑨

Relax Bay Resort ⓣ075 684194, ⓦwww.relaxbay.com. Sharing its own tiny bay south around the next rocky point (and quite a hike) from *Lanta Marina*, with just one other set of bungalows, the style of this French-managed place is affordable rustic chic. Accommodation is in forty tastefully simple thatched bungalows, all with large sea-view decks and beds for three. Choose between fan and air-con. Also has a luxury African-safari style "romantic" en-suite tent on stilts. There's a pool, and yoga classes during high season (see p.755). Open all year. Fan ⑤, air-con ⑥–⑧

Sayang Beach Resort ⓣ075 684156, ⓦwww.sayangbeach.com. Very welcoming, family-run, mid-range place whose thirty fan and air-con bungalows are nicely spaced beneath the palm trees in the expansive shorefront grounds. Some bungalows are designed for families and there's also a beachfront suite. Prices include buffet breakfasts and there's a very good restaurant here too. Fan ⑤, air-con ⑥–⑧

Somewhere Else ⓣ081 536 0858. Located in the heart of the liveliest part of Ao Phra-Ae, with beach bars left, right and seaward, this is one of the main travellers centres on the beach, with the cheapest rooms, and correspondingly hectic. It has just sixteen spacious, unusually designed hexagonal bungalows made of tightly woven bamboo and with pretty bathrooms. Price depends on the size. The drawback is that most are close together and lack a sense of privacy, though many have sea views. ③–④

Eating and drinking

Most of Ao Phra-Ae's most interesting **restaurants** are along the main road, while down on the beach you get small, mellow **bars**.

Klapa Klum Near *Lanta Palm* bungalows. There are bamboo love-booths and private seating areas at this beachfront bar plus happy hours (6–8pm), cheap cocktails all night long and weekly on-the-beach parties.

Moonwalk Bar One of the livelier spots on the far southern beach, with cushion seating on a beautifully sited deck that offers good sea views and breezes, weekly parties with fireshows and music that's mostly trance and techno, barbecues and discounted beer until sunset.

Out to Lunch Next to *Ozone*. Accurately named, this is indeed a good place for lunch, right on the beach and with a range of breads and fillings: paninis and baguettes (mostly B140) topped or filled with imported cheeses – mozzarella, edam, cheddar – and cold meats. Also does burgers and salads.

Ozone Bar On the beach, near *Somewhere Else* bungalows. One of the most famous bars on the beach, especially for its weekly beach parties, which usually draw a lively crowd.

Red Snapper On the main road, inland from *Lanta Marina* bungalows at the southern end of Phra-Ae. Tapas and creative European cuisine are the hallmarks of this highly rated Dutch-run restaurant and bar, where the mid-priced menu changes every couple of months. Daily from 6pm.

Sayang Beach Resort On the beach, at *Sayang Beach Resort*. This is a lovely spot for dinner, with tables set out under shoreside casuarinas strung with fairy lights. The kitchen here has a tandoori oven and serves a long menu of authentic Indian dishes, including sheesh, masalas and dhal, as well as Thai and Western food, plus fresh seafood nightly and a big veggie menu. Mains B70–220.

Thai Cuisine On the main road, inland from *Layana*. Very popular, outdoor place that serves some deliciously authentic Thai food (B60–180), from thick *matsaman* curries to fiery *kway tiaw phat kii maew* (drunkard's fried noodles, so called because the liberal use of chilli is meant to sober you up). Also has plenty of seafood plus some more unusual choices including a surprisingly delicious rice fried with banana. Daily from 6pm.

Hat Khlong Khong

The luxuriously long beach at **HAT KHLONG KHONG**, 2km south of Ao Phra-Ae's *Relax Bay Resort*, is peppered with rocks and in most parts only really swimmable at high tide, though the snorkelling is good. Another big draw is the traveller-oriented bungalows, among them the most creatively designed places to stay on the island. There are several funky little **beach-bars** too, with the inevitable "special" mushroom omelettes on the menu.

Accommodation

Bee Bee Bungalow ⓣ081 537 9932, ⓔbeebeepiya02@hotmail.com, ⓦwww.diigii.de/sugarbeebee. A special, friendly place that stands out for its thirteen highly individual huts, each one a charmingly idiosyncratic experiment in bamboo architecture. All the bungalows are simple but comfortably furnished, given style with batik fabric flourishes, and have fans, mosquito nets and partially open-air bathrooms; some have an upstairs room as well. Closed early May to mid-Oct; unlike most other places on the beach it keeps its prices constant throughout the season. ③–④

Fisherman's Cottage ⓣ081 476 1529, ⓦwww.fishermanscottage.biz. This quiet, low-key chummy place at the southern end of the beach has just eleven thatched-roof and concrete bungalows, each with big windows, quite spartan one-off beach-modern interiors – whitewashed concrete, nutty mural artworks, splashes of strong colour – mosquito nets, fans and good bathrooms. Free wi-fi throughout. Closed mid-may–Oct. ④

Lanta Riviera ⓣ075 667043, ⓦwww.lantariviera.net. There are rows and rows of good, standard-issue, comfortably furnished fan and air-con concrete bungalows here, plus a few rooms in a two-storey building, set among shady beds of shrubs and flowers at the far northern end of the beach. Many of the rooms sleep three so it's popular with families. Also has a small pool near the shore. Fan ④, air-con ⑤–⑦

Lanta New Coconut ⓣ081 537 7590, ⓔnewcoconut@hotmail.com. A range of options here, including sturdy wooden bungalows with fan, plus stone and concrete versions with TVs and hot water and the option of fan or air-con. ③–⑤

Where Else? ⓣ081 536 4870, ⓦwww.lanta-where-else.com. As you might expect from the name, this charming collection of 22 bungalows has a laid-back vibe and lots of personality, though it's more of a party place than *Bee Bee*. The artfully and individually designed bamboo and coconut-wood bungalows all have fans, mosquito nets and open-air bathrooms filled with plants, and there are shell mobiles, driftwood sculptures and pot plants all over the place. The pricier bungalows are larger and nearer the sea, and some even have bamboo sunroofs and turrets. ③–⑥

Hat Khlong Nin

About 4km south of Hat Khlong Khong the road forks at kilometre-stone 13, at the edge of the village of **Ban Khlong Nin**. The left-hand, east-bound arm runs across to Ko Lanta Yai's east coast, via the caves and viewpoint (see p.763). The right-hand fork is the route to the southern beaches and continues southwards along the west coast for 14km to the southern tip.

Just beyond the junction, the little enclave of bungalows, restaurants, bars and tour agents at **HAT KHLONG NIN** lend this beach more of a village atmosphere than the northern beaches. The beach itself is lovely: long and sandy and good for swimming, and free of visible commercial tat; although the road runs close alongside it, the traffic is pretty light. There are several reasonably priced places to stay here, with the cheapest beds in some hotels located in separate little garden compounds on the inland side of the road, and a low-key collection of shoreside bar-restaurants with plenty of character and mellow vibes.

There's a minimarket, **ATM** and clinic at the Ban Khlong Nin junction, and *Atcha Hut* has a **hammam** steam room. Taxis to Sala Dan should cost about B80 per person and you can walk the 3km to the Tham Mai Kaew caves from Khlong Nin in about an hour.

Accommodation

Atcha Hut ⓣ089 470 4607, ⓔjuneto14@hotmail.com. A truly individual, alternative spot at the northern end of the beach, where a couple of adobe caravanserai-style dormitory buildings have B150 beds, the cheapest singles on the island, each in their own little concrete, open-sided cubbyhole, screened by a curtain. Also has six dinky, en-suite wooden bungalows and a hammam and massage service. ❸

Chalee Bar and Bungalows ⓣ087 685 0080. Cute, homely place of just half-a-dozen simple, rickety but en-suite fan-cooled bamboo bungalows, all with decks and shell mobiles, set in a pretty little sandy garden that's right by the road but also right on the shore. Also has four even more basic rooms, sharing a bathroom, above the restaurant. ❶–❷

Lanta Nature Beach Resort ⓣ075 662560, ⓦwww.lantanaturebeachresort.com. In the cluster of concrete bungalow operations right on the beach at the southern end of Khlong Nin, this one has rows of cream-and-lilac painted fan and air concrete huts, with spacious tiled interiors. There are even bigger, cheaper bungalows in a garden inland, across the road. Fan ❹–❻, air-con ❺–❼

Lanta Paradise ⓣ075 662569, ⓦwww.lantaparadiseresort.com. Though the shorefront concrete bungalows here are packed uncomfortably close together, they feel spacious inside; they lack style and are plain but are all air-con, and there's a pool here too. There are cheaper fan bungalows in a garden across the road. Fan ❸, air-con ❺–❼

Otto Bungalow ⓣ084 051 7180, ⓔotto_lanta@hotmail.com. Run by the same people behind the *Bar and Grill* 300m south along the beach, there are just four shorefront A-frame cabins here, with thatched roofs, concrete walls, mosquito nets and fans. Also has an air-con room in a converted bus, beside the small swimming pool, plus a deluxe air-con beachside villa. The drawback is it's right by the road. Fan ❹, air-con ❻

Eating and drinking

A dozen or so mellow little beachfront **bar–restaurants** make inviting places to while away a few hours, day or night, with mats and cushions on the sand, tables under the shade of the spiky shoreside pandanus trees, and appropriately chilled sounds. *Jai-Dee*, in the northerly cluster, has a lovely shady deck, internet access and free wi-fi, a massage service and a good menu of Thai curries and sandwiches. Larger, more formal, beach-view *Otto Bar and Grill*, serves seafood and Thai and European dishes, while *Cook Kai* restaurant, diagonally north across the road from *Nice Beach* bungalows, does hearty portions of all the Thai classics, plus famous hotplate dishes including sizzling squid with garlic and pepper, for B80–170.

Hat Khlong Nam Jud

Just over 1km south of Hat Khlong Nin, the road passes the two tiny little bays known as **HAT KHLONG NAM JUD**. The northerly one is the domain of *The Narima* (ⓣ075 662668, ⓦwww.narima-lanta.com; ❼–❽), a very quiet but welcoming, elegantly designed, environmentally conscious resort of 32 posh but unadorned thatch-roofed bamboo bungalows set in three rows in a palm-filled garden. The bungalows all have polished wood floors, verandas with sea view, and fans as well as air-con (but no TV); there's also a three-tiered pool (with kids' level), a spa and a dive centre, and staff rent out jeeps.

A brief scramble around the rocky point to the south, the next tiny cove is rocky in parts but enjoys a swimmable beach and one set of bungalows, *Lanta Coral Beach* (ⓣ075 62535; fan ❸–❹, air-con ❺; closed May–Oct). The twenty good-sized plain but very clean bamboo and concrete huts here are scattered among the palms (some of which are hung with hammocks) and come with fan or air-con.

Ao Kantiang

The secluded cove of **AO KANTIANG**, some 7km beyond Hat Khlong Nam Jud, is an impressively long curve, backed by jungle-clad hillsides and dominated by one luxury hotel, which keeps the southern half of the beach in pristine condition. Unusually for Lanta, the bay is protected enough to be good for swimming year-round, and there's some coral at the northern end; snorkelling and fishing trips are easily arranged. The small but lively roadside village covers most necessities, including tours, onward transport, motorbike rental and internet access. There's also a clinic a little further south, between *Kantiang Bay View* and *Pimalai*. Wherever you're staying on Ao Kantiang, it's well worth heading down to *Same Same But Different*, a tranquil haven of a **restaurant** on the beach to the south of *Pimalai*, where the tables are set beneath a tangled growth of shrubs and vines, surrounded by shell-mobiles and driftwood sculptures; it's run by the man behind the renowned *Ruen Mai* restaurant in Krabi, and the mid-priced menu of mainly Thai and seafood dishes is of a similarly high standard.

The thirty or so **bungalows** at the buzzing *Lanta Marine Park View* (ⓣ081 956 2935, ⓦwww.lantamarine.com; fan ❹, air-con ❺–❼) are ranged up the slope at the northern end of the beach: steps lead down to the shore. The best of the bungalows, though pricey, are great value as they're on stilts and enjoy glorious bay views from their balconies and glass-fronted interiors, and the furnishings are chic and modern. The cheap fan-cooled bamboo bungalows sit further back and are plain and not especially interesting for the price. There's also a small cliffside bar affording great views, plus internet access and a tour agency. Down at sea level, the southern end of Ao Kantiang is the province of one of Ko Lanta's poshest hotels, the *Pimalai Resort and Spa* (ⓣ075 607999, ⓦwww.pimalai.com; ❾; published rates from B11,500), which spreads over such an extensive area that guests are shuttled around in golf buggies. All rooms are luxuriously and elegantly designed in contemporary style, and there's a delightful spa, a swimming pool and dive centre. However, only the more expensive accommodation gets a sea view (the walled beach villas are particularly stunning). From November to April, guests are transferred direct to the resort by boat, landing at the *Pimalai*'s private floating jetty.

Ao Khlong Jaak and Ao Mai Phai

The paved road terminates at the *Pimalai* boundary at the southern end of Ao Kantiang, so from here to Lanta's southern tip, about 4km away, access is via a steeply undulating, rutted and potholed track that's either dusty or muddy depending on the season – take care on a motorbike as it's extremely challenging. The next bay south of Ao Kantiang is **AO KHLONG JAAK**, site of the lively, buzzing *Anda Lanta Resort* (ⓣ075 665018, ⓦwww.andalanta.com; ❼–❽), which offers two-dozen well-furnished, well-maintained air-con bungalows and rooms (with wi-fi) set around the shorefront garden and swimming pool. It's popular with families and has kayaks and plenty of day-tripping options, though be prepared for a long drive if you want to go to the village facilities of Ban Saladan, for example. Sharing the bay, but right at the other end, convivial, traveller-oriented *Khlong Jaak Bungalows* (ⓣ075 665016; ❸–❹) has fan-cooled bamboo huts nicely located by the sea, plus some less interesting concrete air-con boxes, and a few rooms in a building at the back of the plot. The staff do regular beach barbecues and rent motorbikes.

South around the headland from *Klong Jaak Bungalows*, western Lanta plays its final card in the shape of handsome white-sand **AO MAI PHAI**, a peaceful getaway because of its remote position on the unmade road. There's good coral close to shore here, but this makes it too rocky for low-tide swimming, when you'll need to kayak up to Ao Klong Jaak instead. At the northern end of the bay, the welcoming and very popular Thai-Danish *Bamboo Bay Resort* (ⓣ075 665023, ⓦwww.bamboobay.net; fan ❹, air-con ❻–❼) offers 21 concrete bungalows, with fan or air-con, stepped up the cliffside above the headland, plus a few just across the narrow road. Nearly all have great sea views and interiors are spacious and of a high standard. Its *pièce de resistance* is its idyllically sited deck restaurant and bar, which jut out over the rocks just above the water. Occupying the centre of the bay, the tastefully camp *Baan Phu Lae* (ⓣ081 201 1704, ⓦwww.baanphulae.net; fan ❺, air-con ❻; closed May to mid-Oct) manages to combine a whiff of Bangkok sophistication with laid-back island charm. Its nine fan-cooled bamboo bungalows are stylishly simple and nearly all enjoy direct sea views; the four air-con rooms high above the shore are less interesting. The most luxurious of the trio on this beach is *La Lanta Hideaway Resort* (ⓣ087 883 9966, ⓦwww.lalaanta.com; ❼–❾) at the far southern end; it's very well liked for its attentive staff and comfortable wooden-floored villas – all with air-con, DVD players, low beds and wi-fi – built to a cosy, village-style layout, around two pools and a beachfront garden.

The interior and the east coast

Although the **east coast** lacks decent beaches, it's got plenty of other attractions, including an impressive series of caves at **Tham Mai Kaew**, a jaw-droppingly great **view over islands and coastlines** at the viewpoint (worth an early rise), an atmospheric neighbourhood in **Lanta Old Town**, and cultural interest at its museum. The tiny island of Ko Bubu is also reached from here. Access to the east coast is easy as the road is good: it starts at the Ban Klong Nin junction halfway down the west coast at kilometre-stone 13. Alternatively, most tour agencies offer guided day-trips covering this area.

Tham Mai Kaew caves

The myriad chambers at **Tham Mai Kaew caves**, some of which you can only just crawl into, are Ko Lanta's biggest inland attraction. They are filled with stalactites and interesting rock formations, and there's a creepy cave pool too, as well as the inevitable bats. Access to the cave, 3km from the Khlong Nin junction, is regulated by the local family who first properly explored the cave system in the 1980s: they now act as caretakers and guides, in conjunction with the national park authorities, and charge B200 for a two-hour tour (elephant rides, longer cave tours, and overnight jungle treks are also available). Most of Thailand's countless caves are underwhelming and certainly not worth B200, but this is one of the better ones, not least because the caretakers have resisted stringing it with electric lights so you're left to wonder both at what you catch with your torch and at what you don't see. Among its star features are crystallized waterfalls, fossils and ammonites embedded in the cave walls and overhangs, stalagmites and stalactites young and old and a tangible sense of there being endless passageways to explore. In the rainy season it's a more slippery, challenging experience, with some wading likely and the option of a dip in the wet-season-only lagoon. Even in the dry season it's moderately arduous and best done in sensible shoes and clothes you're happy to get grubby in. If you don't have your own transport, a motorcycle taxi costs about B200 each way from Khlong Dao or Ao Phra-Ae.

The viewpoint

Three kilometres beyond the turn-off to the caves, the eastbound road drops down over the central spine of hills and you pass *Viewpoint* café (daily 6am–9pm), where nearly everyone stops for a drink and a gawp at the stunning panorama. The **view over the east coast** is glorious, encompassing the southeast coast of mangrove-fringed Ko Lanta Noi, dozens of islets – including Ko Bubu and Ko Por – adrift in the milky blue sea, and the hilly profile of the mainland along the horizon. It's an unbeatable spot for a sunrise breakfast.

Lanta Old Town (Ban Si Raya)

Once back down at sea level, follow the east-coast road (Route 4245) south for a few kilometres to reach, at kilometre-stone 20, the seductively atmospheric little waterfront settlement of **LANTA OLD TOWN** (Ⓦwww.lantaoldtown.com), officially known as **Ban Si Raya**. Ko Lanta's oldest town, it began life as a sheltered staging post for ships sailing between China and Penang and served as the island's administrative capital from 1901 to 1998. The government offices have since moved to Ko Lanta Noi, and Ban Sala Dan has assumed the role of harbour, island gateway and commercial hub, so Ban Si Raya has been left much as it was a century ago, with its historic charm intact. There's little more to the Old Town than its peaceful main street, which runs right along the coast and is lined with traditional, hundred-year-old sea- and wind-blasted wooden homes and shops, many of them constructed on stilted jetties over the sea, their first-floor overhangs shading the pavements and plant-filled doorways. The Chinese shrine midway down the street is evidence of the town's cultural mix: Ban Si Raya is home to a long-established Buddhist Chinese-Thai community as well as to Muslims and, in its southern neighbourhood, communities of animist Urak Lawoy *chao ley* ("sea gypsies").

The **Urak Lawoy** *chao ley* (see box, p.663) are thought to have been Ko Lanta's first inhabitants, perhaps as long as five hundred years ago, living along the shoreline during the monsoon season and setting off along the coast again when the winds abated. They have now settled permanently in their own villages on the island, including at **Ban Sang-Ga-U**, 4km to the south of the Lanta Old Town; other Urak Lawoy living elsewhere in the Andaman Sea, around Trang and beyond, consider Ko Lanta their capital and will always stop at Sang-Ga-U when making a journey. One of the accessible elements of Urak Lawoy culture is their **music**, an interesting fusion of far-flung influences, featuring violins (from the Dutch East Indies), drums (from Persia), and gongs (from China), as well as singing, dancing and ritual elements. A good time to hear their music is at one of their twice-yearly three-day full-moon **festivals**, or at the Laanta Lanta Festival (see p.753).

There's an attempt to introduce the cultures of Ban Si Raya's three distinct but peaceable communities at the **Koh Lanta Community Museum** (daily 9am–5pm; B40), which is housed in the attractive 1901 wooden building that used to serve as the local district office, across the small grassy park from the pier and parking lot. Archive photos and the odd English-language caption describe the main occupations for the communities, including fishing, trading and making charcoal from mangrove wood; there's also a fair bit on post-tsunami projects and an interesting video in which villagers air their concerns about the recent explosion in tourism on the island and the effect that the influx of incomers and investors is having on traditional lifestyles and livelihoods.

Practicalities

As an additional incentive to linger among the wooden architecture of main street there are several browsable **shops** selling batik sarongs and souvenirs, plus the charming Hammock House (Ⓦwww.jumbohammock.com), whose amazing range of hammocks include ones woven by people of the endangered Mrabri tribe of northern Thailand (see p.374). South across the bridge from the pier, Sun Island Tours sells watercolours of Ko Lanta and modern batik sarongs, as well as doing longtail boat tours (see p.756).

There are several enticing **restaurants** in the old town too: the dining area at locally popular *Kroua Lanta Yai Seafood* is on a jetty over the seafront, while sophisticated little *Mango House Seafront Villas, Bar and Café* is all done out in stylish dark wood and does burgers, salads and sandwiches. Its waterside **rooms** (Ⓣ086 948 6836, Ⓦwww.bestofkolanta.com; ❼) are delightful and would make an attractive and unusual Ko Lanta base. Three stilted century-old wooden buildings, one of them a former charcoal store, have been charmingly converted into guest homes that can each sleep three; interiors are furnished in fishing-village chic, with elegant contemporary bathrooms, fans, TV, free wi-fi and kitchenette. The big draw though is the large waterside deck, which affords fine views of seven islands. Enjoying a similarly mesmerizing view are the three guest-house rooms at nearby *Orange House* (Ⓣ083 104 3109, Ⓦwww.lantamarineservices.com; ❹–❺), which also does boat trips, charters and transfers.

There's **internet** access and wi-fi on the main street plus an **ATM**, and a fuel station on the edge of town. The hourly Krabi minibus service starts from and terminates in Lanta Old Town.

Ko Bubu

If you really want to get away from everything, the minuscule, wooded island of **Ko Bubu**, with a radius of just 500m, is the place to head for. There's little to do here other than enjoy the pretty beach, swing in a hammock and stroll the round-island trail. Ko Bubu is 7km northeast off Lanta Old Town and is the sole preserve of *Bubu Island Resort* (Ⓣ075 618066, B400–1000; closed May–Oct), which has just fifteen en-suite bungalows and a restaurant. It's twenty minutes' chartered **longtail** ride (B200 per person) from Lanta Old Town.

Travel details

Buses

Cheow Lan Lake (Ratchabrapa Dam, Khao Sok) to: Phunphin (Surat Thani train station; every 2hr; 1hr).
Khao Lak to: Khao Sok (9 daily; 1hr 30min); Phuket (20 daily; 2hr 30min); Ranong (8 daily; 2hr 30min–3hr); Surat Thani (9 daily; 3hr 30min); Takua Pa (18 daily; 30min).
Khao Sok to: Khao Lak (9 daily; 1hr 30min); Surat Thani (every 90min; 2hr); Takua Pa (every 90min; 50min).
Khuraburi to: Khao Lak (5 daily; 1hr 45min); Phuket (5 daily; 3hr 30min–4hr); Ranong (5 daily; 2hr); Takua Pa (5 daily; 1hr);
Krabi to: Bangkok (10 daily; 12hr); Hat Yai (13 daily; 4–5hr); Ko Lanta (hourly; 2hr); Nakhon Si Thammarat (at least hourly; 3hr); Phang Nga (at least hourly; 2hr); Phattalung (7 daily; 3hr); Phuket (at least hourly; 4hr); Ranong (4 daily; 5hr); Satun (2 daily; 5hr); Sungai Kolok (3 daily; 9hr); Surat Thani (at least hourly; 2hr); Takua Pa (4 daily; 3hr 30min–4hr 30min); Trang (at least hourly; 2–3hr).
Phang Nga to: Bangkok (5 daily; 11hr); Krabi (at least hourly; 1hr 30min–2hr); Phuket (at least hourly; 1hr 30min–2hr 30min); Surat Thani (5 daily; 4hr); Takua Pa (at least hourly; 1hr); Trang (at least hourly; 3hr).
Phuket to: Bangkok (34 daily; 10–14hr); Chumphon (20 daily; 6hr 30min); Hat Yai (24 daily; 7hr); Khao Lak (17 daily; 2hr 30min); Khao Sok (13 daily; 3–4hr); Khuraburi (17 daily; 3hr 30min–4hr); Krabi (27 daily; 3hr–4hr 30min); Nakhon Si Thammarat (8 daily; 7hr); Phang Nga (27 daily; 1hr 30min–2hr 30min); Phattalung (20 daily; 6hr); Ranong (17 daily; 5hr 30min); Satun (5 daily; 7hr); Sungai Kolok (3 daily; 11hr); Surat Thani (13 daily; 4hr 30min); Takua Pa (17 daily; 2hr 30min–3hr); Trang (20 daily; 5–6hr).
Ranong to: Bangkok (12 daily; 9hr); Chumphon (hourly; 2–3hr); Hat Yai (3 daily; 5hr); Khao Lak (6 daily; 3hr 45min); Khuraburi (6 daily; 2hr); Krabi (5 daily; 5hr); Phang Nga (5 daily; 4hr); Phuket (6 daily; 5hr 30min); Surat Thani (10 daily; 3–5hr); Takua Pa (6 daily; 3hr).
Takua Pa to: Bangkok (10 daily; 12–13hr); Khuraburi (at least 8 daily; 1hr); Krabi (at least 4 daily; 3hr); Phang Nga (hourly; 1hr); Phuket (hourly; 3hr); Ranong (5 daily; 3hr 30min–4hr); Surat Thani (11 daily; 3hr 15min).

Ferries

Ao Nang to: Ko Lanta Yai (Nov–May 1 daily; 2hr 30min); Ko Phi Phi Don (Nov–May 1 daily; 2hr 30min); Phuket (Nov–May 1 daily; 3hr).
Khuraburi to: Ko Surin (Nov–May 1–2 daily; 1hr 15min–3hr).
Ko Chang to: Ranong (June–Oct 3 weekly; Nov–May 2 daily; 1hr).
Ko Jum to: Ko Lanta Yai (mid-Oct to mid-May 1–2 daily; 1hr); Krabi (mid-Oct to mid-May 1–2 daily; 1hr 30min); Laem Kruat (at least 4 daily; 45min–1hr).
Ko Lanta Yai to: Ao Nang (Nov–May 1 daily; 2hr 30min); Ko Phi Phi Don (Nov–May 1–2 daily; 1hr 30min); Krabi (mid-Oct to mid-May 1–2 daily; 2hr 30min); Phuket (Nov–May 1–2 daily; 4hr 30min).
Ko Phayam to: Ranong (1–4 daily; 40min–3hr).
Ko Phi Phi Don to: Ao Nang and West Railay (Nov–May 1 daily; 2hr 30min); Ko Lanta Yai (Nov–May 1–2 daily; 1hr 30min); Krabi (2–4 daily; 2hr); Phuket (at least 2 daily; 1hr 30min–2hr 30min).
Ko Yao Noi to: Krabi (Ao Thalen; 5 daily; 1hr); Phang Nga (daily; 90min); Phuket (8 daily; 1hr 10min).
Krabi to: Ko Jum (mid-Oct to mid-May 1–2 daily; 1hr 30min–2hr); Ko Lanta Yai (mid-Oct to mid-May 1– 2 daily; 2hr 30min); Ko Phi Phi Don (2–4 daily; 2hr); Ko Yao Noi (departs Ao Thalen; 5 daily; 1hr).
Laem Kruat to: Ko Jum (at least every 2hr; 45min–1hr).
Phang Nga (Tha Dan) to: Ko Yao Noi (daily; 90min).
Phuket to: Ao Nang (Nov–May 1 daily; 2hr); Ko Lanta Yai (Nov–May 1 daily; 4hr 30min); Ko Phi Phi Don (2–3 daily; 1hr 30min–2hr 30min); Ko Yao Noi (hourly; 1hr 10min).
Ranong to: Ko Chang (June–Oct 3 weekly; Nov–May 3 daily; 1hr); Ko Phayam (1–4 daily; 40min–3hr).
Thap Lamu (Khao Lak) to: Ko Similan (Nov–May 1 daily; 2hr).

Flights

Krabi to: Bangkok (up to 6 daily; 1hr 20min); Ko Samui (3 weekly; 50min).
Phuket to: Bangkok (up to 27 daily; 1hr 20min); Ko Samui (2 daily; 55min); Pattaya/ U-Tapao (1–2 daily; 1hr 35min–2hr 55min).
Ranong to: Bangkok (3 weekly; 1hr 5min).

8

The deep south

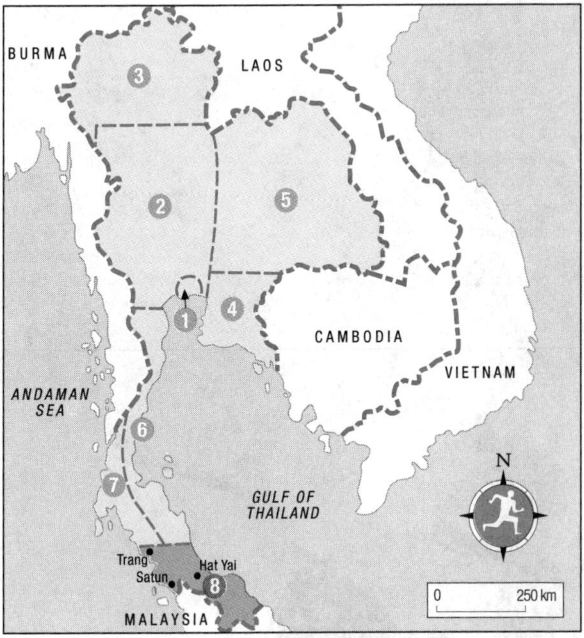

CHAPTER 8 Highlights

* **Nature Resorts** Not-for-profit resorts, great tours and nice people, at Ban Chao Mai, on Ko Mook and Ko Libong. See p.775, p.779 & p.781

* **Ko Hai** A variety of good resorts for all budgets and gorgeous views. See p.776

* **Tham Morakhot** Ko Mook's Emerald Cave, with its inland beach at the base of a natural chimney, is best visited by kayak. See p.778

* **Ko Sukorn** For a glimpse of how islanders live and an outstanding beach resort. See p.781

* **Ko Tarutao National Marine Park** A largely undisturbed haven – bar fast-developing Ko Lipe – of beautiful land- and seascapes. See p.783

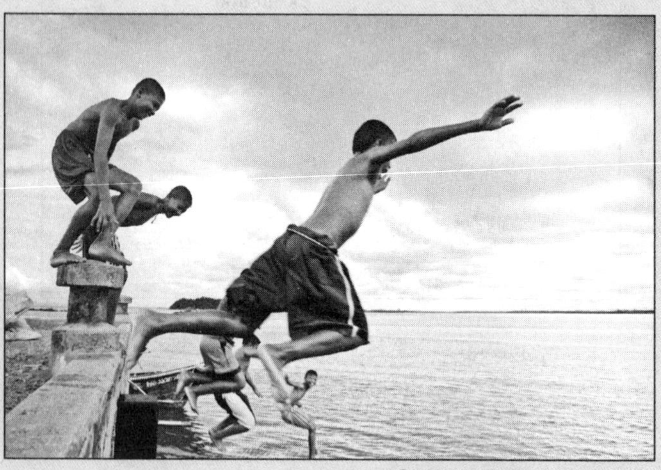

▲ Boys leaping from a pier on Ko Sukorn

8

The deep south

The frontier between Thailand and Malaysia carves across the peninsula six degrees north of the equator, but the cultures of the two countries shade into each other much further north. According to official divisions, the southern Thais – the *thai pak tai* – begin around Chumphon, and as you move further down the peninsula you'll see ever more sarongs, yashmaks and towering mosques, and hear with increasing frequency a staccato dialect that baffles many Thais. Here too, you'll come across caged singing doves outside many houses, as well as strange-looking areas spiked with tall metal poles, on which the cages are hung during regular cooing competitions; and you'll spot huge, hump-backed Brahma bulls on the back of pick-up trucks, on their way to bullfights (in the Thai version, beast is pitted against beast, and the first to back off is the loser). In Trang and Phatthalung provinces, the Muslim population is generally accepted as being Thai, but the inhabitants of the southernmost provinces – Satun, Pattani, Yala, Narathiwat and most of Songkhla – are ethnically more akin to the Malays: most of the 1.5 million followers of Islam here speak Yawi, an old Malay dialect. To add to the ethnic confusion, the deep south has a large urban population of Chinese, whose comparative wealth makes them stand out sharply from the Muslim farmers and fishermen.

Travel warning

Because of the ongoing **violence** in the deep south (see p.771), all major Western governments are currently advising people **not to travel** to or through Songkhla, Pattani, Yala and Narathiwat provinces, unless essential; following on from this, insurance companies are refusing to cover travel in these areas. The four provinces encompass the city and transport hub of **Hat Yai** and several of the main border crossings to Malaysia: by rail from Hat Yai (and Bangkok) to Butterworth via Padang Besar and to Sungai Kolok; and by road from Hat Yai via Sadao, from Yala via Betong, and down the east coast to Kota Bharu.

The routes to Sungai Kolok, Betong and Kota Bharu pass through particularly volatile territory, with **martial law** declared in Pattani, Yala and Narathiwat provinces; however, martial law is not in effect in Hat Yai itself or the districts of Songkhla province through which the Bangkok–Butterworth rail line or the Hat Yai–Sadao road pass.

The provinces of **Trang** and **Satun** are not affected, and it's still perfectly possible to continue overland via Satun: by air-con minibus from nearby Ban Khuan to Kangar, or by ferry from Thammalang to Kuala Perlis or the Malaysian island of Langkawi (see p.789); or by boat from Ko Lipe to Langkawi (see p.784). For up-to-the-minute advice, consult your government travel advisory (see p.63).

The touristic interest in the deep south is currently all over on the beautiful **west coast**, where sheer limestone outcrops, pristine sands and fish-laden coral stretch down to the Malaysian border. The spread of tourism outwards from Phuket has been inching its way south towards **Trang** and **Satun** for some time now, but they remain largely undeveloped. Along Trang's mainland **coast**, there's a thirty-kilometre stretch of attractive beaches, dotted with mangroves and impressive caves that can be explored by sea canoe, but the real draw down here is the offshore **islands**, which offer gorgeous panoramas and beaches, great snorkelling and at least a modicum of comfort in their small clusters of resorts. An added attraction is the recently introduced, scheduled boat services which have set up the intriguing possibility of **island-hopping**: it would now be possible to work your way down from Phuket as far as Penang without setting foot on the peninsula.

As well as the usual bus services, the area covered in this chapter is served by flights and trains to Trang. The deep south is also the territory of **share-taxis**, which connect towns for about twice the fare of ordinary buses. The cars leave when they're full, which usually means six passengers, and sometimes a long wait, though there's always the option of buying up extra seats if you're in a hurry. They are a quick way of getting around and you should get dropped off at the door of your journey's end. A more recent – and now much more successful – phenomenon, run on almost exactly the same principles at similar prices, is **air-conditioned minibuses**; on these you'll be more comfortable,

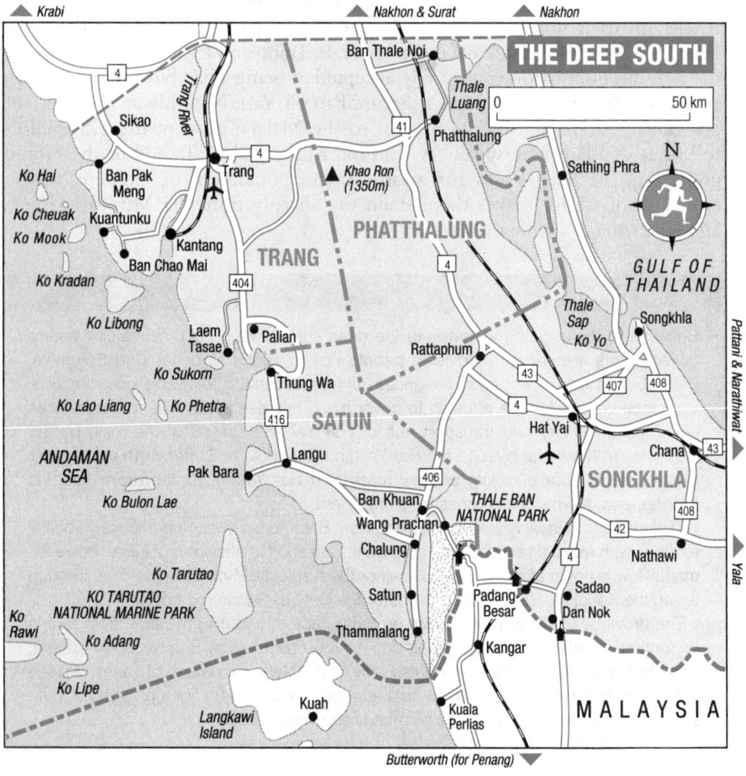

with a seat to yourself, and most of the various ranks publish a rough timetable – though the minibuses also tend to leave as soon as they're full.

Some history

The central area of the Malay peninsula first entered Thai history when it came under the rule of Sukhothai, probably around the beginning of the fourteenth century. Islam was introduced to the area by the end of that century, by which time Ayutthaya was taking a firmer grip on the peninsula. **Songkhla** and **Pattani** then rose to be the major cities, prospering on the goods passed through the two ports across the peninsula to avoid the pirates in the Straits of Malacca between Malaysia and Sumatra. More closely tied to the Muslim Malay states to the south, Pattani began to **rebel** against the central power of Ayutthaya in the sixteenth century, but the fight for self-determination only weakened Pattani's strength. The town's last rebellious fling was in 1902, after which it was definitively and brutally absorbed into the Thai kingdom, while its allies, Kedah, Kelantan and Trengganu, were transferred into the suzerainty of the British in Malaysia.

During World War II the **Communist Party of Malaya** made its home in the jungle around the Thai border to fight the occupying Japanese. After the war they turned their guns against the British colonialists, but having been excluded from power after independence, descended into general banditry and racketeering around Betong. The Thai authorities eventually succeeded in breaking up the bandit gangs in 1989 through a combination of pardons and bribes, but the stability of the region soon faced disruption from another source, a rise in **Islamic militancy**. Armed Muslim resistance to the Thai state had fluctuated at a relatively low level since the 1960s, but in early 2004 the violence escalated dramatically. Since then, there have been thousands of deaths on both sides in the troubles, and barely a day goes by without a fatal incident of one kind or another. The insurgents have viciously targeted Buddhist monks, police, soldiers, teachers and other civil servants, as well as attacking a train on the Hat Yai–Sungai Kolok line and setting off bombs in marketplaces, near tourist hotels and bars and at Hat Yai airport. Increasingly, they have attacked other Muslims who are seen to be too sympathetic to the Thai state. Writing the militants off as bandits, the authorities have stirred up hatred – and undermined moderate Muslim voices – by reacting violently, notably in crushing protests at Tak Bai and the much-revered Krue Se Mosque in Pattani in 2004, in which a total of over two hundred alleged insurgents died. Meanwhile, the army has "subcontracted" much of its work to rangers, untrained village militias, thus inflaming the situation further and deepening the ethnic divide. In 2005, the government announced a **serious state of emergency** in Pattani, Yala and Narathiwat provinces, and imposed **martial law** here and in southeastern parts of Songkhla province. This, however, has exacerbated economic and unemployment problems in what is Thailand's poorest region.

A large part of the problem is that a wide variety of shadowy groups – with names like the Pattani Islamic Mujahideen, the Barisan Revolusi Nasional-Coordinate and New Pulo – are operating against the government, generally working in small cells at village level without central control. Rather than religious issues, the most likely causes of their militancy seem to be disempowerment and resentment towards not only Thais but also the remote and corrupt Muslim elite. However, it's unclear exactly who they are or what they want and, faced with such shifting sands, all attempts to broker a ceasefire have failed.

Trang town

TRANG (also known as Taptieng) is gradually developing as a popular jumping-off point for backpackers drawn south from the crowded sands of Krabi to the pristine beaches and islands of the nearby coast. The town, which prospers on rubber, oil palms, fisheries and – increasingly – tourism, is a sociable place whose wide, clean streets are dotted with crumbling, wooden-shuttered houses. In the evening, restaurant tables sprawl onto the main Thanon Rama VI and Thanon Sathanee, and during the day, many of the town's Chinese inhabitants hang out in the cafés, drinking the local filtered coffee. Trang's Chinese population makes the **Vegetarian Festival** at the beginning of October almost as frenetic as Phuket's (see box, p.686) – and for veggie travellers it's an opportunity to feast at the stalls set up around the temples.

Arrival and information

Nok Air (☎075 212229, at the airport) and One-Two-Go (see p.45) run daily **flights** between Bangkok and Trang airport, which is connected to Trang town 3km to the north by B90 air-conditioned minibuses, operated by, for example, World Travel, 25/2 Thanon Sathanee (☎075 214010–1). Two overnight **trains** from the capital run down a branch of the southern line to Trang. **Buses** arrive at the terminal on Thanon Huay Yod, to the north of the centre, including an air-conditioned service between Satun and Phuket four times daily; many buses also make a stop near the central clocktower. Most **air-conditioned minibus** services have their own offices, as marked on our map, while those for Pak Bara

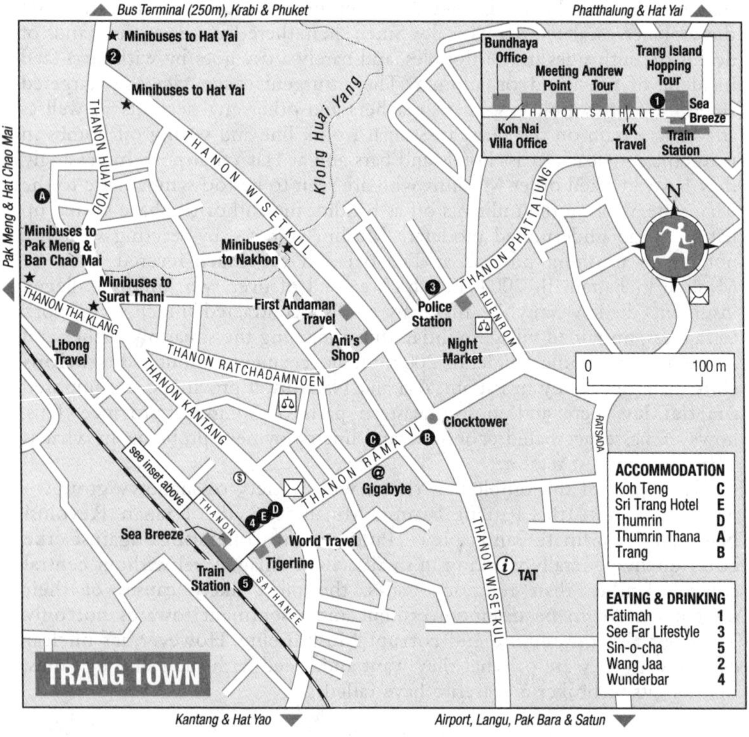

can be found at Andrew Tour travel agency opposite the station (ⓣ075 216110, ⓦwww.andrewlipe.com), those for Ban Saladan on Ko Lanta, KK Travel next door (ⓣ075 211198). **Share taxis** for Pak Bara and Satun congregate on Thanon Ratsada, out on the southeast side of town, for Krabi opposite the bus station.

The best **travel agency** in town is Trang Island Hopping Tour, directly opposite the station at 28/2 Thanon Sathanee (ⓣ075 211457 or 085 888 0898, ⓦwww.trang-islands.com). This well-organized outfit offers a huge range of services, including accommodation booking on any island, boat trips, island and mainland transfers and **car rental** (with or without driver; B1200–1600 per day), as well as one-day treks inland and excursions to waterfalls and **Tham Le** (also known as Khao Kob), a dramatic inland system of caverns accessed by boat. The friendly staff are a great source of impartial information on the area, and their office makes a good first stop in town. Libong Travel, 59/1 Thanon Tha Klang (ⓣ075 214676, ⓦwww.libong-travel.com), offer longer treks and two-night camping trips out to Ko Rok (see p.756) at weekends. **Dive** outfits include Sea Moth at 212/5 Thanon Wisetkul (ⓣ075 225968, ⓦwww.seamoth.com). **Motorbikes** can be rented at *Wunderbar* (see p.774; B150 per day).

TAT have a **tourist office** on Thanon Wisetkul (daily 8.30am–4.30pm; ⓣ075 215867–8, ⓔtattrang@tat.or.th). **Internet** access is available at, among others, *Wunderbar* and Gigabyte opposite the *Koh Teng Hotel* on Thanon Rama VI.

Accommodation

Trang's **hotels** are handily concentrated along Thanon Rama VI.

Koh Teng Hotel 77–79 Thanon Rama VI ⓣ075 218622 or 075 218148. Characterful 1940s Chinese hotel offering large, clean en-suite rooms, some with cable TV and air-con, above a popular restaurant and coffee shop, serving southern Thai and Chinese food and Western breakfasts. Fan ❶, air-con ❷

Only for You Contact Ani's jewellery shop, 285 Thanon Ratchadamnoen ⓣ081 397 4574. Quiet, fan-cooled house with a rear terrace, kitchen and cold-water bathroom, 5min walk from the shop. The owners are a good source of information on the area. B1000 for three nights (minimum), B1500 per week.

Sri Trang Hotel 22 Thanon Sathanee ⓣ075 218122, ⓦwww.sritranghotel.com. Welcoming, recently converted hotel offering spacious rooms with some colourful decorative touches, free wi-fi, hot water, TVs and fridges. Air-con in all but one room. Internet access. ❸

Thumrin Hotel Thanon Rama VI ⓣ075 211011–4, ⓦwww.thumrin.com. Formerly the top hotel in town, now offering international-standard facilities – air-con, hot water, TV, wi-fi and internet access – at bargain prices, in a high-rise block above its popular bakery-cum-coffee shop. ❸

Thumrin Thana Hotel 69/8 Thanon Huay Yod ⓣ075 211211, ⓦwww.thumrin.com. The best hotel in town, though not in the same league as the *Anantara* on the coast (see p.774). Spacious, well-equipped rooms, a pool and health club, wi-fi and internet access. ❼

Trang Hotel 134/2–5 Thanon Wisetkul ⓣ075 218944, ⓕ075 218451. Good, welcoming, moderately priced choice, with large, comfortable twin rooms with air-con, hot water and TV. ❸

Eating and drinking

Trang's streets are dotted with dozens of traditional cafés, which serve up gallons of **kopii** (local filtered coffee) accompanied by various tidbits and light meals. Most famous of these is the local delicacy, **muu yaang**, delicious barbecued pork, which is generally eaten for breakfast. At the excellent **night market**, around the back of the city hall on Thanon Ruenrom, you can try another tasty southern dish, *khanom jiin*, soft noodles topped with hot, sweet or fishy sauces and eaten with crispy greens.

Fatimah Thanon Sathanee. Simple, pink-awninged restaurant that's especially popular in the evenings. Buffet of southern halal curries all day, tasty *pat thai* (3–11pm), *kopii* and tea.

See Far Lifestyle 37 Thanon Phattalung ⓣ075 210139. Excellent, inexpensive restaurant with a varied menu of carefully prepared dishes, specializing in healthy cuisine – fruit and veg sorbets, brown rice – and local food, such as *tom som plakapong*, a light, refreshing soup of sea bass, mushrooms and cumin, and *kao yok*, a Chinese-style dish of steamed pork with taro found only in Trang.

Sin-o-cha Next to the station at 25/25–26 Thanon Sathanee. Very popular, updated traditional café: *kopii* with Thai and Western cakes and main courses, or espresso, various teas, Western breakfasts, and even baguettes and ciabattas. Daily 7am–7pm.

Wang Jaa Thanon Huay Yod, near the Hat Yai minibus office. Simple café open for breakfast and lunch, that's renowned for its *muu yaang*, but also serves *salapao* (Chinese buns), dim sum and, of course, *kopii*.

Wunderbar Bottom end of Thanon Rama VI, near the station ⓣ075 214563, ⓦwww.wunderbar-trang.com. Multi-purpose farang bar-restaurant that serves a wide selection of drinks (including wine), Thai food, and salads, burgers, pizzas and other Western favourites. Also acts as a travel agent, especially for island bookings, and offers internet and reasonably priced overseas calls.

The Trang coast

From **PAK MENG**, 40km due west of Trang town, down to the mouth of the Trang River runs a thirty-kilometre stretch of lovely beaches, broken only by dramatic limestone outcrops. Air-conditioned **minibuses** (roughly every 30min; 45min; B60) run from Thanon Tha Klang in Trang to Pak Meng (as well as to Ban Chao Mai in the south; see opposite), but if you want to explore the whole coastline, you'll need to **rent** a motorbike or car in Trang.

Although it has a fine outlook to the headlands and islands to the west, the beach at Pak Meng itself is not the most attractive on the coast, becoming a rather muddy strip of sand at low tide. At other times, however, it offers quiet, calm swimming, and there's always the possibility of a meal at one of the many tree-shaded foodstalls and restaurants that line the back of the beach. The nicest place **to stay** is *Lay Trang Resort*, a stone's throw from the pier at the far north end of the beach (ⓣ075 274027–8, ⓦwww.laytrang.com; ❹–❺); ranged around a large, peaceful garden, its smart brick rooms come with cold-water bathrooms, air-con and TV, while the bungalows boast fridges and hot water, and it has a pleasant, reasonably priced **restaurant** that's locally renowned for its seafood. Another good, more central restaurant is the popular and helpful *Yok Yor*, less than a kilometre south of the main T-junction where the Trang road hits the beachfront road, which offers carefully presented dishes of fish and seafood under the seaside casuarinas.

Immediately south of Pak Meng's beach is the white sand of **Hat Chang Lang**, famous for its oysters, which shelters at its north end the finest luxury hotel in the province, *Anantara Si Kao* (ⓣ075 205888, ⓦwww.anantara.com; ❾). The low-rise blocks of stylish bedrooms with large balconies, including seven pool suites, are set behind a line of casuarina trees, and facilities encompass a beautiful, large pool, Italian and international restaurants, a fitness centre, and a spa and wellness centre overseen by an Indian naturopathic doctor. Watersports on offer include diving, kayaking, windsurfing and sailing, and there's a huge range of other activities laid on, notably yoga, cooking and Thai-language lessons and some interesting local tours. The hotel also has its own beach club and restaurant on the main strand on Ko Kradan (see p.779), reached by daily boat transfer.

Three kilometres further on is the turning for the headquarters of the **Hat Chao Mai National Park** (entry B200; ⓣ075 213260, ⓦwww.dnp.go.th), which covers 230 square kilometres, including parts of Ko Mook and Ko

Kradan. At the headquarters there's a simple café as well as bungalows and rooms for two to six people (B800–1500), or you can rent a two-person tent to pitch under the casuarinas at the back of the sandy beach (B270 including bedding). From the headquarters a short trail leads to the south end of the beach and a viewpoint partway up a karst pinnacle, from which you can see Ko Mook and occasionally dugongs in the bay below.

Four kilometres south of Hat Chang Lang, beyond Kuantunku, the pier for Ko Mook, is **Hat Yong Ling**. This quiet and attractive convex beach, which shelters a national park ranger station, is probably the nicest along this stretch of coast, with a large cave which you can swim into at high tide or walk into at low tide. Immediately beyond comes **Hat Yao**, which runs in a broad five-kilometre white-sand strip, backed by casuarina trees and some simple restaurants.

Next up is **BAN CHAO MAI** (also called **Ban Hat Yao**), a straggle of houses on stilts, which exists on fishing, especially for crabs. Roughly half-hourly air-conditioned **minibuses** (B60) from Thanon Tha Klang in Trang via Hat Yao take about an hour to reach Ban Chao Mai, from whose harbour boats run regularly across to Ko Libong. By the harbour, *Had Yao Nature Resort* (Ⓣ075 207934 or 081 894 6936, Ⓦwww.trangsea.com; fan ③, air-con ④) is a well-managed, non-profit resort, where your custom will go towards helping local people and the environment (see p.80). The same people own *Libong Nature Beach Resort* (see p.781), *Ko Mook Nature Beach Resort* (see p.779), and an organic farmstay on Highway 4 between Trang and Krabi, where in the low season you can learn to make aloe vera soap, jam and shampoo. Dorm beds in the large house cost B300, and there are also some fan-cooled rooms with shared bath, as well as nicer air-con rooms and bungalows, some with hot water and/or balconies over the canal. The breezy, waterside **restaurant** serves up Western breakfasts, vegetarian food and excellent squid and other seafood dishes; for exploring nearby beaches, **bikes** can be rented for B100 per day, and snorkelling equipment, internet and wi-fi are available. The owners organize tours to the local islands, including highly recommended dugong-watching trips to Ko Libong (available from Ban Chao Mai; see p.780), and through the mangroves to the nearby cave of **Tham Chao Mai**; inside are impressively huge rock pillars and a natural theatre, its stage framed by rock curtains. Tham Chao Mai can be visited on a guided and fully insured trip by longtail and canoe (B1200 per person, including lunch; minimum four people) or you can rent a **kayak** (B800–1200 per day) and guide yourself through the mangroves with a map and torch.

The Trang and Satun islands

Generally blessed with blinding white beaches, great coral and amazing marine life, the islands off the coast of Trang and Satun provinces have managed, mostly with just a handful of resorts on each, to cling onto some of that illusory desert-island atmosphere which better-known places like Phuket and Samui lost long ago. Indeed, islands such as **Ko Hai** and **Ko Kradan** support no permanent settlements other than the bungalow concerns, while on **Ko Tarutao** and **Ko Adang** in the far south, the peace and quiet is maintained by the national parks department; at the other end of the scale, however, nearby **Ko Lipe** is developing at its own merry pace and now boasts over twenty resorts, as well as a substantial *chao ley* village (see p.663). **Access** from a variety of mainland ports is described in the accounts below, but what sets this area apart are the enticing opportunities for **island-hopping**, thanks to regular boat services in the tourist season out of Ko Lanta. Scheduled services are provided by Tigerline, with its office on Thanon Sathanee in Trang (Ⓣ075 590489, Ⓦwww.tigerlinetravel.com), which operates daily ferries between Lanta and Lipe (1 daily; about 5hr; B1500) via Ko Hai, the village on Ko Mook, Ban Chao Mai on the mainland and Ko Lao Liang (on request); and by Satun Pakbara Speedboat Club (Lanta Ⓣ075 684283, Pak Bara Ⓣ074 783643–5, Lipe Ⓣ074 750388, Ⓦwww.tarutaolipeisland.com), which sails from Lanta to Lipe (1 daily; about 3hr; B1900) via Ko Hai, Hat Farang on Ko Mook and Ko Bulon Lae once daily in season, with onward services to the Malaysian island of Langkawi. Meanwhile, day-trip boats from Ko Lanta to Ko Hai, Ko Mook and Ko Kradan will drop you at, or transfer you between, any of the islands: Garden Hill (Ⓣ075 684042, Ⓦwww.lantaislandtours.com) sends out a speedboat every day in season (B500 between Ko Hai and Hat Farang on Ko Mook, for example) while Petpailin (Ⓣ075 667033) has a bigger, slower ferry (B400 for the same leg). Resorts such as *Ko Hai Seafood* also put together longtail transfers, which can work out the cheapest option if there are enough takers.

Accommodation on the islands, much of which is mid-priced, is now often fully booked at the very busiest times. Most of the resorts open year round, though in practice many can't be reached out of season (roughly June–Oct) due to treacherous seas. It's sensible to get in touch ahead of time to check whether the resort you're interested in is open or has vacancies, and in many cases to arrange transfers from Trang; many of the resorts maintain offices in Trang town to make this easier.

If you just fancy a day exploring some of the islands, any travel agent in Trang can book you on a **boat trip** (mid-Oct to mid-May only) to Ko Kradan, the Emerald Cave on Ko Mook, and other small nearby islands for snorkelling, for B1050 per person including admission to Hat Chao Mai National Park, packed lunch and soft drinks. More active types might well be tempted by *Lao Liang Resort* (Ⓦwww.laoliangresort.com; ❽; closed May to mid-Oct), the only habitation on **Ko Lao Liang**, beautiful, twin desert islands to the west of Ko Sukorn that can be reached on the Tigerline ferry. All-in costs include meals, kayaks, snorkelling gear and camping in luxury tents; diving, rock-climbing, yoga and snorkelling tours are extra. **Scuba-diving** is also available on Ko Hai, Ko Mook, Ko Libong and Ko Lipe, while Paddle Asia run **sea-kayaking** trips around the Trang and Tarutao islands (see p.75).

Ko Hai (Ko Ngai)

KO HAI (also known as **KO NGAI**), 16km southwest of Pak Meng, is the most developed of the Trang islands, though it's still decidedly low-key. The island's action, such as it is, centres on the east coast, where half a dozen resorts enjoy a dreamy panorama of jagged limestone outcrops, whose crags glow pink and blue against the setting sun, stretching across the sea to the mainland behind. The gently sloping beach of fine, white sand here runs unbroken for over 2km (though at low tide, swimming is not so good at the northern end, which is scattered with dead coral), and there's some good snorkelling in the shallow, clear water off the island's southeastern tip. For the best snorkelling in the region, the resorts run **boat trips** every day in high season (from B250 per person at *Coco Cottage*, for example) to Ko Cheuak and Ko Maa, just off Ko Hai to the east, where you can swim into caverns and explore a fantastic variety of multi-coloured soft and hard coral; it's also possible to add Ko Mook's Emerald Cave to these trips. As well as all manner of transfers to other islands, the resorts also offer day-trips to the popular snorkelling and diving site of Ko Rok (see p.756), 30km southwest in the Mu Ko Lanta National Park (from B700 per

▲ Longtail boat on Ko Hai

person by longtail, B1300 by speedboat, at *Coco Cottage*), while *Seafood* does overnighters on Ko Rok for B2300 per person.

Ko Hai's resorts lay on **boats** for their guests from Pak Meng, charging from B300 per person in a longtail (45min–1hr), B450 per person in a speedboat (20min), fed by transfers from Trang town or airport for B150 (some also offer pick-ups from Krabi airport). Otherwise, you can book a minibus-and-longtail transfer from Trang town (daily in season; B450) through agents such as Trang Island Hopping Tour (see p.773). Hat Chao Mai National Park maintains a booth at Pak Meng pier, where you'll be charged B200 entrance fee (if the rangers have bothered to show up for work). **Snorkelling equipment** (B100 per day at *Coco Cottage*, for example) and **kayaks** (around B700 per day for a two-seater) can be rented at most of the resorts. Towards the southern end of the beach, *Fantasy Resort* has a well-organized **dive shop**, the German-run Rainbow Divers (Ⓣ075 206962, Ⓦwww.rainbow-diver.com; Nov–April).

Accommodation

Ko Hai now has the whole gamut of **accommodation**, from simple, en-suite bamboo bungalows to swanky, air-con cottages.

Coco Cottage Towards the northern end of the beach Ⓣ089 724 9225 or 087 898 6522, Ⓦwww.coco-cottage.com. Charming, helpful and family-friendly resort in a grassy palm grove, where the stylish, thatched wooden bungalows sport verandas, mosquito nets and outdoor bathrooms with wooden basins and bamboo showers. Very good restaurant and beach bar, internet access, occasional yoga courses and a particularly wide range of boat trips and transfers at cheap prices. Breakfast included. Fan ❻–❼, air-con ❽

Ko Hai Paradise Resort Ao Kauntong on the south coast Ⓣ075 203024, Ⓦwww.kohhaiparadise.com; Trang office at *The Meeting Point* restaurant opposite the station Ⓣ075 216420. With a tranquil bay all to themselves, the simple en-suite bungalows at this friendly resort are sheltered by tall palms in spacious, grassy grounds. The food's good and the long, white-sand beach slopes down towards some great coral for snorkelling right in front of the resort. The resort has opened sporadically over the last couple of years, tending to operate only at the height of the high season. ❸–❺

Ko Hai Seafood Near the centre of the beach, north of *Villa* Ⓣ081 538 0980 or 081 367 8497. Large, well-built, thatched bungalows with wall fans, mosquito screens and well-equipped bathrooms, in a single row parallel to the beach. Substantial discounts in shoulder season. Breakfast included. ❻

Koh Ngai Villa Near the centre of the main beach ⓣ075 203263 or 086 279 4487, ⓦwww.kohngaivillathai.com; Trang office opposite the station ⓣ075 210496. Friendly, old-style beach resort with plenty of space. Simple, well-organized bamboo bungalows boast verandas and small toilets, or you could opt for a large room with two double beds in a concrete longhouse or a smart concrete bungalow with air-con, or even a two-person tent (B300, including bedding). Breakfast included with most rooms. Fan ❸–❺, air-con ❻

Thanya South end of the beach ⓣ075 206965–7, ⓦwww.kohngaithanyaresort.com. A large, very attractive beachside swimming pool with jacuzzis is the main draw here. As well as 24hr air-con, hot water and fridges, the villas feature verandas, big French windows and lots of polished teak, while the restaurant has a varied menu of Thai food, including some interesting seafood dishes. Just opened at the time of research, but looks promising: a spa is planned, though prices may rise. Breakfast included. ❼–❽

Thapwarin Resort Towards the northern end of the main beach, next to *Coco Cottage* ⓣ081 894 3585, ⓦwww.thapwarin.com; Trang office at 140/2 Thanon Rongrien ⓣ075 218153. Welcoming, shady resort, where you can choose between well-appointed bamboo and rattan cottages with outdoor bathrooms, and large, very smart, beach-front wooden bungalows boasting air-con as well as miniature gardens in their spacious bathrooms; all have hot showers. There's internet access, a massage spa, beach bar and good restaurant, serving Thai and Western food and espresso coffee. Breakfast included. Fan ❼, air-con ❽–❾

Ko Mook

KO MOOK, about 8km southeast of Ko Hai, supports a comparatively busy fishing village on its eastern side, around which – apart from the sandbar that runs out to the very pricey *Sivalai Resort* – most of the beaches are disappointing, reduced to dirty mud flats when the tide goes out. However, across on the island's west coast lies beautiful **Hat Farang**, with gently shelving white sand, crystal-clear water that's good for swimming and snorkelling, and gorgeous sunsets.

The island's main source of renown is **Tham Morakhot** (part of Hat Chao Mai National Park and closed July–Sept), the stunning "Emerald Cave" further north on the west coast, which can only be visited by boat, but shouldn't be missed. An eighty-metre swim through the cave – 10m or so of which is in pitch darkness – brings you to a *hong* (see p.716) with an inland beach of powdery sand open to the sky, at the base of a spectacular natural chimney whose walls are coated with dripping vegetation. Chartering your own longtail is preferable to taking one of the big day-trip boats that originate on Lanta or Pak Meng: if you time it right, you'll get the inland beach all to yourself, an experience not to be forgotten. It's also easy enough to **kayak** there from Hat Farang (from B100 per hr from *Sawaddee/Mookies*), and at low tide you can paddle right through to the inland beach: buoys mark the cave entrance, from where a tunnel heads straight back into the rock; about halfway along, there's a small, right-hand kink in the tunnel which will plunge you briefly into darkness, but you should soon be able to see light ahead from the *hong*. Mid-afternoon is often a good time to paddle off on this trip, after the tour boats have left and providing the tide is right. If you fancy a **boat trip** to the cave and Kradan, Chuak and Ma islands in one day, take your custom to *Ko Mook Nature Beach Resort*, where tours are fully insured and licensed and the revenue (B1500 per person; twenty-percent discount for guests) goes to help local people. Meanwhile, *Rubber Tree* put together three-day, two-night trips to Ko Rok for B4000 per person (minimum six people).

The easiest way to **get to Ko Mook** is to book a minibus-and-boat package to Hat Farang through a travel agent in Trang, which costs B350, including the thirty-minute longtail ride. Otherwise, there's a pretty reliable public boat (B60) at around midday to Ko Mook's village from Kuantunku pier, 8km south of Pak Meng, between Hat Chang Lang and Hat Yong Ling; Ban Chao Mai air-con minibuses from Trang (see p.775) will usually detour to Kuantunku if asked (around B100 per person from Trang); once landed at the village, you're left with a thirty-minute walk or B50 motorbike-taxi ride over to Hat Farang.

There's an English-run **dive shop** at *Charlie's Resort* on Hat Farang, Princess Divers (Ⓦwww.divekohmook.com; Nov–early May), offering PADI courses from Bubblemaker up to Divemaster, local dives including a World War II wreck off Ko Kradan and the rock pinnacle of Hin Nok, and trips by speedboat to sites such as Ko Rok, Hin Daeng and Hin Muang.

Accommodation

Most of Hat Farang is unfortunately occupied by the disappointing *Charlie's Resort*, while there are rumours that the Centara hotel chain will take over what's left from *Sawaddee*. However, *Rubber Tree* and *Mookies* make the best of the attractive, shady slopes behind the beach, while *Ko Mook Nature Beach Resort* is away on the east side of the island near the village.

Ko Mook Nature Beach Resort Recently opened branch of the non-profit *Had Yao Nature Resort*, which promotes conservation and sustainable tourism (see p.775; Ⓣ089 647 7030). On the south-facing shore of the sandbar that ends at *Sivalai Resort*, two-person tents with mosquito screens, beds, tables, lights and fans, sharing cold-water bathrooms (B150–200, or B100 with your own tent). Bicycles, kayaks, snorkels, internet and wi-fi available. There are also imminent plans for eco-friendly villas for long stays (minimum one week), each with a kitchen, living room, TV, hot water and air-con. (❻)

Mookies Ⓣ087 275 6533. Welcome to the "tentalows": comfortable tents, each pitched under a semi-permanent shelter with a bed, table, light, fan and mosquito screens. Shared toilets and hot showers. Good, inexpensive Thai and Western food at the popular, often raucous, Thai-Australian bar-restaurant. Free pick-ups from the village. At the lower end of this price range. ❷

Rubber Tree Ⓣ081 270 4148, Ⓦwww.mookrubbertree.com; or contact *Sea Breeze* restaurant in front of the station in Trang Ⓣ075 215972. On a well-tended, landscaped slope that's also a working rubber plantation, fan bungalows with cold-water bathrooms and crisp, white linen, or spacious, smartly designed air-con versions with rubber-wood furniture and hot showers. Breakfast included. Fan ❹, air-con ❻

Sawaddee Ⓣ075 207964–5, Ⓔsawaddeeresort64@yahoo.com; or contact *Wunderbar* in Trang (see p.774). Laid-back, old-style, concrete or stilted wooden bungalows parallel to the beach, which enjoy en-suite bathrooms, plenty of shade and largely uninterrupted sea views. Internet access. At the lower end of this price range. ❹

Ko Kradan

About 6km to the southwest of Ko Mook, **KO KRADAN** is the remotest of the inhabited islands off Trang, and one of the most beautiful, with crystal-clear waters. On this slender triangle of thick jungle, the main beach is a long strand of steeply sloping, powdery sand on the east coast, with fine views of Ko Mook, Ko Libong and the karst-strewn mainland, and an offshore reef to the north with a great variety of hard coral; such beauty, however, has not escaped the attention of the day-trip boats from Ko Lanta, who turn the beach into a lunchtime picnic ground most days in summer. From a short way north of the *Anantara's* beach club (see p.774), towards the south end of this beach, a path across the island will bring you after about fifteen minutes to Sunset Beach, another lovely stretch of fine, white sand in a cove; a branch off this path at *Paradise Lost* (see p.780) leads to a beach on the short south coast, which enjoys good reef snorkelling (also about 15min from the *Anantara* beach club).

Practicalities

Minibus-and-longtail **transfers** from Trang town (daily in season; B450) can be booked through agencies such as Trang Island Hopping Tour (see p.773). Kradan's best-value **accommodation** option is the American-run *Paradise Lost* (Ⓣ089 587 2409, Ⓔkokradan@yahoo.com; ④–⑤), in the middle of the island, roughly halfway along the path to Sunset Beach. In a grassy, palm-shaded grove, it offers simple, clean, thatched rattan bungalows with shared bathrooms or larger, wooden affairs (either en suite or sharing), as well as an open-sided dorm with mosquito nets and fans (B250 per person), kayaks, snorkels and good Thai and Western food. By far the best of several mostly forgettable resorts on the east coast is *Seven Seas* (Ⓣ075 203389–90, Ⓦwww.sevenseasresorts.com; ⑨ breakfast included), which adds a surprising splash of contemporary luxury to this remote spot. Behind a small, black, infinity pool, the large bungalows and rooms with outdoor warm-water bathrooms are stylishly done out in greys and whites, and sport air-con, wi-fi, fridges, TVs and DVDs. At the south end of the main beach there's a Hat Chao Mai National Park ranger station, with a few tents to rent (B200–300 for two to three people, including bedding; contact the park's headquarters for information; see p.774).

Ko Libong

The largest of the Trang islands with a population of six thousand, **KO LIBONG** lies 10km southeast of Ko Mook, opposite Ban Chao Mai on the mainland. Less visited than its northern neighbours, it's known mostly for its wildlife, although it has its fair share of golden beaches too. Libong is one of the most significant remaining refuges in Thailand of the **dugong**, a large marine mammal similar to the manatee, which feeds on sea grasses growing on the sea floor – the sea-grass meadow around Libong is reckoned to be the largest in Southeast Asia. Sadly, dugongs are now an endangered species, traditionally hunted for their blubber (used as fuel) and meat, and increasingly affected by fishing practices such as scooping, and by coastal pollution which destroys their source of food. The dugong has now been adopted as one of fifteen "reserved animals" of Thailand and is the official mascot of Trang province.

Libong is also well known for its migratory **birds**, which stop off here on their way south from Siberia, drawn by the island's food-rich mud flats (now protected by the Libong Archipelago Sanctuary, which covers the eastern third of the island). For those seriously interested in ornithology, the best time to come is during March and April, when you can expect to see brown-winged kingfishers, masked finfoots and even the rare black-necked stork, not seen elsewhere on the Thai–Malay peninsula.

As well as tours of local islands, *Libong Nature Beach Resort* runs award-winning, day-long **boat trips around Libong** itself (B1200 per person, including lunch, in a group of four or more; twenty percent discount for guests), which are safe, insured and licensed with TAT, and staffed by local sea gypsies who know the dugong well. As well as visiting a *chao ley* village, these give you the chance to kayak into the sanctuary to observe the rare birds and to snorkel at the sea-grass beds – with, they reckon, an eighty percent chance of seeing a dugong.

Practicalities

You can arrange a direct **boat** transfer from Ban Chao Mai (see p.775) to *Libong Nature Beach Resort* for about B1000 per boat. Alternatively, public longtails depart daily year-round from Ban Chao Mai when full (most frequent in the morning and around lunchtime; B50 per person), arriving twenty minutes later at Ban Phrao on Ko Libong's north side. From here motorbike taxis (B100) transport you across to the fishing village of **Ban Lan Khao** on the south-western coast, where the island's handful of resorts occupy a long, thin strip of golden sand. At low tide here, the sea retreats for hundreds of metres, exposing rock pools that are great for splashing about in but not so good for a dip.

By far the best of the island's **resorts** is *Libong Nature Beach Resort*, which is run by the same charitable foundation that operates the *Had Yao Nature Resort* (see p.775; ⓣ075 207934 or 081 894 6936, ⓦwww.trangsea.com; ❹–❺). Its neat, en-suite bungalows, all with wi-fi and some with hot water and air-con, stretch back from a secluded part of the beach, a ten-minute walk south of Ban Lan Khao, and there's another sheltered cove a further five minutes' walk (or kayak) to the south. There's a good restaurant attached too, with internet access, and mountain bikes and snorkelling gear are available to rent. Guided or unguided treks into the national park jungle behind the resort include a three-hour walk to a good viewpoint at the southwestern end of the island. There's a **dive shop** at *Libong Beach Resort* on the north side of Ban Lan Khao (ⓣ086 297 9747, ⓦwww.jollyrogerdive.com).

Ko Sukorn

A good way south of the other Trang islands, low-lying **KO SUKORN** lacks the white-sand beaches and beautiful coral of its neighbours, but makes up for it with its friendly inhabitants, laid-back ambience and one excellent resort; for a glimpse of how islanders live and work, this is the place to come.

The lush interior is mainly given over to rubber plantations, interspersed with rice paddies, banana and coconut palms; the island also produces famously delicious watermelons, which are plentiful in March and April. Hat Talo Yai, the main **beach** – 500m of gently shelving brown sand, backed by coconut palms – runs along the southwestern shore. It's here you'll find the outstanding *Sukorn Beach Bungalows* (represented in Trang by Trang Island Hopping Tours, see p.773; ⓣ075 207707, ⓦwww.sukorn-island-trang.com; fan ❹–❺, air-con ❺–❼, breakfast included), one of the few Trang resorts that's reliably accessible all year round (discounts of up to fifty percent are available in low season). The clued-up and congenial Thai-Dutch duo who run the place are keen to keep the resort low-key and quiet (no children under 7), and work with the locals as much as possible, something that's reflected in the friendly welcome you get all over the island. Attractively decorated and well-designed bungalows and rooms – all spotlessly clean and with en-suite bathrooms, most with hot water – are set around a lush garden dotted with deckchairs and umbrellas, and there's an excellent, well-priced **restaurant**. At the resort, you can access the internet (including wi-fi), make overseas calls, exchange money and get a good massage, and you're free to paddle around in kayaks.

Boat excursions from the resort include trips out to Ko Lao Liang and Ko Takieng, which are part of the Mu Ko Phetra National Marine Park, for some excellent snorkelling. These run nearly every day from November to May; at other times of year, the sea is sometimes calm enough but you're usually restricted to fishing trips – and to looking round the island itself, which, at thirty square kilometres, is a good size for exploring. The resort offers **guided tours** (B250 per person), or it has motorbikes (B300 per day) and mountain bikes (half-day B150) for rent, as well as a handy map that marks all the sights, including the three villages and seafood market.

A songthaew-and-boat **transfer to the island** (B175 per person), via the public ferry from Laem Ta Sae, leaves Trang Island Hopping Tours daily at 11.30am and takes a couple of hours, or you can arrange a private transfer. The resort can also organize pricey longtail-boat transfers to or from any of the nearby islands, and can even put together very appealing, five-night island-hopping packages (from B11,000 per person).

The best of the rest of the island's handful of resorts is the friendly and peaceful *Ko Sukorn Cabana* (ⓣ089 724 2326, ⓦwww.sukorncabana.com;

fan ④–⑤, air-con ⑤–⑥, breakfast included), offering stilted bungalows with attractive bathrooms and large, well-appointed log cabins on a secluded beach to the north of Hat Talo Yai. Day-trips to Lao Liang and Takieng, kayaks, motorbikes, internet and wi-fi are also available; private transfers from Trang can be arranged for B2100 all-in.

Ko Bulon Lae

The scenery at tiny **KO BULON LAE**, 20km west of Pak Bara in Satun province, isn't as beautiful as that generally found in Ko Tarutao National Park just to the south, but it's not at all bad: a two-kilometre strip of fine white sand runs the length of the casuarina-lined east coast, while *chao ley* fishermen make their ramshackle homes in the tight coves of the rest of the island. A reef of curiously shaped hard coral closely parallels the eastern beach, while **White Rock** to the south of the island has beautifully coloured soft coral and equally dazzling fish. **Snorkelling** gear, as well as **boats** for trips to White Rock and around the island (around B1700 per boat for 4–5hr), can be rented at *Pansand* resort, while *Bulone* has **kayaks**.

Ferries for Ko Bulon Lae currently leave Pak Bara (see below) daily at about 1.30pm (1hr 30min; B350 one way, B500 return). As there's no pier on Bulon Lae, the inter-island boats are met by longtails to transfer visitors to shore (B50). Boats return from Bulon Lae to Pak Bara at around 9am.

Accommodation

The island's **resorts** are open roughly from mid-October to early May. The largest and best of them is *Pansand* on the east-coast beach (Ⓣ074 728132 or 083 1726812, Ⓦwww.pansand-resort.com; Trang office at First Andaman Travel, 82–84 Thanon Wisetkul Ⓣ075 218035; ⑤–⑥ breakfast included), where large, smart cottages come with verandas, cold-water bathrooms and plenty of room to breathe. On the beach side of the shady, well-tended grounds, there's a sociable restaurant serving up good seafood and other Thai dishes; internet access is also available, and wi-fi is planned. The best of several cheaper resorts is friendly *Bulone* (Ⓣ081 897 9084 or 086 960 0468, Ⓦwww.bulone-resort.net; ③–⑤), a huge grassy compound under the casuarinas at the north end of the main beach. En-suite accommodation ranges from airy, bamboo-walled bungalows to large, white, clapboard affairs, and be sure to eat

En route to Bulon Lae, Tarutao and Lipe: Pak Bara

The main port for Bulon Lae, Tarutao and Lipe is **PAK BARA**, towards the north end of Satun province. **From Trang**, Andrew Tour (see p.773; in Pak Bara Ⓣ074 783459) offer direct air-con minibuses to Pak Bara (2 daily, more in high season; 1hr 30min–2hr); otherwise you'll need to take a Satun-bound bus (2hr–2hr 30min) or a share-taxi from Thanon Ratsada (1hr 30min) to the inland town of **Langu** and change there to a red songthaew for the ten-kilometre hop to the port. Andrew Tour also lay on one air-con minibus a day all the way through **from Krabi** in high season (4hr). Frequent buses, air-con minibuses and taxis **from Satun** make the fifty-kilometre trip to Langu.

If you need a place **to stay** in Pak Bara, try *Bara Guesthouse* (Ⓣ089 654 2801; ②), 200m before the pier on the west side of the main road, which offers large but slightly gloomy, tiled, concrete rooms with their own bathrooms in a garden running down to the sea. There are no banks on the Tarutao islands or Bulon Lae, but Krung Thai Bank send a minibus to Pak Bara pier every day in high season, with an on-board **ATM** and currency exchange facilities.

at the restaurant, which features a small selection of tasty Italian favourites, as well as internet access.

Ko Tarutao National Marine Park

The unspoilt **KO TARUTAO NATIONAL MARINE PARK** is probably the most beautiful of all Thailand's accessible beach destinations. Occupying 1400 square kilometres of the Andaman Sea in Satun province, the park covers 51 mostly uninhabited islands, of which three are easy to reach from the mainland and offer accommodation for visitors. Site of the park headquarters, **Ko Tarutao** offers a variety of government-issue accommodation and things to do, while **Ko Adang** is much more low-key and a springboard to some excellent snorkelling. Home to a population of around a thousand *chao ley*, tiny **Ko Lipe** is something of a frontier maverick, attracting ever more travellers with one dazzling beach, twenty or so private bungalow resorts and a rough-and-ready atmosphere. The port of **Pak Bara** (see opposite) is the main jumping-off point for the park, and houses a **national park visitor centre** (ⓣ074 783485, ⓦwww.dnp.go.th), set back on the left just before the pier, where you can gather information and book a room on Tarutao or Adang before boarding your boat.

The park's forests and seas support an incredible variety of **fauna**: langurs, crab-eating macaques and wild pigs are common on the islands, which also shelter several unique subspecies of squirrel, tree shrew and lesser mouse deer; among the hundred-plus bird species found here, reef egrets and hornbills are regularly seen, while white-bellied sea eagles, frigate birds and pied imperial pigeons are more rarely encountered; and the park is the habitat of about 25 percent of the world's tropical fish species, as well as dugongs, sperm whales, dolphins and a dwindling population of turtles.

The park amenities on Adang, though not on Tarutao, are officially closed to tourists in the monsoon season from mid-May to mid-November (the exact dates vary from year to year). Many of the resorts on Ko Lipe close at this time too, and the frequency of the ferry service is reduced. Accommodation is especially likely

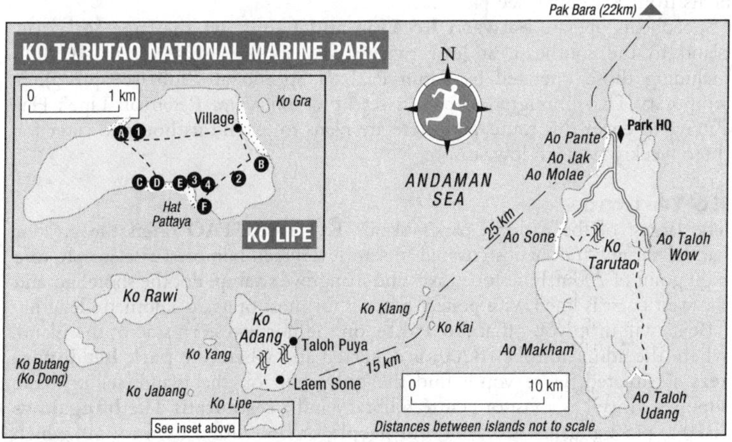

ACCOMMODATION						EATING & DRINKING			
Bundhaya	F	Castaway	B	Pattaya Song	C	Café Lipe	3	Kafair	4
Blue Tribes	F	Daya	D	Porn	A	Flour Power Bakery	1	Pattaya Song	C
		Family	E					Pooh's	2

to get full around the three New Years (Thai, Chinese and Western), when it's best to book national park rooms in advance (see p.52).

The prime **diving sites** in the park, served by several dive shops on Ko Lipe, are to the west of Ko Tarutao, around Ko Klang, Ko Adang, Ko Rawi and Ko Dong, where encounters with reef and even whale sharks, dolphins and stingrays are not uncommon. **Snorkelling gear** can be rented at Pak Bara or on Ko Adang for around B50 per day, and is widely available from the private bungalow outfits or dive shops on Ko Lipe.

Ferries

Ferry services into the park seem to change by the year, due to competition between the boat companies and local politicking. For up-to-date **information**, call the Pak Bara National Park Visitor Centre or contact Koh Lipe Thailand.com (see p.786). There is no pier on Adang or Lipe, so boats anchor in the channel between the islands or off Hat Pattaya, where they're met by **longtails** (B50 to any beach on Lipe or B100 to the Adang park station). The pier at Ao Pante on Tarutao is inaccessible at low tide, when longtails (B30) shuttle people to shore.

Among ferry and speedboat companies from **Pak Bara**, the most reliable are currently Adang Sea Ferry (ⓣ074 783338 or 081 609 2604, ⓦwww.adangseatour.com) and Lipeh Speedboat Co. (ⓣ089 464 7816, ⓦwww.lipehferry-speedboat.com), who each run at least one daily service year-round. In high season, the former has sailings at around 11am and 1.30pm for Ao Pante on Ko Tarutao (1hr; B350 one way, B600 return), before continuing to Ko Adang and Ko Lipe (from Pak Bara: 3hr; B500 one way, B900 return); the latter operates faster boats at 11.30am and 1.30pm to Adang/Lipe (1hr 30min; B650 one way, B1200 return), which usually stop at Ao Pante (30min; B350 each way). With either company, a return ticket to Adang/Lipe will allow you to stop off at Tarutao. Satun Pakbara Speedboat Club (see p.775; in Pak Bara ⓣ074 783643–5) also covers this route in high season. There have also been services in the past from Thammalang pier, 10km south of Satun town, which may possibly reappear; for island-hopping boats from Ko Lanta, see p.775.

Speedboats operate **between Ko Lipe and Langkawi**, the large Malaysian island to the southeast, at least twice a day in high season (1hr; B1200), including those operated by Satun Pakbara Speedboat Club (see p.775). A temporary Thai immigration post is set up at *Bundhaya Resort* on Lipe's Hat Pattaya to cover this route, and there are plans to extend its hours to cater for three weekly boats in low season.

Ko Tarutao

The largest of the national park's islands, **KO TARUTAO** offers the greatest natural variety: mountains covered in semi-evergreen rainforest rise steeply to a high point of 700m; limestone caves and mangrove swamps dot the shoreline; and the west coast is lined with perfect beaches for most of its 26-kilometre length.

Boats will drop you off at **Ao Pante**, on the northwestern side of the island, where the admission fee (B200) is collected and where the **park headquarters** is situated. Here you'll find the only shop on the island, selling basic supplies, as well as a visitor centre, a library and a **restaurant**. The **bungalows** (B1000 per bungalow sleeping four people, or B600 for a twin room), which are spread over a large, quiet park behind the beach, are for the main part national park standard issue with cold-water bathrooms, but there are also some basic mattress-on-floor four-person rooms in **longhouses**, sharing bathrooms (B500 per room). Two/three-person **tents** can be rented for B225 per night (plus B50 per person for bedding). The visitor centre can arrange **transport** by car to several of the island's beaches, as detailed below; transfers to the same places by boat cost at least twice as much, though you may be tempted by a **round-island boat trip** for B3000.

Behind the settlement, the steep, half-hour climb to **To-Boo cliff** is a must, especially at sunset, for the view of the surrounding islands and the crocodile's-head cape at the north end of the bay. A fun ninety-minute boat trip (B500 per boat; contact the visitor centre to book) can also be made near Ao Pante, up the canal which leads 2km inland from the pier, through a bird-filled mangrove swamp, to **Crocodile Cave** – where you're unlikely to see any of the big snappers, reported sightings being highly dubious.

A half-hour walk south from Ao Pante brings you to the two quiet bays of **Ao Jak** and **Ao Molae**, fringed by coconut palms and filled with fine white sand; the latter now sports some **bungalows** (from B600 for an en-suite twin room), tents for rent and a small restaurant. Transfers by car from Ao Pante to Ao Molae are free if you're staying here, B200 per car otherwise. Beyond the next headland lies **Ao Sone** (which gets its name from the casuarina trees that fringe the beach), where a pretty freshwater stream runs past the ranger station at the north end of the bay, a good place for peaceful camping; bungalows and a restaurant may be built here in the future. Transfers to Ao Sone from Ao Pante cost B400 per car, or else it's a two-hour walk. The main part of the bay is a three-kilometre sweep of flawless sand, with a one-hour trail leading up to Lu Du Waterfall at the north end, a ninety-minute trail to Lo Po Waterfall in the middle and a mangrove swamp at the far south end.

On the east side of the island, **Ao Taloh Wow** is a rocky bay with a ranger station, shop and campsite, connected to Ao Pante by a twelve-kilometre road (B600 per car transfer) through old rubber plantations and evergreen forest. Beyond Taloh Wow, a trail (5hr return) cuts through the forest to **Ao Taloh Udang**, a sandy bay on the south side where you can pitch a tent. Here the remnants of a penal colony for political prisoners are just visible: the plotters of two failed coup attempts – including the author of the first English–Thai dictionary and a grandson of Rama VII – were imprisoned here in the 1930s before returning to high government posts. The ordinary convicts, who used to be imprisoned here and at Ao Taloh Wow, had a much harsher time, and during World War II, when supplies from the mainland dried up, prisoners and guards ganged together to turn to piracy. This turned into a lucrative business, which was not suppressed until 1946 when the Thai government asked the British in Malaysia to send in three hundred troops. Pirates and smugglers still occasionally hide out in the Tarutao archipelago, but the main problem now is illegal trawlers fishing in national park waters.

Ko Adang

At **KO ADANG**, a wild, rugged island covered in tropical rainforest 40km west of Ko Tarutao, the park station is at **Laem Sone** on the southern shore, where the beach is steep and narrow and backed by a thick canopy of pines. There are **rooms** in bamboo longhouses (B400 per room sleeping four), **bungalows** sleeping up to eight people (B600–1800), and two/three-person **tents** can be rented (B150 per night). There's a **restaurant** here, too.

The half-hour climb to **Sha-do** cliff on the steep slope above Laem Sone gives good views over Ko Lipe to the south, while about 2km west along the coast from the park station, a twenty-minute trail leads inland to the small **Pirate Waterfall**. You can rent **longtail boats** (as well as snorkels and masks) through the rangers for excellent snorkelling trips to nearby islands such as Ko Rawi and Ko Jabang (around B1500–2500 for up to ten people, depending on how far you want to go).

Ko Lipe

KO LIPE, 2km south of Adang, makes a busy contrast to the other islands. A small, flat triangle, it's covered in coconut plantations and inhabited by *chao ley*, with shops, a school and a health centre in the village on the eastern side. By rights, such a settlement shouldn't be allowed within the national park boundaries, but the *chao ley* on Lipe are well entrenched: Satun's governor forced the community to move here from Phuket and Ko Lanta between the world wars, to reinforce the island's Thai character and prevent the British rulers of Malaya from laying claim to it. More recently, a diverse influx of tourists – Westerners and Thais, families and backpackers – has been enticed here by the gorgeous beach of **Hat Pattaya**, a shining crescent of squeaky-soft white sand with an offshore reef to explore on its eastern side, as well as by the relaxed, anything-goes atmosphere and mellow nightlife. Many of Lipe's *chao ley* have now sold their beachfront land to Thai-Chinese speculators from the mainland, who have increased the island's capacity to nearly two thousand guest rooms – with further developments, including spas and swimming pools, planned. Lipe's main drag is a paved path between the eastern end of Hat Pattaya and the village, lined with tattoo parlours, shops advertising guitars for rent and even a small, so-far-unoccupied mall. The other island path that's most likely to be useful is from *Daya Resort* at the west end of Pattaya across to Sunset beach in around ten minutes.

The best **travel agent** and source of **information** on the island, including a good, regularly updated **website**, is Koh Lipe Thailand.com (ⓣ089 464 5854 or 081 541 4489, ⓦwww.kohlipethailand.com), which currently has three outlets on the path between Hat Pattaya and the village, with the main one hard by the beach. On offer are accommodation bookings (including on the website), transport tickets, **internet** access (B3 per minute), **currency exchange** and **snorkelling trips** to the best sites around the islands on the west side of Ko Adang (B550–650 per person). On the east side of *Porn Resort* on Sunset beach is Canadian-run Sabye Sports (ⓣ081 897 8725, ⓦwww.sabye-sports.com), Lipe's oldest **dive shop**, which offers daily trips and PADI courses from Discover Scuba up to Divemaster, as well as specialities such as photography, naturalist and deep diving. Sabye also does snorkel rental (B150 per day including fins) and trips (B750 per person including lunch). **Mountain bikes** can be rented, for example, from the shop opposite *Pooh's* (see opposite) for B300 per day.

Accommodation

The majority of Lipe's bungalows are on **Hat Pattaya**, the prettiest but most crowded beach on the island. *Porn Resort* has **Sunset** beach on the northwest side to itself, a shady, attractive spot with good views of Ko Adang. Several resorts have set up shop on **Sunrise**, on the east side near the village, an exposed, largely featureless beach that gives access to some good snorkelling around Ko Gra.

If you get stuck for somewhere to stay, you could try *Pooh's* (ⓣ074 750345, ⓦwww.poohlipe.com; ❸) or *Café Lipe* (ⓣ086 969 9472, ⓦwww.cafe-lipe.com; ❹), which both have a few **rooms** behind their restaurants (see opposite).

Bundhaya Hat Pattaya ⓣ074 750248–9, ⓦwww.bundhayaresort.com; offices at Pak Bara pier and 66/24 Thanon Sathanee, Trang ⓣ075 219802. Over a hundred comfortable but tightly packed units, ranging from deluxe family bungalows with air-con, hot water and fridges down to basic, en-suite, fan rooms. Wide array of facilities including a popular restaurant, currency exchange, kayak rental and massages; a spa is planned, and perhaps a fitness centre. Breakfast included. ❺–❾

Blue Tribes Hat Pattaya ⓣ083 654 0316, ⓦwww.bluetribeslipe.com. Congenial spot with very spacious, well-spread bungalows in lovely dark wood, sporting attractive tiled bathrooms; some are two-storied with a balcony and chill-out room/extra bedroom upstairs. Mediterranean restaurant planned. 5–6

Castaway Sunrise ⓣ083 138 7472, ⓦwww.castaway-resorts.com. Airy, thatched, two-storey villas with well-equipped, cold-water bathrooms, ceiling fans and a certain amount of style, mostly bestowed by the distinctive red Indonesian hardwood that they're made from. On a sandy patch with a dive shop, a mellow, multi-tiered bar-restaurant and a massage spa; kayaks and snorkels for rent. 8

Daya Hat Pattaya; book through Koh Lipe Thailand.com (see opposite). *Chao ley*-owned resort with over thirty colourful rooms and bungalows in a large, shady, flower-strewn garden, ranging from simple bamboo huts to clapboard bungalows in a great position on the beach. 2–5

Family (Mit's) Hat Pattaya ⓣ084 633 8332. Good-value, *chao ley*-owned resort, offering basic but sturdy wooden, en-suite bungalows with mosquito nets, in plenty of space and under a little shade, behind a simple, popular restaurant. 3

Pattaya Song Hat Pattaya ⓣ074 728034, ⓦwww.pattayasongresort.com. Italian-run resort, the oldest on the beach (the name means "Pattaya no. 2"), where plain, en-suite bamboo or concrete bungalows are strung out behind the beach or in a lovely location up on a steep promontory with great views of the bay; kayaks for rent.

Porn Sunset ⓣ087 394 4972 or 084 691 8743. Attractive, welcoming and well-run spot in a pleasant, spacious setting under the trees on the beach. Well-designed bungalows come with verandas, mosquito nets and en-suite bathrooms, or there are two-person tents for rent (B200), which might be useful while waiting for a bungalow to become free. Internet access planned. 4

Eating and drinking

Besides the **eating places** reviewed below, there are about half a dozen largely indistinguishable resort restaurants on Hat Pattaya, such as *Daya*, that lay out seafood barbecues and tables on the beach at night. Pattaya supports a similar number of **beach bars**, with low candlelit tables sprawled on the sand and names like *Time to Chill*. The *Navy Club* at the far east end of Pattaya – actually a jerry-built bar with a few wooden benches – is the best spot for a quiet, reasonably priced beer watching the sun set.

Café Lipe Hat Pattaya. Eco-conscious, solar-powered place that rustles up communal Thai dinners if booked in advance, as well as home-made bread and muesli.

Flour Power Bakery Sunset, under the trees behind Sabye Sports. Delicious home-made brownies, apple pies, cookies and iced coffee, as well as sandwiches and other Western and Thai dishes. Daily 7am–5.30pm.

Kafair 100m from Hat Pattaya on the paved trail to Sunrise. Mellow, welcoming café serving deli sandwiches, breakfasts, chicken biryani and good espressos, using coffee from Doi Chang in northern Thailand. Internet access and wi-fi planned.

Pattaya Song Hat Pattaya. Not the best location, set back a little from the sand, but in the evenings they do great home-made pastas, pizzas and bruschetta.

Pooh's On the paved trail between Sunrise and Hat Pattaya. Well-run and welcoming bar-restaurant that's a popular hive of activity, with an attached travel agency and dive school (ⓦwww.lotusdive.com). On offer are great Thai and Western food, including a wide choice of breakfasts and espresso coffees, internet access, big-screen DVDs and live music in the evenings; also has a new bakery, two doors away.

Satun town

Nestling in the last wedge of Thailand's west coast, the remote town of **SATUN** is served by just one road, Highway 406, which approaches through forbidding karst outcrops. Set in a green valley bordered by limestone hills, the town is leafy and relaxing but not especially interesting: the boat services to and from Kuala Perlis and Langkawi in Malaysia are the main reason for foreigners to come here.

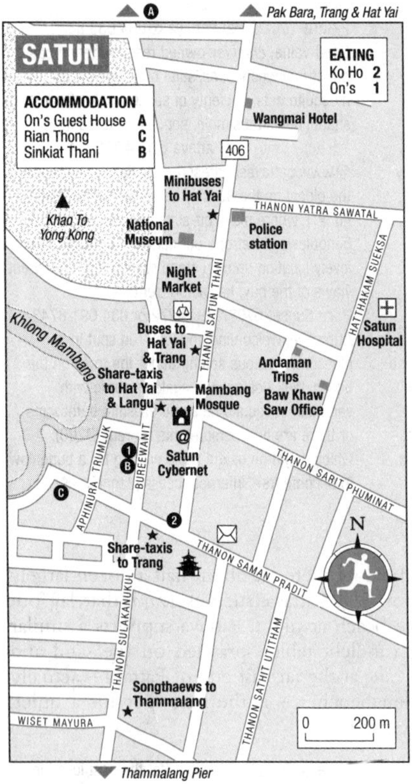

If you find yourself with time on your hands in Satun, it's worth seeking out the **National Museum** (Wed–Sun 9am–4pm; B30) on Soi 5, Thanon Satun Thani, on the north side of the centre. It's memorable, as much as anything else, for its setting, in the graceful **Kuden Mansion**, which was built in British colonial style, with some Thai and Malay features, by craftsmen from Penang, and inaugurated in 1902 as the Satun governor's official residence. The exhibits and audiovisuals in English have a distinctive anthropological tone, but are diverting enough, notably concerning Thai Muslims, the *chao ley* on Ko Lipe, and the **Sakai**, a dwindling band of nomadic hunter-gatherers who still live in the jungle of southern Thailand.

Practicalities

Satun's new **bus station** is far to the southeast of the centre on the new bypass, but Hat Yai and non-air-con Trang buses make a stop at the 7-Eleven on Thanon Satun Thani in both directions; incoming air-con buses from Phuket via Trang (4 daily) will set you down further north on the same road by the *Wangmai* hotel; and you can book tickets in advance at the central Baw Khaw Saw office on Thanon Hatthakam Sueksa. **Share-taxis** and **air-con minibuses** have a variety of bases in town, as marked on our map (minibuses for Langu use the bus station). **Internet access** and overseas calls are available at Satun Cybernet, 136 Thanon Satun Thani. From her restaurant next to the *Sinkiat Thani Hotel* at 48 Thanon Bureewanit, On Kongnual (T074 730469 or 081 097 9783, Eonmarch13@hotmail.com) offers **motorbike** (B150 per day) and **car rental** (B1200 per day), as well as local **tourist information**. The other good fixer in town is Bon Satarat at Andaman Trips, 68 Soi 6, Thanon Satun Thani (T074 722988 or 086 287 6745, Eandamantrips@hotmail.com), who can provide local tours and transfers.

Your best bet for budget **accommodation** is *On's Guest House*, 1km north of the centre at 49 Thanon Kuhaprawed – contact On at her restaurant (see above). In a leafy part of town, the airy wooden house shelters four clean fan rooms (1) sharing a toilet and hot shower, a kitchen and a spacious living area. Just on the west side of the centre at 4 Thanon Saman Pradit, *Rian Thong* (T074 711036; 1) is a decent budget **hotel** with friendly owners, where some of the clean, large, en-suite rooms overlook the canal. Moving upmarket as far as Satun will go, the nearby *Sinkiat Thani*, 50 Thanon Bureewanit (T074 721055–8, Esinkiathotel@hotmail.com; 4), offers large, carpeted bedrooms with air-con, hot water, fridges and good views over the surrounding countryside.

Moving on to Malaysia from Satun

From **Thammalang** pier, 10km south of Satun at the mouth of the river, boats leave when full on regular, 45-minute trips (B120 per person) to **Kuala Perlis** on the northwest tip of Malaysia, from where there are plentiful transport connections down the west coast. Two or three ferry boats a day cross from Thammalang to the Malaysian island of **Langkawi** (1hr 15min; B300 weekdays, B320 weekends; ⓣ074 725294 or 081 959 7053, ⓦwww.langkawi-ferry.com). Songthaews (B60) run to Thammalang from near the 7-Eleven supermarket on Thanon Sulakanukul, while motorbike taxis (B60) can be picked up near the junction of Thanon Saman Pradit and Thanon Bureewanit and around town. It's also possible to cross by road to Malaysia's **Kangar** through Thale Ban National Park, though a little tricky as the air-con minibuses depart from Ban Khuan, 20km or so up Highway 406 from Satun – contact local fixers On or Bon (see opposite) to arrange this.

On's (The Living Room) bar-restaurant (see opposite) offers a wide array of Western **food**, including good breakfasts and sandwiches, a short menu of typical Thai dishes, wi-fi and internet access. For a meal in the evening, however, you can't do much better than the lively and popular night market, north of the centre on the west side of Thanon Satun Thani, or try *Ko Ho*, on Thanon Saman Pradit opposite the Chinese temple, a cheap, busy, friendly restaurant that serves tasty Thai and Chinese food, including plenty of fish, seafood and salads.

Hat Yai

Travelling to or through **HAT YAI**, the biggest city in the region, is currently **not recommended** because of the troubles in the south (see p.769). To be honest you're not missing much, but as it's a major transport axis, we've provided a few, rudimentary practicalities and a map of the city, in case you get stuck there.

The **TAT office** is at 1/1 Soi 2, Thanon Niphat Uthit 3 (daily 8.30am–4.30pm; ⓣ074 243747 or 074 238518, ⓔtatsgkhl@tat.or.th). The **tourist police** have an office just south of here on Thanon Niphat Uthit 3 (ⓣ074 246733 or 1155). The three central Niphat Uthit roads are known locally as *sai neung, sai sawng* and *sai saam*.

The **train station** is on the west side of the centre at the end of Thanon Thamnoon Vithi; the **bus terminal** is far to the southeast of the centre on Thanon Kanchanawanit, while the new **air-con minibus terminal** at Talat Kaset is about 5km west of town towards the airport, both leaving you with a songthaew ride to the centre. The helpful Cathay Tour (ⓣ074 235044, ⓔcathay_ontours@hotmail.com), a **travel agency** on the ground floor of the guest house of the same name, handles onward flight, bus, share taxi and air-con minibus bookings, both within Thailand and into Malaysia.

Accommodation

Cathay Guest House 93 Thanon Niphat Uthit 2 ⓣ074 243815, ⓔcathay_ontours@hotmail.com. This friendly place in the heart of town has long been Hat Yai's main travellers' hub; the café acts as a sociable meeting-place, and the rooms have en-suite cold-water bathrooms. ❶

Lee Gardens Plaza Hotel 29 Thanon Prachatipat ⓣ074 261111, ⓦwww.leeplaza.com. Characterless but good-value and central upmarket option with great views of the city from its four hundred comfortable rooms. Facilities include a fitness centre, a rooftop pool and a 33rd-floor panoramic restaurant. ❻

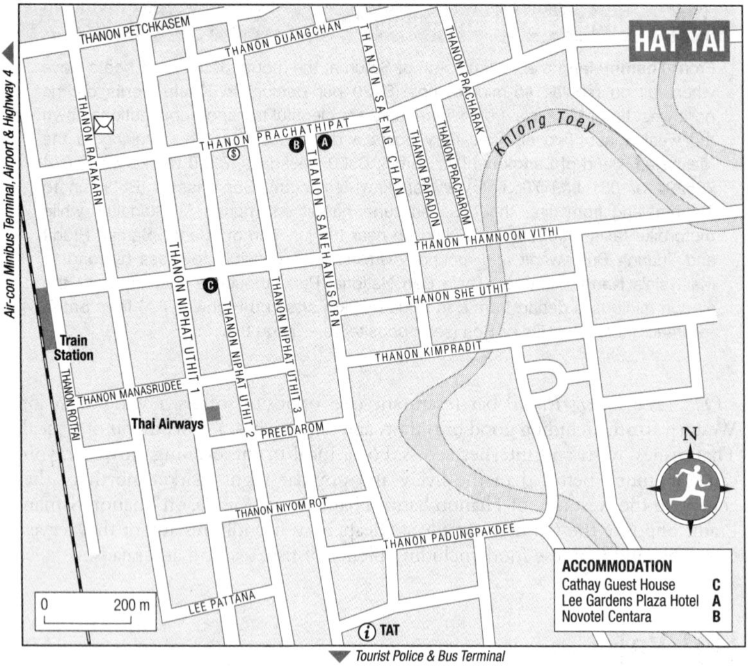

Novotel Centara 3 Thanon Sanehanusorn ⓣ074 352222, ⓦwww.centarahotelsresorts.com. Luxury hotel in a good location next to the Central Department Store, with spa, fitness centre, sauna, swimming pool and Thai, Chinese and Japanese restaurants. Substantial discounts often available on their website. ⑧

Travel details

Trains

Trang to: Bangkok (2 daily; 15–16hr).

Buses

Satun to: Bangkok (5 daily; 16hr); Phuket (4 daily; 7hr); Trang (every 30min; 2hr 30min–3hr).

Trang to: Bangkok (11 daily; 12–14hr); Krabi (roughly every 30min; 2hr); Phuket (hourly; 5hr); Satun (every 30min; 2hr 30min–3hr).

Flights

Trang to: Bangkok (2 daily; 1hr 30min).

Contexts

Contexts

History

As long as forty thousand years ago, Thailand was inhabited by **hunter-gatherers** who lived in semi-permanent settlements and used tools made of wood, bamboo and stone. By the end of the last Ice Age, around ten thousand years ago, these groups had become **farmers**, keeping chickens, pigs and cattle, and – as evidenced by the seeds and plant husks which have been discovered in caves in northern Thailand – cultivating rice and beans. This drift into an agricultural society gave rise to further technological developments: the earliest **pottery** found in Thailand has been dated to 6800 BC, while the recent excavations at **Ban Chiang** in the northeast have shown that **bronze** was being worked at least as early as 2000 BC. By two thousand years ago, the peoples of Southeast Asia had settled in small villages, among which there was regular communication and trade, but they had split into several broad families, differentiated by language and culture. At this time, the ancestors of the Thais, speaking proto-Thai languages, were still far away in southeastern China, whereas Thailand itself was inhabited by Austroasiatic speakers, among whom the Mon were to establish the region's first distinctive civilization, Dvaravati.

Dvaravati and Srivijaya

The history of **Dvaravati** is ill-defined to say the least, but the name is applied to a distinctive culture complex which shared the **Mon** language and **Theravada Buddhism**. This form of religion probably entered Thailand during the second or third centuries BC, when Indian missionaries were sent to Suvarnabhumi, "land of gold", which seems to correspond roughly to mainland Southeast Asia.

From the discovery of monastery boundary stones (*sema*), clay votive tablets and Indian-influenced Buddhist sculpture, it's clear that Dvaravati was an extensive and prosperous Buddhist civilization which had its greatest flourishing between the sixth and ninth centuries AD. No strong evidence has turned up, however, for the existence of a single capital – rather than an empire, Dvaravati seems to have been a collection of city-states, which, at least in their early history, came under the lax suzerainty of **Funan**, a poorly documented kingdom centred in Cambodia. Nakhon Pathom, Lopburi, Si Thep and Muang Sema were among the most important Dvaravati sites, and their concentration around the Chao Phraya valley would seem to show that they gained much of their prosperity, and maintained religious and cultural contacts with India, via the **trade route** from the Indian Ocean over the Three Pagodas Pass.

Although they passed on aspects of their heavily Indianized art, religion and government to later rulers of Thailand, these Mon city-states were politically fragile and from the ninth century onwards succumbed to the domination of the invading Khmers from Cambodia. One northern outpost, the state of **Haripunjaya**, centred on Lamphun, which had been set up on the trade route with southern China, maintained its independence probably until the beginning of the eleventh century.

Meanwhile, to the south of Dvaravati, the shadowy Indianized state of Lankasuka had grown up in the second century, centred on Ligor (now Nakhon Si Thammarat) and covering an area of the Malay peninsula which included the important trade crossings at Chaiya and Trang. In the eighth century, it came under the control of the **Srivijaya** empire, a Mahayana

Buddhist state centred on Sumatra, which had strong ties with India and a complex but uneasy relationship with neighbouring Java. Thriving on seaborne trade between Persia and China, Srivijaya extended its influence as far north as Chaiya, its regional capital, where discoveries of temple remains and some of the finest stone and bronze statues ever produced in Thailand have borne witness to the cultural vitality of this crossroads empire. In the tenth century the northern part of Lankasuka, under the name **Tambralinga**, regained a measure of independence, although it seems still to have come under the influence of Srivijaya as well as owing some form of allegiance to Dvaravati. By the beginning of the eleventh century, however, peninsular Thailand had come under the sway of the Khmer empire, with a Cambodian prince ruling over a community of Khmer settlers and soldiers at Tambralinga.

The Khmers

The history of central Southeast Asia comes into sharper focus with the emergence of the **Khmers**, vigorous empire-builders whose political history can be pieced together from the numerous stone inscriptions they left. Originally vassal subjects of Funan, the Khmers of **Chenla** – to the north of Cambodia – seized power in the latter half of the sixth century during a period of economic decline in the area. Chenla's rise to power was knocked back by a punitive expedition conducted by the Srivijaya empire in the eighth century, but was reconsolidated during the watershed reign of **Jayavarman II** (802–50), who succeeded in conquering the whole of Kambuja, an area which roughly corresponds to modern-day Cambodia. In order to establish the authority of his monarchy and of his country, Jayavarman II had himself initiated as a *chakravartin*, or universal ruler, the living embodiment of the **devaraja**, the divine essence of kingship – a concept which was adopted by later Thai rulers. Taking as the symbol of his authority the phallic lingam, the king was thus identified with the god Shiva, although the Khmer concept of kingship and thus the religious mix of the state as a whole was not confined to Hinduism: elements of ancestor worship were also included, and Mahayana Buddhism gradually increased its hold over the next four centuries.

It was Jayavarman II who moved the Khmer capital to **Angkor** in northern Cambodia, which he and later kings, especially after the eleventh century, embellished with a series of prodigiously beautiful temples. Jayavarman II also recognized the advantages of the lakes around Angkor for irrigating rice fields and providing fish, and thus for feeding a large population. His successors developed this idea and gave the state a sound economic core with a remarkably complex system of **reservoirs** (*baray*) and water channels, which were copied and adapted in later Thai cities.

In the ninth and tenth centuries, Jayavarman II and his imperialistic successors, especially **Yasovarman I** (889–900), confirmed Angkor as the major power in Southeast Asia. They pushed into Vietnam, Laos, southern China and into northeastern Thailand, where the Khmers left dozens of Angkor-style temple complexes, as seen today at Prasat Phanom Rung and Prasat Hin Phimai. To the west and northwest, Angkor took control over central Thailand, with its most important outpost at Lopburi, and even established a strong presence to the south on the Malay peninsula. As a result of this expansion, the Khmers were masters of the most important trade routes between India and China, and indeed nearly every communications link in the region, from which they were able to derive huge income and strength.

The reign of **Jayavarman VII** (1181–1219), a Mahayana Buddhist who firmly believed in his royal destiny as a *bodhisattva*, sowed the seeds of Angkor's downfall. Nearly half of all the surviving great religious monuments of the empire were erected under his supervision, but the ambitious scale of these building projects and the upkeep they demanded – some 300,000 priests and temple servants of 20,000 shrines consumed 38,000 tons of rice per year – along with a series of wars against Vietnam, terminally exhausted the economy.

In subsequent reigns, much of the life-giving irrigation system around Angkor turned into malarial swamp through neglect, and the rise of the more democratic creed of Theravada Buddhism undermined the divine authority which the Khmer kings had derived from the hierarchical Mahayana creed. As a result of all these factors, the Khmers were in no position to resist the onslaught between the thirteenth and fifteenth centuries of the vibrant new force in Southeast Asia, the Thais.

The earliest Thais

The earliest traceable history of the **Thai people** picks them up in southern China around the fifth century AD, when they were squeezed by Chinese and Vietnamese expansionism into sparsely inhabited northeastern Laos and neighbouring areas. The first entry of a significant number of Thais onto what is now Thailand's soil seems to have happened in the region of Chiang Saen, where it appears that some time after the seventh century the Thais formed a state in an area then known as **Yonok**. A development which can be more accurately dated and which had immense cultural significance was the spread of Theravada Buddhism to Yonok via Dvaravati around the end of the tenth century, which served not only to unify the Thais but also to link them to Mon civilization and give them a sense of belonging to the community of Buddhists.

The Thais' political development was also assisted by **Nan-chao**, a well-organized military state comprising a huge variety of ethnic groups, which established itself as a major player on the southern fringes of the Chinese empire from the beginning of the eighth century. As far as can be gathered, Nan-chao permitted the rise of Thai *muang* or small principalities on its periphery, especially in the area immediately to the south known as **Sipsong Panna**.

Thai infiltration continued until, by the end of the twelfth century, they seem to have formed the majority of the population in Thailand, then under the control of the Khmer empire. The Khmers' main outpost, at Lopburi, was by then regarded as the administrative capital of a land called "Syam" (possibly from the Sanskrit *syam*, meaning swarthy) – a mid-twelfth-century bas-relief at Angkor Wat, portraying the troops of Lopburi preceded by a large group of self-confident Syam Kuk mercenaries, shows that the Thais were becoming a force to be reckoned with.

Sukhothai

By the middle of the thirteenth century, the Thais, thanks largely to the decline of Angkor and the inspiring effect of Theravada Buddhism, were poised on the verge of autonomous power. The final catalyst was the invasion by Qubilai Khan's Mongol armies of China and Nan-chao, which began around 1215 and was completed in the 1250s. Demanding that the whole world should acknowledge the primacy of the Great Khan, the Mongols set their hearts on the "pacification" of the "barbarians" to the south of China, which obliged the Thais to form a broad powerbase to meet the threat.

The founding of the first Thai kingdom at **Sukhothai**, now popularly viewed as the cornerstone of the country's development, was in fact a small-scale piece of opportunism which almost fell at the first hurdle. At some time around 1238, the princes of two small Thai principalities in the upper Chao Phraya valley joined forces to capture the main Khmer outpost in the region at Sukhothai. One of the princes, **Intradit**, was crowned king, but for the first forty years Sukhothai remained merely a local power, whose existence was threatened by the ambitions of neighbouring princes. When attacked by the ruler of Mae Sot, Intradit's army was only saved by the grand entrance of Sukhothai's most dynamic leader: the king's 19-year-old son, Rama, held his ground and pushed forward to defeat the opposing commander, earning himself the name **Ramkhamhaeng**, "Rama the Bold".

When Ramkhamhaeng came to the throne around 1278, he saw the south as his most promising avenue for expansion and, copying the formidable military organization of the Mongols, seized control of much of the Chao Phraya valley. Over the next twenty years, largely by diplomacy rather than military action, Ramkhamhaeng gained the submission of most of the rulers of Thailand, who entered the **new empire**'s complex tributary system either through the pressure of the Sukhothai king's personal connections or out of recognition of his superior military strength and moral prestige. To the east, Ramkhamhaeng pushed as far as Vientiane in Laos; by marrying his daughter to a Mon ruler to the west, he obtained the allegiance of parts of southern Burma; and to the south his vassals stretched down the peninsula at least as far as Nakhon Si Thammarat. To the north, Sukhothai concluded an alliance with the parallel Thai states of Lanna and Phayao in 1287 for mutual protection against the Mongols – though it appears that Ramkhamhaeng managed to pinch several *muang* on their eastern periphery as tribute states.

Meanwhile **Lopburi**, which had wrested itself free from Angkor sometime in the middle of the thirteenth century, was able to keep its independence and its control of the eastern side of the Chao Phraya valley. Having been first a major cultural and religious centre for the Mon, then the Khmers' provincial capital, and now a state dominated by migrating Thais, Lopburi was a strong and vibrant place mixing the best of the three cultures, as evidenced by the numerous original works of art produced at this time.

Although the empire of Sukhothai extended Thai control over a vast area, its greatest contribution to the Thais' development was at home, in cultural and political matters. A famous **inscription** by Ramkhamhaeng, now housed in the Bangkok National Museum, describes a prosperous era of benevolent rule: "In the time of King Ramkhamhaeng this land of Sukhothai is thriving. There is fish in the water and rice in the fields … [The King] has hung a bell in the opening of the gate over there: if any commoner has a grievance which sickens his belly and gripes his heart … he goes and strikes the bell … [and King Ramkhamhaeng] questions the man, examines the case, and decides it justly for him." Although this plainly smacks of self-promotion, it seems to contain at least a kernel of truth: in deliberate contrast to the Khmer god-kings, Ramkhamhaeng styled himself as a **dhammaraja**, a king who ruled justly according to Theravada Buddhist doctrine and made himself accessible to his people. To honour the state religion, the city's temples were lavishly endowed: as original as Sukhothai's political systems were its religious **architecture and sculpture**, which, though bound to borrow from existing Khmer and Sri Lankan styles, show the greatest leap of creativity at any stage in the history of art in Thailand. A further sign of the Thais' new self-confidence was the invention of a new **script** to make their tonal language understood by the non-Thai inhabitants of the land.

All this was achieved in a remarkably short period of time. After the death of Ramkhamhaeng around 1299, his successors took their Buddhism so seriously that they neglected affairs of state. The empire quickly fell apart, and by 1320 Sukhothai had regressed to being a kingdom of only local significance.

Lanna

Almost simultaneous with the birth of Sukhothai was the establishment of a less momentous but longer-lasting kingdom to the north, called **Lanna**. Its founding father was **Mengrai**, chief of Ngon Yang, a small principality on the banks of the Mekhong near modern-day Chiang Saen. Around 1259 he set out to unify the squabbling Thai principalities of the region, first building a strategically placed city at Chiang Rai in 1262, and then forging alliances with Ngam Muang, the Thai king of Phayao, and with Ramkhamhaeng of Sukhothai.

In 1281, after ten years of guileful preparations, Mengrai conquered the Mon kingdom of Haripunjaya based at Lamphun, and was now master of northern Thailand. Taking advice from Ngam Muang and Ramkhamhaeng, in 1292 he selected a site for an impressive new capital of Lanna at **Chiang Mai**, which remains the centre of the north to the present day. Mengrai concluded further alliances in Burma and Laos, making him strong enough to successfully resist further Mongol attacks, although he was eventually obliged to bow to the superiority of the Mongols by sending them small tributes from 1312 onwards. When Mengrai died after a sixty-year reign in 1317, supposedly struck by a bolt of lightning, he had built up an extensive and powerful kingdom. But although he began a tradition of humane, reasonable laws, probably borrowed from the Mons, he had found little time to set up sound political and administrative institutions. His death severely destabilized Lanna, which quickly shrank in size and influence.

It was only in the reign of **Ku Na** (1355–85) that Lanna's development regained momentum. A well-educated and effective ruler, Ku Na enticed the venerable monk Sumana from Sukhothai, to establish an ascetic Sri Lankan sect in Lanna in 1369. Sumana brought a number of Buddha images with him, inspiring a new school of art that flourished for over a century, but more importantly his sect became a cultural force that had a profound unifying effect on the kingdom. The influence of Buddhism was further strengthened under **King Tilok** (1441–87), who built many great monuments at Chiang Mai and cast huge numbers of bronze seated Buddhas in the style of the central image at Bodh Gaya in India, the scene of the Buddha's enlightenment. Tilok, however, is best remembered as a great warrior, who spent most of his reign resisting the advances of Ayutthaya, by now the strongest Thai kingdom.

Under continuing pressure both from Ayutthaya and from Burma, Lanna went into rapid decline in the second quarter of the sixteenth century. For a short period after 1546, Chiang Mai came under the control of Setthathirat, the king of Lan Sang (Laos), but, unable to cope with Lanna's warring factions, he then abdicated, purloining the talismanic Emerald Buddha for his own capital at Louang Phabang. In 1558, Burma decisively captured Chiang Mai, and the Mengrai dynasty came to an end. For most of the next two centuries, the Burmese maintained control through a succession of puppet rulers, and Lanna again became much as it had been before Mengrai, little more than a chain of competing principalities.

Ayutthaya

While Lanna was fighting for its place as a marginalized kingdom, from the fourteenth century onwards the seeds of a full-blown Thai nation were being sown to the south at **Ayutthaya**. The city of Ayutthaya itself was founded on its present site in 1351 by U Thong ("Golden Cradle") when his own town, Lopburi, was ravaged by smallpox. Taking the title **Ramathibodi**, he soon united the principalities of the lower Chao Phraya valley, which had formed the western provinces of the Khmer empire. When he recruited his bureaucracy from the urban elite of Lopburi, Ramathibodi set the **style of government** at Ayutthaya – the elaborate etiquette, language and rituals of Angkor were adopted, and, most importantly, the conception of the ruler as *devaraja*. The king became sacred and remote, an object of awe and dread, with none of the accessibility of the kings of Sukhothai: when he processed through the town, ordinary people were forbidden to look at him and had to be silent while he passed. This hierarchical system also provided the state with much-needed manpower, as all freemen were obliged to give up six months of each year to the Crown either on public works or military service.

The site chosen by Ramathibodi turned out to be the best in the region for an international port, and so began Ayutthaya's rise to prosperity, based on its ability to exploit the upswing in **trade** in the middle of the fourteenth century along the routes between India and China. Flushed with economic success, Ramathibodi's successors were able to expand their control over the ailing states in the region. After a long period of subjugation, Sukhothai became a province of the kingdom of Ayutthaya in 1438, six years after Boromraja II had powerfully demonstrated Ayutthaya's pre-eminence by capturing the once-mighty Angkor, enslaving large numbers of its subjects and looting the Khmer royal regalia. (The Cambodian royal family were forced to abandon the palace forever and to found a new capital near Phnom Penh.)

Although a century of nearly continuous warfare against Lanna was less decisive, success generally bred success, and Ayutthaya's increasing wealth through trade brought ever greater power over its neighbouring states. To streamline the functioning of his unwieldy empire, **Trailok** (1448–88) found it necessary to make reforms to its administration. His **Law of Civil Hierarchy** formally entrenched the inequality of Ayutthayan society, defining the status of every individual by assigning him or her an imaginary number of rice fields – for example, 25 for an ordinary freeman and 10,000 for the highest ministers of state. Trailok's legacy is found in today's unofficial but fiendishly complex status system, by which everyone in Thailand knows their place.

Ramathibodi II (1491–1529), almost at a loss as to what to do with his enormous wealth, undertook an extensive programme of public works. In the 1490s he built several major religious monuments, and between 1500 and 1503 cast the largest standing metal image of the Buddha ever known, the Phra Si Sanphet, which gave its name to the temple of the royal palace. By 1540, the kingdom of Ayutthaya had grown to cover most of the area of modern-day Thailand.

Burmese wars and European trade

In the sixteenth century recurring tensions with Burma led **Chakkraphat** (1548–69) to improve his army and build brick ramparts around the capital. This was to no avail however: in 1568 the Burmese besieged Ayutthaya with a huge army, said by later accounts to have consisted of 1,400,000 men. The Thais held out until August 8, 1569, when treachery within their own ranks helped the Burmese break through the defences. The Burmese looted the city, took thousands of prisoners and installed a vassal king to keep control.

The decisive character who broke the Burmese stranglehold twenty years later and re-established Ayutthaya's economic growth was **Naresuan** (1590–1605), who defied the Burmese by amassing a large army. The enemy sent a punitive expedition, which was conclusively defeated at Nong Sarai near modern-day Suphanburi on January 18, 1593, Naresuan himself turning the battle by killing the Burmese crown prince. Historians have praised Naresuan for his personal bravery and his dynamic leadership, although the chronicles of the time record a strong streak of tyranny – in his fifteen years as king he had eighty thousand people killed, excluding the victims of war. A favoured means of punishment was to slice off pieces of the offender's flesh, which he was then made to eat in the king's presence.

The period following Naresuan's reign was characterized by a more sophisticated engagement in **foreign trade**. In 1511 the Portuguese had become the first Western power to trade with Ayutthaya, and Naresuan himself concluded a treaty with Spain in 1598; relations with Holland and England were initiated in 1608 and 1612 respectively. For most of the seventeenth century, European merchants flocked to Thailand, not only to buy Thai products, but also to gain access to Chinese and Japanese goods on sale there. The role of foreigners at Ayutthaya reached its peak under **Narai** (1656–88), but he overstepped the mark in cultivating close links with Louis XIV of France, who secretly harboured the notion of converting Ayutthaya to Christianity. On Narai's death, relations with Westerners were severely cut back.

Despite this reduction of trade and prolonged civil strife over the succession to the throne whenever a king died – then, as now, there wasn't a fixed principle of primogeniture – Ayutthaya continued to flourish for much of the eighteenth century. The reign of **Borommakot** (1733–58) was particularly prosperous, producing many works of drama and poetry. Furthermore, Thai Buddhism had by then achieved such prestige that Sri Lanka, from where the Thais had originally imported their form of religion in the thirteenth century, requested Thai aid in restoring their monastic orders in 1751.

However, immediately after the death of Borommakot the rumbling in the Burmese jungle to the north began to make itself heard again. Alaunghpaya of Burma, apparently a blindly aggressive country bumpkin, first recaptured the south of his country from the Mon, and then turned his attentions to Ayutthaya. A siege in 1760 was unsuccessful, with Alaunghpaya dying of wounds sustained there, but the scene was set. In February 1766 the Burmese descended upon Ayutthaya for the last time. The Thais held out for over a year, during which they were afflicted by famine, epidemics and a terrible fire which destroyed ten thousand houses. Finally, in **April 1767**, the walls were breached and the city taken. The Burmese razed everything to the ground and tens of thousands of prisoners were led off to Burma, including most of the royal family. The king, Suriyamarin, is said to have escaped from the city in a boat and starved to death ten days later. As one observer has said, the Burmese laid waste to Ayutthaya "in such a savage manner that it is hard to imagine that they shared the same religion with the Siamese". The city was abandoned to the jungle, but with remarkable speed the Thais regrouped and established a new seat of power, further down the Chao Phraya River at Bangkok.

The early Bangkok empire

As the bulk of the Burmese army was obliged by war with China to withdraw almost immediately, Thailand was left to descend into banditry. Out of this lawless mess several centres of power arose, the most significant being at Chanthaburi, commanded by **Phraya Taksin**. A charismatic, brave and able general who had been unfairly blamed for a failed counter attack against the Burmese at Ayutthaya, Taksin had anticipated the fall of the besieged city and quietly slipped away with a force of five hundred men. In June 1767 he took control of the east-coast strip around Chanthaburi and very rapidly expanded his power across central Thailand.

Blessed with the financial backing of the Chinese trading community, to whom he was connected through his father, Taksin was crowned king in December 1768 at his new capital of Thonburi, on the opposite bank of the river from modern-day Bangkok. One by one the new king defeated his rivals, and within two years he had restored all of Ayutthaya's territories. More remarkably, by the end of the next decade Taksin had outdone his Ayutthayan predecessors by bringing Lanna, Cambodia and much of Laos into a huge new empire. During this period of expansionism, Taksin left most of the fighting to Thong Duang, an ambitious soldier and descendant of an Ayutthayan noble family, who became the *chakri*, the military commander, and took the title **Chao Phraya Chakri**.

However, by 1779 all was not well with the king. Being an outsider, who had risen from an ordinary family on the fringes of society, Taksin became paranoid about plots against him, a delusion that drove him to imprison and torture even his wife and sons. At the same time he sank into religious excesses, demanding that the monkhood worship him as a god. By March 1782, public outrage at his sadism and dangerously irrational behaviour had reached such fervour that he was ousted in a coup.

Chao Phraya Chakri was invited to take power and had Taksin executed. In accordance with ancient etiquette, this had to be done without royal blood touching the earth: the mad king was duly wrapped in a black velvet sack and struck on the back of the neck with a sandalwood club. (Popular tradition has it that even this form of execution was too much: an unfortunate substitute got the velvet sack treatment, while Taksin was whisked away to a palace in the hills near Nakhon Si Thammarat, where he is said to have lived until 1825.)

Rama I

With the support of the Ayutthayan aristocracy, Chakri – reigning as **Rama I** (1782–1809) – set about consolidating the Thai kingdom. His first act was to move the capital across the river to Bangkok, a better defensive position against any Burmese attack from the west. Borrowing from the layout of Ayutthaya, he built a new royal palace and impressive monasteries, and enshrined in the palace wat the Emerald Buddha, which he had snatched back during his campaigns in Laos.

As all the state records had disappeared in the destruction of Ayutthaya, religious and legal texts had to be written afresh and historical chronicles reconstituted – with some very sketchy guesswork. The monkhood was in such a state of crisis that it was widely held that moral decay had been partly responsible for Ayutthaya's downfall. Within a month of becoming king, Rama I issued a series of religious laws and made appointments to the leadership of the monkhood, to restore discipline and confidence after the excesses of Taksin's reign. Many works of drama and poetry had also been lost in the sacking of Ayutthaya, so Rama I set about rebuilding the Thais' literary heritage, at the same time attempting to make it more cosmopolitan and populist. His main contribution was the *Ramakien*, a dramatic version of the Indian epic *Ramayana*, which is said to have been set to verse by the king himself, with a little help from his courtiers, in 1797. Heavily adapted to its Thai setting, the

Ramakien served as an affirmation of the new monarchy and its divine links, and has since become the national epic.

In the early part of Rama I's reign, the Burmese reopened hostilities on several occasions, the biggest attempted invasion coming in 1785, but the emphatic manner in which the Thais repulsed them only served to knit together the young kingdom. Trade with China revived, and the king addressed the besetting problem of manpower by ordering every man to be tattooed with the name of his master and his town, so that avoiding royal service became almost impossible. On a more general note, Rama I put the style of government in Thailand on a modern footing: while retaining many of the features of a *devaraja*, he shared more responsibility with his courtiers, as a first among equals.

Rama II and Rama III

The peaceful accession of his son as **Rama II** (1809–24) signalled the establishment of the **Chakri dynasty**, which is still in place today. This Second Reign was a quiet interlude, best remembered as a fertile period for Thai literature. The king, himself one of the great Thai poets, gathered round him a group of writers including the famous Sunthorn Phu, who produced scores of masterly love poems, travel accounts and narrative songs.

In contrast, **Rama III** (1824–51) actively discouraged literary development – probably in reaction against his father – and was a vigorous defender of conservative values. To this end, he embarked on an extraordinary redevelopment of Wat Pho, the oldest temple in Bangkok. Hundreds of educational inscriptions and mural paintings, on all manner of secular and religious subjects, were put on show, apparently to preserve traditional culture against the rapid change which the king saw corroding the country. In foreign affairs, Rama III faced a serious threat from the vassal states of Laos, who in 1827 sent an invading army from Vientiane, which got as far as Saraburi, only three days' march from Bangkok. The king's response was savage: having repelled the initial invasion, he ordered his army to destroy everything in Vientiane apart from Buddhist temples and to forcibly resettle huge numbers of Lao in Isaan. Shortly after, the king was forced to go to war in Cambodia, to save Buddhism and its traditional institutions from the attentions of the newly powerful, non-Buddhist Vietnamese. A series of campaigns in the 1830s and 1840s culminated in the peace treaty of 1845–46, which again established Thailand as the dominant influence in Cambodia.

More significant in the long run was the danger posed by the increase in Western influence that began in the Third Reign. As early as 1825, the Thais were sufficiently alarmed at British colonialism to strengthen Bangkok's defences by stretching a great iron chain across the mouth of the Chao Phraya River, to which every blacksmith in the area had to donate a certain number of links. In 1826 Rama III was obliged to sign a limited trade agreement with the British, the **Burney Treaty**, by which the Thais won some political security in return for reducing their taxes on goods passing through Bangkok. British and American missions in 1850 unsuccessfully demanded more radical concessions, but by this time Rama III was seriously ill, and it was left to his far-sighted and progressive successors to reach a decisive accommodation with the Western powers.

Mongkut and Chulalongkorn

Rama IV (1851–68), commonly known to foreigners as **Mongkut** (in Thai, *Phra Chom Klao*), had been a Buddhist monk for 27 years when he succeeded his brother. But far from leading a cloistered life, Mongkut had travelled widely throughout Thailand, had maintained scholarly contacts with French and American missionaries and, like most of the country's new generation of leaders, had taken an interest in Western learning, studying English, Latin and the sciences. He had also turned his mind to the condition of Buddhism in Thailand, which seemed to him to have descended into little more than popular superstition; indeed, after a study of the Buddhist scriptures in Pali, he was horrified to find that Thai ordinations were probably invalid. So in the late 1830s he set up the rigorously fundamentalist Thammayut sect (the "Order Adhering to the Teachings of the Buddha") and as abbot of the order he oversaw the training of a generation of scholarly leaders for Thai Buddhism from his base at Bangkok's Wat Bowonniwet, which became a major centre of Western learning and is still sponsored by the royal family.

When his kingship faced its first major test, in the form of a threatening British mission in 1855 led by **Sir John Bowring**, the Governor of Hong Kong, Mongkut dealt with it confidently. Realizing that Thailand was unable to resist the military might of the British, the king reduced import and export taxes, allowed British subjects to live and own land in Thailand and granted them freedom of trade. Of the **government monopolies**, which had long been the mainstay of the Thai economy, only that on opium was retained. After making up the loss in revenue through internal taxation, Mongkut quickly made it known that he would welcome diplomatic contacts from other Western countries: within a decade, agreements similar to the Bowring Treaty had been signed with France, the US and a score of other nations. Thus by skilful diplomacy the king avoided a close relationship with only one power, which could easily have led to Thailand's annexation.

While all around the colonial powers were carving up Southeast Asia amongst themselves, Thailand suffered nothing more than the weakening of its influence over Cambodia, which in 1863 the French brought under their protection. As a result of the open-door policy, foreign trade boomed, financing the redevelopment of Bangkok's waterfront and, for the first time, the building of paved roads. However, Mongkut ran out of time for instituting the far-reaching domestic reforms which he saw were needed to drag Thailand into the modern world.

The modernization of Thailand

Mongkut's son, **Chulalongkorn**, took the throne as Rama V (1868–1910) at the age of only 15, but he was well prepared by an excellent education which mixed traditional Thai and modern Western elements – provided by Mrs Anna Leonowens, subject of *The King and I*. When Chulalongkorn reached his majority after a five-year regency, he set to work on the reforms envisaged by his father. One of his first acts was to scrap the custom by which subjects were required to prostrate themselves in the presence of the king, which he followed up in 1874 with a series of decrees announcing the gradual abolition of slavery. The speed of his financial and administrative reforms, however, proved too much for the "**Ancients**" (*hua boran*), the old guard of ministers and officials inherited from his father. Their opposition culminated in the Front Palace Crisis of 1875, when a show of military strength almost plunged the country into civil war, and, although Chulalongkorn skilfully defused the crisis, many of his reforms had to be quietly shelved for the time being.

An important administrative reform which did go through, necessitated by the threat of colonial expansionism, concerned the former kingdom of Lanna. British exploitation of teak had recently spread into northern Thailand from neighbouring Burma, so in 1874 Chulalongkorn sent a commissioner to Chiang Mai to keep an eye on the prince of Chiang Mai and make sure that he avoided any collision with the British. The commissioner was gradually able to limit the power of the princes and integrate the region more fully into the kingdom.

In the 1880s prospects for reform brightened as many of the "Ancients" died or retired. This allowed Chulalongkorn to **restructure the government** to meet the country's needs: the Royal Audit Office made possible the proper control of revenue and finance; the Department of the Army became the nucleus of a modern armed services; and a host of other departments were set up, for justice, education, public health and the like. To fill these new positions, the king appointed many of his younger brothers, who had all received a modern education, while scores of foreign technicians and advisers were brought in to help with everything from foreign affairs to rail lines.

Throughout this period, however, the Western powers maintained their pressure on the region. The most serious threat to Thai sovereignty was the **Franco–Siamese Crisis** of 1893, which culminated in the French, based in Vietnam, sending gunboats up the Chao Phraya River to Bangkok. Flouting numerous international laws, France claimed control over Laos and made other outrageous demands, which Chulalongkorn had no option but to concede. In 1907 Thailand was also forced to relinquish Cambodia to the French, and in 1909 three Malay states fell to the British (while Thailand retained a fourth Muslim state, Pattani). In order to preserve its independence, the country ceded almost half of its territory and forewent huge sums of tax revenue. But from the end of the Fifth Reign, the frontiers were fixed as they are today.

By the time of the king's death in 1910, Thailand could not yet be called a modern nation-state – corruption and nepotism were still grave problems, for example. However, Chulalongkorn had made remarkable advances, and, almost from scratch, had established the political institutions to cope with twentieth-century development.

The end of absolute monarchy

Chulalongkorn was succeeded by a flamboyant, British-educated prince, **Vajiravudh**, who was crowned Rama VI (1910–25). The new king found it difficult to shake the dominance of his father's appointees in the government, who formed an extremely narrow elite, comprised almost entirely of members of Chulalongkorn's family. In an attempt to build up a personal following, Vajiravudh created, in May 1911, the **Wild Tigers**, a nationwide paramilitary corps recruited widely from the civil service. However, in 1912 a group of young army lieutenants, disillusioned by the absolute monarchy and upset at the downgrading of the regular army in favour of the Wild Tigers, plotted a **coup**. The conspirators were easily broken up before any trouble began, but this was something new in Thai history: the country was used to in-fighting among the royal family, but not to military intrigue from men from comparatively ordinary backgrounds.

Vajiravudh's response to the coup was a series of modernizing **reforms**, including the introduction of compulsory primary education and an attempt to better the status of women by supporting monogamy in place of the widespread practice of polygamy. His huge output of writings invariably encouraged people to live as modern Westerners, and he brought large numbers of commoners into high positions in government. Nonetheless, he would not relinquish his strong opposition to constitutional democracy.

When **World War I** broke out in 1914, the Thais were generally sympathetic to the Germans out of resentment over their loss of territory to the French and

British. The king, however, was in favour of neutrality, until the US entered the war in 1917, when Thailand followed the expedient policy of joining the winning side and sent an expeditionary force of 1300 men to France in June 1918. The goodwill earned by this gesture enabled the Thais, between 1920 and 1926, to negotiate away the unequal treaties which had been imposed on them by the Western powers. Foreigners on Thai soil were no longer exempted from Thai laws, and the Thais were allowed to set reasonable rates of import and export taxes.

Yet Vajiravudh's extravagant lifestyle – during his reign, royal expenditure amounted to as much as ten percent of the state budget – left severe financial problems for his successor. Vajiravudh died without leaving a son, and as three better-placed contenders to the crown all died in the 1920s, **Prajadhipok** – the seventy-sixth child and last son of Chulalongkorn – was catapulted to the throne as Rama VII (1925–35). Young and inexperienced, he responded to the country's crisis by creating a Supreme Council of State, seen by many as a return to Chulalongkorn's absolutist "government by princes".

Prajadhipok himself seems to have been in favour of constitutional government, but the weakness of his personality and the opposition of the old guard in the Supreme Council prevented him from introducing it. Meanwhile a vigorous community of Western-educated intellectuals had emerged in the lower echelons of the bureaucracy, who were increasingly dissatisfied with the injustices of monarchical government. The final shock to the Thai system came with the Great Depression, which from 1930 onwards ravaged the economy. On June 24, 1932, a small group of middle-ranking officials, led by a lawyer, Pridi Phanomyong, and an army major, Luang Phibunsongkhram, staged a **coup** with only a handful of troops. Prajadhipok weakly submitted to the conspirators, or "Promoters", and 150 years of absolute monarchy in Bangkok came to a sudden end. The king was sidelined to a position of symbolic significance and in 1935 he abdicated in favour of his 10-year-old nephew, **Ananda**, then a schoolboy living in Switzerland.

To the 1957 coup

The success of the 1932 coup was in large measure attributable to the army officers who gave the conspirators credibility, and it was they who were to dominate the constitutional regimes that followed. The Promoters' first worry was that the French or British might attempt to restore the monarchy to full power. To deflect such intervention, they appointed a government under a provisional constitution and espoused a wide range of liberal Western-type reforms, including freedom of the press and social equality, few of which ever saw the light of day.

The regime's first crisis came early in 1933 when **Pridi Phanomyong**, by now leader of the government's civilian faction, put forward a socialist economic plan based on the nationalization of land and labour. The proposal was denounced as communistic by the military, Pridi was forced into temporary exile and an anti-communist law was passed. Then, in October, a royalist coup was mounted which brought the kingdom close to civil war. After intense fighting, the rebels were defeated by Lieutenant-Colonel **Luang Phibunsongkhram** (or Phibun), so strengthening the government and bringing Phibun to the fore as the leading light of the military faction.

Pridi was rehabilitated in 1934 and remained powerful and popular, especially among the intelligentsia, but it was Phibun who became prime minister after the decisive **elections of 1938**, presiding over a cabinet dominated by military men. Phibun encouraged a wave of nationalistic feeling with such measures as the official institution of the name Thailand in 1939 – Siam, it was argued, was a name bestowed by external forces, and the new title made it clear that the country belonged to the Thais rather than the economically dominant Chinese. This latter sentiment was reinforced with a series of harsh laws against the Chinese, who faced discriminatory taxes on income and commerce.

World War II

The outbreak of **World War II** gave the Thais the chance to avenge the humiliation of the 1893 Franco–Siamese Crisis. When France was occupied by Germany in June 1940, Phibun seized the opportunity to invade western Cambodia and the area of Laos lying to the west of the Mekong River. In the following year, however, the threat of a Japanese attack on Thailand loomed. On December 8, 1941, almost at the same time as the assault on Pearl Harbour, the Japanese invaded the country at nine points, most of them along the east coast of the peninsula. The Thais at first resisted fiercely, but realizing that the position was hopeless, Phibun quickly ordered a ceasefire. Meanwhile the British sent a force from Malaysia to try to stop the Japanese at Songkhla, but were held up in a fight with Thai border police. The Japanese had time to establish themselves, before pushing down the peninsula to take Singapore.

The Thai government concluded a military alliance with Japan and declared war against the US and Great Britain in January 1942, probably in the belief that the Japanese would win the war. However, the Thai minister in Washington, Seni Pramoj, refused to deliver the declaration of war against the US and, in co operation with the Americans, began organizing a resistance movement called **Seri Thai**. Pridi, now acting as regent to the young king, furtively co ordinated the movement under the noses of the occupying Japanese, smuggling in American agents and housing them in a European prison camp in Bangkok.

By 1944 Japan's final defeat looked likely, and Phibun, who had been most closely associated with them, was forced to resign by the National Assembly in July. A civilian, Khuang Aphaiwong, was chosen as prime minister, while Seri Thai became well established in the government under the control of Pridi. At the end of the war, Thailand was forced to restore the annexed Cambodian and Lao provinces to French Indochina, but American support prevented the British from imposing heavy punishments for the alliance with Japan.

Postwar upheavals

With the fading of the military, the election of January 1946 was for the first time contested by organized political parties, resulting in Pridi becoming prime minister. A new constitution was drafted and the outlook for democratic, civilian government seemed bright.

Hopes were shattered, however, on June 9, 1946, when King Ananda was found dead in his bed, with a bullet wound in his forehead. Three palace servants were hurriedly tried and executed, but the murder has never been satisfactorily explained, and public opinion attached at least indirect responsibility for the killing to Pridi, who had in the past shown strong anti-royalist feeling. He resigned as prime minister, and in April 1948 the military made a decisive return: playing on the threat of communism, with Pridi pictured as a Red bogeyman, Phibun took over the premiership.

After the bloody suppression of two attempted coups in favour of Pridi, the main feature of Phibun's second regime was its heavy involvement with the US. As communism developed its hold in the region, with the takeover of China in

1949 and the French defeat in Indochina in 1954, the US increasingly viewed Thailand as a bulwark against the Red menace. Between 1951 and 1957, when its annual state budget was only about $200 million a year, Thailand received a total $149 million in American economic aid and $222 million in military aid. This strengthened Phibun's dictatorship, while enabling leading military figures to divert American money and other funds into their own pockets.

In 1955, his position threatened by two rival generals, Phibun experienced a sudden conversion to the cause of democracy. He narrowly won a general election in 1957, but only by blatant vote-rigging and coercion. Although there's a strong tradition of foul play in Thai elections, this is remembered as the dirtiest ever: after vehement public outcry, **General Sarit**, the commander-in-chief of the army, overthrew the new government in September 1957.

To the present day

Believing that Thailand would prosper best under a unifying authority – an ideology that still has its supporters – Sarit set about re-establishing the monarchy as the head of the social hierarchy and the source of legitimacy for the government. Ananda's successor, **King Bhumibol** (Rama IX), was pushed into an active role while Sarit ruthlessly silenced critics and pressed ahead with a plan for economic development. These policies achieved a large measure of stability and prosperity at home, although from 1960 onwards the international situation worsened. With the Marxist Pathet Lao making considerable advances in Laos, and Cambodia's ruler, Prince Sihanouk, drawing into closer relations with China, Sarit turned again to the US. The Americans obliged by sharply increasing military aid and by stationing troops in Thailand.

The Vietnam War

Sarit died in 1963, whereupon the military succession passed to **General Thanom**, closely aided by his deputy prime minister, **General Praphas**. Neither man had anything of Sarit's charisma and during a decade in power they followed his political philosophies largely unchanged. Their most pressing problem was the resumption of open hostilities between North and South Vietnam in the early 1960s – the **Vietnam War**. Both Laos and Cambodia became involved on the side of the communists by allowing the North Vietnamese to supply their troops in the south along the Ho Chi Minh Trail, which passed through southern Laos and northeastern Cambodia. The Thais, with the backing of the US, quietly began to conduct military operations in Laos, to which North Vietnam and China responded by supporting anti-government insurgency in Thailand.

The more the Thais felt threatened by the spread of communism, the more they looked to the Americans for help – by 1968 around 45,000 US military personnel were on Thai soil, which became the base for US bombing raids against North Vietnam and Laos, and for covert operations into Laos and beyond.

The effects of the **American presence in Thailand** were profound. The economy swelled with dollars, and hundreds of thousands of Thais became reliant on the Americans for a living, with a consequent proliferation of corruption and prostitution. What's more, the sudden exposure to Western culture led many to question traditional Thai values and the political status quo.

The democracy movement and civil unrest

At the same time, poor farmers were becoming disillusioned with their lot, and during the 1960s many turned against the Bangkok government. At the end of 1964, the **Communist Party of Thailand** and other groups formed a **broad**

left coalition that soon had the support of several thousand insurgents in remote areas of the northeast. By 1967, the problem had spread to Chiang Rai and Nan provinces, and a separate threat had arisen in southern Thailand, involving **Muslim dissidents** and the Chinese-dominated **Communist Party of Malaya**, as well as local Thais.

Thanom was now facing a major security crisis, especially as the war in Vietnam was going badly. In 1969 he held elections which produced a majority for the government party but, still worried about national stability, the general got cold feet. In November 1971 he reimposed repressive military rule, under a triumvirate of himself, his son Colonel Narong and Praphas, who became known as the "Three Tyrants". However, the 1969 experiment with democracy had heightened expectations of power-sharing among the middle classes, especially in the universities. **Student demonstrations** began in June 1973, and in October as many as 500,000 people turned out at Thammasat University in Bangkok to demand a new constitution. King Bhumibol intervened with apparent success, and indeed the demonstrators were starting to disperse on the morning of October 14, when the police tried to control the flow of people away. Tensions quickly mounted and soon a full-scale riot was under way, during which over 350 people were reported killed. The army, however, refused to provide enough troops to suppress this massive uprising, and later the same day, Thanom, Narong and Praphas were forced to resign and leave the country.

In a new climate of openness, **Kukrit Pramoj** (see p.170) managed to form a coalition of seventeen elected parties and secured a promise of US withdrawal from Thailand, but his government was riven with feuding. Meanwhile, the king and much of the middle class, alarmed at the unchecked radicalism of the students, began to support new, often violent, right-wing organizations. In October 1976, the students demonstrated again, protesting against the return of Thanom to Thailand to become a monk at Wat Bowonniwet. Supported by elements of the military and the government, the police and reactionary students launched a massive assault on Thammasat University. On October 6, hundreds of students were brutally beaten, scores were lynched and some even burnt alive; the military took control and suspended the constitution.

General Prem

Soon after, the military-appointed prime minister, **Thanin Kraivichien**, imposed rigid censorship and forced dissidents to undergo anti-communist indoctrination, but his measures seem to have been too repressive even for the military, who forced him to resign in October 1977. General Kriangsak Chomanand took over, and began to break up the insurgency with shrewd offers of amnesty. His power base was weak, however, and although Kriangsak won the elections of 1979, he was displaced in February 1980 by **General Prem Tinsulanonda**, who was backed by a broad parliamentary coalition.

Untainted by corruption, Prem achieved widespread support, including that of the monarchy. Parliamentary elections in 1983 returned the military to power and legitimized Prem's rule. Overseeing a period of strong foreign investment and rapid economic growth, the general maintained the premiership until 1988, with a unique mixture of dictatorship and democracy sometimes called **Premocracy**: although never standing for parliament himself, Prem was asked by the legislature after every election to become prime minister. He eventually stepped down (though he remains a powerful privy councillor) because, he said, it was time for the country's leader to be chosen from among its elected representatives.

The 1992 demonstrations and the 1997 constitution

The new prime minister was indeed an elected MP, **Chatichai Choonhavan**, a retired general with a long civilian career in public office. He pursued a vigorous policy of economic development, but this fostered widespread corruption, in which members of the government were often implicated. Following an economic downturn and Chatichai's attempts to downgrade the political role of the military, the armed forces staged a bloodless **coup** on February 23, 1991, led by Supreme Commander Sunthorn and General Suchinda, the army commander-in-chief, who became premier.

When Suchinda reneged on promises to make democratic amendments to the constitution, hundreds of thousands of ordinary Thais poured onto the streets around Bangkok's Democracy Monument in **mass demonstrations** between May 17 and 20, 1992. Hopelessly misjudging the mood of the country, Suchinda brutally crushed the protests, leaving hundreds dead or injured. Having justified the massacre on the grounds that he was protecting the king from communist agitators, Suchinda was forced to resign when King Bhumibol expressed his disapproval in a ticking-off that was broadcast on world television.

Elections were held in September, with the **Democrat Party**, led by Chuan Leekpai, a noted upholder of democracy and the rule of law, emerging victorious. Chuan was succeeded in turn by Banharn Silpa-archa – nicknamed by the local press "the walking ATM", a reference to his reputation for buying votes – and General Chavalit Yongchaiyudh. The most significant positive event of the latter's tenure was the approval of a **new constitution** in 1997. Drawn up by an independent drafting assembly, its main points included: direct elections to the senate, rather than appointment of senators by the prime minister; acceptance of the right of assembly as the basis of a democratic society and guarantees of individual rights and freedoms; greater public accountability; and increased popular participation in local administration. The eventual aim of the new charter was to end the traditional system of patronage, vested interests and vote buying.

Tom yam kung: the 1997 economic crisis

In February 1997 foreign-exchange dealers began to mount speculative attacks on the **baht**, alarmed at the size of Thailand's private foreign debt – 250 billion baht in the unproductive property sector alone, much of it accrued through the proliferation of prestigious skyscrapers in Bangkok. Chavalit's government defended the pegged exchange rate, spending $23 billion of the country's formerly healthy foreign-exchange reserves, but at the beginning of July was forced to give up the ghost – the baht was floated and soon went into free fall. Thailand was forced to seek help from the **IMF**, who in August put together a $17-billion **rescue package**, coupled with severe austerity measures.

In November, the inept Chavalit was replaced by Chuan Leekpai, who immediately took a hard line in following the IMF's advice, which involved maintaining cripplingly high interest rates to protect the baht and slashing government budgets. Although this played well abroad, at home the government encountered increasing hostility from its newly impoverished citizens – the downturn struck with such speed and severity that it was dubbed the **tom yam kung crisis**, after the searingly hot Thai soup. Chuan's tough stance paid off, however, with the baht stabilizing and inflation falling back, and in October 1999 he announced that he was forgoing almost $4 billion of the IMF's package.

Thaksin

The general election of January 2001 was the first to be held under the 1997 constitution, which was intended to take the traditionally crucial role of money, especially for vote-buying, out of politics. However, this election coincided with the emergence of a new party, **Thai Rak Thai** (TRT; "Thai Loves Thai"), formed by one of Thailand's wealthiest men, **Thaksin Shinawatra**, an ex-policeman who had made a personal fortune from government telecommunications concessions.

TRT duly won the election but, instead of a move towards greater democracy, as envisaged by the new constitution, Thaksin's government seemed to represent a full-blown merger between politics and big business, concentrating economic power in even fewer hands. Furthermore, the prime minister began to apply commercial and legal pressure, including several lawsuits, to try to silence critics in the media and parliament, and to manipulate the Senate and supposedly independent institutions such as the Election Commission to consolidate his own power. As his standing became more firmly entrenched, he rejected constitutional reforms designed to rein in his power – famously declaring that "democracy is only a tool" for achieving other goals.

Thaksin did, however, maintain his profile as a populist reformer by carrying through nearly all of his controversial election promises. He issued a three-year loan moratorium for perennially indebted farmers and set up a one-million-baht development fund for each of the country's seventy thousand villages – though many villages just used the money as a lending tool to cover past debts, rather than creating productive projects for the future as intended. To improve public health access, a standard charge of B30 per hospital visit was introduced nationwide. However, too little was invested in the health service to cope with the increased demand that was generated.

Despite a sharp escalation of violence in the Islamic southern provinces in early 2004 (see p.771), but bolstered by his high-profile response to the tsunami on December 26, 2004 (see p.672), Thaksin breezed through the February 2005 election, becoming the first prime minister in Thai history to win an outright majority at the polls. The prospect of such a one-party state, however, alarmed a wide spectrum of opposition. When Thaksin's relatives sold their shares in the family's Shin Corporation in January 2006 for £1.1 billion, without paying tax, tens of thousands of mostly middle-class Thais flocked to Bangkok to take part in protracted but peaceful demonstrations, under the umbrella of the **People's Alliance for Democracy** (**PAD**). After further allegations of corruption and cronyism, in September Thaksin, while on official business in the United States, was ousted by a military government in a benign **coup**.

Thaksin set up home in London, but in May 2007 his party, TRT, was found guilty of electoral fraud and dissolved. Undeterred, his supporters formed the People's Power Party (PPP), which despite its ill-concealed opposition to the royalist-military elite, won the December 2007 general election; its leader, Samak Sundaravej, an irascible, right-wing TV chef, openly confessed to being a proxy for Thaksin. In response, the PAD – its trademark yellow shirts (the colour of the king) now firmly established – restarted and stepped up its mass protests, eventually occupying the government's offices for several months. Meanwhile, the merry-go-round of tribunals and court cases continued, including the disqualification of Samak from political office – only to be replaced as prime minister by Thaksin's brother-in-law. Much more significantly, Thaksin was finally convicted *in absentia* of corruption and, as a fugitive from justice, was refused a visa extension by the UK.

Matters came to a head in November and December 2008: PAD seized and closed down Bangkok's Suvarnabhumi and Don Muang airports; the ruling

People's Power Party was declared illegal, which persuaded the yellow shirts to lift their sit-in; and Peua Thai, the PPP's swift reincarnation, found itself unable to form a new coalition government. Instead, led by the young, charismatic **Abhisit Vejjajiva** who was born in Newcastle-upon-Tyne and educated at Eton and Oxford, the Democratic Party jumped into bed with the Friends of Newin (aka the Bhumjaithai Party), formerly staunch supporters of Thaksin, to take the helm. At the time of writing, however, the divisions between the pro- and anti-Thaksin camps have not been resolved. Thaksin's supporters, now red-shirted and organized into the **UDD** (United Front for Democracy against Dictatorship), have taken their turn to hold mass protest meetings; in April 2009 they forced the ASEAN (Association of Southeast Asian Nations) summit meeting in Pattaya to be embarrassingly abandoned and closed down central Bangkok for several days before being dispersed by the army. Meanwhile the PAD, who have blotted their copybook internationally by advocating a part-elected, part-appointed system of government for Thailand to try to minimize corruption, have decided to form a political party; they've changed their colours to yellow and green (to display their environmentalist credentials) and renamed themselves the **New Politics Party**.

Religion: Thai Buddhism

Over 85 percent of Thais consider themselves **Theravada Buddhists**, followers of the teachings of a holy man usually referred to as the Buddha (Enlightened One), though more precisely known as Gautama Buddha to distinguish him from lesser-known Buddhas who preceded him. Theravada Buddhism is one of the two main schools of Buddhism practised in Asia, and in Thailand it has absorbed an eclectic assortment of animist and Hindu elements.

Islam is the biggest of the minority religions in Thailand, practised by between five and ten percent of the population. Most Muslims live in the south, especially in the deep-south provinces of Yala, Pattani and Narithiwat, along the Malaysian border, whose populations are over seventy percent Muslim. The separatist violence in this region has caused great tension between local Buddhist and Muslim communities, which have traditionally co-existed peacefully; it has not, however, obviously affected inter-faith relationships elsewhere in Thailand. The rest of the Thai population comprises Mahayana Buddhists, Hindus, Sikhs, Christians and animists.

The Buddha: his life and beliefs

Gautama Buddha was born in Nepal as **Prince Gautama Siddhartha** in either the sixth or seventh century BC. At his birth, astrologers predicted that he would become either a famous king or a celebrated holy man, depending on which path he chose. Much preferring the former, the prince's father forbade the boy from leaving the palace grounds, and set about educating Gautama in all aspects of the high life. Most statues of the Buddha depict him with elongated earlobes, which is a reference to this early pampered existence, when he would have worn heavy precious stones in his ears.

The prince married and became a father, but at the age of 29 he flouted his father's authority and sneaked out into the world beyond the palace. On this fateful trip he encountered successively an old man, a sick man, a corpse and a hermit, and thus for the first time was made aware that pain and suffering were intrinsic to human life. Contemplation seemed the only means of discovering why this was so – and therefore Gautama decided to leave the palace and become a **Hindu ascetic**.

For several years he wandered the countryside leading a life of self-denial and self-mortification, but failed to come any closer to the answer. Eventually concluding that the best course of action must be to follow a "Middle Way" – neither indulgent nor overly ascetic – Gautama sat down beneath the famous riverside bodhi tree at **Bodh Gaya** in India, facing the rising sun, to **meditate** until he achieved enlightenment. For 49 days he sat cross-legged in the "lotus position", contemplating the causes of suffering and wrestling with temptations that materialized to distract him. Most of these were sent by **Mara**, the Evil One, who was finally subdued when Gautama summoned the earth goddess **Mae Toranee** by pointing the fingers of his right hand at the ground – the gesture known as **Calling the Earth to Witness**, or *Bhumisparsa Mudra*, which has been immortalized by thousands of Thai sculptors. Mae Toranee wrung torrents of water from her hair and engulfed Mara's demonic emissaries in a flood, an episode that's also commonly reproduced, most famously in the statue in Bangkok's Sanam Luang.

Temptations dealt with, Gautama soon came to attain **enlightenment** and so become a Buddha. As the place of his enlightenment, the **bodhi tree** (or bo tree) has assumed special significance for Buddhists: not only does it appear in many Buddhist paintings, but there's often a real bodhi tree (*Ficus religiosa*) planted in temple compounds as well. In addition, the bot is nearly always built facing either a body of water or facing east (preferably both).

The Buddha preached his **first sermon** in a deer park in India, where he characterized his doctrine, or **Dharma**, as a wheel. From this episode comes the early Buddhist symbol the **Dharmachakra**, known as the Wheel of Law, which is often accompanied by a statue of a deer. Thais celebrate this first sermon with a public holiday in July known as **Asanha Puja**. On another occasion 1250 people spontaneously gathered to hear the Buddha speak, an event remembered in Thailand as **Maha Puja** and marked by a public holiday in February.

For the next forty-odd years the Buddha travelled the region converting non believers and performing miracles. One rainy season he even ascended into the **Tavatimsa heaven** (Heaven of the 33 Gods) to visit his mother and to preach the doctrine to her. His descent from this heaven is quite a common theme of paintings and sculptures, and the **Standing Buddha** pose of numerous Buddha statues comes from this story.

The Buddha "died" at the age of eighty on the banks of a river at Kusinari in India – an event often dated to 543 BC, which is why the **Thai calendar** is 543 years out of synch with the Western one, so that the year 2010 AD becomes 2553 BE (Buddhist Era). Lying on his side, propping up his head on his hand, the Buddha passed into **Nirvana** (giving rise to another classic pose, the **Reclining Buddha**), the unimaginable state of nothingness which knows no suffering and from which there is no reincarnation. Buddhists believe that the day the Buddha entered Nirvana was the same date on which he was born and on which he achieved enlightenment, a triply significant day that Thais honour with the **Visakha Puja** festival in May.

Buddhists believe that Gautama Buddha was the five-hundredth incarnation of a single being: the stories of these five hundred lives, collectively known as the **Jataka**, provide the inspiration for much Thai art. Hindus also accept Gautama Buddha into their pantheon, perceiving him as the ninth manifestation of their god Vishnu.

The spread of Buddhism

After the Buddha entered Nirvana, his **doctrine** spread relatively quickly across India, and probably was first promulgated in Thailand in about the third century BC. His teachings, the *Tripitaka*, were written down in the Pali language – a derivative of Sanskrit – in a form that became known as **Theravada**, or "The Doctrine of the Elders".

By the beginning of the first millennium, a new movement called **Mahayana** (Great Vehicle) had emerged within the Theravada school, attempting to make Buddhism more accessible by introducing a pantheon of **bodhisattva**, or Buddhist saints, who, although they had achieved enlightenment, postponed entering Nirvana in order to inspire the populace. Mahayana Buddhism spread north into China, Korea, Vietnam and Japan, also entering southern Thailand via the Srivijayan empire around the eighth century and parts of Khmer Cambodia in about the eleventh century. Meanwhile Theravada Buddhism (which the Mahayanists disparagingly renamed "Hinayana" or "Lesser Vehicle") established itself most significantly in Sri Lanka, northern and central Thailand and Burma.

Buddhist doctrine and practice

Central to Theravada Buddhism is a belief in **karma** – every action has a consequence – and **reincarnation**, along with an understanding that craving is at the root of human suffering. The ultimate aim for a Buddhist is to get off the cycle of perpetual reincarnation and suffering and to instead enter the blissful state of non-being that is **Nirvana**. This enlightened state can take many lifetimes to achieve so the more realistic goal for most is to be reborn slightly higher up the karmic ladder each time. As Thai Buddhists see it, animals are at the bottom of the karmic scale and monks at the top, with women on a lower rung than men.

Living a good life, specifically a life of "pure intention", creates good karma and Buddhist doctrine focuses a great deal on how to achieve this. Psychology and an understanding of human weaknesses play a big part. Key is the concept of *dukka*, which holds that **craving is the root cause of all suffering** or, to put it simplistically, human unhappiness is caused by the unquenchable dissatisfaction experienced when one's sensual, spiritual or material desires are not met. Accepting the truth of this is known as the **Four Noble Truths** of Buddhism. The route to enlightenment depends on a person being sufficiently detached from earthly desires so that *dukka* can't take hold. One acknowledges that the physical world is impermanent and ever changing, and that all things – including the self – are therefore not worth craving. A Buddhist works towards this realization by following the **Eightfold Path**, or **Middle Way**, that is by developing a set of highly moral personal qualities such as "right speech", "right action" and "right mindfulness". Meditation is particularly helpful in this.

A devout Thai Buddhist commits to the **five basic precepts**, namely not to kill or steal, to refrain from sexual misconduct and incorrect speech (lies, gossip and abuse) and to eschew intoxicating liquor and drugs. There are **three extra precepts** for special *wan phra* holy days and for those laypeople including foreign students who study meditation at Thai temples: no eating after noon, no entertainment (including TV and music) and no sleeping on a soft bed; in addition, the no-sexual-misconduct precept turns into no sex at all.

Making merit

Merit-making in popular Thai Buddhism has become slightly skewed, so that some people act on the assumption that they'll climb the karmic ladder faster if they make bigger and better offerings to the temple and its monks. However, it is of course the purity of the intention behind one's **merit-making** (*tham bun*) that's fundamental.

Merit can be made in many ways, from giving a monk his breakfast to attending a Buddhist service or donating money and gifts to the neighbourhood temple, and most **festivals** are essentially communal merit-making opportunities. Between the big festivals, the most common days for making merit and visiting the temple are **wan phra** (holy days), which are determined by the phase of the moon and occur four times a month. The simplest **offering** inside a temple consists of lotus buds, candles and three incense sticks (representing the three gems of Buddhism – the Buddha himself, the Dharma or doctrine, and the monkhood). One of the more bizarre but common merit-making activities involves **releasing caged birds**: worshippers buy tiny finches from vendors at wat compounds and, by liberating them from their cage, prove their Buddhist compassion towards all living things. The fact that the birds were free until netted earlier that morning doesn't seem to detract from the ritual. In riverside and seaside wats, fish or even baby turtles are released instead.

For an insightful introduction to the philosophy and practice of Thai Buddhism, see www.thaibuddhism.net. Details of Thai temples that welcome foreign students of Buddhism and meditation are on p.71.

The monkhood

It's the duty of Thailand's 200,000-strong **Sangha** (monkhood) to set an example to the Theravada Buddhist community by living a life as close to the Middle Way as possible and by preaching the Dharma to the people. The life of a monk (*bhikkhu*) is governed by 227 precepts that include celibacy and the rejection of all personal possessions except gifts.

Each day begins with an alms round in the neighbourhood so that the laity can donate food and thereby gain themselves merit, and then is chiefly spent in meditation, chanting, teaching and study. As the most respected members of any community, monks act as teachers, counsellors and arbiters in local disputes, and sometimes become spokesmen for villagers' rights. They also perform rituals at cremations, weddings and other events, such as the launching of a new business or even the purchase of a new car. Many young boys from poor families find themselves almost obliged to become either a *dek wat* (temple boy) or a **novice monk** because that's the only way they can get accommodation, food and, crucially, an education. This is provided free in exchange for duties around the wat, and novices are required to adhere to ten rather than 227 Buddhist precepts.

Monkhood doesn't have to be for life: a man may leave the Sangha three times without stigma and in fact every Thai male (including royalty) is expected to **enter the monkhood** for a short period, ideally between leaving school and marrying, as a rite of passage into adulthood. Thai government departments and some private companies grant their employees paid leave for their time as a monk, but the custom is in decline as young men increasingly have to consider the effect their absence may have on their career prospects. Instead, many men now enter the monkhood for a brief period after the death of a parent, to make merit both for the deceased and for the rest of the family. The most popular time for temporary ordination is the three-month Buddhist retreat period – **Pansa**, sometimes referred to as "Buddhist Lent" – which begins in July and lasts for the duration of the rainy season. (The monks' confinement is said to originate from the earliest years of Buddhist history, when farmers complained that perambulating monks were squashing their sprouting rice crops.)

Monks in contemporary society

Some monks extend their role as village spokesmen to become influential activists: Wat Tham Krabok near Lopburi and Wat Nong Sam Pran in Kanchanaburi are among a growing number of temples that have established themselves as successful drug rehabilitation centres; monks at Wat Phra Bat Nam Pu in Lopburi run a hospice for people with HIV/Aids as well as a famously hard-hitting AIDS-awareness museum; monks at Wat Phai Lom near Bangkok have developed the country's largest breeding colony of Asian open-billed storks; and the monks at Wat Pa Luang Ta Bua Yannasampanno in Kanchanaburi (see p.241) have hit the headlines with their tiger sanctuary. Other monks, such as the famous octogenarian Luang Pho Khoon of Wat Ban Rai in Nakhon Ratchasima province, have acquired such a reputation for giving wise counsel and bringing good fortune to their followers that they have become national gurus and their temples now generate great wealth through the production of specially blessed amulets and photographs.

Though the increasing involvement of many monks in the secular world has not met with unanimous approval, far more disappointing to the laity are those monks who **flout the precepts** of the Sangha by succumbing to the temptations of a consumer society, flaunting Raybans, Rolexes and Mercedes (in some cases actually bought with temple funds), chain-smoking and flirting, even making pocket money from predicting lottery results and practising faith-healing. With so much national pride and integrity riding on the sanctity of the Sangha, any whiff of a deeper scandal is bound to strike deep into the national psyche. Cases of monks involved in drug dealing, gun running, even rape and murder have prompted a stream of editorials on the state of the Sangha and the collapse of spiritual values at the heart of Thai society. The inclusivity of the monkhood – which is open to just about any male who wants to join – has been highlighted as a particularly vulnerable aspect, not least because donning saffron robes has always been an accepted way for criminals, reformed or otherwise, to repent of their past deeds.

Interestingly, back in the late 1980s, the influential monk Phra Bodhirak (Photirak) was defrocked after criticizing what he saw as a tide of decadence infecting Thai Buddhism. He now preaches his ascetic code of anti-materialism through his breakaway **Santi Asoke** sect, famous across the country for its cheap vegetarian restaurants, its philosophy of self-sufficiency and for the simple blue farmers' shirts worn by many of its followers.

Women and the monkhood

Although the Theravada Buddhist hierarchy in some countries permits the ordination of **female monks**, or *bhikkhuni*, the Thai Sangha does not. Instead, Thai women are officially only allowed to become **nuns**, or *mae chii*, shaving their heads, donning white robes and keeping eight rather than 227 precepts. Their status is lower than that of the monks and they are chiefly occupied with temple upkeep rather than conducting religious ceremonies.

However, the progressives are becoming more vocal, and in 2002 a Thai woman became the first of several to break with the Buddhist authorities and get **ordained** as a novice *bhikkhuni* on Thai soil. Thailand's Sangha Council, however, still recognizes neither her ordination nor the temple, Watra Song dhammakalyani in Nakhon Pathom, where the ordination took place. The Watra (rather than Wat) is run by another Thai *bhikkhuni*, Dhammananda Bhikkhuni, the author of several books in English about **women and Buddhism** and of an informative website, Ⓦwww.thaibhikkhunis.org.

Hindu deities and animist spirits

The complicated history of the area now known as Thailand has made Thai Buddhism a confusingly syncretic faith, as you'll realize when you enter a Buddhist temple compound to be confronted by a statue of a Hindu deity. While regular Buddhist merit-making insures a Thai for the next life, there are certain **Hindu gods and animist spirits** that many Thais – sophisticated Bangkokians and illiterate farmers alike – also cultivate for help with more immediate problems; and as often as not it's a Buddhist monk who is called in to exorcize a malevolent spirit. Even the Buddhist King Bhumibol employs Brahmin priests and astrologers to determine auspicious days and officiate at certain royal ceremonies and, like his royal predecessors of the Chakri dynasty, he also associates himself with the Hindu god Vishnu by assuming the title Rama IX – Rama, hero of the Hindu epic the *Ramayana*, having been Vishnu's seventh manifestation on earth.

If a Thai wants help in achieving a short-term goal, like passing an exam, becoming pregnant or winning the lottery, he or she will quite likely turn to the **Hindu pantheon**, visiting an enshrined statue of Brahma, Vishnu, Shiva or Ganesh, and making offerings of flowers, incense and maybe food. If the outcome is favourable, the devotee will probably come back to show thanks, bringing more offerings and maybe even hiring a dance troupe to perform a celebratory *lakhon chatri*. Built in honour of Brahma, Bangkok's Erawan Shrine is the most famous place of Hindu-inspired worship in the country.

Spirits and spirit houses

Whereas Hindu deities tend to be benevolent, **spirits** (or *phi*) are not nearly as reliable and need to be mollified more frequently. They come in hundreds of varieties, some more malign than others, and inhabit everything from trees, rivers and caves to public buildings and private homes – even taking over people if they feel like it.

So that these *phi* don't pester human inhabitants, each building has a special **spirit house** (*saan phra phum*) in its vicinity, as a dwelling for spirits ousted by the building's construction. Usually raised on a short column to set it at or above eye-level, the spirit house must occupy an auspicious location – not, for example, in the shadow of the main building. It's generally about the size of a dolls' house and designed to look like a wat or a traditional Thai house, but its ornamentation is supposed to reflect the status of the humans' building, so if that building is enlarged or refurbished, the spirit house should be improved accordingly. And as architects become increasingly bold in their designs, so modernist spirit houses are also beginning to appear, especially in Bangkok where an eyecatching new skyscraper might be graced by a spirit house of glass or polished concrete. **Figurines** representing the relevant guardian spirit and his aides are sometimes put inside, and daily offerings of incense, lighted candles and garlands of jasmine are placed alongside them to keep the *phi* happy – a disgruntled spirit is a dangerous spirit, liable to cause sickness, accidents and even death. As with any religious building or icon in Thailand, an unwanted or crumbling spirit house should never be dismantled or destroyed, which is why you'll often see damaged spirit houses placed around the base of a sacred banyan tree, where they are able to rest in peace.

Art and architecture

Aside from pockets of Hindu-inspired statuary and architecture, the vast majority of historical Thai culture takes its inspiration from Theravada Buddhism and, though the country does have some excellent museums, to understand fully the evolution of Thai art you have to visit its temples. Artists, sculptors and architects have tended to see their work as a way of making spiritual merit rather than as a means of self-expression or self-promotion, so pre-twentieth-century Thai art history is all about evolving styles rather than individual artists. This section, in conjunction with our colour section on the **wat**, which explains the typical temple layout, is designed to help make sense of the most common aspects of Thai art and architecture at their various stages of development.

Buddhist iconography

In the early days of Buddhism, image-making was considered inadequate to convey the faith's abstract philosophies, so the only approved iconography comprised doctrinal **symbols** such as the *Dharmachakra* (Wheel of Law, also known as Wheel of Doctrine or Wheel of Life). Gradually these symbols were displaced by **images of the Buddha**, construed chiefly as physical embodiments of the Buddha's teachings rather than as portraits of the man. Sculptors took their guidance from the Pali texts which ordained the Buddha's most common postures (*asanha*) and gestures (*mudra*).

All three-dimensional Buddha images are objects of reverence, but some are more esteemed than others. Some are alleged to have reacted in a particular way to unusual events, others have performed miracles, or are simply admired for their beauty, their phenomenal size or even their material value – if made of solid gold or jade, for example. Most Thais are familiar with these exceptional images, all of which have been given special names, always prefixed by the honorific "Phra", and many of which have spawned thousands of miniaturized copies in the form of amulets. Pilgrimages are made to see the most famous originals.

Postures and gestures of the Buddha

Of the **four postures** – sitting, standing, walking and reclining – the **seated Buddha**, which represents him in meditation, is the most common in Thailand. A popular variation shows the Buddha seated on a coiled serpent, protected by the serpent's hood: a reference to the story about the Buddha meditating during the rainy season, when a serpent offered to raise him off the wet ground and shelter him from the storms. The **reclining** pose symbolizes the Buddha entering Nirvana at his death, while the **standing** and **walking** images both represent his descent from heaven.

The most common **hand gestures** include:

Dhyana Mudra (Meditation), in which the hands rest on the lap, palms upwards.

Bhumisparsa Mudra (Calling the Earth to Witness, a reference to the Buddha resisting temptation), with the left hand upturned in the lap and the right-hand fingers resting on the right knee and pointing to the earth.

Vitarkha Mudra (Teaching), with one or both hands held at chest height with the thumb and forefinger touching.

Abhaya Mudra (Dispelling Fear), showing the right hand (occasionally both hands) raised in a flat-palmed "stop" gesture.

It was in the Sukhothai era that the craze for producing **Buddha footprints** really took off. Harking back to the time when images were allusive rather than representative, these footprints were generally moulded from stucco to depict the 108 auspicious signs or *lakshanas* (which included references to the sixteen Buddhist heavens, the traditional four great continents and seven great rivers and lakes) and housed in a special mondop. Few of the Sukhothai footprints remain, but Ayutthaya–Ratanakosin-era examples are found all over the country, the most famous being Phra Phutthabat near Lopburi, the object of pilgrimages throughout the year. The feet of the famous Reclining Buddha in Bangkok's Wat Po are also inscribed with the 108 *lakshanas*, beautifully depicted in mother-of-pearl inlay.

Hindu iconography

Hindu images tend to be a lot livelier than Buddhist ones; there are countless gods to choose from and many have mischievous personalities and multiple inventive incarnations. In Hindu philosophy any object can be viewed as the temporal residence, embodiment or symbol of the deity so you get abstract representations such as the phallic lingam (pillar) for Shiva, as well as figurative images. Though pure Hinduism receded from Thailand with the collapse of the Khmer empire, Buddhist Thais have incorporated some Hindu and Brahmin concepts into the national belief system and have continued to create statues of the three chief Hindu deities – Brahma, Vishnu and Shiva – as well as using many mythological creatures in modern designs.

Vishnu has always been a favourite: in his role of "Preserver" he embodies the status quo, representing both stability and the notion of altruistic love. He is most often depicted as the deity, but has ten manifestations in all, of which **Rama** (number seven) is by far the most popular in Thailand. The epitome of ideal manhood, Rama is the super hero of the epic story the *Ramayana* (in Thai, the *Ramakien*; see box, p.135) and appears in storytelling reliefs and murals in every Hindu temple in Thailand; in painted portraits you can usually recognize him by his green face. Manifestation number eight is **Krishna**, more widely known than Rama in the West, but slightly less common in Thailand. Krishna is usually characterized as a flirtatious, flute-playing, blue-skinned cowherd, but he is also a crucial moral figure in the lengthy moral epic poem, the *Mahabharata*. Confusingly, Vishnu's ninth avatar is the **Buddha** – a manifestation adopted many centuries ago to minimize defection to the Buddhist faith. When represented as **the deity**, Vishnu is generally shown sporting a crown and four arms, his hands holding a conch shell (whose music wards off demons), a discus (used as a weapon), a club (symbolizing the power of nature and time), and a lotus (symbol of joyful flowering and renewal). He is often depicted astride a **garuda**, a half-man, half-bird. Even without Vishnu on its back, the garuda is a very important beast: a symbol of strength, it's often shown "supporting" temple buildings.

Statues and representations of **Brahma** (the Creator) are rare. He too has four arms, but holds no objects; he has four faces (sometimes painted red), is generally borne by a goose-like creature called a *hamsa*, and is associated with the direction north.

Shiva (the Destroyer) is the most volatile member of the pantheon. He stands for extreme behaviour, for beginnings and endings, as enacted in his frenzied Dance of Destruction, and for fertility, and is a symbol of great energy and power. His godlike form typically has four, eight or ten arms, sometimes holding a trident (representing creation, protection and destruction) and a drum (to beat the rhythm of creation). In his most famous role, as **Nataraja**, or Lord of the Dance, he is usually shown in stylized standing position with legs bent into a balletic position, and the full complement of arms outstretched above his head. Three stripes on a figure's forehead also indicate Shiva, or one of his followers. In abstract form, he is represented by a **lingam** (once found at the heart of every Khmer temple in the northeast). Primarily a symbol of energy and godly power, the lingam also embodies fertility, particularly when set upright in a vulva-shaped vessel known as a **yoni**. The yoni doubles as a receptacle for the holy water that worshippers pour over the lingam.

Close associates of Shiva include **Parvati**, his wife, and **Ganesh**, his elephant-headed son. As the god of knowledge and overcomer of obstacles (in the path of learning), Ganesh is used as the symbol of the Fine Arts Department so his image features on all entrance tickets to national museums and historical parks.

The royal, three-headed elephant, **Erawan**, usually only appears as the favourite mount of the god **Indra**, the king of the gods, with specific power over the elements (particularly rain) and over the east. Other **Hindu gods of direction**, which are commonly found on the appropriate antefix in Khmer temples, include **Yama** on a buffalo (south); **Varuna** on a naga (mythical serpent) or a *hamsa* (west); Brahma (north); and **Isaana** on a bull (northeast).

Lesser mythological figures, which originated as Hindu symbols but feature frequently in wats and other Buddhist contexts, include the **yaksha** giants who ward off evil spirits (like the enormous freestanding ones guarding Bangkok's Wat Phra Kaeo); the graceful half-woman, half-bird **kinnari**; and the ubiquitous **naga**, or serpent king of the underworld, often with as many as seven heads, whose reptilian body most frequently appears as staircase balustrades in Hindu and Buddhist temples.

The schools

In the 1920s art historians and academics began compiling a classification system for Thai art and architecture which was modelled along the lines of the country's historical periods; these are the guidelines followed below. The following brief overview starts in the sixth century, when Buddhism began to take a hold on the country; few examples of art from before that time have survived, and there are no known, earlier architectural relics.

Dvaravati (sixth to eleventh centuries)

Centred around Nakhon Pathom, U Thong and Lopburi in the Chao Phraya basin and in the smaller northern enclave of Haripunjaya (modern-day Lamphun), the **Dvaravati** state was populated by Theravada Buddhists who were strongly influenced by Indian culture.

The only known surviving Dvaravati-era **building** is the pyramidal laterite chedi at Lamphun's Wat Chama Thevi, but the national museums in Nakhon Pathom and Lamphun both house quite extensive collections of Buddha **images** from that period. To make the best of the poor-quality limestone at their disposal, Dvaravati sculptors made their Buddhas quite stocky, cleverly dressing the figures in a sheet-like drape that dropped down to ankle level from each raised wrist, forming a U-shaped hemline – a style which they used when casting in bronze as well. Where the faces have survived, they are strikingly naturalistic, distinguished by their thick lips, flattened noses and wide cheekbones.

Nakhon Pathom, a target of Buddhist missionaries from India since before the first century AD, has also yielded many **dharmachakra**, originating in the period when the Buddha could not be directly represented. These metre-high carved stone wheels symbolize the cycles of life and reincarnation, and in Dvaravati examples are often accompanied by a small statue of a deer, which refers to the Buddha preaching his first sermon in a deer park.

Srivijaya (eighth to thirteenth centuries)

While Dvaravati's Theravada Buddhists were influencing the central plains and, to a limited extent, areas further to the north, southern Thailand was paying allegiance to the Mahayana Buddhists of the **Srivijayan** empire. Mahayanists believe that those who have achieved enlightenment – known as **bodhisattva** – should postpone their entry into Nirvana in order to help others along the way, and depictions of these saint-like beings were the mainstay of Srivijayan art.

The finest Srivijayan *bodhisattva* statues were cast in bronze and are among the most graceful and sinuous ever produced in Thailand. Many are lavishly adorned, and some were even bedecked in real jewels when first made. By far the most popular *bodhisattva* subject was **Avalokitesvara**, worshipped as compassion incarnate. Generally shown with four or more arms and with an animal skin over the left shoulder or tied at the waist, Avalokitesvara is also sometimes depicted with his torso covered in tiny Buddha images. Bangkok's National Museum holds the most beautiful Avalokitesvara, found in Chaiya, but there's a good sandstone example in situ at Prasat Muang Singh near Kanchanaburi.

The most typical intact example of a Srivijayan **temple** is the heavily restored Javanese-style chedi at Chaiya's Wat Phra Boromathat, with its highly ornamented, stepped chedi featuring mini-chedis at each corner.

Khmer and Lopburi (tenth to fourteenth centuries)

By the end of the ninth century the **Khmers** of Cambodia were starting to expand from their capital at Angkor into the Dvaravati states, bringing with them the Hindu faith and the cult of the god-king (*devaraja*). They built hundreds of imposing stone **sanctuaries** across their newly acquired territory, most notably within southern Isaan, at Phimai, Phanom Rung, and Khao Phra Viharn.

Each magnificent castle-temple – known in Khmer as a **prasat** – was constructed primarily as a shrine for a Shiva lingam, the phallic representation of the god Shiva. They followed a similar pattern, centred on at least one pyramidal or corn cob-shaped tower, or **prang**, which represented Mount Meru (the gods' heavenly abode) and housed the lingam. Prangs were surrounded by concentric rectangular **galleries**, whose **gopura** (entrance chambers) at the cardinal points were usually approached by staircases flanked with **naga balustrades**; in Khmer temples, nagas generally appear as symbolic bridges between the human world and that of the gods. Most compounds enclosed ponds between their outer and inner walls, and many were surrounded by a network of moats and **reservoirs**: historians attribute the Khmers' political success in part to their skill in designing highly efficient irrigation systems.

Exuberant **carvings** ornamented almost every surface of the prasat. Usually gouged from sandstone, but frequently moulded in stucco, they depict Hindu deities, incarnations and stories, especially episodes from the *Ramayana*. Towards the end of the twelfth century, the Khmer leadership became Mahayana Buddhist, commissioning Buddhist carvings to be installed alongside the Hindu ones, and replacing the Shiva lingam with a Buddha or *bodhisattva* image.

The temples built in the former Theravada Buddhist principality of **Lopburi** during the Khmer period are much smaller than those in Isaan; the triple-pranged temple of Phra Prang Sam Yot is typical. Broad-faced and muscular, the classic Lopburi-era Buddha **statue** wears a diadem or ornamental headband – a nod to the Khmers' ideological fusion of earthly and heavenly power – and the *ushnisha* (the sign of enlightenment) becomes distinctly conical rather than a mere bump on the head. Early Lopburi Buddhas also come garlanded with necklaces and ornamental belts. As you'd expect, Lopburi National Museum houses a good selection.

Sukhothai (thirteenth to fifteenth centuries)

Capitalizing on the Khmers' weakening hold over central Thailand, two Thai generals established the first real Thai kingdom in **Sukhothai** in 1238, and over the next two hundred years its citizens produced some of Thailand's most refined art. Sukhothai's artistic reputation rests above all on its **sculpture**. More sinuous even than the Srivijayan images, Sukhothai Buddhas tend towards elegant androgyny, with slim oval faces and slender curvaceous bodies usually clad in a plain, skintight robe that fastens with a tassel close to the navel. The sculptors favoured the seated pose, with hands in the *Bhumisparsa Mudra*, most expertly executed in the Phra Buddha Chinnarat image, now housed in Phitsanulok's Wat Si Ratana Mahathat (replicated at Bangkok's Wat Benjamabophit) and in the enormous Phra Sri Sakyamuni, now enshrined in Bangkok's Wat Suthat. They were also the first to represent the **walking Buddha**, a supremely graceful figure with his right leg poised to move forwards and his left arm in the *Vitarkha Mudra*, as seen at Sukhothai's Wat Sra Si.

Rather than pull down the sacred prangs of their predecessors, Sukhothai builders added bots, viharns and chedis to the existing structures, as well as conceiving quite separate **temple complexes**. Their viharns and bots are the earliest halls of worship still standing in Thailand (the Khmers didn't go in for large public assemblies), but in most cases only the stone pillars and their platforms remain, the wooden roofs having long since disintegrated. The best examples can be seen in the historical parks at Sukhothai, Si Satchanalai and Kamphaeng Phet.

Most of the **chedis** are in much better shape. Many were modelled on the Sri Lankan bell-shaped reliquary tower (symbolizing the Buddha's teachings ringing out far and wide), often set atop a one- or two-tiered square base surrounded by elephant buttresses; Si Satchanalai's Wat Chang Lom is a good example. The architects also devised the **lotus-bud chedi**, a slender tower topped with a tapered finial that was to become a hallmark of the Sukhothai era; in Sukhothai both Wat Mahathat and Wat Trapang Ngoen display classic examples.

Ancient Sukhothai is also renowned for the skill of its potters, who produced **ceramic ware** known as Sawankhalok, after the name of one of the nearby kiln towns. Most museum ceramics collections are dominated by Sawankhalok ware, which is distinguished by its grey-green celadon glazes and by the fish and chrysanthemum motifs used to decorate bowls and plates; there's a dedicated Sawankhalok museum in Sukhothai.

Lanna (thirteenth to sixteenth centuries)

Meanwhile, to the north of Sukhothai, the independent Theravada Buddhist kingdom of **Lanna** was flourishing. Its art styles – known interchangeably as **Chiang Saen** and Lanna – built on the Dvaravati heritage of Haripunjaya, copying direct from Indian sources and incorporating Sukhothai and Sri Lankan ideas from the south.

The earliest surviving Lanna **monument** is the Dvaravati-style Chedi Si Liam at Wiang Kum Kam near Chiang Mai, built to the pyramidal form characteristic of Mon builders. Also in Chiang Mai, Wat Jet Yot replicates the temple built at

Bodh Gaya in India to commemorate the seven sites where the Buddha meditated in the first seven weeks after attaining enlightenment.

Lanna **sculpture** also drew some inspiration from Bodh Gaya, echoing the plumpness of the Buddha image, and its broad shoulders and prominent hair curls. The later works are slimmer, probably as a result of Sukhothai influence, and one of the most famous examples of this type is the Phra Singh Buddha, enshrined in Chiang Mai's Wat Phra Singh. Other good illustrations of both styles are housed in Chiang Mai's National Museum.

Ayutthaya (fourteenth to eighteenth centuries)

From 1351 Thailand's central plains came under the thrall of a new power centred on **Ayutthaya** and ruled by a former prince of Lopburi. Over the next four centuries, the Ayutthayan capital became one of the most prosperous and ostentatious cities in Asia, its rulers commissioning some four hundred grand wats as symbols of their wealth and power. Though essentially Theravada Buddhists, the kings also adopted some Hindu and Brahmin beliefs from the Khmers – most significantly the concept of *devaraja* or god-kingship, whereby the monarch became a mediator between the people and the Hindu gods. The religious buildings and sculptures of this era reflected this new composite ideology, both by fusing the architectural styles inherited from the Khmers and from Sukhothai and by dressing their Buddhas to look like regents.

Retaining the concentric layout of the typical Khmer **temple complex**, Ayutthayan builders refined and elongated the prang into a **corncob-shaped tower**, rounding it off at the top and introducing vertical incisions around its circumference. As a spire they often added a bronze thunderbolt, and into niches within the prang walls they placed Buddha images. In Ayutthaya itself, the ruined complexes of Wat Phra Mahathat and Wat Ratburana both include these corncob prangs, but the most famous example is Bangkok's Wat Arun, which though built during the subsequent Bangkok period is a classic Ayutthayan structure.

Ayutthaya's architects also adapted the Sri Lankan **chedi** favoured by their Sukhothai predecessors, stretching the bell-shaped base and tapering it into a very graceful conical spire, as at Wat Phra Si Sanphet in Ayutthaya. The **viharns** of this era are characterized by walls pierced by slit-like windows, designed to foster a mysterious atmosphere by limiting the amount of light inside the building. As with all of Ayutthaya's buildings, few viharns survived the brutal 1767 sacking, with the notable exception of Wat Na Phra Mane. Phitsanulok's Wat Phra Si Ratana Mahathat was built to a similar plan – and in Phetchaburi, Wat Yai Suwannaram has no windows at all.

From Sukhothai's Buddha **sculptures** the Ayutthayans copied the soft oval face, adding an earthlier demeanour to the features and imbuing them with a hauteur in tune with the *devaraja* ideology. Early Ayutthayan statues wear crowns to associate kingship with Buddhahood; as the court became ever more lavish, so these figures became increasingly adorned, until – as in the monumental bronze at Wat Na Phra Mane – they appeared in earrings, armlets, anklets, bandoliers and coronets. The artists justified these luscious portraits of the Buddha – who was, after all, supposed to have given up worldly possessions – by pointing to an episode when the Buddha transformed himself into a well-dressed nobleman to gain the ear of a proud emperor, whereupon he scolded the man into entering the monkhood.

While a couple of wats in Sukhothai show hints of painted decoration, religious **painting** in Thailand really dates from the Ayutthayan era. Unfortunately most of

Ayutthaya's own paintings were destroyed in 1767, but several temples elsewhere have well-preserved murals, in particular Wat Yai Suwannaram in Phetchaburi. By all accounts typical of late seventeenth-century painting, Phetchaburi's murals depict rows of *thep*, or divinities, paying homage to the Buddha, in scenes presented without shadow or perspective, and mainly executed in dark reds and cream.

Ratanakosin (eighteenth century to the 1930s)

When **Bangkok** emerged as Ayutthaya's successor in 1782, the new capital's founder was determined to revive the old city's grandeur, and the **Ratanakosin** (or Bangkok) period began by aping what the Ayutthayans had done. Since then neither wat architecture nor religious sculpture has evolved much further.

The first Ratanakosin **building** was the bot of Bangkok's Wat Phra Kaeo, built to enshrine the Emerald Buddha. Designed to a typical Ayutthayan plan, it's coated in glittering mirrors and gold leaf, with roofs ranged in multiple tiers and tiled in green and orange. To this day, most newly built bots and viharns follow a more economical version of this paradigm, whitewashing the outside walls but decorating the pediment in gilded ornaments and mosaics of coloured glass. Tiered temple roofs still taper off into the slender bird-like finials called *chofa*, and naga staircases – a Khmer feature inherited by Ayutthaya – have become almost obligatory. The result is that modern wats are often almost indistinguishable from each other, though Bangkok does have a few exceptions, including Wat Benjamabophit, which uses marble cladding for its walls and incorporates Victorian-style stained-glass windows, and Wat Rajabophit, which is covered all over in Chinese ceramics. The most dramatic chedi of the Ratanokosin era – one of the tallest in the world – was constructed in the mid-nineteenth century in Nakhon Pathom to the original Sri Lankan style, but minus the elephant buttresses found in Sukhothai.

Early Ratanakosin sculptors produced adorned **Buddha images** very much in the Ayutthayan vein. The obsession with size, first apparent in the Sukhothai period, has since plumbed new depths, with graceless concrete statues up to 60m high becoming the norm, often painted brown or a dull yellow. Most small images are cast from or patterned on older models, mostly Sukhothai or Ayutthayan in origin.

Painting has fared much better, with the *Ramayana* murals in Bangkok's Wat Phra Kaeo a shining example of how Ayutthayan techniques and traditional subject matters could be adapted into something fantastic, imaginative and beautiful.

Contemporary

Following the democratization of Thailand in the 1930s, artists increasingly became recognized as individuals, and took to signing their work for the first time. In 1933 the first school of fine art (now Bangkok's Silpakorn University) was established under the Italian sculptor **Corrado Feroci** (later Silpa Bhirasri), designer of the capital's Democracy Monument and, as the new generation experimented with secular themes and styles adapted from the West, Thai art began to look a lot more "**modern**". As for subject matter, the leading artistic preoccupation of the past eighty years has been Thailand's spiritual heritage and its role in contemporary society. Since 1985, a number of Thailand's more established contemporary artists have earned the title **National Artist**, an honour that's bestowed annually on notable artists working in all disciplines, including fine art, performing arts, film and literature.

Art galleries and exhibitions

Bangkok has a near-monopoly on Thailand's **art galleries**. While the permanent collections at the capital's National Gallery (Ⓦwww.thailandmuseum.com; see p.143) are disappointing, regular exhibitions of more challenging contemporary work appear at the huge, ambitious **Bangkok Art and Cultural Centre** (Ⓦwww.bacc.or.th; see p.164); the main art school, Silpakorn University Art Centre (Ⓦwww.art-centre.su.ac.th; see p.144); the Queen's Gallery (Ⓦwww.queengallery.org; see p.149); and at smaller gallery spaces around the city. The excellent monthly *Bangkok Art Map* (Ⓦbangkokartmap.com), an annotated map of the capital's galleries, carries exhibition listings and is available free from galleries. Large-scale art museums in the provinces include the Art and Cultural Centre, part of Silpakorn University's secondary campus in Nakhon Pathom (see p.219), and Chiang Mai University Art Museum (see p.339). For a preview of works by Thailand's best modern artists, visit the virtual Rama IX Art Museum at Ⓦwww.rama9art.org.

One of the first modern artists to adapt traditional styles and themes was **Angkarn Kalayanapongsa** (b. 1926), an early recipient of the title National Artist. He has been employed as a temple muralist and many of his paintings, some of which are on show in Bangkok's National Gallery, reflect this experience, typically featuring casts of two-dimensional Ayutthayan-style figures and flying *thep* in a surreal setting laced with Buddhist symbols and nods to contemporary culture.

Taking this fusion a step further, one-time cinema billboard artist **Chalermchai Kositpipat** (b. 1955) specializes in temple murals with a modern, controversial, twist. Outside Thailand his most famous work enlivens the interior walls of London's Wat Buddhapadipa with strong colours and startling imagery. At home his latest project is the unconventional and highly ornate all-white Wat Rong Khun in his native Chiang Rai province (see p.410).

Aiming for the more secular environments of the gallery and the private home, National Artist **Pichai Nirand** (b. 1936) rejects the traditional mural style and makes more selective choices of Buddhist imagery, appropriating religious objects and icons and reinterpreting their significance. He's particularly well known for his fine-detail canvases of Buddha footprints, many of which can be seen in Bangkok galleries and public spaces.

Pratuang Emjaroen (b. 1935) is famous for his social commentary, as epitomized by his huge and powerful canvas *Dharma and Adharma; The Days of Disaster*, which he painted in response to the vicious clashes between the military and students in 1973. The 5m x 2m picture depicts severed limbs, screaming faces and bloody gun barrels amid shadowy images of the Buddha's face, a spiked *dharmachakra* and other religious symbols. Many of Pratuang's subsequent works have addressed the issue of social injustice, using his trademark strong shafts of light and bold colour in a mix of Buddhist iconography and abstract imagery.

Prolific traditionalist **Chakrabhand Posayakrit** (b. 1943) is also inspired by Thailand's Buddhist culture; he is famously proud of his country's cultural heritage, which infuses much of his work and has led to him being honoured as a National Artist. He is best known for his series of 33 *Life of the Buddha* paintings, and for his portraits, including many of members of the Thai royal family.

More controversial, and more of a household name, **Thawan Duchanee** (b. 1939) has tended to examine the spiritual tensions of modern life. His surreal juxtaposition of religious icons with fantastical Bosch-like characters and explicitly sexual images prompted a group of outraged students to slash ten of his early paintings in 1971 – an unprecedented reaction to a work of Thai art. Since then, Thawan has continued to produce allegorical investigations into the individual's struggles against the obstacles that dog the Middle Way, prominent among them lust and violence, but since the 1980s his street cred has waned as his saleability has mushroomed. Critics have questioned his integrity at accepting commissions from corporate clients, and his neo-conservative image cannot have been enhanced when he was honoured as a National Artist in 2001.

Complacency is not a criticism that could be levelled at **Vasan Sitthiket** (b. 1957), Thailand's most outspoken and iconoclastic artist, whose uncompromising pictures are shown at – and still occasionally banned from – large and small galleries around the capital. A persistent crusader against the hypocrisies of establishment figures such as monks, politicians, CEOs and military leaders, Vasan's is one of the loudest and most aggressive political voices on the contemporary art scene, expressed on canvas, in multimedia works and in performance art. His significance is well established and he was one of the seven artists to represent Thailand at the 2003 Venice Biennale, where Thailand had its own pavilion for the first time.

Equally confrontational is fellow Biennale exhibitor, the photographer, performance artist and social activist **Manit Sriwanichpoom** (b. 1961). Manit is best known for his "Pink Man" series of photographs in which he places a Thai man (his collaborator Sompong Thawee), dressed in a flashy pink suit and pushing a pink shopping trolley, into different scenes and situations in Thailand and elsewhere. The Pink Man represents thoughtless, dangerous consumerism and his backdrop might be an impoverished hill-tribe village (*Pink Man on Tour*, 1998), or black-and-white shots from the political violence of 1973, 1976 and 1992 (*Horror in Pink*; 2001).

Women artists tend to be less high profile in Thailand, but in 2007 **Pinaree Sanpitak** (b. 1961) became the first female recipient of the annual Silpathorn Awards for established artists, sharing the honour that year with, among others, notorious bad-boy Vasan Sitthiket. Pinaree is known for her interest in gender issues and for her recurrent use of a female iconography in the form of vessels and mounds, often exploring the overlap with Buddhist stupa imagery. She works mainly in multimedia; her "Vessels and Mounds" show of 2001, for example, featured installations of huge, breast-shaped floor cushions, candles and bowls.

Among the younger faces on the Thai art scene, **Thaweesak Srithongdee** (b. 1970) blends surrealism and pop culture with the erotic and the figurative, to cartoonlike effect. He is preoccupied with popular culture, as is **Jirapat Tatsanasomboon** (b. 1971), whose work plays around with superheroes and cultural icons from East and West, pitting the *Ramayana*'s monkey king, Hanuman, against Spiderman in *Hanuman vs Spiderman*, and fusing mythologies in *The Transformation of Sita (after Botticelli)*.

Flora, fauna and environmental issues

Spanning some 1650km north to south, Thailand lies in the heart of Southeast Asia's tropical zone, its northernmost region just a few degrees south of the Tropic of Cancer, its southern border running less than seven degrees north of the Equator. As with other tropical regions, Thailand's climate is characterized by high humidity and even higher temperatures, a fertile combination which nourishes a huge diversity of flora and fauna in a vast range of habitats, from mixed deciduous and dry dipterocarp forests in the mountainous north to wet tropical rainforests in the steamy south. At least six percent of the world's vascular plants are found here, with over 15,000 species so far recorded.

The best places to appreciate Thailand's biodiversity are its national parks, the most accessible of which include Khao Yai in the northeast, Doi Inthanon and Doi Suthep in the north, and Khao Sam Roi Yot, Khao Sok and Ko Tarutao in the south. General practical information on national parks is given in Basics on p.74.

The geography of Thailand

Thailand has a **tropical monsoon climate**. Most rain is brought from the Indian Ocean by the southwest monsoon from May to October, the so-called rainy season. From November to February the northeast monsoon brings a much cooler and drier climate from China: the cold, dry season. However, this northeastern monsoon hits the peninsular east coast after crossing the South China Sea, loading up with moist air and therefore extending this region's rainy season until January or later. The north–south divide is generally considered to lie just north of Ranong (10°N) – the capital of Thailand's wettest province – at the Kra Isthmus.

Agriculture plays a significant role in Thailand's economy, and some forty percent of Thais live off the land or the sea. Waterlogged rice paddies characterize the central plains; cassava, tapioca and eucalyptus are grown as cash crops on the scrubby plateau of the northeast; and rubber and palm-oil plantations dominate the commercial land-use of the south. Dotted along Thailand's coastline are mangrove swamps and palm forests.

Mixed deciduous and dry dipterocarp forests

An estimated 65 percent of Thailand's forests are **deciduous**, sometimes referred to as monsoon forest because they have to survive periods of up to six months with minimal rainfall, so the trees shed their leaves to conserve water. Deciduous forests are often light and open, with canopies of 10–40m and dense undergrowth. They are dominated by trees of the **Dipterocarpaceae** family, a group of tropical hardwoods prized for their timber and, in places, their resin. **Teak** was also once common in northern deciduous forests, but its solid, unwarpable timber is so sought after that nearly all the teak forests have been felled. Since teak trees take around two hundred years to mature, logging them was banned in Thailand in 1989 and these days most of Thailand's teak comes in from Burma.

Bamboo thrives in a monsoon climate, shooting up at a remarkable rate during the wet season, often in soils too poor for other species; it often predominates in secondary forests, where logging or clearing has previously taken place. The smooth, hollow stem characteristic of all varieties of bamboo is a fantastically adaptable material, used by the Thais for constructing everything from outside walls to chairs to water pipes (in hill-tribe villages) and musical instruments; and the bamboo shoot is common in Thai-Chinese cuisine.

Tropical rainforests

Thailand's **tropical rainforests** occur in areas of high and prolonged rainfall in the southern peninsula, most accessibly in the national parks of Khao Sok, Tarutao and Khao Luang. Some areas contain as many as two hundred species of tree within a single hectare. Characteristic of a tropical rainforest is the multi-layered series of **canopies**. The uppermost storey sometimes reaches 60m, and these towering trees often have enormous buttressed roots for support; beneath this, the dense canopy of 25–35m is often festooned with climbers and epiphytes such as ferns, lianas, mosses and orchids; then comes an uneven layer 5–10m high consisting of palms, rattans, shrubs and small trees. The forest floor in tropical rainforests tends to be relatively open and free of dense undergrowth, owing to the intense filtering of light by the upper three layers. Again, members of the *Dipterocarpaceae* family are dominant, playing an important role as nesting sites for hornbills, as lookout posts for gibbons – and as timber.

Semi-evergreen and montane forests

Semi-evergreen forests are the halfway house between tropical rainforests and dry deciduous forests and include all lowland and submontane evergreen forests from the plains to about 1000m. They thrive in regions with distinctly seasonal rainfall and fine examples can be found at Khao Yai and Kaeng Krachan national parks, and all along the Burmese border, all of which are potentially good places to observe large mammals, including elephants, gaurs, tigers and bears.

Above 1000m, the canopy of tall trees gives way to hardy **evergreen montane forest** growth such as oaks, chestnuts and laurels, many with twisted trunks and comparatively small leaves. Frequent rainfall means plenty of moss and a dense undergrowth of epiphytes, rhododendrons and tree ferns. Good examples can be seen in Doi Inthanon and Phu Kradung national parks, and in parts of Doi Suthep and Khao Yai national parks.

Mangrove swamps and coastal forests

Mangrove swamps are an important habitat for a wide variety of marine life (including 204 species of bird, 74 species of fish and 54 types of crab) but, as with much of Thailand's inland forest, they have been significantly degraded by encroachment and large-scale prawn farming. Huge swathes of Thailand's littoral used to be fringed with mangrove swamps, but now they are mainly found only along the west peninsular coast, between Ranong and Satun, though Chanthaburi's Ao Khung Kraben is a notable east-coast exception. On Phuket, the Thachatchai Nature Trail leads you on a guided tour through a patch of mangrove swamp, but an even better way of **exploring the swamps** is to paddle a kayak through the mangrove-clogged inlets and island-lagoons of Ao Phang Nga. Not only do mangrove swamps harbour a rich and important ecosystem of their own, but they also help prevent coastal erosion; in certain areas of the tsunami-hit Andaman coast intact mangrove forest absorbed some of the waves' impact, protecting land and homes from even worse damage.

Nipa palms share the mangrove's penchant for brackish water, and these stubby-stemmed palm trees grow in abundance in the south, though commercial plantations are now replacing the natural colonies. Like most other species of palm indigenous to Thailand, the nipa is a versatile plant that's exploited to the full: alcohol is distilled from its sugary sap, and its fronds are woven into roofs (especially for beach huts and village homes), sticky-rice baskets and chair-backs.

The hardy **coconut palm** is also very tolerant of salty, sandy soil, and is equally useful. On islands such as Ko Kood, it's the backbone of the local economy, with millions of coconuts harvested every month for their milk, their oil-producing meat (copra), and their fibrous husks or coir (used for making ropes, matting, brushes and mattress stuffing); the palm fronds are woven into roof thatching and baskets, and the wood has an attractive grain.

Casuarinas (also known as she-oaks or ironwoods) also flourish in sandy soils and are common on beaches throughout Thailand; fast-growing and tall (up to 20m), they are quite often planted as wind breaks. Though its feathery profile makes it look like a pine, it's actually made up of tiny twigs, not needles.

The wildlife

Thailand lies in an exceptionally rich "transition zone" of the Indo-Malayan realm, its forests, mountains and national parks attracting wildlife from both Indochina and Indonesia. In all, Thailand is home to three hundred species of mammal (36 of which are considered to be endangered) and 971 species of bird (42 of them endangered).

Mammals

In the major national parks such as Khao Yai, Doi Inthanon and Khao Sok, the animals you're most likely to encounter are **primates**, particularly macaques and gibbons. The latter spend much of their time foraging for food in the forest canopy, while the former often descend closer to the ground to rest and to socialize.

The gibbons are responsible for the distinctive hooting that echoes through the forests. Chief noise-maker is the **white-handed** or **lar gibbon**, a beige- or black-bodied, white-faced animal whose cute appearance, intelligence and dexterity unfortunately make it a popular pet. The poaching and maltreatment of lar gibbons has become so severe that several organizations are now dedicated to protecting them (see box, p.833).

Similarly chatty, macaques hang out in gangs of twenty or more. The **long-tailed** or **crab-eating macaque** lives in the lowlands, near rivers, lakes and coasts as at Ao Phang Nga, Krabi, Ko Tarutao, Ang Thong and Khao Sam Roi Yot. It eats not only crabs, but mussels, other small animals and fruit, transporting and storing food in its big cheek pouch when swimming and diving. The **pig-tailed macaque**, named after its short curly tail, excels at scaling the tall trees of Erawan, Khao Yai, Doi Inthanon and other national parks, a skill which has resulted in many of the males being captured and trained to pick coconuts.

Much more elusive is the **Indochinese tiger**, which lives under constant threat from both poachers and the destruction of its habitat by logging interests, which together have reduced the current population to probably fewer than one hundred; for now Khao Yai and Khao Sok are the two likeliest places for sightings. The medium-sized arboreal **clouded leopard** is also on the endangered list, and is hard to spot anyway as it only comes out to feed on birds and monkeys under cover of darkness, rarely venturing out in moonlight let alone daylight.

The shy, nocturnal **tapir**, an ungulate with three-toed hind legs and four-toed front ones, lives deep in the forest of peninsular Thailand but is occasionally spotted in daylight. A relative of both the horse and the rhino, it's the size of a pony, with a stubby trunk-like snout and distinctive two-tone colouring to confuse predators: its front half and all four legs are black, its rear half is white.

It's thought there are now as few as two thousand wild **elephants** left in Thailand: small-eared Asian elephants found mainly in Khao Yai and Khao Sok (see box, p.366).

Birds

Because of its location at the zoogeographical crossroads of Southeast Asia, Thailand boasts a huge diversity of **bird** species. The forests of continental Thailand are home to many of the same birds that inhabit India, Burma and Indochina, while the mountains of the north share species with the Himalayas and Tibet, and the peninsular forests are home to birds found also in Malaysia and Indonesia. Khao Yai and Khao Nor Chuchi are prime year-round sites for bird-spotting, and, during the dry season, Doi Inthanon is a good place for flycatchers and warblers, and Khao Sam Roi Yot and Thale Noi Waterbird Park are rewarding areas to see migrant waders and waterfowl. For exhaustive information on specific **birdwatching** locations throughout Thailand see ⓦwww.thaibirding.com; for guided birding tours contact Thailand Bird Watching (ⓦwww.thailandbirdwatching.com) and for birdwatching guidebooks see p.858.

There are twelve species of **hornbill** in Thailand, all majestic with massive, powerful wings (the flapping of which can be heard for long distances) and huge beaks surmounted by bizarre horny casques. Khao Yai is one of the easiest place to spot the plain black-and-white **oriental pied hornbill** and the flashier **great hornbill**, whose monochromic body and head are broken up with jaunty splashes of yellow; the little islands of Ko Phayam and Ko Chang in Ranong province also have many resident oriental pied hornbills.

The shyness of the gorgeous **pitta** makes a sighting all the more rewarding. Usually seen hopping around on the floor of evergreen forests, especially in Doi Inthanon, Doi Suthep and Khao Yai, these plump little birds – varieties of which include the **rusty-naped**, the **blue** and the **eared** – have dazzling markings in iridescent reds, yellows, blues and blacks. The one pitta you might see outside a rainforest is the **blue-winged** pitta, which occasionally migrates to drier bamboo forests. Thailand is also home to the extremely rare **Gurney's pitta**, found only in Khlong Thom National Park, in Krabi province.

Members of the pheasant family can be just as shy as the pittas, and are similarly striking. The black-and-white-chevron-marked **silver pheasant**, and the **green peafowl** are particularly fine birds, and the commonly seen **red jungle fowl** is the ancestor to all domestic chickens.

Thailand's **rice fields** attract a host of different birds including the various species of **munia**, a chubby relative of the finch, whose chunky, conical beak is ideally suited to cracking unripened rice seeds. **Egrets** and **herons** also frequent the fields, wading through the waterlogged furrows or perching on the backs of water buffaloes and pecking at cattle insects, while from November to April, thousands of **Asian open-billed storks** descend on agricultural land as well, building nests in sugar-palm trees and bamboos and feeding on pira snails.

Coastal areas also attract storks, egrets and herons, and Thale Noi Waterbird Park and the mud flats of Khao Sam Roi Yot are breeding grounds for the large, long-necked **purple heron**. The magnificent **white-bellied sea eagle** haunts the Thai coast, nesting in the forbidding crags around Krabi, Ao Phang Nga and Ko Tarutao and preying on fish and sea snakes. The tiny **edible nest swiftlet**

The gecko

Whether you're staying on a beach, in a national park or in a town, chances are you'll be sharing your room with a few **geckos**. These pale green tropical lizards, which are harmless to humans and usually measure a cute four to ten centimetres in length, mostly appear at night, high up on walls and ceilings, where they feed on insects. Because the undersides of their flat toes are covered with hundreds of microscopic hairs that catch at the tiniest of irregularities, geckos are able to scale almost any surface, including glass, which is why you usually see them in strange, gravity-defying positions. The largest and most vociferous gecko is known as the **tokay** in Thai, named after the disconcertingly loud sound it makes. *Tokays* can grow to an alarming 35cm, but are welcomed by most householders, as they devour insects and mice; Thais also consider it auspicious if a baby is born within earshot of a crowing *tokay*.

makes its eponymous nest – the major ingredient of the luxury food, bird's-nest soup – in the limestone crags, too; for more on these swiftlets and their nests see the box on p.746.

Snakes

Thailand is home to around 175 different species and subspecies of **snake**, 56 of them dangerously venomous. Death by snakebite is not common, however, but all hospitals should keep a stock of serum, produced at the Snake Farm in Bangkok (see p.167).

Found everywhere and highly venomous, the two-metre, nocturnal, yellow-and-black-striped **banded krait** is one to avoid, as is the shorter but equally poisonous **Thai** or **monocled cobra**, which lurks in low-lying humid areas and close to human habitation and sports a distinctive "eye" mark on its hood. The other most widespread poisonous snake is the sixty-centimetre **Malayan pit viper**, which has an unnerving ability to camouflage its pinky-brown and black-marked body. Non-venomous, but typically measuring an amazing 7.5m (maximum 10m) and with a top weight of 140kg, the **reticulated python** frequents human habitation all over Thailand and feeds on rats, pigs, cats and dogs, strangling them to death; it will do the same to humans if provoked.

Marine species

The Indian Ocean (Andaman Sea) and the South China Sea (Gulf of Thailand) together play host to over 850 species of open-water fish, more than one hundred species of reef fish and some 250 species of hard coral. Forty percent of Thailand's coral reef is protected within **national marine parks**, and these offer the best snorkelling and diving, particularly around Ko Similan, Ko Surin and Ko Tarutao (see p.73).

Coral reefs are living organisms composed of a huge variety of marine life forms, but the foundation of every reef is its ostensibly inanimate **stony coral** – hard constructions such as boulder, mushroom, bushy staghorn and brain coral. Stony coral is composed of colonies of polyps – minuscule invertebrates which feed on plankton, depend on algae and direct sunlight for photosynthesis, and extract calcium carbonate (limestone) from sea water in order to reproduce. The polyps use this calcium carbonate to build new skeletons outside their bodies (an asexual reproductive process known as budding) and this is how a reef is formed. It's an extraordinarily slow process, with colony growth averaging somewhere between 5mm and 30mm a year.

The fleshy plant-like **soft coral**, such as dead man's fingers and elephant's ear, generally establishes itself on and around these banks of stony coral, swaying with the currents and using tentacles to trap micro organisms. Soft coral is also composed of polyps, but a variety with flaccid internal skeletons built from protein rather than calcium. **Horny coral**, like sea whips and intricate sea fans, looks like a cross between the stony and the soft varieties, while **sea anemones** have the most obvious, and poisonous, tentacles of any member of the coral family, using them to trap fish and other large prey.

The algae and plankton that accumulate around coral colonies attract a huge variety of **reef fish**. Most are small in stature, with vibrant colours that serve as camouflage against the coral, and flattened bodies and broad tails for easy manoeuvring around the reef.

Among the most easily recognizable is the **emperor angel fish**, which boasts spectacular horizontal stripes in bright blue and orange, and an orange tail. The bizarrely shaped **moorish idol** trails a pennant fin from its dorsal fin and has a pronounced snout and dramatic black, yellow and white bands of colour; the ovoid **powder-blue surgeon fish** has a light blue body, a bright yellow dorsal fin and a white "chinstrap". The commonly spotted **long-nosed butterfly fish** is named for the butterfly-like movements of its yellow-banded silver body as it darts in and out of crevices looking for food. The bright orange **clown fish**, whose thick white stripes make it resemble a clown's ruff, is more properly known as the anemone fish because of its mutually protective relationship with the sea anemone, near which it can usually be sighted.

Some reef fish, among them the ubiquitous turquoise and purple **parrot fish**, eat coral. With the help of a bird-like beak, which is in fact several teeth fused together, the parrot fish scrapes away at the coral and then grinds the fragments down with another set of back teeth – a practice reputedly responsible for the erosion of a great deal of Thailand's reef. The magnificent mauve and burgundy **crown-of-thorns starfish**, named for its "arms" covered in highly venomous spines, also feeds on coral, laying waste to as much as fifty square centimetres of stony coral in a 24-hour period.

Larger, less frequent visitors to Thailand's offshore reefs include the **moray eel**, whose elongated jaws of viciously pointed teeth make it a deadly predator, and the similarly equipped **barracuda**, the world's fastest-swimming fish. **Sharks** are quite common off the reefs, where it's also sometimes possible to swim with a **manta ray**, whose extraordinary flatness, strange wing-like fins and massive size – up to 6m across and weighing some 1600kg – make it an astonishing presence. **Turtles** sometimes paddle around reef waters, too, but all four local species – leatherback, Olive Ridley, green and hawksbill – are fast becoming endangered in Thailand.

Environmental issues

Thailand's rapid economic growth has had a significant effect on its environment. Huge new infrastructure projects, an explosion in real-estate developments and the constantly expanding tourist industry have all played a part, and the effects of the subsequent **deforestation** and pollution have been felt nationwide. Such was the devastation caused by floods and mud slides in Surat Thani in 1988 that the government banned commercial logging the following year, though land continues to be denuded for other purposes. There is also the endemic problem of "influence" so that when a big shot wants to clear a previously pristine area for a new property development, for example, it is virtually impossible for a lowly provincial civil servant to reject their plan, or money. Thailand lost nine percent of its forest cover between 1990 and 2005 (2005 figures show just over 28 percent of Thailand's total land area as forested).

Flooding has always been a feature of the Thai environment, crucial to the fertility of its soil, and its worst effects are obviated by the stilted design of the traditional Thai house. In recent times, however, far more dangerous **flash floods** have recurred with depressing frequency, most dramatically around the northern town of Pai in 2005, where many homes and guest houses were washed away, and along the Mekong River in 2008. More mundanely there is now an almost annual inundation in certain riverside town centres, and of roads and railways, particularly along the Gulf coast. The link between deforestation and flash floods is disputed, though encroaching cement and tarmac on Thai flood plains surely play a part, as does the clogging of exit channels by garbage and other pollutants, and of course climate change.

Reefs and shorelines

A number of Thailand's **coral reefs** – some of which are thought to be around 450 million years old – are being destroyed by factors attributable to tourism, most significantly the pollution generated by coastal hotels with inadequate sewage systems. Longtail boats that anchor on reefs, souvenirs made from coral, and the use of harpoon guns by irresponsible dive leaders all have a cumulative effect, dwarfed however by the local practice of using dynamite to gather fish, including reef fish for sale to aquariums.

The 2004 **tsunami** also caused significant damage to coastal and marine environments the length of the Andaman coast. Reefs close to shore were crushed by debris (furniture, machinery, even cars) and buried under displaced soil; the sea was temporarily polluted by extensive damage to sewage systems; and tracts of shorefront farmland were rendered unusable by salt water.

National parks

Although Thailand has since the 1970s been protecting some of its natural resources within **national parks**, these have long been caught between commercial and conservationist aims, an issue which the government addressed in 2002 by establishing a new National Park, Wildlife and Plant Conservation Department (DNP; www.dnp.go.th), separate from the Royal Forestry Department and its parent Ministry of Agriculture.

With 103 national parks across the country, plus 26 national marine parks, as well as various other protected zones, over thirteen percent of the country is now, in theory at least, protected from encroachment and hunting (a high proportion compared to other nations, such as Japan at 6.5 percent, and the US at 10.5 percent).

However, the **touristification** of certain national parks endures; Ko Phi Phi and Ko Samet in particular have both suffered irreversible environmental damage as a direct result of the number of overnight visitors they receive. While most people understand that the role of the national parks is to conserve vulnerable and precious resources, the dramatic hike in entrance fees payable by foreigner visitors to national parks – from B20 up to B200 in 2000 and up again to B400 for a few special parks – was greeted with cynicism and anger, not least because there is often little sign of anything tangible being done on site with the money.

Elephant trekking and the wildlife trade

espite the efforts of local and international conservation and wildlife-protec-
on organizations, **animal rights** issues often meet with a confused response

Wildlife charities and volunteer projects

The Golden Triangle Asian Elephant Foundation *Anantara Resort and Spa*, Sop Ruak ⓦwww.helpingelephants.org. Elephant welfare is the primary concern at the well-regarded Anantara Elephant Camp, which offers elephant treks and mahout courses. Profits support the foundation's baby elephant rescue centre. See p.418.

Elephant Nature Park Near Chiang Mai ⓦwww.elephantnaturefoundation.org. Famous conservation-education centre and sanctuary for elephants that's open to pre-booked visitors, overnight guests and volunteers. See p.401.

Gibbon Rehabilitation Project Phuket ⓦwww.gibbonproject.org. Resocializes abused pet gibbons before releasing them back into the forests. Visitors and volunteers welcome. See p.707.

Highland Farm Gibbon Sanctuary Near Mae Sot ⓦwww.highland-farm.org. Day-trippers and home-stay guests are welcome at this haven caring for over forty injured and abandoned gibbons. One-month placements are also possible. See p.302.

Wild Animal Rescue Foundation of Thailand (WAR) ⓦwww.warthai.org. A campaigning organization that runs animal rescue sanctuaries, hospitals and research centres in various locations across Thailand and is open to unskilled paying volunteers.

in Thailand. The muddled thinking behind the launch of the Chiang Mai Night Safari park was typical: not only was this commercial animal park erected on land appropriated from a national park, but early publicity trumpeted the fact that meat from many of the exotic animals kept in the park – including tigers, lions and elephants – would be available in the park's restaurant. Negative comment soon quashed that, but exotic meats from endangered animals are served, albeit clandestinely, all over Thailand.

Some of Thailand's many **zoos**, such as those in Bangkok and Chiang Mai, are legitimate, reasonably decent places, but a number of the country's other private wildlife theme parks and zoos – especially those majoring in tigers and crocodiles – have more dubious purposes and some have been targeted by international animal welfare organizations such as Born Free.

There is also increasing concern about the **ethics of elephant trekking**, a fast-growing and lucrative arm of the tourist industry that some consider has got out of hand. What began as a canny way for elephants to earn their (very expensive) keep after the 1989 ban on logging rendered most working elephants unemployed is now endangering Southeast Asia's dwindling population of wild elephants as more and more are captured for the trekking trade (see also p.366). Burmese elephants are particularly vulnerable and reportedly get smuggled across the border in significant numbers. In addition, welfare standards at these elephant trekking centres vary enormously. On the positive front, there's an increasing number of **animal sanctuaries** working to look after abused and endangered animals, especially elephants and gibbons (see box above), which operate both as safe havens and as educational visitor attractions.

The wildlife trade

Though Thailand signed the Convention on the International Trade in Endangered Species – **CITES** – in 1983, and hosted the annual CITES conference in 2004, the business of imported animals and animal products continues.

Most of the trade in **endangered species** is focused along the borders with Cambodia and Burma, where Thai middle-merchants can apparently easily acquire any number of creatures. Some will be sold as pets and to zoos, while others are destined for dining tables and medicine cabinets. **Tiger** body-parts are especially lucrative and mostly end up on the black markets of China, Korea, Taiwan and Hong Kong, where bones, skin, teeth, whiskers and penis are prized for their "medicinal" properties; it's thought that much of Thailand's dwindling tiger population ends up this way. **Bear** paws and gall bladders are considered to have similar potency and are a star feature, along with other endangered species, at certain clandestine restaurants in Thailand catering to "gourmet" tourists from China and Korea; the traditional custom of slicing paws off a living bear and enhancing gall-bladder flavour by taking it from an animal that is literally scared to death make this practice particularly vile. The Burmese border market at Thachileik near Mae Sai is a notorious outlet for tiger and bear body-parts, while Chatuchak Weekend Market in Bangkok has long had a thriving trade in live animals – everything from hornbills to slow loris – despite occasional crackdowns.

Music

Music is an important part of Thai culture, whether related to Buddhist activities in the local temple (still a focal point for many communities), animist rituals, Brahmanic ceremonies or the wide range of popular song styles. While local forms of Thai popular music such as *luk thung* and *mor lam* remain very popular and distinctively Thai in character, a lively, ever-changing rock, indie, DJ/clubbing and underground scene is also fast developing.

The classical tradition

Thai classical dance and music can be traced back to stone engravings from the Sukhothai period (thirteenth to fifteenth centuries), which show ensembles of musicians playing traditional instruments, called **phipat**. The *phipat* ensembles include many percussion instruments, rather like Indonesian gamelan – gong circles, xylophones and drums – plus a raucous oboe called the *phinai*. The music was developed to accompany classical dance-drama (*khon* or *lakhon*) or shadow-puppet theatre (*nang*): a shadow-puppet show is depicted in the magnificent *Ramayana* murals at Wat Phra Kaeo in Bangkok's Grand Palace complex.

Phipat music sounds strange to Western ears as the seven equal notes of the Thai scale fall between the cracks of the piano keyboard. But heard in the right environment – in a temple, at a dance performance or at a Thai boxing match – it can be entrancing. As there is no notation, everything is memorized. And, as in all Thai music, elements have been assimilated over the years from diverse sources, and synthesized into something new. Check out any of the international albums by the Prasit Thawon Ensemble (Thawon was a National Artist).

Despite the country's rapid Westernization, Thai classical music has been undergoing something of a revival in the past few years, partly as a result of royal patronage. There have been recent experiments, too, at blending Thai classical and Western styles – often jazz or rock – led by groups like **Kangsadan** and **Fong Naam**. **Boy Thai** followed their lead, albeit with a more pop-oriented sound, and have had some mainstream success with two albums. The two *ranat* (xylophone) playing brothers from Boy Thai, Chaiyoot and Narongrit Tosa-ngan have their own bands now: Chaiyoot with his huge **Bangkok Xylophone Orchestra** and Narongrit as **Khun-In and Off-Beat Siam**. The 2004 biopic *Homrong* (*The Overture*) features a character called Khun-In (played by Narongrit) who duels on the *ranat* against Thailand's greatest classical musician Luang Pradit Pairoh.

There are dance and classical music **performances** in Bangkok at the Sala Chalermkrung Theatre and the Thailand Cultural Centre (see p.191), and you may also come across some more lacklustre examples at the Erawan Shrine on Thanon Rama I and the *lak muang* shrine behind the Grand Palace, where people give thanks to deities by paying for the temple musicians and dancers to go through a routine. A number of Bangkok restaurants also feature music and dance shows for tourists, including regular shows by Bruce Gaston of Fong Naam at the *Tawandang German Brewery* (see p.189), and **Duriyapraneet**, the latter being the country's longest-established classical band.

Folk music

Thailand's folk music is called **pleng pheun bahn**, and different styles are found in the country's four distinct regions (central, north, northeast and south). Despite Thailand's rush to modernity, numerous folk styles are still enthusiastically played, from the hill-tribe New Year dances in the far north to the *saw* vocals and *fon lep* (fingernail dance) of Chiang Mai, from the all-night singing jousts of northeastern *lam glawn*, to the haunting Muslim vocals of *likay wolou* in the deep south.

Most Thais are familiar with the exciting central folk styles like *lam tad*, *pleng choi* and *pleng I-saw*, which often feature raunchy verbal jousting between male and female singers. Styles like these and the ever-popular *mor lam* from the northeast (see p.840) are incorporated into modern popular styles such as *luk thung* (see p.838).

One notable folk style to have grown in popularity in recent years is the up-tempo and danceable northeastern instrumental style known as **bong lang** (a wooden xylophone that is attached vertically to a tree and was originally used to keep birds off crops). *Bong lang* is ancient, predating Indian-Thai culture, and was updated by National Artist Pleung Chairaasamee in the 1970s. A few years ago, **Pong-Lang Sa-Orn** emerged with an action-packed comedy show that propelled the band to national fame, million-selling albums and movies.

The best place to see *bong lang* is upcountry, especially in Kalasin province in central Isaan in the dry season between November and March. Folk music also features prominently at the major festivals (see p.65) held in the northeastern cities of Khon Kaen, Ubon Ratchathani and Udon Thani, particularly during Songkhran (April), the Bun Bang Fai rocket festival (May), and the Asanha Puja candle festival (July). Generally, any national holiday or religious festival is a good time to look out for folk music, in any region.

Popular styles

Thailand is the second biggest Southeast Asian music market after Indonesia, and Bangkok is a major and increasingly important regional hub for pop music and popular culture.

Western orchestration for Thai melodies was introduced in the 1920s and 1930s and this led to the development of *pleng Thai sakon*, or modern Thai music, in the form of big band and swing, country and western, Hollywood film music, rock'n'roll, and so on. In the early days, two distinctive Thai genres developed: *pleng luk grung*, a romantic ballad form, popularized by Thailand's most beloved composer and bandleader Euah Sunthornsanan and his Sunthara-porn band; and *pleng luk thung* (Thai country music). **Luk grung**, with its clearly enunciated singing style and romantic fantasies, was long associated with the rich strata of Bangkok society; it's the kind of music that is played by state organs such as Radio Thailand. However, it was largely transformed during the 1960s by the popularity of Western stars like Cliff Richard; as musicians started to mimic the new Western music, a new term was coined, *wong shadow* (*wong* meaning group, *shadow* from the British group The Shadows).

String

The term **string** came into use as Thai-language pop music rapidly developed in the economic boom times of the 1980s. *String* encompasses ballads, rock and alternative, indie, disco, techno/house, J-Pop and K-Pop (Japan and Korea), heavy metal, reggae, ska, rap and underground; whatever trend is popular internationally is picked up and put into the Thai cultural blender. Currently popular are all things Korean – boy bands, girl bands, fashion styles and haircuts, megastars Rain and F4, teen TV shows, soap operas, food and comics.

Megastars such as veteran **Thongchai "Bird" Macintyre** generally record on either of the two major labels, GMM Grammy and RS Promotion, though another major star, **Tata Young**, is now signed to BEC-Tero and has a cult following in other Asian markets including Japan, Hong Kong and the rest of Southeast Asia. Grammy, which controls more than half the market, has an umbrella of labels that release everything from soft rockers **Mai Chareonpura** to *luk thung* star "Got" Chakrapand Arbkornburi. Their most famous Thai rock act, though, are the talented brothers **Asanee and Wasan** (**Chotikul**), now producing a new generation of rockers on their own label; the two brothers toured the worldwide Thai diaspora in 2008.

The Thai alternative rock scene developed in the mid-1990s with the emergence, on the then-indie Bakery label (now part of BMG), of **Modern Dog**, whose latest album *Ting Nong Noy* swept various Thai rock awards in 2009. Bakery helped kick-start indie rock and rap with the mercurial **Joey Boy** (the hip only buy his profane and savage MP3 underground songs). At the moment, **Loso** are probably the most popular rock band, with leader **Sek Loso** enjoying a serious solo career and iconic status.

Recently, more Western and Asian musicians have joined their Thai counterparts – as with electro-clash band **Futon** (Thai-Japanese-Western). And no list of current Thai pop stars and rockers would be complete without mentioning **Ebola** (metal plus rap), **Big Ass** (hardcore punk/pop), **Bodyslam** (heavy rock), **Thaitanium** (hip-hop from US-raised Thais), **Tattoo Colour** and **Silly Fools** (both indie rock) and **Apartment Khun Pa** (funk plus indie rock).

Thailand, and in particular Bangkok, is developing its own musical identity, partly as a result of many high-profile **festivals**, such as the Hua Hin Jazz Festival and the Pattaya Music Festival, which showcases Asian bands, and partly because of the explosion of new genres and the emergence of a busy underground and **live scene**. You'll find Thai, foreign and mixed bands and DJs playing in Bangkok's many clubs and bars, and dynamic scenes in Chiang Mai, Khorat and Ko Samui.

Campuses such as Ramkhamhaeng University are good places to get information on upcoming **events**, as are radio stations (especially Fat Radio FM). Bangkok is the best place to catch gigs – check ⓦwww.bangkokgigguide.com for comprehensive listings, or browse websites and the *Nation* and *Bangkok Post* newspapers.

Songs for Life and reggae

Another important genre is **pleng phua chiwit**, or "**Songs for Life**", which started as a kind of progressive rock in the early 1970s, with bands like **Caravan** (no relation to the British songsters) blending *pleng pheun bahn* (folk songs) with Western folk and rock. Caravan were at the forefront of the left-wing campaign for democracy with songs like *Khon Gap Kwai* (*Human with Buffaloes*):

Greed eats our labour and divides people into classes
The rice farmers fall to the bottom
Insulted as backward and ignorant brutes
With one important and sure thing: death.

Although an elected government survived from 1973 to 1976, the military returned soon after and Caravan, like many of the student activists, went into hiding in the jungle. There they performed to villagers and hill-tribe people and gave the occasional concert. When the government offered an amnesty in 1979, most of the students, and Caravan too, disillusioned with the Communist Party's support for the Khmer Rouge in Cambodia, returned to normal life.

In the 1980s a new group emerged to carry on Caravan's work, **Carabao**. The band split up but has had several reunions, most recently for their 25th anniversary; their influence is still strong, with leader Ad Carabao still in the limelight but now more as a businessman hawking his "energy" drink, Carabao Daeng, via the band's gigs and nasty nationalistic TV ad campaigns. However, despite the bloody street riots of 1992 (in protest at the then military-installed government) once again bringing Songs for Life artists out to support the pro-democracy protests, since the 1980s the strong social activism of Caravan's early years has generally been replaced by more individual and personal themes. The current top act is fresh-faced singer-songwriter **Pongsit Kamphee**, whose earnest approach and rise through the ranks (he was reportedly once a stagehand for Caravan) have garnered him a sizeable following.

Musically, the genre has changed little in 25 years, remaining strongly rooted in Western folk-rock styles. Recently, however, this has begun to change as musicians have belatedly discovered that **reggae** riddims work well with Songs for Life vocals; perhaps they were inspired by **T-Bone**, for so long the only reggae band in the kingdom. Best of this new sub-genre is Southerner **Job** of the **Job 2 Do** band, while the best classic Marley-style reggae band is the **Srirajah Rockers**. There's a weekend reggae festival held in the north in Pai every winter (Ⓦwww.paireggaefest.com). For ska bands, check out **Teddy Ska and Skalaxy**.

Songs for Life fans should check out CD stalls at Bangkok's Chatuchak Weekend Market, several of which specialize in this genre.

Luk thung

Go to one of the huge **luk thung** shows held in a temple or local stadium on the outskirts of Bangkok, or to any temple fair in the countryside, and you'll hear one of the great undiscovered popular musics of Asia. The shows, amid the bright lights, foodstalls and fairground games, last several hours and involve dozens of dancers and costume changes. In contrast with *luk grung*, *luk thung* (literally, "child of the field") has always been associated with the rural and urban poor, and because of this has gained nationwide popularity over the past forty years.

According to *luk thung* DJ Jenpope Jobkrabunwan, the term was first coined by Jamnong Rangsitkuhn in 1964, but the first song in the style was *Oh Jow Sow Chao Rai* (Oh, the Vegetable Grower's Bride), recorded in 1937, and the genre's first big singer, **Kamrot Samboonanon**, emerged in the mid-1940s. Originally called *pleng talat* (market songs) or *pleng chiwit* (songs of life), the style blended together folk songs, central Thai classical music and Thai folk dances. Malay strings and fiddles were added in the 1950s, as were Latin brass and rhythms like the cha-cha-cha and mambo (Asian tours by Xavier Cugat influenced many Asian pop styles during the 1950s), as well as elements from Hollywood movie music and "yodelling" country and western vocal styles from the likes of Gene Autry and Hank Williams. In 1952, a new singer, **Suraphon Sombatjalern**, made his debut with a song entitled *Nam Da Sow Vienne* (Tears of the Vientiane Girl) and became the undisputed king of the style until his untimely murder (for serious womanizing, rumour has it) in 1967. Suraphon helped develop the music into a mature form, and was known as the "King" of the genre, along with his Queen, sweet-voiced Pongsri Woranut.

Today, *luk thung* is a mix of Thai folk music and traditional entertainment forms like *likay* (travelling popular theatre), as well as a range of Western styles. There are certainly some strong musical affinities with other regional pop styles like Indonesian *dangdut* and Japanese *enka*, but what is distinctly Thai – quite apart from the spectacular live shows – are the singing styles and the content of the lyrics. Vocal styles are full of heavy ornamentation (*luk khor*) and sustained notes (*auen* or "note-bending"). A singer must have a wide vocal range, as the late *luk thung* megastar **Pompuang Duangjan** explained: "Making the *luk thung* sound is difficult, you must handle the high and low notes well. And because the emotional content is stronger than in *luk grung*, you must also be able to create a strongly charged atmosphere."

Pompuang had the kind of voice that turns the spine to jelly. She rose to prominence during the late 1970s, joining **Sayan Sanya** as the biggest male and female names in the business. Like Suraphon Sombatjalern, both came from the rural peasantry, making identification with themes and stories that related directly to the audience much easier. Songs narrate mini-novellas, based around typical characters like the lorry driver, peasant lad or girl, poor farmer, prostitute or maid; and the themes are those of going away to the big city, infidelity, grief, tragedy and sexual pleasure. Interestingly, it is not always the lyrics that carry the sexual charge of the song (and if lyrics are deemed too risqué by the authorities the song will be subject to strict censorship) but rather the vocal style and the stage presentation, which can be very bawdy indeed.

With the advent of TV and the rise in popularity of *string*, the number of large upcountry *luk thung* shows has declined. It's not easy, said Pompuang, to tour with over a hundred staff, including the dancers in the *hang kruang* (chorus). "We play for over four hours, but *string* bands, with only a few staff members, play a paltry two hours!" Her response to the advent of *string* and the increasing importance of promotional videos was to develop a dance-floor-oriented sound – **electronic luk thung** (**Grand X** had already experimented with *luk thung* and disco a few years earlier). Few *luk thung* singers are capable of this, but Pompuang had the vocal range to tackle both ballad forms and the up-tempo dance numbers. Her musical diversification increased her popularity enormously, and when she died in 1992, aged only 31, up to 200,000 people, ranging from royalty to the rural poor, made their way to her funeral in her home town of Suphanburi.

Pompuang's death pushed ongoing political problems (the 1992 coup) off the front pages of newspapers, a situation that was repeated in 2008 when **Yodrak Salakjai** died. Yodrak was the most recorded *luk thung* star of all time, with some three thousand songs and five hundred albums to his credit.

Since Pompuang's death, the top *luk thung* slot has been occupied by "**Got**" **Chakrapand Arbkornburi**, whose switch from pop to full-time *luk thung* has brought many younger listeners to the style, while the reigning female singer was **Sunaree Ratchasima**, but she has been superseded by the perkier **Arpaporn Nakornsawan**. **Mike Piromporn**, originally a *mor lam* man, is Got's main challenger. Bangkok's first 24-hour *luk thung* radio station, Luk Thung FM (at 90 FM), was launched in 1997, and it's even hip for the middle class to like *luk thung* these days. A new generation of singers has also emerged, including **Monsit Kamsoi**, **Yingyong Yodbuangarm**, **Dao Mayuri**, **Yui Yardyuh**, **Tai Orathai** and **Fon Thanasunthorn**. There is some truth, however, in the criticism that some new *luk thung* stars are being artificially manufactured just like their pop and rock counterparts, and there's a tendency to rate a pretty face over vocal expertise.

For many years, *luk thung* was sung by performers from the Suphanburi area in the central plains, but more regional voices are being heard in the genre now, with northeasterners now outnumbering these singers. A slightly faster rhythm, *luk thung Isaan*, has been developed, initially by **"Khru" (Teacher) Saleh Kunavudh** in the 1980s. The south, too, has its own *luk thung* star, in the enormously popular **Ekachai Srivichai**.

As well as at temple fairs, fairs at district offices in provincial capitals, national holiday events at Bangkok's Sanam Luang by companies like Waitee Thai and New Year celebrations are the best places to catch *luk thung* shows.

Mor lam

Mor lam is the folk style from the poor, dry northeastern region of Isaan, an area famed for droughts, hot spicy food, good boxers and great music. Over the past 25 years, the modern pop form of this style has risen dramatically. Traditionally, a *mor lam* is a master of the *lam* singing style (sung in the Isaan dialect, which is actually Lao), and is accompanied by the *khaen* (bamboo mouth organ), the *phin* (two- to four-string guitar) and *ching* (small temple cymbals). Modern **mor lam** developed from *mor lam glawn*, a narrative form where all-night singing jousts are held between male and female singers, and from *mor lam soeng*, the group-dance form. Both still play an important part in many social events like weddings, births and deaths, festivals and temple fairs. A *mor lam* may sing intricate fixed-metre Lao epic poems or may relate current affairs in a spontaneous rap. In the large groups, Western instruments like guitar (replacing the *phin*) and synthesizer (for the *khaen*) are used.

The style came to national prominence more than twenty years ago, when a female *mor lam* singer, **Banyen Rakgan**, appeared on national TV. In the early 1980s the music was heard not only in Isaan but also in the growing slums of Bangkok, as rural migrants poured into the capital in search of work. By the end of the decade stars like **Jintara Poonlarp** (with her hit song *Isaan Woman Far From Home*) and **Pornsak Songsaeng** could command the same sell-out concerts as their *luk thung* counterparts. Jintara remains one of the biggest stars and her shows mix both *luk thung* and *lam*; for a big raucous show, **Nok Noi Ulaiporn** and Pong-Lang Sa-Orn (see p.836) are probably the hottest acts. **Siriporn Ampaiporn**, whose strong vocals burst upon the *lam* scene with the monster-selling *Bor Rak Si Dam* album, mainly records *luk thung* these days.

The format of a *mor lam* **performance** is similar to that of *luk thung* shows – lots of dancers in wild costumes, comedy skits and a large backing orchestra – as is the subject matter. The music is definitely hot, especially if you see it live, when bands will often play through the night, never missing the groove for a minute, driven on by the relentless *phin* and *khaen* playing. To some people, the fast plucking style of the *phin* gives a West African or Celtic tinge; the *khaen* has a rich sound – over a bass drone players improvise around the melody, while at the same time vamping the basic rhythm. Male and female singers rotate or duet humorous love songs, which often start with one of the *mor khaen* setting up the beat. They sing about topical issues, bits of news, crack lewd jokes or make fun of the audience – all very tongue-in-cheek.

Musically, however, *mor lam* and *luk thung* are very different; *mor lam* has a much faster, relentless rhythm and the vocal delivery is rapid-fire, rather like a rap. You'll immediately recognize a *mor lam* song with its introductory wailing moan "*Oh la naw*", meaning "fortune". *Mor lam* artists, brought up bilingually, can easily switch from *luk thung* to *mor lam*, but *luk thung* artists, who often only speak the national central Thai dialect, cannot branch out so easily.

In the 1990s, *mor lam* musicians headed off the challenge of increasingly popular *string* bands by creating **mor lam sing**, a turbo-charged modern version of *mor lam glawn* played by small electric combos. The number of large touring *luk thung* or *mor lam* shows has declined in recent years, owing to high overheads, TV entertainment and the popularity of *string* bands, so *mor lam sing* satisfies the need for local music with a modern edge.

Mor lam sing was followed quickly by a more rock-oriented *mor lam* sound (this is a little similar to Grand X in the 1980s, which played a mix of rock and *luk thung*), led by funky little combos like **Rocksadert** and **Rock Saleang**, actually much better live than on recordings, although the latter had a hilarious hit in 2006 with *Motorcy Hoy*.

Kantrum: Thai-Cambodian pop

"Isaan *neua* (north) has *mor lam*, Isaan *dai* (south) has *kantrum*," sings **Darkie**, the first star of **kantrum**, Thai-Cambodian pop, in his song *Isaan Dai Sah Muk Kee* (Southern Isaan Unity). His music is a very specific offshoot, from the southern part of Isaan, where Thai-Cambodians mix with ethnic Lao and Thais. So far *kantrum* is only popular in Isaan in Thailand but it has spread over the border to nearby Cambodian towns like Siem Reap where the style is known as Khmer Ler or Khmer Surin.

Modern *kantrum* has developed from Cambodian folk and classical music, played in a small group consisting of fiddle, small hand-drums and *krab* (pieces of hardwood bashed together rather like claves). This traditional style is now quite hard to find in Thailand; twenty years ago, musicians started to electrify the music, using both traditional and Western instruments. Shunning the synthesizer preferred by his competitors such as **Khong Khoi**, Oh-Yot and Samanchai, Darkie added the wailing fiddle centre-stage and cranked up the rhythms (*kantrum* has a harder beat than even *mor lam*). In 1997, he broke new ground with *Darkie Rock II: Buk Jah*, the first *kantrum* crossover album to have success in the mainstream pop market. Sadly, in 2001, Darkie died aged 35, but a new generation of *kantrum* stars is now emerging, led by **Songsaeng Lungluangchai**, who has recorded several excellent albums of Darkie covers.

Discography

CDs have taken over from cassettes, even in the provinces (where the mix is seventy percent *luk thung*, 25 percent *string* and five percent international). In Bangkok, ask the vendors at the day and night markets, or the stores on Thanon Charoen Krung (New Road) or at Sunday's Klong Thom market (in the small sois behind Thanon Charoen Krung, between Plaplachai and Mahachak intersections). Most major *luk thung* or *mor lam* artists release a CD every three months, which is often given an artist's series number. Old-style recordings of Suraphon Sombatjalern and the like can be found on the ground floor of the Mah Boon Krong Shopping Centre at the Bangkok Cassette Co. store (label name in Thai is Mere Mai Mere Pleng) or at Panthip Plaza. Nearly all of the releases listed here are on CD, apart from one or two *kantrum* and other recordings that are on cassette.

In addition, several **DVDs** are well worth seeking out: Jeremy Marre's episode on music in Thailand, *Two Faces of Thailand: A Musical Portrait* (Shanachie, US), from his award-winning *Beats of the Heart* music-TV documentary series; *Homrong* (see p.835); and *Mon Rak Transistor* (see p.843).

For music on the **internet**, try ⓦthaimuzic.com, ⓦthaiclassicalmusic.com, ⓦthainetcity.com and ⓦethaimusic.com; the last is also a good site to learn the language as it features lyrics in Thai and English, from a large archive of popular songs. Music sites such as ⓦtruemusic.truelife.com and the sites of GMM Grammy and RS Promotion are also worth browsing for info on major stars.

Classical

Fong Naam *The Hang Hong Suite* (Nimbus, UK). A good introduction to the vivacious and glittering sound of classical Thai music, this CD includes some upbeat funeral music and parodies of the musical languages of neighbouring cultures. *The Sleeping Angel* (Nimbus, UK) is also a splendid recording.

Lai Muang Ensemble *The Spirit of Lanna: Music From the North of Thailand* (AMI Records, Thailand). Top-quality recording, featuring multi-instrumentalist Somboon Kawichai on the *peejum* (bamboo pipes) and the eerie-sounding *pin pia*, a chest-resonated oboe.

The Prasit Thawon Ensemble *Thai Classical Music* (Nimbus, UK). Brilliant playing (and outstanding recording quality) from some of Thailand's best performers, mainly of *phipat* style. Includes the overture *Homrong Sornthong* and, on *Cherd Chin*, some scintillating dialogues between different instruments.

Folk music

David Fanshawe *Music From Thailand and Laos: Southeast Asia Recordings* (Arc Music, UK). Excellent range of folk music from different regions of both countries.

Various *Sea Gypsies of the Andaman Sea* (Topic, UK). The traditional music of nomadic Moken (*chao ley*) fisherfolk in southern Thailand, mostly recorded in the Surin islands.

Various *Thailand: Musiques et Chants des Peuples du Triangle d'Or* (Globe Music, France). Recordings of the traditional music of Thailand's main hill-tribe groups: Hmong, Lisu, Lahu, Yao, Akha and Karen, as well as Shan (Thai Yai).

Modern music (Thai sakon)

Euah Sunthornsanan *Chabab Derm* ("Old Songs") Vols 1–5, 6–10 (Bangkok Cassette, Thailand). Modern Thai music was popularized by the late master Euah. Some of the most popular Thai songs ever were performed by the Suntharaporn band and a bevy of singers.

String and Songs for Life

Carabao *Made in Thailand* and *Ameri-koi* (both Krabue, Thailand). Two classic albums from the Songs for Life giants. *Made in Thailand* was right in tune with the times and targeted social problems like consumerism, the sex trade and a failing education system. *Ameri-koi* (*Greedy America*) is even more nationalistic than the previous one, but it also hits out at Thai migrant workers exploited by labour brokers.

Futon *Never Mind the Botox* (Rehab, Thailand). Electro-clash with a punk attitude from the kingdom's favourite underground band. Excellent cover of Iggy Pop's *I Wanna Be Your Dog*.

Loso/Sek Loso The best compilation of Loso's music is the

2001 release *The Red* album, while the solo work of Sek Loso is best captured on the same year's *Black & White* (both GMM Grammy, Thailand) and live on the VCD *10 Years of Rock Volumes 1 & 2*.

Modern Dog *Modern Dog* (Bakery Music, Thailand). This album of alternative rock marked an important change of direction for the Thai rock scene. Also see albums *Love Me Love My Life*, *That Song* and their newest, *Ting Nong Noy*.

Luk thung

If you can't find any of the albums below, go for a compilation of past albums, usually under a title like *Luam Hits* (*Mixed Hits*).

"Got" Chakrapand Arbkornburi *12 Years of Grammy Gold* (GMM Grammy, Thailand). Packed with slow ballads, this is one for the ladies from *luk thung*'s heartthrob.

Pompuang Duangjan In Thailand, the best of many albums to go for is *Pompuang Lai Por Sor* ("Pompuang's Many Eras"; Topline, Thailand). Her early spine-tingling hits can be found on several CD compilations from Bangkok Cassette, some recorded when she was known as Nampung Petsupan (Honey Diamond from Suphanburi).

Sayan Sanya *Sayan Dao Thong* ("Sayan Golden Star"; Bangkok Cassette, Thailand). Classic 1970s *luk thung* featuring the "honey-voiced" master. As Yodrak said, "Women cry when he [Sayan] sings."

Suraphon Sombatjalern *Luam Pleng* ("Mixed Songs") Vols 1–4 (Bangkok Cassette, Thailand). Greatest hits by the king of *luk thung*. Great voice, great songs, great backing – Siamese soul.

Various *Mon Rak Transistor* ("A Transistor Love Story"; UFO, Thailand). From the hit movie about a young country boy who tries to make it in the big city as a *luk thung* singer. Includes Suraphon's wonderful theme song, *Mai Lerm* ("Don't Forget").

Various *The Rough Guide to the Music of Thailand* (World Music Network, UK). Good review of some current *mor lam* and *luk thung*, despite confusing liner notes, elephants, and the odd pop group.

Mor lam/northeastern music

Chalard Songserm *Rhythms of I-Sarn Vols 1 & 2* (AMI Records, Thailand). Top-quality album from National Artist Chalard, *khaen* maestro Sombat Simlao and a band of great musicians, covering many styles of Lao music in the region. Sombat's train-sounding *khaen* solo is a standout.

Isan Slété *Songs and Music from North East Thailand* (Globestyle, UK). Excellent selection of traditional *mor lam*. Vocal and instrumental numbers, played by a band of master musicians.

Jintara Poonlarp *Luam Hit 19 Pii Tawng Chut* (Master Tape, Thailand). Nineteen years at the top on two killer volumes. Vol. 1 features haunting *mor lam*.

Various *Instrumental Music of Northeast Thailand* (King, Japan). Wonderful collection of *bong lang* and related instrumental northeastern styles. Lively and fun.

Various, featuring Chaweewan Damnoen *Mor Lam Singing of Northeast Thailand* (King, Japan). Female *mor lam* National Artist,

Chaweewan, headlines this fine collection of many *lam* styles. Most *mor lam glawn* narrative and dance styles, even spirit-possession rituals, are included.

Kantrum

Darkie *Darkie, Rock II: Buk Jah* (Movie Music, Thailand). The first-ever *kantrum* crossover album achieved nationwide stardom for the King of Kantrum. Darkie's booming voice moves from rap-like delivery to moans and wails, shadowed closely by the fiddle and some funky riddims. Unmissable.

Darkie *Kantrum Rock Vols I & II* (available on separate cassettes). Benchmark recordings by *kantrum*'s only major star: Darkie's fine wailing voice is featured in rock-*kantrum*, *kantrum* and *kantrum luk thung*.

Songsaeng Lungluangchai *Songsaeng Kantrum Rock: Chut Ta Don Duay* (PK Sound, Thailand). Fast-rising star set to replace Darkie. Keyboardless, rootsy sound. Look out for his tribute album to Darkie, *Kantrum Rock* (PK Sound, Thailand).

John Clewley

(Adapted from *The Rough Guide to World Music*)

The hill tribes

Originating in various parts of China and Southeast Asia, the hill tribes are sometimes termed Fourth World people, in that they are migrants who continue to migrate without regard for established national boundaries. Most arrived in Thailand during the last century, and many of the hill peoples are still found in other parts of Southeast Asia – in Vietnam, for example, where the French used the *montagnards* ("mountain dwellers") in their fight against communism. Since 1975, a large percentage of the one million refugees that Thailand has accepted from Burma, Laos and Cambodia has been hill-tribe people. Some, however, have been around for much longer, like the Lawa, who are thought to have been the first settlers in northern Thailand, though these days they have largely been assimilated into mainstream Thai culture.

Called **chao khao** (mountain people) by the Thais, the tribes are mostly pre-literate societies, whose sophisticated systems of customs, laws and beliefs have developed to harmonize relationships between individuals and their environment. In recent years their ancient culture has come under threat, faced with the effects of rapid population growth and the ensuing competition for land, discrimination and exploitation by lowland Thais, and tourism. However, the integrity of their way of life is as yet largely undamaged, and what follows is the briefest of introductions to an immensely complex subject. If you want to learn more, visit the Tribal Museum in Chiang Mai (see p.336), or the Hill Tribe Museum and Handicrafts Shop in Chiang Rai (see p.409) before setting out on a trek.

Agriculture

Although the hill tribes keep some livestock, such as pigs, poultry and elephants, the base of their economy is **swidden agriculture**, a crude form of shifting cultivation also practised by many Thai lowland farmers. At the beginning of the season an area of jungle is cleared and burned, producing ash to fertilize rice, corn, chillies and other vegetables, which are replanted in succeeding years until the soil's nutrients are exhausted. This system is sustainable with a low population density, which allows the jungle time to recover before it is used again. However, with the increase in population over recent decades, ever greater areas are being exhausted, and the decreasing forest cover is leading to erosion and micro climatic change.

As a result, many villages took up the large-scale production of **opium** to supplement the traditional subsistence crops, though the Thai government has now largely eradicated opium production in the north. However, the cash crops which have been introduced in its place have often led to further environmental damage, as these low-profit crops require larger areas of cultivation, and thus greater deforestation. Furthermore, the water supplies have become polluted with chemical pesticides, and, although more environmentally sensitive agricultural techniques are being introduced, they have yet to achieve widespread acceptance.

Religion and festivals

Although some tribes have taken up Buddhism and others – especially among the Karen, Mien and Lahu – have been converted by Christian missionaries bringing the incentives of education and modern medicine, the hill tribes are predominantly **animists**. In this belief system, all natural objects are inhabited by spirits which, along with the tribe's ancestor spirits and the supreme divine spirit, must be propitiated to prevent harm to the family or village. Most villages have one or more religious leaders, which may include a priest who looks after the ritual life of the community, and at least one shaman who has the power to mediate with the spirits and prescribe what has to be done to keep them happy. If a member of the community is sick, for example, the shaman will be consulted to determine what action has insulted which spirit, and will then carry out the correct sacrifice.

The most important festival, celebrated by all the tribes, is at **New Year**, when whole communities take part in dancing, music and rituals particular to each tribe: Hmong boys and girls, for instance, take part in a courting ritual at this time, while playing catch with a ball. The New Year festivals are not held on fixed dates, but at various times during the cool-season slack period in the agricultural cycle from January to March.

Costumes and handicrafts

The most conspicuous characteristics of the hill tribes are their exquisitely crafted **costumes** and adornments, the styles and colours of which are particular to each group. Although many men and children now adopt Western clothes for everyday wear, with boys in particular more often running around in long shorts and T-shirts with logos, most women and girls still wear the traditional attire at all times. It's the women who make the clothes too – some still spin their own cotton, though many Hmong, Lisu and Mien women are prosperous enough to buy materials from itinerant traders. Other distinctive hill-tribe artefacts – tools, jewellery, weapons and musical instruments – are the domain of the men, and specialist **blacksmiths** and **silversmiths** have such high status that some attract business from villages many kilometres away. Jewellery, the chief outward proof of a family's wealth, is displayed most obviously by Lisu women at the New Year festivals, and is commonly made from silver melted down from Indian and Burmese coins, though brass, copper and aluminium are also used.

Clothing and **handicrafts** were not regarded as marketable products until the early 1980s, when co-operatives were set up to manufacture and market these goods, which are now big business in the shops of Thailand. The hill tribes' deep-dyed coarse cloth, embroidered with simple geometric patterns in bright colours, has become popular among middle-class Thais as well as farang visitors. Mien material, dyed indigo or black with bright snowflake embroidery, is on sale in many shops, as is the simple but very distinctive Akha work – coarse black cotton, with triangular patterns of stitching and small fabric patches in rainbow colours, usually made up into bags and hats. The Hmong's much more sophisticated **embroidery** and **appliqué**, added to jacket lapels and cuffs and skirt hems, is also widely seen – Blue Hmong skirts, made on a base of indigo-dyed cotton with a white geometric batik design and embroidered in loud primary colours, are particularly attractive.

Besides clothing, the hill tribes' other handicrafts, such as knives and wooden or bamboo musical pipes, have found a market amongst farangs, the most saleable product being the intricate engraving work of their silversmiths, especially in the form of chunky bracelets. For a sizeable minority of villages, handicrafts now provide the security of a steady income to supplement what they make from farming.

The main tribes

Within the small geographical area of northern Thailand there are at least ten different hill tribes, many of them divided into distinct subgroups – the following are the main seven, listed in order of population and under their own names, rather than the sometimes derogatory names used by Thais. (The Thai Yai – or Shan – the dominant group in Mae Hong Son province, are not a hill tribe, but a subgroup of Thais.) Beyond the broad similarities outlined above, this section sketches their differences in terms of history, economy and religion, and describes elements of dress by which they can be distinguished.

Karen

The **Karen** (called Kaliang or Yang in Thai) form by far the largest hill-tribe group in Thailand with a population of about 500,000, and are the second oldest after the Lawa, having begun to arrive here from Burma and China in the seventeenth century. The Thai Karen, many of them refugees from Burma (see box, p.298), mostly live in a broad tract of land west of Chiang Mai, which stretches along the border from Mae Hong Son province all the way down to Kanchanaburi, with scattered pockets in Chiang Mai, Chiang Rai and Phayao provinces.

The Karen traditionally practise a system of **rotating cultivation** – ecologically far more sensitive than slash-and-burn – in the valleys of this region and on low hills. Their houses, very similar to those of lowland Thais, are small (they do not live in extended family groups), built on stilts and made of bamboo or teak; they're often surrounded by fruit gardens and neat fences. As well as farming their own land, the Karen often hire out their labour to Thais and other hill tribes, and keep a variety of livestock including elephants, which used to be employed in the teak trade but are now often found giving rides to trekking parties.

Unmarried Karen women wear loose white or undyed V-necked shift dresses, often decorated with grass seeds at the seams. Some subgroups decorate them more elaborately, Sgaw girls with a woven red or pink band above the waist, and Pwo girls with woven red patterns in the lower half of the shift. Married women wear blouses and skirts in bold colours, predominantly red or blue. Men generally wear blue, baggy trousers with red or blue shirts, a simplified version of the women's blouse.

Hmong

Called the Meo ("barbarians") by the Thais, the **Hmong** ("free people") originated in central China or Mongolia and are now found widely in northern Thailand; they are still the most widespread minority group in south China. There are two subgroups: the **Blue Hmong**, who live around and to the west of Chiang Mai; and the **White Hmong**, who are found to the east. Their overall population in Thailand is about 110,000, making them the second-largest hill-tribe group.

Of all the hill tribes, the Hmong have been the quickest to move away from subsistence farming. In the past, Hmong people were more involved in opium production than most other tribes in Thailand, though now many have eagerly embraced the newer cash crops. Hmong clothing has become much in demand in Thailand, and Hmong women will often be seen at markets throughout the country selling their handicrafts. The women, in fact, are expected to do most of the work on the land and in the home.

Hmong **villages** are usually built at high altitudes, below the crest of a protecting hill. Although wealthier families sometimes build the more comfortable Thai-style houses, most stick to the traditional house, with its dirt floor and a roof descending almost to ground level. They live together in extended families, with two or more bedrooms and a large guest platform.

The Blue Hmong dress in especially striking **clothes**. The women wear intricately embroidered pleated skirts decorated with parallel horizontal bands of red, pink, blue and white; their jackets are of black satin, with wide orange and yellow embroidered cuffs and lapels. White Hmong women wear black baggy trousers and simple jackets with blue cuffs. Men of both groups generally wear baggy black pants with colourful sashes round the waist, and embroidered jackets closing over the chest with a button at the left shoulder. All the Hmong are famous for their chunky **silver jewellery**, which the women wear every day, the men only on special occasions: they believe silver binds a person's spirits together, and wear a heavy neck-ring to keep the spirits weighed down in the body.

Lahu

The **Lahu**, who originated in the Tibetan highlands, migrated to southern China, Burma and Laos centuries ago; only since the end of the nineteenth century did they begin to come into Thailand from northern Burma. They're called Muser – from the Burmese word for "hunter" – by the Thais, because many of the first Lahu to reach northern Thailand were professional hunters. With a population of about 80,000, they are the third-largest hill-tribe group: most of their settlements are concentrated close to the Burmese border, in Chiang Rai, northern Chiang Mai and Mae Hong Son provinces, but families and villages change locations frequently. The Lahu language has become a *lingua franca* among the hill tribes, since the Lahu often hire out their labour. About one-third of Lahu have been converted to Christianity (through exposure in colonial Burma), and many have abandoned their traditional way of life as a result. The remaining animist Lahu believe in a village guardian spirit, who is often worshipped at a central temple that is surrounded by banners and streamers of white and yellow flags. Village houses are built on high stilts with walls of bamboo or wooden planks, thatched with grass. While subsistence farming is still common, sustainable agriculture – plantations of orchards, tea or coffee – is becoming more prevalent, and cash crops such as corn and cotton have taken the place of opium.

Some Lahu women wear a distinctive black cloak with diagonal white stripes, decorated in bold red and yellow at the top of the sleeve, but traditional costume has been supplanted by the Thai shirt and sarong amongst many Lahu groups. The tribe is famous for its richly embroidered **yaam** (shoulder bags), which are widely available in Chiang Mai.

Akha

The poorest of the hill tribes, the **Akha** (Kaw or Eekaw in Thai) migrated from Tibet over two thousand years ago to Yunnan in China, where at some stage they had an organized state and kept written chronicles of their history – these chronicles, like the Akha written language, are now lost. From the 1910s the tribe began to settle in Thailand and is found in four provinces – Chiang Rai, Chiang Mai, Lampang and Phrae – with a population of nearly 50,000 in about 250 villages. The greatest concentration of Akha villages is in Chiang Rai province followed by northern Chiang Mai, near the Burmese border – recently many Akha have fled persecution in politically unstable Burma. A large Akha population still lives in Yunnan and there are communities in neighbouring Laos as well as in Burma.

The Akha are less open to change than the other hill tribes, and have maintained their old agricultural methods of **shifting cultivation**. The Akha's form of animism – *Akhazang*, "the way of life of the Akha" – has also survived in uncompromised form. As well as spirits in the natural world, *Akhazang* encompasses the worship of ancestor spirits: some Akha can recite the names of over sixty generations of forebears.

Every Akha village is entered through ceremonial **gates** decorated with carvings depicting human activities and attributes – even cars and aeroplanes – to indicate to the spirit world that beyond here only humans should pass. To touch any of these carvings, or to show any lack of respect to them, is punishable by fines or sacrifices. The gates are rebuilt every year, so many villages have a series of gates, the older ones in a state of disintegration. Another characteristic of Akha villages is a giant **swing** (also replaced each year), and used every August or early September in a swinging festival in which the whole population takes part.

Akha **houses** are recognizable by their low stilts and steeply pitched roofs, though some may use higher stilts to reflect higher status. Even more distinctive is the elaborate **headgear** which women wear all day; it frames the entire face and usually features white beads interspersed with silver coins, topped with plumes of red taffeta and framed by dangling, hollow silver balls and other jewellery or strings of beads. The rest of their heavy costume is made up of decorated tube-shaped ankle-to-knee leggings, an above-the-knee black skirt with a white beaded centrepiece, and a loose-fitting black jacket with heavily embroidered cuffs and lapels.

Mien

The **Mien** (called Yao in Thai) consider themselves the aristocrats of the hill tribes. Originating in central China, they began migrating southward more than two thousand years ago to southern China, Vietnam, Laos and Thailand; in southern China they used to have such power that at one time a Mien princess was married to a Chinese emperor. In Thailand today the Mien are widely scattered throughout the north, with concentrations around Nan, Phayao and Chiang Rai, and a population of about 40,000. They are the only hill tribe to have a written language, and a codified religion based on medieval Chinese Taoism, although in recent years there have been many Mien converts to Christianity and Buddhism. In general, the Mien strike a balance between integration into Thai life and maintenance of their separate cultural base. Many earn extra cash by selling exquisite embroidery and religious scrolls, painted in bold Chinese style.

Mien villages are not especially distinctive: their houses are usually built of wooden planks on a dirt floor, with a guest platform of bamboo in the communal living area. The **clothes** of the women, however, are instantly recognizable: long black jackets with glamorous looking stole-like lapels of bright scarlet wool, heavily embroidered loose trousers in intricate designs which can take up to two years to complete, and a similarly embroidered black turban. The caps of babies are also very beautiful, richly embroidered with red or pink pom-poms. On special occasions, like weddings, women and children wear silver neck-rings, with silver chains decorated with silver ornaments extending down the back, and even their turbans are crossed with lengths of silver. A Mien woman's wedding headdress is quite extraordinary, a carefully constructed platform with arched supports which are covered with red fabric and heirlooms of embroidered cloth. Two burgundy-coloured fringes create side curtains obscuring her face, and the only concession to modernity is the black insulating tape that holds the structure to her head.

Lisu

The **Lisu** (Lisaw in Thai), who originated in eastern Tibet, first arrived in Thailand in 1921 and are found mostly in the west, particularly between Chiang Mai and Mae Hong Son, but also in western Chiang Rai, Chiang Mai and Phayao provinces, with a population of around 30,000. Whereas the other hill tribes are led by the village headman or shaman, the Lisu are organized into patriarchal clans which have authority over many villages, and their strong sense of clan rivalry often results in public violence.

The Lisu live in extended families at moderate to high altitudes, in houses built on the ground, with dirt floors and bamboo walls. Both men and women dress colourfully; the women wear a blue or green parti-coloured knee-length tunic, split up the sides to the waist, with a wide black belt and blue or green pants. At New Year, the women don dazzling outfits, including waistcoats and belts of intricately fashioned silver and turbans with multicoloured pom-poms and streamers; traditionally, the men wear green, pink or yellow baggy pants and a blue jacket.

Lawa

The history of the **Lawa** people (Lua in Thai) is poorly understood, but it seems very likely that they have inhabited Thailand since at least the eighth century; they were certainly here when the Thais arrived around eight hundred years ago. The Lawa people are found only in Thailand; they believe that they migrated from Cambodia and linguistically they are certainly closely related to Mon-Khmer, but some archeologists think that their origins lie in Micronesia, which they left perhaps two thousand years back.

This lengthy cohabitation with the Thais has produced large-scale integration, so that most Lawa villages are indistinguishable from Thai settlements and most Lawa speak Thai as their first language. However, in an area of about 500 square kilometres between Hot, Mae Sariang and Mae Hong Son, the Lawa still live a largely traditional life, although even here the majority have adopted Buddhism and Thai-style houses. The basis of their economy is subsistence agriculture, with rice grown on terraces according to a sophisticated rotation system. Those identified as Lawa number just over ten thousand.

Unmarried Lawa women wear distinctive strings of orange and yellow beads, loose white blouses edged with pink, and tight skirts in parallel bands of blue, black, yellow and pink. After marriage, these brightly coloured clothes are replaced with a long fawn dress, but the beads are still worn. All the women wear their hair tied in a turban, and the men wear light-coloured baggy pants and tunics or, more commonly, Western clothes.

Film

Until recently, Thai cinema was almost impenetrable to the outside world. But the West began to take notice in 2000, when films such as *Iron Ladies*, *Tears of the Black Tiger* and later *The Legend of Suriyothai* showed that Thai directors had the style and wit to entertain non-Thai-speaking audiences. Many larger-budget Thai films are now released outside Thailand and with English subtitles.

A brief history

Thailand's first **cinema** was built in 1905 in Bangkok, behind Wat Tuk on Thanon Charoen Krung, and for a couple of decades screened only short, silent films from America, Europe and Japan. Though nothing remains of the earliest film-theatres, the renovated Art Deco Sala Chalermkrung, which was built in 1933 in Bangkok's Chinatown, is still in use today as a venue for live theatre and the occasional screening.

The **first home-grown film**, *Chok Sorng Chan* (*Double Luck*), made by the Wasuwat brothers of the Bangkok Film Company, didn't emerge until 1927, and it was another five years before *Long Thang* (*Going Astray*), the first Thai film with sound followed.

During the 1920s, a few foreign film companies came to Thailand to film the local culture and wildlife. One early classic from this period is *Chang* (1927; available on video), which tells the simple story, in documentary style, of a family who live on the edge of the forest in Nan province. *Chang*'s American directors Merian Cooper and Ernest B. Schoedsack later drew on their experiences in the Thai jungle for their 1933 classic, *King Kong*.

Though Thai film-making continued throughout the 1930s and 1940s, it was virtually suspended during World War II, before re-emerging with a flourish in the 1950s. The **1950s, 1960s and 1970s** were golden years for the production of large numbers of hastily made but hugely popular low-budget escapist films, mainly action melodramas featuring stereotypical characters, gangsters and corny love interest. Many of these films starred **Mitr Chaibancha**, Thailand's greatest-ever film star. He played the handsome hero in 265 films, in many of them performing opposite former beauty queen **Petchara Chaowarat**. Of the 165 movies they made together, their most famous was *Mon Rak Luk Thung* (*Enchanting Countryside*, 1969), a folk-musical about life and love in the countryside that played continuously in Bangkok for six months and later spawned a bestselling soundtrack album. Nearly every Thai adult can recall the days when Mitr co-starred with Petchara, and when Mitr fell to a dramatic death in 1970 during a stunt involving a rope ladder suspended from a helicopter – it caused nationwide mourning. He was cremated at Wat Thepsirin in Bangkok (off Thanon Luang in Chinatown), where photos of the cremation ceremony and the crowds of fans who attended are still on display. Though non-Thai speakers are denied the pleasure of seeing Mitr and Petchara in action, you can get a good idea of the general tone of their films from the 2000 hit *Tears of the Black Tiger* (see p.853), which affectionately parodies the films of this period.

For many years after Mitr's death, Thai cinema continued to be dominated by action melodramas, though a notable exception was *Khao Cheu Karn* (*His Name is Karn*), the first Thai film to tackle corruption in the civil service – it was released in 1973, not long before mass student demonstrations led to the ousting of the military government, and was made by Chatri Chalerm Yukol, who went on to direct the 2001 epic *The Legend of Suriyothai* (see opposite). The other stand out film of the 1970s is *Phlae Khao* (*The Old Scar*, 1977), in which director Cherd Songsri uses traditional rural Thailand as a potent setting for a tragic romance that ends with the heroine's death.

With competition from television and large numbers of imported Hollywood films, Thai film production dwindled during the 1980s, but in 1984 the **Thai National Film Archive** was set up to preserve not only Thai films but also many of the wonderful posters used to promote them. A rare gem from the 1980s is Yuttana Mukdasanit's coming-of-age drama *Butterflies and Flowers* (*Pee Sua Lae Dok Mai*, 1986), which is set in a Muslim community in southern Thailand and looks at the pressures on a poor teenager who ends up smuggling rice across the nearby Malaysian border. The film won an award at the Hawaii International Film Festival.

By the 1990s, the Thai film industry was in a rather sorry state and the few films still produced were mainly trite melodramas aimed at an undiscerning teenage audience. But everything started to change for the better in 1997.

Modern Thai cinema

The rebirth of the Thai film industry started in 1997 with the release of Pen-Ek Ratanaruang's *Fun Boy Karaoke* and Nonzee Nimibutr's *Daeng Bireley's and the Young Gangsters*. Fuelled by a **new wave** of talented directors and writers, including Nonzee and Pen-Ek, this resurgence has seen Thai films benefiting from larger budgets and achieving international acclaim. The new breed of Thai film-makers has moved away from traditional action melodramas and soap operas to create films that are more imaginative, realistic and stylish. With a new emphasis on production values, they also look very good, yet it is the fresh, distinctly Thai flavour that most charms Western audiences, a style summed up by one Thai film commentator as "neo-unrealist", and by another as being influenced by the popular *likay* genre of bawdy, over-the-top Thai street-theatre, where actors use song and dance as well as speech to tell their story.

Posters and billboards

Until the 1990s, domestic and foreign films were always promoted in Thailand with **original Thai artwork**, especially commissioned to hang as billboards and to be reproduced on posters. The artists who produced them really poured their hearts into these images, interpreting the film in their own style and always including an extraordinary amount of detail, usually as montage. Unlike the films themselves, Thai film posters were rarely subject to any censorship and as a result they were often far more eye-catchingly graphic and explicit than Western artwork for the same films. Posters for horror films (always very big in Thailand) depicted particularly gruesome, blood-drenched images, while ads for the (illegal) screenings of soft-porn movies often displayed a surprising amount of naked flesh.

Locally produced posters are still used to advertise films in Thailand, but for over a decade now they have featured photographic images instead of original artwork. However, there's still a chance to admire the exuberant creativity of Thai cinema art because many provincial cinemas continue to employ local artists to produce their own **billboard** paintings every week. Look for these giant works of art above cinema doors, at key locations around town, and on the sides of the megaphone trucks that circulate around town screeching out the times and plot lines of the next show. In seven days' time they will have been dismantled, reduced to a pile of planks and painted over with the artwork for next week's film.

Directors of the new wave

Daeng Bireley's and the Young Gangsters (*Antaphan Krong Muang*) was the surprise hit of 1997; **Nonzee Nimibutr** showed in this story of 1950s gangsters that he was able to appeal to the international festival circuit as well as local cinema goers. He followed it up with the even more successful *Nang Nak* in 1999, giving the big-budget treatment to a traditional nineteenth-century Thai ghost story about a woman who dies while in labour, along with her unborn child. In *Jan Dara* (2001), the 1930s story of a young man who despises his womanizing stepfather, yet eventually becomes just such a person, Nonzee pushed the envelope of what was acceptable in Thai cinema by including scenes of rape and lesbianism that would not have been permitted a decade earlier. *Queens of Lungkasuka (Puen Yai Jom Salad*, 2008) saw him turning to the more conservative genre of historical action fantasy, complete with sumptuous costumes, pirates, sea gypsies and sorcerers.

In a wry tale of messages received from beyond the grave, **Pen-Ek Ratanaruang**'s first film *Fun Bar Karaoke* (1997) looked at how the lives of modern middle-class Thais are still affected by traditional superstitions. His next film *6ixtynin9* (*Ruang Talok 69*, 1999) was a fast-paced thriller set during the Asian financial crisis, with a down-on-her-luck woman stumbling upon a horde of money. Pen-Ek followed this with *Mon Rak Transistor: A Transistor Love Story* (2003), a bitter sweet love story about a naïve boy from the country with ambitions to be a *luk thung* singer. It's full of charm and the popular soundtrack is available on CD (see p.843). Pen-Ek's *Last Life in the Universe* (2003) is a much darker, more melancholy affair, following two very different personalities – a suicidal Japanese man and a Thai girl – who are brought together in grief. In *Ploy* (2007), a jet-lagged night in a Bangkok hotel sees the marriage of an expat Thai couple unravel, with sex scenes deemed too explicit by Thai censors.

The scriptwriter on Nonzee's *Daeng Bireley's* and *Nang Nak* was Wisit Sasanatieng who, in 2000, directed **Tears of the Black Tiger** (*Fah Talai Jone*). This gentle send-up of the old Thai action films of the 1960s and 1970s uses exaggerated acting styles and irresistible comic-book colours to tell the story of handsome bandit Dum and his love for upper-class Rumpoey. Writer-director Wisit grew up watching the spaghetti westerns of Sergio Leone and includes more than a few passing references to those films. His **Citizen Dog** (*Mah Nakorn*, 2004) is an even more surreal colour-saturated satire, both comic and pointed, about a country boy looking for work and romance in Bangkok.

Blockbusters at home and abroad

Among other high-profile international successes, the warm and off-beat comedy **Iron Ladies** (*Satri Lek*, 2000) charts the often hilarious true-life adventures of a Lampang volleyball team made up of transsexuals and transvestites. **Beautiful Boxer** (2003) fashions a sensitive, insightful biopic out of a similar subject – the true story of transvestite *muay thai* champion Nong Toom who fights in order to win money for sex-change surgery. **Bangkok Dangerous** (*Krung Thep Antharai*, 2000) is a riveting John Woo-style thriller directed by brothers Oxide and Danny Pang; both a brutal tale about a deaf hitman and the story of his love affair with a girl innocent of his occupation, it features several scenes shot in the streets of Bangkok.

The visually stunning historical blockbuster **The Legend of Suriyothai** (2001) tells the true story of a sixteenth-century queen of the Ayutthayan court who gave her life defending her husband during a Burmese invasion. Keen to give international appeal to this complex portrait of court intrigue and rather partisan take on Thai-Burmese relations, director Chatrichalerm Yukol brought

Thai film festivals

Interest in Thai films has become so significant that since 1998 Thailand has hosted regular film festivals, most notably the **Bangkok International Film Festival**, though in recent years it's moved from January to July to September, so check Ⓦwww.bangkokfilm.org for scheduling details. Meanwhile, entire festivals of Thai films have also been held in London and Tokyo, and Thai films have been enthusiastically received at many international film festivals, including Cannes.

For the latest reviews and archive stories on all aspects of Thai cinema, see Ⓦwww.thaicinema.org, the website of leading Thai film critic Anchalee Chaiworaporn.

in Frances Ford Coppola to edit a shortened version for Western audiences. He followed it with the even more epic three-part biography of King Naresuan, a national hero who ruled Thailand from Ayutthaya in the sixteenth century. At a reported cost of B700 million, the most expensive Thai film to date, **The Legend of King Naresuan** (*Tamnan Somdej Phra Naresuan*, 2007) was filmed at the purpose-built Prommitr Film Studios just outside Kanchanaburi, whose period sets and resident troupe of elephants are now open to the public (Ⓦwww.prommitrfilmstudio.com).

Prachya Pinkaew's martial arts action flick **Ong Bak** (2003) was such a huge box-office hit around the world that its star **Tony Jaa** – who performed all his own extraordinary stunts – was appointed Cultural Ambassador for Thailand. Director and star teamed up again in the similarly testosterone-fuelled **Tom Yum Goong** (2005), in which Tony Jaa's fight skills lead him to Australia on the trail of a stolen elephant. Elephants also feature big time in the action-spectacular *Ong Bak 2* (2008), set in the fifteenth-century Ayutthaya period and with Tony Jaa co-directing this time, as well as starring. At the other end of the spectrum, Thai art house also went international with the success of **Apichatpong Weerasethakul**'s challenging **Tropical Malady** (*Sud Pralad*, 2004), which won the Jury Prize at Cannes in 2004. Part gay romance, part trippy jungle ghost story, it was for some a pioneering experiment in Thai storytelling, to others an inaccessible bore. His *Syndromes and a Century* (*Sang Sattawat*, 2006) was Thailand's first film to be entered in competition at the Venice Film Festival but failed to impress the Thai censors who, among other reasons, banned it for its depiction of a guitar-playing Buddhist monk. Apichatpong responded by joining a protest against the introduction of a new, reactionary film-ratings system, but to no avail.

Many of the films that get widespread international release are unrepresentative of the crowd-pleasers that play week in, week out at most Thai cinemas. These tend to feature lots of laughs, slapstick, gangsters, likeably corny romance and much poking of fun at authority figures. The domestic blockbuster of 2008, however, was the high-school romantic comedy **Hormones** (*Pidtermyai Huajai Wawoon*, 2008), a quartet of interlinked stories directed by Songyos Sukmaganan and starring that year's biggest teen pin-ups to a soundtrack by hit Thai rock band Big Ass. The four spooky horror stories of **4Bia** "*Phobia*" (*See Prang*, 2008), each by a different director (including **Yongyoot Thongkongtoon**, who made *Iron Ladies*), were woven round a much more tenuous link but proved that while ghosts still do it for a Thai audience, they can intrigue foreign film-goers too.

Neil Pettigrew

Books

We have included publishers' details for books that may be hard to find outside Thailand, though some of them can be ordered online through www.dcothai.com. Other titles should be available worldwide. Titles marked 🏃 are particularly recommended.

Travelogues

Carl Bock *Temples and Elephants* (Orchid Press, Bangkok). Nineteenth-century account of a rough journey from Bangkok to the far north, dotted with vivid descriptions of rural life and court ceremonial.

Karen Connelly *Touch the Dragon.* Evocative and humorous journal of an impressionable Canadian teenager, sent on an exchange programme to Den Chai in northern Thailand for a year.

Charles Nicholl *Borderlines.* Entertaining adventures and dangerous romance in the "Golden Triangle" form the core of this slightly hackneyed traveller's tale, interwoven with stimulating and well-informed cultural diversions.

James O'Reilly and Larry Habegger (eds) *Travelers' Tales: Thailand.* Absorbing anthology of contemporary writings about Thailand, by Thailand experts, social commentators, travel writers and first-time visitors.

Steve Van Beek *Slithering South* (Wind and Water, Hong Kong). An expat writer tells how he single-handedly paddled his wooden boat down the entire 1100-kilometre course of the Chao Phraya River, and reveals a side of Thailand that's rarely written about in English.

Tom Vater *Beyond the Pancake Trench: Road Tales from the Wild East.* Adventures, insights and encounters on the margins of twenty-first-century Thailand. Also covers Cambodia, Laos, Vietnam and India.

Culture and society

Michael Carrithers *The Buddha: A Very Short Introduction.* Accessible account of the life of the Buddha, and the development and significance of his thought.

🏃 **Philip Cornwel-Smith and John Goss** *Very Thai.* Why do Thais decant their soft drinks into plastic bags, and how does one sniff-kiss? Answers and insights aplenty in this intriguingly observant, fully illustrated guide to contemporary Thai culture.

James Eckardt *Bangkok People.* The collected articles of a renowned expat journalist, whose encounters with a varied cast of Bangkokians – from construction-site workers and street vendors to boxers and political candidates – add texture and context to the city.

Sandra Gregory with Michael Tierney *Forget You Had a Daughter: Doing Time in the "Bangkok Hilton" – Sandra Gregory's Story.* The frank and shocking account of a young British woman's term in Bangkok's notorious Lard Yao prison after being caught trying to smuggle 89 grammes of heroin out of Thailand.

Roger Jones *Culture Smart! Thailand.* Handy little primer on Thailand's social and cultural mores, with plenty of refreshingly up-to-date insights.

Erich Krauss *Wave of Destruction: One Thai Village and Its Battle with the Tsunami.* A sad and often shocking, clear-eyed account of what Ban Nam Khen went through before, during and after the tsunami. Fills in many gaps left unanswered by news reports at the time.

Elaine and Paul Lewis *Peoples of the Golden Triangle.* Hefty, exhaustive work illustrated with excellent photographs, describing every aspect of hill-tribe life.

Father Joe Maier *Welcome to the Bangkok Slaughterhouse: The Battle for Human Dignity in Bangkok's Bleakest Slums.* Catholic priest Father Joe shares the stories of some of the Bangkok street kids and slum-dwellers that his charitable foundation has been supporting since 1972 (see p.80).

Trilok Chandra Majupuria *Erawan Shrine and Brahma Worship in Thailand* (Tecpress, Bangkok). The most concise introduction to the complexities of Thai religion, with a much wider scope than the title implies.

Cleo Odzer *Patpong Sisters.* An American anthropologist's funny and touching account of her life with the prostitutes and bar girls of Bangkok's notorious red-light district.

Phra Peter Pannapadipo *Little Angels: The Real-Life Stories of Twelve Thai Novice Monks.* A dozen young boys, many of them from desperate backgrounds, tell the often poignant stories of why they became novice monks. For some, funding from the Students Education Trust (p.81) has changed their lives.

Phra Peter Pannapadipo *Phra Farang: An English Monk in Thailand.* Behind the scenes in a Thai monastery: the frank, funny and illuminating account of a UK-born former businessman's life as a Thai monk.

Pasuk Phongpaichit and Sungsidh Piriyarangsan *Corruption and Democracy in Thailand.* Fascinating academic study, revealing the nuts and bolts of corruption in Thailand and its links with all levels of political life, and suggesting a route to a stronger society. Their sequel, a study of Thailand's illegal economy, *Guns, Girls, Gambling, Ganja*, co-written with Nualnoi Treerat, makes equally eye-opening and depressing reading.

Denis Segaller *Thai Ways.* Fascinating collection of short pieces on Thai customs and traditions written by a long-term English resident of Bangkok.

Pira Sudham *People of Esarn.* Wry and touching, potted life stories of villagers who live in, leave and return to the poverty-stricken northeast, compiled by a northeastern lad turned author.

Phil Thornton *Restless Souls: Rebels, Refugees, Medics and Misfits on the Thai–Burma Border.* An Australian journalist brings to light the terrible and complicated plight of the Karen, thousands of whom live as refugees in and around his adopted town of Mae Sot on the Thai–Burma border.

Richard Totman *The Third Sex: Kathoey – Thailand's Ladyboys.* As several *kathoey* share their life stories with him, social scientist Totman examines their place in modern Thai society and explores the theory, supported by Buddhist philosophy, that *kathoey* are members of a third sex whose transgendered make-up is pre determined from birth.

William Warren *Living in Thailand.* Luscious gallery of traditional houses, with an emphasis on the homes of Thailand's rich and famous; seductively photographed by Luca Invernizzi Tettoni.

Daniel Ziv and Guy Sharett *Bangkok Inside Out*. This A–Z of Bangkok quirks and cultural substrates is full of slick photography and sparky observations but was deemed offensive by Thailand's Ministry of Culture, so some Thai bookshops won't stock it.

History

Anna Leonowens *The English Governess at the Siamese Court*. The mendacious memoirs of the nineteenth-century English governess that inspired the infamous Yul Brynner film *The King and I*; low on accuracy, high on inside-palace gossip.

Michael Smithies *Old Bangkok*. Brief, anecdotal history of the capital's early development, emphasizing what remains to be seen of bygone Bangkok.

William Stevenson *The Revolutionary King*. Fascinating biography of the normally secretive King Bhumibol, by a British journalist who was given unprecedented access to the monarch and his family. The overall approach is fairly uncritical, but lots of revealing insights emerge along the way.

John Stewart *To the River Kwai: Two Journeys – 1943, 1979*. A survivor of the horrific World War II POW camps along the River Kwai returns to the region, interlacing his wartime reminiscences with observations on how he feels 36 years later.

William Warren *Jim Thompson: the Legendary American of Thailand*. The engrossing biography of the ex-intelligence agent, art collector and Thai silk magnate whose disappearance in Malaysia in 1967 has never been satisfactorily resolved.

David K. Wyatt *Thailand: A Short History*. An excellent treatment, scholarly but highly readable, with a good eye for witty, telling details. Good chapters on the story of the Thais before they reached what's now Thailand, and on more recent developments. His *Siam in Mind* (Silkworm Books, Chiang Mai) is a wide-ranging and intriguing collection of sketches and short reflections that point towards an intellectual history of Thailand.

Art, architecture and film

Jean Boisselier *The Heritage of Thai Sculpture*. Expensive but accessible, seminal tome by influential French art historian.

Susan Conway *Thai Textiles*. A fascinating, richly illustrated work which draws on sculptures and temple murals to trace the evolution of Thai weaving techniques and costume styles, and to examine the functional and ceremonial uses of textiles.

Sumet Jumsai *Naga: Cultural Origins in Siam and the West Pacific*. Wide-ranging discussion of water symbols in Thailand and other parts of Asia, offering a stimulating mix of art, architecture, mythology and cosmology.

Bastian Meiresonne (ed) *Thai Cinema* (®www.asiexpo.com). Anthology of twenty short essays on Thai cinema up to 2006, published to accompany a film festival in France, including pieces on art house, shorts and censorship. In French and English.

Steven Pettifor *Flavours: Thai Contemporary Art*. Takes up the baton from Poshyananda (see below) to look at the newly invigorated art scene in Thailand from 1992 to 2004, with profiles of 23 leading lights, including painters, multi media and performance artists.

Apinan Poshyananda *Modern Art In Thailand*. Excellent introduction which extends up to the early 1990s, with very readable discussions on dozens of individual artists, and lots of colour plates.

Dome Sukwong and Sawasdi Suwannapak *A Century of Thai Cinema*. Full-colour history of the Thai film industry and the promotional artwork (billboards, posters, magazines and cigarette cards) associated with it.

Steve Van Beek *The Arts of Thailand*. Lavishly produced and perfectly pitched introduction to the history of Thai architecture, sculpture and painting, with superb photographs by Luca Invernizzi Tettoni.

William Warren and Luca Invernizzi Tettoni *Arts and Crafts of Thailand*. Good-value large-format paperback, setting the wealth of Thai arts and crafts in cultural context, with plenty of attractive illustrations and colour photographs.

Natural history and ecology

Ashley J. Boyd and Collin Piprell *Diving in Thailand*. A thorough guide to 84 dive sites, plus general introductory sections on Thailand's marine life, conservation and photography tips.

Boonsong Lekagul and Philip D. Round *Guide to the Birds of Thailand*. Unparalleled illustrated guide to Thailand's birds. Worth scouring secondhand sellers for.

Craig Robson *A Field Guide to the Birds of Thailand*. Expert and beautifully illustrated guide to Thailand's top 950 bird species, with locator maps.

Eric Valli and Diane Summers *The Shadow Hunters*. Beautifully photographed photo-essay on the birds'-nest collectors of southern Thailand, with whom the authors spent over a year, together scaling the phenomenal heights of the sheer limestone walls.

Literature

Alastair Dingwall (ed) *Traveller's Literary Companion: Southeast Asia*. A useful though rather dry reference, with a large section on Thailand, including a book list, well-chosen extracts, biographical details of authors and other literary notes.

M.L. Manich Jumsai *Thai Ramayana* (Chalermnit, Bangkok). Slightly stilted, abridged prose translation of King Rama I's version of the epic Hindu narrative, full of gleeful descriptions of bizarre mythological characters and supernatural battles. Essential reading for a full appreciation of Thai painting, carving and classical dance.

Chart Korbjitti *The Judgement* (Howling Books). Sobering modern-day tragedy about a good-hearted Thai villager who is ostracized by his hypocritical neighbours. Contains lots of interesting details on village life and traditions, and thought-provoking passages on the stifling conservatism of rural communities. Winner of the S.E.A. Write Award in 1982.

Rattawut Lapcharoensap *Sightseeing*. This outstanding debut collection of short stories by a young Thai-born author now living overseas highlights big, pertinent themes – cruelty, corruption, racism, pride – in its neighbourhood tales of randy teenagers, bullyboys, a child's friendship with a Cambodian refugee, a young man who uses family influence to dodge the draft.

Nitaya Masavisut (ed) *The S.E.A. Write Anthology of Thai Short Stories and Poems* (Silkworm Books, Chiang Mai). Interesting medley of short stories and poems by Thai writers who have won Southeast Asian Writers' Awards, providing a good introduction to the contemporary literary scene.

Kukrit Pramoj *Si Phaendin: Four Reigns* (Silkworm Books, Chiang Mai). A kind of historical romance spanning the four reigns of Ramas V to VIII (1892–1946). Written by former prime minister Kukrit Pramoj, the story has become a modern classic in Thailand, made into films, plays and TV dramas, with heroine Ploi as the archetypal feminine role model.

S.P. Somtow *Jasmine Nights*. An engaging and humorous rites-of-passage tale, of an upper-class boy learning what it is to be Thai. *Dragon's Fin Soup and Other Modern Siamese Fables* is an imaginative and entertaining collection of often supernatural short stories, focusing on the collision of East and West.

Khamsing Srinawk *The Politician and Other Stories*. A collection of brilliantly satiric short stories, full of pithy moral observation and biting irony, which capture the vulnerability of peasant farmers in the north and northeast, as they try to come to grips with the modern world. Written by an insider from a peasant family, who was educated at Chulalongkorn University, became a hero of the left, and joined the communist insurgents after the 1976 clampdown.

Atsiri Thammachoat *Of Time and Tide* (Thai Modern Classics). Set in a fishing village near Hua Hin, this poetically written novella looks at how Thailand's fishing industry is changing, charting the effects on its fisherfolk and their communities.

Klaus Wenk *Thai Literature – An Introduction* (White Lotus, Bangkok). Dry, but useful, short overview of the last seven hundred years by a noted German scholar, with plenty of extracts.

Thailand in foreign literature

Dean Barrett *Kingdom of Make-Believe*. Despite the clichéd ingredients – the Patpong go-go bar scene, opium smuggling in the Golden Triangle, Vietnam veterans – this novel about a return to Thailand following a twenty-year absence turns out to be a rewardingly multi-dimensional take on the farang experience.

Mischa Berlinski *Fieldwork*. Anthropology versus evangelism, a battle played out over an imaginary hill tribe in the hills of Chiang Rai by a fascinating cast of characters, as wrily and vividly told by an eponymous narrator.

Botan *Letters from Thailand*. Probably the best introduction to the Chinese community in Bangkok, presented in the form of letters written over a twenty-year period by a Chinese emigrant to his mother. Branded as both anti-Chinese and anti-Thai, this 1969 prize-winning book is now mandatory reading in school social studies' classes.

Pierre Boulle *The Bridge Over the River Kwai*. The World War II novel that inspired the David Lean movie and kicked off the Kanchanaburi tourist industry.

John Burdett *Bangkok 8*. Riveting Bangkok thriller that takes in Buddhism, plastic surgery, police corruption, the *yaa baa* drugs trade, hookers, jade smuggling and the spirit world.

Alex Garland *The Beach.* Gripping cult thriller (later made into a film, shot partly on Ko Phi Phi Leh) that uses a Thai setting to explore the way in which travellers' ceaseless quest for "undiscovered" utopias inevitably leads to them despoiling the idyll.

Andrew Hicks *Thai Girl.* A British backpacker falls for a reticent young beach masseuse on Ko Samet but struggles with age-old cross-cultural confusion in this sensitive attempt at a different kind of expat novel.

Michel Houellebecq *Platform.* Sex tourism in Thailand provides the nucleus of this brilliantly provocative (some would say offensive) novel, in which Houellebecq presents a ferocious critique of Western decadence and cultural colonialism, and of radical Islam too.

Christopher G. Moore *God of Darkness.* Thailand's best-selling expat novelist sets his most intriguing thriller during the economic crisis of 1997 and includes plenty of meat on endemic corruption and the desperate struggle for power within family and society.

Darin Strauss *Chang & Eng.* An intriguing, imagined autobiography of the famous nineteenth-century Siamese twins (see p.221), from their impoverished Thai childhood via the freak shows of New York and London to married life in small-town North Carolina. Unfortunately marred by lazy research and a confused grasp of Thai geography and culture.

Food and cookery

Vatcharin Bhumichitr *The Taste of Thailand.* Another glossy introduction to this eminently photogenic country, this time through its food. The author runs a Thai restaurant in London and provides background colour as well as about 150 recipes adapted for Western kitchens.

Jacqueline M. Piper *Fruits of South-East Asia.* An exploration of the bounteous fruits of the region, tracing their role in cooking, medicine, handicrafts and rituals. Well illustrated with photos, watercolours and early botanical drawings.

David Thompson *Thai Food.* Comprehensive, impeccably researched celebration of the cuisine, with over 300 recipes, by the owner of the first Thai restaurant ever to earn a Michelin star.

Travel guides

Oliver Hargreaves *Exploring Phuket & Phi Phi: From Tin to Tourism.* Fascinating, thoroughly researched guide to the Andaman coast's big touristic honeypots; especially good on Phuket's history.

Thom Henley *Krabi: Caught in the Spell – A Guide to Thailand's Enchanted Province* (Thai Nature Education, Phuket). Highly readable features and observations on the attractions and people of south Thailand's most beautiful region, written by an expat environmentalist.

Dawn F. Rooney *Ancient Sukhothai.* Lively and beautifully photographed full-colour guide to the ruins of the northern plains: Sukhothai, Si Satchanalai and Kamphaeng Phet.

William Warren *Bangkok.* An engaging portrait of the unwieldy capital, weaving together anecdotes and character sketches from Bangkok's past and present.

Language

Language

Language

Thai belongs to one of the oldest families of languages in the world, Austro-Thai, and is radically different from most of the other tongues of Southeast Asia. Being tonal, Thai is extremely difficult for Westerners to master, but by building up from a small core of set phrases, you should soon have enough to get by. Most Thais who deal with tourists speak some English, but once you stray off the beaten track you'll probably need at least a little Thai. Anywhere you go, you'll impress and get better treatment if you at least make an effort to speak a few words.

Distinct dialects are spoken in the north, the northeast and the south, which can increase the difficulty of comprehending what's said to you. **Thai script** is even more of a problem to Westerners, with 44 consonants and 32 vowels. However, street signs in touristed areas are nearly always written in Roman script as well as Thai, and in other circumstances you're better off asking than trying to unscramble the swirling mess of symbols, signs and accents. For more information on transliteration into Roman script, see the box in this book's introduction.

Among **language books**, *Thai: The Rough Guide Phrasebook* covers the essential phrases and expressions in both Thai script and phonetic equivalents, as well as dipping into grammar and providing a menu reader and fuller vocabulary in dictionary format (English-Thai and Thai-English). Probably the best pocket dictionary is Paiboon Publishing's (Ⓦwww.ThaiLao.com) *Thai-English, English-Thai Dictionary*, which lists words in phonetic Thai as well as Thai script, and features a very handy table of the Thai alphabet in a dozen different fonts.

The best **teach-yourself course** is the expensive *Linguaphone Thai* (including six cassettes), which also has a shorter, cheaper beginner-level PDQI version (with four CDs). *Thai for Beginners* by Benjawan Poomsan Becker (Paiboon Publishing) is a cheaper, more manageable textbook and is especially good for getting to grips with the Thai writing system; you can also buy accompanying CDs to help with listening skills, or get the whole thing in CD-ROM format. For a more traditional textbook, try Stuart Campbell and Chuan Shaweevongse's *The Fundamentals of the Thai Language*, which is comprehensive, though hard going. G.H. Allison's *Easy Thai* is best for those who feel the urge to learn the alphabet. The **website** Ⓦwww.thai-language.com is an amazing free resource, featuring a searchable dictionary of over 40,000 Thai words, complete with Thai script and audio clips, plus a guide to the language and forums.

Pronunciation

Mastering **tones** is probably the most difficult part of learning Thai. Five different tones are used – low, middle, high, falling, and rising – by which the meaning of a single syllable can be altered in five different ways. Thus, using four of the five tones, you can make a sentence from just one syllable: "mái mài mâi ma˘i" meaning "New wood burns, doesn't it?" As well as the natural difficulty in becoming attuned to speaking and listening to these different tones, Western efforts are complicated by our habit of denoting the overall meaning of a sentence by modulating our tones – for example, turning a statement into a question through a shift of stress and tone. Listen to native Thai speakers and you'll soon begin to pick up the different approach to tone.

The pitch of each tone is gauged in relation to your vocal range when speaking, but they should all lie within a narrow band, separated by gaps just big enough to differentiate them. The **low tones** (syllables marked ̀), **middle tones** (unmarked syllables), and **high tones** (syllables marked ́) should each be pronounced evenly and with no inflection. The **falling tone** (syllables marked ^) is spoken with an obvious drop in pitch, as if you were sharply emphasizing a word in English. The **rising tone** (marked ̌) is pronounced as if you were asking an exaggerated question in English.

As well as the unfamiliar tones, you'll find that, despite the best efforts of the transliterators, there is no precise English equivalent to many **vowel and consonant sounds** in the Thai language. The lists below give a simplified idea of pronunciation.

Vowels

a	as in dad
aa	has no precise equivalent, but is pronounced as it looks, with the vowel elongated
ae	as in there
ai	as in buy
ao	as in now
aw	as in awe
ay	as in pay
e	as in pen
eu	as in sir, but heavily nasalized
i	as in tip
ii	as in feet
o	as in knock
oe	as in hurt, but more closed
oh	as in toe
u	as in loot
uu	as in pool

Consonants

r	as in rip, but with the tongue flapped quickly against the palate – in everyday speech, it's often pronounced like "l"
kh	as in keep
ph	as in put
th	as in time
k	is unaspirated and unvoiced, and closer to "g"
p	is also unaspirated and unvoiced, and closer to "b"
t	is also unaspirated and unvoiced, and closer to "d".

General words and phrases

Greetings and basic phrases

When you speak to a stranger in Thailand, you should generally end your sentence in *khráp* if you're a man, *khâ* if you're a woman – these untranslatable politening syllables will gain goodwill, and are nearly always used after *sawàt dii* (hello/goodbye) and *khàwp khun* (thank you). *Khráp* and *khâ* are also often used to answer "yes" to a question, though the most common way is to repeat the verb of the question (precede it with *mâi* for "no"). *Châi* (yes) and *mâi châi* (no) are less frequently used than their English equivalents.

Hello	sawàt dii
Where are you going?	pai năi? (not always meant literally, but used as a general greeting)
I'm out having fun/ I'm travelling	pai thîaw (answer to pai năi, almost indefinable pleasantry)
Goodbye	sawàt dii/la kàwn
Good luck/cheers	chôhk dii
Excuse me	khăw thâwt
Thank you	khàwp khun
It's nothing/it doesn't matter	mâi pen rai
How are you?	sabai dii reŭ?
I'm fine	sabai dii

What's your name?	khun chêu arai?
My name is…	phŏm (men)/ diichăn (women) chêu…
I come from…	phŏm/diichăn maa jàak…
I don't understand	mâi khâo jai
Do you speak English?	khun phûut phasăa angkrìt dâi măi?
Do you have…?	mii…măi?
Is…possible?	…dâi măi?
Can you help me?	chûay phŏm/ diichăn dâi măi?
(I) want…	ao…
(I) would like to…	yàak jà…
(I) like…	châwp…
What is this called in Thai?	níi phasăa thai rîak wâa arai?

Getting around

Where is the…?	…yùu thîi năi?
How far?	klai thâo rai?
I would like to go to…	yàak jà pai…
Where have you been?	pai năi maa?
Where is this bus going?	rót níi pai năi?
When will the bus leave?	rót jà àwk mêua rai?
What time does the bus arrive in…?	rót theŭng…kìi mohng?
Stop here	jàwt thîi nîi
here	thîi nîi
there/over there	thîi nâan/thîi nôhn
right	khwăa
left	sái
straight	trong
north	neŭa

south	tâi
east	tawan àwk
west	tawan tòk
near/far	klâi/klai
street	thanŏn
train station	sathàanii rót fai
bus station	sathàanii rót mae
airport	sanăam bin
ticket	tŭa
hotel	rohng raem
post office	praisanii
restaurant	raan ahăan
shop	raan
market	talàat
hospital	rohng pha-yaabaan
motorbike	rót mohtoesai
taxi	rót táksîi
boat	reua
bicycle	jàkràyaan

Accommodation and shopping

How much is…?	…thâo rai/kìi bàat?
I don't want a plastic bag, thanks	mâi ao thŭng khráp/ khâ

How much is a room here per night?	hâwng thîi nîi kheun lá thâo rai?
Do you have a cheaper room?	mii hâwng thùuk kwàa măi?

Can I/we look at the room?	duu hâwng dâi măi?	**cheap/expensive**	thùuk/phaeng
I/We'll stay two nights	jà yùu săwng kheun	**air-con room**	hăwng ae
Can you reduce the price?	lót raakhaa dâi măi?	**ordinary room**	hăwng thammadaa
Can I store my bag here?	fàak krapăo wái thîi nîi dâi măi?	**telephone**	thohrásàp
		laundry	sák phâa
		blanket	phâa hòm
		fan	phát lom

General adjectives

alone	khon diaw	**easy**	ngâi
another	ìik…nèung	**fun**	sanùk
bad	mâi dii	**hot (temperature)**	ráwn
big	yài	**hot (spicy)**	phèt
clean	sa-àat	**hungry**	hiŭ khâo
closed	pìt	**ill**	mâi sabai
cold (object)	yen	**open**	pòet
cold (person or weather)	năo	**pretty**	sŭay
delicious	aròi	**small**	lek
difficult	yâak	**thirsty**	hiŭ nám
dirty	sokaprok	**tired**	nèu-ay
		very	mâak

General nouns

Nouns have no plurals or genders, and don't require an article.

bathroom/toilet	hăwng nám	**foreigner**	fàràng
boyfriend or girlfriend	faen	**friend**	phêuan
food	ahăan	**money**	ngoen
		water/liquid	nám

General verbs

Thai verbs do not conjugate at all, and also often double up as nouns and adjectives, which means that foreigners' most unidiomatic attempts to construct sentences are often readily understood.

come	maa	**go**	pai
do	tham	**sit**	nâng
eat	kin/thaan khâo	**sleep**	nawn làp
give	hâi	**walk**	doen pai

Numbers

zero	sŭun	**four**	sìi
one	nèung	**five**	hâa
two	săwng	**six**	hòk
three	săam	**seven**	jèt

eight	pàet	twenty-two, twenty-three…	yîi sìp săwng, yîi sìp săam…
nine	kâo	thirty, forty, etc	săam sìp, sìi sìp…
ten	sìp	one hundred, two hundred…	nèung rói, săwng rói…
eleven	sìp èt	one thousand	nèung phan
twelve, thirteen…	sìp săwng, sìp săam…	ten thousand	nèung mèun
twenty	yîi sìp/yiip		
twenty-one	yîi sìp èt		

Time

The commonest system for telling the time, as outlined below, is actually a confusing mix of several different systems. The State Railway and government officials use the 24-hour clock (9am is *kâo naalikaa*, 10am *sìp naalikaa*, and so on), which is always worth trying if you get stuck.

1–5am	tii nèung–tii hâa	hour	chûa mohng
6–11am	hòk mohng cháo–sìp èt mohng cháo	day	wan
noon	thîang	week	aathít
1pm	bài mohng	month	deuan
2–4pm	bài săwng mohng–bài sìi mohng	year	pii
5–6pm	hâa mohng yen–hòk mohng yen	today	wan níi
7–11pm	nèung thûm–hâa thûm	tomorrow	phrûng níi
midnight	thîang kheun	yesterday	mêua wan níi
What time is it?	kii mohng láew?	now	diăw níi
How many hours?	kìi chûa mohng?	next week	aathít nâa
How long?	naan thâo rai?	last week	aathít kàwn
minute	naathii	morning	cháo
		afternoon	bài
		evening	yen
		night	kheun

Days

Sunday	wan aathít	Thursday	wan pháréuhàt
Monday	wan jan	Friday	wan sùk
Tuesday	wan angkhaan	Saturday	wan săo
Wednesday	wan phút		

Food and drink

Basic ingredients

kài	chicken	ahăan thalay	seafood
mŭu	pork	plaa	fish
néua	beef, meat	plaa dùk	catfish
pèt	duck	plaa mèuk	squid

kûng	prawn, shrimp
hŏy	shellfish
hŏy nang rom	oyster
puu	crab
khài	egg
phàk	vegetables

Vegetables

makĕua	aubergine
makĕua thêt	tomato
nàw mái	bamboo shoots
tùa ngâwk	bean sprouts
phrík	chilli
man faràng	potato
man faràng thâwt	chips
taeng kwaa	cucumber
phrík yùak	green pepper
krathiam	garlic
hèt	mushroom
tùa	peas, beans or lentils
tôn hŏrm	spring onions

Noodles

ba mìi	egg noodles
kwáy tiăw (sên yai/sên lék)	white rice noodles (wide/thin)
khanŏm jiin nám yaa	noodles topped with fish curry
kwáy tiăw/ ba mìi haêng	rice noodle/egg noodles fried with egg, small pieces of meat and a few vegetables
kwáy tiăw/ba mìi nám (mŭu)	rice noodle/egg noodle soup, made with chicken broth (and pork balls)
kwáy tiăw/ ba mìi rât nâ (mŭu)	rice noodles/egg noodles fried in gravy-like sauce with vegetables (and pork slices)
mìi kràwp	crisp fried egg noodles with small pieces of meat and a few vegetables
phàt thai	thin noodles fried with egg, bean sprouts and tofu, topped with ground peanuts
phàt siyú	wide or thin noodles fried with soy sauce, egg and meat

Rice

khâo	rice
khâo man kài	slices of chicken served over marinated rice
khâo mŭu daeng	red pork with rice
khâo nâ kài/pèt	chicken/duck served with sauce over rice
khâo niăw	sticky rice
khâo phàt	fried rice
khâo kaeng	curry over rice
khâo tôm	rice soup (usually for breakfast)

Curries and soups

kaeng phèt	hot, red curry
kaeng phánaeng	thick, savoury curry
kaeng khĭaw wan	green curry
kaeng mátsàman	rich muslim-style curry, usually with beef and potatoes
kaeng karìi	mild, indian-style curry
hàw mòk thalay	seafood curry soufflé
kaeng liang	peppery vegetable soup
kaeng sôm	tamarind soup
tôm khà kài	chicken, coconut and galangal soup
tôm yam kûng	hot and sour prawn soup
kaeng jèut	mild soup with vegetables and usually pork

Salads

lâap	spicy ground meat salad
nám tòk	grilled beef or pork salad
sôm tam	spicy papaya salad
yam hua plee	banana flower salad
yam néua	grilled beef salad
yam plaa mèuk	squid salad
yam sôm oh	pomelo salad
yam plaa dùk foo	crispy fried catfish salad
yam thùa phuu	wing-bean salad
yam wun sen	noodle and pork salad

Other dishes

hâwy thâwt	omelette stuffed with mussels
kài phàt bai kraprao	chicken fried with holy basil leaves
kài phàt nàw mái	chicken with bamboo shoots
kài phàt mét mámûang	chicken with cashew nuts
kài phàt khĭng	chicken with ginger
kài yâang	grilled chicken
khài yát sài	omelette with pork and vegetables
kûng chúp paêng thâwt	prawns fried in batter
mŭu prîaw wăan	sweet and sour pork
néua phàt krathiam phrík thai	beef fried with garlic and pepper
néua phàt nám man hâwy	beef in oyster sauce
phàt phàk bûng fai daeng	morning glory fried in garlic and bean sauce
phàt phàk ruam	stir-fried vegetables
pàw pía	spring rolls
plaa nêung páe sá	whole fish steamed with vegetables and ginger
plaa rât phrík	whole fish cooked with chillies
plaa thâwt	fried whole fish
sàté	satay
thâwt man plaa	fish cake

Thai desserts (khanŏm)

khanŏm beuang	small crispy pancake folded over with coconut cream and strands of sweet egg inside
khâo lăam	sticky rice, coconut cream and black beans cooked and served in bamboo tubes
khâo niăw daeng	sticky red rice mixed with coconut cream
khâo niăw thúrian/ mámûang	sticky rice mixed with coconut cream and durian/mango
klûay khàek	fried banana
lûk taan chêum	sweet palm kernels served in syrup
săngkhayaa	coconut custard
tàkôh	squares of transparent jelly (jello) topped with coconut cream

Drinks (khreûang deùm)

bia	beer
chaa ráwn	hot tea
chaa yen	iced tea
kaafae ráwn	hot coffee
kâew	glass
khúat	bottle
mâekhŏng (or anglicized Mekong)	thai brand-name rice whisky
klûay pan	banana shake
nám mánao/sôm	fresh, bottled or fizzy lemon/orange juice
nám plào	drinking water (boiled or filtered)
nám sŏdaa	soda water
nám taan	sugar
kleua	salt
nám yen	cold water
nom jeùd	milk
ohlíang	iced black coffee
thûay	cup

Ordering

I am vegetarian/vegan	**Phŏm (male)/ diichăn (female) kin ahăan mangsàwirát/jeh**
Can I see the menu?	**Khăw duù menu nóy?**
I would like…	**Khăw…**
with/without…	**Saì/mâi saì…**
Can I have the bill please?	**Khăw check bin?**

LANGUAGE | Food and drink

Glossary

Amphoe District.

Amphoe muang Provincial capital.

Ao Bay.

Apsara Female deity.

Avalokitesvara Bodhisattva representing compassion.

Avatar Earthly manifestation of a deity.

Ban Village or house.

Bang Village by a river or the sea.

Bencharong Polychromatic ceramics made in China for the Thai market.

Bhumisparsa mudra Most common gesture of Buddha images; symbolizes the Buddha's victory over temptation.

Bodhisattva In Mahayana Buddhism, an enlightened being who postpones his or her entry into Nirvana.

Bot Main sanctuary of a Buddhist temple.

Brahma One of the Hindu trinity – "The Creator". Usually depicted with four faces and four arms.

Celadon Porcelain with grey-green glaze.

Changwat Province.

Chao ley/chao nam "Sea gypsies" – nomadic fisherfolk of south Thailand.

Chedi Reliquary tower in Buddhist temple.

Chofa Finial on temple roof.

Deva Mythical deity.

Devaraja God-king.

Dharma The teachings or doctrine of the Buddha.

Dharmachakra Buddhist Wheel of Law (also known as Wheel of Doctrine or Wheel of Life).

Doi Mountain.

Erawan Mythical three-headed elephant; Indra's vehicle.

Farang Foreigner/foreign.

Ganesh Hindu elephant-headed deity, remover of obstacles and god of knowledge.

Garuda Mythical Hindu creature – half-man half-bird; Vishnu's vehicle.

Gopura Entrance pavilion to temple precinct (especially Khmer).

Hamsa Sacred mythical goose; Brahma's vehicle.

Hanuman Monkey god and chief of the monkey army in the Ramayana; ally of Rama.

Hat Beach.

Hin Stone.

Hinayana Pejorative term for Theravada school of Buddhism, literally "Lesser Vehicle".

Ho trai A scripture library.

Indra Hindu king of the gods and, in Buddhism, devotee of the Buddha; usually carries a thunderbolt.

Isaan Northeast Thailand.

Jataka Stories of the Buddha's five hundred lives.

Khaen Reed and wood pipe; the characteristic musical instrument of Isaan.

Khao Hill, mountain.

Khlong Canal.

Khon Classical dance-drama.

Kinnari Mythical creature – half woman, half bird.

Kirtimukha Very powerful deity depicted as a lion-head.

Ko Island.

Ku The Lao word for prang; a tower in a temple complex.

Laem Headland or cape.

Lakhon Classical dance-drama.

Lak muang City pillar; revered home for the city's guardian spirit.

Lakshaman/Phra Lak Rama's younger brother.

Lakshana Auspicious signs or "marks of greatness" displayed by the Buddha.

Lanna Northern Thai kingdom that lasted from the thirteenth to the sixteenth century.

Likay Popular folk theatre.

Longyi Burmese sarong.

Luang Pho Abbot or especially revered monk.

Maenam River.

Mahathat Chedi containing relics of the Buddha.

Mahayana School of Buddhism now practised mainly in China, Japan and Korea; literally "the Great Vehicle".

Mara The Evil One; tempter of the Buddha.

Mawn khwaan Traditional triangular or "axe-head" pillow.

Meru/Sineru Mythical mountain at the centre of Hindu and Buddhist cosmologies.

Mondop Small, square temple building to house minor images or religious texts.

Moo/muu Neighbourhood.

Muang City or town.

Muay thai Thai boxing.

Mudra Symbolic gesture of the Buddha.

Mut mee Tie-dyed cotton or silk.

Naga Mythical dragon-headed serpent in Buddhism and Hinduism.

Nakhon Honorific title for a city.

Nam Water.

Nam tok Waterfall.

Nang thalung Shadow-puppet entertainment, found in southern Thailand.

Nielloware Engraved metalwork.

Nirvana Final liberation from the cycle of rebirths; state of non-being to which Buddhists aspire.

Pak Tai Southern Thailand.

Pali Language of ancient India; the script of the original Buddhist scriptures.

Pha sin Woman's sarong.

Phi Animist spirit.

Phra Honorific term – literally "excellent".

Phu Mountain.

Prang Central tower in a Khmer temple.

Prasat Khmer temple complex or central shrine.

Rama/Phra Ram Human manifestation of Hindu deity Vishnu; hero of the Ramayana.

Ramakien Thai version of the Ramayana.

Ramayana Hindu epic of good versus evil: chief characters include Rama, Sita, Ravana, Hanuman.

Ravana see Totsagan.

Reua hang yao Longtail boat.

Rishi Ascetic hermit.

Rot ae/rot tua Air-conditioned bus.

Rot thammadaa Ordinary bus.

Sala Meeting hall, pavilion, bus stop – or any open-sided structure.

Samlor Three-wheeled passenger tricycle.

Sanskrit Sacred language of Hinduism; also used in Buddhism.

Sanuk Fun.

Sema Boundary stone to mark consecrated ground within temple complex.

Shiva One of the Hindu trinity – "The Destroyer".

Shiva lingam Phallic representation of Shiva.

Soi Lane or side road.

Songkhran Thai New Year.

Songthaew Public transport pick-up vehicle; means "two rows", after its two facing benches.

Takraw Game played with a rattan ball.

Talat Market.

Talat nam Floating market.

Talat yen Night market.

Tambon Subdistrict.

Tavatimsa Buddhist heaven.

Tha Pier.

Thale Sea or lake.

Tham Cave.

Thanon Road.

That Chedi.

Thep A divinity.

Theravada Main school of Buddhist thought in Thailand; also known as Hinayana.

Totsagan Rama's evil rival in the Ramayana; also known as Ravana.

Tripitaka Buddhist scriptures.

Trok Alley.

Tuk-tuk Motorized three-wheeled taxi.

Uma Shiva's consort.

Ushnisha Cranial protuberance on Buddha images, signifying an enlightened being.

Viharn Temple assembly hall for the laity; usually contains the principal Buddha image.

Vipassana Buddhist meditation technique; literally "insight".

Vishnu One of the Hindu trinity – "The Preserver". Usually shown with four arms, holding a disc, a conch, a lotus and a club.

Wai Thai greeting expressed by a prayer-like gesture with the hands.

Wang Palace.

Wat Temple.

Wiang Fortified town.

Yaksha Mythical giant.

Yantra Magical combination of numbers and letters, used to ward off danger.

Small print and

Index

A Rough Guide to Rough Guides

Published in 1982, the first Rough Guide – to Greece – was a student scheme that became a publishing phenomenon. Mark Ellingham, a recent graduate in English from Bristol University, had been travelling in Greece the previous summer and couldn't find the right guidebook. With a small group of friends he wrote his own guide, combining a highly contemporary, journalistic style with a thoroughly practical approach to travellers' needs.

The immediate success of the book spawned a series that rapidly covered dozens of destinations. And, in addition to impecunious backpackers, Rough Guides soon acquired a much broader and older readership that relished the guides' wit and inquisitiveness as much as their enthusiastic, critical approach and value-for-money ethos.

These days, Rough Guides include recommendations from shoestring to luxury and cover more than 200 destinations around the globe, including almost every country in the Americas and Europe, more than half of Africa and most of Asia and Australasia. Our ever-growing team of authors and photographers is spread all over the world, particularly in Europe, the US and Australia.

In the early 1990s, Rough Guides branched out of travel, with the publication of Rough Guides to World Music, Classical Music and the Internet. All three have become benchmark titles in their fields, spearheading the publication of a wide range of books under the Rough Guide name.

Including the travel series, Rough Guides now number more than 350 titles, covering: phrasebooks, waterproof maps, music guides from Opera to Heavy Metal, reference works as diverse as Conspiracy Theories and Shakespeare, and popular culture books from iPods to Poker. Rough Guides also produce a series of more than 120 World Music CDs in partnership with World Music Network.

Visit www.roughguides.com to see our latest publications.

Rough Guide travel images are available for commercial licensing at www.roughguidespictures.com

Rough Guide credits

Text editor: Alice Park
Layout: Ankur Guha
Cartography: Jasbir Sandhu, Rajesh Chhibber
Picture editor: Sarah Cummins
Production: Rebecca Short
Proofreaders: Diane Margolis and Margaret Doyle
Cover design: Chloë Roberts
Photographers: Martin Richardson and Karen Trist
Editorial: Ruth Blackmore, Andy Turner, Keith Drew, Edward Aves, Lucy White, Jo Kirby, James Smart, Natasha Foges, Róisín Cameron, Emma Traynor, Emma Gibbs, Kathryn Lane, Monica Woods, Mani Ramaswamy, Harry Wilson, Lucy Cowie, Amanda Howard, Lara Kavanagh, Alison Roberts, Joe Staines, Peter Buckley, Matthew Milton, Tracy Hopkins, Ruth Tidball; **Delhi** Madhavi Singh, Karen D'Souza, Lubna Shaheen
Design & Pictures: **London** Scott Stickland, Dan May, Diana Jarvis, Mark Thomas, Nicole Newman, Emily Taylor; **Delhi** Umesh Aggarwal, Ajay Verma, Jessica Subramanian, Pradeep Thapliyal, Sachin Tanwar, Anita Singh, Nikhil Agarwal, Sachin Gupta
Production: Vicky Baldwin
Cartography: **London** Maxine Repath, Ed Wright, Katie Lloyd-Jones; **Delhi** Ashutosh Bharti, Rajesh Mishra, Animesh Pathak, Karobi Gogoi, Alakananda Bhattacharya, Swati Handoo, Deshpal Dabas
Online: **London** George Atwell, Faye Hellon, Jeanette Angell, Fergus Day, Justine Bright, Clare Bryson, Aine Fearon, Adrian Low, Ezgi Celebi, Amber Bloomfield; **Delhi** Amit Verma, Rahul Kumar, Narender Kumar, Ravi Yadav, Debojit Borah, Rakesh Kumar, Ganesh Sharma, Shisir Basumatari
Marketing & Publicity: **London** Liz Statham, Niki Hanmer, Louise Maher, Jess Carter, Vanessa Godden, Vivienne Watton, Anna Paynton, Rachel Sprackett, Libby Jellie, Laura Vipond, Vanessa McDonald; **New York** Katy Ball, Judi Powers, Nancy Lambert; **Delhi** Ragini Govind
Manager India: Punita Singh
Reference Director: Andrew Lockett
Operations Manager: Helen Phillips
PA to Publishing Director: Nicola Henderson
Publishing Director: Martin Dunford
Commercial Manager: Gino Magnotta
Managing Director: John Duhigg

Publishing information

This seventh edition published October 2009 by
Rough Guides Ltd,
80 Strand, London WC2R 0RL
14 Local Shopping Centre, Panchsheel Park,
New Delhi 110017, India
Distributed by the Penguin Group
Penguin Books Ltd,
80 Strand, London WC2R 0RL
Penguin Group (USA)
375 Hudson Street, NY 10014, USA
Penguin Group (Australia)
250 Camberwell Road, Camberwell,
Victoria 3124, Australia
Penguin Group (Canada)
195 Harry Walker Parkway N, Newmarket, ON,
L3Y 7B3 Canada
Penguin Group (NZ)
67 Apollo Drive, Mairangi Bay, Auckland 1310,
New Zealand
Cover concept by Peter Dyer.
Typeset in Bembo and Helvetica to an original design by Henry Iles.
Printed in Italy by L.E.G.O. S.p.A, Lavis (TN)

888pp includes index
A catalogue record for this book is available from the British Library
ISBN: 978-1-84836-092-1

1 3 5 7 9 8 6 4 2

Help us update

We've gone to a lot of effort to ensure that the seventh edition of **The Rough Guide to Thailand** is accurate and up-to-date. However, things change – places get "discovered", opening hours are notoriously fickle, restaurants and rooms raise prices or lower standards. If you feel we've got it wrong or left something out, we'd like to know, and if you can remember the address, the price, the hours, the phone number, so much the better.

Please send your comments with the subject line "**Rough Guide Thailand Update**" to Ⓔmail@roughguides.com. We'll credit all contributions and send a copy of the next edition (or any other Rough Guide if you prefer) for the very best emails.

Have your questions answered and tell others about your trip at Ⓦwww.roughguides.com

Acknowledgements

The **authors** jointly would like to thank: Abigail Silver at London TAT; staff at TAT offices in Ayutthaya, Phitsanulok, Mae Hong Son, Chiang Rai, Surat Thani, Ko Samui, Hat Yai and Nakhon Si Thammarat; Felix Hude for the original section on cycling; John Clewley for his piece on Thai music and Camilla Mitchell for her advice on elephants.

From **Lucy**, thanks to: Serge and Morn in Trat; Charlie, Apple, Noi, Sam and Steve Nye in Kanchanaburi; Tan and Khun Naa in Sukhothai; Bronwen in Chanthaburi; Ian on Ko Chang; Stuart and Ball on Ko Mak; Gai on Ko Kood; Tom and Aroon; Aung on Ko Samet; Paul Embrechts; Heather and Kitty on Ko Yao Noi; Richard on Ko Phayam; Ray and Sao on Ko Jum; Panja in Bangkok; and Mai and Maree in Krabi. This edition is dedicated to Seonai Gordon, always an inspiration.

From **Paul**, very special thanks to Gade Taraksa. Thanks also to: Bill Gray; Jack Grassby; Mike Barraclough, Ron Emmons and Khun Sin in Chiang Mai; Anne Scott in Chiang Rai; Khun Wat in Chiang Khong; Rashi and Bambi on Ko Pha Ngan; Ekkachai Binwaha, Dick te Brake, Anita and all the Siaws in Trang; Bon Satarat and Ratana Kongnual in Satun; Nikki Busuttil, Wannapa Rakkeo, Maria Kuhn and Marion Walsh in Bangkok; on Ko Tao, Matt Bolton, Nathan Cook, Dev and Don; Aekkasan in Mae Sariang; on Ko Lipe, Luca, Boi and Johann; Tom in Phetchaburi; Suda in Chumphon; and Tuppadit Thaiarry at Avis.

From **Ron**, thanks to: Arjin Sookkaseam in Khao Yai National Park; Pirom and Aree in Surin; Payungsak Inchay in Ubon Ratchathani

Readers' letters

Thanks to all the readers who have taken the time to write in with comments and suggestions (and apologies if we've inadvertently omitted or misspelt anyone's name):

Carla Anderson, Julien Anseau, Luis F Arévalogarcia, John Archibald, Jane Barnett, Alison Batley, Marcel Bokhorst, Paul Bonner, Michelle Brodie, Margo Burgers, Phil Cairns, Adam Cathro, Katie Clare, G Clegg, John & Maggie Coaton, Ryan Collins, Cian Connolly, Diana Coode & Lee J Barnett, Melanie Cook, David Cunningham, Conrad Davies, Kieran Dignam, Chris Eichler, Mike Fletcher, Michael Gardham, Joanne Gardiner, David Gaukrodger, Chris Goward, Bernd Greiner, Kimberley Anne Gray, Pelle Gustafson, John & Shirley Harper, Anna Harrison, Paul Hie, Benjamin L Hilditch, Charlie Hogan, Andrew Hunt, Clare Johnson & Peter Lawrie, Steven Jolly, Grace Kenny, Helen Keynes, Majid Khan, A.G. Klei & Ruth Campbell-Page, Jan Kling, Viviana & Allister Levy, Jason Lewis, Rob van Loo, Bridget MacDonald, Aiden MacFarlane, Monica Mackaness & John Garratt, Anita & Hamish McFarlane, Jim McNalis, Regine De Naegel, Matt Nicholls, Jan van Oort, Megan Murphy O'Connell, James Newton, John, Phil & Sinead O'Reilly, John & Saw Payne, Jan Pennington, Por Fl Pharo, Allan and Margaret Rickmann, Paul Robson, Kimberley Ross, Simon Rowley, Vanessa Ryan & Russ Nash, Riccardo Sai, Beat & Anaida Schmid, Peter Searl, Keith Shaw, Alex Shields, Clayton Smith, Ray Smith, Andrea Spescha, Dave Stark, Jeff Stone, Vicky Stone, Sarah Stuteville, Will Swainson, Neal Teplitz, Robin & Matt Thomsen, Sue Thornton, Nick Trautmann, Wayne Turner, Charlotte Underwood, Gillian Walker, John Weldon, David Whiting, Moritz Winnen, Lisa Wortley

Photo credits

All photos © Rough Guides except the following:

Things not to miss

06 Procession of the Vegetarian Festival, Phuket © Luca Tettoni/Photolibrary
11 National Museum, Bangkok © Robert Harding Picture Library/Alamy
14 Diving, Ko Tao © Simon Podgorsek/istock
15 Thai cookery classes courtesy of Chiang Mai Cookery School
16 Fish, Similan Islands © Dejan Sarman/istock
18 Fishing, Mekong River © Michael Jung/istock
22 Nakhon Si Thammarat © Avatra images/Alamy
24 Mural, Nan province © Chris Hellier/Alamy
25 Umphang province © Crystite licenced/Alamy
26 Full moon party, Ko Pha Ngan © Chris Mclennan/Photolibrary
27 Ko Tarutao National Park, Ko Lipe © travelib asia/Alamy
28 Ko Kood Island © Body Philippe/Photolibrary
32 Rock climbing, Laem Phra Nang Railay © Ingolf Pompe 17/Alamy
34 Songkhran Festival, Bangkok © Caro/Alamy
35 Wat Phu Tok, Isaan © Jack Barker/Alamy

Black and whites

p.227 The Bridge over the River Kwai, Kanchanaburi courtesy of Sam's Guest House
p.307 Tee Lor Su waterfall © Yvan Cohen/OnAsia .com
p.768 Ko Sukorn © Andrew Woodley/Alamy
p.777 Longtail boat on Ko Hai © Simon Attrill/ Alamy

Index

Map entries are in colour.

C

INDEX

D

E

F

G

R

S

INDEX

Map symbols

maps are listed in the full index using coloured text

- International boundary
- Province boundary
- Chapter division boundary
- Expressway
- Pedestrianized road
- Road
- Steps
- Unpaved road
- Path
- Railway
- Ferry route
- River/Canal
- Wall
- Cable car & station
- Footbridge
- Bridge
- Accommodation
- Restaurants & bars
- Border crossing
- Peak
- Mountains
- Cave
- Waterfall
- Spring
- Rocks
- Lighthouse
- Viewpoint
- Gate
- Arch
- One-way street
- Statue
- Airport
- Transport stop
- Point of interest
- Museum
- Bank/ATM
- Internet access
- Tourist information
- Telephone office
- Hospital
- Post office
- Market
- Mosque
- Temple
- Chinese temple/Pagoda
- Stadium
- Church
- Building
- Christian cemetery
- Swamps/marshes
- Park/forest
- Beach

About the authors

Paul Gray has been a regular visitor to Thailand since working as an English teacher at the British Council in Chiang Mai in the late 1980s. He is co-author of the *Rough Guide to Bangkok* and the *Rough Guide to Thailand's Beaches & Islands*, as well as the *Rough Guide to Ireland* and *Dublin Directions*, and has edited and contributed to many other guidebooks, including updating his native Northeast for the *Rough Guide to England*.

Lucy Ridout has spent all her working life travelling in and writing about Asia. She is co-author of the *Rough Guide to Bangkok*, the *Rough Guide to Thailand's Beaches & Islands* and the *Rough Guide to Bali and Lombok*, and has also co-written *First-Time Asia*, a handbook for travellers making their first visit to the region.

…used the Rough
…lishments our
…perfectly sited
… restaurant. The
…k recommendations
… us your own
…ll be happy to check
out for future editions.

Accommodation price codes

Throughout this guide, guest houses, bungalows and hotels have been categorized according to the price codes given below. These categories represent the minimum you can expect to pay in the high season (roughly July, Aug and Nov–Feb) for a double room. For full details see p.50.

❶ B250 and under	❹ B601–900	❼ B2001–3000
❷ B251–400	❺ B901–1400	❽ B3001–4500
❸ B401–600	❻ B1401–2000	❾ B4501 and over

Front cover image: Tuk Tuks, Hua Hin © Cris Haigh/Alamy
Back cover image: Sino-Portuguese doorway, Phuket © Martin Richardson/Rough Guides
Right: Young monks, Mae Hong Son © Martin Richardson/Rough Guides